W9-ACH-171

The Geography of Modern Africa

MAURITANIA
SENEGAL
MALI
UPPER VOLTA
NIGER
CHAD
(EGYPT)
FEDERATION OF
BECHUANALAND

The Geography of Modern Africa

by William A. Hance

Columbia University Press
New York and London 1964

William A. Hance, Professor of Economic Geography at Columbia University, is also the author of *African Economic Development* (1958).

Library of Congress Catalog Card Number: 64-14239

Printed in the United States of America

To Nicholas McD. McKnight, Robert F. Moore,
and the memory of
Richard Herpers *and* John E. Orchard

Preface

Africa has become in recent years one of the keystones of the world-wide struggle for independence. The rapid evolution from colonial status to independence has received the greatest attention in the flood of reports and scholarly documents focusing upon that great continent. The fact is, however, that the "struggle," for almost all countries, has been far less difficult than the problems of development that these countries now face. The demand for independence has been met for most of the continent; nobody knows the secret of achieving rapid economic advance for the peoples of Africa.

The purposes of this book are to present the major features of the economy of Africa, to analyze the handicaps and attributes that affect economic development, and to assess some of the potentialities for growth in the years ahead. Since variety is one of the keynotes of Africa, the continent is approached on a regional basis, with all but the first five background chapters being devoted to individual countries or groups of countries.

Africa has been changing with sometimes startling rapidity. This contributes to its fascination, but greatly increases the task of reporting on it. Assessments such as are attempted here require constant revision as knowledge of the continent is broadened and deepened. Nonetheless, many of the problems and conditions affecting economic development are more or less timeless and others will remain for many years to come.

It cannot be too forcefully noted that most African statistics must be approached with caution. Demographic data are often of highly questionable validity. Figures on such things as production or acreage of subsistence crops, numbers of livestock, and per capita incomes are especially suspect. Subjects that are more accurately covered include production and sales of export crops, output of minerals, and commodity exports and imports, but even here one runs into baffling contradictions and numerous missing links.

It is impossible to know the continent as well as one should to write a book such as this. The author's preparation has involved studying Africa since 1941, teaching courses about the continent since 1949, and four field trips including an extended one in 1962–63. All of the major countries have been visited at one time or another, and return visits to many of them have proved valuable in assessing the growth of various economic sectors and regions. The debt to others who have studied the continent and its parts is enormous, however, and is acknowledged with gratitude.

Many people have been generous in the help extended in preparation of this book. Academic colleagues, government officials, persons in business and industry, and citizens of African, European, Asian, and American origin have gone beyond the call of duty in attempting to supply the material requested. Their personal kindnesses and unfailing cooperation are deeply appreciated. I am indebted to the Rockefeller Foundation, the Graduate School of Business of Columbia University, and the Liberia Mining Company for research grants which made possible the latest field trip to Africa. I have enjoyed working with my friends at the Columbia University Press, including William F. Bernhardt, Eugenia Porter, Nancy Dixon, and Robert J. Tilley, and with the cartographer Vaughn Gray. Particular thanks go to my assistant, Donald A. Measner, who showed great perseverance and intelligence in ferreting out data required to complete a number of the sections and tables. My wife suffered through several typings and proofreadings, and accompanied me on a trip of considerable difficulty and occasional hazard. My thankfulness to and for her cannot be measured.

William A. Hance

Columbia University
February, 1964

Contents

Maps

Tables

Charts

Part One INTRODUCTION

Freight train ascending the east side of the Great Rift Valley about 40 miles from Nairobi in Kenya
Mt. Longonot, an extinct volcano lying within the Rift Valley, is seen in the background.

CHAPTER ONE

The Interest in Africa

Africa has been catapulted into the consciousness of the developed world with startling impact just since World War II. American "discovery" of the continent has been even more recent. The Mau Mau uprising in Kenya, the long and bloody Algerian revolt, the collapse of effective rule in Congo, the flood of African nations achieving independence, the seeming intransigence of colonial and racial positions in southern Africa—these and other dominantly political problems have moved successively or simultaneously into the international limelight. Much less attention has been given to some of the possibly more basic social, economic, and physical conditions and problems, to forces which may in the long run prove to be more decisive in shaping the future of African nations.

The objective of this book is to assemble and analyze material which will contribute to a better understanding of the African economic scene. Specifically, it focuses upon two main questions: What is the present state of economic development? and what are the potentialities for development in the coming decades? Generalizing about a continent as vast as Africa is a hazardous undertaking. Hence the bulk of this study is devoted to analyses of African regions and subregions. Only the first five chapters are devoted to the continent as a whole.

Reference has already been made to the recency of widespread interest in Africa and we know that, except for very ancient contacts in the north, it was the last of the inhabited continents to be explored and developed. Why this retarded opening up? and why the enormously increased interest in postwar years? A brief answer to these questions will serve to introduce the continent and will reveal some of the fundamental features which affect actual and potential development of the area.

EXPLANATIONS FOR LATENESS IN DEVELOPMENT

Northern Africa is largely an exception to the following discussion, which focuses upon the enormous sub-Saharan portion of the continent. The northern fringe, tied by a land bridge to the Near East, separated from Europe by only very narrow bands of water, open to navigation on the great, inland Mediterranean Sea, participated in and contributed to the advance of civilization over many centuries. It has always had more important ties with Europe and Asia than with Black Africa, though the lack of contact between north and south must not be exaggerated, witness the historic dhow traffic along the east coast and the movement of peoples along the Nile and later by caravan across the Sahara.

ISOLATION

In sub-Saharan Africa, one of the important factors which contributed to a retarded development is isolation, explained by the location, the difficulty of access from the sea, and the massive character of the continent.

Africa is the continental southward extension of the great Afro-Eurasian land mass. Africa south of the Sahara, surrounded by seas and the great sea of the Sahara, has no marked orientation geographically toward any other continent

Map 1. Globe focused on Africa

Relief Map Copyright Aero Service Corporation

(Map 1). It stands in a position of at least partial isolation. It may be noted, however, that the bulge of West Africa results in the larger part of sub-Saharan Africa being oriented toward the Atlantic rather than toward the Indian Ocean.

A second factor explaining the long isolation of the area was the typically difficult access from sea to land, occasioned in turn by the general shortage of indentations giving protection for vessels, by the frequent blocking of river mouths and estuaries by sand bars, and by the unfortunate circumstance that some of the best natural harbors were found adjacent to unproductive hinterlands. There are exceptions to these rules, such as the huge harbor of Freetown or the protected bays of Angola and Mozambique, but the subcontinent, particularly along the Guinea Coast, compared very unfavorably with western Europe and other continents in accessibility by sea.

The massiveness of the continent is a third explanation for its long isolation. With a total area of 11.6 million square miles, of which two thirds is below the northern tier of countries, Africa has the shortest coastline in relation to its area of any of the continents. Only Asia has a larger interior area remote from the sea.

DIFFICULTY OF OVERLAND MOVEMENT

A second major contributor to the slowness of penetration and economic development of tropical Africa was the difficulty of overland movement. Africa is often called the plateau continent, which immediately conveys the impression of difficult landforms inhibiting penetration (see frontispiece map). A coastal zone averaging only twenty miles in width is typically backed by steep scarps or scarp zones which

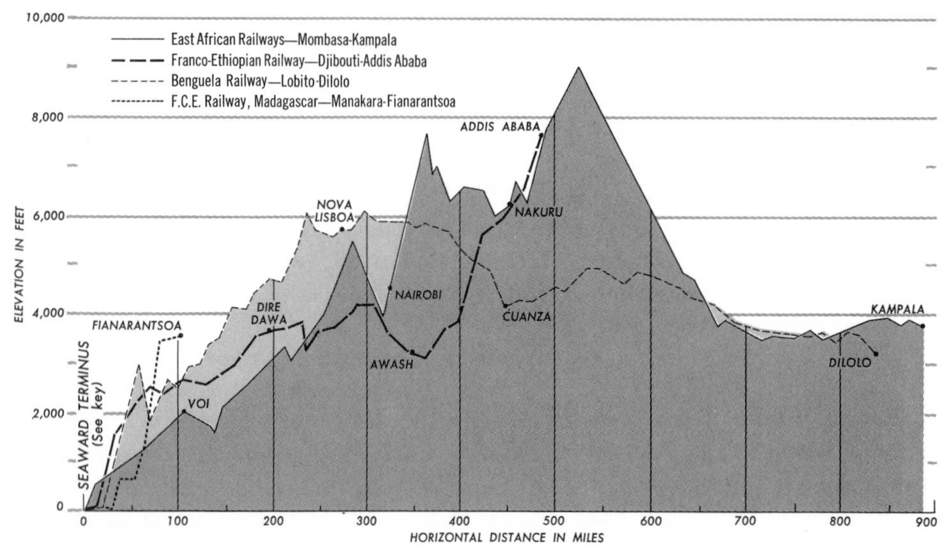

Chart 1. Profiles of four African railways
Difficult scarps often impede overland movements on the continent.

make road and rail construction difficult and costly.

The profiles of many African railroads reflect this adverse topographic pattern (Chart 1). The Djibouti–Addis Ababa line, for example, requires 475 miles to cover a distance of 360 miles. In the first 60 miles it rises 2,320 feet, and in the final 180 miles, 4,625 feet. There are 1,426 bridges, numerous tunnels, and many viaducts on the line, which has maximum gradients that usually do not exceed 18 per thousand but that occasionally reach 28 per thousand. (Minimum radii on curves are generally greater than 1000 feet but go as low as 500 feet.) It is said to cost as much to ship an automobile from Djibouti to Addis Ababa as it does to ship it from Detroit to Djibouti. The Benguela Railway provides a second example. So steep were the gradients on this line that it was first built with a 5-mile rack-and-pinion section which was not converted to normal track until 1948. Even so, the minimum curve radii on the new line are 325 feet and gradients go up to 25 per thousand. The powerful Beyer-Garatt locomotives have their maximum load capacity reduced from the 1,720 metric tons prevailing on the coastal stretch between Lobito and Benguela to 520 metric tons on the scarp section.

A concomitant of the plateau character of the continent is a characteristic stream profile having rapids close to the coast. With few exceptions, such as the Niger and the Senegal, rivers have not provided access to the interior, and river valleys, unlike those of Europe and North America, have not been the natural routeways for road and rail penetration. The fact that the Congo was first traced from upstream rather than by following its course from the mouth illustrates the extreme inhospitality of river routes descending across the plateau edges.

But landform problems are not confined to coastal scarp zones. In eastern Africa, from Ethiopia to Mozambique, are the great rift zones, providing some of the most difficult landform barriers anywhere in the world (see frontispiece map). Also in East Africa there tends to be a series of antithetic scarps, so that what has been laboriously gained in mounting the steep, seaward facing slopes is gradually lost on the plateau surface and a repetition of scarps must be overcome. Examination of the same map will also reveal that the plateau is divided into several high basins, requiring that an elevated rim, often more like a mountain, be negotiated before proceeding to the flatter plateau surfaces at somewhat lower elevations.

A scarp road in eastern Congo
The difficulty of overland movement long impeded the penetration of Africa and contributes to the high cost of transportation today.

A variety of other impediments to overland movement may also be listed: the heavy seasonal rainfall over most of the area, which makes a large number of the roads dangerous or impassable during parts of the year; the dense forest growth in the rainforest regions; the absence of ballast, especially where it is most needed, in the constantly humid areas; the scarcity of water in some areas, requiring the use of special condensers or expensive supply installations; sand blowing in desert and steppe areas; the general deficiency of coal for locomotives which required the more costly and wasteful use of wood and now requires expenditure of foreign exchange for diesel oil imports; and, lastly, the vast areas of low productivity which must often be crossed before reaching economically attractive regions.

HISTORICAL AND SOCIAL FACTORS

But physical factors were not alone in repulsing the opening of Africa; certain political, social, and economic considerations were also of significance. From an historical standpoint, lines of communication and transportation—of development—advanced eastward and westward from older centers in the Northern Hemisphere. True, this involved the navigation of African coasts at a fairly early date, but interest was primarily in the securing of a route to India and the East, not in Africa. Slaves, gold, and ivory from Africa played minor roles in world commerce.

In the nineteenth century the Northern Hemisphere axis showed signs of becoming saturated. Again, the tropics were by-passed in favor of peopling the more poleward areas of the continents in the Southern Hemisphere. It was only after these newer areas in both hemispheres had been partially filled, after some of them had begun competing with Europe, and after the continuing industrial growth of Europe had created a desire for new markets and new sources of raw materials that Europeans began to look with interest toward Africa and that its partition by European powers was assured. Africa, then, got a late start on the path to modern economic development in part because of the greater attractiveness of opportunities in other areas.

Nor was the status of the peoples inhabiting tropical Africa conducive to early contact. Backward by Western standards, often warlike, and of low average stamina, they were not as attractive as laborers used in situ as were various Asian peoples, nor were the opportunities for interchange present that existed in other parts of the world.

Finally, the conditions of health and the prevalence of insects and diseases were enormous repulsing factors. From 1835 to 1907, 62 of 225 Wesleyan Methodist missionaries died in Africa; from 1878 to 1888, half of the Baptist missionaries in the Congo succumbed to tropical disease.

For all of these reasons, and others not mentioned which will become apparent in later sections, Africa was not generally an attractive area for great concentrations of economic activity. We know, however, that this situation has changed, first slowly, and then with dramatic speed. Why? And how have the liabilities and impediments been overcome to permit or command a greatly expanded interest and attention?

EXPLANATIONS FOR THE HEIGHTENED INTEREST IN AFRICA

CHANGING COMPETITIVE POSITION OF THE AREA

It has already been noted that a growing need for markets and raw materials was among the factors leading to partitioning of the continent in the late nineteenth century. These needs expanded in the twentieth century and particularly after World War II. In the immediate postwar years, most of colonial Asia, which had been the prime source of tropical staples, became independent, and much of it was troubled by continuing unrest. South America was largely composed of independent nations which were often somewhat reluctant to have outsiders develop their resources. As a consequence, Africa became, instead of a stepchild, the chief focus of interest of metropolitan powers concerned with tropical development or needing new supplies of minerals. It inherited a considerable part of the interest that had previously been oriented elsewhere.

SCIENTIFIC AND TECHNOLOGIC DEVELOPMENTS

In the meantime, certain advances have overcome or reduced the impediments that had previously been retarding development. For example, a series of new deepwater ports and marked improvements and extensions to most other ports have greatly reduced the difficulty of accessibility to and from the sea. Just since the war, new deepwater facilities have been provided where none existed before at the following ports: Freetown, Sierra Leone; Monrovia

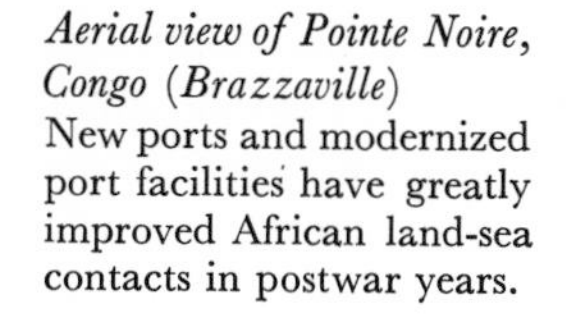

Aerial view of Pointe Noire, Congo (Brazzaville)
New ports and modernized port facilities have greatly improved African land-sea contacts in postwar years.

and Buchanan, Liberia; Abidjan, Ivory Coast; Tema, Ghana; Moçâmedes, Angola; Nacala, Mozambique; and Mtwara and Dar es Salaam in Tanganyika. While some areas are still inadequately served and there is still congestion in other ports, it is no longer accurate to generalize that Africa is characterized by difficulty of access from the sea.

The construction and extension of roads and railroads have similarly greatly reduced the impact of factors inhibiting overland movement. A difficult scarp zone is no longer so formidable once a route has been built across it. In postwar years, railway extensions have been constructed in seventeen countries, providing one of the world's more dynamic railroad building programs. Roads have also been given renewed attention; they have assumed an ever larger share in the total transport picture and have brought fairly extensive areas into the orbit of an exchange economy. Airways have been greatly expanded, particularly for the movement of personnel within Africa and between it and Europe.

This is not to say that the problems of overland movement have been solved. Far from it. Experts from a variety of disciplines continue to repeat that adequate transport is one of the top requirements for an expanding African economy. But inadequate transport facilities and difficult landforms are certainly not the retarding influence they were 10, 25, or 50 years ago. And airways have, of course, permitted rapid movement of persons and high-class freight over the most difficult terrain features.

In the control of disease, again a staggering problem, wide control has been achieved over great epidemics, there has been considerable local success in fighting malaria, and it is now quite reasonably safe from the health standpoint for non-Africans to visit and work in the area providing standard precautions are taken. The effect of disease control on the indigenous population is seen in the greatly reduced death rates in most African countries.

Numerous other technological advances might also be listed, such as the spread of modern telephonic, radio, and other means of communication, the expansion of electricity production, and the introduction of earth-moving equipment, mechanical saws, and some agricultural machinery. It should be noted, however, that these scientific and technological changes are permissive in character and not direct incentives for African advancement.

EXPANDED ECONOMIC INCENTIVES

Third among the factors that explain the heightened interest in Africa has been the greatly enlarged economic incentives of European metropoles. This reflects the declining raw material position of older areas plus the growing demands of a substantially enlarged industrial establishment, as well as higher standards of living and consumption in that area.

Table 1 shows the variety of minerals for which Africa has become an important world source. It promises to become even more important in these minerals, particularly in iron ore, manganese, copper, petroleum, and natural gas, and to move into a position of world significance in the production of bauxite and other minerals. The continent also has stature in the production of numerous vegetable commodities, the more important of which are listed in Table 1.

Enlarging the demand for raw materials from Africa has been the desire on the part of the European nations to secure them from their own currency areas, a desire greatly strengthened by the postwar balance of payment difficulties of these European countries. On the one hand, there has been an emphasis on the output of "dollar savers," commodities which had previously been purchased in hard currency areas and whose production in Africa would result in the conserving of an inadequate dollar supply. The most successful switch was made with tobacco from Southern Rhodesia, but cotton and oil seeds also received emphasis in response to this financial situation. On the other hand, there has been an emphasis on "dollar earners," commodities which might be sold in hard currency markets to the benefit of the central dollar holdings of the sterling, franc, and escudo blocs. Cocoa, pyrethrum, sisal, rubber, coffee, and many minerals have been dollar earners of significance.

Another strong economic incentive was the expanded necessity to find markets for European manufactured products. The most important single solution for European balance of payment problems was the securing of markets for its items of specialization. The marked diminution of invisible receipts occasioned by wartime liquidation of foreign holdings meant that exports had to be expanded to cover a larger part of import expenditures. The deficit position of Europe in food, energy, and mineral and vegetable raw materials means that there is a continuing necessity to expand foreign sales if the standard of living in western Europe is to continue to rise. Africa, of course, was only one market area, but an increasingly important one for Europe.

STRATEGIC CONSIDERATIONS

Fourth among the elements explaining the greater interest in Africa in postwar years was its increased strategic value. North Africa stands in a flanking position with regard to western Europe and to the Mediterranean route. Northeast Africa occupies a special position vis-à-vis the Middle East. The loss of the British base in the Suez Isthmus and nationalization of the Canal created a desire for alternate strength, focusing attention on Cyprus and Libya, the latter receiving a substantial share of its governmental revenues in return for payments for British and American bases.

Also along the north were the French naval bases at Bizerte in Tunisia and Mers-el-Kebir in Algeria, American naval and air bases in Morocco, and an important United States communications center in Eritrea. Other bases of more than purely local significance have been Dakar, the British military bases in Kenya, the former Belgian base at Kamina in eastern Congo, the minor French naval bases at Djibouti in French Somaliland and Diégo-Suarez at the northern tip of Madagascar, and the naval base at Simonstown in the Republic of South Africa.

In more recent years there has been a considerable rethinking with respect to the value and necessity of many of these bases. African

Table 1. African share of world production and exports of selected commodities[a]

MINERALS

	Percent of world production		
	1938	*Ave. 1955–57*	*1961*
Base metals			
Copper	18.0	23.9	22.2
Tin	12.0	14.9	9.9
Lead	3.2	11.5	8.2
Zinc	1.3	8.9	7.3
Ferroalloys			
Columbium-tantalum	nil	75.5	82.3
Cobalt	87.0	67.0	76.9[b]
Chromite	35.0	35.0	34.5
Vanadium	47.5	8.7	30.9[b]
Manganese	22.0	21.8	21.8
Antimony	4.0	30.8	21.7
Cadmium	0.3	3.6	5.6
Tungsten	1.9	5.6	2.5
Nickel	0.5	1.3	0.8
Precious metals and stones			
Diamonds			
Industrial	98.5	99.9	97.4
Gem		78.8	94.4
Gold	40.0	62.7	52.2
Platinum	9.2	47.8	30.0
Silver	0.3	4.3	4.7[b]
Other metallic minerals			
Lithium ores	nil	97.6	98.7[b,e]
Beryl		39.8	40.3
Uranium ores			15.2[b]
Zirconium		3.9	8.3
Bauxite	nil	3.1	6.7
Titanium concentrates			
Ilmenite		2.1	6.6
Rutile		0.4	4.5
Barite	0.4	2.0	4.2
Iron ore	3.5	3.7	3.2
Energy minerals			
Coal	1.0	3.4	2.3
Petroleum	0.1	0.2	2.2
Other nonmetallics			
Kyanite			68.6[e]
Phosphates	33.0	34.0	26.4
Vermiculite		23.6	25.6
Asbestos	16.0	19.6	14.1
Graphite	7.4	6.2	4.0
Mica	6.1	2.7	2.2

AGRICULTURAL, FOREST, AND FISHERY PRODUCTS

	Percent of world production		Percent of world exports	
	Ave. 1950–58	*1961*[c]	*Ave. 1950–58*	*1961*
Vegetable oils and oilseeds				
Palm kernels	82.8		93.0	92.5
Palm oil	81.0		65.3	62.4
Peanuts	25.4[d]	29.9	74.4[d]	86.9
Olive oil	8.7[d]	13.4	43.2[d]	22.5
Cashew nuts				
Sesame seed	11.7[d]	21.4	44.4[d]	75.5
Castor beans		34.1	18.9[d]	40.0[e]
Cotton seed	9.3[f]	7.2		
Copra	3.8[d]	2.9	4.6[d]	4.7[e]
Stimulants and spices				
Cloves	c. 98.	c. 98.	c. 98.	c. 98.
Vanilla	c. 98.	c. 98.	c. 98.	c. 98.
Coffee	16.0	21.2	19.4	25.3
Tea	3.2[d]	4.7	2.0[d]	8.2
Wine	9.9[b]	9.4	67.3[d]	64.3[e]
Tobacco	4.2[b]	4.7	13.1	14.0[e]
Chat				
Other food products				
Cocoa beans	64.2	74.3	62.9	79.8
Citrus fruit	7.1[d]	8.9	21.4[d]	26.2[e]
Bananas	5.1[d]	5.2	9.5[d]	14.3
Sugar (cane)	5.4[d]	7.6	6.5[d]	6.4[e]
Corn	5.8[d]	5.4	8.2[d]	7.5[e]
Cassava	50.6			
Sweet potatoes and yams	50.8			
Fibers				
Cotton	11.6	7.6	22.8	21.8[e]
Sisal	67.5	49.3	52.9	61.2
Piassava				
Raffia				
Urena and punga				
Wool	9.4		9.2[d]	8.6[e]
Other industrial products				
Pyrethrum				
Quinine				
Rubber	3.4[d]	7.1	2.7[d]	6.1[e]
Forest products				
Timber				
Cork				
Wattle				
Gum arabic				
Fish products				
Fish oil				16.2
Fish meal				17.4[e]

Sources: U.S. Department of Agriculture, commodity publications; U.S. Department of Interior, Bureau of Mines, *Minerals Yearbook, 1961*; U.N., *Statistical Yearbook, 1962* (New York, 1963); U.N., *Economic Survey of Africa since 1950* (New York, 1959); U.N., *International Action for Commodity Stabilization and the Role of Africa* (Addis Ababa, 1962).

[a] Some commodities are listed for which data are not available, but for which Africa is known to have a significant production. [b] Excluding Sino-Soviet bloc. [c] Or crop year ending in 1961.

[d] Average of 1948/49–1952/53 crop years. [e] 1960. [f] Average for 1948–52.

states have tended to resent perpetuating foreign military bases as a partial infringement on their complete autonomy and as undesirable vestiges of colonialism. The desire to expedite French withdrawal from Bizerte, for example, led to brief but bloody attacks in 1961, settled temporarily by Tunisia's offer to permit continued occupance during the Berlin crisis. Morocco has negotiated for the release of American strategic air bases and of the Franco-American naval base at Kenitra (formerly Port Lyautey). In the former French territories south of the Sahara, bilateral agreements at the time of independence provided for continuing specific French military rights. Evidence suggests that these rights are likely to be gradually withdrawn, although some nations may wish to retain them as protection against their neighbors, because they reduce the expenditures that might otherwise be necessary from national budgets, and because of employment and income advantages resulting from the presence of French military personnel.

An additional strategic concern of the West has been to assure the maintenance of strategic exports, of which uranium ores and ferro-alloys are perhaps the most significant.

Lastly may be listed the desire to minimize Soviet penetration and impact in the area. Western trade policies and actions have not always been consistent with this objective, however, providing convenient openings for the opportunistic entry of missions from the Communist nations. Guinea, in particular, has received aid and technical delegations from eastern Europe. The USSR has provided the bulk of funds so far utilized for construction of the High Dam in Egypt and has concluded aid and trade agreements with the Sudan, Somalia, Ethiopia, Mali, Ghana, and other nations. Numerous individual Africans have stated that they will accept aid from East or West; others have expressed considerable interest in the techniques that Communist China has adopted to speed its material development. The relative poverty of Africa, plus real and imagined objections to the former colonialism of western Europe, would appear to make Africa a potentially very attractive and receptive theater for Communist activities. But one should not underestimate the sophistication of independent African leaders in this regard, nor their resolution to retain national independence once it has been achieved.

CHANGING ATTITUDES OF COLONIAL POWERS

Thus far the explanations for heightened interest in Africa that have been given are very largely in the materialistic sphere. Taken alone, they present an incomplete and misleading picture.

Moral considerations have, of course, long been important in the attitudes of colonial powers toward their territories. As examples, the following may be cited: the opposition toward Arab slaving in East Africa, which was partially responsible for the British acquisition of Kenya and Uganda; the extension of rule to inland areas along the Guinea Gulf, which was often carried out more to end barbaric practices or intertribal warfare than with the goal of immediate economic development; and the often selfless contributions of missionaries and government servants. It is difficult for Africans to assess colonialism objectively at the present juncture, but future indigenous historians will doubtless give greater credit to the colonial period than the present emphasis on exploitative relations might suggest.

The point to be made here, however, is that the evolution of colonial philosophy was greatly accelerated after World War II. The metropolitan powers assumed far greater responsibilities for development of their territories and displayed greater concern with educational and social advance as well as with economic goals. Markedly increased aid, together with enlarged revenues resulting from higher prices received for sale of African staples, permitted a rapid expansion of medical and educational facilities, substantial expenditures on the infrastructure of African countries, greater attention to remote areas that had previously been largely neglected, and a general improvement in the standard of living of many Africans. The most important change, however, was the decision to expedite the moves toward independence. It became increasingly clear that prolonged refusal to grant self-rule and national freedom would lead to resentment and to the exacerbation of relations after independence, possibly destroying the long-run ability of the metropole to carry on effective relations with its former territories. The increasing expenditures required of the metropole may also have contributed to the desire for a more rapid evolution toward independence.

AFRICAN INITIATIVE

Most of the reasons thus far given for stimulated interest in Africa have been concerned with the needs and attitudes of ruling and former ruling powers. These considerations have first contributed to and then been eclipsed by the rising initiative of the Africans themselves. Possibly the most important single factor in the rapid political evolution which has focused so much attention on Africa in recent years was the growing body of educated Africans who quite logically demanded that Western goals respecting political and human liberties be applied to Africa. The pace of the political changes that have resulted has exceeded most expectations of 1950 or even 1958. The very dynamism of the political scene has enormously enlarged interest in the continent. The acquisition of independent status has naturally brought increased American concern. And certainly the will of the Africans to develop their own countries will play the prime role from now on.

CHAPTER TWO

The Physical Background

The physical environment assumes a prominent role in African economic development—more persistent and pervasive than one would encounter in a more advanced area. Certain of the continent's physical features have been touched upon in Chapter I. A brief overview of some of the other natural factors affecting the present and potential economies of Africa will serve as essential background for the succeeding discussions of individual areas. These include climate, natural vegetation, soils, and energy and mineral resources.

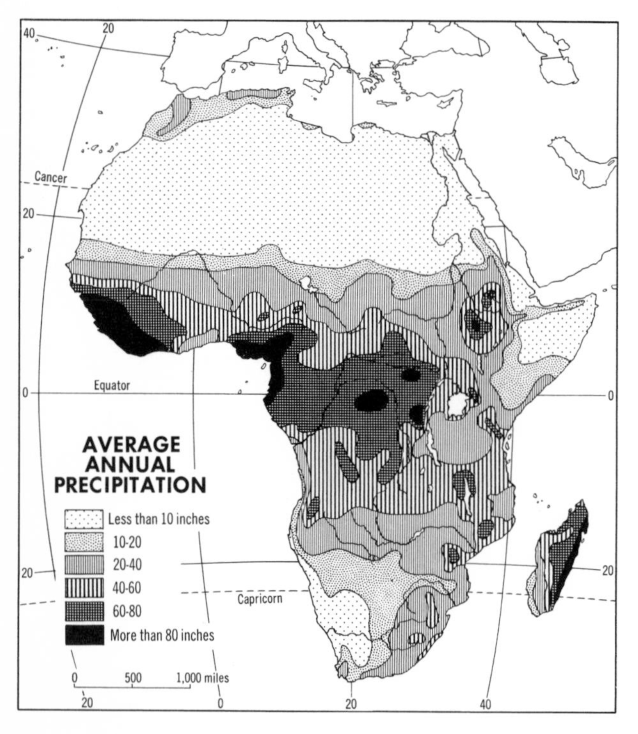

Map 2. Average annual precipitation, Africa

CLIMATE

While landform features were more important in impeding penetration in earlier years, climate is the most important physical factor retarding present economic development. Africa lies astride the equator, with Tunis 2,400 miles to the north and Cape Town 2,600 miles to the south. This gives to the continent the maximum expression of tropical conditions; about 90 percent may be classified as tropical, the highest percentage for any continent. It also results in a certain symmetry in the pattern of climate, vegetation, and soil regions, and hence, to a considerable degree, in land use regions.

The equatorial position also means that temperatures are high over the bulk of the continent. This being so, it follows that the element of climate which is of most significance is precipitation (Map 2). There are numerous systems of classifying African climates, three of which are shown in Map 3. It should be noted that boundaries dividing the several regions are arbitrary except where topographic features make for sharp distinctions; elsewhere, as for example in West Africa or in the Sudan, one region grades into another imperceptibly, and annual differences would show marked alterations in the arbitrary lines selected. Map 4, containing climographs for selected stations, is helpful in showing the seasonal patterns of temperature and precipitation on the continent.

As far as human utility is concerned, the climatic pattern of Africa means that a very large proportion has low productivity. On a continental basis Africa leads the world in the

Map 3. African climatic regions according to three systems

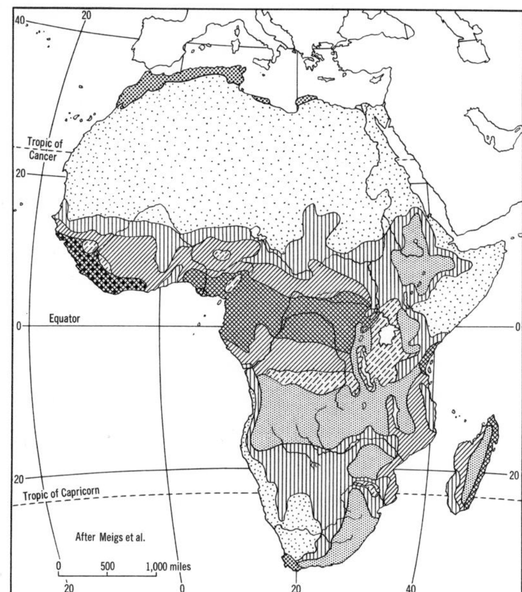

(a) After Meigs *et al.*

- Equatorial wet
- Equatorial monsoon
- Tropical wet-dry
- Semi-arid
- Desert
- Tropical highland
- Temperate highland
- Dry subtropical

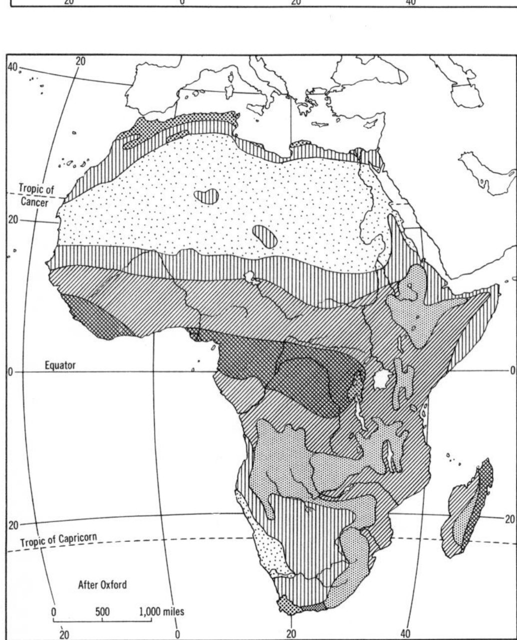

(b) After Oxford

- Tropical rainforest and monsoon rainforest
- Tropical savanna
- Tropical and subtropical steppe
- Tropical desert

Temperate, Warm, Rainy:

- dry winters
- dry summers
- no dry season

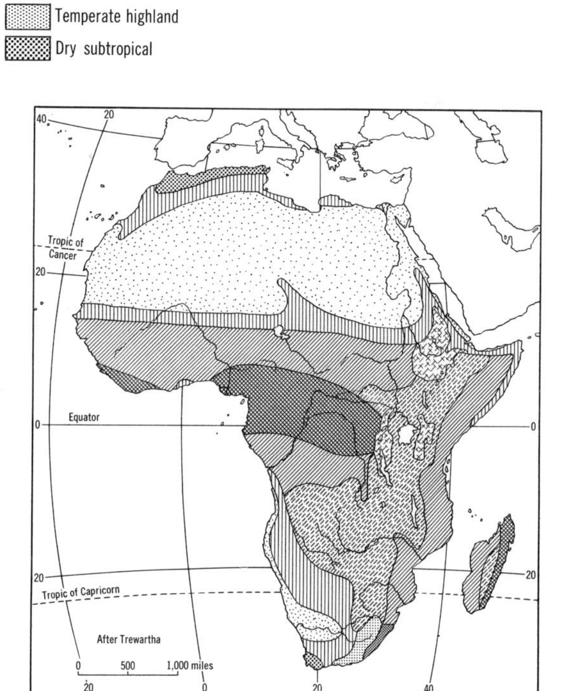

(c) After Trewartha

- Tropical rainforest
- Tropical savanna
- Tropical savanna highlands
- Tropical and subtropical steppe
- Tropical desert
- Dry summer subtropical
- Humid subtropical
- Marine west coast
- Undifferentiated highlands

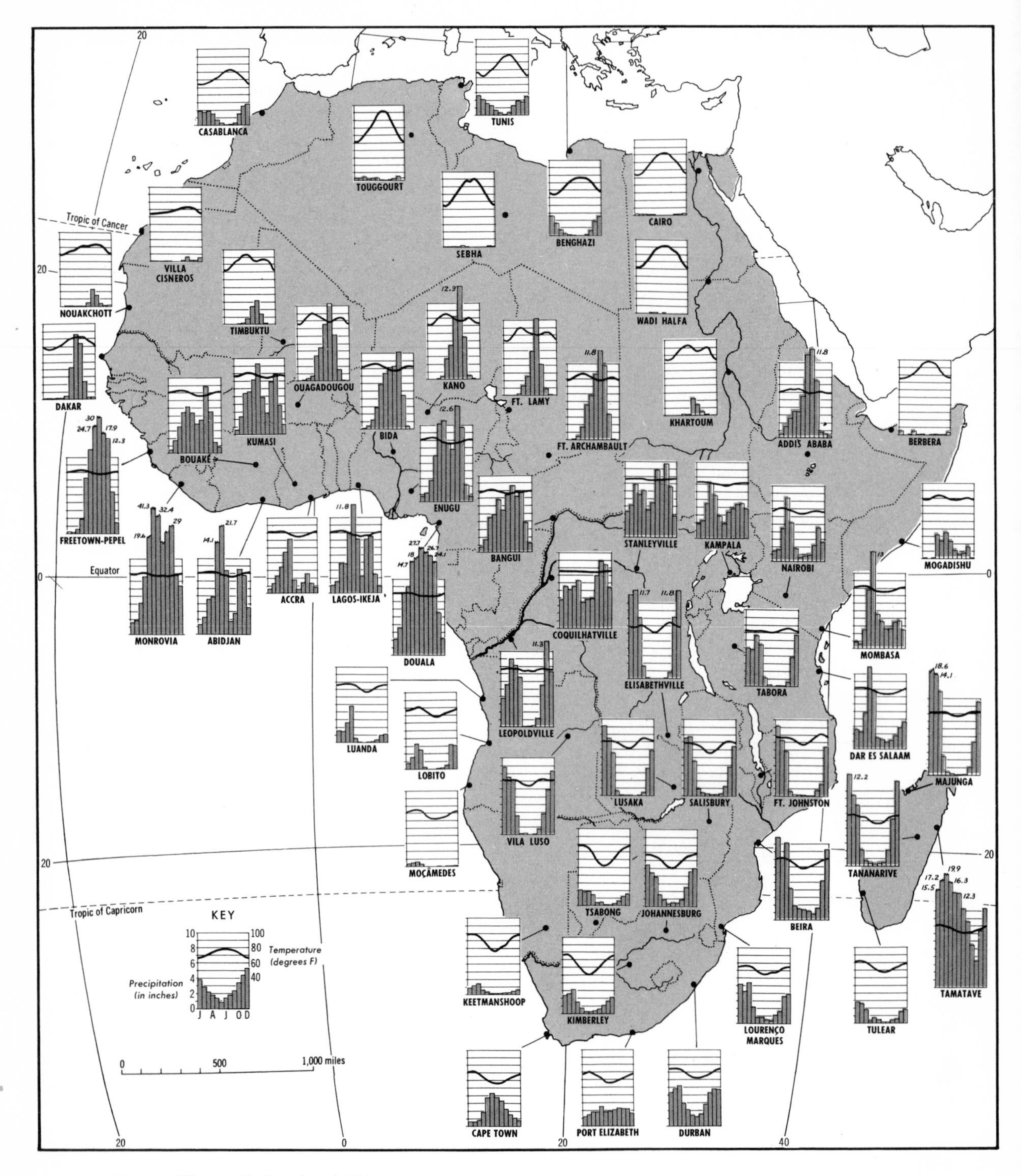

Map 4. Climographs for selected African stations

extent of dry climates, possessing about a third of the arid lands of the world and having the highest percentage of arid lands of any continent except Australia. Meigs[1] estimates the position as follows:

	Million square miles	*Percent of total area*
Hyperarid	1.76	15.2
Arid	2.82	24.3
Semiarid	2.35	20.2
Total arid	6.93	59.7

Worthington[2] states that precipitation is scanty in about 75 percent of sub-Saharan Africa, and that in over half of Africa water is *the* principal physical factor limiting advance. Not only is there inadequate precipitation in these regions, but they suffer also from great fluctuations within individual seasons and from year to year.

Moving from the arid and semiarid areas toward the equator, we find that the savanna climate type occupies about 20 percent of the continent. Characterized by a long rainy season and a short dry season, climate is not so strong a limiting factor as in the arid areas. But regions in this climate type are again plagued by uncertainty, and the torrential character of much of the precipitation is another disadvantage. And new problems arise in these zones—the presence of the tsetse fly and poorer soils.

About 8 percent of Africa has a tropical rainy climate, marked by a ten to twelve-month rainy season. Much of this area might be said to be too wet for optimum utility, at least under present known techniques. Its constantly high temperatures and high rainfall do present climatic conditions of great potential productivity, however.

Much of the more favorable land of Africa from the climatic standpoint falls in the highland climate regions. Precipitation in these areas may have the characteristics of any of the other types depending upon exposure, distance from the equator and from the sea, and specific landform features. Temperatures are moderated by elevation. There are some fairly extensive areas with highland climates, such as the Ethiopian Massif or the highveld of the Rhodesias, but many are small, irregular, and separated from one another by other climate types. There is no large tropical highland area comparable to the Brazilian Highlands. Additional disadvantages stem from the difficult landforms which must be expected in highland areas and from the fact that many of the tropical highlands suffer from remoteness of location, as, for example, those of the eastern Congo or of southwestern Tanganyika.

The regions of subtropical climate are relatively small, and their utilizable portions are further restricted by difficult landform conditions.

About 92 percent of the continent may be said to suffer from one or another climatic disability—surely one of the most important facts concerning Africa. It presents a picture, as far as water is concerned, of plenty where it cannot be used and of paucity where it is most needed. It should also be noted that the climate is often considered undesirable from the standpoint of human health and energy, though there is little scientific evidence to support this hypothesis. In fact, Lee states that "apart from a reduced desire for activity, there seem to be no permanent deleterious *direct* effects in healthy persons living under natural conditions in the tropics."[3] We do know, however, that it is very difficult to acclimatize quality middle latitude livestock to the high temperatures of tropical lands, one of the many factors which has kept the livestock industry in a low state of commercial development. An indirect effect of climate of considerable weight is the conduciveness of the constant warmth and, in the rainy tropics, of the constant humidity to promotion of insect pests and bacteriological life, to the detriment of man, plants, and animals.

[1] Peveril Meigs, "Arid and Semi-arid Climatic Types of the World," in *Proceedings, Seventeenth International Geographic Congress* (Washington, 1952), p. 137.

[2] Edgar B. Worthington, *Science in the Development of Africa* (London, 1958), p. 23.

[3] Douglas H. K. Lee, *Climate and Economic Development in the Tropics* (New York, Harper, 1957), p. 99.

VEGETATION

The striking fact regarding the vegetation of Africa from the standpoint of human use is the marginal utility of much of it. About 27 percent of Africa is classified as in forest, a lower percentage than for South America, but covering an area about equal in size. But much of the total is in savanna woodlands, whose trees, with few exceptions, are not suitable for lumbering. Nor are the trees of the tropical rainforest comparable in utility to those of the middle latitude forests, while they cannot be as easily exploited because of the necessity to maintain some canopy and some pioneer or nurse communities. Most of the grasses of the savannas and steppes are of relatively low nutritive value. And fire has degraded an enormous part of African vegetation.

Map 5, based upon a map prepared for the Commission for Technical Cooperation in Africa, is the best available depiction of vegetation distribution in Africa. But much more intensive surveys will be required before greater certainty can be attached to vegetation zones. In West Africa, for example, there are differences on almost every map produced regarding the landward boundary of the rainforest regions. The accompanying photographs show some of the more important vegetation types of Africa.

SOILS

The picture with regard to soils is not quite so bleak, but the tropical latosols rate negatively, the soils of steppe areas do not compare in fertility and structure to the grassland soils of the middle latitudes, there are proportionately fewer young, rich, alluvial soils than on any other continent, and soil erosion has reached very serious proportions over broad areas. Latosolic soils provide the main reason for the dominance of shifting agriculture in tropical rainy and savanna areas, a system which presents severe limitations to raising rural standards.

There are, of course, some good to excellent soils, among which may be mentioned the exceptionally rich alluvial soils of the Nile floodplain and delta, the soils of isolated volcanic peaks such as Mt. Kilimanjaro and Mt. Meru, and lowland soils of the Mediterranean regions. The soils of many highland areas are also relatively favorable, and the soils of swampy areas are worthy of greater study.

It is obvious that much more attention must be given to studying and protecting African soils. As Worthington states: "Soil can . . . be regarded as a kind of fulcrum on which the whole of land ecology is balanced, the physical environment on the one side and the biological environment on the other."[4] Despite its deficiencies, the soil of Africa is still its most valuable physical resource.

FAUNA

The cataloguing of African faunal species is not pertinent to this brief overview, which is designed to summarize in the broadest terms the most significant influences of the several physical elements on the human utility of the continent. The most important disadvantages regarding animal life would include: the existence of large numbers of deleterious insects and organisms, such as termites, the anopheles mosquito, and locusts; the fact that organized agriculture or the concentration upon one crop in a limited area almost assuredly leads to increasing plant disease; the fact that cattle, with minor exceptions, cannot be raised over the vast tsetse-ridden savanna and rainy tropical regions, an area totaling at least four million square miles; and the fact that indigenous livestock is characteristically of low utility.

On the favorable side there are, of course, possibilities for meeting some of these problems through eradication or control of specific insects and organisms, perfection and dissemination of drugs and serums, adoption of better livestock practices, and other means. In limited areas of Africa, the existence of big game provides an important attraction for the tourist industry as well as a potentially very great source of much-needed proteins. The coasts and inland waters

[4] Worthington, *Science in the Development of Africa*, p. 138.

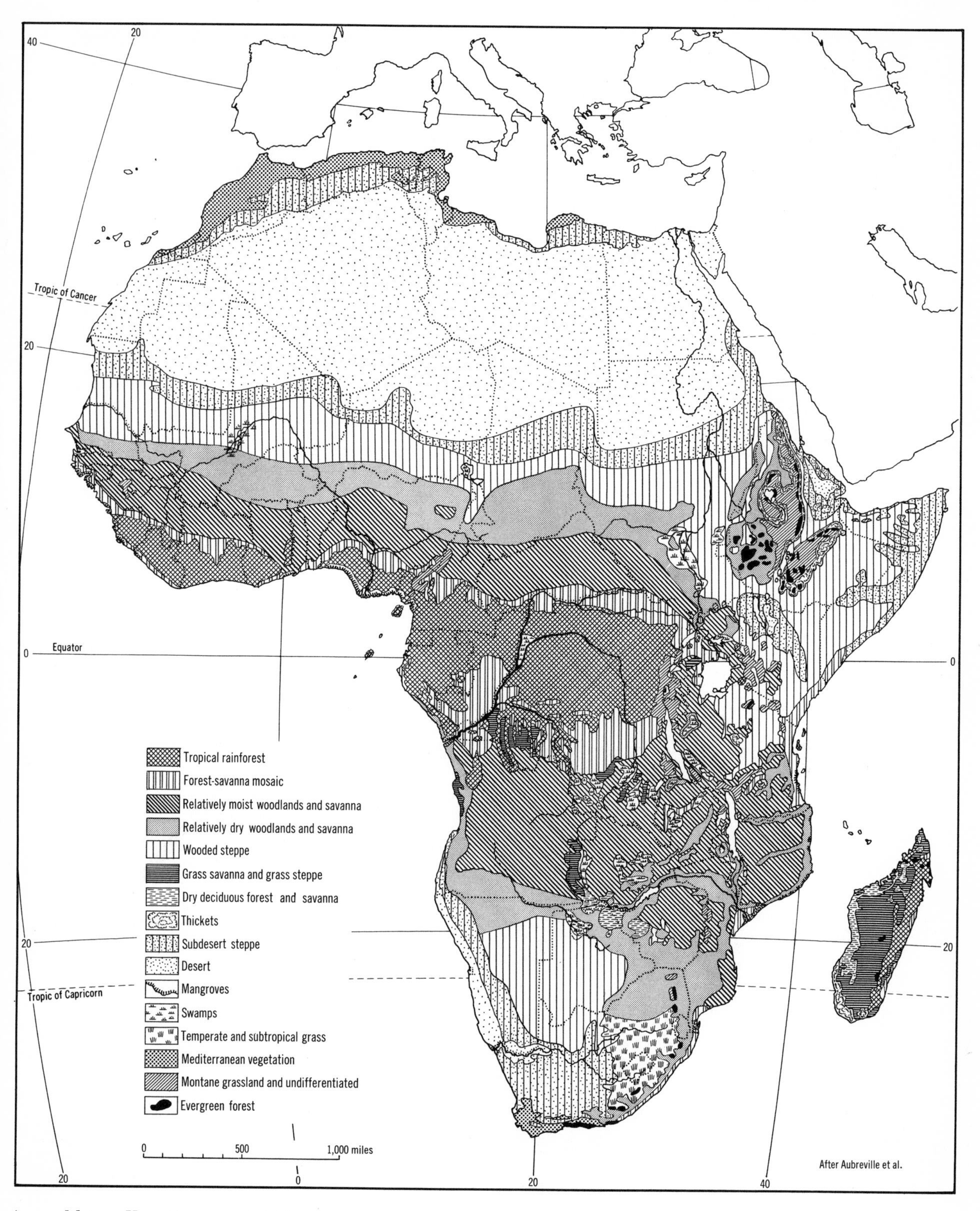

Map 5. Vegetation zones of Africa

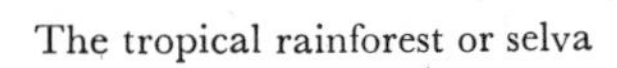

The tropical rainforest or selva

Savanna woodlands

Four major vegetational types of tropical Africa

Savanna grasslands

Steppe grasslands

provide opportunities for the fishing industry, which is, however, poorly developed except in the Republic of South Africa, South-West Africa, Angola, and Morocco.

It is evident from the foregoing summaries that the physical environment in Africa has great force; it is not so permissively favorable as in Europe or North America. This reflects, in part, the fact that man does not yet know how properly and effectively to utilize the environment. Two dilemmas that characterize Africa result. One is the need to increase the production of agricultural commodities to provide more food and larger exports, which is faced by the danger of permanently damaging the land unless proper techniques are employed. The second is that political and population pressures call for speed, whereas the scientific study required to solve or ameliorate the land use problems takes time.

The physical elements thus far summarized concern mainly the utilization of the surface resources of Africa. Brief statements regarding the energy and mineral position of Africa will conclude this introductory section.

ENERGY RESOURCES

The dominant facts with regard to energy resources are the relative weakness in coal and, except for parts of the Sahara and the Niger Delta, petroleum, and the great wealth of water power and fissionable raw materials.

Some good coal is found in the Republic of South Africa, Mozambique, and Southern Rhodesia. But most of the known coal is of poor quality, both in these three countries and in North Africa, Nigeria, Congo, and Madagascar. Except for the Republic of South Africa, production remains low and may even be expected to decline in some countries with the provision of hydroelectric facilities or through replacement by imported and domestic petroleum. The meagerness of coal resources must be considered a major handicap to certain types of industrial development.

In petroleum and natural gas, the Libyan and southern Algerian finds rate the Sahara as a major field, and the Niger Delta appears to have substantial resources. Smaller fields are being tapped in Morocco, Egypt, Gabon, Congo (Brazzaville), and Angola and exploration is progressing in many new areas, particularly along the coasts. But most of Africa is a basement rock area where petroleum and natural gas are not likely to be found. It must be expected, therefore, that most countries will be required to make greater expenditures of foreign exchange as their consumption of petroleum products continues to increase.

The water power resources of Africa are tremendous and are estimated at about 40 percent of the world's total (275 of 688 million horsepower). It is somewhat ironic that this continent, plagued with aridity over such great areas, should at the same time have such a magnificent hydroelectric potential. The high rainfall in the rainforest and savanna areas, and their high average elevation, combine to explain this wealth. About 18 percent of the world total and 45 percent of the total African potential is in the Congo Basin. The 217-mile stretch of the Lower Congo River from Leopoldville to Matadi has an estimated potential of 85 million horsepower.

There were still relatively few hydroelectric installations in 1963, their total capacity being less than 1 percent of the world total. But numerous projects are under study and some are being developed, so that it may confidently be predicted that the African position in production of hydroelectricity will greatly improve in the years ahead.

South Africa and the Congo have been the chief producers to date of fissionable raw materials. The Congo's Shinkolobwe deposit, possessing unusually rich ores, held a leading position during World War II and the early postwar years. South Africa's production occurs as a by-product of the gold ores. Many other African countries are known to have deposits of fissionable ores, including Nigeria, Northern Rhodesia, and Mozambique, while Gabon has entered the list of producers in the last few years.

The Republic of South Africa, Madagascar, and Senegal have large reserves of monazite sands. While these fissionable resources are not significant now in the field of energy production, they may give substantial bargaining power in the securing of nuclear electric plants in the years ahead and are a potential domestic raw material of no small dimensions.

NONENERGY MINERALS

It is a commonplace that Africa is a mineral storehouse, and it has already been seen that the continent accounts for important shares of world production in a variety of minerals. But one must be careful not to exaggerate the present significance of mineral output. Surprisingly few countries have more than a small part of their exports in minerals. Five or six countries account for a high percentage of the total value of mineral production. And only about eight countries have higher than the average world output on a per square mile or per capita basis.

Early exploitation of mineral resources tended to be confined to precious minerals—gold and diamonds. Other minerals with a relatively high value per unit weight followed, though the enormous size of some bodies was another attracting factor of importance. Coal was the first low-value mineral to be mined and was unique in being produced primarily for domestic use.

So far, the bulk of mineral output has been for export and this pattern is likely to continue for many years. It is far easier to increase productivity rapidly in mining than in agriculture, and African countries which are important mineral producers usually compare favorably in economic strength with those which are not. Postwar years have witnessed greatly increased geological mapping and prospecting for minerals. Numerous finds have been made, and several countries are about to join the ranks of mineral producers. But enormous areas remain to be scientifically mapped and explored, hence our knowledge of African mineral resources is often very incomplete.

For some years, the chief contributions made by the mining industry will be the employment opportunities it creates, the increased tax revenues it provides, and the foreign exchange it earns. Most minerals will not be used as raw materials for African industries, except for the primary processing plants which concentrate and refine the mineral. In the long run, possibly the most important minerals which would support manufacturing in Africa are coal and iron ore, needed for the iron and steel industry.

Table 2. Estimated reserve position of Africa in selected minerals

Very large	*Large*	*Average*	*Small*
Bauxite	Asbestos	Antimony	Coal
Chromium	Beryllium	Barite	Molybdenum
Cobalt	Columbium	Cadmium	Nickel
Copper	Graphite	Fluorine	Potash
Diamonds	Lead	Silver	Quartz crystal
Gold	Mica	Tin	Sulfur
Iron	Natural gas	Titanium	Tungsten
Manganese	Petroleum		Zinc
Phosphates	Uranium		
Platinum	Vanadium		
	Vermiculite		

The weak position of most territories in coal has already been noted. In iron ore, the continent is very well endowed. Iron ores are now exploited in the Maghrib, Egypt, Mauritania, Liberia, Guinea, Sierra Leone, Angola, Southern Rhodesia, and South Africa. Large bodies are known to exist in Nigeria, Gabon, Congo, Swaziland, and elsewhere. Some ores are very high grade, such as those of the Bomi Hills in Liberia, but the bulk of reserves is probably low grade.

Minerals now being mined in significant quantities in Africa are listed in Table 1. Table 2 gives the estimated position of African reserves in major minerals based upon present knowledge. Obviously, Africa rates favorably in quantity and variety of mineral resources. Production of minerals can be expected to be of very great importance in helping to finance development in the years ahead.

THE UNKNOWN AND THE LITTLE KNOWN

In concluding this chapter it is well to emphasize that the physical background of Africa is still very inadequately mapped and catalogued and still very imperfectly understood. There is a need for intensive and continuing resource surveys. There is a need for scientific research and application. Answers to such questions as the following are required:

How can the limited fertility of the leached tropical latosols be preserved or how can it be improved?

How can the basic system of shifting agriculture, whether it be the *chitemene* of Central Africa, the coppicing of Iboland, or the bush fallow of the Congo, be altered to increase yields and productivity?

How can the menace of the tsetse fly, which precludes keeping cattle in an area larger than the United States, be removed to encourage the introduction of a mixed agriculture and to help balance the protein-deficient diet?

In the widely represented steppe areas, what measures can be taken to prevent runoff, increase soak-in, utilize ground water, control the highly erratic and often silt-laden flow of wadis and mountain khors, prevent the more damaging effects of grass burning, improve the quality of the typically unnutritious and unpalatable grasses, and increase productivity by introduction of mechanical cultivation?

How can the livestock of the continent be improved through application of appropriate breeding, feeding, pasture management, and disease control practices?

Many of the brief analyses given earlier in this chapter reveal that Africa rates unfavorably with respect to several important physical factors. This does not mean, however, that there are not enormous potentialities for improvement. The productive capacity of much of the area has neither been scientifically measured nor adequately tested. Many of the possible avenues for enlarging the production and realizing the productivity of the area will be examined in the ensuing chapters.

CHAPTER THREE

The Economic Setting

There is tremendous diversity in the economic position of individual African countries. There is also great variation and contrast from region to region within most countries. By some economic criteria, the Republic of South Africa is an exception, but certain generalizations may be made in the economic sphere which have wide validity on the continental scale.

UNDERDEVELOPMENT

By almost any measure, Africa rates low on the scale of economic development. There is low production per man and low productivity per area in the agricultural realm. A large part of the continent is still devoted to subsistence production. The dominant activity is extractive; energy production and manufacturing output rate poorly. There is a shortage of skilled and semiskilled workers, of entrepreneurs, and of managers. The needs in education are great, most countries still having relatively few high schools and only a small number of college graduates. Rates of illiteracy, incidence of disease, infant mortality, and death are high. The infrastructure often remains grossly inadequate despite very real improvements that have been made, in postwar years at a markedly accelerated rate.

Recent estimates suggest that the average annual income per capita for Africa as a whole is about $122. But incomes vary from a high of $427 (1961) for the Republic of South Africa to a low of under $50 for the Central African Republic, Chad, Congo (Brazzaville), Dahomey, Ethiopia, Niger, Rwanda, Somali Republic, and Upper Volta. Tropical African countries, with the exceptions of Gabon ($200 in 1961), Ghana ($199 in 1961), the Rhodesias and Nyasaland ($163 in 1961), Ivory Coast ($184), Mauritius ($226), and Senegal ($175), have per capita incomes below $150. In the countries of the Maghrib they ranged from about $150 to $281 per person.

Somba men tilling the land in northern Dahomey
In some areas, commercialization has been brought about chiefly by transformation of the traditional economy, usually by peasant production of export crops.

In 1961 Africa accounted for only 5.6 percent of free-world imports and 5.4 percent of free-world exports. The export figure did, however, represent a 14.9 percent improvement over pre-war years, when the area accounted for only about 4.8 percent of free-world exports.

SUBSISTENCE AND EXCHANGE ECONOMIES

Africa is marked by the coexistence, often the juxtaposition, of heterogeneous economies. Most of it is in transition from a subsistence to an exchange economy, but there are relatively few people who have not been affected in some way, however slight, by modern economic forces. It was estimated in 1954 that 69 percent of the total cultivated area of tropical Africa was devoted to subsistence production, which occupied about 60 percent of the male population over fifteen years of age.[1] These percentages have declined in the ensuing years, but not significantly.

In the *Economic Survey of Africa since 1950*,[2] two prototype extremes are recognized, between which most African economies lie. In both extremes there is a modern and a traditional economy. In the first, commercialization has been brought about chiefly by the transformation of part or parts of the traditional economy, usually by peasant production of export crops; there is relatively little foreign investment in large-scale enterprise; and the movement of workers to the modern economy remains relatively small. Falling largely in this type would be such countries as Gambia, Ivory Coast, Mali, Upper Volta, Niger, Nigeria, Chad, the Central African Republic, Uganda, and Tanganyika.

The second prototype is characterized by an exchange economy brought about largely by foreign capital and enterprise, operating with a high capitalization and advanced techniques, mainly in mining and agricultural enterprises; it depends heavily on non-African and foreign capital; and there is a relatively large flow of workers from the traditional to the modern economy. South Africa, the Rhodesias, and Kenya fall into this group.

The transition to a modern economy frequently involves the development of economic distortions and social and political tensions. Traditional systems of tenure and land use frequently conflict not only with preservation of the soil but with the most economic disposition of land. Tribalism often directly opposes modernist tendencies, leading to some of the most dynamic of African political problems. The migration of labor from traditional areas may result on the one hand in deterioration of subsistence agricultural production, and on the other in all of the problems associated with urbanization, a relatively recent phenomenon in Africa but one of rapidly growing dimensions.

[1] U.N., *Enlargement of the Exchange Economy in Tropical Africa* (1954), pp. 14, 17.

[2] U.N., *Economic Survey of Africa since 1950* (1959), p. 12.

A sugar plantation near Jinja, Uganda
In other areas, an exchange economy has been brought about largely by foreign capital and enterprise.

In countries falling in the first prototype, movement into a modern economy is likely to result in transformation of the traditional economy; in countries of prototype two, the result is more likely to be disruption and disintegration of previous forms.

THE DOMINANCE OF EXTRACTIVE ACTIVITY

The importance of primary production is a dominant feature of the modern economy of Africa (Table 3). The largest part of commercial production is destined for shipment outside the continent, there being relatively little exchange among African countries and poorly developed domestic markets. The trend is, however, away from both these characteristics, and particularly toward an expansion of the domestic African economies.

Table 3. Exports of Africa and tropical Africa by commodity realm as a percentage of the total value of exports, 1961

	Africa[a]	*Tropical Africa*[b]
Vegetable products	45.2	61.2
Mineral products	35.9	28.6
Animal products	5.9	3.2
Manufactured products	4.4	1.0
Unaccounted	8.6	6.0
Total	100.0	100.0

Source: Compiled from national trade statistics.

[a] Includes islands in the Bight of Biafra, Madagascar, and the Mascarenes.

[b] Excludes Morocco, Algeria, Tunisia, Libya, Egypt, South Africa, and the territories which are in customs union with South Africa.

The dominance of extractive activity has meant that Africa has suffered rather severely from the generally declining prices for raw materials which started between 1951 and 1955. In late 1962 the price index of raw materials from the developing countries of the world fell to 85 (1950 = 100), whereas the price index for manufactured products had risen to about 125. Efforts of African countries to redress the balance by increasing the volume and variety of exports have been reasonably successful, but are increasingly faced by inadequate market demand and by restrictions on output under international commodity agreements. In some cases, increased foreign aid has not been adequate to offset declining revenues from the foreign sale of African staples. And, since long-run prognostications are not favorable, the price and market limitations on increased sales of African produce in world markets present one of the most serious development problems on the continent.

AGRICULTURE

As would be expected, agriculture is the main sector of economic activity. In tropical Africa about 90 percent of the population is rural and usually over 75 percent is agricultural. There is great variation in institutional agricultural forms. Commercial crops are produced primarily in modified traditional systems in such countries as Senegal, Ghana, Nigeria, Uganda, and Ethiopia. Plantations are important in the production of rubber in Liberia, palm products, rubber, cocoa, and other crops in Congo, sisal and tea in East Africa, and sugar in Angola, Uganda, and elsewhere. European farms and estates account for a high percentage of commercial agricultural output in Morocco, Kenya, Southern Rhodesia, and South Africa. Peasant cultivation of irrigated crops is dominant in Egypt, while a large part of Sudanese cotton is produced under a somewhat unique partnership arrangement.

Africa's total agricultural production is estimated to have increased by about 54 percent from prewar years to 1961–62 as compared to a 41 percent increase for the world, but per capita output in Africa actually decreased slightly during this period. In food production, African output rose only 49 percent from prewar years to 1960–61 as compared to a 56 percent increase in world food supplies. These figures suggest a certain imbalance in crop emphases and a partial failure in achieving more desirable subsistence levels.

Since a large part of Africa is semiarid, pastoral activities occupy a great portion of the continent, and in 1962 Africa was estimated to have about 118.6 million cattle or 11.5 percent of the world total. But in tropical Africa, cattle are often kept largely as a store of value or for prestige, and are relatively very unimportant commercially. Indigenous livestock are typically very poor milkers and have a low dressed weight as well. Livestock products comprise a very small part of total exports, though hides and skins do figure among the commodities shipped from most countries. The fact that the tsetse fly prevents keeping cattle in about half of tropical Africa helps to explain why most African countries are net importers of meat.

FISHING

A second primary activity, fishing, is well developed commercially only in South Africa, South-West Africa, Angola, and Morocco, all of which have relatively valuable exports of fish and other products of the sea. Fishing in the great lakes of eastern Africa is of some significance and many rivers are sources of fish for local areas. A number of territories have promoted the establishment of fish ponds in which *tilapia*, in particular, are raised to produce a welcome addition to the characteristically protein-deficient diets.

FORESTRY

Although Africa is estimated to have 27 percent of the total forest area of the world, her share of the world production of forest products was estimated in 1955 at 0.2 percent of industrial softwood, 4.9 percent of industrial hardwood, 1.8 percent of plywood, and 0.2 percent of wood pulp. About nine tenths of the total recorded cuttings plus large unrecorded cuttings are consumed as fuel. Only in a few areas, such as southeast Ivory Coast, southwest Ghana, parts of southern Nigeria, Gabon, and Congo (Brazzaville), does forestry make more than a small contribution to the money economy. Still a net importer of forest products, Africa does have great potentialities for an intensified utilization of its forests. At present, only about an eighth of the valuable forests are under exploitation.

MINING

Mining ranks after agriculture among extractive activities in value of production. Employing about a million people, including perhaps 100,000 non-Africans, mining is the most highly organized and capitalized sector of the modern economy, of which it has sometimes been a decisive initiator. But the mining industry is very unevenly distributed. South and South-West Africa, the Rhodesias, and Congo have normally accounted for over three quarters of the gross value of African mineral output, with South Africa alone accounting for over two fifths of the total value of mineral production. For Africa as a whole, minerals accounted for about 35.9 percent of the total value of exports in 1961; the comparable figure for tropical Africa was about 28.6 percent. The African share of total world exports of metalliferous ores and metal scrap was estimated at 10.4 percent in 1961; its share of base metal exports was 6.3 percent.

NONEXTRACTIVE ACTIVITIES

Nonextractive activities are thus far poorly represented in most of Africa. Much of manufacturing is still closely associated with extractive pursuits, being concerned with the primary processing of mining, agricultural, forest, and fishing products. South Africa accounts for perhaps two fifths of the manufactured output of Africa and is the only country whose economic structure is strongly affected by its industrial sector.

North Africa and Egypt have a large number of persons employed in handicraft industries and in the beginnings of modern manufacturing. In tropical Africa, Southern Rhodesia is the only country which shows at least minimal development in all major divisions of manufacturing; the Congo also had a relatively well-developed manufactural sector. Most other countries have only a rudimentary industrial development. Manufacturing in Africa is like mining in the importance of non-African capital, skill, and entrepreneurship. With the exception of a few large forestry plants and large-scale smelters and refiners, industry is composed mainly of small-scale plants using relatively simple manufacturing processes. In recent years, most African countries have taken steps to expand the industrial segments of their economies and efforts to build up this sector may be expected to accelerate in the years ahead.

Public administration and defense, trading activities, and domestic service figure importantly among other nonextractive activities. They account for a substantial percent of wage employees in many countries but their contribution to the gross domestic product is still relatively small.

THE "ONE-PRODUCT" CHARACTER OF AFRICAN ECONOMIES

Just as there is emphasis upon the extractive end of the economic spectrum, so there tends to be heavy dependence on a limited number of commodities as far as exports are concerned. Chart 2 shows the small number of products required to account for the bulk of exports in African countries. This "one-product" character has numerous actual and potential disadvantages. It makes the economy of an individual country excessively vulnerable to fluctuations in prices and in the size of market for its staple products, fluctuations which are very largely or completely beyond its control.

According to one report,[3] the degree of fluctuation in unit value is larger for African commodities than for the world as a whole. In the period 1948–58 the purchasing power of exports from Ghana fluctuated by 12.8 percent, in British East Africa by 9.3 percent, in Nigeria by 10.3 percent, and in the Rhodesias and Nyasaland by 9.7 percent. In the past few years, price drops have been particularly notable in some major commodities. Between 1959 and 1961, for example, the average price of Ghanaian cocoa dropped 32.4 percent, of Ugandan coffee 36.1 percent, and of Nigerian palm kernels 29.0 percent. On the other hand, there have been slight increases in the average prices for bananas, cotton, peanut oil, and sisal.

Reductions in price and volume will cause reductions not only in export earnings but also in revenues to government, characteristically highly dependent on export and import taxes. For example, these duties accounted in recent years for the following percentages of government revenues: Ghana, 68; Nigeria, 62; Ivory Coast, 58; Uganda, 56; Cameroon, 55; Togo, 45; and the Rhodesias and Nyasaland, 21. A marked decline in export tax receipts can significantly affect development programs.

"One-product" emphases may create further difficulties in pursuing an effective labor market policy, cause serious unemployment, and lead to political unrest. They may also have physical disadvantages, including soil deterioration, increased insect and disease attack, and neglect of proper dietal standards.

Table 4 shows the major exports from Africa and tropical Africa in 1961 by percent of the total value of exports from these areas, revealing how the continent or a large part of it, and not just individual countries, is characterized by dependence upon a limited number of commodities. In 1961 the five leading commodities in the vegetable realm accounted for 24.5 percent of total African exports by value; the comparable figure for tropical Africa was 38.8 percent. In the mineral realm, the five leading items accounted for 27.9 percent of total African exports, while the five leading mineral exports from tropical Africa made up 22.2 percent of shipments from that area. Taking all commodities, it required only the nine leaders to account for 50.8 percent of the total value of African exports in 1961, while the top twenty accounted for 68.8 percent. For tropical Africa, exports of the six leaders totaled 52.6 percent of all exports while the first twenty exports comprised 80.4 percent of total exports by value.

[3] U.N. Economic Commission for Africa, *International Action for Commodity Stabilization and the Role of Africa* (Addis Ababa, 1962).

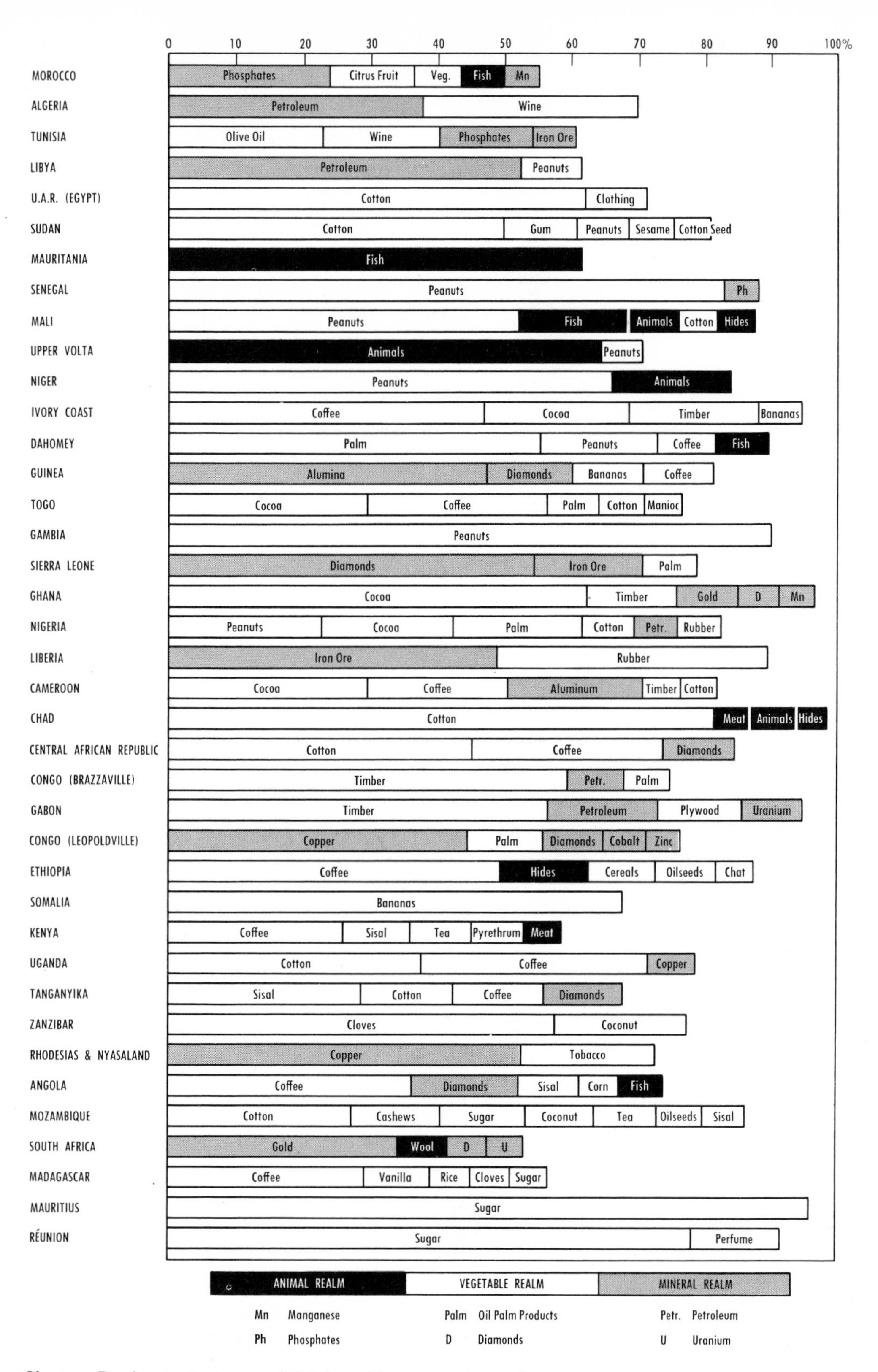

Chart 2. Dominant export commodities from African countries, 1961, as a percentage of total exports by value
Only commodities with 5 percent or over of exports from a country are included.

Table 4. Main exports of Africa and tropical Africa, 1961[a]

	Africa			Tropical Africa		
Rank	Commodity	Percent of total value	Cumulative totals	Commodity	Percent of total value	Cumulative totals
1	Gold	10.3		Copper	13.8	
2	Copper	7.5	17.8	Cocoa	10.8	24.6
3	Cotton	7.3	25.1	Coffee	9.3	33.9
4	Cocoa	5.4	30.5	Peanut products	7.2	41.1
5	Coffee	4.7	35.2	Cotton	7.0	48.1
6	Petroleum	4.7	39.9	Logs and lumber	4.5	52.6
7	Peanut products	4.0	43.9	Palm products	4.4	57.0
8	Diamonds	3.8	47.7	Diamonds	4.2	61.2
9	Wine	3.1	50.8	Tobacco	3.3	64.5
10	Logs and lumber	2.3	53.1	Sugar	2.9	67.4
11	Palm products	2.2	55.3	Rubber	2.0	69.4
12	Sugar	1.9	57.2	Sisal	1.9	71.3
13	Tobacco	1.9	59.1	Gold	1.6	72.9
14	Atomic materials	1.6	60.7	Iron ore	1.4	74.3
15	Fish and products	1.5	62.2	Petroleum	1.2	75.5
16	Phosphates	1.5	63.7	Tea	1.1	76.6
17	Citrus fruit	1.4	65.1	Tin	1.1	77.7
18	Iron ore	1.4	66.5	Bananas	1.0	78.7
19	Hides and skins	1.2	67.7	Hides and skins	0.9	79.6
20	Corn	1.1	68.8	Alumina	0.8	80.4

Source: Compiled from national trade statistics.
[a] See notes at end of Table 3.

There is, of course, considerable variation from territory to territory, as may be seen from Chart 2. Gambia, Niger, Chad, Somalia, and Mauritius have an exceptional dependence on one product; 19 countries have only one commodity represented in the first 50 percent of exports by value; and 30 countries have only two commodities in the first 50 percent of exports. Congo, Kenya, Tanganyika, and Madagascar, as well as the countries of the Maghrib and South Africa outside tropical Africa, have greater variety among their exports. It cannot be said, however, that there is any close correlation between breadth of exports and strength of the economy because several of the more nearly "one-product" countries are considerably healthier than those with multiple exports.

Concern over the fragility of "one-product" economies has led to a variety of measures and programs designed to reduce the impact of their undesirable features. On the one hand, these measures have been applied to the major commodities involved, with the goal of reducing price fluctuations and evening out returns to the primary producer and to the country. On the national scene, there has been introduction of production quotas, controlled marketing, and some control by taxation. On the international level, there has been increased interest in international commodity arrangements designed to stabilize raw material prices. None of these measures has been particularly effective. On the other hand, efforts have been made to diversify the economies of African countries by introduction of new cash crops, building up domestic markets, developing mineral production, attracting new industries, promoting tourism, and so on. While some of these measures are beneficial to individual countries, they may actually increase the difficulties for the continent as a whole, since the new crops or minerals from one area may already be in surplus production from others. Attention is also being given to the upgrading of African produce with the goal of commanding higher prices for what is sold on world markets. All of the measures outlined above may be expected to receive increased attention in the coming decades, and non-African countries are likely to be more strongly persuaded to take steps designed to counteract the impact of unstable conditions in the world market for raw materials.

THE INADEQUATE INFRASTRUCTURE

While commendable progress has been made in developing the basic public services of African countries, in no case is the provision of transportation facilities, power, water supply, communications, and other services adequate. Transport facilities are of such pervasive importance in Africa that they are deserving of special consideration.

TRANSPORTATION

The provision of transport is fundamental to all other forms of development. Substantial improvements have been made in postwar years in this field, which has received much larger allocations than before the war. Table 5 gives a few comparative figures to show the position of Africa in relation to other continental areas. Table 6 reveals the position of individual countries in railway mileage and traffic, road mileage, vehicle numbers, ocean freight movements, and aviation passenger traffic in 1961.

Americans and Europeans are inclined to take transport for granted.[4] They have available well-developed road, rail, air, and waterway systems which offer a choice of routes and of modes of transport. Service is usually regular and is interrupted only by major storms and floods. In these circumstances one forgets the tremendous significance of transport, not only

[4] A part of this section is based upon Chapter 3 in William A. Hance, *African Economic Development* (New York, Harper, 1958), and is used by kind permission of the Council on Foreign Relations.

Table 5. Africa's position in world transport and trade, 1961

	Railway traffic (percent of ton-miles)	*Motor vehicles in use (percent)*	*International seaborne shipping (percent of goods loaded and unloaded)*	*World trade*	
				Imports (percent of total)	*Exports (percent of total)*
Africa	1.8	2.0	5.9	5.6	5.4
South America	1.0	2.3	10.6	5.3	5.1
Asia	11.9	3.4	24.3	12.5	9.7
North America	28.8	62.3	22.4	16.8	21.9
Western Europe	49.4	23.5	34.7	43.2	41.2
Eastern Europe (incl. USSR)	6.6	3.8	—	11.7[a]	11.8[a]
Oceania	0.5	2.7	2.1	3.3	3.2
Unaccounted				1.6	1.7
Total, in percent	100.0	100.0	100.0[b]	100.0	100.0
Total, actual	2,016 billion ton-miles	133 million	2,319 million metric tons	$140.2 billion	$133.4 billion

Sources: U.N., *Statistical Yearbook, 1962* (New York, 1963); compilations from national statistical sources for African exports.

[a] Includes China Mainland.

[b] Eastern Europe (including USSR) not included.

Table 6. Selected transport data for African countries, 1961

	RAILWAYS				ROADS[a]			MOTOR VEHICLES	OVERSEAS SEABORNE FREIGHT		AVIATION TRAFFIC[d]
		Traffic									
Country	Track miles (in miles)	Freight (in million ton-mi.)	passenger (in million pass. mi.)	Locomotives (in units)	Total (in miles)	Paved (in miles)	Third-class tracks (in miles)	(in thousands)	loaded (in thousand M.T.)	unloaded (in thousand M.T.)	passengers loaded and unloaded (in thousands)
Morocco	1,093	1,140	296	106[b]	38,440	6,500	23,300	245	10,116	2,897	212
Algeria	2,608	911	410	284[d]	34,000	5,523	18,000	275	15,112	6,687	1,134
Tunisia	1,256	592	226	145	9,650	4,625	3,650	73	3,605	1,754	162
Libya	213	1	4	20	5,971	3,540	...	31	698	801	71
U.A.R. (Egypt)	2,397	1,273	2,402	1,004	22,000	7.637	4,700	93	6,625	7,259	...
Sudan	2,902	1,084	...	219	30,000	...	...	32	661	1,151	51
Mauritania	419	—	—	...	...	...	...	2	10	142	5
Senegal	615	88	122	79	6,500	600	4,500	38	1,282	2,073	120
Mali	401	...	...	...	6,420	279	5,270	5	—	—	25
Upper Volta[e]	335	—	—	—	9,600	...	6,200	6	—	—	9
Niger	—	—	—	—	5,265	48	3,400	3	—	—	28
Ivory Coast	401	207	201	53	19,300	491	11,925	31	1,431	1,087	74
Dahomey	359	35	41	37	3,230	213	745	5	117	161	16
Guinea	501	25[c]	29[c]	...	4,100	124	...	16	1,455	450	...
Togo	273	4	50	7	2,666	76	1,430	5	57	86	6
Gambia	—	—	—	—	730	50	624	2	67	56	...
Sierra Leone	369	16	61	67	3,600	250	...	12	1,943	757	15
Ghana	762	231	155	194[c]	...	2,014	...	50	2,524	1,924	96
Nigeria	1,887	1,412	481	312	...	6,908	...	71	4,718	3,186	60
Portuguese Guinea	—	—	—	—	2,040	60	1,132	...	...	...	...
Liberia	260	...	...	...	1,163	129	293	8	3,109	372	...
Cameroon	329	84	60	50	8,500	372	4,100	45	678	555	83
Chad	—	—	—	—	11,540	...	11,178	7	—	—	38
Central African Republic	—	—	—	—	10,905	...	6,064	7	—	—	22
Congo (Brazzaville)	497	146	45	52	4,190	124	1,863	8	357	436	98
Gabon	—	—	—	—	2,431	...	1,459	6	1,428	122	53

Congo (Leopoldville)	3,214	1,029[b]	...	482[b]	79,360	960	29,000	61[e]	607	636	...
Rwanda and Burundi	—	—	—	—	6,600	20	...	6[d]	—	—	75
Ethiopia	711	119[f]	41[f]	54[f]	10,700	...	7,800	35	254	266	...
French Somaliland[g]	60				495	...	...	2	1,260	1,327	...
Somalia	—	—	—	—	5,490	390	5,100	6	...	...	5
Kenya	1,872 (Kenya and Uganda)				26,000	746	15,844	74	1,033	1,739	133
Uganda		1,647[h] (Kenya, Uganda and Tanganyika)	2,459[h]	470	13,000	680	...	42	—	—	14
Tanganyika	1,617				27,150	...	8,000	41	711	792	90
Zanzibar and Pemba	—	—	—	—	803	357	...	2	56	86	...
Northern Rhodesia	2,604 (Northern and Southern Rhodesia)	4,186	2,594	424	19,853			48	—	—	...
Southern Rhodesia					36,270	5,000 (Northern Rhodesia, Southern Rhodesia and Nyasaland)	41,000	135	—	—	...
Nyasaland	497	83	...	32	6,896			13	—	—	...
Angola	1,931	...	...	203	21,050	...	17,092	52	1,906	653[d]	44
Mozambique	1,708	1,318	134	250[d]	23,600	...	16,519	50	5,687[k]	4,600[k]	35
South Africa	13,595	25,383	...	3,416	234,000	8,730	...	1,267	9,118	9,539	366
High Comm. Terr.	395	...	...	...	3,600	...	2,400	...	—	—	...
Madagascar	532	85	83	76	16,000	1,200	7,680	42	270	432	137
Réunion	79	2	5	...	1,240	310	...	11	212[d]	260[d]	15
Mauritius	77	5	—	42	807	500	—	15	593	478	...
Total[l]	46,769	41,290	...	...	865,000	57,000	...	2,990	77,760	52,834	...

Sources: Mainly from national statistical sources; also U.N., *Statistical Yearbook, 1961* (New York, 1962).

... = not available. — = nil or insignificant.

[a] Estimates often of questionable validity.

[b] 1957 or 1958.

[c] 1959.

[d] 1960.

[e] Figures for railway traffic and locomotives included under Ivory Coast.

[f] Franco-Ethiopian Railway only; figures apply to whole line.

[g] Figures for railway traffic and locomotives included under Ethiopia.

[h] Includes some lake and road services of E.A.R. and H.

[k] Includes coastwise shipping.

[l] Partly estimated.

in economic life, but in making possible social and political intercourse. One must approach African transportation with an entirely different outlook. Its shortcomings and problems intrude constantly in the study of other matters. There are still vast areas without any regular service, while it would be difficult to claim that any region is adequately served. A few illustrations will show the great power of improved transport to quicken the economic pulse of a region.

Before construction of the Dahomey rail line, carriage of goods from Cotonou to Niamey required 70 days by human porterage. When the line reached Parakou in 1934, the time was reduced to three days, and an air service now covers the route in three to four hours. The transport of 4,200 tons of cereals in the Ivory Coast during World War I required 2,500,000 man days and 125,000 porters. It is estimated that an average African train can perform the work of 15,000–20,000 human porters for one fifth to one tenth the cost, and that one 5-ton truck can replace 500 head bearers. Before the rail line was built in northern Nigeria, two- or four-wheeled carts were used between Zungeru and Kano, requiring 25 days to cover 250 miles at a cost of £42 per ton, and even this service was confined to the dry season. After the line was completed the 25 days were reduced to less than that number of hours.[5] The most spectacular result of this line was a quite unexpected and rapid increase in the export of peanuts, now one of the leading exports of the country.

A more recent example of the high cost of primitive transport is from Kenya. Before a new road was completed in the coastal belt of northern Kenya in 1953, it cost $1.00–$1.75 per ton-mile to bring market crops by porter or by donkey to coastal villages. Trucks now handle this produce at a charge of 50 to 75 cents per ton-mile. The earlier charges effectively confined the production of marketable crops to a belt only six to eight miles inland from the coast, which resulted in premature soil exhaustion in the area. That the cost of transport is still a heavy charge upon remote areas is indicated by the fact that a ton of cement costs four and a half times as much at Niamey as at Dakar.

Almost nowhere in tropical Africa is there a fully integrated transport complex permitting a rational selection of either road, rail, or air transport. Transport has to a considerable degree developed without proper planning. Political factors often outweighed economic considerations, to the detriment of some of the transport agencies, individual territories, and particular regions which were forced to use longer, higher-cost routes than might have been necessary. More recent years have, however, witnessed more rational planning and greater international cooperation and coordination in the field of transportation.

PORTS. Most of Africa is notoriously poor in good natural harbors. The Guinea Gulf countries, Tanganyika, and Somalia were particularly handicapped by the absence of desirable sites for ports. Lighterage ports and surf ports are still important in numerous countries. Some are situated in protected waters, but many are completely open roadsteads, and their piers have more than once been partially or entirely destroyed by storms. In any case, surf loading is slow, expensive, inefficient, and dangerous. Waves frequently preclude working the two end hatches by surf boats, further slowing the operation and requiring special arrangements in loading cargo.

Great progress has been made, however, in improving the port situation of Africa. There are now first-class ports along most coastal stretches, extensions of existing ports are under way, and new ports are being constructed or planned in several territories. It is no longer sound to generalize that African development is hampered by the absence of ports, though certain countries are still handicapped in this regard, and some areas still suffer from congestion in the ports which handle their traffic.

An important feature of postwar port traffic which has contributed to congestion has been

[5] Most of these examples come from R. J. Harrison Church, *Modern Colonization* (London, Hutchinson, 1951), pp. 84, 101, and also "The Transport Pattern of British West Africa," in *Geographical Essays on British Tropical Lands* (London, Philip, 1956), pp. 70–71.

The Stanley *pushing barges loaded with cotton on Lake Kioga, Uganda*
The East African lakes are of some importance as inland waterways, but the long, narrow, steep-sided Rift Valley lakes often impede contact rather than assist it.

the much greater increase in goods landed than in goods embarked from African ports. The tremendous variety of import packages makes them much more difficult to handle than most export cargoes, which typically contain a large proportion of homogeneous produce such as sisal, cocoa, cotton, palm oil, or metallic ores.

Map 6 shows the relative importance of African ports as measured by tonnages handled in 1961.

WATERWAYS. The plateau character of Africa and the high seasonality of precipitation away from the equatorial core have meant that navigable waterways have only limited importance in most African areas. Other handicaps to river transport are the floating vegetation known as "sudd" on the Upper Nile, the water hyacinth which has required intensive control measures on the Congo and parts of the Nile system, and low-hanging vegetation on minor streams. In the north, only the Nile is of importance. In West Africa, the Niger continues to be significant for bulk shipments; the Senegal is only locally important; the Gambia, which might have been a major routeway, has had circumscribed use because of preference by the French for use of the national routes in Senegal. Of considerable benefit to several territories in West Africa are the systems of coastal lagoons and tidal creeks.

In middle Africa, the estuaries and coastal indentations of Cameroon and Gabon are important in floating logs to shipping points. The Congo system is the most important inland waterway of tropical Africa and the natural feeding system of the Matadi-Leopoldville and Brazzaville–Pointe Noire axes. The East African lakes are of some importance in inland navigation, particularly Lake Victoria. The value of the long, narrow, rift-valley lakes can easily be exaggerated, however, for they are, to a considerable degree, impediments to transport rather than aids. Lake Tanganyika, for example, is the only break in a transcontinental rail route from Lobito to Dar es Salaam. A few of the rivers flowing into the Indian Ocean, such as the Zambezi, the Rufiji, and the Tana, are navigable for short stretches, but none are important routeways. In South Africa, inland waterways are almost entirely lacking.

The further development of inland waterways is not a crucial need in improvement of the African infrastructure, though some interesting possibilities present themselves. The blasting of rock shelves can sometimes extend the navigability of streams, as it has below Bangui on the Ubangi. Lock systems may some day permit the elimination of short trans-shipments on the Niger and the Congo. Lakes created by some of the great hydroelectric dams may become locally significant as routeways, in some cases opening up possibilities for the carriage of bulk timber that would not otherwise be practicable.

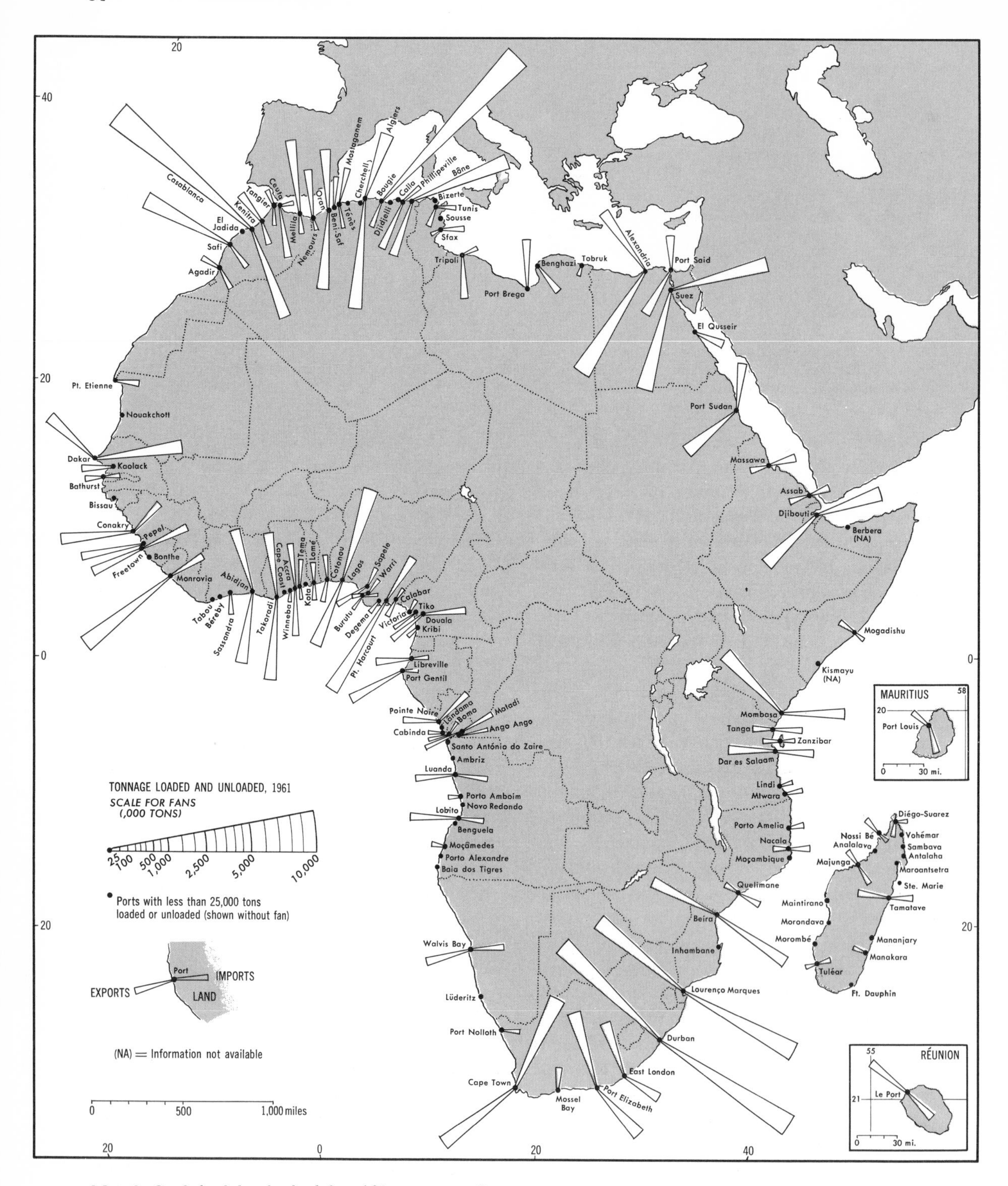

Map 6. Goods loaded and unloaded at African ports, 1961

A road in the Central African Republic near the Sudan border

The need for new and improved roads continues to be a major requirement for African economic development. The road shown here was classified as one of the "seven excellent main roads" of the country in literature distributed by the government.

RAILWAYS. The railway map of Africa is notable chiefly for its emptiness (Map 7). The Maghrib does have a skeletal system and South Africa has at least an embryonic network. But in most areas, single-track routes stretch inland with few branch lines and fewer connecting links with other lines. The only point on the west coast that is connected by rail to the east coast is Lobito; only Beira, Lourenço Marques, and Durban are so connected on the east. However, railways are still the most important means of transport in Africa as far as import and export traffic is concerned though road traffic is growing with greater rapidity. Rail traffic has expanded in Africa more rapidly than in other continental areas with the exception of the USSR, and rail extensions have been built in postwar years in numerous African countries.

There has also been a marked improvement in the efficiency of the railways in Africa, revealed by the fact that there has been a much lower percentage increase in freight rates than for other expenses in postwar years in most countries. But the needs for railway extension and improvement remain very large indeed.

ROADS. It was very roughly estimated that Africa had a total of 865,000 miles of roads in 1961, of which about 57,000 miles were paved. This gives the continent only about 3.5 to 4 percent of the free world's paved highways and streets and 10 percent of its total road mileage. The roads of Africa are inadequately mapped, and information regarding their negotiability is often not available in advance. Thomas has prepared a series of valuable maps on West African routeways,[6] indicating their serviceability on a month-by-month basis, but even such maps can only show average conditions, since the variability of precipitation in most areas of the continent defies accurate forecasting.

On some African maps "main roads" represented by bold red lines often turn out to be more like tracks; on other maps such lines represent planned networks, there being no roads at all where some are indicated. The aptness of the term "road" for some routeways is questionable: the unimproved tracks in Ethiopia have been described as the only roads where pedestrians overtake vehicles.

Roads in the tropical rainy areas are more likely to be built for year-round service because the constant rainfall requires it, but they may still be periodically or even chronically impassable or so rough that only powerful vehicles are capable of using them. Laterite is often a satisfactory surface when traffic is light, having a tendency to harden upon exposure, but it tends to corrugate or break down with heavier use. In areas that are alternately wet and dry, only the roads of greatest importance are likely to be open in the rainy season, and in the dry season it is sometimes more practical and more comfortable to drive alongside the road than in the rutted route. Wadis which are bone dry in the dry period may become raging torrents in the rainy season, but building bridges across them is often not justified at the present level of economic activity. Washouts are a regular occurrence, even on the permanent roads.

[6] Benjamin E. Thomas, *Transportation and Physical Geography in West Africa* (University of California at Los Angeles, Department of Geography, 1960).

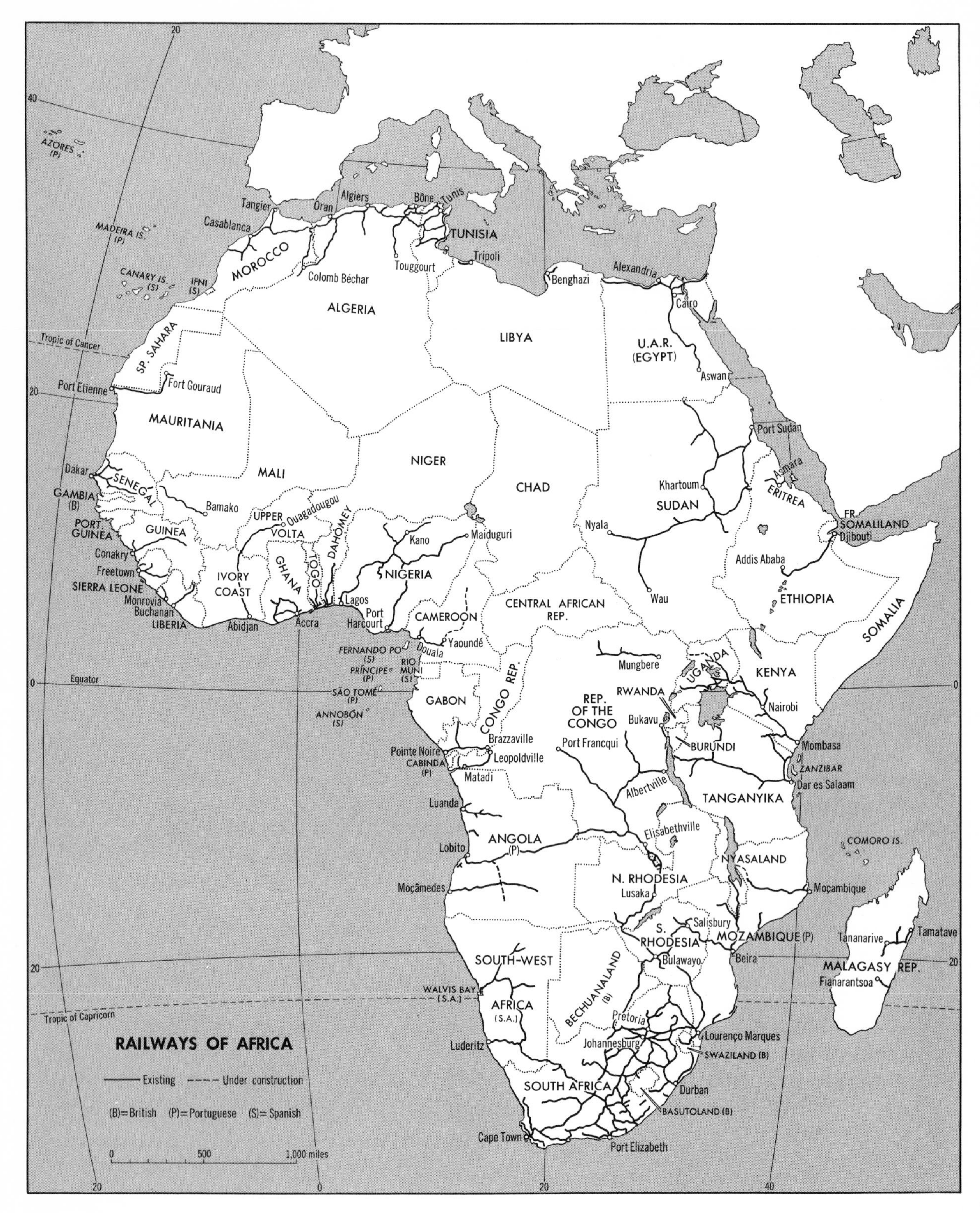

Map 7. Railways of Africa, 1963

In middle Africa it is generally accepted that a car using cross-country roads has a life expectancy of about 40,000 miles. It may go further, but the repair time and expense mount rapidly beyond this approximate level. Dust and dirty gasoline are a menace to vehicles in many areas though great progress has been made in recent years in the bulk handling and retail distribution of gasoline.

Much consideration has been given in postwar years to the comparative costs and values of roads and railroads. The view of many experts was well summarized in an economic report on a proposed north-south rail link between the Rhodesias and East Africa:

> In the past before the advent of the internal combustion engine and the heavy duty road vehicle, development, particularly of the remote areas of Africa, stood or fell on the construction of a rail line.... The railways of the early days of African development were competing with the ox wagon.... It may well be that today the correct approach to the problem is to allow road transport to carry the burden hitherto borne by the low cost line and to postpone rail construction until traffic has begun to build up to such a point that higher standards of rail construction are warranted, and their sound economics assured. A special advantage of road transport, particularly during the early phases of development, lies in its greater flexibility and in the fact that the roads themselves can be constructed and vehicles obtained more quickly.[7]

Yet road construction has also proved more expensive than was thought likely in the immediate postwar years. In Liberia, the average cost per mile for a primary road has been $48,684 in recent years; the cost of a minimum road in that country is set at $18,000 per mile. The average cost of $36,400 per mile of 520 miles of paved and high-standard gravel roads in Tanganyika was considered so high in the early 1950s that it was decided not to build additional roads of this standard, because such an expenditure prevented the improvement and construction of roads serving productive and potentially productive areas. The paved road from Douala to N'Kongsamba in Cameroon cost an average of $117,000 per mile, yet it required major maintenance efforts in 1963. In Ghana, reconstruction of roads to full Public Works Department trunk road standards costs $56,000 to $61,000 a mile. In Ethiopia, preparation of an all-weather road costs about $10,000 per mile. For the future, improved soil stabilization techniques may permit low-cost construction of roads; soil stabilization involves the mixing of cement, lime, bitumen, or synthetic resins with soil to make a more durable and water-resistant surface.

The benefits of improved roads can only be roughly estimated. A recent study suggests that costs per ton-mile can frequently be reduced by 15 percent if a dry-weather road is upgraded to a gravel surface or 25 percent if it is paved.[8]

Only a careful study of each region can reveal the appropriate choice among modes of transport. Water transport, where available, is still normally the cheapest means; railways provide the best transport for bulk and long-distance movements; roads are generally most suitable for shorter-distance hauls and in newly developing regions or areas with a low-productive potential. The average charge of transport in pence per ton-mile in certain West African services is revealing: ocean steamer, 0.33d; the Niger River Fleet, 2.34d; the Nigerian Railway, 2.73d; the Ghana Railway, 3.65d; and the Nigerian Railway road feeder services, 7.25d.[9] The last figure undoubtedly exaggerates the average cost of road transport, because it is confined to a regular service often operating in areas of low traffic density. Trucks have been very successful in carrying goods in the south of Ghana and Nigeria and elsewhere in competition with the railways.

PROBLEMS OF TRANSPORTATION. Many handicaps to the development of transport have been given in this and the first chapter. Size and

[7] Quoted in Territory of Tanganyika, *Development Plan 1955–1960* (Dar es Salaam, Government Printer, 1955), p. 12.

[8] U.N. Economic Commission for Africa, *Transport Problems in Relation to Economic Development in East Africa* (Addis Ababa, July 27, 1962), p. 5.

[9] "Port Capacity and Shipping Turnaround in West Africa," United Africa Company Limited, *Statistical and Economic Review*, No. 19 (March, 1957), p. 10.

distance must be stressed in any discussion of difficulties facing African transport. The continent is 3.22 times the size of the United States; tropical Africa alone is about 2.35 times as large. To provide an integrated transport system for so vast a region is obviously a staggering task. Many of the productive areas are far from the coast; to meet their needs, long routes traversing low-productive regions with poor traffic potential must be constructed. For example, on the western Nigerian line there is practically no freight traffic between Oshogbo, 180 miles from Lagos, and Zaria, at 618 miles. On the eastern line, little traffic develops between Enugu, 151 miles from Port Harcourt, and the Kafanchan junction at 459 miles.[10] A large part of the navigable portions of the lower Niger and the Benue traverse a relatively sparsely populated and low-productive middle savanna belt; it would be much more advantageous to Nigeria if the river tapped the cotton and peanut belts to the north. The Central Tanganyika line traverses great stretches of wasteland in crossing the country from Dar es Salaam to Lake Tanganyika, while the Kenya line produces little seaward freight before Nairobi.

Distance also means time. Therefore, perishable crops cannot be grown for export in some favored areas. Sometimes air transport can meet this problem. Considerable quantities of meat are shipped from steppe areas to the protein-deficit cities of the rainy tropics such as Douala, Brazzaville, and Leopoldville. But air freight, although it has grown tremendously in postwar years, cannot be more than a limited solution. The greatest significance of airways is the annihilation of time in moving people.

African transport has also been plagued with problems of equipment and personnel. Expansion and replacement of power, rolling stock, and facilities proceeded slowly in postwar years. It was often not possible to increase rail capacity simply by using more powerful locomotives because track weights were too light and bridge capacities too low. Congestion at ports and on the railroads contributed to further congestion, for the slower the turn-around time the greater was the need for more trains and ships.

The cost of maintaining African road, rail, and harbor equipment has often been very high. It becomes disproportionately high on short rail lines, especially where there is a variety of locomotives in use. A considerably higher portion of the working life of a locomotive is spent in the repair shops, because of more rapid deterioration under tropical conditions, poor water and fuel consumed, outmoded repair facilities, and inadequately trained engineers. Maintenance difficulties largely explain the switch to diesel engines on numerous African lines in more recent years; dieselization may result in savings of up to 40 or 50 percent in operating and maintenance costs.

Personnel problems go a long way toward explaining the inability of African transport systems to cope with the greatly increased traffic of postwar years. Management has sometimes been unimaginative and shortsighted, failing to develop adequate plans for a continuing growth of traffic. Shortcomings are also present at the middle and lower levels, where inadequate training and lack of interest are often apparent. In a few countries, such as South Africa and the Rhodesias, certain jobs on the railways were reserved for whites, but all too often it was the less qualified whites who were employed. Elsewhere there has been too rapid Africanization, resulting in the assumption of posts by persons who were inadequately prepared to discharge their functions. These difficulties will, of course, be removed in time. Nor should the shortcomings be permitted to obscure the very real achievements that have often been made under most difficult conditions.

Many of the rail lines of tropical Africa "were built as acts of faith in the hope that traffic would later justify the cost."[11] This is true of the nonmineral lines in West Africa. The Central line in Tanganyika was built primarily

[10] R. J. Harrison Church, *West Africa* (London, Longmans, Green & Company, 1957), cited, p. 155.

[11] F. J. Pedlar, *Economic Geography of West Africa* (London, Longmans, Green & Company, 1955), p. 113.

for strategic reasons and the Kenya-Uganda Railway was constructed partially to suppress the slave trade. When sufficient traffic developed it was not difficult to pay interest charges on capital borrowed for construction, but in some cases the rail lines ran at a loss for decades, and many are still a financial drain on their territories. As a consequence, they are sometimes not properly maintained, and the allocation of funds to cover operating costs precludes allotments to other development projects. There frequently was, at least until recent years, a more or less chronic shortage of capital for investment in railways, ports, and roads.

The precarious position of some of the railways, plus the importance of others as sources of governmental income, helps to explain a number of the transport policies adopted by African territories. The preoccupation with railways often resulted in a failure to develop an adequate road network and, more often, in failure to develop an over-all plan in which each means of transport would be used where it was most practical.

In a number of cases, the policy was so weighted in favor of railways that road building was deliberately obstructed or made to follow devious routes that minimized possible competition with railways. Elsewhere, laws and licensing arrangements have been instituted to keep trucks from taking traffic away from the railroads. Sometimes, as in Nigeria, the railways were given tax relief by excusing them from payment of taxes on diesel fuel. In some areas long-standing agreements have bound important users to specific transport routes.

Closely interwoven with the social, economic, and financial factors influencing transport in Africa are strong forces operating to favor national ports, roads, and railways even when extranational routes are cheaper, shorter, or less congested. The techniques employed are highly diverse and often very difficult to uncover. Construction contracts may include clauses requiring shipment by vessels of a specific flag; contracts for purchase of African goods may prescribe the routes of shipment to be followed. There are understandable reasons for the desire to focus upon national routes—support of the territorial economy, assistance to sometimes

Table 7. Production of coal and petroleum in Africa, 1948, 1961, and 1962 (in thousand metric tons)

	Coal production			Petroleum production		
	1948	*1961*	*1962*	*1948*	*1961*	*1962*
Morocco	290	410	370	13	80	127
Algeria	226	78	53	—	15,659	20,508
Libya	—	—	—	—	684	8,097
U.A.R. (Egypt)	—	—	—	2,092	3,819	4,668
Senegal	—	—	—	—	2	...
Nigeria	615	607	634	—	2,303	3,372
Congo (Brazzaville)	—	—	—	—	103	123
Gabon	—	—	—	—	774	827
Congo (Leopoldville)	117	73	...	—	—	—
Tanganyika	—	2	...	—	—	—
Southern Rhodesia	1,696	3,073	2,820	—	—	—
Angola	—	—	—	—	104	471
Mozambique	9	321	...	—	—	—
South Africa	24,017	39,564	41,280	—	—	—
Madagascar	16	2	...	—	—	—
Total	26,986	44,130	...	2,105	23,528	38,195

Source: Same as Table 8. — = None or negligible. ... = Not available.

Table 8. Electricity production and energy consumption in Africa, 1948 and 1961

	ELECTRICITY PRODUCTION				ENERGY CONSUMPTION	
	Total (in millions of kwh)		*Hydro (in millions of kwh)*		*Total (in millions of metric tons of coal equivalent), 1961*	*Per capita (in kg. of coal equivalent), 1961*
	1948	*1961*	*1948*	*1961*		
Morocco	377	1,053	204	951	1.73	145
Algeria	461	1,435	90	344	2.86	254
Tunisia	120	282	...	19	.73	172
Libya	...	110	—	—	.38	307
U.A.R. (Egypt)	...	3,722	—	1,012	7.90	297
Sudan	17	103	—	—	.64	52
Former French West Africa[a]	34	c. 300	...	c. 84	.89	37
Togo	1	6	—	...	.04	28
Gambia	1	6	—	—	.01	41
Sierra Leone	5	50	—	—	.13	52
Ghana	171	390	19	176	.64	92
Nigeria	108	662	57	101	1.71	47
Liberia	10	120	6	20	.08	56
Cameroon	2	920	—	910	.28	66
Former French Equatorial Africa[b]	...	71	—	40	.27	49
Congo (Leopoldville)	497	2,600	...	2,500	1.25	64
Ethiopia	34	124	15	69	.19	9
French Somaliland	1	10	—	—	.02	278
Somalia	...	11	—	—	.05	24
Kenya	59	215	...	132		
Uganda	8	435	—	435	1.64	69
Tanganyika	30	164	17	93		
Zanzibar	2	12	—	—	.02	51
Northern Rhodesia	...	659	...	233		
Southern Rhodesia	230	2,782	—	2,206[c]	3.92	460
Nyasaland	...	35	—	2		
Angola	23	160	—	130	.35	71
Mozambique	39	220	18	110	.82	124
South Africa	9,259	24,556	—	—	43.52	2,414
Madagascar	27	113	—	82	.18	32
Réunion	1	20	—	—	.04	114
Mauritius	16	63	15	20	.08	115
Totals[d]	13,400	43,100	...	9,670	70.37	

Sources: U.N., *Statistical Yearbook, 1962* (New York, 1963); U.N., *Monthly Bulletin of Statistics* (May, 1963); U.N., *World Energy Supplies, 1958–1961* (New York, 1963).

[a] 1961 output of electricity in million kwh was as follows: Senegal, 152; Niger, 9.2; Dahomey, 9.6; Upper Volta, 10; Ivory Coast, 92.8 (of which, hydro 73.8). Output for Mali in 1960 was 15.3. No figures available for Mauritania or Guinea.

[b] 1961 output of electricity in million kwh was as follows: Chad, 9.0; Congo (Brazzaville), 30.9; C.A.R., 9.4 (of which, hydro 9.3); Gabon, 21.7.

[c] Federal Power Board (Kariba).

[d] Includes estimates where data are not given and for countries not listed.

... = Data not available.

— = Nil or negligible.

shakily financed transport companies, and desire to save on expenditure of foreign exchange. But the result has been that some areas have had to pay excessively for their transport services, thus in some degree inhibiting their development.

The shortcomings of African transport are, then, numerous and weighty. The density of routes is typically low, the quality is often inferior, there are shortages of equipment, and there is inadequate planning and coordination within and among the individual countries. The difficulties of ameliorating and eliminating these shortcomings are formidable. Despite the difficulties, however, very considerable progress has been achieved, witness the new ports, rail lines, and roads in every country. Very large expenditures have been made on transport, which usually receives one of the two largest allocations in national and developmental budgets.

But a glance at any modern map of transport routes in Africa reveals the continuing need. Ten countries with a total area of 1.6 million square miles have no railways. Six or seven transshipments are typical in forwarding freight from Europe to Rwanda or Burundi. Congestion is still present in many ports and on many railways. Many regions are not adequately served to permit their operating within the modern exchange economy. Heavy expenditures must obviously continue to be made in the transportation field, on which all basic development must in the last resort depend.

The Komatipoort Electric Station, Republic of South Africa
Africa accounts for less than 2 percent of total world production of electricity. South Africa produces about three fifths of the African total.

OTHER FEATURES OF THE INFRASTRUCTURE

With the exception of the Republic of South Africa, the continent also ranks poorly in other infrastructural aspects, in piped water supply and sewage disposal, telephonic and radio systems, electricity supply, and energy available for industrial enterprises.

The resource position of Africa in energy raw materials was briefly summarized in Chapter II. The picture with regard to production and consumption of energy in selected years is given in Tables 7 and 8. Table 9 reveals the energy position of Africa in the world, showing its very minor share of production and consumption. In output of electricity, Africa accounts for only 1.75 percent of the world total, and one country, South Africa, produces about three fifths of the African total. In per capita consumption of energy, only South Africa, with 172 percent of the world average, rates favorably. The Rhodesias and Nyasaland rank second, with a per caput consumption about a third of the world average. Most tropical African countries have less than 5 percent of the world figure.

The characteristic position with regard to energy production and consumption varies among territories according to their mining and industrial development. Where these activities are important, a few large consumers, particularly those concerned with the processing of

Table 9. African energy production and consumption as a percentage of world totals, selected years, 1948–1961

	1948	*1953*	*1961*
Coal	1.91		2.26
Petroleum	.43		2.05
Electric energy	1.60		1.75
Total energy production		1.15	1.58
Total energy consumption		1.50	1.41
Per capita consumption		20.1	22.1

Source: U.N., *Statistical Yearbook, 1962* (New York, 1963).

minerals, are likely to account for a high percentage of the total. In predominantly agricultural countries, aside from the fuels consumed in transportation, the consumption is represented by power plants confined to the leading cities. In Nigeria, for example, there were only 30 cities with electric power plants in 1961 and 34.7 percent of the total output served the capital city, Lagos.

A few countries have had spectacular rates of increase in electricity production in recent years. The experience of Uganda, whose production rose from 8 million kwh in 1948 to 278 million kwh in 1958 and 435 million kwh in 1961, reveals both an unrequited demand that previously existed and the attraction of power for new industrial pursuits. With the enormous hydroelectric resources of Africa, and considering the low stage of present development, it is reasonable to expect marked advances in energy production in the future.

SHORTAGES OF CAPITAL AND SKILL

Another major characteristic of African economies is the inadequacy of capital resources and of skill. The situation regarding sources of capital varies markedly from country to country with respect to both public and private funds. One thing that is clear is that the formidable character of African development problems requires securing contributions from all sources. Governments alone are incapable of expending amounts adequate to achieve desired expansion rates; economies are not likely to grow unless the private sectors in agriculture, trade, industry, and mining are improving. Indeed, private industry is needed to pay for government expenses which face marked increases to meet rising social requirements.

In British African territories and former territories, fiscal policy has aimed at accumulating public savings in the form of budgetary surpluses, marketing board funds, and certain reserve funds from prosperous years. Before the war, it was policy that each territory pay its own way in so far as possible. In postwar years, however, substantial assistance has been provided under the Colonial Development and Welfare Acts (CD and W) and through the Colonial Development Corporation (CDC). After independence, a country is no longer eligible for CD and W funds except for completion of projects under way; in 1961–62 CD and W expenditures in Africa totaled $31.6 million. The CDC, which has since been renamed the Commonwealth Development Corporation and which can initiate projects in independent countries, had commitments totaling $168 million in Africa in early 1963. In 1961–62, $46.8 million was made available for participation in such developments as electricity generation, water supply, housing, industrial assistance, land development, and plantations. Five independent members of the Commonwealth (Nigeria, Ghana, Sierra Leone, Tanganyika, and Uganda) had been offered $110.6 million in Commonwealth Assistance Loans by the end of 1962, while $44.8 million in government loans for specific development projects was extended to dependent territories in 1961–62. Special grants are also made to countries becoming independent. Technical assistance includes substantial programs for training of Africans in Britain, provision of 262 specialized advisers from Britain (1962) under short-term programs, and meeting the additional costs of retaining expatriate public servants in the independent East African countries.

The total foreign aid of the United Kingdom in 1962 was about $504 million, but less than half of this went to Africa. While Britain's aid expenditures compare unfavorably with those of France, there has been a much greater private investment over the years in present and former British African areas. Trade policies and the larger British market also gave greater stimulus to development. The results may be roughly measured by the superior infrastructure and greater economic output of most British-connected areas. In 1960 the Special Commonwealth African Assistance Plan was set up, which has elicited aid from non-African members of the Commonwealth, including a $10 million three-year grant from Canada.

In postwar years France has contributed more than any other metropolitan power to the development of its African territories, and it has continued to be the largest supplier of foreign aid following independence. In the 1950s public capital from France accounted for three fourths of the total funds available for capital formation in French territories, financing over four fifths of new investment in the public sector and over two fifths of the total capital formation of the territories. In 1961 it was estimated that France allotted 2.41 percent of its gross national product to foreign aid as compared to 1.32 percent for the United Kingdom, and 0.97 percent for the United States. In 1962 France extended about $327 million to the former French territories south of the Sahara and to Madagascar, in addition to large-scale aid to North Africa, especially Algeria, and subventions to French Somaliland and Réunion. Independent countries which were formerly part of the French Community are aided through "contractual cooperation," the bulk of funds being assigned to the Fund for Aid and Cooperation (FAC) and administered by the Central Bank for Economic Cooperation (CCCE). Unlike most other countries, former French territories often receive direct subventions to current budgetary expenditures. In addition, they receive preferences ranging from about 8 to 15 percent on most commodities and guaranteed market quotas for some staples at prices well above world prices. Some aid, particularly in the military and transport fields, comes directly from the metropolitan budget. In 1961 some 25,345 French were taking part in technical aid to all African countries; in mid-1962 there were about 8,500 French technical assistants in Africa south of the Sahara and Madagascar. The most difficult problems in the years ahead will be moving away from the closed-circuit character of Franco-African trade to conform to the goals of the European Economic Community and withdrawing from direct budgetary subventions, which are likely to be considered as neocolonialist.

The Bank of India, Kampala, Uganda
Most banks in Africa are branches of banks with headquarters on other continents. East Africa has adequate banking facilities for present requirements, but the financial infrastructure of some areas is poorly developed.

Congo, the Rhodesias and Nyasaland, and South Africa financed a large proportion of development expenditures by borrowing abroad, while reinvestment of earnings by the larger companies has also been important. Internal savings in Belgian Africa were $215 million in 1950 and $170 million in 1958; external contributions grew in these years from $61 million to $86 million. From 1958 to independence, declining Congo revenues forced Belgium to contribute more heavily to the development budget. It is quite likely that Belgian contributions to Congo will increase as the U.N. operation is phased out, but Belgium is reluctant to participate in any program which might subject her to the charge of neocolonialism.

Development in Portuguese Africa was largely financed by earnings of the overseas territories, but Portugal has made increasing contributions in recent years under the joint six-year plans for metropolitan and overseas areas. Portugal's ability to extend aid is limited, however, while its policies are not conducive to attracting help from other nations. Should Portugal be forced by developments in Africa to change its general attitude regarding independence there will be a need for large-scale aid from other sources.

Aid from international agencies and from

nonmetropolitan countries has increased with some rapidity in recent years and may be expected to rise even more rapidly as more African countries become independent.

The United States extended its first direct aid under the Point Four program in 1949, though almost every dependent country in tropical Africa had been aided indirectly before that under the Marshall Plan. In the period 1945–62, Africa received about 1.8 percent of the total of $97.7 billion allotted to foreign aid. The percentages of total net overseas credits and grants in recent years have been 3.3 percent in 1959–60 and 8.5 percent in fiscal 1962. The aid in 1963 totaled about $400 million as compared with $267 million in 1961. Aid is not likely to increase markedly in the immediate future, particularly if the 1963 recommendations of the Clay Committee are accepted. That committee noted that security interests are less evident in Africa than elsewhere and that Africa is an area where western European countries should bear most of the aid burden. The minor part of U.S. exports taken by Africa, only 4.3 percent of the total in 1961, also decreases interest to a degree. American private investment in Africa is about 3 percent of the overseas total. About 44 percent of the total of $925 million U.S. private investment in Africa in 1960 was in petroleum; another 27 percent was in mining and smelting.

Western European countries other than the colonial powers have substantially increased contributions to Africa in recent years, particularly West Germany and Italy. Other free-world assistance has come from Egypt, Israel, and Nationalist China. In 1960 or 1961, Egypt extended $11 million each to Somalia and Mali and $17 million to Guinea. It has also provided a considerable number of teachers and religious workers, while some 1,100 students from other African countries are on scholarships in Egypt. Israel has compiled an excellent record for effective aid in the field of technical assistance. In 1962 most of its $20 million direct aid to Africa represented salaries for over 400 technical experts assigned in Africa or scholarships for students from 20 African countries, whose numbers increased from 250 in 1959 to 1,150 in 1962. Aid from Nationalist China began in 1960 and has accelerated in succeeding years. It has included the establishment of a successful model rice farm in Liberia, help with irrigation in Dahomey, instruction on tuna fishing in Madagascar, and training in rice cultivation on Formosa of 25 Africans from eleven countries.

Aid from Communist-bloc nations has involved grants, low-interest, long-term loans, technical assistance, and provision of scholarships for students attending universities in those countries. Aid has been concentrated in a number of countries, especially Algeria, Egypt, Ethiopia, Guinea, Mali, and Ghana. The Soviet Union, in particular, has not proved very effective in its assistance to African nations, even in those countries where it was most openly welcomed. Complaints have included the inappropriateness of equipment for tropical conditions, the lack of convertibility of Eastern currencies, language barriers, and efforts at political subversion. As of early 1963 only $2 million of a $100 million loan to Ethiopia had been drawn, none of the turn-key factories that had been promised Ghana had been delivered, and relations had weakened with many of the recipient nations, including Guinea and Egypt. It would be unrealistic, however, to expect that the Communist nations would not benefit from their mistakes or that they would fail to take advantage of new possibilities which may develop in Africa.

Multilateral aid has been particularly important from the European Economic Community (EEC) and from the U.N. Associate members of the EEC (see Map 18) received a total of about $486 million in the five years ending with 1962 through the European Development Fund. Signing of a new convention of association between the EEC and the 18 independent African associated countries, slated for late 1962 when the first agreement expired, was delayed in protest against France's vetoing the invitation to the United Kingdom to join the EEC. The Development Fund will, however, probably have about $620 million available in the five-year period to 1968 for grants and $110 million in loans for African states. About 60 percent of expenditures has thus far been allocated to economic projects, of which transport and communications accounted for two thirds of the total, and 40 percent has gone to social projects, particularly for health and education. Allocations by the member states are supposed to be over and above their normal aid commitments.

The Development Assistance Group (DAG), formed in 1960 by what is now the Organization for Economic Cooperation and Development, has as its purpose the promotion of greater commitments to aid of underdeveloped areas and the coordination of planning of aid programs.

Some nine U.N. agencies are contributing to African development in one way or another, including the Technical Assistance Board, the Special Fund, and the International Bank for Reconstruction and Development (IBRD or World Bank). Africa's share in U.N. technical assistance increased from 10 percent in 1956 to 20.2 percent in 1961; expenditures for this form of aid to Africa totaled $6.3 million in 1961 and about $9 million in 1962. The Special Fund concentrates on surveys and studies of pre-investment projects which might later attract capital investment. The IBRD is now the world's most important source of multilateral development aid; from its formation in 1946 to 1961 its loans totaled $5.67 billion of which 14 percent went to Africa. From 1950 to April, 1963, it made 43 loans to 16 African countries totaling $954 million. Loans are heavily concentrated on transport, electric power, and industry, but several more recent loans have been made to aid African agricultural advancement. The Bank has two affiliates. The International Development Association, started in 1961, makes long-term no-interest or low-interest rate loans to projects which may be expected to require a relatively long period to become self-liquidating; from June, 1961, to March, 1963, it made four loans in Africa totaling $34.3 million. The second affiliate, the International Finance Corporation, is designed to help finance private enterprise; as of mid-1963 it had invested or loaned $7.8 million in Africa for three projects. The World Bank has assumed important functions beyond that of extending loans. Its country studies have provided valuable guidelines for economic planning; its Economic Development Institute provides high-level instruction to senior officials of member countries concerned with economic development; and it has even become involved in the mediation of international economic disputes including settlements arising from the Suez incidents of 1956.

It is obvious that a multiplicity of agencies and nations are now concerned with assisting African development through grants, loans, provision of technical assistance, etc. In fact, one of the criticisms of aid programs is their excessive number. It is extremely difficult for a small underdeveloped country to know which agency to approach for assistance and to maintain adequate liaison with the multitude of national and international aid organizations.

The importance of governmental and multilateral assistance should not be permitted to obscure the significance of private investment, even if the public sector usually accounts for 50 percent or more of total investment. The high requirements for types of economic and social developments which are not likely to attract foreign private capital explain the significance of public investment. But all African countries have taken steps to encourage private investment, including constitutional stipulations regarding payment in the event of nationalization, formulation of laws designed to attract foreign enterprise, and organization of governmental assistance boards. Some countries are prepared to participate in specific projects as an inducement to the inflow of foreign capital. Just how significant foreign private investment proves to be will depend in large part on the assessment of the climate for investment in specific countries; it does appear, however, despite anticolonialist and anticapitalistic emanations from some countries, that there is increasing awareness on the part of African governments of the need to increase funds from private sources, to create more favorable conditions for expatriate participation in commerce and industry.

Turning to the other great shortage, that of skill, it should be noted that this applies to workers, entrepreneurs, technicians, and managers. Until very recently almost all major managerial and technical posts have been held by non-Africans. In the newly independent countries, the top government jobs are being filled by Africans with increasing rapidity, as are the administrative posts on a local and regional level, but there continues to be heavy reliance on expatriates in scientific and technical work, in education, and in advisory managerial capacities. The transitional period from predominantly European to African management is a most difficult one and has been marked by a temporary running-down in the efficiency of governmental operations. In fact, an international symposium on the economic development problems of Africa held in Nyasaland in mid-1962 concluded that the biggest obstacle to African development at the present time is African inexperience in the political, administrative, and industrial fields.

The basic features of the Africans among the economically active population are lack of specialization, a small but growing number of skilled persons, and a high degree of occupational instability. The last feature is reflected both in the rapidity of job changes in urban areas and in the large number of migrant workers employed in agriculture, mining, and industry. In South Africa, for example, it is estimated that 45 percent of the able-bodied males are outside the reserves; in the Rhodesias and Nyasaland, 60–70 percent are away from the indigenous villages at one time or another during the year.

The resolution of these problems may be expected to accelerate as rates of turnover in employment decrease, as educational facilities expand, and, in the territories where they exist or existed, as various bars to African advancement are removed. But skill is only acquired in time, and it will take many years to build up a cadre of skilled workers, technicians, engineers, and other trained personnel. Thus the inadequacy of skilled persons will remain a major problem for at least several decades.

THE ISLANDIC PATTERN OF ECONOMIC ACTIVITY

The final characteristic of African economies to be discussed in this chapter is the distributional pattern of economic activity. Available data do not permit mapping the entire modern economy, but a map prepared by the author and two colleagues[12] showing the source areas of exports from tropical Africa presents a visual picture from which one can obtain quickly an impression of the relative importance of various regions. Since the export economies of tropical Africa represent a high percentage of the total money economies of the area the map gives a fairly good idea of the important economic regions of that area, particularly if it is supplemented by a map of urban areas which shows the main commercial, administrative, and industrial centers. Map 8, based upon the export map cited above but extended to other areas of Africa, is intended to portray the more significant modern productive regions of the continent. Map 10 depicts the cities of Africa with over 30,000 people.

The map of economic regions displays a pattern of productive "islands" often set in vast seas of emptiness. There is no solid frontier such as characterized the economic opening of North America or Australia. There is great unevenness in the size and distribution of these "islands" and the individual nodes are often either completely separated from each other or joined by only very tenuous links. These "islands" may be classified into a limited number of categories.

The coastal or peripheral "islands" provide one of the dominant patterns of important economic areas, a pattern which is heavily reinforced

[12] William A. Hance, Vincent Kotschar, and Richard J. Peterec, "Source Areas of Export Production in Tropical Africa," *The Geographical Review* (October, 1961), pp. 487–99, with map in rear pocket.

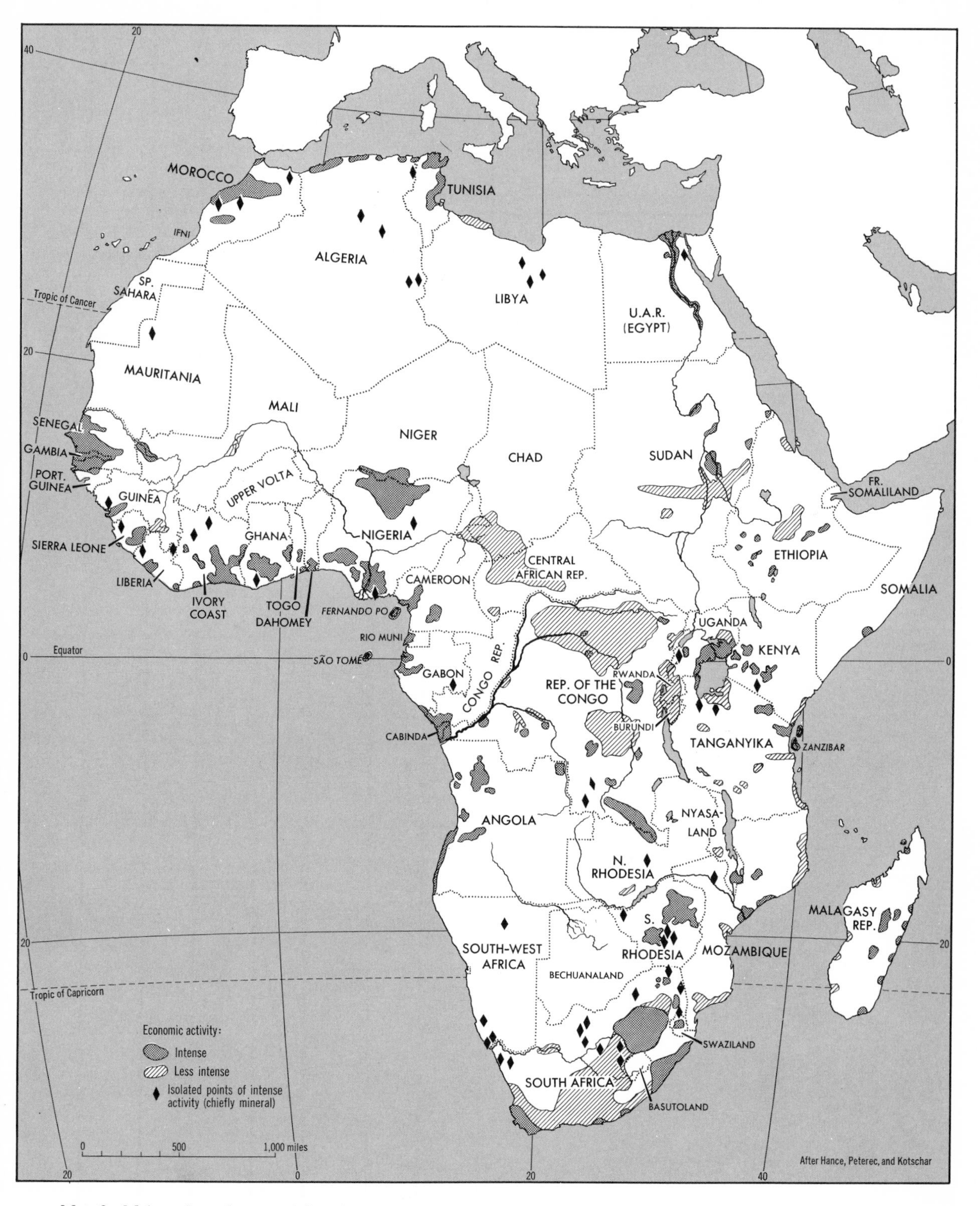

Map 8. Main regions of commercial production in Africa

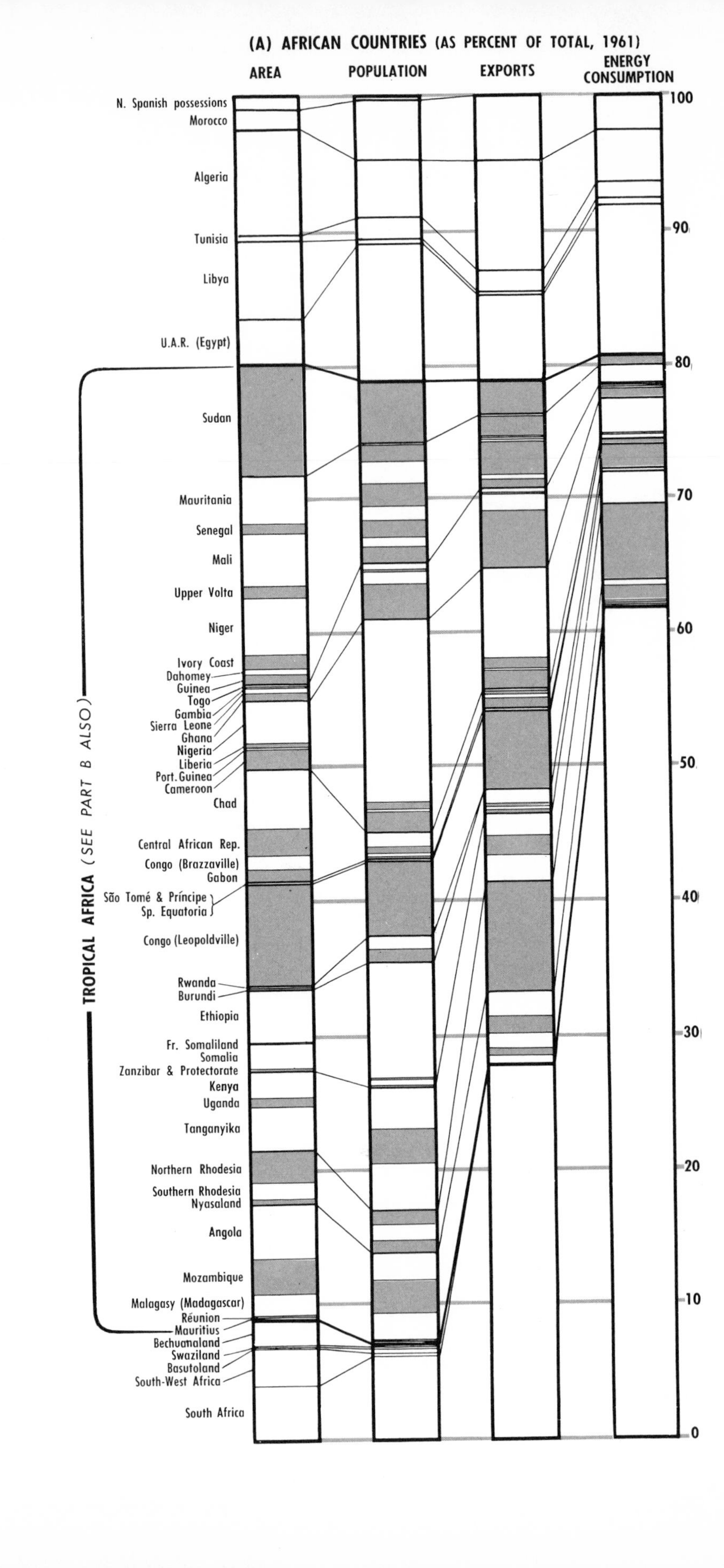
(A) AFRICAN COUNTRIES (AS PERCENT OF TOTAL, 1961)
AREA
POPULATION
EXPORTS
ENERGY CONSUMPTION
N. Spanish possessions
Morocco
Algeria
Tunisia
Libya
U.A.R. (Egypt)
Sudan
Mauritania
Senegal
Mali
Upper Volta
Niger
Ivory Coast
Dahomey
Guinea
Togo
Gambia
Sierra Leone
Ghana
Nigeria
Liberia
Port. Guinea
Cameroon
Chad
Central African Rep.
Congo (Brazzaville)
Gabon
São Tomé & Príncipe
Sp. Equatoria
Congo (Leopoldville)
Rwanda
Burundi
Ethiopia
Fr. Somaliland
Somalia
Zanzibar & Protectorate
Kenya
Uganda
Tanganyika
Northern Rhodesia
Southern Rhodesia
Nyasaland
Angola
Mozambique
Malagasy (Madagascar)
Réunion
Mauritius
Bechuanaland
Swaziland
Basutoland
South-West Africa
South Africa
TROPICAL AFRICA (SEE PART B ALSO)
100
90
80
70
60
50
40
30
20
10
0

by the high percentage of important cities which are coastal points. It is estimated that 18.3 percent of tropical African exports in 1957 came from within 50 miles of the coast, 29.5 percent from within 100 miles. Conversely, possibly the most striking feature in the entire pattern is the emptiness of the vast, remote areas.

Perhaps the most important explanation for this group of "islands" is the factor of accessibility, the relative ease of moving goods to export points. But the factor of climate is also of great importance. Rainforest climate areas occur along the Guinea Gulf coast, providing areas ecologically suitable for the production of cocoa, robusta coffee, bananas, palm oil, timber, rubber, and other products. The historical fact of earlier contact may be credited for some of the significance of coastal areas. The cool Benguela Current helps to explain exports of fish from the Angolan coast. And finally, the division of Africa into numerous political units led to efforts by each metropole to produce the various tropical products from its own territories, a factor helping to account for the pattern along the coasts of West Africa, including the way in which empty areas often coincide with boundary lines.

A second category, the highland "islands," is explained by a variety of factors: rich volcanic soils; ameliorated temperature and humidity; lower incidence of insects and disease; attractiveness for white settlement; greater population densities; and ecological suitability for the production of high value crops such as coffee, particularly arabica coffee, tea, tobacco, and pyrethrum. Almost a quarter of the value of animal and vegetable exports of tropical Africa is estimated to come from tropical highland climate areas.

There are a few areas classified as irrigation "islands," where the intensity permitted through irrigation is the prime factor in their importance. Often, too, these areas have excellent azonal soils. The Nile floodplain and Delta, irrigated areas in the Maghrib and South Africa, and the Gezira in the Sudan, the only outstanding irrigated area in tropical Africa, are important examples of irrigation "islands."

Mineral output is usually characterized by high productivity in a limited area. The so-called mineral "islands" may, therefore, consist of only one mine, though several are considerably larger and produce a variety of minerals. While the mining of relatively low value minerals such as iron ore, phosphates, and bauxite is favored by closeness to the coast and it is the more accessible bodies of these minerals which have been opened up, much of African mineral production comes from places far in the interior. This is disadvantageous to the mining industries themselves but it has benefited the regions involved by justifying far better transport services than would otherwise be expected and by providing funds for social and economic development which certainly could not have come so quickly from agricultural improvements.

There are a few producing areas of importance which do not fit into the four classifications given above: southeast Sierra Leone, the peanut and cotton areas of northern Nigeria, the cotton belt of the Central African Republic and Chad, the vegetable producing areas of the Congo Basin, and the belt of gum arabic, grain, peanut, and animal product exports in central Sudan. A complex of factors explains their importance, among which the availability of transport plays a decisive role. The unusual dispersion of production in the Congo Basin reflects the availability of an extended network of inland waterways. The rather large area of sparse production in Chad and the Central African Republic is explained in part by early administrative requirements regarding the planting of cotton by peasant cultivators.

Chart 3 shows the relative position of African countries in area, population, and two key economic criteria, consumption of energy and value of exports, providing an incomplete but nonetheless valuable index to the present level of economic development of the many national entities on the continent.

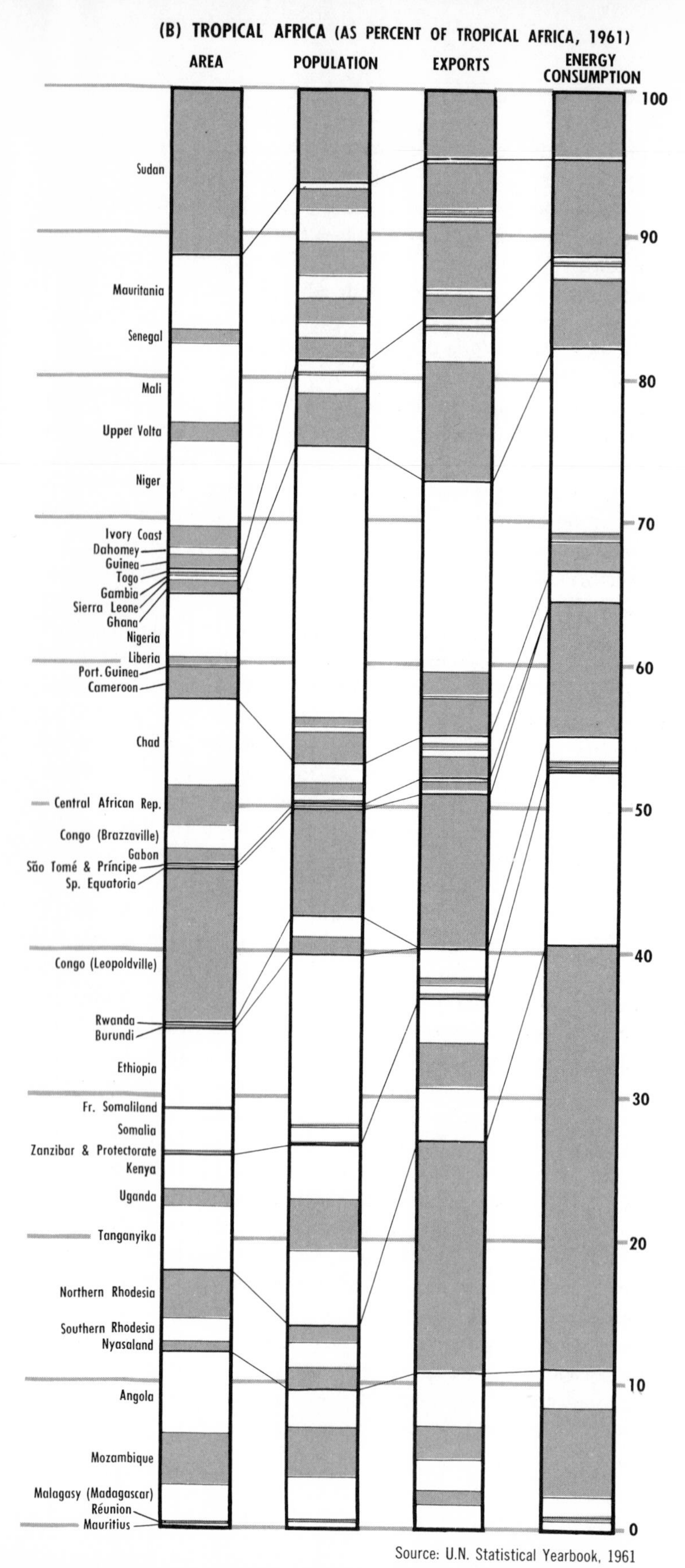

Chart 3. The comparative position of African countries in area, population, energy consumption, and exports, 1961

CHAPTER FOUR

The Population and Peoples of Africa

The population of Africa in 1961 was probably somewhere between 260 and 290 million. No accurate figure can be given because no censuses have ever been taken in many areas and some that have been taken cannot be accepted as reliable. Estimates for some countries are no more than sheer administrative guesses. Where censuses have been taken in recent years for the first time the prior estimates have characteristically been revealed as low, sometimes by as much as 20–25 percent.

Obtaining accurate demographic data is beset by great difficulties in many African areas. There are no base maps upon which a proper census must be based; there is a shortage of personnel trained in modern survey methods; and governments have frequently been loath to allot the funds and administrative talent required. The response of Africans also sometimes precludes accurate results. In a Brazzaville survey, for example, one man claimed to be 430 years old, another to be 35 and to have a 30-year-old son. One tribal group refused to have data recorded on forms of a particular color, and in one location where the individuals had no final names there were 2,000 persons with the same name. Elsewhere, Africans believe that it is sacrilegious or unlucky to count anything, while many fear that the census taker is simply securing data to justify the imposition of higher taxes.

Pons, in writing about a social survey in Stanleyville, reported a generally favorable reception but that

> In a number of cases interviewees expressed fears concerning the motives of the investigation. Often these were in the realm of the supernatural. There were people who thought that the sponsors of the investigation were too friendly to be "normal" Europeans and that they were ancestral spirits who, having lost touch with their descendants, were seeking to re-establish contact; others expressed the fear that by answering questions they were being recruited to work in Europe after death.[1]

In 1962 the Nigerian census ran into difficulties because of accusations that regional totals had been exaggerated to gain increased representation in the Federal legislature. Political considerations also prevented publication of census figures in Liberia.

POPULATION DENSITIES

If a total of 263 million is taken as the population of Africa in 1961, this gives an over-all density of 22.6 per square mile, the second lowest of any inhabited continent. It is frequently held that Africa is sparsely populated. In the U.N. *Survey of Africa since 1950* it is stated that "in tropical and southern Africa, except for a few specific cases, the population in relation to land resources is sparse" (p. 1); and in the Northwestern University report to the Senate Committee on Foreign Relations the following statement appears: "Subsaharan Africa . . . is but lightly peopled, so that the question of pressure of population against the land enters only in a few regions."[2]

[1] V. G. Pons, "The Growth of Stanleyville and the Composition of Its African Population," in UNESCO, *Social Implications of Industrialization and Urbanization in Africa South of the Sahara* (Paris, 1956), p. 249.

[2] Senate Committee on Foreign Relations, *United States Foreign Policy, Africa: A Study by Program of African Studies Northwestern University*, No. 4 (October 23, 1959), p. 18.

These claims may overstate the case. Of course, there are great difficulties in defining overpopulation. Should it be calculated on the basis of existing practices or on known and potential improvements? How much allowance should be made for absorption in such activities as industry, mining, and services? What standard of living should be envisaged? And how productive is the soil of Africa?

Admittedly basing my results on subjective analysis, but trying to be reasonably conservative, I would estimate that 28 percent of the whole continent is now overpopulated and, more important, that 38 percent of the present population resides in overpopulated areas. Areas considered to be overpopulated include most of Mediterranean Africa, discontinuous belts in the steppe and coastal regions of West Africa, many of the highland areas of eastern Africa, Rwanda and Burundi and adjacent parts of Congo, Nyasaland, Basutoland, Mauritius, and Réunion.

Map 9 shows the distribution of population in Africa. Closer analyses will be made in regional chapters, but it may be noted here that there are numerous anomalies discernible in the over-all pattern. While the effect of aridity is quite apparent in the low population of the Sahara and Namib deserts and the steppes of East Africa and the Kalahari, other areas with long dry seasons have unexpectedly high densities, such as parts of northern Nigeria, the Mossi country of Upper Volta, Senegal, and Gambia. Savanna lands, with longer rainy seasons, typically have lower densities than the steppes. Rainy tropical areas show great variation, parts of the West African belt being densely populated, while the bulk of the rainforest belt of Cameroon, Gabon, and the two Congos has low densities.

RURAL AND URBAN DISTRIBUTION

Africa is the least urbanized of all the continents. The rural population of most countries exceeds 80 percent of the total. South Africa and Egypt stand out as important exceptions, with from 32.9 to 45.6 percent of their populations urbanized. The Maghrib, both because of its traditional Muslim cities and because of the significance of its modern development, also has a relatively high percentage of its population residing in cities, about 23 percent in 1961 in cities of 30,000 and over. Nigeria has a special situation in tropical Africa owing to the great number of large Yoruba towns, but still has only about 11 percent of its total population in centers of over 30,000. In Africa as a whole, 13 percent of the total population resided in cities of over 30,000 in 1961, while 9.2 percent inhabited cities of over 100,000. For tropical Africa the comparable figures were about 6.8 percent and 4.0 percent.

Except for northern Africa, where numerous cities have existed for centuries, the growth of urban communities is a very recent phenomenon. Table 10 illustrates this point for a number of African cities. The estimates included in this table must be taken with considerable caution because accurate data are rarely available and it is not always clear whether the city proper or its agglomeration is being numbered. The recency of growth, not only in tropical Africa but in the modern cities of the Maghrib, is tied to the establishment of public administration, to the growth of nonindigenous enterprises, and to the growth of exchange economies. Non-African populations are usually heavily concentrated in the cities and have an impact on them far greater than their percentage of the country populations would suggest.

A complex of advantages and disadvantages is associated with the rise of urbanism in Africa. On the one hand, it tends to expedite the evolution to a modern economy, to loosen the hold of traditional beliefs and values, to permit a greater degree of specialization through the acquiring of new skills, to provide incentive for developing more diversified economies, and to develop concentrated markets for domestic produce. On the other hand, it may lead to the development of bidonvilles and shanty towns; in some cases it subjects the urbanite to new forms of discrimination; it favors inflationary prices and construction; and it may result in

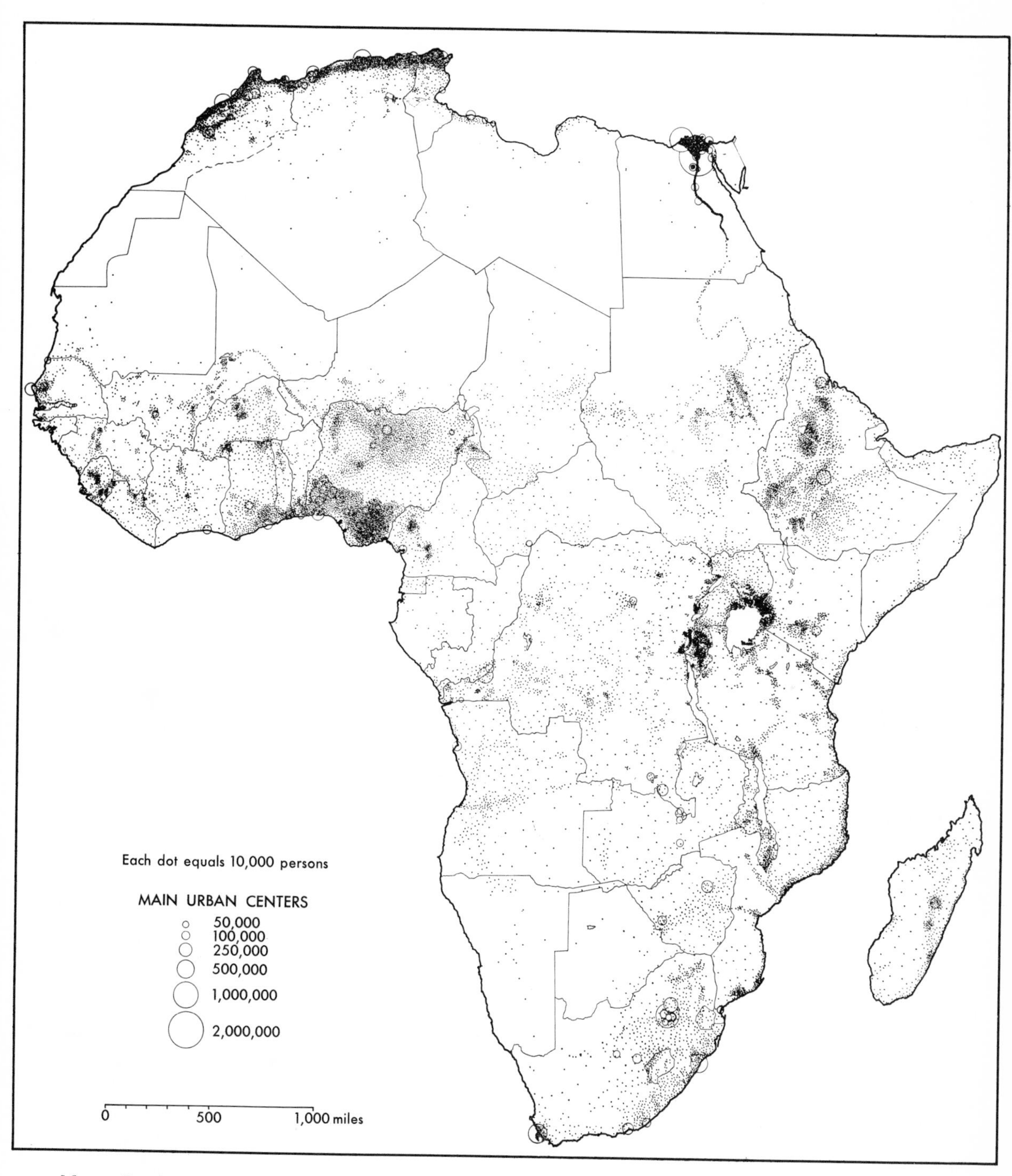

Map 9. Population distribution of Africa
Courtesy University of Stellenbosch

Table 10. Estimated population of selected African cities, 1900–1962 (population in thousands)

	1900–9		*1910–19*		*1920–29*		*1930–39*		*1940–49*		*1950–59*		*1960–62*	
City	*Yr.*	*Pop.*	*Yr.*	*Pop.*	*Yr.*	*Pop.*	*Yr.*	*Pop.*	*Yr.*	*Pop.*	*Yr.*	*Pop.*	*Yr.*	*Pop.*
NORTHERN AFRICA														
Casablanca							1936	257			1952	682	1960	961
Algiers							1936	264	1948	489			1960	834
Tunis							1936	220	1946	365	1956	410	1960	748
Alexandria							1937	686	1947	919	1959	1,335	1962	2,000
Cairo							1937	1,312	1947	2,091	1959	2,852	1962	3,500
SUB-SAHARAN AFRICA														
Khartoum-Omdurman	1905	77			1928	123	1938	176	1948	210	1956	235	1960	315
Dakar	1904	18	1910	25			1936	92	1945	132	1955	300	1960	383
Bamako			1910	7			1931	20	1945	37	1955	68	1960	120
Bobo Dioulasso			1910	8			1931	11	1945	28	1955	45	1960	45
Conakry			1910	6			1936	13	1945	26	1951	50	1960	113
Freetown									1947	65	1959	100	1960	125
Abidjan			1910	1			1936	17			1955	127	1960	180
Accra	1901	18			1921	19	1931	61					1960	491
Kumasi			1911	19							1955	75	1960	190
Cotonou			1910	2			1931	8	1945	19	1955	57	1961	68
Lagos	1901	18	1910	74	1921	100	1931	127			1955	270	1960	364
Ibadan	1900	210					1931	387			1952	459	1960	600
Kano	1903	30					1931	89					1960	176
Douala							1931	28			1954	118	1961	150
Brazzaville							1936	24			1959	100	1961	129
Leopoldville	1908	5			1923	18	1935	27	1946	110	1955	340	1961	420
Elisabethville					1923	16	1935	23			1959	184	1961	190
Addis Ababa	1908	35			1928	70	1938	300					1961	449
Mombasa	1906	30			1926	40			1948	85			1960	190
Nairobi	1906	12			1928	30			1948	119	1959	248	1962	267
Dar es Salaam	1906	25					1931	23	1948	69	1957	129	1962	140
Salisbury							1931	26			1956	168	1961	300
Bulawayo					1927	27			1946	53	1959	190	1961	195
Luanda					1923	23	1930	51			1955	190	1960	220
Lourenço Marques	1907	10			1927	37	1935	47			1950	94	1961	184
Johannesburg							1931	283			1957	1,030	1960	1,097
Tananarive	1900	50			1925	70			1945	142			1960	248

heavy unemployment with accompanying problems of prostitution, corruption, and indebtedness. Furthermore, the local economies are often slow in rising to the new opportunities and needs created by urbanism, particularly in capitalizing on new market possibilities. The whole gamut of urban problems requires far more attention than it has received in the past.

Map 10 is of value in showing the general distribution of cities of 30,000 and over on the continent. Several dominant patterns may be delineated. First is the large number of agglomerations which are port cities. Seventy-two cities, with 39.4 percent of the population of the 239 cities mapped, are ports. In tropical Africa, with the exception of Nigeria, 35 of the 93 cities with over 30,000 are ports and have 40.9 percent of the total city population of their countries. In the 32 countries of Africa which front on the sea, all but 8 have their largest city on the coast.

The explanations for this dominant pattern, which exists despite the massiveness of the continent, are historical and economic.[3] European

[3] Part of this discussion is based upon William A. Hance, "The Economic Location and Functions of Tropical African Cities," *Human Organization* (Fall, 1960), pp. 132–33, 135–36.

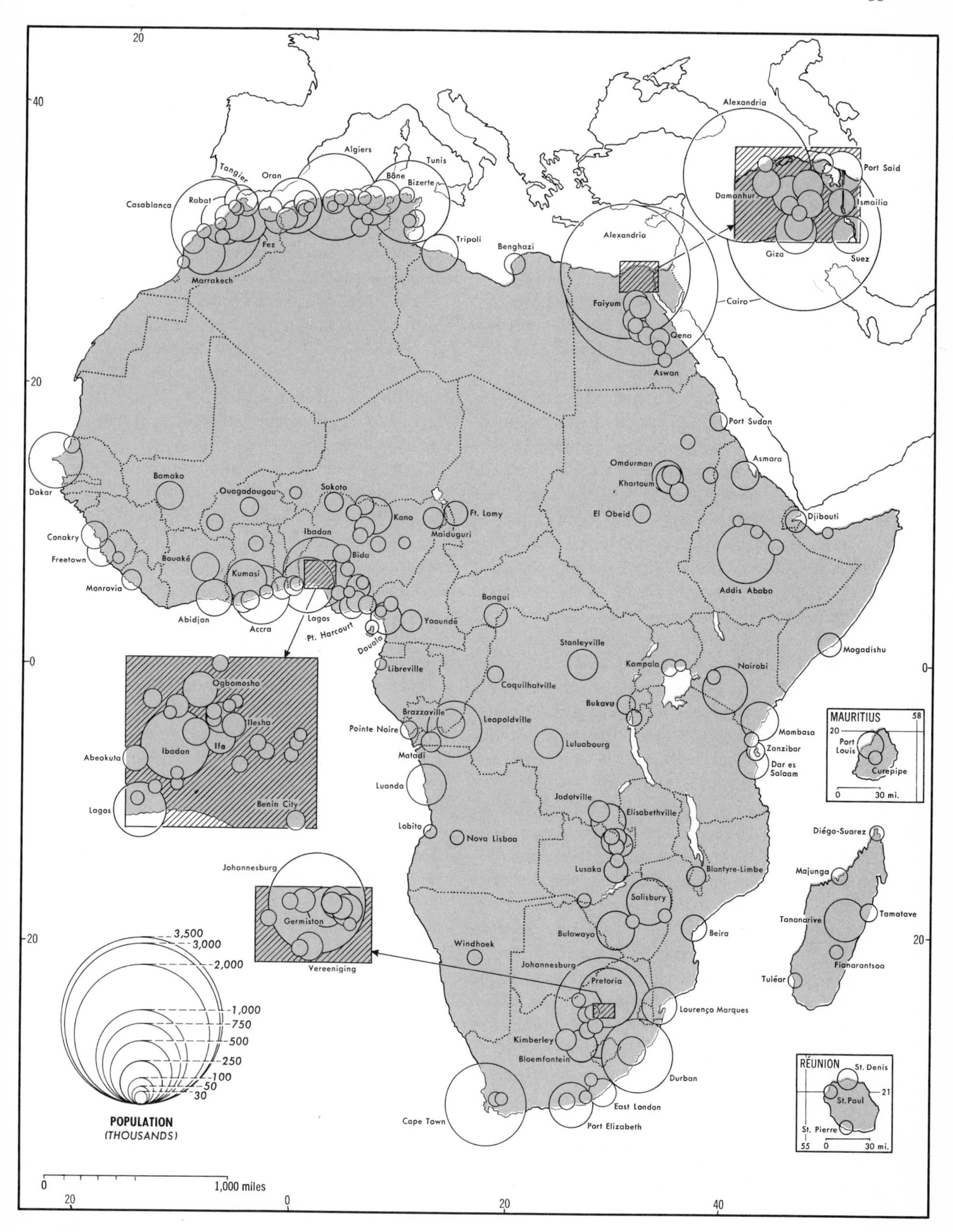

Map 10. Cities of Africa with populations exceeding 30,000

interest in sub-Saharan Africa was for decades confined to coastal points, where trade in gold, ivory, and slaves could be conducted and which could be more readily supplied and protected. These points became foci of pathways and later roads and finally the coastal termini of the tentaclelike African railways. As commerce expanded they became the gathering points for domestic staple exports and the break-of-bulk centers for the greater variety of imported goods. In view of the high proportion of the total money economy of tropical Africa that is assumed by the export-import economy, it is not surprising that ports have so frequently become the leading cities.

It was logical that many of these cities be selected as colonial capitals. Both the commercial and the political functions resulted in disproportionate concentrations of the expatriates in these countries. This, in turn, gave many of the port-capitals considerable significance as consuming centers, well illustrated by Casablanca, Dakar, Luanda, Lourenço Marques, and Dar es Salaam, which absorb some potential exports and a considerable percentage of total domestic imports within their urban boundaries.

All of these factors resulted in the provision of better services and amenities than are found in lesser communities—electricity, water, telephones, paved roads, superior housing, schools, and entertainment facilities. Once started, the development was self-generating.

A second group of important cities are inland ports—river and lake ports—which owe their location and their significance to the same assemblage and break-of-bulk functions that caused the coastal ports to grow. Seven of these, Bamako, Niamey, Bangui, Fort Lamy, Brazzaville, Leopoldville, and the conurbation of Khartoum-Omdurman, are the prime economic cities and the capitals of their countries. Cairo might also be included, though its history is more complex.

A third group of African cities also owes its importance largely to the commercial function—the cities situated at important nodes of land routes. This category includes some of the inland cities of the Maghrib, Ouagadougou, Sokoto, Kano, Lusaka, Salisbury, and Bulawayo. Some of these cities have grown up from indigenous market towns which existed in precolonial times.

It is apparent from the number of leading African cities that fall into the first three categories—coastal ports, inland ports, and crossroad cities—that the most important explanation for their significance and their location is the commercial functions they fulfill.

The climatic factor is significant in centers of European settlement areas in tropical Africa. These areas are found where elevation moderates the heat of tropical coasts and lowlands. Examples are Nova Lisboa, Salisbury, Bulawayo, Gwelo, Umtali, Nairobi, Nakuru, and formerly Bukavu.

Next are a number of cities which have been built up because of mining activities, including Jos and Enugu in Nigeria, Elisabethville, Jadotville, Kolwezi, and Manono in Congo, Ndola and the smaller Copperbelt towns of Northern Rhodesia, and the great string of cities based upon gold in the Transvaal and Orange Free State. These assume particular significance when processing of ores occurs before shipment.

The remaining cities are less easily classifiable economically. Those of southwestern Nigeria, some of which reach surprising size, are descendants from the great agrotowns of the Yoruba and are perhaps not too unlike the former large rural agglomerations of Hungary. The element of security was important in causing both these agglomerations and those of the walled cities of the Hausa Emirates. Kampala, Kumasi, Benin, Addis Ababa, Tananarive, and Fianarantsoa all grew from their positions as the residences of important tribal chiefs, Tananarive having been selected in part because of its easily defensible site on a rock knoll rising above the Betsimitatatra Plains. Nairobi was located largely by chance, growing from a railroad construction camp; if an objective choice could be made again, this capital and most important city of Kenya would probably be located elsewhere.

With respect to the growth and rise of cities

in the future, it is likely that inland cities may expand as internal exchange increases, that cities will develop where new mineral and hydroelectric resources are exploited, and that some cities will be built as centers of developing agricultural regions.

But several factors appear to be leading toward the greatest growth occurring in the already important cities. On the coasts, for example, there is a tendency to suppress minor ports and concentrate upon fewer cities. This trend is apparent in Senegal, Ghana, Nigeria, Angola, East Africa, and Madagascar. The high cost of modern harbor installations, plus improvements that are being made in overland links to the better ports, explains these consolidations.

A second factor tending to enlarge the present big cities is the increasing importance of governmental functions, Parkinson's Law being just as applicable in Africa as in Europe or America.

A third important factor tending to increase the importance of existent major economic centers is the new trend in industrialization toward the rise of consumer-oriented industries. Almost all of these industries want to be situated in large urban areas and in centers which possess the best means of communication with the rest of the country.

The conclusion may be hazarded that the basic distributional pattern of African cities is now fairly well delineated and that the most dynamic growth will take place in those agglomerations which are already the leading cities.

GROWTH OF THE POPULATION

United Nations estimates of population growth, slightly adjusted for 1961, are shown in Table 11. The Food and Agricultural Organization (FAO) has estimated that population totals will reach 295 million by 1980 and at least 485 million by the year 2000.[4] Almost all population data for Africa must be used with reservation, but it is particularly hazardous to estimate rates of population growth, especially where past estimates are of highly questionable validity. But such statistics as are available indicate that African countries generally have extremely high birth rates, death rates, and rates of infant mortality. The U.N. *Demographic Yearbook 1961* estimated that the birth rate in the period 1956–60 in Africa was 47 per thousand; the highest rate for any continent, this figure compared with a world average estimated at 36. The crude death rate of 25 per thousand for the same period compared with a world average of 18 and was also higher than for any other continent. Only Middle and South America had crude rates of natural increase exceeding that of Africa's 22 per thousand.

Improved sanitation, expanded health services, and increased control of disease are rapidly reducing the death rates, sometimes in a remarkably short period. It follows that the rates of increase are mounting with some rapidity. In Congo, for example, where great concern was expressed not many years ago that the weak growth pattern threatened future development, it is now predicted that the population

[4] The Food and Agricultural Organization of the United Nations, *FAO Africa Survey* (1961), p. 17.

Table 11. Estimated population in Africa, 1920–1961 (in millions)

	1920	*1930*	*1940*	*1950*	*1960*	*1961*
North Africa	47	53	61	71	88	90
Tropical and South Africa	94	104	115	135	166	173
Total	141	157	176	206	254	263
Decennial percent increase		11.3	12.1	17.0	23.3	
African percent of world population	7.9	7.8	7.8	8.2	8.5	8.6

Sources: U.N., *1961 Demographic Yearbook* (New York, 1962); U.N., *Statistical Yearbook, 1962* (New York, 1963).
N.B. Area defined as North Africa includes Ethiopia and Sudan.

A Moslem sheik on pilgrimage in Cameroon

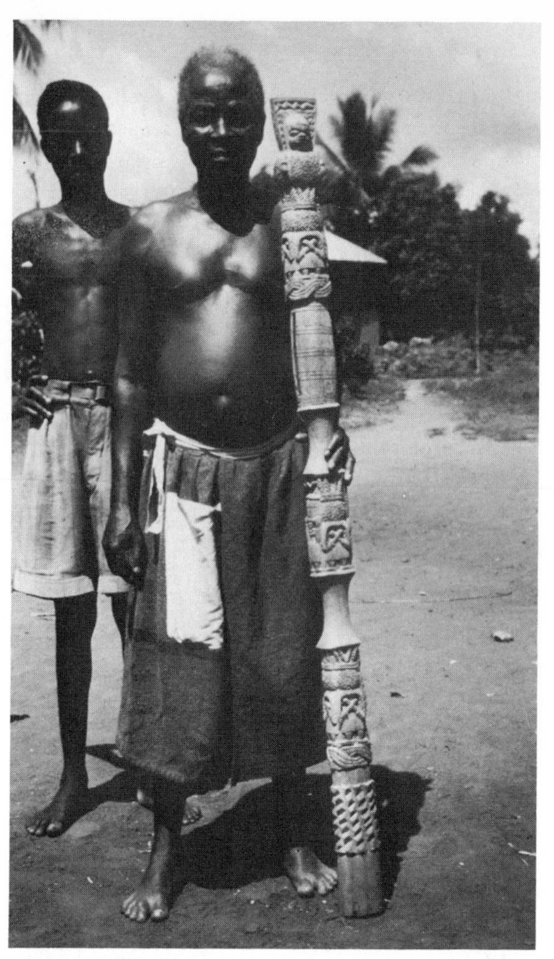

Chief of a woodcarving clan in Benin City, southern Nigeria

A small Azande village near Obo, Central African Republic, gathered to meet a provincial political officer

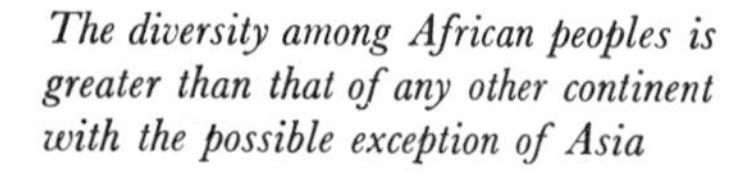

The diversity among African peoples is greater than that of any other continent with the possible exception of Asia

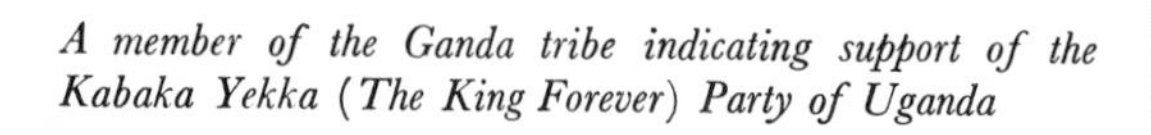

A member of the Ganda tribe indicating support of the Kabaka Yekka (The King Forever) Party of Uganda

will double in about thirty years. In Madagascar, as a second example, the excess of births over deaths has grown from 20,666 in 1948 to 123,019 in 1961. It is obvious that the results of these population "explosions" will have a formidable impact on economic development. The typically very youthful populations mean that the need for expenditures on education is greatly increased, and that each productive individual is responsible for maintaining a larger number of unproductive persons than is characteristic of developed areas. It calls for much more vigorous development if desirable economic growth rates are to be achieved.

THE PEOPLES OF AFRICA

About 97 percent of the total population of Africa is of African origin. In 1958 there were some 5.7 million persons of European origin and 1.4 million of Asian descent. The large-scale exodus of Europeans from Algeria since that time has more than offset gains by natural increase and net immigration in other areas since that date. The terms "European" and "Asian" and "of European or Asian origin" are not entirely satisfactory because they include persons who have been born in Africa or whose forebears were born in Africa from one to many generations back. Other difficulties arise in the failure to differentiate among persons of Asian origin belonging to the yellow, brown, and white races and in the various ways of recording mixed ancestry. A major problem exists for Madagascar, where it is not certain what portion of the population is descended from early Asian migrants and what portion from Africans.

EUROPEANS

The population of Africa of European origin is very unevenly distributed, over half being in the Republic of South Africa. In the Republic, Europeans comprise about 20 percent of the total population; in Algeria they represented about 10 percent until 1961. In tropical Africa, Southern Rhodesia has the highest percentage of whites, 6.9 percent, and relatively large numbers are recorded for Angola, Congo, and Kenya, but most territories have less than .02 percent of Europeans.

Many Europeans consider themselves only temporary residents, including most colonial officials or advisers to new African governments, missionaries, and commercial representatives. It is not possible to define the permanent residents of European origin with any accuracy because the changing political stature of the African may result in a large exodus of persons who had previously been considered part of the permanent populace.

Other characteristics of the European population in Africa include the dominance of urban dwellers, true even in countries where European farmers account for a high percentage of the total value of commercial crop production, the large percent who are salaried or wage earning, their heavy concentration in services, particularly the government, and the very large economic contribution they make in proportion to their numbers.

The dominant position that Europeans have held in almost every sphere until recent years has engendered considerable resentment, which all too often leads to racial antagonism. Many new countries, as a result, have tended to concentrate excessively on the negative aspects of Eurafrican relations. In fact, there is a greater need today than ever before for persons of all races to work together, for Africa needs the skill and capital that expatriates can supply. There can be little excuse for racialism no matter in what direction it is applied.

ASIANS

Persons of Asian origin are concentrated in the east and the south of the continent, on Madagascar, and in the Mascarene Islands. Many Asians were first brought as plantation workers, particularly on the sugar estates of Mauritius and Réunion, or to assist in the construction of ports and rail lines. Today they generally occupy a disproportionate number of intermediate positions as artisans, skilled and semiskilled workers, and clerks. They also have great importance in merchandising, including the operation of small shops in remote areas. Some have been extremely successful, being owners of large plantations (particularly sisal plantations in Tanganyika), hotels, movie houses, and large stores in urban centers. They have, however, frequently been the subject of calumny on the part of Africans and Europeans or been legally restricted from certain areas and occupations. Europeans have tended to resent their penuriousness and their willingness to work excessively long hours; Africans have seen them as blocking their advance on the next rung of the ladder.

Such racial considerations tend to stultify and inhibit economic growth. They are based upon the notion that the size of the pie is limited and, therefore, that its pieces must be rigidly divided and assigned. In fact, the development of African economies needs the full contribution of all its peoples to the best of their abilities.

AFRICANS

While it is possible to generalize that most of the indigenous population of African origin is rural, relatively unskilled, and still influenced largely by traditional ways of life, it must be noted emphatically that there is no such thing as *the* African. There is enormous ethnic variety. There are hundreds of tribes, about 800 distinct languages, numerous religions, and marked differentiation in occupation and land use. Each group is advancing at a different pace; persons from within most groups have moved varying distances away from traditional patterns. In some cases the tribal pattern has remained dominant, elsewhere it appears to be crumbling. The resultant patterns are, therefore, complex in the extreme.

Ethnographers do not agree regarding the classification of African groups. But whatever the correct groupings may be, there is no question regarding the variety of peoples of the African continent, a variety far greater than in Europe, the Americas, or Oceania, to some extent even greater than in Asia, which has strong unifying cultural elements over broad regions.

CHAPTER FIVE

The Political Scene in Africa

A brief survey of certain features of the African political scene which have importance in economic and geographic terms will serve to conclude these introductory chapters. Tremendous dynamism and rapid acceleration are keynotes of the political arena. And while it is possible to delineate some of the trends and many of the forces involved in the political field it is well to expect the unexpected in Africa.

INDEPENDENT AND DEPENDENT COUNTRIES

The dominant trend of recent years has been that toward the independence of African countries (Maps 11–14). Before World War II, only Egypt, Liberia, and South Africa were independent, though Ethiopia had been one of the oldest nations in Africa until the Italian occupation of 1936. Ethiopia became nominally independent again during the war and was subsequently federated with Eritrea. Libya joined the small group of independent states in 1951. The extension of this status to Libya by the U.N., which was motivated by the desire to exclude the USSR from becoming one of the trustees of an African territory, had far greater significance than the importance of that country might have suggested. It had fewer than twenty

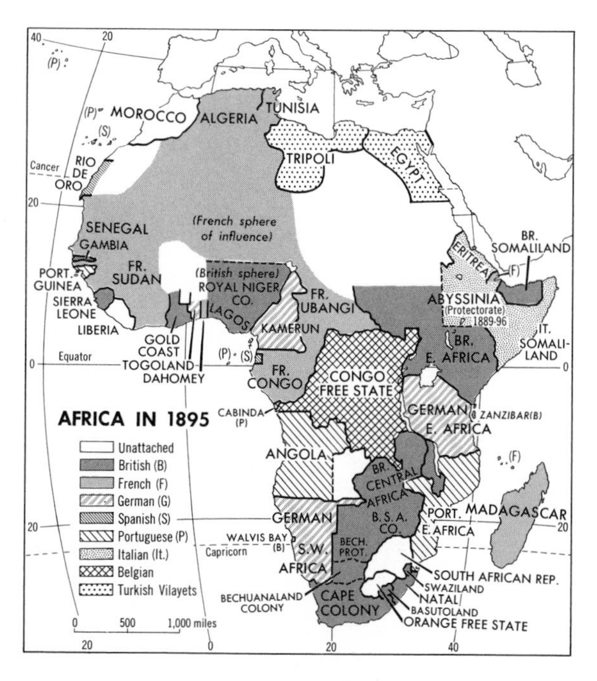

Map 11. Africa in 1895 (after Stamp)

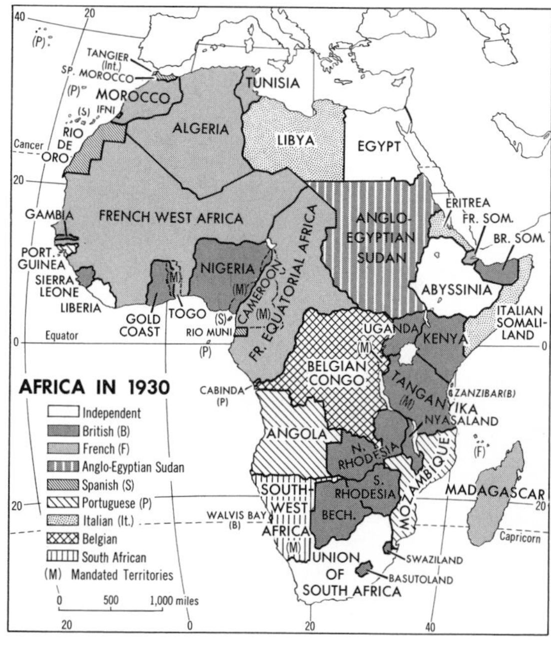

Map 12. Africa in 1930 (after Stamp)

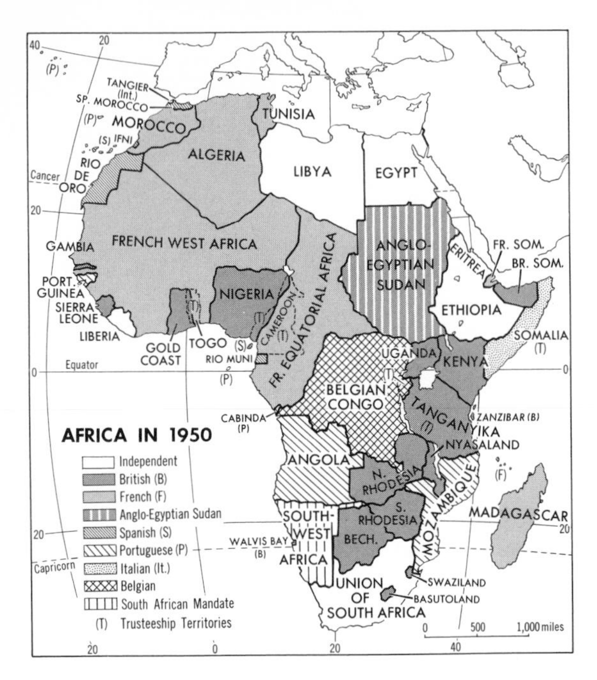

Map 13. Africa in 1950 (after Stamp)

college graduates at the time, and the argument that African territories must have a large number of educated persons before achieving self-government was, therefore, effectively undermined. But it was the strengthening will of the Africans, appealing to the basic precepts gained from their Western education, that was the most powerful force leading to the rapid evolution to independence beginning in the 1950s. Most of the colonial powers conceded the weakness of their philosophical positions and, as the African position matured, it became increasingly clear that effective continuing relationships could best be maintained with countries that were independent, that holding out against the inevitable and irreversible trend toward independence would only cause exacerbation.

In 1956 Morocco, Tunisia, and Sudan became independent; in the following year the Gold Coast became the first colony of Black Africa to achieve this status, joining with the trusteeship area of British Togoland to form Ghana. Guinea was the only territory to opt for independence in the French referendum of 1958 and was summarily abandoned by France. In 1960 the remaining states of French West Africa, those of French Equatorial Africa, Madagascar, the trustee territories of Togoland, Cameroon, and Somalia, Nigeria, Congo, and British Somaliland became independent, the last joining with the Italian-administered Somaliland to form the new Republic of Somalia. In 1961 Sierra Leone, Tanganyika, and the Cameroons achieved independence, the Southern Cameroons federating with the Republic of Cameroon and Northern Cameroons joining with Nigeria. In 1962 Ruanda-Urundi became Rwanda and

Uhuru or Independence celebration at Kampala, Uganda, October 9, 1962
In postwar years to 1964 thirty-two African nations achieved independence.

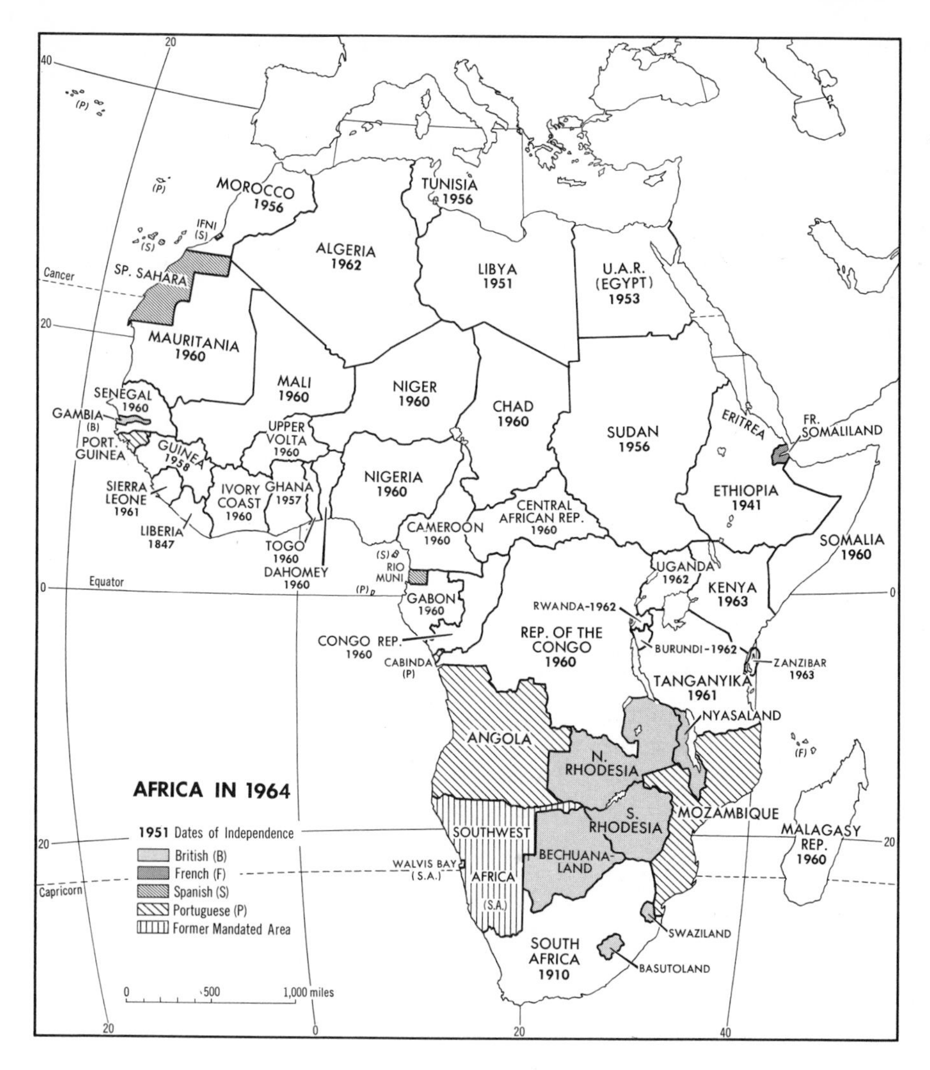

Map 14. Africa on January 1, 1964

Burundi and Uganda reached "uhuru" or independence, as did Algeria. Kenya and Zanzibar followed in late 1963. Thus by 1964, about four fifths of the area and nine tenths of the people of Africa were independent, and other countries were far on the road, including Gambia, Nyasaland, Northern Rhodesia, and even the High Commission Territories. It is more difficult to predict the timing for Southern Rhodesia and for Spanish and Portuguese areas. But pressure for rule by the African has reached explosive proportions, at least in Southern Rhodesia and Angola. And accession to independence of each new nation stimulates moves toward self-government in the remaining dependent territories.

The most difficult position exists in the Republic of South Africa, classified as independent, but containing a majority of Africans who are denied representation and who are subject to economic and social restrictions that are a contradiction of the whole Western ethos. Nor does the present program for the formation of Bantustans from the existing tribal reserves, even if they were intended eventually to receive independence, solve the problem.

Certain generalizations regarding the newly independent states may be hazarded: most have elected to continue association with their former metropoles; many have one-party systems whose leaders have assumed greater authority than originally envisaged in their constitutions; most are friendly to the West but have adopted positions of neutrality or noninvolvement in the East-West conflict; many have expressed interest in the formation of associations of African states. Perhaps the greatest contrast is between those states where the modernist element appears to have superseded the traditional, such as Senegal, Guinea, Ghana, Togo, and the Malagasy Republic, and those where the tribal heritage appears to continue dominant, including Nigeria, Congo, and Uganda.

Independence is likely to involve a complex of economic advantages and disadvantages. Advantages include, first, the elimination of such inhibiting restrictions as tariff barriers and quotas designed to favor the metropole; obligations to use European companies for construction work; requirements to ship via the fleet of the governing power; restrictions on the level of industrial production in Africa; restrictions on the production and sale by Africans of agricultural produce competitive to that from European farms, ostensibly to preserve foreign markets through quality control (happily, this type of regulation is fast disappearing in the colonial territories); and restrictions on the advancement of Africans in civil service, industrial, and technical employment. Second, the enthusiasm unleashed by gaining independence, if sustained and properly channeled, can have a distinctly favorable impact. Third, achievement of autonomous status may go a long way toward removing racialism and colonialism as issues in economics. And fourth, indigenous leaders are sometimes able to institute programs or to enforce desirable regulations which colonial officers were not, witness the reinstituted cut-out program for diseased cocoa trees in Ghana or disease-prevention activities in Nyasaland.

Numerous potential economic disadvantages may also accrue from independence. These cl ude a possible reduction in public and private capital flowing from the former metropoles to Africa; the loss of skilled personnel, so desperately required in Africa; the diminution in contacts between scientific organizations in Africa and those in Europe; possible disruption in trading and monetary arrangements; an increased intrusion of Communist nations; the reemergence of tribal antagonisms which had been held in check; and the danger that African nationalism will adopt undesirable economic policies such as those western Europe has been struggling to eliminate in postwar years. African nations are becoming independent at a time when political independence is possible but when economic independence is not. Their high dependence on outside powers for capital, skill, markets, and for industrial and other equipment is likely to persist for many years and even to increase in the short run.

THE GEOGRAPHIC PATTERN OF POLITICAL UNITS

The pattern of present national units in Africa presents several important characteristics. First, it tends to be peripheral; many countries, particularly in West Africa, represent extensions from previously held coastal strips or nodes. This reflects the way-station character of early interests, the difficulty of exploration and penetration, the desire to control river mouths for more effective control of inland trade (e.g., Gambia and Nigeria), and the degree of competition among imperial powers.

Second, political boundaries bear little relation to natural regions. Examples would include the former French Equatorial Africa, extending from south of the equator to the middle of the Sahara; the inhibitive boundary situation of the lower Congo; the High Commission Territories.

Third, the political pattern was superimposed on the area with almost no regard to tribal or ethnographic distribution. Almost every boundary divides several tribes among two or more countries. The Ewe, Hausa, Zande, Bakongo, Masai, and Somali, to name but a few, are so divided. While this has created problems in certain areas, in the longer run it may prove to have been desirable; certainly the history of Europe reveals the disadvantages of attempting to divide an area on ethnographic and linguistic bases.

Fourth, it was characteristic for the imperial powers to have holdings in more than one part of the continent, for each major region to be divided among several powers (Maps 11–13). This probably aided development to a degree in that each metropole strove to secure raw materials from its own areas, but it also resulted in some cases in unnecessary duplication of facilities, particularly in the field of transportation.

POLITICAL CONSOLIDATION AND FRAGMENTATION

It would be a mistake to assume that the future political pattern of Africa will be the same as that today. As has been indicated, the boundaries are largely artificial. Indeed, a few changes have already been made in postwar years: Spanish and French Morocco and Tangier have been incorporated in Morocco, British Togoland

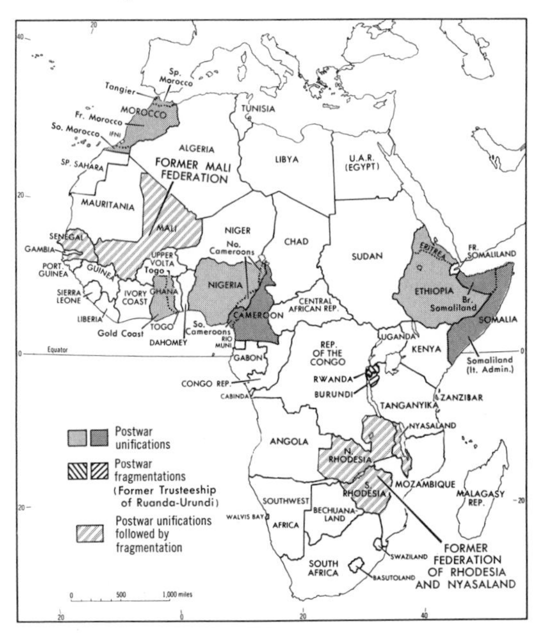

Map 15. Modern boundary changes in Africa involving political consolidations or fragmentations

Chief Pokkam, Chef Superieure de Bangangté, Cameroon
While "indirect rule" is more closely associated with British colonial rule, it was also practiced in French areas. The position of chiefs in Africa is in a period of rapid transition as they now often find themselves in direct conflict with modernist forces.

and British Cameroons have disappeared, British Somaliland has become a part of Somalia, Eritrea and Ethiopia have been federated (Map 15), and Kenya, Uganda, and Tanganyika planned to federate at the end of 1963. In addition, Egypt has developed varyingly close relationships with Syria and Iraq, while Ghana, Guinea, and Mali formed a new union, now ended, which was so tenuous that it could not be classified with the consolidations noted above. Examples of fragmentation include the early breakup of the Mali Federation into Senegal and Mali, the demise of the Federation of Rhodesia and Nyasaland and Egypt's various unions, and the split of Ruanda-Urundi into two nations. But neither the obliteration of old boundaries nor the drawing of new boundaries has been particularly notable—most nations have the same boundaries which they had as colonies and have expressed their firm intention not to relinquish any of their soil to other nations. Even the expansionist ambitions on the part of several powers, including Morocco, Tunisia, Somalia, Ghana, and Egypt, have been rather effectively restrained to date.

The strongest force motivating tendencies to Balkanize the area is tribalism. For some years it threatened to destroy the unitary government in independent Ghana. It accounts for selection of federal forms of government for Nigeria, Congo, and Uganda. It explains rioting in French Congo in 1958–59 and in the Kasai Province of Congo in 1959–60. It slowed the move toward independence in Uganda because the Ganda, occupying about a quarter of the area, are strongly tribalistic and had relatively little interest in other parts of the country. It provided a major stumbling block in the prolonged and complex negotiations for extending authority to the Africans in Kenya.

Other factors which tend to be divisive include the lack of geographic cohesion in many areas; the desire of richer areas not to share their wealth with poorer neighbors, a separatist factor in Katanga or Northern Rhodesia; and the desire to remain dissociated from territories where whites are dominant, the strongest force disrupting the Federation of Rhodesia and Nyasaland.

Factors which do not necessarily favor Balkanization but which tend to work against the formation of larger political units involve linguistic, economic, and political considerations, many of which represent carry-overs from colonial introductions. Former French territories, for example, find it difficult to withdraw from special trade, monetary, and aid relationships with France in favor of achieving closer ties with other African countries. The partial acquisition of French, British, or other cultures by the elite of African nations, the adoption of European languages as lingua francas, and the possession of administrative forms characteristic of the former metropole also would appear to militate against the elimination of existing boundaries. Furthermore, once power is achieved it is likely to be jealously guarded, whereas joining with other powers might lead to the subordination of some political leaders. Defense agreements with the former metropole may be motivated in considerable part by this consideration and are doubtless significant in curbing some expansionist ambitions.

There are, however, factors favoring consolidation rather than Balkanization or maintenance of the status quo. The very absurdity of some present boundaries and the desire of tribal groups to be reunited would tend to contribute to consolidation. Modernists have sought to reaffirm the solidarity among all Africans and have been supported by intellectual efforts to establish the African personality. The example of the United States has influenced many supporters of the pan-Africanist movement and a United States of Africa is frequently cited as a goal for the continent. The economic motives for consolidation, less often cited by African leaders, include the avoidance of waste and duplication in several fields including administration, transportation, research, and technical and advanced education; the avoidance of creating landlocked states; and the greater ability of larger political units to achieve economic viability, develop interregional exchange, attract foreign capital, and justify the establishment of market-oriented manufacturing plants.

POLITICAL, ECONOMIC, AND TECHNICAL GROUPINGS

Looking next at what political, economic, and technical groupings have been established to achieve greater unity and cooperation in Africa, one may distinguish between those associations which are entirely African and those which involve relationships with Europe. Among the former, perhaps the most important until 1963 were the Casablanca and Monrovia Groups (Map 16). The Casablanca Group, which first met in January, 1961, held that a political

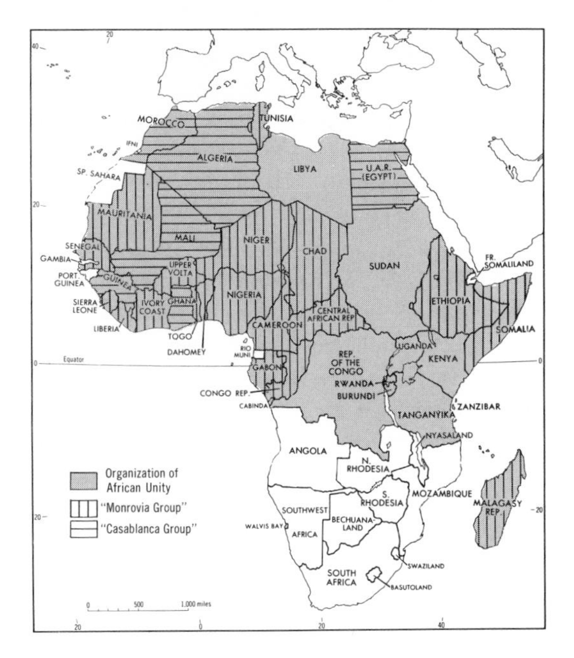

Map 16. The Organization of African Unity; the former Monrovia and Casablanca Groups

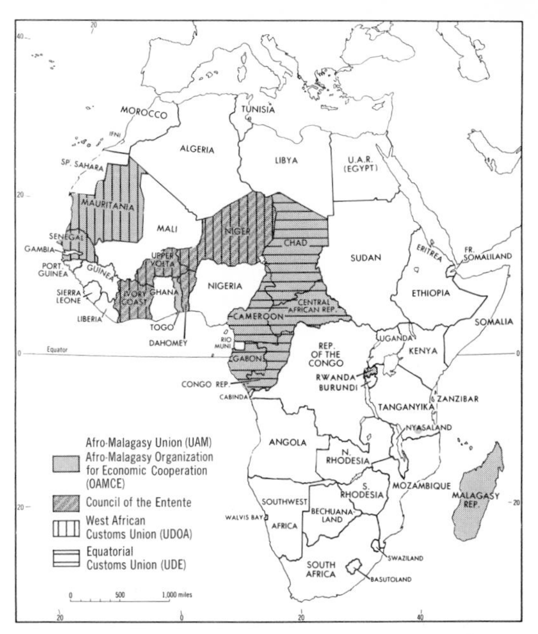

Map 17. The Brazzaville Group and organizations within it

unity must come first. It typically adopted a somewhat more expansionist and militant stand and a more radical anticolonial, anti-European position. It agreed to form an "African Common Market" in 1962, having discussed numerous other forms of cooperation. Within it, Ghana and Guinea formed a union in November, 1958, which was joined by Mali in December, 1960, but the union did not result in any political changes of consequence. The Monrovia Group, which first met in the Liberian capital in May, 1961, held that existing political boundaries must be respected, that cooperation in economic and technical spheres must be effected before political unity could be achieved. Its specific objectives included the formation of a regional customs union, a common organization of social and health affairs, development of a connecting network of roads and other communications, and working toward the harmonization of educational systems and the removal of language barriers.

All of the former sub-Saharan territories of France except Guinea are joined with Madagascar and Rwanda in the Brazzaville Group, forming the Afro-Malagasy Union (UAM) and the Afro-Malagasy Organization for Economic Cooperation (OAMCE) (Map 17). Several subgroups and bodies were included within the Brazzaville Group, including the Council of the Entente, a fairly tenuous association of four former French West African states, and customs unions among the former members of French West Africa (UDOA) and French Equatorial Africa (UDE).

In May, 1963, the first really effective efforts to weld these several groups together was made at Addis Ababa, where thirty-one African nations signed a charter setting up the Organization of African Unity (OAU) (Map 16). Many of the stipulations of this charter were common to the Casablanca and Monrovia Groups, but the position with respect to achieving unity followed closely the moderate pattern of the Monrovia Group. While the Casablanca and Monrovia Groups have essentially been absorbed within the OAU, it is likely that the previous differences among them will be reflected in the positions adopted within the newer body. Efforts have been made to discontinue

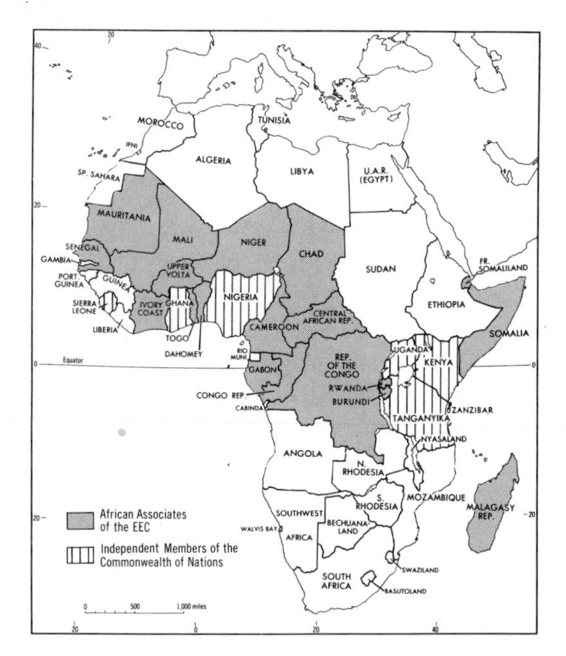

Map 18. Associate members of the European Economic Community and members of the Commonwealth of Nations

the Brazzaville Group, but the involvement of that group or parts of it in various transport, scientific, and customs organizations, as well as the special relations of all of its members except Rwanda with France, gives it purposes which are not yet adequately covered by the OAU.

The concrete achievements of these various pan-African bodies cannot be said to be very dramatic as yet. But they have provided the groundwork for increasing cooperation in the future, and the efforts to unite several of the groups and to reduce the anomalies among them have displayed considerable statesmanship. The strong appeal of pan-Africanism, particularly to most younger politicians, should help to sustain the advances that have already been made. Real tests remain, however, especially in satisfying the radicalism of the younger generation and in resolving disputes of potential magnitude among African nations.

Relationships among African and European states have been continued in a variety of formal and informal ways. Some former French territories continue as members of the remodeled French Community but most of them have concluded bilateral agreements, protocols, or agreements of cooperation with France. All of the former British territories of tropical Africa which are now independent have become members of the Commonwealth.

The association of eighteen independent African nations, plus dependent French Somaliland, with the six nations of the European Economic Community (EEC) provides one of the most important Eurafrican connections (Map 18). This association began in 1958 under a five-year agreement, and is extended by a Convention of Association. The chief benefits to the African territories involved are, first, that it gives them a larger, protected market for their staples and, second, that it makes available capital resources for social and economic development. In return, the associated countries agreed in principle to reduce their tariffs on imports from the Common Market six by 15 percent annually, though tariffs may be retained or instituted to protect infant industries, to avoid balance of payments difficulties, or to yield budget revenues. They also contracted to eliminate any discrimination in trade relations with the EEC countries within four years.

This association, which is administered by three joint institutions, raises several serious problems for African states. The removal of discriminatory conditions affecting trade between Africa and each member of the EEC means that the former French areas must forego their guaranteed markets at above world prices in the French market and that France must lose its reciprocally favored position in their markets. In order to ease the transitional difficulties, $230 million of the total financial aid of $800 million promised over a five-year period is allotted to the financing of projects which are designed to permit the products of the association to be marketed at competitive prices. Each associated state is expected to submit a five-year plan designed to eliminate present artificially high prices. The largest share of the sum allotted will go to eleven countries which are not now able to sell their products at competitive world prices and whose price supports will gradually be abolished, the last no later than four years after implementation of the convention. While some associated territories may have little trouble in meeting this schedule, the loss of subsidies and guaranteed markets may be very painful to others and it is not unlikely that some kind of extended special treatment may prove necessary.

Perhaps a more serious problem raised by the association of some African states to the EEC is the damaging impact that achievement of the community's goals may have on other African nations. Commonwealth countries (Map 18) have been particularly concerned about their potential losses in the markets of the six, though Ghana and Nigeria in particular have stated that they did not wish to join the associates, even if Britain were admitted to the Community. As most industrial raw materials will enter the EEC duty and quota free, some nonmember countries would suffer very little from being outside the group, but Angola, Ghana, Kenya, Uganda, and Tanganyika, relying heavily on coffee and cocoa sales, a not inconsiderable share of which goes to the EEC, are in fairly vulnerable positions. Nigeria would also be hurt, but less so because its vegetable oil exports would not be subject to tariff preferences. It is highly unfortunate that the failure of western European efforts at unification should result in emphasizing a divisive element in Africa that is not even of African origin.

Other multilateral agencies include those primarily concerned with technical assistance. The Economic Commission for Africa (ECA), one of the regional economic commissions of the United Nations, was organized in 1958 and has its offices in Addis Ababa. It gives priority to studies and conferences on development problems and techniques, the improvement of statistical services, and staff training. The Commission for Technical Cooperation in Africa (CCTA) was created in 1950 to coordinate the exchange of scientific and technological information, primarily in the natural sciences. A number of its committees focus upon specific fields such as disease control, soils, and animal

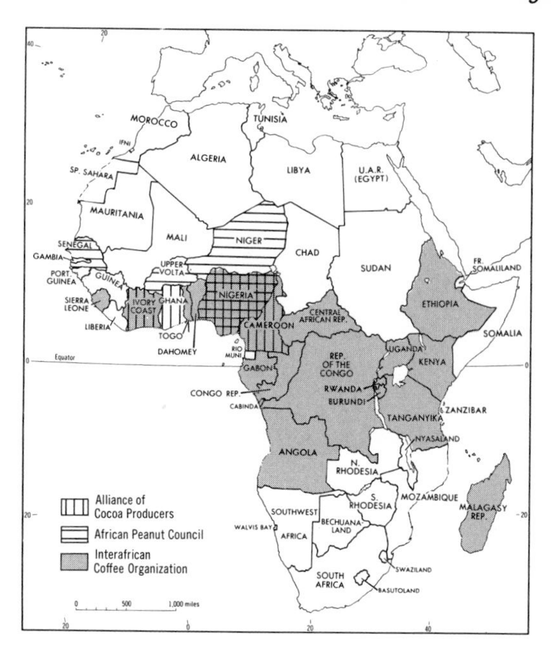

Map 19. African members of international commodity agreements

health. It is advised by the Scientific Council for Africa (CSA), composed of experts responsible only to the Commission.

Additional organizations concerned with cooperation among African states include the Pan African Freedom Movement of East, Central, and South Africa (PAFMECSA), a number of organizations concerned with technical control of insects and diseases, and several bodies which have been formed to reach agreements among commodity producers (Map 19).

COLONIAL POLICIES

Each of the metropolitan powers developed over the years a distinctive colonial policy, certain features of which are likely to have an impact continuing for many years after independence. Certainly in 1964 the heritage of the several colonial legacies was very apparent in the political and economic structures of the independent African nations.

Despite the unique character of each metropole's approach, certain common denominators, particularly in the postwar years, may be delineated. These include the greatly increased attention and expenditure focused upon African territories; a very considerable expansion of allotments for education and social improvements; strenuous efforts to improve the infrastructure of African countries; a general shift, with important exceptions, from tribal authorities to the modern elite as the main intermediaries; and a trend toward less directing and more advising. It is also apparent that, whatever the differences in colonial policies may have been, they made little difference in the desire of Africans for ultimate self-rule.

FRENCH COLONIAL POLICIES

Until recent years France was committed to the goal of assimilation of African territories in a French Union in which all the citizens would become citizens of France. In postwar years that country moved from the aim of assimilation to one of association in three big steps: the Brazzaville Conference of 1944, the Loi Cadre of 1956, and the New Constitution of 1958. The last, ratified by 14 of the 15 French African areas, made each ratifying territory a member of the French Community with certain governmental institutions common to all, including France, and with certain powers reserved to the Community in which France had a special position. In 1960 this Constitution was amended to permit assumption of complete independence without becoming dissociated from the Community, thus establishing a relationship more comparable with that of the Commonwealth. The new status was defined by President De Gaulle as "independence-association," but even this arrangement was rapidly liberalized to permit withdrawal from the Community without impairment of relations with France. Perhaps the two most important explanations for the continued strong ties of most former French African colonies to France are the genuine acceptance and admiration of French culture by their African leaders and their realization of the continuing need for economic and technical aid from France.

France was also largely responsible for including the overseas territories of the EEC member nations on an associative basis with the six, a part of the original agreement upon which French ratification was stated to depend.

In the field of education, which is one of those most likely to have carry-over value following independence, the goal was to make the African a Frenchman. Relatively little attention was paid to the local culture and language. In prewar decades emphasis was placed upon the training of a small elite who were used in the government as auxiliaries. The French were somewhat more successful in this regard than the British, where numerous educated unemployed joined the ranks of the malcontents. In postwar years, education was greatly expanded and, in addition to many new primary and secondary schools, there are now four universities in what was French Afrique Noire, while about 10,000 Africans are pursuing higher education in France.

Socially, the French extended far more personal and political freedom to their dependents than was characteristic of the other powers. There was much less of a color bar. In such places as Dakar, Abidjan, Madagascar, and, of course, North Africa, Frenchmen occupied some of the low-level and intermediate positions which would have been filled by Africans or Asians in other territories.

From the economic standpoint, French trade policies always favored exchange with the metropole and about 70 percent of exports and imports of the overseas territories were normally so routed. Aided by various laws and agreements and constricted by mutual inflation, the French franc block tended to become more and more a closed circuit. While African territories were benefited by guaranteed markets at high prices they were disadvantaged by the narrowness of the market and by the reciprocal obligation to purchase their imports at high prices. This situation has been ameliorated by devaluation of the franc in December, 1958, and by the African association of the EEC. Table 12 shows the 1961 trade position of African countries grouped according to their 1955 political

Table 12. The 1961 exports of Africa and tropical Africa by 1955 political affiliation

1955 political affiliation		Africa (percent of total value), 1961	Tropical Africa (percent of total value), 1961
Commonwealth countries		57.6	58.6
Of which, South Africa	28.1		
French Community		23.9	18.5
Of which, North Africa	14.6		
Belgian Africa		5.6	11.0
Portuguese Africa		3.3	6.5
Spanish Africa		0.5	0.9
Somalia (Italian administration)		0.2	0.5
Independent countries not included above		8.9	4.0
Total		100.0	100.0

Source: Compiled from national trade statistics.

Africa includes all continental countries, islands in the Bight of Biafra, Zanzibar and Pemba, Madagascar, and the Mascarenes.

Tropical Africa includes all above except Morocco, Algeria, Tunisia, Libya, Egypt, South Africa, and the territories which are in customs union with South Africa.

affiliations, revealing the relatively less favorable position of former French areas as compared with those of the Commonwealth and Belgium. Investment in sub-Saharan French territories was very limited in prewar years, totaling an estimated $127 million in 1938 in French West and Equatorial Africa, and tended to be concentrated in a few places, especially in Senegal and the Ivory Coast. The greatly expanded effort of postwar years, making France the largest contributor of aid to Africa, has already been noted, but even these great expenditures did not permit development of infrastructures comparable with those of most former British territories.

White settlement was relatively unimportant in sub-Saharan French Africa. There are numbers of permanent French residents in Dakar and other major cities, a few in the Cameroon Mountains, and some on Madagascar and Réunion, where there are a substantial number of persons of mixed blood. But there were no territories in this part of the continent which had a racial problem comparable to that of Kenya or Southern Rhodesia.

BRITISH POLICIES

Britain was long committed to the policy of evolution from colony to commonwealth or independence and could point to evidence of the completed cycle on several continents. In Africa the most rapid progress toward self-government occurred in territories where no permanent white minority existed. In countries like Kenya and the Rhodesias, however, where Europeans were jealous of their rights and fearful of being swamped by an illiterate majority, the pace has been slower. And geographic juxtaposition with these areas tended to delay, albeit not for long, the evolution of Uganda, Tanganyika, and Nyasaland. Nonetheless, in recent years the factor of white settlement has been overruled in favor of African advancement in all countries except the self-governing colony of Southern Rhodesia.

British colonial administration was very decentralized. The governor could override the Secretary of State for the Colonies; each territory had its own constitution adapted to its peculiar circumstances, and there was a bewildering variety of franchise systems and legislative bodies.

One of the important features of British colonialism in Africa was "indirect rule," which tried to make systematic use of the customary institutions of the people as agencies for local and regional rule. While its application assumed a great variety of forms, certain common features can be recognized. Indirect rule had the advantages of fostering the retention of indigenous culture, permitting control without undue usurpation of power, and allowing considerable areas to be administered by a small number of officials. Its disadvantages included the retention of some undesirable features of the indigenous culture, the fact that it was not easily applied where tribal political forms were poorly developed, the anomalous position in which it placed the chiefs who were forced to serve two masters, and the inability to take care of the *évolué* by associating him with the administration. Where it was most purely applied it often resulted in undue conservatism, as in northern Nigeria. While its effect will long be felt in parts of Africa, its inherent undemocratic character and its repression of modernist ambitions spelled its gradual demise. The period of transition, however, is a difficult one.

The British deserve particular commendation for their approach to the training of indigenous police forces, which are less authoritarian, less inclined to the use of force in the maintenance of law and order. The somewhat aggressive stance adopted by the *gendarmerie* in various French areas has probably prolonged some conflicts, such as the Bamiléké revolt in Cameroon, while the breakdown of police discipline in Congo was a major factor in the collapse of authority after independence.

In the economic sphere the British nominally applied the open-door policy in Africa from 1860 to 1919. After that, preferential trade arrangements grew, but sales of African products continued to be ruled primarily by world markets and prices. The investment in British Africa was much greater over the long run than in the territories of other powers. This is reflected in the greater importance of present and former British territories in tropical African production and trade. In 1961 these countries accounted for 58.6 percent of the total value of exports from tropical Africa.

With respect to economic aid, the traditional prewar policy was for the colony to pay its own way with only occasional subsidy from the metropole. In postwar years local sources financed about two thirds of total investment, the British government providing substantially increased grant and loan funds, while a considerable flow of private investment was maintained.

In the social sphere the position of the African has varied greatly. In areas with few if any permanent white settlers restrictive bars were fairly rapidly removed. In other areas such as Kenya, Southern Rhodesia, and parts of Northern Rhodesia, where white settlement was encouraged, the juxtaposition of modern economies with indigenous subsistence economies is striking. Here various color bars have existed, though they have been progressively or entirely removed in recent years.

The British educational policy favored the training of an elite, though the educated were not always utilized well. African languages were normally used in primary grades and sometimes in secondary schools. Technical education was probably underprovided. University education was encouraged in African institutions such as Fourah Bay College in Sierra Leone and Makerere College in Uganda. At present there are a dozen universities, while in 1961 about 15,000 Africans were enrolled in institutions of higher education in Britain. The bulk of the approximately 2,800 African students in the United States in 1962 were also from former British areas.

BELGIAN POLICIES

Until about 1958, Belgium envisaged that the goal for her African territories of eventual self-government with some association with Belgium would require many years for fruition, and her over-all policy was predicated on a deliberate evolutionary pace. Control was highly centralized in Belgium, laws for the Congo being made by the Belgian Parliament which had no representatives from the Congo. The Governor had less power than his British but more than his French counterpart. Until the late 1950s neither the Africans nor white settlers had a vote nor were there any legislative bodies.

The franchise was first extended to a few cities for election of local officials. Rather than concerning themselves with urban affairs as had been expected, however, they quickly turned to the larger sphere of Belgian-African relations and of independence for the Congo. The situation deteriorated in 1958–59 with great rapidity, and early in 1960 the Belgians, quite surprisingly, offered complete independence by June 30 of that year to the Congo. While this speed has been interpreted as displaying commendable realism, it must be admitted that this large, potentially wealthy, and heterogenous country moved into independence with far less experience of government than most other territories had had.

The Belgian colonial policies had given first priority to the economic sphere, maintaining that all other forms of development must rest on a sound economic base. Their main forte was in the systematic and scientific development of the resources of the area, and there were few territories where a better effort had been made to use Africans in technical and industrial employment. Investments were considerable and substantial earnings within the colony were reinvested to expand production. Large semi-state companies played an important role in mining, plantation agriculture, and transportation. While the Congo, under the Congo Basin Treaty and the Treaty of Saint-Germain-en-Laye, was nominally open equally to all investors, in actuality the virtual monopolies of some of the large corporations discouraged non-Belgian interest.

The educational policy of the Belgians fit logically into their over-all plans. It called for a broad base and for some emphasis on technical education, and the Belgians claimed that Congo had the highest literacy rate in Africa. No effort was made to educate an elite; there were no universities in the country until 1954 and very few Africans attended universities in the metropole. Today there are two universities, Lovanium at Leopoldville and the State University at Elisabethville, but Congo will require many years before it has an educated group comparable to that of many African nations.

In the social sphere the efforts were much like those of the good industrialist who strives to improve the working and living conditions of his men, realizing the mutual advantage that results. While it was claimed that no color bar existed, not all Europeans in the colony respected this official position. The government made increasing efforts in the years before independence, however, to eliminate all racial barriers.

PORTUGUESE POLICIES

The political goal of the Portuguese has been assimilation. African territories are considered to be an integral part of the Portuguese Union, authority over all parts of which is highly centralized in Lisbon.

The Portuguese territories were among the least developed in Africa in prewar years, reflecting the poverty of Portugal plus a certain unwillingness to encourage outside investment. In postwar years, under joint development plans for metropolitan and overseas Portugal, investment has been substantially increased to the benefit of economic development in all territories. Angola and Mozambique benefit considerably from their positions as outlets for interior areas of adjacent countries, thus providing the base for important transit services and for a large-scale migration of labor from the latter to Central and South Africa.

In attitude toward the African there are contradictions in Portuguese policy and practice. On the one hand, there is less apparent color bar than in many African countries, and there is a liberal *évolué* system in which all persons of mixed blood have equality of status with Europeans. More recently it has been declared that racial intermixture is an official goal. On the other hand, there is little real personal political freedom, no toleration of troublemakers, and a strict control of African movements. Some claim that the regulations respecting labor are akin to a forced labor system.

There are a substantial number of white settlers in Portuguese territories, especially in Angola. Some settlement has been promoted on demographic grounds to relieve pressure in the metropole. And in certain areas Portuguese farmers are forbidden to utilize African laborers, thus fostering a pattern of farming comparable with that in Portugal itself, but atypical in Africa.

SPANISH AND ITALIAN POLICIES

Little need be said regarding the policies of other colonial powers. The remaining Spanish possessions are small bits of land or islands, plus a sizable bit of the Sahara in Rio de Oro. Plantations and estates are well developed in the Spanish Equatorial Region; the Spanish Sahara is relatively untouched. Rule is centralized in Madrid and few provisions have thus far been made for devolution of authority to the Africans.

Italy enlarged its African possessions in the 1930s on the grounds of demographic necessity. Only a few thousands of Italians were ever effectively settled in the countries seized at that time and even this required large and continuing subsidization. After the war, Italy was given trusteeship of Somalia until 1960. Substantial efforts were devoted to preparing that country for independence, but the natural poverty of the area was not conducive to spectacular results. Italy continues to assist Somalia by special trade agreements and through monetary and technical assistance.

CONCLUSION

The foregoing chapters have been designed to sketch in the background for succeeding discussions of specific regions and countries. In them a considerable number of generalizations have been assayed, but it is well to repeat three points which are pervasive: Africa is a continent of enormous diversity; there is very much that is not known or adequately understood in all branches of African studies; the dynamic character of the African political and economic scene makes prediction very hazardous.

Part Two NORTHERN AFRICA

Zelten, Libya
Gathering lines approaching the operating plant. Discovery of oil and natural gas in Algeria and Libya has been one of the most dynamic economic developments in North Africa in recent years.

CHAPTER SIX

The Maghrib and Northwest Africa

The northwest segment of Africa has numerous characteristics, physical and cultural, which distinguish it from other parts of the continent. No criteria for defining the boundaries of the region are entirely satisfactory, but political boundaries permit a more effective use of statistical and other data (Map 20). The political units include three major ones: Morocco, which incorporated the French and Spanish Moroccan protectorates and Tangier, and which became an independent kingdom in 1956; Algeria, which attained independence in 1962 after a prolonged revolt; and Tunisia, which became a republic in 1957, the year after it had achieved independence. The main boundaries of these three countries, except for those of Algerian Sahara, date from the Turkish conquest over 400 years ago; Morocco, however, had existed as an independent state for a millennium before the inception of the modern French and Spanish protectorates. Minor political units of the region are Spanish Sahara; Ifni, the Spanish enclave in southern Morocco; and the "plazas" of Ceuta and Melilla and

Map 20. Political units and railways of Northwest Africa

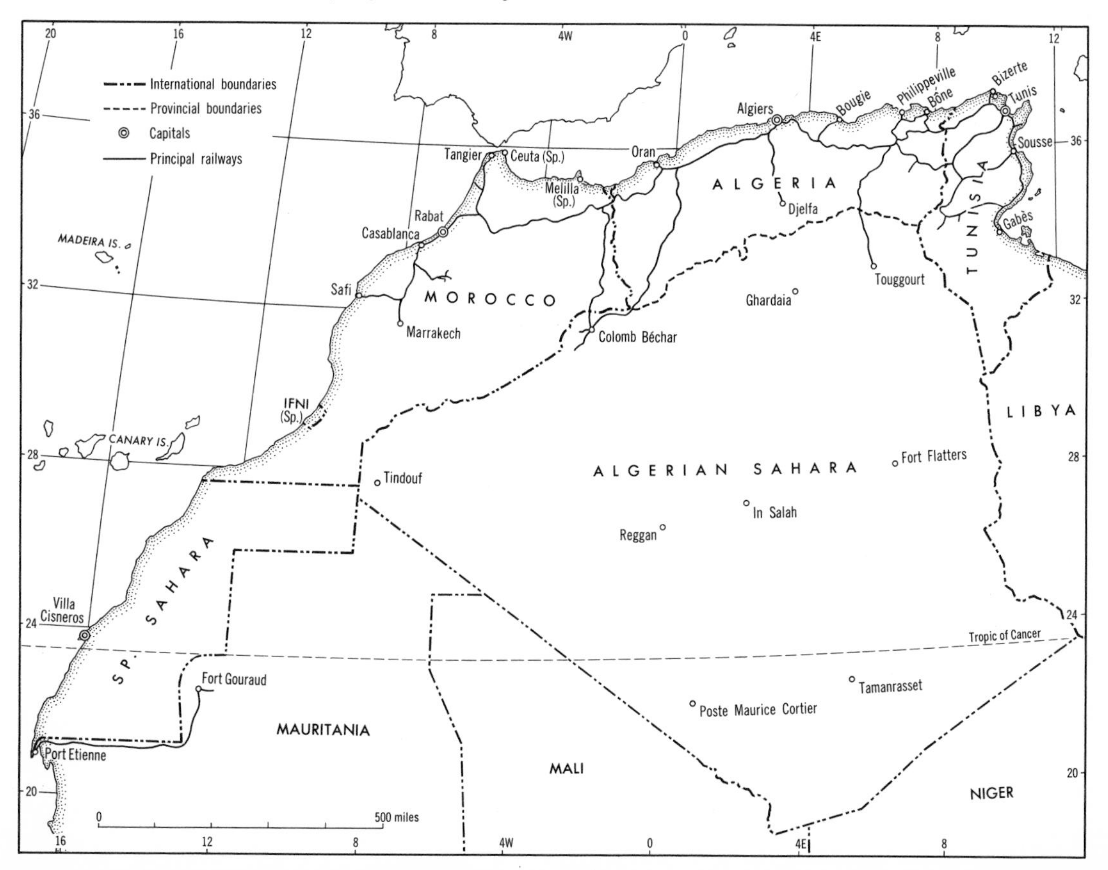

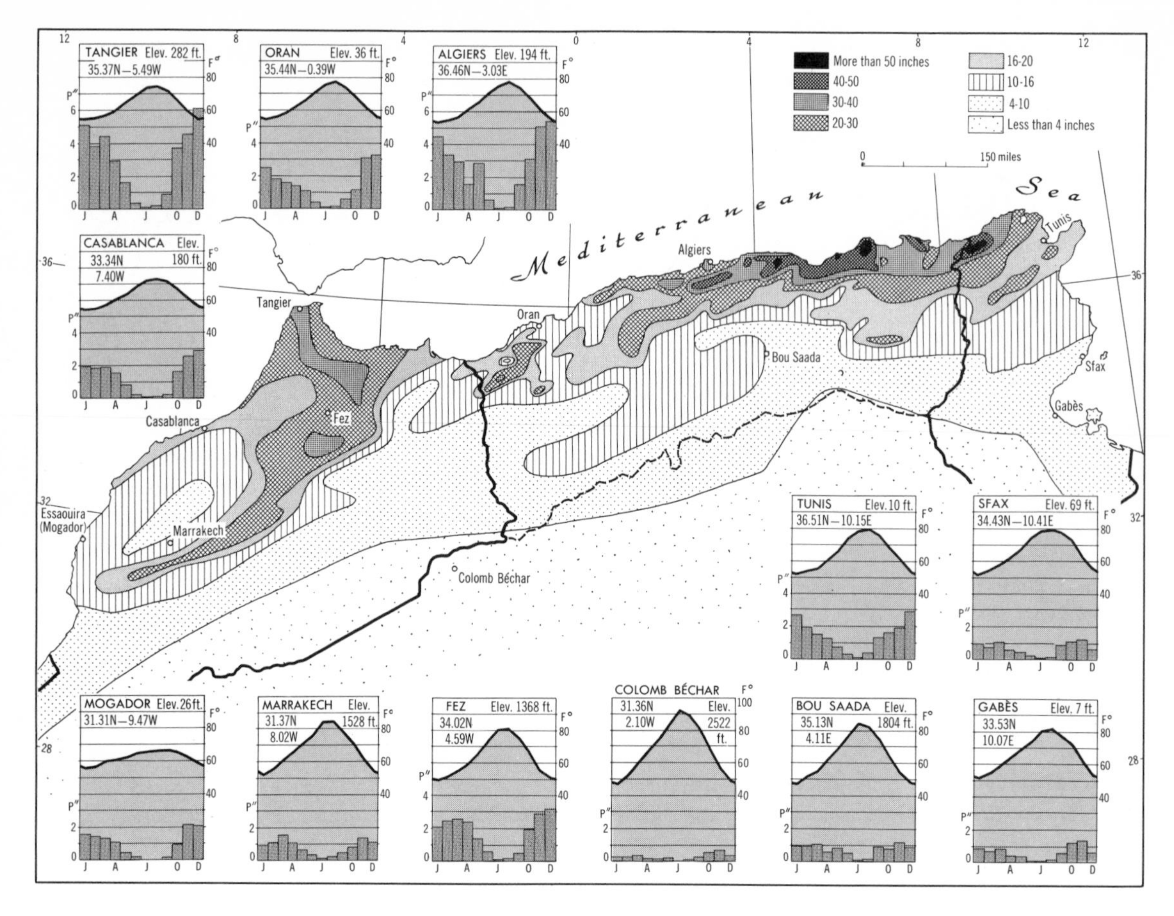

Map 21. Precipitation of the Maghrib and climographs for selected stations

adjacent islands, considered as integral parts of Spain. With the important exception of oil and natural gas in the Sahara, economic development is concentrated in the lands north and west of the high Atlas Mountains, in what is often referred to as Mediterranean Africa or the Maghrib.

SIMILARITIES WITH OTHER MEDITERRANEAN LANDS

The Maghrib is largely Mediterranean from the physical standpoint and it has many characteristics of other such lands. First, it faces the sea, which has permitted contacts for several millennia with other Mediterranean lands. Intermingling has also been facilitated by the closeness of Iberia and Sicily, and by movements along the northern coast of Africa from the Middle East. Second, much of it has a climate with Mediterranean influences, either the true dry subtropical or the Mediterranean steppe. Exceptions include some of the high plateaus and mountains, whose elevation results in a temperature regime marked by sharp seasonal contrasts, and the Sahara, which has a tropical desert climate (Map 21). The three main characteristics of the Mediterranean climate are moderate and unreliable precipitation concentrated in the winter with consequent droughts in summer; hot summers and warm winters; and reception of a high percentage of the possible sunshine.

Third, there is a similarity in landforms

between this area and the lands north of the Mediterranean, particularly in the existence of youthful mountain ranges. They are, in fact, sections of the western, or Alpide, portion of the Alpine system which may be traced down the boot of Italy, across Sicily, and into North Africa (Map 22). The northern range bifurcates in northern Morocco, one branch curving around in the Rif Atlas and in the Sierra Nevada of Spain, eventually to reappear in the Balearic Islands, the other curving south in the Middle Atlas. The southern range, known as the Saharan Atlas in Algeria, becomes the High Atlas in Morocco. South of it in Morocco is the Anti-Atlas. As in the Mediterranean lands of Europe, the steepness of these mountains limits their utility, though there are surprisingly high population densities within them. A second topographic similarity is the existence of alluvial-filled piedmont and coastal plains which are the sites of intensive irrigation agriculture. Fourth, the natural vegetation of the area is also Mediterranean.

The physical characteristics of the Maghrib result in a fifth similarity, that of land use. There are three distinct crop associations found in these and other Mediterranean lands, defined in accordance with the supply of moisture to the plants: (1) The rain-grown crops, which depend upon the winter precipitation. These crops, chiefly wheat and barley, cover by far the largest cultivated area. (2) The drought-tolerant crops, perennials which are adapted in one way or another to withstand the summer drought. These include the olive, fig, cork, and certain nut trees—some of the most distinctly Mediterranean plants. (3) The irrigated crops, which depend upon a supply of water beyond that from natural precipitation. They may be perennials, such as citrus and deciduous fruit or the vine, or annuals, such as vegetables and flowers. While occupying only a small portion of the total cultivated area they account for a large percentage of the value of export crops. It may be seen, then, that the major crops and crop specialities of North Africa are the same as those of other Mediterranean lands.

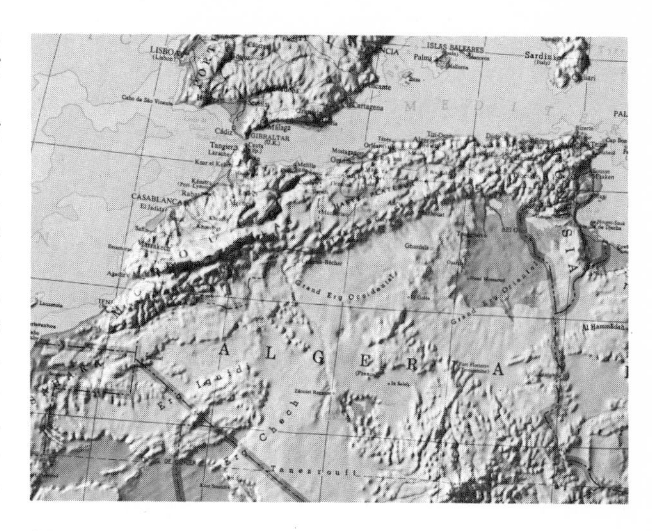

Map 22. Landforms of Northwest Africa
Relief Map Copyright Aero Service Corporation

Other similarities with northern Mediterranea are seen in the considerable number of European residents in the area, the fact that the general trend is toward Westernization, especially in Tunisia and Algeria, and the European character of modern industry and urbanization in such cities as Casablanca, Oran, Algiers, Bône, and Tunis.

Overpopulation is a final similarity. It threatens to be even more serious in North Africa than in other lands around the sea, however. In Algeria, for example, there are about 600,000 landless peasants, about 40 percent of the active agricultural force is un- or underemployed, at least 800,000 people were totally unemployed in mid-1963, five million people are said to be victims of poverty, and the population is increasing at a rate of somewhere between 2.6 and 3.0 percent per annum, which will double the total in less than 25 years. In Tunisia, about a third of the population may be considered as unemployed. Morocco is somewhat better off, but poverty is the lot of a large segment of the population. Overpopulation is at the base of the severe economic problems which beset the area, and, with the high rates of increase that characterize the Maghrib, it presents a frightening dilemma for the future. Furthermore, the extreme youth of the population (50 percent of Tunisians are under 20 years of age and 42 percent of Moroccans are under 14) means that the relatively small population of working age must support a large number of dependents and that educational requirements are unusually high.

CONTRASTS WITH OTHER MEDITERRANEAN LANDS

While there are significant similarities between North Africa and other Mediterranean countries, the contrasts are also quite striking. First, from the physical standpoint, Morocco was less influenced by sea contacts than most Mediterranean countries, partly because of the inhospitable character of its coasts. Climatic contrasts stem from the facts that the area is further south and hence is both hotter and has less reliable precipitation, and that there are considerable areas of high plateaus which are colder in winter and more steppelike. Furthermore, the Mediterranean climate graduates into desert, while north of the Sea it borders more productive, humid climates. Hydrographically, therefore, the area is less favorably endowed. Only Morocco has permanent streams, and the opportunities for irrigation in each of the countries compare unfavorably with their counterparts in Europe.

There are also important human differences; the culture of the indigenous peoples of North Africa is in sharp contrast with the cultures of northern Mediterranea. The Maghrib is the western wing of the Muslim world, if the Nile axis be the body and southwest Asia the eastern wing. While one often thinks of the lands east of Suez as the Muslim or Arab world, in fact, the countries from Egypt to Morocco have a Muslim population over twice as great as those of Asia Minor.

The true "natives" of the Maghrib are the Berbers, a northern Hamitic group whose origin is not known but who are believed to have come from the east, and some of the Jews, who were probably converted Berbers. While there has been very considerable admixture with the Arabs and adoption of the Islamic religion everywhere, the Berbers remain dominant in some areas, particularly the highland redoubts of Morocco and the Kabyle and Aures Mountain areas of Algeria.

The largest number of peoples of the area are Arabs, descended from groups which came across Egypt and Libya in several waves from the eighth to the thirteenth century. About three quarters of the population has Arabic as its mother tongue, a quarter Berber. In coastal areas there has been mixture of Arabs and Berbers with other stock, while admixture with Negro blood has occurred in the oases and elsewhere.

The Jewish population of the Maghrib totaled about 500,000 in early postwar years but is now estimated at fewer than 150,000, of which 105,000 remain in Morocco, 30,000 in Tunisia, and 10,000 in Algeria. The emigration of Jews, largely to Israel and France, has had an impact on virtually every aspect of Jewish communal life in North Africa. The Jewish population of the area has been characterized by a very high degree of urbanization and by greater Europeanization than other indigenous peoples.

The European population of the Maghrib can only be estimated because of rapid emigration since 1956 in Morocco and Tunisia and since 1961 in Algeria. In 1956 there were about 400,000 Europeans in Morocco, a million in Algeria, and 255,000 in Tunisia. In 1963, about 140,000 remained in Morocco, perhaps 130,000 in Algeria, and 40,000 in Tunisia. Evidence suggests that these numbers may be cut by two thirds in the next five years. The exodus of Europeans represents some gains for the indigenous peoples; it also entails severe losses in skill, managerial ability, capital, and market capacity, and has resulted in serious economic recessions in each of the countries.

Another important sphere of contrasts with northern Mediterranea is in land use patterns. These reflect in part a response to the less favorable climate, but more importantly to the cultural heritage of the peoples of the Maghrib. The most significant contrasts include a greater concern with livestock grazing, especially the nomadic grazing of sheep and goats; an overweening interest in grains among the cultivated crops; the relatively minor position of Arab and Berber peoples in irrigation agriculture and in production of high-value export crops; and the much poorer methods employed by the indigenous peoples. There is relatively greater dependence on agriculture in all its forms than in European Mediterranea but a higher proportion of it is at the subsistence level.

THE IMPORTANCE OF THE MAGHRIB

North Africa, like other parts of the continent, is underdeveloped. But it does compare favorably with other regions by several measures. Morocco, non-Saharan Algeria, and Tunisia, with only 2.6 percent of the total area and 10.1 percent of the total population, accounted for about 12.5 percent of total exports and 21.4 percent of African imports in 1961. Incomes are well above average for the continent. The infrastructures of each of the main countries are distinctly superior to those of tropical African countries.

The three major countries have also had great significance for France. Algeria ranked second among French markets in 1961; it normally took 70 to 80 percent of its imports from France. Forty to 60 percent of Moroccan and Tunisian imports are normally French. Some exports of North Africa have been important to France, including phosphates, citrus fruit, and now oil, but many are competitive rather than complementary, such as iron ore, vegetables, deciduous fruit, and wine in recent decades.

At one time it was thought that colonization would be the most important contribution of North Africa, but the stabilizing population of France reduced the necessity for and interest in emigration. The area also had military significance for France, on the one hand as a source of recruits, on the other in the provision of naval and air bases.

History can be perverse, however, and developments in North Africa have largely negated earlier expectations held by the French. Rather than making a net economic contribution to France, North Africa became an increasing burden on the French taxpayer through expenses for budgetary deficits, developmental contributions, and military campaigns. Emigration from France was considerably offset by a countermigration of Algerians to France and has, in any case, now been reversed. In the military sphere, North Africans with experience in the French forces were often among the leaders of nationalist revolts, while in the years immediately before independence there were as many as 500,000 French soldiers stationed in Algeria, weakening the whole strategic position of NATO.

MOROCCO

Morocco, with an area of 171,305 square miles, had a total population of 12.2 million in 1962. About 140,000 Europeans and 105,000 Jews remained in 1963, the rest of the populace being almost entirely Arab or Berber. About 2.6 million Muslims still speak Berber, though many of these are Arabized to a greater or lesser degree. Both the Moroccan and non-Moroccan populations are characterized by extreme youth, and the crude rate of increase may be as high as 3.0 percent per annum.

Morocco probably has the greatest land use potential of the main countries, but it is the least advanced in development. This is explained by the greater physical isolation of the area, behind the mountain ramparts of the Rif and High Atlas and with an inhospitable coast, by the proportionately small European population in earlier years, and by the lateness of the date at which modern economic forces began to be introduced. The French protectorate was acquired only in 1912; the country was not pacified until 1934. On the other hand, Morocco progressed more rapidly from World War II to 1956 than its sister countries.

Morocco is the most strongly individual of all the Barbary states. It is part European, part

Arab, part African in character. Fez is Arabic, Casablanca French, and Marrakech almost Sudanese. From the human standpoint there is a greater division between Arab and Berber, fewer educated *évolué*, and a greater retention of medieval culture and methods. The tribe is a more significant unit than in Algeria or Tunisia, inter- and intratribal conflicts being a highly complex and dynamic element in the scene. The main factor of unity in the country is the king; the elements of disunity include the differences between Arabs and Berbers, the rivalries of the several political parties, and the sometimes conflicting position among various groups within the country such as the labor unions, the modernized and urbanized European and indigenous population, the proletariat occupying the bidonvilles of Casablanca and other cities, the nomads, the mountain dwellers, and the inhabitants of the north who were under a Spanish rather than a French protectorate.

Morocco differs from the other North African countries physically in having considerably larger plains, in having the highest mountains, and in largely facing the Atlantic rather than the Mediterranean. The fact that the mountains more directly face the prevailing winter winds results in heavier precipitation; their greater height brings more snow; together these give the area a better river system, including several permanent watercourses, and thus greater hydroelectric and irrigation potentialities.

THE REGIONS OF MOROCCO

THE COASTAL PLAIN. A 20 to 30-mile-wide coastal plain (Map 23) extends from Rabat to Essaouria (Mogador), itself divided into two parallel belts, the sandy Sahel along the sea with littoral dunes marking former shores of the ocean and the "tirs," a black-soiled region suitable for grain production. The agricultural usefulness of the plain is somewhat restricted by the drying influence of the cool Canaries Current, though there are some irrigation communities and production of winter vegetables in favored zones and rain-growing of cereals in the "tirs." Behind Rabat and Kenitra (Port Lyautey) are fairly extensive dry woodland areas contributing to the cork production of the country, and Rabat has one of the largest cork factories in the world. The cork forests were not exploited until arrival of the Europeans, who first destructively overstripped the trees. Cutting of the bark is now controlled and the forests, which are state owned, have been sufficiently regenerated to permit an increased production. The cork oak has a second value in some areas—helping to control soil erosion.

While the Canaries Current decreases the utility of the littoral zone it is advantageous in

Map 23. Regions of the Maghrib

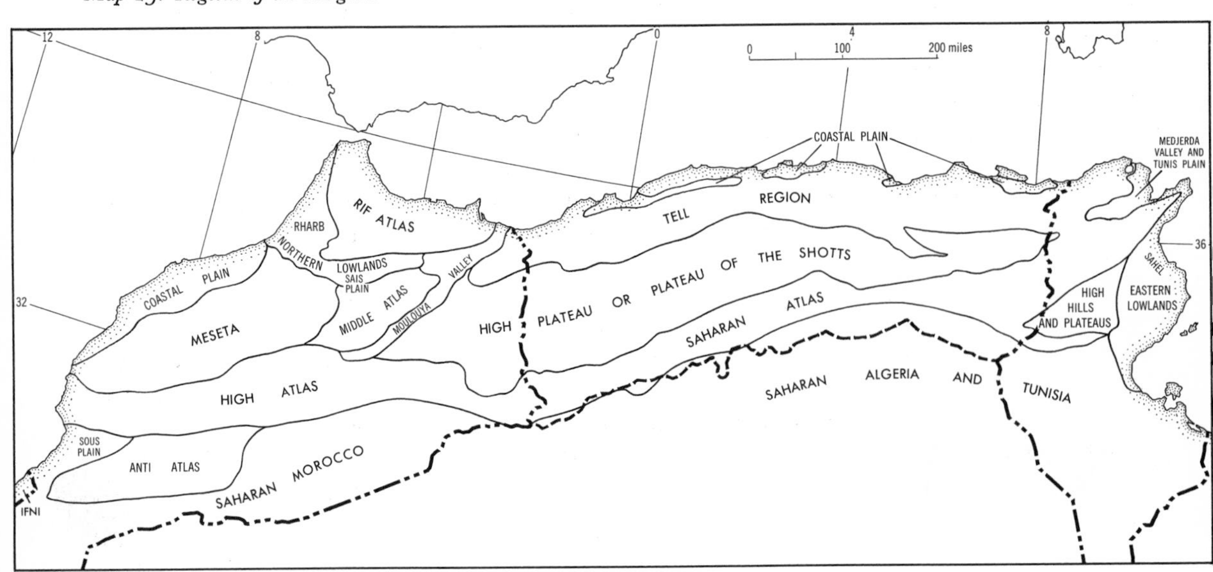

Production of winter vegetables on the coast south of Casablanca
Much of Morocco's coastal zone is made more arid by the effects of the cool Canaries Current, but in favored areas an intensive agriculture is possible.

supporting large schools of fish, which provide the base for one of the important fishing industries of Africa. Safi is the main port for the landing of sardines, which comprised 138,000 tons of the record 1961 catch of 182,000 tons valued at $12.2 million. Casablanca has the largest fish canning establishment; El Jadida (Mazagan) is a secondary center of importance. Morocco ranks second to Portugal in the production of sardines; other fish of importance are tunny and anchovies.

The coastal belt also contains the leading ports of Morocco. That country is disadvantaged by the lack of natural harbors, particularly the absence of havens at river mouths which are impeded by heavy silt deposition, and by the characteristically large ocean swell. The construction of an artificial port at Casablanca enormously improved the situation and that city now accounts for about 75 percent of the seaborne trade of the country. It possesses almost four miles of quays with alongside depths of 30 feet and its cargo handled grew from 200,000 tons in 1914, the year after creation of its artificial port, to 5,600,000 tons in 1949 and 9,486,000 tons in 1961, making it one of the leading ports of Africa. It is favorably situated with regard to mineral areas, and phosphates from Khourigba make up a large part of its export tonnages. Casablanca, which is the most

Casablanca, Morocco
The port handles about 75 percent of the seaborne trade of the country, while approximately 70 percent of the modern industrial establishments of Morocco are located at Casablanca.

Pastoralism in Morocco
The greater part of the Meseta and many of the mountain areas of the country are inhabited by seminomadic pastoralists. Physical conditions are very difficult and practices are poor in all regards.

Plowing a wheat field in Morocco
Barley and wheat are the chief rain-grown crops, occupying about 85 percent of the total cultivated area. Average yields are low and disastrous harvests are periodic.

modern of Moroccan cities, has a large part of the remaining European and Jewish populations and about 70 percent of the modern industrial establishments of the country.

Safi, 120 miles to the southwest, is Morocco's second port. It leads in shipments of sardines, but its exports are mainly phosphates from Louis Gentil. Other Atlantic ports include Kenitra, a river port and Franco-American naval base, and Agadir, where new port works will provide capacity to handle a million tons a year.

The main rail line and one of the major road routes of the country follow the coast (Map 20). The main railway runs from Marrakech to Casablanca, Rabat, Fez, Oujda, and then connects with the Algerian line. Branch lines run from Tangier to Fez and from the phosphate deposits to their ports. The rail net totals 1,091 miles.

THE MESETA. Inland from the coastal plain a 60- to 80-mile-wide raised platform of primitive rock overlaid with sedimentaries extends to the Atlas Mountains. With an average elevation of about 1,000 feet, the meseta is dry and almost treeless except in the rugged northern part with its forests of holly and cork oak. The southernmost portion of the meseta is the foundered plain of Marrakech, the valley of the Haouz River.

The greater part of the meseta is inhabited by seminomadic pastoralists. Pastoralism, in fact, is *the* economy of the meseta and a large part of the mountains as well. Practices are poor in all respects: in breeding, in lack of shelter provided, in feeding, and in proper stocking. In areas with such variable precipitation stocking is, at best, extremely difficult. In arid years the grazier may lose or be forced to slaughter 40 percent or more of his flock. Sheep and goats are the most common livestock; camels, asses, and horses are kept as draught animals and beasts of burden.

Tillage agriculture on the meseta is found only on the better watered areas, in areas where orographic influences bring greater precipitation, in the incised valleys where water is available for irrigation, and around Marrakech where underground supplies are tapped. Although the Haouz Plain is in a region of low humidity, with inadequate and variable rainfall, and subject to desiccating summer winds, the snows and the nearness of the Atlas provide surface and underground water. A system of open canals or "seguias" distributes the surface water; "khettaras" or subterranean channels, dug and maintained at an enormous expense of labor, control the underground supplies. Large date palm groves are supported in this area, which also produces olives, citrus fruit, and vegetables.

The chief crops of the meseta, and of Morocco, are rain-grown barley and wheat, which occupy 85 percent of the total cultivated area, estimated at 12.5 million acres. About 96 percent of the total acreage in cereals is under dry farming. In five years, one very good harvest may be expected, three good to poor, and one bad to disastrous. Yields of only half the average are common; in the worst years only one fifth to one seventh of the average yields may be won. And average yields are themselves quite low, about 9 bushels per acre for the country as a whole as compared with about 16 bushels per acre for the world. In some years there is a substantial export of grains, in others Morocco is a net importer.

Moroccan farming has been described as "a traditional world still enslaved by the conditions of a capricious climate." Methods of the Muslim farmers are very poor. The wooden plow is employed; there is little if any fertilization; dry-farming techniques are inadequately applied; there is very little mechanization. It is no wonder that 60 percent of Moroccans may be classified as indigent.

Landownership is characterized by great unevenness in land distribution, including a large number of excessively small holdings, and by a very difficult and complex land tenurial situation. The approximately one million Muslim cultivators own about 80 percent of the farm land, but about 10 percent of these own 60 percent of the total. About 40 percent own less than 1¼ acres, while 60 percent of the rural residents are landless wage laborers or "khames," sharecroppers usually entitled to one fifth of the harvest. It has been estimated that the average peasant is unemployed 200 days a year, that 50 percent of the rural labor force works less than four months a year. Only about 30 percent of total production from the traditional sector is commercialized, so subsistence farming is still the norm in Moroccan agriculture.

European farming, on the other hand, is characteristically modern, large scale, and concentrated upon higher value crops and commercial production. There are about 3,500 holdings with 1.3 million cultivated acres, 70 percent of which is in the relatively well-watered and populated regions of Rabat, the Rharb, and Casablanca. Europeans account for about half of the total commercial production, for 85 percent of the citrus fruit, 80 percent of tobacco, 75 percent of the wine, and most of the peas, beans, and tomatoes produced. The disproportionate share of European farms in production of export crops, their significance as employers of about 60,000 workers, and the present inability of Moroccan farmers to take over these farms effectively have led the government to adopt a conservative approach to conversion of European holdings. Only about a seventh of European farms had reverted to Moroccan ownership by 1963, but pressure for nationalization and subdivision may be expected to increase, especially in view of the more dynamic programs adopted in Algeria and Tunisia.

Moroccan agriculture is, then, beset with

Vineyards on European farm inland from Rabat, Morocco
There were about 3,500 European holdings in Morocco in 1963, accounting for about half of total commercial production. They are characteristically large-scale operations and focus where possible on higher value crops.

The Bin el Ouidane Dam on the Oued el Abid
This is Morocco's largest dam, permitting control of about 370,000 acres for irrigation and production of about 550 million kwh of electricity yearly.

serious problems. Despite substantially enlarged production of citrus fruit, fresh vegetables, and wine in recent years agricultural output has advanced much less rapidly than the population has increased and per capita production of cereals is no better than it was thirty-five years ago.

Efforts to improve the situation have included a variety of programs, sometimes quite massive, but results to date have been far from spectacular. In 1957 "Operation Plow" was instituted, involving the mechanical preparation of a large acreage of lands in small holdings. Hundreds of tractors were used to plow almost a million acres, but by 1962 the operation was considered a failure and emphasis had shifted from it. Problems included the difficulty of shifting peasants to a new type of farming, inadequate arrangements for maintenance of machinery, costs which were considered greater than were justified by the increased yields, corruption, and pressure resulting from the large concealed and actual unemployment in the countryside. An associated tractor factory also was forced to close.

In 1961 the Rural Promotion Program was announced. Patterned after a similar plan in Tunisia, it was designed to mobilize unused labor by compulsory work on such projects as water and soil conservation, irrigation, tree planting, pest control, and construction of schools. It is in part a self-help program since wages are very low, though supplemented by surplus American food. Its greatest success has apparently been in the building of schools and roads, but the agricultural impact has not been impressive, the free supply of food having sometimes led to decreased local production.

Another program of considerable interest is concerned with the development of irrigation (Map 24). At present about 1,000,000 acres are irrigated, but only a quarter of the total is modern and with good yields. Plans call for increasing the area by about 37,000 acres a year. The largest project to date, instituted by the French on the Oued el Abid tributary of the Rebia River, involved construction of the world's tenth largest dam, Bin el Ouidane, which permits irrigation control of 370,500 acres and has a hydroelectric capacity of 212,000 kw. Thus far, about 100,000 acres in the Beni Amir–Beni Moussa area are controlled by the dam. The distribution of holdings there involved direction of the crops grown and the rotation program adopted, but, as in other newer irrigation schemes, there have been great problems of training the inhabitants to an entirely new system of agriculture.

It is estimated that about 2.3 million acres could be brought under irrigation in the country. Irrigation projects are important to Morocco because that country is incapable of feeding itself in dry years and because its population, increasing by some 300,000 people yearly, requires that agriculture be intensified wherever possible. Irrigation development is not unaccompanied with problems, however. The use of deep plows on areas formerly in grass or only scratched by primitive plows can lead to serious erosion; there is the necessity to protect against the silting of reservoirs and canals; there are great difficulties in shifting untrained peasants to a more evolved agricultural system; and there are problems in securing adequate capital and developing schemes which justify the expenditure involved.

Other measures designed to advance agriculture have included efforts to introduce collective forms of farming, despite the overwhelming evidence that these have not worked in other countries, programs to increase production of specific crops such as tobacco, sugar beets, and cotton, and a plan to increase the output of preserved meats, which has failed. Despite the lack of success thus far obtained, it must not be concluded that there are not substantial opportunities remaining. Possibly the greatest single handicap which must be overcome is the attitude of Moroccan peasants and landlords. Far more individual initiative must be developed; the desire to secure leisure and prestige by employing labor or leasing land must be abandoned. There are very great potentialities in increasing livestock and poultry output and in the extension of fruit and vegetable production. Subdivision of lands will undoubtedly involve first the disposition of government lands, then those of corporate ownership, and finally the large estates. As for so many advances in Africa, education holds the key; little real progress can be expected from a largely illiterate peasantry confined by traditional habits and institutions.

REGIONS OF NORTHERN MOROCCO. North of the meseta is the basin of the Sebou River, richer and more populous than other parts of the country. Stretching inland from the sea is the Rharb Plain, an ancient marine gulf filled with alluvium from the Sebou. This flat and sometimes marshy plain, a considerable part of which has been developed by European farmers, has immense fields of wheat and barley and accounts for about 40 percent of citrus production. The country's acreage in citrus trees increased from only 27,000 acres before World War II to over 147,000 acres in 1958, presenting one of the more dynamic aspects of Moroccan agriculture. One large marshy area of over 600,000 acres north of Rabat has been almost completely drained in recent years and is becoming an important area for intensive production. In 1962–63, however, great floods caused heavy damage throughout the Rharb.

The central plain of the Sebou, or Sais Plain, an ancient lake drained by the Sebou, is densely populated. Cereals and fruit trees are grown and there is a considerable number of European farms in the areas around Fez and Meknès. Fez, the religious and intellectual capital of Morocco, and Meknès, an important commercial crossroads point, are the chief cities of this subregion. The plain is enclosed by small massifs on the north and by a plateau attached to the Middle Atlas on the south. To the east, the Taza corridor, which provided the routeway for early invasions, permits relatively easy passage to Algeria.

In what was formerly Spanish Morocco the Rif Atlas is the dominant physiographic feature. Only pacified in 1927, this region never received the attention accorded more favored areas, and the fiercely independent mountain tribes largely maintain their traditional systems. Some sections are very densely populated, especially considering the difficult landforms, and the region is constantly threatened with famine. The only area with good possibilities is the valley of the Moulouya River. One dam completed in 1956 and the Mechra Khila Dam under construction will control some 160,000 acres for irrigation, permit production of about 150 million kwh yearly, and provide an estimated 50,000 new agricultural jobs.

The northern coast of Morocco is the site of several cities of some importance. Tangier, whose international status had attracted numerous phantom corporations and monetary manipulations, was fully integrated with Morocco in 1960, after a period during which special monetary concessions had resulted in a big currency drain from the country. With the loss of about three fifths of its commercial activity, the city faces a somewhat uncertain future, but it should continue to benefit from tourism, from rerouting of traffic as it is developed to be the main outlet for the north, from its selection as the summer capital, and as several industrial plans for the area come to fruition. Tangier is more easily tied to the rest of Morocco than the other northern ports because a zone of low hills and plains extends west of the Rif arc to the Atlantic.

Ceuta and Melilla are Spanish "plazas" with somewhat precarious economic bases. Melilla, with a population of about 79,000, does ship iron ore. Ceuta (73,000 population) has a good harbor and handles some bunkerage trade. The population of both is mainly Spanish. Morocco has stated that it wishes to incorporate them as well as the Spanish areas to the south of Morocco and parts of Mauritania.

THE ATLAS MOUNTAINS. With the exception of the Rif, the mountains of Morocco consist of several roughly parallel Alpine ranges. The Middle Atlas, rising to 11,000 feet, is like the Jura in having high plateaus, limestone soils, subterranean drainage, and great forests. Plans call for doubling the output of cedar, establishing several new eucalyptus plantations, and developing chipboard, pulp, and box factories. The Middle and High Atlas are the reservoir of Morocco, their heavier orographic precipitation feeding the most important streams. The High Atlas extends from sea cliffs north of Agadir to Algeria, where it becomes the Saharan Atlas. Over 9,800 feet high in the center and culminating in the highest point of Morocco (Djebel Toubkal, 13,661 feet), the High Atlas is covered with vegetation on the north, rocky and bare in the south. The Anti-Atlas is formed of ancient rock, part of the Saharan shield, more recently uplifted and subjected to volcanic action.

The Atlas chains are an immense physical barrier, not so difficult to cross but more important in protecting the northwest of Morocco from desiccating Saharan winds. Some valuable timber is shipped from the north, but the mountains, which harbor some remarkable population densities in the wetter areas, have local self-sufficiency as their economic keynote.

SOUTHERN AND EASTERN MOROCCO. South and east of the Atlas ranges is Saharan Morocco, largely composed of "hammadas," dry, bare, rocky plateaus. While the Atlas ranges protect seaward Morocco from the Sahara they also shut off the inland areas from marine influences; hence most of the region is suitable only for nomadism and extensive stock breeding. Palm groves are supported close to the mountains in wadi type oases which usually suffer from overpopulation, having densities as high as 1,600 per square mile. The northeastern segments of the country prolong the regions of Algeria. High plateaus, with a semidesert climate, support some large herds of camels and sheep and yield a minor output of alfa grass.

Moroccan land use, then, presents a scene of great contrasts. While it is now generally poor, there are distinct possibilities for agricultural development, better indeed than those possessed by the other two major states of the Maghrib. Mineral and industrial developments of the area are discussed in a later section.

IFNI AND SPANISH SAHARA

Before we turn to Algeria and Tunisia, the remaining minor political units of northwestern Africa may be briefly examined. Ifni, classified as an African province of Spain, is a 579-square mile enclave in southern Morocco. Its major interest was apparently as a potential fishery base and possibly as landward protection for the Canary Islands. Effective occupation dates from 1934, but it has little economic significance except to its population of about 50,000, most of whom are Berbers. Livestock remains the primary source of wealth among the rural inhabitants, many of whom are still nomadic. Aridity and rugged relief limit tillage agriculture to production of barley, plus small quantities of olives, dates, cotton, and tobacco. Sidi Ifni, the capital, has about a quarter of the population and owes its significance to the political function plus its position as a "free port." Exports of Ifni are valued at only about $28,000 yearly.

Spanish Sahara, with an area of about 102,703 square miles and a population of 25,000, is largely a desert wasteland. Most of it is inhabited by impoverished nomads; farming takes place in a few scattered areas estimated to total only 1,430 acres. The main productive economy of the province is fishing; 540 fishing boats were based on its coastal stations in a recent year yielding exports valued at about $100,000. Following the oil boom in Algerian Sahara, seventeen oil companies rushed into Spanish Sahara prepared to spend $200 million in six years. Operations proceeded under some difficulties, both political (eleven technicians were kidnapped at gun point and later released in Rabat in 1961 and oil teams work under protection against Moroccan incursions) and physical, but results were disappointing as of mid-1963, when several companies abandoned the search and others were proceeding at a less enthusiastic pace. There has also been some interest in other minerals, including phosphates south of El Aaium, the capital, iron ore, and uranium. There is some production of salt by evaporation at Villa Cisneros.

ALGERIA

Algeria may best be divided for examination into northern and Saharan Algeria. The north, formerly "departmental Algeria," covers an area of 115,537 square miles and had a population in 1963 of about 10,612,000. Stretching for 620 miles along the Mediterranean and 120 to 210 miles southward to the desert side of the Saharan Atlas, it is a land of mountains, interior plateaus, and limited coastal plains, subject to even greater climatic handicaps than Morocco.

Algeria long occupied the prime position among French overseas areas in investment, number of "colons," and general cultural attachment. Until 1957 France claimed that Algeria was an integral part of that country, but its special administrative regime, inequality of representation, and certain economic restrictions belied this assertion. Dissatisfied with the position of the Muslim majority, several leaders instituted a revolt in November, 1954, which continued for seven years, led to the collapse of the Fourth French Republic in 1958, and finally to independence for the country on July 3, 1962.

The French followed two courses in meeting the revolt: military repression and enormously increased expenditures for economic and social development, but years were required before the French realized that only the granting of independent status would satisfy Algerian demands. The war is estimated to have cost France over $10 billion; over 200,000 persons were killed, including 14,000 members of the French forces and 18,500 European civilians in Algeria; over a million Muslims were displaced; and the country suffered enormous material damage.

The Constantine Plan, announced in 1958 and effectively started the following year, represented the nonmilitary effort to win Algerian support. It called for expenditures of about $1 billion yearly for ten years, about one third from public and two thirds from private sources. While many of its ambitious goals were not met, particularly in rural areas where military conditions precluded its application, substantial progress was made on improvement of roads, construction of houses, soil conservation, hydroelectric installations, development of industries, and expansion of schools.

The end of the war, however, created an entirely new situation in Algeria. Rivalry among various political and military leaders resulted in a chaotic period before effective control was achieved. Most of the Europeans fled, so that by mid-1963 their numbers had declined from over a million to perhaps 130,000. This meant that some three million acres were abandoned, including a large part of the more productive part of the country; hundreds of small businesses and industries were closed, representing an estimated 70 percent of such establishments; construction declined so steeply that only 15,000 of the 120,000 workers normally employed were active by the end of 1962; total unemployment reached over 2 million, while the government stated that 4.5 million were without resources and dependent entirely or in part on food shipments coming from abroad, mainly from the United States.

Thus in 1963 Algeria was a country in dire economic straits. It possessed an unusually well-developed infrastructure but had neither the means nor the know-how to exploit it. French aid, while still very substantial, was down to about $200 million a year; aid from other countries, including a $100 million long-term loan announced in September, 1963, from the Soviet Union, was not sufficient to replace the former funds; the exodus of Europeans meant that the largest source of tax revenues was greatly reduced; government expenditures, despite efforts at austerity, were running well ahead of receipts, thus necessitating several emergency loans; and yields from Saharan oil, totaling about $39,760,000 in 1962, were far from adequate to fill the gap. It will require several years before something approaching normalcy can be achieved, perhaps several decades before economic advances comparable to those of the 1950s can be expected.

ALGERIAN AGRICULTURE

Agriculture normally supports about two thirds of the Algerian population and accounts for one third of the national income. An estimated 73.4 percent of northern Algeria is considered useful, but much of this is of low productivity. Although a third of the total is cultivated, 36 percent of that is suitable only for dry farming and 79 percent of the remaining productive acreage is devoted to grain crops of relatively low value and low yield. Only about 13.5 percent of the productive lands or 2.9 percent of the country is devoted to higher value crops such as the vine, vegetables, fruit, and modern olive orchards.

Contrasts between the traditional and modern segments of agriculture have been striking. Most of the modern farms were European, accounting for about 38.6 percent of the total cultivated area and supporting about 21,000 Europeans. The size of these holdings varied greatly: there were a few enormous individual and company estates, 3,800 proprietors had over 500 acres, and over a third had less than 25 acres. The European holdings tended to be concentrated in the more favored areas—in the coastal lowlands and in the better-watered northern section of the plateau. By no means did all of the European farmers employ advanced farming practices; many were small holders transplanted from the poorer sections of France. But techniques were generally good and yields of grain were over double those on Muslim holdings, only partly because of superior natural conditions.

By mid-1963 between 2½ and 3 million acres of European holdings had been abandoned, and in October, 1963, the Algerian government announced that all remaining European lands would be expropriated. Most of the abandoned or nationalized farms have been turned over to workers' and farmers' collectives which have been subject to several organizational arrangements including tenant management committees. Only time will tell the impact of this revolution in landownership, but serious losses in production of cash crops must be expected in the immediate future. In the meantime a part of French aid allotted to Algeria is being diverted to reimburse dispossessed French farmers.

The traditional sector of agriculture is characterized by features similar to those prevailing in Morocco. Before independence, about 630,000 Muslim proprietors held about 10.75 million acres of cultivated land. Most holdings were not adequate, as about 50 acres of unirrigated land are required for the support of a family. Over 700,000 peasants were completely landless, while 200,000 engaged in sharecropping. The situation was no better among the graziers, most of whom were seminomadic and largely in the self-subsistent realm.

In postwar years, greater efforts were made to improve indigenous agriculture. There was some large-scale resettlement; major antierosion schemes were undertaken; various loan arrangements were instituted; and programs of reclamation and subdivision of large estates were instituted. But even if all the cultivable land were subdivided there does not appear to be adequate land to support the present rural population, let alone the additional numbers born each year. The increasing pressure on the land is dramatically revealed by examining the production per inhabitant of major crops, which shows a drastic decline since 1911 or since 1938 in such things as wheat, barley, potatoes, and dry vegetables. If wine is excluded, the country is, in fact, a net importer of foodstuffs. The number of animals per inhabitant has also decreased markedly; indeed there were only 55 percent as many cattle and 64 percent as many sheep in 1959 as in 1911. And in April, 1963, Algerians were asked to refrain from eating mutton during a traditional Muslim feast because the sheep population had declined from 10 million in 1954 to 3 million in 1963.

A large European estate in one of the coastal plains of Algeria
The future of Algerian vineyards is problematical because of the large European exodus and recently imposed tariffs on wine imports to France.

THE REGIONS OF ALGERIA

COASTAL LOWLANDS. The coastal lowlands of Algeria occur as a series of pockets or valleys between the enecheloned prongs of the maritime Atlas. From west to east the important lowlands are the plains around Oran and along the Sig River, the Chelif Valley, the plains of Algiers and the Metidja, and those near Bougie and Bône. Together, these comprise one of the quality areas of Africa. On only 2 to 3 percent of the area of Algeria they contain over half its population and most of the 1.3 million irrigated acres in the country, and account for a major share in the value of agricultural production and exports. Population densities range from 180 to 1,200 per square mile and there are over two million urban residents.

Advantages of these separated plains include the presence of excellent alluvial soils, a relatively favorable Mediterranean climate, and the availability of water for irrigation. Insalubrious marshes formerly covered large tracts, but most of these have been reclaimed and are among the most productive parts of the country. The major crops of the coastal plains are the vine, citrus fruit, and vegetables; cotton, tobacco, and deciduous fruit are also produced.

To the French, the vine was the "soul of Algeria" and it was the most powerful attraction for many "colons." In recent years it occupied almost a million acres in the country; three quarters of the acreage was in thirteen private or company estates, but many small holdings existed at the opposite extreme. About 400,000 people were dependent on the vine, and wine accounted for about 51 percent of the total value of exports excluding oil. Algeria has been producing about 30 percent as much wine, mostly *vin ordinaire*, as France itself. This permitted it to rank as the leading exporter of wine in the world, large quantities going by tanker to the ports of southern France, partly for mixing with French wines. Overproduction in France in postwar years raised the question whether the vine should not be partially replaced by other crops. It would not be easy, however, to find a substitute of similar value; vineyards involve a high investment in capital and know-how and require over four times as many man days per acre as grains. The vineyards of Algeria face a somewhat precarious future, first because of some transferral from European to Muslim ownership with a consequent loss in skill, and second because wine producers in France have been successful in their efforts to have imports restricted in view of the surplus production in that country.

Citrus fruit, whose production increased considerably over prewar years but failed to keep up with the dynamic advances in other Mediterranean countries in the 1950s, has a potentially more hopeful future because of the expanding markets in western Europe. It does, however, require more irrigation water than the vine.

The production of vegetables is markedly concentrated around Algiers because of the high dependence on speed of transport. As for Morocco, early vegetables have the economic advantage of reaching the Paris market before production from any French region. Sometimes two crops are grown in a year, one irrigated, the other on the winter rains. As is the case for wine, the size of the market appears to be the limiting factor in production.

Irrigation is important in considerable areas of the coastal plains (Map 24). A total of about 1,300,000 acres is under irrigation in northern Algeria, over twenty storage dams having been constructed since 1920. Irrigation involves even more serious problems than in Morocco because so many factors compound to make for erosion: the extreme steepness of the Tell Atlas, the softness of its rocks, the sparse vegetation cover, and the seasonal rain pattern, particularly the characteristic deluges of autumn and spring. Older dams are already badly silted and multipronged prevention campaigns are required for all projects, programs involving large-scale reforestation, terracing of tilled lands, control of overgrazing, and, in extreme cases, the movement of peoples from particularly vulnerable areas. Forced migration is difficult to impose; terracing is costly; and protection of forests is hindered by indiscriminate cutting of trees for firewood, tent poles, and production of extract tannin, by destructive grazing, and by fires.

The coastal lowlands are the sites of the major cities of Algeria, somewhat in contrast to Morocco which has a considerable number of large inland cities. The present population of Algerian cities is highly conjectural because of the enormous exodus of Europeans, over 80 percent of whom were urban residents. In 1960 about 22 percent of the Muslim population lived in the cities, but one fifth of these were unemployed. Algiers, with about 834,000 people in 1960, is the principal city commercially, industrially, culturally, and politically. It does not handle the high percentage of national trade that Casablanca does for Morocco because of the scattered nature of producing areas along

Map 24. Major dams and irrigated areas in the Maghrib

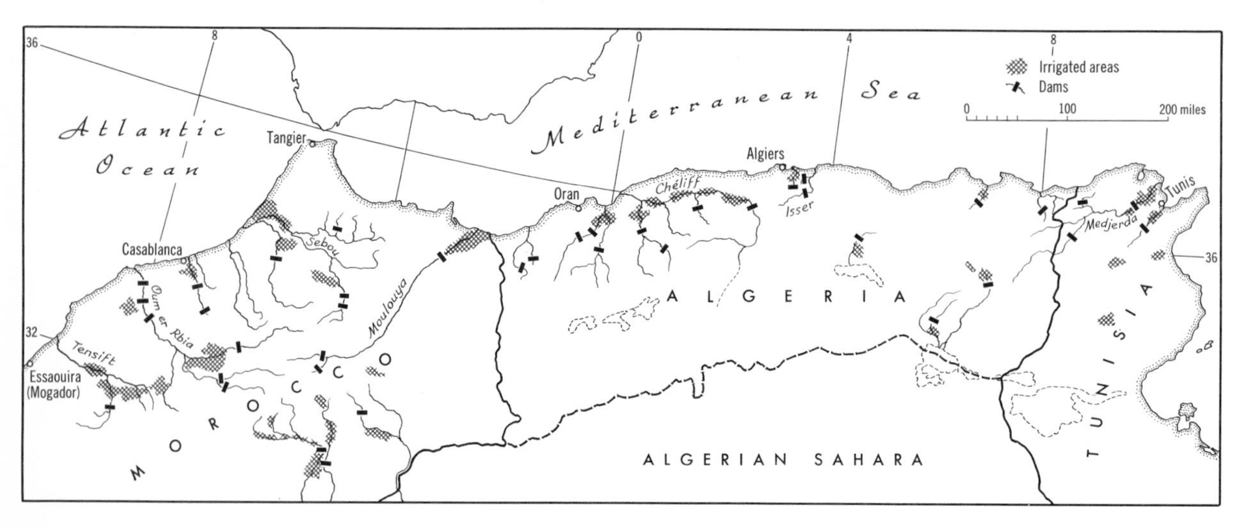

the extended coastline and the greater importance of other outlets for mineral traffic, including oil from the Sahara. Oran, with 393,000 people, has a better natural harbor than Algiers; in addition to serving its own productive hinterland it exports iron ore and has a rail link to oases and the Colomb Béchar mineral area in the south. Bône also handles an important mineral traffic, while Bougie, the seaward terminus of a pipeline from Hassi Messaoud, is the major petroleum port of the country. The coastal cities are connected by a modern and well-equipped rail line; the north-south connections, however, which carry greater tonnages, are not as well developed as they should be. Despite the difficult terrain, the highway network is superior by African standards.

Harvesting grain on a large farm in Algeria
Barley and wheat are the main crops in the Tell Atlas and in those areas of the Plateau of the Shotts where precipitation is adequate to support crops. These cereals occupy about seven eighths of the total cultivated area of the country.

THE COASTAL TELL. This region may be divided into three zones: the littoral band where hills, known as the Sahels, plunge brusquely to the sea; the coastal plains and associated valleys already covered; and the Tell Atlas. The Sahels are intensively used where possible for gardening, vineyards, and orchards; elsewhere they are tree covered or in maquis, the characteristic scrub vegetation of Mediterranean areas.

The Tell Atlas consists of large tabular plateaus with some mountainous massifs often cut by profound valleys; it joins with the Saharan Atlas in Tunisia. Despite the inhospitable character of these mountains they are often densely populated. Kabylia, with about 4 percent of the area of Algeria, has an estimated 15 percent of its population. It is in these mountainous areas that the worst problems of soil erosion exist, where land is being lost more rapidly than it is being reclaimed.

The main crops of the mountains are barley and wheat, which occupy 87 percent of the cultivated area of the country. Grains face many climatic handicaps in the Tell Atlas: cold winters, late frosts lasting even to May, damaging hailstorms, torrential rains, uncertain and widely fluctuating precipitation, and the desiccating sirocco. Also important in the mountains are viticulture in the west and olives and figs in the east. In Kabylia every fragment of usable land is employed. In the lower areas the land use pattern is comparable to that in the littoral zone; at middle elevations figs and olives become dominant; the highest lands are in cork oak or grasslands. The production of olives and figs, carried on mostly by Berbers, who tend to be better farmers than the Arabs, still suffers from archaic methods. Failure to prune and spray the trees and to replant with younger stock, plus the inadequate application of quality selection or of attractive packaging means that the market for these crops is more limited than it might be.

PLATEAU OF THE SHOTTS. Stretching across the country between the Tell Atlas and the Saharan Atlas is a region of semiarid high plateaus with an elevation of about 3,300 feet. About 125 miles wide on the west, it breaks up into a series of small valleys on the east and is only the width of a river valley at the Tunisian border. The elevation of the plateau makes for cool winters, while the mountains on the north condemn it to steppelike conditions and over-all low productivity. The over-all density of the region is about 11 per square mile.

Along the north of the plateau are large areas used for grain production. Here and there areas of more intensive use are found, usually associated with a stream bringing water off the back slopes of the Tell or in oases along the northern flanks of the Saharan Atlas.

Nomadic and seminomadic herding is the most widespread activity of the plateau and becomes increasingly dominant toward the dryer south. A large number of wells were sunk in postwar years to improve the domestic and stock water supply of the area. Considerable tonnages of alfa or esparto grass are cut. This grass covers an estimated 10 million acres in the country, and about 1.7 million acres are held in concessions which approximate a monopoly. Most of it is baled for export and used for the production of high-grade paper.

The Plateau of the Shotts derives its name from the basins of interior drainage occupied by ephemeral lakes and salt flats. These shotts have little utility at the present time though it may prove possible to tap water beneath them in the future and even to develop hydropower by utilizing the drop from the higher to the lower plateaus.

THE SAHARAN ATLAS. The greatest significance of this southern range is the protection it gives to Algeria from the drying Saharan winds. It does support extensive grazing and some alfa grass production; its streams supply oases along both flanks and a few which stretch far into the desert. High-quality dates are exported from some of these oases, which have the advantage of relative nearness to coastal points and sometimes very good transport facilities. These factors normally stimulate the tourist trade as well, as the oases along the Atlas flanks can be reached in a matter of a few hours from the cities of Europe or Algeria.

THE ALGERIAN SAHARA. South of the Saharan Atlas is the enormous region of the Saharan Departments with an area of 804,053 square miles and a population in 1960 of 589,505. The political disposition of this area provided a stumbling block in negotiations for the independence of Algeria, but in 1961 De Gaulle offered political sovereignty over the area providing conditions for the satisfactory exploitation of oil and natural gas were preserved, and it subsequently became part of Algeria in July, 1962. The story of oil and gas developments in the Algerian Sahara is given in the section under minerals. At this point, a brief survey will be made of the physical, human, and land-use characteristics of the area. These characteristics are similar to those in other parts of the Sahara, which covers an area astride the Tropic of Cancer larger than the United States and extending from the Atlantic to the Red Sea.

Physically, the most significant factor is, of course, the insufficiency of rainfall, which is under 4 inches a year over most of the area. Averages are meaningless, however, because extreme variability is characteristic; a period of years may be rainless, but when rain does fall it is likely to be torrential. While these rains may be destructive to clay houses and wadi farming, they are necessary to feed the subterranean reserves of water upon which many oases depend. Rain falling in gentle showers would be quickly lost to evaporation. Other climatic characteristics include a very low relative humidity, usually no more than 4 to 5 percent, very rarely above 20 percent; wide annual ranges in temperature with frosts not uncommon in winter, consistently low night temperatures in winter, and very high summer temperatures; great diurnal temperature ranges, running as high as 60 to 70 degrees F.; and frequent winds of considerable velocity, often with great desiccating power and charged with sand and dust. These often brutal climatic conditions mean that man must be hardy, that he must be prepared in clothing and shelter for quick changes.

Topographically, the Sahara is mostly dry plains and plateaus with occasional mountains such as the Ahaggar, the Aïr and the Tibesti. Characteristic surfaces include sand dunes or ergs, such as the Eastern and Western Ergs of Algeria each of which is about 20,000 square miles in extent, or the Libyan Erg, which is larger than France; regs, or plains of stones and boulders; hammadas, or tables of denuded rock often with a polished surface; and basins of interior drainage which may have salt pans within them. Gradational forces operate very differently in desert areas as compared to humid regions, giving special characteristics to both large and small features. Angularity is common, and may be seen in mesalike forms and in wadi profiles.

The vegetation of the Sahara is characterized by one common feature—adaptation to withstand the lack of moisture over long periods. Illustrations would include the sparsity of leaves, low habit, enormous root systems, wide spacing between plants, and the ability to go through the life processes with great speed once water is available.

The major result of the harsh physical conditions of the Sahara is to limit severely the utilizable areas. In the whole Sahara, excluding the Nile oasis, there are perhaps 500,000 acres under irrigation or less than 0.03 percent of the total area. In the Algerian Sahara about 62,500 acres are cultivated or about 0.012 percent of the total. This means that there is only about one tenth of an acre of cultivated land per capita. Overpopulation is, then, a feature of most oases, some of which have densities of 2,500 per square mile. This in turn leads to standards of living "about as low as the average rainfall" and to a fairly heavy exodus to coastal cities. In recent years, new employment opportunities in the petroleum industry have developed and incomes in some oases have been greatly increased.

Inhabitants of the Algerian Sahara include Berbers, the oldest historically known white group, who are both nomads and sedentary oasis dwellers; Arab-Berbers, who inhabit the northern regions; Negroid peoples who are descendants of the first Saharan settlers and of slaves brought as workers to the oases; and Haratin, dark-skinned people who really represent a social class, between the slaves and the upper classes. Widely distributed, they are usually engaged in cultivation. For centuries it was the nomads, mostly Berbers and Arabs who controlled the oases through their control of the routes connecting them. The highly developed social stratification of desert life was severely disrupted by modern developments: French forces assumed the military function, while trade by auto, truck, train to a few oases, and airplane broke down the caravan trade, since one truck alone could replace hundreds of camels. The effect on the nomads was to create much unemployment. Many oases also declined: political changes cut some of them off from former orientations; some which had only been way stations on caravan routes found that their purpose for existence had disappeared; meanwhile the commodities which oases could produce in surplus became of decreasing importance in a changing world. There were exceptions to these generalizations; some of the more accessible oases were greatly aided by modern transport, both for the export of high-quality dates and in the attraction of a fairly lucrative tourist trade.

The land use patterns of the desert are noted by a marked contrast. On the one hand, there is very extensive nomadic grazing of goats, sheep, and camels, particularly on the margins. On the other hand, there is the highly intensive irrigation agriculture of the oases. It is estimated that about two thirds of the inhabitants are oasis dwellers, one third nomads. The oases of the Algerian Sahara support an estimated 4 million date palms producing about 67,000 tons of dates yearly, of which about 18,000 tons of the high-quality Deglet Nour dates are exported. Gardening is also very important and involves a notable variety of fruits, vegetables, and cereals, all produced mainly for local consumption. Agriculture is extremely backward; the land tenurial system is highly complex; concealed unemployment is enormous.

Considerable attention has been given to the potentialities for increasing the irrigated areas of the Sahara as a solution to its population problems. Oases may receive their water supply in a variety of ways:

(1) Water is sometimes led from wadis to the gardens.

(2) Catch cultivation may be practiced in wadi floors after flooding. Sometimes small

bunds or dikes are built to increase the soak-in. Usually only drought-tolerant crops can be grown, such as barley or wheat.

(3) Water is often spring fed, springs being found characteristically along faults, at the contact of permeable and impermeable beds, or where an aquifer comes to the surface.

(4) Wells dug to the water-bearing strata support numerous oases. Some are fortunate to have artesian or partly artesian wells, but in most the water must be laboriously drawn to the surface. This has been frequently done by manual power, sometimes by animal power, but at least until recently, seldom by mechanical pumps. It is ironic that in areas underlain by millions of tons of petroleum, the high cost of fuel has been a prime limiting factor in obtaining water.

(5) Foggaras, or horizontal tunnels, are used to gather and direct water from under fans or from aquifers to surface gardens at lower elevations. Some foggaras are highly intricate and exceptionally well built, but the difficulty of maintaining them is leading to the decline of some oases.

(6) Under the bour system, which is found only where the water table is close to the surface, fields are excavated to sufficient depth to permit date palm roots to tap the table directly, though other crops may require supplementary watering. Here the main problem is keeping the sand out of the fields, which requires more or less constant attention.

The enormous effort expended to provide water and to maintain some oases is scarcely justified by the returns, a factor to remember

El Oued, in the Algerian Sahara
Fields are maintained at such a level as to permit the date palm roots to tap the shallow water table.

in assessing the potentialities for increasing irrigation in the desert. No accurate estimate of the possibilities can be made without very careful study of the underground supply. Numerous examples exist of oases being expanded through well drilling only to be depleted later through overdrafts on the available supply. Elsewhere, drawing of water for a new oasis has resulted in the loss of water for existing oases, sometimes many miles away. Some concept of the difficulties of replacing water is gained when it is realized that it may require 100,000 years for water feeding the northern Egyptian oases to travel underground from its source in the Sudan belt.

Since 1950 a number of deep boreholes have been sunk in the Algerian Sahara, particularly into the Albienne Nappe, a thick aquifer extending southward from the Atlas Mountains. These deep wells are likely to be very costly (one 3,500 feet deep at Ouargla cost $280,000), and hence they cannot always be justified. Furthermore, some water tapped is of ancient origin and once used is gone forever, while other water is excessively mineralized or too deep to permit economic pumping. Nonetheless, enough is known to suggest that the cultivated area of Saharan Algeria could probably be doubled. But even if all sources of available water were tapped the irrigated area would still be only a tiny fraction of the total surface, scarcely enough to alter greatly the economic position of the desert or its inhabitants. Some day, of course, it may prove possible to use desalinized sea water, but the cost will have to be markedly reduced before this can be economically applicable for agricultural purposes.

While the Sahara has undergone several revolutionary changes in the past, including the introduction of the dromedary camel in Roman times, the subsequent replacement of cereals and animals by the date palm as the major concern of oases, the decline of caravan routes which was made certain by the development of sea trade, the abolition of slavery, the changing position of the previously dominant nomad, and the introduction of mechanical transport, the most dynamic change of all has come from the discovery and exploitation of oil and natural gas within the last decade. Never before has so much attention been focused upon the Sahara, and no period has seen equal changes in transport or in the socioeconomic position of many desert dwellers.

The Algerian Sahara, for example, now has three major highways to the south, to Colomb Béchar, El Goléa, and Hassi Messaoud, and a total of 1,100 miles of surfaced roads. New vehicles have been constructed specifically for desert use. Twenty commercial airfields and 80 private fields for use by the petroleum companies now exist. Pipelines have already carried tonnages in excess of the total movements across the Sahara in all of history. Greatly increased attention has also been accorded housing, social work, and education, and to the provision of electricity and additional water supplies to a considerable number of oases. Many of these developments were handled by the Common Organization of Saharan Regions, which was also concerned with the desert portions of Niger and Chad. In 1961 the budget for the Algerian Sahara was about $80 million, $25 million of which came from petroleum royalties, the remainder from the French budget. Whether the Algerian government will be able and willing to continue this intensified effort remains to be seen.

TUNISIA

Tunisia has much in common with the other countries of the Maghrib: its western Arab culture, its experience of French rule, its Mediterranean and Saharan climates, and its basic land use patterns. But there are also profound differences. It is much smaller, less favored climatically because of its situation in the rain shadow of the Atlas ranges, more favored topographically because plains cover a very extensive part of the whole giving a higher degree of penetrability. Culturally, it is more advanced, exhibiting markedly bourgeois and secular tendencies, and it is more solidly unified under its strongly centralized government, which has placed emphasis upon cultural as well as economic modernization. The president has instituted various programs to alter traditional Islamic customs, insisting, for example, that work requirements must take precedence over the religious duty of fasting in Ramadan. Self-help programs have worked with considerable success, resulting in a large amount of terracing, reforestation, planting of fruit trees, construction of roads, and community development.

The population of Tunisia was 4,295,000 in 1962, just over half being under 20 years of age, and is increasing by about 1.7 percent per annum. All but a small minority are Muslims, relatively few of whom are of Berber stock. The Jewish population declined from 58,000 in 1956 to about 30,000 in 1963; it is largely concentrated in Tunis. European numbers were reduced from 255,000 in 1956, when 71 percent were classified as French and 26 percent as Italians, to about 85,000 in 1961 and perhaps 40,000 in 1963. Nearly a third of Tunisians are urbanized; indeed the great age and importance of urban life and the significant commercial development of the eastern coastal communities are characteristics which stand in contrast with neighboring Algeria. Tunis and its suburbs alone have about a fifth of the total population.

About 65 percent of Tunisian Muslims are dependent for their living on the land, and agriculture provides about one third of the national income. In good years a substantial surplus is available; in bad years yields may be very low and as much as half of the livestock may be lost. For example, the average yearly production of wheat and barley in the ten years ending with 1957 was 670,000 metric tons, but in 1961 it was only 265,000 tons. Such shortfalls reduce exports, necessitating large imports of grain, and seriously affect the balance of payments of the country. The needs for modern methods and for rural credit have been attacked by organization of rural extension schools and by establishment of an Agricultural Bank; some cooperative mechanization has been instituted; and agriculture has received realistic attention in the ten-year development plan.

Europeans held about 1,853,000 acres in 1957, 1,250,000 acres in 1959, and 1,000,000 acres in late 1961, including some of the best land in the country. France has assisted Tunisia in purchasing large sections of these lands; the latest agreement, signed in March, 1963, called for the purchase of 375,000 acres in 1963, while the government planned to purchase a further 125,000 acres in 1964. By 1965 European-owned lands will probably be reduced to about 300,000 acres.

Tunisian lands have been held under a complex system of ownership including *melk* or freehold lands, *habous* lands endowed according to customary Muslim institutions, and tribal common lands. Three big changes have occurred since independence which have substantially altered the distribution of land: about a million acres of *habous* lands, which accounted for about a quarter of the cultivated area, have been split into individual holdings; about 5.5 million acres of tribal land have been subdivided as part of the effort to have the Bedouin population become sedentary; and the purchased European lands have been redistributed among Tunisians.

The major economic dilemma of Tunisia is how to expand production and opportunities for employment enough to absorb the large numbers of people who are unemployed or underemployed and to improve the general standard of living, which is particularly low in the southern regions. Agricultural improvements are certainly possible, and redistribution of lands will benefit many Muslim farmers, but climatic and areal limitations are severe. Nonetheless, it is planned that grain production be increased two thirds by 1971 on an acreage reduced by 24 percent from the present 3.68 million acres. The released lands would then be used for other crops or for animal husbandry. The unemployment problem has been attacked by mobilizing workers for road, dam, and canal construction and digging wells, the laborers receiving about 48¢ a day plus a ration of grain supplied by the United States. In 1962 about

Irrigation conduits on the Medjerda plain in Tunisia
The Medjerda Valley and the Tunis plain are the most important areas of Tunisia for production of high-value irrigated crops.

half the unemployed were engaged in this program, which has had much greater success than the comparable program in Morocco. Nonetheless, about 300,000 people are still without work and the mobilization scheme does not provide a satisfactory permanent solution to the problem.

THE REGIONS OF TUNISIA

Tunisia may be divided most broadly into a relatively well-watered region north of the Atlas, where Mediterranean influences are dominant, and the semiarid to arid south where Saharan influences are increasingly felt. About 70 percent of the population is concentrated in the northern third of the country, and there continues to be heavy migration to that area from the less favored south.

THE NORTH. In the northwest mountainous area, cork oak and eucalyptus forests are important, while subsistence crops are produced in the valleys, and goats and sheep are grazed wherever possible. Opportunities in this region include intensification of forest output, protection of forests from indiscriminate grazing, planting of more deciduous fruit trees, installation of drainage works in the valleys, and development of summer crops in the valleys, including tobacco, corn, sorghum, and forage crops.

The richest and most intensively used areas of the country are the Medjerda Valley and the plains around Tunis and Cape Bon. It is in these areas that the vast bulk of European estates were located and that the higher value Mediterranean crops are largely produced. A sort of Medjerda Valley Authority has been set up to develop the full potential of this river system, the most important in Tunisia. Plans call for irrigating 125,000 acres, draining 130,000 acres, protecting 130,000 acres by flood control projects, and instituting erosion control practices on 300,000 acres in the watershed. Three dams are now in existence and others will be constructed. Some "cooperative farms" have been set up in the valley which follow rather authoritarian direction in the planting of crops and even in the movement of their members. In addition to extending irrigation in the valley it should be possible to improve farming on about 1,250,000 acres of rain-fed land by substituting for the present cereal monoculture the mixed cultivation of pulses, forage crops, and such industrial crops as flax, sugar beets, and cotton. Stock farming could also be intensified by harmonizing it with tillage agriculture.

The Medjerda Valley and the Tunis plain account for a substantial percentage of the country's wheat production and most of its wine and

Olive orchards in the Sfax region
Olive oil ranks as Tunisia's third export by value. Although the trees are spaced farther apart than in the more humid north, yields per acre are higher because the trees are younger and better tended.

citrus fruit. Wine exports have risen sharply in recent years, from $5.4 million in 1950 to $18.5 million in 1961, but may decline with the continued emigration of European farmers. Citrus production has also grown, and there have been concerted efforts in recent years to plant peach, pear, plum, and nut trees. These richer cultures normally show fluctuations far less severe in production and exports than are seen for the cereals and the olive.

The largest cities of the country are in this northern zone. Tunis occupies a position comparable to that of Algiers as the center of commercial, political, cultural, and industrial activity. Much of the country's individuality is, in fact, a product of Tunis City. The port of Tunis is well equipped and handles about three fourths of the country's imports and half of its exports. It is the terminus of the national railway system, which is reasonably well developed but in need of some modernization and eventually standardization of the narrow-gauge lines.

SOUTHERN TUNISIA. Covering by far the largest area of Tunisia, this zone may be divided into several subregions. The eastern plain or "Sahel" stretches southward along the coast and is steppelike in character. The areas around Sousse and Sfax have the greatest olive orchards of Tunisia, the million acres tributary to Sfax having some of the finest in the world. With some 26 million trees in the country there is still room for expansion and for replacement of senile stock. Tunisia normally ranks third among exporters of olive oil, which is one of the leading agricultural exports of the country. Olive trees bear fruit in a two-year cycle which, together with climatically induced changes, results in great fluctuation in output. In the 1950s production ranged from a low of 20,000 tons to a high of 130,000 tons, but there has been a definite long-term upward trend. Many of the groves of the Sahel were introduced under the *m'gharça* system whereby a Tunisian peasant would acquire half of an area in return for tending the trees for fifteen years until they ripened. Trees in the south are normally spaced about 75 feet apart as compared with a 30-foot spacing in the north, but yields per acre are superior because many trees in the north are older and less well tended.

There are some opportunities for small-scale irrigation of vegetables, forage crops, pomegranates, and dates in the Sahel and one relatively large-scale development under construction. This project involves erection of a dam on the Oued Nebhana; it was undertaken without adequate study of stream flow or of the area to be controlled, and may prove to have been excessively expensive in relation to the benefits reaped. National fervor, which does not always provide the wisest counsel, demanded that the project be consummated.

West of the plains are steppelike plateaus and hill lands, the domain of extensive livestock raising and dry farming. About a quarter of the total population of the country lives in the central south, but this region is witnessing an alarming northward drift. Stock breeding accounts for about a fifth of agricultural income in Tunisia and occupies about two fifths of the productive lands. The broad-tailed sheep, a specialty of the country, is the basis of pastoralism in the central and southern zones; goats are of some significance, but the government is attempting to reduce their numbers as an erosion control measure. Wool, skins, and hides are important bases for the handicraft industry but are minor among the country's exports. Alfa grass covers some 4,700 square miles of Tunisia, especially in the steppelike west. A pulping factory has recently been constructed in the Kasserine area.

South of Gafsa only sporadic grazing is possible, especially of camels. There are also a few oases around the immense Shott el Jerid and near Gabès. The waters off Gabès are the most important fisheries area for Tunisia; operations are usually small scale and concentrated on inshore waters. Sfax and Jerba Island have small sponge collecting industries.

MINING IN THE MAGHRIB COUNTRIES

North Africa has a significant production of petroleum, natural gas, phosphates, iron ore, manganese, lead, and zinc, and a minor output of various other minerals. In Morocco there are about 60 mines, many of which are distinctly marginal and about a quarter of which account for the vast bulk of production. About 40,000 persons, including several thousand Europeans, are employed in mining. The state owns a 15 to 49 percent share of many mines and all of the phosphate mines. Royalties, earnings, and taxes from mining account for about 11 percent of the ordinary government revenues; mineral carriage assures the profitability of the railways; the industry is the largest consumer of electricity in the country; and mineral exports account for about three eighths of the total value of exports.

The mineral position of Algeria is marked by spectacular wealth of petroleum and natural gas in the Sahara, but relatively meager resources in the north, where production was lower in 1961 than in 1938 partly because of interruptions caused by the revolt.

In Tunisia about 14,000 people are employed in mining; mineral traffic accounts for about 70 per cent of total railway freight and 80 percent of port tonnages; and mineral exports comprise about 25 percent of the total value of exports.

PHOSPHATES

North Africa ranks as the world's leading exporter of phosphates, shipments going primarily to western Europe, the main consuming area of fertilizers in the world. Morocco, with the largest reserves of any nation and with good quality rock, has become the Maghrib's main producer in postwar years, its output having grown from 1.5 million tons in 1937 to 2.9 million tons in 1947 and 8.29 million tons in 1962. Phosphates account for almost a quarter of Moroccan exports by value, about three eighths of rail traffic, and two thirds of tonnage exports from all ports, and provide about one twelfth of

Storage of phosphate rock at Louis Gentil, inland from Port Safi
Louis Gentil is the second ranking phosphate producing area of Morocco. A 3.6-mile telpher system brings the rock from the mine.

the country's budgetary receipts. The Khourigba area is the major producer; most operations are underground and the 80–82 percent tricalcium phosphate produced is shipped about 87 miles to Casablanca where three ships can be loaded at the rate of 1,500 tons per hour at a special quay. In 1961 a new mine in this area began the exploitation of podzolized phosphate of relatively low content but capable of enrichment to 82 percent by simple washing. Later, all of the rock may be enriched by a new, more complex process to 85–86 percent quality rock. The second main area is at Louis Gentil where lower grade but more readily dried rock is shipped 51 miles to Safi for processing or export. A major new chemical complex is under construction at Safi designed to produce 400,000 tons of sulfuric acid, 150,000 tons of phosphoric acid, and 200,000 tons of triple superphosphate. Operations are scheduled to begin in 1964 and Morocco plans to increase its sales of phosphate to 12 or 13 million tons by 1965.

Algerian phosphates are of poor quality except for those at Kouif which are approaching exhaustion. In order to sustain exports an investment of about $27 million has been made to develop an enormous low-grade body at Djebel Onk, 205 miles from Bône. While this deposit has been known since 1906, its exploitation was long delayed because of the distance from the sea, the necessity to construct a 62-mile rail extension, and the low grade of the body. Eventually a process was developed permitting treatment to reach the 75 percent grade. The need for substantial quantities of fuel and water was met by use of oil and bringing water from a find 42 miles to the northwest.

Phosphate rock covers about 380 square miles in central Tunisia, with Gafsa having the main deposits. The relatively low-grade phosphates are shipped 150 miles to Sfax where a new $14.1 million triple superphosphate plant, started in 1962, will process increasing quantities prior to shipment. At M'Dilla, south of Gafsa, production of 75 percent quality rock using impregnation and calcination processes has begun.

IRON ORE

Most of the iron ore of North Africa is hematite and limonite of good purity and with from 51 to 63 percent metal content. It is shipped to western Europe, with the United Kingdom normally ranking as the largest customer. In 1961 Algeria produced 1,491,000 tons measured by iron content, Morocco 815,000, and Tunisia 453,000 tons. Deposits are widely scattered in

Algeria; the largest production comes from Ouenza near the Tunisian border and lesser amounts from Zaccar, tributary to Algiers, and Beni-Saf, dependent upon Oran. An important iron ore deposit has also been under study at Gara-Djebilet, 84 miles southeast of Tindouf in the Sahara. Tunisian ore comes from the north and west where there are known reserves of 35–40 million tons. In Morocco, iron ore is mined near Melilla and north of Khourigba. These deposits will probably be exhausted in 30 years, but other unexploited deposits, particularly at Khenifra, may permit extended production.

LESSER MINERALS

Morocco produces a considerable variety of other minerals of which manganese and lead figure with some significance in world figures. Exploitation of manganese began in 1929 at Bou-Arfa, south of Nemours, while more important bodies were opened up shortly before World War II in the High Atlas southeast of Marrakech. In the peak year, 1961, 261,300 tons (manganese content) were produced, placing Morocco second among African and fifth among world producers. Heavy transport costs make production somewhat marginal, but known reserves are adequate to sustain production for many years. Lead, for which Morocco ranks tenth in the world, and zinc are produced in widely scattered areas of the east, especially in the Oujda district near the Algerian border. Cobalt, tin, copper, iron pyrites, and tungsten also exist.

Algeria has a number of small lead and zinc mines, two antimony mines in the east, and an iron pyrite mine at Aïn Ben Merouane. A small manganese body is known at Guettara in the Sahara. Pyrites are used to produce sulfuric acid which is then employed in the production of superphosphates. In Tunisia, lead has been mined since Punic times, but the remaining ores are of inferior quality, occur in small deposits, and can only be produced at a relatively high cost. Zinc, potash, mercury, and magnesium deposits also exist, while Tunisia exports 90 percent of its salt production, which comes mainly from salt pans at Tunis and Monastir.

ENERGY MINERALS

Until the discovery of major resources of petroleum and natural gas in the Sahara, production of energy minerals in North Africa occurred in a series of deposits of coal, oil, and gas whose combined production was inadequate to meet the needs of the area.

Anthracite coal of good quality but costly to mine because of the thinness of seams comes from Djerada in Morocco and low-grade coal has been mined at Kenadza in the Colomb Béchar area of Algeria. The latter is 360 miles from the nearest port and production has required subsidization since imported coal could be delivered to seaboard at a lower cost. The known reserves at Kenadza are not large, seams average only 16 inches in thickness, and output per manshift has been only about half that of France. Plans to develop a metallurgical and industrial complex based upon this coal were abandoned after natural gas from Hassi R'Mel provided a far more attractive fuel.

A small output of petroleum comes from the Rharb in Morocco, particularly near Sidi Kassem (Petit Jean), where a refinery has been erected, and natural gas has been discovered at Essaouria. Algeria developed a small deposit near Aumale in the plateau south of Algiers, while in Tunisia a minor natural gas deposit on Cape Bon augments the energy supply of Tunis.

The enormous deposits of petroleum and natural gas in the Sahara have, however, provided a most dynamic change in the mineral and energy scene in North Africa, particularly for Algeria.

OIL AND GAS IN SAHARAN ALGERIA

The story of finding and developing petroleum and natural gas in the Sahara provides a striking example of how a changing resource picture can stimulate activity and provide a major socioeconomic impact on an area. Serious efforts to find oil in North Africa began only in

1946 and were rewarded with a first strike in 1949 in the north of Algeria. In the Sahara itself the first concessions date from 1952; four years later two important discoveries were made, the first at Edjeleh, the second at Hassi Messaoud. These were followed by discovery after discovery, including enormous reserves of natural gas at Hassi R'Mel and Hassi el Gassi. Six years after the original find, at least 700 million tons of recoverable petroleum had been proved plus 800 billion cubic meters of natural gas. There was no longer any question that this was a major area of world reserves or that large additional reserves remained to be proved.

Geologists predicted many years ago that, if oil ever were found in the Sahara, it would be found in large quantities because of the enormous size of the geological structures of the area. The comparative richness may be seen from the facts that it has required only 21 wells to prove 50 million barrels as contrasted with 1,000 wells in the United States and that the ratio of reserves to the number of feet drilled is 4,000 barrels per foot in the Sahara and only 12 barrels per foot in the United States. High production levels have also been achieved in a remarkably short period, rising from about 450,000 tons in 1958 to 8.6 million tons in 1960, about 16 million tons in 1961, and 20.5 million tons in 1962. In 1963 production was limited by pipeline capacity to about 24 million tons.

Drilling equipment at Edjeleh
The first major find of petroleum in the Algerian Sahara was made in the Edjeleh field. It is now connected by pipeline to Sekhira in Tunisia.

Development in the Sahara has required very large capital expense. The French alone invested about $96 million from 1951 to 1956 and over a billion dollars in the following five years. The need for large amounts of capital prompted the French to invite participation of foreign companies though a 50 percent French ownership was required for all concessions. Today most of the large international petroleum corporations are involved in Saharan operations.

Numerous problems have accompanied development. The Saharan environment is a difficult one: crews can work at full tempo only eight months of the year, they must be changed frequently, and heat and sand expose machinery to tremendous wear and tear. These factors result in costs of drilling being four to six times those in Europe, though the results, of course, are likely to be far more rewarding. The securing of an adequate water supply, recruitment of labor, and difficult transport to and from coastal points are other problems common to all sites. Security was another difficulty during the revolt, though the only major interruption occurred in 1961 when Tunisia closed down the pipeline from Edjeleh at the time of the Bizerte crisis.

At the present time, three areas are of greatest interest in production. Hassi Messaoud, south of Touggourt and 375 miles from the coast (Map 25), is the most important. High-grade oil, free of sulfur, occurs in a 500-foot layer extending over at least 77 square miles at a depth of about 11,000 feet. In 1957, the year after discovery, the first oil was transported by a 6-inch "baby" pipe 110 miles to Touggourt and then 250 miles by rail to Philippeville. This inadequate and costly system was soon replaced by a 24-inch pipeline extending 410 miles to the port of Bougie. Its capacity was raised from 10 to 14 million tons a year in 1961. Hassi Messaoud has also been tied by pipelines to other Algerian fields, as is shown on Map 25. The 8-inch line from Hassi R'Mel carries gas condensates, while gas from Gassi-Touil, discovered in 1961, will be used to assist recovery of oil at Hassi Messaoud.

There are a series of fields in the east near the Libyan border, four of which are tied by a 24-inch, 484-mile line from In Amenas to Sekhira on the Gulf of Gabès in Tunisia. Its capacity is 9.5 million tons a year. A connection was made from this line to the Ohanet–Hassi Messaoud line as a result of the closure of the main pipe, but its capacity is limited to 2 million tons per annum. Oil is found about 1,500 feet below the surface in the eastern fields, which are believed to have only average reserves.

Hassi R'Mel is believed to be one of the largest natural gas reserves in the world. It is linked by a 24-inch pipe to Arzew in northern Algeria, and by 15-inch branch lines to Oran and Algiers, for a total of 515 miles. To date, the output of Hassi R'Mel has been restricted by the size of the Algerian market, which consumed 215 million cubic meters in 1961 and about 500 million cubic meters in 1962.

Fears that an independent Algeria might nationalize operations in the Sahara were greatly reduced by the signing of accords between France and Algeria in 1962. Under these agreements all concessions and permits for exploration that had been granted remained valid, the Saharan Petroleum Code continued operative, French companies were promised priority for six years in exploration and development if equal offers were made, and payment for sale of oil in the French franc areas was to be in French francs. The Saharan Petroleum Code, which is now administered by a Franco-Algerian body with equal representation, provides for a 50-50 profit ratio, for 50-year concessions, and guarantees against tax changes for 25 years. New concessions, however, may not be available at such favorable terms as in the past, when little was known about the wealth of the region. French and other interests concede that the Algerians have accepted very fair commitments; they hope that the oil companies will conduct their relations with the new government in such a way as to assure continuing harmony.

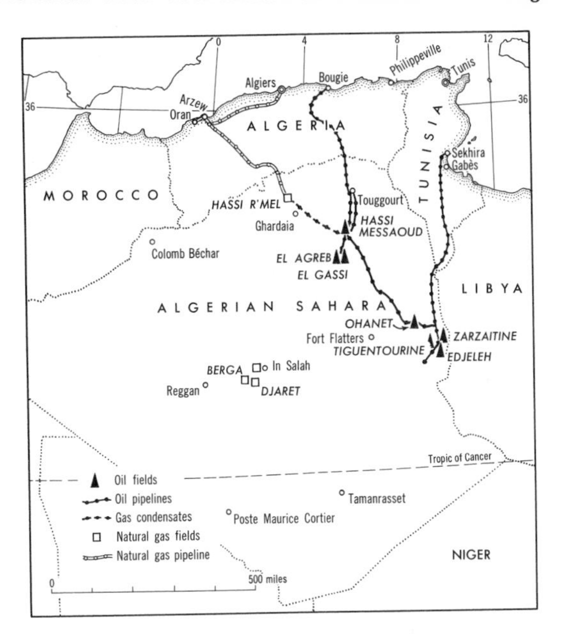

Map 25. Petroleum and natural gas in Algeria

The French have seen petroleum and natural gas developments in the Sahara as bringing an economic revolution to three areas: the Saharan region, Algeria, and France. As noted earlier, the impact on Saharan communities has been very great, but this area cannot absorb more than a tiny fraction of output and is not likely to be allotted more than a minor part of profits. Algeria can realize a variety of substantial benefits. Very low-cost natural gas permits reducing the cost of electricity in areas served and provides an attraction for chemical and other industries. The export of oil and later gas will yield valuable exchange as well as substantial budgetary receipts from taxes, pipeline profits, and royalties. The Algerian government also inherited a 40.51 percent share in SN Repal, which holds the largest stake in Saharan petroleum. Total returns to Algeria, which were about $40 million in 1961 and $50 million in 1962, are far from adequate, however, to solve the nation's economic needs.

France's gains from Saharan oil include the saving of about $350 million yearly in hard currency, a reduction in dependence on the Middle East, a saving in cost of delivery to markets in France which can be accomplished at from one-tenth to one-third the cost of transporting crude from Kuwait, and profits received by the French companies in Algeria, which are frequently part-owned by the government.

One of the major problems respecting Saharan oil and gas developments is that of the market, particularly as there is a surplus available in the world. This has been partially met by requiring French refineries to accept specified quotas of Algerian oil, despite the fact that many of them were ill equipped to take the light oils delivered. The assured French market, which, like others in western Europe, has been expanding with notable rapidity, is of considerable value to Algeria and was doubtless a factor in acceptance of the Franco-Algerian accords. France cannot afford, however, to ignore its commitments to the international oil companies operating in France nor those it has in the Middle East, particularly in Iran and Iraq. It has sought, therefore, to secure a special position for Saharan oil in the EEC and probably will intensify this effort as capacity for production increases. The world surplus of oil, to which Saharan output contributes, does tend to weaken the price structure. In 1963 a small reduction was applied to the artificially high price of about $2.40 a barrel, and some oil was sold at 60¢ to 75¢ off the stated price. The markets for oil in North Africa are, of course, fairly limited, though adequate to support the construction of several new refineries in recent years. In Morocco, a refinery was opened in 1962 at Mohammadia, north of Casablanca. Built with Italian cooperation, it has a capacity of 1.25 million tons of crude a year. The Italians are also constructing a 1-million-ton refinery at Bizerte in Tunisia while a 2-million-ton plant is to be completed by 1964 at Algiers. A 165,000-ton refinery was built at Hassi Messaoud in 1961.

Part of the petrochemical complex at Arzew, Algeria
A number of installations based upon natural gas from Hassi R'Mel are planned for this site.

The market for natural gas provides interesting possibilities. Within Algeria, the French planned that it be used to support a large chemical complex at Arzew and to provide a large share of energy needs for a cement mill and for the new metallurgical complex at Bône. In November, 1961, Britain contracted to take 700,000 tons of liquid methane over a 15-year period beginning in 1964. A Franco-British society undertook the construction of a big methane plant at Arzew, while special insulated vessels will carry the liquefied gas at −160°C. Eventually these imports are expected to cover about a tenth of British gas requirements. A really large-scale market will be tapped if it proves feasible to lay pipelines under the Mediterranean to various European countries. The possible routes and technical aspects of such a scheme have been under study for some time, the most frequently mentioned routes being to Malaga and across Spain and to Italy, Switzerland, and West Germany via Sicily.

INDUSTRIAL DEVELOPMENTS

Industry is in an early stage of development in the Maghrib, but is ahead of that in most African countries. Algeria was estimated to account for 8.0 percent of the value added by manufacturing for all of Africa and Morocco for 7.2 percent in 1958. Industrial production increased two-and-a-quarter-fold in Algeria from 1948 to 1961 and three-fold for Morocco in the same period. Unemployment, pressure on the land, sizable urban populations, and the demographic surge in each country create strong desires to expand and diversify industry, but many barriers impede a rapid build-up. Since independence, Tunisia has witnessed the most satisfactory progress in manufacturing; Morocco has sustained a 3 percent growth per annum, but in 1962–63 Algerian industry was in a state of near collapse resulting from the withdrawal of European capital and management and the chaotic economic condition of the country.

In no case has industry actually fulfilled the objectives of country planners. In Morocco the numbers engaged in industry increased only 3.6 percent from 1958 to 1961, and at the end of 1961 it was estimated that only 40 percent of industry was operating at capacity while 16 percent was functioning at less than half of capacity. The ambitious Constantine Plan for Algeria planned to create 400,000 new jobs in industry in ten years. After three years some 30,000 new jobs existed; the goals for establishing small establishments were not fulfilled, but some rather notable achievements were made in starting large new industrial complexes. Just how viable some of these will prove to be under the radically changed situation in Algeria remains to be seen.

TYPES OF INDUSTRY

TRADITIONAL HANDICRAFTS. Industry may first be divided into the long-standing artisanal workshops and modern manufacturing. Despite competition of mass-produced items, the handicraft industries, almost entirely carried on by Muslims, retain very considerable importance, especially in Morocco and Tunisia. Both artistic and utility goods are produced, the latter having suffered most severely from rising competition, the former having actually increased in value of exports from Morocco. Much of the work is carried on in the *souks* or markets or in the homes of the craftsmen. Some fine leather goods, rugs, woolens, metal articles, and pottery are produced, but much of the handcrafted output is inferior in quality. Artisans are often grouped into guilds according to their specialities; in Morocco 115 corporations of handcraftsmen have been created.

In Morocco some 155 to 160 thousand artisans are engaged in handicraft production, with the textile and leather fields employing about two thirds of the total. It is estimated, however, that about 60 percent of artisans are underemployed. Comparable figures are not available for Algeria where modern industry had the greatest impact on traditional output, which was, in any case, less well developed. In Tunisia it has been estimated that 600,000 people are supported by 23,000 craft establishments. In both Morocco and Tunisia the number engaged is greater than the number employed in modern manufacturing.

MODERN MANUFACTURING. The largest segment of modern industry, which has been characterized by the primary importance of foreign investment and expatriate management, is concerned with the processing of extractive output. Included are plants associated with the upgrading of phosphate exports, metal concentrators and smelters, and salines in the mineral sphere; modern fish canneries; cork factories and alfa grass pulp mills; and, in the agricultural field, flour and oil mills, wineries, vegetable and fruit canning establishments, modern tobacco factories, and tanneries. A large number of plants in this category produce mainly for the export market.

The construction industry enjoyed a real boom in the first postwar decade with enlarged expenditures for development. In Morocco the industry has not recuperated from the depressed conditions resulting from the European exodus after 1956, but in Tunisia, after a temporary setback, the number of both residential and nonresidential buildings under construction increased 100 percent from 1956 to 1961. Algeria's construction industry continued to expand with vigor until 1960; cement production increased 235 percent from 1953 to 1960 and building permits more than trebled in this period. In 1963, however, almost 85 percent of construction workers were unemployed.

Production of consumer goods in modern

A truck assembly plant at Casablanca, Morocco
Assembly of vehicles is an appropriate industry for the larger countries of Africa because of the substantial savings in transport cost that may be realized.

factories is not well developed in the Maghrib, although it is this type of industry which has been especially fostered in postwar years. Initial production of many items began during World War II when goods could not be supplied from Europe, but many factories built at that time were unable to compete after the war with the larger and better established European plants or continued to work below capacity. Nonetheless, substantial progress was made in establishing market-oriented industries, particularly with government assistance and stimulation. Almost all of these industries suffered severely with the loss of relatively high income Europeans from the domestic market, while the dependence of a considerable segment of Algerian industry on government contracts was a factor of weakness.

Consumer-oriented industries in the Maghrib include a variety of food and beverage plants; the beginnings of a modern textile complex; production of glass, plastic, wooden, and paper containers; output of simple chemicals such as soap, perfume, paint and varnish, and some pharmaceuticals; and a fair representation in the field of metal fabrication. The last category includes several automobile and truck assembly plants, now operating well below capacity; production of household appliances, metal furniture, and communications equipment in Algeria; an armament factory at Fez; and small shipyards and ship-repairing installations.

Like other underdeveloped countries, those of the Maghrib have been interested in establishing iron and steel mills as evidence of their maturity and to base metal fabrication industries. Tunisia has a small Bessemer steel plant operated by the national railways to manufacture precision articles. A $167 million steel mill with a capacity of about 400,000 tons was under construction at Bône at the time of independence, but shortages of capital have delayed its completion indefinitely. Its economies were highly doubtful, the associated French companies having required heavy subsidization to encourage their participation, the mill having been designed as proof of French intentions to develop the Algerian economy. Morocco is interested in constructing a steel mill at Nador, on the coast near Melilla, where it would be close to the Rif iron mines and relatively near the coal of Djerada. Designed with a capacity of 165,000 tons of steel and 20,000 tons of ferromanganese, the plant would cost an estimated $112 million. Disadvantages of the proposal include the high cost which is likely to result from the small scale of operations, and the necessity to import coke to supplement the noncoking domestic coal. There has also been talk of a 125,000-ton steel mill being placed at the abandoned American air base at Nouasseur.

Algeria has placed considerable hopes for industrial expansion on the availability of very low-cost natural gas from the Sahara, not only to provide cheap power but to base a number of petrochemical industries. A variety of plants have been proposed for the chemical complex at Arzew: liquefaction of methane, nitrogen fixation, synthetic rubber, and a range of petrochemicals.

FACTORS INFLUENCING INDUSTRIALIZATION

While considerable progress has been made in establishing modern industries in North Africa, there are numerous handicaps retarding a rapid expansion. The size of the market is restrictive, not only in numbers but in purchasing power, and has been seriously reduced in all countries by the loss of Europeans with a high purchasing power. The range of industries which might be appropriate to the area could be increased by formation of a Maghrib customs union, but at present each country is intent upon its own needs and there has been no joint planning or coordination. Tariff protection does assist the inception of some specific industries in each of the countries.

The flight of expatriates created additional problems for industry, especially in Algeria, particularly through the repatriation of capital and the loss of skilled labor and managerial ability. It will require many years before the availability of a trained and reliable labor force and an adequate supply of managers is no longer an important impeding factor. Governments are striving to meet these problems and have become the leading sources of investment capital for manufacturing.

In the past, the shortage and high cost of power was an additional handicap, but the immense reserves of petroleum and natural gas in the Algerian Sahara promise a dynamic change, even a reversal in this field, for some industries may be attracted to the area specifically to utilize these assets. Tunisia and Morocco also hope to benefit by effecting connections with the natural gas fields. Production of power from domestic sources covered considerably less than total energy consumed in all of the countries until 1960, when Algeria became a net exporter; the percentage of consumption provided by domestic sources in the other two countries has continued to decline despite new hydroelectric installations. Hydropower did provide 90 percent of electricity produced in Morocco in 1961, 24 percent of that in Algeria, and about 7 percent in Tunisia. Morocco's linked plants on the Oued el Abid, Bin el Ouidane and Afourer, account for almost two thirds of that country's hydroelectric production.

LOCATION OF INDUSTRY

Modern manufacturing is heavily concentrated in each of the Maghrib countries in a limited number of localities. In Morocco it is estimated that 68 percent of total industrial employees are in the coastal strip from Casablanca to Rabat. In Algeria about two thirds of the establishments are concentrated in Algiers and a quarter in Oran, while Tunis has two thirds of the industry in that country.

Concern has been expressed regarding the excessive movement of new plants to these same centers and some steps have been taken to encourage dispersion. Morocco, for example, is prepared to assist approved industrial projects by grants of up to 15 percent if they locate outside the Casablanca-Rabat zone or 20 percent if they select Tangier, whose economy has been particularly depressed. Plans are also being developed for establishing industrial estates at the evacuated American air bases of Nouasseur near Casablanca and Sidi Slimane in north-central Morocco, utilizing several hundred permanent buildings left intact at the bases.

The Constantine Plan called for the development of fifteen big cities and forty medium-sized towns in Algeria over a period of twenty-five years, including construction of satellite industrial communities around the large urban centers. In the early years of the plan, however, two thirds of new industry located in Algiers. There is some question, in fact, as to whether market-oriented industry should be asked to forego the advantage of proximity to a country's largest market, especially at such an early stage of industrial development.

CHAPTER SEVEN

Libya

Libya became independent by U.N. decree in 1951. At the time it was incapable of supporting itself, had one of the lowest income levels in the world, a considerable annual budgetary deficit, a serious imbalance in trade, and no visible resources which could be developed readily to alter the situation. It was also incapable of governing itself, over 90 percent of the population being illiterate, there being almost no indigenous professional or technical workers and less than a score of college graduates. As a former Italian colony, Libya had become the responsibility of the United Nations, where the only positive majority agreements were that the USSR should not become one of the trustees and that the alternate solution was the granting of independence. One can only speculate what the disposition might have been if there had been knowledge of the wealth of oil resources beneath the miserably poor surface.

For centuries before the Italians moved into Libya it had been ruled by the Turks, who were satisfied to hold the coastal cities and collect such taxes as were forthcoming. The Italians occupied Tripolitania in 1912 and Cyrenaica thereafter, though rule in the latter did not become fully effective until 1929. More ambitious than the Turks, they built up a considerable administration and, as the years progressed, gave increasing attention to economic and social improvements, particularly in the coastal belts where a reasonably good infrastructure was developed. They also promoted Italian migration, either to private concessions or in public or "demographic settlements," involving the somewhat questionable transfer of people from one overpopulated country to another. By 1939, about 100,000 Italians were resident in Libya, a majority in the cities rather than on the land. During World War II, the Germans, Italians, and British seesawed back and forth across the country. Very considerable destruction occurred in the cities and elsewhere and, since Libya was the territory of a defeated belligerent, damages could not be collected after the war and reconstruction came very slowly despite increasingly generous contributions made by Western nations. After the war the country remained under British and French military rule until a U.N. commission was set up to organize its independence.

Libya had one valuable natural resource which directly and indirectly supported its regular and development expenses in this period, namely its location. This factor gave it value as the site of military and air bases and the country survived by subsidies received in return for the rights to these bases. In the period 1951 to 1957, Libya received $96.9 million in foreign assistance and about $40 million a year in succeeding years. At present the United Kingdom makes an annual grant of $9.1 million to the Libyan budget, while the United States will pay $10 million a year for Wheelus Field until 1965 plus unspecified contributions for development expenses. The U.N. has been expending about $800,000 yearly in Libya, and Italy has made contributions, particularly to assist in the transfer of Italian-owned assets and the purchase of Italian farms. A rather intricate series of joint Libyan and foreign agencies, perforce staffed largely by expatriates, administered the foreign commitments until 1960 when a Development Council was created by Libya to supervise all projects and coordinate the various agencies.

Within Libya there are strong centrifugal forces, sustained to a degree until 1963 by the structure of the federal government, which inhibited a truly national approach to many problems. The more conservative Bedouins of Cyrenaica often disagree with the Berbers of Tripolitania; the Fezzan has yet to be brought into the scene effectively. The separation of the two main provinces by nearly 500 miles of desert and the remoteness of the oases in Fezzan and southern Cyrenaica are factors of importance. Succession to the throne may involve disputes, while other problems include the short work week resulting from traditional attitudes toward work, an unfortunate degree of family and tribal preferences in appointments, and, despite great improvements in education, the continuing lack of skilled administrative and technical personnel. Rivalry between Tripoli and Benghazi, which were to alternate as the capital city every two years, has been partly met by creation of a third capital city, Beida, now in an advanced stage of construction in the Jebel Akhdar of Cyrenaica.

THE POPULATION OF LIBYA

The population of Libya was estimated to be 1,244,000 in mid-1962. About 70 percent of the total, including almost all of the remaining non-Muslims, reside in Tripolitania, about 22 percent in Cyrenaica, and the remainder in Fezzan, which has recently been credited with about 100,000 inhabitants, a substantially larger number than had previously been given. The Muslims of Libya have been, at least until recently, essentially static and conservative, a condition which was fostered by their religion, their tribal society, the meager development of education, and the lack of opportunity for economic change.

The original inhabitants of northern Libya were Berbers; Arabs arrived in successive waves in the seventh, ninth, and eleventh centuries, displacing and assimilating their predecessors, while there was an admixture with Greeks in Cyrenaica in the fourteenth century. Today almost the entire population is Muslim and is Arabic-speaking. In recent decades the position of minority groups has changed with great rapidity. Italians have contributed to the economy of Libya out of all proportion to their numbers: their better-developed farms figure significantly in the production of commercial crops; most of what industry there is is in their hands; while they occupy an important position in a variety of commercial, artisanal, and professional services. Their significance is declining, however, and this trend is likely to continue as Libyans become capable of assuming their functions and as remaining farms are transferred to local ownership. Their numbers have gone from a peak of 110,000 in 1941 to 38,000 in 1954, and an estimated 29,000 in 1962. The Jewish population, which was about 30,000 in 1948, was only 3,200 in 1961.

About 24 percent of Libya's population is urban, and the main cities of Tripoli and Benghazi are mushrooming rapidly in response to new economic conditions including the oil boom. About 40 percent of the population are sedentary rural dwellers, 19 percent seminomads, and 18 percent nomads.

LAND USE IN LIBYA

The area of Libya is 679,358 square miles or about 2½ times the size of Texas. Ninety-five percent of the country is classified as desert and not much more than 5 percent can be put to economic use. Permanent cultivation is now confined to less than ½ of 1 percent of the total area and probably cannot be more than doubled, though varying areas can be used for catch cultivation depending on precipitation. There are three regions of more intensive use: the coastal plain and Jefara of Tripolitania in the west, the Cyrenaican plateau to the east, and the scattered oases of the south.

TRIPOLITANIA

Tripolitania, with at least three times the population of Cyrenaica, contains the best-developed regions of the country. With far more habitable space and a more socially advanced populace, it accounts for about two thirds of the nation's cultivated acreage and the bulk of its agricultural production, including a greater variety of crops than the other regions. Its inhabited area consists of three parts. First is a broken line of oases extending for about 200 miles along the coast between Zuara on the west and Misurata on the east (Map 26) and inland only six miles or less. The resources of ground water here are fairly abundant, with one water table found only 15 to 50 feet below the surface along the coast and another at 50 to 70 feet depth which is partially artesian. This permits Tripolitania, which has a total of about 247,000 acres under irrigation, to have the most stable agriculture of Libya. The main crops include cereals and vegetables, peanuts, the vine, and tree crops such as olives, figs, dates, almonds, and citrus fruit. Many of the higher value crops were concentrated on Italian farms, which required subsidy even after Libya became independent. This anachronistic position is gradually being eliminated as Libyans are assisted to purchase the Italian holdings.

A small mechanical pump drawing water from an old well at Taguira, about 11 miles east of Tripoli
The introduction of a large number of such pumps in recent years has helped to stabilize agricultural output in favored areas.

In recent years there has been a considerably expanded acreage put to tree crops, not all of which are as yet yielding. A large number of mechanical pumps has also been installed, which has had a stabilizing effect on output in the favored areas. Peanuts have become the leading agricultural export of the country; the fact that they are grown under irrigation has contributed to their becoming the most consistently successful crop. Olive oil ranks second among agricultural exports but yields fluctuate markedly. The 1961 record sales, for example, were succeeded in 1962 by a yield which was inadequate to meet domestic requirements. None of the agricultural exports of Libya have any great significance in world markets, their total value having been only about $2.9 million in 1961. Practices are still generally archaic, while the single greatest cultural obstacle to development of agriculture in parts of Tripolitania and in Cyrenaica is the complicated and insecure tenurial system which creates a disincentive for improving land and increasing yields.

The second inhabited area is a triangular open plain behind the coastal oases called the Jefara and covering about 6,000 square miles. The main characteristic here, as in other areas of Libya outside the oases, is instability. Dry farming is concentrated upon grains, particularly barley, which has enormous fluctuations in yields from year to year. The Libyan barley crop, for example, totaled 1,800, 22,000, and 141,000 tons in three recent years. Winds compound the difficulties occasioned from aridity;

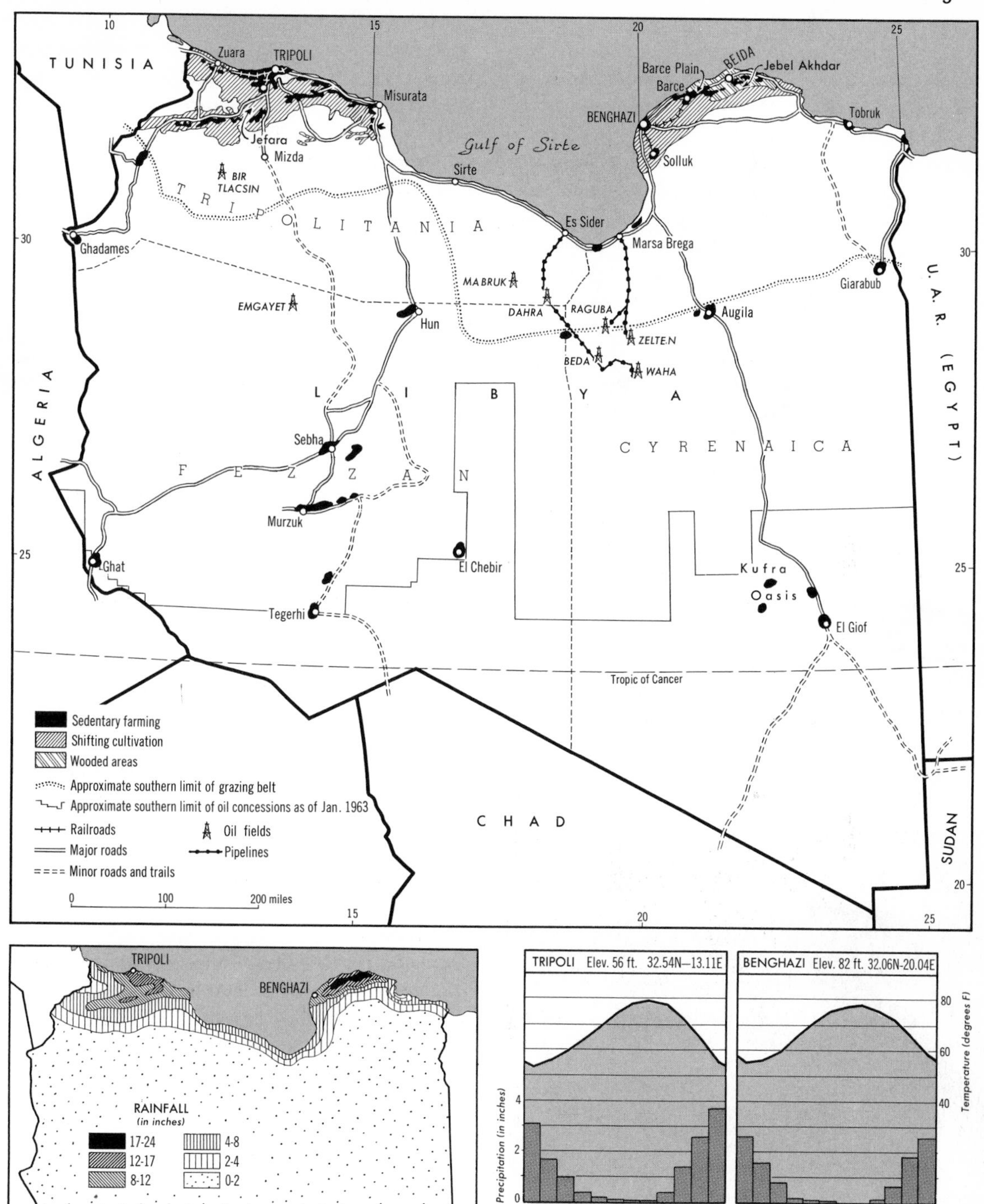

Map 26. Economic map of Libya; precipitation and selected climographs

the hot, desiccating "ghibli" may raise the temperature of the Jefara well above 110° F. for days and cause additional damage by driving sand. Dry farming may benefit in Libya if the present experiments in dune stabilization through spraying with petroleum-based mixtures prove effective and economic. The Jefara is the main olive producing region of the country and almonds, which are often planted alternately with olive trees, have been doing well. Grazing is also important in the Jefara, as is the collection of alfa grass.

Last of the inhabited zones of Tripolitania is the Jebel, a plateau of 2,000- to 3,000-foot elevation whose scarp bounds the Jefara on the interior. Relatively well watered in the east where it carries a modest vegetation, it is increasingly arid to the west. It is used mainly for grazing and the collection of alfa grass, but overexploitation of this resource has been a major cause of soil erosion in the Jebel.

CYRENAICA

The main area of this province is the Barce Plain, a low limestone plateau running in a 150-mile crescent along the coast and having a maximum extension inland of only about 30 miles. The highest elevation is about 3,000 feet and the plateau falls abruptly to the sea in the north. To the east and west it is fringed by coastal steppes which in turn merge into the desert. Behind the Barce lies the Jebel Akhdar or Green Mountain, a Mediterranean steppe area which supports the juniper bush and a few conifers and which supports some production of cereals. But the water sources in Cyrenaica are very deep and difficult to find, hence that province has only one eighth the area suitable for sedentary farming that Tripolitania has. Grazing, therefore, is almost universal, its dominance also being explained by the existence of more Arabs than Berbers in Cyrenaica. Many of the ancient water control works, in fact, were permitted to decay or remained unused because of the lack of interest in tillage agriculture. In recent years a major effort has been made to rehabilitate and extend various storage and supply systems; by 1963, in all of Libya about 300 small reservoirs had been repaired, 160 wells drilled, 3,000 ancient rainwater cisterns cleared and renewed, and increased attention given to construction of dikes across the wadis. Improvements in the livestock economy have included efforts to crossbreed the local sheep with Turkish Barbary or Karaman sheep to develop a better wooled sheep for support of the carpet industry and increase exports of lamb and mutton. Nomads along the desert edge have been assisted by the sinking of wells for stockwater; when these sources are visited on the seasonal trek the animals are dipped, drenched, and treated with insecticide to reduce the losses from disease. Animal products were formerly the leading export of the country, but improved living standards have resulted in a heavier domestic consumption and in 1962 Libya was, for the first time, a net importer of meat.

Sheep grazing near the coast east of Tripoli
Nomadic and seminomadic grazing involves about 37 percent of the population of Libya.

THE SOUTHERN OASES

The oases of Fezzan and of southern Cyrenaica have little economic significance at the present time. Their most important crop is dates, but yields and total production are low and only a small export is possible. A paved road is nearing completion to Sebha and is to be continued into Chad; whether this stimulates commercial production remains to be seen.

SECONDARY ACTIVITIES

Libya has about 240 boats, mostly owned by Italians, Greeks, and Maltese, engaged in fishing along the Mediterranean. The main catch is tunny and sardines, and canning operations are concentrated in Tripoli. Collection of sponges has been carried on for over 2,000 years; in modern years the Greeks have monopolized the industry and efforts to break their grip have apparently led to a marked decline in production.

Manufacturing has only a very limited development. There are numerous small craft shops run by one man or a family, the better handicraft output consisting of Misurata rugs and Tripoli silver and leather. Modern industry is almost exclusively concerned with the provision of services and the processing of agricultural produce. It is heavily concentrated in two cities, with about two thirds of the establishments being in Tripoli and a quarter in Benghazi. All of the important towns and most of the coastal area of Tripolitania are served by electric plants. A serious shortage in Tripoli was met by construction of a new plant in 1961 which brought the capacity there to 42,150 kw.

Mineral production, with the exception of oil, has been confined to about 30,000 tons of marine salt yearly, building materials, and a small output of natron salt from Fezzan and sulfur from Cyrenaica. Exploitation of potash deposits at Marada began in 1963. It is hoped that exploration for petroleum as well as other geological investigation will lead to the discovery of other significant mineral bodies.

Until the discovery of oil, then, it is apparent that there was no economic sector in the country with adequate production and no visible undeveloped resources which could have been expected markedly to raise the standard of living or alter the serious trade imbalance. The finding of oil provides a striking and very recent postscript to the account of Libyan economic development.

PETROLEUM IN LIBYA

The development of Libyan oil resources has been even more recent and more rapid than that of Algeria. It began in 1955 with the promulgation of a liberal law allowing for a 50-50 ratio plus depletion allowances to producing companies. United States companies obtained the first prospecting rights and the first discovery was reported two years later in the Fezzan 560 miles south of Tripoli. The first large find came in 1959 at Zelten in Cyrenaica only 95 miles south of the Gulf of Sirte coast, after which a series of important fields have been discovered in widely scattered areas of the country. The dynamic nature of operations in Libya is revealed by the following data:

Oil camp at Zelten
Oil was discovered at Zelten in 1959 and it is now one of the major producing fields of the country. Gathering lines from producing wells lead to gas-oil separation tanks in center.

	As of Sept., 1960	*As of Sept., 1961*	*As of Sept., 1962*	*As of July, 1963*
Number of wells completed	99	338	553	790
Number of producing wells	26	137	231	344
Number of gas wells		2	2	2
Number of dry holes		199	320	444
Tested rate of production, in thousand barrels per day		219	351	489

At the present time 11 companies are drilling and 19 companies hold concessions in Libya covering almost three fifths of the country and five marine concession areas in the Gulf of Sirte. Expenditures increased from $12.6 million in 1956 to $220 million in 1962 and totaled about $800 million from 1956 to the end of 1962. The rapidity which has characterized operations in Libya is explained not only by the apparent great wealth of the area but by a provision in the petroleum law requiring that the concession be reduced to 75 percent of its original size after five years, to 50 percent after eight years, and to 25–33⅓ percent of its original extent after the first ten years. This stimulates exploration because each holder wishes to retain the best section of his concession.

Libyan oil is comparable in quality to that of Algeria; costs of operation are also relatively high, largely because of desert conditions. But the Libyan finds appear to have two important advantages over those of Algeria: first, that some important finds are closer to the coast and have no mountain barriers to cross, and second, that oil is found at comparatively shallow depth, usually between 5,000 and 10,000 feet. Production costs are, therefore, considerably lower than in Algeria.

The most important producing areas to date are the Zelten field of Esso Libya and the Dahra field of Oasis Petroleum Company, a combination of three American companies. Zelten is connected by a 106-mile, 30-inch pipeline to Marsa Brega, opened in October, 1961. A small refinery, whose capacity is adequate to meet domestic requirements, has been built at the terminal. An 88-mile, 30-inch pipe was completed the following year from Dahra to another new outlet on the Gulf of Sirte, Es Sider. Other fields have since been connected to these pipelines, as shown on Map 26. The Zelten field is also being connected by a 36-inch pipeline to carry partially desalinized seawater from the coast for use in maintenance of pressure in the field. Natural gas cannot be used because the oil is unsaturated and it would simply be absorbed. The cost of this pipeline with accompanying power stations is about $50 million, but it may double the eventual yield. It is expected that a third major pipeline 270 miles in length will be constructed from southern Cyrenaica to Tobruk. Production of oil from Libya went from about 643,000 tons in 1961 to 8,097,000 tons in 1962 and was expected to reach 18 million tons in 1963.

Libya faces a more difficult market situation than Algeria and is the first North African producer to compete on wholly commercial terms. Efforts have been made to secure assured markets, in part by agreements to construct refineries, as, for example, in Spain. So far, no great difficulties have been met, but Libyan crude must be sold at a price markedly lower than the price set for French receipts from Algeria. The main hope is that consumption in the major market area of western Europe will continue to expand as vigorously as it has.

The impact of oil on the Libyan economy has been startling. It gives the country, for the first time in many centuries, the chance to be self-sustaining. In 1962 receipts from royalties totaled only $33.6 million, but may well reach $500 million in the period from 1963 to 1967. Budgetary expenses of the government were increased 35 percent from 1960–61 to the $48.4 million level of 1961–62. The national economy has been greatly stimulated by the enormous expenditures for petroleum development, about 30 percent of which are spent locally. About 11,000 people have found employment and the per capita income has increased from about $50 in 1951 to an estimated $150 in 1961. The construction industry has had a particularly notable expansion.

On the other hand, petroleum developments have brought new problems to the country. It will not be easy to spend the money effectively; a whole new set of plans will be required to allocate the 70 percent of royalties that has been earmarked for development. The inability of Libya to staff the required bureaucracy and the inhibiting character of what has been an essentially static society are factors which cannot be overcome as rapidly as oil can be developed. Additional problems that have been created include inflationary forces which have brought great increases in the price of food, rents, city land, and construction. Local production has not been able to take full advantage of the new developments; indeed they have had a depressing effect on agriculture, leading to abandonment of some farms, excessive migration to the cities, and a shortage of seasonal workers, while the dependence on and expenditures for imported food have risen sharply. Nor has industry yet responded to the newly created possibilities. The petroleum industry, furthermore, cannot be expected to provide large-scale employment; it will probably never directly support more than 5 percent of the population. Meanwhile, the high wages offered by the industry have attracted some of the few educated Libyans from the government, thus slowing the pace of Libyanization. Many of these distortions may be only temporary, but great skill will be required to meet the new challenges rationally. New political concerns have also been aroused now that Libya has such apparent wealth. Egyptian intrusion in Yemen and continued machinating with respect to Jordan and Saudi Arabia do not go unheeded in Libya, which has a long common frontier with its expansionist neighbor. It is not unlikely that this concern will increase Libya's interest in the retention of Western bases.

Petroleum loading terminal at Marsa Brega
The special bow mooring permits ships to swing a full 360 degrees while loading. Tug controls loading arm at right.

TRANSPORTATION AND TRADE

Libya has a reasonably good road system, especially considering its previous poverty. A surfaced road runs 1,140 miles along the coast; about 2,400 additional miles of paved road exist in the north, while the new 390-mile road to Sebha in Fezzan has already been noted. Aside from these highways and linking roads, however, there are mostly only tracks of variable negotiability. Two narrow-gauge railways exist, one tying Barce and Solluk with Benghazi in Cyrenaica, the other serving the towns adjacent to Tripoli. Both lines run at a loss and carry only minor tonnages, mostly comprising agricultural produce.

Tripoli handles over three fourths of the general port cargo of the country. It has a good harbor capable of receiving vessels of about 26-foot draught. Benghazi is the main port for Cyrenaica; it is being completely renovated and deepened to 30 feet at a cost of about $13.2

million. Tobruk, which has one of the best natural harbors in North Africa, has been partially restored and will be further rehabilitated and used as a third oil-exporting port, but its barren hinterland greatly reduces its potential value. The two existing petroleum terminals have, of course, become the biggest shippers in Libya, and their connecting pipelines provide a new feature in the transportation picture. Libya has three international airports, of which Idris Field near Tripoli has become of increasing importance as a stopping point on international routes.

Libyan trade has been noted by a marked imbalance for many years and a stagnation in exports of most crop and livestock products. The total value of exports was only $13 million in 1951 and $11 million in 1960, while imports were $28 million and $169 million in these two years. Before discovery of oil, invisible receipts, particularly in the form of foreign aid, covered the trade deficit. Petroleum investments resulted in an over-all favorable balance of payments in later years, despite enormously increased imports required by that industry. Greatly increasing oil exports should rapidly reverse the trade imbalance in the years ahead, when exports will be far above those of earlier years. In 1962 total exports reached $141 million, almost thirteen times the 1960 level; the trade deficit in 1962 of $65 million compared with one of $158 million in 1960.

CHAPTER EIGHT

The United Arab Republic (Egypt)

With the exception of about 36,000 inhabitants of the western oases, some thousands supporting the Suez Canal, and the meagerly supported refugees in Asian Egypt, the 27.9 million (1963) people of Egypt are basically dependent on the Nile. A fortuitous combination of physical features makes possible this greatest of all oases. First is the river, second longest in the world, with its headwaters in regions of abundant precipitation. One main branch has its source in equatorial lands 4,000 miles from the Mediterranean, though the Nile proper measures 3,473 miles from the outlet of Lake Victoria; the others, which contribute more water to Egypt, come in a tremendous seasonal flow from the Ethiopian Massif. Second is the presence of a topographic channel which the Nile occupies in its lower course, which permits the Nile to flow all the way across the Sahara instead of spreading out largely to be lost by seepage and evaporation. Third is the existence of low-lying areas along the Nile and in its delta, suitable, indeed magnificent, for cultivation under irrigation. And last is the excellent temperature regime permitting double and even triple cropping.

The utilized area of Egypt is about 15,000 square miles, an area about as large as Switzerland, and only 4 percent of the total area of the country. This gives an over-all density of 1,860 per square mile in the inhabited areas, but rural densities of 2,500 per square mile are not uncommon. The farmed area of the Nile Valley is given as about 6 million acres, resulting in a man-to-arable-land ratio of about 2,976 per square mile or one person per 0.20 acres, compared to 0.90 acres per capita in Europe and 3.90 in the United States.

The raw figures of population density are impressive enough in their own right, but reveal only part of the story. The evidence of extreme poverty, the high disease rate, the high infant mortality rate, and the low dietal standards reveal the consequences of such great densities, while a glance at the rates of increase of the population and an understanding of the improvements that are being made in certain health and disease conditions present a frightening prospect for the future.

The per capita income is estimated at about $134 per annum, but since there is extreme disparity the poorest peasants receive very much less than this. A survey conducted in 1948–52, based in so far as possible on quantitative terms so that comparison could be made with areas in India, South America, and elsewhere where similar surveys were conducted, rated the Egyptian village as the most insanitary place to live of any civilized part of the world, ranking far below the villages of India. In the five villages studied, 100 percent of the population had amoebic dysentery, 92 percent bilharzia, 89 percent trachoma, 64 percent intestinal worms, 6.5 percent syphilis, 5 percent pellagra, and 2 percent tuberculosis; 6 percent were typhoid carriers and 6.4 percent were blind in one eye; 12 percent of the residents lived entirely on unleavened bread plus skim milk and cheese; 56 percent lived on these foods plus fresh vegetables about once a week.

The death rate for Egypt as a whole was estimated to be 15.8 per thousand in 1961, while the infant mortality rate was 108.0 per thousand. While these figures are still high, they have been markedly reduced in the past few decades, the death rate having been 27 per thousand before the war. Medical facilities, still grossly inadequate, have been improved. The use of DDT, cutting down the malaria rate, is more and more common. In 1951 a typhoid epidemic, which would previously have caused an untold number of deaths, was met by international teams which reduced the losses to a fraction of what they might have been. Each year now sees over 650,000 more mouths to feed and the population may well reach 43 million by 1980.

While the death rate has declined, the birth rate has continued high, which means that the rate of increase has gone up. In 1920–24 and 1930–34 the crude rate of increase was 1.6 percent; it was 2.74 percent in 1952 and 2.81 percent in 1961.

What can be done to meet this fantastic population problem? There are perhaps five major possible solutions:

1. Extend the land under cultivation, principally by more effective control of the waters of the Nile.
2. Intensify production on the already existing acreage.
3. Absorb the excess population in nonagricultural pursuits—mining, industry, tourism, etc.
4. Promote emigration.
5. Promote the conscious limitation of population growth.

EXTENDING THE LAND UNDER CULTIVATION: CONTROL OF THE NILE

Some conception of the possibilities offered by control of the Nile may be seen from the fact that about 32 billion cubic meters of the average annual flow of 84 billion cubic meters normally flows to the sea without being used. The hydrography of the Nile has been the subject of study and speculation for at least six millennia; the height of the Nili, or flood Nile, has been recorded since 3600 B.C. Today, with the tremendous population pressure existing, its study is as important as it has ever been. The problems of how best to protect the waters from dissipation and wastage, how best to conserve them for effective use, involve tremendous hydrographic, engineering, political, economic, and human problems. By tracing the course of the main streams and noting the actual and possible improvements, a more accurate assessment of this answer to Egypt's problem may be obtained.

THE WHITE NILE

The White Nile begins at Lake Victoria, whose most important feeding river is the Kagera rising in the uplands of Rwanda at about 2° S latitude (Map 27). Lake Victoria, which is the size of Eire and the second largest lake in the world, is unlike the other great lakes of Central Africa in that it occupies a relatively shallow uplifted plateau basin rather than an elongated rift valley. Located in a region of great and fairly evenly distributed rainfall, it is significant as far as Egypt is concerned in that it acts as a huge reservoir, evening the discharge into the Nile at Jinja. The big disadvantage, explained by its size and equatorial position, is the high loss from evaporation, which exceeds 80 percent of the amount received by the lake in precipitation and from tributaries. Just below the outlet of the lake we find one of the more recent engineering structures which influence the Nile flow to Egypt, the Owen Falls Dam. Completed in 1954, this dam raises the level of the lake only three to four feet, but adds 200 billion cubic meters to its storage capacity, the resultant benefit to Egypt accounting for her willingness to contribute to the cost of the dam. The Owen Falls Dam is a good example of international cooperation, an element all too often lacking in the 1,107,000-square-mile basin of the Nile. Egypt gained by more effective control; Uganda and Kenya gained through the production of low-cost hydroelectricity; Britain gained through the improved economy of two of its dependent territories.

The river is called the Victoria Nile through Lake Kioga to Lake Albert, a distance of 254 miles in which the river drops 1,400 feet. The hydrography of these sections, particularly the influence of Lake Kioga, is imperfectly known. Eventually several power and storage dams may be placed along these stretches, but other projects are likely to receive higher priority for many years. Lake Albert, being a narrow, steep-sided, rift-valley lake, provides a suitable place for storage without excessive evaporation loss, but its ownership by two nations and the fact that some utilized areas would be flooded are impediments to such use. From this lake the Mountain Nile or Bahr el Jebel descends to the plains of southern Sudan, to the region known as the Bahr el Ghazal or "the Sudd." About a hundred miles below the lake and just inside the Sudan border, at Nimule, is another site appropriate for a future dam.

In the Bahr el Ghazal the gradient of the Nile is so reduced that it forms tortuous and bifurcated passages creating a vast swampy area for about 200 miles, full of papyrus reeds and of floating vegetation called "sudd," which denotes blockage. This vegetation contributes to the water's spreading and interferes with navigation on the river. And in recent years the water hyacinth has found its way into the Nile system, threatening additional difficulties. While the Bahr el Ghazal swamps act as a regulator, evening the flow of the river below them, their far greater significance is in the enormous losses from evaporation that occur as the high waters spread over vast stretches of the region. One of the main functions of dams above this area would be to prevent such wide spreading by evening the flow into the Bahr el Ghazal. More effective would be the Jonglei Diversion Scheme or Equatorial Nile Project, which would involve cutting one or more 16-foot-deep, 390-foot-wide, 175-mile-long canals across the area that would carry a portion of the flow while the main passages would continue to carry the rest, thus preventing the present dispersion with its consequent high losses to the sun. It is estimated that, with stabilization of flow into the area, the loss to evaporation in the region could be reduced to one tenth of the present level. This scheme, which has been the subject of intensive study off and on since 1904, represents one of the few ways in which larger quantities of water could be passed down the river for later use in irrigation; most of the other control schemes are designed to even out the flow in Egypt or the Sudan. While they increase the so-called timely water, that is, water coming in the period when it can be used, they usually result in some actual loss in total flow owing to increased evaporation losses. Bringing the Jonglei Scheme to fruition will entail large expenses, political agreement between Egypt and Sudan, and provision for some alternative method of livelihood for the indigenous peoples of the Bahr el Ghazal, whose way of living is closely coordinated with the seasonal ebb and flow of the Nile. The question should also be raised whether the waters saved should not be used in this area rather than further downstream. The remoteness of the area, its relatively sparse population, and the backward nature of the inhabitants argue against large-scale expenditure on intensive irrigation in this area, but it may also be held that control of these waters permits the development of an otherwise poor area which should not be condemned to poverty.

Where the Bahr el Ghazal and the Bahr el Jebel meet, the true White Nile begins. Map 27 presents in the inset water accounts a picture of the gains and losses at specific points along the Nile, and it may be seen that the river emerges from the Sudd region with only about 56 percent of its entering volume despite the precipitation which falls on the area and the existence of several tributaries. Soon the White Nile is joined by its first major eastern affluent, the Sobat, which rises in southwest Ethiopia. The rains in that area are highly seasonal, concentrated in the months of April to October, and when the peak flow of the Sobat reaches the Nile in November and December its height acts as a dam to the main Nile, ponding its waters upstream from the confluence. The flow chart for Khartoum in Map 27, showing the seasonal flow of the White and Blue Niles at their confluence, reveals the much more even regimen of the White Nile, explained by the more even precipitation in its equatorial headwaters, the reservoir effect of the lakes and swamps through which it passes, and the ponding effect of the Sobat. It is the White Nile which supplies the bulk of water to Egypt in spring and early summer, when it is most valuable, and hence it provides more than a proportional contribution to the multiple cropping possibilities in Egypt. Even so, there is considerable variation in the flow of the White Nile, from a low in May to an average high three times as great in October and a maximum flow from five to six times as great.

Not far above the confluence of the White and Blue Niles is the Jebel Auliya Dam, completed in 1937. Its purpose is to conserve the White Nile waters during the high flow period of the Blue Nile. It serves Egypt rather than the country in which it is situated, though the Sudan is compensated for the lands which are flooded and cannot be used, and has recently installed a hydroelectric plant at the dam.

THE BLUE NILE

It is the Blue Nile which provides the spectacular element to the main Nile, contributing about four sevenths of the total volume, or twice the amount from the White Nile. Its flow is highly seasonal, reaching a low in spring but rising from June to September to an average flow thirty times as great; the maximum flow can be 4,000 times the minimum. The Blue Nile causes the annual flood or Nili, provides the chief supply of water to Egypt in August-September, and brings down the tremendous quantities of invaluable reddish brown alluvial silt which is the soil of Egypt. It rises in the Gojjam Highlands near Lake Tana, from which it flows through precipitous gorges onto the Sudan Plain near Roseires. Increased storage capacity in its headwaters would be highly desirable, and construction of a dam at Lake Tana has been discussed for many years, but, again, the difficulty of completing international accords has delayed fruition. The existence of shrines and religious monuments which would be flooded, the remoteness of the area, and Ethiopia's lack of interest in major hydroelectric production are factors which have militated against an effective concern by that country.

Descending to the Sudan we find a new dam near Roseires which permits a large additional supply to the irrigated areas of Sudan, while at Sennar is the dam which stores most of the water for the Sudan Gezira. Under the 1929 Nile Waters Agreement the amount of water that could be utilized by the Sudan was strictly limited. This agreement, which was completed when Britain was acting as the "protector" for Sudan and when little need was seen for supplying water to an underpopulated country, threatened in recent years to exacerbate Egyptian-Sudanese relations and to make "the unity of the Nile" an empty phrase. After several abortive negotiations, however, a new agreement was concluded in late 1959. The allocation of water under these agreements is shown below, the 1959 distributions actually referring to the situation which will exist upon completion of the High Dam.

Distribution of Nile waters (billion cubic meters)

	1929 Agreement	*1959 Agreement*
Egypt	48.0	55.5
Sudan	4.0	18.5
Flow to sea	32.0	
Loss to evaporation		10.0
Total average flow	84.0	84.0

At present about 32 billion cubic meters are wasted each year; about 22 billion cubic meters of this will be utilizable after construction of the High Dam, while some 10 billion cubic meters will be lost through evaporation. The 1959 Agreement also provided for the formation of a permanent commission to supervise the distribution and for payment of $43 million by Egypt for the evacuation and resettlement of about 70,000 Sudanese residing in the area of

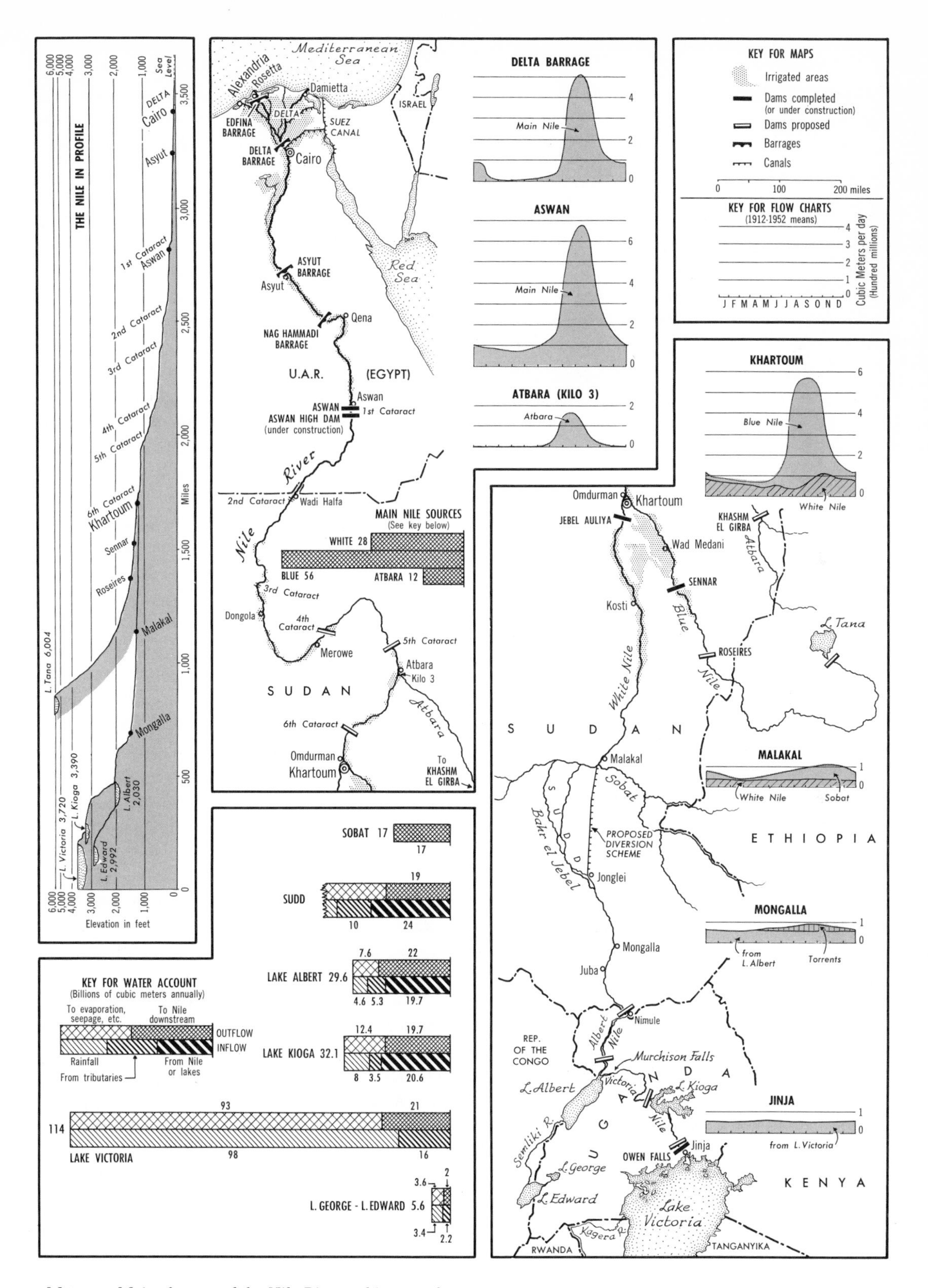

Map 27. Major features of the Nile River and its control

The Aswan Dam, Egypt
First of the major control works on the Nile, this dam will be superseded by the High Dam about five miles to the south.

Sudan which will be flooded by the High Dam reservoir.

THE MAIN NILE

At Khartoum, which means "elephant trunk," the two mighty branches of the Nile converge, though for many miles the waters of the streams, one heavy with silt, fail to mix. Two hundred miles downstream the last of the great east bank tributaries, the Atbara, joins the main stream. Its regime shows the same marked variations as the Blue Nile; its contribution to the river provides about an eighth of its average flow at the confluence. From that point the Nile flows 1,600 miles to the Mediterranean without a single tributary other than wadis with only very irregular if any flow.

The Nile traverses the Nubian Desert in a great S curve. In places there are high and barren cliffs and the desert comes right to the river's edge; elsewhere there are narrow bands of irrigated lands, especially in the Dongolo region between the third and fourth cataracts. The sixth to the third cataracts occur before the S bend ends; the second cataract ends just above Wadi Halfa. Aswan, 216 miles below the border, is at the first cataract. The river formerly fell here 16½ feet in three miles, but the Aswan Dam, first of the major storage dams to be constructed, ponded back the waters over 100 miles when full. First built in 1902, the dam was later raised twice in height to a maximum head of 76 feet to provide greater storage capacity. The flow at Aswan has both great seasonal range and great variation from year to year. In a 50-year period, the flow has varied from 42 to 130 billion cubic meters. The storage capacity of the dam is only 5.3 billion cubic meters, which has permitted an average wastage to the sea of 32 billion cubic meters.

Most of the present and prospective storage dams thus far mentioned were parts of the so-called Century Storage Plan, worked out by the Egyptian Water Department. Designed to conserve waters from evaporation loss and to even out the flow not only within each year but from year to year and over extended cycles of high or low flow, this plan would probably represent the most effective control system for the Nile. But it would have required intricate international negotiation and many years to complete. Faced with the need to provide more water to extend irrigation rapidly, Egypt was naturally attracted by the grandiose High Dam, which could increase the irrigated acreage by about 1.3 million acres in ten years or less. This does not mean that the other projects are all passé, though certainly the need for them will be postponed. The dams above the Sudd region and the Jonglei Scheme, however, have no alternates and, as noted earlier, would add to the volume of water available for the Sudan and Egypt.

The High Dam, which is being constructed about five miles south of the present dam, calls for the use of many superlatives. It will be 2.6 miles long, 346 feet high, 3,900 feet thick at the base, and 126 feet wide at the top, thus being the world's largest earth-filled structure. When full it will store 130 billion cubic meters of water in a 2,000-square-mile lake extending southward some 310 miles. Unlike the Aswan Dam it will not have sluices, the water being carried around the dam in huge tunnels cut into the buttressing cliffs. While the dam is under construction, a mile-long, 240-foot-wide canal will carry the waters past the site.

It is claimed that the dam will have the following effects: (1) permit extending the cultivated area by 1.3 million acres; (2) permit the application of permanent irrigation on 700,000 acres now using the basin system (see below, p. 127); (3) make all of Egypt secure from floods; (4) permit improved drainage on existent land; (5) provide a considerable amount of hydroelectric capacity (see below, p. 133); and (6) improve navigation below the dam.

The dam does have certain disadvantages. It is not absolutely certain that it would preclude the highest floods from wreaking havoc and, strategically, it presents a target to potential enemies which could wash away the country. Other disadvantages include the flooding of some utilized areas, particularly in the Sudan; the high loss through evaporation in this mid-desert area, perhaps 10 billion cubic meters a year or almost double the present capacity of the Aswan Dam; the fact that the huge lake will act as a desilting basin, depriving the country of its yearly supply of enriching silt and gradually filling the reservoir; the possible erosional effect of the clarified water passed around the dam; and the complete interruption to navigation created by the dam. Not too much can be done to prevent the deposition of silt; each new storage reservoir reduces the amount carried downstream. The earlier dams, however, had sluices all the way across the river permitting the reservoirs to be flushed out each year. At Aswan, storage did not begin until the most silt-laden waters had moved through the dam. Despite the heavy deposition expected in the new lake, however, it is estimated that it would take 500 years to fill the reservoir with silt.

The High Dam has figured importantly in Egyptian and international politics. Angered by withdrawal of offers to extend loans for construction of the dam by the United States and Britain, who felt that Egyptian commitments to purchase arms from the East precluded its covering the loan, Egypt nationalized the Suez Canal. This, in turn, led to the aborted United Kingdom-French-Israeli invasion of Egypt in late 1956. The Soviet Union then extended

A model of the hydroelectric plant and part of the High Dam at Aswan, Egypt
When completed, this dam will be the world's largest earth-filled structure and will have a storage capacity about 25 times that of the Aswan Dam.

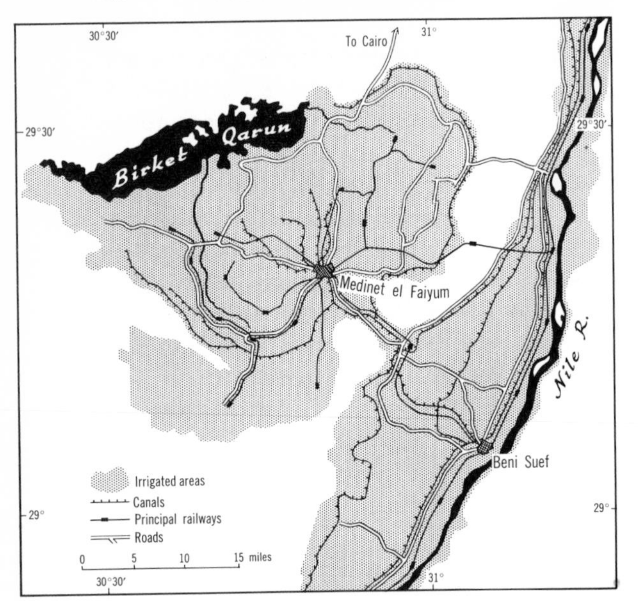

Map 28. The Faiyum oasis

loans to assist in the initial stages of construction of the High Dam plus all necessary technical assistance and later offered to help complete the dam on an accelerated schedule. The dam and irrigation works are scheduled for completion between 1970 and 1972, though it will take until 1975 for the reservoir to fill. Its estimated cost is $1.12 billion.

From Aswan to the Delta the river flows 605 miles with an average gradient of 1 in 13,000. High cliffs rise on each side confining the irrigable area to from only a few yards to 10 miles in width; the long band of green is divided with razor sharpness from the desert. There are no more storage dams below Aswan, only a series of barrages which raise the level of the river high enough to feed the canals on either bank and, later, in the interdistributary areas of the delta. Egypt has a total of 8,500 miles of large canals and about 45,000 miles of small canals and ditches.

About 60 miles south of Cairo, a canal takes off from the left-bank canal and cuts through the narrow gravel ridge separating the Nile Valley from the Faiyum Depression (Map 28), one of a number of structural depressions whose surface had probably been further lowered by the wind. At a period 3,600 years ago one of the Pharaohs conceived of using the depression as a kind of safety valve in the event of excessively high floods and had the canal connection dug. Some thousand years later it was decided to make the Faiyum an integral part of the Nile and the necessary canals were constructed. Meanwhile, many feet of rich Nile mud had been deposited. Today, over 870,000 live on the 700-square-mile irrigated area of the Faiyum, which has the distinct advantage that most irrigation can be done by gravity as the basin slopes gradually toward the lake, Birket el Qarun, which is 140 feet below sea level. A second depression, Wadi Natrun, lying southwest of the Faiyum, has been the subject of study to determine whether it might be developed on a basis comparable to that of Faiyum.

Just below Cairo the Sweetwater Canal leads northeastward and across the desert to the Suez Canal area. Utilizing in part the bed of an early canal connecting the Red Sea via the Nile with the Mediterranean, this canal provides water for support of the communities along the Suez and to permit the planting of trees along the canal to act as a shelter belt against windblown sands. With minor exceptions, the Faiyum and Sweetwater Canals are the only offtakes from the river in Egypt which do not supply either the floodplain or the delta.

Twelve miles below Cairo are the Mohammed Ali or Delta Barrages, the first constructed in 1835 and no longer used, its replacement dating from 1884. Canals from above serve each side of the Rosetta and Damietta distributaries. These barrages are of particular interest not only because of their age but because the delta contains 60 percent of the cultivated land of the Egyptian Nile.

One other barrage remains, the Edfina, near the mouth of the Rosetta Branch. This barrage has somewhat different functions from the run-of-river barrages; in addition to raising the level to ease irrigation it must hold the sea waters out at low water periods and, by slowing the flow of the river, increase the deposition of silt to help build up the delta.

To return to the original question—how much land can be added to the irrigable area by improved control of the Nile?—it is not possible to give precise figures because the investigations have not been sufficiently exact. The High Dam will add about 1.3 million acres to the control area. The present area controlled is 6.0 million acres, so this represents an increase of 21.7 percent. A good part of this will be in the sandy area west of the delta, which will presumably require a greater application of water than the depositional soils of the floodplain and delta. By improving the drainage pattern it may also expedite the reclamation of swampy lands along the seaward margins of the delta. These lands are saline and their recovery requires flushing out the salts and early planting with saline-tolerant crops before a characteristic rotation can be adopted. The High Dam will also permit intensification on a considerable acreage, a point covered in a later section of this chapter. It is estimated that the Jonglei Scheme would add 5.2 billion cubic meters to the flow of the Nile. Assuming that this were divided by the present ratio, which may certainly not be the case in view of the fact that it would be entirely on Sudanese territory, this would add perhaps 7 percent to the water available to Egypt. The possibilities are, then, substantial. But when one projects them against the population growth it becomes apparent that they are nothing but stopgap measures. Indeed, the population will have increased by a higher percentage than will be added to the irrigable area of Egypt by the High Dam just over the period of its construction. The Jonglei and other schemes would obviously only give additional short-period respite to the inexorable population pressure.

EXTENDING THE LAND UNDER CULTIVATION: OTHER METHODS

There are other possibilities for extending the cultivated acreage of Egypt. One is the so-called New Valley Project, which would involve tapping the ground-water supplies in the desert between the Kharga and Dakhla oases. One estimate holds that 3 million acres could be added, but hydrologic studies would have to be far more intensive before this or any figure could be accepted with safety.

A second possibility would be to tap the underground water of the Nile itself, which is probably substantial. Again, however, relatively little study has been made, so no firm estimates can be assayed. In the meantime, this subterranean water is being tapped to provide potable water; a five-year program calls for drilling 500 wells to serve 900 communities. In view of the present practice of taking water from the Nile, which is also used for sewage disposal and bathing, these wells should contribute mightily to the improvement of health conditions.

Third, there is some possibility of increasing the utility of the narrow steppelike band along the Mediterranean west of the delta, formerly a granary of considerable significance.

Lastly, there is the longer-term potentiality of desalinizing sea water and pumping it on the land. Just when this may become practicable is a matter for speculation, but it quite obviously provides the only really substantial solution to extending the productive area of the country.

INTENSIFYING PRODUCTION ON THE EXISTING AREAS

Increasing the output per acre on the areas that are now subject to irrigation may be accomplished in several ways: by extending perennial irrigation, by avoiding wasteful application of water, and by intensifying methods on these areas.

PERENNIAL AND BASIN IRRIGATION

With the exception of a minor production of catch crops sown on areas along the river as the high waters recede, there are two systems of irrigation employed in Egypt. Before the barrages and the Aswan Dam were constructed, back to time immemorial, the basin system was

Fields irrigated under the basin system about 60 miles south of Cairo
With increased control from the High Dam the 700,000 acres now using the basin system will be converted to perennial irrigation, permitting multiple cropping and production of higher value crops.

dominant. Each year the Nile flooded carefully prepared basins; when control was possible, the water was drained off, usually after two to three weeks; and, as soon as the soil could be tilled, the crop was planted and grew solely on the basis of the moisture which the soil was capable of retaining. This system permitted only one crop a year and only drought-tolerant crops such as wheat or barley. The modern engineering development, occurring mainly after 1900, brought an agricultural revolution to Egypt by permitting the widespread application of the perennial system. By storing the waters and releasing them as required, lands could be irrigated all year, permitting multiple cropping with such crops as corn and cotton grown in the summer and grains and bersim (Egyptian clover) grown in the winter. This system permitted a striking increase in production but also, unfortunately, an even greater increase in population.

Perennial irrigation also brought other problems. As has been noted, storage of waters increased the evaporation losses and decreased the supply of silt. It also increased the incidence of disease, particularly bilharzia. This disease, which affects about 80 percent of the population, is caused by the larvae of a tiny mollusc carried by snails entering the body through the skin. While the disease is normally not fatal, the parasite undermines the whole organism, greatly debilitating its human hosts.

At present there are about 6.0 million acres of land subject to irrigation. About 700,000 acres are still using the basin system. The annual crop acreage is 9.5 million, which would mean that the equivalent of two thirds of the area under perennial irrigation is double cropped each year. One of the important contributions of the High Dam will be virtual elimination of the basin system, permitting more intensive use and the planting of higher yielding crops on some 700,000 acres.

The more even year-round supply of water should also lead to less wasteful application of water. The tendency of the fellah is now to take more than is required when it is available; this leads to waterlogging, reduced yields per acre, and higher incidence of plant diseases.

MORE INTENSIVE PRACTICES

A second way to increase production is through more intensive agricultural practices: increased fertilization, improved plant disease and insect control, more careful seed selection, etc. Perhaps the most effective of these would be application of larger quantities of fertilizer. The Nile silt is itself very rich, adequate in potash, phosphates, and trace minerals but deficient in nitrates and extremely low in organic content. Under the basin system, eight or nine tons of silt might be added each year to each acre, but increased control, particularly the new reservoir, will greatly decrease this application, requiring heavier fertilization just to sustain present yields.

Egypt already consumes large and increasing quantities of fertilizers, particularly nitrogenous fertilizers, the use of which has more than doubled in the past decade. Nitrogenous fertilizer plants are situated at Suez, where a very modern plant is based on use of refinery gas, and at Helwan, while the new $60 million Kema fertilizer plant on the east bank of the Nile near Aswan, using electricity from the old dam, will have a capacity of about 300,000 to 480,000 tons of fertilizer a year. In addition, local fertilizing agents are used as available: silt cleaned from canals, mixed with grass; stable manure, but never human excrement; rubbish mounds from dead cities; material taken from the neighboring cliffs in Upper Egypt; and pigeon droppings from the huge rookeries which are often the most noble edifices in the rural landscape. These rookeries may yield as much as one to six tons of extremely rich manure each year. The possibilities of treating sewage from Cairo and other large cities should be studied as an additional source of fertilization.

Plant insect and disease control presents some significant possibilities. At present, cotton is protected by children meticulously picking affected leaves. Although extremely labor intensive, this system was considered superior to spraying with disinfectants, at least until the severe attacks of leaf worm resulted in a loss of about one third of the crop in 1961 at a cost of about $150 million in foreign sales. Insect control is made more difficult by the practice of storing cotton twigs and corn stalks on house roofs, but the absence of other sources of fuel makes it impracticable to destroy these breeding sources.

Other ways of increasing yields are to switch the crop emphasis to more intensive crops and to intensify the rotation. Adequate waters, as noted, will permit switching to more intensive crops in the present basin areas and will, in particular, lead to an increased production of rice; corn may also replace wheat and sorghum to some degree. The present use of the cropped area is roughly as follows:

Percent of cropped area in major crops

Crop	Percent	Crop	Percent	Crop	Percent
Bersim	22	Cotton	16	Lentils	1
Corn	17	Rice	9	Sugar	1
Wheat	17	Sorghum	6	Other	11

There are numerous rotational systems used in Egypt, but a common one would be: April to October, cotton; November to April, wheat; May to November, corn; and December to March, bersim. It would be possible to further intensify this rotation, but that would probably result in greater loss from insects and would require considerably heavier fertilization.

It is sometimes suggested that cotton and other cash crops be replaced by food crops in view of the growing population and the present necessity to import foodstuffs. On a large scale, this would tend toward a low-level subsistence economy by reducing the ability to export and thus to earn exchange which, if properly expended, could be used to introduce development programs and improvements. Cotton and cottonseed now provide about 70 to 80 percent of export revenues. Rice, sugar, potatoes, peanuts, onions, and fruit account for an additional 10 percent. The almost unique quality of Egyptian cotton, with $1\frac{1}{2}$–2″ staples, gives it high value. That country accounts for a major share of the world's long and extra-long staple cotton. The dependence of the economy on one crop has the usual weakness of concentration, as has been proved several times in the past decade, but it is not easy to find substitutes of equal value.

A pigeon rookery in the Faiyum oasis
Such large rookeries may yield from one to six tons of guano yearly and are a locally important source of fertilizers in Egypt.

A market at Tanta in the Nile Delta
The size of the cabbages illustrates the fertility of the soils, which rank among the richest in the world.

REPLACEMENT OF ANIMAL POWER

Still another way of increasing the food production of Egypt would be to substitute mechanical power for animal power, thus releasing the area now devoted to feedstuff production, particularly bersim, to other crops. There are an enormous number of animals in Egypt: the water buffalo or *gamoose* is used in plowing and for drawing water; sheep and goats supply meat, milk, wool, and hides; the camel is a beast of burden and a source of meat; and the ass is used for human and other transport.

The application of power pumps would have a considerable effect on the need for animal power, but would also markedly increase the amount of rural underemployment. Despite the modern development of large-scale engineering works, the methods of lifting water to the fields are still very primitive. The most rudimentary system employs the *nattâla*, a shallow vessel about 18 inches in diameter suspended on ropes; two men dipping it into the water, raising it, and emptying it into the irrigation runnel can irrigate about one acre in 12 hours of strenuous labor. The *shaduf*, of which there are some 50,000, is a crude balanced-weight lift which permits two fellaheen working in two- to three-hour shifts to water about an eighth of an acre in a 12-hour day. In upper Egypt, two or three shadufs may be used in tandem to get the water to the necessary height. Where water need be raised only about 30–40 inches the Archimedes screw is commonly used, there being about 250,000 in the country. This is a wooden cylinder about six to nine feet long hooped with iron; inside is a spiral or helix in which the water rises as the cylinder is turned. While the Archimedes screw costs more and is heavier to work, it can irrigate two or three times as much as the shaduf. The most complex of the ancient water-lifting systems is the *saquia* (*sakieh*), used since the time of the Ptolemies, consisting of a horizontal cogged wheel turned by an ox, buffalo, or donkey which engages a vertical wheel with wooden or galvanized iron pots or pockets which in turn pick up water at the bottom and tip it out at the top into channels running to the field. The saquia, being expensive, is often owned by several fellaheen who bring their animals in turn; it can water about 5 acres. There are said to be about 16,000 saquias in Egypt.

Pumps are surprisingly few, perhaps 2,500 in number. The average fellah can neither afford to purchase one nor to buy the fuel to keep it running. It is planned, however, that about a fifth of the power from Aswan will be used for lifting water, reducing the cost of irrigating an acre from $42 to $12 a year.

There is also much excess use of man and animal power in plowing the fields. Plows which are no better than those used thousands of years ago, except for the metal edge on the share, are employed. While replacement with mechanical pumps and tractors would undoubtedly release land now used to support the animal population of Egypt, there are numerous difficulties inhibiting their wider use: the lack of capital, the extremely low wages of labor, the cost of fuel, the often tiny holding, and the impediment of numerous ditches and canals. Examples have been cited of tractors being purchased as a threat to peasant laborers and then not being used in the fields.

MORE EQUITABLE LAND DISTRIBUTION

It has often been suggested that subdivision of large holdings would result in more intensive use, through the greater care that would be taken by individual owners. Certainly the distribution of agricultural holdings appeared to be highly inequitable before the land reforms of the past decade. In 1952 less than 0.1 percent of owners held more land than the 72 percent with the smallest holdings; the 1.2 percent with over 20 feddans (1 feddan equals 1.038 acres) held about 45 percent of the land. In 1952 a land reform program was initiated which restricted holdings to a maximum of 200 feddans, though a large holder could give in addition no more than two 50-feddan holdings to his sons. While politically very popular, this reform did not have spectacular results; in 1956 the 1.2 percent holding over 20 feddans still had 42.5 percent of the feddanage. One of the most important objectives of the program was to divert capital into industry by purchase of land above the legal limit at requisition prices and selling it to new owners at prices which would yield a net profit to the government. This objective was apparently not met, because in 1961 the government found it necessary to reduce debts incurred under the first land reform by 50 percent.

In 1961 the maximum holding permitted was reduced to 100 feddans, while steps were taken to make land available to about 6,000 farmers and farm workers who were either landless or had less than 5 feddans. It is estimated that some 750,000 feddans had been taken from large landlords between 1952 and mid-1962, while 180,000 feddans were confiscated from the royal family. Possibly about 9 percent of Egyptian fellaheen have been affected by the several land reform measures, which have gone far to destroy the political feudalism in the country. Their provisions have also attacked the problem of fragmentation by restricting the size below which it is illegal to split a farm. Accompanying programs have also attempted to correct the problems of subletting at usurious rates, rural indebtedness, and absentee landlords.

Actually, it would be impossible to divide the land so that each holder had enough to support a family. It is estimated that five feddans are required to support a family of eight. An equal division among rural families of eight each would result in farms about three-fifths that size. It is difficult to determine what effect on yields the subdivision that has taken place has had. In fact, the system of agriculture, the rotations, and the yields appear to differ very little between small and large farms. The land reform program has had a more noticeable effect on distribution of earnings, the big landowners receiving an estimated 21 percent of rural income in 1951 and 11 percent in 1955. Politically, the program had great value in that it represented the first land reform undertaken in modern times.

To summarize the possibilities of increasing

A saquia in use in the Nile Delta
About 16,000 of these devices are used to raise water to the fields in Egypt. Each saquia can supply water to about five acres.

Egyptian agricultural production, it would appear that the greatest gains will result from extending the irrigated area, converting to perennial irrigation, intensifying the rotation, and increasing fertilization. Other measures are likely to have minor significance, and some may simply contribute to greater rural self-sufficiency. The following data very roughly estimate the possible production gains from control of the Nile and from intensification:

	Feddans
Present irrigated area	6,000,000
Area added by High Dam	1,300,000
Possible area added by other control schemes	600,000
Total area to be controlled by Nile	7,900,000
Present crop feddanage	9,500,000
Crop feddanage assuming 100 percent double cropping and total control as above	15,800,000

Estimated gains in agricultural output	*Percent*
From increased feddanage	31.7
From closer cropping	54.7
From other intensification (assuming 25 percent increase in yields on all lands)	41.6
Total projected gains	128.0

Assuming that the gains indicated above were achieved, and assuming a population increase of 2.8 percent per annum, it would take about 30 years before the gains would have been completely offset. When it is recalled that there is already great poverty, great rural unemployment, and great concealed unemployment, it may be concluded that the agricultural field can provide only a temporary palliative to the population problem.

PROMOTION OF NONAGRICULTURAL EMPLOYMENT

What, then, are the opportunities for meeting the Egyptian population problem by the development of other economic sectors? The significance of nonagricultural employment is already relatively high by African standards. Whereas agriculture accounted for 55.9 percent of the 1957–58 labor force of 7,029,000, services and public administration accounted for 18.3 percent, transport, communications, and commerce for 12.9 percent, industry and construction for 10.7 percent, mining for 0.2 percent, and other activities for 2.0 percent. The population of urban areas has increased slowly from 19 percent of the total in 1882 and 1907 to 25 percent in 1937 and 33 percent in 1957. This increases the pressure to develop secondary activities and, since a continued exodus from the land may be expected, it is a trend which is likely to accelerate in the years ahead.

MINING

The mining industry is not of great significance in the Egyptian economy; it employed only 13,000 people in 1957–58 and mineral exports total only about $13 million yearly. Small quantities of lead, zinc, and gold are produced; low-grade manganese ore comes from the Sinai Province, phosphate rock from deposits along the Red Sea, salt from salines along the coast; and there is a substantial output of nonmetallic construction materials.

Iron ore to supply the steel mill at Helwan is mined near Aswan, but its quality is low and reserves are very limited. A larger body has recently been discovered in the Bahariya Oasis in the west, much closer to Helwan than is Aswan, and shipments may be made from this area in the near future, while Krupps and Demag of Western Germany are helping to develop iron ore in the Red Sea area.

The most important mineral is petroleum, which was produced first in the Suez area. The Ras Gharib field on the western shore of the Red Sea was the most productive field until recently, but the Sinai Peninsula has now become the more promising area, particularly the Belayim and Abu Radais fields. Operations in Egypt have been frustrated to a degree by partial or complete nationalization and by various decrees regarding composition of boards of directors, labor participation in profits, and employment of nationals. Oil may be present in the

Western Desert, but United States oil companies discontinued prospecting there in 1958 after 4½ years and an expenditure of $30 million. Prospecting continues in the Red Sea area, however, and in 1961 the Italian E.N.I. secured two new concession areas, one covering the Nile delta east of the Rosetta branch; it agreed to a 75-25 distribution of profits from these two concessions and extended a $50 million credit for the construction of petrochemical plants near Suez to use by-products from the existent refinery. Domestic production meets a declining share of the country's needs despite increasing output. In 1958 Egyptian production was equal to three quarters of consumption, but much of the Sinai crude is unsuitable for direct distillation and has been exported to Italy for special desulfurizing treatment; in 1961 domestic production provided little more than half of requirements. Refinery through-put has increased substantially in recent years and new plants are nearing completion at Alexandria (a one-million-ton atmospheric distillery financed under USSR credits) and at Suez, where an Italian company is constructing plants to extract middle distillates from Egyptian crude, improve the quality of refinery output, recover sulfur, and produce industrial detergents at a total cost of $25.8 million.

The Egyptian second five-year plan included thirty-seven mining projects to be completed by 1965 involving a threefold increase in mineral output. Intensified aerial and surface surveying may reveal additional mineral raw materials, but at present this sector does not appear to promise much additional employment nor to be able to cover the cost of mineral imports required by industry.

INDUSTRY

Egypt places major emphasis on expansion of manufacturing, which now contributes about 10 percent of the national income, or one third as much as agriculture. There was a 50 percent increase in industrial production from 1953 to 1959; in 1958 Egypt accounted for an estimated 6.1 percent of African industrial production, ranking fourth among manufacturing countries of that continent. In the uncompleted first five-year plan, 105 industrial projects valued at $239.6 million were inaugurated, providing an estimated 42,000 new jobs; the second plan, running to mid-1965, calls for about seven times as many projects involving a total investment of $1.7 billion. At the end of the first two years, contracts totaling about $450 million had been signed for 306 industrial projects.

HANDICAPS TO INDUSTRY. Egypt faces severe problems in its drive to industrialize. Its energy resources are not at present adequate. About a half of petroleum products must be imported; imported coal and coke is costly and the coke brought from Poland and the Soviet Union has proved to be of poor quality. Power costs from 1¼ to 2½ times as much as in western Europe. A substantial improvement will come with completion of the High Dam, while hydroelectric installations at the old dam have contributed to sharply increased output in recent years. It is claimed that firm production from the High Dam will be 1.9 billion kwh yearly and that total production capacity will first be 6 billion kwh and later 10 billion kwh. These figures would compare with a total electricity production of 3.7 billion kwh in 1961. Power from Aswan will be used in the Kema fertilizer plant, for pumping irrigation water, and to supply part of the needs of Cairo, to which it will be connected by a 600-mile high voltage line, which will have a further extension to Alexandria. A serious disadvantage of the High Dam hydroelectric installation will be the substantial seasonal decline in production as stored water is released in the period of lower reception. Additional developments in the energy field include the construction of two sizable thermoelectric plants at Cairo and a 21,000-kw gas-turbine plant at Zeneima in Sinai whose output will supply that town and a ferromanganese ore concentrator, and whose exhaust gases will be used in two 600,000-gallon per day seawater distilleries.

The lack of raw materials is a second major handicap to industry. The list of minerals is not impressive as far as basing large-scale industry is concerned, though the existence of iron ore is helpful, at least in saving valuable foreign exchange. Some agricultural commodities do support processing industries. Cane sugar and some beet sugar, which is high cost, a little flax, and some grains are processed in modern factories, but much grain is ground into meal and flour by primitive domestic techniques. Cotton, which might be thought to be of great importance, is actually too high value to justify its use for most domestic fabrics though the medium-staple cottons are frequently so used. The cotton textile industry is, however, pushing the sale of its products on the world market, and the value of exports of cotton yarn and fabrics reached $46 million in 1961. Eventually it may produce special high grade cloth or cotton garments for export. The fairly important tobacco industry, which could be based on domestic output of leaf, uses imported tobacco because the government feels that it can be assured of benefiting from this source of tax revenue only by forbidding the growing of tobacco. A decade ago, tobacco provided 35 percent of total customs receipts and 16 percent of total government revenue. Fruits and vegetables could provide the raw materials for a large canning industry if adequate markets could be secured.

A third problem stems from the shortage of skilled labor and managerial talent in Egypt. The number of skilled workers has increased, however, and the large number of handcraftsmen provides a potential source of employees with some training for modern manufacturing. Considerable attention is also being directed to vocational training and to provisions for on-job training of Egyptian personnel. Limitations of no small dimensions are the restrictions on employment of foreign workers and managers and policies favoring the Muslim population over Greek and other minorities who have greater entrepreneurial experience. The situation of most minority groups has, in fact, become precarious: all but about 30,000 Greeks have left the country, whereas Alexandria alone had 100,000 only a few years ago; Italians, who formerly numbered 40 to 50 thousand, have all but disappeared; the Jewish population has declined from 60,000 to about 5,000; and even the 4,000,000 Coptic Christians who are native Egyptians are subject to increasing discrimination. Nonetheless, the position regarding scientific and engineering talent, semiskilled and skilled labor, and even managerial ability is much better than for most African countries and a very sizable number of graduates are coming each year from scientific and engineering departments of Egyptian universities.

Shortage of capital also slows industrial expansion, but the government has succeeded in channeling rather large sums into manufacturing in recent years. Governmental policies have discouraged much private investment: about 82 percent of business and industry was estimated to be nationalized by mid-1962 and in August, 1963, an additional 500 manufacturing and service establishments were socialized; regulations regarding removal of profits from the country and representation of Egyptian capital have been excessively rigid, though they are periodically relaxed and apparently subject to negotiation. Nationalization of the Suez Canal in 1956 and increasing intrusion of eastern European representation in the area in the years thereafter were not conducive to investment by American and West European companies, but in the late 1950s and early 1960s Egypt made fairly strenuous efforts to attract Western capital, in part because of some disappointment with the results of trade and aid arrangements with the Soviet bloc. Most foreign participation is now in the form of loans on a contractual basis, though some foreign private investment is still forthcoming. Egyptian ability to finance industry is restricted by a traditional lack of interest in manufacturing investments on the part of most private sources, and, as far as government is concerned, by heavy military expenditures and the cost of a swollen bureaucracy. Nonetheless, most of the industrial investments for the present five-year plan are coming from the government, which had concluded 215 contracts totaling $285 million with Western countries and 91 contracts totaling $164.1 million in Communist countries by mid-1962. The evidence suggests that Egypt will find it possible to continue to allocate substantial sums to industrial development.

Perhaps the most severe handicap to industrial development is the relatively small domestic market. Most fellaheen and industrial workers have such low incomes that they can afford little beyond the bare necessities, while the moneyed Egyptian has generally preferred foreign over domestic manufactured products. Certain industries are probably already overdeveloped in relation to the home market, there being excess capacity in brewing, soap making, canning, and other industries. Nevertheless, with the second largest population in Africa and a per capita income of about $134, Egypt has a considerable market for basic consumer goods. It has, for example, the largest national textile market in Africa and its industrial consumption of cotton in 1961–62 was almost five times that of South Africa and more than half that of the United Kingdom.

ADVANTAGES FOR INDUSTRY. While the position of Egyptian manufacturing with respect to raw materials, energy, markets, capital, and availability of skilled labor and management may compare unfavorably with more advanced nations and hence be considered as a handicap to industrial development, it is apparent from the foregoing discussion that there are two sides to every coin and that later analyses may be able to reclassify several of these categories. Egyptian industry, however, does have several positive advantages at the present time. One is the very low wages of labor, only slightly above those of India. (There is also much child labor in the country, both on the farms and in the factories. A child of nine may be employed for a seven-hour day; children above twelve may work a full day, six days a week.) To date, these low wages have not resulted in much export of manufactured goods except for some handicraft products, plus some textiles. But there is little question that a considerable portion of industry is at least temporarily benefited by low wage labor. The continuing influx to the main manufacturing centers promises to sustain labor docility and pressure to depress wages. The reverse of this coin is, of course, the low purchasing power of the average worker.

An Egyptian textile mill
Egypt has the largest production of cotton textiles in Africa. Most production is for domestic sale but efforts are being made to enlarge foreign markets.

Certain industries are advantaged by government protection, and might not otherwise be justified by the size of the domestic market. This is true for tire, automobile assembly, iron and steel, and other establishments. Whether such protection is beneficial to the economy as a whole is subject to question. If tariffs were used to stimulate infant industries which became progressively more competitive they would surely be justified, but all too frequently, as in many other countries, tariffs are used to protect inappropriate industries and the infants require bottle feeding to senility.

The greatest force making for industrial expansion is the aggressive government investment program. The 1958–62 plan, which was ended after promulgation of a new plan in 1960, resulted in the construction of 115 new plants, while the present plan calls for establishing 733 projects in mining, electricity, and manufacturing. On the other hand, governmental interference has doubtlessly inhibited private investment and led to certain distortions in the manufacturing sector.

THE INDUSTRIAL PATTERN. The most important segment of industry in Egypt is the textile and clothing industry, which employs perhaps 40 percent of workers in medium and large plants and accounts for about 35 percent of the total value added in manufacturing. In addition to plants in Cairo and Alexandria, a model plant and community exists in Melhalla el Kubra in the delta 60 miles north of Cairo. Spinning mills are among the largest plants in Egypt; the two plants at Kafr el Dawar and Melhalla el Kubra have 30,000 workers, which is about double the number that would be required for a comparable output in Europe. Weaving is done in hundreds of small shops. In fact, a considerable part of clothing, shoe, blanket, and rug production is still on a handicraft basis.

Food, beverages, and tobacco rank second, with about 22 percent of the total value added by manufacturing. This category includes sugar refining, in which Egypt is self-sufficient, flour milling, canning, brewing, and cigarette manufacturing.

Metal and metal fabricating industries, which are better represented than in most African countries, probably account for about 12 to 15 percent of value added in manufacturing. In 1958 the first blast furnace of the Egyptian Iron and Steel Company mill at Helwan was completed and the plant now has a capacity of 220,000 tons of steel. The raw material situation for this plant condemns it to high-cost production, while the limited market prevents diversification of output. The only advantages the mill has are to free the country from complete dependence on imports and to provide a feeling of pride to Egyptians of all classes. Like the great ancient monuments it has become a place of pilgrimage, but whether this justifies paying higher prices for crude steel is open to question. Output of the plant in 1960 was 118,000 tons of pig and 90,000 tons of steel, levels which were to be doubled by 1962. Egypt has recently acquired an industrial forgings plant at Cairo to produce forged iron parts primarily for transport equipment. Metal fabrication establishments include automobile, tractor, and truck assembly, including a new Fiat plant and a large factory at Helwan; production of sewing machines, washing machines, refrigerators, radios, diesel engines, and elevators; shipbuilding at Alexandria, Port Said, Ismailia, and Suez; and production of military equipment.

The construction industry is fairly well represented, but the fact that most Egyptians live in houses of sun-baked clay means that markets are confined mainly to the large cities and new industrial projects. The capacity of cement mills was raised to two million tons upon completion of a factory south of Helwan, and higher than that by plants built to supply the High Dam. Output of cement reached 2,141,000 tons in 1961, second only to South Africa among the continent's producers. This permitted an export of cement valued at about $8.1 million.

The chemical industry has seen a considerable expansion in recent years. In addition to the petroleum refineries and fertilizer plants, Egypt produces soap, perfume, caustic soda and chlorine, petrochemicals, and pharmaceuticals. Miscellaneous industries include production of pulp and paper (new components of which include a $25.8 million factory at Alexandria, a kraft paper factory at Suez, and a plant at Edfu in Upper Egypt to make 18,000 tons of pulp yearly from bagasse), printing and publishing, leatherworking, and production of pressed wood.

Cairo and Alexandria, with estimated populations of 3½ million and 2 million in 1962, are credited with about 25 and 22 percent respectively of Egyptian industry. Helwan, formerly a high-class suburb of Cairo, is increasingly important as a center of heavy industry. Suez may be considered as the leading chemical producer.

SUMMARY. Whether industry can continue to expand with sufficient rapidity to reduce pressure upon the land is open to serious question. With a population increase of over 750,000 yearly it would require an enormous expansion to absorb the new workers coming on the market each year. It is difficult to assess the gains in employment to date because of inadequate data. One estimate is that persons engaged in industry increased from 235,000 in 1937 to 299,000 in 1947, 397,000 in 1954, and 497,000 in 1960. This would mean that industrial employment increased 66 percent between 1947 and 1960, while the population increased 36 percent. In recent years new jobs in industry could support perhaps about one sixth of the yearly increase in population. Some modern manufacturing will have a depressing effect on employment, particularly if more productive techniques are applied in agriculture and if the large handicraft segment is seriously reduced.

Part of the Egyptian Iron and Steel Company plant at Helwan

The small capacity of this plant and its difficult raw material position condemn it to high-cost production.

OTHER ACTIVITIES

The possibilities of increasing employment substantially in other occupations do not appear to be very great. There is already an excessive number of government employees and low-paid domestic servants. Fishing and collection of sponges and shells are minor activities. Fishing is carried on in adjoining waters, in Birket el Qarun of the Faiyum Oasis, and in the Nile. The huge reservoir created by the High Dam may present new opportunities in that area.

The unique attractions of Egypt for tourism need not be belabored. The major cities and such spots as Luxor are well equipped and, under propitious conditions, thousands of Egyptians cater, sometimes excessively, to the wishes of the visitor. Some day a Pan-Mediterranean Highway might open the country to the rapidly increasing travel-conscious motorists of western Europe. Meanwhile, the crossroads position of Egypt for air traffic and the importance of passenger traffic through the Suez contribute considerably to the opportunities for developing the tourist industry.

PROMOTION OF EMIGRATION

Emigration as a means of easing the population pressure does not now appear to offer much hope. Adjacent countries are often themselves overpopulated. The Sudan, while friendly to Egypt, would not be likely to welcome any large-scale influx of peoples. Syria and Yemen, with which Egypt has had special relations, do not possess undeveloped resources capable of supporting large numbers of Egyptians.

Nor do Egyptians show great propensities for migrating from their homeland or rural community. Even when opportunities are known to exist in other parts of Egypt it is sometimes difficult to get Egyptians to move from their grossly overpopulated villages. The only significant emigration that has occurred in recent years is that of several minority groups who could be welcomed or accepted in other countries.

CONSCIOUS LIMITATION OF GROWTH

It is difficult to see how any solution other than deliberate limitation of the birth rate can do anything but temporarily alleviate the population pressure of Egypt. But it will take time before any significant changes can be expected in such a program. Many Muslims object on religious grounds to birth control. And the average fellah continues to consider a large family a must, his only hope of assistance in the arduous work of raising water, controlling cotton insects, tilling the soil, and harvesting the crop.

Nonetheless, a change could come about with some rapidity under a properly directed program inspired by a respected government. Certain steps have, in fact, been taken which would tend to reduce the number of births: birth control clinics were opened in 1958; nursing homes have been set up where abortion may be legally practiced; polygamy is being suppressed; and the divorce laws no longer make it easy for a man to secure a new wife in a matter of hours. Some Muslim leaders claim that the Koran does not prohibit birth control if it is used to prevent poverty.

The greatest hope may be seen in the rapid extension of educational facilities, not only in this sphere but for many aspects of Egyptian life. In the late 1950s, 76 percent of the population and 95 percent of the fellaheen were illiterate. In 1961, 3½ million students were enrolled in educational establishments or 13 percent of the population, and plans called for achieving universal compulsory primary education in about five years. Egyptian universities graduate a proportionately larger number of students than the United Kingdom or the Scandinavian states, and the total university population was 113,000 students in 1961.

TIMELESSNESS AND CHANGE

One tends to think of Egypt as a place of timelessness. Certainly the fellaheen remain much as they probably were in the years when the Great Pyramids were built. They use the same implements: the sickle, the shaduf, the straw basket. They still level the fields and dig the runnels as their ancestors did; they still keep the same jealous, even selfish, watch on the water supply. An Egyptian woman striding gracefully along the banks of a canal carrying a water jug on her head is mindful of scenes depicted in bas-relief on the walls of the great temples. This imperviousness to change, this stability, this intractability, has been explained as stemming from their close association with an element no less uniform and stable—the soil of Egypt.

Yet further analysis reveals that many important changes have been effected. The masters of the fellaheen have changed from Persians to Greeks, Romans, Byzantines, Arabs, Turks, French and British, to Egyptians. The main religion has changed from totemism to Christianity to Islam, the language from Egyptian to Arabic. Corn was introduced in the nineteenth century; cotton assumed its great importance even later. The buffalo became a major beast of burden in recent times and the main perennial system of irrigation is largely a product of the present century. Modern social experiments also suggest that the fellah is quite prepared to change once the reason for change becomes apparent, but it has not been many years since any interest was taken in his education or betterment. Here may hopefully be the greatest potential contribution of the postmonarchical government: it has imbued the country with a national pride, has adopted programs designed to move away from an inequitable status quo, has fostered a massive educational program which cannot fail to have profound effects on the entire Egyptian milieu.

THE SUEZ CANAL

One additional aspect of the Egyptian economy requires attention—the Suez Canal, entirely within the country but not "of" it. Its importance as one of the world's great arteries stems from the savings in time and distance which it permits (Map 29). Completion of the Suez Canal in 1869 was not the first time that the Red Sea had been linked with the Mediterranean. An inscription at Karnak suggests that a canal connected the Nile with what was then the head of the Red Sea, now the Bitter Lakes, via Wadi Tumilat in 1380 B.C. Darius constructed another canal in 520 B.C. and Amr, the Arab conqueror of Egypt, had a third excavated in the seventh century. All of these went via the Nile rather than directly across the Isthmus; part of the last canal still flowed in the nineteenth century and was used in building the Sweetwater Canal to supply domestic, irrigation, and industrial water to the canal zone.

The present 103-mile canal could accommodate vessels of 24.6-foot draught when first completed. Eight improvement programs under the Suez Canal Company and continued dredging after nationalization in 1956 gradually increased the depth and width to permit the passage in 1961 of vessels of 35.5-foot draught or about 36,000 deadweight tons. A program costing $107.9 million, of which $56.5 million was loaned by the IBRD and nine private institutions, will soon permit ships with 37-foot draught and 46,000 deadweight tons to negotiate the canal, but already plans are being made further to deepen the waterway so it can take ships of 38-foot draught. Additional improvements have been made to expedite movement through the canal, and the present program also involves deepening the harbor at Port Said to relieve congestion, providing berths for cargo and passenger ships there, and construction of roads and bridges at Port Said and at Port Tewfik at the southern end of the canal. The so-called Nasser Program calls for providing two-way passage in ten years through the entire canal.

Control of ships, keeping vessels of different size and speed going through the canal with maximum efficiency, is handled by seventeen stations along the canal with the nerve center at Ismailia. Despite the many improvements that have been made, several problems persist with respect to use and maintenance of the canal: a rail bridge and piles of a former bridge are obstacles, the latter having been hit by the U.S.S. *World Peace* on Christmas, 1954, holding up 150 ships; pilotage is tricky in the confined waters; two large suction dredges and 30 or 40 other dredges must operate continuously to keep the canal free of sand; and maintenance of the walls becomes more and more difficult as the average size of vessels using the canal increases. Large ships take a third of the canal section, creating great suction even at low speeds with the result of drawing sand from behind the stone revetments until they slip into the canal. No easy answer has yet been found to this problem.

While use of the canal has increased more or less continuously since its opening, the sensational Middle East oil developments in postwar years brought canal traffic to record levels almost every year. In 1958, three fifths of all oil tankers of over 4,000 gross tons passed through the canal at least once. South-to-north cargo tonnage, including crude oil, minerals, oilseeds, rubber, textiles, fibres, and soya beans, greatly exceeds that moving toward the south because 70 percent of all cargo is oil from the Middle East. Major cargoes moving southward are manufactured metal products, metals, cement, pulp and paper, and cereals. The interest of

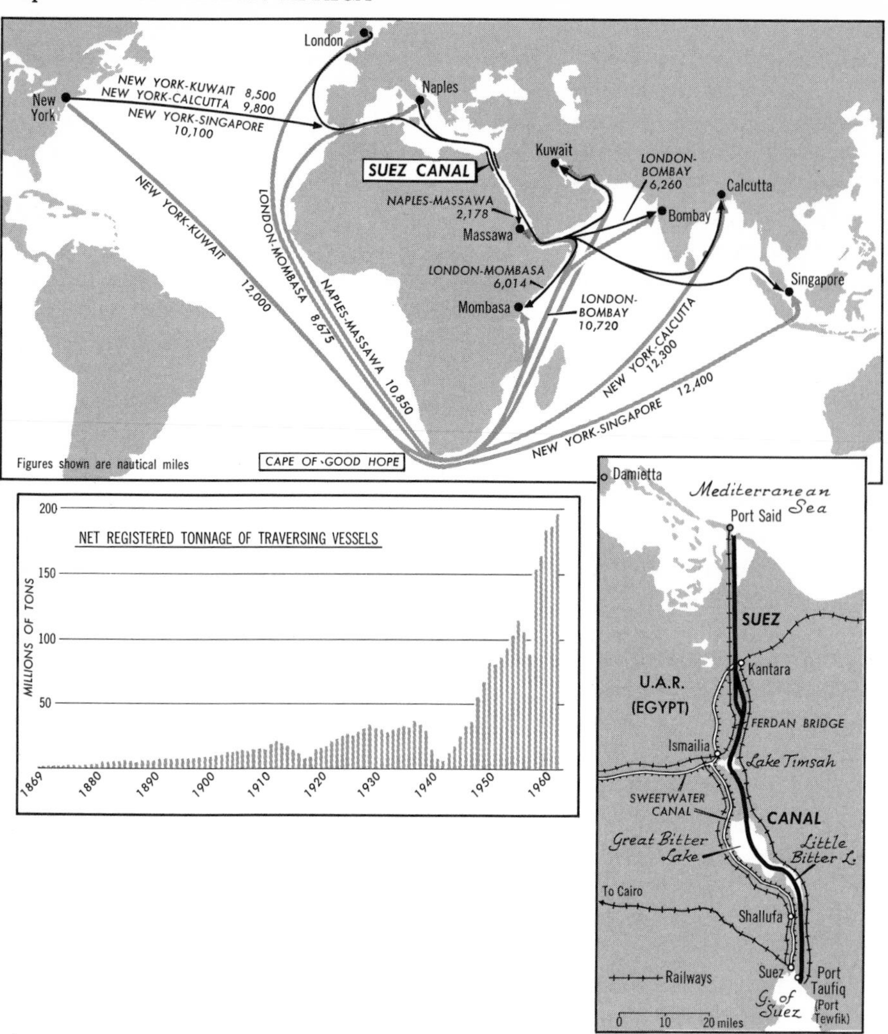

Map 29. The Suez Canal

the United States in the canal has greatly expanded: before the war, cargo to and from the U.S. totaled only one million tons in the record year. In 1954, 9 million tons, mostly minerals, moved through the canal toward the United States, 2 million tons away. Development of oil in Libya and the Algerian Sahara may slow the rate of growth in the years ahead.

Despite the cost of improvements, canal tolls have been reduced twenty-seven times since its opening, twice since the war. In spite of some fears to the contrary, tolls have not been raised since the canal was nationalized; in 1960 they were 98¢ a ton for loaded ships and 55¢ a ton for ships in ballast. The gross revenue to Egypt from canal tolls in 1961 was $147 million. This source of revenue has particular importance because it is primarily in freely convertible currencies. After payment for operating expenses is made and about one quarter of revenues is allocated for canal improvements, some $20–25 million a year in profits are remitted to the Egyptian treasury.

The geographic position and economic importance of the Suez Canal involve it in important political and strategic considerations. When the canal was first opened, an international agreement provided for free passage for all nations in peace and in war. This was adhered to by the Suez Canal Company and by the Western allies, but, of course, control of international waters in the Mediterranean and Red Seas prevented its use by the Germans in both world wars. The Germans bombed the canal and dropped mines into it. Nor is it expected that the canal could be kept open in any future conflict. The strategic significance of the zone is that the isthmus constitutes a land bridge between Eurasia and Africa which can be supplied either from the Mediterranean or from the Indian Ocean. No base in or behind the area is as favorably placed from this standpoint, so even a considerable build-up of bases on Cyprus, Libya, Eritrea, and Kenya could not offset the loss of the British base in the canal zone.

In postwar years the Egyptians have precluded the passage of ships to and from Israel and state that they will continue to do so as long as a state of war exists with that country, this despite the United Nations Security Council voting unanimously that free passage should be resumed. As noted earlier, the canal was nationalized in 1956, twelve years before it was scheduled to become Egyptian property. Despite predictions to the contrary, Egyptian operation of the canal has been efficient and improvements have been continued. After several years in which relations between Egypt and the West were rather strained, new agreements were negotiated whereby Egypt agreed to pay $65 million to compensate the stockholders of the Suez Canal Company for nationalization of the canal in return for loans from the IBRD and other sources. In 1963 Egypt paid the final installment on this debt one year ahead of schedule.

While relations between the West and Egypt are now set fair, western European countries often consider their high dependence upon Middle East oil and upon the Suez Canal strategically precarious. Developments which tend to reduce reliance upon the Middle East for oil include exploitation of Saharan oil and promotion of nuclear-electric capacity. Alternatives to use of the canal include construction of additional pipelines to the Mediterranean, particularly via Turkey rather than through Syria, which now controls all the pipelines; and the routing of super-tankers around Africa. But no alternative to the canal is entirely satisfactory; while the profit per voyage of a 45,000-ton tanker moving between the Persian Gulf and the United States east coast would be approximately the same via the Cape or the canal, the yearly profit via the canal would be about 40 percent greater because of the additional number of voyages possible along the shorter route.

Injection of concrete behind the revetments of the Suez Canal
Stabilization of the banks becomes increasingly difficult as the average size of vessels using the canal increases.

CHAPTER NINE

The Republic of the Sudan

The Sudan, with an area of 967,498 square miles, is the largest of African countries. Its population was recorded as 10.3 million in the 1956 census and was estimated to be 12.1 million in 1961. This gives an over-all density of 12.6 per square mile, but there is very uneven distribution, the highest densities being found along the Nile, including the Gezira area between the Blue and White Niles, and in an east-west belt from Gedaref to El Fasher.

The term "Sudan" has several applications in Africa: there were two countries with that name until 1960, and it is used to describe a climatic-vegetation belt lying between the desert and the higher grass savannas stretching across Africa from the Atlantic to the Red Sea and the Ethiopian Massif. The country which is considered in this chapter is like others sharing the same latitudes in containing climatic, vegetational, and land use regions which range from desert and steppe to savanna and rainforest; it is like them also in having an Islamized north and a pagan or Christian south. But it differs from the lands to the west in the presence of a great through-flowing river, in its eastward transport orientation, in the great isolation of its south, and in the relative position of its northerners and southerners. Here the former are the more evolved, the more politically conscious, and have had longer and greater contact with the outside world. In the former French Equatorial Africa and in the great bulge of West Africa, with the exception of Senegal, the situation is reversed.

From 1899, after the crushing of the Mahdist revolt, until 1956 the Sudan was ruled nominally by an Anglo-Egyptian Condominium. It was the British, however, who actually administered the country through the Sudan Office, which was not a part of the Colonial Office. Egyptian influence was felt primarily in the sphere of water control. While the Sudan Office, like the colonial services of all the powers, did not foresee the rapidity with which independence would be achieved and hence did not sufficiently prepare the Sudanese for self-government, it was in many ways an outstanding colonial administration. Recruiting and promoting its members with care, it inaugurated many important development projects, placed emphasis upon studies and written reports which would be beneficial in later years, and brought the country from an impoverished and largely self-sufficient state into the modern economic world.

The first election in the country, in 1953, brought to power the party which favored a political connection with Egypt, but in succeeding years and after independence on January 1, 1956, deteriorating relations between the two countries negated the earlier desires. The new Sudanese government operated reasonably well until the economic and political crisis of 1958, when General Ibrahim Abboud seized power in a bloodless military coup. Relations with Egypt, which had become particularly exacerbated in 1957–58, were rationalized and negotiations for a new Nile Waters Agreement were successfully concluded in 1959, which permitted the country to move forward with important extensions to its irrigation program.

While this most significant political problem has been met, others, of course, remain.

Difficulties associated with marketing of its staple export, cotton, led to conclusion of barter agreements with seven Communist nations, restricting to a degree the country's policy of free multilateral trade. Suppression in 1958 of trade unions, the largest of which, the 24,000-member Railway Workers Union, had been sympathetic to the Communist Federation of Trade Unions, has delayed the formation of an effective labor force. Within the country, the major political problem is the development of some sense of unity between the pagan, Negro, remote, undeveloped, suspicious south and the Islamic, partly Arab, more politically and economically developed north. Prior to independence rioting occurred in the south and in 1958 the southern delegates walked out of the Assembly to protest the failure to publish the constitution in English, their lingua franca. In succeeding years the government has taken steps to Islamize the south, whose residents have seen their basic freedoms increasingly restricted. Certain conflicts between northern city and rural residents are another factor of disunity.

Other problems have been associated with Sudanization of the government, which was applied at an excessive rate in the years immediately following independence. The efficiency of the administration was drastically reduced; important reports ceased to be published and technical studies were severely curtailed. Very slowly and with the help of advisers from foreign countries and international agencies the bureaucracy is being brought to an effective level, and this problem should gradually disappear in the years ahead.

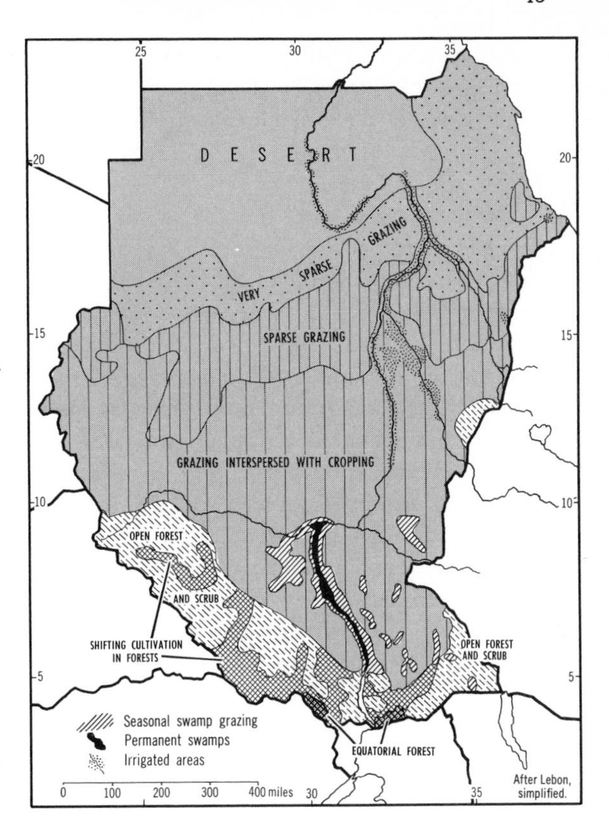

Map 30. Major land use regions of the Sudan

REGIONS OF THE SUDAN

The fact that the vast bulk of the Sudan is an immense plain means that land use is primarily affected by climatic factors and that the major regions are vegetation-climatic belts running roughly east-west across the country (Map 30).

THE DESERT

The northern 30 percent of the Sudan is desert or semidesert, including almost all of the Northern Province, northern Darfur, and the northern half of Kassala Province (see Map 35 for provincial boundaries). This section of the country is largely empty except for a few oases, a discontinuous strip along the Nile, and the southern part, which is used by nomadic pastoralists in the rainy season.

Cultivation along the 1,000-mile stretch of the Nile from Khartoum to the border is restricted to a narrow and disconnected belt varying in width from a few feet to a maximum of 2½ miles. A total of only about 500 square miles supports over 600,000 people. Part of this is *seluka* land, that is land along the banks and on islands which is flooded in the high water period and subsequently used for a catch crop; some is saquia or shaduf land, subject in considerable measure to the vagaries of the river; basin irrigation is utilized on an average of about 80,000 acres but the area flooded may vary enormously from year to year; and much land is now irrigated by diesel pumps. Recent years have seen a marked increase in the number of pumps employed; they now control over half of the irrigated area.

Despite having date and citrus soil par excellence, described as "the dream of perfection," most of the inhabitants of this belt live on the verge of poverty, if not starvation. Land fractionation, jealously maintained, "has a stranglehold on agricultural advancement" and rural indebtedness is almost universal. The date palm provides food, drink, construction material, and cash income for about two thirds of the people, and conditions for its growth are ideal in much of the belt. But failure to replace old trees with higher yielding stock and to adopt modern marketing practices has reduced the total production and the commercial possibilities of the crop. At Kareima, 200 miles north of Khartoum, a scheme is devoted to remedying this situation and to the development of new outlets for the region's products. It is estimated that about 30,000 tons of dates are produced yearly in the 560 miles between Ed Damer and the northern border, of which about one fifth are normally shipped out. A new factory has introduced grading, selection, and packing in cellophane, which permits shipment abroad and to other parts of the Sudan without the previously destructive losses. It has also experimented with making alcohol and liqueurs from dates, with a mixed date and grapefruit juice for canning, and canning of other local produce such as tomatoes, mangoes, and vegetables. In the past, the distance from markets has precluded the expansion of citrus fruit production.

When the reservoir behind the High Dam at Aswan is filled it will stretch southward beyond the Second Cataract to Kosha in Sudan, covering about 200,000 acres of the country, including 4,000 acres of cultivated soil. An estimated 11,000 persons will be flooded out at Wadi Halfa, plus about 30,000 in the district. Dozens of monuments in Egypt and the Sudan will be buried beneath the lake, a problem with which UNESCO has been concerned. Under its guidance at least intensive photographic records will be made available. A new Wadi Halfa port will be built a few miles south of the old city and the possibility of cultivating a strip along the lake shore will be investigated.

Numerous resettlement projects for the bulk of the displaced population were studied before selection of the main solution—construction of a dam at Khashm el Girba on the Atbara east of Khartoum. Capable of storing 500 million cubic meters to control about 500,000 acres, the dam, which is due for completion in 1965, will cost about $20 million. Twenty-six new villages are being constructed at a cost of $36 million, so that the total cost is well above the $42 million compensation payment made by Egypt. A $28 million sugar factory will be constructed at Khashm el Girba to process the main commercial crop planned for the area. The heavy water requirements of this crop may force a reduction in the area brought under irrigation.

Other possibilities for intensification of agriculture exist along the Nile in northern Sudan. An excellent site for a storage dam exists between the Fifth and Fourth Cataracts; its waters could be used to supply pump schemes downriver while hydroelectricity could supply Atbara and replace the need for diesel imports. The 1959 Nile Waters Agreement should also permit converting some of the basins to perennial use. Attention must also be given to eliminating excessively small tenancies, usurious financing, and land fragmentation, and to reducing the unusually high incidence of human diseases in the region.

ACACIA DESERT SCRUB BELT

South of the desert proper is a semidesert belt with erratic precipitation averaging between about 4 and 14 inches yearly. Covering the northern part of Kordofan, central Darfur, and much of southern Kassala provinces, the bulk of this area is inhabited by seminomads who settle in the winter near a permanent water source around which a wide belt of grass has been carefully left ungrazed during the summer. Seldom able to save enough fodder, however, they characteristically bring their animals through the dry winter on a semistarvation basis. When the rains begin to move up from the south, the tribal units split up, first moving southward and then swinging around and proceeding as far northward into the desert as the rains permit, sometimes to 18° N latitude. Only when there is no more forage available do they return to the *dammars* or settled areas. Although this is a largely self-sufficient economy, there is some sale of sheep, wool, skins, and camels, the last sometimes being driven overland to markets in southern Egypt.

Gum arabic
The Sudan accounts for over three fourths of total world exports of gum arabic, which is obtained from a species of *Acacia* tree.

ACACIA GRASS STEPPE AND SAVANNA

Paralleling the previous belt is a broad region of steppe and savanna with from 14 to 30 inches of average precipitation a year. This includes southern Darfur, most of Kordofan and Blue Nile provinces, and part of southern Kassala to the east of the Blue Nile. This belt contains the most developed parts of the country including major irrigation schemes based on the Nile which have, of course, an atypical land use pattern within the whole region. It also includes several mountain massifs rising above the generally monotonously flat terrain. While most tribes in this area are still seminomadic because of the precarious precipitation, rain cultivation becomes important and accounts for the growing value of Sudanese commercial and export production.

Dura, which is a sorghum-millet, millet, corn, sesame, and peanuts are grown on the *qoz* lands, former sand dunes which have been fixed by vegetation, while the areas in between are used for grazing livestock. Remoteness of the western portion of the belt restricts the possibilities for sale of crops and livestock, though some tobacco is shipped to Omdurman while cattle are driven to El Obeid. Commercial production becomes more significant in Kordofan where better transport is available both to the largest domestic market and to Port Sudan for export. In addition to sale of the major staples, gum arabic and melon seeds are sold at auction in the markets of El Obeid, the latter being exported in considerable quantities to Egypt. Gum arabic, of which the Sudan accounts for 75 to 85 percent of total world exports, is a major source of income. Most of the good quality gum is collected from trees in enclosed tracts called *geneinas*. It is sold at auction under government supervision, cleaned, and shipped in bags to Port Sudan. Used mainly in candy, but also for adhesives and in the production of textile sizing, ink, polishes, insecticides, medicinal oil, and beverages, gum arabic ranks as Sudan's second export, but production fluctuates rather widely in relation to the precipitation of the previous rainy period and in response to prices offered. In the Kordofan plateau, American upland rain-grown cotton is produced.

The separated islands of higher land, the Nuba Mountains south of El Obeid and Jebel Marra in Darfur, were places of refuge for the Nuba and Fur tribes, who were driven to these redoubts in the Arab invasions eight or nine centuries ago. Some intensive practices were developed such as terracing on the higher slopes,

A gum suk *or market in central Sudan*
Gum is sold at auction, cleaned, and shipped in bags to Port Sudan.

but overuse led to soil erosion and eventual deterioration of the terraces. The Fur, who have converted to Islam, now ship peppers and small tomatoes to Sudanese markets. The Nuba have remained largely pagan and isolated from adjoining groups but have moved, partly by British direction, from their fortified hill villages to lower areas where water is available. Practicing a rather complex agricultural system, they produce a considerable part of the cotton in Kordofan. The Baggara, formerly entirely nomadic, also inhabit the Nuba Mountains, grazing their livestock on the clay plains among the hills and growing cotton and grains where permanent water supplies are available.

Nomadic and seminomadic tribes also utilize the very favorable conditions for grazing along the White Nile, and the less favorable lands along the Blue Nile, but there is increasing settlement and tillage agriculture in much of this whole area.

The special *harig* system of farming is practiced in several parts of this belt, and efforts by the government to extend it have been made especially in the lands east of the Blue Nile. Under this system, old grass is saved for several years until a dense mat is formed; after new grass has sprouted with the first summer rains the old grass is fired; this controlled firing kills off the new shoots and provides an ash into which grain or cotton seeds are immediately planted. Specialists feel that most of the disadvantages of grass firing are avoided by burning at this time. A grain crop can then come up without further attention until harvesting, while the indigenous tribes move off with their flocks until that time approaches. One of the problems associated with harig cultivation is the danger of accidental fires burning off the dry grasses, thus leaving nothing to kill off the new shoots, in which case planting is impractical. To restrict such damages, two 30-foot lanes are plowed about 240 feet apart and the intervening stretch is burned to make a 300-foot fire break. Harig planting, which provides an improved food supply and more fodder for the dry winter, is being extended, particularly as new wells provide adequate domestic and stock water to areas where its absence was previously a strong limiting factor.

In 1944 the so-called Mechanized Agricultural Scheme was started in an area northwest of Gedaref where the natural grasses could be easily cleared. This area proved to be too dry, but as the isohyet gradient is rather steep in this region a relatively short move southward permitted a more successful application, and a similar scheme has since been introduced in Kordofan. Until 1953 the scheme involved expropriation of the land by the government, which was responsible for mechanical discing and sowing; the cultivator handled the remaining operations and shared equally with the government in the proceeds. This arrangement, which was patterned in part on the partnership prevailing in the Gezira, proved too expensive for low-value crops such as dura and sesame and was abandoned in favor of the present private schemes. At present, over a million acres are involved, with dura produced in the north, dura, sesame, and some short-staple cotton in the south. Land allotments are still made by the government. While the scheme may be considered to have had considerable success, and while it has contributed to making the region around Gedaref the granary of the country and that city the country's leading grain market, certain problems remain to be adequately solved. The most severe limiting factor has been the shortage of hand labor. This might have been met by mechanical harvesting, but the grains tended to shatter when combine harvested and species developed to overcome this problem proved unacceptable in taste. A second problem was that inadequate provision was made for rotation, required after about four years. The later allotments have provided for this by allocation of 2,000 feddans to a holder, half of which is left in grass. There is, finally, a need for greater integration of livestock grazing to provide enrichening manures. The scheme has shown that mechanical cultivation is possible in this region and that incomes can be increased if adequate land is available in each holding.

THE PROBLEM OF WATER SUPPLY. As in other steppe and dry savanna areas of Africa, the availability of water is a factor of prime importance in most of the region under consideration. Around El Obeid some man-dug wells are 250 feet deep, though most are 60 to 100 feet deep. To the west, where there are fewer wells, the baobab or tebeldi tree is sometimes used as a storage tank. During the rainy season, water is collected in depressions dug around the tree, then raised in buckets and poured into the hollowed trunk, which can hold up to 1,000 gallons of water. The wood of the baobab is not suitable for lumber, but the rather astringent fruit is sometimes eaten and the bark may be used for making rope. The Dar Hamar are said to be so saving of water that they make children whose heads are to be shaved run around until they are perspiring heavily.

In postwar years much attention has been given to increasing and conserving water in many of the semiarid areas of Africa, by techniques which it is appropriate to summarize at this point because the Sudan has applied most of them in a variety of areas and programs.

A baobab or tebeldi *tree*
The hollowed trunk of the baobab, which is found in tropical steppe areas throughout Africa and Madagascar, is sometimes used to store water for the dry season.

Securing subsurface water from the stream bed of the Bubu River, Tanganyika
This illustrates the difficulty of finding adequate water for domestic and stock use in the arid and semiarid areas of Africa. In some cases such pits are so deep that two or three men working at different levels are needed to lift the water to the surface.

A newly constructed well in northern Nigeria
Thousands of such wells have been dug in postwar years, greatly improving the supply of sanitary drinking and stock water.

Thousands of wells and boreholes have been dug in many African countries in recent years, some much deeper than earlier sources. In Uganda, for example, it is planned that there be at least one well every five miles. Africans must often walk miles to secure water; frequently it is impure, which contributes to the high incidence of internal diseases. One of the most valuable material improvements that can be provided is a certain and clean supply of domestic water at a reasonable distance, although Africans sometimes complain that clear water lacks the taste of their previous supply. The multifaceted aspect of many African problems is well illustrated by these simple wells. On the one hand, they bring safer water, reduce disease, often permit the grazing of livestock where it would otherwise not be possible because of an inadequate stock or human water supply, and sometimes permit the growth of fodder so badly needed in the dry season and required for a real upgrading of the livestock. On the other hand, they may contribute to greater soil erosion, degradation of the vegetation, and to possible overpopulation. In all too many cases micro-deserts have been created by failure to control the use of new wells. The point is that African problems need attacking on a broad front; an effort must be made to envisage the results of even the simplest of development projects so that their undesirable effects may be minimized.

Important techniques of conserving surface water include bunding, digging of surface reservoirs, construction of small dams both above and below the beds of streams and wadis, and larger scale irrigation projects utilizing traditional control works. In the Sudan, *terūs* or earth banks are used extensively on the clay plains to decrease runoff and increase soak-in. A large number of surface reservoirs, called *hafirs*, have been provided in an ambitious program. These large rectangular basins about 15–20 feet deep may be hand dug but are now usually machine excavated; used to collect surface water in the rainy season, a hafir of 15,000-cubic-meter capacity can meet the minimum

A wadi near Omdurman, Sudan
Conservation of water from intermittent streams is one method of improving water supplies. Small surface and subsurface dams may be used, but heavy silting often presents a serious problem.

water requirements for about 2,500 people for an initial cost of about $15,000. Built by teams using scrapers, tractors, bulldozers, and other modern equipment day and night during the dry season, several thousand hafirs have been provided in the Sudan in postwar years and a seven-year program starting in November, 1961, at an estimated cost of $12.6 million is designed to provide additional hafirs and small dams throughout the central Sudan. Problems connected with hafirs are the prevention of silting or provision of desilting basins, protection of the banks from destruction by men and animals, and avoidance of water pollution. The last two problems can be avoided by fencing, piping of water to a nearby tank, and control of numbers using the hafir, which is often very difficult. Loss from evaporation is another problem which requires attention; a possible solution is the use of monomolecular films, but this involves a degree of supervision which is not always available. A somewhat specialized type of water collection is the use of inselberges as a sort of roof supply, water being captured at the base to serve local communities.

The construction of small earth and stone dams in wadis and streams is receiving attention in many parts of Africa. A successful example cited by Worthington is in the N'Cema catchment in Southern Rhodesia, involving the construction of one main dam to supply Bulawayo and 464 smaller dams in a 264-square-mile area. These dams reduced the loss of soil by an estimated 90 percent, greatly lengthened the life of the main reservoir, and caused several small streams which had previously been seasonal to flow year round. Control of wadis is, however, often very difficult because of the enormous quantities of water and silt they may carry when in spate. Another technique of conserving water in wadi beds is the provision of "subsand dams," cement dams situated over impervious sills which result in storing water in the sandy bed, thus reducing losses from evaporation, increasing the seasonal life of springs, and sometimes extending the possibilities of catch crop production.

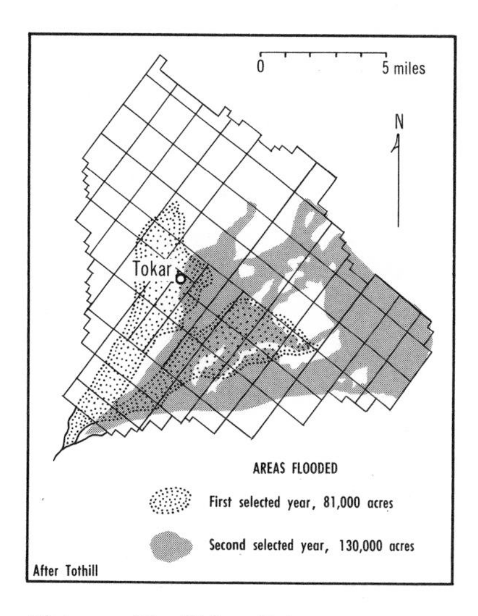

Map 31. The Tokar Delta

The Sudan has several very interesting examples of mountain streams whose waters have been more effectively utilized with minor engineering works, though in some cases no control is considered feasible. The Tokar and Gash deltas are important examples of flush irrigation. The former, situated near the Red Sea south of Suakin, is fed by the Baraka River, which drains a large part of the Eritrean Highlands (Map 31). It is dry most of the year, but from mid-July to mid-September spates arrive, sometimes lasting only a few hours, sometimes a few days. The silt carried by the Baraka may reach one part in 10, or 48 times as much as is carried by the Blue Nile. Irrigation on the Tokar Delta is an example of wild or uncontrolled flooding, there being only a slight control at the apex of the delta to give initial direction to the flow. The area watered varies from about 30 to 125 thousand acres a year, but the soils are so rich and so remarkable in water-holding capacity that cotton can be grown after only ten days of flooding. Land on the delta is allocated by a local committee before the flood, each tenant normally being assigned five feddans. In the past, three fifths of this was planted in cotton, most of the remainder in dura, the government receiving 25 percent of receipts from cotton sales. In recent years, however, bollworms have caused considerable damage to the cotton crop and efforts have been made to switch to castor seed. Other problems of the Tokar Delta are the prevalence of dust-laden winds and the shortage of manual labor, which has sometimes resulted in a portion of the crop going unpicked.

A similar but larger area is that of the Gash Delta, north of Kassala and due east of Khartoum (Map 32). An average of about 50,000 acres a year are flooded, though the delta area is about 700,000 acres of which about half is available for irrigation. Unlike the Tokar Delta, no water ever reaches the sea from the Gash. Although there is a greater control of the flow of the Gash, this is still irrigation in its simplest and roughest form. The flow, which is highly variable and which lasts from 68 to 111 days, is carried down the eastern side of the delta in a natural watercourse; five main canals leading across the delta take off the relatively silt-free top water, and channels with masonry headwork lead from there to the fields. In recent years, about half the irrigated area has been sown to cotton, two fifths to dura, and the remainder to castor seed. Because of the isolation of the area and its sharp dry period, both of which have given relative freedom from disease, the Gash Delta has been used to provide seed for the Gezira Scheme. The soils of the delta are an exceptionally rich silt capable of holding moisture for six months after 23 to 30 days of flooding. The cotton produced is very high grade, but yields under this type of irrigation are only about half those of the Gezira. Land in the Gash Delta is distributed among the tenants by lot after the area that has been flooded has been delineated; tenants receive 50 percent of cotton proceeds, the managing Gash Board and the government the other half. About three quarters of the tenancies are held by Hadendowa, most of the rest by "westerners," Africans from as far away as Nigeria who have for years stopped in the Sudan on the way to or returning from Mecca. Over 400 gardens drawing water from shallow wells are located on silt terraces of the Gash; fairly substantial quantities of fruit and some vegetables are marketed in the cities and more populous areas of Sudan.

A third flush irrigation scheme has been developed in postwar years on the Khor Abu Habl which drains the northern portion of the Nuba Mountains. Two small dams and canals permit the flush irrigation of about 10,000 acres. But the soils did not permit cropping comparable to that of the Gash and Tokar deltas and it was decided to provide a series of basins not

Map 32. The Gash Delta

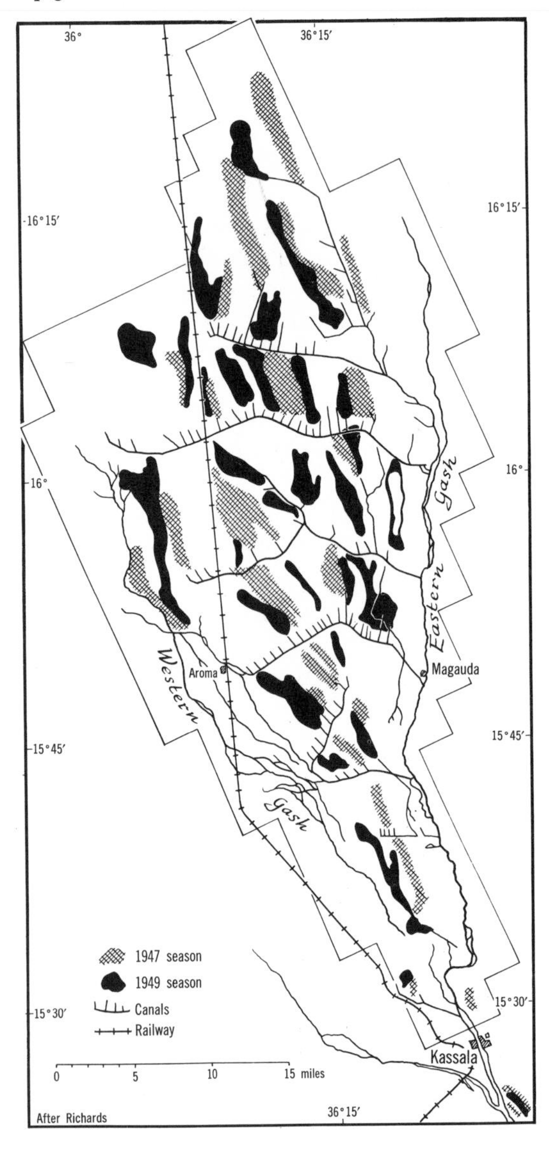

exceeding 30 feddan where, after thorough flooding, cotton could be produced. The relatively low incidence of cotton pests has led to the use of the area in providing seed for the Nuba Mountains.

Another method of conserving water is the rejuvenation of underground storage both natural and artificial, the second procedure being particularly applicable to North Africa. Some of the techniques noted above, such as bunding and catchment schemes, contribute to underground supply. It has been suggested that "billiger," which are natural subsurface openings found in northern Ghana, be restored and used as underground storage tanks.

There are, too, large- and small-scale irrigation projects based upon gravity flow from permanently flowing streams. Development of these projects is receiving increasing attention in many parts of Africa because of the great extent of semiarid lands and the needs to intensify output. The Sudan has, in the Gezira Scheme and its extensions, by far the most important irrigation project in sub-Saharan Africa, as well as several lesser but still important developments such as Khashm el Girba, the Guneid Scheme, and an increasing number of pump schemes dependent upon the Nile.

THE GEZIRA SCHEME. The most important economic "island" of the Sudan is the area of the Gezira Scheme, which took its name from "the gezira" or "island" lying between the Blue and White Niles south of Khartoum. In the ten year period 1951–60, cotton and cottonseed accounted for 65 percent of the value of Sudanese exports; the Gezira accounted for about 58 percent of total cotton production in this period and for a considerably higher percentage of the value of production because of the high quality of its output. The Sudan accounts for only 1 to 2 percent of world cotton production but about 35 percent of extra-long staple production.

Before the scheme was begun the semipastoral population of the area lived a traditional life, still enslaved by the requirements of a capricious climate.[1] Average annual precipitation in this

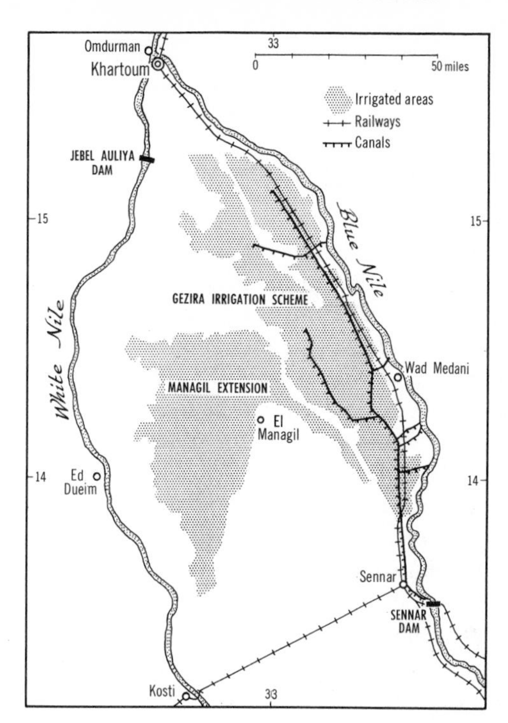

Map 33. The Gezira Scheme

steppe area varied from about 7 inches in the north to about 18 inches in the south, with a pronounced maximum in July and August and at least five winter months of absolute aridity. The rainfall permitted the planting of drought-tolerant grains, but at least two years in five produced poor crops. In the winter, the pastoralist-cultivators were forced to migrate southward to better grazing areas. Water for man and beast had to be hauled night and day from 120-foot-deep, hand-dug wells.

Today the gross cultivable area of the Gezira Scheme, including the new Managil extension, is 1.87 million acres and the annual area in cotton is over 515,000 acres (Map 33). Cotton is the economic mainstay of the operation, but there is also an assured production of food and fodder. A highly organized, highly productive irrigation system has replaced a low-productive,

[1] A portion of this section is based upon previous writings of the author: "The Gezira: An Example in Development," *The Geographical Review* (April, 1954), pp. 253–70, and Chapter 2, *African Economic Development* (New York, Harper, 1958), pp. 18–45.

precarious semipastoralism. The ability to support people has been enormously increased, and per capita incomes in the area are about three times the average for the country and second only to those of the "Three Towns" of Khartoum, Khartoum North, and Omdurman.

Despite certain problems associated with environment, there can be no doubt that the Gezira has important physical advantages. Topographically, the gentle downward slope from the Blue Nile practically eliminated expenses of leveling and permitted gravity irrigation, while the banks of the Blue Nile were sufficiently high to make practicable the Sennar control and storage dam. Climatically, the prolonged winter aridity permitted a far more effective control of plant pests and diseases than would have otherwise existed. During the dry period, strenuous efforts are made to uproot and destroy all cotton plants. The dry period also causes the soil to crack, so that greater permeation of water and air is possible. The soil, deposited many years ago in great depth when the Blue Nile flooded annually across the Gezira plain, is high in minerals, and its high impermeability permits negligible loss by seepage and makes unnecessary the lining of canals. Its cracking quality in the dry period, however, allows adequate permeation of water and air. Difficulties associated with the physical environment have included the effect of summer rain on weed growth and incidence of plant diseases, the constant battle against pests and diseases, the danger of waterlogged soils, and the necessity to provide drainage, especially from the lower lying areas.

The principal engineering feature of the project is the Sennar Dam, about 18 miles above the irrigated area, used to store water after the Blue Nile flood has passed. The 1929 Nile Waters Agreement prescribed the amount that could be withdrawn, thus strictly limiting the area that could be cultivated and the period during which water was available. The 1959 Agreement opened up new possibilities which are being met by construction of an $89 million dam near Roseires, 66 miles from the Ethiopian border. With a 3,600-foot-long, 196-foot-high central section and long earth-filled embankments bringing the total length of the structure to 10 miles, the Roseires Dam, which is scheduled for completion in 1967, will have a storage capacity of 2.7 billion cubic meters, or over five times the amount previously stored at Sennar. This will permit irrigating an additional 300,000 acres in the Gezira, plus about 900,000 acres elsewhere, probably in the Keneina area to the south. Emphasis in these other areas will be in crops other than cotton, including citrus fruit.

The total area so far brought under the Gezira Scheme is about 1.87 million acres of which about 56 percent is irrigated each year. Flow of water is continuous during the irrigation season in the canals and major distributaries, which command almost the entire area by gravity flow. A unique system of "night storage" is employed whereby water is fed to the minor distributary canals only by day, which assures easy flow, simplifies supervision, and prevents wastage. Continuous watering has been tried on half of the 100,000-acre northwestern extension. Water is applied to the individual fields on a carefully controlled and scheduled basis.

The main Gezira employs an 8-course crop rotation so that in any year about $\frac{1}{4}$ is in cotton, $\frac{1}{4}$ in food and fodder crops, and $\frac{1}{2}$ is fallow. A 6-course rotation is applied in the Managil extension: $\frac{1}{3}$ cotton, $\frac{1}{3}$ food and fodder, and $\frac{1}{3}$ fallow. All of the cotton grown is derivative of Egyptian cotton, the ecological suitability of the area to these long-staple, high-value cottons being an important element in the economic success of the scheme. Yields vary rather sharply depending upon differences in precipitation and the incidence of pests and diseases. The fight against the chief diseases, black arm and leaf curl, has been one of the most interesting and successful phases of the operation. Dura and lubia, a leguminous fodder crop, have been the other major crops, but the latter has been increasingly replaced in more recent years by wheat, peanuts, and vegetables. The open rotation system permits resting the soil and cleaning the land thoroughly between cotton crops.

Some of the farming processes in the Gezira are mechanized, including most of the cultivation, spraying from the air and on the ground, and the digging of field irrigation channels. Most of the work, however, is done by hand with the use of relatively primitive equipment. The cotton is ginned in factories at Meringan and Hassa Heissa run by the Sudan Gezira Board, which has the largest such enterprise under single management in the world. The ginned cotton and most of the cottonseed are exported via Port Sudan.

Two of the most important features of the Gezira Scheme are the tenurial arrangements and the tripartite partnership under which it has operated. The land of the scheme was first nationalized, the owners receiving thereafter a rent equivalent to highest market rate before the scheme started; tenancies were then allotted, with priorities going to the former owners and their relatives. The tenants' real return comes from their share of the work, not through ground rent, and security exists so long as practices are kept to prevailing standards. These arrangements permitted direction of land use and prevented land speculation. Under the partnership arrangements, the tenants received a 40 percent share in the cotton crop plus full right to the other crops; the government also received a 40 percent share in the cotton crop, and the managing board, first operated by private companies who were replaced by the government's Sudan Gezira Board when their concession expired in 1950, received a 20 percent share. The present distribution of gross profits is 42 percent to the government, 44 percent to the tenants (including a 2 percent allotment to a reserve fund), 10 percent to the manager, 2 percent to local councils, and 2 percent to a social development fund.

The advantages of the original partnership arrangement were that it protected the interests of the indigenous people, permitted the long-term financing of capital expenditures, and secured the services, for a specific period, of an

Mechanical plowing in the Gezira Scheme
Under the tripartite arrangement used in the scheme the managing Sudan Gezira Board is responsible for most of the cultivation, spraying from the air and on the ground, provision of field irrigation channels, ginning, and marketing of the cotton.

Picking cotton in the Gezira
The tenants are responsible for providing the labor required in production of the crops. They receive a 44 percent share in the cotton produced plus full right to the other crops.

outside, independent, commercial organization with managerial skill and experience. The government got about 25 percent of its revenues from the scheme before the war and over half of its revenues in postwar years, the managing board made a reasonable profit, and the tenants raised their standards from one of poverty and uncertainty to a level that compares favorably with that of other peasants in Africa and the Middle East.

The scheme, however, cannot be considered an unmitigated success. Particularly in the human aspects, certain features have proved undesirable, while traditional attitudes threaten to negate real possibilities for improvement. The scheme has been likened to a huge cotton factory where workers are so subject to managerial direction that there is little chance to develop initiative and independence. Efforts have been made in more recent years to win more intelligent participation by the devolution of some responsibilities to the tenants and to local councils, but the strict physical requirements of a highly organized irrigation project and the potential damage that might result from failure to control disease limit the opportunities severely. Criticism has also been directed at the government and the managing boards for failure to give adequate concern to the social growth of the community; the 2 percent allocation of profits to the Social Development Fund now permits giving greater attention to such things as education, training, public health, housing, and various village amenities. The most serious difficulty facing the area is the danger of overpopulation resulting from the practice by tenants of employing workers to do agricultural work which is considered as socially demeaning.[2] About 90,000 tenancies exist on the whole scheme, but it is not unlikely that tenancy-splitting will raise this number to nearer 150,000 in not too many years. In addition, the wage labor force is likely to exceed 300,000, about 40 percent of whom would probably reside permanently in the area. While the aversion to work may have the effect of leveling incomes, it also results in greater production costs, failure to realize the possible benefits of the operation, the development of an absentee landlord pattern, a shortage of labor for other development projects, and the persistence of a rigidly class-conscious social system. It has been estimated that twice as much labor is now required to produce a given output of cotton or grain as was required twenty years ago. Nor can many of the workers hope to improve their status in the Gezira, for westerners, who provide half the labor output, were disallowed from securing tenancies about eight years ago. Possibly the smaller tenancies of the Managil extension (15 feddans as compared to 40 in the main area) may reduce these tendencies, but the long-ingrained social attitudes of many Sudanese will probably continue to prevent realization of the really substantial potentialities for improved standards that exist in the area.

PUMP SCHEMES ON THE NILE. The first pump schemes of significance in the Sudan were developed between 1917 and 1928, during which period seven projects were installed in the north of the country on the main Nile. The first pump scheme on the White Nile was started in 1927, while development was slower on the Blue Nile because of its relatively deep valley and restrictions on cotton production to protect the Gezira from infestation. By 1939 some 244 pump schemes had been installed in the Sudan, and in 1944 this number had increased to 372 containing a gross cultivable area of 181,000 acres. Postwar years have witnessed a remarkable extension of pump schemes largely under private investment. By 1960 there were 2,267 pump schemes, 793 of which were cotton producers, the remainder being classified as gardens. In 1961–62 pump schemes accounted for about 28 percent of total cotton production in the Sudan as compared with 3 percent in 1940; in 1962–63 the total acreage within them exceeded 1.25 million acres and the acreage devoted to cotton was 236,352 or 22 percent of the total for the country. Over 90 percent of these pump

[2] Peter F. M. McLoughlin, "Economic Development and the Heritage of Slavery in the Sudan Republic," *Africa* (October, 1962), pp. 355–91.

schemes are privately owned; about 46,000 tenants are employed on them under arrangements comparable to those in the Gezira as far as allocation of the crops is concerned. In addition to the cotton produced, millet and lubia are also grown as are a variety of food crops marketed in the great conurbation of Khartoum–Khartoum North–Omdurman.

Of particular interest is the Guneid Scheme, started in 1955 on the right bank of the Blue Nile across from the Gezira. With a gross area of about 32,500 acres, which is being increased by a third, it is supplied by the largest pumping station in Africa. As water must be raised as much as 65 feet, the cost of supplying water at Guneid is relatively high. At first, each tenant in the scheme was allotted 15.6 acres, one third of which was to be planted to cotton, one third to dura and lubia, and one third left in fallow. In recent years it has been decided to concentrate upon production of sugar, partly to move away from the high dependence on cotton, partly to save an estimated $11.2 million on foreign exchange yearly. A 60,000-ton sugar factory has been constructed and production began on a limited scale in 1962, but tenants have resented the new crop and it is not yet possible to determine whether the switch to sugar will prove successful. Another crop change has involved substitution of peanuts on about one third of the lubia acreage, considered desirable both from the standpoint of their value in rotation and from the resultant improvement of tenant incomes. There is considerable question regarding the economic justification for the Guneid Scheme: the investment cost per unit area was over twice that for the Massara Scheme, a private project of comparable size in the Sennar area; the high water lift makes operating costs expensive; and sugar will probably require a subsidy for some years. More careful cost studies would prevent such questionable investments and permit focusing available capital where returns could be considerably greater.

There are substantial possibilities for increasing the acreage under pump schemes along the Blue and White Niles, and the continued attraction of private domestic capital to this type of project is a healthy aspect of the Sudan economy.

SOUTHERN SUDAN

The bulk of the remaining area of the country is savanna, sometimes predominantly grassy, elsewhere mainly savanna woodlands, plus the enormous area of the Bahr el Ghazal subject to seasonal flooding and bits of rainforest in the extreme south. Most of it is remote and very undeveloped, contributing very little to the economy of the Sudan and less to the exports of the country.

Nilotic tribes such as the Dinka, Nuer, and Shilluk occupy the lands along the Nile and the great swamp of the Bahr el Ghazal. All of them have a "cattle culture," which is characteristic of pastoral tribes in most semiarid areas of sub-Saharan Africa. The common feature of the cattle culture is the consideration of cattle as a sign of wealth and prestige, only rarely as a source of meat or an item for commercial sale. Cattle have particular significance in payment of the "bride price" and in ceremonial functions. The milk, which often has a high butterfat content, is drunk, though yields are typically low, averaging perhaps about five pints a day. Some tribes also draw blood from their cattle and use this as a regular item of their diet.

The Dinka and Nuer live on the huge, flat, grassy plains between the watercourses of the Bahr el Ghazal, building their huts and grazing their livestock on the higher parts and using the lower lands when the water recedes. Some of their practices reveal an excellent adaptation to the environment, such as a knowledgeable selection of soil and the tethering of cattle so that land is evenly fertilized for the planting of dura. But the remoteness of this area and the character of the inhabitants suggest that the region will remain one of the more backward parts of Africa for some years, though there are possibilities for very considerable intensification and particularly for the production of rice and sugar. Two experimental rice centers have

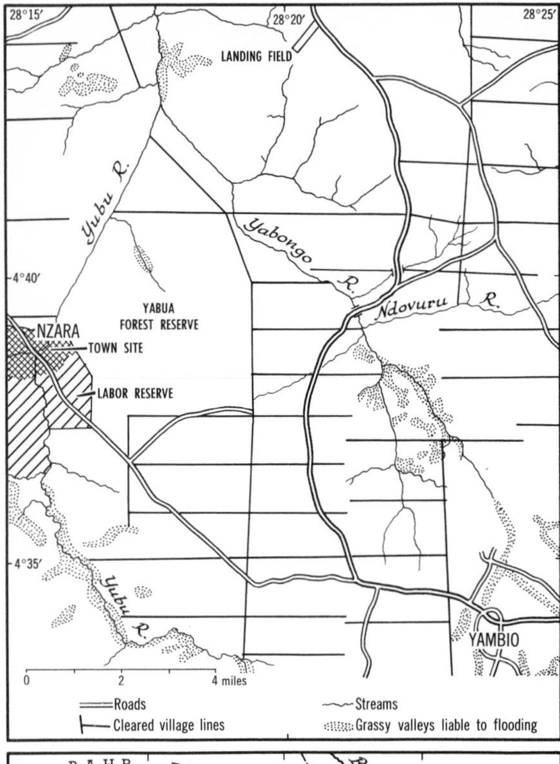

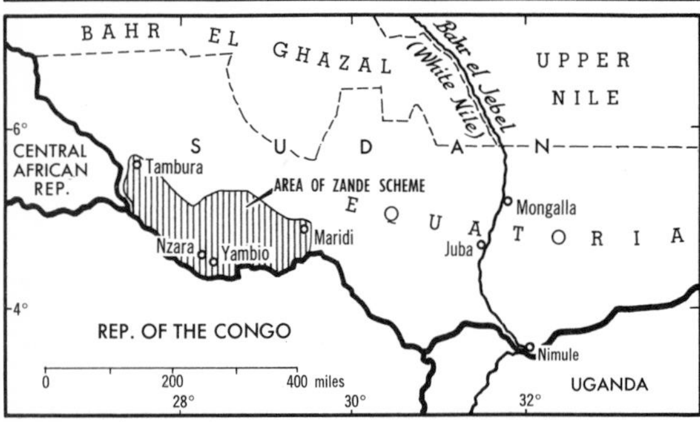

Map 34. The Zande Scheme

Above: Layout for application of organized shifting agriculture
Below: Location of the Zande Scheme area in southern Sudan

recently been set up at Wau and Aweil with the aid of FAO technicians.

Equatoria Province, largely low, undulating plateau country rising in the southwest to the watershed between the Nile and Congo systems, is the wettest part of the Sudan, having an annual precipitation ranging from about 24 to 80 inches. A great melange of tribes inhabits the province, of which the largest is the Zande, who are also found in adjacent parts of Congo and the Central African Republic. This is largely a region of shifting agriculture (see pp. 202–3), with the major crops being those typical of rainforest and wet savanna regions elsewhere in Africa. Its extreme remoteness meant for years that it received minimal attention, expatriates being limited to a few missionaries and district officers. Juba is over 900 miles and 12 days by river from Kosti; it requires two or three days by road to reach Nzara from Juba, while the region to the east of the river is very poorly served by any transport. Today the area is undergoing a process of Sudanization which also involves Islamization. Christian missions are finding it increasingly difficult to operate in the region and some of their educational and agricultural programs are being curtailed. The government is attempting to introduce tobacco and coffee as cash crops, but it is too early to foretell the results. Chilies have been produced near Juba for export for some years.

The rather interesting Zande Scheme, situated in about 20,000 square miles of the remotest part of Equatoria around Yambio, represented the only major effort to upgrade the area (Map 34). Begun in 1946 as "an experiment for the social emergence of indigenous races in remote areas," it was allocated $2.8 million over the first five years. About 220,000 Zande occupy this high grass-woodland area with poor, laterized soil and about 55 inches of rain concentrated in nine months. Practicing a shifting agriculture, they were prevented from keeping cattle by the presence of the tsetse fly, their need for proteins being partially met by eating rodents, occasional game, and termites. Termites are collected in the flying stage by attracting them to torches which burn their wings.

The goals of the scheme were substantially to improve the standards of local self-sufficiency and to provide for the purchase of those few necessities that cannot be produced domestically through a limited exchange with the north. It was thought that production for export was not practicable because of the great distance to the seaboard. Agriculturally, a system of organized shifting agriculture was applied under which the area was subdivided into rectangular blocks and each householder was allotted from 25 to 40 acres laid out in long, narrow plots with about 150-foot frontage and running at right angles to the roads or cycle tracks on which the huts were erected. Each holding was further subdivided by distinctive hedge strips into a series of fields which were successively opened up, used for a few years, and then permitted to revert to a bush fallow. Farmers in each block opened up the same plots each year, which at least made it possible to contemplate the use of machinery.

The economic mainstay of the scheme was to be American upland cotton, and acceptance of a tenancy required the planting of at least one-half acre to this crop, plus another one-tenth acre for each additional wife. In the first years it proved possible to sell some of the cotton on the world market, which had not been expected. Rather, it was planned that the cotton would be sold to the mill at Nzara, which would produce cloth for both local needs and for shipment to the north. Subsistence crops were similar to those already grown, but special efforts were made to introduce higher yielding varieties, while scattered community oil palm plantations were set out and numerous experiments were made with other crops.

While the Yambio Agricultural Station is still making contributions to improving the farming in this remote area, the scheme has not continued to receive the intensive attention required and there has been a considerable regression from earlier achievements. A major difficulty is the problem of selling the cloth produced at Nzara in the north, particularly with the recent introduction of large modern mills at Khartoum. In 1961–62 Equatoria produced only 6,000 bales of cotton or 0.52 percent of the Sudan total; yields are only about half those for rain-grown cotton in Nuba or one-fifth the average for the country. The small sugar and soap mills built for the Scheme were closed some years ago.

MINERAL PRODUCTION

There is at present very little production or export of minerals from the Sudan. Claims of

A Zande man and his wife carrying cotton to market

Cotton production in this remote area of Equatoria Province was stimulated by the Zande Scheme, designed to improve the local self-sufficiency of the area and to provide for the purchase of limited necessities through sale of cotton cloth in the north of Sudan.

A crude sesame seed oil press at Khartoum
Handicraft production contributes about three times as much as modern manufacturing to the gross domestic product of Sudan.

Scene in modern cotton textile mill
A new $20 million mill at Khartoum North with a capacity of 70 million yards a year is said to be the largest single textile mill in the Middle East.

important mineral finds have not been accompanied by sufficient evidence to assess their significance and much of the area has not been more than cursorily prospected. Italian and American companies have been looking for oil in the Red Sea Hills and Shell holds a concession along the Libyan border in the northwest. Small shipments have been made in recent years of gold, manganese ore, and iron ore from the Red Sea area. Iron ore is also known to occur near Wadi Halfa, while an Italian concern has shown interest in a copper body in the Jebel Marra area of Darfur.

INDUSTRIAL DEVELOPMENT

Manufacturing is in an embryonic stage in the Sudan, though a good number of modern plants have been constructed during the past decades. In 1960 some 88 modern plants were in operation employing 18,462 persons. The gross value added by manufacturing in 1959–60 was estimated to be $14.5 million, of which 63 percent came from the food, beverage, and tobacco industries. Modern manufacturing was estimated to account for 2 percent of the gross domestic product in 1960–61. Industrial output increased 90 percent from 1956 to 1960. There is also still considerable handicraft production; the latest estimates available indicate that it contributed $3\frac{1}{2}$ times as much to the gross domestic product in 1955–56 as did modern manufacturing. In that year, about 5 percent of the population was dependent upon all types of industry as compared to 86 percent dependent upon agriculture.

As in other parts of Africa, most modern plants are owned and managed by outsiders, though the government owns an increasing number of establishments, most of which it hopes will eventually be bought by private capital. The government attempts to attract new industries by import duty concessions, reduced rail freight rates, freedom from profit taxes for five years, easy repatriation of dividends and capital, and assistance in financing by the newly created Industrial Bank. The United States, Yugoslavia, and the Soviet Union have aided a number of new plants by extension of loans and technical assistance.

Industries based upon the processing of domestic raw materials include cotton ginning, flour milling, sugar refining (Guneid and later

Khashm el Girba), meat packing, tanning (an industrial tannery said to be the largest in Africa was opened in Khartoum in 1962 but is not yet operating at capacity), production of cardboard from waste cotton stalks of the Gash Delta, and a button factory using pearl shell from the Red Sea Coast. Plans call for the erection of fish, fruit, and vegetable canneries and for the production of paper using papyrus from Lake No as the raw material.

Most of the plants which are essentially market-oriented have been constructed during the last five years, and it is this category which has seen the greatest growth since the war. Industries of this type include two relatively large breweries and producers of soft drinks; a new and very modern soap plant; several shoe factories including a 1962 Bata plant at Khartoum North; appliance and assembly plants; the manufacture of tires, batteries, paint, enamelware, aluminum ware, pharmaceuticals, matches, containers, hardware, bricks and tiles, and cement; and several textile mills. By far the largest cloth producer is the new $20 million Sudan American Textile Mill at Khartoum North, which, with a capacity of 70 million yards per year, is reported to be the largest single mill in the Middle East. It is expected to employ 3,000 workers within the near future. The most important plant in the service industries is the railway workshop at Atbara, which not only overhauls all locomotives every 90,000 miles but also builds passenger and freight cars for the Sudan Railways.

Production of electricity in the country is still at a low level, but rose from 16.7 million kwh in 1948 to 103.1 million kwh in 1961. Generally only the major towns have distribution of electricity and many factories must supply their own power. Installation in 1962 of a $13.5 million hydroelectric station at the Sennar Dam added 15,000 kw to the capacity of electric plants, which is now about 66,000 kw. The new dam at Khashm el Girba will have a hydroelectric installation, as will the Roseires Dam, where output may be partly directed to a proposed nitrogenous fertilizer factory. For the future, it is estimated that about 1.3 million kw could be developed on the Nile between the Sixth Cataract and the border on a firm basis plus about 1.1 million kw seasonally.

The "Three Towns" have the lion's share of consumer-oriented manufacturing, with the industrial estate at Khartoum North being particularly significant. This great conurbation at the confluence of the Blue and White Niles has the advantages of a central location, existence of the country's largest market in the cities themselves and in the nearby Gezira and pump schemes, relatively good transport links with the rest of the country, and proximity to the national administration. This triumvirate of cities had an estimated population of 315,000 in 1961. Atbara has special importance because of the railway workshops and the cement plant whose capacity has recently been enlarged. The raw material processing plants are much more dispersed, the Gezira having the most important segments of the cotton ginning industry, which ranks first among this type of manufacturing.

TRANSPORTATION

The Sudan is relatively well off by sub-Saharan standards in the provision of transport routes and particularly in its considerable mileage of railways, totaling 4,137 route miles in 1962. By all odds the most important means of physical communication, the railways are run by the largely autonomous Sudan Railways, which also operates Port Sudan and services on the Nile. In 1960 it had a staff of 27,564 or about a fifth of all the wage employees in the country. Handling almost all the foreign trade of the Sudan, the railways usually operate at a profit if not always on time. Among the reasons for their overwhelming importance, especially as contrasted to road transport, are the great distances of producing areas from each other and from the port, the bulk character of the main exports, the relative ease of constructing lines across the vast plains of the country, and deliberate suppression of roads which might compete with the railways.

The railways were begun as a military line from the Egyptian border to Atbara in 1898 and Khartoum was connected with Port Sudan at a relatively early date. Map 35 shows the major components of the present transport picture, including the rail system. Recent additions include the extension from El Obeid west to Nyala, opened in 1959, the branch from Babanusa on this line to Wau, completed in 1962 and providing a year-round outlet for the Bahr el Ghazal region, plus short extensions to the Roseires and Khashm el Girba dam sites. It is hoped that the line to Wau will be extended to Juba and that the line to Nyala will be carried to Geneina in the extreme west of Darfur within the next ten years; eventually a connection might be effected from there across Chad to Maiduguri in northeastern Nigeria, thus creating one of the few transcontinental links in Africa.

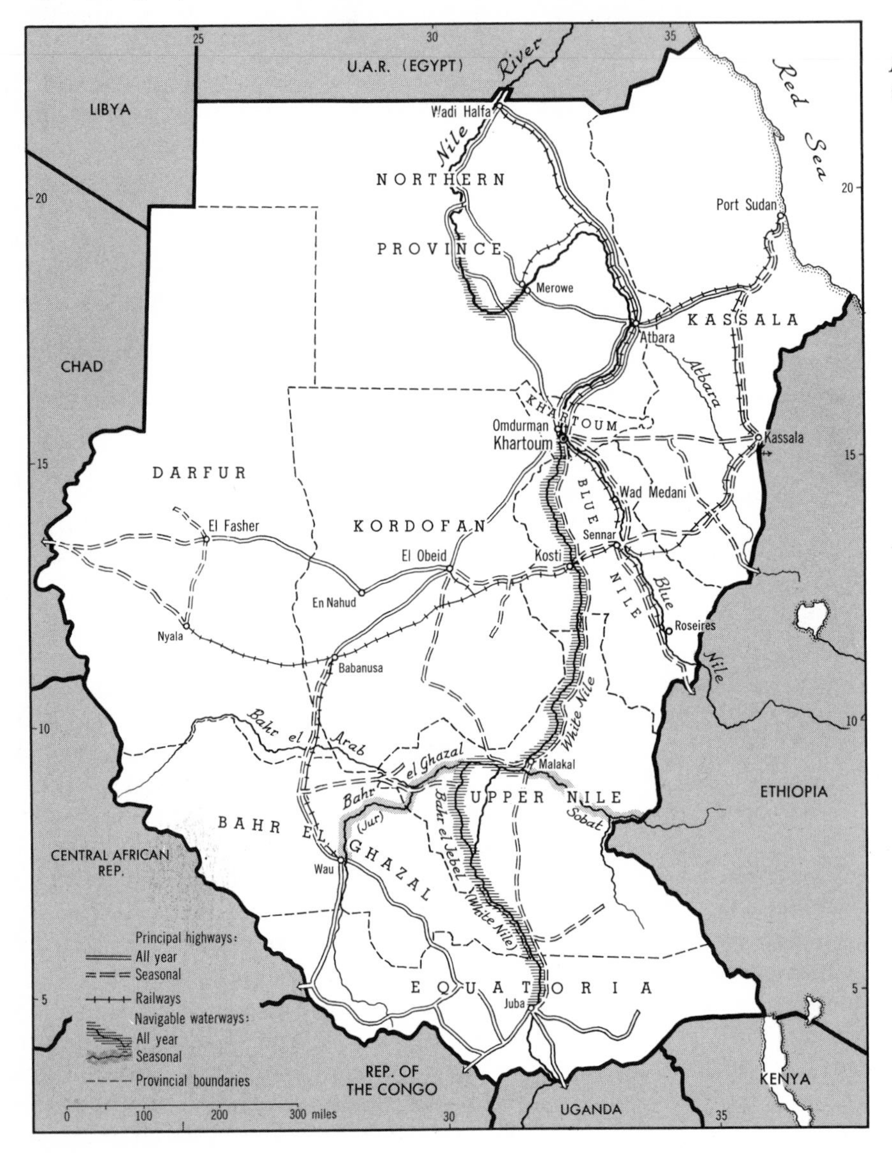

Map 35. Transport in the Sudan

The Sudan has a total of about 2,325 miles of inland navigable waterways, of which 1,500 are opened year round. Steamer services operate all year on the White Nile between Kosti and Juba and on the main Nile in the north between Merowe and Kerma, and seasonally on the Sobat to Gambeila in Ethiopia and via the Bahr el Ghazal and Jur rivers to Wau. Other navigable stretches are not regularly served. Water transportation has always provided the chief link between central and southern Sudan, but the services are run at a loss primarily because of the small amount of traffic generated in the south. Operation in the Bahr el Ghazal is sometimes rendered difficult by floating vegetation, while the appearance of the water hyacinth on the Bahr el Jebel in the winter of 1957–58 represented a potential catastrophe to the Sudan.

Few countries are so lacking in roads as the Sudan. Only around and within the main cities and in the south from Juba to the Central African Republic and to Uganda are there all-weather roads. In the dry season, however, vehicles can travel over large parts of the country. In the past, road connections between some cities, such as Khartoum and Wad Medani, were deliberately neglected in order to preserve traffic for the railways. A paved road is now under construction between these very important cities, and plans are being developed for a surfaced road between Khartoum and Port Sudan. Camels and other animals are still significant in the movement of goods to railheads and in the more remote areas of the country but their high cost results in a progressive replacement by motor vehicles. It is estimated that the ton-mileage cost of camel transport is three to seven times greater than by truck; carriage by other animals is four to nine times as costly.

Port Sudan handles a very high percentage of the total foreign shipments of the Sudan. Constructed to replace Suakin, which was inadequate except for dhows and small ships, it can accommodate 14 ships at quayside. It has

Aerial view of part of Port Sudan
This port is the only major ocean terminal of the Sudan, though plans call for constructing a second major port at the present dhow harbor of Suakin.

been handling from 1.3 to 1.9 million tons per annum in recent years. Plans call for constructing a second modern port for the country at Suakin; half of the estimated cost of $16.8 million will be provided by a long-term loan from Yugoslavia. Like many other countries in Africa, the Sudan is attempting to build up its own merchant marine and has purchased two 4,800-ton vessels to begin the fleet.

Thirty-seven airfields in the Sudan are served by scheduled or charter service. The Sudan Airways, which functions as a government department with its own budget, was formed in 1946 with the aid of Airwork, a British company.

Part Three WEST AFRICA

Ganvié, Dahomey, a lagoon fishing village

CHAPTER TEN

West Africa: Introduction

With some 15 countries covering 20 percent of the continent, having about 29 percent of the population of Africa and 19.1 percent of its exports by value, West Africa is one of the most interesting and most important parts of the continent. The tremendous diversity, especially in the political sphere, creates difficulties in writing about the area. A region-by-region or country-by-country approach would be excessively lengthy and repetitive; the functional approach is not entirely satisfactory. In this and the next three chapters a compromise is attempted: certain features, such as transportation, land use, mining, and industry, are treated in separate sections for the whole of West Africa, but analysis is given of the relative importance of individual nations and subregions in various economic activities.

West Africa, parts of which have had long contact with the Western world, has important contrasts with other areas of the continent, including its greater political subdivision, an earlier political evolution, the minor importance of white agriculturalists, and its relatively unimportant position in mining, though rapid progress is now occurring in this field in several states.

THE AREA AND ITS POLITICAL UNITS

West Africa, if taken to include all of the former territories of French West Africa and the other countries from Gambia to Nigeria, covers a total area of about 2.38 million square miles. Considerable parts of the three largest countries, Mauritania, Mali, and Niger, are desert, however, so that the utilizable area is roughly about 40 percent the size of the United States. The area measures about 2,100 miles from Dakar to Lake Chad, equivalent to the distance from Madrid to Moscow or from Boston to Salt Lake City; the usable north-south distance is about 600–700 miles. Politically, the region is made up of fifteen countries, all independent except Gambia and Portuguese Guinea. Eight of these countries were, until 1958, part of French West Africa; four were at one time under British rule.

FORMER FRENCH COUNTRIES

MAURITANIA. The Islamic Republic of Mauritania is a sparsely populated part of the Sahara, characterized, at least until recently, by a very meager commercial development. Its northern Moors, comprising about 75 to 80 percent of the population, are mainly nomadic pastoralists; the Negro tribes of the south depend on the production of grains, especially along the banks of the Senegal. Welding these two groups and suppressing the somewhat anarchical tendencies of the scattered Moorish tribes are major political tasks which appear thus far to have been approached with skill and resolution. The main hope for securing increased funds for economic and social requirements rests upon the newly opened iron ore mines at Fort Gouraud. Fears that Mauritania might become part of Morocco appear to be dissipating as a national consciousness develops and since Morocco has failed to win the support of other African nations for its pretensions. Continuing French economic and military support has also contributed to the survival of Mauritanian independence.

SENEGAL. One of the two most important economic units of former French West Africa, Senegal accounts for a very high percentage of peanut-product exports from this area, and these account for the bulk of Senegalese exports by value. Indeed, the overwhelming dependence upon one crop, which has been only moderately reduced by new mining and fishing developments, is a major economic problem of the country. A notable factor in the importance of Senegal is the presence of Dakar, which has the bulk of the country's 62,000 non-Africans, a disproportionate share of manufacturing industry in the former French areas, and a commercially very strategic position in ocean and air transport. Dakar's position as the capital of the huge French West Africa, together with its unusually attractive climate, accounts in considerable part for its having so large an expatriate populace and such a relatively well-developed interest in manufacturing. But, despite continuing heavy subsidization of the Senegalese economy by France, the economy of that country has been somewhat stagnant in recent years and Dakar possesses a degree of artificiality which results in a marked sense of uncertainty regarding its economic future. Like interwar Vienna, it is the decapitated head of a much larger body; like Casablanca, it will probably suffer severely from the exodus of Europeans who occupy numerous positions which Senegalese either could occupy today or will be able to occupy in the years ahead. When the Dakar balloon bursts, the economy of Senegal will be seriously affected, but it seems inevitable that it will burst in the not too distant future. Another serious problem which the country faces is the elimination of subsidized prices for its major export by 1965; amounting to about 20 percent of the world price for peanuts, this subsidy and the guaranteed French market for a high percentage of Senegalese production are assets which may prove very painful to forego.

MALI. Largely desert and steppe, Mali is one of the poorest areas of Africa, though it has interesting potentials in mining and in further irrigation of the interior Niger River delta. A federation of Mali and Senegal foundered after nineteen months in August, 1960, resulting in the severing of all contacts between the two, including cutting of the main access route via Dakar. In the ensuing years, Mali turned increasingly to the East, joined the leftish Casablanca Group and the Ghana-Guinea Union, and set itself resolutely upon a course designed to create a planned, highly centralized, and socialistic economy. Despite considerable aid from the USSR, Czechoslovakia, and Yugoslavia, however, ties continued strong with France, while the United States and West Germany have extended loans and grants to Mali. In 1963, cordial relations with Senegal were reestablished and Mali appeared less enamored of its previous "dynamic" line, more interested in restoring relations with its sister republics of French expression. Mali is another of the countries of West Africa which depends heavily upon peanuts as its dominant export.

UPPER VOLTA. The Republic of Upper Volta, like Mali, participates to only a minor degree in the commercial economy of West Africa. Since the country is generally unsuited for tillage agriculture, its predominantly grassy vegetation is used for grazing, and meats and hides provide the major part of its small exports. Densely populated in some sections, it obtains some relief by a relatively large seasonal migration of workers to the Ivory Coast and Ghana. The value of its exports is one of the lowest in Africa, being about one-third those of Gambia, which is about 4 percent as large. While Upper Volta was a province of French West Africa, Bobo Dioulasso, at the focus of trade routes, was the main economic center of the country. Since independence, this city has suffered an economic decline resulting from the exodus of Europeans, evacuation of French military forces from the nearby camp, and removal of major offices to the capital at Ouagadougou, which is also the residence of the emperor of the Mossi, the country's most important tribe.

NIGER. The Republic of Niger, like Mauritania and Mali, is mainly desert. Its economically important area is limited to the lands along the Niger River and bordering Nigeria, where peanuts, the main export, and grains are produced. About 52 percent of the population is concentrated upon 8 percent of the area having over 21.5 inches of precipitation yearly; 83 percent of it is found in the 24 percent having over 13.7 inches of rain. Grazing of livestock is the major activity of its inhabitants, cultivation occupying only about 2 percent of the total surface, which is the largest but one of the poorest in West Africa.

GUINEA. This country was the only French African area which opted for independence in the plebiscite of September, 1958. Angered by this election result, the French government abruptly withdrew its aid, its technicians, and its administrators. The Soviet Union and other Communist nations immediately shipped goods and dispatched missions to Guinea and by 1961 had about 1,200 technicians at work in the country. The United States, having failed to reply to Guinea's early request for aid, found its position more difficult than it need have been. Guinea, meanwhile, declared itself a revolutionary socialist state; much of industry, services, and retail trading and almost all of wholesale trading and banking were nationalized, and more and more trade was tied up in barter and other agreements. Trade with France declined from $56.3 million in 1959 to $20.4 million in 1961.

Guinea's first years as an independent state provided many harsh lessons. Lacking the necessary administrative and technical skill, the government was unable to run the country on an efficient basis. There has been almost no maintenance of public buildings, roads, or service establishments; repair of mechanical apparatus is extremely difficult. Efforts to increase output from the rural areas have failed and a program requiring twenty days of work a year in community projects has been downgraded because of the disillusioning results. While party discipline was in many ways highly developed and broadly based, it has not proved adequate to prevent corruption, black marketeering, and the growth of clandestine exports or to arrest a decline in productivity throughout the economy. Relations with the East-bloc nations also proved less helpful than had been anticipated. Barter agreements were restrictive; equipment and products received were not made for tropical conditions; only one productive enterprise was established from October, 1958, to 1962; and Soviet aides were accused of fomenting dissatisfaction and engaging in internal political machinations. Several Communist representatives, including the Russian ambassador, were asked to leave the country. By 1961 Guinea had reached a position of economic and political crisis from which it is still endeavoring to recuperate.

In the years 1961–63 Guinea has gradually altered its position to a more moderate and thoughtful one. It has rather slowly and painfully reestablished its relations with France, has sought greater assistance from Western nations, has promulgated a new investment law in April, 1962, designed to attract foreign private investment, and has attempted to draw up somewhat more realistic programs for development. But it is not an easy task to switch directions on the internal front, where fewer signs of change are apparent.

As to its relations with other African states, Guinea, together with Ghana, anxious to display the solidarity of independent African nations after Guinea's rude abandonment by France, formed a "union" which called for cooperation in various spheres. Later Mali joined this union, whose members were also in the militant Casablanca Group. In 1963, however, Guinea and Mali appeared less attracted by the dynamic but somewhat ephemeral goals of this group and willingly supported the more moderate approach to pan-Africanism adopted by the UAS in Addis Ababa. It is ironic that less than two years after France summarily withdrew from Guinea because of that country's choice of independence, it had granted independence to all of the other parts of French West Africa.

Guinea was not a particularly rich member of French West Africa, but it had been the most important mineral producer, and its vast resources of iron ore, bauxite, and diamonds, coupled with substantial hydroelectric potential, gave it great promise for the future. The iron ore mine and the Fria alumina works, completed after independence, have not been nationalized, and represent the two best functioning enterprises in the country; the foreign exchange they earn has provided an element of stability of very great value to the otherwise precarious economy. Coffee, palm kernels, and bananas have been Guinea's main agricultural exports.

Guinea provides important and fascinating lessons for other developing African nations. Nowhere else has there been a situation more hospitable toward the Communist bloc; nowhere else have those nations made so many errors and so misused their opportunities. No other country has Africanized to such a high degree as Guinea; no other country has such a crying need for semiskilled, skilled, and administrative talent. But neither the West nor proponents of colonialism can take pride or pleasure from the Guinean experience; had France been able to make as rapid adjustments to the changing demands of African nations as it later proved capable of making, much wasted time and anguish might have been avoided and Guinea would probably have been functioning reasonably well instead of on a basis in which many of the crucial financial and economic facts are not known to anyone and hence not available to assist in proper economic planning or assessment.

IVORY COAST. This republic, which became independent in 1960, is the richest of all the former French areas in sub-Saharan Africa, producing large tonnages of coffee and cocoa and supplementary output of tropical woods, bananas, and palm products, plus an increasing amount of minerals, particularly diamonds and manganese. In sharp contrast with Guinea, but even in comparison with most other former French areas, the Ivory Coast has retained the assistance of expatriate personnel in government, commerce, and industry. French influence remains extremely strong; the cultural attachment of educated Ivoriens to France persists despite a growing national awareness; 12,000 Europeans, most of whom are French, continue to reside in the country; and France contributes about $50 million yearly in the form of technical assistance, an amount equal to about one third of annual expenses. Also in contrast with Guinea, the Ivory Coast has fostered the establishment of a capitalistic society committed to the West. The economy of the country has benefited but it is far from having reached a take-off point. Progress in the rural areas has been slow; there has been a marked inflationary tendency; and excessive emphasis has been focused upon Abidjan, whose modernity and dynamism fade out rapidly in the hinterland. Nonetheless, the inclusion of an unusual number of trained expatriates in the government permits a smoother transition and provides a chance to unify the diverse ethnic groups of the country before any one of them achieves a dominant position.

DAHOMEY AND TOGO. Dahomey, the last and smallest of the former French West African countries, is a minor producer of palm products and miscellaneous other tropical commodities. There remains one other previously French-administered area, the former U.N. Trustee Territory of Togo, which became independent in April, 1960. A small sliver of territory between Ghana and Dahomey, Togo relies mainly on sales of coffee, cocoa, and, more recently, phosphates for its international exchange. Despite suggestions from its western neighbor that Togo represented an undesirable example of Balkanization, that country has expressed its resolution to remain independent and to achieve economic viability.

COMMONWEALTH WEST AFRICA

GAMBIA. Next among the political units of West Africa are four countries of the Commonwealth. Gambia, a riverain enclave in Senegal, was one of the two remaining colonial areas in West Africa in 1963. It has been called the peanut colony, a term which is apt for its size as well as for its overwhelming dependence on that crop. Too small readily to become a viable independent unit, it may effect some kind of ties with Senegal.

SIERRA LEONE. Achieving independence in April, 1961, Sierra Leone is a member of the Commonwealth. Freetown was established in 1788 by British philanthropy as a settlement for liberated African slaves, and the "Creoles" who live there are descended from those settlers. They speak English as their native language and consider themselves more advanced than the tribal peoples of the protectorate. The transition period before and after independence has represented a difficult period as its increasing democratization has weakened their position. Relatively poor economically despite a broad range of exports, Sierra Leone will require continuing aid and technical assistance for some years. Illicit diamond operations during the 1950s frequently disturbed the Sierra Leone economy, which has remained rather stagnant in the agricultural field despite various efforts to increase cash and subsistence crops.

GHANA. The first British colony in tropical Africa to achieve independence, having become an independent member of the Commonwealth on March 6, 1957, Ghana replaced the Gold Coast and the British Trustee Territory of Togoland. While its public posture and the emanations from its press and radio suggest that it is Marxist, anti-Western, anti-European, and violently anticolonialist, its actions have generally been considerably more conservative. With a per capita income of about $198, Ghana is one of the richest of tropical African countries. The world's leading producer of cocoa, it has also been West Africa's major mineral exporter, shipping gold, manganese, diamonds, and bauxite to world markets.

Ghana has proved rather adept at eliciting aid from both East and West. The USSR and Ghana signed their first economic and technical cooperation agreement in 1960; in 1961 Mainland China extended a $19.6 million interest-free loan; Czechoslovakia has also agreed to build a variety of factories and four hydroelectric plants. As of early 1963 there was little tangible evidence of this aid, but several turnkey factories were reported to be ready for shipment. Ghana has also elected to follow the Russian example in agriculture; the Soviet Union is organizing three state farms, while twenty agricultural stations are also being transformed into state farms. The West has contributed heavily to the huge Volta hydroelectric and aluminum scheme, to a considerable number of new industrial establishments, and to the extension of plantations. Ghana had very substantial reserves of its own at the time of independence, totaling some $700 million. These have been heavily drawn upon, there being only $280 million remaining at the end of 1961. Austerity and new revenue-producing measures adopted in 1961 have not proved adequate; inflation has become a serious threat; and hopes for continued heavy foreign investment have not been realized in the last few years. While the government has professed a desire for continued investment from private sources, militant pronouncements by the government have undoubtedly been a deterrent to such aid. Ghana has important assets in its favor, including a relatively high average income, a good infrastructure in the south, and a much larger number of college graduates than most African countries; its leadership has not utilized these assets as wisely as it might.

NIGERIA. With the largest population of any African country and almost half of the population of all West Africa, Nigeria became an independent member of the Commonwealth on October 1, 1960, and later was joined by two sections of the former British Trustee Territory of the Cameroons. Comprised of many diverse regions and a multitude of tribal groups, Nigeria has a constitution that provides for a federal form of government, and it is one of the few African countries which does not have a one-party state.

The political regions[1] of Nigeria have a considerable degree of authority in the economic

[1] In July, 1963, a referendum held in Benin and Delta provinces in the Western Region overwhelmingly supported the formation of a fourth region—the Midwest Region.

realm; the older three had set up development corporations responsible for planning economic advance but these plans are incorporated in the 1962–68 Development Plan for Nigeria, which calls for a total expenditure of $1.89 billion. Each region has a dominant tribal grouping: the Hausa and Fulani in the north, the Ibo in the east, the Yoruba in the west, and the Edo in the midwest. The huge Northern Region has over half the population; the government has thus far been a coalition of the north and east. Tribal jealousies still threaten to disrupt the federation or to lead to the formation of an increased number of regions, but Nigeria has succeeded in developing a sense of national rather than just regional or tribal identification in an increasing number of its citizens and talk of a possible split into several independent countries has largely disappeared. There has been, particularly in 1962–63, a certain running-down in governmental efficiency owing to rapid Africanization. This is delaying the implementation of some development projects, but the government has shown skill and moderation in many of its major decisions.

While the per capita incomes of Nigeria are well below those of Ghana, being estimated at $84 in 1961, its much greater population makes it one of the leading economic units of tropical Africa. Three crops comprise its main agricultural exports: palm products, for which it is the world's leading exporter; cocoa, for which it ranks after Ghana and Brazil; and peanut products. It also has significant exports of rubber, tropical woods, tin, and, in recent years, petroleum from the Niger Delta. Nigeria has experienced a rather dynamic industrial growth in recent years. It is greatly advantaged by its size and population in the attraction of foreign capital.

PORTUGUESE GUINEA AND LIBERIA

PORTUGUESE GUINEA. Two countries remain to be noted. Portuguese Guinea is the only remaining of many earlier Portuguese interests in West Africa and it may be the only non-self-governing territory in that area in the near future. Suffering from the superior attraction of the larger Angola and Mozambique, it also lacks the desirable climate which has drawn settlers to the latter areas. Its exports are mainly palm and peanut products.

LIBERIA. This country is one of the oldest independent states in Africa, Monrovia and other coastal points having been settled with American aid by freed slaves whose descendants are called Americo-Liberians. Until after World War II there was very little economic and social development, with the exception of the large Firestone rubber plantations. In postwar years, greatly increased American aid and investment has brought it very rapidly into contact with the economic world and, for the first time in its history, efforts have been made to bring the tribal interior into the national economy. The "open-door" policy adopted by the government has also attracted investment by many West European companies.

The most sensational development has been in the opening of iron mines which are likely to make Liberia one of the leading exporters of iron ore in the world. Efforts to expand agricultural output have been less successful. Forestry, fishing, and industrial developments have been started where almost none existed before. The country has also seen great improvements in its infrastructure and in its social services. Much work remains to be accomplished, of course, especially in bringing the tribal hinterland into the picture, but Liberia has made remarkable strides and is no longer the butt for criticism of other African countries. Government revenues increased from $4 million in 1950 to $32.4 million in 1960; the economic growth of the country in the decade to 1961 was unsurpassed by any other country except Japan.

THE PATTERN OF POLITICAL UNITS IN WEST AFRICA

West Africa has the greatest political fragmentation of any African area, explained in part by its length of contact with Europe. European countries were early interested primarily in coastal points where trade might be effected;

if there had been an interest in colonization some of the larger powers might well have absorbed the holdings of lesser nations. Division of the interior came partly in response to demands to quell tribal wars and to prevent what were considered to be barbaric practices; during the period of division the French displayed the greatest initiative, moving behind the coastal extensions of other powers to consolidate the large, contiguous French West Africa.

The superimposed political pattern has had significant effects on the economy of the area, aside from its failures to divide the area into logical physical units or to recognize the various tribal areas, which were often split by artificial boundaries. One of the unfortunate effects has been the projection of economic nationalism from Europe to West Africa, seen best in trade and transport policies. Differing administrative, legal, educational, and economic systems and a differing lingua franca also tend to divide the area. With the exceptions of the aborted Mali Federation and the somewhat nebulous and now dead Ghana-Guinea-Mali Union, the former British and French territories have tended to eschew any changes of their artificially superimposed boundaries.

The rate of economic progress in the several countries shows important correlations with the metropolitan connection. Commonwealth West Africa developed most rapidly and remains far ahead of other countries; only in postwar years did the French attempt to make up for lost time; neglected Liberia progressed the least until postwar years.

Another important effect of differing political policies in West Africa is seen in the position of plantations. With minor exceptions, they were forbidden in British territories, where the vast bulk of agricultural produce has come from indigenous farmers. Plantations were favored in French territories though their output did not compare with that from native farms; the Firestone Plantations Company accounted for the lion's share of Liberian exports for many years.

Despite these and other contrasts stemming from the political differences in West Africa, the basic land use and economic pattern is much more affected by the climate. Broadly speaking, the same products and the same type of agriculture are found in the similar climatic belts of the various countries. These climatic belts run predominantly east-west, more or less counter to the direction of most political boundaries, especially along the Guinea Gulf.

PHYSICAL OVERVIEW OF THE AREA

LANDFORMS

While West Africa may be divided into hundreds of fairly well-defined topographic units, the over-all pattern is fairly simple, most of it being plains and low plateaus under 1,500 feet in elevation. A typical traverse from south to north would cross, first, a relatively narrow, low-lying zone, consisting of sandbars often backed by lagoons and mangrove swamps; second, a coastal plain varying in width and rising gradually inland to a more or less well-marked escarpment; third, the West African Plateau, composed primarily of an erosion plain of pre-Cambrian rock bordered by plateaus whose sandstone layers form scarps falling abruptly to areas of less resistant rock; and fourth, a lower basin of immense alluvial plains occupied in part by the Senegal and Upper Niger rivers and often marked by volcanic inselberge. Only in a few areas do higher lands occur: the cuestal Fouta Djalon Plateaus and Guinea Highlands on the west, rising to over 6,000 feet; the Jos Plateau in Nigeria; and the series of mountains and high plateaus running along the eastern border.

From the landform standpoint alone, West Africa is one of the more favored of African areas. There are relatively few landform barriers; scarps are not as formidable as in the remaining portion of the west coast and most of the Indian Ocean coast. The average relatively low elevation also suggests the easier overland movement which characterizes the area, while it further explains in considerable part the paucity of white settlements, which have led to difficult political problems in other parts of the continent. Perhaps the greatest topographic handicap of the area has been the absence of good natural harbors or of protected bays along much of the coast, particularly along the Gulf of Guinea.

CLIMATE

The most important physical factor in explaining the general pattern of commercial agriculture of West Africa is climate, and, more particularly, precipitation. Some climatic regions are relatively well defined because of topographic conditions, but there is a gradual transition from zone to zone in most of the area (see Maps 2–4). A certain arbitrariness, therefore, attaches to delineating specific regions, particularly because precipitation may vary greatly from year to year or in cycles of several years.

The major characteristics of precipitation are as follows:

(1) A progressive decrease as one goes from south to north. Rainfall is especially heavy where the land rises to create an orographic influence. The average annual precipitation drops off relatively rapidly towards the interior, for example, from 110 inches on the Niger Delta coast to 80 inches at Benin, 65 miles inland, 49 inches at Bida, and 33 inches at Kano. Rainfall on the coast of Liberia is 120 inches, while at the eastern boundary it is down to 60 to 80 inches. An exception to this general pattern is seen in the corridor of dryer climate extending to the Gulf of Guinea coast from Cape Three Points in Ghana eastward to Dahomey. It is not completely understood why this exception exists, but the facts that winds at this section of the coast are more parallel to the coast and that cool waters upwell along the coast probably are important.

(2) A progressive decrease in the length of the rainy season toward the interior. Along most of the southern coast it lasts from 11 to 12 months; about 150 miles inland it is only about 9 months, while at Kano it is down to five or six months' duration. In some sections, double maxima occur as the sun's direct rays move north and south in the summer. The length of the rainy season is a critical factor for vegetation and crops. For example, crops associated with the tropical rainy climate may be grown when precipitation is no more than 40 to 60 inches if the dry season is of moderate duration and not entirely dry.

(3) A decrease in dependability of precipitation toward the north. The generalization that the dryer the climate the greater is the variability of precipitation applies to this area as it does to most parts of the world, but there is somewhat greater dependability owing to the monsoonal influence which affects the area. It is this influence which also explains the short dry period in the southern portions of the area.

Temperature conditions are of minor importance in influencing land use in West Africa. Temperatures tend to be high throughout, but there are contrasts between coastal and interior regions. In tropical rainy areas temperatures are high year round, averaging about 85° F. Coupled with the characteristic high humidity, they produce high sensible temperatures and hence considerable discomfort. During the short period when the winter monsoon, the harmattan, is blowing, humidity is somewhat reduced.

In the interior, a slight seasonal temperature curve appears, but the summer rains have a cooling effect which flattens the curve in that season. The diminution of vegetation, clear skies, and low humidity make for high diurnal temperature ranges. Nights can be uncomfortably cold; days may have temperatures rising to 110°–120° F.

VEGETATION

The vegetation zones of West Africa show the same transition as the climate (see Map 5). The neat transitions suggested by any of the systems of classification used often do not exist in fact. Use by man and the effects of fire, usually set by man, often distort the pattern, resulting particularly in a sharp division between grasslands and the tropical rainforests. Several interesting problems pertaining to the vegetational pattern of West Africa exist: How rapidly is the rainforest disappearing and with what results? How serious is grass burning? How can the vegetation and soils of the area best be preserved? What human practices are tending to cause deterioration in the natural landscape? Is West Africa suffering from progressive desiccation with a consequent invasion of desert conditions into the steppes, steppe conditions into the savanna, and so on? Most of these questions will be examined in conjunction with discussion of the land use regions to which they apply. The last question may be briefly examined at this point.

Until a few decades ago it was quite generally accepted that climatic desiccation was taking place here and in other parts of the continent, and some students continue to maintain that West Africa is suffering from progressive desiccation. In support of the contention it is claimed that the long period of tribal southward migration has been required by desiccation, that sand is actively drifting in some areas, that Saharan drift is gradually filling the Lake Chad basin, and that alluvial soils underlie sands in parts of Senegal. It is further pointed out that ancient rock engravings in the Tibesti Mountains and other parts of the Sahara depict elephants, hippopotamuses, and other animals which could no longer be supported there, and that stream profiles in the desert are characteristic of such profiles in more humid areas.

Much of this evidence is not questioned by those who believe that climatic desiccation is not now taking place in the area. There is agreement, for example, that the desert was wetter in Quaternary times, 10,000–15,000 years ago. But many question whether it is a continuing phenomenon, noting that rain-eroded dunes may be seen along the desert border, that a blanket of sand found from the Sahara to about 10° 30′ N and presumably blown there, is everywhere fixed by vegetation, and that the extreme youth and infantile character of stream lines in the Fouta Djalon, one of the wettest areas in Africa, suggests that this region was dryer in the past than it now is.

Whatever the fact may be, and more evidence is needed for certainty, it is agreed that bad human practices have led to degradation of vegetation, which would give the impression that there was desiccation. These malpractices, which will be covered later, include deforestation, overcropping, overgrazing, and grass burning. There is little question that man is slowly, and in some areas not so slowly, downgrading a vast part of the West African environment.

SOILS

The generalities regarding tropical soils given in Chapter II pertain to West Africa and need not be repeated here. It should be stressed, however, that increasing evidence suggests the necessity for more detailed soil studies, including analysis of the association of important cash crop areas with distinctive soil regions and examination of some fairly intricate soil selection systems.

POPULATION PATTERNS

The population of West Africa in 1961 was given at 71.3 million but may have been considerably higher than that estimate. For example, the population of Nigeria in 1961 was 35,752,000 according to official estimates, but the nullified census of 1962 would have given the figure of 43,200,000. Just how much this marked disparity may be explained by underestimation of the earlier census and by deliberate distortion of the 1962 figures for the purpose of gaining greater political representation is impossible to tell. On the other hand, the 1961 estimate for Liberia of 1.32 million may be exaggerated, since it is rumored that that country's census was suppressed because it revealed a population considerably lower than had been expected. Still other countries have never had a modern census.

The distributional pattern of the population is not easily discernible or readily explained (see Map 9). Population is, however, heavier in the east, and it is possible to delineate two discontinuous east-west belts of greater density

Part of Ibadan, Nigeria
This is the largest of the many towns of the Yoruba, who characteristically live in large agglomerated settlements.

separated by a belt of rather low densities. Nodes within these belts include some of the more densely populated parts of the continent. The southern belt, which is predominantly in the tropical rainy climate and wetter savanna areas, includes, first, the very densely populated Iboland of the Eastern Region of Nigeria. According to the 1952 census the region had an average density of 269 per square mile, but 10 percent of the region had over 500 per square mile and parts had as high as 1,700 per square mile.

Second is the heavily populated Yoruba area of the Western Region. One of the important features here is the high percentage of people living in towns and cities (Map 10), quite in contrast with the pattern among the Ibo.

A view in Katsina, northern Nigeria
Large walled cities are characteristic of the Hausa emirates. The vegetation-covered pond is a borrow pit from which clay has been taken to build the houses.

Ibadan has a population over 600,000; there are four other cities with over 100,000; and about 50 percent of the total population of the Western Region lives in towns of 5,000 or more. The large communities of the area are not urban centers in the Western sense; about three quarters of their inhabitants are farmers, some of whom commute on a weekly basis to their rather distant holdings. Other nodes along the south include those in southern Ghana and in southeastern Ivory Coast.

The northern belt includes numerous clusters of great density, many of which are associated with the great Hausa emirates. From east to west, there are in Nigeria the nodes centered on Maiduguri, Kano, Katsina, and Sokoto. Kano has an estimated 176,000, while densities of 500 per square mile are found in a considerable radius around it. Westward from Nigeria there are additional densely populated areas in northern Ghana, in the Mossi country centered on Ouagadougou in Upper Volta, in the Fouta Djalon, and in Senegal and Gambia. Senegal has an urban population of over 700,000 or over a quarter of the total.

Chance migrations are undoubtedly of great importance in explaining the over-all distribution of population. Other explanations for the heavier concentrations in the south as compared to the relatively empty middle belt include the comparative ease of producing food in tropical rainy areas, the attraction of the border zone between savanna and rainforest where fire could readily be employed, and the greater commercialization of this zone. In the northern belt concentrations are explained in part by the existence of several areas with unusually shallow water tables which could be tapped by primitive techniques, the availability of some relatively good soils which could be tilled repeatedly, and exploitation of some surface water. The low densities of the middle belt are explained by early slaving in the area from both north and south, the agglomeration of peoples on both sides as a protection against intertribal wars, the fact that the tsetse fly made cattle rearing impractical while crop production was easier to the south, and the greater prevalence of human trypanosomiasis in this belt. But much additional research is required before the population patterns of West Africa are better understood.

There are relatively few non-Africans in West Africa, the only large group being found in Senegal and totaling about 62,000. Europeans among the non-Africans in West Africa are concerned primarily with technical, educational, and administrative services in government, with the larger commercial houses, with mining, except for small diamond workings, with modern industry, and with the numerous missions in the area. Lebanese and other Mediterraneans are important in some large and many small commercial operations.

TRANSPORTATION

Transportation is of such fundamental importance to economic development in West Africa that a survey of its major components will reveal many features of significance to land use in the area. Before we turn to the specific ports and land transport routes, a few generalizations may be made:

(1) The area was not favored so far as access by sea is concerned owing to the prevalence of offshore bars, silted river channels, and heavy movement of sand along the Guinea Coast. Several solutions to this problem will be detailed below. It is interesting that Britain secured most of the superior coastal points, including the Gambia, the estuaries of Sierra Leone, and the distributaries of the Niger.

(2) The inland waterways are also navigable only with difficulty. Most streams flowing south have only short negotiable stretches. Even the better waterways are usually troubled with great seasonal fluctuations, shifting channels, and interrupting rapids.

(3) Overland movement is not generally difficult so far as landforms are concerned, except for the high expense of bridging the numerous streams. Great vegetational and climatic handicaps do exist.

(4) The growth of traffic on roads and railways and at ports has been extremely rapid in postwar years, and it is no wonder that some of the railroads and ports have suffered from great congestion. Road traffic has been gaining relatively over rail, especially on short hauls. While this helps relieve congestion, it may also cause financial difficulties for railways, many of which, including those of the French-speaking states in West Africa, of Sierra Leone, and of Togo, have always run at a loss. An example of the shift to road use is seen at Apapa, Nigeria, where only 51.5 percent of transport traffic moved by rail in 1958–59 as compared to 92 percent in 1948–49; 67.5 percent of export traffic was received by rail in 1958–59 as compared to 94 percent a decade earlier. Heavier use of roads has also required an accelerated program of paving, as the laterite or gravel surface becomes inadequate.

(5) Improvements to existing transport means and extensions of routes, particularly roads, have also been very great. The position with regard to ports has improved enormously. Nigeria's road mileage, for example, has increased over 60 percent since the war and bitumenized roads have increased from 500 miles in 1946 to 6,908 miles in 1961, though a substantial part of these roads is in poor condition. Bridge construction in many territories has eliminated traffic bottlenecks which previously existed. Some of the more important of these new structures are the Volta River Bridge providing a direct road link between the Eastern Province and Trans-Volta Togo in Ghana, the Houphouët-Boigny Bridge connecting the parts of Abidjan, and a bridge under construction on the River Niger between Asaba and Onitsha providing the first direct road access between the Eastern and Western Regions of that country. There has been increasing attention in most territories to the construction of access roads, which have made a principal contribution to expanded production and exchange of export crops and domestic foodstuffs. While there have been relatively few extensions to rail lines, there has been much replacement with heavier track, some realignments, heavy purchase of rolling stock, improved

signalization, and dieselization. All of the French Community lines are dieselized and those of Ghana and Nigeria are rapidly replacing their steam locomotives. Diesel locomotives cost more than steam engines but can haul heavier loads, require less maintenance and servicing, are cheaper to run, and can save time because they do not have to stop to pick up water.

Expenditures on the transport infrastructures of West African countries have perforce absorbed a substantial percentage of development funds. In Nigeria and Ghana, transport and communications were allotted 36 percent of development expenditures from World War II to 1959; in French West Africa 64 percent of such funds were allotted to transport between 1948 and 1952. From 1946 to 1960, 25 percent of CD and W grants went to transport, while a very large share of all of the IBRD loans to Africa have been for transport developments.

Map 36. Transport in Mauritania, Senegal, Gambia, and Portuguese Guinea

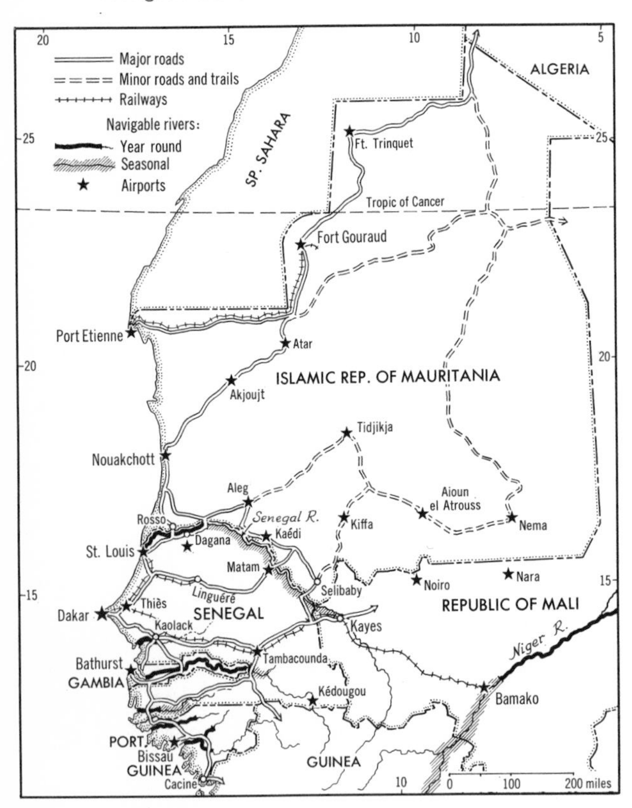

(6) There has been a sensational increase in air transportation in postwar years. By 1950, arrivals and departures by air had exceeded those by ship. Domestic routes have been markedly expanded in many countries. In recent years numerous countries have set up their own national air lines, but some of these appear to be overequipped and to require excessive subsidization from the national budgets.

(7) Despite the expenditure of large sums of money, often the largest single segment of government allocations, the needs in the field of transport are still very great. Some areas remain remote from any modern means of communication. Only three of the rail lines penetrate very far inland: the Dakar-Niger, the Abidjan-Niger, and the Nigerian lines. Much remains to be done before an adequate transport structure has been achieved.

NATIONAL TRANSPORT SYSTEMS

In the presentation of specific features of the transport picture of each territory which follows, the focus will be upon the ports and their connecting routes, moving from the west to the east.

MAURITANIA. Most of Mauritania's small international trade formerly moved through Dakar, except for fish landed at Port Etienne. Two developments are altering this position: the selection of Port Etienne as the outlet for large tonnages of iron ore from Fort Gouraud, and the desire of the independent country to have its own outlet nearer the south. To meet this latter concern, a small pier has been constructed at the new capital of Nouakchott (Map 36). At Port Etienne, which possesses the only protected bay between Casablanca and Dakar and which has exceptionally fine site features for a port, a lighter pier and new fishing facilities are being installed, while six miles south ore-loading equipment has been provided at an 810-foot pier attached to the mainland by a 1,395-foot jetty. Vessels drawing 44 feet will be able to use this facility, which has a storage capacity of one million tons of ore. A 419-mile rail line connects Port Etienne with the iron mines. Most of the roads of Mauritania, even those classed as "major," are little better than tracks.

SENEGAL. The first port encountered is St. Louis, near the mouth of the Senegal River. It would appear to be the natural outlet for the lands along the river, but its very difficult entrance, plus seasonal limitations of river navigation, has greatly reduced its importance. The Senegal River is navigable to Podor year round for boats drawing 8 feet and to Kayes, 574 miles from St. Louis, from July to October. While the river is regularly used by steamboats and canoes, the traffic, especially from Kayes, has never been very great.

Dakar ranks as one of the great ports of Africa. It is not just a port, however, it is the leading city of the states of French expression in West Africa, the capital of Senegal, an important industrial center, and a focus of educational and research institutions. It contains a large part of the European population of West Africa, which gives it great importance as a consumer of imported goods. In addition it has naval facilities and an international airport which serves not only Eurafrican routes but some of those between Europe and South America. Its position at the extremity of the West African bulge gives it strategic value for both air and sea routes.

Dakar is largely an artificial port enclosed by breakwaters, though the Cap Vert peninsula does give natural protection from the west and north (Map 37). Quay space exists for 33 vessels; many of the quays are very modern, as is the mechanical equipment of the port. Bunkerage facilities are well developed and new phosphate loading installations have recently been built. The harbor is now being dredged to permit use by 33,000-ton tankers at all times and a new fishing pier is also being built.

The high tonnages handled at Dakar tend to exaggerate its importance in the West African economy, a large part normally being bunker fuel which concerns only the port and low-value phosphate rock. The hinterland is a big producer of peanuts and phosphate, but of not much else, though Dakar does ship some manufactured goods. It is not unlikely that Abidjan, with a potentially much richer hinterland, will surpass Dakar as the leading port of former French West Africa in the not too distant future.

The Dakar-Niger Railway extends to Bamako and Koulikoro on the Niger River in Mali, while branches run to St. Louis and Linguéré. The line was severed for three years at the Mali border following the split of the Mali Federation. The French originally planned that rail lines would extend from points on the West African coast to navigable stretches on the Niger and Senegal rivers, which would serve as the backbone of the whole transport system. In fact, neither river is very adequate, nor are the interior areas along the Niger generators of important traffic.

There remain several minor outlets in Senegal: Kaolack, situated 75 miles up the Saloum, which is an arm of the sea, and Ziguinchor, on the navigable estuary of the Casamance. Kaolack handles fairly substantial tonnages of peanuts; both suffer from restrictions on the depth of vessels which can enter.

MALI. The major outlets of this huge landlocked country have been the Dakar-Niger

Dakar, Senegal
The general cargo piers are shown with the main part of the city in the background. See Map 37.

Railway and the Senegal River. During the political crisis between Mali and Senegal, traffic was rerouted via Abidjan, which greatly increased the cost of transport, particularly of peanuts which are produced in the west. The cost of cement delivered at Bamako doubled. There was talk of extending the line from Conakry to Bamako, but this would be a more difficult route and the poorly maintained Guinean line would make it a less attractive outlet than Dakar. Fortunately, Mali and Senegal reestablished relations in mid-1963 and earlier traffic patterns were soon regained.

Mali has two navigable stretches of the Niger River, connected by the Sotuba Canal around the rapids between Bamako and Koulikoro. The 217-mile stretch from Bamako to Kouroussa in Guinea is open from about mid-June to mid-December. Tugs can pull barges of 40-ton capacity and drawing about 3 feet in this section, but only about 1,000 tons of traffic is handled yearly. Eastward the Niger is navigable on a very uneven basis to Gao and sometimes to Ansongo, a total distance of 869 miles. Despite the difficulties of operating on the river, the main river ports have been improved and the

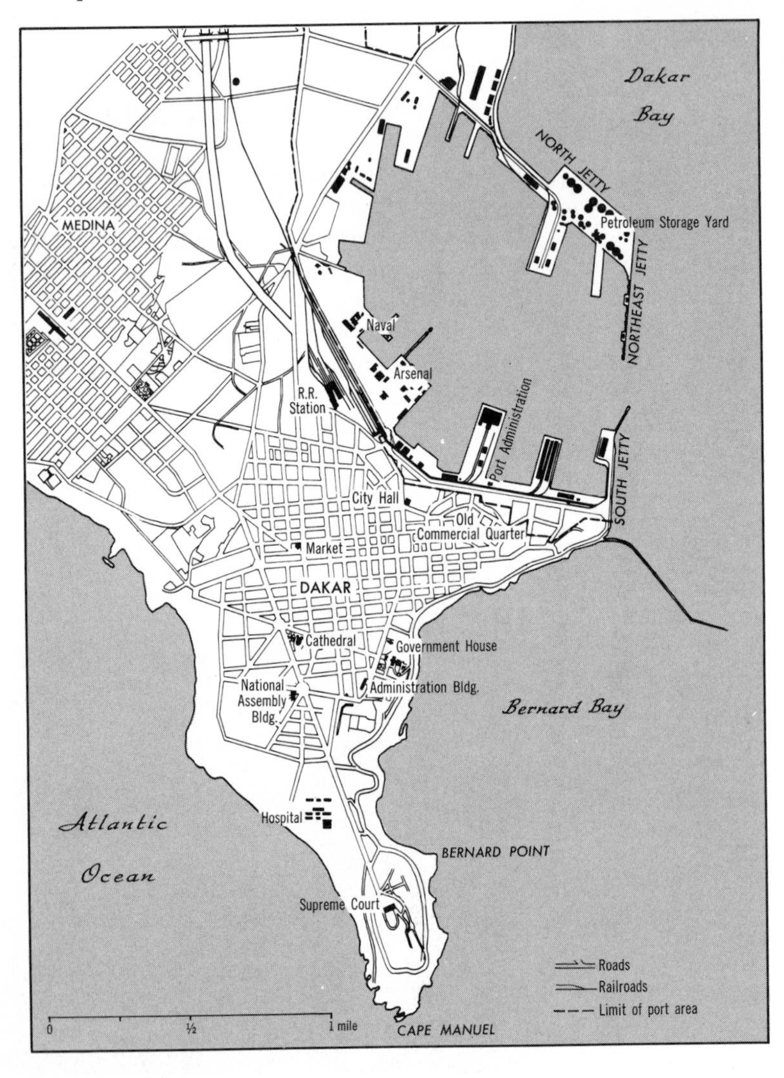

Map 37. The port of Dakar

total river traffic in Mali runs around 16,000–21,000 tons downstream, mainly cement and petroleum products, and 28,000–36,000 tons upstream, chiefly rice and peanuts.

GAMBIA. Bathurst is the only significant ocean port for this small country; it has one 290-foot quay which can accommodate one vessel, considered adequate for present traffic. The Gambia River, navigable to the eastern border, handles almost all of the country's peanut traffic and distributes imports not consumed in the capital city itself; of its 30 river wharfs, 23 had been rebuilt by 1961. The Gambia should probably have been the main outlet for most of the peanut zone of Senegal and Mali, but desire to develop and support national transport organizations has precluded more than domestic use of the river. The Dakar-Niger Railway, it may be noted, parallels the river for a considerable distance. What realignment of traffic would result from a possible federation of Senegal and Gambia is difficult to say, but the Gambia River and Bathurst would probably attract peanuts from adjacent sections of Senegal, particularly in Casamance. At present this remote part of the country uses less suitable local outlets or the trans-Gambian highway to Dakar.

PORTUGUESE GUINEA. The main port of this country is Bissau, a lighterage port. Many such ports existed in Africa in the past and a substantial though decreasing number are still utilized. They vary from completely open roadsteads to protected bays and inlets where vessels can anchor in safety. Ships may be loaded and unloaded by surfboats paddled by a crew which doubles as stevedores, or by modern motor lighters. Installations at the shore may be almost nonexistent, the surfboats landing on the beach through the surf, or there may be a metal or wooden jetty along which lighters may tie up to take on or discharge their cargoes. Sometimes small cranes are available to assist with heavier goods. Such ports are an anachronism in modern times, being slow, dangerous, and expensive as far as cost of handling is concerned. Where the surf is likely to be high, as in the Guinea Gulf, it is also difficult to work the two end hatches of a large vessel with surfboats, requiring special loading if such ports are to be visited and further reducing the speed of moving a given tonnage. Lack of protection for piers is another disadvantage; numerous examples exist of partial or severe damage from heavy storms to such installations.

GUINEA. Conakry is the dominant port of this country (Map 38). Situated on one of the few segments of hard rock providing a firm base along this coastal stretch, it is a fairly modern

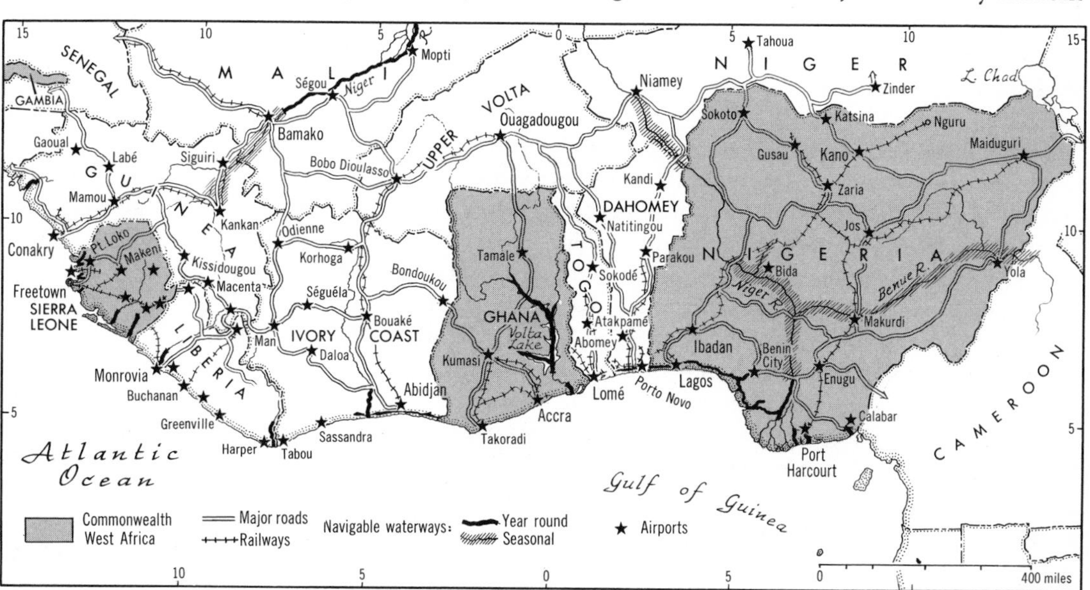

Map 38. Transport in the southern part of West Africa

port which has recently been improved to handle larger tonnages of iron ore and alumina. Its protection is not as good on the north as would be desirable, and its problem of shallowing depths has required the hiring of two Dutch dredges to work on a continuous basis. Capable of taking six vessels of up to 25-foot draught, it is to be extended under a Guinea-Polish contract.

Guinea has a 375-mile narrow-gauge rail line running from Conakry to Kankan on the Niger and a new 87-mile extension to the bauxite and alumina operation at Fria. The main line runs through very difficult, precipitous country, much of which is not highly productive. The Guinea railway has not been adequately maintained since independence; much equipment is very old; and operations have suffered greatly in efficiency. The Russians have expressed a willingness to rebuild the railway to wide-gauge standards; rebuilding might be desirable, but conversion to anything but standard African gauge would be unwise. The arcuate shape of Guinea means that a large part of the interior is far removed from a national port. The natural outlets for much of southeastern Guinea would be Freetown or Monrovia; the latter port is handling increasing Guinean traffic as a result of improvement of the trunk road to Ganta. But strenuous efforts have been made to route traffic from interior Guinea by truck to Kankan and Dabola and then by rail to Conakry. This does contribute to support of domestic transport routes and of the port and saves exchange, but it places a considerable burden on the remote region, which must reduce its ability to trade to some degree. Construction of a new port in the north was begun to serve the proposed bauxite-alumina complex at Bóké.

Guinean roads are very inadequate for a country of its size, the shortage and poor quality of overland routes being one of the main limiting factors in the economic development of the hinterland. Yet road construction has been given low priority and existing roads are more often than not poorly maintained.

SIERRA LEONE. Freetown, capital of Sierra Leone, has one of the finest natural harbors in Africa and the third largest in the world, created by drowning along this segment of the coast. Nonetheless, it was only a lighterage port until as late as 1952 when the 1,203-foot Queen Elizabeth Quay, capable of berthing two or three vessels, was completed. Growth in traffic has led to plans for additional space and efforts may be made to develop it as a bunkerage port to compete with Las Palmas, Dakar, and St. Vincent in the Cape Verde Islands.

Freetown is the seaward terminus of a 227-mile rail line to Pendembu, in the southeastern part of the country, with an 84-mile branch line to Makeni in the center. Narrow gauge and devious, the railway has an average of forty derailments a year and has always operated at a loss. In recent years the government subsidy has actually exceeded the revenue from freight traffic. Recently trucks have been carrying an increasing share of agricultural exports, from an estimated 39 percent in 1950 to 70 percent in 1956; moreover, they tend to skim the cream of high-value traffic. Despite these facts the government has been reluctant to scrap the railway, which provides the main link for some parts of the country, and has decided to realign some of the worst sections, relay a portion of the line with heavier track, and gradually replace steam traction by diesel power. It is difficult to see how this compromise can prevent continued, even accelerating, losses.

Across the bay from Freetown is Pepel, a private port belonging to the iron mining company which it serves. Construction of a new pier at Pepel and deepening of the Freetown-Pepel channel will permit entry of 35,000-ton ore carriers. A 3-foot–6-inch gauge rail line extends from Pepel 57 miles to the iron mines at Marampa. Devoted primarily to handling iron ore, Pepel can load a greater tonnage in an hour than most ports in Africa load in a day. General cargo is, of course, much more difficult to load and unload, and an important explanation for congestion in African ports in postwar years has been the relative gain of imports over exports; imports are comprised of hundreds of commodities while exports are characteristically made up of only a limited number of staples.

Sierra Leone's drowned coastline provides opportunities for coastal navigation; there are at least 680 miles of navigable waterways along the coast and on the lower courses of the rivers, though some are only utilizable a part of the year. About 500 miles of launch routes are delineated and over 1,000 small craft are believed to be operating in these waters, while a considerable number of "Bullom boats" transport produce and passengers from the shores opposite Freetown. This small-boat traffic is, incidentally, one of the few areas in which Africans play a dominant role in ownership and operation.

Roads were given minor attention in Sierra Leone before the war but under a greatly accelerated program the road mileage was doubled between 1948 and 1960. A problem of increasing proportions is how to maintain the typical laterite roads under the increasing traffic they are called upon to bear. Some sections with 500 vehicles a day are estimated to be handling five times their suitable capacity. Sierra Leone roads are among the most poorly marked in Africa and connections with adjacent countries are poorly developed.

LIBERIA. Before the war, Liberia's port facilities were practically nonexistent; since then it has had one of the more dynamic construction programs in Africa. Its first modern port was constructed by the United States at Monrovia during the war; an artificial port, it has berthing for three large ships, two mechanical ore-loading piers completed in 1961 and 1962, a T-head pier used by tuna boats, a new oil jetty and pipeline facility, and a 150-foot drydock. It was originally feared that the port's capacity would prove excessive, but the enormously accelerated expenditures for development, exploitation of iron ore, and coastal transshipment of rubber have increased traffic to such an extent that congestion has sometimes been severe in recent years. Even the new facilities listed above, which doubled the capacity of the port, may prove inadequate shortly, at least for servicing dry-cargo vessels.

Farrell Lines, Inc., the leading American shipper between Africa and the United States, operates a number of coastal vessels on the Liberian coast. Two 250-ton latex vessels and one 400-ton cargo boat serve the Harbel Plantation of the Firestone Company. Loading a vessel with rubber, which used to require seven or eight days, now takes only one or two. A fourth general cargo vessel operates between Monrovia and Cape Palmas.

Monrovia is connected by a private rail line with the Bomi Hills iron mine of the Liberia Mining Company, a distance of 41 miles. This line has more recently been extended northward to the mine of the National Iron Ore Company near the Sierra Leone border. A 50-mile line is planned to connect the Bong Range with Monrovia. The new road across the country to Ganta and Sanniquellie and into Guinea has brought additional traffic to Monrovia, as the other planned road extensions may be expected to do.

The port of Monrovia, Liberia
This completely artificial port was built during World War II. Liberian trade has increased so rapidly that new facilities are now required. Iron ore shipments are mechanically handled at finger piers.

The main highway from Monrovia to Ganta
The new major roads of Liberia are built to a higher standard than most roads in West Africa.

Three other ports have been built or started in recent years in Liberia. A major port is nearing completion at Buchanan, near the mouth of the St. Johns River, primarily to serve the LAMCO iron ore operations. Built at a cost of about $45 million, it will be able to load 45,000-ton vessels at the rate of 6,000 tons per hour and may later be deepened to permit entry of 60,000-ton ore carriers. A 984-foot quay will handle general cargo. Buchanan will have a 175-mile rail line running almost across the country to the LAMCO mine in the Nimba Mountains. Part of the track and equipment for this line, which will open up a huge untouched part of the country, was obtained from the liquidated Lehigh and New England Railroad. Later a spur may be run to the Bassa Hills, where a second holding exists.

At Sinoe, across the river from Greenville, a new 24-foot draught harbor has been built by a German company on behalf of the government. The banana plantations which Sinoe was designed to serve were abandoned after severe disease attack and are to be replaced by rubber production and forest exploitation. The third new port installation is in the extreme southeast of Liberia, at Harper, where a 14-foot draught harbor is under construction.

In 1945 Liberia had no paved highway and only 206 miles of unimproved roads. A major effort to correct this situation began in 1952, and by mid-1961 a total of 2,082 miles of road existed, of which 741 miles were surfaced and 129 miles were paved. The number of vehicles in the country has increased from 560 in 1949 to 7,900 in 1961. Criticism has been made of the practice of building main roads to American standards, which, it is maintained, results in the neglect of local access roads. Roads have cost an average of $48,684 per mile and a total of $30 million was spent on their construction from 1952 to 1961. On the other hand, this investment is estimated to support roughly $400 million in private investment and to have cut in half the time required to open up the Nimba iron mines. The new roads have also expedited the opening of independent rubber estates and forest exploitations, but the opportunities they have created for exchange have thus far adversely affected the production of subsistence crops.

An interesting feature of the transport industry of Liberia is its growth in postwar years as a place of registry for foreign-owned ocean-going vessels. This concentration upon Liberia as a "flag of convenience" was stimulated by very attractive laws and rates, said to have been suggested by the Farrell Lines. The original registration charge is $1.20 per ton, while the government undertook not to make any change in these fees for twenty years. In 1948 Liberia had a registered fleet of 1,000 gross registered tons; by 1959 a peak of 11,936,000 tons was reached, giving that country the third largest registration in the world; in 1962 the total had declined to 10,573,000 tons, owing largely to pressure from American maritime unions, and Liberia dropped into fourth place after the United States, the United Kingdom, and Norway. In 1958, receipts from registry and fees accounted for 13 percent of the national revenue.

The use of "flags of convenience" has met strong opposition in recent years. Countries such as Norway and the United Kingdom, whose shipping earnings are an important source of revenue, consider registration in such countries as Liberia and Panama as a thinly veiled subterfuge to escape taxation, laws regarding training of and provisions for the crew, and safety regulations. Various seamen's unions have also attacked such registration as a threat to wage levels and employment. Owners of ships registered in Liberia, most of whom are Americans, answer these criticisms by saying that their wage rates and safety regulations maintain accepted standards. They claim that subsidization of many national fleets makes competition impossible unless some way is found to reduce tax burdens, that "flags of convenience" are really "flags of necessity," and that, rather than reducing the fleet available in the event of war, they actually permit maintenance of a much larger tonnage than would otherwise be possible.

IVORY COAST. This country had no modern port facilities until the 1950s, when Abidjan was opened to ocean-going vessels. Its coast is the epitome for West Africa: straight, sandbar-ridden, and subject to enormous movements of sand. The western stretch is served only by lighter ports, of which Sassandra is the leading example. It has a pier jutting into the sea and several cranes, including one of 20-ton capacity. Its cargo is mainly bananas and lumber. Southwest Ivory Coast is poorly developed at the present time yet probably has potentials equivalent to those of the southeast; any very substantial growth in production in the region will require improved port facilities, and plans are now being made to construct a port at San Pedro.

The port of Abidjan was finally opened to ocean traffic by cutting the Vridi Canal through the coastal bar (Map 39), thus giving access to the large and well-protected Ebrié Lagoon. The problem of silting by longshore currents, the curse of the whole Guinea Coast, was met by extending the canal's western dike further than the eastern dike and by narrowing the seaward lip of the canal, thus creating a current to direct any sand deposited at the mouth to a deep offshore fosse known as the *trou sans fond*. Some concept of the nature of the problem may be gained from earlier experiences in cutting through the bar at Abidjan. The first attempt, made in 1904–7, was badly sited and the canal silted up in a few months. In 1933 a yard-wide ditch was cut along the abandoned canal to

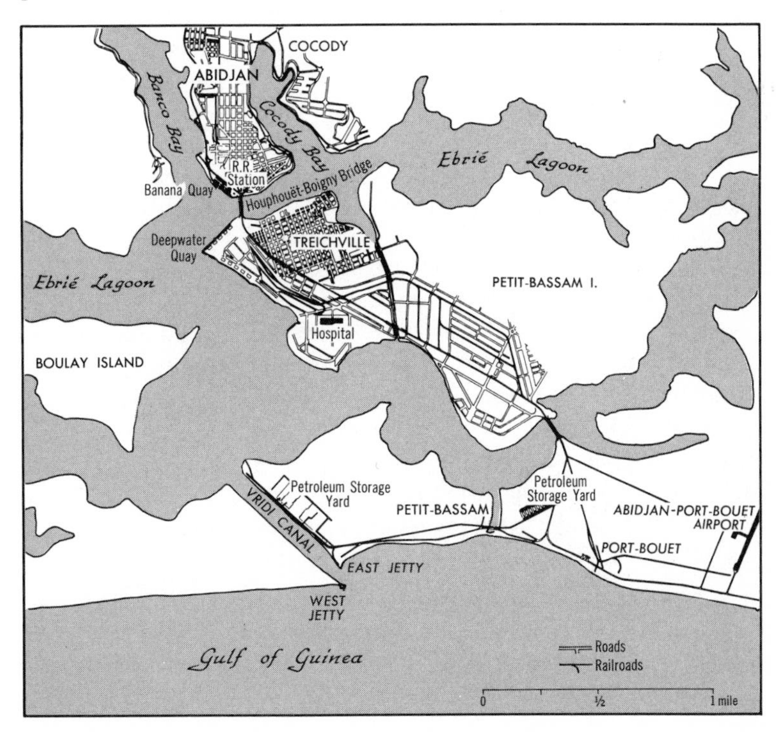

Map 39. The port of Abidjan

Aerial view of Abidjan, Ivory Coast
Opening of the Vridi Canal, seen in the extreme center background, led to a spectacular growth in the population and economic importance of the capital city.

release unusually high flood waters from the lagoon. In eight days the ditch had widened to 375 yards, but six months later the outlet had already been blocked by the action of the sea.[2] The port of Abidjan has been equipped with two main quays capable of berthing 10 ships, two banana piers, a mineral loading post, a fuel dock on the east bank of the Vridi Canal, a wood depot, and a fishing port which has proved to be inadequate.

These improvements illustrate well the stimulation that modern facilities can bring. Between 1948 and 1952, Abidjan had a threefold increase in population and it has since grown to 190,000 in 1961, or twelve times its prewar population. Port facilities were originally planned to handle 850,000 tons a year; the million-ton level was reached in 1954 and total cargo handled in 1961 was 2,300,000 tons. Particularly notable has been the increase in log and timber exports, which comprised 54 percent of the 1961 tonnage; without modern facilities it would have been impractical to move such quantities of this bulky cargo. Plans now call for constructing five new berths to help handle an expected continued growth in traffic.

Abidjan's ability to serve its hinterland is greatly aided by the series of lagoons extending about 180 miles along the coast, which have been interconnected and each of which has rivers navigable for distances inland not exceeding about 30 miles.

The Ivory Coast has one rail line, the Abidjan-Niger Railway, which traverses the country and extends into Upper Volta to Bobo Dioulasso and, in a postwar extension, to Ouagadougou. Traffic is not adequate to permit operating at a profit and the railway suffers from increasing competition from road traffic. It was estimated that in 1959 roads handled five eighths of total overland movements, including much of the high-value coffee and cocoa traffic of the country but also a very heavy tonnage of logs. The Ivory Coast has the best system of roads of any of the former French West African countries, a system which is being extended and improved with considerable rapidity.

UPPER VOLTA. This landlocked territory is served by the railway to Abidjan plus trunk-road connections to the four countries lying between it and the sea. In 1961 it contributed 22 percent to the tonnage handled by the Abidjan-Niger Railway, but part of this represented Mali traffic which will probably revert to the more normal and shorter route via Dakar. But the total traffic of Upper Volta is not impressive because the country does not produce a large tonnage of exports and is too poor to support a heavy import traffic.

GHANA. Ghana's first modern port was Takoradi, an artificial port where two breakwaters enclose 220 acres of water, constructed in 1928 and extended in 1956. It now has nine berths for large vessels, five for small, and one for mechanical loading of manganese. A jetty has been built in recent years to unload clinker imported to make cement in a nearby plant, while a 1,400-foot lighter wharf at the inner end of the harbor handles all cocoa and sawn timber to be loaded on ocean vessels from lighters.

[2] R. J. Harrison Church, *West Africa* (London, Longmans, Green & Company, 1957), p. 12.

Logs are frequently floated alongside vessels for loading by the ships' gear. Takoradi's traffic has been about 3 million tons a year in recent years, making it one of the leading ports in West Africa. It serves the main mineral and forest areas of Ghana as well as a large part of the cocoa traffic.

Until recently, all the other ports of Ghana were surf ports, which handled a surprising tonnage. Accra was the most important, with no less than 600,000 tons in 1958. The opening in 1962 of Tema, 17 miles east of Accra, gives Ghana a second modern port with deepwater facilities. While Tema was originally conceived as a port for the Volta Scheme, it became increasingly clear that eastern Ghana needed improved facilities regardless of that scheme. Tema, entirely artificial and protected from the sea by 7,200-foot and 4,800-foot breakwaters (Map 40), was designed to permit an eventual capacity of 5 million tons, with 20 deepwater berths. At present there are 10 berths totaling 6,000 feet in length, one 350-foot lighter berth, and 1,319 feet of fishing quays which are being extended to accommodate long-range trawlers. Cocoa, which is the main export cargo, is delivered to quayside from large storage sheds by overhead closed conveyors. Tema will be the port for Accra and will obviate the necessity of either using the beach there or bringing goods unsuitable for surfboat operations across country from Takoradi. Tema has already been selected as the site for a variety of industrial establishments and it has been decided that plans must be drawn up for a city of 250,000 instead of the original estimate of 80,000.

Ghana's 617 miles of rail lines are concentrated south of the Kumasi parallel, the main lines forming a triangle with Takoradi, Tema, and Kumasi at the angles. Branch lines serve the mining towns in the southwest. While roads have been of increasing importance in Ghanaian traffic, the railways operate at a profit in considerable part because of the mineral carriage on the western lines. Several rail extensions have been planned. Early in 1962 it was announced that the USSR would assist in constructing a line from Kumasi to Ouagadougou in Upper Volta; it is difficult to justify this line on the basis of present traffic generated in northern Ghana or Upper Volta. Other plans call for a 110-mile direct line from Takoradi to Accra and for short extensions to mining sites.

Surf boats working at Accra, Ghana
The new port of Tema will all but eliminate this slow, expensive, and sometimes hazardous method of handling cargo.

Ghana also has an unusually dense network of roads in the south, a considerable mileage

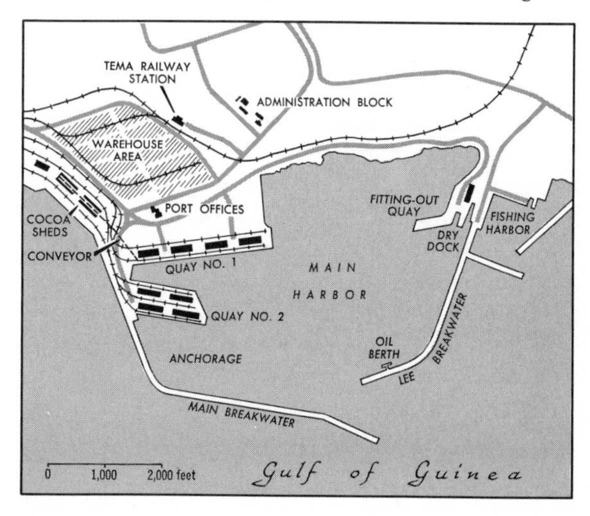

Map 40. The port of Tema

Port of Cotonou, Dahomey
A roadstead port served by lighters which move back and forth between the vessels anchored offshore and the metal pier projecting from the mainland in unprotected waters. Modern deepwater facilities are now being constructed about a mile west of the city.

being paved. The middle section of the country is sparsely served, its roads largely being links with the more populated but still undeveloped north, more important in migration than in movement of goods.

Navigable waters are of very minor importance. Plans call for opening a canal linking the Tano River with the sea at Half-Assini in the west. Mainly planned to serve the $4.5 million cement plant at Bonyeri, hopefully the canal would also facilitate the shipment of agricultural products from that region. Completion of the Volta Scheme will greatly improve navigability on the Volta River, creating possibilities of increasing traffic between north and south.

Ghana was among the first African countries to establish a national airline and merchant marine. By 1963, its Black Star Line, operated jointly with Zim Israel Navigation Company, had 10 vessels (5 chartered) and 7 new ships on order. Its airline has proved to be a costly venture; distances between the major southern cities are not so great as to encourage air travel, traffic with the north is poorly developed, and some of the planes acquired are not suitable for the average length of flights or the level of passenger and freight traffic.

TOGO. Lomé is the capital and major gateway of this small territory. It is a lighter port with a simple pier extending from the shore in protected waters. Both the wharf and the rail lines of the country, which are operated as a unit, run at a deficit. While the efficiency of the port measured by tonnage handled per day doubled after installation of several cranes, it is still very poor, totaling only 700 to 800 tons per day. Togo is, however, slated to have a new modern port by 1968, probably about five miles east of Lomé. A 3,280-foot metal wharf has recently been constructed at Kpémé to handle phosphates from Lake Togo on a fully mechanized basis.

Togo's railways total only 275 miles and only one line extends as far inland as 172 miles; hence the railways do not penetrate to the developed sections in the north. To correct this, two extensions are planned from the northern terminus of Blitta to Bassari and Sokodé. Two other branches are planned in the south, one to Anécho to serve the oil palm belt and tapioca industry and one from Anécho to Grand Popo to provide a direct rail contact with the new port of Cotonou in Dahomey. Togo's road system includes only about 800 miles of all-weather roads, of which only about 77 miles are paved.

DAHOMEY. Cotonou, the major port of Dahomey, has long been dependent on a 1,476-foot wharf and lighters. In recent years the level of traffic has been sufficient to justify consideration of improved facilities; the marked seasonality of export shipments, concentrated in a four- to five-month period, also contributed to the need for more facilities. In addition, about 40,000 tons a year, mostly petroleum products, are brought by lagoon from Lagos in Nigeria. During some periods in recent years, conditions became so congested at Cotonou that shipping companies were forced to impose a 100 percent surcharge on goods moving through the port.

An intensive study began in 1952 to determine where a new port to serve Togo and Dahomey might be placed and how the problem of coastal sand movement might be met. Marked by sometimes bitter rivalry among various localities and interests, the debate ended in 1957 with a decision to construct a new artificial port at Cotonou. The major physical difficulties were the shallow coastal waters and the movement of about $1\frac{1}{2}$ million tons of sand from west to east a year. Three types of installations were studied: placing the port on an artificial island connected with the mainland by bridges which would permit the sand to move freely along the coast; a port protected by projecting jetties with a continuous piping of sand around it; and a port with projecting jetties west of which sand would simply be permitted to accumulate. The first two solutions were rejected as being too expensive, the first having the additional disadvantage of congested access to the port area. After the sand has accumulated for some years, it will be necessary to extend the west jetty further out to sea. Protective works to the east of the port are designed to protect that coast from erosion. Started in 1959, the new port is scheduled for completion in 1964 at a cost of $30 million, $20 million of which will be provided by France.

The port will be protected by a 5,512-foot western jetty and a 2,611-foot eastern jetty enclosing 162 acres of water. Four quay posts will be provided; the port's capacity will first be about 400,000 tons, but may later be raised to about 1 million tons. It is estimated that the new port will save $2.68 per ton in reduced freight rates plus a total of $830,000 a year on cargoes of oil and gasoline. It is hoped that the port will not only stimulate increased shipments from Dahomey, including iron ore from the north, but that traffic with parts of Upper Volta and Niger will contribute to its growth.

Cotonou is the starting point of the 273-mile Benin-Niger Railway, which ends about in the middle of the country at Parakou, and of shorter lines which serve the south. The railway operates at a heavy loss. Completion of the new port may justify extending the rail to Niamey in Niger, finally achieving the original goal of the now misnamed line.

NIGER. Most of Niger is best tied to the sea by routes through Nigeria, but efforts have been made to secure as large a portion as possible of its traffic for Dahomey through "Operation Hirondelle" (Operation Swallow). Started in 1953, it involves subsidization of traffic moving by road via the railhead at Parakou. In recent years, 26,000 to 29,000 tons of peanuts, or about 40 percent of Niger's exports, have used this route and about 21,000–28,000 tons of merchandise have moved into Niger via "Hirondelle." But Nigeria is the most economic outlet for the richest zone of Niger, toward the east. Maradi is connected by a well-surfaced road to Kano; other goods move to Nigerian railheads at Kaura Namoda and Nguru and some may later move to Maiduguri.

A considerable amount of clandestine traffic moves across the Nigerian border to the disadvantage of government income by loss of customs duties. The high transport charges which this landlocked country is forced to pay are indicated by the fact that cement delivered at Niamey costs 94 percent more than at Abidjan; imported goods cost from 11 to 60 percent more than at Cotonou.

Southwestern Niger has been benefited by the Niger River, which is navigable from October to March between Niamey and Gaya. Formerly carrying about 250,000 tons a year, the river route lost most of its attraction when construction of a bridge at Gaya cut the delivery time to Niamey to a half day as compared to two days by water.

NIGERIA. Lagos is the leading port of the Federation (Map 41), although petroleum shipments from Port Harcourt–Bonny have greatly reduced its share of total tonnage exports of the country in recent years. Despite improvements and extensions in postwar years, Lagos was still plagued by congestion in 1963, the monthly average of days lost by ships awaiting space having increased from 22 in 1960 to 159 in 1962. The port consists of the old Customs Quay on Lagos Island, used mainly for incoming general cargo, and Apapa Quay on the mainland, which now has nine berths. To meet

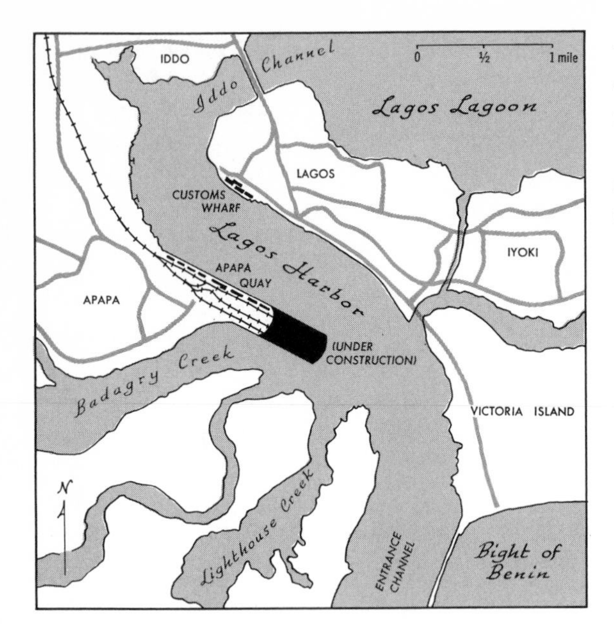

Map 41. The port of Lagos

a projected increase of about 50 percent in exports and 100 percent in imports by 1967, the Apapa Quay is being further extended to provide four additional berths. Eventually, a quay connecting Apapa with the Customs Wharf would provide for a total of 30 berths but would require extensive reclamation works. Lagos, as the name implies, is a lagoon harbor whose access to the sea is protected by several jetties. Physical problems associated with the port include erosion of Victoria Island to the east and a relatively shallow depth; the latter is being attacked by a vigorous dredging program begun several years ago.

Port Harcourt, 41 miles up the Bonny River, ranks second to Lagos. There was heavy congestion at Port Harcourt during the 1950s, leading to the adoption of improvement programs, including dredging to permit the entry of 13,000-ton vessels instead of the approximate 9,000-ton previous limit, straightening the river at the port site to reduce congestion, and increasing the berth spaces to seven including a bulk palm oil berth. Four additional berths are now under construction. At Bonny, near the mouth of the river, Shell-BP has constructed a petroleum terminal to dispatch crude gathered from the delta fields. The Bonny bar was first experimentally dredged to a depth of 28 feet to accept 18,000-ton tankers at a cost of about $2.8 million; gradual silting did follow but to a degree considered maintainable by normal dredging, so that plans now call for deepening the channel to 35 feet to permit 35,000- to 40,000-ton tankers to call at the terminal.

Next, there is a series of lesser ports on various watercourses of the Niger Delta. Sapele is owned by the United Africa Company and is the site of that company's large lumber mill and plywood plant; the heavy tonnage of these products permits Sapele to rank third among Nigerian ports. Burutu is the base of the Niger River fleet of the United Africa Company; Warri serves the same function for John Holt and Company; Koko has recently been reopened and provided with facilities. These ports are all controlled by the Escravos and Forcados bars, which, despite several dredgings, were gradually filling in. In 1899, for example, there were 20 feet of water at the Forcados bar, in 1934 only 12 feet, and in postwar years favoring of other outlets by the Niger threatened further to close the Forcados channel. Shallowing of these bars meant that access to the delta ports was limited to smaller vessels, or that larger vessels could use them only if partially loaded. This led to the transshipment of considerable cargo by barge to and from Lagos, raising the cost by about $1.75 to $2.10 per ton; this provided no solution for the high-bulk, low-value timber shipments.

The firm of NEDECO, Netherlands Engineering Consultants, was hired to study the problem and, after six years of research including the testing of various alternatives in hydrographic laboratory scale models, it presented its recommendations to the Nigerian government in 1959. These were adopted and have involved focusing upon the Escravos bar, over which 20 feet of water is to be maintained at all tides, permitting the loading of up to 5,000 tons instead of the previous 1,200–1,400 ton limit. This has required a major engineering works, a five-mile mole on the south side of the Escravos Estuary, plus extensive dredging of the channel. Scheduled for completion in 1964, the project will cost about $22.4 million. In addition to saving lighterage charges it will relieve pressure on Lagos and Port Harcourt. NEDECO has also studied the eastern part of the delta. The minor port of Calabar is found to the east of the Niger Delta.

Nigeria is something of an exception to the rule as far as the availability of inland waterways is concerned. A network of navigable creeks in the south makes it possible to maintain passenger and cargo movement all the way from Dahomey to Eket, sixty miles from the border of Cameroon. The Cross River is also used to bring exports to Calabar. But it is the Niger and its main eastern affluent, the Benue, which are the leading interior waterways. The Niger is navigable from June to March to the confluence of these streams at Lokoja, 360 miles from the sea, but depths vary greatly above Onitsha. Above the confluence the Niger is navigable from August to March a further 206 miles to Jebba, beyond which rapids preclude further navigation, but boats seldom go farther than Baro, 74 miles from Lokoja, where a rail branch permits more direct contact with the north.

The Benue is navigable 150 miles to Makurdi from June to November, 520 miles to Yola, near the border, from July to October, and for 6 to 10 weeks between July and October to Garoua in Cameroon, a distance of 612 miles from Lokoja and 972 miles from the sea. In addition to an intensive canoe and barge traffic, three private companies having a combined fleet of over 30,000 tons maintain river fleets. In recent years, about 180,000 tons a year have been handled by this fleet on the Niger and about 78,000 tons on the Benue, with about two thirds of the total moving seaward and one third moving upstream.

But difficulties of navigation, its limitation to daytime hours, and problems of integrating the traffic flow result in high freight rates, not far below those on the railways, whereas waterway rates in more developed countries are normally only a quarter to a half of rail tariffs.

Petroleum barges with the tug Adama *on the Niger River*
The Niger River may one day become the Rhine of Nigeria, but regular traffic now totals only about 200,000 tons a year.

A five-year survey, again assigned to NEDECO and completed in 1959, resulted in a series of recommendations for multipurpose development of the Niger and Benue rivers. The proposal was reviewed in succeeding years and a somewhat revised scheme was included in the First National Plan of 1962–68. Several decades will be required to complete the scheme, which is divided into three stages and the central purpose

A switching engine at Kano, northern Nigeria
Nigeria will have about 2,200 miles of railway by 1965.

of which is the development of hydroelectric power. As far as navigation on the river is concerned, the proposed second dam at Jebba, to be completed by 1982, will provide complete navigable control to the confluence of the Benue. The first dam at Kainji would also permit nine months' use of the river above that dam to Niamey in Niger. Later, dams above Yola and near Makurdi on the Benue could be built to extend the navigable season on that river.

It is estimated that these dams plus introduction of night navigation, dredging on some stretches, installation of training works, buoyage, and charting would bring costs of transport on the river to from one third to one half of rail rates, hopefully stimulating production in the areas served. Part of the gain would result from greater use of the existing fleet, which is now used only about 30 percent of the time, part from the ability to use larger boats. While the Niger River Scheme will not influence navigation on the river until completion of the first dam in 1968, an allotment of $4.2 million was made for the 1962–65 period to expand and improve buoyage and patrolling on the river. One rather unfortunate feature of the river system of Nigeria is that the Niger and the Benue above Lokoja traverse the relatively low productive middle belt.

Nigeria had 1,887 miles of rail lines in 1962 and will have 2,210 miles upon completion of the Bornu extension in 1964. One western main line runs 700 miles from Apapa through the cocoa area of the Western Region, across the Niger at Jebba, and via Kaduna and Zaria to Kano, its main terminus in the north, thus tapping the main cotton and peanut zones. Branches run from Zaria northwest to Kaura Namoda, from Kano east to Nguru, and from Minna to the river port of Baro. The other main line runs 569 miles from Port Harcourt via the oil palm district, the Enugu coal fields, and Makurdi on the Benue, to Kaduna, where it joins the western line. The Bornu or Maiduguri extension starts at Kuru on a branch line and runs to the tin producing area of Jos. It will serve areas in which about five million people live and should stimulate large increases in exports of peanuts, cotton, and livestock products. The line, which will probably not run at a profit in early years, will also tap traffic from eastern Niger, from Chad, and from northern Cameroon.

Nigerian Railways was hard pressed in postwar years to handle the increased traffic available. Designed and equipped to handle 1.5 million tons of paying traffic, it regularly carried much more and still could not move the enormous peanut exports, which accumulated in great mounds at Kano and other centers after all but the poorest harvests. Improvement was delayed by inability to obtain additional stock, low track capacities, old age of equipment, and a very rapid program of Nigerianization. After 1953 the situation improved, aided particularly by a program of dieselization; in 1960–61 the total savings credited to diesel locomotives over 1956–57 when diesel engine mileage was about 25 percent of the total was $1.75 million, savings in fuel cost representing 68 percent of this figure. A feature of the postwar traffic picture has been a marked loss of short-haul freight to road haulers, reflected in a much higher average haul per ton handled but also in considerable losses to working revenues. Nigerian Railways is, in fact, finding it increasingly difficult to avoid operating in the red.

Nigeria has greatly improved its highway

Table 13. Exports from West Africa by commodity, 1961 (in million $ U.S.)

	Mauritania	*Senegal*	*Mali*	*Upper Volta*	*Niger*	*Ivory Coast*	*Dahomey*	*Guinea*	*Togo*	*Portuguese Guinea*[a]	*Liberia*	*Gambia*	*Sierra Leone*	*Ghana*	*Nigeria*	*Total*
AGRICULTURAL PRODUCTS																
Palm products		.55				1.41	7.13	2.63	1.42	.03	1.13	.22	6.83		92.71	114.06
Peanut products		102.87	5.07	.19	5.92		2.25	1.68	.62	2.74		8.62			109.64	239.6 0
Other vegetable oil products			.10		.04		.44	.19	.98						4.52	6.27
Coffee						81.68	1.12	6.39	5.04		.35		1.67			96.25
Cocoa						39.71			5.22		.23		.83	197.10	94.49	337.58
Bananas						11.76		6.51								18.27
Other food products						2.53		1.49	1.22	.88			.34	2.91	1.33	10.70
Cotton			.57				.26		1.26						36.47	38.56
Piassava											.13		.80		.63	1.56
ANIMAL PRODUCTS																
Live animals		} 1.18	.72	2.13	1.60		.04		.08							5.16
Hides and skins		}	.55	.04	.38			.21		.18		.02			1.24	3.21
Fish and products	1.08		1.60	.02	.28		.97		.05							4.00
FOREST PRODUCTS																
Logs, lumber, plywood						33.75	.01			.37				42.78	22.15	99.06
Gum arabic		.64	.06		.02										.83	1.55
Rubber								.02		.07	26.80				30.85	57.74
MINERALS AND METALS																
Alumina								28.94								28.94
Bauxite								2.46						1.30		3.76
Coal															.68	.68
Columbite															3.26	3.26
Diamonds						3.25		7.74			2.20		44.71	20.02		77.92
Gold														29.10		29.10
Iron ore								1.60			32.40		13.08			47.08
Manganese						2.57								16.87		19.44
Petroleum															32.33	32.33
Phosphates		6.50							.63							7.13
Tin															18.60	18.60
Other minerals		.67			.01		.01									.69
MISCELLANEOUS																
Shoes		.55														.55
Others	.67	11.16	1.05	.91	.70	.34	.78	1.17	2.16	.11	2.96	.60	.56		22.68	52.05
Re-exports													13.18	6.20	9.59	22.77
Total exports	1.75	124.12	9.72	3.29	8.95	177.00	13.01	61.03	18.68	4.38	66.20	9.46	82.00	316.28	482.00	1,377.87

Source: National trade statistics.

[a] 1960.

network since the war and now has 6,908 miles of paved road and 38,000 miles of gravel and earth roads, a 57 percent increase since the war. The number of motor vehicles increased from 14,200 in 1950 to 42,050 in 1958 and 71,000 in 1961. Traffic on considerable stretches of the main roads is excessive for the quality of the road, which has led to serious deterioration and unsafe motoring conditions. While Liberia may have built its roads to unnecessarily high standards, Nigeria has erred in the other direction, which may possibly prove to be more costly in the long run. In recent years many access roads have been constructed under communal programs, proof that there is considerable initiative in the countryside.

Nigeria, like Ghana, has its own merchant fleet, the Nigeria National Line, with 10 ships, of which 5 are chartered, and its own Nigeria Airways, which is being expanded with the aid of Air India technical assistance under a $43 million 10-year plan running to 1972.

One feature deserving of note in concluding this section on West African transport is the markedly national orientation of almost every country's transport system. There is no road connecting the major coastal cities; there is no easy route from Dakar to Lagos. And despite numerous agreements designed to "unify" the area, protestations favoring pan-Africanism, and desires to develop the tourist industry, the red tape involved in moving across boundaries in West Africa is often appalling. An agreement was reached in 1961 to establish a net of all-weather roads totaling 14,000 miles and serving all of the countries of the region; few countries have thus far implemented their parts of this commitment.

A "mammy wagon" near Kumasi, Ghana
Such buses are very important in West Africa for transport of persons and country produce.

TRADE AND COMMERCE

Space prohibits examining the foreign trade and domestic commercial patterns of West African countries in detail, though many specific features will appear in the following discussions. West Africa is like other parts of the continent in the high dependence of its money economies on foreign trade, in the limited number of commodities appearing on the list of exports, and in the almost complete dependence of exports on extractive industries (Table 13). There continues to be a marked orientation of trade with western Europe and with the former colonial powers. The seven former French countries which are now members of the UDOA take about 71 percent of their imports from the franc zone and ship about 73 percent of their exports to that zone, with France itself accounting for the vast bulk of such trade. The share of the United Kingdom in the trade of Ghana and Nigeria is considerably lower than that of France with its former colonies, being about 36–40 percent of imports and 30–45 percent of exports. The United States supplies only a small part of West African imports, except in Liberia, but takes about 8–10 percent of exports except for Liberia and Ghana. In 1961 it received 23.5 percent of Ghanaian exports, almost entirely cocoa. Almost all West African countries have had unfavorable trade balances in recent years (Table 14), owing in part to reduced prices of

Table 14. Imports and exports of West African countries for selected years, 1938–1961 (in million $ U.S.)

	Mauritania[a]	*Senegal*	*Mali*[a]	*Upper Volta*[c]	*Niger*	*Ivory Coast*	*Dahomey*	*Guinea*	*Togo*	*Portuguese Guinea*	*Liberia*	*Gambia*	*Sierra Leone*	*Ghana*	*Nigeria*
Imports															
1938		29[b]			1	9[d]	3	5	2	1	2	2	7	38	42
1948		115[b]			3	34[d]	10	16	7	7	9	9	20	127	169
1958		208[b]		9	11	109	21	73	18	8	38	11	67	237	466
1960		172[b]		8	14	120	31	50	26	11	69	9	74	362	604
1961	31	155	36	28	19	150	25		26		91	13	91	394	623
Exports															
1938		19[b]			1	11	3	3	2	1	2	2	11	32	47
1948		84[b]			6	42	12	10	10	5	16	9	22	202	252
1958		137[b]		5	18	150	16	25	15	7	54	12	55	263	380
1960		113[b]		4	13	151	18	55	15	4	83	8	83	294	475
1961	2	124	10	3	9	177	13	61	19		66	9	82	316	482

Sources: U.N., *Statistical Yearbook, 1961* (New York, 1962); national trade statistics.
[a] Figures for 1938–60 included under Senegal.
[b] Includes Mauritania and Mali.
[c] Figures for 1938 and 1948 included under Ivory Coast.
[d] Includes Upper Volta.

staple exports, in part to increased developmental expenditures.

Features of the domestic commerce are the very large number of petty traders found in most countries and the great importance of expatriate companies in wholesale trade, importing, and exporting. The purchasing of domestic staples has, however, been removed to a considerable degree from such companies and placed under governmental boards, while the larger trading concerns are tending, particularly in the former British countries, to move toward specialized trading and to redeploy their capital to industry. The largest trading companies are the United Africa Company group (including G. B. Ollivant, Pickering and Berthoud, Paterson Zochonis, and Kingsway Stores), Compagnie Française de l'Afrique Occidentale (CFAO), and Société Commercial de l'Ouest Afrique (SCOA). Syrians and Lebanese also play a significant role in commerce, while Indians are relatively poorly represented, except in Sierra Leone. Some African traders, particularly some of the "market mammies" of the southern regions, have developed very substantial businesses, and, as African experience grows, it may be expected that the role of the expatriate firm in trade and commerce will continue to diminish.

CHAPTER ELEVEN

West Africa: Land Use

With the background provided by the previous chapter, it is now appropriate to examine the major land use patterns of West Africa, in which large climatic-vegetation regions will be used as the basic units. Emphasis is upon commercial development and potentialities, but it should not be forgotten that there is a high degree of self-sufficiency in the agricultural pattern and that production for domestic sale and for export remains only a part of total production.

COASTAL AREAS

The coastal regions have certain economic uses with which they may be associated, including, in addition to the port functions already discussed, ocean and lagoon fisheries, the growth of swamp rice for domestic use, and some production of coconut products.

FISHING

There is a considerable and growing interest in fishing along many parts of the West African coast, some tribes being almost solely devoted to this activity. In Ghana, for example, it is estimated that 250,000 people are involved in some branch of the fishing industry, including 67,000 fishermen who man a fleet of 9,000 canoes. Senegal is estimated to have 3,000 canoes manned by 10,000 fishermen.

Methods are largely primitive, fishing usually being carried on from pirogues launched through the surf and paddled by hand. The catch per man and per boat is very low, being estimated at one ton per year per fisherman in Nigeria. Wastage on shore is very high owing to inadequate preservation, storage, and marketing arrangements. Traditional techniques of conservation include sun drying, charring, and smoking; fish which are to be sold locally for consumption in three or four days are smoked for about eight hours, while those destined for the interior may be smoked for several days. The high demand for fish and the desirability of promoting their consumption as a means of increasing the protein intake have led to efforts to rationalize the industry.

Emphasis has been placed, as far as fishing itself is concerned, on the use of bigger boats, on the introduction of powered vessels or outboard motors for canoes, and on the adoption of better and bigger nets, particularly shark, set, and encircling nets. And a notable development of recent years has been the attraction of tuna vessels from France, Spain, Japan, and the United States which are fishing for tuna off the shore from Senegal to Sierra Leone and Cape Three Points to west of Fernando Po, operating out of Dakar, Freetown, Monrovia, Abidjan, Tema, and Cotonou. Some conception of the progress made in securing larger, more modern vessels may be derived from the following: in Senegal the number of boats operating in tuna fishing increased from 5 in 1954 to 57 in 1960; 8 vessels are owned by a state company in Guinea where Poles are training local crews in modern fishing practices; the Mesurado Fishing Company is operating several trawlers from Monrovia; the number of fishing vessels operating from Abidjan increased from 2 in 1950 to 48 in 1962; 243 vessels were based on Ghana in 1961 operating chiefly along the coast; the number of canoes fitted with outboard motors in Ghana increased from 205 in 1960 to 1,700 in 1961; 10 commercial trawlers worked out of Nigerian ports in 1962 as compared to 1 in 1956. Ghana, which has one of the more dynamic fisheries development programs, has attempted to expedite the acquisition of power vessels and modern gear by extension of credit, is building several score of fishing vessels at Sekondi, and has ordered a fleet of trawlers from Britain and ten from the USSR, plus a 929-ton trawler whose catch will be frozen aboard ship before landing.

Provision of better port facilities for fishing vessels is receiving increased attention in several countries. Ports which are scheduled to have improved fish harbors include Port Etienne, Monrovia, Elmina (Ghana), Tema, Cotonou, and Lagos. Tuna fishing, in particular, requires large-scale and modern shore facilities, but any real improvement in any kind of fishing requires better and safer port installations.

Relatively little is known regarding the potential of the ocean waters off West Africa, particularly those beyond the immediate coastal waters to which the smaller boats and canoes are perforce restricted. Early in 1959, an East German research expedition surveyed the grounds along part of the Guinea Gulf; in 1963 surveys were completed by Star-Kist International and by the Russians indicating that Ghanaian offshore waters are rich in tuna and sardinella, while Japanese and Ghanaian experts began a study to determine the variety and quantity of fish available in coastal waters. While there is increasing evidence that tropical waters are far richer than previously believed and that resources off West Africa are very substantial, not all signs are optimistic. Ivory Coast fisheries, for example, had a sharply decreased catch in 1961 attributed to overfishing of inshore waters; the size of fish caught along the Nigerian waters is apparently declining; and there are said to be too many vessels operating off Senegal in relation to the desirable catch.

With regard to improvements in processing,

Pirogues and nets used in ocean fishing in Togo
At present most fishing is primitive and characterized by low production per man and per boat. Efforts are being made in many West African countries to introduce larger powered vessels and modern fishing gear.

attention is being given to the erection of canning, processing, and freezing establishments which could avoid most of the loss associated with the marketing of fresh fish. Port Etienne is slated to receive a freezing plant, fish flour mill, and lobster cannery. Dakar got a large fish freezing plant in 1957; its canneries, however, are small and poorly equipped. In Guinea, a West German company is operating a fish smoking plant, while a cold store is under construction with a capacity of 100 tons of fish daily. Sierra Leone has begun the erèction at a cost of $280,000 of brine storage tanks and an ice-making plant to supply catchers. Ghana has completed a $2.24 million fish cold-storage plant at Tema and proposes to erect canneries for sardines and other fish. Nigeria plans new facilities at Lagos. Despite the advantages of reduced losses and an increased widening of the market permitted by canning and proper preservation, some plants have had great difficulty in operating at a profit, partly because supply has been erratic, partly because marketing facilities have not been sufficiently advanced to accept the improved product. Here the effort is to introduce refrigerated trucks and fish depots capable of handling fresh frozen fish. Ghana, for example, plans to establish 36 receiving stations throughout the country, and the Ivory Coast is

Fish traps used in seasonally inundated land in northern Nigeria
Despite relatively meager total catches, the steppe areas of West Africa ship fish to cities in the rainforest belt.

setting up a chain of freezers to permit delivery up to 250 miles from Abidjan.

Statistics are not readily available on the size and value of fish catches since much of the industry is conducted on a small-scale and strictly local basis. It is estimated that about 100,000 tons of fish a year are caught off Mauritania but only 7 to 10 percent are treated there, the rest going directly to Europe. It is hoped that new facilities there will increase the tonnage processed at Port Etienne to 40,000 tons a year by 1970.

About 7,500 tons of tuna were landed at Dakar in 1959. The Liberian catch increased from 940 tons in 1956 to 2,266 tons in 1961, while the Ivory Coast catch was 50,000 tons in 1960 but declined sharply in 1961. Ghana's total domestic catch is estimated at 33,000 tons and Nigeria's trawler catch totaled 3,441 tons in 1961. That there is ample room for improvement is indicated by the facts that most countries are still net importers of fish; in 1961 Ghana imported 83 percent of its consumption, while Nigeria and Sierra Leone import an estimated 70 percent of their fish supplies.

While sea fishing contributes the greatest share of the total fish catch in West Africa, fishing is also widespread in the lagoons, lakes, rivers, and seasonally inundated lands throughout West Africa. In addition to fishing from canoes, hand lining, seining, and draining of ponds, crude raffia fish traps are used in inland waters. In Dahomey, where much of the sea fishing is in the hands of Ghanaians and Nigerians, there are unusually well-developed inland fisheries employing over 100,000 people, of whom 25,000 live exclusively on this activity. Niger exports about two thirds of its estimated 2,000-ton commercialized catch. Upper Volta has a catch estimated at 6,000 tons exclusive of fish caught by Ashantis in the upper Volta River. Nigeria's inland catch is thought to be about equal to that of its marine fisheries.

In postwar years many countries of tropical

Constructing a large fishpond in northern Nigeria
When properly maintained, these ponds can yield a significant contribution to local protein supplies.

Africa have had large-scale programs devoted to the building of fishponds and their stocking with fish. The favorite species is *tilapia*, which has numerous advantages: it multiplies rapidly, provides good eating, reduces the mosquito population, and keeps the pond free of weeds. These ponds serve multiple purposes, particularly in the dryer savanna and steppe areas; in addition to providing an important source of protein, they can improve the domestic and stock water supply, help the retention of a high water table, and reduce soil erosion. Some idea of their potentialities may be obtained from the record of a fish pond in West Africa: before provision of a dam, a pool measuring 240 yards long and 6 to 15 inches deep remained in the dry season in this small stream, from which 13.5 pounds of fish were obtained; the dam created a pool six feet deep from which 3,250 pounds of fish were obtained. Experiments continue in many areas to determine the best stocking practices, the value of fertilization, and other information, but it is safe to predict that these ponds will become integral parts of improved land use in many parts of the continent. In West Africa, Liberia now has 68 producing fish ponds, Upper Volta has 62, and numerous others have been provided in the Ivory Coast, Ghana, and Nigeria.

THE USE OF COASTAL MANGROVE SWAMPS

The mangrove forested areas of West Africa are normally very sparsely populated, and are used only to a minor degree for fuel or small construction timber or for production of tanning bark and extract. Sierra Leone has done the most to reclaim littoral swamps and now has about 163,000 acres in rice in tidal and riverain swamps. This type of production covers about a quarter of the total area in rice and accounts for about 39 percent of the country's output. Liberia has also had a swamp rice program, assisted by American aid and technicians. The mangrove trees are difficult to clear and, so far, most reclamation has been by hand, though mechanical means were employed on 16,000 acres in Sierra Leone. Attention should perhaps be given to adapting swamp buggies such as are used in petroleum exploration in the bayous of Louisiana to the large-scale clearing of swamp areas. A second problem is the necessity to construct bunds to keep out salt water and protect against tidal scour. There must then be an adequate flow of fresh water to flush out the salt and prevent a toxic accumulation on the empoldered land. Finally, production of wet rice tends to result in a greater incidence of bilharzia and malaria.

There are enormous potentialities for the extension of rice cultivation in coastal swamps. Sierra Leone, which, despite increased rice production, still finds it necessary to import large quantities, has possibly 500,000 acres which could be reclaimed. The Niger Delta presents an immense area and one which is close to regions of increasing deficit in food production. Advantages of these areas include the presence of some good to excellent soils which, being under water most of the time, are not subject to erosion, and the ability to obtain a considerably higher yield per acre from rice than from other major food crops. The FAO has recommended the extension of wet rice cultivation where possible because rice is almost universally acceptable, can be more readily prepared than many staple foods, is comparatively easy to store, and is nutritionally much superior to yams or cassava. An American expert studying the mangrove swamp area of the Niger Delta, however, recently concluded that large-scale reclamation was not now practicable because of an inadequate number of residents, difficult working conditions, and problems of weed growth, insects, birds, and poor soils.

THE COCONUT

The coconut is best adapted to coastal lands and in West Africa it is concentrated in various places along the margin of the sea. The Portuguese introduced the coconut to Dahomey in the sixteenth century and the Germans and French promoted its production in Togo and Dahomey in the present century. Production has declined in recent years, however, owing to failure to replace older trees. Output of coconut products is not large in any country and is absorbed primarily in local markets.

HUMID TROPICAL REGIONS

Extending inland from the coastal zone, which in part also has a humid tropical climate, is a belt of varying width including the remaining portions of the tropical rainy climate plus the wetter portions of the tropical savanna climate region of West Africa (see Map 3c). This belt accounts for a very large part of the vegetable exports of the area, particularly of the important tree crops such as cocoa, coffee, palm products, and rubber. The rainforests are also included in this zone, which was, presumably, originally covered with this type of vegetation.

EXPLOITATION OF THE TROPICAL RAINFORESTS

The extent of the rainforest in West Africa is inadequately mapped. Furthermore, much of the area depicted as forested is no longer so covered and from one third to two thirds of what is forested is in inferior, secondary growth. Some experts maintain, in fact, that the forest never completely recovers after it has been cropped. Factors that are working toward a reduction of the total area under forest are primarily the following: (1) the increasing population, forcing the use of a greater area for subsistence plots and adoption of a shorter regeneration period in the bush fallow system of agriculture; (2) the extension of commercial crop production; and (3) the damage caused by fire, particularly on the savanna margin. Burning the grasses of that zone causes fires to eat back into the forest area, creating channels for further damage in ensuing years. As a consequence, there is often a sharp line between the high tree zone and the high grasses, without the more gradual transition that would otherwise exist. The extension of both subsistence and commercial production has meant in more recent years that a great deal of "salvage" timber has been available, trees that are cut down to make room for agricultural use and which would be unused and destroyed if not very shortly removed. Their inclusion in forest production conveys an erroneous impression of the productivity of an area in so far as these areas are not concerned with the forest industry per se. Removal of the forest for farming has gone especially far in such regions as the Ibo and Yoruba country of Nigeria, the Eastern and Ashanti regions of Ghana, and the original forested area of Sierra Leone, of which only 5 percent still remains.

Stripping logs prior to shipment near Kumasi, Ghana
Removing the bark reduces the loss from insect attack.

Despite the diminishing extent of tropical rainforests, a very large area still is available for exploitation in West Africa. The FAO estimates that Africa has 17 percent of the total forest area of the world but only 9 percent of the world forest area in use, 7 percent of total forest removals, and 1.5 percent of world output of industrial woods. In West Africa, Liberia is estimated to be 37 percent covered by high forests with an estimated quantity of standing timber placed at 140 billion board feet. The Ivory Coast has an estimated 27,000 square miles in forest; Ghana has 32,000 square miles, of which 9,427 remain as potentially productive forests; and Nigeria has 139,000 square miles of forest, of which only about 14,000 square miles are in tropical rainforest.

Exploitation of West African forests has been

characterized in postwar years by the following:

(1) A great increase in production both for export and for local use. Very large but unmeasured quantities are used for fuel, and many areas have an urgent need for more fuelwood plantations, which are often difficult to introduce because of tenurial conditions. But the focus here is upon commercial production, where the rate of increase has been the highest of any vegetable product from the area. Liberia, which is really just starting with exploitation of its forests, has had a 250 percent increase in output of logs from 1956 to 1961; export of logs from the Ivory Coast increased tenfold from 1947 to 1957 and continued to grow rapidly in succeeding years; Ghana's timber exports increased in value almost a hundred fold from 1939 to 1957; and Nigeria's output of timber products increased one third from 1951 to 1961. Timber exports, however, account for a relatively small percentage of the total value of exports from most West African countries. Only the Ivory Coast, Ghana, and Nigeria have significant shipments; in 1961, timber exports ranked second to cocoa in Ghana, accounting for 14.7 percent of the total value of exports, third in the Ivory Coast with a 19.1 percent share of the total exports, and sixth in Nigeria at 4.6 percent of the total value of exports. Liberia should soon join this group since six timber concessions have been granted including a 500,000-acre holding 60 miles from Cape Palmas.

(2) The acceptance of a wider variety of species than before the war. Rainforests are characterized by a large number of species, it being not uncommon to find 100 species in a relatively small area. The total number of species is very great; some have probably not yet been recorded. For example, 225 species are known in the Ivory Coast and over 200 in Ghana. In prewar years mahogany accounted for over 90 percent of timber exports; its percentage has now dropped to below 20 and to 8 percent in Ghana. Today about 25 species are regularly marketed, of which ten are sold in substantial volumes. Most of these were practically unknown before the war. Not only are fine hardwoods exported, but there is an increasing sale of general purpose timbers. Most important in West Africa are obeche, abura, mahogany, and sapele. Obeche, also called arere and wawa, is the main export timber of Ghana (64.5 percent of the total in 1960) and Nigeria (over 50 percent). It is one of the largest trees in height and up to 5 feet in diameter. Having good natural regeneration, it is outstandingly light for a tropical hardwood, strong in relation to its weight, and very easy to work because of its comparative softness. African mahogany is probably the most widely used of the true mahoganies, as it is the cheapest and is obtainable in all sizes; sapele is also a true mahogany.

Storage and loading of logs at Abidjan, Ivory Coast
Brought to the port by truck, the logs are rolled and jacked into the lagoon, then taken alongside vessels for loading by the ships' gear.

(3) An increasing use of mechanization in cutting, hauling, and shipping. Logging is not easy in the tropical rainforest environment. Dense undergrowth often matted together by creepers, swampy terrain, the absence of waterways, the high cost of providing and maintaining roads or railways, and the highly selective cutting that market acceptance requires, all contribute to make tropical forestry generally high

cost as compared to its counterpart in middle and higher latitudes despite the low wages of labor and the great total volume available per acre. The buttresses, which many species have and which may rise to 10 or 15 feet on the trunk, make cutting more difficult. Most trees are still cut by axe, from stages that are nailed to the tree to permit cutting above the buttresses. Sawed into manageable lengths, the logs are hauled by caterpillar tractor and "logging arch" to the nearest road, rail, or river. This part of the operation was formerly carried on by large gangs of men who hauled the logs to loading or floating points. In Ghana and the Ivory Coast, most logs are moved overland to sawmills or to port. In Nigeria, most are rafted and towed by special 150 hp diesel-engine tugs. The average delivery time to Sapele has thus been reduced from about five weeks for simple floating to less than a week for towing. Very dense logs or "sinkers" were formerly attached to two "floaters"; they are now often lightered to plant or port. Transport savings are of great importance for this bulkiest of exports; even with postwar improvements in handling, transport takes 50 to 100 percent (depending upon the species) of the f.o.b. price in the Ivory Coast.

(4) An increased processing of timber products. A large part of exports is still in logs, the best logs usually being rafted or lightered alongside ships, though the giant hardwood logs may first be squared to remove most of the sapwood, thus reducing the danger of insect attack and permitting better stowage aboard ship. But an increasing percentage is exported as sawn lumber, plywood, and veneer (Map 49). In 1946, only 7 percent of timber exports from Ghana were sawn; in 1951, 35 percent were in this category, whose value was equal to that of logs. In Nigeria, no sawn wood was exported in prewar years; by 1961, 2.2 million cubic feet of sawn wood were being shipped as compared to 20.3 million cubic feet in logs, and the value of lumber exports was 22.7 percent that for logs. The Ivory Coast presents something of an exception; log exports increased 250 percent from 1956 to 1961 while sawn timber only increased 50 percent.

A sawmill in Ghana
While a substantial export of logs still takes place, the trend is toward shipment of lumber, plywood, and veneer.

The number of sawmills has greatly increased in postwar years, though some pit sawing still takes place, whereby one man standing above and one below the log laboriously saw it from end to end. Most of the sawmills are small and often cater primarily to the domestic market. Liberia has 12 mills, the Ivory Coast 35 with an annual capacity over 100,000 cubic meters, and there are dozens in Ghana and Nigeria. The largest mill is the United Africa Company plant at Sapele in the Western Region of Nigeria, which also produces plywood. Other large plants include the Public Works Department sawmill at Ijora, Lagos, the Omo Sawmills of Nigeria Ltd. near Ijebu-Ode, which was partially financed by CDC; the UAC mill and plywood plant at Samreboi, Ghana; and four of the Ivory Coast mills which handle half of the total sawn wood. After sawing, the lumber is air- or kiln-seasoned, tropical hardwoods usually being stacked for one or two years and then put in the kilns.

Production of plywood and veneer represents new phases of processing introduced since the war. The Sapele and Samreboi plants, plus factories in the Ivory Coast, are leading in this production. Ghana's exports of plywood and veneers were valued at $824,000 in 1961, Nigeria's at $3,329,200. While there is a strong incentive to produce such commodities close to the forests because of the large waste that need not be shipped, there are difficulties associated with their production in West Africa. The high temperatures and humidities require a more expensive glue between the plywood layers, which makes it more costly, while shipping of veneers is more difficult than the basic log as far as protection from damage and insect attack is concerned.

There are interesting potentialities for continued growth and evolution of the forest industries. The increased activity of postwar years reflects a rising demand and the application of improved technology has made forestry under tropical conditions more attractive. Considering the rate of cutting elsewhere and the new uses for forest products that are constantly being developed, demand should continue to increase despite the offsetting substitution of metal, plastic, ceramic, and other materials. As far as reserves are concerned, enormous opportunities remain. Liberia's reserve is adequate for 7,000 years at the 1962 rate of cutting with no allowance for regrowth; half of the Ivory Coast's forested area remains untapped; and large resources remain in western Ghana and Nigeria. It will not be possible, however, to continue the present rate of cutting of several species in the main producing areas. In the meantime, increasing attention will doubtless be given to establishing forest reserves, replanting, adoption of sustained yield practices, and pushing the acceptance of other species. In Ghana, 62 percent of the remaining productive forest area has been placed in a forest reserve where sustained and improved yield practices are required; in the Western Region of Nigeria, which has been the major producing zone, 35 percent of the area under exploitation has been similarly controlled, while plantings increased to 600,000 acres in 1962. A more intensive attack on insect pests would also save timber now wasted. The loss in West Africa attributed to the ambrosia beetle alone is estimated at 15 percent of the value of forest products. Methods of attack include spraying from the air, dipping, and incorporation of chemicals in the glue used in plywood manufacture. Establishment of plantations of selected woods is another possibility. It holds the advantages of preferred location with respect to transportation and of avoiding the high cost of selective logging; its main disadvantages are the higher cost of artificial planting and the increased danger of insect attack when one species is dominant in an area. The existence of programs to train forest workers and specialists in several West African countries augurs well for the accelerated adoption of improved practices.

A great advance would be achieved if it became practicable to exploit forests for the production of pulp. The characteristically shorter fibers and the hardness of tropical woods militates against such use, but a pilot plant near Abidjan did show that it is possible to produce pulp and paper from mixed tropical woods. This plant, which was too small for optimum operations, has been closed down, but the ability to produce pulp economically in large-scale plants situated where power is cheap may not be too far distant. Perfection of such a process would permit great savings through the rationalization of forest operations. An area of appropriate size to permit natural regeneration could be cut over, the better logs being used for lumber, plywood, and veneer, the other logs for pulping. The forest industry will also benefit from improved transport, including the laying of roads and rail lines not intended primarily for that industry, such as the new mineral lines in Liberia and Guinea. Finally, the industry in the Ivory Coast should benefit from freer access to the EEC, while reduction of U.S. tariffs, which are particularly high for plywood, would expand potential markets.

AGRICULTURE OF THE HUMID TROPICAL REGIONS

Agriculture, including the production of tree crops, is the main activity of the bulk of the inhabitants of West Africa and especially of humid tropical areas. But it does not occupy a high percentage of the area except in the more densely populated regions.

SHIFTING AGRICULTURE. The basic agricultural system was originally a self-sufficient bush fallow on small farms with a great variety of crops often grown on the same patch and with a considerable interest in tree crops. Planted crops included corn, yams, cassava, vegetables, and pineapple. Tree crops which were used for food were palm oil, coconuts, bananas, and citrus fruit. For the annual crops, openings were laboriously cleared in the forests and planted. Care had to be taken to assure a continuous supply of food because storage was extremely difficult. After from two to five years the soil would be exhausted, forcing the clearing of new patches and permitting the abandoned plot to revert to bush.

The explanation for this shifting agriculture is the poverty of the regional latosolic soil. While it supports the world's most vigorous vegetation growth—the tropical rainforest—continuing to mislead uninformed observers regarding its fertility, it is actually one of the world's poorest soil types. This seeming contradiction is readily explained by the different character of forest and cultivated vegetation. Under forest, the cycle of decay maintains an adequate supply of humus to support rapid growth, while tree roots extend sufficiently far below the surface to secure the necessary minerals. Cut the forest down and replace it with annual plants, however, and this cycle is destroyed. Shallow roots cannot supply minerals from below, the available humus is rapidly used up, exposure to the sun and rain speeds up decomposition and increases leaching. Yields drop off rapidly, usually making it desirable to abandon the plot in less than five years. This process is one of the most fundamental factors limiting African agricultural production.

Under present conditions, a number of changes have been made in the basic pattern of shifting agriculture resulting from the superimposing of a money economy on a primarily subsistence agriculture and from an expanding population. Production of some commercial crops has developed monocultural tendencies resulting in soil depletion if not in its actual erosion. Overemphasis on commercial crops has sometimes led to a narrower range of food production, again leading to accelerated depletion and, incidentally, to a lowered dietal standard. Expanding populations have forced a lengthening of the growing period and a reduction of the bush fallow period. In Sierra Leone, for example, the average fallow period has been reduced from seven to four years.

It is generally accepted that shifting agriculture is poor agriculture, even with a full fallow and despite the fact that it displays a reasonably good adaptation to the physical environment. In addition to its physical disadvantages, it also requires so much labor in relation to what is produced that it almost precludes the high productivity that would be required to raise living standards beyond a certain level. Yet no really effective alternative has been discovered, so the proper utilization of tropical latosols continues to be a prime problem for Africa.

Research institutions and experimental farms are devoting increasing attention to this problem, but to date only palliatives have been developed. These practices include:

(1) Green manuring, which involves the turning under of a leguminous crop. This is beneficial, but not adequate, and it is often unpopular because the indigenous farmer cannot see the value of planting a nonproductive crop.

(2) Composting, which is often better, but which is seldom practiced.

(3) The use of legumes, which is not as beneficial as in the middle latitudes since local legumes do not have the nitrogen-fixing power of middle latitude legumes.

(4) Litter farming or the planting of cover crops to reduce leaching and direct exposure to the sun.

(5) Termite farming.

(6) Application of inorganic fertilizers, which is increasing, particularly on commercial operations, but which is usually too expensive to permit adoption by peasant cultivators. Relatively

little is yet known regarding the effect of various chemical fertilizers, but the rapid leaching in tropical rainy areas does require heavier doses than would be required in the middle latitude. It is believed, however, that they may prove to be more effective than organic manures, but fertilizers alone cannot maintain soil productivity.

(7) Application of organic fertilizers. Rapid oxidation and leaching reduce the value of organic applications, but it is the inability to keep cattle, other than dwarf species such as the N'Dama and West African Shorthorn, in the humid tropics that prevents the development of a mixed agriculture comparable to that of the middle latitudes. Use of animal manures has permitted continuous cultivation on home gardens.

(8) Copying the natural pattern as closely as possible. This involves a concentration on tree crops, among which the oil palm is least demanding on the soil.

(9) Coppicing, which is an adaptation of bush fallowing. A rosaceous bush is employed which is cut back when planting takes place and permitted to grow again in the fallow period. Its deep roots secure minerals, while it is easier to cut than large trees and has the additional advantage of checking gullying in badly eroded country. Coppicing is now practiced in some densely populated parts of Iboland.

In addition to the basically physical problem of farming tropical soils, a host of human problems beset West African agriculture including ignorance and apathy, the scattered nature and small size of holdings farmed, problems associated with tenurial arrangements and common ownership of land, excessive reliance on female labor, and market difficulties. Results of a pilot agricultural survey conducted in the Ivory Coast in 1959–60 provide an interesting quantitative measure of many of these problems (Table 15).

Table 15. Results of a pilot agricultural survey in Ivory Coast, 1959–1960

	Savanna region	*Southwest forest*	*Southeast forest*
Percentage employing paid labor	20	30	57
Percentage employing fertilizer			3
Percentage employing insecticides		6	19
Percentage not knowing about fertilizer	19	36	20
Percentage not knowing about insecticides	13	20	5
Number of parcels by tenant	1.4	1.4	1.6
Size of parcels by percent of total			
.01–.49 hectare (1 ha. = 2.47 acres)	52	32	41
.5–.99 hectare	23	26	28
1.0–1.99 hectares	17	28	19
2.0–4.99 hectares	7	13	10
5.0 and over hectares	1	1	2
Percent of parcels far from village	41	49	41

Source: *Resultats de l'Enquete Agricole par Sondage* (*Côte d'Ivoire 1959–60*), *Supplement Trimestriel au Bulletin Mensuel de Statistique* (2d year, 4th quarter, 1960).

COMMERCIAL CROP PRODUCTION

The vast bulk of crops produced for sale in West Africa comes from African small holdings, probably less than 5 percent being produced on plantations and estates. The area ranks as one of the most important in the world in commercial tropical tree crop production, particularly in cocoa and palm products. The three outstanding crops of the humid regions are these two, plus coffee.

OIL PALM. The oil palm, native to West Africa, is found in a belt varying from a few miles to 150 miles in width from eastern Nigeria

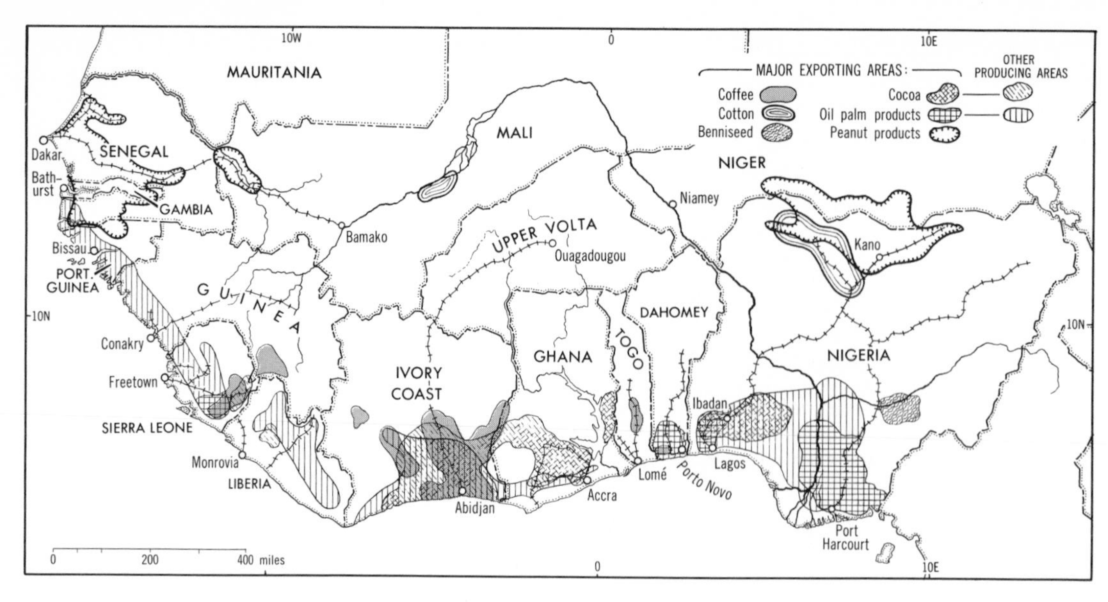

Map 42. Producing areas of major commercial crops in West Africa

to Ghana and in a less concentrated belt from Ghana to Guinea (Map 42). The oil palm finds its ideal habitat in a belt 5 degrees each side of the equator, with heavy precipitation, no marked dry season, and average high temperatures and humidity. Selected trees grown on plantations yield in the fourth year, reach a productive peak at about the tenth year, and are normally replaced at age 30 to 35. The wild palm takes about 10 to 12 years before bearing fruit and yields much less than plantation trees. Oil is secured both from the outer fruit and from the palm kernel. The two major uses of palm oil are in soap and in edible oils and fats.

The fruit of the oil palm
Nigeria accounts for about 30 percent of the world's palm oil exports and over 50 percent of its palm kernel exports.

The leading producing areas in West Africa are in Nigeria: the so-called Oil Rivers District of the Eastern Region, where palm production often amounts to a monoculture, and the Western Region. The Eastern Region exports most of the palm oil of Nigeria, which accounts for about 30 percent of the world's palm oil exports; the Western Region sells mainly kernels, of which Nigeria exports over 50 percent of the world total. Plantations produce only about 7 percent of the total, but their share may be expected to increase as newer plantings reach bearing age.

Dahomey is the leading producer among the former French West African countries; indeed palm products are the fundamental richness of the country and account for over half of the total value of that country's exports. Efforts to arrest a general decline in palm oil exports and stagnating shipments of palm kernels have included provision of seedlings to permit rejuvenation of older areas and increasing the number of plantations, especially in the Adjohon Region.

Production is relatively small in Togo, Ghana, and the Ivory Coast where higher value cocoa and coffee greatly reduced the interest in palm products. Liberia exported about $1.13 million of palm products in 1961 but production has continued to decline despite introduction of hand presses, mills, and some plantation output.

Palm kernels have been the main export crop of Sierra Leone for over 60 years, and were long the main export of any kind. The harvest is not very efficient and exports have declined since 1951 despite efforts to rationalize production. Explanations for this include a switch to alternative crops in some regions, the disrupting influences of the diamond rush, and failure of farmers to participate in the government's expansion program. Inadequate attention has led to heavy losses of new seedlings of higher yielding trees, of which as many as 100,000 have been issued yearly; many farmers consider the wild palm as a gift of God which need not be tended or cultivated and hence show little interest in planting new trees. The government also introduced nine pioneer oil mills, comparable to those successfully set up in Nigeria, but thus far only one has operated at a profit and that because it was associated with a 2,000-acre government plantation at Masanki. Similarly, efforts to encourage farmers to establish small plantations have failed, while foreign capital has not been forthcoming upon invitation to organize larger oil palm plantations. In Guinea, palm produce has accounted for about 4 to 6 percent of exports in recent years.

Local factors other than the physical environment which influence the production pattern and the sales of palm produce include the following:

(1) The use of palm oil for food. Palm oil is an important subsistence crop, as much as 100 pounds per person per year being consumed in some areas. The kernel, being too hard to crack without a machine, is almost always exported. As a result, the local demand for oil may confine exports to kernels.

(2) Competition from other crops. Cocoa, for example, is a favored crop in Yoruba country, in Ghana, and in the Ivory Coast; coffee is preferred in the Ivory Coast and parts of Sierra Leone and Guinea.

(3) Bulkiness of the crop tends to concentrate production where transport is readily available. Exports are more important from the coastal side of the oil palm belt and come from interior points only when a river, road, or railway provides superior conditions. There have been considerable improvements in postwar years in the handling of palm products, including the use of bulking stations, tank trucks, and pipelines for loading palm oil in the tank holds of vessels equipped for this trade.

(4) Quality improvement has aided some areas more than others. The introduction of Pioneer Mills, hand presses, and the use of incentive payments resulted in sensational increases in the percentage of Nigerian oil qualifying as top grade. In 1950, only 0.2 percent of palm oil was Special Grade; in 1958 and 1962, the percentage was 77. Pioneer Mills can extract 85 percent of the oil content of the fruit as compared to 60–65 percent for hand presses and only 45–60 percent by traditional techniques. Speed in delivery of the fruit is important in retaining a low free fatty-acid content.

(5) Some governments have had active programs to expand production, while others have not. Ghana and the Ivory Coast are interested in reviving palm production as one way of broadening exports. The lack of success of Liberian and Sierra Leone efforts has been noted. Nigeria, however, has the most intensive program, involving the subsidized sale of seedlings, informational programs regarding the preferred practices of production, continued distribution of mechanical presses, promotion of the use of potash to increase yields, and the organization of regional plantations with a total area of 52,000 acres, of which 33,000 acres had been planted by 1962.

In the early 1920s almost all of the palm products entering world trade came from their native West Africa. The oil palm was introduced to Malaya and Indonesia on a plantation basis and by 1939 Asia was producing about 40 percent of the world supply. Plantation methods resulted in higher yields, a higher extraction rate, and a better grade oil. Yields on southeast Asian plantations were as much as twenty times those from West African small holdings. The Belgian Congo also became a strong competitor, most of its oil coming from large plantations. Despite strong presentations from commercial operators, the British refused to permit the introduction of plantations in West Africa, a decision which explains the concentration of United Africa Company oil palm plantations in the Congo, operated by the subsidiary Huileries du Congo Belge. With the interruption of World War II and continued postwar difficulties in Asia, Africa partially regained some of the palm product sales previously lost. In the meantime, improvements in the quality of peasant production made it more competitive, thus helping to sustain the importance of Nigeria in total production. The advantages of the plantation system (see pp. 321–322 for discussion) have led Nigeria and Ghana, in particular, to experiment with cooperative and partnership plantations, which may be of increasing importance in the years ahead, or may lead to modifications in the traditional small-holder practices.

A cocoa tree with mature pods
Because cocoa trees are usually grown under the shade of partially cleared forests and in untilled land, the appearance of a "cocoa farm" bears little resemblance to the usual concept of a farm.

Palm oil is only one of many sources of vegetable oil. Butter, lard, and whale oil among animal products, peanuts, coconuts, benniseed, cotton seed, shea nuts among vegetable products, and synthetic detergents made from petroleum are all competitors for one or another end use of palm and kernel oil. This makes for an immensely complex competitive position and means that market limitations are the main factor restricting expansion. But the oil palm gives the highest yields per acre of any oil-bearing plant and the consumption of edible oils has been increasing with sufficient rapidity to offset losses to detergents in the manufacture of soap. A rapidly increasing world population also presages increased consumption of vegetable oils, which have not yet suffered from the excess production characteristic of many tropical products.

COCOA. By common usage the plant cacao and its product the cacao bean have become cocoa in African terminology. Cocoa is produced in the tropical rainforests and the transition zone to the savanna. Its needs for well-drained soil keep it away from low-lying coastal lands. A short dry period is desirable to permit harvesting, and drying in the sun is aided by the winter monsoon wind or harmattan. Other requirements are protection from winds, considerable shade, and high temperature. Production is greatly affected from year to year by weather conditions.

Today, Africa accounts for over 70 percent of total world cocoa production, West Africa for over 60 percent of global output. But cocoa was not introduced to the mainland until 1879 when it was brought from Fernando Po to what is now Ghana. The first exports of that country were in 1896, when 100 tons were shipped; tonnages increased thereafter from 1,000 in 1901 to 40,000 in 1911, 118,200 in 1921, 226,600 in 1931, and to a prewar record of 311,151 tons in 1936. It was not until 1959 that this figure was surpassed and in 1961 a new record of 435,000 tons was set. Cocoa is the cash crop par excellence in Ghana, the chief source of the comparative wealth of that country, and Ghana in turn accounts for 30 to 36 percent of total world production. Nearly 40 percent of the population is said to be directly dependent on cocoa and exports usually account for three fifths to two thirds of the total value of exports. Within the country the center of production has been shifting from the Eastern Region to the Ashanti and Western regions owing to losses from disease in the older areas and opening of virgin lands to the west; Trans-Volta Togoland Region also has an important production.

An estimated 3.95 million acres are now in cocoa in Ghana, but a "cocoa farm" bears little resemblance to the concept of a farm in the middle latitudes. Trees are often more or less haphazardly placed under natural shade trees, and underbrush may contribute to the general appearance of a woodland landscape. There are many types and sizes of cocoa farms: in the oldest areas a farmer may have one or more cocoa holdings varying from about ½ to 3 acres in size while his wives may have smaller holdings of their own; in the formerly uninhabited forest of southern Ghana farms were opened by strangers; elsewhere, groups or companies of farmers developed cocoa farms, some of very considerable extent. Laborers from the north of Ghana and from Upper Volta are nearly equal to the farmers themselves in its production; they may operate on a sharecrop basis, as annual, contract, or daily workers. While they are perhaps fortunate to share in the wealth of this crop they also reflect the desire of owners to avoid work themselves and often to reside away from their farm holdings.

Cocoa is also the leading crop of the Western Region of Nigeria and ranks as the second or third export of that country. Of the approximately one million acres in cocoa in Nigeria, 98 percent are in the Western Region, with the heaviest concentration in Oyo and Ondo districts. Cocoa was for years the leading export of the Ivory Coast but has been surpassed by coffee in recent years. At present, about 662,000 acres are planted to cocoa and an early postwar trend toward stagnation appears to have been overcome with the planting of new stock, the improvement of quality (only 2.7 percent of output sold as top grade in 1955 as compared to 84 percent in 1961), and a substantial increase in production. Other countries of West Africa are minor producers.

Cocoa in West Africa presents an excellent example of the ever-present danger of serious losses from pests and diseases which characterizes the production of crops in tropical areas much more than in areas where winter cold results in at least a seasonal halt to their attack. The more concentrated production becomes, the more likely it is that disease will strike.

Swollen shoot has been the most serious of cocoa diseases, threatening for a time to wipe out the industry in Ghana. A virus disease carried by the mealy bug, it gradually kills the tree and spreads rapidly from tree to tree. Despite much research, no solution was found to swollen shoot disease other than to cut out and destroy the diseased trees and to replant with disease-resistant species. As the tree continues to yield for some years following attack, cocoa farmers were bitterly opposed to compulsory cutting programs initiated by the government, despite partial compensation and provision of superior stock for replanting. The whole program became enmeshed in politics and was one of the factors causing strained relations between the British colonial officials and Gold Coast politicians in the years preceding independence. Nkrumah gained support by promising that there would be no compulsory cutting, but following independence in 1957, after it became apparent that a voluntary program would not work, he too adopted a compulsory program. By 1961, no less than one hundred million trees had been cut out; in 1961, 3.57 million trees were cut, mostly in the Eastern Region.

The Cocoa Research Institute at Tafo, while unsuccessful in finding an antidote to swollen shoot disease, did show the way to increased production of cocoa. It was found that seedlings brought from the Amazon were resistant to swollen shoot; these have been propagated and improved so that it is now possible to replant with stock which yields in four instead of seven years, is disease resistant, and gives a higher yield per tree. In Ghana, the distribution of Amazon pods increased from 64,000 in 1955 to a peak of 2.39 million in 1959, and was about 1.3 million in 1961. The distribution of seedlings is subsidized; in Nigeria they are sold at one quarter of cost. Governments have also promoted the adoption of better methods which farmers are gradually accepting in caring for the cocoa tree. It is believed that farmers could treble yields with proper methods, instead of practicing what sometimes amounts to little more than a gather economy. Recently, initial experiments in injecting swollen shoot virus into young seedlings to provide immunity to that disease have shown some success.

Spraying against the capsid bug on a cocoa farm in Ghana Losses from insect and disease attack have been enormous in postwar years. In Ghana alone, over a hundred million trees were cut out in an effort to prevent the spread of "swollen shoot." The capsid bug causes a second major disease which has resulted in heavy losses in some recent years.

A second serious disease is caused by the capsid bug and has resulted in the loss of as much as a quarter of the Ghanaian crop in some recent years. An insecticide which destroys the capsid has been perfected and the Ghana and Nigerian governments have instituted large-scale programs to combat that insect. In Ghana, mature cocoa is sprayed with Gamalin 20 at government expense, about 700,000 acres being covered twice a year. In addition, the insecticide and 20,000 hand sprayers have been sold to farmers at subsidized prices to spray young cocoa trees. After the record yield of 1961, however, there was a slackening in the capsid campaign, and there is evidence that the bug is gaining resistance to Gamalin. Fungicides have been developed to cope with a third enemy of the cocoa tree, blackpod disease.

The high dependence of Ghana and southwest Nigeria on cocoa is a good example of the "one crop" character of many African economies, already seen in the concentration of Egypt and the Sudan on cotton. Such dependence contains both physical and economic dangers. From the physical standpoint, it is likely to deplete the soil and lead to soil erosion, and plant disease is more likely to occur and to be more damaging when it does occur. From the economic standpoint, the economy of the country is subject to erratic world markets as to both volume and price, markets over which it has very little, if any, control. The price fluctuations for cocoa have been very great in the past decade, having ranged from $420 to $1,568 per ton, while in the first three months of 1963 the range was from $456 to $574 per ton.

The supply of cocoa is relatively inelastic, as new plantings cannot affect the market for from four to seven years, while supply from any given area may be seriously affected by noneconomic factors such as weather and disease. Demand for cocoa is more elastic, as high prices will cause confectioners to turn to substitutes, reduce the amount of cocoa in a candy bar, or reduce the size of the bar. Low prices will not only reduce the producer's income, unless there is some cushioning arrangement, but will greatly affect government revenues, which are likely to be highly dependent on export taxes and on duties on imports which will automatically be curtailed. During the depression of the 1930s, for example, revenue in the Gold Coast was reduced one third and it was necessary to cut back European personnel from 1,200 to 400 officers. More recently, receipts have been cut by amounts which have been greater than the total of foreign aid to some countries. Evils of a "one crop" economy are not confined entirely to periods of low sales and prices; high prices may result in an overemphasis on the cash crop to the detriment of the local food supply and may introduce inflationary conditions which curtail development. And conspicuous consumption is favored by the lack of tradition for saving that is likely in an underdeveloped community.

All African countries are now cognizant of the dangers of a "one crop" economy and most have adopted measures to alleviate them. Four main avenues have been taken: (1) diversification of the economy, hence the emphasis on introduction of new crops, on development of mining and industry; (2) promoting a better balance between domestic and export production; (3) attempting to emphasize quality production so that the individual country will not be as seriously affected as its competitors in the event of reduced markets; and (4) the establishment of marketing boards to even out receipts of the producers.

Many if not most African countries have adopted some kind of marketing arrangement in postwar years designed to sustain the income level of peasant farmers at a fairly constant level. In Commonwealth West Africa the major staples come under statutory marketing boards which usually announce a fixed minimum price before the buying season. The former French countries have adopted somewhat similar measures, but have more frequently depended upon subsidized prices and guaranteed markets in France.

There is difference of opinion regarding the suitability and economic justification for marketing boards. Those opposed to them claim that the lower price paid to the farmer reduces his incentive to expand and improve production, since he does not receive the full benefit of his labors; that the indigenous producer does not understand the arrangements, which leads to resentment and even to political difficulties; that they tend toward maintenance of the status quo regardless of dynamic world conditions; that they can lead to an incorrect crop emphasis in that the farmer might get more for an unstabilized crop though the country would be disadvantaged by such a shift; and that marketing boards, having control over a large supply, are tempted to manipulate the world prices.

Those favoring marketing boards maintain that they assure a more steady income to the farmer through provision of reserve funds which are used to subsidize payments to farmers in low price periods; prevent inflation; tend to smooth fluctuations in production; permit sale of the crop by experts who can take advantage of market opportunities not known or understood by the individual producer; reduce the costs of marketing the crop through middlemen; and create funds which may be used in a variety of ways for the benefit of the producer and the country and which could not be provided by direct taxes.

The funds accumulated by West African marketing boards were very substantial during many postwar years, as prices paid to producers were usually well below market prices. In 1960, for example, the Ghana cocoa farmer was receiving $336 per ton while the market price was $616. Funds accumulated by the boards became so large that governments were tempted to extract substantial sums for various purposes other than creating a stabilization fund. The original purpose of the boards thus became more and more obscured and the fixed price to the producer soon represented more of a tax than an insurance against bad years. Accumulated funds have been used in three main ways:

(1) For research on problems of crop disease, plant selection, and improved methods pertaining to the crop involved. In the decade of the 1950s, for example, the Ghana Cocoa Marketing Board provided $40.6 million to combat swollen shoot and capsid diseases. The marked quality improvements characterizing staple production in West Africa have also been stimulated by incentive payments provided by

A small coffee plantation near Abidjan, Ivory Coast
The Ivory Coast vies with Angola among African coffee producers and ranks second or third in the world in tonnage exports of coffee.

the boards. The notable increase in percentage of Special Grade palm oil in Nigeria has already been noted. Similarly, Special Grade peanuts in the Kano area increased from 22 percent in 1955–56 to 97.7 percent in 1957–58, and after 1959–60 only Special Grade peanuts have been purchased. Grade I cocoa in Nigeria increased from 23 percent of the total in 1947 to the present level of 99 percent, and top-grade cocoa in the Ivory Coast grew from 2 percent in 1955 to 84 percent in 1961.

(2) For general development and assistance in the producing regions. Roads, schools, and hospitals have been constructed; diversification of crops has been assisted; and scholarships have been provided for residents of the areas involved. In Ghana, for example, the Marketing Board is providing 280 scholarships for use within Ghana and 400 for study in overseas institutions.

(3) For support of regional and national government budgets. Marketing boards have provided a substantial part of the funds expended by the several development corporations in Nigeria and they are now required to set aside 22.5 percent of their net trading profits for these corporations in each region. In 1961–62 Ghana introduced a new method of acquiring funds through the Ghana Agricultural Produce Marketing Board, successor to the Cocoa Marketing Board, whereby about one tenth of the price paid to producers is in the form of 10-year National Development Bonds.

The increasing surplus in world cocoa production in recent years, amounting to about 100,000 tons in 1959–60 and 200,000 tons in 1960–61, has led to efforts to conclude some kind of international control scheme. Twenty-one major producers held meetings in 1962 and 1963 and asked the U.N. to assist them in drawing up an agreement comparable to that achieved for coffee. While the urge to secure some degree of stability in world prices for tropical staples is very great, the complexities of international commodity agreements are enormous and the efficacy of past agricultural schemes has not been very encouraging.

COFFEE. Coffee grows wild in the forest area of West Africa up to about 8° N, but exported coffee comes from small farms and a few plantations. Most coffee produced is robusta, which is more suitable to lower tropical areas than the higher value arabica, which is the main type grown at higher elevations in Africa. Africa has assumed much greater significance as a coffee producer in postwar years. In 1934–38 it accounted for about 5.1 percent of world production; by 1953 the percentage had increased to 12.8 and it was 17.3 in 1961–62. Africa's share of exportable coffee is now about one quarter of the world total. Coffee is now the leading export by value in seven African countries and a major export from eight additional countries. Imports of African coffee to the United States, which is the world's largest consumer, have increased from less than 2 percent of the total in 1949 to 11 percent in 1955 and 22 percent in 1962. Two factors have been of particular importance in permitting this marked increase: the lower price of African robustas than of Latin American coffees, and the increased use of solubles, for which robustas are as good or better than higher priced coffees.

Ivory Coast is by far the leading coffee producer in West Africa; it vies with Angola for first place among African producers and for third place in world output. Coffee was introduced to the Ivory Coast in 1880 but saw its first important expansion in 1926; today, coffee occupies about 1,262,000 acres and accounts for about 46 percent of the total value of exports. Production is in the hands of African small holders with the exception of about 16,000 acres in European estates. While the marked increase in production in recent years has shown commendable vigor, yields are still quite low, being only a third those of Congo; there is a need to rejuvenate old plantings and to mount a more intensive campaign against plant pests. There has been a marked improvement in quality in recent years, prima and superior grades having accounted for 79 percent of production in 1961 as compared to 18 percent in 1959. A problem which is common to other former French areas is the necessity to work away from the heavily subsidized prices obtained in the French market; the 1960 prices were, for example, about 64 percent above prevailing world prices and that portion of coffee sold by Togo to the United States received a lower price than was paid to the producer.

Other West African producers include Guinea, which doubled production from 1955 to 1962; Togo, which trebled output in the past decade, and where coffee now ranks as the leading export; Sierra Leone, where a dramatic increase occurred after 1953; Ghana, which has increased production from 518 tons in 1958 to 3,446 tons in 1961 as part of its effort to diversify production; and, on a quite minor scale, Dahomey and Liberia.

During most of the 1950s, coffee appeared to be a white hope for Africa, but increasing world surpluses have reduced prices and restricted possibilities for further extension. Concerned about this problem, ten countries organized the Interafrican Coffee Organization in 1960 and thirteen joined the rather elaborate 1962 International Coffee Agreement. Africa's quota under this agreement is to be 12.92 million bags of 60 kg. each, a figure slightly below the exportable production of 1960–61 and 1962–63. Just how effective this scheme will be remains to be seen, but the existence of a surplus equivalent to about one and a half years' world consumption gives reason for participating powers to restrain exports. Furthermore, all signs point to a continuing surplus for some years. This situation means that no dynamic increase such as typified the scene in earlier postwar years may be expected; the agreement should, however, provide somewhat greater stability in the prices received.

SECONDARY COMMERCIAL CROPS

Palm oil, cocoa, and coffee are the big three among commercial vegetable crops coming from the humid tropical areas of West Africa. Two crops, bananas and rubber, may be considered in a second range, and a long list of lesser crops have tertiary importance.

BANANAS. The plantain or cooking banana is grown over a large part of West Africa for subsistence purposes though it nowhere assumes the importance that it does in parts of East Africa. Bananas produced for export include the dwarf or finger banana and the Gros Michel. The needs for strict quality control, for a well-coordinated delivery to port, and for special handling facilities have tended to restrict the areas of production and to give European estates a major share in output. Excepting British Cameroons, which is now a

Bananas being grown under partial irrigation near Kindia, Guinea

Almost all bananas exported from West Africa are produced on plantations and estates rather than on indigenous farms.

part of the equatorial African region, the main West African producer in prewar years was French Guinea, which had almost doubled exports by 1958. Guinea bananas come mostly from small European plantations about 60 miles inland from Conakry in the Kindia district and from around Mamou, being grown under a system of partial irrigation. Following independence, production dropped sharply because of the exodus of French managers and the lack of knowledge of African producers. The creation of two state-owned plantations has not saved the situation, but about 100 French managers remain in the area on a somewhat precarious basis and bananas still rank as the main agricultural export of the country.

The Ivory Coast has inherited much of the interest focused upon Guinea and now ranks second only to the Canary Islands among African producers. Its 1961 exports were almost eight times the prewar level and over three times those of 1951–55, and Cobafruit, the banana producers' association, expects to increase exports by 50 percent between 1961 and 1965. About 140 European plantations, concentrated relatively close to Abidjan, cover about 112,000 acres and account for the bulk of production, but about 1,600 African small holders are also engaged in the commercial production of bananas.

Lesser amounts come from several countries. Liberia had hoped to become a large-scale producer with the opening of the African Fruit Company of Hamburg plantations in Sinoe County, but most of the early plantings were lost to Panama disease and the company has turned to other crops. Ghana has increased its exports from an average of 9,000 stems in 1951–55 to 211,000 in 1961.

RUBBER. Stimulated by uncertainties regarding supplies from the Far East, especially as a result of nationalization of Indonesian plantations, and by a continuing increase in the world consumption of rubber, various African countries have been promoting the production of rubber with some intensity in postwar years. The African share of natural rubber supplies has increased from 1.3 percent in 1938 to 2.7 percent in 1948 and 6.6 percent in 1961. Four countries account for the bulk of output, Nigeria, Cameroon, Liberia, and Congo, but several other countries have acreages in rubber which were not yet yielding in 1961.

The Firestone Plantations Company has played a notable part in the history of Liberia, having been the largest employer, exporter, and trainer of skills in the country. The company's decision to produce natural rubber in Liberia resulted largely from a desire to escape the Stevenson Plan of 1922–28, which regulated rubber exports from British producing areas with the aim of sustaining world prices. After

Tappers in the Firestone rubber plantation at Harbel in Liberia
About 80,000 acres are planted to rubber in this estate, which employs over 20,000 Liberians. Until iron ore developments were started, rubber from the Firestone plantations accounted for the vast bulk of Liberian exports.

some difficulties, Firestone secured in late 1926 a 99-year concession on one million acres. During the period of negotiation, Liberia was in a precarious financial state, and Liberia's interest in Firestone resulted from its belief that a large investment would help in securing the financial assistance so desperately needed and would strengthen the United States resolution to protect Liberian independence. Firestone's payments were first an annual rental fee of 6 cents an acre plus a 1 percent tax on the gross value of its exports, but these were replaced by an income tax in 1950 which has since been paid at the maximum rate of 25 percent. Despite numerous difficulties, some 72,500 acres had been planted by 1940, 54 percent of which were yielding. The importance of Firestone Plantations increased enormously during the war and production, with some emergency overtapping, reached 20,000 tons in 1945. A major planting program was again undertaken in 1950 and a regular replanting with higher-yielding stock began in 1954. Today, about 90,000 acres are under rubber in the two Firestone plantations, about nine tenths at Harbel and one tenth at Cavalla.

The Harbel plantation is said to be the finest and most modern rubber plantation in the world, yields being the highest in the world. About 20,400 Liberians, including 3,000 classed as skilled or semiskilled workers, are employed on the plantation and in its associated factories, including the world's largest latex processing plant, a hydroelectric installation, a sawmill, a brick and tile factory, and a small workshop making latex cups, soap, and rubber sandals. Before the development of iron mining, Firestone was responsible for as much as 85 percent of total Liberian exports and 39 percent of government revenues.

B. F. Goodrich has invested about $8 million in a 58,000-acre rubber plantation north of Monrovia which began yielding in 1963. The six rubber concessions now existing in the country are expected to increase Liberia's production of rubber by more than 35 percent in the decade to 1972.

Firestone has encouraged the production of rubber by Liberian nationals by providing seedlings and technical advice free of charge and by extending credit against future sales. Until 1962 it purchased all of the rubber independently produced; four concessionaires are now prepared to handle this function, but Firestone has spent $1 million to expand processing facilities to accept the increasing flow from private farms. The number of independent producing farms has grown from 150 in 1941 to 777 in 1951 and 2,705 in 1961; they now cover about 51,200 acres and employ a labor force of about 10,400. Few have expert managers and yields are rarely as high as half the average Firestone yield. There is great disparity in the size and earnings of individual farms; in 1960 0.1 percent of farms accounted for 21.9 percent of gross sales from independent farms, 15.0 percent for 85 percent, and 79.0 percent of the farms at the other extreme for only 11.2 percent of gross sales. Small farms have been plagued with a shortage of labor in recent years, resulting in a considerable acreage going untapped. Most independent farms are relatively near the Firestone plantations, but the country's new roads have also attracted many of the more recent holdings. It is relatively easy to enter rubber production; land costs 50¢ an acre, rubber stumps can be obtained at little or no cost, and wage rate tappers receive about 50¢ a day or less. Maintenance costs in the six to eight years prior to maturity are estimated at $5 per acre per year. In 1960, independent farms accounted for about 14.5 percent of total Liberian rubber production.

In Nigeria there are several European-owned estates in the Delta area and native small holdings in the Sapele-Warri-Benin area. Yields on the African holdings have been low and grade of production inferior, but the government hopes to improve conditions through a replanting program and establishment of modern processing plants at Benin, Araromi, and Umutu. From 1960, about 2.5 million seedlings yearly have been made available to replace old trees and extend rubber production. The most dynamic program, however, has been the promotion of partnership estates in both the Eastern and Western regions. The Regional Development Corporations, the CDC, and several private companies have invested in these plantations. By 1961, 47,127 acres of a total of 75,846 acres available had been planted to rubber, with slightly more than half being in the Western Region. Rubber exports from Nigeria (including Southern Cameroon) increased from 8,100 tons in 1948 to 55,700 tons in 1961, and, since much acreage has not reached tapping age, a continued growth may be expected. By 1970, in fact, rubber may be one of the major exports of that country.

Other West African states have lesser but growing interests in rubber. By the end of 1962, about 25,000 acres had been planted in the Ivory Coast in two large plantations, one west of Ono and the other in Dabou, while a 600-acre experimental station has been established at Bimbresso. Exports are expected to reach 3,500 tons by 1965 and 10,000 to 12,000 tons by 1970.

Ghana has a 2,500-acre joint Danish-Ghanaian estate starting production in 1963, a 1,400-acre estate at Prestea owned by the Agricultural Development Corporation, plus a number of small holdings. The government attempts to stimulate the last by offering farmers a 6-year subsidy on the first 500 acres planted. It has also selected four areas in the Western Region for cooperative rubber plantations. A research station has been set up at Ainyinase, 75 miles west of Takoradi.

The greatest deterrent to increasing rubber plantings is the fear of intensifying competition from synthetic rubbers. The new polydiene synthetics are said to be equal in quality to natural rubber and large-scale expansion of artificial rubber production is planned in the United States and elsewhere. To date, increased consumption of rubber has provided a market both for enlarged synthetic and natural rubber output; just what share of the market each of these will hold in another decade is difficult to predict.

COMMERCIAL CROPS OF LESS IMPORTANCE

A number of lesser commercial crops are produced in the humid tropical regions of West Africa. They will receive only brief attention at this point.

KOLA NUTS. One of the few items shipped in quantity from the humid south of West Africa to the dryer north is kola nuts. Chewing these nuts releases caffeine and theobromine, which are mild stimulants but which also reduce the feeling of hunger. Also used in extract for soft drinks, kola nuts are exported in minor quantities from Sierra Leone, Liberia, the Ivory Coast, and Ghana.

GINGER. Sierra Leone has a fairly significant export of this crop.

PIASSAVA FIBER. Taken from the leaves of the raffia palm, this fiber is used for making brooms. The Sherbro district of Sierre Leone has practically a world monopoly in the sale of best-quality piassava fiber, whose marketing is handled by a successful African cooperative.

FRUIT. There is a considerable local trade in citrus fruit and pineapples in West Africa and a small export of fruit, preserves, and extract from Guinea, Sierre Leone, the Ivory Coast, Ghana, and Nigeria. The quality and appearance of much of the fruit will require improvement before any substantial growth in production can be expected. Canning establishments have had considerable difficulty in securing sufficiently continuous supplies to permit their rational operation.

CASHEW NUTS. Produced in considerable quantities in eastern Africa, the cashew nut has been introduced to West Africa as one of several crops which would help to diversify crop emphasis. The Eastern Region Development Corporation in Nigeria has established over 1,800 acres of cashew nut plantations at Oji, Mbala, and Ajali; the comparable corporation in the west has planted 1,922 acres of an allotted 2,408; and Ghana has also experimented with this crop. The crop is to be used primarily for industrial oil, the nut containing about 30 percent oil.

TOBACCO. With a large increase in consumption of cigarettes, many nations of West Africa have wished to increase domestic production in order to save foreign exchange and to provide a new cash crop for peasant farmers. Tobacco manufacturers have assisted in promoting production. Much of West African tobacco is grown in the dryer north, but several humid tropical regions now produce and intend to expand output of tobacco. Dahomey, the Ivory Coast, Ghana, and the Western Region of Nigeria all have plans to expand tobacco production in southern regions.

SUGAR. Ghana is establishing sugar estates near Komenda which, when in full production, are expected to employ 3,000 to 4,000 Ghanaians and to reduce that country's sugar imports by 60 percent or more.

RICE. Rice is the favored staple in the countries from Liberia to Senegal, most of which do not produce adequate quantities to meet their needs. Various efforts have been made to expand output with varying results. In Sierra Leone about 39 percent of domestic rice comes from tidal and riverain swamps, 12 percent from inland swamps, and 49 percent from upland areas. The government's rice policy has been to discourage production of upland rice, which is conducive to soil erosion and yields poorly, and to encourage expansion of swamp rice, with total output being meant to increase. In fact, production has decreased and consumption increased and from 1954 on imports have tended to expand. Considering the expenditures involved, this has been a discouraging record. Professor Jack estimated the cost of the rice program in one year to have been $943,600, 14 percent to direct government expenditure and 86 percent representing the cost to the consumer resulting from the subsidized price set at 25 percent above the world price.

Liberia has enlisted the help of Taiwanese experts in establishing a rice project at Gbedin, where it has been shown that yields can be increased 50 to 100 percent by using varieties of seed imported from Taiwan and carefully controlling irrigation. Furthermore, crops mature in 3½ months instead of the 6 months required for swamp rice. But Liberia's rice output fell 40 percent in the five years to 1962 owing to migration from the farms, and imports of rice increased 30 percent in 1961 alone.

Ghana and Nigeria, where rice is not a major staple, have also decided to expand production. Ghana plans to construct a dam at Dawhenya, 25 miles east of Accra, part of whose 200-million-gallon capacity would be used for irrigating rice paddies, and to increase total acreage in rice to 60,000 acres by 1964. Nigeria is studying the opportunities of growing rice along the rivers of the Western Region.

ANIMAL INDUSTRIES

The humid tropical regions of West Africa are heavy deficit producers of animal products, chiefly because the tsetse fly precludes keeping most species of cattle. Most goats, pigs, chickens, and other livestock are kept on a haphazard basis with little thought for improvement or commercialization. There is often a shortage of meat, dairy produce, and eggs in urban centers. Efforts to correct this situation have thus far been inadequate. They include the setting up of poultry and pig farms, and the upgrading of dwarf cattle, which are resistant to trypanosomiasis. The dwarf N'Dama and African Shorthorn are very poor milkers and have very low carcass weights, but with proper selective breeding they might be bred up to more satisfactory weights and milking yields. There are an estimated 400,000 N'Dama cattle in the Fouta Djalon massif, 150,000 to 200,000 in northern Sierra Leone, where the breed may have originated, and fairly sizable numbers along the Gulf of Guinea coast.

ORGANIZATIONAL APPROACHES TO AGRICULTURAL DEVELOPMENT

The recognized inefficiencies and limitations of traditional farming practices have led to a variety of experiments with new approaches to farming in West Africa. Efforts vary from simple extension work to state farms comparable to the sovkhoz of the Soviet Union. Many of the programs have not been clearly thought out and seem to represent more a desire to start something new than to face up to the real problems of African agriculture.

Cooperative farming is being tried in Sierra Leone, Ghana, and Nigeria. Cooperatives have been successful in the marketing of agricultural crops but will probably prove less satisfactory on the production side. A cooperative mechanical scheme has recently been introduced in Ghana at a cost of about $7 million. The first consignment of 400 tractors arrived from Czechoslovakia in early 1963 and additional equipment has been ordered from Czechoslovakia and Yugoslavia. Repair stations are to be set up at Kumasi and Winneba in the south and at Tamale in the north. Past experience with the use of mechanical equipment in West Africa suggests that it is only economic under optimum conditions, and one cannot be very optimistic with respect to the success of this scheme.

The Eastern and Western regions of Nigeria have placed considerable emphasis on resettlement schemes. The goals of these schemes are to establish modern farming communities, expedite crop diversification, reduce the drift from the land to urban centers, provide employment for school leavers, and increase farm incomes. In the Eastern Region each of seven 12,000-acre settlements is divided into six villages of 120 settler families grouped around a common center where administrative buildings, quarters for supervisory staff, processing plants, social and health centers, schools, and markets are to be sited. Each settler is allotted a 2½-acre plot for food farming and a poultry house for 50 birds. Plots are arranged to permit the maximum use of mechanical equipment. The major crop, in which each settler will have a 15-acre interest, will vary: one farm will specialize in irrigated rice, two in oil palms and citrus fruit, one in cocoa and oil palms, and three in oil palms and rubber. An estimated 5,040 settlers, the first of whom were recruited in late 1962, will be associated with the seven schemes, whose over-all cost will be about $17.2 million. This works out to about $3,400 per settler, which represents a very substantial figure for so poor a country. The Western Region resettlement schemes, 18 of which have been planned, vary from 8,000 to 12,000 acres with each family getting 30 acres. The cost of settling each farmer will be about $3,100 and the total cost about $56 million. These resettlement schemes are excessively costly and tie up too great a share of limited available funds.

Still another approach is the promotion of partnership plantations, sometimes using outside capital and managerial skill. The two southern regions of Nigeria had completed about 96,000 acres of plantings on 161,000 acres allotted to plantations by 1961. So far the bulk of investment has come from the two development corporations. Other characteristics have been an emphasis on crops other than the present staples, though both regions have included cocoa and oil palm plantations, and a tendency toward nucleus plantations around which outgrowers will be encouraged to produce the same crop. The partnership basis of many of these plantations removes one of the major objections to this type of organization. The fact that they occupy only a tiny fraction of the available land also reduces the possible criticism.

The task of modernizing indigenous agriculture in Africa is a formidable one to which no one has as yet found an easy answer. Just how well the various schemes being tried in West Africa will work remains to be seen, but it may be predicted with some confidence that neither the state nor the collective farm type will work any better than they have in the Soviet Union, while the high expense of settlement schemes almost condemns them to failure in an area where land and labor are relatively cheap. Greater effort to develop initiative and the knowledge of the individual farmer and to provide adequate incentive for improvement will hold the key in the long run to better farming practices and higher farm incomes.

TRANSITION ZONE TO THE DRYER SAVANNA

The middle belt of West Africa, lying between the humid tropics and the dryer savannas and steppes, is of very little significance as far as commercial production is concerned. As already noted, it is less densely populated than the zones to the north or south. It cannot participate easily in livestock production because of the tsetse fly; most tropical crops can be more readily grown in the rainy areas. It is often further disadvantaged by inadequate transportation. But even in Nigeria, where two great rivers plus roads and rail lines linking the north and south are available, there is relatively little production for sale outside the area. To some extent, the middle areas have the disadvantages of lands on both their equatorial and sudanic sides: the leached latosolic soils, tsetse flies, and heavy downpours of the south, and lower dependability of precipitation characteristic of the north.

Crops that are produced for export from this belt include small quantities of grains, tobacco, cotton, and sugar. The area inhabited by the Tiv along the Benue in east-central Nigeria is an important producer of beniseed, a source of vegetable oil. A major sugar plantation is planned for 20,000 acres of marshy land on the south bank of the Niger in Nigeria.

THE DRYER SAVANNA AND STEPPE BELT

The regional occupation of this area is grazing, pastoralism covering a far wider area than sedentary agriculture. Its contribution to the money economies of West Africa, however, is much less than that of the cultivators. The large number of tillage farmers, far more concentrated than the graziers, produce the bulk of the food consumed in the area and of the goods exported from the region. Even in a dry country such as Niger, with only 2 percent of its area under cultivation, tillage agriculture provides the main occupation of about two thirds of the population.

Most of the inhabitants of this belt are Islamic, though clusters of pagan peoples reside in the higher sections. With the exception of Senegal, the area has been less influenced by contact with modern forces than southern zones; traditional life gives it a conservatism which contrasts with the dynamism of the south.

PASTORALISM

Pastoral tribes of West Africa, of which the Fulani or Peuhl is the most important, range widely over the dry savanna-steppe belt and into the desert, keeping cattle, sheep, and goats in large numbers. Some sedentary tribes also keep cattle and smaller livestock. Asses are commonly used in the north and camels are used to carry produce to and from the great market cities.

Graziers may be broadly divided into three groups:

(1) The true nomads, such as the Fulani Bororo or Bush Fulani, who are the most tradition-bound. On the move with their large herds almost continuously, they consider sedentary graziers and tillage agriculturalists to be practicing inferior occupations. Theirs is a largely self-sufficient existence and cattle are sold only with great reluctance.

Fulani cattle in northern Nigeria
While some Fulani are true nomads, others are transhumants who graze their cattle in the dry period on the stubble and fallow fields of the sedentary farmers, and some have settled permanently, continuing to keep animals on their farms.

(2) The transhumants, including certain Fulani, who congregate around rivers, lakes, and marshes during the dry months and disperse for the summer. Many transhumants are involved in a symbiotic relation with sedentary farmers. In northern Nigeria, for example, many Fulani spend part or all of the dry period grazing their herds on the stubble or the fallow fields of the Hausa, being paid a small amount for the enriching manures provided.

(3) Sedentary graziers, who are largely settled Fulani or mixed Fulani groups who have converted to tillage agriculture but who continue to keep as many animals as can be supported in their area.

The problems of these pastoralists are legend and may be considered as typical of those besetting graziers in most of the dryer areas of tropical Africa.

PHYSICAL PROBLEMS. Climatic difficulties are among the most severe handicaps to grazing in steppe areas. Water supply is highly irregular, there being a period of often violent showers followed by a longer period with no rain at all. This means that not only is stock water often in short supply in the dry period but that vegetation drys up, becoming palatable only to indigenous beasts. Almost as serious, precipitation is unreliable, resulting in wholesale loss of animals in dry years. Not only does the rainfall vary from season to season, but it is likely to fall very unevenly within the rainy period, whose start and ending are not readily predictable. Relatively little can be done about these natural conditions; the major palliative is to provide better stock water supplies by one or more of the techniques noted in the chapter on the Sudan. Temperatures are also a handicap, being generally too hot for quality animals from the middle latitudes, which cannot sweat adequately, develop an artificial fever, lose their appetites, and become more susceptible to disease.

The vegetation of steppe areas also leaves much to be desired. Some grasses have a high protein content when they sprout after the early rains, but as they grow older the fiber content increases and the protein and water content decreases. They tend to be high in silica and low in phosphorus and calcium and are coarse and hard, unpalatable for quality animals, particularly in the dry season. Shrub vegetation, particularly thorn bush, also covers large expanses and, while eaten by sheep and goats and even by cattle when grass is not available, it also is poor animal fodder. It would obviously be very difficult to improve indigenous grasses, the low value of lands not justifying the expenditure required. Very little study has been made of tropical grasses, though some superior species have been delineated. Under controlled conditions it might be possible to sow superior grasses under a system comparable to that of *harig* farming in the Sudan, while eventually it may prove practical to carry on a large-scale program of replanting if a sufficiently cheap method of tearing out brush vegetation becomes available. One of the most effective improvements that could be made with regard to cattle feeding would be the provision of larger quantities of fodder in the dry season. This would require development of a kind of mixed agriculture whereby sorghum and millet could be ensilaged for winter consumption while livestock was grazed on the natural vegetation in the summer.

A great variety of diseases, parasites, and insects afflict tropical livestock, presenting one of the greatest physical barriers to improvement. In the past, epidemics of catastrophic proportions have hit the livestock of Africa, influencing the whole history of certain areas, such as parts of the East African highlands. Very considerable progress has been made in combating animal diseases. Efficient vaccines now exist for rinderpest, bovine pleuro-pneumonia, and other diseases; tick-borne diseases are being controlled by regular dipping and spraying, which is compulsory in some areas. But it is an enormous task to treat every animal in the huge grazing areas and success has been by no means complete. Furthermore, effective treatments have not yet been developed for certain diseases. The most limiting of such diseases, not necessarily in the steppe areas but in the continent as a whole, is bovine trypanosomiasis, otherwise known as nagana or sleeping sickness.

Carried by the tsetse fly, trypanosomiasis makes vast stretches of Africa untenable for man and beast, affecting in one way or another the livelihood of perhaps 35 million people in West Africa alone. As may be seen from Map 43, various species of the tsetse fly are found in a broad belt of Africa from about 12° N to 15° S, with certain areas within, especially at higher elevations, being tsetse free. Generally speaking, cattle cannot move into tsetse-ridden areas except on a seasonal basis, hence in West Africa grazing is rather effectively restricted to steppe areas and to higher lands such as the Jos Plateau. As has been noted, this restricts the possibility of developing a soil-conserving mixed agriculture in tropical rainy and savanna areas.

Numerous techniques have been tried in the battle against the tsetse fly. Biological control has been studied, for example, via the fly's parasites and predators such as an ant which favors the pupa of the tsetse, by interbreeding of related species to promote sterile offspring, and by bombarding flies with gamma rays in the hope of rendering them sterile. Destruction of game which carry the trypanosome or fencing to protect cattle from close contact with wild game may be helpful in limited areas. Spraying with DDT is too expensive, even when limited to spraying tracks every 200 yards or so, and painting cattle with DDT solutions did not prove effective. In the late 1940s it was believed that a serum had been discovered, atabrine, which would give immunity. But it proved not to last sufficiently long to be a success and it was considered impossible under present conditions to inoculate every beast as often as would be necessary to give protection. Further experimentation may, of course, result in the improvement of atabrine, but results to date have been disappointing. It has, however, brought one considerable advantage in that it greatly reduces the losses of animals walked to market within the tsetse belt.

Thus far the only effective answer to the tsetse fly appears to be the clearing of bush where

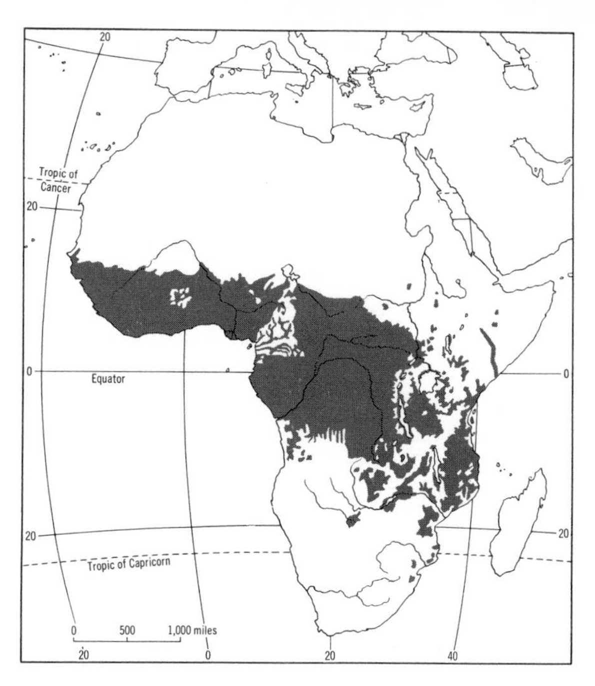

Map 43. Areas infested by the tsetse fly in Africa

breeding occurs and the immediate use of the area to prevent reversion. This applies more to human trypanosomiasis than to nagana, for there must be the intensity of use involved in tillage agriculture to stem the renewed invasion of the tsetse. Clearing of bush is likely to be expensive, however, and cannot be considered a practical method of opening the savanna grasslands to cattle raising. In East Africa there has been considerable success in the selective clearing of bush preparatory to the occupation of an area, but a solution in one area is not necessarily translatable to other regions because different species of the fly present different problems.

That no real solution to the tsetse fly has been found is not entirely to be regretted, because opening of the huge areas now infested would subject these lands to the same destructive practices that characterize the steppe regions. To prevent this, it will be necessary, when a remedy is found, to mount a multifaceted campaign to ensure that proper land use is practiced in the newly opened areas.

Returning to the physical difficulties affecting

grazing in the steppe lands, we find that poor quality of the indigenous livestock is also a major deterrent to advancement. This applies to all types of livestock, about the only quality product coming from West Africa being goatskins from the Red Sokoto or Maridi goats from Nigeria and Niger. Indigenous breeds of cattle, sheep, and goats do have the advantages of adaptability to local conditions, an instinctive avoidance of toxic and other undesirable vegetation, a high butter-fat milk, and resistance to some diseases. But they also have slow growth and breeding rates, low carcass weights and milk yields, and high mortality rates in young animals. The poor quality of livestock in West Africa and other parts of the tropics stems from both physical deficiencies of the area, already noted, and poor human practices. Considering the lack of attention livestock receive, the poor quality is not surprising; evidence shows that there is a favorable response to simple improvements in husbandry.

For years it was believed that crossbreeding with quality animals from other areas would be the best method of upgrading tropical breeds. But the new note in animal husbandry is that adaptability to the tropical environment is as important as production per se. Animals vary greatly in heat tolerance and heat tolerance is highly inherited. The best chance for improving tropical livestock would appear to be in the upgrading of beef cattle. What they consume is relatively abundant as compared to fodder for dairy cows, hogs, and chickens; they occupy the cheaper lands; dietal deficiencies can be corrected with minor additives; and the heritability of meat production is high. Improvement of dairy cows is much more difficult, and yields comparable to those of the middle latitudes, say 10,000 pounds per year per cow, can probably never be attained except under strictly controlled artificial conditions. Such levels require full feeding, three to four times more than maintenance feeding, but under tropical conditions such feeding increases the heat burden on the animal, increases its discomfort, and results in the loss of appetite.

HUMAN PROBLEMS. While the physical problems influencing livestock raising are obviously enormous, the human problems are equally impressive. Lack of knowledge and certain cultural practices lead either to serious malpractices or to lack of interest in improving livestock or in commercializing their production. As has already been noted, most pastoral tribes of tropical Africa practice a "cattle culture." While the nomadic Fulani, for example, may ostensibly pay a great deal of attention to their cattle, calling each by name, and may even practice a kind of selective breeding, their practices are anything but modern and selection is for shape of horn, not for meat or milk. Furthermore, communal grazing makes it very difficult to apply many of the improvements required to increase productivity.

Grass burning is one of the most widespread of malpractices in Africa. Believed to be beneficial to the soil and vegetation through the supply of ash, it is also practiced to destroy the breeding ground of insects and thus reduce the insect population. The ash does provide some nourishment to new shoots, but increasing evidence suggests that grass burning is harmful. Burning out the humus in the upper soil is detrimental to soil structure, which is none too good anyway; this in turn makes the soil more subject to erosion. Burning is also harmful to the vegetation because it favors the spread of fire-resistant bush and poorer grasses. Finally, it destroys helpful worms and organisms along with the undesirable species.

No adequate alternative for grass burning is yet known, and despite having been declared illegal in most countries, it is still very widely practiced as the only way to keep the insect population under control and to control bush growth. Carefully timed late burning might reduce its harmful effects, and burning once in four years is probably adequate to control bush, but this would require no grazing in the previous season to provide sufficient combustible material for a fierce fire. Here is another good example of the close interplay of physical factors in Africa, the need for attacking a problem from

Stock water tanks at Gajiram, northern Nigeria
Overuse of the tanks has led to destruction and degradation of the vegetation over a considerable area.

many angles, and the need for scientific research to find a solution to physical problems before human problems can be satisfactorily met.

Overgrazing is another malpractice prevailing over most grazing lands in Africa. It has contributed greatly to degradation of vegetation in the steppes and dry savannas and to its destruction along the desert margins. Livestock are selective eaters, choosing the more palatable and nutritious grasses, which, unless proper stocking is practiced, are gradually replaced by less nourishing plants. The accelerating expansion of woody, and often thorny, growth is a curse in many grazing areas of Africa. Overstocking is explained by lack of knowledge, failure to allow for periodic and certain droughts, presence of the "cattle culture" with its emphasis on numbers rather than quality, and by the practice of bringing cattle through the dry period on a near-starvation basis. Any stocking practice based on wet season carrying capacity is bound to impair growth and productivity in the wet season and be destructive in the dry period. Overgrazing has become so severe in certain parts of Africa that governments have had to introduce voluntary or compulsory culling to prevent outright destruction. This is often very difficult because it runs counter to the traditions of the cattle culturalists, but by working carefully through local chiefs, considerable progress is being made. In West Africa, where the "cattle culture" has been broken down more than elsewhere and there is, therefore, a greater willingness to sell cattle, it is estimated that there are still about twice as many animals as there should be, and a large proportion of herds is made up of unproductive animals.

Skinning and drying of hides and skins is also characterized by inadequate techniques, though agriculture departments have succeeded in introducing improved methods in some areas, including the stretching of hides on frames rather than on the ground and provision of shade drying. Improvements in these and other practices are more difficult because of the small number of agricultural officers. Northern Nigeria, for example, has only one for every 22,000 farmers.

Despite the many problems that exist, livestock grazing remains the most widespread activity of the western Sudan, and there is some export of hides and skins from all countries whose territory falls within it. There has also been an increasing sale of live animals and meat, both within the region and to the protein-deficient humid tropical areas. Much of the sale goes unrecorded and international movements are difficult to estimate because of clandestine crossings, especially from former French areas to Commonwealth West African countries. Efforts to increase commercialization include the installation of modern abattoirs, provision for shipping frozen carcasses by air to southern cities, and the setting up of a few ranching schemes. Senegal, for example, is launching a 220,000-acre ranch in the Linguéré region which will purchase local beasts and fatten them prior to marketing. The total exports of livestock products from West Africa remain very small, however, and imports of meat often greatly exceed the shipment of all livestock products from individual countries. That livestock represent a substantial potential resource, however, is indicated by the estimate that West African countries have over 23 million head of cattle, or about one fifth of the African total.

Aerial view of a small village and surrounding fields near Katsina, northern Nigeria
Peanuts are the main cash crop in this region; sorghum and millet are important subsistence crops. The regular field pattern contrasts strongly with that of the rainforest and wetter savanna areas.

SEDENTARY AGRICULTURE

Tillage agriculture in the dryer savannas and steppes contrasts strongly with that of the humid tropical regions, the tilled fields being more comparable to those of the middle latitudes than the cleared patches in the south. The staple crops are sorghum, millet, sorghum-millet (guinea corn or dura), and peanuts, plus sweet potatoes, cassava, sesame, beans, and cowpeas.

Peanuts being collected in southern Senegal for shipment to an oil factory
Peanut products normally account for over 80 percent of Senegal's exports by value, over 2½ million acres being devoted to that crop.

In limited areas, where water is available, rice is a leading crop, while tomatoes, onions, and sugarcane are also produced. The calabash vine is grown, often on the huts, to provide containers and utensils of varied size and shape; henna produces a favored dye; peppers and tobacco are commonly grown for local consumption. Much more labor is required than in the humid areas, where cassava can be grown by sticking shoots in the ground and many cash and food items are tree crops. A considerable effort has been made to introduce more modern plows and, in some regions, to encourage the use of cattle as draft animals. In northern Nigeria, for example, 20,000 farmers were using plows drawn by cattle in 1960, a ten-fold increase over early postwar years.

COMMERCIAL CROPS. There are two major export crops of the dryer north: peanuts, by all odds the most important, and cotton. Other crops sold on the world market are of minor significance. In postwar years there has been an increasing interregional sale of country produce—grains, fruit, and vegetables—to the markets of the humid tropical areas.

Peanuts. West Africa ranks as the largest exporter of peanuts in the world, accounting for about 70 percent of world exports. Shipments have grown from an average of about 1.0 million tons in terms of unshelled peanut equivalent in 1950–54 to over 2.2 million tons in 1962, and are expected to continue to increase in the years ahead since consumption is steadily expanding. In production, the area ranks well below India and accounts for only about 20 percent of total world output of peanuts.

Two major production zones may be delineated: that of Senegal and Gambia extending inland to Mali, and the several nodes of production in northern Nigeria and adjacent Niger (Map 42). In the western area peanut production is monocultural, which has led to such degradation that it has been necessary to move progressively further inland to find suitable conditions for production. Peanut production started in Senegal in the mid-1800s, and that country was producing about 125,000 tons in the early 1900s.

The output had increased to 550,000 tons before the war and has ranged around 800,000 to 875,000 tons in recent years. Peanuts have provided over 40 percent of that country's budget receipts and about 82 to 90 percent of its exports. In 1962, over 2.5 million acres were planted to peanuts, but as yields are characteristically quite low and holdings small the average cultivator gets only a small return. Disturbed by the high dependence upon this one crop, the detrimental effect its continuous cultivation has had on soil fertility, and the neglect of other crops which has occurred with the growth of peanut production, the government has been attempting to rationalize peanut production and to stimulate the interest in other crops. Efforts respecting peanuts include the distribution of better-yielding varieties, encouragement to use fertilizers by making them available at one half their cost, and reorganization of marketing arrangements to eliminate some of the grossly excessive number of intermediaries. Almost all of the peanuts of West Africa are produced by small holders, though one scheme in the Casamance area of Senegal has involved the mechanical cultivation by a central organization of several hundreds of individual 15-acre plots one half of which were planted to peanuts, one quarter to cereals, and one quarter to a green manure crop. Gambia has had similar problems and is attempting to replace its shifting agriculture with a more intensive system of farming. The present system is, with decreasing reserves of fallow land, reaching a stage where soil fertility and production have fallen to a level considered to be threatening to the livelihood of the populace.

In the eastern producing zone, the area around Kano is most important, accounting for about two thirds of Nigeria's export of peanut products. This is a roughly triangular area with apexes at Kaduna, Nguru, and Kaura Namoda. A second node is centered on Sokoto, while completion of the Bornu Line may create a third node of intensity in the northeast. Peanuts provide about two thirds of the exports of Nigeria's northern neighbor, Niger. Produced along the southern borders, particularly in the east, peanuts have increased substantially in output during the past decade but exports have required subsidization in the French market and there has been some fear that further extension of peanut production will threaten the domestic food supply. But peanuts play such a significant role in the nation's economy, supporting the transport organs and providing a large share of government revenues and exchange, that no alternative is readily available.

Cotton at Bole, Mali
Cotton ranks second to peanuts among cash crops from the dryer savanna and steppe areas of West Africa.

A large share of peanuts from West Africa are decorticated and exported in bags, this being the predominant method in the east and in Gambia. In Senegal, about half of the peanuts are treated in mills, the largest of which are in Dakar, and exported as oil and cake. An agreement with French oil mills has prevented processing of further quantities. Four privately owned mills have more recently been established at Kano and exports of oil have been about one tenth by weight of shelled exports.

Cotton. A considerable part of the cotton produced in West Africa is consumed locally. Hopes that the inner delta of the Niger in Mali would become a second Nile have thus far been frustrated and the whole area remains a very minor world producer and exporter of this crop. The most important producing region is around Zaria in north-central Nigeria, and that country exported about 1.1 percent of world cotton shipments in the period 1957–61. Nigerian cotton, 98 percent of which comes from the Northern Region, corresponds to American Middling. Increasing acreages and improved methods point to further expansion in the future, while the local textile industry, which is growing apace, should also provide a much-enlarged domestic market. Crop improvement can be more rapid than for most crops because 90 percent of the seed is provided by the ginneries which provide selected seeds to the producers. About half of the seed has also been dressed against bacterial blight in recent years, resulting in an estimated 6 percent increase in yields. There is still much room for improvement, however, as yields under optimum practices can be 1,900 pounds of seed cotton per acre as compared to the present average of 250 pounds, and it has been shown that higher profits will justify the increased inputs required to achieve better yields.

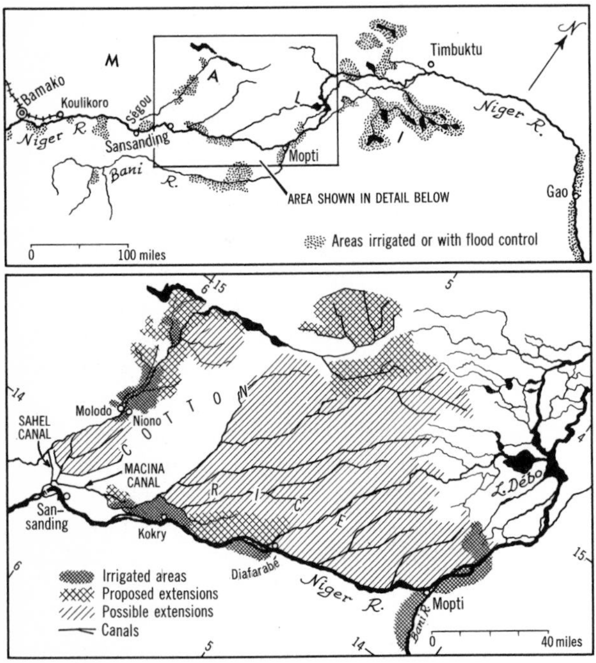

Map 44. The interior Niger Delta area in Mali

Above: Location of the Niger Delta and areas now irrigated or under flood control

Below: Detail of the indicated section of upper map showing location of the main features of the Niger Scheme

Mali has been the chief cotton producer in former French West Africa, much of it coming from the Office du Niger, noted below. Upper Volta produces several thousand tons of cotton, which provides about one tenth of that country's exports. Elsewhere cotton is grown only for local use.

Other cash crops. Other crops of the northern zone are definitely of minor importance. They include sisal, gum arabic, kapok, shea products, tobacco, market garden produce, sugar, and rice. Sisal is grown on three plantations along the Senegal, in Mali, and at Diakandapé in the Bobo Dioulasso region of Upper Volta. Several countries export small quantities of gum arabic, for which Podor in Senegal is the most important market. Kapok is ginned in three mills in Mali and produced in northern Dahomey and Niger. Shea products come from the shea butter tree which is native to the savanna and steppe areas and is another of the many sources of vegetable oil. The existence of many trees across the area periodically leads to suggestions that the tree be more intensively commercialized. But its oil is not as rich as palm oil; its extraction requires much labor; and long distances to shipping points further increase the costs of marketing. Tobacco is produced in increasing quantities for local and domestic consumption; the areas around Zaria and Sokoto are important in Nigeria. Rice is produced in several special scheme areas, discussed below, but also in swamp and valley areas scattered throughout the area. Gambia has increased its acreage under rice to about 50,000; Mali produces about seven tenths of its rice outside the Office du Niger, output also coming from the live delta of the Niger, the high valley near Bamako, and from along the valleys of smaller rivers; Upper Volta has increased its production of rice from the swampy areas of the west where a considerable potential exists for further development. Most of the rice produced is high cost and cannot compete with rice imported from Indo-China.

SPECIAL DEVELOPMENT SCHEMES

The northern belt is the scene of a number of special projects of considerable interest, most of them associated with development of river basins in the area.

OFFICE DU NIGER. The Niger Project was the largest single agricultural development scheme in all of the French areas south of the Sahara, over $100 million having been devoted to it up to 1959 (Map 44). At one time the Upper Niger, rising in the Fouta Djalon, flowed northeast and spread over a large area below Ségou, where it was lost to seepage and evaporation. It apparently supported a much larger population than that inhabiting the region in recent times. The Lower Niger, cutting backward from the southeast, captured the other stream, creating an outlet to the sea for part of its waters. The interior delta formed by the Upper Niger was divided in two parts, the dead delta on the right bank and the live delta, subject to annual flooding by the Niger. M. Bélime, a French engineer, first studied the possibilities of utilizing the inner delta, devoting ten years to an examination of the river's regime and of the soils in the area and then to a pilot canal and agricultural center at Baguineda. In 1932 the Office du Niger was created, with headquarters at Ségou, with a plan to revivify the dead delta and to use the live delta in a rational fashion. The major engineering work is the 8,580-foot-long, 16-foot-high Sansanding Dam, started before the war and completed in 1947; it is situated at the apex of the delta. Its reservoir feeds the canals, which utilize in part the channels of former distributaries and lead to the irrigated areas. A five-mile main canal divides into the 16-mile Sahel and 37-mile Macina canals, while a 43-mile dike protects the irrigated areas from the seasonal flooding of the Niger. About 130,000 acres are now irrigated in the Niger scheme. The original plan was to concentrate upon cotton and the various tasks were to be shared by the administration and the tenants. The administration leveled the area, built and equipped the villages, provided the tenants with equipment, undertook to teach them improved methods of farming, and mechanically prepared the land. The African colonists were responsible for the remaining operations except at Molodo, where rice was grown mechanically with paid labor. Approximately 33,000 colonists grouped in 3,800 families have been involved in the scheme. Rice became the major crop of the area, its production reaching 42,721 tons of paddy in 1959; cotton proved too difficult to produce and output only reached about 3,000–4,000 tons. Originally it was thought that 2½ million acres might be brought under control in the inner delta; the achievement has fallen far short of what now appears to have been an excessively optimistic goal.

The major explanation for the disappointing results of the Office du Niger is probably the poor quality of much of the soil in the delta area, which is far from matching the fabulous Nile mud. Several large areas, in fact, had to be abandoned because of the difficulties with the soil. Other physical problems have included the attack of cotton parasites, which has been successfully met by spraying from the air, and attack by locusts and quelea birds. The quelea-quelea or weaver bird, which inhabits the dry savanna and steppe areas of Africa, has become a rising menace to crops in a fifth of the continent. Swarms of millions devour crops, sometimes obliterating harvests, and are particularly injurious to grain crops, it being estimated that hundreds of millions of birds consume as much as 200,000 tons of cultivated grain annually in the Senegal Valley alone. As many as 300 to 2,000 nests may be found in one tree and some swarms number in the billions. Thus far, noise, low-flying aircraft with smoke producers, poison bait, biological control, explosive charges, and flame throwers have failed to meet the attack. The spraying of chemical poisons from the air has been the most effective method of control.

Human problems have included the difficulty of training tenants to a new system of agriculture, and a certain apathy in the production of the major cash crops. Economically, the scheme has been excessively costly both in relation to the numbers of persons involved and in the output levels achieved. Mechanical operations appear to have been very expensive, while some control has been applied outside the scheme's area at a fraction of the capital expenditures involved in the scheme.

In 1961 the Office du Niger became a Malian public entity and in 1962 a five-year plan was announced calling for an increase in the cultivated area to 162,000 acres or about 43 percent of the area commanded by the present dam. Two important shifts in emphasis were also announced: from extensive mechanical to manual operations and from rice to cotton with some introduction of sugar cane. Rice had proved to be high cost and the political feud with Senegal had resulted in the loss of a guaranteed market for this staple.

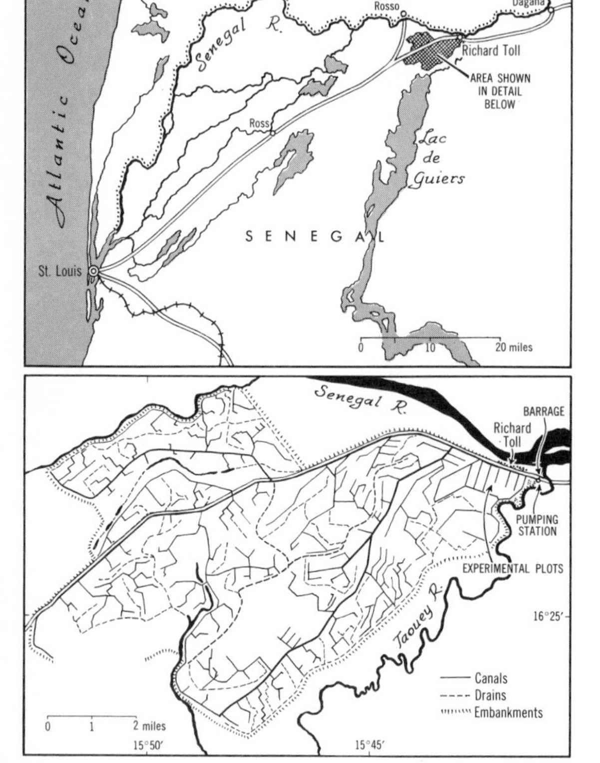

Map 45. The Richard-Toll Scheme in Senegal

Above: Location of the scheme
Below: Detail of the controlled area

The Niger Project may be considered as part of the development of the whole Niger basin. The Niger River within former French West Africa has been the subject of study by a team headed by geographer Pierre Gourou. Preliminary recommendations call for (1) construction of a dam in the Fouta Djalon headwaters which would improve supplies on 100,000 acres of the Niger Project; (2) improvements of the Koulikoro-Ségou navigable stretch of the river; and (3) control of the water flow to Lake Faguibine on the right bank in the Goundam region, southwest of Timbuktu (Tombouctou). The lake, 48 miles in length and 6 miles wide, has no outlet. When it is covered by a low flood, a large area can be used for cropping; after high floods, only a narrow band can be cultivated. It is proposed that the inflow be controlled, permitting the regular cropping of about 37,500 acres. Improved navigation on the river would require removal of sand banks, possibly by the use of anchored boats and panels to direct the flow as desired.

RICHARD-TOLL SCHEME. This project, one of the most important investments in former French West Africa, is dependent on the Senegal River. It involves using Lac de Guiers, between St. Louis and Dagana, which fills up during the high water period, as a reservoir from which water is pumped to irrigate an area along the river (Map 45). The project was begun in 1947 to provide domestic rice; about 15,000 acres of saline, infertile soil have gradually been developed and are now producing about 15,000 to 20,000 tons of rice yearly. The fields are mechanically cultivated and artificially fertilized. This project has proved very costly, but the government, which took over its management in 1961, continues to operate it to reduce the dependence on imported rice, because it represents some diversification away from peanuts, and because it possesses the only experimental center in the Senegal Valley. Despite production of 15,000 to 20,000 tons of paddy at Richard-Toll and 25,000 to 50,000 tons in Casamance, Senegalese imports of rice total about 80,000 to 130,000 tons yearly. In addition to difficulties with the soil, the Richard-Toll Scheme has been plagued by quelea birds, ducks, locusts, and other pests. From 1947 to 1961, a total of $15.5 million had been invested in the scheme.

As the Office du Niger represents only one part of development on the Niger River, so the Richard-Toll represents the beginnings of control on the Senegal. The Mission d'Amenagement du Senegal, with aid from the FAC and the EEC Development Fund, is preparing a 20–30 year plan for extending control on this river. It is estimated that about 6,000 square miles of the 77,000-square-mile basin is capable of supporting more intensive use. The 388-mile section from Bakel to Dagana, usually called "the Valley," is considered to have the finest economic potential of the entire Senegal River region. With an average width of about 12 miles, this section now supports some 400,000 people, but the waters are poorly used and support mainly some catch cultivation. The delta area, now almost uninhabited, presents additional possibilities but the problems of control are considerably greater. In years of high rainfall the river fills the numerous abandoned channels and floods over almost the entire area; in the dry season salt waters encroach and result in soil salinity. Thus special draining works would be required followed by heavy flushing to remove the salt.

Tentative plans call for a large upstream regulatory dam, possibly near Gouina, and three submersion dams near Bakel, Cascas, and Dagana to assist in local irrigation and transport. The dam at Dagana would be built first, which would permit the development of additional land in the Richard-Toll area. In addition to supporting more intensive land use, the several control works would also permit year-round navigation for vessels drawing up to 10 feet at least as far as Matam.

Rice fields in the Richard-Toll Scheme, Senegal
About 15,000–20,000 tons of rice are produced annually using mechanical methods and irrigation waters from the Senegal River stored in Lac de Guiers.

SOKOTO RICE SCHEME. Another specialized scheme for the production of rice is the Sokoto Rice Scheme in northwest Nigeria. Each year large sections of the floodplain of the Sokoto River and some of its tributaries, especially the Rima, are inundated in the rainy season. After the water recedes, crops are grown on the saturated soils, but the amount of available lands that farmers could cultivate with primitive techniques was strictly limited. The Sokoto Rice Scheme simply involved the mechanical plowing of as much riverain land as possible, after which the local farmers performed the rest of the work. Each year's plowing campaign was an intensive operation. Starting on the river north of Sokoto as soon as the lands were sufficiently dry to support the bulldozer-type tractors, the machines worked night and day moving downstream in a great arc toward the confluence with the Niger. The campaign completed, the tractors were "walked" back overland to the park at Sokoto, which had to be reached before the onset of the summer rains. There the machines were completely overhauled in preparation for the following year's operation. It is estimated that some 500,000 acres of fadamas, or seasonally inundated lands, could be developed in this area. The inhabitants along the Sokoto first lacked enthusiasm for the scheme but supported it more willingly after it had been proved that an increased production permitted not only an improved local food supply but also a surplus for sale within the region. In more recent years, however, and for reasons which are not entirely clear, the scheme has been diminishing in importance. The traditional conservatism of local farmers, interference with the raising of cattle, and objection to the $8.40 per acre charge for plowing are given as reasons for the declining interest.

GONJA OR DAMONGO SCHEME. A postwar project designed to determine the possibilities of mechanical operations in a bush area of northern Ghana and to resettle farmers from a congested area, the Gonja or Damongo Scheme was situated 76 miles west of Tamale in northern Ghana. The scheme was not successful. From the human standpoint, the participants did not welcome the opportunity to resettle and objected to the freehold tenurial arrangements, which did not result in the expected increase in initiative since the earnings of one man continued to be shared by his whole kinship group. From the physical standpoint, the soils turned out to be very poor, resulting in lower yields than had been predicted. From the economic standpoint, the expenses of resettlement were very high and the costs of operating the mechanical equipment, which were to be borne by a share of the production, were out of proportion to the opportunities for sale of commercial crops. The isolation of the area was a factor in the scheme's disappointing results.

THE LAKE CHAD BORDERS. The Lake Chad area, shared by Nigeria, Niger, Chad, and Cameroon, has been the subject of preliminary investigation. The lake, in an area of interior drainage, expands greatly during the rainy season, and it is suggested that part of the shore area be diked and irrigated by controlled flow of the lake waters. One project that has been started involves the sinking of several deep boreholes to tap what is believed to be the very considerable underground resources of the Chad Basin.

WEST AFRICAN DESERT AREAS

Most of Mauritania, Mali, and Niger are parts of the Sahara, all of their northern boundaries extending to or beyond the Tropic of Cancer. The southern margins are invaded each year by nomads; scattered oases support a sedentary agriculture whose chief resource is the date palm; and a few higher massifs, such as the Aïr or the Adrar des Iforas, give meager sustenance to permanent but possibly declining populations. The effect of increasing aridity towards the heart of the desert is strikingly illustrated by the case of Niger, where only 3.33 percent of the total population resides on that half of the country which receives less than 100 mm. of precipitation yearly. The greatest potential of these areas would appear to be in the mineral realm.

CHAPTER TWELVE

West Africa: Minerals and Mining

West Africa is less important than other mineral-producing regions of the continent, though mining has been increasing rapidly in significance in several countries and accounted in 1961 for about a fifth of the total value of exports from the region. Minerals play a more significant role in transport, sustaining several rail lines and contributing to the profitability of port installations. Only in Sierra Leone, Guinea, and Liberia do minerals provide more than half of exports by value, 70.5, 66.7, and 52.3 percent respectively in 1961.

Commonwealth West African countries were far ahead of other West African producers until 1950, and still accounted for two thirds of all mineral exports from the region in 1961. Attention to mineral possibilities in French-speaking West Africa was largely neglected until postwar years, but production has increased rapidly in recent years, especially in Guinea, the Ivory Coast, Senegal, and Togo, and Mauritania has just joined the group of producing nations. Geological prospecting has been pursued with increasing vigor throughout the area; new deposits have been brought into production and others are nearing this stage. There is little question that minerals will make an increasing contribution, actually and relatively, to many West African economies.

The most important minerals now produced, in order of value of exports, are diamonds, iron ore, bauxite and alumina, petroleum, gold, manganese, and tin. Lesser minerals include phosphates, columbium, and coal. Almost all mining output is exported except for coal in Nigeria and production of common building materials. A country-by-country analysis will provide a better basis for estimating the present importance and some of the future potentialities of the mining industry in West Africa. Table 16 shows production figures for West African minerals in selected years.

MAURITANIA

IRON ORE

The story of opening the iron ore deposits near Fort Gouraud illustrates well the time lag that often occurs between discovery and development of an ore deposit and the difficulties associated with such development, especially in the Sahara. The existence of a mountain of iron was noted in 1912 and confirmed in 1937. In 1949 Bethlehem Steel made an appraisal of the body, which was followed by a new survey in 1951. In 1952 a company was formed, Miferma, to proceed with development of the body. It was not until 1960, however, that preparations were finally begun; by this time Miferma was owned 62 percent by French interests, including the government, 20 percent by British, 15 percent by Italian, and 3 percent by German shareholders, including several steel companies. A $66 million loan from the World Bank sparked implementation of the preparatory work.

Iron ore occurs in three bodies atop a range of mountains known as Khédia d'Idjil near Fort Gouraud. Reserves of 63–64 percent iron-content ore were placed at 215 million tons in 1962 and reserves of 40–45 percent ore were estimated at 8 billion tons; both these figures may be very conservative. Mining will be entirely from open pits.

Table 16. West African mineral production in selected years, 1937–1961

Mineral and Country	*Unit*	*1937*	*1948*	*1958*	*1961*
Diamonds	thousand metric carats				
Guinea		—	80	117	1,117[a]
Sierra Leone		...	466	1,490	2,076
Liberia		—	—	824	1,005[a]
Ivory Coast		—	9	164	549
Ghana		...	786	3,132	3,214
Iron ore (Fe content)	thousand metric tons				
Guinea		—	—	212	242
Sierra Leone		386	567	832	1,107[b]
Liberia		—	—	1,453	2,178
Bauxite and alumina	thousand metric tons				
Guinea: Bauxite		—	—	351	352
Alumina		—	—	—	390
Ghana: Bauxite		—	133	210	199[b]
Petroleum	thousand metric tons				
Senegal		—	—	—	2
Nigeria		—	—	256	2,303
Gold	kg.				
Upper Volta		—	—	—	482
Sierra Leone		1,100	75	—	—
Liberia		80	429[b]	12	65
Ghana		17,400	20,895	26,525	25,909
Nigeria		80	90	20	17
Manganese (Mn content)	thousand metric tons				
Ivory Coast		—	—	—	54
Ghana[b]		172	314	250	188
Tin (Sn content)	metric tons				
Niger		—	3	62	48
Nigeria		11,000	9,384	6,330	7,904
Phosphates	thousand metric tons				
Senegal		—	—	—	567
Togo		—	—	—	57
Chrome ore (Cr_2O_3 content)	thousand metric tons				
Sierra Leone		0.3	3.4	6.1	—[c]
Lead ore (Pb content)	thousand metric tons				
Nigeria		0.6	0.3	0.6	0.3[a]
Coal	thousand metric tons				
Nigeria		315	615	939	607

Sources: U.N., *Statistical Yearbook, 1962* (New York, 1963); national statistical sources.

[a] 1960.

[b] Exports.

[c] 9.4 in 1962.

... = Not available.

— = None or negligible.

Problems encountered in opening up the body, in addition to the difficulty of enlisting the $190 million capital investment required, include those of water supply, very high summer temperatures, transportation, and availability of a market. From the standpoint of transportation, the easiest and shortest rail route would have been via Villa Cisneros in Spanish Sahara, second easiest to Port Etienne cutting across the southeast corner of Spanish Sahara. Spanish demands for either of these routes were considered excessive, so the alternative was to dig a 5,900-foot tunnel and keep the line within Mauritania (Map 36). Agreement to have 8 miles of line in Rio de Oro would have avoided an expenditure of about $8.4 million. Other transport problems included the absence of ballast near the seaward terminus, which was met by laying the rail 42 miles to the first source and then reworking that section, and two stretches of sand dunes which will hopefully be fixed by spraying with oil. The water problem has been solved by finding one source between the mine and Fort Gouraud and by bringing water by tank car to Port Etienne from wells located 66 miles inland along the line. During the four hottest months mining will be cut back by 50 percent; to ensure a steady rhythm at the port, provision is made there for storing 650,000 tons. The problem of finding markets was solved when steel companies participated in the venture and agreed to take specific shares of output. Mining began in 1960; the first shipments were made in 1963. A level of 4.2 million tons is planned in 1964 and 6 million tons by 1967.

The Fort Gouraud operation will have a very important impact on the economy of Mauritania. Approximately 470 Europeans and 1,520 Africans will be employed at the mine, where a village to accommodate 6,250 people has been built. Budgetary revenues, which, at $5.6 million in 1960, were the lowest of any former French area, will be increased by $4 million in the first year and by at least $8 million in succeeding years. The government receives a 50 percent share of net profits plus duties on the exported ore amounting to between 6 and 9 percent of the f.o.b. price; in return the government agrees to spend 35 percent of these revenues on development schemes which will dovetail with Miferma's projects. The value of Mauritania's exports will increase about fivefold. Other benefits are associated with improvement of Port Etienne.

COPPER

Two deposits of copper have been the subject of considerable attention at Gueld Moghrein, near Akjoujt, to which a 125-mile branch line might be extended from the railway to Fort Gouraud. Reserves of 600,000 tons have been proved, but probable reserves are placed at 18.5 million tons of 1.5 percent ore and 9 million tons of 2.5 percent ore which could be mined at the surface, plus 4.5 million tons of 1.5 percent ore requiring underground removal. Enough gold occurs as a by-product to permit Mauritania to become the leading gold producer among former French African countries. Several iron ore bodies are known to exist within 30 miles of Akjoujt.

OTHER MINERALS

In 1961 geophysical work was begun by petroleum companies in three sedimentary basins along the coast and in the Senegal Valley; eleven companies held 14 exploration leases at that time. Salt has been mined for many years but its production has declined to about 500 tons a year. Some gypsum has been mined north of the capital and used for plaster in construction of that city. Titanium occurs in sands along the coast and could be shipped from the Nouakchott pier.

SENEGAL

PHOSPHATES

Senegal has two phosphate deposits under exploitation (Map 46). At Pallo, near Thiés, a reserve of aluminum phosphate estimated at over 100 million tons is being worked by a

Pechiney subsidiary, which has invested $3.6 million in mining and transport of the rock. After removal of up to 13 feet of overburden the rock is blasted, loaded aboard freight cars, and hauled 51 miles to Dakar where it is loaded aboard ships by mechanical gear having a capacity of 200 tons per hour. Most of the output has been used in fertilizers but studies are being made of the possibility of extracting aluminum.

At Taiba, some 70 miles from Dakar, a vast phosphate deposit has been worked since 1960 by a company which had invested $25.4 million by the end of 1961, partly from public sources and partly from a private consortium with a large American participation. Again, mining is very simple. After removal of a 50- to 80-foot burden of sand a layer of phosphate rock averaging 20 feet in thickness is extracted, both of these operations employing draglines; the rock is then treated in a concentrator, the 82 percent concentrate being railed to Dakar where it is mechanically loaded at the rate of 1,000 tons per hour.

OTHER MINERALS

Several companies have been prospecting for oil in Senegal for some years. Some strikes of natural gas and petroleum have been made and 2,000 tons of petroleum were produced in 1961, but results have been somewhat discouraging to date. An ore containing ilmenite, rutile, and zircon is found widely in Senegal and has been mined in recent years at the mouth of the Saloum. After concentration it is loaded at a wharf, but the shallow bar of the Saloum restricts vessels to only 1,500 tons. Because of this poor siting, the company plans to shift operations to the Cap Vert peninsula in 1964. Salt is produced in the salines of Sine-Saloum, the 1961 level having been 43,445 tons.

Phosphate concentration plant at Taiba, Senegal
This installation, involving an investment of about $25 million, was started in 1960. After concentration, the product is railed 70 miles to Dakar.

MALI, UPPER VOLTA, AND NIGER

The remoteness of these three landlocked countries has had a depressing effect even on the exploration for minerals, which was not undertaken with any intensity until the late 1950s. Deposits of all but the higher value minerals would have to be more than average in quality to justify the heavy cost of transport to seaboard.

In Mali a manganese body is situated near Ansongo on the Niger and copper is known to occur in the Adrar des Iforas. Five companies were authorized to search for oil at the end of 1961 and several other companies were prospecting for metallic minerals.

Upper Volta started the production of gold in 1961 from a deposit at Poura, south-southeast of Bobo Dioulasso; numerous other indications of gold have been located. A large 35 percent manganese body has been found at Kiéré, 8 miles from the rail line east of Bobo Dioulasso; bauxite has been discovered in several areas, and there are indications of titanium, iron, copper, tin, and other metallic minerals.

Small quantities of tin have been mined in the Aïr Massif in Niger since 1948, the 1962 output having been about 42 tons, measured by metal content. Tungsten and wolfram are also known to exist in this remote Saharan region. Prospecting for oil began in 1960 and there was a marked increase in geological activity in 1961–62. A deposit of medium-grade iron ore has been reported at Say, 40 miles south of Niamey.

GAMBIA AND PORTUGUESE GUINEA

Ilmenite was mined briefly in Gambia and processed in a modern plant owned by Imperial Chemical Industries, but this operation was discontinued in 1959 because the deposits proved smaller than had been predicted and because of lower world prices. Exploration for oil has not as yet resulted in any finds.

No minerals now come from Portuguese Guinea, but Standard of New Jersey has been granted concessions to search for oil. In 1961 a $45 million project was reported to be under negotiation with Krupp's to develop iron and manganese deposits and to construct a rail line and port facilities. Bauxite deposits have also been under study.

GUINEA

Guinea appears to be one of the more favored mineral areas in West Africa and could be one of the leading bauxite producers in the world. The withdrawal of Guinea from the French Community and later from the franc zone, plus the nationalization of many segments of its economy including one producer of bauxite, has caused concern among foreign investors and doubtless reduced interest among potential sources of capital. Contracts of the large Fria bauxite-alumina complex and the iron ore producer have continued to be honored by the government, however, though special arrangements have had to be made to handle compensation of senior employees at Fria. The very significant contribution of mining companies to government receipts and in convertible currencies makes their continued operation a matter of considerable importance to Guinea. In fact, one of the few bright spots in the Guinean economy in recent years has been the increased output at Fria.

BAUXITE

Bauxite has been mined since 1952 on Kassa Island, one of the Iles de Los, just off Conakry (see inset, Map 46). A subsidiary of Aluminium Ltd. of Canada operated this extremely favorably located, 53 percent surface deposit until 1962. After mining, the ore was washed and loaded from a 450-foot pier onto 10,000- to 15,000-ton vessels. Production at this site, which has reserves limited to only four or five million tons, increased from 60,000 tons in 1952 to a record of 540,000 tons in 1960, the bulk of shipments going to Canada. In February, 1962, the operation was nationalized and Communist-bloc technicians were reported to have taken over management; shipments appear to have been very restricted in succeeding months.

One of the world's most important deposits occurs at Sangaridi, inland from the northern coast near Boké, reserves being placed at over 700 million tons of 45 percent or better ore, with a low silica content. In May, 1958, a long-term convention was signed between the then colonial government and Bauxites du Midi, the Alcan subsidiary, calling for development of bauxite and alumina production at Boké. The original plan was to export a million tons of bauxite a year and treat another half-million tons, both of which would be shipped about 75 miles by a company rail line to a new outlet, Port Kakandé. While $23 million had been invested in this project and construction had proceeded on the port and railway, the company was unable to secure sufficient capital to proceed with development on the schedule demanded by Guinea, which, because of this failure, nationalized both the Boké and Kassa Island concessions. Harvey Aluminum Company, an American firm, has negotiated a new contract for Boké.

A reserve of 300 million tons of 42–44 percent bauxite occurs at Fria and is under exploitation by an international consortium owned 48.5 percent by Olin Mathieson, 26.5 percent by Pechiney-Ugine of France, 10 percent by British Aluminium Company, Ltd., 10 percent by a Swiss concern, and 5 percent by a West German company. Mining is open pit and heavily mechanized. In 1960 a $150 million alumina plant was completed at Kimba near Fria with a capacity of 480,000 tons a year. In 1961, 390,000

A portion of the Fria alumina plant, Guinea
Shown here are evaporators and red mud settling tanks in the foreground, a conical water-cooling tower in the center, and the powerhouse to the right. This plant is part of a $150 million bauxite mining and processing project at Fria.

tons of alumina valued at $29 million were exported from the Kimba plant plus several hundred thousand tons of bauxite; the alumina exports accounted for 47.4 percent of total Guinean exports by value in 1961. Bauxite and alumina are moved 93 miles by rail to Conakry, where new installations handle the mechanical loading aboard ore carriers. Part of the alumina has been shipped to Edéa in Cameroon and part to Norway for refining.

The final stage of development would involve construction of a dam on the Konkouré at Souapiti and the erection of an aluminum refinery with a capacity of 150,000–200,000 tons. The dam, about 3,275 feet long and 394 feet high, would create a lake about the size of Lake Geneva and would permit the production of about three billion kwh of electricity a year.

Guinea is apparently extremely rich in bauxite, for additional deposits are known in the lower Kondouré Valley, near Kindia, and around Dabola on the east side of the Fouta Djalon. Total reserves are conservatively put at about 2 billion tons.

IRON ORE

French and British capital is involved in the exploitation of a large iron deposit situated on the Kaloum Peninsula, only seven miles from Conakry. Laterite ores of 48–55 percent metal content occur at the surface with no overburden and are underlain with hematite; 200 million tons have been proved but probable reserves are put at 2,000 million tons. Exports from this favorably situated deposit were 400,000 tons in 1957, but only 534,243 tons in 1961. A decline of 200,000 tons from 1960 to 1961 was attributed to technical difficulties associated with new machinery and the lack of spare parts. Additional iron ore bodies exist in lower Guinea.

Considerable interest has been focused upon iron ores in the Nimba Mountains area of extreme southern Guinea, across the border from deposits being developed in Liberia. The Guinean sector of the Nimba range contains 150 to 200 million tons of 60–65 percent ore, while preliminary prospecting in the adjacent Simandou range suggests reserves two or three times as great. In mid-1961 a consortium of European banks and Japanese companies formed a company (Consafrique) in which the Guinea government has a holding to develop these deposits at an initial expense of perhaps $100 million, which might later be doubled. In January, 1962, an accord in principle was reached with Liberia to permit shipment of ore from the region via the LAMCO line in that country.

DIAMONDS

Diamonds come from the interior southeast of Guinea where exploitation of surface deposits was first undertaken by two companies. In 1956, when thousands of Guineans who had been digging for diamonds in Sierra Leone were expelled from that country, many of them descended on the Kerouane region and began potholing there. Much of their output was illegally exported through Liberia, but greatly increased official sales in succeeding years suggested that much of the clandestine trade had ceased, or that large quantities were being illegally moved into Guinea from adjacent countries. A sharp drop in 1962 sales has not been adequately explained.

GOLD

From 70,000 to 100,000 African panners participate in the search for gold in the Siguiri area near the northeast corner of the country. In the years preceding independence, exports of gold had been declining, but production is believed now to be increasing, though figures are not available.

SIERRA LEONE

The growth of mining in Sierra Leone in post-war years has been spectacular. In 1929 the value of mineral exports was about $1,000 for 26 ounces of coarse platinum; the next year it increased to $30,000 with the addition of gold exports. Diamonds were first produced in 1932, iron ore in 1933, and chrome ore in 1937, but total exports were only about $8 million in 1940 and $9.2 million in 1950. By 1959, however, exports had increased to $38.4 million and continued sharply upward to $72.6 million in 1960, falling to about $58 million in 1961. In these last three years, minerals accounted for 70 to 84 percent of the total value of domestic exports, the highest relative dependence of any West African country. Mining is also the main source of government revenues, while mining companies generate a considerable activity through their expenditures.

Unfortunately, as will be shown, the impact of mining has not been entirely favorable, though the country appears to be moving into a period of greater stability and more rational exploitation and marketing. Mapping and exploration of the country are proceeding with vigor, although, as elsewhere, it is difficult to fill the posts open in geology.

DIAMONDS

Diamonds rank first among Sierra Leone minerals, accounting for about 65 percent of total domestic exports in 1961. Very widespread alluvial diamond deposits occur on the surface of Sierra Leone. Some fields are unusually rich, containing up to 250 carats per cubic yard, and some exceptionally large stones, from 50 to 100 carats, have been secured from them. In January, 1945, a 770-carat stone was found, believed to be the largest ever from an alluvial deposit. Diamonds were first discovered at

Map 46. Mining and mineral localities in West Africa

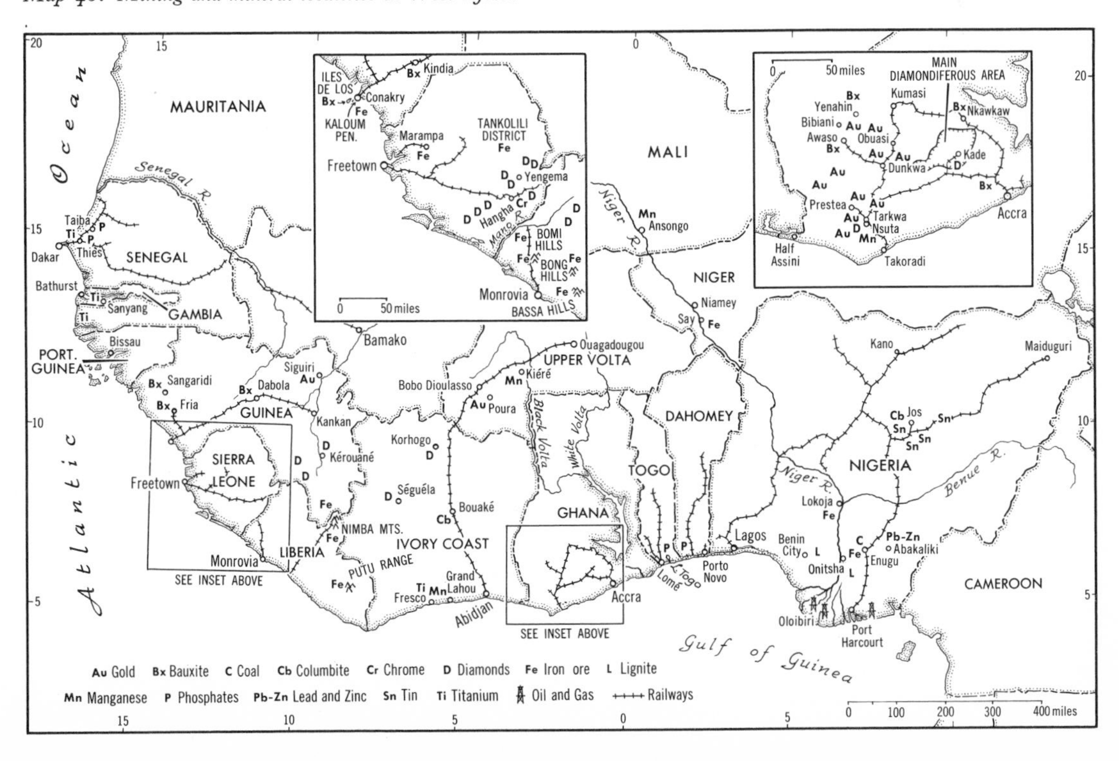

Potholing for diamonds in Sierra Leone
Diamonds occur close to the surface over large areas of Sierra Leone. During the 1950s thousands of Africans engaged in illegal mining, leading to serious distortions in the Sierra Leone economy.

Kono and it was thought that they were confined to that area. Mining began in 1932 after the Sierra Leone Selection Trust (SLST) had been given exclusive rights for diamond prospection and exploitation over the entire colony. Production grew to an average of 748,000 carats in 1936–38 and went on normally until 1952 when Africans began potholing, or surface digging, which led to a veritable diamond rush and to a great increase in illicit sales. By October, 1956, about 75,000 Africans were involved, but some 20,000 Liberian and Guinean diggers were later expelled. Various methods of dealing with this mining, which abrogated the agreement with SLST, were attempted. But powerless to stop it, the government finally concluded a new agreement with the company, whose rights were reduced to a 450-square-mile area in Kenema and Kono districts in compensation for which it was paid $4.4 million and was promised that illegal mining would be controlled within its remaining area. The rest of the diamond area, covering at least 9,000 square miles, was opened to Africans who were supposed to deal exclusively with the official purchasing organization.

Illegal mining and sales continued apace, however, being estimated at $12–17 million in 1955, $30–50 million in 1957, and $123 million for the period 1956 to 1959, the last figure comparing with $72.8 million in legal sales. From 1957 there were varying periods during which the situation became almost chaotic; pitched battles took place with the police, numerous potholers were expelled from the company area, and several Lebanese were arrested and deported. Although 600,000 carats were recovered in one haul and lesser quantities in others, the government could by no means control activities and diamonds continued to be smuggled wholesale out of the country.

These operations had numerous disadvantages. First, potholing is deficient as a mining method. It picks the eyes out of the deposit, recovering only an estimated one quarter to one half of the stones, but rendering the deposit uneconomic for further working. The company, using modern methods, extracts about 90 percent of the stones. Second, a large number of people were attracted to the mining areas and were living under most primitive conditions. Their removal from customary areas led to a decline in farming output and standards, reflected in declining exports of staples, increased imports of foodstuffs, and probably in a poorer dietal intake. Third, illegal mining created a strong tendency towards inflation and conspicuous consumption. And fourth, losses to the government were very great, including a loss in prestige resulting from its inability to enforce laws or even maintain peace. From the monetary standpoint, the government was forced to use capital resources to compensate for a reduced leasehold, while there was an indeterminate loss owing to failure to collect taxes and export duties on smuggled stones. The government gets 50 percent of SLST profits plus returns from a 7.5 percent export tax.

The diamond rush did have at least one substantially favorable result. It put money into tribal areas of the hinterland, which probably contributed to greater unity between these areas and the Creoles of the Freetown area. It also demonstrated, contrary to numerous statements, that many Africans have considerable initiative in response to economic motivation.

Finally, after organized illicit operations had increased to an alarming rate on the SLST lease in August, 1958, the government increased police activity, imposed heavier sanctions on offenders, put stricter controls on movements into the diamond areas, and managed to restore law and order. In late 1959, a Government Diamond Office, managed but not controlled by the Diamond Corporation, was set up. If Africans were dissatisfied with the price offered by this office they could ship their diamonds to London for sale at auction. Some 9,000 square miles have been officially declared alluvial mining areas and an estimated 16,000 to 35,000 diggers are employed at any one time in extracting diamonds. The result of these several measures was a marked increase in the value of African-won diamonds sold through the official market.

In the meantime, the Selection Trust has been developing a new part of its concession and has erected two additional plants at a cost of $1.4 million, while its earth-moving equipment is working lands thought uneconomic just a few years ago. SLST is also aiding the government in stimulating the use of simple equipment on the part of African diggers which will permit winning a higher percentage of the diamonds in the alluvial deposits worked, and is studying the possibility of reworking old areas.

IRON ORE

Iron ore has supplied a less spectacular but much steadier support to the Sierra Leone economy. It is mined by the Sierra Leone Development Company (Delco) from two deposits located 52 miles from Pepel in the Ghafal and Massaboin Hills of the Marampa chiefdom. The rich, hard-lump laterite hematite there, with 58.4 percent metal content, is now practically exhausted, but the 45 percent "powder" ore still has substantial reserves and is readily concentrated to about 66 percent. All operations at Marampa are highly mechanized and about 2,000 workers are employed.

Delco has been investing about $24 million in an expansion and modernization program scheduled for completion in 1964. Two new mills will increase capacity to 3 million tons; the company's railway is being relaid with heavier track, and a new half-mile long pier will expedite loading and permit use of larger vessels. Production in 1962 was 2 million tons. Sizable sums have been spent on examining an iron ore body at Tonkolili, larger but less rich than the Marampa reserve. Tentative plans for producing about 3–4 million tons at this site, which would have involved an investment of $69 million, were abandoned in 1961 when a German steel company decided not to participate in the financing or enter into long-term purchase contracts, presumably because higher grade ores are becoming available elsewhere in Africa.

MINOR MINERALS

Chrome is found in Sierra Leone near Hangha. High transport costs, a high silica content, and the necessity to turn to underground mining made extraction a marginal proposition, and increased competition resulted in closing operations in 1961, but exports were resumed and totaled 9,357 tons in 1962. Gold production has practically disappeared in postwar years.

In 1962 an agreement was reached with the Sierra Leone Ore and Metal Company, a subsidiary of the largest Swiss aluminum company, to mine bauxite at Mokanji Hill in the southwest. An output of 100,000–200,000 tons is planned, which may be shipped from a site on the Bonthe River. A bauxite deposit of comparable size has more recently been reported from the Pujehun District.

Other minerals of possible interest in Sierra Leone include corundum, columbium, and molybdenum. For titanium-bearing minerals, a 1.5-million-ton rutile deposit has been proved, while another estimate suggests that 100,000 tons of ilmenite could be dredged yearly in the coastal areas.

LIBERIA

Liberia presents an excellent illustration of the great dynamism which mining can introduce to an economy. In a country with no mineral output of significance before 1950, iron ore accounted for 47.4 percent of the value of all exports in 1961 and promises to be considerably more important as additional projects reach the shipping stage. With diamonds included, mineral exports now account for over half of total exports from the country.

IRON ORE

The Liberia Mining Company (LMC), with mining operations at Bomi Hills, 42 miles north of Monrovia, was the first of four companies to enter iron mining in Liberia. The reserve is stated to have 50 million tons of 66 percent ore plus 150 million tons of 43 percent milling-grade ore which must be concentrated before shipment. Operations, which began in 1951, are conducted at the surface and are highly mechanized. The lower grade ore is beneficiated to a 65–66 percent product in a 1.2-million-ton capacity plant erected at a cost of $11 million in 1958. Ores and concentrates are then shipped by the company's rail line to Monrovia for mechanical loading. About 2,700 persons, including 165 Europeans and Americans, were employed at the mine in 1961, when output was about 3 million tons.

The Bomi Hills iron mine, Liberia
The rich 66 percent metal content ores are shipped directly to Monrovia; lower-grade 43 percent ores are concentrated in the plant shown at the right. All mining is open pit.

The Liberia Mining Company and its president, Lansdell K. Christie of New York, have participated heavily in the second development, that of the National Iron Ore Company (NIOC), holding an 80-year lease from 1958 on a concession on the Mano River forty miles inland from Bomi Hills. This ore, with given reserves of 165 million tons, has a 54 percent metal content which is raised to 57–58 percent by scrubbing and washing before the ore is shipped by a 52-mile line joining the Bomi Hills line 39½ miles from Monrovia. About 1,300 employees, including 50 foreigners, are engaged at the mine. While the operation had difficulty in starting on schedule, owing in part to serious washouts, it was expected to ship about 5 million tons a year by 1964.

The largest venture to date is that of the Liberian-American-Swedish Minerals Company (LAMCO), managed by the Grängesberg Company of Sweden and including a 25 percent share of Bethlehem Steel. LAMCO is developing the largest known iron ore reserve in Liberia in the Nimba Mountains, 165 miles across the country from its new port at Buchanan. The operation involves a total investment of about $200 million. The 66 percent hematite is bench mined, crushed, and conveyed to railhead at the base of the mountain. Production began in late 1963 at an initial rate of 7.5 million tons. Bethlehem has contracted to take one quarter of output, which may be raised to 12 million tons within a few years, and has an option on additional quantities; other purchase commitments have been made with German, French, Belgian, and Italian companies. In early 1962, 3,650 African laborers and 50 African and 368 foreign staff were employed by LAMCO. The company also has the largest sawmill in the country, used so far to prepare ties and lumber consumed by the company itself.

Lastly, the German-Liberian Mining Company (Delimco), with German and Italian participation, is preparing to mine iron ore in the Bong Range, 50 miles east of Monrovia. Here a 230-million-ton reserve of relatively low-grade (37 percent) ore will support a planned output of 4 to 5 million tons a year starting about 1967. The ore will be fine-ground and concentrated to 65 percent before shipment by a proposed rail line to Monrovia. The development costs, estimated at $126 million, and expected production costs for this operation are relatively high, but Delimco has the advantage of assured markets among its shareholders.

With these four projects all producing, Liberian output of iron ore may reach 18.5 to 26 million tons by 1967, which would place it among the top exporters in the world. Other known bodies might later increase production to even higher levels: LAMCO has concessions in two additional areas in the Putu Range and Bassa Hills; Liberian Enterprises is investigating a 54 percent deposit in the Bie Range; and iron ore is also known to exist in the Wolo-Gisi Range.

Contracts of the various mining companies with the Liberian government have a number of features of interest. LMC's first contract, calling for a basic royalty of 5 cents per ton shipped, was renegotiated by mutual consent to give Liberia a 25 percent share of profits for 5 years, 35 percent for the succeeding 10 years, and 50 percent thereafter. NIOC is owned 50 percent by the Liberian government, whose share was provided mainly by loans from the Bank of Monrovia, owned by the First National City Bank of New York, 15 percent by LMC, the managing company, and 35 percent by Liberian Enterprises, an investment company formed by Mr. Christie to handle stock sales to Liberian citizens who, it was hoped, would gain knowledge of the free enterprise system by participation as shareholders in such a company. By 1963 an estimated 1,700 Liberians had invested in NIOC but there had been great difficulty in attracting small investors. One criticism of the NIOC arrangement has been that Liberia might well have made a comparable return through taxation without investing funds. On the other hand, the investment might not have been forthcoming at all without governmental participation, while there is a certain pride and prestige associated with domestic ownership. Liberia will get a 50 percent share of LAMCO and 50 percent of the net profits of Delimco as a tax.

DIAMONDS

Like Sierra Leone, Liberia has a large area where alluvial diamonds may be dug close to the surface, principally along the Lofa River in the north. Real interest in their mining began in 1953 and reached proportions of a diamond rush in 1957. The attraction of laborers to the workings threatened the Firestone and Bomi Hills operations, forcing President Tubman to close down the area to diamond mining in order to protect the main sources of governmental revenue. The fields have since been reopened to small prospectors and miners on a controlled basis. It is very difficult to estimate the output of diamonds, partly because of illegal marketing of Liberian stones, partly because of a substantial illicit import to Liberia from Sierra Leone and Guinea, but official diamond exports were listed at $2.2 million in 1961. It has been estimated that a rich deposit in the Bopolu region of the Western Province could add $3 to $60 million to annual export earnings, but more intensive investigation is required to test the validity of this projection.

Deposits of bauxite, lead, graphite, manganese, and mica have been reported from various localities in Liberia but little is known about them.

IVORY COAST

The Ivory Coast is a relative late-comer among African mineral producers, but has seen its production of diamonds and manganese increase greatly in recent years.

DIAMONDS

Two companies exploit diamond deposits, one 60 miles north of Katiola in the north-central

Surface installations at a gold mine near Tarkwa, Ghana
Gold has been mined in this area since the tenth century, but modern mining began about 1880. Ghana now ranks as the fifth largest world producer of gold.

part of the country, the other at Seguéla in west-central Ivory Coast, while African potholers operate in the latter district. Production increased gradually from 33,700 carats in 1949 to 199,880 carats in 1960, then jumped to 539,420 carats in 1961, this increase being explained by a rash of illegal mining in 1961 plus a system of controls which apparently greatly reduced smuggling to Liberia. Whereas potholing accounted for 40 percent of output in 1960, its share of 1961 production was 74 percent. New diamond finds, including one kimberlite pipe, strengthen the outlook for increased production in the future.

MANGANESE

A deposit totaling 1.6 million tons of 36 to 52 percent manganese ore has been exploited in recent years at Grand-Lahou along the southern coast. Shipped by lagoon to special loading facilities on the Vridi Canal at Abidjan, exports from this site totaled 114,000 tons in 1961. Other manganese deposits are known to occur west of Tiebessou and near Odienne.

OTHER MINERALS

The Ivory Coast exports a small but declining amount of gold. Some columbo-tantalite has been produced near Bouaké for some years, but it was not exported until 1962, when 8 tons were shipped. Active prospecting is going on for bauxite and iron ore, for which several medium-grade deposits have been located in the Sassandra region and west of Man. Indications of several other minerals have been found: titanium west of Abidjan, copper near Man, chrome at Bouaké, and gold. Prospecting for oil began in 1957 near Port Bouet but results have been discouraging.

GHANA

Ghana was for long the leading mineral producer in West Africa, though the great value of its cocoa production tended to obscure the significance of mining output. Mining and quarrying employed an estimated 43,000 in 1961, when exports of minerals were valued at $67 million, or 23 percent of the total. Gold, diamonds, and manganese are the big three of Ghanaian minerals; bauxite is of less present significance but of great potential importance to the economy.

GOLD

Gold has been worked in Ghana since the tenth century and the Portuguese traded for it as early as 1471. In the early 1700's, the British, Dutch, and Danes are estimated to have secured about £250,000 a year from the area, giving an obvious justification for the name Gold Coast. Modern mining began in 1880 and total production to April, 1962, has been valued at $649 million. Today Ghana ranks as the fifth largest gold producer in the free world. The industry employed 21,119 Africans and 533 Europeans in 1961–62.

While gold is found in many areas of the country, about 90 percent of mining is within a 60-mile radius of Dunkwa; seven mines are now producing (see inset, Map 46). Obouasi has been called "the richest square mile in Africa"; it may be the world's richest mine based on yield per ton, and it produced about $84 million in gold from World War II to 1962, paying over $19.2 million in taxes to the government. A feature of interest with some of the mines is the occurrence of gold in bankets comparable to those in South Africa, which has permitted these areas to benefit from each other's technical developments.

In February, 1961, Ghana took over five producing mines which had been unable to find the necessary capital to continue development. A 30 percent wage increase awarded miners in 1960 had made some ores unpayable and further development inadvisable. The prices offered in buying out these properties were considered eminently fair in the London market.

DIAMONDS

Ghana produces mainly industrial stones, accounting for about 10 percent by weight of the free-world output and ranking second only to Congo in production of industrial diamonds. Most of the stones are produced by mining companies, but the output of African potholers increased to 38 percent of the total in 1961–62. In that year, 2,927 Africans and 105 Europeans were employed by the companies, while some 12,000 Africans were engaged in local operations. The value of output has been increasing in recent years and is expected to continue upward in the future.

MANGANESE

One of the largest single manganese mines in the world is situated at Nsuta, within sight of the gold mines at Tarkwa. The ore, with 50–57 percent metal content, occurs in 100-foot-thick beds along the tops of five disconnected ridges over two miles long, permitting very low-cost bench operations. Output began in 1916 and reached a peak in 1953; despite a fairly notable decline in recent years the country still ranks fourth among free world producers. About 4,500 Africans and 40 Europeans are employed in manganese operations.

BAUXITE

At present there is only one mine producing bauxite, at Kanayerebo, 50 miles from Dunkwa in the Western Region. The ore is bench mined from the top of a hill, moved after breaking by aerial ropeway to a washing plant at Awaso, and then railed to Takoradi where special mechanical gear loads it aboard ore carriers.

Future hopes for exploiting bauxite are associated with the Volta Scheme, whose main object is the harnessing of hydropower for production of aluminum. The large deposit at Aya, 35 miles west of Kumasi, where ore occurs as 20- to 50-foot-thick cappings on the flat tops of hills permitting low-cost surface operations and

A diamond dredge at work on the River Ankobra in Ghana
Ghana ranks second only to Congo (Leopoldville) in the production of industrial diamonds.

gravity loading, will sooner or later be developed, while other deposits are known at Mt. Ejuanema and in the Kibi region, 37 miles northwest of Accra.

OTHER MINERALS

Gulf Oil began prospecting for oil in 1956 in the Half-Assini district in southwest Ghana; no successful wells have as yet been reported. Indications of a variety of metallic minerals have been noted in various sections of the country.

TOGO AND DAHOMEY

PHOSPHATES

The only important mineral operation in these two countries is the exploitation of phosphates behind Lake Togo between Lomé and Anécho; shipments were begun in September, 1961. The mining company, which is owned 20 percent by the Togo government and 80 percent by six French concerns, has invested about $24.5 million in the infrastructure of extraction and transport. Reserves estimated at over 50 billion tons are found in two bodies; mining capacity is 600,000 tons a year, which may later be raised to 1,000,000 tons; the rock is moved 13 miles by rail to a plant at Kpémé on the coast where it is washed, dried, and purified before being taken to a metallic wharf at the end of which two mechanical loaders have a capacity of 2,000 tons per hour. The product is an unusually pure 80–82 percent tricalcium phosphate. About 500 people are employed in this phosphate operation.

OTHER MINERALS

There are numerous indications of other minerals in Togo, including graphite, southwest of Atakpamé; modest reserves of chromite at Mt. Ahito and some bauxite at Mt. Agou, both in the Palimé area; iron at Bangeli near Bassari. The Togo American Oil Company, Ltd. has concessions for exploration along the coast.

A dragline scooping out tin-bearing ore on the Jos Plateau, northern Nigeria
After the ore is washed, the resulting mud is passed over sluices and a shaking table, the metal bearing product then going to a factory for extraction of tin and columbite.

Dahomey is still in the prospecting stage except for output of building materials.

NIGERIA

Minerals contributed only a little over 1 percent to the net income of Nigeria in 1959 and accounted for 11.4 percent of exports by value in 1961. Nigeria occupies an outstanding position in the world in the output of columbium and is a minor producer of tin. It has an outstanding position in West Africa in production of mineral fuels and sufficient known but unexploited mineral deposits to suggest that output will increase in the years ahead.

TIN

Tin was long the backbone of mining in Nigeria, cassiterite having been exported for over 50 years. Alluvial tin deposits are found on or near the Jos Plateau. Tin was early collected by primitive methods from river beds, hillside runnels, and water-washed channels, and some is still produced by small pit operations. Methods of prospecting and mining have become increasingly modern and most ore now comes from large-scale hydraulic mining similar to that in southeast Asia. Reserves have been listed at 135,000 tons for over a decade and all major companies are estimated to have adequate reserves for another 15 years, but large undetermined reserves lie below a basalt capping and may become of interest in the future. Some 74 firms are engaged in tin mining, which employed about 33,000 Africans and 257 Europeans in 1961.

Since Nigeria is a subscriber to the International Tin Agreement, its foreign sales fluctuate according to the allotments it receives from the Council. This results in wide fluctuations in employment; in 1959, for example, when restrictions were severe, output was only 53 percent of the 1957 level and employment was reduced from 63,000 to 28,000. At present, restrictions on output have been removed and the industry is operating at full capacity.

In 1961 the first tin smelter was opened in the area at Makeri, near Jos. A second large smelter is planned by the Consolidated Tin Smelters of London for the Jos Plateau. These two would have adequate capacity for all production, which suggests that three other smelters which are slated to be installed will create a serious overcapacity in the area and represent a somewhat questionable capital investment.

COLUMBITE

About 95 percent of the world's columbite, the ore of niobium or columbium, is normally produced in Nigeria, the bulk as a by-product of tin mining. Output reached peaks in 1954 and 1956 when large quantities were purchased by the United States for stockpiling. After these demands were satisfied, exports dropped drastically and in some recent years no exports have been recorded. Reserves are very substantial, as columbite is widely disseminated in the younger granites of the area.

OTHER METALLIC MINERALS

An important lead and zinc deposit is found near Abakaliki in the Eastern Province, containing 9.9 percent lead, 10.3 percent zinc, plus 2.5 to 3.5 ounces of silver per ton, but capital has not yet been forthcoming to develop this body. In 1961 a small lead and zinc mine near Zurak yielded 522 tons valued at $77,000. Iron ore bodies exist in several areas: a 100-million-ton reserve of 45–50.8 percent content has been proved on the Agbaja Plateau near the confluence of the Benue and Niger rivers; 30 million tons have been proved at Mt. Patti, near Lokoja, but the body may total several billion tons; and 45 million tons of 43 percent ore have been proved in a deposit near Enugu. In addition to having only moderate metallic contents, some of the iron ores of Nigeria are also disadvantaged by a high phosphorus and sulfur content. A small output of gold comes from Nigeria.

COAL AND LIGNITE

Nigeria has indicated reserves of subbituminous, noncoking coals totaling 242 million tons, 170 million tons in the Northern Region remote from the rail line, 32 million tons in the Eastern Region, and 40 million tons in Benin Province of the Midwest Region. Coal has been mined for over 45 years near Enugu, where four mines are now in operation employing about 3,300 people. Coal was the basic fuel of the country until recently and has also been exported to Ghana in sizable quantities. The conversion of the railroads to diesel locomotives (in 1959 over half of production went to the Nigerian Railways) and increasing competition from imported and domestic petroleum (oil can be delivered to Lagos for about 60 percent of the cost of coal) have caused a substantial decline in production, from a peak of 924,000 tons in 1958 to 597,000 tons in 1961. The chief hopes for continuing production would appear to be an increasing market for electricity in the Eastern Region, expansion of cement and glass industries, and the possible erection of an iron and steel mill.

Nigeria also possesses substantial deposits of lignite on both sides of the Niger in Benin and Onitsha provinces. The fact that lignite cannot be economically produced by opencast methods means that it will probably not be exploited for some years.

OIL AND NATURAL GAS

The search for oil began in Nigeria in 1937 and was renewed after the war, but it was not until 1957 that the first finds were made, at Oloibiri in the delta area 45 miles west of Port Harcourt and at Afam, 25 miles east of Port Harcourt. All of the first finds were made in the Eastern Region, but in 1959 oil was found in the Midwest Region, notably at Ughelli, a few miles east of Warri. A Shell-BP subsidiary played the dominant role in exploration and had invested about $200 million by the end of 1962; it has been joined more recently by Mobil, Gulf, and several other American companies. In 1960, offshore areas were opened for concession. The center of operations has been Port Harcourt, which is linked by pipe to the exporting terminal at Bonny. Eleme, 14 miles from Port Harcourt, has been selected as the site of Nigeria's first refinery, a 1.9-million-ton plant completed in

Aerial view of an oil camp at Oloibiri, Nigeria
Nigerian oil was first discovered in this part of the Niger Delta.

1964 at a cost of $28 million. It will produce enough gasoline and kerosene for domestic needs and at prices considerably below the present costs.

Development of oil resources in Nigeria has been a long, difficult, and costly affair. Operations are difficult because of the highly complex subsurface geology, the depth of oil-bearing strata, the quite low percentage of successful wells, and the very inhospitable environment, largely swampy, hot, humid, and insect infested. The use of water-borne rigs has improved the speed and efficiency of exploration, however, and Nigeria is further advantaged by the low sulfur content of its petroleum and by lower transport costs to Europe than for the Middle East. And prospects for finding oil are now considered sufficiently favorable for Nigeria to require substantial premiums before granting prospecting licenses.

Daily production levels increased from 7,000 barrels in 1958 to 65,000 by the end of 1961. In that year exports reached 2.3 million tons valued at $32.3 million; in 1962 they were valued at about $45 million. Shell-BP alone hope to achieve a level of production by 1975 of 10 million tons. It is now apparent that the reserves of Nigeria are very substantial, though not necessarily comparable to those of the Sahara.

Major finds of natural gas have also been made and represent a valuable resource for the country. A part of gas production is being used in a $4 million gas turbine generating plant at Afam which transmits electricity to the Aba–Port Harcourt area.

CHAPTER THIRTEEN

Industrialization in West Africa

While the industry that now exists in West Africa is rather insignificant from the world standpoint, the intense interest of many nations in expanding the manufacturing sector of their economies and the considerable number of new industries that are being set up in the area make it important to analyze the present and potential industrialization of the area. In doing so, West Africa will be used as a case study for manufacturing development in all of tropical Africa.[1]

INCENTIVES TO INDUSTRIALIZATION

There are many explanations for the keen desire of African nations to expand industry: (1) such development presents a major avenue for strengthening the economy by broadening its base and reducing the overwhelming dependence upon agriculture; (2) the desire to provide employment for an expanding population, a valid objective but one whose significance may be easily exaggerated because of the relatively small numbers required to operate a modern factory and losses in employment which may result in the handicraft industries; (3) the wish to earn more foreign exchange by the further processing of raw materials and export of higher valued products; (4) the wish to save foreign exchange by substituting domestically produced items for goods which were previously imported; (5) the realization that it is usually easier to increase productivity in manufacturing than in agriculture; and (6) the desire to have industry as evidence of the modernity of their economies.

The last reason, which stems from a simple comparison of developed and underdeveloped nations, may be more emotional than logical. If the desire to emulate advanced manufacturing nations leads either to neglect of agriculture or to the establishment of inappropriate industries it is likely to be detrimental rather than helpful to the economy. Agriculture is the primary activity in most African countries and the first manufacturing industries have often been concerned with the processing of agricultural exports. Agriculture can continue to stimulate industrial growth by providing the main market for consumer-oriented industries, labor, exchange for the capital equipment and imported raw materials needed in new industries, and funds for investment in industry itself or in the infrastructure which manufacturing requires.

What is required is a rational development which involves the selection and stimulation of industries that are most suitable at a given time in a given country, and, conversely, the eschewing of investment in, subsidization, and protection of industries which are likely to become a charge on the national economy. A great deal can be learned from studying industries that are already in place in underdeveloped countries, from analyzing the factors that justify their presence or that have caused their lack of success. By examining the list of industries in the somewhat more developed countries, it is often possible to secure suggestions which may be appropriate for study by the nation seeking to broaden its manufactural base.

[1] A portion of this chapter is based upon the author's "West African Industry: An Analysis of Locational Orientation," *Journal of International Affairs*, XV, No. 1 (1961), 3-15.

It is also necessary, of course, to know the economy of the country as thoroughly as possible, including its resources, its transportation and power facilities, its position with respect to labor and management, the availability of capital, the size, wealth, and stage of development of the market, the governmental attitude toward industry, and many other elements. Each of these factors changes in time, and hence continuing or periodic surveys are required; an industry which is inappropriate today may become justified by the discovery of new resources, by the provision of additional or lower cost energy, by a developing agriculture, by improved standards of living, and by many other dynamic conditions.

Dyeing vats at Katsina, northern Nigeria
Handicraft industries continue to have considerable significance in many parts of West Africa and employ a larger number of people than modern manufacturing.

STATUS OF INDUSTRY IN WEST AFRICA

Manufacturing in West Africa may be broadly divided into African craft industry and modern industry. There is a great variety of craft industries, including spinning, weaving, dyeing, pottery work, wood cutting and carving, production of furniture and household utensils, gold- and silversmithing, ironworking, tanning, leatherworking, preparation of calabash containers and utensils, raffia weaving, etc. Specialties vary from tribe to tribe and from area to area. Certain of the handicraft work displays a high level of skill and artistic taste, but much is relatively crude. Handicraft production has survived remarkably well in the face of low-cost manufactured imports and output from new domestic plants. Its contribution to national income in Nigeria, for example, is probably still greater than that of modern industry. A 1959 survey of seven communes in Togo revealed that there were 7,000 artisans in the total of 76,000 persons of both sexes over 15 years of age.

Methods employed in the making of handicraft items are usually fairly primitive, with only hand tools being used. There are few "transition workshops" where some mechanical power equipment replaces traditional hand operations. Perhaps the major exception is the ubiquitous Singer sewing machine found in the markets and bazaars all over Africa and used to sew up simple garments on demand.

Modern industry is in an early stage of development in West Africa, though each year sees the introduction of new manufacturing establishments. Data are not available to permit a statistical comparison of all of the countries; in fact, the inadequacy of statistical information is one of the handicaps facing prospective industrialists. The following fragmentary data will, however, help to suggest the status of manufacturing in West Africa. Senegal, the Ivory Coast, Ghana, and Nigeria have the largest developments in manufacturing.

In Senegal, there are approximately 320 manufacturing firms employing about 30,000, but one industry, peanut oil, accounts for half of the total value added by manufacturing, and six establishments account for half of the business turnover. The total value of industrial production increased 75 percent from 1956 to the estimated level of $304 million in 1962, when the value added by manufacturing was about $91 million. It is estimated that Senegalese industry now provides 100 percent of the country's consumption of vegetable oils, flour, biscuits, and soft drinks, 80 percent of confectionery, beer, tobacco, and cement, 65 percent of shoes, and 20–30 percent of sugar, chocolate, and textile yarns.

In the Ivory Coast, business turnover increased threefold from 1954 to 1961, when it was about $49 million; value added by manufacturing was placed at $24 million in 1961. Manufacturing employed 13,392 persons in 1960 or 7.6 percent of the total salaried working force. It is estimated to produce about 30 percent of manufactured goods consumed in the domestic market.

Ghana's industrial census of 1959 gave the total turnover in manufacturing at $61 million, the value added at $33.6 million, and total wages and salaries at $11.5 million. Industrial establishments reporting totaled 234, of which 9 employed over 500 workers, and accounted for half of total sales and 56.4 percent of total value added. In December, 1960, the number of employees in manufacturing was placed at 24,145; in that month the wage bill was at the yearly rate of $16.4 million. The rate of growth in industrial production has been estimated to have been 32 percent in 1960 and 26 percent in 1961.

In Nigeria, 48,216 persons were employed in manufacturing and electricity production in September, 1960, or 9.7 percent of total wage employees. At 1957 prices, the value added by manufacturing rose from $8.7 million in 1951 to $44 million in 1960. In all other West African countries, the level of output and employment in industry is very much lower than in the four major countries.

Most of the modern manufacturing establishments are owned by European companies. The largest are usually associated with the processing of agricultural, forestry, or mineral output, and, for the two latter fields, are owned by the company having the forest or mining concession. In Commonwealth West Africa, particularly in Ghana and Nigeria, the large trading company, United Africa Company, has increased its interest in industrial investment in recent years while tending to withdraw from commerce. Increasingly important, also, are plants owned by governments or in which governments have provided a portion of the capital investment in some kind of partnership arrangement.

Almost all plants are managed by expatriate personnel, though the number of African staff workers is increasing. But a rapid or total replacement of European personnel cannot be expected, primarily because it takes time to develop technical and managerial talent, but also because relatively few Africans are as yet able or willing to invest in their own establishments.

INDUSTRIAL REPRESENTATION

There are numerous ways by which the industries of West Africa may be classified: by product (shoes, beer, lumber, etc.); by end use of product (food, clothing, industrial raw material, etc.); by industrial group (forest, textile, mining, chemical, metal and mechanical, etc.); by source of raw material (domestic or foreign); or by major locational orientation (market, raw material, power, labor). There are lessons to be learned from any of these systems, but the last, which is relatively little used, is particularly revealing in that it involves explaining the presence of specific industries. While many industries have a complex of factors which influence their placement, it is usually possible to distinguish among primary, secondary, and tertiary attracting forces.

RAW MATERIAL ORIENTED INDUSTRIES

The earliest and still the most important group of industries in West Africa is that concerned with the primary processing of raw materials. Since such a high proportion of the economies of these countries is involved in the export of staples, and since the production of raw materials usually requires at least some preliminary processing, this fact is not surprising. Because it is often claimed that manufacturing should be carried forward to the finished product stage, however, it is important to seek the specific explanations for raw material orientation.

Raw materials tend to be processed in situ for several reasons: (1) to make the product less perishable; examples would include the canning of fish, fruit, and vegetables, or the extraction of oil from palm fruit, where speed is essential in avoiding a too high free fatty-acid content; (2) to reduce the bulk of the product and thus save on transport costs; examples are the processing of meat and the squaring of logs; (3) to reduce the weight of the material shipped for the same reason, as, for example, in the decortication of peanuts, the extraction of vegetable oils, ginning of cotton, concentration of minerals, and production of sawn timber, plywood, and veneers. In some cases, manufacturing reduces bulk, weight, and perishability, as in the case of canning pineapples or tuna.

PROCESSING OF AGRICULTURAL RAW MATERIALS. Most of the plants in West Africa devoted to the processing of agricultural products confine their operations to the early stages of processing. Exceptions include the production of certain food items such as canned fish, processed meat, and flour where there is essentially only one step between raw material and finished product, or the manufacture of soap and margarine which may be produced very simply in adjuncts to an oil extraction plant.

The most important industries in West Africa concerned with the processing of agricultural raw materials are the oil extraction mills, particularly for peanuts and palm oil. In Senegal, eight peanut oil mills accounted for over one half of the value of industrial production and employed 17.3 percent of all wage earners in industry in 1961 (Map 47). Sale of peanut oil to France is regulated by agreement with metropolitan oil processors; without this restriction a higher percentage of oil as compared to decorticated peanuts would probably be exported because there is a substantial reduction in weight through extraction. A factor which does give some justification for shipping the unprocessed nut, however, is the lack of a market for oil cake in the producing area. Peanut oil mills are a relatively recent introduction in Nigeria.

Processing of oil palm products other than by primitive methods or hand presses is usually confined to small plants such as the pioneer oil mills in Nigeria, where there are about 116 in the Eastern Region (Map 47). Unlike Congo, West African mills do not as yet process the palm kernel, which requires large-scale and heavy equipment. A few small mills in scattered localities also process shea nuts, cashew nuts, coconuts, and cottonseed. Soap and margarine

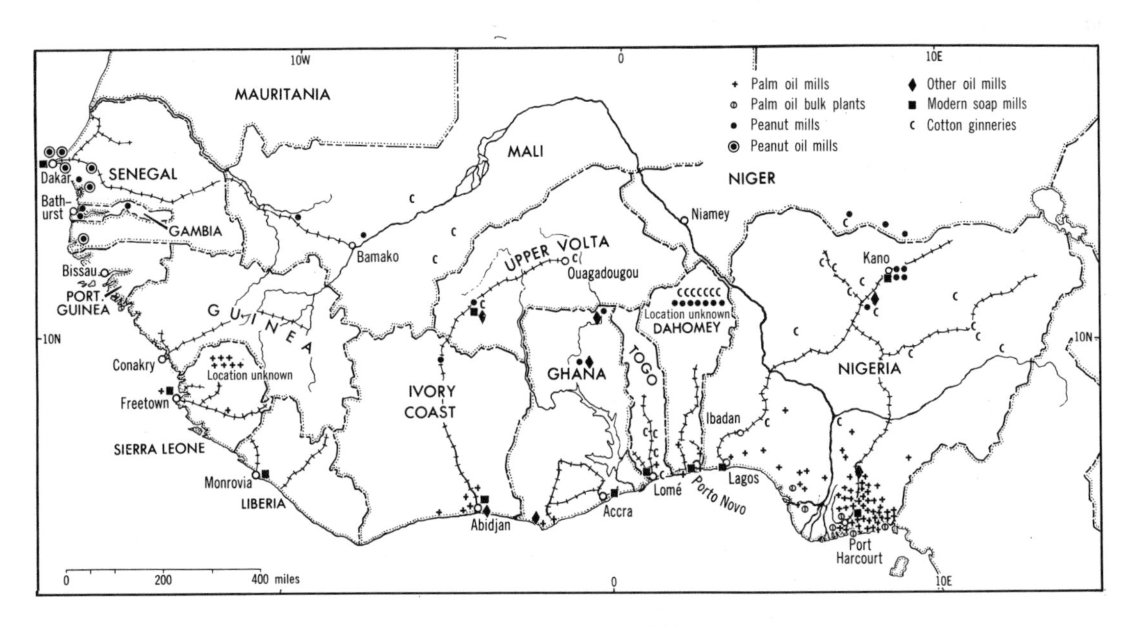

Map 47. Vegetable oil processing plants and cotton ginneries in West Africa

A peanut oil mill at Zaria, northern Nigeria
Palm oil and peanut oil mills are among the most important raw material oriented industries in West Africa.

are occasionally produced in conjunction with oil-milling operations, but the newer factory-scale soap plants tend to locate in market areas.

Other relatively important processing industries in this category include rubber processing (Harbel, Liberia; Bingerville and Pakidie, Ivory Coast; Sapele, Calabar, and Benin City, Nigeria; and other plants scheduled for the new plantations in various countries); cotton ginning; rice mills (Map 48); meat packing and processing; and tanning. Modern abattoirs and tanning establishments are not as important as the traditional, more primitive methods in output of meat, hides, and skins.

Less important industries processing agricultural produce include: (1) Canning of fruits and vegetables, which is attracting a number of new plants (Map 48). Pineapples and citrus fruit are the most common fruits canned; tomatoes rank first among vegetables. Despite the advantages of a raw material location for canning, several of the canneries introduced in postwar years have had considerable difficulty in operating at a profit, largely because of inability to develop a sustained supply of good quality fruit and vegetables. (2) Kapok cleaning and sisal decortication. (3) Processing of manioc. The plant at Ganavé in Togo ranks second

Map 48. Rice mills, canning of fruits and vegetables, meat processing, and tanning establishments in West Africa

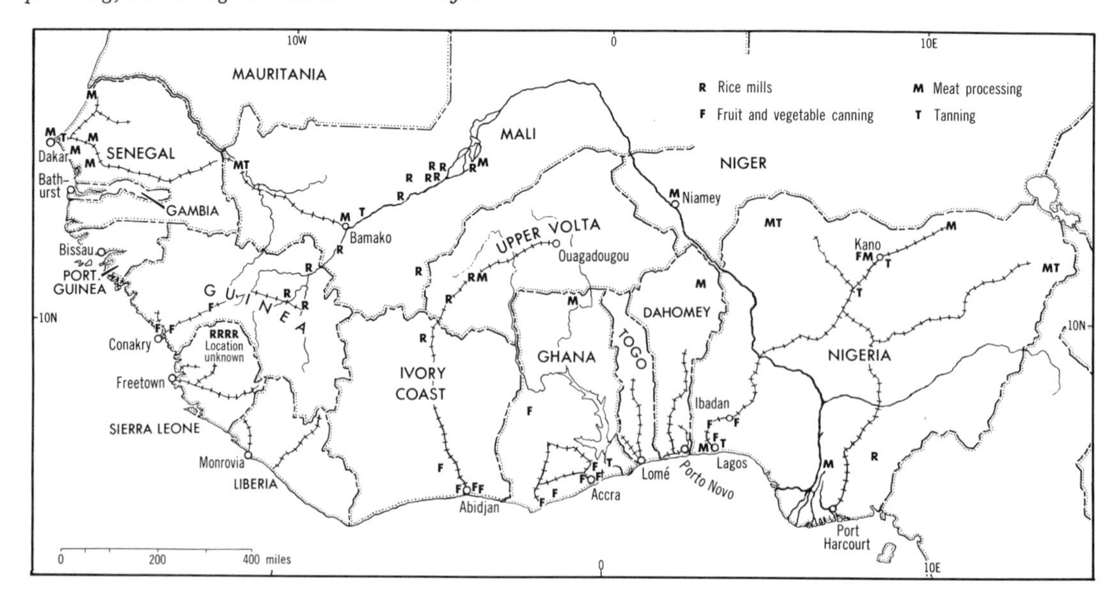

only to the phosphate works among manufacturing establishments in that country, all of the product being exported. (4) Extraction of perfume essences at Labé, Guinea, which may no longer be in operation.

PROCESSING OF FISH AND FOREST PRODUCTS As has been noted, a number of tuna fish canneries have been set up at various places along the coast of West Africa. Opportunities in this area should increase as the industry is modernized and marketing facilities improved. One or two canneries have had the same difficulties experienced by fruit canning establishments.

The growth and broadening of forest industries has already been described. The savings in bulk and weight are particularly notable in this group, which is concerned with the bulkiest of West African exports. Usually at least half of the weight is lost, sometimes more. While most of the sawmills of West Africa are small scale (Map 49), many of them catering to the domestic market, this category includes several of the largest plants in the area, particularly the Sapele and Samreboi sawmills and plywood plants of the United Africa Company in Nigeria and Ghana. A plant at Grand Bassam in the Ivory Coast produces prefabricated wooden houses.

The United Africa Company lumber and plywood plant at Sapele, Nigeria
This ranks as one of the largest industrial establishments in West Africa.

PROCESSING OF MINERALS. Most ores contain a relatively low percentage of metal, the remainder being waste. There may be, for example, only from $\frac{1}{4}$ to 1 ounce of gold per ton of ore, while diamonds occur in even lower ratios to the surrounding rock or alluvium. The original concentration, therefore, usually takes place as close to the mineral deposit as possible. In

Map 49. Sawmills, plywood and veneer plants in West Africa

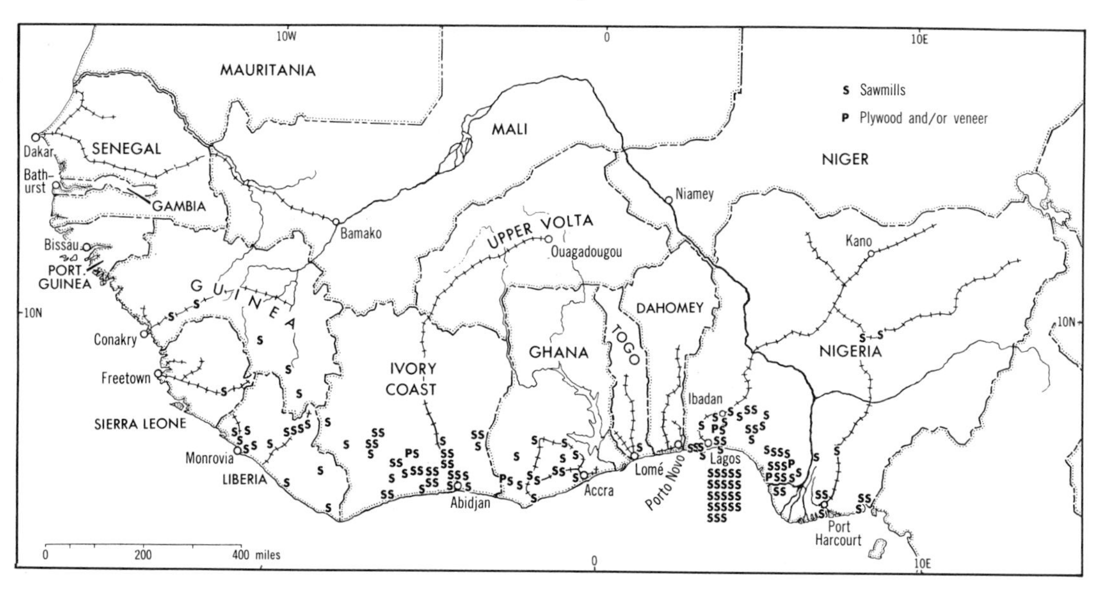

the case of alluvial gold and diamonds, the process is sufficiently simple to permit separation by African diggers, but the separation of gold from lode ores or mining a higher percentage of diamonds from alluvial material requires more elaborate equipment. Significant plants for concentration, washing, and sorting of minerals in West Africa include (Map 46) those for phosphates in Senegal and Togo; the very important Fria alumina plant in Guinea; iron ore beneficiation plants at Bomi Hills, Liberia, and Marampa, Sierra Leone; plants for extraction of gold at Tarkwa, Dunkwa, and Obuasi, Ghana; the collieries at Enugu; and tin smelters on the Jos Plateau.

As it happens, however, several of the more important minerals in West Africa are frequently shipped raw, or only after simple crushing and washing, including much of the iron ore, bauxite, and manganese, as well as crude oil from Nigeria. The three metallic mineral ores above have a sufficiently high metal content to permit direct shipping, though there is a distinct trend towards beneficiation of iron ores and production of alumina within the producing countries. There is every expectation that mineral processing industries will increase in significance as mineral output from present bodies expands and as new deposits are opened up.

LABOR-ORIENTED INDUSTRIES

Industry is attracted to labor for two rather different reasons. First, if labor costs represent a high percentage of the total cost of production and if relatively unskilled labor can be utilized, the industry will tend to be attracted to areas of low-cost labor. Examples are attraction of the textile industry to Japan and India, or from New England to the American South. Second, if unusual skill is required, the industry will tend to locate where that skill, which is usually rather immobile, is available. Examples are the production of optical goods in Rochester or New York City, the production of watches in Switzerland, or the manufacture of high-grade steel products in Sheffield and Solingen.

One would not expect to find the latter type of industry represented in West Africa, but it may be surprising that examples of low-cost labor orientation are not present. This is not to say that the low wages of labor are not a significant consideration, but there are no real examples of attraction of plants to the area specifically to take advantage of low-cost labor. If this were an asset of the region one would expect to find industries producing consumer goods for sale in foreign markets. Instead, protection is required for many industries even to sell their goods in the domestic market. One should not, of course, confuse low-wage labor with low-cost labor. And by the time that West African labor has gained experience, it may be hoped that wages will have improved sufficiently so that the area will not have to rely on low-cost labor to attract further industry. With the possible exception of Nigeria, it is difficult to see why the area should be comparable to such countries as Japan and India.

MARKET-ORIENTED INDUSTRIES

Almost all of the remaining manufacturing establishments in West Africa may be classified as market-oriented industries. And it has been in this category that the greatest advances have been made in the past decade. Manufacturing tends to be drawn to the market under a variety of circumstances: (1) if the product is made more perishable by manufacturing; (2) if the product is more bulky than the raw materials from which it is made; (3) if the product is more fragile than its raw materials; (4) if the industry is a service activity; and (5) if it is cheaper to import the raw materials than the finished product because of lower transport or lower tariff rates on the raw materials. The last factor, be it noted, may be a largely artificial one, whereas the first four are based upon physical factors. The strength of the pull toward market, raw material, power, or other orientation varies from product to product, and an examination of the industrial representation in any tropical African area will reveal that those industries which are most strongly affected by a specific locational factor are the ones which

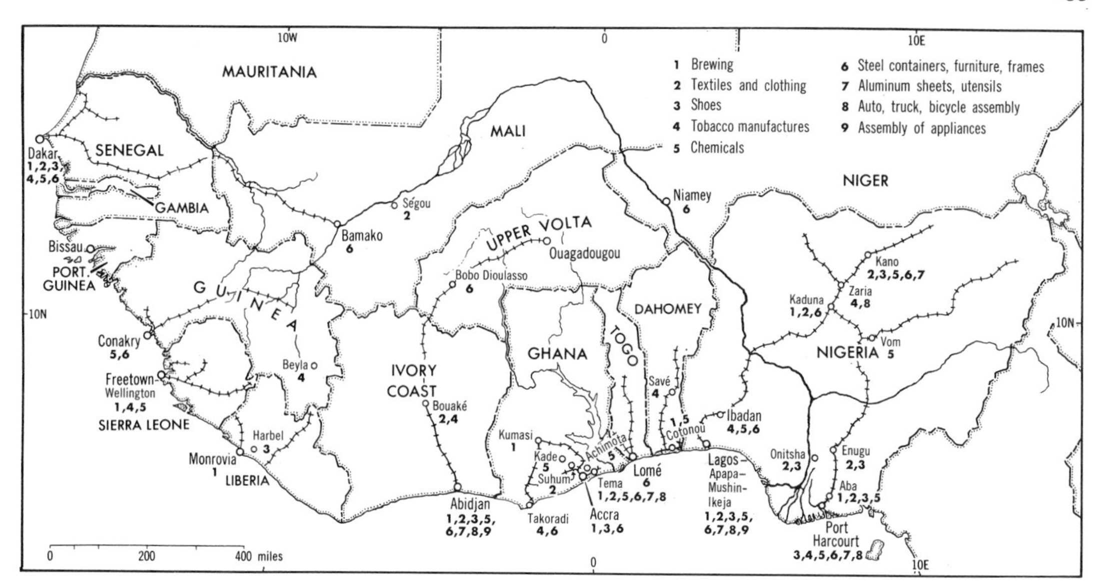

Map 50. Selected market-oriented industries in West Africa

appear first in the industrial roster and are also the ones which are likely to be more widely spread within individual countries. Good examples of this point would be cotton gins for the raw material category and carbonated beverages for the market-oriented group of industries. The large number of market-oriented establishments makes it desirable to subdivide this category.

FOOD AND BEVERAGE MANUFACTURE. Examples of industries whose products become more perishable after manufacture include baking and ice cream making. The first is often carried on in small shops, but larger, mechanical bread and biscuit factories have been introduced in recent years at Dakar, Abidjan, Accra, Kumasi, Apapa, Ikeja, and Lagos. Ice cream is produced in many of the larger cities.

Beer and carbonated beverages are examples of products which, because of the large content of water, offer substantial transport savings if good water is available in the market area. It is not surprising, therefore, that many of the largest cities of Africa have big breweries (Map 50). The production of carbon dioxide as a by-product makes it logical to have associated facilities to produce carbonated beverages, but the much lower capital and skill required in producing soft drinks and their lower value per bottle as contrasted with beer have permitted and led to a much wider distribution of plants producing colas, lemonades, and other such bottled drinks.

Other market-oriented food industries include (1) flour mills (often more because of protection than transport savings, however); modern flour

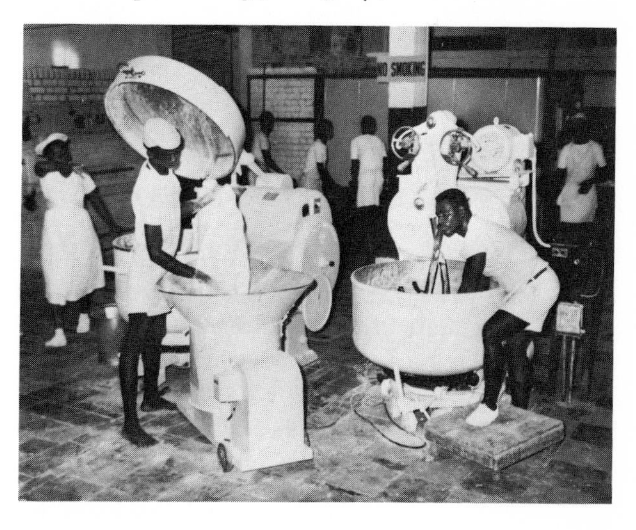

A modern bakery near Lagos, Nigeria
An example of an industry whose product is more perishable than its raw material and which must, therefore, be situated close to its market.

Bottling soft drinks at a plant in Salisbury, Southern Rhodesia
The high content of water in such products gives them a very strong market orientation because large savings in transport costs are possible.

mills, usually based on imported grain, are found at Dakar, Freetown, Abidjan, Apapa, and Port Harcourt; (2) chocolates and other candy (Dakar, Niamey, Tema, Lagos, and Kano); and (3) milk processing (Ikeja and Mushin, Nigeria).

TOBACCO PRODUCTS. The production of cigarettes and pipe tobacco in the market is favored by transport savings resulting from use of domestic leaf or imported leaf in bulk and from the protection accorded this industry, whose significance as a source of governmental revenue contributes to the desire to reap the full benefit of its manufacture. It is not unusual for the tobacco manufacturer to agree to assist the domestic tobacco growers in order to reduce the expenditure of foreign exchange and to stimulate the production of a new cash crop. Map 50 shows the cities with modern cigarette factories in West Africa.

TEXTILES AND CLOTHING. At the present stage of economic development in West Africa cloth and simple clothing are two of the most important items of expenditure by the average citizen and they frequently loom very large on the import list. There is a natural desire, therefore, to produce them domestically. Permissive factors which help to make this possible include the relatively small capital investment required, the fact that labor can be relatively easily trained to the necessary tasks, the low wage levels prevailing, and, in some cases, the existence of domestic supplies of cotton and the remoteness of some market areas (e.g., northern Nigeria) from textile producers in Europe and Asia. An advantage of the textile industry over many others is the relatively large number of persons required to produce a given value of output, a factor of some significance in densely populated areas such as parts of Nigeria. Despite these considerations, the textile industries of West Africa would probably find it very difficult to operate without some tariff protection, though it should prove possible to reduce this assistance after the industries become well established.

Dakar and Rufisque in Senegal and Bouaké and Abidjan in the Ivory Coast are the leading textile centers in former French West Africa. The spinning and weaving mill at Bouaké, which had 16,915 spindles in 1962, is one of the earliest such plants in tropical Africa, having been started shortly after World War I. Employing about 1,100 workers, it markets half of its output in the Ivory Coast and the other half in other West African countries of French expression. Abidjan has several plants in this field producing clothing, knitted goods, and cotton hosiery. The eleven textile and clothing mills of Dakar-Rufisque are estimated to produce about 40 percent of the Senegalese consumption of these goods, but also export over half of their production, chiefly to other parts of former French West Africa. Ségou in Mali is stated to have a textile mill with 25,000 spindles and 500 looms with the aid of Czech loans and technicians.

Nigeria has seen a particularly rapid build-up of the textile industry in the past few years. Kano had a small, modern cloth mill in 1952 which now produces about 1½ million square yards of drills a year. Kaduna received a $7 million spinning and weaving mill in 1957 producing about 42 million square yards of baft yearly; a second mill costing $2.8 million is planned for the northern capital in the near future, plus a third by 1965. In the Lagos area, Mushin has had a small cloth factory since 1948, Lagos has several clothing factories, Ikeja has a $4.9 million mill with a capacity of 18 million square yards a year, and a spinning mill is planned for Lagos. In the Eastern Region, Enugu has a new $2.8 million plant producing cloth for that region's first clothing factory, a $14 million textile mill with a 30 million square yard capacity is planned for Onitsha, and a $5.6 million mill is scheduled for placement at Aba. Whether there is an excessively rapid build-up in Nigeria remains to be seen, but some concern has been expressed that there may be a surplus capacity if all of the plants under consideration actually are constructed.

Ghana was relatively slow in getting into the textile industry, but Tema now has a textile printing plant and a small Chinese-Ghanaian mill; a third $8 million plant to produce 20 million square yards is scheduled for operation in 1965, while a clothing factory is to be placed at Sulum.

In addition to the cotton and rayon mills noted above, sisal products are manufactured at Dakar and Bouaké; a state-owned factory at Kumasi, Ghana, produces jute bags; and a plant at Badagry, west of Lagos, uses coir fiber as its raw material.

SHOES. Many shoes are produced by artisans in West Africa, but several modern plants are also found in the area. The Bata Shoe Company has had particular success in introducing the relatively complex processes of shoe manufacture into several African countries, primarily by breaking the processes down into individual operations and by careful attention to adequate training of personnel. It opened a factory at Rufisque in 1940 which now produces about 2 million pairs a year of leather and rubber shoes; a second Bata factory is located at Apapa. Map 50 gives the other cities which have shoe factories, though some of these are relatively small and produce only plastic shoes.

HOUSEHOLD FURNISHINGS. It is primarily the great increase in bulk after manufacture that makes it appropriate to produce many household furnishings in the market area. Certain items, such as wooden furniture, can also be produced on a semihandicraft basis. Wooden furniture has been produced for many years in West Africa and almost every large city has some shops engaged in this industry; a more recent introduction is the manufacture of metal furniture. Steel utensils, enamelware, and aluminum hollow ware and utensils are other household furnishings produced in a number of relatively new plants.

Metal doors and window frames, desirable because of their freedom from warping and from insect attack, have been among the first metal products manufactured in tropical Africa. They are easily assembled and their bulk is enormous in relation to the space occupied by the metal strips and sheets of which they are

A small Ghanaian-owned furniture factory at Accra
The great increase in bulk after manufacture makes it appropriate to produce many household articles in the market areas.

Assembly of bicycles at Tema, Ghana
About five such plants in West Africa take advantage of the savings in transport made possible by shipping partially assembled bicycles.

made. Plastic goods are manufactured at Conakry, Abidjan, Takoradi, Ibadan, and Apapa. Such things as combs, cups, buckets, garden hose, etc., can be readily produced, have a wide market, and are frequently bulky in relation to their weight.

An automobile and truck assembly plant at Tema, Ghana
Such plants represent a new introduction to West Africa.

METAL AND MECHANICAL INDUSTRIES. In addition to the steel and aluminum furnishings noted above, there are a few metal fabricating industries and a small but growing number of plants assembling vehicles and appliances. The explanation for these latter industries is the ability to save on transport costs by packing many more items in the space that a fully assembled product would occupy. The three main vehicle assembly industries of West Africa are the new Régie Renault plant at Abidjan with a capacity of 25 trucks or cars daily, and sizable UAC plants at Tema and Apapa. Bicycles are assembled at Abidjan, Tema, Mushin, Port Harcourt, and Zaria. A few plants assemble sewing machines, radios, and other household appliances.

Metal drums, cans, and other containers were among the earliest metal items produced in West Africa since it is particularly costly to ship empty containers. In more recent years, pipes, storage tanks, metal boxes, nails, and wire products have been added. Corrugated iron and aluminum sheets, used widely for roofing, and metal gutters are also produced in a few plants.

Two small steel-rolling mills are situated at Tema and Emene, near Enugu, using local scrap as the raw material, and a third such plant is planned for Senegal by 1965.

CONSTRUCTION MATERIALS. Because of their great weight in relation to their value, there is a strong incentive to produce materials such as bricks, tiles, cement, and concrete shapes as close to their markets as possible. Bricks and tiles can usually be readily produced near their markets since clay is common and only a small-scale operation is required. Cement cannot be so readily decentralized: a large investment is required if the plant is to be economic, suitable limestone is not as widespread as clay, fuel should be available at a reasonable cost, and there must be good transport facilities to the market. These sometimes conflicting requirements have meant that the number of cement plants in tropical Africa is usually limited to one or two mills in a country, but that a cement plant is likely to be established as soon as the size of the market justifies its operation. Cement plants in West Africa are situated at Rufisque, Takoradi, Nkalagu (Eastern Region, Nigeria, near Enugu), and Ewekoro (Western Region, near Abeokuta), while new mills are planned for Bobo Dioulasso, Upper Volta, and Kalambaina, near Sokoto in the Northern Region of Nigeria. The selection of this last site may have been prompted more by political considerations than by any analysis of locational advantages. In addition to these cement mills, clinker-grinding plants occur at Wellington, Takoradi, and Port Harcourt, while factories producing asbestos cement sheets and pipes are situated at Ikeja, near Lagos, and Emene, near Enugu.

CHEMICAL PRODUCTS. In addition to plastic products already noted, a variety of chemical products is produced in West Africa including perfumes and pomades, paints and varnishes, ink, industrial gases, matches, insecticides, pharmaceuticals, and explosives. In recent years there has been increased interest in petroleum refining in the area; a Shell-BP plant is under construction near Port Harcourt, the only one based on domestic resources, while other refineries are scheduled for Mbao, near Dakar, Monrovia, Abidjan, and Tema.

MISCELLANEOUS PRODUCTS. A few products manufactured in West Africa do not fit conveniently into any of the above categories. These include paper containers, stationery, neon signs, phonograph records, and ceramics. A new industry in the area is glass bottles, tumblers, and sheets to be produced at a state-owned plant at Tarkwa, Ghana, and at a factory in Port Harcourt.

SERVICE INDUSTRIES. Industries in this category, if they are to exist at all, must be in the market area, for a variety of obvious reasons. The largest such establishments in West Africa are the railway workshops. The shop at Ebute Metta, just outside Apapa, for example, is the largest industrial plant in Nigeria. The shops of the Public Works Departments, equipped to repair many types of mechanical gear, but particularly vehicles, are a similar type of service industry. Some of them make bus and truck bodies, which permits substantial transport savings by making it necessary to import only the chassis of such vehicles. Vessel and aircraft repair facilities are also in this category.

Other service establishments include refrigeration and ice plants, printing works, carpentry shops, and tire retreading plants. There is a fairly wide representation of ice-making, printing, and joinery works; tire retreading on a factory scale is much less common, but there

The Nkalagu cement mill, Eastern Region, Nigeria
The low value of cement in relation to its bulk makes it desirable to produce it close to the market, but the high investment required and the needs for fuel restrict the number of such plants found in underdeveloped areas.

are establishments at Monrovia, Ibadan, Aba, and Jos.

ELECTRICITY. Perhaps the most important of all service industries is the manufacturing of electric power, an essential part of the infrastructure of any nation which wishes to industrialize. The availability of power for general industry is not to be confused with large-scale production of low-cost hydroelectricity to attract power-oriented industry. Power consumption may represent only a small fraction of the inputs in most industries and need not necessarily be especially low in cost; but it must be available either from public lines or by private installation.

Power in West Africa is usually confined to the larger cities and the mining communities, but new installations are gradually being placed in the lesser cities and in a few rural areas. Illustrative of the concentration of capacity and output is the case of Sierra Leone, where 40 percent of the total capacity of the country is at Freetown, or the example of Nigeria, where Lagos accounted for 35 percent of electric output in 1961–62. Electricity is relatively expensive at most points, but is becoming less costly in some of the bigger cities as larger and more efficient plants become practical. Diesel oil is the most common fuel, there being only a few coal-burning plants remaining in Nigeria. The Afam plant, based on natural gas, is being increased to a capacity of 60,000 kw; it is slated for further expansion to 80,000 kw and a new 60,000-kw plant is earmarked for Ughelli under the 1962–68 plan. Some of the sawmills and peanut mills use plant waste for a portion or all of their fuel requirements.

Though the capacity and the production of electric plants are now small in all countries, both are expanding rapidly and new installations are being made each year. For example, the Ivory Coast got its first important electric plant only in 1950 at Abidjan, but by 1962 twelve internal communities had received plants; total production of electricity increased from 1.8 million kwh in 1952 to 120.0 million kwh in 1962. As a second example, Nigerian output of electricity increased from 97 million kwh in 1947 to 662 million kwh in 1961–62, and the Electricity Supply Commission now has four major plants and thirty additional plants serving as many communities.

A number of small hydroelectric plants are now in being and others are in advanced planning stages, while two very large schemes are under development. Opportunities for development in the northern tier of countries are restricted because of their aridity, but Mali plans a 5,000-kw plant on the Niger five miles downstream from Bamako and equipping of the Markala Dam with a 1,000-kw installation. Upper Volta has studied a site at Dédougou on the Black Volta halfway between Bobo Dioulasso and Ouagadougou which would have a capacity of 5,000 kw and could aid in the extension of irrigation. Niger could install seven 3,500-kw sets at the site called W, 75 miles downstream from Niamey on the Niger.

Guinea has a 10,000-kw plant at Grand Chutes on the Samou River whose capacity could be increased to 18,000 kw. In 1961 it signed an agreement with Yugoslavia to construct a dam ten miles above the present dam which would permit doubling the power to Kindia and Conakry. Sierra Leone will produce some power from its Guma Valley Dam, which is intended primarily as a water supply scheme for the capital area. In 1961 a team of German scientists investigated the hydroelectric potential on five rivers in that country. In Liberia, a $22 million project is under development at Mount Coffee on the St. Paul River whose capacity should be about 7,500 kw, while the U.S. Agency for International Development authorized a $24.3 million loan in 1963 to finance a run-of-river plant near Monrovia with a capacity of 15,000 kw. In the Ivory Coast, a 19,800-kw plant, Ayamé I on the Bia River, started producing in 1960, and a second plant, Ayamé II, is under construction 2½ miles above the first installation and will have a capacity of 30,000 kw. A 68-mile transmission line connects these sites with Abidjan, which is also getting a new

36,000-kw thermoelectric plant. A 100,000- to 120,000-kw hydro station is under study on the Bandama River about 43 miles west of Bouaké.

While most of these and other small hydroelectric plants now in being have been or will be developed primarily to serve existent consuming centers, the huge Volta Scheme in Ghana and the Niger River Scheme in Nigeria represent the development of resources which will have attraction for industry in their own right, though some of their output will be transmitted to urban areas. Both are discussed under the section on power-oriented industries. In addition to the Volta Scheme, Ghana may develop hydropower at Bui, 120 miles northwest of Kumasi on the Black Volta, and surveys have recently been completed of the Pra, Ankobra, and Tano rivers in the Western Region of that country.

In Togo, the Yugoslavs are constructing a 1,600-kw station at Kpimé near Palimé, about 65 miles from Lomé, under a $1.5 million 5-year loan. In Nigeria there are four hydroelectric plants with a total capacity of 18,000 kw serving the tin mines on the Jos Plateau, three on the Kura River and one on the Gyel River.

POWER-ORIENTED INDUSTRIES

Industries are attracted to sources of low-cost power if the cost of energy represents a considerable fraction of the total cost of the finished product. Examples are the refining of aluminum, which is an enormous consumer of electricity, and the production of nitrogenous fertilizers, ferroalloys and other electro-metals, and electro-chemicals such as calcium carbide and abrasives.

At present there are no examples of strictly power-oriented industries in West Africa. The Afam gas-turbine electric plant in Nigeria may be considered something of an exception, though it could not be justified if a market for its output were not available within a reasonable transmission distance. The proposed glass works at Port Harcourt will also be partially power-oriented. For the future, several large-scale projects will introduce power-oriented industries to West Africa, particularly the refining of aluminum at Tema based upon the Volta River Project and, later, a similar development harnessing the Konkouré in Guinea. West Africa's hydroelectric resources, however, do not compare with those of equatorial Africa, especially on the Kouilou and Congo rivers.

THE VOLTA SCHEME. The Volta River Project is a multifaceted scheme involving mining of bauxite, its reduction to aluminum using the power from a large installation on the Volta, irrigation of a part of the Accra Plains, improvement of transport, provision of power for urban and industrial uses, and minor additional features. The backbone of the project is the aluminum smelter, since it will be the only consumer large enough to justify a scheme of the dimensions involved.[2]

The Volta Scheme had a long gestation period before it finally got under way in 1962. The possibility of harnessing the Volta River was suggested as long ago as 1924 and a general plan was drawn up in the 1930s. In 1945 private interests formed a company to move forward with the scheme, which was joined by Aluminium Ltd. in 1949. From 1949 to 1951 the first intensive study was made, followed in 1953 by the appointment of a preparatory commission which published a voluminous report in 1956. Uncertainty with respect to the political situation in Ghana plus lower prices for aluminum reduced interest in the scheme and Alcan withdrew from it subsequently. Ghana meanwhile placed greater and greater emphasis on the project as a cornerstone of its whole plans for development, and, after several additional studies and much difficult negotiation, the Volta Aluminium Company Ltd. (VALCO) was formed at the end of 1959 and enough capital had been aggregated by the end of 1961 to permit moving forward with the project. Cold-war considerations probably played a role in

[2] See Chapter 3, "The Proposed Volta River Project, a Study in Industrial Development," in William A. Hance, *African Economic Development* (New York, Harper, 1958), for a fuller discussion of the earlier negotiations and plans for this scheme.

the several substantial loans made by the United States to VALCO and to Ghana for construction of the dam.

The Volta River Authority (VRA) is responsible for construction of the dam, the electric grid system, and the hydroelectric station, and for peripheral expenses such as compensation in the flooded areas. The estimated $196 million required for this work is being provided by a $47 million loan from the World Bank, $51 million in loans from three U.S. agencies, and up to $98 million from Ghanaian reserves. VALCO, which is a consortium of two American companies, Kaiser Aluminum and Reynolds Metals, is responsible for the aluminum smelter, which will cost not less than $129 million; it will provide one quarter of this amount and the other three quarters has been provided by an Ex-Im Bank loan. Involving a total expense of at least $325 million, the Volta project represents one of the largest single investments in tropical Africa.

The Volta is a large stream, even by African standards, with a catchment area of some 150,000 square miles and a main course length of about 1,000 miles. But most of the tributaries, with the exception of the Black Volta, are dry for about seven months of the year, while from May to October they are in flood. The flow of the river varies at the dam site from below 1,000 cubic feet per second to a peak which may be from 125,000 to 390,000 cubic feet per second, hence the need for a storage reservoir, while the need to create a suitable head of water dictated placing the dam and power station where the stream has a steep gradient as it cuts through the Akwapim Hills.

The rockfill dam being built at Akosombo will rise 370 feet above its foundation and 244 feet above river level and will measure 2,100 feet in length at the crest; a second dam, 120 feet high and 1,200 feet long, is required to close a valley on the left bank. The reservoir created will extend upriver for about 250 miles and have an estimated surface of 3,275 square miles, making it the third largest man-made lake in the world. The lake will be of some value as a transport route, but should have very considerable value for inland fisheries and eventually for recreation.

The power station will have an initial capacity by about 1967 of 589,000 kw and an eventual capacity of 883,000 kw, while an 86,000-kw station can later be installed at Kpong. These levels compare with a total installed capacity of all electric plants in Ghana in 1961 of 121,000 kw. VALCO will pay 0.193 cents per unit for electricity and has contracted to take 60 percent of output for thirty years. Electricity will first be transmitted to Tema, 44 miles away, then to Accra, 18 miles west, while a separate 400-mile circuit will serve the cities, villages, and mines of southern Ghana, including Kumasi and Takoradi.

The aluminum smelter will be situated at Tema and will have a capacity rising from 120,000 to 220,000 tons. It has been estimated that aluminum exports will be valued at about $84 million yearly, which would have added 28.8 percent to the value of exports in 1961. VALCO has been given pioneer status for ten years, exempting it from all taxes, and has been guaranteed for the next twenty years the present level of corporation taxes. Its payments to VRA for electricity will be paid in foreign exchange and will give the authority an assured revenue by the sixth year of about $7 million. Imported bauxite may first be used at the plant, but eventually it will probably be supplied from the several known reserves of bauxite in the country.

The U.N. Special Fund has been studying the possibilities of developing irrigation on the Accra plain based on water from the Volta, including the control of numerous creeks in the area which flood in the high-water period.

Final realization of the Volta project will represent a very considerable achievement for Ghana and will have an important impact on several aspects of its economy. It may well be followed by comparable developments elsewhere in Africa and hence will be watched with considerable interest by all parties concerned.

THE NIGER RIVER SCHEME, NIGERIA. Not to

be outdone by Ghana, Nigeria has included the first stage of development on the Niger River as the keystone of its 1962–68 plan. This will involve construction of a dam at Kainji, near Kurwasa and upstream from Jebba. Initial capacity will be 280,000 kw but may be raised to 980,000 kw when additional units are installed. The dam, power station with first-stage capacity, and transmission lines are estimated to cost $191 million. Power from this site, it is thought, will be fully utilized by 1980; a second dam is projected for Jebba by 1982 with a total capacity of 500,000 kw, while a third dam would follow in the Shiroro Gorge of the tributary Kaduna River south of Shiroro with a capacity of 250,000 kw. Electricity from the first dam will be transmitted north to Kano and south as far as Lagos; earnings from this sale are calculated to pay for the second and third dams.

The Niger River project will have a variety of subsidiary advantages. Control at Kainji will permit use of the floodplain below Jebba not now utilizable because of annual flooding, plus irrigation on higher ground above the level of present floods. Locks around the Kainji Dam and around the Awuru rapids would permit river navigation to Niamey in Niger and help to regularize navigation below, but any real improvement downstream would require additional dams on the Niger and the Benue. The crest of the dam will be used by a new road improving contacts north and south of the river. Finally, it is estimated that about 10,000 tons of fish could be produced yearly from the lake created by the dam. It is hoped that the first stage of the scheme may be completed by 1968.

LOCATION OF INDUSTRY IN WEST AFRICA

A clear distinction between the locational pattern of raw material and of market-oriented establishments is apparent in West Africa. The processing of agricultural, forestry, and mineral raw materials tends to be in or very close to the producing area or mine. The locational pattern for these industries, therefore, shows considerable dispersion, as is shown in Maps 47 to 49. With the major exceptions of Dakar, with its large peanut mills, and Lagos, with many small lumber mills, most such industries are found outside the major urban communities.

The market-oriented industries, on the other hand, are markedly concentrated in the major cities, which also are often ports and capitals of their countries (Map 50). Dakar, for example, had over half of industry in the former French West Africa, and Abidjan ranked second; these two cities continue to lead, though Abidjan has attracted more new industries than its older rival. Accra has the largest number of consumer industries in Ghana, though Tema appears to be getting a major share of new establishments and may even be considered as a port and industrial satellite of the capital city. Takoradi is also of significance.

Lagos and its adjoining towns, Apapa, Ebute Metta, Mushin, and Ikeja, comprise the largest industrial nucleus of Nigeria. But the very substantial regional authority in the Nigerian Federation has resulted in a greater dispersion of industry than would otherwise have occurred. There is even a degree of regional "me-too-ism" seen in the growth of some industries, such as textiles and cement. Each region appears to have a number of rising industrial centers, of which the more important are Ibadan and Abeokuta in the Western Region; Enugu, Onitsha, Aba, and Port Harcourt in the Eastern Region; and Kano and Kaduna in the Northern Region.

In the smaller countries, the capital city usually has the bulk of market-oriented manufacturing establishments: Conakry, Freetown, Monrovia, Lomé, and Cotonou, which are also the leading ports in their respective countries, and Bamako, Ouagadougou, and Niamey for the landlocked countries where development is very much lower.

The present most important industrial centers are likely to continue to attract a major share of new plants in the years ahead. They typically have the largest markets in their countries, the best transport facilities both for import and for distribution to the hinterland, the best-developed power facilities, the greatest number of semiskilled laborers, and the advantage of proximity to government departments.

FACTORS INFLUENCING DEVELOPMENT OF INDUSTRY

There are differences of opinion regarding the suitability of West Africa for industry. One fact that is certain, however, is that there will be continuing political pressure for the extension of manufacturing. The preceding analysis of existent industry has pointed to several important considerations pertaining to the suitability of specific industries for the stage of development now existent in West Africa. Now, an examination of the major factors influencing manufacturing will permit a more accurate assessment of the potentialities and limitations for continued industrial development in the area.

RAW MATERIALS

Developments already noted suggest that there are further opportunities for the exploitation and processing of raw materials. Particularly important are the new mineral bodies coming into use, the expansion of rubber production, increased processing of forest output, and extension of plants expressing oil from peanuts, palm fruit, and palm kernels. It is often assumed that, because the raw material is available, the producer should not only perform the preliminary processing but should manufacture the finished product as well and export it to the world market.

Several examples will illustrate the necessity of examining the appropriateness of each successive stage of manufacture, for the locational factors may be entirely different from one to the next. It is sometimes suggested, for instance, that Ghana, the world's largest producer of cocoa, should make chocolate and other finished products in which cocoa is consumed. There are numerous reasons why this is not practicable, except in so far as the chocolate would be marketed within Ghana itself: the storage of raw cocoa is difficult, of the finished product even more so, especially under tropical conditions; cocoa is only one raw material in chocolate, sugar and milk being more important from the standpoint of volume; there is only a very small internal demand; the finished product requires greater space in shipment, is more perishable, and is subject to greater damage in handling; and the skill required in manufacture is not yet available in Ghana.

A second example is that of veneers. The fact that only 25–30 percent of the log is used in veneering creates a very strong incentive to manufacture at the raw material site, but veneering demands considerable skill and the veneers need very careful packing and are subject to greater damage from insect attack. As has already been noted, even a plywood plant has certain difficulties because of the higher-cost glue required under tropical heat and humidity. These industries have, however, become more practical as special techniques and greater skill have been developed.

A third example is the iron and steel industry, whose appropriateness for Nigeria has been the subject of three major investigations. There is no question that it is physically possible to produce steel from the raw materials in Nigeria. But the iron ore is only of moderate grade and the coal is low quality, subbituminous, and noncoking. Natural gas might be used for a substantial part of the fuel requirements but would not satisfy the needs of a blast furnace. Here the alternatives would appear to be making the Enugu coal capable of being coked by the addition of pitch, a by-product of oil refineries, coking the lignites of southern Nigeria, or using a process which does not require coke. Westinghouse has recommended that Nigeria employ the Strategic Udy process, which requires neither scrap nor coke; a steel mill would consist of a rotary kiln, two electric reduction furnaces, a basic oxygen converter, a continuous casting machine, and two 25,000-kw generators. It has been estimated that such a plant with a 97,000-ton capacity would cost $72.5 million.

The Ferrostaal proposal suggested constructing a mill with 100,000-ton capacity consisting of a coking plant, lime kilns, blast furnace, oxygen converter, and power plant, the whole estimated to cost $63 million. This recommendation presupposed that Enugu coal could be coked by the addition of pitch. There is one major drawback to both of these recommendations, namely that the small scale of the plant is likely to result in high cost for the finished product. A disadvantage of the Strategic Udy process is that it has not been commercially operated and therefore there is inadequate experience upon which Nigeria might base a decision. The Nigerian market is too small to justify a mill large enough to permit savings by quantity production, and the record of other small mills in Africa, South America, and elsewhere indicates that their output is not competitive with the imported product. Unlike cotton textile mills, which can be constructed at relatively low cost, utilize unskilled labor, and have a market for the finished product, a steel mill involves a very heavy investment, requires an investment in iron, coal, and limestone mining, needs a substantial number of skilled workers, and has a ready market only for simple products such as sheets, bars, and rails. A fully integrated mill presupposes a substantial build-up in metal fabricating industries. It might well be more advantageous for a country at the stage of industrial development at which Nigeria now is to stimulate the growth of metal fabricating industries by using the lowest-cost steel available, even by subsidizing the purchase of imported steel. After some years, the market for steel would very probably justify the construction of a domestic steel mill. In the meantime, small rolling mills such as those at Tema and Emene based upon domestic scrap might satisfy the desire for possession of some steel-making capacity. Unfortunately, the establishment of an integrated works is often considered important to the national prestige, and this subjective view may dictate that a political rather than an economic decision be made with respect to a very large capital outlay.

POWER

Little need be added to what has already been noted regarding the energy position and potentials of West Africa. Provision of power for small industries is proceeding satisfactorily; development of large-scale projects will introduce an entirely new type of industry to West Africa. Nigerian resources of natural gas may prove attractive for a number of industries requiring low-cost energy, while oil and natural gas finds in the southern Sahara might eventually transform the energy position of portions of the area.

MARKET

In numbers, only Nigeria has a sizable market, though various customs unions create reasonably large market populations. Little effort has thus far been made to harmonize industrial development programs among the countries of West Africa, but a first exploratory meeting to examine such possibilities was held in September, 1962, with Nigeria, Niger, Dahomey, Upper Volta, and Mali in attendance. Countries such as Gambia, Sierra Leone, Liberia, Togo, Dahomey, Mauritania, and the three landlocked countries are distinctly handicapped by the small size of their national markets. The wide dispersion of peoples, particularly in former French countries, is disadvantageous as far as distributional costs are concerned, and transport facilities are often far from optimal as far as marketing is concerned. The marked concentrations of people in some parts of West Africa, on the other hand, favor the development there of consumer-oriented establishments. Most favored from this standpoint are the three clusters in Nigeria, the south of Ghana, and the area dependent upon Dakar.

From the standpoint of purchasing power the average per capita incomes are very low, which means, as far as market-oriented industries are concerned, that emphasis should be on relatively simple items which enjoy a broad market—items of clothing, canvas and leather shoes, household goods, etc. Ghana has the highest average income, which helps to explain its relatively good position among West African countries in industrial development. Senegal, with about 62,000 non-Africans, most of whom are in Dakar and who have relatively high per capita incomes, has a special market position of considerable actual and potential value to manufacturers.

LABOR

The main characteristics of the labor supply in tropical Africa have been impermanence, instability, low productivity, and low wages.[3] All but the last are not conducive to industrialization, and the advantage of low wages is offset in part by the resultant low purchasing capacity. These characteristics apply to labor in mining, agriculture, and other activities as well as to industrial workers.

IMPERMANENCE AND INSTABILITY. These characteristics reflect the evolving socioeconomic stage in which the African frequently has "one foot in the tribal area, one in the modern economy." While increasing numbers are detribalized and permanently urbanized, more so in some West African countries than in other parts of tropical Africa, greater numbers are still migratory.

Migrations are a long-standing feature in Africa; most movements take place on African initiative, though some are now subject to a degree of control. The duration and character of migrations vary greatly. Some Africans migrate to cities, some to seek employment on farms, both those of Europeans and Africans, some to mines or to engage in gold and diamond digging on their own; other forms of migration are those associated with nomadic grazing, with pilgrimages to Mecca, with service on freighters handling timber products, with coastal fishing, and with marketing of handicrafts. Some movements involve very substantial numbers. For example, it is estimated that about 100,000 people migrate from Upper Volta every year to Ghana and 150,000 to the Ivory Coast, while about 120,000 Voltarians are more or less permanently settled in Ghana and additional large numbers are semipermanent residents of the Ivory Coast. Other large-scale migrations include those from Rwanda to Uganda, from Mozambique to the Rhodesias and South Africa, and from the Bantu reserves and High Commission Territories to the places of employment in South Africa. Migration to the large cities has been intensifying, contributing to the many problems associated with rapid urbanization that is a characteristic of most countries.

Relatively few intensive studies have been made of migration, but it now appears that the incentives and explanations for it are highly complex. They include deterioration of the traditional subsistence agriculture in customary areas; the imbalance between population and resources in some areas; the desire to break away from the traditional rule and discipline of tribal society, including the wish to escape from continual requests from relatives for money or to get away from a reactionary chief; the fear of witchcraft in the home village; the development of new habits and needs; the social prestige stemming from certain types of employment; the psychological attractions of urban life; the desire to move where educational facilities are available; and the need to earn money to pay personal taxes. The relative weight of each of these depends upon many factors including who is making the assessment. Some see certain migrations, such as that from Mozambique to South Africa, as akin to forced labor; others claim that among some Mozambique tribes the man is hardly considered a man unless he has been off to work in the mines, this experience replacing to a degree the previous necessity to have killed a lion or stolen someone else's cattle as proof of maturity. Many migrants are considered to be "target workers"; as soon as earnings are adequate to buy the desired article, say a bicycle, or to meet the bride-price, the worker returns to his native village. Whatever the incentive or the duration, however, it is obvious that a largely migrant population is a disadvantage to industrial operations, greatly increasing the problems of training and promotion.

[3] See I.L.O., *African Labour Survey* (Geneva, 1958).

Instability is also explained by other factors. The cultural and mental factors conditioning the attitude of the African to work in general and to employee work in particular are not necessarily those of an American or European. African tribal life provides no particular conditioning for acceptance of the demands inherent in factory employment. Incentives may differ considerably from those of Europeans, there being numerous examples of workers, rather than being attracted to stay longer by higher wages, quitting sooner.

The conditions under which the African has to work and live also contribute to instability. The lack of security and the strangeness of a new environment contribute to the schizophrenic attitude created by the desire to retain ties in the tribal area. The lack of decent accommodations should also be mentioned, and many cities have been growing so rapidly that it has not been possible to keep up with the demand for housing. In certain parts of Africa there are also the irritations of Pass Laws and the restrictions on access to specific types of jobs which contribute to instability.

LOW PRODUCTIVITY. There is no basis for questioning the inherent abilities of the African to perform factory work; indeed there are examples, usually involving relatively simple repetitive operations, where his productivity is higher than that of the European. But with the present level of education and training it is not surprising that productivity is frequently only one-quarter to one-half as high as that of his European counterpart.

Low productivity is explained not only by the lack of an industrial heritage and inadequate training but by all the factors of instability noted above, and by climatic, health, and nutritional conditions. The evidence shows that the African is no better able to cope with high humidity than the European, while he frequently does not have proper clothing for the cold, wet, misty weather prevailing seasonally in some areas. The greatest single cause of absenteeism is poor health. There is abundant evidence that the typical worker's capacity is continuously impaired and often interrupted by endemic disease.

It is not surprising that high turnover and high absentee rates are characteristic of many enterprises engaging numbers of African wage earners. At the Wankie Collieries in Southern Rhodesia, turnover has been as high as 100 percent a year; in Salisbury, it is estimated to be about 80 percent in all types of occupations. A study[4] made by Peter Kilby in Nigeria indicates that some of the generalizations frequently made regarding African worker performance are not necessarily applicable in Nigeria. After studying 29 establishments employing 30,935 workers, he concluded that voluntary absence and voluntary turnover are low, that there is a high tolerance for continuous and demanding labor, and that productivity was often superior to that of the European in work involving simple repetitive motions. He also found a positive correlation between wages, hours, and distance from work on the one hand and absenteeism and turnover on the other, and a productivity about one-third to one-half the normal English standard in work requiring coordination of various operations.

Efforts to improve the output and stability of labor have received much greater attention in recent years. Increased emphasis has been placed on the selection of workers, sometimes involving the use of aptitude tests. Both government and individual employers have expanded technical training facilities. Much attention is given to health improvement, a field in which the big companies have often made notable contributions. New employees are examined and treated, efforts are made to acclimatize the worker, diet is sometimes improved by the provision of one hot meal free or by the subsidization of food. Tests made when employment is severed show that the vast bulk of workers have distinctly improved health conditions even after short periods of employment. An objection to special provisions respecting dietal intake is that they are a form of paternalism, that the worker

[4] Peter Kilby, "African Labour Productivity Reconsidered," *The Economic Journal* (June, 1961), pp. 273–91.

would prefer to receive additional cash payments rather than extra food.

Another technique of stimulating output and stability is through some kind of incentive payment such as bonuses for steady attendance, extra payments based on length of service, or payment on a piece-rate basis. Such incentives have not always proved successful, but probably will be increasingly effective as work experience increases. Amenity incentives are also used, including provision of better housing and food and recreational facilities.

The availability of managerial and technical ability is also of great importance in assessing the potentialities for industrialization. At present, tropical African countries must rely almost entirely on expatriate managers and technicians. This tends to make management costs higher than in other manufacturing countries because most such personnel will demand higher wages and provision of more amenities than they would expect at home. As Africans gain experience in the industrial world this differential can gradually be reduced, but under present circumstances it is good economics to pay sufficiently well to attract capable managers.

LOW WAGES. The subject of wage rates in Africa must be studied in the context of African conditions. Direct comparison of wages in Europe or North America with those in Africa is misleading. Purchasing power should be calculated in terms of local food and housing, and industrial wages should bear some relation to earning capacity in subsistence and commercial agriculture. Low wages also, of course, reflect low skill and low productivity. If wages are artificially forced to too high a level the economy is likely to be distorted and the chances for introducing new activities in many segments will be reduced.

Government can protect against exploitative wages and practices by various regulations, including the setting of minimum wages in various sections of the country, minima which are raised as productivity and the general economic position of the country improve. Particular attention is required to the introduction of a family rate rather than a bachelor rate if stability is to be attained.

PROVISION OF CAPITAL

The securing of adequate capital is another problem for African countries wishing to industrialize. Capital available from domestic sources is usually quite inadequate, though increasing amounts are being allocated from governmental revenues for investment in industry. In the former French territories, joint companies, with both private and government participation, have long been a common feature. The governments of Ghana and the first three Nigerian regions have been encouraging investment by providing a portion of the capital required for new industries in partnership with foreign and domestic companies.

Practically all African governments have taken steps in recent years to attract additional foreign capital, particularly for new industrial undertakings. The incentives include temporary exemptions from taxation, allowances for depreciation, remission of customs duties on imported equipment and raw materials, increased tariff protection for the product manufactured, and free transfer of dividends and repatriation of capital. In addition, attention is given to improved financial and advisory services, to the creation of a financial infrastructure more responsive to the needs of modern industry, and to the setting-up of industrial estates which obviate the necessity for prospective industrialists to worry about otherwise difficult tribal tenurial systems. Finally, efforts have been made to provide economic resource surveys and other data of importance to potential investors. The U.N. and its subsidiary, the IBRD, have been particularly important in publishing background studies of several tropical African countries.

The climate for investment, of course, differs widely from one country to another. One would not have expected private capital to move to Guinea or Mali, which were nationalizing enterprises in a variety of fields and were set upon a course of state socialism. The antipathy toward Western institutions expressed by the

Ghanaian press and radio must also weaken the response from potential investors. It is interesting to note, however, that Guinea and Ghana have both enacted recent laws which are designed to welcome foreign capital. These countries have come to realize that the task of development requires utilizing all resources available, that private enterprise can often operate more efficiently than state-run establishments, and without so great a commitment from the limited funds available to the government.

In conclusion, it is apparent that many difficulties exist to inhibit the rapid expansion of African industry, but that constructive steps are being made to reduce their dimensions. The opportunities for growth are undoubtedly very substantial, and there is no permanent impediment to the achievement of a fully integrated industrial establishment in the area. Nigeria would appear to have the greatest potentialities, and may some day see its Niger Valley develop as the Ruhr of West Africa.

Part Four EQUATORIAL AFRICA

Forest operations in Gabon
The largest area of rainforest in Africa is situated in the equatorial belt facing the Atlantic. Gabon and Congo (Brazzaville) have a particularly high dependence on the forest industries.

CHAPTER FOURTEEN

Middle Africa from Chad to Congo (Brazzaville)

There is no convenient term for the group of nations and territories covered in this chapter (Table 17). Included are four republics derived from the former French Equatorial Africa, the Federal Republic of Cameroon, comprised of the former French Trusteeship Territory and a part of the former British Southern Cameroons, the Spanish Equatorial Region, consisting of the mainland enclave of Rio Muni and the island of Fernando Po (Fernando Póo), and the Portuguese overseas province made up of São Tomé and Príncipe. The common heritage of five of these countries under French administration and the actual or near juxtaposition of the remaining territories make it appropriate to include them in one grouping. The former French countries also have in common adherence to the franc zone and membership in the UAM, OAMCE, and UDE. For convenience in this chapter the Republic of Congo (Brazzaville) will be referred to as Congo except where it is necessary to differentiate it specifically from the Republic of Congo (Leopoldville). The islandic portions are treated in subsections and do not necessarily share in the generalizations made for the continental regions.

GENERAL CHARACTERISTICS OF THE AREA

Certain keynotes and generalizations may appropriately be made regarding the continental part of the area covered in this chapter before an examination of the regional economies is begun. These are the enormous heterogeneity of the area; the marked isolation characterizing much of the region; the generally low densities of population; the relatively low stage of economic

Table 17. Areas and populations of middle African countries, 1961 and 1962

Country	Area in square miles	Population (in thousands) 1961	1962
Federal Republic of Cameroon	183,567	4,261	4,326
Republic of Chad	495,952	2,680	2,755
Central African Republic	238,224	1,227	1,255
Republic of Congo (Brazzaville)	132,046		820
Republic of Gabon	103,089	448	452
Spanish Equatorial Region			
Fernando Po	785	64	
Rio Muni	10,045	185	
São Tomé and Príncipe	372	64	

Sources: U.N. *Statistical Yearbook, 1962* (New York, 1963); U.N., *Monthly Bulletin of Statistics* (August, 1963).

development over large parts, even by African standards; the marked concentration of commercial activities into limited sections; and the rapidity with which political evolution to independence was achieved.

HETEROGENEITY OF THE AREA

While there is justification from the political standpoint for grouping together the five former French areas, there is a general lack of unity in almost all other respects. From the physical standpoint there is exceptional heterogeneity, not surprising when it is noted that the region comprises an area almost a third the size of the United States and extends from about 5° South to 20° 20′ North, and from the Atlantic deep into the interior of the continent. Geologically, it has portions of the Congo and Chad basins, of the pre-Cambrian basement complex, of recent volcanics, and of the Atlantic coastal plain. As regards climate and vegetation, it stretches from the equatorial rainforest through savanna and steppes to the heart of the Sahara. Precipitation varies from 400 inches to almost nil. Some areas have a surplus of water and wood; in others the scarcity of both presents major problems. Even the individual nations have relatively little homogeneity.

The human aspects of the area show similar diversity. There are, for example, an estimated 140 tribal groups in Cameroon, 40 in Congo, and 40 in Gabon, though often only a few tribes are of major importance. Ethnic groups range from Negrillos in the rainforests to groups of Negro, Bantu, and Hamitic stock. Contrasts in stage of development and degree of contact with modern forces are as sharp as anywhere in Africa. These contrasts tend to accentuate tribal differences and help to explain some of the political problems of the area. In Congo, for example, the Bakongo assume a position of dominance resented by other groups; in Gabon, the Fang, with about a quarter of the total population, are prominent; in Cameroon, the Bamiléké have been a particularly dynamic but also deviant group. The Central African Republic, however, has no dominant tribe among its multiplicity of ethnic groups. Chad is beset by tribal and other antagonisms and the position of chiefs is a problem sometimes of acute proportions. While not a factor of serious concern, white settlement in the mountains of western Cameroon and in the Niari Valley of Congo further complicates the human pattern.

IMPORTANCE OF ISOLATION

Chad and the Central African Republic lie close to the center of Africa and it is not surprising that they suffer from isolation. Fort Lamy is almost 700 miles from the sea and still possesses no easy routeway to it. Chad, the Central African Republic, Gabon, and Rio Muni have not a single mile of railway and the region as a whole has only 1 mile for every 1,400 square miles of area. Over three quarters of the population of former French Equatorial Africa resided over 600 miles from the sea. And large parts of Cameroon, Gabon, and Congo, all of which front on the sea, also suffer from isolation. The allocation to transport of 52 percent of FIDES funds available to French Equatorial Africa in the first ten-year plan, and continuing heavy expenditures in this field, suggest the overwhelming need to reduce this isolation.

LOW DENSITY OF POPULATION

Most of the region stands in strong contrast with many of the countries thus far examined from the standpoint of population density. Over-all densities, among the lowest of the continent, are greatest on the islands (111 per square mile) and Cameroon (23.5 per square mile) but average only 5.4 per square mile in the remaining nations. The shortage of manpower is considered particularly serious in Gabon and Congo, where it has made considerably more difficult the development of a rounded economy. Over-all density figures, however, conceal marked disparities within each nation.

In Congo, 70 percent of the population resides in the southern half. The Brazzaville district, with about 44 per square mile, is most heavily populated, followed by the coastal regions with 15 per square mile, while the forest zones of the north and the Batéké Plateaus, with average densities of only about 1 per square mile, are practically uninhabited over large stretches. Congo also has a higher percentage of urbanized peoples, over 19 percent of the total, with about 14 percent in Brazzaville alone.

Gabon has a somewhat more evenly distributed population, though there is clustering in the areas close to roads and waterways. Its only sizable urban areas are Libreville and Port Gentil. The Central African Republic has no densely populated areas with the exception of a few regions along the Ubangi River and on the border with Chad. The eastern three eighths of the country, however, has only one sixteenth of the population. Over 90 percent of the population is rural. Bangui, with about 90,000 people, is by far the largest agglomeration; its rapid growth in postwar years is considered to have been excessive in relation to the need for rural improvement.

Chad has the lowest urban population of the area, only 3.5 percent of the total. The Chari-Logone Basin in the southwest has the greatest densities; north of the 15° N parallel there is only one person for every 4 to 5 square miles.

Cameroon has an over-all density of 23.5 per square mile, but two thirds of the total is concentrated in three areas: in the north, from the Benue to Lake Chad; in the western highlands; and in the southwest, which includes the two cities of Douala and Yaoundé.

The population of the Spanish Equatorial Region is very unevenly distributed between the more developed island of Fernando Po and the mainland Rio Muni. Fernando Po, with an area of 779 square miles has a density of about 79 per square mile; Rio Muni, with an area of 10,045 square miles, has only about 18 per square mile. About 2,000 people inhabit the smaller islands of the Spanish Equatorial Region. São Tomé and Príncipe have a density of about 172 per square mile.

It should be emphasized that population figures for the region are estimated. Only the Spanish area has had a classic census; other figures were derived from administrative surveys. This means that it is not possible to estimate with any accuracy the rate of population growth. It was long believed that the population of Congo and Gabon was actually declining, but this was never substantiated. With a marked increase in health services in postwar years, it is reasonable to expect a rapidly lowering death rate throughout most of the area, which is likely to mean a nearly comparable increase in the rate of growth.

RELATIVE UNDERDEVELOPMENT

By most measurements, this middle African area rates low on the scale of economic development. French Equatorial Africa and Cameroon long remained the Cinderellas of the French Empire. This is explained only in part by the disappointing failures of many early concession companies, by the low population, difficulty of transport, and generally unhealthy conditions of the coastal stations. Other French overseas areas were considerably more attractive for the fairly limited prewar investments, particularly Indo-China, but also Senegal, the Ivory Coast, and Madagascar. Except for a few limited areas, no real effort was made to develop the economies of these areas until after World War II. As late as 1936 there were only 4,749 Europeans in all of French Equatorial Africa. The Congo-Ocean Railway was not completed until 1934; the modern port of Pointe Noire came into operation in 1939.

And despite a very considerable effort in postwar years, the economic positions of the several countries rate poorly. French Equatorial Africa and Cameroon accounted for only 0.5 percent of imports and 1.4 percent of exports of the continent in 1938. In 1961 they still accounted for only 3.3 percent of imports and 3.1 percent of African exports. Exports in 1961 from the whole area were less than those from Ghana and about equal to those from Angola and Mozambique combined. The remoter areas had very moderate levels of exchange; exports from the Central African Republic were valued at only $13 million, while Chad's totaled only $21 million.

In no commodity, except okoumé logs, lumber, and aluminum ingots, does any of the countries occupy a position of world importance. For its two leading exports, Cameroon produced about 6.7 percent of the world's cocoa and 1.2 percent of its coffee in 1961–62. The former French Equatorial Africa's leading export was forest products, especially okoumé; it produced only 0.25 percent of the world output of its second leading export, cotton. The element of isolation helps to explain why it is still accurate to state that this section of middle Africa is one of the least well-known regions of the world.

MARKED CONCENTRATION OF COMMERCIAL PRODUCTION

This keynote will have begun to be apparent by inference from the statements regarding varying population densities, isolation, and the relatively minor importance of the remoter countries in export trade. It will be illustrated more fully in connection with the regional discussions below.

RAPID POLITICAL EVOLUTION

While it is true that the now independent countries of this part of middle Africa achieved that status at about the same time as much of the rest of Africa, it must be said that independence came with great rapidity in relation to the levels of educational and economic development. The four states of French Equatorial Africa became internally autonomous republics within the French Community in 1958 and fully independent in August, 1960. Cameroon was declared independent by the U.N. on January 1, 1960, and became the Federal Republic of Cameroon on October 1, 1961, when it was joined by what is now West Cameroon.

The transition to independence was marked by considerable unrest in several of the countries. Tribal conflicts occurred in Congo, especially in 1959. But Cameroon has seen the longest and most severe troubles, dating from as early as 1955 and still not fully under control by 1963. French troops have been stationed in the area even since independence, and their presence probably prevented an anarchical situation. The most seriously affected area has been within a triangle with apexes at Dschang, Bafoussam, and Bafang, though the two main cities of Yaoundé and Douala were periodically placed under curfew. In the Bamiléké country there was a considerable destruction of banana, coffee, and cocoa plantations, while in December, 1962, while the author was visiting the area, the farmers were being made to cut vegetation 25 meters back on both sides of the road as a preventive measure against ambush, a truckload of soldiers having been killed in a carefully prepared ambush the previous week.

A complex situation was posed by the decision of part of the British trusteeship area of Southern Cameroons to join the Cameroon Republic, taken in the plebiscite of February, 1961, when the vote was 233,571 for and 97,741 against such a move. West Cameroon had been governed as a part of Nigeria and hence did not have the political and financial administrations needed by a federated state with a considerable degree of autonomy. Its money, system of taxation, prevailing wage rates, price levels, form of aid from the metropole, and relative lack of inflation were all in contrast with East Cameroon, as was its lingua franca. The last problem has been met by declaring both English and French to be official languages, making Cameroon the only country in Africa with two European languages officially accepted. Coordination of the economies has been phased in West Cameroon by a series of steps which have meant the gradual adoption of the East Cameroon system, but at least temporary retention of special trading relationships with Britain. Fears that the revolt might spread to West Cameroon and lead to a chaotic political situation in that area did not materialize.

The rapidity of political evolution is reflected at the governmental level by very serious shortages of qualified Africans, a shortcoming which has slowed the formation of effective bureaucracies. France, however, continues to pay for expatriates working with the several governments and Gabon, in particular, has elected to retain a large number of foreign advisers and administrators. The rapidity of political evolution is reflected in parts of the countryside by a general running-down of economic activity; in some areas the local residents stopped working on the roads, maintaining community plantations, and planting cash crops after independence. The problems faced by the African administration in attempting to improve the economy of an area as remote as the Central African Republic, where even subsidized prices bring poor returns to the average producer, are formidable, made particularly difficult by the fact that a large part of the populace has not reached the stage of having a real interest in and understanding of economic development.

LAND USE REGIONS

THE PREDOMINANTLY RAINFOREST SOUTH

Much of Congo, almost all of Gabon and Rio Muni, a narrow strip along the southwestern border of the Central African Republic, and a large swath across the south of Cameroon are in tropical rainforest and may be considered as the first major region (Maps 51, 54, and 55). The only large savanna areas within this section occur in Congo, where the coastal plain is largely untimbered, as are the Niari Valley, the hilly region around Stanley Pool, and the Batéké Plateaus toward the north.

TOPOGRAPHY. This whole area may be fairly easily divided into a number of roughly parallel topographic regions. First is a generally narrow low coastal plain, extending about 40 miles inland in Congo, from 18 to 125 miles inland in Gabon, and from a few miles in the extreme south of Cameroon to about 60 miles in width in the Douala area. South of Kribi the crystalline massif comes out to the sea and two tongues extend to the coast at Pointe Indienne and Pointe Noire in Congo. Except for Douala Bay, which is partly closed by sand, and the deeply indented northern shore of Gabon, the coasts are generally straight and sandy and often bordered with lagoons, frequently quite large and enclosed by mangrove swamps. The coastal region is the area of petroleum exploitation and continued exploration, the scene of the greatest activity in forestry, and the site of the few ports serving this part of middle Africa.

Inland from the coastal plain the land rises more or less abruptly to a series of hills, mountains, and plateaus, running parallel to the coast. In southern Congo this is the Mayombé Massif, consisting of a succession of sharp ridges with elevations from 1,600 to 2,600 feet cut deeply by the gorges of the Kouilou. In Gabon, almost all of which lies in the Ogooué Basin, mountains rise in various parts above the plateau extending over a portion of the south and all of the northern and eastern sections of the country. North of the Mayombé in Congo and extending into Gabon are the Chaillu Mountains, forming Gabon's main watershed and giving it, in Mount Iboudji, its highest elevation (5,186 feet). In the north of Gabon the Crystal Massif lies inland from the coastal plain. The plateau of Cameroon has an average elevation of about 1,600 feet but is quite hilly over large stretches. Much of this zone is deeply carved by the numerous rivers of the area.

On its interior side, this region of mountains and plateaus forms the western margin of the Congo Basin. The terrain along the Congo River is quite hilly where it cuts through the system at Stanley Pool. This gives way northward to the monotonous Batéké Plateaus separated from each other by the deep valleys of the northern tributaries of the Congo, while northeast of the Sangha River in Congo is a part of the true Congo Basin, where the rivers form a jumble of branches linked with one another and often flowing through a dense forest which is seasonally inundated.

TRANSPORTATION. This southern region, enjoying the best contacts with the sea, contains, with the exception of the western highlands of Cameroon, the most important actual and potential economic regions, accounting for a very large portion of the exports of the whole area. Before examining the specific economic interests, a discussion of the transport pattern of the area is appropriate.

There are six ports along this coast worthy of attention. Starting in the south, the first is Pointe Noire, the best equipped of the ports. An entirely artificial port protected by dikes, Pointe Noire was not started until the early thirties and only completed in 1939. The occurrence of a submarine rock spur along an otherwise difficult coastal stretch facilitated jetty and pier construction and accounts for the exact positioning of this port. With 3,600 feet of quays and 409,000 square feet of transit sheds, Pointe Noire has an estimated general cargo capacity of 600,000 tons, but this is now being doubled by the construction of two new piers.

French hopes that Pointe Noire would become the "Dakar of the South Atlantic" have by no means been achieved. It has been one of the few ports of tropical Africa possessing excess capacity, despite ranking as the main gateway of former French Equatorial Africa. Its traffic has, however, grown from 100,000 tons in 1947 to 793,000 tons in 1961, but this includes about 100,000 tons of petroleum exports. About one fourth of its tonnage is transit traffic from other nations of the former French Equatorial Africa, from the Congo (Leopoldville), and from the Cabinda Enclave of Angola.

Pointe Noire is connected with Brazzaville by the 317-mile Congo-Ocean Railway (CFCO). This single-track, standard-gauge line was started in 1921 and was finished at an immense cost in lives and money in 1934. It provides, like the Matadi-Leopoldville line in former Belgian Congo, an outlet from the areas tributary to the Congo River, whose extensive inland navigable stretches begin at Stanley Pool. Part of the produce of eastern Gabon uses the so-called Federal Route via the Congo system and the CFCO; most of the trade of the Central African Republic, and part of that of Chad, also employs this somewhat lengthy route. The CFCO follows a difficult route through the Mayombé Massif, necessitating 12 tunnels, one about a mile long, 92 bridges, steep gradients, and excessively narrow curves. Shortage of funds accounts for the somewhat inadequate trajectory of the line, which has required slow operating speeds and which helps to explain the

The port and part of the city of Pointe Noire, Congo (Brazzaville) This artificial harbor is expected to increase greatly in importance with new mining and industrial enterprises in its hinterland.

fact that the line has normally operated at a deficit.

Although the CFCO and Pointe Noire had excess capacity available while the Leopoldville-Matadi line was severely taxed, almost no traffic from the Congo (Leopoldville) was permitted to escape via the French line until the mid-1950s; in 1958, 30,000 tons of copper from the Katanga moved over the CFCO. Over a third of the total tonnage is normally comprised of low-paying forest products; cotton and peanuts moving downline and cement and petroleum products moving inland are other important tonnage items.

The city of Brazzaville has grown with great rapidity in postwar years, first as a governmental center, second as a nascent industrial community, and third as a river port. It has been improved in postwar years by construction of quays and provision of cranes and other mechanical gear but its cargo tonnage is far below its counterpart on the other side of the Pool. About three eighths of its traffic is in transit for other nations.

The Congo and Ubangi rivers form the border of Congo (Brazzaville) and the Central African Republic with Congo (Leopoldville). They are navigable to Bangui, a distance of 740 miles from Brazzaville. A shelf at Zinga, 60 miles below Bangui, which inhibited navigability in low flow periods, has been removed to make Bangui accessible all year. Here the Ubangi is interrupted by rapids, upstream from which the river is not well suited for regular traffic. Many of the right-bank tributaries of the Congo in Congo (Brazzaville) are navigable for some distances at least seasonally. The Sangha, which is the most important of these, is open to smaller boats as far as Ouesso. At present, however, the regions served by these streams are generally unproductive and the streams continue to be used mainly by dugout canoes for local interchanges.

The rail-river route from Pointe Noire to Brazzaville to Bangui, called the Federal Route, is, then, one of the main routeways of our whole region. The relatively low levels of river traffic, about 140,000 tons at Bangui and 200,000 tons at Brazzaville, reflect one of the previously mentioned keynotes—the relatively low stage of economic development in the areas served. They also suggest the significance of Brazzaville as a consuming center and the importance of the seaward areas as producers. These include, in particular, the Niari Valley and the forest reserves of Congo. And, while Pointe Noire has failed thus far to warrant the title of "Dakar of the South Atlantic," there are excellent prospects for a very marked growth in the decades ahead. As will be noted later, Pointe Noire is slated to become an important shipper of manganese; new roads and railways should stimulate its timber shipments; continued development in the Niari Valley should increase agricultural exports; and, finally, construction of the Kouilou hydroelectric project will make it an important center for electro-process industries. In the long run, it could well handle an increased share of traffic from the Congo (Leopoldville). The Federal Route is, finally, one of the few economic assets of Congo of major importance.

Port Gentil and Libreville are the main ports of Gabon, which has one of the least adequate transport systems in Africa. Port Gentil is a lighterage port, equipped with a new 1,110-foot pier in the late 1950s, while a wharf for loading crude oil and receiving general cargo is under construction. Except for petroleum, the bulk of traffic at Port Gentil is okoumé logs, brought down the Ogooué system in rafts, or plywood and veneers from a large mill in operation since 1950. Libreville is also a lighterage port, situated along the northern shore of the Gabon Estuary, actually a deeply indented bay. The city itself, possessing three wharves of which one is modern and well equipped, handles a relatively small tonnage. Okoumé roundwood, which accounts for over 90 percent of outgoing traffic of the estuary, is handled at Owendo, 10 miles upstream from Libreville. Rafts of 40 to 60 logs brought to Owendo are sorted and reassembled into larger rafts called *dromes* which are then pulled by tugs alongside the ships lying

Assemblage of dromes *of okoumé logs at Owendo, Gabon* These rafts are hauled to vessels lying at anchor. Okoumé is particularly favored for production of plywood.

at anchor. Loading is carried on by experienced Kru seamen picked up and let off at such points as Monrovia and Sassandra on each voyage. A study is now under way to determine whether Libreville or Pointe Pongara on the south bank of the estuary should be the terminus of a rail line to be built to the Mékambo region in the northeast corner of Gabon. Gabon benefits considerably from the presence of navigable waterways, whose total length is over 620 miles. The Lower Ogooué, the main lifeline of the country, is navigable 150 miles to Lambaréné year round, while 170- and 190-mile stretches are seasonally open to shallow-draught river boats. The Ogooué's main affluent, the Ngounié, is navigable 50 miles to Sindara by 5-foot draught vessels and 65 miles between Fougamou and Mouila from October to June. North of Cape Lopez the Gabon Estuary, Mondah Bay, and Rio Muni offer good access for deepsea vessels but their tributaries are fairly restricted even for shallow craft. The Gabon Estuary is not a true estuary and the absence of any sizable streams flowing into it reduces its value considerably.

The roads of Congo and Gabon provide only a rudimentary system, open only limited distances to heavy-duty traffic. Construction and maintenance costs are very high, especially in the rainforest regions. Most of Gabon's roads date from World War II, there having been only about 60 miles open in 1936. A main north-south highway connects with Douala in Cameroon and Dolisie in Congo and a road runs from this highway to Libreville. Several of the main towns along the coast are still accessible only by water, however. Congo has an international airport at Brazzaville and an excellent field at Pointe Noire plus 12 local airports. In Gabon, Libreville and Port Gentil have large airports and lesser towns are served by minor fields.

Moving up the coast, Rio Muni's main gateway is Bata, a lighterage port using a small concrete jetty. Some of the rivers of the country are used for floating logs. Roads are generally good, in part because the villages along them are responsible for maintaining them. A good airport exists at Bata.

Cameroon has one major and three minor ports. Kribi is a small lighterage port at the mouth of the Kienké with a 460-foot pier used primarily for shipment of logs and of cocoa from the Boulou district. It handled 37,000 tons in 1961. The main gateway is Douala on the estuary of the Wouri River. It is accessible by a channel which requires periodic deepening but which is now capable of taking the largest cargo vessels used in west African trade; it may eventually be further deepened to take larger tankers. Douala now has seven quay posts for ocean vessels, one especially equipped to handle forest products, one used for unloading petroleum which is pumped by a 2.5-mile pipeline to storage tanks at Bassa, and five used for general cargo. Four old berths are being reconstructed with the aid of a grant from the EEC and new fishing facilities are also being built. Bananas are often shipped from Bonaberi, across the estuary. Douala-Bonaberi, which accounts for the vast bulk of East Cameroonian imports and exports, handled 646,000 tons in 1955 and 937,000 tons in 1961. Importation of alumina for refining at Edéa and export of aluminum ingots have increased traffic at Douala in recent years. A small tonnage traffic for the

Central African Republic, some of it moving by air, uses the port of Douala.

Douala is now the terminus of the two short rail-lines of Cameroon. Both of these meter-gauge lines were largely completed by the Germans before World War I. They were not joined until 1955, when the Wouri Bridge permitted using a common terminus and workshops at Bassa, just outside Douala. In postwar years, both lines were modernized and largely dieselized, and rolling stock was more than doubled. Despite this and an increasing traffic, the Cameroon lines are a high-cost operation and high rates are required to cover expenses. Their limited lengths contribute to the high costs, making them particularly susceptible to road competition, which is an intensifying problem. The railway authorities have, however, succeeded in discouraging road transport between Douala and Yaoundé by preventing improvement of the road beyond Edéa.

The Northern Line runs 99 miles from Bonaberi to N'Kongsamba, serving the most important banana and coffee producing areas of East Cameroon. It was originally intended that it be continued northward, but the extremely difficult terrain of the western mountains led to abandonment of this goal. There is now talk of laying a 19-mile branch to Kumba in West Cameroon, whose connections with East Cameroon were still in a deplorable state in 1963. The Central Line runs 191 miles from Douala to Yaoundé and has a 24-mile branch to Mbalmayo on the Nyong River. It serves the industrial town of Edéa, the capital of Yaoundé, and the main cocoa producing area of the southern plateaus.

In 1962 a decision was made to begin construction of a rail line from Yaoundé which should eventually extend to the north of the country. The first section, built under loans and grants totaling $35 million from France, the United States, and the EEC, will extend 205 miles from the capital to Goyoum. It is intended that the line later be carried to N'Gaoundéré on the Adamoua Plateau and then to Moundou in Chad. A branch might be connected to Bangui. This new rail activity should contribute to continued growth at Douala, though the only known resource near the new line whose development could yield really large-scale tonnage increases is bauxite in the Martap region.

The roads of southern Cameroon are sparsely distributed and often in extremely poor condition. As in other rainforest areas, road construction is very expensive; the 110-mile road from Bonaberi to N'Kongsamba cost $117,466 a mile and requires a yearly expense of $2,415 per mile for maintenance. Eventually, two trunk roads are planned to connect with the northern part of the country. The rivers of southern Cameroon are only of local interest.

West Cameroon has two very inadequate ports. Tiko has a quay capable of taking 460-foot vessels with a maximum draught of 20 feet, while logs are floated to ships tied up at two official posts in the harbor. The narrow, winding access to Tiko greatly restricts its utility. Bota (Victoria) is a lighterage port with four recognized anchorages in Ambas Bay. Studies are being made of possible overland connections between these ports and Douala which might eventually lead to their suppression. The roads in the extreme south of West Cameroon are

Loading bananas on a lighter at Victoria, West Cameroon
Hovercraft, capable of moving smoothly over rough-cut roads and over water, may be adopted here to reduce damage to and handling of bananas.

paved, but their use by large trucks hauling logs to port has often destroyed the surface; elsewhere the roads are generally poor and seasonally impassable. Plans have been announced to utilize Hovercraft for the transportation of bananas from plantations via rough throughways made by bulldozers to shipping points.

THE SUBSISTENCE ECONOMY. Although the rainforest areas of the middle African region have the greatest commercial development of any parts, and although a considerable number of the available workers have been attracted to employment in the forest areas and commercial-urban centers, a high percentage of the population is still engaged primarily in subsistence production. In Congo, an estimated 75 percent of agricultural production is for subsistence and 60 percent of the active population is engaged in farming, but agricultural exports are of very minor importance. In Congo, 69 percent of the population is still dependent upon agriculture.

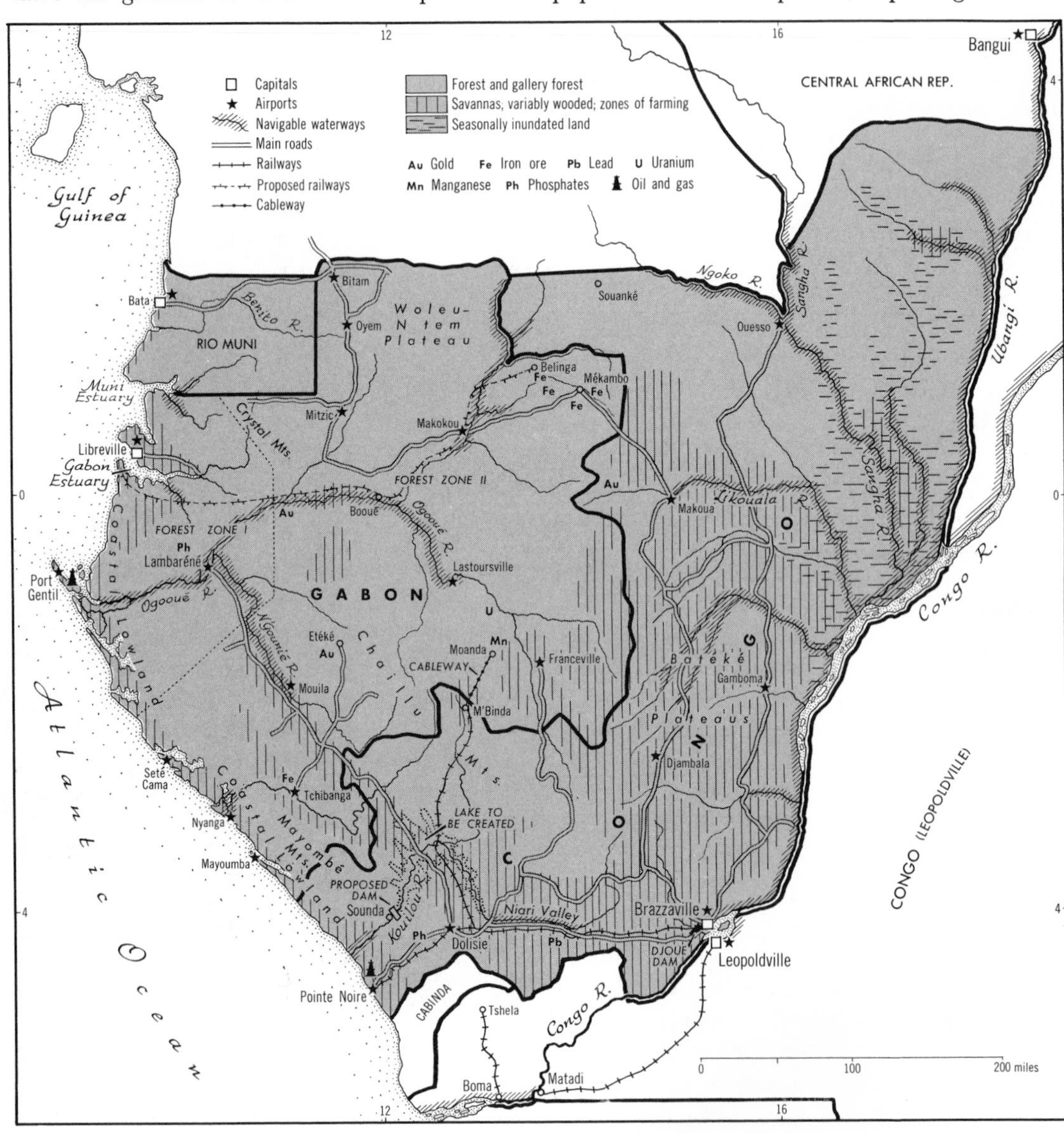

Map 51. Economic map of Gabon and Congo (Brazzaville)

The small Negrillo population follows a semi-gather economy, but the more widespread agricultural system is the traditional shifting agriculture, which, in some of the more remote areas, is probably as little changed as anywhere in Africa. Production from the laboriously cleared forest plots is supplemented, where possible, by products gathered directly from the forest, by fishing, and by hunting. Fish are obtained by seining with fiber nets, by poisoning pools, and by draining pools, particularly in the low-water season.

FORESTRY. Forests cover half of Congo and almost all of Gabon (Map 51), providing the major source of income for both countries. In 1961, forest products accounted for almost 70 percent of the exports by value of Gabon and 61 percent of those of Congo. The Central African Republic exports some logs and lumber to Congo (Leopoldville). Cameroon has a less important share in the forest industry, but production and exports have increased rapidly in recent years, and exploitation in West Cameroon is quite intensive.

In general, the countries of this region which have tropical rainforests have the same limitations and potentialities as those detailed for West Africa and it is unnecessary to repeat them here. There are, however, certain characteristics which distinguish this region from West Africa.

First, the forest area is greater and less degenerated than that along the coasts of West Africa. This is explained in part by a much lower density of population in the forest zone. Nonetheless, there has been such intensive exploitation in the so-called Forest Zone I in Gabon, particularly of the favored okoumé species, that five big operators had been forced to move to the second zone by 1963, which increases their costs because of the greater distance from the coast, the more rugged terrain, and the reduced ability to use navigable waterways in moving the logs to seaboard. Okoumé, which is a tropical softwood particularly suitable for peeling to produce plywood, accounts for 85 percent of Gabon's timber exports. While the present level of output cannot be sustained in Forest Zone I, it is estimated that the total exploitable area is twenty times the area now being used. In Congo, exploitation of the interior area around Betou up the Ubangi River began in 1962, this being the first major development of any kind in a region considered unusually rich in fine tropical woods. In Cameroon, an area over ten times the size of the present exploited area is available.

Second, the labor supply in this region is much more limiting than in West Africa and has often been considered the major factor restricting production. Third, some species occur in greater concentrations than is typical of most tropical forests, a marked advantage in view of the characteristic high selectivity of logging operations. Particularly favorable is the extent of okoumé, which is not found in other tropical forests and the attributes of which have already been noted. Okoumé stands are particularly important in Gabon, Congo's main timber export being *limba.* Nevertheless, the high concentration upon okoumé is a concern to Gabonese and Congolese officials who would like to promote the use of other species, particularly *ozigo* and *azobé.* There are also plans for extensive artificial plantings of okoumé, with one such experiment being located at N'Koulounga. Experts have recommended that about 7,500 acres should be planted to okoumé each year in Gabon, suggesting that the trees might be interplanted with bananas or oil palms. Experimental plantings in Gabon have shown that one could obtain about 100 tons per acre in 50–60 years instead of the natural yield of 1 to 4 tons per acre, while wood for cellulose would also be available ten years after planting.

Fourth, some areas of this region are particularly favored by the existence of an intricate system of waterways. The northern embayments and the Ogooué River system in Gabon are especially favored in this regard, helping to explain why that country has the greatest interest in the forest industry. Cameroon is less favored in this regard, though a very large modern sawmill at Eseka uses water transport

A heating press used at the large plywood factory at Port Gentil, Gabon
This plant has a capacity of 10 million board feet a month but has had difficulty in securing adequate markets to permit operating at that level.

Cocoa growing in a partially cleared rainforest area near Yaoundé, Cameroon
Cameroon ranks fifth among world cocoa producers and cocoa is its leading export.

on the Wouri. The rail line in Congo is important in stimulating forest exploitation in that country, and new mineral lines in both Congo and Gabon will open up possibilities for intensified forest activity in new areas.

Other special features of forestry in this area include the existence of a large hardwood plywood plant at Port Gentil and of a pulp mill twelve miles from Pointe Noire producing cellulose. The plywood plant, with a capacity of 10 million board feet a month, was built in 1948 by U.S. Plywood for French interests, the Compagnie Française du Gabon. The mill is one of the largest in the world, but the available market, limited in Europe because of protection secured by metropolitan plywood interests, has never permitted its full-scale operation. Nonetheless, it ranks as Gabon's fourth largest enterprise with an output of 590,000 square feet in 1961 valued at about $8 million. The cellulose plant, owned by a Danish and French company, is relatively small but represents, it is hoped, the beginnings of much larger scale operations, based also on low-cost power. Gabon, for example, hopes to establish a mill with a capacity of 100,000 tons a year. Other somewhat specialized plants include a new mill at Dimbrako in south-central Cameroon designed primarily to produce knocked-down wooden fruit and vegetable crates for sale in France, and the Eseka plant of Les Bois du Cameroun which mass-produces prefabricated houses, almost all of which have thus far been marketed in adjacent countries.

Despite the existence of these and other plants, most of the forest products of the region are exported undressed or only semifinished, though Congo has seen a sharp rise in output of lumber and plywood in recent years. In Gabon, only the large sawmill at Foulenzem is equipped to handle hardwoods; it produces railroad ties and other timbers for France's state railways. None of the 22 sawmills in Gabon is operated to capacity.

COMMERCIAL CROP PRODUCTION. Small tonnages of various tropical vegetable products are commercialized in the rainforest region under consideration, but only cocoa, palm products, and bananas are of any great importance.

The major producing area for cocoa is the region around Yaoundé in southern Cameroon, though plantings are found in a much wider belt across the south. An estimated 180,000 to 200,000 planters produce about 70,000 to 75,000 tons yearly on small holdings, often intermixed with bananas and cassava. Yields are low and quality has tended to decline in recent years. Nonetheless, cocoa has long been the prime export of the country, which ranks fifth among world cocoa producers. Its output, however, is less than a fifth that of Ghana. Efforts to improve quality and yields have involved the distribution of improved seedlings, premium payments for higher grade beans, and education concerning planting and conditioning practices. The bulk of the cocoa region falls within the purview of the Secteur de Modernisation du Centre (Semcentre), whose efforts have not been very successful in recent years. Cocoa prices have been subject to a price stabilization scheme since 1955, but the farmer often gets only a fraction of the f.o.b. Douala price, the remainder being absorbed by middlemen, taxes, and transport operators.

Gabon produces about 2,500 to 4,000 tons of cocoa yearly from the Woleu-N'Tem and Ogooué-Ivindo regions in the north. Production began under a compulsory planting program but gradually caught on and now these regions are about the only areas of Gabon with a stable and relatively prosperous indigenous agriculture. A very small output of cocoa comes from around Souanké and Ouesso in the north of Congo. The remoteness of the Gabon-Congo areas is a continuing handicap; Gabon cocoa is shipped via Douala, Congo's over the Federal Route.

Banana production is concentrated mainly on European plantations in a narrow band along the Northern Line of the Cameroon railway. Two main problems have affected the planter in recent years: chronic overproduction and the increasing incidence of Panama disease, which started in 1956. A possible solution to the latter problem would be to switch from the predominant Gros Michel variety to the disease-resistant Poyo variety, which has the additional advantage of yielding three times as much. But a rapid switchover is deemed inappropriate because of preferences for the Gros Michel in the traditional markets, especially Western Germany. About 56 percent of export bananas from East Cameroon come from industrial estates, the remainder from small holdings.

Bananas being loaded for transport to Douala, Cameroon
In East Cameroon bananas are produced mainly on European plantations along the Northern Line of the Cameroon Railway. Plant disease problems have plagued the industry in recent years.

Palm products account for a small percent of exports from Cameroon and Gabon; they rank first among agricultural exports from Congo but account for only about 7 percent of the total value of exports. Shortage of manpower and keen competition in the French market from Senegalese-Malien peanut production tend to suppress interest, though some new plantations have been started in Congo and Gabon. Oil palms are found in three main centers in Congo: the very large but isolated natural grove of Moabi, a small natural stand at Kango, and around Lambaréné, where plantations are expanding. Young plantations are situated at Etoumbi and Lebango in the Likouala-Mossaka

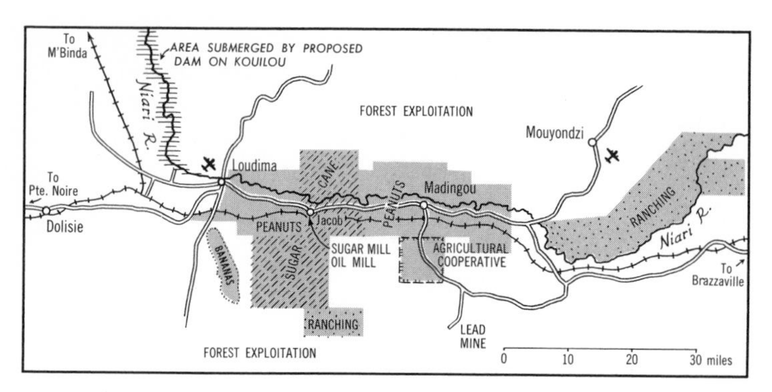

Map 52. The Niari Valley in Congo (Brazzaville)

region and at Ouesso. Congo now has about 37 palm oil mills, 22 of which are privately owned.

There is a small commercial production of numerous other tropical crops which may be briefly summarized as follows: (1) about 4,000 tons of rubber come from a 22,000-acre plantation at Dizangué on the banks of the Sanaga near Douala; (2) 400 tons of tobacco were exported from Congo in 1959, coming from the Djambala and Batéké Plateau regions; (3) coffee is produced in scattered areas of the rainforest, but the main coffee areas of both Cameroon and the Central African Republic are outside this region. Six thousand acres have been planted in Gabon in recent years with French aid.

Gabon and Congo have such poorly developed agricultural bases that they are quite heavily dependent on food imports. Production for the domestic market is restrained by the difficulty of farming in rainforest areas, by the shortage of labor, by the poor transport facilities, and by the aversion to farm work on the part of adult males. Efforts to stabilize rural communities and to expand production of food crops have frequently been frustrated, but a number of "paysannats" had relatively good success. Paysannats, which were started in 1952, involved a multifaceted effort to improve village life and farming practices. Requiring a heavy expenditure per capita and much supervision, they are difficult for African governments to promote. Congo has been attempting to improve its agriculture by introducing "mutuels" or incipient cooperatives, agricultural credit, and rural training centers. In Gabon, some success in developing paddy cultivation has been had in the Tchibanga district but, illustrating the transport difficulties, it is necessary to fly rice to coastal markets where it can only be sold at prices above those prevailing on imports. A great hope in Gabon is that mining and industrial expansion will stimulate "light agriculture" to provide food for the supporting communities. A specific example of such stimulation is seen in the recent signing of a contract by the company developing petroleum in the area for production of local produce near Port Gentil.

FISHING. Relatively little is known regarding the fish population of the offshore waters. Small whales have been caught off Congo and Gabon for production of oil, but the catch has had to be restricted in recent years to permit regeneration. Fishing in rivers and lagoons provides local supplies of valuable protein food and some thousands of fishponds have been created and stocked with tilapia. The presence of the Benguela Current suggests that ocean fishing might be intensified, but no accurate estimate can be given of the potential until further research has been conducted. Pointe Noire has a modern fish canning establishment which was enlarged in 1962 to a capacity of about 1.5 million cans of tuna and pilchards monthly, and Douala is improving its fishing port, but most fishing is still handled by pirogues.

THE NIARI VALLEY SUBREGION. The Niari Valley (Map 52), situated inland from Pointe Noire below the main scarp, rates particular attention because of its special physical features and because of the concentration of government-assisted projects in the region. The advantages which account for this special interest are (1) the climatic regime, marked by a dry season from May to October and two rainy seasons from October to January and March to May which make two planting cycles possible and permit production of a wide variety of crops including corn, rice, and peanuts. Topographical conditions and the presence of the cool Benguela Current explain the somewhat atypical climate of the region. (2) There is a substantial flattish area possessing soils with good structure and depth, making the valley the only truly fertile region of Congo. Soil scientists estimate that 600,000 acres are suitable for cultivation. (3) The natural vegetation over most of the area was tall grass, much easier to clear than tropical rainforests. (4) The Niari River, actually the upper part of the Kouilou, provides potentialities for irrigation. (5) There is a somewhat greater density of population in the region, reducing the problem of securing laborers. (6) The valley is well served by means of transport, being along the route of the Congo-Ocean Railway and one of the main roads of Congo. (7) There has been an unusual concentration of research and experimental activities in the valley. In addition to the work of the agricultural research station at Loudima, studies are being made there and at Sibiti and Madingou on vegetable oils, cotton, fruits and vegetables, and forest and water resources including fishponds. (8) The periphery of the valley may be of future importance in mineral production as there are known deposits of lead, zinc, tin, gold, and diamonds. At the present time, however, only the marginal M'Fouati lead-zinc mine is of any significance.

A great variety of crops have been introduced in the valley, including vegetables, bananas, corn, manioc, and tobacco. Dry rice is produced in part by cooperative mechanical cultivation. The region accounted for a large share of peanut exports from French Equatorial Africa, though its production was far below that of the north.

Major attention has been focused upon sugar cane. La Société Industrielle et Agricole de la Vallée du Niari (SIAN) has, at Jacob, the only sugar factory in all of former French Equatorial Africa. SIAN has been operating since the 1940s and has three separate farms employing about 2,000 Africans and 70 Europeans. In 1959, 5,750 acres of cane were cut, treated, and refined, and acreages in sugar have continued to expand. The total production is sold in middle Africa, where the market has been expanding with some rapidity, but costs of production are still high, requiring protection for sugar in the domestic market. In 1961, SIAN gave up planting manioc and began experimentation with rubber.

In addition to tillage agriculture, cattle are raised on several ranches and are grazed on the savanna hills bordering the valley. The tsetse-resistant N'Dama cattle have been introduced from West Africa, and Congo had about 22,000 head by 1961 plus a few Montbeliard cattle on ten small European farms and one semipublic ranch between Mouyondzi and Mindouli. Pigs and chickens are also kept, but output of all animal products is far below demand.

A large field of mechanically cultivated peanuts in the Niari Valley, Congo (Brazzaville)
This favored subregion has been the scene of intensive development in postwar years.

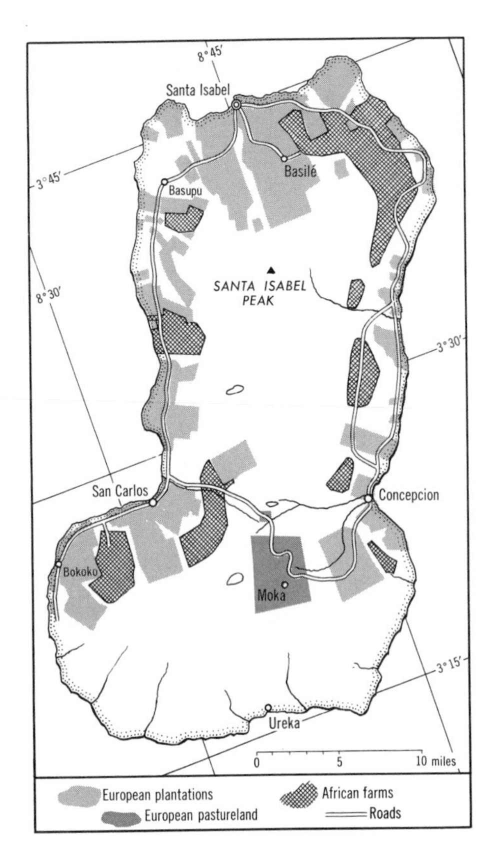

Map 53. Land use of Fernando Po

The Niari Valley has several types of agricultural holdings, ranging from large industrial estates of around 10,000 acres to individual European farms of 1,250 to 2,500 acres, small "colonats" of 125 to 250 acres, and "paysannat indigènes." The first paysannat was created at Divenié, where African farmers have been encouraged to grow oil palms and coffee on the edge of their traditional holdings. The success of operations in the Niari Valley is still far from assured except possibly for the paysannats and the cattle ranches. Many of the small colons and the bigger operators have had great difficulty in achieving a reasonable profit.

SPANISH AND PORTUGUESE POSSESSIONS

As both the mainland and islandic portions of the Spanish Equatorial Region and the Portuguese islands of São Tomé and Príncipe have tropical rainy climates, it is appropriate to examine them briefly at this point. The Spanish region consists of Rio Muni, an enclave between Cameroon and Gabon, Fernando Po, Annobón, and about a dozen islands and islets adjacent to the two main islands. Since the region is considered to be a province of Spain, all the inhabitants are citizens of that country. The region has thus far been free of serious political difficulties, despite the fact that Rio Muni is now bounded by independent countries. This has been explained by the thoroughgoing Spanish paternalism, by the practice of limited assimilation, and by the absence of strong incentive or the means for political activity or protest. Complaints of exploitative use of labor on Fernando Po have not been substantiated by investigations.

Rio Muni, with an area of 10,045 square miles, long remained largely untouched because of the more attractive character of Fernando Po. It has, however, witnessed a considerable boom in postwar years. Its main interest is focused upon timber products and coffee. Some twenty concessionaires hold rights over 300,000 acres of forests; operations are concentrated near the coasts, to which the Benito River and Muni Estuary are used to float logs. Europeans and Africans produce the coffee, which has been robusta and liberica, but arabica is now replacing the latter. Palm products and bananas are also grown on large plantations.

Fernando Po, about 44 miles long and 22 miles wide and with an area of 779 square miles, is the more important part of Spanish Guinea (Map 53). The smaller islands, some of which were formerly infamous as slaving depots, are now of little economic importance. The islands are of volcanic origin and are related to the Cameroon Mountain system. A narrow coastal plain rises gradually behind steep shores to mountain slopes culminating in the 9,350-foot Pico de Santa Isabel.

Cocoa is the main crop of Fernando Po, which was one of the first areas of Africa to become interested in its production. Despite its small size, it accounts for about 2.3 percent of the world's output. Most of the cocoa comes from large farms (*fincos*) ranging from 100 to 2,000 acres situated all along the western, northern, and eastern coasts, and up to 2,000 feet above sea level. Quality of the beans is high and the island has remained free from swollen shoot.

Fernando Po also produces about a third of the coffee from the Spanish Equatorial Region. Coffee ranks third after cocoa and forest products among the province's exports; it is grown up to about 3,000 feet elevation and almost entirely on European estates. Beginning at about 3,300 feet, but largely between 4,000 and 5,350 feet, is a region of pasturelands, frequently enveloped in mist, which have for the most part been carved from the forests. Their output permits Fernando Po to be self-sufficient in dairy products, but it is still necessary to import meat.

Fernando Po has a population of about 64,000, including about 6,000 Europeans. The local tribes provide an inadequate labor supply and, normally, about 20,000 to 25,000 West Africans, mostly Nigerians, migrate to the island to work on the estates. Santa Isabel, on the northern tip of the island, is the capital, commercial and financial center, and main port. It has docking facilities for two freighters, which is considered adequate for the foreseeable future. San Carlos is also a port of call. The island is well served with hard surfaced roads and there is an airport near Santa Isabel.

About three quarters of Spanish Guinean trade is with Spain. Exports have increased markedly in postwar years and were valued at $33.5 million in 1961. Spain pays above world prices for Guinean produce, has permitted Guinea to have lower customs duties than for the metropole, and has been generous in its allowance of foreign exchange. It is quite obvious that this province benefits from being the sole member of the Spanish Equatorial Region for which the Spanish market, while not large, is certainly adequate enough to stimulate production, even in so small an area. Pride of possession and the desire to demonstrate the benefits of Spanish rule have undoubtedly also accounted for the special attention given to educational, health, and other social services.

São Tomé and Príncipe are situated about 180 miles off the coast. Discovered by the Portuguese in 1470, they depended for their early development on sugar and slaves. Cocoa was introduced in 1822 and the two islands ranked as the second world exporter in 1907; annual production is now about three-eighths that of the Spanish Equatorial Region. Coffee is the second main crop, and there is a small output of coconuts, palm oil, cinchona, vanilla, rubber, cinnamon, and kola nuts.

Despite a population density of 171 per square mile on the 330-square-mile São Tomé and of 179 per square mile on the 42-square-mile Príncipe, there is a shortage of farm workers, and about 25,000 contract laborers recruited from Angola, Mozambique, and Cape Verde Islands are employed on the cocoa and coffee plantations.

Both islands are volcanic, which explains both the richness of their soils and the high percentage of lands in steep slopes. Precipitation varies from 100 inches to 12 inches depending on aspect of slope and elevation. The lower and most intensively used sections, which are on the northeastern part of both islands, have densities reaching 650 per square mile.

THE REGIONS OF SOUTHWESTERN CAMEROON

The southwestern regions of Cameroon are distinguished by their elevation, their volcanic heritage, and by population densities considerably higher than in most of the middle African area. Starting with Mt. Cameroon (13,370 ft) there is a whole line of volcanoes running northeastward, sometimes rising from and bounded by high crystalline and volcanic plateaus. Many of the volcanic soils are superior in quality, while the area is ecologically suitable for a great variety of tropical crops including those of higher value usually associated with tropical highlands. Development in the former French and former British parts of the area differs greatly, making it desirable to divide the area into two regions (Map 54).

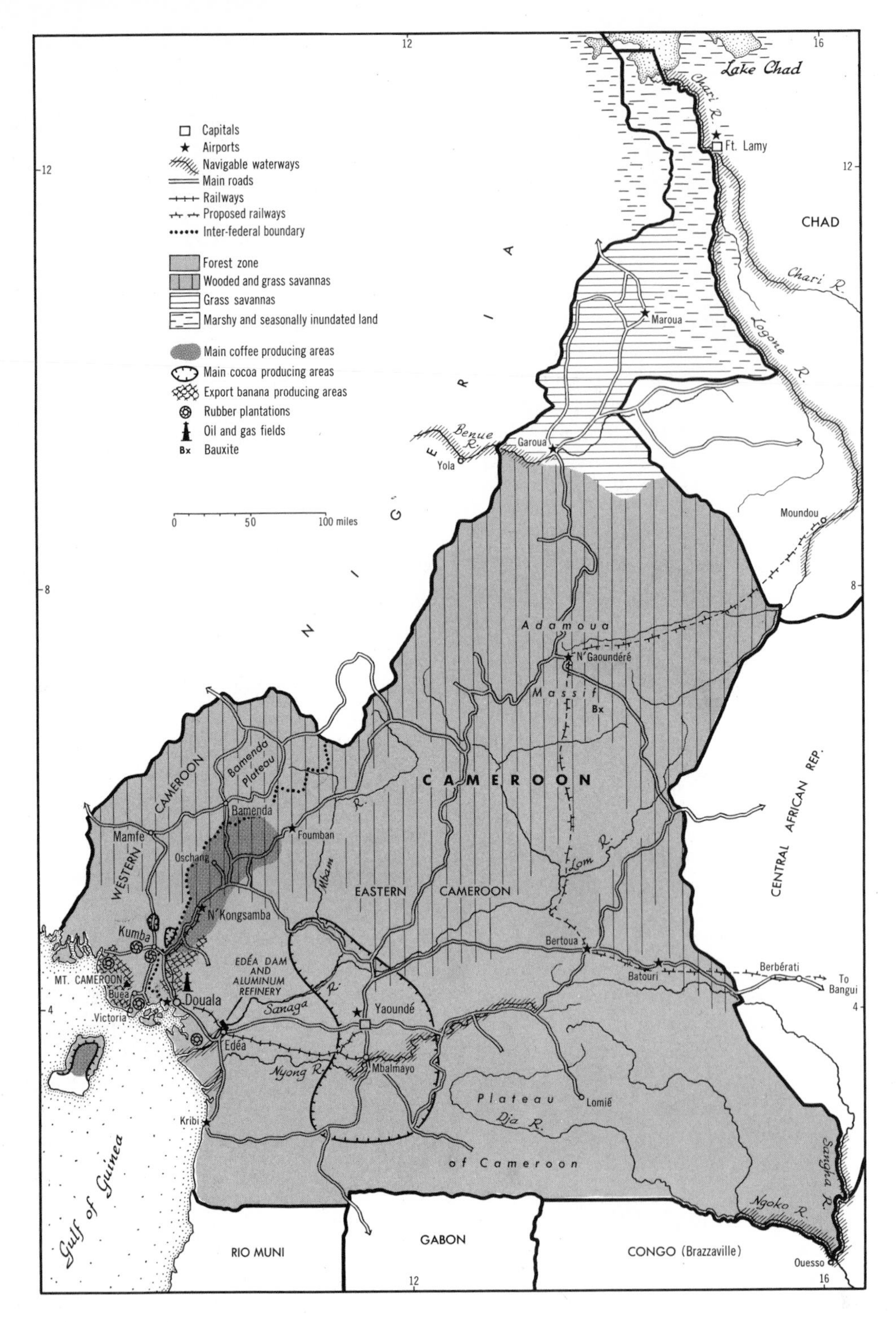

Map 54. Economic map of Cameroon

FORMER FRENCH SECTION. That portion of the southwestern highlands within the former French area comprises less than 5 percent of the area of East Cameroon, but has close to 22 percent of its total population. The major tribal group is the Bamiléké, who occupy a series of plateaus with an average elevation of 4,000 to 5,000 feet. About 500,000 members of this tribe live in an area of 2,084 square miles, giving an average density of 240 per square mile, while some parts have densities up to 750 per square mile. It is no wonder that there is heavy emigration from the region, there being an estimated 30,000 Bamiléké in Douala and 45,000 in the Mungo area.

The major problem in the Bamiléké country is to protect the equilibrium of the people and the land. This calls for reforesting the steepest slopes, terracing the hills and valleys, protecting the common pasturelands from overgrazing, and probably stimulating continued emigration. North of the Bamiléké country is the Bamoun Region, which represents a prolongment of the plateaus to the north. It is less humid and less densely populated, being occupied by the Bamoun, an Islamized tribe of Sudanic origin.

Commercial production in the region includes coffee, palm products, cinchona, cola, bananas, and tea. The area centered on N'Kongsamba is excellent for coffee, both from the standpoint of climate and because of the presence of some very fertile soils. Robusta, excelsa, and arabica coffees are produced. The region produces 80 percent of Cameroon's coffee and all of the higher value arabica coffee. Production was reduced by the revolt, which necessitated closing some of the European holdings, but has recovered well in recent years. In 1955 there were 780 Europeans and 1,068 African planters of arabica plus 4,829 European and 7,139 African robusta planters; the number of European planters has been substantially reduced since that date. The oil palm was formerly much more important to the Bamiléké and large groves remain in the low parts, but exports, confined largely to kernels, are now only of minor importance. Cinchona has been grown on European estates near Dschang, a former rest station, where a small quinine plant was located. Kola nuts are marketed in the north. Tea and pepper are recent introductions which the government would like to see extended in the area.

An intensively farmed area in the Bamiléké country near Bangangté

A major problem in this area is to protect the equilibrium of the people and the land.

WEST CAMEROON. That section of the British Cameroons which is now West Cameroon has an area of about 16,791 square miles. Its

Robusta coffee growing under bananas in the Bamiléké country near N'Kongsamba

Residents were required in late 1962 to cut the vegetation bordering the roads as a precaution against ambushes. A revolt has flared here sporadically since 1959.

Workers' housing on an oil palm plantation in West Cameroon
The Cameroons Development Corporation plantations form the backbone of the economy of this region, which was formerly under British trusteeship.

topography is very accentuated. North of Mt. Cameroon is a lower region extending to Kumba and corresponding to the valley of the Mongo across the border; the land then rises to the high grasslands of the Bamenda Plateau, while the frontier with East Cameroon starting about 60 miles north of Douala is the chain of extinct volcanoes already noted.

The population of West Cameroon is about 900,000; it contains a complex of tribes speaking over 100 vernaculars and the demographic scene is further complicated by several migratory patterns including Fulani from northern Nigeria to the high plateaus, plantation workers from the densely populated parts of eastern Nigeria, and movements of indigenous peoples to the more developed south. The over-all density of population is only about 54 per square mile, and, in contrast to the Bamiléké country, there are large areas of unused land of good quality.

The backbone of the West Cameroonian economy has been the plantations of the Cameroons Development Corporation (C.D.C.). Plantations were introduced to the area before World War I by the Germans. Taken over by the British during that war, they were sold back to their previous owners by 1924. Again taken over in World War II, they were put under a statutory corporation, the C.D.C., in 1947. The C.D.C. now directs 18 plantations covering about 58,000 acres in 1962 and plans to increase this to from 76,000 to 84,000 acres by 1975. About 16,000 workers are employed by the C.D.C., which furnishes roads, houses, schools, and medical facilities in its zone of operation and remits profits and taxes to the government. Its budget is normally greater than that of both the central and local governments combined. The Cameroons Development Corporation lacked capital in the late 1950s to proceed with expansion and replacement of bananas and an arrangement was concluded whereby the Colonial Development Corporation supplied $8.4 million in capital in return for a share of profits and the right to manage the C.D.C. for 10 years. Plans now call for focusing upon rubber, but also upon diversifying output on the corporation's holdings.

In 1962, production from the C.D.C. estates included 33,120 tons of bananas, 3,800 tons of rubber, 6,230 tons of palm oil, 2,400 tons of palm kernels, 155 tons of cocoa, 83 tons of tea, and a few tons of pepper. These provided a substantial portion of total exports from West Cameroon, which have been about one quarter those of East Cameroon in recent years. The success of C.D.C. in stimulating the economy of West Cameroon has prompted East Cameroon to suggest that its activities might be extended to that part of the Federation in the years ahead.

Bananas normally rank as the prime export of West Cameroon, accounting for at least two thirds of the total value of exports. In addition to the C.D.C. plantations, bananas are grown on private plantations owned by Elders and Fyffes and other concerns, and by African small holders, whose Bakweni Cooperative Union has marketed about as many bananas as C.D.C. in recent years. Sigatoka, "Cigar End," and Panama disease have driven most of the private plantations out in the last few years and have begun to affect small holder production. Efforts by C.D.C. scientists to develop strains which are resistant to these diseases continue, but the ravages of disease plus a difficult market position have resulted in declining interest among peasant farmers and a decision by the C.D.C. to reduce acreage in bananas by at least one half.

Rubber is grown mainly on C.D.C. and Pamol plantations, though the interest of local farmers has increased in recent years. Rubber exports rose from about 2,000 tons in 1957 to 3,590 tons in 1961 and should continue to increase as immature plantings of new, high-yielding clones reach tapping age. Palm oil comes almost exclusively from plantations, while peasants account for about half of kernel exports.

The C.D.C. has also been increasing tea plantings on the slopes of Mt. Cameroon and in the Bamenda area, where fairly sizable areas are considered suitable for its production. Production from the Tole estate of the C.D.C. increased from 101,000 pounds in 1960 to 185,000 pounds in 1961, and the corporation's tea factory is to be expanded to handle 1,200,000 pounds by 1971. A coffee estate has been started in an old volcanic crater in the Bamenda Highlands but poor soils and the extremely poor communications to that area have limited its success to date. Both robusta and arabica coffees could be widely grown in West Cameroon.

Other cash crops grown in the region include cocoa, which had record exports of 9,073 tons in 1961, pepper, and cashew nuts. The most intensive developments in West Cameroon are found within 50 miles of the coast, an area which has experienced boom conditions in the past decade. The Bamenda Plateau, which could be an important surplus producer of corn, peanuts, and cattle, is inhibited by poor roads, as is the area between Kumba and Mamfe.

A very great increase in timber output has taken place since 1956. Over 2,000 people are now employed in logging, which has a good future so long as access roads are made available. It is questionable whether forest concessionaires are now paying an adequate share of road building and maintenance costs in view of the heavy damage caused by log haulers.

One of the great uncertainties facing West Cameroon is the question of maintaining traditional markets in the United Kingdom. Preferences have been extended several times since federation with East Cameroon and ties with Britain have been maintained through the presence of expatriate managers and advisers, continuing commercial relations, and the presence of over 100 West Cameroonian students in British universities, but how long the West Cameroon can have a foot in both camps remains to be seen.

THE ADAMOUA MASSIF

This plateau, ranging in elevation from 2,500 to 4,500 feet, extends more or less east-west across Cameroon and into the Central African Republic. Beginning north of the Sanaga River and dropping off abruptly in the north to the Benue Basin, it extends between about 6° and 8° N, occupying a total area in Cameroon of about 26,000 square miles. This massif, which is essentially granite with basaltic outflows in the highest part near N'Gaoundéré, forms a formidable barrier between the north and south of the country. It is a savanna region, with rather heavy precipitation owing to its elevation, but with a more clearly marked dry season than in the south.

Population densities on the Adamoua Massif are low, only about 6 to 10 per square mile. It is like northern Nigeria in having two distinct population groups: Mboums, agriculturalists of Sudanic origin related to the Hausas, and Peuls and Bororos, Hamitic people related to the Fulani pastoralists. The main richness of the massif is its approximately 600,000 animals, which are only poorly commercialized, though some are moved south for sale in the protein-deficient rainforest areas. A local company, La Pastorelle, runs a 45,000-acre ranch and has an abattoir at N'Gaoundéré, from which refrigerated carcasses are flown to Douala, Yaoundé, and Brazzaville. The capacity of the abattoir has not as yet been reached. There are also eleven European ranches, only a few of which are well managed. Unlike many livestock areas of Africa, the plateau is apparently not overstocked. It is also favored, more so than the north, in its freedom from rinderpest and foot-and-mouth disease, probably owing to its elevation. It is also tsetse free, but there is a high incidence of parasitic infestation. Efforts have been made to upgrade the stock by crossbreeding with French Montbeliard and Texas Brahman cattle, to introduce better pasture plants, and to control grass firing. With continued improvement in practices and particularly in pastures and with better transport facilities this region could become a favored area.

THE LOWER SAVANNAS AND STEPPES OF MIDDLE AFRICA

Included within this region is all of the Central African Republic except the small tropical

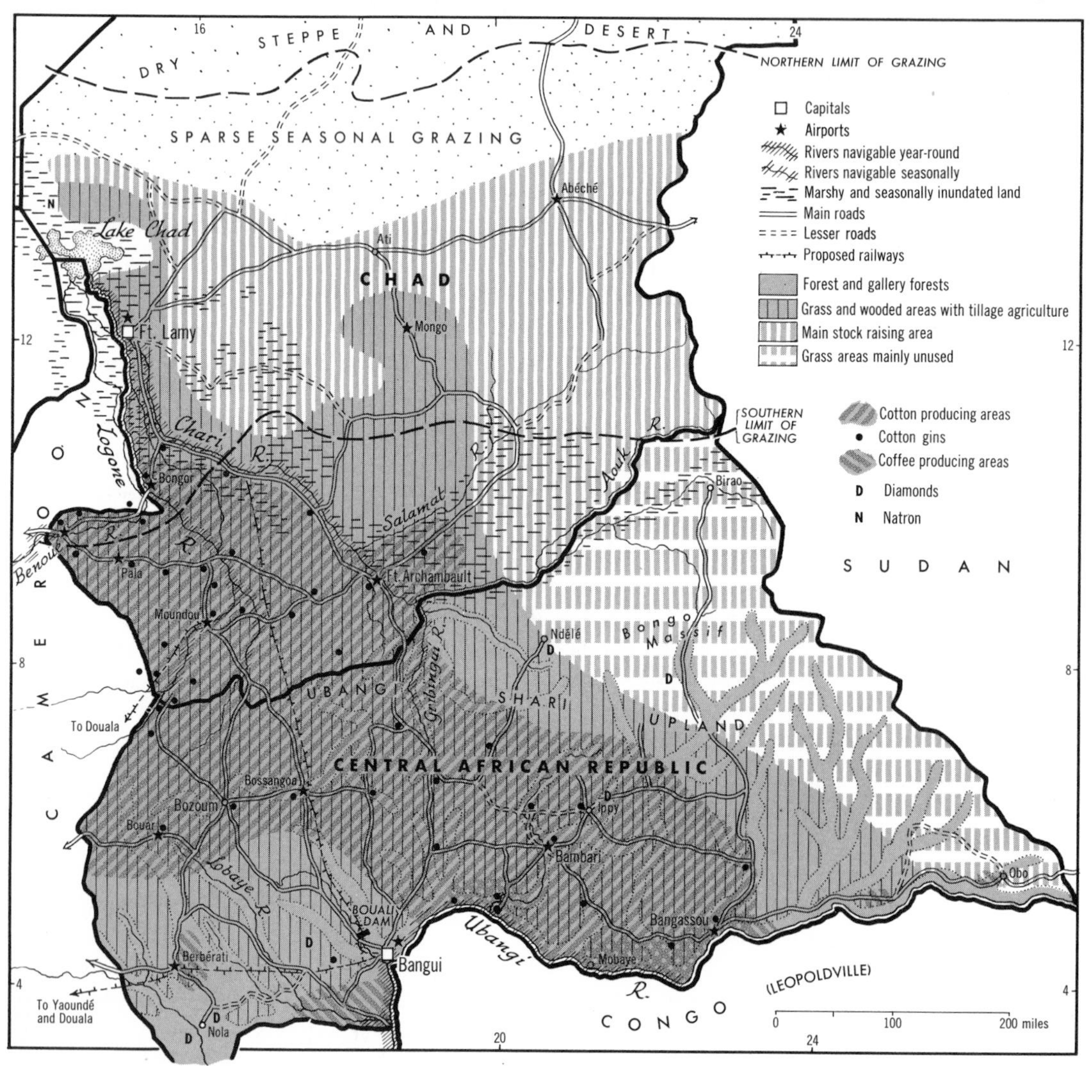

Map 55. Economic map of Chad and the Central African Republic

rain-forest zone in the southwest, the southern half of Chad, and the area of Cameroon north of the Adamoua Plateau (Map 55).

THE CENTRAL AFRICAN REPUBLIC. The dominant topographic feature of the republic is an undulating plateau with elevations ranging from 2,000 to 3,300 feet which is a sill between the two great river systems of the Chad and Congo basins. A number of massifs rise above the general level, the Bongo Massif attaining the highest elevation, 4,590 feet. Vegetation varies from gallery forests along the southern rivers to savanna woodlands and grasslands which gradually decline in height and become more sparse toward the north. Most of the country is plagued with the tsetse fly, and soils are generally poor.

While the republic is larger than France and the Low Countries combined, its population is less than that of the Pas-de-Calais Department, being estimated at 1,227,000 in 1961. The Central African Republic is one of the most remote and least-developed parts of Africa. The infant mortality rate is still about 191 per 1,000 and the life expectancy 35.3 years; about 40 percent of the population is under 14 years of age. The average income is placed at $55, which may be an exaggeration. In any case, there is an enormous disparity in incomes of government employees and peasants, which contributes to a generally poor contact between the government and the people. The 1961 governmental budget totaled only $15.4 million, which, however, did not include certain direct contributions from France, whose total support was estimated to be about $12 million in the same year. Exports, almost all of which have required French subsidization, have been about $14 million yearly, while imports have been about $20–21 million.

The Central African Republic is essentially an agricultural country. Cotton and coffee are the major commercial crops, accounting for about three fourths of the country's exports. Cotton production began between 1926 and 1930 on a compulsory basis, which, together with the laborious work involved in its cultivation and harvesting, made it a chronically unpopular crop.

A cotton market in northern Cameroon
Cotton is the main export crop of the Central African Republic, Chad, and northern Cameroon, but remoteness makes its production very marginal.

Cotton production was organized here and in Chad by four concessionaires who employed African supervisors, or "boys coton," in local areas to enforce planting requirements. Africans who failed to obey instructions were fined and on occasion physically punished, a procedure which contributed to a sizable migration from the countryside. The companies were charged with collecting, processing, transporting, and exporting cotton from their respective zones; purchase prices and profit percentages were set each year by the government. No profits were, in fact, earned until 1936.

Despite the objectionable features associated with the introduction of cotton, it gradually caught on and its output was sustained and increased after abolition of forced labor in 1946. Today it is indispensable to the economies of the Central African Republic and Chad, whose African governments are attempting to promote a continued increase in production, though without much success to date in the former. Cotton illustrates well the precarious nature of the economies of these two countries. On the one hand, technical progress has trebled yields to the present average of 264 pounds of lint per acre and has improved quality, and at least 1.5 million people in the Central African Republic and Chad are wholly or partly dependent on cotton for whatever cash income they enjoy. On the other hand, returns to the farmers are low and the market is dependent on French benevolence. In 1956, even with subsidies of the Cotton Price Stabilization Fund, it was estimated that the individual farmer received only about $18 per acre for approximately 40 days of work. Still, the cost of production plus shipment to market makes the local cotton unsalable at world prices, France absorbing the exports at artificially high prices.

Cotton is now cultivated on about 250,000 acres by about 320,000 planters in the Central African Republic, which ranks second among former French African countries in cotton production. Its exports, however, are only about one-thirtieth those of Egypt or one-tenth those of the Sudan. The producing zone of the Central African Republic and Chad is indicated on Map 55, which also shows the location of cotton ginneries. The ginneries in the two countries employ about 175 Europeans and 4,000 to 8,000 Africans, depending upon the season. Some cotton is absorbed by the textile mill at Bouali in the Central African Republic.

Coffee ranks second among exports of the republic. Its production was begun about 1925 by European farmers and by 1936 some 50,000 acres were devoted to the crop, mostly excelsa coffee. A serious blight then largely eliminated African production, but a second boom occurred in the postwar years, this time concentrating upon robustas. By 1958, Europeans had 41,150 acres in coffee and Africans 7,945 acres, which represented a total increase of 138 percent over the 1945 level. Coffee is grown in scattered areas along the southern margins of the Central African Republic, from Berberati on the west to Obo on the east.

The only other commercial crops of any significance in the Central African Republic are sisal and peanuts, which together account for about 2.6 percent of total exports by value. Six sisal plantations covering about 7,500 acres are situated around Kouango in the east, where a sisal product factory was built in 1953. Despite excellent organization and suitable growing conditions, sisal proved uncompetitive in the world markets after a break in prices in the early 1950s. Most of the republic's peanuts are grown in the northwest and in the central south, and two modern mills have been placed at Bohina and Alindao, but again the high cost of transport limits the chances of exporting to world markets. Both coffee and peanuts are more popular than cotton among African producers.

French efforts to improve rural standards in the Central African Republic were focused upon the organization of paysannats, which were started in 1936 and were modeled after similar schemes in the Belgian Congo. Designed to substitute family tenure for tribal systems and to stimulate production of cash crops, they failed because of strong tribal resentment and because they appeared during the war to be vehicles for the imposition of forced labor. In 1953 they were reinstituted under a program designed to avoid past errors and concentrating upon both subsistence and export crops, the latter being guaranteed against price drops. Production was organized by research stations and technical services, with roving agronomists and monitors being responsible for specific regions. The first results were a marked increase in output of cotton and coffee, but advances have not been maintained in succeeding years and many local plantations appear to be reverting to bush. The present government has neither the money nor the technical staff to move forward with a similar program.

Only a few parts of the Central African Republic are free from tsetse fly and the livestock population is inadequate to meet local demands, the deficit normally being filled from Chad. A barter agreement with the Sudan for exchange of cattle and coffee for the remote eastern part has proved difficult to maintain because of reduced coffee output and inadequate communications. In 1961, 650 N'Dama cattle were imported, bringing the total of trypanosomiasis-resistant cattle to about 3,500.

CHAD. Southern Chad is a vast peneplain cut by the valleys of the Chari and Logone rivers, with a low sedimentary basin around Lake Chad. Around that lake, which varies in size from about 4,000 to 10,000 square miles, and between the Chari and Logone rivers enormous swamplands modify the scene and are inundated for about half the year. Several massifs rise above the plain, though the highest are found in the Sahara.

The modest level of the economy is revealed in the 30-year development plan drawn up in 1960 calling for investments increasing from only $16.2 million in the first year to $60.7 million in the thirtieth, this for an area five times the size of the United Kingdom and with a population half that of the former French Equatorial African countries. The somewhat precarious balance is suggested by the unfavorable trade position, with imports usually exceeding exports by about 50 percent, which would be only partially redressed by an unrecorded and partially clandestine export of about $5 million yearly. The year 1961 was an unusually prosperous one owing to a record cotton crop, but it was followed by a relatively poor year in 1962.

Chad has an almost exclusively agricultural economy, with a high percentage still concerned with local subsistence. This area and northern Cameroon are like the Adamoua Plateau or northern Nigeria in being strongly Islamic, in having tribes ranging from purely cultivators to purely pastoralists, and in having scattered pagan elements. Its remoteness and the very late date at which any real concern was given to its development have meant that it remains much less changed by modern forces than most African countries.

Cotton is even more important to Chad than to the Central African Republic, for it accounts for about 80 percent of Chadian exports and one third of budget resources. It was introduced in 1929 on the same basis as in the Central African Republic. An estimated 700,000 acres farmed by 400,000 families are now planted to cotton, which is usually grown in rotation with peanuts. New varieties and the use of insecticides have

Livestock near Fort Lamy, Chad
Commercialization of livestock products is poorly developed and distance from markets limits the possibilities for rapid change.

brought about a 30 percent increase in yields in recent years, which are, however, still only about 220 to 300 pounds per acre. Some cotton is grown under irrigation in the Chari-Logone region, where, with more effective control, a rather intensive agricultural region could be developed, but most is grown in the southwest on a basis entirely comparable to that of the Central African Republic.

Livestock products rank second among exports from the Chad Republic, which is estimated to have some 4 million cattle, 600,000 sheep and goats, 300,000 camels, and 450,000 donkeys and horses. Some 290,000 people are engaged in stock raising, which is faced with all the problems noted in the discussion of livestock in West Africa, plus the additional deterrent of an unusually remote location.

Postwar efforts to improve the livestock economy have included an intensive and generally successful anti-disease program, crossbreeding with imported stock, digging of numerous wells, and promotion of air transport to equatorial markets. In 1948, 59 tons of meat were shipped by air; by 1959, shipments totaled 3,433 tons, but have declined following the troubles in Congo (Leopoldville), which formerly took about half of the exports. The difficulties facing a marked increase in such movements include the different sales prices prevailing in the several markets, the competition from fish in some places, the difficulty of getting return cargo, and, most important, the transport charges, which double the cost of meat shipped, for example, to Brazzaville and hence limit the sales severely. Some 50,000 head of cattle are walked into Nigeria through customs stations and an estimated 200,000 head are moved clandestinely to that country each year.

It was hoped that modern refrigerated abattoirs located in a suburb of Fort Lamy and at Fort Archambault would stimulate export of beef from Chad and greatly reduce illegal movements to Nigeria, but excessively high costs of operation have actually worsened the situation. Nor did the well-digging program turn out to be an unmixed blessing. Those wells dug in the south attracted settlement by nomads, which was resented by the residents of the area; in the north, problems arose because the nomads refused to pay for the new supplies despite the fact that some of the wells permitted grazing of areas otherwise useless because of lack of surface water, and despite the fact that others reduced the necessity for migrating to the south each year, a procedure which often resulted in the loss of a quarter of the herd. Two private ranches have been established in Chad with French and American aid, one now having a herd of 3,000. In addition to live cattle and meat, Chad exports hides and skins, which account for 4 to 5 percent of total exports.

Peanuts are the only crop besides cotton that is exported, but distance handicaps the ability to compete with other producing areas. A recent introduction is rice, grown on 56,000 acres yielding 36,000 tons of paddy. About 20,000 to 30,000 individuals produce rice in the Logone area, but primitive methods and inadequate control result in poor yields. The Chari-Logone area is the scene of a special development scheme. Initially, it was planned to dike all the Chad bank of the Logone from Lai to Katoa, but in fact a much shorter dike originally built by Africans north of Bongor was reinforced, giving flood protection to over 142,500 acres. The northern, underpopulated portion is held under concession by a company producing cotton and rice; the southern, more populous part is inhabited by over 18,000 Massa producing millet and rice. A rice-growing scheme also exists on the Cameroon side of the river. Eventually, some 425,000 acres might be brought under control for rice production in the Bongor area, 212,000 acres in the Lai area, and two million acres in the Léré region.

Chad also produces a great variety of cereals, millet being the basic food crop. Corn and wheat are grown in the Lake Chad area. There is some sale of poor-quality dates from the wadis bordering that lake.

Fish are a resource of some value in Chad and adjacent parts of northern Cameroon, the rivers and lakes having an abundant population. From 60,000 to 80,000 tons of fish a year are taken from the Logone and Chari rivers and from Lake Chad by about 10,000 Chadian fishermen, while about 40,000 to 80,000 tons are taken in the Chari-Logone system by Cameroonian fishermen. Some tribes specialize entirely in fishing, but their methods are primitive. A modern fish drying installation sixty miles above Fort Lamy on the Chari has given promising results.

NORTH CAMEROON. The northern part of Cameroon consists of the Benue Valley, a gentle rise between that and the basin of the Logone River and Lake Chad, and the Massif of Mandara along the Nigerian frontier, which is a continuation of the Jos Plateau. Running southwest-northeast, it rises to 3,700 feet and is prolonged towards the east by large and small massifs rising above the plain.

This region is quite comparable to adjacent areas of Chad and the Central African Republic in tribal, physical, and economic conditions. Cotton, introduced in the early 1950s, has caught on well and is now produced by about 75,000 families. Some peanuts are exported, and there is a fairly dense livestock population only meagerly commercialized. The factor of remoteness is well illustrated by the difference in the statutory minimum wage here and in Douala in a recent year—4¢ an hour as compared with 10.85¢ an hour.

TRANSPORT IN THE NORTH. The element of isolation is such a marked keynote of this entire region that it is deserving of re-emphasis. There are four major outlets available to the region, none of them particularly favorable or adequately developed at the present time.

1) The Federal Route, involving road transport to Bangui, a distance of 740 miles from Fort Lamy, a 740-mile river stretch to Brazzaville, and 317 miles on the Congo-Ocean Railway. While this route is of undoubted historic interest, it is difficult to see it as of more than temporary value to most of the northern region.

2) West and south via road to Yaoundé and rail or road to Douala. Douala is the closest port to most of the interior north but is poorly connected by roads, which are capable of handling only light traffic. From Fort Lamy the distance by road to Douala is 973 miles, or by road to Yaoundé and rail to Douala, 1,175 miles.

3) The western route by road to Garoua and then by river to Nigerian ports. From Garoua to Burutu is a distance of 930 miles. This is the cheapest route for much of the area but has severe disadvantages: first, the upper Benue is navigable only 7 to 10 weeks a year, thus requiring expensive storage facilities; second, it is very difficult for the Niger River fleet to provide adequate services to Garoua and too expensive to provide Cameroonian barges, which would only be used on a seasonal basis; and third, the route is an extremely slow one for vegetable exports. Gautier gives the example of cotton bought at Moundou in December, baled in January, sent by truck to Garoua where it was stored until August 1. Arriving at Burutu in September, it was stored up to a month and finally reached French ports about November 1, eleven months after purchase. Involving several transshipments, storage charges, and a long period when capital is immobilized, the Benue

The river port of Bangui, Central African Republic
Situated at the head of navigation on the Ubangi tributary of the Congo River, Bangui is a major transit point on the so-called Federal Route in former French Equatorial Africa.

The Benue River near Garoua, Cameroon
Open to navigation only 7 to 10 weeks a year, the Benue nonetheless handles a substantial share of foreign trade for northern Cameroon and adjacent parts of Chad.

route obviously is less than adequate to stimulate development. Nevertheless, Garoua has handled between 25,000 and 52,000 tons in recent years.

4) The western route via Maiduguri in northeastern Nigeria. Some cattle, hides, skins, and peanuts move by highway into Nigeria, eventually reaching the railheads for shipment to port. Completion of the Bornu rail line to Maiduguri may increase the value of this routeway, while there is some talk of extending the line to the Chad border.

Numerous studies and much debate have been devoted to the possible ameliorations of the transport situation of this immense area of middle Africa. Most frequently mentioned for years was a rail line from Bangui to Chad, which was favored by the federal authorities in the former French Equatorial Africa; the most recent proposal called for construction of a .60-meter gauge, 539-mile railway to Berbéré, 155 miles southeast of Fort Lamy. The viability of such a line, which would probably cost more than the estimated $37 million, would depend upon a marked increase in peanut shipments plus gaining much of the traffic now following alternative routes.

A second proposal was to construct a railway terminating at Douala, and it is this alternative which has recently been selected. While construction of the first section has begun, it will be many years before the northern regions are reached at Moundou, an important cotton center in southern Chad on the navigable Logone. This route will be the shortest to seaboard and will have the advantage over the Federal Route of not involving transshipments en route.

A branch line from the Cameroon Railway to Bangui would further reduce the significance of the Federal Route. It has been estimated that this line would carry 170,000 tons the first year, and that traffic would increase by 8 to 10 percent annually in succeeding years. In 1961, only about 6,000 tons moved to and from the Central African Republic via Cameroon roads.

Other possibilities include controlling the flow of the Benue to permit its use for 130 days, extending the rail line from Nigeria across Chad to link with the Sudan Railways, and constructing heavier duty roads to various railheads or to Douala. It has also been suggested that a market for meat could be tapped in the Saharan oil fields by constructing a road suitable for use by refrigerated trucks.

The internal transport net of the northern regions is only reasonably satisfactory, though the long dry season permits use of readily constructed routes. The Central African Republic has the best network, but its claim of having "seven excellent main roads" is grossly exaggerated. Roads in the bulk of the area are poorly maintained, bridges are hazardous, and some ferry service is rather rudimentary. Waterways are of local and seasonal significance. The Chari may be used from July to February on the 480 miles between Fort Archambault and Fort Lamy and from the latter to Lake Chad all year. The Logone is generally too winding, though it is navigable for some distance above Fort Lamy. The rivers of the Central African Republic are not particularly valuable except, of course, for the Ubangi to Bangui; some are overgrown with thick vegetation, and their flow is quite irregular and frequently interrupted by shallows.

Both the Central African Republic and Chad hope to capitalize on the centrality of their location in the field of air transport. A large new field may be constructed at Bangui; the field at Fort Lamy can already accommodate the largest planes now in service.

THE DESERT OF NORTHERN CHAD

Almost half of Chad is desert, inhabited by perhaps 50,000 people, mostly nomads, whose contribution to the economy of the country is minute. The Tibesti Mountains attain 11,204 feet in Emi Koussi and have sufficient orographic precipitation to support a small permanent populace, a mere remnant of what the area apparently supported several millennia ago.

MINING IN MIDDLE AFRICA

The countries of middle Africa treated in this chapter have ranked far down the scale of

African mineral producers. But one of them, Gabon, has recently become a leading world producer of manganese and may achieve this status in iron ore in the years ahead, while numerous mineral finds have been under study in recent years both in Gabon and in other middle African countries.

PETROLEUM AND NATURAL GAS

Basins totaling about 17,300 square miles occur in the coastal belt and there are interesting potentials for exploiting offshore areas. Finds to date have been somewhat disappointing, though small exports of petroleum are important to Congo and Gabon. Exploration along much of the coast was difficult because of the lack of topographic and geologic maps, the forest vegetation, and the general absence of roads. The region is advantaged, on the other hand, by its proximity to the sea and, in some areas, by an intricate system of waterways.

In Gabon and Congo, the Petroleum Society of Equatorial Africa (SPAFE) inaugurated exploration and is now continuing the search in conjunction with subsidiaries of Royal Dutch-Shell and Socony Mobil. The first discovery was made in 1956 near Port Gentil and exports began in 1957. The largest expenditures were made in 1959 and 1960, including allotments for a mole at Port Gentil, a pipeline from Ozouri to Cape Lopez where the main terminal is situated, pumping installations, and quarters for personnel. Production increased from 143,000 tons in 1957 to 774,500 tons in 1961. Five fields, four of modest and one of small dimensions, are now producing in Gabon and in 1961 the first offshore wells in the entire franc zone were begun. Natural gas is piped to Port Gentil, where it is used in producing electricity; additional quantities may be available for industrial use.

In Congo, the first discovery was made in 1957 and production began in 1960 when eight wells produced 100,000 tons, most of which came from Pointe Indienne, 12 miles from Pointe Noire. Exports are expected to be limited to about 150,000 tons yearly for some years, barring additional finds, particularly in offshore areas where exploration began in 1962.

Gulf Oil and the Spanish CEPSA agreed to explore for oil on a concession in Rio Muni starting in 1961. In Cameroon, a small natural gas find was made at Logbaba, 6 miles from Douala, in 1955; there has been discussion of using this to fuel a cement plant in the area.

MANGANESE

One of the largest bodies of manganese ore in the world is situated at Moanda near Franceville in interior Gabon. Proved reserves total 200 million tons of 48 percent metallic content. The deposits cover four plateaus and are very favorably disposed for open pit operations. Development is in the hands of La Compagnie Minière de l'Ogooué (Comilog), in which United States Steel, the French government, and private French interests hold 49, 22, and 29 percent of the shares respectively. U.S. Steel has agreed to take 50 percent of the output; the remainder will go to France and other European Coal-Steel Community nations. Development of the Moanda manganese was assured in 1959 when the IBRD advanced $35 million to Comilog, the total investment being about $99 million.

The area around Moanda is very sparsely populated, covered with dense forest, and very

Mechanical gear for loading manganese ore at Pointe Noire, Congo (Brazzaville)
The source of this ore is the new mine at Moanda, Gabon, which is expected to become one of the largest producers of manganese ore in the world.

rugged. This helps to explain two features of the operation, the highly mechanized mining and the use of a 47-mile cableway from the mine to M'Binda. From there the ore moves on a 180-mile rail extension to Dolisie and 125 miles on the Congo-Ocean Railway to Pointe Noire, where storage space and special loading gear have been installed. The provisions for transport absorbed about 67.5 percent of the total investment. Shipments began in 1962 and were expected to total some 500,000 tons in 1963, rising thereafter to 850,000 or 1,000,000 tons depending on the market.

Both Gabon and Congo will benefit from the manganese operation. Exports from Gabon will increase by about $16 million yearly. Some 400 Africans and 60 Europeans will be employed. Taxes and duties will yield about $1.60–$2.00 per ton shipped, which will be divided between Gabon and Congo. Gabon will be the third or fourth world exporter of manganese at the level of production planned.

IRON ORE

The iron ores of the Makokou-Mékambo region of northeast Gabon have been known since 1895. Reserves are estimated at one billion tons of 60 to 63 percent metallic content ore. These high-grade ores, mostly hematite with a low silica content and only traces of sulfur and phosphorous, occur to a depth of 100 to 200 feet on the crests of a series of elongated hills rising over 1,640 feet above the surrounding peneplain, and are underlain by 45 percent ores.

The company which will work the Mékambo ores is 50 percent owned by Bethlehem Steel, 34 percent by nine French companies, and 16 percent by Italian, Belgian, West German, and Dutch interests. Exploitation, which is slated to begin at Belinga, will require construction of a 435-mile railway to the coast, where special gear would be erected. At present, a study is being made of two alternative routes: the first, preferred by Bethlehem, would lead to Pointe Pongara on the south side of the Gabon Estuary; the second, preferred by the government, would lead to Libreville and thus help to sustain the importance of that city. To maintain a planned annual output of 10 million tons, about 2,000 Africans and 400 Europeans would be required. Capital expenses for the mine, railway, and port would total about $315 million. The time required to complete the infrastructure means that shipments may not begin for five to ten years.

Several other iron ore bodies are known in the countries covered in this chapter. A 100-million-ton reserve is situated at Tchibanga in southern Gabon which could be opened quite readily by construction of a 30-mile cableway. An iron deposit at Zanaga, 135 miles northwest of Brazzaville in Congo, is said to have at least 400 million tons of 65 percent ore, while a 100-million-ton body has been discovered near Kribi in Cameroon, where prospecting is continuing.

URANIUM ORE

Exploitation of uranium ores, found at Mounana in the Franceville region of Gabon in the largest known deposit in areas of French expression, began in 1961. It is planned that 75,000 to 90,000 tons of mineral be concentrated yearly, the 1961 shipments having been valued at $4.95 million. After five years of surface operations it will be necessary to go underground.

OTHER MINERALS

Numerous other mineral finds have been made in these middle African countries and organization of modern mapping, geologic, and mining services suggests that additional deposits will be found in coming years.

CONGO. Except for petroleum, the only mineral of any importance now produced in Congo is lead from the M'Fouati and Hapilo mines in the Niari Valley. The operations are marginal, however, and a search for other bodies in that area has not been successful. A very small amount of tin, copper, and gold is mined by primitive techniques. In 1963 a major bauxite find was reported in the Divenié region near the Gabon border, and uranium ores occur at Nboko-Songo, about a hundred miles west of Brazzaville. Extensive phosphate deposits have been found in the Hollé region at the foot of the Mayombé escarpment near the Congo-Ocean Railway and elsewhere.

GABON. In addition to petroleum, manganese, iron ore, and uranium ore, Gabon is known to have deposits of lead, colombo-tantalite, bauxite, potassium, nickel, and coal, and has a small output of gold and diamonds. Potash from deposits in the Lake Azingo district could be readily shipped from Owendo.

CAMEROON. This country produces very small quantities of gold, cassiterite, and titanium. Of interest for the future is a huge bauxite deposit at Minim-Martap on the Adamoua Plateau, estimated to have 1 to 2 billion tons of 43 percent alumina. Whether this deposit will be opened up by the new rail line remains to be seen. Another bauxite deposit, totaling 45 million tons of about 45 percent alumina content, occurs in the Fongo-Tongo area, near Dschang. Indications of numerous other minerals have been reported, including molybdenum, magnesium, diamonds, graphite, and mica.

CENTRAL AFRICAN REPUBLIC. The only mineral of present interest in the Central African Republic is diamonds. Four companies produce in widely separated parts of the country, but their output appears to be decreasing. African diggers sold 62,930 carats to the official purchasing agents in 1961 but are believed also to be smuggling large quantities. The peak production was 147,103 carats in 1954; total recorded output in 1961 was 111,480 carats.

CHAD. The only mineral produced in Chad is natron (sodium carbonate), used for cattle licks. Production is probably several thousand tons above the 2,000–4,000 tons officially listed each year. Tungsten deposits have been located in the Tibesti Mountains, and in 1961 the first permit to explore for oil in Chad was granted.

INDUSTRY

Manufacturing plays only a minor role in the economies of the countries covered in this chapter. In Cameroon, which has the greatest development, industry was estimated to account for 3.0 percent of the gross domestic product in 1958, when about 12,300 people were employed in manufacturing industry and shops. The value of output increased from $24.3 million in 1956 to $52.6 million in 1961, but the bulk of the increase was attributed to the opening of one factory, the Alucam aluminum smelter. In Congo, industry and mining were estimated to support 4.4 percent of the African population and 6.3 percent of the non-African population in 1958–59. In both Congo and Gabon, the forest industries are the largest and most significant branch.

The types of industry represented in this part of middle Africa are very comparable to those in West Africa except that there is not so broad a range. The locational pattern is also similar, with primary processing establishments being dispersed and the newer, market-oriented factories being heavily concentrated in the ports and capital cities. Cameroon is unique among tropical African countries in having an aluminum refinery attracted by low-cost hydroelectric power, undoubtedly the forerunner of several such plants.

PRIMARY PROCESSING

Industries represented in this category are indicated in Table 18. A brief examination will reveal the close relationship between these plants and the major commercial interests of each of the countries. Most of the processing plants are small, the major exceptions being the plywood mill at Port Gentil, a few sawmills, and the SIAN sugar refinery in the Niari Valley.

POWER-ORIENTED INDUSTRY

In the plant of Alucam at Edéa, Cameroon has the first important low-cost power-oriented plant in Africa south of the Sahara. The simple run-of-stream dam on the Sanaga River was built in the early 1950s, partly on faith, with an original capacity of 22,000 kw; success of this venture was not assured until erection of the aluminum refinery. Built by a subsidiary of Pechiney-Ugine, the refinery has permitted

Table 18. Raw material processing industries of middle Africa, 1962

	Cameroon	*Congo (Brazzaville)*	*Gabon*	*Central African Republic*	*Chad*
Vegetable oils					
Palm oil mills	9 }	30	Y	Y	—
Peanut oil mills	3 }		—	2	...
Cotton oil mills	1	—	—	1	1
Sesame oil mill	—	—	—	1	—
Fibers					
Cotton ginning	4	—	—	20	24
Sisal	—	—	—	1	—
Coffee cleaning	Y	Y	Y	Y	—
Tea factories	2	—	—	—	—
Food crops					
Cocoa butter	1	—	—	—	—
Rice mills	3	Y	Y	—	3
Tapioca	—	1	—	—	—
Sugar	—	1	—	—	—
Quinine	1	—	—	—	—
Rubber	5	—	—	—	—
Forest products					
Sawmills	33	17	22	Y	—
Plywood	—	1	1	—	—
Cellulose	—	1	—	—	—
Animal products					
Meat packing	4	—	—	—	2
Tanning	—	2	—	—	Y
Fish canning and processing	2	1	—	—	1
Whale oil processing	—	—	1	—	—

— = None.
Y = Is represented, details not known.
... = Data not available.

The aluminum smelter of Alucam at Edéa, Cameroon
This plant uses 80 percent of the electricity produced by the 159,760-kw Edéa hydroelectric station and represents one of the very few low-cost power-oriented industries in Africa.

Cameroon to rank fifth among free-world aluminum producers in recent years with an output of about 46,000 tons yearly. This required raising the capacity of the hydroelectric plant to 159,760 kw, 80 percent of the output being taken by Alucam. The plant has had to close down on a number of occasions owing to low water on the Sanaga River, and a study is being made of a possible storage dam on the upper Sanaga near Tibati to obviate this necessity. Capacity could also be greatly enlarged by installation of hydroelectric facilities up to 400,000 kw upstream from Edéa at Hebert Falls.

Alumina for the refinery has come from Provence and Marseilles factories and from the Fria

Table 19. Market-oriented industries of middle Africa, 1962

Cameroon		*Congo (Brazzaville)*	*Central African Republic*
Douala	*Yaoundé*	*Brazzaville*	*Bangui*
Beer	Beer	Beer	Beer
Carbonated beverages	Cigarettes	Carbonated beverages	Carbonated beverages
Food pastes	Textiles	Cigarettes	Textiles
Flour	Nails, nuts, bolts	Textiles (2)	Shoes
Textiles (4)		Shoes	Bicycle assembly
Shoes (2)	*Edéa*	Wooden furniture	
Wooden furniture	Aluminum sheets	Metal drums and furniture	*Bouali*
Metal drums and furniture (2)		Matches	Textiles
Nails, nuts, bolts	*Foumban*		
Bicycle assembly and parts	Chocolates	*Pointe Noire*	
Aluminum utensils		Sheet metal	
Plastic containers		Pipes	
Matches		Aluminum utensils	
Disinfectants		Industrial gases	
Industrial gases			
Cement shapes			

plant in Guinea; originally it was imported in bags but later in liquid form in an 8,000-ton cargo vessel specially constructed by Pechiney to service the Edéa plant. Cameroon would, of course, prefer to see domestic bauxite and alumina used at Alucam, but this would require at least considerably improved transport facilities as well as a substantial investment. Alucam is the largest industry in Cameroon, with a value of output of about $11.5 million yearly. It employs about 650 Africans and 75 Europeans.

A white hope for future industrialization in Congo is development of the Kouilou River. Studies of the potentialities of this scheme began in 1954 and have been pursued with varying intensity ever since. The Kouilou-Niari system drains about 20,000 square miles of Congo and has an average flow at the proposed dam site of 1,000 cubic meters per second. Plans call for construction of a dam 410 feet high where the Kouilou leaves the Crystal Mountains in the Sounda Gorge. Creating a lake twice the size of Lake Geneva, the dam would support a hydroelectric station with a capacity of 820,000 kw, larger than any plant in France.

A variety of consuming establishments have been suggested, most of which would be placed at Pointe Noire, which is only 80 miles by road from Sounda. These include, in the electrometallurgical category, a 200,000- to 250,000-ton aluminum refinery permitting an output larger than France, a ferromanganese plant using iron ore from Belinga and manganese from Moanda, a ferrosilicon plant using quartz from Mayombé, and a ferrochrome plant using chrome imported from Rhodesia or South Africa. In the electrochemical field, suggested plants include a calcium carbide factory obtaining calcium from the Niari Valley, a nitrogenous fertilizer factory, a superphosphate plant using phosphates from Hollé, an ammonia plant, and a heavy water plant. Finally, it is hoped that cheap power would justify erection of a large cellulose plant, which would also be based upon the extensive forest resources of the region or upon eucalyptus plantations. Subsidiary benefits would include stimulation of the forest industry by the improved transport on the lake and the possibility of establishing a fishing industry.

Repeated delays in moving forward with the development of the Kouilou scheme are explained by fear that the power would not be readily absorbed and by uncertainties regarding investment of the large funds required in a new nation whose political stability could not be accurately foreseen.

MARKET-ORIENTED INDUSTRY

Most of the consumer industries of the area have been installed in postwar years and are concentrated in a very limited number of centers (Table 19). Most of them require aid or protection to permit profitable operation. Douala is the single most important center and has continued to attract new industries. Brazzaville owes its significance as the second-ranking center of the area to its previous position as capital of French Equatorial Africa. While the Equatorial Customs Union (UDE) theoretically permits Brazzaville to service the entire area, it is poorly placed with respect to Gabon and Cameroon, and may lose a good share of its trade with the Central African Republic and Chad as the routeways to Douala supersede the Federal Route. Pointe Noire would appear to have greater attraction than the capital of Congo, particularly when the Kouilou is developed. Yaoundé is a center of secondary importance in Cameroon, while Bangui has all of the consumer industries in the Central African Republic except the textile mill at Bouali. Gabon and Chad have no industries in this category.

POWER FOR INDUSTRY

The situation in the main manufacturing centers with respect to availability of power is quite satisfactory at the present time. In addition to the larger scale Edéa plant, which serves Douala, and the Kouilou scheme, which will more than cover Pointe Noire, there are a number of small hydroelectric plants in being in the area. Brazzaville receives power from the 15,000-kw plant on the Djoué River, which flows into the Congo just west of the city; there has been surplus capacity available ever since completion of the plant in the early 1950s. Bangui and Bouali in the Central African Republic are served by the 3,200-kw Bouali Power Station, about 65 miles northwest of Bangui, now being enlarged. Dschang has a small 330-kw station. Production of electricity is even more heavily concentrated in the main cities than in West Africa. In Congo, for example, Brazzaville accounted for 65.3 percent of recorded electric production in the Central African Republic and the Edéa plant for 98.4 percent of production from central stations in Cameroon in 1961. Away from these few plants, electricity is likely to be high cost and in short supply.

As already noted, the electric plant at Port Gentil is fueled by natural gas. L'Électricité de France earlier proposed construction of a 5,000-kw nuclear-electric plant at Fort Lamy, Chad, where high delivery costs of fuel make production of electricity very expensive. There is adequate water in the Chari River to provide the quantities required by such a plant.

CONCLUSION

This very large, heterogenous, largely undeveloped area of middle Africa is one of the most fascinating in Africa because of the sharp contrasts from region to region in ethnic makeup and in stage of economic development. There are sufficient known and undeveloped resources to justify optimism regarding its future, particularly that of mineral-rich Gabon. The greatest possibilities for the area appear to be in opening up its mineral reserves, developing its immense hydroelectric resources, and further exploiting its forest wealth. An improved transport net is a requirement for the whole area, but particularly for the landlocked Chad and Central African Republic.

The Congo Republic (Leopoldville)

The decision to grant independence to the Belgian Congo on July 1, 1960, came with great abruptness and represented a drastic change in the Belgian position vis-à-vis the Congo. To some extent it represented an abrogation of responsibility because the Congolese were very inadequately trained to assume the responsibilities of self-government in such a large, economically complex, and culturally heterogenous area. Two grave errors were made by the Belgians: first, the failure to change their colonial approach in consonance with the rapidly evolving political scene in Africa in postwar years, and second, having decided in 1959 that such an error had been made, the failure to institute a crash program to prepare Congolese leaders for independence after a period of perhaps five to seven years.

THE POLITICAL BACKGROUND

Until 1959 the primary emphasis of the Belgians was on developing the Congolese economy, the contention being that this must precede extension of political rights. And great credit is due the Belgians for the achievements made in the economic sphere, as well as for the attention given to primary and technical education, health and medical advances, and other social betterments. It is true that the eventual objective was self-government, hopefully with some more or less formal relation with Belgium, but, even in the 1950s, officials usually spoke of reaching this goal in 50 to 100 years.

The first cracks in this policy came with the introduction of the *carte d'immatriculation* and the *carte de merite* in 1952, the permission to form labor unions in 1957, the opening of two universities in 1954 and 1956, and the introduction in 1958 of a system of elected councils in the three main cities. These councils proved to be the turning point. The Belgians had envisaged their dealing with such mundane urban problems as water supply and sewage disposal; instead, the elected African officials talked about further and rapid extension of political rights. Almost overnight the Congo moved from its rather tranquil state to one of political turbulence and dynamism. It is possible, of course, to relate this apparently abrupt metamorphosis to earlier experiences and conditions. Dispatch of Congolese troops outside the area in World War II was important, nor had the Congolese remained politically unconscious of the rapid strides being made in other African areas, including those in French Africa across the river. A few Belgian voices warned of the necessity to move with the times, a Congolese manifesto was issued calling for dramatic change, but the official policy hewed rather strictly to its emphasis on nonpolitical advancement.

In 1958 the Belgians apparently decided that the pace of devolution must be accelerated and in January, 1959, they announced a program under which local, provincial, and central legislative bodies and administrative institutions would have been successively introduced. Riots occurred just prior to and following this pronouncement. In December, 1959, the Belgians promised to grant independence by July, 1960. They were doubtless influenced by the relatively uneventful evolutions that had taken place and were occurring in British and French territories. They believed that this massive gesture would win the confidence of the Congolese, who would continue to rely heavily on Belgian administrative, technical, and financial support following independence. But the Congolese lacked political experience and the number of potential leaders was pitifully small. In 1959 there were only 16 college graduates in the African population; one graduated from a Belgian university and two from the universities in the Congo in that year; and there were only 247 Africans enrolled at Lovanium University at Leopoldville and 14 studying at the Official University at Elisabethville. In 1960 only 161 Congolese graduated from secondary schools.

Within a week of independence on July 1, 1960, there was a collapse of authority, made particularly dangerous by inability to control the Force Publique. The Belgians resumed police authority to protect the European population, most of whom were evacuated in July and August. The power vacuum created threatened to attract unilateral attempts to intercede in the Congo, which were only controlled after the United Nations, upon invitation by the President of Congo, moved into the country to maintain order and assist in its administration.

Separate administrations were set up by rival factions in various parts of the Congo. There was no real national leader who commanded the respect of all regions, nor could it have been expected that one would have appeared under the previous policies. As a result, tribalism became paramount in many regions, and the Congo was only tenuously held together by the presence of the U.N. force. In the ensuing months and years, numerous efforts were made to bring the various regional leaders together with only partial success, until U.N. military action in late 1962 and early 1963 brought Katanga back into the fold.

By mid-1963 it appeared that secessionist tendencies had been effectively suppressed and that national plans could be developed with some confidence. Partly to satisfy local demands and partly to reduce the authority of secessionist leaders, a total of some twenty provinces had been created, replacing the six which had existed under Belgian rule. The overpaid and underdisciplined army continued as a major problem, absorbing about 20 percent of government revenues and creating uncertainty with respect to the efficacy of civilian authority. The U.N. force, which totaled 18,900 at the beginning of 1963, had been reduced to 8,700 by July and was slated for virtual elimination by the end of the year. Refusal of several countries to pay their share of U.N. expenses in Congo represented a serious threat to continuing aid from the United Nations. It was apparent, however, that U.N. action had preserved the unity of Congo, prevented its becoming a theater for the cold war, and avoided a complete breakdown of the economy.

THE PRESENT ECONOMIC POSITION

The economic situation in Congo three years after independence had developed less satisfactorily than the political scene. The central government was expending two to three times its receipts. The U.N. was finding it increasingly difficult to secure funds required to maintain its technical assistance. The retail price index, with June 30, 1960, as the base, stood in early 1963 in Leopoldville stores at 192.2 and in the Leopoldville markets at 278.3. The Congolese franc declined from 50 per U.S. dollar to a black-market rate of 350 to the dollar, and was devalued in November, 1963. Unemployment had reached serious proportions, being estimated at half the regular labor force in the capital and the agricultural regions.

Full information is not available with regard to the productive economy, but some indications are available. Agricultural exports declined from about 695,000 tons in 1959 to about 393,000 in 1962; wood exports decreased from 163,000 tons to 115,000 tons. Most seriously affected has been the production of African export crops, which declined an estimated 61 percent from 1959 to 1962. Numerous small

European farms have been abandoned and many will probably never be reoccupied. The large plantations and bigger estates maintained production reasonably well, however, except in Oriental Province, which was closed off from the remainder of the country for many months; there was only a 22 percent decline in the exports from organized agricultural operations from 1959 to 1962.

Mining in the High Katanga, on the other hand, has achieved new record levels in several minerals. But revenues from Katanga, which had normally provided about 40 percent of Congo revenues including 57 percent of tax receipts, were not available to the central government until 1963, when it appeared that even Katanga had no funds left from its previous years' receipts. In Kasai, output of the diamond mines has been severely cut back. The country's major rail lines, waterways, and ports have suffered from sporadic destruction of bridges and from inability to obtain parts required for maintenance, but were in reasonably good operating condition in mid-1963. The road system, however, was suffering severely from lack of attention, and in some regions private companies had assumed the task of maintaining public roads.

It is not possible to determine the losses sustained by Belgium that were due to the Congo events, but an indication of the significance of the former colony to the Belgian economy may be derived from the following: an estimated 3.5 percent of the Belgian economy was directed to the Congo; trade with Congo accounted for 4.3 percent of Belgian exports in 1957 and 2.7 percent in 1959, while imports from Congo were 5.5 percent of the total in both years; Belgian investments in Congo totaled about $3.5 billion, of which $2 billion was from private sources. Belgian losses have included the expenses of some 90,000 refugees, pension payments, payments on Congolese loans guaranteed by Belgium, a reduction in tax returns of about 5 percent, and depreciation of the market value of Congolese securities. An agreement regarding the economic commitments of the two countries has yet to be reached, but Belgium will probably have to write off a substantial portion of the sums it claims to be owed by Congo. At present, it does not appear that the long-run losses of Belgium will be very great; most of the larger enterprises are continuing to operate and relationships between Congo and its former metropole have been increasingly improved in recent months.

THE REQUIREMENTS FOR ECONOMIC STABILITY

The elements needed to get the Congo economy functioning again are easy to delineate, but may not prove very simple to apply. First, of course, there must be an establishment of state authority, of order and security in all parts of the country. Good progress has been made in this sphere, but whether order will be maintained after withdrawal of the U.N. forces remains to be seen.

Second, there is the need for a large number of advisers, and it would appear that Belgium was the most likely source for their recruitment. The U.N. staff was not meant to be a shadow government and was not authorized to manage the economy. Efforts to recruit non-Belgians have not met with success, but the number of Europeans, which fell from 115,000 to 20,000 after the July, 1960, crisis, had increased to 35,000 by April, 1961, including some 28,000 Belgians, and was about 60,000 in mid-1963. Actually, the need is for administrators, not just advisers, because the Congolese are not yet trained to manage most of the economic and other enterprises of the country. Fortunately, Congolese leaders appear to be realistic regarding the need for foreign aides and most of them welcome the return of Belgian advisers. But the expatriate advisers must act in full cognizance of the independent status of Congo, of the authority of African government officials, and must be prepared to accelerate programs to train Africans progressively to assume the positions held by Europeans.

Third, there is a need to attract new capital.

This looks like a formidable task at the present time, but should not prove too difficult if political stability and unity are maintained. Investors will also wish to be assured that the government has regularized its operations, is striving to achieve a balanced budget, and can control the army. In 1963 the United Nations, the United States, Belgium, and other Western nations were forced to threaten withdrawal of large aid funds unless the government succeeded in achieving a more rational financial program. The United States has estimated that Congo will need $175 million yearly for the next few years in foreign aid, and has been itself contributing about $62 million annually. In the long run, Belgium may be expected to provide a substantial part of the capital required for renewed development, while other EEC countries may also participate in large-scale financial assistance. The Congo is not a poor country; on the basis of 1958 values, it had $711 million in portfolio shares of the big parastatal companies, of which about one half is represented by shares in Union Minière du Haut Katanga (UMHK) and Géomines, with other large holdings being in Otraco, Sabena, and electricity companies.

Given peaceful conditions, it should not prove too difficult to regenerate activity in a reasonable period of time in the mines, factories, estates, and plantations of the country. It will probably be much more difficult to reinstitute a program for advancing indigenous agriculture and to develop initiative in this sphere. It will also be very difficult to rekindle the momentum required to equal or exceed the rate of growth enjoyed by Congo from 1945 to 1960. Investments from 1947 to 1957 are estimated at $148 per capita, an amount exceeded in Africa only by the two Rhodesias (c. $200 per capita). Gross investment in that period was about 34 percent of national income, an excellent record.

One problem which will have to be faced in the years ahead is associated with the organizational arrangements characteristic of much of the Belgian development in Congo. Parastatal societies are particularly important and are involved in an unusual range of activities, from mining and agriculture to transportation, power, urban development, scientific research, and native welfare. In three cases there was transfer of certain powers of sovereignty: the Comité Spécial du Katanga (CSK), the Comité des Chemins de Fer du Congo Supérieur aux Grands Lacs Africains (CFL), and the Comité National du Kivu (CNKi). Each of these enterprises was created to stimulate rapid development in the vast regions under their supervision, in considerable measure by attracting private capital when government funds were not adequate. CSK was organized in 1900 to rationalize the exploration of the remote and little-touched Katanga Province where British expansion from the south was feared. Its political powers were withdrawn in 1910 but its economic and technical powers in Katanga remained very extensive, particularly through its subsidiary, Union Minière. CFL, created in 1902, received grants of land and mining rights in return for constructing certain rail lines. CNKi, dating from 1928, was granted large concessions over land and mining in Kivu with the particular goal of encouraging settlement by Belgian colons. While Congolese part-ownership of these companies removes them from some criticism, they have two disadvantages: first, they represent a highly evolved economic and financial system which is not easily comprehensible to Congolese and which tends to favor the big operator, and, second, they are subject to criticism as being neocolonial, sustaining a degree of economic control which is unpopular among African nationalists. Whatever the criticisms, however, it has been the big companies which have had the best record in sustaining the economy of the Congo since independence.

THE ECONOMIC-GEOGRAPHIC KEYNOTES OF CONGO

Before examining the several segments of the Congolese economy, it is desirable to present certain keynotes of its economic geography.

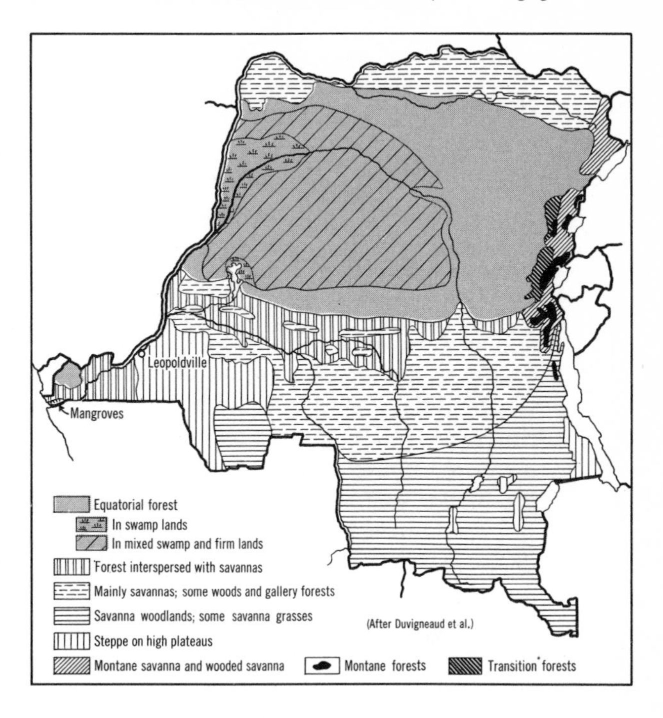

Map 56. Vegetation of Congo

Certain of these special features will serve to introduce additional background information required to understand the country.

EQUATORIAL POSITION

About a third of Congo lies north of the equator and two-thirds south. This latitudinal location is the most important factor in setting the climatic pattern; it is a strong indirect determinant in the gross distribution of vegetation and soils, and, hence, greatly influences the land use pattern of the country.

Climatically, a large tropical rainy area straddles the equator, skewed somewhat to the Northern Hemisphere because of the greater land mass. A small region of similar climate is found in Lower Congo. Precipitation in these regions ranges from 50 to 60 inches a year up to about 80 inches, and 10 to 12 months are humid. Most of the remainder of the country is tropical savanna except for zones of tropical highland climate along the eastern margins. Only very small areas of tropical steppe climate are found, in the deep rift valleys along part of the eastern border.

The vegetation pattern of Congo is shown in Map 56, adapted from several sources. Again there is a marked symmetry to north and south of the equator. The southern savanna zone is predominantly grassy in a belt south of the rainforest, but mainly savanna woodlands in southern Leopoldville Province and in Katanga.

Latosols are dominant among the soils of Congo, which means that the country is poorly endowed in this resource. Only limited areas have good soils: alluvials in the central basin and along some of the main watercourses; soils regenerated by erosion in the Mayumbe, Lower Congo, and in the east; and especially the volcanic lands of Kivu, which are periodically enriched by volcanic ash carried by the wind.

HYDROGRAPHIC UNITY

A second keynote is the hydrographic unity of the country, which gives Congo greater geo-

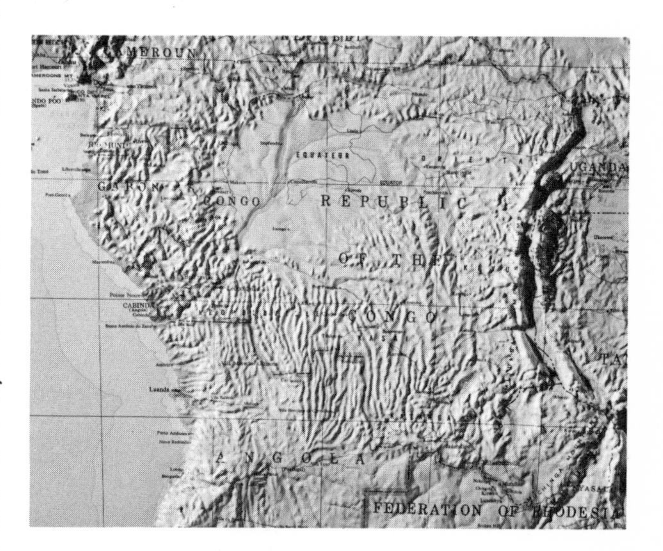

Map 57. Landforms of Congo
Relief Map Copyright Aero Service Corporation

graphic unity than most of the other areas of the continent. The vast bulk of Congo is within the Congo River Basin and the bulk of that basin is within the Congo (Map 57). Much of the area is a huge fan-shaped, shallow saucer, covering about 400,000 square miles, whose base is at the point where the Congo breaches the Crystal Highlands just below Stanley Pool. The fact that this basin also straddles the equator contributes further and importantly to the symmetrical pattern already noted for climate, vegetation, soil, and land use patterns.

From the geological standpoint, Congo rests on an ancient foundation, revealed in the mountainous rim circling the vast depression of the central Congo basin. Most of the mineral wealth of the country is found in the peripheral rim. The basin is covered by more recent sediments of varying thickness deposited in the last 200 million years. The effects of erosion during this period have left great accumulations in the depressions and sometimes terraced plateaus, especially in the south.

The geological history of Congo explains its relief features and the hydrographic basin. The central depression has an average elevation of about 1,300 feet. It is lowest in the Lac Tumbo and Lac Leopold II region, both lakes being the remnants of a once vast inland sea. Plains and terraced plateaus extend to the rim of the basin. The rim consists of more or less dislocated plateaus, lowest on the west and north but rising progressively as they approach Katanga to heights of 5,500 to 6,500 feet in several masses. On the east, the great longitudinal fractures of the Central Rift, 875 miles long and 25 to 30 miles wide, distinguish that area from the remainder of the country. The rift valley is bordered on both sides by uplifted mountains, while extinct and semi-active volcanic formations exist, particularly near Lake Kivu. The magnitude of the fractures is suggested from the height of the block mountain, Ruwenzori, with general elevations of 6,500 to 13,000 feet and a maximum elevation of 16,800 feet in Mt. Marguerite, and from Lake Tanganyika's maximum depth of 4,800 feet.

The country may, then, be broadly divided into three landform regions: (1) the concave central plain, containing some higher parts such as the hills of Zongo and Banzyville; (2) the rather circumscribed coastal zone consisting of an elevated plateau west of the Crystal Mountains which terminates in an escarpment, sometimes quite high, along the Atlantic beaches; and (3) the peripheral higher hills, mountains, and plateaus. This pattern provides generally well-marked boundaries, accentuating the geographic unity created particularly by the cuvette of the Congo.

THE EXISTENCE OF A GREAT SYSTEM OF INLAND WATERWAYS

Closely related to the previous keynote is the presence, within the Congo Basin, of the most important system of inland waterways in Africa (Map 59). Although by no means perfect, the Congo has permitted greater ease of access than in most interior African areas and, just as important, rather cheap means of communication. The series of thirty rapids and falls in the 217-mile stretch between Matadi and Leopoldville where the Congo cuts through the Crystal Mountains did, however, long discourage penetration, and the potential value of the Middle Congo was not appreciated until Stanley, on his second trip, came down it from the east. Navigable stretches on the 3,000-mile-long Congo total about 1,700 miles, the most important being the 80-mile maritime section to Matadi and the 1,085-mile section between Leopoldville and Stanleyville. The total mileage of navigable waterways within the Congo Basin is about 7,200. Contributing to the suitability of the Congo for navigation is the unusual evenness of its flow, explained by the presence of tributaries on both sides of the equator. The average flow at Leopoldville is 40,000 cubic meters per second; the ratio of low to high flow is only 1 to 3 as compared to 1 to 20 on the Mississippi or 1 to 48 on the Nile. The development of commerce on the Congo and its position within the whole transport complex of the republic is treated in a later section.

GREAT MINERAL AND HYDROELECTRIC WEALTH

The final physical keynote of Congo is its great richness in minerals, including the "white gold" of falling water. Congo ranks among the three leading mineral producers of Africa: it is fifth in the free world in output of copper, its most important mineral, and normally fifth in tin; it leads the world in production of industrial diamonds and cobalt; and it has an important output of a variety of other minerals. Exports of minerals normally account for over half of total Congolese exports by value, and the mining industry makes important contributions to the revenue of the country. In hydroelectric power, the country has the greatest potential of any nation in the world and some 40 percent of the estimated total for Africa. While developed facilities have harnessed only a fractional part of the enormous potential, Congo has witnessed one of the more dynamic hydropower programs in Africa. The details of mining and hydroelectric development are given below.

LOW AVERAGE DENSITY OF POPULATION

The final keynote to be presented in these preliminary notes is the generally low density of population, averaging about 16.0 per square mile in 1961, based on extrapolation from the 1956–57 census. The low population of Congo has presented certain problems in the development of agriculture, mining, and industry, particularly for plantation interests in the equatorial rainforest zone and for mining companies in Katanga, and the literature on Congo gives frequent reference to what was long considered a population crisis. At the end of the nineteenth century Stanley made a purely speculative estimate of the population, placing it at 28 million. This and other equally unscientific estimates were frequently cited as fact and contributed to the rather widely accepted belief that the population was actually declining, threatening the whole base for economic development. It is probably true that the death rate was extremely high, especially during the Leopold period when there were few restrictions on the use of labor, when men were frequently removed from their communities for long periods, and when the incidence of disease was heightened by migrations and the introduction of previously absent maladies. Experts now calculate that the population was about 9 million in 1900 and about the same in 1925.

The rate of growth of the population is estimated to have been 0.6 percent per annum from 1925–40, 1 percent in the period 1940–50, and 1.9 percent per year in the period from 1950

A landing stage on a small tributary of the Congo
Congo is unusual among African countries in the vast extent of its inland waterway system, totaling about 1,700 miles.

to the 1956–57 census. At that time the crude rate of increase was calculated to be 2.3 percent per annum, the birth rate being 43 per thousand and the death rate 20 per thousand. It is not unlikely that the very high rate of increase of 3.0 percent will soon be reached; indeed it already has been in Katanga, where the death rate is still fairly high and subject to rapid improvement.

The dramatic change that has taken place in the demographic position is explained in considerable part by the Belgian concern with what was considered a serious population problem. Having decided that such a problem existed, Belgium took strong measures to correct it by promulgating a number of protective laws and by instituting a number of positive programs designed to promote population growth. Limitations were placed on the numbers of workers that could be recruited from any tribal area; workers were encouraged to settle in the employment areas; and recruitment was often made on a family basis. The large compounds for bachelor migrants characteristic of the South African mines were not seen in the Katanga mining communities. Employers were also required to maintain certain standards of rations, medical facilities, housing, and sanitation in the nontribal areas. The health program was also progressively improved, and compared favorably with that of other African countries; special emphasis was given to reducing the originally high infant mortality rate.

While the crisis of 1960 and particularly the exodus of medical personnel thereafter may lead to a setback in the health situation in the Congo, it is not unreasonable to expect that the population will reach 25 million by 1980. There is also some question whether the problem of worker shortage was not exaggerated. There are some real advantages that can be delineated: it encouraged the adoption of labor-saving equipment, which incidentally permitted the training of more technicians; it stimulated the desire to upgrade agricultural methods; and, for the future, there is a greater possibility of achieving a good standard of living rather than simply that of a glorified peasantry. When labor is cheap there is a great temptation to use it poorly—to cut the grass with knives, to mine with pickaxes and shovels, or to build roads by hand. In the Congo, where there are great development potentialities, it is easier, with a low population, to set the sights higher than it is, say, in Nigeria or Rwanda and Burundi, where population increases frequently press against available resources. Even with its present low average density, the Congo may prove to have a greater problem in its very rapid rate of increase than it faced in adjusting to real and imagined shortages of manpower. The fact that 40 percent of the population is under 14 years of age suggests that problems of absorption will grow apace in the years ahead.

With regard to the distribution of population within Congo, the highest densities occur in the eastern highlands and in Lower Congo, the lowest in the former provinces of Katanga, Equator, and Oriental. The increase in urban communities has been particularly striking in the last two decades. Leopoldville, for example, had 17,825 people in 1923, 22,000 in 1933, 368,000 in 1958, and an estimated 420,000 in 1961. The four largest cities in Katanga, all mining centers, had a total population of 325,644 in 1958—none of them existed in 1900.

The Belgians for some years recorded the number of Congolese living outside of their customary tribal milieus; while these figures cannot be taken as indicative of urban growth, they do suggest the extent of migrations and do represent an approximation of the numbers residing where economic activity has been more intensified. Their greatest value, of course, is in giving a crude index of persons who are more concerned with the monetary than the subsistence economy. In 1935, 6 percent, and in 1945, 9.8 percent of the African population was "non coutumière"; by 1957 this percentage had increased to 23.

A great mosaic of tribes exists in the Congo, but the vast bulk of the population is classified as Bantu. Of the 69 more important tribes,

49 are Bantu, 16 located along the northern border are Sudanese, one each in the east is Nilotic and Hamitic in origin, and, finally, there are four groups of pygmies and pygmoids with an estimated 1.5 percent of the total population. While there are several hundreds of dialects, four African languages are spoken or understood by most of the people: Kikongo, Kiluba, Lingala, and Kiswahili. French is, of course, the lingua franca for the country. The significance of tribalism has already been noted with respect to the regional differences that developed after independence.

The non-African population in Congo totaled 118,003 in 1958. Only a small number were Asian in origin. The European population increased from 17,000 in 1926 and 28,500 in 1939 to 66,078 in 1952 and 112,757 in 1958. In the last of these years, some 78.2 percent of the non-Africans were Belgians, while Portuguese and Greeks were the next best represented. Of the 46,441 non-Africans gainfully occupied in 1958, company personnel represented 43.7 percent, government employees 20.2 percent, "colonists" 20.7 percent, and missionaries 15.4 percent. These figures reflect the great importance of parastatal companies and also the significant part played by religious groups in the educational and social work of the colony. The term "colonists" included small businessmen and manufacturers, storekeepers, craftsmen, and independent professional people as well as farmers and cattle breeders who represented only about 20 percent of all the colons. As is typical of tropical Africa, most Europeans lived in the large urban centers. In Congo, one third of the total resided in Leopoldville Province and 18 percent in the city itself; another third was in Katanga, with almost 20 percent of the total in the four largest cities. As has already been seen, most of the European population left the Congo in 1960, though a sizable number have since returned. What the European population will be in the decades ahead can only be speculated; its composition will doubtless include a somewhat lower percentage of Belgians and of "colons."

THE TRANSPORT COMPLEX

An appreciation of the main features of the transport network of Congo can be gained by tracing the major routes of access into and from the area, noting the major break of bulk points when appropriate (see Maps 59 and 60).

THE MATADI-LEOPOLDVILLE AXIS

It is logical to start with Matadi, the only port of real importance within the national territory. The republic has a very small coastline on the Atlantic, the use of which is further restricted by the freak boundary situation in the area in relation to the topography. Most of the southern shore of the Congo River in its lower navigable stretch belongs to Angola (Map 58). Congo has the northern bank in this stretch but to use it for a major port would require either a bridge at Leopoldville and a rail line running through Brazzaville Congo territory or a bridge at Matadi, either of which would be very costly. A third alternative would be to use the river port of Brazzaville and the Congo-Ocean Railway to Pointe Noire, but the Belgians

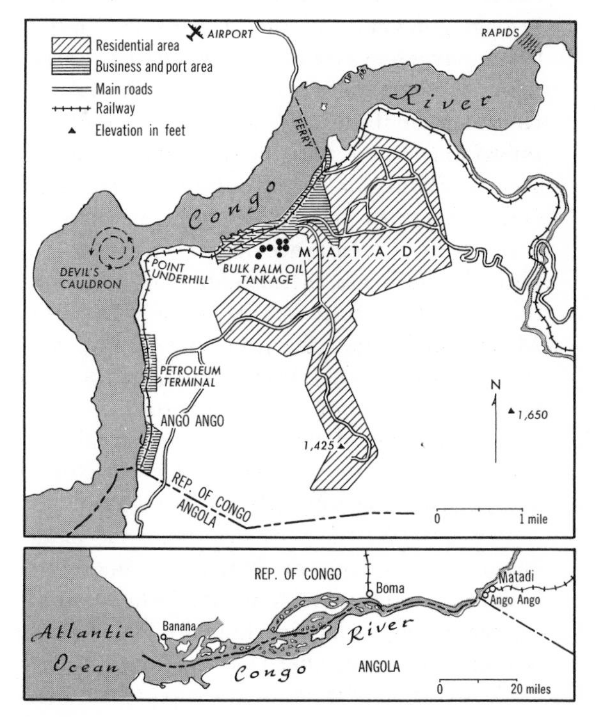

Map 58. The port of Matadi and the Congo approaches to it

The ocean port of Matadi on the lower Congo River
Matadi is the main port for Congo and efforts have long been made to use it for as much of Congo traffic as was practicable. It is, however, disadvantaged by difficult site features and by the necessity for numerous transshipments for freight of southern and eastern Congo.

had constructed the Matadi-Leopoldville line long before this alternative route was completed and adopted policies designed to use the national route as much as possible.

Located 80 miles up the maritime section of the river, Matadi occupies the very small area belonging to Congo on the left bank and on the lower navigable stretch. This site has three main disadvantages: (1) the impediments to navigation on the lower Congo; (2) the difficult topography at the port; and (3) the restricted area available for possible future expansion. Impediments to navigation include powerful currents at the entrance to the estuary; the unstable sandbanks, silt accumulation, and sand islands characteristic of the section between Malela and Boma; sharp turnings in the constricted rocky passage below the port; and the whirlpools of the Devil's Cauldron between Ango Ango and Matadi, which are difficult for smaller vessels to negotiate. The maritime stretch has, however, been considerably improved over the years by deepening the main channel, continuous dredging, and improved channel markings, including the installation of luminous buoys which permitted night navigation under pilotage after 1955.

Construction of facilities at the port itself first required extension of the very limited flat land along the river by blasting it from the steep hills rising abruptly from the river. The narrow width and the velocity of the river at Matadi precluded anything but marginal quays, which could not be extended continuously downstream because of the proximity of the Devil's Cauldron at Ango Ango, whose site features are comparable to those at the main port.

Matadi now has three deepwater quays totaling 1,750 yards in length, 10 transit sheds, and bulk palm oil storage facilities. It is well equipped with cranes and mobile mechanical handling equipment. Lighters are extensively used at Matadi; they permit savings in construction of additional sheds and expedite loading and unloading operations when worked on the outboard side of berthed vessels, but they do have the disadvantage of increasing handling at the port. The annex of Ango Ango, seven miles downstream, serves as the petroleum port; its tank depot is connected by 4-inch and 6-inch pipelines to Leopoldville. Ango Ango also has some bulk palm oil tankage, a small pier for ships unable to pass the cauldron, and a fish processing installation.

Traffic at Matadi and Ango Ango increased from 531,000 metric tons in 1938 to 1,746,000 in 1959, but declined to 1,057,000 tons in 1962 (Map 60). Congestion was severe between 1946 and the mid-fifties, forcing the Belgians to use foreign outlets to an increasing degree despite the strong desire to use the "voie nationale." In 1959, despite the handicaps, the port and its annex handled 61.3 percent of Congolese imports and 48.3 percent of exports. It would be possible to expand capacity at the port by further extension of quays to the Angolan border, but sooner or later it will probably become necessary to bridge the Congo at Matadi and construct a rail line across difficult terrain on the north shore to Boma or Banana. Outbound shipments at Matadi are chiefly agricultural and forestry products; it normally handles the bulk of high-value general cargo imports for the country as well as most of its needs in petroleum products. Belgian vessels typically handled close to three fifths of the traffic at Matadi, a share which was partially assured by setting port charges on the basis of total tonnage of ships calling and by various tie-in agreements in contracts involving sales and construction in the Congo.

The immediate hinterland of Matadi is extremely restricted; its traffic largely comes from and is destined to the interior Congo Basin. It may, in fact, almost be classified as an outport of Leopoldville, the inland terminus of the Matadi-Leopoldville Railway (CFML), and the base of navigation for the whole middle Congo River system. The ports of Matadi and Leopoldville, the connecting railway, and much of the river transport are managed by Otraco (Office d'Exploitation des Transports Coloniaux), one of the great parastatal transport organizations in the Congo.

Of the cargo handled at Matadi, 95 percent normally moves over the CFML. This single-track, 227-mile line cuts laboriously through the Crystal Mountains on a route that involved much cutting, filling, and bridging. Despite

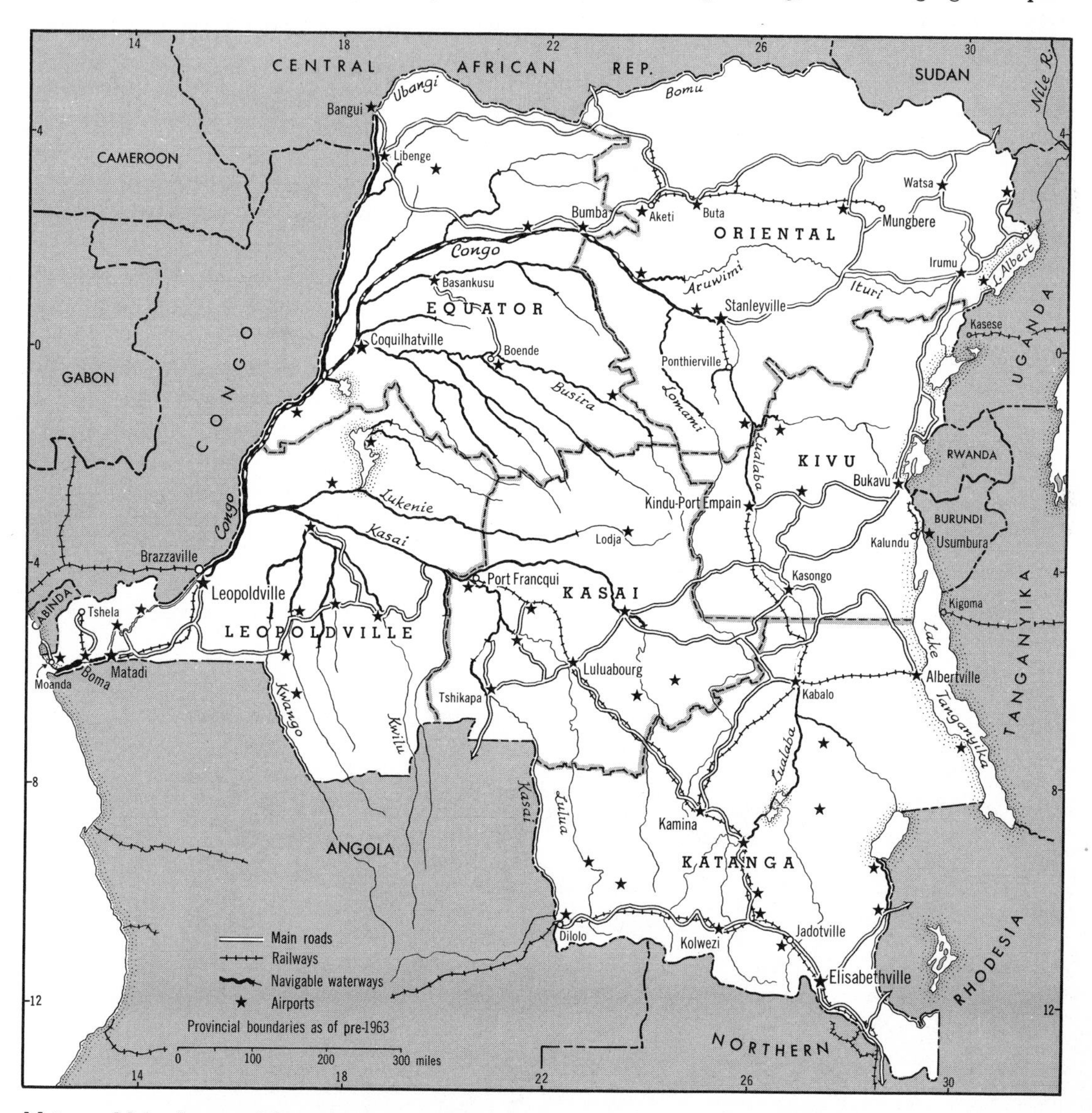

Map 59. Major features of the transport net in Congo

marked improvements, train speeds are still limited to 37 miles per hour and axle loads to 18 metric tons. Traffic on the CFML was 2.13 million metric tons in 1959 and 1.12 million metric tons in 1962.

Leopoldville, the interior terminus of the axis, is situated on Stanley Pool, where the vast fanlike interior Congo River system converges. It is Africa's most important river port, handling 1.59 million tons in 1959, more than most ocean terminals in Africa; its 1962 traffic was only 855,000 tons. Its port facilities include 1,070 yards of public quays, large bulk storage for palm and palm kernel oil and for petroleum products, smaller private beaches, and shipbuilding and ship repair yards. The port is well equipped with mechanical gear, but does suffer from inadequate space behind the river front because of placement of the business section immediately adjacent to the early port facilities. If traffic increases greatly in the future, it may be necessary to consider construction of new facilities at Kimpoko, 21 miles upstream. Leopoldville, with a population of over 420,000, is an important consuming center both for goods moving inland from Matadi and for those coming down the Congo River. Almost all of its transit traffic moves on the river.

The river port of Leopoldville
Leopoldville is situated at the base of navigation of the inland Congo River system. Its traffic is greater than that of most African seaports.

THE CONGO WATERWAY SYSTEM

Almost the whole transport system of the Congo was originally designed to take advantage of the extensive navigable waterways of the great Congo Basin. The particular features of the road and rail system were, generally speaking, determined by the specific features of the Congo and its tributaries; since water transport cost less than overland movement, the roads and railways were frequently built to supplement the waterways. Rail lines were placed at breaks in the navigable river or were directed to it from regions which were not served by navigable streams.

The Belgians were also interested in focusing traffic on the Congo because use of that route involved support for the national port. Special rates were instituted on combined routeways to induce Congo trade to use the "voie nationale" instead of shorter and less costly foreign routes. Waterborne traffic maintained its 40 percent share of total ton-kilometer traffic from prewar to postwar years, but must be expected to decline relatively in the decades ahead when the road system is improved and extended.

The two most important sections of the middle Congo are the 1,085-mile stretch from Leopoldville to Stanleyville and the 378 miles of the Kasai River from its confluence to Port Francqui. Map 59 shows the navigable streams of the Congo. In the early years of traffic on the Congo River little was done to improve

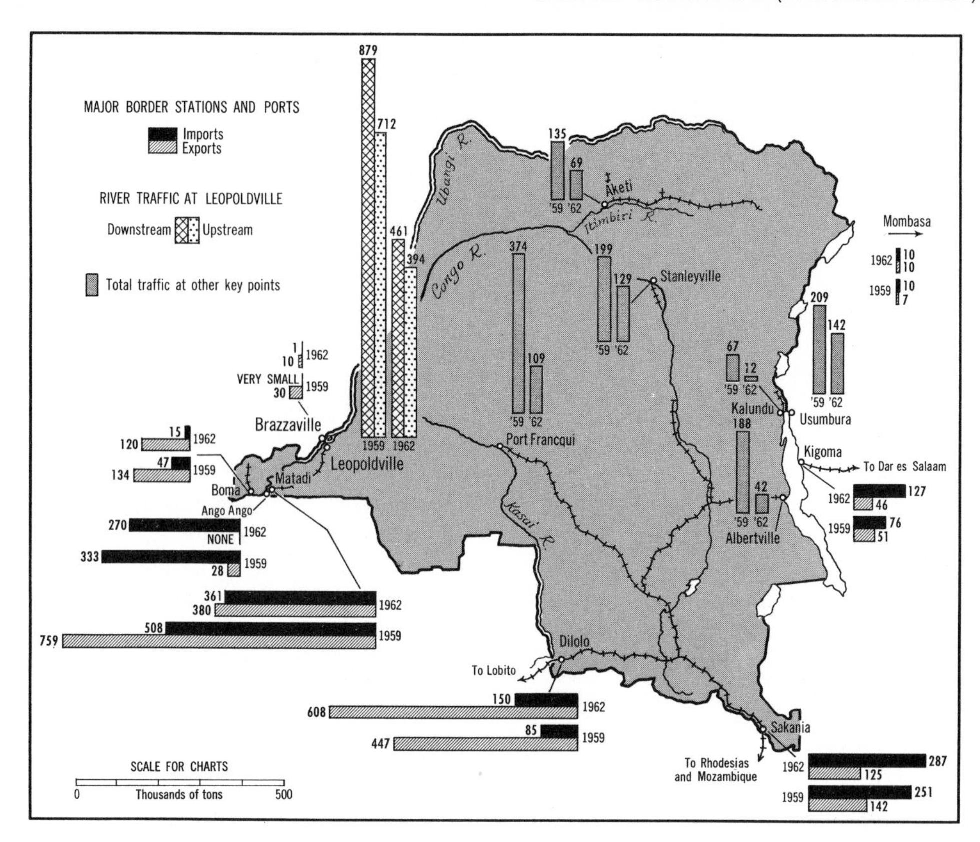

Map 60. Traffic at ports, border stations, and key transshipment points in Congo, 1959 and 1962

navigability. Flat-bottomed stern-wheelers towing strings of low draft barges operated on the main streams; small tugs drawing less than 2 feet picked up those barges which were directed to the shallower streams at junctions and towed them to their destinations. Important changes to this general pattern were not made until after World War II and included the installation of luminous beacons and of mirrors on the main sections; equipment of vessels with radar; introduction of diesel-powered vessels; use of the integrated pushtow system as used on the Mississippi; and removal of some of the more restricting shoals. Towing power was more than doubled from 1948 to 1958, as was capacity of cargo carriers. A new problem in recent years has been the appearance of water hyacinth on the river; spraying with chemical weed killers appears to have kept this rapidly multiplying floating vegetation under control on the major streams.

Many shipping points, some well equipped and others only landing stages, have sprung up along the waterways. Stanleyville and Port Francqui are the two most important, the latter being mainly a transshipment point between the rail system of the south and the river. Stanleyville, an important regional capital, occurs where the Stanley Falls, a series of seven rapids, interrupt navigation. Eventually they may be canalized, for there is not a very great drop and no serious engineering problem exists. At present, however, they are by-passed via a 78-mile rail line to Ponthierville. Above the Falls, the Upper Congo, which is sometimes called the Lualaba, is navigable to Kindu and again from Kongolo to Bukama, a distance of 240 miles. The river flows across a vast plain in this region and spreads out each year into numerous lakes, some of which are permanent. It has been necessary to cut and maintain a passageway through the floating vegetation and papyrus on these stretches. A portion of the Chemins de Fer du Congo Supérieur aux Grands Lacs Africains (CFL), running from Kindu to Kabalo, connects the two navigable sections of the Upper Congo, and other sections continue from the latter town to Albertville on Lake Tanganyika and connect with Kamina on the Katanga line (Map 59). When the Kabalo-Bukama link was completed in 1956, most of the CFL system was converted from meter gauge to 3-foot–6-inch track. The CFL river-rail system was seriously interrupted in 1961 and 1962 owing to the blockade of Oriental Province and to sporadic fighting in the area.

The Vicicongo rail system in the northeast of the country was also built largely as a feeder to the Congo system. This 2-foot gauge line is of local importance, particularly to the Uele cotton producing region, but it has suffered severely in post-independence years because of interruption of traffic with Oriental Province, abandonment of cotton and other plantings, the poor state of feeder roads, and inadequate maintenance of the line itself. In many parts of the Congo Basin, roads link interfluvial areas to available river shipping points.

It may be seen, then, that the Congo waterway system and its supplementary road and rail connections cover a very large portion of the country, even servicing portions of the south via the Kasai and Upper Lualaba routes. But the use of the Congo routeway is not entirely appropriate for some sections of eastern Congo, which are nearer the Indian Ocean seaboard than they are to the Atlantic.

ROUTEWAYS TO THE EAST

Several routes leading to ports on the eastern seaboard are open to use for Congo traffic but are normally of only minor significance. The eastern edge of the Congo is the most remote area of the country; 1½ to 2 years may elapse before goods ordered in Europe reach their destinations in that region. The Kivu area may be taken as an example of the inadequacy of the national routes, which are, however, frequently used. Goods moving from Bukavu, for example, would go by (*a*) truck to Usumbura or Uvira on Lake Tanganyika, (*b*) lake vessel to Albertville, (*c*) rail to Kindu, (*d*) river boat to Ponthierville, (*e*) rail to Stanleyville, (*f*) boat to Leopoldville, (*g*) rail to Matadi, and (*h*) ship to Europe or other destination. An alternative national route, reducing the number of transshipments, became available after 1956, namely, rail from Albertville via the Kabalo-Kamina link to Port Francqui, boat to Leopoldville, and so on. Improved roads in the east, particularly the heavy-duty road from Stanleyville to Goma on Lake Kivu, may prove to be more efficient in serving the Kivu area in the long run.

Possible extranational routes available to various parts of eastern Congo include (1) road to the Nile in southern Sudan and hence via boat and Sudan Railways to Port Sudan, very seldom used; (2) road to Mahagi or Kasenyi on Lake Albert, steamer across the lake, road to Kampala, and rail to Mombasa; (3) road to the railhead of Kasese on the Uganda line and hence to Mombasa; (4) road or rail to Lake Tanganyika, steamer to Kigoma in Tanganyika, and Central Line to Dar es Salaam. The last of these routes is the most important extranational route for eastern Congo; special facilities known as Belbases were formerly maintained at Kigoma and Dar es Salaam to handle transit trade for Congo and Ruanda-Urundi.

TRANSPORT IN SOUTHERN CONGO

As has already been noted, some traffic of southern Congo uses the Congo and Kasai waterways. But this area, and particularly the High Katanga, is least well served by water routes, not only because of their distance from the producing areas but also because transshipments are more difficult for bulk mineral traffic than for other types of cargo. The transport backbone of Katanga is the Chemin de Fer du Bas-Congo au Katanga (BCK), which has 1,587 miles of 3-foot–6-inch gauge rail lines including its connection with the CFL at Kabalo, its line to Port Francqui, its line connecting with the Rhodesia Railways to the south, and its branch connecting with the Benguela Railway in Angola. The BCK leads all Congo railways in ton-mileage and freight volume transported, mainly because much of its traffic is in minerals and metals. The BCK raised its capacity greatly in postwar years by reequipping and relaying with heavier track and by electrifying the 421-mile section west of Elisabethville.

The BCK and the Benguela Railway to Lobito is the most direct outlet for Katanga, which results in that Angolan port normally ranking second among African ports in tonnage of Congolese traffic handled. After the 1960 crisis and Katanga's defection, it was even more important because Katanga would not permit utilization of the national route to Matadi. In 1962 the Benguela Railway handled 758,000 tons of Katanga cargo, minerals from that province comprising 95 percent of the down-line traffic. In 1963 the BCK was finally brought back into the national system and traffic between Leopoldville and Katanga was resumed.

There has been much discussion over the years of connecting the Katanga line with the Matadi-Leopoldville line, which would eliminate the necessity of transshipment at Port Francqui and Leopoldville. But the distance from Elisabethville to Matadi would be 1,751 miles as compared to 1,308 miles to Lobito.

Some traffic of Katanga moves over the Rhodesian Railways to and from the Mozambique ports of Beira and Lourenço Marques, the former being 1,619 miles from Elisabethville.

A train operating on the electrified section of the BCK Railway near Jadotville

The BCK handles almost all of the mineral traffic of Katanga. It has connections with the Benguela Railway, the Rhodesia Railways, and river services of the Congo and Kasai rivers.

TRANSPORT IN MAYUMBE

Matadi handles some traffic brought by ferry from the section of Congo lying north of the maritime Congo River, Mayumbe, but that rather productive area is more tied to the port of Boma. Boma has 770 yards of deepwater quay and handles about 180,000 tons of cargo annually. The narrow-gauge, 87-mile Mayumbe Railway running to Tshela is inadequate to serve the region's needs and was being augmented by a first-class highway when Congo became independent.

SUMMARY

It is probable that the basic pattern of Congolese freight movement has now largely been set: dependence of the center and north on the Congo, of the south on the Katanga Railway. A particular feature of Congolese transport has been the very limited importance of trucking, measured by percent of total ton-mileage of freight carried. A number of factors disfavor the use of roads more in Congo than in most African countries: its interior location, which means that trucks have less chance of competing with railways and waterways in conveying goods imported and exported via distant coastal points; the considerable bulk of much of the traffic; the fact that a substantial part of the highest value agricultural traffic is generated in the more remote eastern reaches; the unusual extent of navigable waterways; and the usual physical problems which beset road building in all tropical areas. Construction of a major east-west routeway across the south, which was planned but not carried out in the first ten-year plan, is rendered particularly costly because such a route runs counter to the general north-south grain of the country and involves a multitude of expensive bridges.

Despite all these difficulties, however, there was a marked expansion of road mileage in postwar years and the motor vehicle park increased from 7,623 cars and trucks in 1938 to 17,671 in 1948 and 68,750 in 1959.

Congo was well served by internal and external air routes before the 1960 crisis and by 1963 it was possible to maintain regular schedules to 33 airports in the country. Leopoldville has one of the busiest airports on the continent, its new field meeting all international requirements. Congo holds a part-interest in Sabena Airlines, which manages the internal services for Air Congo.

AGRICULTURE IN CONGO

A high degree of local self-sufficiency is still characteristic of Congo agriculture though a higher percentage of farmers had been brought into the money economy than in most of tropical Africa. The most important subsistence crops are cassava, by far the leader; plantain; corn, which is the major basic crop in the southwest; and millet. Livestock are relatively unimportant to the Africans except in the higher, tsetse-free Kibali-Ituri area. In postwar years, intensified efforts were directed toward upgrading indigenous agriculture, particularly by introduction of paysannats, and by greater African production of commercial crops. Plantations are more important in Congo than in any of the countries thus far studied, while European estates also figured significantly in commercial production. Agricultural exports normally accounted for about 40 to 50 percent of total exports by value, a not unimpressive share in view of the great importance of the mining industry.

DEVELOPMENT OF PLANTATIONS

European plantations and estates exploited over 1,500 square miles of crop lands and 450 square miles of forests and pasturelands in 1959, employing a labor force of about 300,000 Africans. Large companies were especially important in the production of palm products, rubber, coffee, and cocoa; colons were concerned with cattle and specialized crops.

Plantations had their debut in 1890 when the governor prescribed to each of his district commissioners that cocoa plantations be established at each post. Although over 4,500 acres were planted to cocoa by 1898, the results of this program were disappointing owing to the lack of knowledge and of qualified personnel and to the fact that some areas were not ecologically suitable to the cocoa tree. In succeeding years, efforts were made to introduce plantation production of rubber, sisal, ramie, and cotton with only limited success, despite the issuance of various decrees from 1891 to 1903 requiring the local chiefs to supply labor to produce plantation crops on lands belonging to the state.

Early efforts to stimulate African output of commercial crops were also disappointing, owing to indifference, lack of skill, and inadequate knowledge regarding suitable crops. Convinced of the inability of moving forward with sufficient rapidity by this method, the government adopted a policy favoring the introduction of company operations. In 1911 a convention was signed with Lever Brothers involving rights of exploitation of natural and planted oil palms

A three-year-old oil palm plantation at Yaligimba, Congo
Foreign-owned plantations and estates normally account for about three fourths of Congo agricultural exports by value.

in large blocks of land. The spectacular results of this entente, which increased exports of palm oil and palm kernels with great rapidity, were a dominant factor in the continuing emphasis given to plantation production. The period from 1925 to 1930 witnessed a particularly rapid increase in extension of plantations; banana plantations were started in Mayumbe, sugar in Lower Congo, and acreages were considerably increased in rubber, coffee, cocoa, and other crops. Many of these new plantations were closed during the great depression, despite government aid through reduction in taxes, lowered freight rates, and provision of assistance funds. In the late 1930s and particularly after World War II, there was renewed interest in plantations, with an especially notable increase taking place between 1950 and 1957 in the acreage devoted to coffee. In 1959, production on European plantations and estates accounted for about 75 percent of the value of agricultural exports.

The question whether plantations should be promoted in underdeveloped areas has been a subject of discussion for many years and is worthy of parenthetical attention at this point. The physical and economic advantages weigh heavily in favor of plantation methods. First, it is much easier to apply scientific techniques on plantations, including careful seed selection, proper rotational and fertilization practices, and scientific disease control. As a consequence of using more advanced methods, plantations typically have crop yields ranging from two to ten times those of indigenous producers. They also often bear fruit earlier and have a longer productive life.

Second, the use of large-scale techniques often permits lower cost production. Orderliness facilitates control of competing growth; harvesting can be systematic, swift, and cheap; special transport can be provided, such as narrow-gauge lines or overhead conveyors; assurance of a regular supply may justify provision of processing mills, which, in the case of palm oil, for example, permit cleaner, richer oil and extraction of about twice as much oil as is normally obtained by cruder indigenous methods; processing plants may also be able to utilize by-products which would otherwise be wasted; and, finally, there is usually a marked saving in manpower. The United Africa Company, for example, states that only one-third as many laborers are required on its plantations to produce a given amount of oil as would be required in indigenous production.

Plantation operators claim that there are also social benefits of considerable value associated with the plantation system. Governments usually stipulate that certain standards of schooling, medical facilities, housing, and food supply be maintained and many plantation companies make such provisions on a level superior to the legal requirements.

The arguments are by no means all in favor of plantations. From the physical standpoint, there is somewhat greater possibility of disease devastating a plantation than the scattered, mixed holdings of indigenous farmers. The United Africa Company states rather strongly that "new diseases, not found in natural circumstances, are bound to attack." Also, concentration on one crop is often harder on the soil than the mixed agriculture of the peasant.

From the economic standpoint, there is the disadvantage of too great dependence on one crop. Also, overhead expenses may offset economic advantages of plantations as compared with indigenous production. And there is the danger that too great a portion of earnings will leave the country.

From the social standpoint, there is disruption of the existing way of life, detribalization, sometimes the separation of families when labor is recruited from a distance, and there may be interference with local land tenure systems.

From the political standpoint, enterprises run by outside companies are always open to charges of exploitation, no matter how justified or unjustified the charge may be. In many areas of the world where plantations were important they have been the subject of increasing resentment as nationalism increases. This is perhaps the most cogent argument against them.

Yet to eliminate plantations because of their political objections is possibly to deny oneself the advantages of what can be a highly efficient and competitive way of increasing production and productivity. Possible answers to this dilemma include the organizing of partnership or cooperative plantations or simply accepting plantations as one form of outside investment but reaching some agreement with regard to such factors as local representation on the company board of directors and appropriate limitations on profits. The whole matter of organization of production of tropical commodities is an interesting and important one to watch.

ESTATE AGRICULTURE

The term "estate agriculture" is used here to refer to farms owned and run by colons, as opposed to the usually much larger plantation operations which are typically company-owned and managed by a paid staff. The first effort to promote colonization was made in Katanga. Mining brought a big influx of Europeans and Africans to the High Katanga after 1908, a region which was sparsely populated, did not have agricultural surpluses available for provisioning the mining communities, and whose remoteness made importing of food very costly. To stimulate local food production, and also to neutralize what was then considered the serious danger that Katanga might be attracted to Britain by penetration from the south, it was decided in 1910 that Belgian colonists would be encouraged to settle in the area. These colonists were to be aided by assistance in laying out their farms and by subsidized passage; 18 farms were occupied in 1910, but they met with very disappointing results. Katanga soils are generally poor, precipitation is less regular than in other Congo areas, labor was hard to find, and it proved difficult for the produce of the colons to compete either with that of local Africans or with imports from South Africa. By 1926, however, some 115 colons had become established in Katanga, which remained one of the two centers for European agricultural colonization.

The second area for European colons was in the higher, eastern part of the country, in Kivu and Ituri (Map 61). Settlement began there with the establishment of a farm at Irumu early in the century; in 1959, most of the 1,899 colons in agriculture in the country were in the east.

A European-owned market garden near Elisabethville, Katanga
European farms in this area were promoted to provide food supplies for the large mining communities.

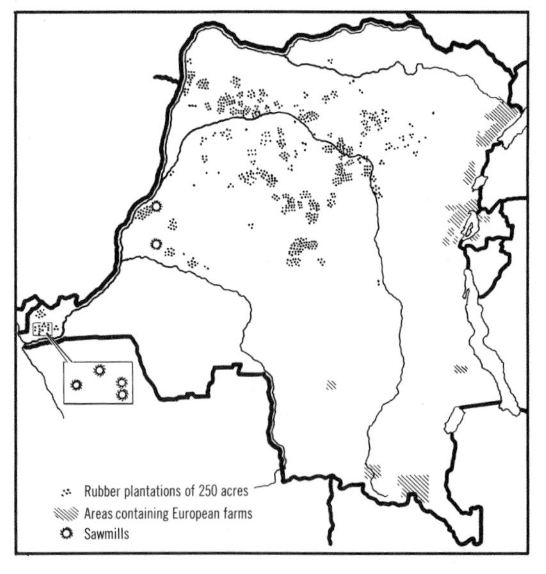

Map 61. European estates, rubber plantations, and sawmills in Congo

A European coffee estate in the east
Colonization in eastern Congo was concerned with the production of high-value export crops.

A variety of assistance programs inaugurated in 1945 had helped to increase their number from 657 immediately after the war, but colonization in Congo was usually carried on by settlers who had substantial personal financial resources; it bore little relation to pioneer farming in the American West.

Colonization in the east was in strong contrast to that in Katanga. In Katanga, the farmers raised cattle and hogs and produced food crops for sale to the large mining communities. Settlers in the east concentrated on high-value, low-bulk crops, many of which were destined for foreign markets. The remoteness of the area required such an emphasis, but the region was also ecologically well suited for specialized tropical crops. Possessing some excellent soils and having a tropical highland climate with moderate temperatures, it was far more attractive for European settlement than other parts of the Congo. Labor was also much less of a problem, the east frequently having a high density of population. Coffee was the prime crop on European estates in the east; tea, medicinals, pyrethrum, perfume plants, and tobacco were also of importance, while some farms specialized in the raising of cattle. What percentage of these estates were still functioning in 1963 is not known.

DEVELOPMENT OF INDIGENOUS AGRICULTURE

The first effort to stimulate African peasant farming in Congo, both for production of commercial crops and for improved local standards, was the imposition of obligatory duties. This system led to abuses which, after severe criticism, were gradually removed. The reform, however, led to what the Belgians considered economic disaster in that many Africans simply stopped working. Obligatory duties were reinstituted during World War I with the provision, however, that they were to have an educational goal and that the work was to be for the exclusive profit of the indigenous producer. From 1927 to 1930 each African was required to plant 10 palm trees a year around his village; after 1935, increased efforts were made to stimulate African production of coffee and systematically to establish indigenous palm plantations. While required work did lead to a big increase in production of cotton and other crops, achievement of the educational goal was only moderately successful.

In 1936 an experiment was undertaken near the Gandajika station of INEAC, the agricultural research organization of Congo. In the experimental area each volunteer was allotted a plot divided into yearly pieces to be cultivated according to a rotational system determined by the station. This modest effort is important in that it presaged the large-scale introduction of paysannats after the war.

After World War II, under the influence of changing conditions during the war and in other colonial areas after the war and the general improvement in economic conditions, the Congolese gradually abandoned their attitude of passivity and took increasing initiative in their own advancement. Imposition of duties was necessarily replaced by persuasion and demonstration; the duration of *travaux educatifs* was reduced to 45 days a year in 1955 and they were largely suppressed after 1957. But indigenous methods evolved relatively little and increased production was offset by losses to erosion, deforestation, and degradation of soils. It was with these considerations in mind that the Belgians decided to institute a system of paysannats. Paysannats involved all manner of technical and social improvements in the indigenous agricultural system, but the distinctive feature in the Congo was the institution of organized shifting agriculture, sometimes called the "corridor" system. While there are several variants of this system, basically it involves organizing land into corridors whose fields are systematically opened and permitted successively to revert to bush on an over-all 20-year cycle. The advantages of the corridor system, which represents a compromise between technical agronomy and the natural regenerative capacity of the soil, are that it tends to stabilize the rural population, permits an orderly rotation, makes plant protection easier, can be conducive to the introduction of mechanization, and may be instituted without drastically changing the indigenous approach to land and agriculture. Resettlement of farmers along roads or tracks may also facilitate improvements in transport and provision of social amenities.

A few examples will illustrate some of the major features of Congolese paysannats. The Turumbu system was typical of forest paysannats producing annual crops. East-west corridors of 328-foot width were laid out and cultivation took place in two bands separated by a forested band of equal depth. The initial cycle involved three years of cultivation followed by 15 to 20 years in bush fallow, a period which it was later possible to reduce by technical improvements. Holdings were not assigned on a permanent individual basis but were divided annually according to tribal custom and reverted to the community after the cultivation period. An effort was also made to rationalize the preparation and conservation of the annuals grown at Turumbu. In 1958, 1,925 peasants were involved with the Turumbu paysannat system, which covered about 44,000 acres.

Terraced agriculture in Kivu Province
Much attention was given in the higher eastern lands to the application of practices which would prevent soil erosion.

The Babua paysannat system, which had 12,356 participants in 1958, was another system applied in forest areas for production of annual crops. It differed from the Turumbu system in that it entailed the assignment of individual holdings with tenure, which required complete mapping before it could be applied. The corridor plots had a rotation based on cotton and peanuts and the main food crops, while perennials were placed on special parcels of land reserved for their production.

The Gandajika paysannat is an example of a paysannat located in low-altitude savanna country. Assignment of plots was on an individual basis; the rotation was based on cotton and peanuts but also included cassava, corn, beans, and other crops. Over 15,000 acres in various areas were under this type of paysannat in 1958. In some it was possible to use machines and fertilizers economically, while protection against fire permitted shortening the fallow period.

Application of the system in high-altitude savannas was often more complex because of the dominant need to protect the soil and the necessity to provide space for subsistence crops, perennial cultures (especially arabica coffee), reforestation, and livestock grazing. Installation of paysannats required, therefore, careful preparation of land use maps. By 1959, 7,828 peasants were included in paysannats in Ituri and Kivu.

The paysannat system was also applied in areas where perennials were the dominant interest. A variety of allotments was tried: individual plots, grouped areas, progressively opened corridors, etc.

By the end of 1958, some 194,000 peasants were associated with the entire paysannat program. It was, of course, not an unqualified success. In some cases there was a poor choice of land, of crops, or of timing; a few had to be abandoned or remodeled. But the paysannats were responsible for a disproportionate share of indigenous agricultural production; in 1957, when they included less than one tenth of the agricultural population, they produced 15 percent of the corn, 22 percent of the paddy rice, and 27 percent of the cotton. Incomes of paysannat members were typically well above those of nonmembers in the same areas. In addition, thousands of miles of roads had been constructed to serve the paysannats, hundreds of wells had been sunk, and thousands of fishponds had also been prepared and stocked. The second ten-year plan called for the accelerated application of the paysannat system. Following the collapse of authority in Congo, all of the monitors who were responsible for scheduling work on the paysannats were dismissed, very few Belgians who had been associated with them remained after the first few months, and those operations which had used machinery have had increasing difficulties with maintenance. Just what attitude the former paysannat members and the government would take toward a possible reintroduction of paysannats remains to be seen; possibly the need for supervisors and skilled technical advisers will militate against any such attempt.

The paysannat system was designed to stimulate development of an independent, indigenous peasantry. As such it embodied a multipronged approach. But certain other programs for agricultural improvement, some regional and some general in character, were also instituted. Special programs were begun, for example, in Mayumbe and Kwilu, densely populated areas with rugged relief and often poor soils which are not capable of supporting high-yielding palms but whose richness, nonetheless, is based on large production of palm products from the natural palmeries. These programs were designed to control deforestation and erosion, to rationalize the exploitation of oil palms, to increase the cultivation of coffee and rubber, and to upgrade the Dahomey cattle that were earlier brought to the regions. Programs of a more general nature include the training and distribution of draft animals, tried especially in Katanga in the late 1950s; extension of agricultural credit; support for development of cooperatives; and soil protection programs, including the granting of power to agricultural officials to prescribe antierosion practices. Special note should be made of the research and development work of the Institut National pour l'Étude Agronomique du Congo Belge (INEAC), established in 1933. One of the leading tropical research institutes of the world, it numbered among its accomplishments the development of selected seeds which permitted tripling of coffee yields and doubling of yields of rice, corn, and cotton from 1934 to 1957. Its work, of course, benefited both European and African agriculture.

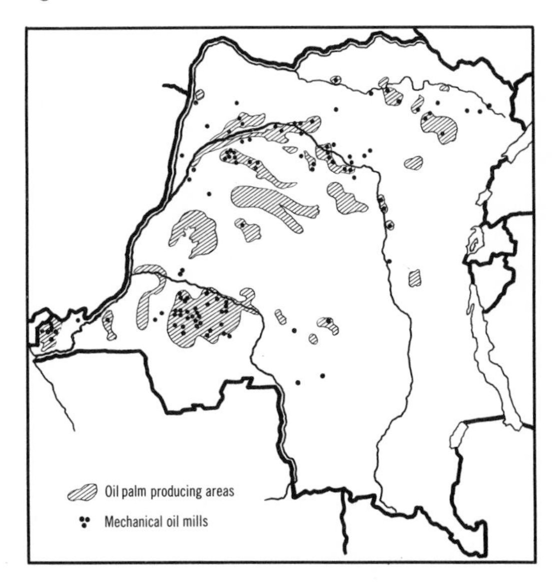

Map 62. Oil palm producing areas in Congo

THE COMMERCIAL CROP AND LIVESTOCK PATTERN

All of the major tropical crops are produced in Congo, giving that country a somewhat broader range of exports than is enjoyed by most African countries. But four products—coffee, palm oil and kernels, cotton, and rubber—have been of outstanding importance among vegetable-product exports.

PALM PRODUCTS. Palm oil and kernels have been the leading vegetable export by tonnage and value since at least 1887. In the late 1950s exports of coffee from the customs area of Congo and Ruanda-Urundi did exceed the value of palm exports, but the latter remained the leader in Congo alone. In addition, the oil palm is the chief source of edible fats within the Congo and the raw material for domestic production of soap and margarine.

The oil palm grows wild in the equatorial basin and has also been planted there and in parts of the savanna zones. Kwilu is the single most important area (Map 62); Mayumbe and the Congo Basin are also large producers. Plantations account for about three quarters of output, there being over 500,000 acres in oil palm plantations. The largest holder, Huileries du Congo Belge (HCB), a subsidiary of Unilever, normally accounted for over 40 percent of production. In 1961 it had 150,000 acres under cultivation in plantations varying in size from 8,000 to 35,000 acres and it also was responsible for harvesting 250,000 acres of natural palmeries, there being 50,000 people on the payroll at the plantation and in the palmeries.

Table 20. Tonnage exports of agricultural and forest products from Congo (Leopoldville), selected years, 1930–1962 (in thousand tons)

	1930	*1939*	*1950*	*1959*	*1960*[a]	*1961*[a]	*1962*[a]
Palm oil	37.0	72.5	132.0	185.5	168.9	153.5	151.9
Palm kernels	66.4	84.9	85.8	40.2	20.5	12.7	18.9
Palm kernel oil	—	.1	14.6	60.7	52.5	49.9	41.9
Oil cake	—	—	20.8	100.2	77.6	61.2	53.0
Coffee	1.5	20.4	33.2	93.4	60.6	33.3	32.4
Cotton	9.8	36.6	51.0	52.8	42.4	14.8	9.8
Rubber	.5	1.1	8.2	40.2	35.6	37.6	37.5
Bananas	—	2.4	—	31.1	33.6	28.3	28.8
Cassava				50.0	26.5	5.7	2.4
Peanut oil			5.4	7.0	6.0	—	—
Cocoa	1.5	1.2	1.7	3.9	5.8	5.0	6.0
Cotton oil		.1	2.3	6.0	5.2	2.1	.9
Urena and punga				4.2	5.1	5.3	2.2
Tea			.6	3.6	3.9	...	4.0
Copal	16.7	11.1	12.5	4.1	2.7	1.8	2.0
Quinine				1.8	1.6		.5
Corn				8.9	1.4	—	—
Skins				.8	.4		
Pyrethrum and derris root			1.7	.2	.1	...	.1
Logs and sawn wood	13.4	50.0		162.5	135.4	128.0	114.7

Sources: *Bulletin Agricole du Congo et du Ruanda-Urundi*, Volume Jubilaire, pp. 36, 54, 55, 61, 86, 87, 97, 107; Banque Centrale du Congo et du Ruanda-Urundi; *Bulletin Mensuel*, Comité des Transporteurs au Congo (Comitra), June 15, 1963, pp. 1–5.

[a] Does not include Katanga and South Kasai; low producers of agricultural products.

... = Not available.

— = None or negligible.

In 1961 its Mokaria and Elisabetha plantations were severely affected by the political crisis and the internal blockade prevented shipment of their produce. Unilever has a total investment in Congo of about $64.4 million, second only to its investment in Nigeria; in 1960 its Congo plantations, not all in oil palm, yielded produce valued at $19.6 million, while its trading subsidiary, Sedec, had turnovers of about $70 million yearly in the late 1950s.

Congo is the best-equipped country for the treating of palm produce, HCB alone having 17 modern oil plants. Most palm kernels are pressed in the Congo rather than in Europe, as is typical for West African production. This is explained in part by the necessity to reduce transport costs that are due to the relative remoteness of producing areas from the seaboard and in part by the concession system applied in 1933 and modified in 1936. Decrees issued at that time set up zones where concessionaires were given the sole right to buy palm fruit, with the understanding that fair prices would be paid and that all palm produce delivered by Africans would be accepted. This system favored the institution of modern oil mills and the production of high-quality oils.

Palm products rely more heavily on the Congo waterways than any other crop, and the low cost of movement over this system and then by rail to Matadi has been very significant in encouraging the expansion of oil palm exports. In postwar years, considerable attention was given to extending the bulk handling of oil palm shipments. Moving from company-owned, riverside mills, palm products are shipped by barge to Leopoldville where the oil is pumped to storage tanks, then to tank cars for the rail trip to Matadi–Ango Ango where storage and pumping facilities permit bulk loading into ships' tanks. Before the war, palm kernel exports exceeded the tonnage of both palm oil and palm kernel oil; in 1959, shipments of kernels had declined to less than half the prewar tonnage, while kernel oil shipments had increased from 142 tons in 1939 to 60,674 tons in 1959 (Table 20). Palm oil exports in 1959 were 185,549 tons, over 2½ times the prewar level, but declined to 151,949 tons in 1962.

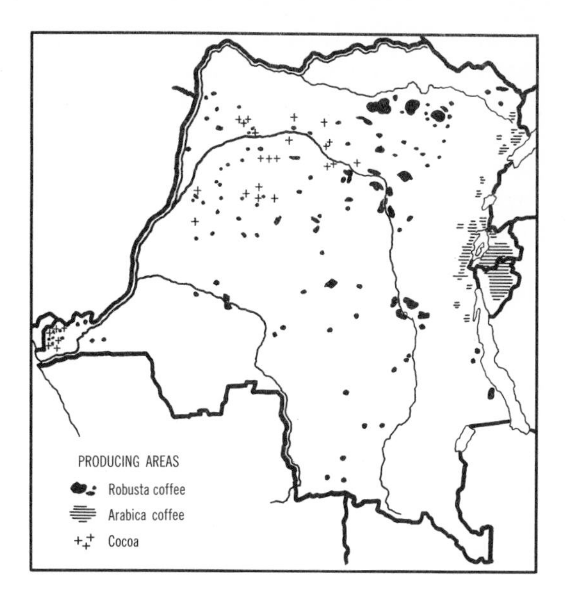

Map 63. Coffee and cocoa producing areas in Congo

Congo normally accounts for about a fifth of world palm oil and about a sixth of palm kernel production, ranking second to Nigeria in both cases; in the period 1957–61, it accounted for 27 to 31 percent of world exports of palm oil.

COFFEE. Production of coffee is more scattered than that of any other export commodity, many producers being at great distances from the national seaboard. Robusta coffee is native

Nursery on a robusta coffee plantation in the Uele district of Oriental Province

Coffee exports from Congo trebled in the period 1943 to 1959.

to the Congo and can be cultivated up to 5,000 feet. It is grown by both Africans and Europeans in the wetter savanna areas of the Congo Basin (Map 63), the region of Uele having witnessed a particularly rapid extension from 1945 to 1958. Arabica coffee, cultivated between 3,300 and 8,300 feet, is mainly grown on European estates in Kivu and Ituri, where it is the main cash crop.

Congo has long had an export of coffee, but it did not become of real importance until after World War II and particularly with the boom in African coffee sales of the 1950s. Coffee exports trebled in tonnage from 1945 to 1959. If the market and internal conditions permitted, there could easily be a continued big increase, because in 1959 only 46 percent of the area in robusta and 33 percent of the area in arabica in Congo and Ruanda-Urundi had as yet reached yielding age; exports of coffee, however, declined markedly after independence.

COTTON. Cotton is normally the most important commercial crop grown primarily by Africans. Its production, which the Belgians considered to be of prime importance in maintaining village life and in introducing the African to the modern economy, was stimulated by provision of selected seed, by encouragement of ginneries, of which there are 125 (Map 64), by eliminating middlemen, and by setting up a marketing board with reserve funds for poor years. Between 1921 and 1947, ginning monopolies were granted in specific regions. Though the monopolies were criticized as an abridgment of free commerce, the Belgians maintained in retrospect that their total effect was favorable through their promotion of cultivation, the regularization of prices, avoidance of excessive ginning charges, and maintenance of the quality and hence the reputation of Congolese cotton sold on the world market. In 1947 a new decree stipulated that ginning was simply to be carried on as a paid service, that the cotton would remain the property of its producers until it was sold.

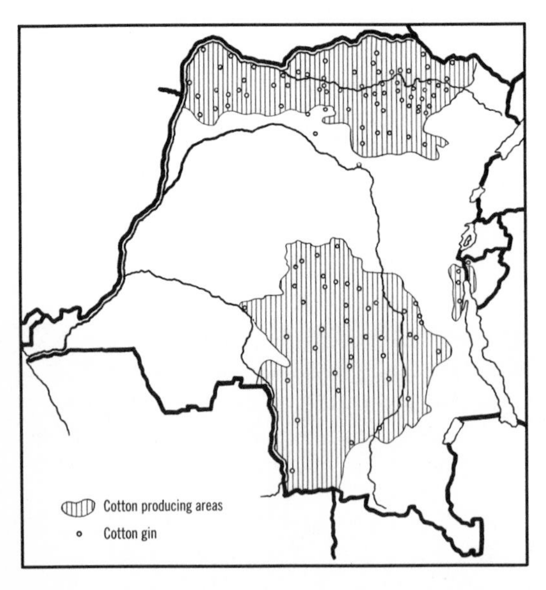

Map 64. Cotton producing areas and cotton ginneries in Congo

In the period to 1960, cotton became an important crop over a large part of the non-equatorial regions. It does best north of 2° 5′ N, where dry seasons permit harvesting in the dry period. About 9,000 miles of access roads were built by cotton societies, as was the Uele Railway (Vicicongo). Cotton oil mills were established at Elisabethville, Katende near Luluabourg, and Tinda near Aketi. By 1960, some 700,000 planters were growing cotton on an estimated 825,000 acres. Yields ranged from 66 to 110 pounds of fiber per acre. About four fifths of production was exported, one fifth being absorbed by Congo cotton spinning factories. Despite the rather special importance of cotton, Congo produced less than Uganda and only about half that of the Sudan, and there has been a distressing drop in production and exports since independence. Exports of cotton in 1962 were only 12.8 percent of the average for 1958 and 1959.

OTHER CROPS OF THE RAINFOREST AND LOW-LYING SAVANNAS. Rubber exports increased from 1,000 metric tons in 1938 to 40,173 in 1959, giving the Congo third place among African rubber producers and a 1.8 percent share of world production; exports have been well maintained and were 37,530 tons in 1962. About 90 percent of rubber is grown on plantations (Map 61); African production, which sometimes takes place on cooperatives or with the assistance of local European interests, did, however, increase considerably in the years preceding independence.

Cocoa proved a very difficult crop for the Congo because of its susceptibility to disease. But its production did increase moderately from 1,300 metric tons in 1938 to 4,958 metric tons in 1957 and 3,874 tons in the bad crop year of 1959. It is one of the few crops whose 1962 exports (6,007 tons) exceeded those of pre-independence years. Almost all cocoa is grown by Europeans (Map 63) on plantations covering about 15,000 acres chiefly in Mayumbe and in the equatorial zone from Lukolela to Stanleyville.

Bananas are grown chiefly on European plantations but also on African collectives in Mayumbe and Lower Congo. Export of Gros Michel bananas increased from 2,354 tons in 1939 to 31,097 tons in 1959, meeting about a quarter of Belgian needs. Sugar, produced at the large plantation near Tumba on the Matadi-Leopoldville line, formerly figured in exports but is now marketed entirely within the country. Urena and punga fibers are grown entirely by Africans in parts of Leopoldville Province, and a bag factory using these fibers is situated at the capital; earlier hopes that Urena would become an important crop have not been met. A small tonnage of peanuts was exported in prewar years but only peanut oil is now shipped out. Finally, a sizable though decreasing tonnage of copal, a fossilized vegetable resin gathered in the marshes of certain equatorial regions, is also exported.

COMMERCIAL CROPS OF THE HIGHER LANDS. Arabica coffee, as has already been noted, is the chief commercial crop of the higher eastern lands (Map 63). Efforts were also made to extend the acreage under tea with considerable success, production having increased from 300 metric tons in 1948–52 to 3,600 tons in 1959. After an extremely poor record in 1961, exports reached 3,962 tons in 1962. Other specialized crops of the eastern highlands have tended to decline since 1945, particularly where synthetic substitutes have increased competition. This is true for cinchona, which does still support the quinine plant of Congokina at Bukavu, pyrethrum, derris root, another natural insecticide, and perfume essences. Tobacco has fared somewhat better and has a growing domestic market. With the exception of tobacco, most of the specialized crops were produced primarily on European estates.

LIVESTOCK. Cattle are precluded from most of the Congo by presence of the tsetse fly but efforts to increase the numbers of cattle and other livestock met with some success and permitted reductions in meat imports. The herd on European holdings increased from 120,000 in 1935 to 201,000 in 1945 and 469,000 in 1958. Most were raised on ranches in Lower Congo, Kivu, Ituri, and the high plateaus of Katanga and Kasai, but standards on many ranches left much to be desired. Cattle are mostly of African breeds, though some farms specialized in European and Asian breeds.

African-owned cattle are concentrated primarily in the northeast; their number increased from 194,000 in 1935 to 514,000 in 1945 and 1,006,000 in 1958. The pig, sheep, and goat population has also increased rapidly in postwar years, but much greater advances will be required before Congo can satisfy its needs in animal products.

FOREST AND FISHERY RESOURCES

Forests, ranging from tropical rainforest to sparsely wooded savannas and montane forests, cover about half of the Congo. Much of the total area is in woodlands whose trees are suitable only for firewood, but straddling the equator is one of the largest zones of selva in the world, while a much smaller region of rainforest exists in Mayumbe (Map 56). It is estimated that only 5 percent of the forested area is now exploitable, partly because of the difficult transport conditions. Only Mayumbe has a location competitively comparable to that of other producing African rainforest regions.

That area has long been the dominant export source, but reserves of *limba*, which usually comprises 80 percent of exports, have been so depleted that it was necessary to impose restrictions on output beginning in 1955. Production from the main forest area of the Congo Basin would require too many transshipments to justify large-scale operations at this time. There is exploitation there, particularly in the Lac Leopold II region, but most of the output is for domestic consumption. Congolese timber exports in recent years have comprised about 20 percent of the tonnage of vegetable-realm exports, but only 4 to 5 percent of their value. While exports have exceeded prewar shipments by more than three times, this rate of increase is moderate in comparison with those of Gabon and West Africa.

Forest exploitation has undergone most of the trends noted for West Africa. Semiprocessed products provide a larger share of exports; new sawmills (Map 61) and plants for peeling and veneering have been installed in several localities; a plywood plant is situated at Lukula in Mayumbe; and investigations were under way before the crisis regarding the possibility of introducing a pulping plant.

The fishery resources of Congo are not inconsiderable and have been expanded through the introduction of fishponds. Sea fisheries, conducted largely from Banana, account for only 4 percent of the total catch. Efforts have been made to modernize the lake fisheries, particularly those of Lakes Albert and Tanganyika, and a score of small European companies were engaged in fishing operations on these lakes and on Lakes Edward and Kivu. Lake fish accounted for almost three fifths of the total catch. River fisheries are particularly important, with the largest yield coming from various sections of the Congo River. Fishponds were increased from 47,000 in 1952 to 122,404 in 1958 covering over 10,000 acres. From 880 to 1,320 pounds can be obtained without difficulty from an acre pond if it is regularly fed with household waste, banana leaves, fresh cassava, etc. Systematic feeding can yield as much as four tons per acre.

MINING AND METALLURGY IN THE CONGO

Mining has been the most dynamic and most important element in the modern Congolese economy. Its output increased tenfold from 1920 to 1950 and doubled again in the next six years. There are some 300 mines and as many quarries in Congo, though a small number of these account for the bulk of output. About 100 processing plants treat the mineral output of the country, which was in the hands of 60 enterprises in 1958.

Mining employs a relatively small number of people considering its importance, usually about 100,000 Africans and 3,500 Europeans; in the rather poor year of 1958, however, there were only 87,000 Africans and 3,359 Europeans employed. Congo mining companies pay above-average salaries, and established their own system of benefits, schools, etc. Mining companies have also greatly stimulated the construction of transport and hydroelectric services. While adding to the problems of the mining industry itself, the fact that the more important producing regions of the Congo are far in the interior has meant that Congo transport is much better developed than it otherwise would have been. It also stimulated the desire to concentrate ores in the area, thus contributing to the expansion of industry in the country.

The Congo holds substantial shares in the big companies and normally derives a very significant share of taxes from their operations. Belgium has held Congo portfolio securities pending resolution of political difficulties in Congo and settlement of counterclaims of the two countries. In 1960, UMHK paid about $25 million each to the Congo central government and the Katanga government; in 1961, it is estimated to have paid $52 million to Katanga; its contribution to the reunited Congo will help to meet budgetary expenses but cannot be expected to meet more than one fifth of needs.

Almost all mining is concentrated in the foundation rock formations girdling the Congo Basin. Minerals are limited in the ancient rock on the edge of the central depression, especially in the north and northeast, but the ranges of strongly folded sediments peripheral to the basin have great mineral wealth, especially in Katanga and the Kibara Mountains. Tin, tungsten, niobium, rare earths, gold, and bismuth occur in these zones. A third element of the Congo's foundation mass is composed of other layers encircling the depression, layers which, like the rest of the base, were folded and dislocated time and again and then peneplained over a long period. The most important portion of this last element is found in Katanga, including systems which are abundantly mineralized with copper and its allied cobalt, uranium, zinc, lead, and silver. The younger sediments of the Congo contain the coal beds of Katanga but are otherwise not significant from the mineral standpoint.

The chief minerals in Congo by percent of the total value of mineral production for one of the last "normal" years, 1958, are shown below:

Copper	47.5%	Tantalo-columbite	1.5%
Diamonds	15.1	Silver	1.2
Cobalt	8.5	Germanium	1.2
Manganese	6.7	Coal	0.8
Tin	6.4	Cadmium	0.5
Zinc	5.2	Beryl	0.1
Gold	4.6	Total of above	99.3%

By grouping certain minerals, the significance of particular mining regions is more apparent. Copper and its associated cobalt, zinc, silver, germanium, and cadmium, for example, give the Katanga copper mines 64.1 percent of the total value of mineral output, while tin and its associated tantalo-columbite and beryl give the eastern tin district 8.0 percent of total output by value.

THE KATANGA COPPER COMPLEX

The Katanga copper mines are distinctly the most important segment of the Congo mining industry. Mineralization occurs discontinuously in a belt about 50 miles wide and extending for about 280 miles along the Northern Rhodesia border. With the continuation in that country, one of the most remarkable metallogenetic zones in the world is formed, second only to the Rand in South Africa among African mineral producing regions. Within tropical Africa, the High Katanga and the Copperbelt of Northern Rhodesia account for no less than 15 percent of the total value of exports, making the combined area the most important economic "island" north of the Union and south of the Sahara.

Union Minière du Haut-Katanga, holding a

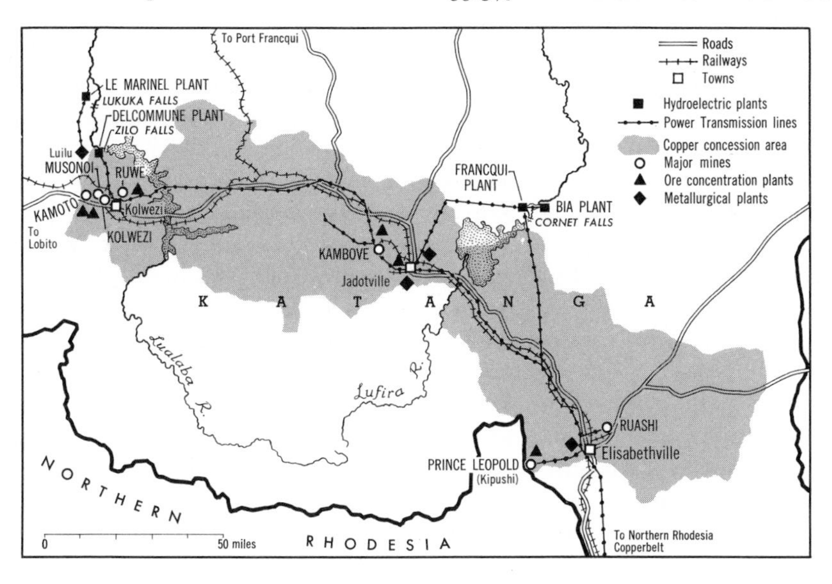

Map 65. The High Katanga mining area

7,700-square-mile concession from CSK, ranks among the 100 most important industrial concerns in the world by virtue of its development of the mines and metallurgical complex of the High Katanga. It was founded in 1906 by CSK, Tanganyika Concessions Ltd., and Société Générale de Belgique.

The mines are divided into three groups (Map 65): Southern, of which the Prince Leopold or Kipushi and the Ruashi mines are most important; Central, including the very large Kambove mine and now defunct Shinkolobwe uranium ore mine; and the newer Western Group, of which Kamoto, Ruwe, Musonoi, and Kolwezi are the chief mines. While the ores are very rich by comparison with most other copper regions, the occurrence of the surface ores in irregular veins means that much interlarded waste must also be mined. Reserve figures are not available, but probably 600–800 million tons of ore have been proved.

The copper ores of the area are divided into sulphides and oxides. Sulphides come from the Kipushi or Prince Leopold mine west of Elisabethville, for long the only underground copper mine in Katanga. An unusually rich vein, containing 11 percent copper, extends almost vertically downward, and mining is now at the 1,600-foot level. Associated with the copper of this mine are zinc, lead, cadmium, and germanium, plus small amounts of gold, silver, platinum, and palladium.

Once brought to the surface, the ore is divided into copper and zinc concentrates by flotation. The copper concentrate is treated at the Lubumbashi plant near Elisabethville, smelted to yield 62 to 64 percent copper matte, and treated in converters to produce 99 percent blister copper, which is shipped to Belgium for electrolytic refining. Part of the zinc concentrate is roasted and then sent to Belgium; part is treated in Katanga, the final product being 99.99 percent pure electrolytic zinc. Sulfureous gases produced in treating the zinc concentrate are used to make sulfuric acid. Cadmium and germanium are recovered in the dust from the Lubumbashi furnaces and in the refuse from the process of electrolyzing zinc; they are either treated on the spot or in Belgium.

The oxide ores, of sedimentary origin and containing 4 to 6 percent copper with which cobalt is associated, come from surface mines, chiefly in the Western Group of mines. Operations are highly mechanized, permitting high productivity per worker. Preparations for underground mining have recently been made at Kambove and Kamoto. The oxide ores of the western mines are either washed at Ruwe or concentrated at Kolwezi or, starting in 1964, at Kamoto to yield copper and copper-cobalt concentrates. These are sent to a large, new copper-cobalt plant at Luilu which includes an automatic electrolytic refinery and which represents a general movement in the center of operations toward the west, where vast reserves have been located. In the central mines, sulfureted ores are concentrated at a new plant at Kambove and treated in the metallurgical complexes at Jadotville-Shituru and Jadotville-Panda. These installations, comprising the most important industrial establishment in Congo, produce 99 percent pure cobalt, 99.95 percent copper, and cobalt-copper alloy which is forwarded to Belgium or the United States for refining. Slag is used to produce metallurgical cement at Jadotville.

UMHK normally employs about 21,000 Africans and 1,700–2,000 Europeans. It has been the epitome of paternalism, providing all manner of amenities and guidance for its employees. In addition to the metallurgical plants noted, UMHK also has workshops, an acetylene plant, a subsidiary producer of mining explosives, and important hydroelectric facilities. Just what part its officials played in the unilateral secession of Katanga in 1960–61 is difficult to say, but the company has insisted that its hands were tied and that it had to abide by the regulations of the *de facto* Katanga government. In any case, production was maintained at high levels throughout the crisis years and the whole establishment survived the final fighting with relatively little damage; it represents one of the great assets of the Congo economy.

The setting up of the whole mining-industrial-urban complex of High Katanga in a remote, sparsely populated part of Africa presents a fascinating story. Numerous problems had to be overcome over the years, to which is now added what may be the most difficult of all—how to adjust from an attitude of paternalism stemming from a position of authority to a posture more appropriate to dealings with an independent people.

One of the major problems faced in developing Katanga was that of securing an adequate labor supply. That province was sparsely populated and could not support the numbers required. A recruitment program was instituted which involved moving workers from distances up to 500 miles away. The shortage was also responsible for the decision made as early as 1927 to recruit on a family basis and doubtless contributed to the efforts to make living and working in the area as attractive as possible by the provision of housing and other amenities. Certainly the record of labor turnover of UMHK compared very favorably with that of comparable enterprises. The labor situation also helps to explain the efforts made to improve productivity, which have made the mining and metallurgical operations as modern as can be found. The very high wages required to attract European employees to this otherwise somewhat unattractive part of the world probably also contributed to the desire to upgrade African employees, who do perform many of the tasks usually assigned to Europeans in other African mining communities.

A second great problem involved the provision of transportation for this area located 1,200 miles from the coast. At the start of operations, the nearest railhead was 425 miles south, and in 1910 only that rail line extended to Elisabethville. With construction of the BCK and then the Benguela Railway, available transport was much improved, but the problem was not really solved until postwar years because Rhodesia Railways was periodically incapable of delivering adequate quantities of coal to Katanga. The Belgian policy of favoring the

The Ruwe copper mine
This large open-pit mine is located in the newer western group of Katanga copper mines.

The Jadotville-Shituru metallurgical complex
The installations at Jadotville produce 99 percent cobalt, 99.95 percent copper, and a copper-cobalt alloy, and comprise the most important industrial complex in Congo.

The electrolysis hall at the Luilu plant
The Luilu copper-cobalt installation was constructed to serve the western group of mines in Katanga.

national route militated against the Katanga mines, because it required costly transshipments at Port Francqui and Leopoldville. This policy had gradually to be relaxed, however, until the bulk of mineral output was permitted to use the direct rail route to Lobito. In 1960 the Katanga government boycotted the Kasai routeway, all exports going to Lobito or via Rhodesia Railways to ports in Mozambique.

A third problem was largely technical and has been solved—namely, the development of new methods required to treat some of the more difficult Katangan ores and concentrates.

Perhaps the most difficult problem was that of providing adequate power and coking coal, the latter required for smelting operations. This continued to be a severe problem until about 1956, occasioning periodic slowdowns and restricting over-all activity for considerable periods. The mines relied first on coal or coke from Europe, then mainly on the Wankie collieries of Southern Rhodesia, but in the first postwar decade the latter usually could not supply sufficient quantities, sometimes because there was inadequate output, sometimes because of congestion on the railways. It was necessary, therefore, to use large tonnages of wood, which is expensive, and to import coking coal from South Africa or the United States via the Benguela Railway, a very costly haul for this bulk commodity.

Penstocks and hydroelectric plant of Le Marinel
This is the largest of the three hydropower stations which have been constructed to serve the Katanga copper mining industry. It has also transmitted power to the Northern Rhodesia Copperbelt in recent years.

To reduce the pressure on over-all energy demands, output of coal from the Luena coal field was increased from about 100,000 tons to about 460,000 tons in 1955, but this coal is of very low grade and could not be used in smelting operations. Its major role was to produce electricity and to provide fuel for the railways and a cement plant at Lubudi, and thus to reduce the need for imports. With the opening of additional hydroelectric plants, partial dieselization of the railways, and removal of bottlenecks on Rhodesian coal, output of coal in the Congo declined to 247,000 tons in 1959 and 164,000 tons in 1960. The Luena area had to be evacuated in early 1961 and production that year totaled only 66,000 tons.

Construction of hydroelectric facilities in Katanga has been the most important solution for energy problems and permitted the extension of electrolytic refining in the region. Four plants are in being (Map 65): (1) the Francqui Power Plant at Mwadingusha, a little northeast of Jadotville, where the Lufira River drops 370 feet in the Cornet Falls; (2) the Bia plant, a few miles below the first; (3) the Delcommune installation at Zilo Gorge on the Lualaba River; and (4) the Marinel plant, twenty miles below the third, which doubled the previous capacity, bringing the total to 468,000 kw as of June 30, 1962. Production was interrupted in early 1963 by destruction of high-tension masts, all of which had been repaired by May of that year. Pending completion of the Kariba Gorge operation in the Rhodesias, a portion of the output of Le Marinel was transmitted to the Copperbelt of Northern Rhodesia with the agreement that it might later be repaid by reverse transmission from Kariba. It is somewhat ironic that over three fourths of Congo electric power should be produced in an area which is not particularly well suited for hydroelectric installations because of the highly seasonal precipitation and the great year-to-year fluctuations in amount, while the magnificent hydroelectric potential of the Congo River below Leopoldville has gone almost untouched. This is explained, of course, by the limitations on economic transmission distances and the great consumption requirements of Katanga, 4,000 to 5,000 kwh being needed to produce one ton of copper or zinc.

OTHER MINERALS IN KATANGA

Uranium-radium was mined until 1961 at Shinkolobwe, 15 miles west of Jadotville. This mine is of great historic importance because it supplied a very important share of uranium ores utilized by the United States in World War II. Its unusually rich pitchblende ores were mined at the surface until 1950, after which it was necessary to turn to underground operations, where reserves were exhausted after about a decade.

Lead is mined at Kengere, 34 miles from the Manika Station of the Katanga railway. As has already been noted, coal of mediocre quality is mined at Luena. The coal measures there are very irregular and have only limited reserves. Small quantities are also won at Lukuga, 8 miles west of Albertville, but this coal, too, is low grade. Salt and iron ore deposits are known but not exploited.

A relative newcomer to Katanga operations is the production of manganese ores at Kisenge and Kasekelesa in the southwest. After washing, a product containing 50 to 52 percent manganese is exported via the Benguela Railway. Output measured in manganese content increased with great rapidity from 6,400 tons in 1948 to a peak of 230,900 tons in 1955; output fell off in 1961 to 159,400 tons, but Congo continued to hold its position as the fifth largest producer of manganese in the free world.

THE EASTERN "TIN ZONE"

A region extending more than 600 miles north from northern Katanga through Maniema, the leading producing area, to northern Kivu and about 200 miles east and west comprises a second mineral region. It has scattered but sometimes rich deposits of tin, tantalum, columbium, tungsten, beryllium, bismuth, gold, and rare earths. Tin is extracted from cassiterite, sometimes in primary mineralized formations, sometimes in alluvial and eluvial sediments. Often associated with it are wolframite, containing tungsten, and tantalo-columbite, containing tantalum and columbium, each of these being extracted and exported as concentrates. For the future, the deposits at Manono and elsewhere may become an important source of lithium. The pegmatites there contain 15 percent spodumene, containing lithium, making the reserve one of the more important in the world.

The tin mine of Géomines at Manono
Congo normally ranks fifth among free-world tin producers.

The tin ores are exploited by several colonists and some twenty companies, the most important being Géomines, with headquarters at Manono, and Symétain in Maniema. Extraction from small detrital deposits is by hand; working of the large detrital and the primary deposits is achieved either by hydraulic mining, or by shovels and draglines. After extraction the ores are concentrated by differential sedimentation, though the pegmatites at Manono must first be reduced by grinding. Most of the output is sold as "marketable" cassiterite, containing 72 to 76 percent tin, though electric foundries produce 99.9 percent ingots at Manono and Lubudi. Some deposits in the "tin zone" are approaching exhaustion, but it would be possible to sustain and increase output by opening up new bodies. This would, however, require a larger investment than has been needed in the past.

Congo ranks after Malaya, Indonesia, Bolivia, and Thailand among free-world tin producers. Its share of the market was determined by the International Tin Agreement, though producers frequently complained that the allotment to Congo was unreasonably low. Production was reduced after independence by sporadic fighting in Kivu and north Katanga, but stood at about 70 percent of pre-independence output in 1961.

THE NORTHEASTERN GOLD AREA

The gold zone of Congo runs in a broad belt along the east, overlapping the "tin zone" in Kivu, but extending across Oriental Province to the Sudan border. About two thirds of production comes from primary deposits, the remainder from alluvial and eluvial deposits. A very small amount of gold is also secured as a by-product of the copper mines. About 15 companies mine gold in widely scattered deposits, but the Société des Mines d'Or de Kilo-Moto, operating in Ituri, and the Compagnie Minière des Grands Lacs Africains account for four fifths of the total. Gold mining normally employs some 26,000 Africans and 276 Europeans. Gold is concentrated and smelted in the Congo and refined largely in Belgium. Output of about 10,000–11,600 kg per year is about 1 percent of the world total; 1961 output was down to 7,260 kg, however.

Diamond washing plant at Bakwanga
Congo usually accounts for 95 percent of the world's total production of industrial diamonds. Mining was seriously interrupted in parts of Kasai in 1961–62 because of political conditions.

THE KASAI DIAMOND AREA

Diamonds are mined in two zones: around Tshikapa on the Kasai River and at Bakwanga on the Bushimaie. Some gem diamonds are obtained at Tshikapa, but Bakwanga, which usually accounts for 95 percent of total production, yields almost entirely industrial stones, especially crushing boart. After independence, operations at Tshikapa became more and more chaotic and uncontrolled. Forminière reduced its workings from a normal 40 to 6 in 1961, its output declining from 425,234 carats in 1959 to 44,000 carats in 1961, and in 1962 it suspended industrial exploitation completely. In the meantime, illicit operations increased by leaps and bounds, losses from smuggling being estimated at $50 million in 1961 and $41.5 million in 1962, when Congo (Brazzaville) suddenly became a fairly significant exporter of diamonds.

Bakwanga also has had its troubles; in mid-1960, about 250,000 Baluba refugees streamed into the area interrupting operations for about four months. However, 1961 and 1962 proved to be record years, but all royalties and taxes in 1961 went to the South Kasai government. The Bakwanga operations, which are run by Sibéka, employed about 150 Europeans and 3,800 Congolese in 1962, when operations appeared to be proceeding quite normally. In 1946, only 46 percent of diamonds at Bakwanga was mechanically extracted; by 1956, over 92 percent was so mined. All processing is highly

Table 21. Number of manufacturing establishments in Congo (Leopoldville) in selected years, 1939–1958

Raw material processing	1939	1950	1957	1958
Crop processing				
Palm oil mills, incl. hand mills				457
Coffee	290	286	502	557
Cocoa	28	31	78	74
Tea			15	16
Bread grain				625
Rice	28	112	171	168
Sugar				2
Cotton gins				74
Fiber cleaning				25
Essential oils				12
Pyrethrum and derris root				2
Rubber	23	59	131	138
Animal products				
Smoked meat				52
Tanneries				7
Milk, butter, cheese				192
Fish	56	198	1,091	1,104
Forest products				
Felling and sawing	349	438	1,252	1,081
Market-oriented industries				
Soap and margarine				54
Macaroni, starch, etc.				3
Brewing	2	3	10	12
Soft drinks	19	27	42	48
Tobacco products		5	8	7
Textiles	1	4		22
Clothing				54
Hosiery				3
Rope				7
Sacking and bagging				4
Shoemaking	14	129	275	
Wood products				1,385
Mattresses				7
Plastic articles				1
Bottles				1
Industrial chemicals	4	8	14	25
Paint and varnish		3	8	9
Pharmaceuticals		1	5	6
Explosives				3
Chemical fertilizers				2
Bottled gas				1
Perfume		3	9	9
Foundries	4	14	20	
Railway workshops				26
Shipyards				20
Sheet iron, wire, nails				18
Barrels, cans, trunks				15
Brick, tile, ceramics	169	471	482	470
Concrete, cement products	6	33	120	136
Cement works	2	2	4	5
Record pressing				1
Electricity plants	71	83	136	

Sources: *Statistics, 1958*, Governor General's Speech; *Bulletin de la Banque Centrale du Congo Belge et du Ruanda-Urundi* (January, 1959); *Industries et Travaux d'Outremer* (April, 1957), p. 250.

mechanized, and a 7,460-kw hydroelectric plant at Tshala, near the Lubilash Falls and 12 miles from Bakwanga, supplies power for the mining operations and communities.

MINOR MINERAL ZONES

Two mineral zones remain: (1) a strip along the Atlantic which has traces of oil and bituminous sands whose 15 percent bitumen is used for asphalting roads, but which is of little significance as a producer, and (2) the folds of the Lower Congo, which contain copper, zinc, lead, vanadium, and gold. Plants near Thysville treat lead and vanadium on a small scale from local deposits. Two bauxite bodies, one with estimated reserves of 100 million tons of 42 percent metal content, are known in Mayumbe and would be of particular significance if the Inga hydroelectric project were developed.

The tremendous mineral wealth of the Congo is, then, apparent. While the crisis interrupted production, particularly of diamonds, tin, and gold, output of minerals in Katanga continued apace. It was estimated shortly before independence that Congolese mineral output could be doubled within a decade without great difficulty except possibly for acquiring new capital needed to expand tin and gold production. In the long run there is even a good possibility of establishing an iron and steel industry based upon the extensive reserves of iron ore in Katanga and the east, on low-cost hydroelectric power, and on Wankie coal.

INDUSTRIALIZATION IN CONGO

Manufacturing increased rapidly in Congo in postwar years, total development comparing favorably with other tropical African countries except Southern Rhodesia. Table 21 indicates the number of African and European establishments existing in various types of industry in selected years. Unfortunately, no distinction is made between handicraft establishments and modern installations, hence the degree of development is exaggerated in some categories. Very little information is available regarding the position of manufacturing in the years after independence.

Estimates of the growth of industrial production are given in Table 22, revealing that the textile industry enjoyed the greatest advance in more recent years, followed by the chemical industry. The only recent estimate available is that industrial output in the Leopoldville area increased about 30 percent from mid-1960 to 1963, but this figure is subject to question. It is estimated that Congolese industry met about

Table 22. Index numbers of industrial production for Congo (Leopoldville), selected years, 1938–1959 (1958 = 100)

Industry	*1938*	*1948*	*1953*	*1956*	*1959*
Food, beverages		35	66	103	111
Textiles		16	71	111	118
Chemicals		16	66	96	89
All manufacturing	8	28	72	100	99

Source: U.N., *Statistical Yearbook, 1962* (New York, 1963), p. 78.

half of the domestic consumption of manufactured products in the late 1950s. Employing some 300,000 Africans and representing an investment of over $20 million, manufacturing was credited with a 14 percent contribution to the gross national product in 1958. It is interesting to note that the index of employment in manufacturing based on 1950 was only 75.6 in 1958, probably because modern establishments were eliminating the smaller-scale handicraft shops. The productivity index in manufacturing stood at 371 in 1958, with 1950 as the base year.

Most industry in Congo is located either in the old Katanga or Leopoldville provinces, with Leopoldville itself having the greatest representation of consumer-oriented industries. Raw material processing establishments, which vary from the great metallurgical plants of Katanga to the smallest oil press, are widely distributed, especially those processing agricultural crops.

It would be redundant to analyze industrial representation and location of Congo industry as in the West African discussion, particularly since relatively little is known about the present status of manufacturing establishments in Congo. It is appropriate to note the outstanding features of the Congolese pattern and the contrasts between it and the industrial development of other tropical African countries:

(1) Mineral processing industries have particular importance. It has already been noted that the Jadotville complex is the leading industrial concentration in the country. Plants there, at Luilu, Lubumbashi, Manono, and elsewhere made the old Katanga the leading province in processing of raw materials. The mining and metallurgical build-up there also explained the rise of subsidiary servicing industries—production of acetylene, sulfuric acid, explosives, and mining tools.

(2) Oil mills represent the largest and most significant processors of agricultural raw materials. Reference has been made to the importance of palm oil mills and to the processing of kernels, unusual in Africa.

(3) Congo had an earlier and somewhat greater development of textile and clothing industries than most African countries. Leopoldville is the main center for this type of industry, as it is for market-oriented manufacturing in general. Utexleo, started in 1932, is the most important producer of cloth, having had an output of 5,700 tons in 1957. Socotex, also at Leopoldville and operating from 1947, produced 1.6 million blankets in 1957. Albertville also has a cloth mill. The cloth factories, which supply only a small part of needs, have had considerable difficulty in meeting competition from foreign imports, especially in printed fabrics, but the workshops and factories producing ready-made clothing, underwear, and knitted goods satisfied the market except for luxury and high-fashion items.

(4) The shoe industry is relatively well developed. The Bata and Splendor shoe factories had a combined production of 728,000 pairs of leather shoes and 2,100,000 pairs of canvas shoes in 1957.

(5) There is a somewhat greater representation of mechanical industries, although the types of metal-fabricated items produced are quite comparable to those of other tropical African countries.

A shoe factory at Leopoldville
Congo has relatively well-developed textile, clothing, and shoe industries, with the most important plants located at the capital.

(6) The chemical industry is also rather better developed than elsewhere. Jadotville plants produce sulfuric acid, sodium chlorate, glycerine, oxygen, hydrochloric acid, and caustic soda. Two powder and explosive factories are situated at Kakontwe. Other chemical works produce paints and varnishes, insecticides, pharmaceuticals, perfumes, and quinine.

(7) The construction industry is notable for a large output of cement, fibro-cement, and various cement and concrete forms including pipes. In 1957, the record year, 464,000 metric tons of cement were produced, giving Congo fifth position among African producers; the 1961 production was only 140,000 tons. Cement plants are situated at Lubudi, Lukala, Jadotville, Albertville, and Bukavu.

(8) There is an unusual development of hydroelectric facilities in Congo. In the period 1950–59, twenty-four stations were either constructed or extended, resulting in an increased generating capacity of 577,000 kw. In addition to the four plants constructed for UMHK and

the installations serving the Manono tin and Bakwanga diamond operations, small and medium-sized plants have been constructed to meet the electricity needs of most of the larger cities. Leopoldville is supplied by two plants, an 11,500-kw one at Sanga on the Inkisi and the newer 26,000-kw plant at Zongo. A small 2,000-kw plant at M'Pozo, 1.2 miles from Matadi, serves that port. Stanleyville's needs are met by a 12,300-kw installation at Tshopo. Albertville receives electricity from the Kijmbi plant, completed in 1959, 73 miles to the north at Bendera; this installation, with a capacity of 17,500 kw, makes use of an unusually high head as the stream falls 2,200 feet in 1.2 miles into Lake Tanganyika. Bukavu is supplied from a 12,600-kw plant on the Ruzizi, which forms part of the border with Rwanda. The total installed hydroelectric capacity in Congo is greater than that of any African country.

Congo's total hydroelectric potential is estimated to be about 110 million hp, about 16 percent of the total for the entire world and 40 percent of the African total. The entire Congo system, which is partly shared with adjacent countries, draining a 1,467,000-square-mile area with an average precipitation of about 63 inches a year, is estimated to have a potential of 125 million hp or about 18 percent of the world total at average minimum flow.

Some 85 million hp are concentrated in the 217-mile stretch of the Congo River between Stanley Pool and Matadi, in which the river drops a total of 886 feet in 30 falls and rapids. A particularly favorable feature of this stretch is the unusual evenness of flow, which varies from a low of 24,000 to a high of 67,000 cubic meters per second. The first scientific studies in the area date from 1887; in 1925 it was examined in connection with a grandiose scheme to canalize the river to Leopoldville, and in 1946 it received some attention under a study concerned with hydroelectric facilities for the whole country. In 1954 a decision was taken to accelerate study of the lower river and from 1955 to 1957 numerous intensive analyses were made. Not long before independence, a decision was made to proceed with a first stage of development, called Inga I, but the disorders of 1960 resulted in the scheme's being shelved indefinitely. The enormous capacity available in the 217-mile section of the Congo, 2.36 times the installed capacity of all the hydroelectric plants in the United States in 1961 or greater than the capacity of all types of electric plants in either the six EEC or seven European Free Trade Association countries in the same year, represents a magnificent resource which must sooner or later attract large-scale development.

The Inga I project involved a relatively simple diversion scheme which would have taken advantage of a 300-foot drop occurring along an immense bend in the river 18 miles above Matadi. In addition to the advantages of nearness to seaboard, immense potential, and simplicity of installations required, Inga had the further asset of permitting development in stages without greatly affecting the eventual total cost. The first stage, which would have had an installed capacity of 1.57 million kw, was scheduled for completion in 1964. It was estimated that the cost of power would be one-third that at Kariba and that the whole section could be developed to produce the cheapest power in the world.

The industries proposed as possible consumers of Inga electricity were very comparable to those suggested for Kouilou in Congo (Brazzaville). The most important would probably have been a 500,000-ton aluminum refinery using alumina derived from the Mayumbe deposits. Other plants considered would produce electrometals and ferroalloys, electrochemicals, heavy water, isotopes, fertilizers, cellulose, and cement. Some electricity would also be used for general purposes in Matadi, to electrify the Matadi-Leopoldville railway, and, possibly later, to help attract consumer industries to the capital city.

TRADE

The major exports of Congo in the vegetable and mineral realms have been shown in Table 20 and on page 27. Congo normally had a favorable balance of trade, but not always a favorable balance of payments. Figures for the entire country for recent years are not available and the total for exports in 1961 of $398 million represents a calculation made by the author. During that year, the country was divided into three or four separate entities as far as trade was concerned.

Congo trade has differed from that of many African countries from the standpoint of its position vis-à-vis the former metropole. In 1958, for example, Belgium took only 18.9 percent of Congo exports, while it supplied 36 percent of its imports. The United States has ranked as one of its leading trading partners, taking 25 percent of Congo exports and supplying 15 percent of its imports in 1958. Unlike former French territories, Congo normally marketed its commodities at prevailing world market prices.

The Congo Basin Treaty and the Treaty of Saint-Germain-en-Laye provided that an open-door policy would be applicable to Congo in trade and investments. In fact, non-Belgian investment played a minor role, and investors were sometimes reluctant to enter the Congo because of the power of the great, interlocking group of parastatal companies and the fear that taxes or transport rates would be altered to the detriment of the foreign investor. Even in trade, the Belgians succeeded in securing a large share of international traffic for their own fleet despite repeated criticisms that their policies were discriminatory and not in accord with treaty obligations.

A multitude of lessons can be drawn from the unfortunate experience of Congo from 1960 to 1964, including the fallacy of giving attention to material development without comparable development in the political sphere, the strength of separatist tendencies in tribal societies where education has been focused essentially on primary grades, the ease with which a going economic proposition can be distorted and partially destroyed, and yet the surprising perseverance of the more highly organized and directed segments of the economy, especially large-scale mining, plantations, and manufacturing industry. In 1963, for the first time since independence, Congo seemed to be in a position to take constructive steps toward reestablishing its economy and planning for renewed economic growth. Time will be required to establish confidence, but possession of a good infrastructure and of great natural wealth should permit Congo to regain its previous important position among African countries.

Rwanda and Burundi

The outstanding feature of the economic geography of Rwanda and Burundi is their great population densities, the highest for any countries in Africa. Rwanda, with an area of 10,169 square miles and about 2,745,000 people, had a density of 270 per square mile in 1961; Burundi, with 10,747 square miles and an estimated 2,262,000 people, had a density of 210 per square mile. With a combined area only one forty-third that of Congo, this former Belgian trusteeship area has a population 34.6 percent as great. In parts of the two countries, such as Ruhengeri, densities reach over 450 per square mile.

Efforts to alleviate the population pressure in Rwanda and Burundi are made more difficult by their rugged topography, by their rather meager known mineral resources, and by the remoteness of their location, about 620 miles as the crow flies from the Indian Ocean and 1,300 miles from the Atlantic.

THE SOCIOPOLITICAL BACKGROUND

Greatly complicating the economic advance of Rwanda and Burundi has been the presence of a feudal relationship between the two main ethnic groups, developed over the 300 or more years from the migration into the area of the Tutsi, who were until 1961 the dominant group in both countries. About 82 percent of the Rwanda population and 88 percent of the Burundi population are Hutu, a Bantu tribe which had developed some superior agricultural practices over the years, such as rudimentary terracing and rational use of fertilizers. Almost all of the remaining population are Tutsi, a pastoral tribe of possible Hamitic origin noted for their unusual height, averaging about 6′3″, but often reaching 6′8″ or even 7′. The Twa, a group of pygmoids living in the west and on the mountains, comprise perhaps 1 percent of the combined population of the two countries.

The Tutsi arrived in the area some three centuries ago and were apparently peacefully accepted by the Hutu because of the long-horned cattle they brought and perhaps because of their imposing height. In any case, a feudal system developed known as *ubuhake* whereby the Hutu were given charge of the Zebu cattle, an allotment of land, and the protection of the Tutsi in return for performing a number of services and offering a number of gifts. The Hutu could use milk from the cows, the male calves, and meat and skin of dead animals, the clientship relation lasting so long as satisfactory relations were maintained with the overlord. Such a system could quite obviously lead to abuses.

The Germans maintained the feudal system when Ruanda-Urundi was part of East Africa, as did the Belgians when that territory was mandated to it under the League of Nations. It became increasingly clear, however, that *ubuhake* was an anachronism with dangerous political overtones and which to a degree prevented rational development of the country. In 1954, therefore, a decree was issued requiring that the chiefs surrender two thirds of their cattle held under *ubuhake* to those who were actually looking after them. It was not possible to enforce the decree, however, and relations between the Hutu and Tutsi deteriorated rapidly, particularly as the Hutu became politically more conscious of their power of numbers.

In Ruanda, following the death of the *mwami* or king in 1959 and during the selection of his successor, the Hutu rose up in a brief but destructive and, from their standpoint, successful revolution. A large number of huts were burned, cattle and coffee plantations were destroyed, there were several hundred casualties, and the new mwami plus some thousands of other Tutsi fled the country. Elections in July, 1960, resulted in the Parmehutu Party (Party of Hutu Emancipation) winning 70.4 percent of electoral seats, while the Tutsi's main supporting party secured only about 17 percent. The Belgians, in agreement with the parties, created the Ruanda Council in October, 1960, to which the Resident General appointed 35 Hutu, 12 Tutsi, and 1 Twa. In January, 1961, came the coup d'état of Gitarama, after which Ruanda was declared a republic with the Parmehutu leader as president. The mwami was exiled and was unsuccessful in several efforts to return. At one time it was estimated that half of the Tutsi of Ruanda had fled, chiefly to Uganda and Kivu.

In the meantime, there had also been rioting in Urundi, but it did not reach the proportions of the Ruanda revolt and the mwami was retained in power with the understanding that his position would be defined. The social distinction between Hutu and Tutsi was less distinct than in Ruanda, the feudal system had been more effectively eroded, and the ruling mwami was a much more acceptable figure than his counterpart to the north.

Several U.N. efforts were made to get the governments of Ruanda and Urundi to agree to political union of the two territories but both were adamant, although agreeing to an economic union. Somewhat reluctantly, the U.N. accepted this compromise and two new countries achieved independence on July 1, 1962, their names being slightly changed to Rwanda and Burundi. Fears that another situation similar to that in Congo might develop after independence were not realized. Rwanda has followed a moderate course, joining the Brazzaville group, and retaining a sizable number of Belgian advisers. Burundi has been more hostile to its former administrator, making special efforts to replace Belgian officers. The Hutu have assumed greater authority there, though Burundi remains a kingdom with a mwami of Tutsi origin.

FEATURES OF THE DEMOGRAPHIC PATTERN

Returning to the demography of the country, there are certain additional features of interest. First is the occupational pattern: the Hutu are primarily cultivators and, as has been indicated, herders of cattle; the Tutsi do not normally concern themselves with cultivation; the Twa, who have been treated as outcasts by the other groups, are artisans, hunters, and farmers. In 1958 there were also 7,105 Europeans and 2,320 Asians in the country, a very small proportion of the total population. Most Europeans were employed in the government or missions; some 811 were colons, including a number of estate holders in the Lake Kivu region and a few who were engaged in mining and commerce. The Asians were mostly clerks, artisans, and small commercialists. The number of Europeans remaining in late 1962 was estimated at 2,800.

A second and highly distinctive aspect of the population pattern is its unusual dispersion, 98 percent of the populace being rural. Almost all the inhabitants live on isolated farms usually on steep slopes, there being almost no organized villages and only one large town, the capital of Burundi, Usumbura. This creates certain problems with respect to provision of amenities and of schools, problems which are offset to some extent by the rather even distribution and average high density of the population. Only the Kagera Park along the east of Rwanda, a section in the southeast of Burundi, the higher mountains in the west of both countries, and the rift valley in Burundi have relatively low densities. The last area was long practically uninhabited because of the presence of sleeping sickness and malaria, the absence of which from the higher parts of the country is important in explaining the high rate of population growth.

In contrast to the Congo, the Belgians long recognized the problems created by a rapidly increasing population. In addition to measures taken to stimulate the domestic economy, attention was given to resettlement in adjacent parts of Congo, but the goal of assisting the permanent migration of 100,000 in the first ten-year plan was not achieved. Some relief is provided by seasonal or specific-period migrations to adjacent countries. There are usually about 15,000 migrants in Congo and 30,000–60,000 in East Africa, the largest number of whom are employed in the production of coffee and cotton on African farms in Uganda, while there may be as many as 300,000 residing more or less permanently in Uganda.

PHYSICAL CONDITIONS

An unbroken chain of mountains forming the eastern side of the Central Rift system runs for about 174 miles along the west of Rwanda-Burundi (Map 57). Forming the watershed between the Congo and Nile waterways in this region, it is nowhere less than 6,500 feet high and has peaks of over 9,800 feet in the north. Eastward from these mountains is a highly dissected plateau sloping gradually towards Lake Victoria and having elevations varying from about 5,900 to 4,500 feet. In the north of Rwanda are the volcanic Birunga Mountains, still active in part, with Mt. Karisimbi rising to 14,788 feet. The vast bulk of both countries is in slopeland. A small portion of Burundi, comprising the Ruzizi and Tanganyikan Plains, lies in the downfaulted rift valley at elevations of 2,540 to about 3,600 feet.

Situated not far south of the equator, the area has two wet and two dry seasons with precipitation ranging from about 40 to 56 inches a year, except within the graben where steppe conditions prevail. There is considerable variability, which, because of the high population, frequently led to famines until an improved road system and food storage programs were provided. The natural forest vegetation has been almost completely removed in the last 500 to 600 years, leaving only about 2.9 percent of the combined areas forested, the largest portion of which is in two reserves. A rather remarkable program of reforestation, using primarily eucalyptus trees, has, however, protected some of the steepest slopes and, by plantings along the roads, has given a more closed appearance to the area than might be expected from the raw figure of forested area.

There are some excellent soils in Rwanda and Burundi, including decomposed lavas in the northwest and alluvials in the valleys, but most soils are light, forest-derived soils overlying lateritic subsoils. The steep slopes, frequency of intense rains, and soil characteristics all favor rapid erosion, which is one of the most serious problems facing the country.

Scene near Ruhengeri, Rwanda
The high population density of Rwanda and Burundi and their accentuated relief result in the farming of an unusually high percent of the total area and the use of unusually steep slopes.

Cattle near Kitega, Burundi
Valued as a measure of wealth and prestige, cattle are poorly commercialized in Rwanda and Burundi and occupy much land which could be used for crops.

TILLAGE AGRICULTURE

An estimated 41.4 percent of the total area is arable, a very high figure by African standards. Valley bottoms are often planted in leguminous crops and potatoes, while an effort has also been made to install fishponds where possible. Corn, cassava, and peas are grown on slopes of as high as 40 degrees. Bananas are another important subsistence crop and are often planted around the huts. Most of the cultivated areas have contour ridges, terracing, and measures to control torrential runoff. An effort has been made to promote the planting of peanuts and soya to alleviate the marked shortage of vegetable oils.

COFFEE

The dominant cash crop is coffee, which has witnessed a remarkable extension in recent years. Introduced in 1920, it took hold very slowly, but by 1938 some 22 million trees had been planted. The big increase occurred after 1945, however, and by 1958 about 560,000 peasants had coffee trees, the total for the area being 65 million on about 100,000 acres. Production totaled 20,500 tons in 1958 and 29,300 tons in the record 1959, while 23,300 tons were produced in 1961 despite damage sustained in the revolt. The exportable production for 1963 is estimated at 11,700 tons for Rwanda and 17,700 tons for Burundi.

Coffee was introduced and extended under a thoroughgoing paternalistic system. The territorial government established nurseries, planted the trees, usually about 60 per holding, supervised their cultivation, established cooperative processing centers, and organized the processing, shipment, and sale. However, it is the African who now grows the coffee, in contrast with the position in Congo, where most of the coffee was grown on European estates. Arabica coffee is grown everywhere except in the Ruzizi Valley, where robusta was introduced in 1956. The arabicas command premium prices in the world market, but returns to the individual farmer are low because of the high cost of shipment from this interior producing region and the small output per grower.

OTHER CASH CROPS

Cash crops of lesser importance include cotton, tobacco, sisal, tea, and pyrethrum, but all cash crops are estimated to occupy only 3 percent of the total cultivated acreage. Pyrethrum, grown chiefly on European farms, is the only crop besides coffee figuring in the exports from Rwanda. The development fund of the EEC is contributing $930,000 to the planting of 12,350 acres of tea plantations.

Cotton is produced mainly in the Ruzizi

Valley, where an area totaling some 425,000 acres has been under development since 1949. Swamps along the north end of Lake Tanganyika were drained and put into rice paddies, but the bulk of the area, which is sandy soiled and arid, was mechanically cleared, provided with water from boreholes, and divided into 25-acre farms for production of cotton and subsistence crops such as cassava, legumes, and peanuts. Communal grazing rights are held in nearby uncultivated lands. Cooperatives assist in the mechanical cultivation of fields and in the sale of cotton, which, despite serious disease problems necessitating free government dusting and spraying, has done reasonably well. This scheme was considered to be largely a social one, designed to relieve overpopulation. By 1958, some 10,000 families had been brought into the scheme, but whether it may be considered to have been a demographic and economic success is questionable.

A tin mine near Kigali, Rwanda
Tin and its associated minerals account for about three eighths of the value of Rwanda exports. Only a few mines are relatively large-scale operations.

LIVESTOCK

Livestock are more a question of socio-politics than of economics in Rwanda and Burundi. They graze on about one third of the total area of the two countries, some of which could profitably be put to crops. Milk yields average 1 to $1\frac{1}{2}$ liters per day and cattle are valued more for magnificently long horns than anything else. Coveted as a sign of wealth and comprising an important element in the culture of both Hutu and Tutsi, yet dangerous to preservation of the soil and preempting some of the better lands, cattle pose an enormous problem, not made easier by difficulties associated with commercialization from this remote area. A program of voluntary reduction had little success, the cattle population increasing from an estimated 874,000 in 1945 to 1,008,052 in 1958, while numbers slaughtered declined from 110,000 to 54,300. In addition to the cattle, of which there are at least double the proper number, there are about 1,750,000 sheep and goats.

BELGIAN AGRICULTURAL POLICIES

The agricultural policies of the Belgian authorities in Ruanda-Urundi differed considerably from those applied in Congo. Here the imperatives were to prevent famines, which formerly occurred in about one of three years, and to provide for a rapidly increasing population. Organizing the country into rural action zones (ZAR), the Belgians devoted their attention particularly to draining marshy valleys, extending soil-control measures, especially terracing, reforesting hill crests, and limiting abuses of cattle raising. The agricultural department also introduced cassava and, as has been seen, participated closely in the extension of coffee plantings. Little was accomplished by way of consolidating the typically fragmented farms except in the Rubona settlement scheme, which involved complete replanning of a small area at an elevation of 6,500 feet. An interesting program on hill pastures was the cutting of infiltration channels, comparable to the "valats" in the French Cevennes or the "irrigations pluviales" in the southern Alps, which permit the rain to impregnate the soil and thus keep the pastures green most of the dry period. By 1961, about 250,000 acres had been provided with these sills.

NONAGRICULTURAL ECONOMIC ACTIVITIES

There are a number of relatively small mining operations, particularly in Rwanda, where mineral exports valued at $4.24 million accounted for 38.1 percent of total exports in 1962. Tin concentrates provide the bulk of output; associated with the tin are tantalite, columbite, beryl, and wolfram. A small quantity of gold is won from alluvial deposits; mica and graphite are known to occur, and iron ore is said to be abundant. It does not appear likely, however, that mining or metallurgical developments will provide many opportunities for absorption of the surplus population.

There are prospects for developing power in this mountainous area. Rwanda now shares the Ruzizi plant with Congo and has a 7,500-kw plant at Taruka serving the needs of the mining enterprises in that region. Methane gas estimated to have an energy potential equivalent to 50 million tons of coal is found in the waters of Lake Kivu and has been the subject of investigation.

The Belgians sometimes talked of making a second Switzerland out of Ruanda-Urundi, basing industry on the readily available labor supply. But present manufacturing is very limited, coffee processing and a brewery at Usumbura being most important, and it is difficult to see how any really significant development can be expected in the foreseeable future considering the deficiencies of raw materials, location, and market.

The area could, however, emulate Switzerland from the standpoint of tourism. Rwanda, Burundi, and the adjacent parts of neighboring countries comprise one of the most beautiful parts of Africa, notable for the diversity of its physical and human characteristics.

Internal transportation is quite well developed, particularly considering the difficult nature of the topography. There are no railways or navigable waterways except for the two peripheral lakes, but the network of roads has greater density than many other tropical African countries. The main outlet of both countries is Usumbura, which has a new 25-mile paved highway leading up to the central plateau and a new modern lake port, both financed by a $4.8 million IBRD loan authorized in 1957. External contacts leave much to be desired. The two leading routeways to the sea both use Usumbura and Lake Tanganyika, one going east from Kigoma to Dar es Salaam, the other west from Albertville, leading by rail and river to Matadi. It is likely that the eastern route will be more favored than in the past, since Belgian pressure to use the Congo routeways no longer exists. Usumbura has an international class airport, the airport serving Bukavu in Congo is on the Rwanda side of Lake Kivu, and a new airport is planned for the capital of the latter country at Kigali.

Rwanda and Burundi, in conclusion, have more than their share of problems. Excessively populated by man and beast, culturally divided, remote, inhibited by rugged terrain, they are at present not economically viable and would appear to require assistance for many years to come. Whether Belgium, which covered the annual budgetary deficits by increasing grants in the years before independence, will be willing to continue aiding both countries in the amounts required remains to be seen. It signed a convention of cooperation and assistance in late 1962 with Rwanda providing for 221 Belgian technicians in 1963, and for assistance in the medical, educational, and agricultural fields. The U.N. and the EEC have provided generous help to both countries in recent years, but one cannot be very optimistic that investments will be sufficiently massive to meet the rapid population growth. And recent tribal clashes have added a new element of insecurity.

Part Five EASTERN AFRICA

Government Road, Nairobi, Kenya

Ethiopia

With the exception of a brief period under Italian rule from 1936 to 1941, Ethiopia has existed as an independent entity for over 750 years, by far the longest modern period for any African country. It cannot be said, however, that the very old traditions of Ethiopia have brought it to a more advanced stage than younger African countries; rather it stands today as one of the least developed nations on the continent, a country whose complex of customs and institutions are incrustations which inhibit economic, social, and political advance. In 1952 Ethiopia was federated with Eritrea, which had been an Italian colony from 1890 to 1941 and under British administration thereafter. In 1962 the federal system of government was abolished, essentially making Eritrea a province of Ethiopia.

St. George's Coptic Christian Church at Addis Ababa
Ethiopia's highly developed religious and feudal institutions have inhibited the introduction of modern economic, social, and political advances.

The cornerstones of Ethiopian society are the church, the emperor, and a feudal land system. The ruling Amhara group have been Christians since the fourth century and Coptic Christianity is the officially established religion of the country. The church has been a major source of national culture and a unifying force for perhaps half of the population, but it is also a source of conservatism and preserver of the archaic land tenurial arrangements, being estimated to own at least one fifth of agricultural lands in the highlands.

The emperor, who is considered to have descended from a divine line, dominates the political and social scene. While the present emperor has been working toward a constitutional form of government, the Parliament is at present only partly elected and its acts are subject to his veto. In 1960 a revolt against the government was put down, following which the emperor took somewhat more vigorous steps toward liberalization of the bureaucracy. The emperor has, in fact, made greater strides toward opening the country to modern influences than any of his predecessors. But the balance he must achieve between the impatient demands of the younger, educated, modernist elite and the representatives of older, deeply entrenched traditions is a delicate one and any step forward is likely to be too little for the former and too great for the latter. Certainly Ethiopia may find it very difficult to replace the present emperor, and a tradition of conflict over imperial succession adds greater uncertainty to the course of events.

The feudal system is highly complex and is intertwined with other components of the culture. It is represented by an unusually conservative titled aristocracy, a notorious system of serfdom, and a castelike social stratification which is dependent upon a notable variety of physical, occupational, religious, and political considerations.

The land tenure systems, which vary greatly from one part of the country to another and which are still very poorly understood, have in common an unusual degree of complexity and the inequitable distribution associated with feudalism. Large parts of the farmlands of Ethiopia are owned by the royal family and the church, the rest by powerful landlords, who are often absentee. Most Ethiopians have their holdings under the *gabar* system, which keeps them subservient to the owner. A beginning toward land reform was made in 1959 and the Second Five-Year Plan starting in 1963 calls for tax and tenure reform, but any effective reform will require more than declarations of intention.

Despite the unifying influences of church and empire there are great divisive forces in Ethiopia. The majority of the population still lives in tribal societies, noted for feuds within and between groups. Amharas, comprising about a third of the population, are the dominant tribe; they and the Tigreans are mostly Semitic but partly Hamitic, speak Semitic languages, are mainly Christians, and have been relatively well united in facing threats from other tribal groups. When the government speaks of unifying the country, it views it as a process of Amharization.

The greatest threats to the Amhara, other than revolts from within, are from the Galla, a partly Christian but mainly Muslim Hamitic tribe somewhat more numerous than Amharas, and from the Somalis, living in the eastern Haud and Ogaden, upon whom the Amharas keep a watchful eye because of the border disputes with Somalia. Most of the remaining tribes are Hamitic, though some Nilotic and Negro tribes live along the low western borderlands, remote from the control or ken of the central government. In all, there are perhaps 100 tribes in Ethiopia, 70 languages, and two important religions.

The early stage of educational development contributes to lack of cohesion. Despite substantial recent developments, about 95 percent of the population is still illiterate. In fact, the vast majority of the people remain practically untouched by outside forces, unaware of the modernizing influences in parts of the country, entirely dependent upon their own efforts for subsistence.

Trying to help this complex and stultified society to move more rapidly into the modern world is a veritable United Nations of assisting groups and countries. The United States has extended over $140 million in loans and grants in the past decade. The USSR made a $100 million loan available in 1959; while very little of it had been drawn upon up to 1963, a part was slated to finance a petroleum refinery under the Second Five-Year Plan. Israel, Norway, Sweden, West Germany, Yugoslavia, and Czechoslovakia have also assisted in one way or another, while the IBRD and its International Development Association made loans totaling $39 million up to mid-1963, mainly for transport developments, but also to cover foreign exchange requirements for small industries. Ethiopia hopes that one third of the $1,062 million expenditures of the Second Plan will be provided by foreign sources, public and private.

Working in Ethiopia has proved a frustrating experience for many foreign technicians and advisers. The government has been described as a tangled combination of modern bureaucracy, feudalism, and primitive society where red tape is a major activity and procrastination a password. But progress is certainly discernible; a uniform legal system has been adopted, provincial tax collection has been reformed, a modern money and banking system has been organized, a rudimentary frame of good roads has been constructed, the country has an excellent airline, exports have been increasing and diversifying, and, most important, education is being sharply extended.

THE PHYSICAL BACKGROUND

The conservatism and relative backwardness of Ethiopia may be attributed in part to the isolation of the country, explained in turn by the topographic pattern of its core areas—highlands and plateaus of high average elevation with difficult access and sharply distinct from adjoining regions.

LANDFORMS OF EASTERN AFRICA

Before looking more closely at Ethiopian topography, it may be noted that it shares certain characteristics of the area extending from the Ethiopian Highlands to the Republic of South Africa. This is high Africa, the bulk of which is a great uplifted land mass. Steep scarps along the coasts and at irregular intervals inland are typical throughout. The landform pattern shows signs of extreme geologic youth: freshness of scarps, steepness of canyons, disturbed drainage patterns including developing areas of inland drainage, and lack of extensive alluvial depositional forms.

Great rift valleys run from north of this region all the way to the Zambezi River (Frontispiece map), giving another similarity in structural character to the area. Occupied in places by long, narrow, deep lakes, the rift valleys are a series of grabens or downfaulted trenches cut in the high plateaus, often bounded by upfaulted blocks or horsts. The Western or Central Rift System runs from the Upper Nile to the Zambezi; it is occupied by Lakes Albert, Edward and George, Kivu, Tanganyika, and Rukwa before joining with the Eastern Rift System just north of Lake Nyasa. Lake Tanganyika, which drains west to the Congo, illustrates an extreme of displacement, the bottom of the lake being 2,172 feet below sea level, the level of the lake about 2,540 feet above sea level, and mountains on both sides attaining elevations of 8,000–9,000 feet. The lake is also a biological enigma, with a unique fauna that has developed in part along independent lines.

The Eastern Rift System begins in the Dead Sea, is occupied by the Red Sea, splits Ethiopia into two massifs of unequal size, and is well marked across Kenya but less easily recognized in central Tanganyika. The system bifurcates south of Mbeya, one branch being along the Luangwa trough, the other extending along Lake Nyasa and the Shire River to the coast of Mozambique. Many of the lakes in the Eastern Rift do not drain to the sea and are becoming increasingly saline.

Another characteristic common to many eastern African areas is the significance of volcanism. However, there is a gradual transition from the north, where recent volcanism has molded the land intensively, as in Ethiopia and much of Kenya, to the center, where mighty volcanic masses lie sometimes far apart, and to the south, where there are no recent magmatic outpourings, as in the Rhodesias and the Republic of South Africa.

The structure of eastern Africa has important effects on use of the area. It often makes road and rail construction difficult; it results in an almost total absence of navigable streams, though the lakes all function to a greater or

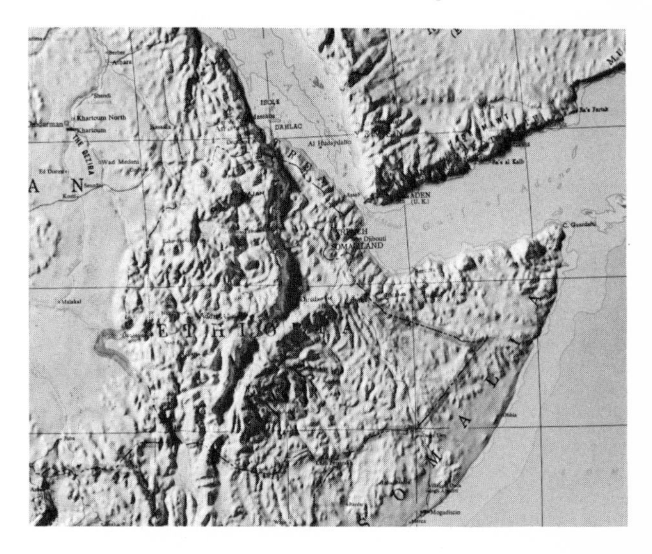

Map 66. Landforms of Ethiopia
Relief Map Copyright Aero Service Corporation

Highlands in the Blue Nile Province of Ethiopia
The Ethiopian massifs comprise the most extensive upland of Africa. Scarps separating them from adjacent regions and a highly accidented topography within them help to explain the isolation which characterized the country for many centuries.

lesser degree as transport arteries; and it has a strong influence on climatic and hence on land use patterns.

LANDFORMS OF ETHIOPIA

The highlands of Ethiopia form the most extensive upland of the entire African continent (Map 66). Most of the main western massif is formed of "plateau basalts" which reach thicknesses of several thousand yards in some places; these are also found in the more thoroughly eroded remnants of the eastern or Harar Massif stretching from Harar to Sidamo. Elsewhere, the highlands are composed of crystalline rocks. Elevations in the north are commonly 8,000 to 9,000 feet but rise to 14,000 and 15,000 feet in the higher peaks; they are several thousand feet lower in the south. While the massifs of Ethiopia are frequently called plateaus, this conveys an erroneous impression of the present topographic situation because their surfaces are rarely flat. Both massifs are broken by hills, mountains, peaks, and cliffs, and are rent by canyons of sometimes great depth. The main highland block is sharply divided from adjacent regions: on the east a 2,000- to 4,000-foot escarpment drops to the Red Sea plains and the Rift Valley; on the west there are a series of terraces and much broken land leading to the Sudan plains. The Harar Massif has similar sharp topographic boundaries on the north and west but slopes fairly gradually toward the southeast, merging into the Somali Plateau, broken and eroded country mainly covered with brush, thornbush, and coarse grasses.

The topographic pattern of the Ethiopian massifs makes them among the most isolated parts of Africa and still among the most poorly known. This isolation is compounded by zones of aridity around the base, the 100-mile-wide belt on the south being one of the sharpest ethnologic divides on the entire continent.

The Rift Valley is a distinct topographic region, dividing the massif into separate sections but also providing, in the Awash Valley, a kind of gateway to the western highland. At the southern border the floor of the valley is about 2,000 feet above sea level, while in the section near Addis Ababa it is about 6,000 feet above sea level. Not much farther north it opens on to the Danakil Plains, which form a sizable region along the northeast of the country. Elevations drop to 381 feet below sea level in the Danakil Depression, east of which the volcanic Red Sea mountains parallel the Red Sea

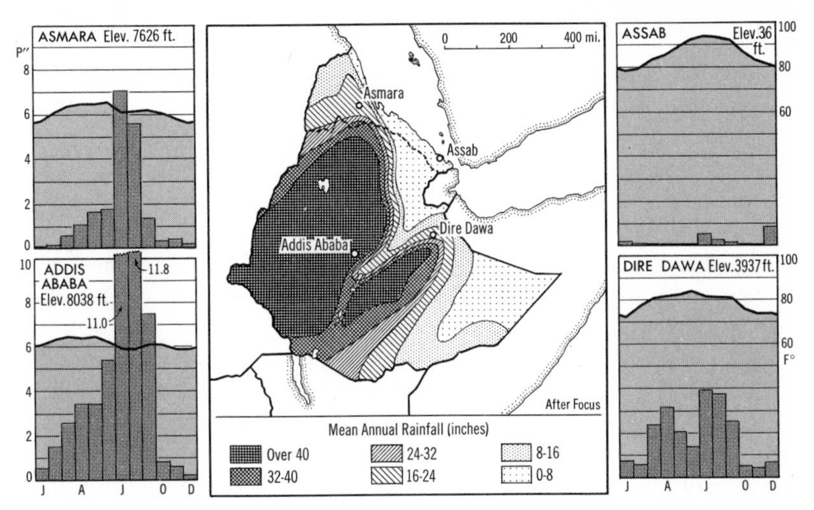

Map 67. Precipitation in Ethiopia; climographs for selected stations

coast, rising to an elevation of 6,700 feet in the south. Along the west of Ethiopia are several small segments of the Sudan plains, vastly different in every way from the other parts of the country.

CLIMATE

The climate zones of Ethiopia are based primarily on elevation, though the use of the several zonal terms is not uniform throughout the country. Lands above about 11,500 feet are called *wirch*; they are of little use and the problem of atmospheric rarefaction is a permanently limiting one. From about 7,900 to 11,500 feet is the *dega*; from about 5,000 to 7,900 feet is the *woina dega*, which would be comparable to the *tierra templada* tropical highland zone. This zone has a very low temperature range but a high diurnal range and contains much of the more favorable lands of Ethiopia from the climatic standpoint. From sea level to about 5,000 feet is the *quolla* zone, which includes the *bereha* or desert areas.

Precipitation varies greatly, but is usually over 40 inches on the highlands (Map 67). There is a marked maximum in the summer of the Northern Hemisphere, but in the highlands the Ethiopian names for the seasons are almost reversed owing to higher temperatures in the clear dry period and lower temperatures, especially sensible temperatures, under the rain and cloud cover of June to September. Much of the moisture reaches Ethiopia from the Atlantic Ocean, which means that the heaviest precipitation is on the southwest facing slopes.

SOILS

Soils formed from the "plateau basalts" are generally young, rich, and of excellent structure, and their sizable representation gives Ethiopia soil conditions superior to most African countries. The soils of the crystalline rock areas are much less favorable. The finest soils of the country are probably the alluvials of the Nile, Awash, and other rivers, but they cover a relatively small total area.

The Ethiopian massifs are, then, generally favored by climate and soils, but much less favored by landforms, which are a major cause of isolation with respect to both the outside world and among internal regions, and which reduce the utility of otherwise high-quality areas. The physical attributes of Ethiopia have led many people to conclude that it could one day be one of the great granaries of the world. Much closer study would be required, however, before this assessment can be accepted, with regard to both the physical elements and the population.

THE POPULATION OF ETHIOPIA

No one knows how many people live in Ethiopia. The Five-Year Plan was based on an estimate of 19.8 million in 1957, increasing at a rate of 1.6 percent per annum. The 1962 U.N. *Statistical Yearbook* gives only a figure for 1958, namely 21,600,000, which was considered to be of questionable validity. United States specialists have used a figure of 17.2 million for 1961, while Mesfin W. Miriam, an Ethiopian geographer, calculates that it was 24.58 million in 1960 and is increasing at the rate of 2 percent per annum. Only Addis Ababa has had a census; this revealed a population of 401,915 in 1961, about 100,000 less than had been predicted. Quite obviously, planning is hazardous when so little is known regarding the vital statistics of the country.

AGRICULTURE

Information is inadequate to permit very much quantification regarding Ethiopian agriculture, and estimates of expert observers vary rather widely. Two estimates of the major land use categories are given below:

	U.S. Department of Agriculture (percent)	*Food and Agriculture Organization (percent)*
Grazing land	49.8	28.0
Bush and thornbush		25.0
Cropland	9.5	8.1
Potentially productive, now unused	6.9	
Forests	3.6	6.9
Wasteland	30.2	32.0
	100	100

Sources: U.S. Department of Agriculture, Foreign Agricultural Service, *The Agricultural Economy of Ethiopia*, by Henrietta M. Holm (November, 1956), p. 9; H. P. Huffnagel, *Agriculture in Ethiopia* (Rome, F.A.O., 1961), p. 136.

Other estimates place the cultivable land at roughly 50 percent of the total area.

About 90 percent of Ethiopians are engaged in agriculture, which accounts for over 90 percent of exports by value, and provided an estimated 62 percent of the gross domestic product in 1961. But most farmers cultivate for subsistence only, much of the main export "crop," coffee, actually being more of a gather product than a cultivated crop. Poor transport, isolation, obscure and inequitable tenure, and lack of knowledge contribute to reduce motivation to produce above subsistence levels.

Ethiopian farms, which are believed to have an average of about 12 to 20 acres of cultivated land, are further characterized by primitive techniques, including the use of crude implements, poor seed selection, lack of integration of livestock and tillage agriculture, and failure to protect against soil erosion, which is frequently of serious proportions. Nonetheless, animal power is used in some plowing and for threshing grain, though the FAO had difficulty in introducing the moldboard plow, and plowing is typically too shallow, which means that fields must frequently be plowed three times in order to prepare a field for planting. The government has given relatively little attention to agriculture in the past, but has assigned it high priority under the present plan. One of the problems which is shared with other underdeveloped areas is illustrated by the Agricultural Technical School at Jimma, managed and staffed by Oklahoma A. and M.; a few students have had to be dropped for refusual to work with their hands, while as of late 1962 none of its graduates had actually gone back into farming.

MAIN CROPS

About half of the cultivated area of Ethiopia is planted to grains, of which teff, a very fine grain cereal, is the most important, particularly on the higher lands. Durra, wheat, and corn are other grains of significance, while barley is grown as a feed. Grain paid as rent to landowners accounts for the bulk of grain reaching the market. Other subsistence crops include a variety of oil seeds, vegetables, and ensete, the false banana, from whose leaves a flour is derived. Considerable quantities of honey are produced, particularly in Gojjam, much of it being used to produce *tej*, a mildly intoxicating beverage. The physical conditions of the *woina dega* zone permit a very wide variety of middle latitude, subtropical, and tropical crops.

A coffee producing forest near Jimma
Much of Ethiopian coffee still comes from plants which grow wild in such forests.

A coffee plantation in the Harar area
Efforts are being pressed to replace wild coffee with regularly planted fields, where yields can be much higher and of better quality.

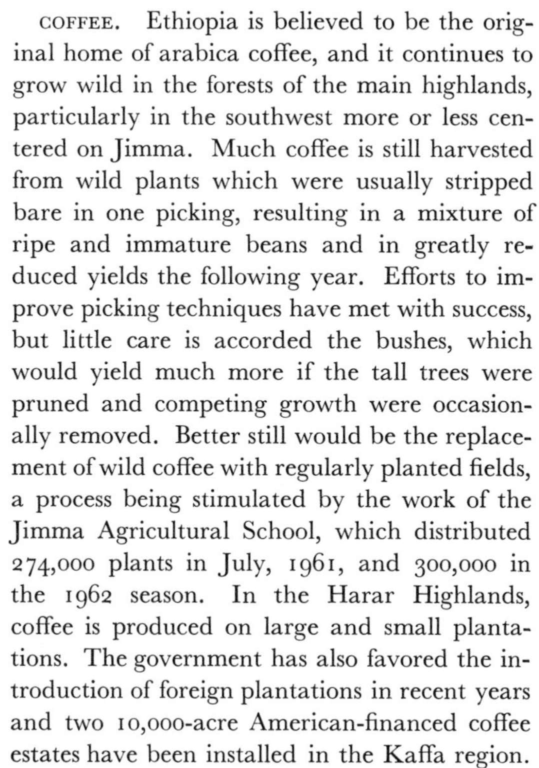

COFFEE. Ethiopia is believed to be the original home of arabica coffee, and it continues to grow wild in the forests of the main highlands, particularly in the southwest more or less centered on Jimma. Much coffee is still harvested from wild plants which were usually stripped bare in one picking, resulting in a mixture of ripe and immature beans and in greatly reduced yields the following year. Efforts to improve picking techniques have met with success, but little care is accorded the bushes, which would yield much more if the tall trees were pruned and competing growth were occasionally removed. Better still would be the replacement of wild coffee with regularly planted fields, a process being stimulated by the work of the Jimma Agricultural School, which distributed 274,000 plants in July, 1961, and 300,000 in the 1962 season. In the Harar Highlands, coffee is produced on large and small plantations. The government has also favored the introduction of foreign plantations in recent years and two 10,000-acre American-financed coffee estates have been installed in the Kaffa region.

Exports of coffee have been rising steadily in recent years, over half normally going to the United States. The record 1962 exports of 65,000 tons were valued at about $45 million, below the value of 1957 returns owing to the lower average selling price. In 1963 Ethiopia exported 64,000 tons of coffee under terms of the International Coffee Agreement. It had previously rejected a suggested quota of 51,000 tons. Ethiopia is concerned about limitations on coffee sales and the increased difficulty of selling to EEC countries, which normally take over 10 percent of exports. In addition to its relatively large recorded exports, which give Ethiopia fourth place among African producers with about 2 percent of total world production, that country is believed to consume about 20,000 to 30,000 tons, while about 5,000 tons are smuggled to Sudan.

OTHER EXPORT CROPS. Pulses and oilseeds have been of increasing importance in recent years among Ethiopian exports. Chat, a mildly narcotic plant whose leaves are a substitute for tea or coffee, is shipped from Harar in substantial quantities to Arabia.

IRRIGATED CROPS. While precipitation is adequate on the highlands to produce raingrown crops, it is quite inadequate in the lowland areas. Since streams flow from the more humid uplands into these areas and there are some excellent soils available, it is logical for Ethiopia to consider development of the more favorable irrigable areas. At present, irrigation is practiced on about 100,000 acres or about one tenth of the area estimated to be irrigable. Recent years have seen the introduction and extension of several projects, particularly in the Awash Valley, for the production of cotton, sugar cane, tomatoes, and other crops.

Cotton. This fiber has been grown for many years by farmers on small plots for their own use, but yields and quality were not good because of poor practices and the prevalence of insects and diseases. About 2,000 tons have been produced on an organized basis in two places, near Tessenei and Metemma near the Sudan border, and in the vicinity of Massawa.

Newer irrigation developments are being made at scattered localities: near Om Ager in the Takayze Valley, which is expanding from a 3,500-acre plantation; near Lake Abbaya toward the south of the Rift Valley; east of Asmara, where an Italian company grows cotton on a 1,250-acre plantation and supplies small cultivators on about 6,250 acres; and at three places in the Awash Valley. The area east of Asmara, which is irrigated from the Zula Dam, is slated to be increased to about 35,000 acres to support 8,000 farmers producing cotton, corn, sorghum, and millet. Since this area is periodically plagued by locust invasions, it was necessary to sow cotton four times in 1958 because of their destructive attacks.

The FAO is conducting a three-year survey of the potentialities of the Awash River Valley and of the Danakil Desert; financed by the U.N. Special Fund, the hydrologic, soil, sedimentation, and other studies will cost about $1.25 million. An important part of the investigation is located at Tendaho, where a large British firm is experimenting with cotton on a 10,000-acre leasehold. If this proves successful, it is proposed that 250,000 acres be developed under a Gezira Scheme pattern with cotton as the main cash crop and legumes, oil seeds, and other subsistence crops being grown in rotation. This would involve an expense of about $14 million for the project, plus about $25 million for a dam at Tendaho and auxiliary irrigation works. It is estimated that the project would make Ethiopia self-sufficient in cotton.

Sugar Cane. The Wonji Plain, downstream from the Koka Dam on the Awash River, is the site of the largest private investment in Ethiopia, two sugar estates and associated mills owned by a Dutch company. The first sugar was produced in 1954 and by 1963 about 59,000 tons of sugar were produced, necessitating enlarging the capacity of the sugar factory. In 1958, development of a second plantation and factory at nearby Shoa was begun at a cost of $10 million; output is expected to satisfy Ethiopian demand and permit some export of sugar. In the 1962 milling season, 7,500 persons were employed at Wonji and Shoa; 20,000 may be employed when the operation is fully developed. The company also built a small confectionery and sugar tablet factory in 1961; it had previously constructed 5,000 accommodations in fifteen villages in the area and a modern hospital to serve the plantation communities.

Fruits and Vegetables. The Awasa Agricultural Concession, situated on the Wando Plain near Lake Awasa about 175 miles south of Addis Ababa, is growing a variety of fruits and vegetables on about 1,000 acres of irrigated land. The main crop has thus far been tomatoes, and a canning factory at the concession is producing a variety of tomato products as well as canned peas, beans, and meat. About 1,500 fruit trees of a planned 20,000 have been planted; the emphasis has been upon avocados, which are expected to provide a new export. The plantation also breeds pigs and has planted 150,000 coffee trees; about 1,500 workers are employed. In Eritrea, there is a fairly sizable output of irrigated fruits and vegetables near the cities and below the eastern escarpment.

LIVESTOCK INTERESTS

Ethiopia has a large livestock population, including 15–20 million cattle, mostly longhorn Zebu, 25–40 million sheep and goats, and $3\frac{1}{2}$ to 6 million horses, mules, donkeys, and camels which provide the main means of transport in most of the country. On the highlands, most farmers keep some animals, but they are not well integrated with tillage farming. At lower elevations grazing is the dominant interest, though carrying capacity tends to decline with elevation. Here nomads and seminomads depend on sheep, goats, and camels, frequently fighting with their neighbors over pasture and water rights. Overgrazing is usual in these areas.

Practices are poor in all regards: feeding, breeding, disease control, use of manure, preparation of hides and skins, etc. Animals are characteristically scrawny, diseased, and poor milkers; most wool is so short and coarse it cannot readily be marketed. No real improvement is possible unless better feeding practices are adopted, while enforcement of vaccination against rinderpest would reduce heavy losses from this disease.

Animal products provide only 5 to 7 percent of the total exports of Ethiopia, though it is estimated that they could equal coffee in value. Hides and skins account for 86 percent of animal product exports. More exotic products include honey, beeswax, and civet, a perfume base taken from the civet cat.

Several foreign firms have an interest in commercialization of Ethiopian livestock. An Israeli firm ships meat from its refrigeration plant at Massawa to Israel. A British firm hopes to ship 100,000 cattle yearly via Djibouti to Egypt and Greece. Another project involves the fattening of livestock at Dire Dawa on oil-cake plus by-product molasses from the Wonji sugar factory. Finally, Mitchell Cotts and Mediterranean Canners, Ltd. were authorized in March, 1962, to establish an Ethiopian company to exploit cattle resources in Arrusi and Sidamo provinces; it is planned that 60 percent of the $2 million capital will be subscribed by nationals and that there will be a yearly output valued at $2.8 million.

MINING

Mining is of only minor significance in Ethiopia, employing an estimated 4,000 people in 1961. Relatively little is known regarding the mineral resources of Ethiopia, a position which should begin to be remedied under the present plan, which gives attention to provision for basic staff and surveys. Gold has been mined for some years, but output has remained small despite the introduction of modern machinery.

In 1957 Sinclair Petroleum quit its search for oil in the Ogaden after 10 years, 17 dry holes, and an expenditure of about $10 million. In 1958 Ethiopia contracted with a Yugoslavian concern to conduct a survey on the Red Sea coast of Eritrea; on the basis of its 1960 report, two concession areas have been made available to private companies. And in 1961 a German oil company secured a concession to explore in the Ogaden area.

In 1955 an American firm, the Ralph M. Parsons Company, was granted a large mining concession and exclusive prospecting rights, except for oil, in certain parts of the country. After exploring in the north end of the Danakil Depression from 1958, it contracted in 1961 to mine, process, and sell potash from the Dallol deposit. A total investment of about $16 million will be required, chiefly for construction of a new deepwater shipping point and a 68-mile railway to the open pit operation. Output may reach 300,000 tons a year, providing employment for over 2,000 Ethiopians.

A little platinum is mined in Wallega province and salt is produced in several salines. Other minerals reported to exist include iron ore, near Massawa, copper, tin, lead, cobalt, molybdenum, mica, graphite, and lignite, but intensive examination would be required before any accurate estimate could be made regarding the mineral potential of the country.

INDUSTRIAL DEVELOPMENT

Manufacturing in Ethiopia is confined to about 200 plants, almost all of which are small scale. In 1957 modern industry was estimated to account for 1.7 percent of the gross domestic product, electrical output for 0.2 percent, and handicrafts for 3.2 percent. A more recent estimate placed the contribution of industry at

11 percent of gross domestic product at factor cost in 1961. There is an old and well-established handicraft and cottage industry, particularly important in spinning and weaving. Table 23 summarizes some of the scanty data available on Ethiopian industry, estimating that the value of output increased 30.7 percent from 1957 to 1961, that capital expenditure increased sixfold from 1957 to 1962, and that employment has grown by about 32 percent from 1957 to 1960. The table further indicates that the food and beverage and textile industries accounted for about eight tenths of the total value of output in 1960, though representing only a third of total capital invested in manufacturing.

A considerable number of establishments are partly or wholly owned by the government, which plans to attract additional industries by capital participation. Italians established many of the industries in Eritrea, which continues to have a disproportionate share of the country's manufacturing plants. Greeks are also represented, while the French firm, A. Besse and Company, which is the country's largest importer and exporter, has a major share in the coffee and grain processing industries. The largest single establishment is the Dutch sugar factory at Wonji, though the Russian-financed refinery at Assab will be the largest when completed about 1966.

Table 24 lists the industrial establishments of Ethiopia by product and location. It may readily be seen that it compares unfavorably with several other African areas thus far studied, particularly in the relatively low development of metal-fabricated items. Addis Ababa and Asmara are by all odds the leading centers, but it is the capital city which has gained the most new industries in postwar years, while Asmara has suffered from the somewhat depressed conditions that have characterized the Eritrean economy.

The textile industry has had a notable expansion in recent years. The largest single plant is a former Italian one at Dire Dawa which is government-owned. A joint Italian-Ethiopian plant at Asmara, started in 1954, was expanded in 1960. Three mills have been opened at Addis Ababa since 1959 and one of these has already been doubled. Finally, the government is constructing a mill at Bahar Dar in the Lake Tana area. Based in part upon a new hydroelectric

Table 23. Selected estimates on Ethiopian industry, 1957–1962

	1957	*1958*	*1959*	*1960*	*1961*	*1962*
Average number employed, in thousands	19.7	20.0	23.1	26.0		
Wages paid, in million $ U.S.	4.8	5.0	5.2	6.0		
Capital expenditure, in million $ U.S.	2.0	2.4	3.9	6.5		12.0
Value of output, in million $ U.S.	33.0	33.4	35.4	43.1	46.0	
	Share of industrial groups in total value of output in industry (in percent)				*Share of total investment in industry (in percent)*	
Food and beverages	49.4	51.7	52.8	47.6	23.0	
Textiles	30.1	25.4	25.2	33.3	10.0	
Leather and shoes	3.8	4.1	4.1	3.8	3.5	
Timber and building material	5.8	7.3	2.6	2.6	16.0	
Tobacco	4.9	5.8	4.6	3.8		
Chemicals					30.0	
Others	6.0	5.7	10.7	8.9	17.5	

Sources: State Bank of Ethiopia, *Report on Economic Conditions and Market Trends* (May, 1962) pp. 7, 9; (April, 1963), p. 5.

Table 24. Industrial representation in Ethiopia, 1963

Industry	Location
Raw material processing	
Vegetable oil extraction	Dessie, Harar, Debre Markos, Addis Ababa, etc.
Coffee cleaning	20 plants in Addis Ababa, others scattered
Grain milling	scattered
Vegetable and fruit canning	Awasa
Sugar	Wonji, Shoa
Meat processing	Asmara, Massawa
Tanning	Addis Ababa, etc.
Dom palm buttons	Asmara
Fish meal	Massawa
Sawmills	details not known, two large mills planned
Plywood	Addis Ababa
Market-oriented industries	
Brewing	Asmara, Addis Ababa
Distilling	Asmara
Carbonated beverages	Addis Ababa, Asmara
Modern dairy	Addis Ababa, Asmara
Macaroni and biscuits	11 plants, location not known
Confectionery	Wonji
Tobacco	Addis Ababa
Soap	Asmara
Bottles	Asmara
Textiles	Addis Ababa (3), Asmara, Dire Dawa, Bahar Dar (under construction)
Clothing	Addis Ababa, Asmara
Shoes	Addis Ababa (2)
Furniture	details not known
Mosaic	Asmara
Cement	Dire Dawa, Addis Ababa (under construction)
Asbestos sheet and tubes	Addis Ababa cement plant
Ammunitions	Addis Ababa
Matches	Asmara
Oil refinery	Assab (under construction)
Nails	location not known
Metal bars, rods	Addis Ababa
Printing	Addis Ababa, Asmara, etc.
Tire retreading	Addis Ababa

plant at the Tesissat (Tis Abbai) Falls on the Blue Nile, it represents a program designed to begin a more intensified development in the Blue Nile Province and to prevent an overconcentration of industry at Addis Ababa. While these goals may have considerable political value, they do not ensure success of the mill, which will be in an isolated, poorly developed part of the country, without roads to some of its potentially most important markets.

The number of spindles in Ethiopia has increased from about 54,000 in 1959 to 101,000 in 1962 and will total 126,000 in 1964. Whereas the industry met about one third of domestic consumption in 1959, it is expected to meet the total demand by 1970.

Other important manufacturing developments include the new $320,000 plywood plant at Addis Ababa, the cement and asbestos cement product plant at Addis, and the oil

The weaving room of the Ethiopian Cotton Company
Ethiopia has seen a rapid build-up of this industry in recent years.

refinery at Assab. There is a serious question regarding the suitability of this last plant from the standpoints of size, capital expenditure required, and location. With a capacity of 500,000 tons, the refinery will have a potential output about 2½ times the present consumption; a smaller plant would have involved a lower cost than the estimated $15.2 million for the Assab refinery. Finally, Assab is connected with the highlands only by road, and delivery of products is likely to be more costly than it would be by rail from Djibouti.

Plants of somewhat unusual interest include the distillery at Asmara, associated with the brewery there, which produces alcohol from the nut of the dom palm, and the match factory at Asmara, which is unique in using Euphorbia candelabra for matches and box covers. Employing about 300 workers, this factory produces about 15 million boxes yearly, some of which are exported. Special note should also be made of the well-organized central workshop of the Ethiopian Air Lines and the central garage of the Imperial Highway Authority, both set up by American firms. A tire-retreading installation is associated with the IHA garage at Addis Ababa.

Ethiopia has ranked very low in per capita consumption of electricity, but is now increasing output rapidly. In 1956, 12 towns were electrified; 21 were served by 1962. Output of electricity has increased from 48.5 million kwh in 1953 to 124.4 million kwh in 1961, 55 percent of which came from hydroelectric plants. By far the most important installation is that of the Koka Dam on the Awash River, about 50 miles from Addis Ababa. Constructed at a cost of $16.4 million, which was met by Italy as a part of its war reparations, the dam is 1,502 feet long and 138 feet high, and its associated plant has a capacity of 54,000 kw. Power is transmitted not only to Addis Ababa but 209 miles to Dire Dawa. Surveying has begun for a possible new dam on the Awash near Sodeire, where a 60,000-kw plant could be erected at an estimated cost of $10–12 million.

A 14,000-kw plant has been constructed on the Blue Nile, intended to spark development in the Lake Tana region. This represents a fraction of the total capacity that could be developed on the Nile between the lake and the Sudan border. The Gibe River has also been studied with a view to placing a small plant there to serve Jimma. The main household fuels are wood and dung. Eucalyptus grows very rapidly on the highlands and numerous small plantings have been made to provide a local source of fuel.

TRANSPORT

The characteristically precipitous edges of the Ethiopian highlands and the highly accidented interior topography make for difficult and expensive transport. Considering the ability to practice local self-sufficiency and the long period of isolation from outside forces it is little wonder that the transport net is greviously inadequate. Italy did construct a fairly good road system in Eritrea, no mean accomplishment in view of the mountainous terrain, and built 4,000 miles of roads in Ethiopia, half of them paved, in its brief period of colonial rule. These roads opened the country for the first time, but most of them were permitted to deteriorate in the 1940s.

A really major program of road building was

begun about 1950 with aid from the World Bank and the United States and by 1963 a total of $63 million had been expended by the Imperial Highway Authority (IHA), a fairly autonomous, American-managed body responsible for surveying, building, and maintaining roads, though much construction is done by private companies under contract. Map 68 shows the approximately 2,900 miles of drivable and maintained roads existing in 1963. A 1963 International Development Association loan of $13.5 million will permit increasing this by 700 miles and resurfacing 500 miles. One of the problems of the IHA has been to convince the government that maintenance is as important as construction. Beyond this very rudimentary main-road system is a sizable length of trails, possibly 7,800 miles of which can be considered jeepable but which are usually in abominable condition. The trails in Ogaden are very inaccurately known and mapped.

Road construction is probably the most important contribution that has been made to Ethiopian economic development. It has provided relatively good contact between most of the major cities, opened up rich agricultural regions, and improved contact among the various ethnic groups. A 1960 study revealed that current transport rates on dry-weather roads were more than twenty times as high as those on maintained all-weather roads. While traffic density is still low, it is increasing; 1960 traffic counts on the improved roads showed a low of 9 vehicles a day and a high of 884, the latter on the Addis Ababa–Debre Zeit road. The number of vehicles in the country has increased from about 10,000 in 1948 to 38,000 in 1962. About 88 percent of the private vehicles are registered in Addis Ababa.

Most of the country remains dependent upon animal transport, which has been estimated still to carry over three fourths of produce to market. The need for secondary access roads is obvious, but many decades will be required to develop an adequate pattern unless local communities become sufficiently interested to participate in their construction.

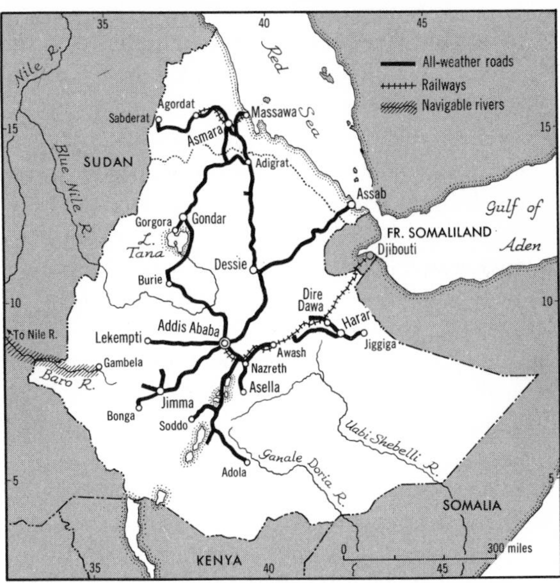

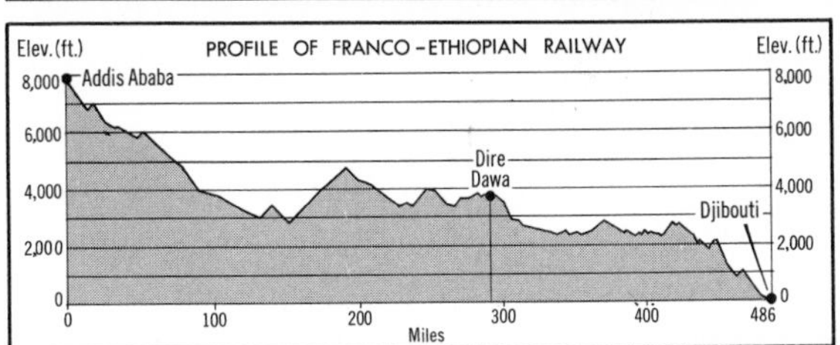

Map 68. Transport in Ethiopia

Above: Rail lines, all-weather roads, and waterways
Below: Profile of the Franco-Ethiopian Railway

RAILROADS

Ethiopia has two of the most spectacular railways in Africa from the standpoint of topographic profile. The narrow-gauge (95 cm) Eritrean line was constructed from 1899 to 1911 between Massawa and Asmara and was extended to Agordat and Biscia by 1932, reaching a total length of about 224 miles. Its most difficult section, between the coast and Asmara, at 7,694 feet, has extremely sharp curves, gradients of 3.3 percent, and 30 tunnels. The line carries only about 200,000 passengers and 120,000–140,000 tons of freight yearly. Early hopes that it might extend into Sudan were negated by construction of the Sudan Railways to Port Sudan.

The most important line serving Ethiopia is

that from Djibouti in French Somaliland to Addis Ababa. Begun in 1896, the line reached Addis Ababa in 1917, but inadequate capital resources of the French company had dictated construction at as low a cost as possible and the railway still suffers from excessively sharp curves and light rails. After 1952, when Ethiopia ceased being a landlocked country because of its federation with Eritrea, Ethiopia favored use of its national ports to the detriment of the line to Djibouti. An agreement was accordingly made with Ethiopia providing that it receive an immediate 25 percent and later a 50 percent interest in the line plus the right to station its own customs inspectors at Djibouti and to have free transit privileges through French Somaliland. These provisions made use of the line, now called the Franco-Ethiopian Railway, more attractive and have resulted in profitable operating years since 1958.

The Franco-Ethiopian Railway is a meter-gauge line totaling 487 miles in length (Map 68). Since World War II it has been modernized and dieselized, and a beginning has been made on replacing with heavier track. It remains, however, as one of the most difficult and most costly lines in the world and transport charges are a heavy burden on both import and export commodities. About 2,500 persons are employed by the railway, which has been 90 percent Africanized in recent years.

PORTS

Massawa is the best developed of Ethiopian ports and has a superior natural harbor to Assab. Providing the major outlet for Eritrea and the north of Ethiopia proper, Massawa has accommodations for 6 large vessels drawing from 17 to 29 feet, plus two posts at petroleum jetties. It is planned that the harbor be deepened to 31 feet.

Assab, situated about 300 miles south, had facilities for only one vessel until its reconstruction by Yugoslav engineers from 1958 to 1961 under a $12.5 million Yugoslavian loan. Now protected by a 2,329-foot mole, the port has accommodations at modern quays for three large vessels and for smaller coastal ships and local boats, giving it an estimated capacity of 800,000 tons yearly. Assab has not lived up to original expectations. In 1962–63 it was underutilized, with equipment and trucks standing idle, the latter unable to get adequate loads to deliver to the highlands. The road up the scarp to Dessie is a difficult one, with curves and gradients that restrict speeds and contribute to the high costs of shipment between Addis and Assab. It has been estimated that these costs could be reduced by more than half if a road were built along the Rift Valley via the easier ascent of the Awash corridor. This would also make contact with the Harar Massif very much easier, a consideration which will be more important upon completion of the Assab refinery.

The special privilages available at Djibouti make that port to all intents and purposes a third port of Ethiopia. Strategic considerations pertaining to Ethiopian-Somali relations also dictate that Ethiopia sustain its friendly ties with France and French Somaliland.

Ethiopia has one river port, Gambeila in the extreme west, which is open to navigation from the White Nile when the Sobat is at the high-water stage.

AIRWAYS

Ethiopian Air Lines was founded in 1945 and has been managed and partly staffed by TWA ever since. EAL maintains a monoply on service in and to Ethiopia, which has permitted charging relatively low rates on internal flights. The network of regularly served airports has been gradually increased to the present rather extensive coverage. The poor surface transport helps to explain the importance of airways, which play a prime role in maintaining contact with some otherwise very remote points. The United States has extended several loans to the government for development of EAL, including two in 1961 for airport construction and for maintenance facilities for new jet aircraft used on international flights.

CHAPTER EIGHTEEN

Somalia

On July 1, 1960, two of the lands inhabited predominantly by Somalis became the independent Republic of Somalia, a country with an area (246,000 square miles) as great as California and Oregon, with a population estimated to be about 2 million in 1962. Despite the low density, 8.1 per square mile, Somalia is probably overpopulated in relation to its meager natural resources.

THE SOMALI PEOPLES

The Somalis are an eastern Hamitic people, relatively homogeneous in religion, language, and culture, but often split by primary loyalty to the clan, by intratribal friction and boundary disputes associated with claims to water holes and pasture rights. The Somalis are noted for their love of fighting, and it has been estimated that tribal wars in the former British Somaliland resulted in killing one third of the population in the three years after 1910 when incessant wars led the British to evacuate the interior.

The Somalis do have a strong tribal consciousness in relation to other groups, which was best represented in the drive to independence and which continues to unite them in the drive toward a Greater Somalia. But the more important trend since independence has, according to Castagno, been toward inexorable fractionalism, strengthened clanism, and fragmentation of political parties.[1]

The Somali flag contains a five-pointed star, each point representing the Somali peoples resident in specific political units: one each for former Italian and British Somalilands, now united in the Republic, and one each for the Somalis in northern Kenya, eastern Ethiopia, and French Somaliland. The unification of all the Somali clans is the one goal which unites all Somalis, though it has not prevented their participation in pan-African movements or ratification of the Convention of African Unity.

Somalia has never had a census and estimates of its population range from around 1.5 to 5 million. Almost no other African country has as high a percentage of its population in one tribal group, for in addition to the Somalis and a few indigenous Negro peoples there are only about 34,000 persons of other national groups, including about 30,000 Arabs, 600 Pakistanis, 200 Indians, and 2,800 Europeans, the largest number of whom are Italians. The minority groups, however, have been responsible for most of the economic and commercial life of the country, particularly its international trade and transactions.

Occupationally, the population may be roughly divided into (1) nomads, comprising about three fourths of the total, and roughly divided in a ratio of 60:40 between nomads and semi-nomads; (2) settled Somali and other agriculturalists, possibly 12 percent of the total; (3) government employees, comprising about 5 percent of the total; (4) traders, about 4 percent, among whom the Arabs handle petty trade, while Pakistanis and Goans participate in much of the more important commercial operations; (5) fishermen, about 1 percent; (6) handcraftsmen, about 1 percent (this group includes most

[1] Alphonso A. Castagno, Jr., "The Somali Republic in Transition," *Africa Report* (December, 1962), p. 8.

of the small Negro population, who are hunters, iron and leather workers, and the chief collectors of gum and resin, and who have generally been considered as inferiors, even outcasts, by the dominant Somalis); and (7) Europeans, who, unlike the other groups, cannot be considered as permanent residents. Italians play a significant role in the larger commercial and transportation services, a dominant role in the banana plantations, and a continuing important role in government advisory services. Other Europeans are associated primarily with diplomatic and aid missions.

The Somalis have long had strong prejudices against certain occupations, considering them fit only for inferior persons, and have been against working with one's hands, which is regarded as undignified. Guided by the principle that Allah will provide, they look upon the economic motive with obvious contempt. Other impediments include a very high rate of illiteracy, over 90 percent; the small number of educational facilities in the country, there having been only 6 secondary schools in the former Italian section in 1960; the fact that Somali is not a written language; and high disease rates. From 20 to 50 percent are believed to have venereal disease; rheumatism and tuberculosis are prevalent; malaria is common on the coasts; and there is a high incidence of other diseases. Both the educational and the medical programs have been greatly accelerated in recent years, but the high percentage of nomads in the population is an inhibiting influence of major dimensions.

Although the urban population of Somalia is still small, perhaps about 11–12 percent of the total, it doubled in the postwar years to 1960 and continues to grow rapidly. This gives Somalia the urban problems that are present in other parts of Africa, but poverty makes the possibilities of meeting them even more difficult. Many city dwellers reside in one of the two main types of indigenous dwellings, the *aqal* or the *arish*. The *aqal*, typical in the country, is a beehive hut of semicircular wooden struts covered with mats of grass and bark fiber which can be easily carried by camel. Quite satisfactory, clean and healthy under nomadism, it quickly deteriorates in the city, creating unhealthy slum conditions. The *arish* is a wattle and daub structure, as unsatisfactory as the *aqal* for permanent dwelling, housing ticks and bugs in the walls and mosquitoes in the rush roof,

Nomads stopping at a new well near Bur Hacaba
About three quarters of the population of Somalia are nomads, who face very difficult physical conditions in this dry country.

and lacking in light and ventilation. It was estimated in 1951 that of 32,000 inhabitants of Hargeisa, 26,000 lived in *aqal* and 2,000 in *arish* dwellings, presenting what seemed to be an almost insuperable housing problem. The population of some towns varies enormously between the seasons, being greatly reduced when the seminomads move away to summer pasture areas.

The new republic, then, faces severe problems. Clanishness must be suppressed in so far as it leads to intra-Somali conflict. The former Italian and British parts, which had differing administrative, educational, and legal systems, and different lingua francas, must be welded together. An effort must be made to create a viable economy with only meager resources available. In the international sphere, the desire for a Greater Somalia overrides other considerations and accounts for a probably excessive expenditure on police and military forces, particularly in view of the serious and continuing imbalance in the national budget and in physical trade plus the numerous requirements for economic and social advance.

PHYSICAL BACKGROUND

Most of Somalia is a low plateau averaging about 3,000 feet in elevation, which rises fairly gradually from the Indian Ocean. In the north, an extension of the Harar Plateau runs in two ranges parallel with the Gulf of Aden coast to Cape Gardafui. Except in the north, landforms are seldom a limiting factor on economic use, climatic conditions being the controlling physical element.

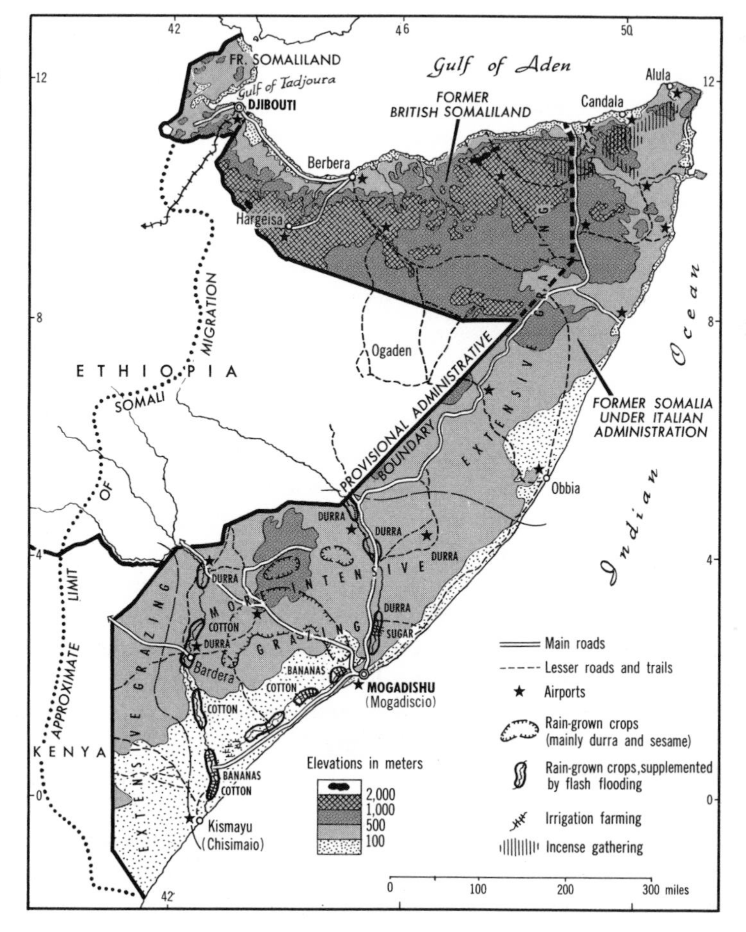

Map 69. Economic map of Somalia

Climatically, the whole area is hot and dry. Summer temperatures average about 80–95° F., but reach over 100° F. for many days. Rainfall is low and irregular, varying from 1 to 5 inches along the coast and in the northern interior to a maximum average of about 24 inches. In the dryland farming area between the two main rivers, the Giuba and the Webi Scebeli (Map 69), precipitation averages about 20 inches. The heavier rains occur from April to June–July, lesser amounts are received in August and September, and almost none falls from December to March. Drought years are common; but occasionally there is excessive precipitation which leads to great destruction and interruption of the normal cycle of farming and grazing, as occurred in 1961. Much of the country is characterized by interior drainage and evaporite sediments, leading to a concentration of salts in both ground and surface water.

Vegetation on the plains is sparse except for thorn bush and other scrub growth. South of the Giuba, however, the brush is often thick and mangrove is found along the coast. In the interior, "orchard bush" country is found—parched grassland with scattered thorny acacia trees. In the hills, incense and myrrh trees give rise to a gather industry of some significance.

GRAZING

Nomadic grazing is the most important activity, and animal products, particularly hides and skins, rank after bananas among the country's exports. Climatic conditions restrict the number of cattle—hence sheep, goats, and camels are the main support. Camels are used for milk and for transport, the Somali nomad having been dubbed by one observer as "the parasite of the camel." Most nomads live on an incredibly low standard, suffering from a multitude of physical problems and being further restricted by cultural attitudes and practices. From the physical standpoint, there is inadequate and uncertain rainfall, which is the basic reason for the overwhelming dependence on pastoralism. About 40 percent of the area is practically useless because of low rainfall; the rest is subject to periodic severe droughts with consequent high stock losses. Low precipitation in turn means that fodder growth is inadequate and of poor quality. Overgrazing of the sparse growth contributes to soil erosion, which is prevalent and increasing throughout the country.

Stock and domestic water supply is often inadequate. Many of the older wells are poorly constructed, dangerous, and unsanitary, and often yield ground water of poor quality. A well-drilling program, involving the sinking of 660 wells from 1954 to 1960 and about 70 in 1961–62, has greatly improved this situation, but some difficulties have resulted from nomad refusal to pay taxes on the new wells and from tribal jealousies, which have required the guarding of wells to prevent their destruction.

Disease and insect pests are additional limiting factors. Some pastures are tsetse-ridden and presence of the fly in the river valleys keeps graziers from the best watered areas. Two locust invasions may be expected each year, and, although international control measures have reduced losses, some tribesmen have bitterly resisted using gammexane-treated bait in the belief that it caused livestock deaths.

Inadequate management, inter- and intra-tribal difficulties, and the usual attitudes associated with a cattle culture are further explanations for the generally low standard of Somali nomads. A pilot project in range management near Afmadu ran into difficulties because its intended beneficiaries did not understand its objectives. The sale of cattle is strongly resisted, though it takes place. Hides and skins are improperly prepared, most being of inferior quality. The skin of the black-headed Somali sheep, the Berbera Blackhead, is, however, acknowledged to be the best of its kind, excellent for the manufacture of gloves.

TILLAGE AGRICULTURE

Tillage agriculture is severely restricted by the low precipitation and relatively meager surface and subsurface water resources. Cultivable land

Preparing the land for plowing near Baidoa
Less than 1 percent of the total area is cultivated and efforts are being made to extend dryland farming in the area between the Giuba and Scebeli rivers.

is variously estimated at 11 to 17.5 percent of the total, but less than a third of 1 percent of the total area is cultivated, and irrigated lands total only about 52,000 acres or 0.033 percent of the total. Yet crops produced under irrigation occupy a dominant role in the country's exports, account for a high percentage of wage laborers, and directly or indirectly supply an important segment of the country's revenue.

The main areas for production of rain-grown crops are along and between the two main rivers, where precipitation is somewhat more certain. A recent survey by the U.S. Agency for International Development (AID) concluded that a further $2\frac{1}{2}$ million acres could be used for dryland farming between the Giuba and the Scebeli. Sorghum is the principal crop; sesame and peanuts are secondary. Yields fluctuate severely, but total production does usually permit some surplus for export. Recent development plans call for extending the production of oil seeds on about 12,500 acres.

Irrigation agriculture in the former British Somaliland is confined to a number of date palm orchards along the coast, which were successfully extended in postwar years. In former Italian Somalia, irrigation is concentrated along the Webi Scebeli and Giuba, which drain large segments of southeastern Ethiopia. The Scebeli is usually dry in February and March, but has an average flood flow of about 5,400 cubic feet per second. The Giuba has a flow about $2\frac{1}{2}$ times the Scebeli and usually has some flow in all months, though there is a high ratio between flood and low-period volumes.

Sugar is the main crop on the Webi Scebeli; it is produced on a modern plantation at Villabruzzi about 100 miles from Mogadishu that is owned by the Societa Agricola Italo-Somalia (SAIS). About 22,240 acres of its total area of 62,000 acres are cultivated and irrigated. The plantation, which is divided into seven farms served by 60 miles of narrow-gauge railways, employs about 90 Italians and 3,500 to 4,500 Somalis. Almost all of the sugar produced is sold in the domestic market, the tax on sugar providing a not unimportant source of government revenue. Costs of production are too high to permit sale at world prices. SAIS also produces some cotton. One of the country's most important development projects, calling for the irrigation of 50,000 acres, is situated on the Scebeli near Genale.

The Giuba River supports most of the country's banana plantations. About 220 plantations are owned and operated by Italians, exporting about 3.4 million stems a year of Cavendish or Giuba bananas, which gives Somalia third or fourth rank among African exporters. Bananas account for over two thirds of Somalia's exports by value, provide a local payroll of about $2 million yearly, and contribute about $500,000 to the national budget through an export duty.

The precarious nature of the Somali economy is clearly revealed by the position with regard to banana exports. Not only is there the typical "one crop" dependence, but the one crop has required subsidization in a preferential market to permit its sale. The Italian banana trade is controlled by that government's Banana Monopoly, which permits the entry of Somali bananas with only a 1 percent customs charge as opposed to a 40 percent duty for bananas from other sources. The monopoly sets a high price to the Italian consumer, the difference giving a substantial return to the government. Just how competitive Somali bananas could be in a free market is uncertain. The Cavendish is a variety that is easily bruised, requiring higher expenditure for packing, but some savings on packing and transport will result from installation of modern facilities at Chisimaio (Kismayu), the exporting point. This should also eliminate the necessity for Somalia to pay a subsidy to vessels stopping at Chisimaio to pick up bananas. Somalia also has a distance handicap as compared with some of its potential competitors. Whether a lower consumer price in Italy would stimulate sales, permitting absorption of Somali and other bananas, can only be hazarded, but fruit growers in Italy are not anxious to stimulate keener competition.

Italy promised that the banana market conditions in existence at the time of independence would remain in force for four years, and that no abrupt changes which might be damaging to Somalia would be made. In late 1962 Italy agreed to increase its banana quota by about 440,000 stems, which will permit increasing exports by about 13 percent.

Other crops grown under irrigation include vegetables and cotton. Cotton is one of the few crops in which Africans are interested, about 60 percent being raised by Somalis; its production may be increased along both rivers as irrigation is extended. One development calls for increasing cotton acreage by 12,500 acres. Another project will concentrate upon citrus fruit to supply a marmalade and fruit juice industry. Finally, the Descek Uamo Project on the lower Giuba has recently been completed, permitting inundation farming on about 49,000 acres as water recedes in natural depressions along the river, and improved watering of livestock. No accurate estimate of the total irrigable area is available.

Digging an irrigation channel for a banana plantation at Genale
Bananas account for over two thirds of Somali exports by value; most are grown on about 220 plantations owned and operated by Italians.

NONAGRICULTURAL ACTIVITIES

Developments in nonagricultural pursuits are of minor importance. The country is the world's leading exporter of frankincense, which, with myrrh, is collected from the woods of the north. Charcoal has also been an export of local significance, though its continued shipment was forbidden in 1961 because of the growing threat to the country's vegetation occasioned by its preparation. A small amount of gum arabic is also tapped, and the nut of the dom palm, called "vegetable ivory," is sold for the production of buttons.

There is a small production of rock lobsters, sponges, and pearls along the coast, while guano is obtained from the island of Mait off the north coast. Though mainly a petty industry, fishing is the chief support of some coastal peoples. The only large venture, a tunny fishery on the Gulf of Aden, is in Italian hands. Hunting yields a small commercial output of hides and skins, leopard skins from the area being considered the best in the world.

Mineral production is almost lacking, though the government hopes that discoveries of oil will provide a major source of revenue in the future. Several American companies and the Italian AGIP have been prospecting in Somalia for several years, but no finds had been reported as of mid-1963. Italian Somaliland had some of the world's largest salt pans before the war; destroyed during the war, they have not been restored, nor does distance from market encourage their reclamation. Gypsum deposits occur near Berbera and phosphates may exist in commercial quantities.

An acute shortage of artisans and an almost absolute lack of technicians, plus the minute domestic market, inhibit the development of manufacturing. There is, of course, some craft production, including leather and iron work by Negro artisans. Modern industry is extremely restricted. The largest plant is the SAIS sugar mill, which accounts for about one half of the value of industrial output and employs about a third of the industrial employees. SAIS also runs an alcohol distillery, a cotton gin, an oil extraction mill, and a soapmaking plant, A cotton textile factory at Mogadishu was forced to close down in 1952 because of high operating costs, but new efforts were being made in 1962 to have this industry represented in Somalia. Tuna canneries at Candala and Abo and beef canneries at Mogadishu and Merca operate below capacity. Small leather and shoe factories are situated at Mogadishu and Brava, while Merca has a small plant producing rope from banana leaf fibers. Most factories are owned by Italian companies. While Somalia has a liberal investment law, little interest has been shown by foreign companies, and the Somalis' dislike of working with their hands does not augur well for the expansion of manufacturing. A recent AID study suggested 17 small-scale plants considered suitable for placement in Somalia. The total capacity of electric plants in the country is under 10,000 kw, but the EEC plans to assist in expanding power plants.

TRANSPORTATION

The Italians built about 450 miles of paved road in Somalia before the war, part of it to support the military campaign against Ethiopia, but much of this has been permitted to deteriorate. In the British protectorate, a trunk road was constructed between Berbera and Hargeisa. Some 1,250 miles of gravel road and several thousand miles of bush track complete the road system, but the flatness of much of the terrain and the long arid season make movement relatively easy over large stretches. There are no railroads, excepting the SAIS plantation lines. Mogadishu, the capital, has an international airport, and lesser fields are available at the more important towns.

None of the ports have had deepwater quays, though this situation is now being remedied. Chisimaio and Merca are important for export of bananas, which have been loaded entirely by hand; only Chisimaio has a protected harbor. A new port is now being constructed there which is expected to stimulate cash crop production along the Giuba.

Mogadishu has had the best-developed facilities and normally handles a large share of the country's import traffic. Its completely artificial port gave shelter for small craft during the northeast monsoon. Under a $5.6 million program financed by the United States, a new port will be completed by 1965 capable of accommodating four freighters and having a capacity twenty times that of the older installation.

Berbera, on the Gulf of Aden, is protected from the sea by a sand spit and has long been a dhow port. A postwar program costing $924,000 provided it with a 30-foot pier for coastal vessels, mooring buoys, and bulk storage facilities with a submarine pipeline from an offshore post. A 1962 loan from the USSR will be used in part to construct a deepwater port at Berbera. Bosaso, also in the north, handles a small dhow traffic with Aden. With three new deepwater installations, Somalia will probably be better equipped than the level of its seaborne traffic justifies.

TRADE AND AID

Both the low level of trade and the unfavorable balance of international payments make Somalia very dependent on foreign aid if any significant development is to occur. For reasons which are not always entirely clear, numerous countries have been prepared to provide rather substantial grant and loan funds.

In the years immediately preceding independence, the British contributed about $3.5 million to British Somaliland, half going to balance the budget, half to development. Italy expended about $15.7 million a year, while U.S. aid from 1952 to 1960 totaled $5.6 million plus a $2 million Development Loan Fund loan. The U.N. estimated that Somalia would need about $6 million a year upon independence and would require aid for about 20 years. Since independence, foreign assistance commitments totaling over $100 million have been made, including a $56.2 million credit from the USSR announced in 1961, from which $55 million is to be drawn for a variety of economic and social projects. This represents the largest loan on a per capita basis that that country has extended. Other loans have been extended from the United Arab Republic, West Germany, Czechoslovakia, and the United States, and direct financial assistance has come from the two former trustee nations, the United States, and the EEC. The U.N. has also provided $700,000 in technical aid plus $830,000 for four-year hydrologic and photogrammetric surveys. Italy is helping to pay for about 300 Italian technicians; the Peace Corps and Egypt are providing teachers; and numerous scholarships have been made available for Somali students to study abroad.

The per capita income of Somalia is placed at about $45 per annum, but 80 percent of the population is outside the money economy. Barring discovery of oil or other minerals, it is difficult to see how any very dramatic advance can be achieved for many years. But the Somalis are a proud and independent people who refuse to be pessimistic about their future.

FRENCH SOMALILAND

With about 68,000 to 83,000 people on 8,494 square miles, French Somaliland is the only remaining French territory on the African continent. It is essentially dependent on the port of Djibouti and the Franco-Ethiopian Railway. The indigenous population is about evenly split between Somalis and Danakil, both Muslim tribes, while there are about 5,000 Arabs and 2,400–3,000 Europeans, mainly French. About half the population resides in Djibouti.

Activities outside of the port are extremely limited. Salines situated south of Djibouti were closed in 1956. About 89 percent of the country is classed as desert and 10 percent as permanent pastureland on whose sparse vegetation a few thousand nomads graze their livestock. Finally, there are a number of irrigated orchards and date palms.

Djibouti, which is one of the hottest points on the globe, has a modern port situated on the deeply indented Gulf of Tadjoura. It has a 3,279-foot jetty and accommodations for six cargo vessels, plus a special fueling pier and a large petroleum storage capacity. A floating dock for repair of tankers is being installed. Traffic figures for the port give an erroneous impression of its importance because of the high percentage of bunkerage traffic. In 1961, for example, 89 percent of the total tonnage of 2,582,000 tons was comprised of petroleum products, 96.5 percent of which was bunker fuel figuring in both imports and exports. The position of Djibouti and of the Franco-Ethiopian Railway in Ethiopian trade was briefly noted in the previous chapter.

French Somaliland, which came under French authority in 1884, is constitutionally a part of the French Republic and its residents seem satisfied with this status at the present time. It receives direct budgetary support from France, and has been regarded as of considerable strategic value to that country.

CHAPTER NINETEEN

East Africa

Four political units are included in East Africa: Kenya, Uganda, Tanganyika, and Zanzibar. The evolution toward independence in this area was slightly retarded as compared to West Africa, in considerable part because of the political importance of the European population in Kenya. But progress toward that goal was greatly accelerated in 1960. Tanganyika, relatively the poorest and least developed, achieved independence in December, 1961; Uganda, despite intertribal friction, followed in October, 1962; Kenya became independent on December 12, 1963, and these three countries contemplate federating in the future. Zanzibar received its independence on December 10, 1963.

In Kenya, the European population felt until the early fifties that a very long period would elapse before their dominant position was seriously challenged. But in 1950 to 1952 various instances of unrest occurred which, in retrospect, presaged the Mau Mau revolt. A state of emergency was declared in October, 1952, and the revolt was not effectively ended until 1956. Some 11,503 terrorists, 1,887 loyal citizens, and 167 members of the security forces were killed to the end of 1956, while some 1,582 members of the forces and 978 loyal citizens were wounded. Of these totals, 224 were Europeans and 77 were Asians, the vast bulk of the casualties being Africans. At the height of the emergency, about one tenth of the area of the colony was affected. Mau Mau members were primarily Kikuyu, but the debased character of the oaths and the stated goals were repulsive to many members of that tribe, which helped to explain the lack of success of the revolt. It has been estimated that the cost of the emergency to June 30, 1959, totaled about $156 million. Its significance in the present context is that it awakened the British and Kenya authorities to the necessity to expedite drastically the efforts to improve African conditions and to work toward a rapid devolution of political authority. Major steps in that direction included introduction of the Swynnerton Plan; a great increase in educational programs; elimination of the racial exclusion policy for the "White Highlands" in 1960; the February, 1961, election, the first on a common roll basis, which elected an African majority to the Legislative Council; and a series of constitutional conferences leading to independence in late 1963.

These changes have not been unaccompanied by problems. There has been a substantial flight of European capital; many Europeans have declared their intention to emigrate; and the Asian population looks to the future with considerable uncertainty. In 1961 the import of agricultural machines declined by 60 percent, the nominal capital of newly registered companies was halved, and bankruptcies increased by one third. In 1963 it was estimated that there were about 300,000 Africans in the ranks of the unemployed.

On the other hand, very real progress had been made in reorganizing African agriculture and in stimulating the production of commercial crops by Africans. In the five years through 1961 the value of African-produced crops doubled, while 261,000 of the estimated 800,000 African farmers had had their farms consolidated. Exports have continued to rise, and record levels have been achieved in several important fields. Many Europeans appeared willing to adjust to the rising power of the Africans and some were continuing to purchase land in the heart of the predominantly European-farmed districts. Responsible African leaders have taken more realistic positions with respect to the presence and value of European farmers, who have accounted for about four fifths of crop exports.

Severe tests remain. An overwhelming victory by the TANU party did not solve the problem of extreme tribal hostility. A rapid running-down in what has been an unusually well-developed government administration is to be expected as experienced officials are replaced by localization, the East African term for Africanization. This raises serious questions regarding the ability to extend land reform rationally and effectively. Another problem is the need for continuing heavy financial support from Britain, which provided about $45 million in loans and grants in 1962.

Uganda, whose racial minority problems were insignificant as compared to those of Kenya, might well have reached independence before 1962 had it been possible to achieve internal unity. The most advanced tribal group, the Ganda,[1] had a highly developed political kingdom before the Europeans arrived, and their hierarchical system was preserved under their status as a British protectorate. The Ganda did not wish this to be weakened by inclusion in a larger, unified area and even declared their separate independence a few years before their actual *uhuru*, a move that was ignored by the British. The Nyoro in the west also had a well-developed kingdom, but lost certain lands to the Ganda for early opposition to the British and had not made as substantial economic advances in the ensuing years; the problem of the "lost counties" was only partly met by preindependence arrangements and continues to threaten relations between the Ganda and Nyoro. British efforts to prevent this already small country from splitting into smaller units and to permit achievement of independence led to the drawing up of a complex constitution whose federal character recognizes the four existent kingdoms within Uganda and, by the formation of ten additional districts, the position of some of the other 24 principal tribes in the country. Despite the relatively small number of non-Africans in Uganda, the attitude toward minority groups, and particularly toward Asians, has sometimes been marked by considerable animosity. Asian ownership of ginneries led to friction before and after the war, and from 1959 to 1961 a boycott of Asian traders adversely affected the whole economy. Nonetheless, it is possible to view the future with optimism. African leaders have generally displayed wisdom and forbearance in their desire to achieve a reasonable compromise between tribal and national loyalties. The relatively favorable educational situation, with about 500 Uganda students receiving degrees each year, should also prove to be a constructive element.

Tanganyika, a former United Nations trusteeship under British supervision, had the smoothest transition to independence, despite its great tribal variety and its relative poverty. The fact that there is no one dominant tribe has helped to reduce the significance of tribal friction. The rather limited number of non-Africans in Tanganyika and the small area of land leased to them also help to explain the easy transition. Tanganyika has faced difficult financial problems, particularly because of its rather stagnant economy in recent years. Additional problems have stemmed from some misdirection in its self-help program that has caused disillusion, and from excessively rapid replacement of expatriate administrators at the insistence of lower party officials.

The three main East African countries have expressed their intention to form a federation, possibly even adopting a common flag and single representation in the United Nations.

[1] Prefixes in East Africa have the following meanings:
Bu—the area inhabited by a tribe, e.g., Buganda
Mu—an individual member of the tribe, e.g., Muganda
Ba—several or all members of the tribe, e.g., Baganda
Lu—the language of the tribe, e.g., Luganda
For the sake of simplicity, root terms are used where possible, e.g., Ganda, Nyoro.

Certain joint services have existed for some years, as has an internal customs union. In 1948 these services were placed under the East Africa High Commission with headquarters in Nairobi, and this became the East African Common Services Organization before the countries became independent. EACSO runs two separate groups of services: (1) the so-called self-contained services, which are supported by charges and fees levied upon their users, and which include the East Africa Railways and Harbour Authority and the postal and communication services; and (2) the "non self-contained" services, which have been supported by grants and reimbursements from the British and East African governments. These services include scientific and technical research, collection of revenue, civil aviation, meteorological offices, statistical studies, and the desert locust survey, which also receives support from other African nations. Achievement of federal status should strengthen these services, some of which have been neglected by the preoccupation with strictly national problems.

Zanzibar and Pemba comprised a sultanate under a United Kingdom protectorate until independence on December 10, 1963. Friction among its heterogeneous peoples, which culminated in a bloody riot in July, 1961, delayed the move toward independence, and only one month after independence the government was overthrown in a Shirazi-dominated revolt.

AREA AND POPULATION

With a total area of 683,020 square miles, East Africa is about a fifth as large as the United States. Tanganyika alone is about four times the size of Great Britain; Kenya is the size of France and Belgium; Uganda is a little smaller than the United Kingdom. Table 25 shows the area and population of the major groups of these countries in 1961. Estimates for 1962 total populations are included because Kenya's census of that year revealed a population about one million larger than had been expected, indicating that the 1961 figures are heavily underestimated, possibly for all countries.

RACIAL GROUPS IN EAST AFRICA

Africans comprise about 97.5 percent of the total population. Numerous language groups and tribes are represented, including some 120 tribes in Tanganyika alone. There is probably as great diversity among them as can be found anywhere in Africa. Some tribes, such as the Ganda and Nyoro, had elaborate heirarchies,

Table 25. Area and population by racial origin of East African countries, 1961, 1962

	Kenya	*Uganda*	*Tanganyika*	*Zanzibar*	*Total*
Total area, in square miles	224,960	92,525[a]	361,800	1,020	680,305
Land area, in square miles	219,789	76,135[a]	341,150	1,020	638,094
1961 population, in thousands					
African	6,998	6,751	9,258	291.6	23,245.5[b]
Arab	39.0	2.1	27.6		121.8[b]
Indo-Pakistani and Goan	178.0	77.4	90.5	19.2	365.1
European	66.0	11.6	22.7	0.6	100.9
Other	6.0	2.5	4.9	0.4	13.8
Total population, 1961, in thousands	7,287.0	6,844.6	9,403.7	311.8	23,847.1
Total population, 1962, in thousands	8,676[c]	7,016[d]	9,560[d]	317[d]	25,569

Source: East African Common Services Organization, the East African Statistical Department, *Economic and Statistical Review*, No. 3 (June, 1962).

[a] Uganda Protectorate, *Statistical Abstract, 1961* gives area as 91,134 square miles, land area as 74,748 square miles.

[b] Zanzibar African and Arab populations calculated on basis of ratio according to 1948 census.

[c] Based upon census of August, 1962.

[d] Mid-year estimates.

well-organized armies, and orderly though sometimes barbarously cruel governments before they were first encountered by Europeans; others had very poorly evolved political systems. Some tribes are predominantly cultivators; others preserve the cattle culture as rigidly as anywhere on the continent. Some tribes have made striking advances in recent decades; others have remained almost untouched. Tribal boundaries tend to be rigid in East Africa, particularly in Kenya and Uganda, and stand as a deterrent in numerous areas to the most rational distribution of population and use of the land.

The term "Indians" is usually used with reference to the second largest group. Actually it includes Hindus, Pakistanis, and Goans, who are further divided by caste and strong religious and sectarian rivalries. Hindus outnumber Pakistanis by about two to one. In the nineteenth century, Indian traders had headquarters in the great entrepôt of Zanzibar, from which they moved to Dar es Salaam and Mombasa as the importance of Zanzibar declined. Indians were first brought to East Africa as soldiers and as indentured railway workers. Many died from diseases or were invalided home in the early years; others chose to remain when the choice was presented. While their part in opening up the areas was welcomed, strong hostility toward them developed later, particularly on the part of white settlers in Kenya, and they have been subjected to various forms of discrimination such as exclusion from farming, segregation in urban areas, inequitable representation in legislative bodies, and restrictions on immigration. Nor have Indians been free of opprobrium on the part of Africans, who have often resented their holding positions which Africans might otherwise fill. Occupying an intermediate stage between the Africans and Europeans, they were sometimes considered the more immediate block to African ambitions.

Despite these unfavorable attitudes, which are usually more emotional than realistic, the Indians have made a contribution to East Africa out of all proportion to their numbers. They occupy a dominant role as traders, being owners of large wholesale organizations and of the ubiquitous Indian store or *duka*, found everywhere from the largest cities to remote localities. Over three fourths of the Indian population, however, reside in the 17 large towns, with particularly large agglomerations in Mombasa, Nairobi, and Dar es Salaam. Some have become quite wealthy, not only in trade, but in motion picture theatre, hotel, and garage businesses, but many eke out a precarious livelihood operating on the narrowest of margins. About a tenth of the Indians are employed by government, particularly as office workers. The railways, manufacturing establishments, and various artisan trades are also heavily dependent on Indians, whose industriousness has sometimes won them more criticism than appreciation. One large Indian investor has financed a sizable part of the modern industry represented in Uganda.

In the agricultural sphere, Indians are particularly important in the sugar and sisal plantations. They developed the large sugar estates in Uganda, and own a considerable share of sisal estates in Tanganyika, where they have enjoyed greater acceptance than in any of the other countries. In Uganda their control of ginning and the sale of cotton led to bitter criticisms on the part of African producers.

Arabs are most numerous in Zanzibar and along the coasts. They had contact with these areas long before the Portuguese explorers arrived and continue to operate dhows between the Arab countries and East Africa, moving back and forth in accord with the alternating monsoon. They own most of the clove and coconut trees on Zanzibar and occupied a special political position because of the sultanate.

Kenya has about two thirds of the European population of East Africa, which cannot be explained simply by the greater importance of European farming in that country. Kenya's position as the leading industrial area of East Africa and its handling of almost all overseas trade for both Kenya and Uganda also help to explain the larger number of Europeans. But the dominance of Europeans in the Kenya economy has had extremely important economic, social, and political repercussions. Since 1960, emigration has exceeded immigration in Kenya by increasing amounts; the net emigration was 185 in 1960, 2,848 in 1961, and 4,423 in 1962.

Over a third of the Europeans in Kenya live in Nairobi, about a twentieth in Mombasa. In Tanganyika, about half of the European population is found in the large towns, and over a fifth in Dar es Salaam. The British comprise the bulk of Europeans in all four countries, but Tanganyika has had a rather important Greek minority which was originally associated with construction of the railways but which has pioneered in several other areas. Italians, Dutch, Germans, and Swiss also have sizable representations in Tanganyika, while Danes have made a special contribution to farming in Kenya.

DISTRIBUTION OF THE POPULATION

In over-all distribution of population the outstanding features are the marked concentrations on the better lands and, conversely, the huge areas that are empty or virtually so. This means that the average densities for each country are rather meaningless. The key factor in the tremendous disparities which exist is the amount of precipitation, in which landforms play an important role through the orographic influence. The distribution of the tsetse fly is also of great importance, particularly in Tanganyika.

In Kenya, about 80 percent of the population is found on the areas of high agricultural potential of the Lake Victoria Basin and of the Highlands, totaling perhaps 15 percent of the country. Densities in these areas average about 215 per square mile; they are probably about 550 per square mile in the Kiambu and Fort Hall districts and sometimes reach 1,000 per square mile.

In Uganda, which has an over-all density on its land areas of 92 per square mile, the population is more evenly distributed because precipitation is better distributed, but the Masaka, Mengo, and Busoga districts have densities of about 150 per square mile, Kigezi in the southwest has about 275 per square mile, parts of the higher lands of the West Nile Province have 440 per square mile, and subcounties on the slopes of Mt. Elgon have over 1,100 per square mile.

In Tanganyika, with an average density of only about 28 per square mile, about two thirds of the population live on the third of the country north of the Central Railway. And, as in the other countries, the greatest densities exist on the superior-soiled, better-watered, and tsetse-free highland areas, densities frequently exceeding 500 per square mile. The lands around Lake Victoria also have above-average densities; it is estimated that the Lake and West Lake provinces have about 25 percent of the total population on about 9 percent of the area.

Cities have been mushrooming as in other parts of Africa. Nairobi, which has been the leading city, had about 119,000 in 1948 and 266,700 in 1962. Dar es Salaam has grown from 69,000 in 1948 to 140,000 in 1961. The highest crude rates of increase in population appear to exist in just those areas which are already the most densely populated.

DIVERSITY OF LAND USE

Diversity is a keynote of East Africa—it is apparent in the physical, cultural, political, and economic fields. It results in a remarkable heterogeneity of land use patterns. But to confound the issue, there is less sense in some of the patterns than in most parts of Africa. Some graziers occupy excellent farming land while some cultivators try to subsist on what should be grazing land. Different tribes use the same physical area in sharply contrasting ways. Rigid boundaries mean that areas of dense population exist side by side with moderately or sparsely populated areas which are otherwise entirely comparable. Much of the area tends to be split into units whose contact one with another varies to a high degree, which function to some extent without regard to neighboring units, and which are advancing at different rates. This crazy-quilt pattern is explained in no small measure by the erection or solidification of artificial barriers, cultural and economic, among the various tribes, including the white tribe. Its existence is a heavy burden economically; what is needed is a breaking down of barriers that separate the many units and a working toward a more integrated whole.

REGIONS OF EAST AFRICA

It is obvious from the foregoing that regionalizing East Africa, except by very small units, is a hazardous proposition. Nonetheless, it will be helpful to break the area down into a number of large regions, within which subregions are delineated where appropriate. As the main focus is upon commercial activities, little attention will be paid to subsistence economies. The five major regions used are essentially delineated by topography (Map 70). Running more or less north-south, they are (1) the coastal belt and Zanzibar, (2) the low eastern plateau, (3) the Eastern Highlands and Rift System, (4) the Lake Victoria or Central Plateau, and (5) the Western Highlands and Rift System, which is shared with Congo, Rwanda, and Burundi.

THE COASTAL BELT

The true coastal belt is a relatively narrow plain except where it broadens in the Tana lowlands of eastern Kenya and the Rufiji Lowland in central Tanganyika. Temperatures are warm and tropical; sensible temperatures are inclined to be high. Precipitation varies from conditions of semiaridity in eastern Kenya, where the plain passes into the similar Giubaland lowlands of Somalia, to about 60 inches in southern Kenya and northern Tanganyika, and declines southward to about 35 inches on the southern Tanganyika coast. Monsoons play a prominent role in the climate of this region and other parts of East Africa; the northeast monsoon blows from December to March, the southeast monsoon from May to October. Much of the area has two rainy seasons.

Many of the coastal lands are formed of coral rocks, and light sandy soils are also characteristic. Coconut woodlands and bush are common vegetational types; mangrove swamps line the coastal creeks and river valleys; only occasionally is dense forest found.

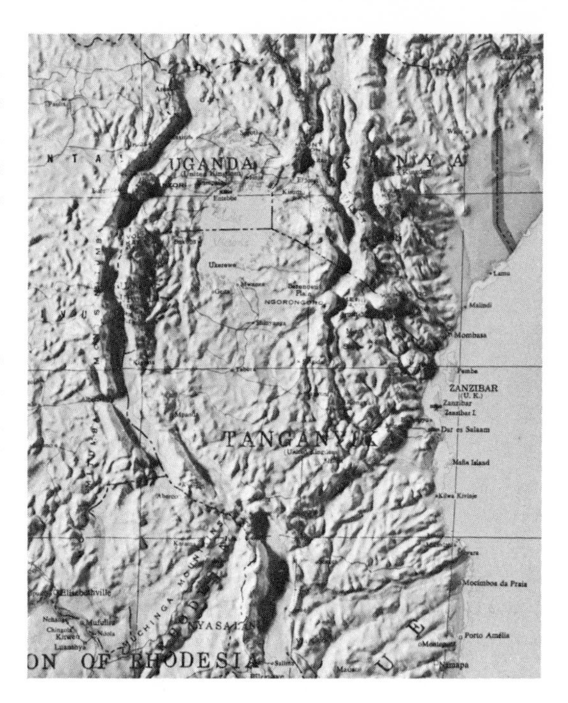

Map 70. Landforms of East Africa
Relief Map Copyright Aero Service Corporation

Coastal peoples have had contact with the Middle East for over a thousand years. In the sixteenth and seventeenth centuries, the Portuguese challenged the position of the Arabs, erecting forts at various points including Fort Jesus at Mombasa, built in 1592. Portuguese influence has long since vanished, but the significance of Arab influence is now seen in the continuing dhow traffic and in the marked concentration of Arabs in the coastal cities. A disproportionate percentage of Indo-Pakistanis also live along the coasts, particularly at Mombasa and Dar es Salaam. Much of the coastal zone has fairly high population densities, not only because of the cities, but because this is a relatively favored and, for the most part, adequately watered zone. About half of the Africans along the coast of Tanganyika work in the estates of Tanga Province.

AGRICULTURE. The most significant agricultural production of the coastal belt is that of sisal, which is particularly important in the area around Tanga and along the Central Railway inland from Mombasa in Tanganyika (Map 74). Its production is not confined to the coastal zone, as it can be grown from sea level up to 6,500 feet. Factors which are important in influencing the location of sisal producing areas include:

(1) Its bulk, particularly before stripping. The usable fiber makes up only 3 to 4 percent of the leaf weight, hence it is necessary to have the decorticating plant adjacent to the producing fields and there is typically a well-organized system of transporting the leaf to the factory—either small rails, overhead mechanical conveyors, or trucks. Even the dried and baled fiber is bulky in relation to its value, hence there is a strong incentive to locate production relatively near the coast and along rail routes leading to the major ports.

(2) The high capitalization of the decorticating plant. Since a decorticating installation is costly it is necessary to keep it in operation as continuously as possible, which means that about 5,000 acres should be allocated to its support with individual fields in various stages of planting, growing, and maturity. The life cycle of sisal is about 10 to 14 years in East Africa, of which during the first 2 to 5 years the plant is immature and yields no revenue. In late maturity the plant sends up a 12- to 15-foot pole containing 2,000 young bulbils from which selected plants are taken to the nursery and then later planted in the fields. Total investment for a minimum-sized estate producing 1,000 tons a year would be somewhere around a million dollars. While sisal is, like sugar, particularly appropriate for plantation-type operations, some is outgrown by Africans and brought to nearby plants, and varying but usually small (1 to 6 percent of total) amounts of hedge sisal are marketed annually depending in considerable part on prevailing prices.

Worker on a sisal estate near Tanga

Sisal, which ranks first among Tanganyika exports, is produced almost entirely on large plantations. About 28,000 Africans are employed on some 172 estates.

(3) The availability of water for decortication, which requires substantial quantities. Experiments have been carried out with dry decorticators but none have as yet been perfected.

(4) The presence of lime soils, which are attractive for sisal production because the plant will yield especially well on such soils.

Sisal is the number-one export of Tanganyika by value. It was brought to that country by an agent of the East Africa Company in 1891 from Florida via Kew Gardens. About 595,000 acres are in 172 sisal plantations owned by various nationals, but the total area planted to sisal is less than half of this figure. About 28,000 Africans are employed on the sisal estates of Tanganyika, of which some 70 percent have permanently settled on or are adjacent to the producing areas, partly as a response to recruitment on a family basis.

Tanga Province, with 71 estates and about 57–60 percent of total production, is Tanganyika's leading sisal area (Map 74). Most plantations are situated along the coast or along the railway to Arusha, that section of the Northern Province having about 5 percent of the country's output. The second major region, accounting for about 26 percent of production, is concentrated along the Central Railway from Dar es Salaam inland to Kilosa, with Morogoro being the main center. An important minor region is found around Lindi in the south. Tanganyika accounts for about 35 percent of total world sisal production, while its share of world hard-fiber production (sisal, henequen, and abaca) has increased from 46 percent in 1935–39 to 71 percent in 1962.

Kenya, which produces about 10 percent of world sisal output, has about 68 sisal plantations owned mainly by Europeans and concentrated close to Nairobi but also found along the rail lines leading to Kisumu and Kitale. Uganda's output is of very minor importance.

Sisal sales and prices have fluctuated very considerably in postwar years, which has resulted in the usual "one-product" difficulties for Tanganyika, which has such heavy dependency on it. Average prices varied in the 1950s from $159.60 per ton delivered at port in Tanganyika in 1955 to $473.98 per ton in 1951; 1962 and 1963 prices have been abnormally high. Exports in 1962 were valued at $44 million in Tanganyika or 30.7 percent of the total; Kenya's sisal exports yielded $12 million or 11.4 percent of that country's total exports. A factor which may result in considerable further increases in production is the development in Tanganyika of a hybrid plant capable of producing three times the existing normal yield. Released from the research station in 1960, it is still considered to be on a trial basis. The chief concern of the industry is the rising cost of production, labor wages having been increased 25 to 40 percent in 1962 and an export levy of 5 percent ad valorem having been introduced in December, 1962. While high prices have offset these increased costs, the chairman of the Kenya Sisal Growers' Association believes that the selling prices are so high as to threaten the long-term well-being of the industry.

Other cash crops that are produced in the coastal belt include cashew nuts, coconuts, wattle, cotton, cassava, kapok, and a variety of fruits and vegetables for the large coastal cities. Production of cashew nuts is particularly important along the south coast of Tanganyika, but it is increasing in the Coast Province of Kenya as well. In 1962 Tanganyika exported cashew nuts to the value of $6.5 million; tonnage of shipments increased from about 4,000–5,000 tons in 1950 to the present level of about 40,000 tons and may be expected to continue to expand in view of plantings which are not yet bearing. Drought-resistant and not requiring very fertile soil, cashew nuts could be grown on a very large area along the coast. Almost all nuts are shipped to India for shelling, a procedure which is extremely labor intensive. If some machine method could be perfected or if Tanganyikan workers performed this task, the contribution of cashew nuts to the economy could be doubled.

None of the other cash crops in the coastal zone are of major importance, though 1962 saw a record production of 10,000 bales of excellent quality cotton from the Rufiji Delta. Cassava is the major subsistence crop followed by corn, while sweet potatoes, sorghum, and rice in limited areas are supplementary crops. In the future, the delta of the Rufiji and other similar but smaller areas could become significant producers of paddy rice.

FISHING. Practiced all along the coast, fishing is almost entirely confined to inshore waters and characterized by primitive techniques. About 1,500 Africans are engaged in coastal fishing, while one European firm is found at Shimoni, south of Mombasa. The introduction of nylon shark nets in 1954 resulted in a notable increase in catch per man, but total landings are still low and the large unrequited market would appear to justify efforts to upgrade the industry and to extend fishing to offshore areas.

THE PORTS OF EAST AFRICA AND THEIR CONNECTING LINKS. The coastal zone is also, of course, the site of the major ports and rail termini of East Africa, so they may appropriately be discussed at this point. The only ocean port of significance in Kenya is Mombasa, which handles almost all of the overseas trade of Kenya and Uganda, plus a portion of trade for two sections of Tanganyika, the high-productive Kilimanjaro-Meru region, and the Bukoba area west of Lake Victoria. Mombasa is situated on an easily defensible island which is now connected by causeways to the mainland. Access

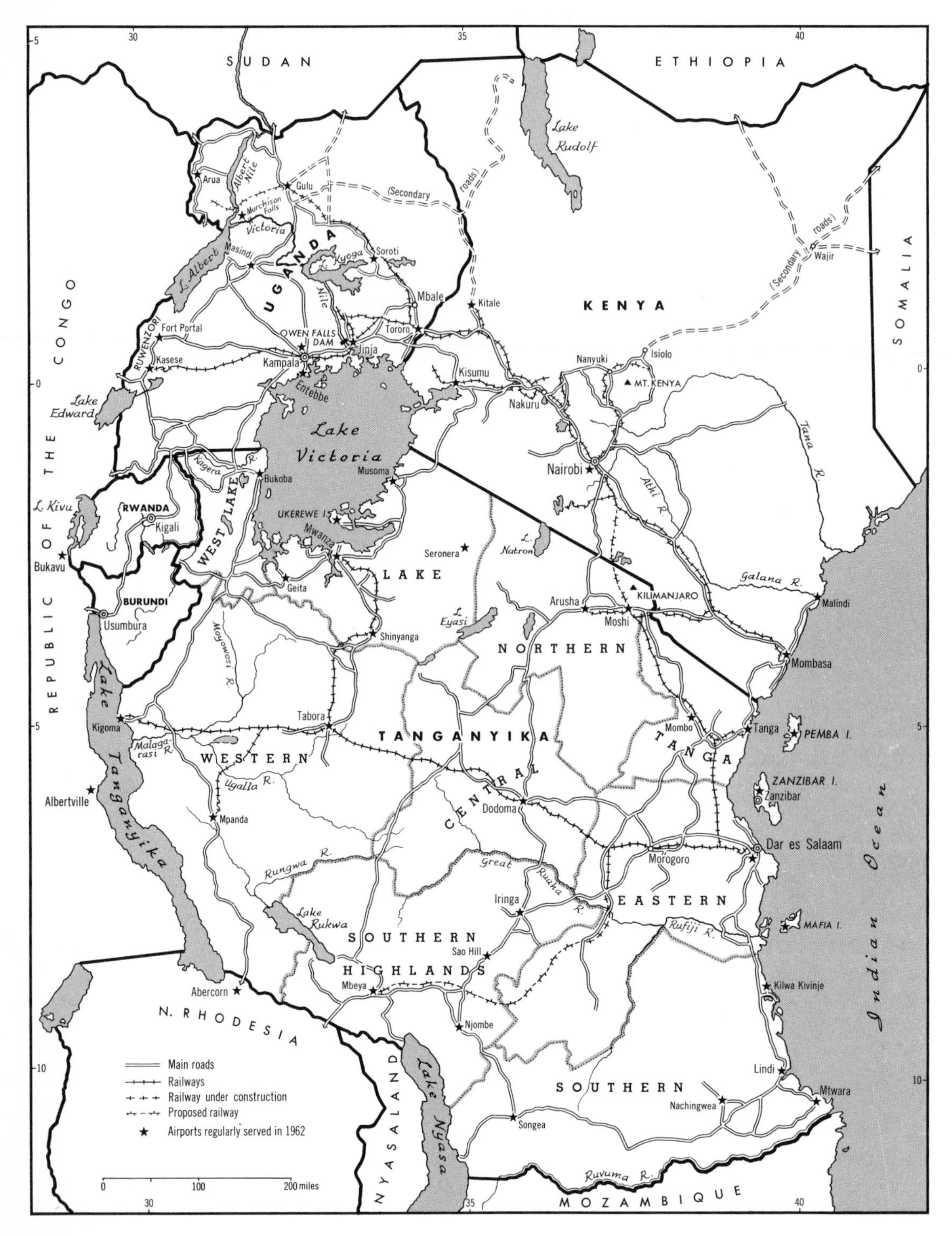

Map 71. Transport in East Africa

to its harbor is via a 1.2-mile-wide opening in the longshore coral shelf.

The original harbor is now used only by dhows and small coastal craft. The first deep-water berths were started in 1921 on the south side of the island on Kilindini ("place of the deep waters") Harbor. Construction was inadequate to handle increased traffic in postwar years, which were marked by severe congestion. Several development programs have greatly extended capacity. The Kilindini Wharf now totals 5,290 feet and can accommodate nine vessels drawing up to 33 feet. All available space having been utilized along the south of Mombasa Island, a newer extension has been constructed on the mainland at Kipevu where a 2,400-foot quay will berth four ships when the second two have been equipped. Other facilities at Mombasa include the Shimanzi oil jetty for bulk unloading, a 1,280-foot lighterage wharf, a coal wharf, and small dockyards. Construction of a large new refinery and storage depot at Changamwe, behind Kipevu, has led to the construction of a new crude oil berth, while a channel is being prepared through Kilindini Harbor to permit access of 65,000-ton tankers. With a traffic of about 3.12 million tons in 1962, Mombasa ranks as third leading port of the Indian Ocean coast of Africa.

Mombasa is the seaward terminus of the Kenya-Uganda portion of the East African Railways (Map 71). Originally called the Uganda Railway and built in part to assist in the military and religious penetration of Uganda, the line has played an unusually potent role in the modern history of East Africa. It was first thought that Kenya was largely an impediment on the route to Uganda, but with the recognition that good, unoccupied lands were available in the Kenya Highlands and particularly with the desire of providing some kind of traffic which would make the railroad a paying proposition, the British and local governments decided to set aside land and to solicit European settlers to move into regions served by the railway. The repercussions of this original and rather innocent policy have obviously been enormous.

Construction of the line began in 1896 and by 1899 it had been carried inland 330 miles to Nairobi, which was nothing but a railway camp. By 1901 the line reached Kisumu on Lake Victoria, whence boat services were run to Entebbe and Port Bell, which was connected by a short line to Kampala. It was not until 1931 that the railway reached Kampala, and in postwar years it has been extended to Kasese near the Congo border, a total of 1,081 miles from Mombasa. The route traversed is a difficult one, rising to 8,000 feet west of Nairobi, descending to 6,000 feet in the Rift Valley only to go up again to over 9,000 feet at Timboroa and 6,878 feet at Eldoret, then to descend to less than 4,000 feet at Kampala. In 1961, a 45-mile cutoff from Jinja to Bukonte reduced the distance of most Uganda stations to the coast by 40 miles.

Aerial view of Mombasa, Kenya
The new Kipevu quay is in the foreground; the older berths lie across Kilindini Harbor on Mombasa Island. Mombasa handles the vast bulk of overseas traffic for Kenya and Uganda as well as some traffic for Tanganyika.

Aerial view of Nairobi, Kenya
The marshaling yard and workshops of the East African Railways and Harbours. Nairobi began as a railway camp when the line to Uganda was being constructed.

A number of branch lines have been constructed over the years, including a 91-mile line to Lake Magadi to serve the soda extraction works, a 146-mile line from Nairobi to Nanyuki at the foot of Mt. Kenya, and a 172-mile branch in Uganda from Tororo to Soroti and Lira to serve the eastern cotton producing area. This last branch is now being extended 60 miles to Gulu and approval has been given for its further extension to Pakwach on the Nile and to Okollo 30 miles beyond the river, 40 miles from Arua, and 30 miles from the Congo border. The great expense of constructing a bridge across the Nile may result in postponement of the West Nile extension. There is, finally, a connection with the Northern Line in Tanganyika from Voi to Kahe, built during World War I to facilitate military operations into what was then German East Africa. Consideration has been given recently to making a direct connection between Moshi in northern Tanganyika and Nairobi, which would permit a reasonably direct route also with Dar es Salaam.

Freight tonnages handled on the Kenya-Uganda line have increased from 190,000 in 1913–14 to 898,000 in 1930, 2,475,000 in 1950, and about 3,345,000 tons in 1961. There have been marked improvements in power equipment, rolling stock, signalization, and terminal facilities, particularly in the last decade. Just as the Kenya-Uganda line handles the giant share of freight traffic on the whole East African system, so does Mombasa account for a large share of port tonnages, about 72 percent in 1961.

The northern port of Tanganyika is Tanga, a lighterage port situated on the south shore of Tanga Bay on a low coral platform protected from the ocean by a headland almost enclosing the harbor. Its improved lighterage quays total 1,250 feet in length, and there is adequate space for vessels lying offshore. It handled 225,000 tons in 1961, the largest part of which was sisal. Tanga is the terminus of a line which was constructed by the Germans to Moshi from 1893 to 1911 and extended by the British in 1927–29 to Arusha, 273 miles from Tanga. It serves not only the leading sisal area of East Africa but also the productive coffee regions of Mts. Kilimanjaro and Meru, though much of the traffic of those areas moves via Mombasa.

Dar es Salaam is the capital and the leading port of Tanganyika. Possessing only a fair natural harbor, it had only lighterage facilities until 1956 when the $12.6 million Princess Margaret Quay was opened, offering a 1,824-foot space for three ocean-going vessels of 30-foot draught; one of its berths was built as a Belbase to handle transit traffic for Congo and Ruanda-Urundi. The lighterage quay has also been extended to 1,929 feet and a new jetty for bulk oil movements has been constructed.

Dar es Salaam replaced the historic ports of Bagamoyo and Kilwa Kisiwani when Germany entered East Africa. Its trade increased only slowly, however, largely because its domestic hinterland is not particularly rich, but also because Belgian policies restricted movement eastward despite the markedly shorter distances from eastern Congo and Ruanda-Urundi. In the interwar years, Tanganyika did not receive as great attention as many other African areas, partly because there was some fear that it might eventually revert to Germany. With the greatly increased interest focused upon it in postwar years, however, the traffic of Dar es Salaam increased rapidly to far beyond the capacity for which the facilities had been constructed leading to severe congestion for extended periods. With the improvements noted above, however, it is now adequately equipped, and handled 955,512 tons in 1959 and 743,000 tons in 1961.

Dar es Salaam is the terminus of the Central Tanganyikan Railway. The main line, completed in 1914, runs across the country 780 miles to Kigoma, following the former Arab slave route most of the way. In 1928 a 236-mile branch was completed to Mwanza on Lake Victoria and in 1950 a 131-mile line was laid to serve the Mpanda mineral complex. Operating at a deficit in prewar years because of the low traffic offering, the Central Railway was incapable of meeting the greatly increased demands placed upon it in postwar years, contributing to the congestion at Dar. Despite considerable improvements, particularly after the first postwar decade, it is still not up to the standards of the Kenya-Uganda line. In 1959 work began on a branch from Kilosa to Mikumi to serve the potentially productive Kilombero Valley, and this is now being extended to Kidatu. It may later be carried to Mbeya and the Southern Highlands and eventually be connected with a line from Northern Rhodesia. In 1962 a 117-mile connection from Ruvu on the Central line to Manyusi on the Tanga line was completed, connecting all the East African lines except the Southern Line for the first time.

In southern Tanganyika there are two minor ports. Lindi is a lighterage port whose harbor can be entered by 17-foot draught vessels. Possessing a landing jetty and seven piers belonging to sisal estates, it handled 38,000 tons in 1961. Mtwara, variously dubbed as the "Cinderella" and "Peanut" port, was equipped with a 1,248-foot deepwater quay with 32-foot alongside depths as the port for large tonnages

Aerial view of Dar es Salaam, Tanganyika
Dar is the capital and leading port of the country. The Princess Margaret Quay, in the middle ground, provided the port's first deepwater berths in 1956.

expected to come from one of the Tanganyika Groundnut Scheme areas. The collapse of that scheme left Mtwara with a substantial surplus capacity. Situated in a spacious and sheltered bay extending over an area of four square miles, it handled 77,000 tons in 1961.

A rail line from Mtwara was also constructed for the Groundnut Scheme, extending 132 miles to Nachingwea with a branch to Masasi. It had been hoped that it would be handling 250,000 tons by 1961; actually, it handled 21,000 tons and ran a deficit of $686,000. A decision was made, therefore, to close the line and to improve the region's roads to handle such traffic as there is.

The railway mileage in East Africa now totals about 3,335 miles, all meter gauge. All the railways and harbors come under the East Africa Railways and Harbour Authority, one of the services of EACSO, which also handles lake and river services and road feeder lines in some areas. One of the largest employers in East Africa, the Railways and Harbour Authority had 1,509 European and 49,691 African and Asian employees at the end of 1961. While the possession of three lines and more than the usual branch lines might appear to be satisfactory, there is in fact only 1 mile of railway for each 191 square miles of land area in East Africa, and several potentially productive areas are still so remote that their ability to trade with the world is severely restricted.

Railroads still form the backbone of the transport complex, but roads form most of the ribs and are the only means of surface transport available over most of the area. The Railways and Harbour Authority operates regular road services over about 2,685 route miles, often feeding into the rail lines. Most East African roads are unpaved gravel and dirt roads. Uganda has a comparatively excellent system, including the longest stretch of macadam highway in East Africa. Its relatively very favorable road net, particularly the pattern of convergence on Kampala, is explained in part by the fact that the Saza (County) chiefs were required to keep a road to the capital in good shape, in part by the rather good surface made from the natural surface material so long as traffic is not too heavy. Certain restrictions have prevented road services from competing freely with the railways, but truck traffic has expanded sufficiently in recent years to require the railways to reduce tariffs on higher-rated freight in order to meet the competition.

Inland waterways are of some significance in East Africa, particularly Lake Victoria. The Railways and Harbour Authority operates 6,311 miles of river and lake services which handled 331,000 tons in 1961, 71 percent on Lake Victoria, 16 percent on Lake Kioga, 11 percent on Lake Albert and the Nile River, and 2 percent on Lake Tanganyika. Kisumu in Kenya is the main port on Lake Victoria, though the improvement of Mwanza has made that Tanganyikan lake port more competitive than it formerly was. In addition to the steamers operated on the main lakes, canoe traffic is often important for local movement.

R.M.S. Victoria *leaving Kenya's Lake Victoria port of Kisumu*

About 235,000 tons of cargo yearly are handled by the regularly scheduled services on Lake Victoria.

ZANZIBAR

Zanzibar has physical similarities with the coastal belt, which makes it appropriate to examine the islands briefly at this point. The country consists of three islands. Zanzibar, the main island, is about 53 miles long and 24 miles wide and has an area of 640 square miles. It lies about 22 miles from the nearest coastal point. The other important island is Pemba, lying about 25 miles to the northeast; it measures about 42 by 14 miles and has an area of 380 square miles. The third is Latham Island, a small, rocky, uninhabited island half-covered with guano lying 40 miles southeast of Zanzibar.

Zanzibar and Pemba are generally rather flat, though the latter has some small, steep hills and valleys. The bulk of the population of Zanzibar lives in the somewhat higher, better-soiled west, the east being a coral plain. Precipitation is relatively high and reliable, averaging about 60 inches on Zanzibar and 73 inches on Pemba. The climate permits a wide variety of crops, but little advantage has been taken of the opportunity for diversification.

Zanzibar and Pemba are inhabited by a motley of peoples. No accurate estimate is available of the make-up, the 1958 census being considered unreliable in its coverage by race. The 1948 census is regarded as accurate for that time but cannot be extrapolated to 1963 without distinct reservations. It showed a population divided as follows: "African," 75.8 percent; Arab, 16.9 percent; Indian, 5.7 percent; Comorian, 1.2 percent; Goan, 0.2 percent; European, 0.1 percent; and Somali and other, 0.1 percent. The over-all population density is about 311 per square mile.

The category "African" includes two main groups which are socially quite distinct: (1) the Shirazi, who claim to be indigenous and to have part-Persian ancestry, and (2) the mainland Africans, who may be descended from slaves brought to the islands by the Arabs or may be more recent migrants. The Shirazi are Muslims and outnumber the mainland Africans by about 3 to 1; the latter are mostly Christians or pagans. Africans are mainly peasant farmers, fishermen, and laborers.

The second largest group are Arabs, who include some descendants of mixed Arab-African unions. Omani Arabs are the chief landowning class; other Arabs are civil servants and merchants. Friction among the several racial groups has sometimes been severe, as was revealed in the election of 1961 and subsequent political conferences.

A cluster of clove blossoms freshly plucked from a clove tree on Zanzibar

Zanzibar and Pemba account for about 80 percent of the world's clove exports.

Once notorious as a slave center, Zanzibar is most noted as the world's greatest producer of cloves. Cloves were introduced to Zanzibar in 1818 from Mauritius and, by order of the sultan, were planted in a ratio of three clove trees for every coconut tree, the penalty for noncompliance being forfeiture of one's estate. Today, about 6 million clove trees occupy about 80,000 acres on the two islands, permitting the country to export about 80 percent of the world's cloves. Nearly all the trees are owned by Arabs, who originally resided on their estates to oversee the work of their slaves; later many moved to Zanzibar Town, entrusting the management of their estates to Swahili overseers. Being poor businessmen, many of them became heavily indebted to Indian moneylenders, but Indian influence in the clove trade was drastically reduced by 1934 under a series of decrees.

About 80 percent of the cloves are produced on Pemba, though Zanzibar Town is still the chief selling and shipping point and the site of the factory which distills oil of cloves, used principally in the preparation of vanillin. The clove industry was seriously threatened in postwar years by two plant diseases. "Die back," caused by a fungal wound parasite, was controlled by careful picking and trimming. "Sudden death" disease killed about half the trees on Zanzibar; no solution was found for it, but it now appears to have passed off in some mysterious cyclical pattern. More recently the industry has been severely hurt by restrictions on imports into two of its main markets, India and Indonesia, while since 1955 there has also been a small but persistent downtrend in prices. From 1957 to 1961 sales of cloves declined from 264,000 to 188,000 centals and their value from $8.7 million to $5.0 million. In 1963 India made a welcome return to the market, but cloves do not appear to have a promising future, since world consumption has increased very little in past decades.

The second major crop of Zanzibar is copra, processed in several oil factories. Coconut trees are planted on about 120,000 acres and are the dominant feature of most landscapes. Copra, coconut oil, oil cake, coconuts, and coir fibers accounted for 19.8 percent of exports in 1961; while this is a significant amount it does not represent a very good return per acre.

Cloves and coconuts both illustrate the major

A coconut nursery on Zanzibar
Coconut products are the second main export of Zanzibar and Pemba.

economic keynote of Zanzibar today—stagnancy.[2] Evidence of stagnancy includes declining clove exports; the fact that coconut and chili exports were higher in 1916 than 1959; a very low rate of investment; a level of re-exports about one-fifth the level of 50 years ago; and a general failure to adopt modern techniques. Only the low-value by-product coir fiber, used in making mattresses, has seen a marked increase in production in recent years. In face of a population increase which has been estimated at from 1 to 1.5 percent, but which may be considerably higher in view of the nearly complete eradication of malaria and lowered incidence of other diseases, this record augurs very poorly for the future.

The main explanation for stagnancy appears to be a general lack of economic initiative. This may, in turn, be explained by a variety of factors: (1) the high dependence on cloves, which give an adequate return in good years; (2) the relative ease of producing many of the major crops such as cloves, coconuts, cassava, and bananas; (3) the social structure, including the prevalence of absentee landlords who consider farm work degrading; (4) a tenurial system which discourages initiative; (5) the excessively small size of many holdings; (6) heavy indebtedness and lack of resources to cover the cost of improvements; (7) political uncertainties; (8) poor marketing facilities except for the main export crops; (9) the small market available on the islands themselves; (10) ignorance of proper farming methods or of the possibilities of switching to other crops; and (11) failure of the government to disseminate the information collected in its first-rate agricultural research station or to have an adequate extension service.

Zanzibar and Pemba stand in contrast with many African countries where physical conditions, remoteness, and lack of scientific understanding inhibit agricultural advance. These readily accessible islands have superior physical assets, including a high proportion of cultivable land, a good infrastructure, and ecological suitability for a wide variety of high-value crops. The question here is not what to do, but how to encourage the inhabitants to do it. With respect to present crops there has been failure to use disease-resistant, better-yielding varieties of cassava made available by the Department of Agriculture, careless picking of cloves, careless preparation and drying of copra, and a failure to replace old trees.

There has also been a general reluctance to plant new crops. Field trials at the research station indicate that a variety of high-value crops could be grown to the benefit of the producer. Chilies, which now account for 0.6 percent of exports, give a very high return, and are soil tolerant. Ylang-ylang, a flower from which perfume essence is extracted, nutmeg, and coffee all could be very profitable. Derris, whose root provides one of the few natural insect repellents, could do well. A CD and W scheme supported the production of limes on about 300 acres; neglect led to successive losses, but it is believed that limes, lime juice, and lime oil could be very remunerative if properly produced.

[2] The authors of an economic survey of Zanzibar write: "Our principal impression of the Protectorate is of a stagnant economy." P. Selwyn and T. Y. Watson, *Report on the Economic Development of the Zanzibar Protectorate* (Zanzibar, Government Printer, 1962), p. 1.

Cocoa has not done well as yet, but it is considered that it has promise if a suitable variety can be found.

Although there is a substantial animal population on the islands, the animals are not well cared for or properly integrated with tillage agriculture. An effort is being made to promote ranching on the eastern, open coral plains, which are now inadequately utilized. Fishing employs about 9,000 people on a rather erratic basis. The catch averages less than one ton per fisherman per year and could be greatly increased. A commercial concern exports lobster, while there is also a small export of shells.

Zanzibar Town possesses one of the world's more romantic names, which doubtless contributes to its significance as a tourist attraction. One of the oldest settlements south of the Sahara, it does have unusual charm and interest. Its population is now about 65,000. Its lighterage port is a port of call for many steamers plying the East African lanes, while dhows carried products to and from the islands valued at a yearly average of $4.65 million in the period 1956 to 1960.

THE LOW EASTERN PLATEAU

Returning to the continent, the next major region consists of a series of low plateaus varying in elevation from 300 to 2,000 feet and rising from the coastal belt by a series of scarps best marked at the Kenya-Uganda border and in the south. On the west it is bounded by the plateaus and mountains associated with the Eastern Rift System, to which the outlying volcanic peaks of Mt. Kilimanjaro and Mt. Meru and the Usambara Mountains more properly belong. It has something of an hourglass shape with the waist occurring near the border of the two countries. The somewhat higher Masai Steppe, almost ringed by higher lands, may be considered as an outlier of this region.

NORTHERN FRONTIER PROVINCE, KENYA. The upper part of the hourglass covers almost all of northern Kenya. The Northern Frontier Province occupies about half of that country; it contains about 600,000 people or less than 6 per square mile. Much of it is a volcanic desert, almost uninhabitable; most of it is an arid thornbush plain supporting only a small nomadic population. There are no Europeans in the area with the exception of a few district officers and missionaries and almost nothing comes out of the region on a commercial basis. The northern border cuts across the tribal lands of the primitive, pagan Borans and of the Somalis. Intertribal skirmishes are not uncommon, while Somali desire to unite with Somalia has required special police action on several occasions in recent years.

In this section of Kenya locusts may be expected to appear in about half of a long run of years; sometimes they are destructive for four or five years in a row. Kenya's northern neighbors are also plagued by locusts, Ethiopia having lost crops in 1958 estimated capable of feeding a million people for a year. Somalia, too, suffers periodically and severely. East Africa has played a key role in control of the locusts not only in its own area but through its contribution to the international locust control campaigns. Great progress has been made in the past decade in fighting this voracious insect, no important locust swarms having entered East Africa for years. Mist sprays containing highly diluted poison are now capable of killing swarms extending over broad areas. But the desert locust is extremely difficult to exterminate because it migrates over tremendous distances and breeds wherever rain occurs. Swarms may contain 75 billion locusts and blacken the sky when in motion. Only the sustained vigilance of the Desert Locust Control Organization of East Africa and quick response to developing swarms prevent locusts from wreaking far more serious destruction than they do.

SOUTHEASTERN KENYA. This section becomes somewhat better watered, but it is still moderately dry and precipitation is very unreliable. Again, it is sparsely inhabited except along the banks of the Tana and in the Teita Hills. Two large game reserves, Tsavo and Amboseli, are situated in this area, having a considerable actual and very great potential value for the Kenya tourist industry.

MASAILAND. Straddling the Kenya-Tanganyika border is the Masai Reserve, occupying about 15,000 square miles in the former, and 26,000 square miles in the latter country. While the reserve is not confined entirely to the low eastern plateau region, most of it is a vast, grass- and bush-covered plain receiving only about 25 inches of rain yearly. The Masai at one time roamed over and dominated a much greater area, including part of what has been until recently the White Highlands. Left very much alone in the past, they have preserved their cattle culture with very few concessions to modernist forces. The Masai are among the richest of African tribes in cattle, and also have several million sheep and goats. They eat little meat, subsisting on milk and on blood drawn from the living cattle, while the women cultivate a little corn and sugar.

It has been particularly difficult to persuade the aristocratic Masai to sell their cattle, even to prevent overgrazing. Their intransigence has presented a dilemma to government not unique to this tribe. If left alone, they may destroy by improper use a large area of satisfactory grazing lands, yet it is difficult to apply the direction required to carry out a good scientific land use.

A Masai herding cattle in southern Kenya
The Masai, who practice a rigid cattle culture, are frequently cited as exemplifying the difficulties associated with achieving economic advance among African graziers.

Efforts are being made, however, to implement a Masai Development Plan, which involves provision for more and better water, a crucial need; improved pasturage and pasture management; clearing of tsetse bush; and provision of areas for expansion.

In recent years there have been some signs of a willingness to change. Masai are appearing in schools in still small but increasing numbers. Milk is sold to the Chagga on Mt. Kilimanjaro. Arrangements have been made for them to participate in and benefit from the preservation of portions of their reserves as game parks. And there has been a greater concern with the political scene, a beginning to the realization that a haughty isolation has reduced their relative power in a world dominated by modern forces.

SOUTHEASTERN TANGANYIKA. Much of the widening low plateau in southern Tanganyika is covered by *miombo* woodlands, baobabs, and thickets. Most of it is tsetse-ridden and sparsely populated and has only been the subject of development plans in recent years.

The Makonde Plateau represents something of an exception to these generalizations. Covering about 1,200 square miles in the southeast just inland from the coastal belt, it is densely populated by the industrious Makonde people who produce cassava and cashew nuts as cash crops. A considerable handicap on the plateau has been the almost complete absence of water sources, requiring as much as a twelve-mile daily walk down to sources in the valley below and back to the plateau. This situation has been greatly improved by the recent installation of a pump scheme which raises spring water 1,300 feet to the living areas; the $840,000 expenditure is to be repaid gradually by a cess on the use of water.

The Tanganyika Groundnut Scheme. Two of the three areas originally selected for the Tanganyika Groundnut Scheme are situated in the eastern plateau region, one at Kongwa, just north of Mpwapwa on the Central Tanganyika Railway and at the southern end of the Masai Steppe, and one at Nachingwea in the far south at the end of the former Southern Line (Map 74). The Groundnut Scheme was started in 1947 with the goal of developing some 3.2 million acres in East and Central Africa for mechanical cultivation of peanuts, largely to help meet what was then considered to be a long-range shortage of vegetable oils in Britain. Initial work was carried out by the United Africa Company, but the whole scheme came under the Overseas Food Corporation (OFC), a British government company, in 1948. The three largest areas were to be in Tanganyika. Doubtless the large scale of the proposal reflected the wartime psychology that if something were big enough it was bound to succeed. The problems, however, turned out to be far greater than the Corporation had envisaged and the scheme had largely failed by 1949 and was eventually written off at a loss of some $72.8 million.

The difficulties encountered were legend and included the following:

(1) Most of the machinery employed was not adequate, particularly the Sherman tanks which were converted to bulldozers and tractors.

(2) No satisfactory method was found to clear the bush, and it took four times as long and cost ten times as much as had been estimated to clear a given area. The use of chains in 1950 proved to be somewhat more effective than earlier techniques.

(3) Great difficulties were encountered in harvesting peanuts from the sun-baked earth. In one area, an estimated 181 pounds per acre had to be left in the ground, and harvesting costs everywhere exceeded the original estimates.

(4) Animal and plant disease pests were encountered. Wild pigs ate the peanuts in one area; giraffes became entangled in the telephone lines; rosette and black spot diseases attacked the peanuts.

(5) The climatic conditions proved to be inadequate. The first area, Kongwa, was the least attractive agriculturally, its only advantage being its nearness to the Central Railway. It was perhaps unfortunate that the first few years were unusually dry, but the evidence suggests that trouble could have been expected sooner or later and periodically because of inadequate precipitation.

(6) Overhead expenses, such as expenses for housing, provision of amenities, rail and port facilities, also were much higher than had been anticipated.

(7) Labor problems resulted from a very rapid turnover among African employees, running as high as 10 percent per month, and from the fact that most of the European supervisors had never had experience in Africa.

(8) Finally, management was not as efficient as it should have been and changes that were necessitated contributed to a general loss of morale among what had been an eager if ill-informed group.

Several lessons have been taught by the rather spectacular failure of the Groundnut Scheme. First, of course, no such large-scale adventure should have been undertaken without adequate knowledge of the area and without a period of pilot operations. Rainfall records were completely inadequate; soil studies were largely lacking.[3] Nor was advantage taken of the knowledge of local experts who knew the environment far better than the OFC people. Second, it demonstrated quite clearly the intransigent character of much of the African environment, revealing that techniques applicable in middle latitudes are not necessarily appropriate elsewhere. It is somewhat ironic that thousands of tons of peanuts were available in northern Nigeria, which could have met the vegetable oils shortage if a sum considerably smaller than that invested in the Groundnut Scheme had been applied to improving the Nigerian transport system.

In 1950 the scheme was placed on an experimental basis and in 1954 the operation was converted into a corporation, half-British and

[3] F. Fraser Darling labels the Groundnut Scheme "a megalomaniac pipe-dream advanced in ignorance of the plainest facts about African soils." "Wildlife Husbandry in Africa," *Science* (November, 1960), p. 124.

half-Tanganyikan, under the name Tanganyika Agricultural Corporation. Field operations were confined to small portions of the original acreages, and a variety of experiments were initiated. It is now allotted money on the basis of a three-year development plan, a portion being earmarked for profitable ranch schemes and the rest for experimental settlement schemes. These schemes are not all in the old Groundnut Scheme areas.

One of the ranches is at Kongwa. Here about 10,330 cattle are maintained, and some success has been had with Boran–Aberdeen Angus crosses. A second ranch is at Ruvu, 50 miles inland from Dar es Salaam. The developed portion of a 78,000-acre holding supports about 6,000 head of cattle, and it is likely that it will later be used as a holding and fattening ground. A third ranch is at Mkata, southeast of Handeni; it had about 8,100 cattle and a net profit of $9,200 in 1961. The market demand is sufficient to absorb a considerably larger turnout than now exists.

Kongwa is also the site of a settlement scheme for African tenant farmers. Low precipitation is a major handicap, and mechanical operations in the earlier years proved excessively costly. The number of tenants has been increased to 113 with a crop area of 960 acres; while the tilled area has declined, the number of tenant-owned cattle has increased. Among the crops, peanuts have done reasonably well but experiments with castor beans have been disappointing.

Nachingwea now has 19 tenants in a settlement scheme, all but one of whom made a profit in 1960–61. Cropping an average of about 14 acres, with peanuts, corn, soya, and sesame, they realized an average profit of $191.38. Nachingwea also has about 14 so-called production farms with a total of 12,393 acres under crops and 1,385 cattle. A variety of crops has been grown, with soya beans covering about 60 percent of the cropped area, peanuts 15 percent, cashew nuts 13 percent, and sorghum, corn, and sesame the remaining 12 percent. While these farms operated at a loss, it is hoped that the new varieties of soya and peanuts adapted to the unfavorable conditions of the area will eventually permit successful yields. The third area of the Groundnut Scheme was at Urambo in the Central Province; it will be noted later.

It would be unfair to say that the Groundnut Scheme had been a total failure. The semiarid areas in which the transferred undertakings are being carried on are representative of a tremendous area of East and Central Africa. If some method can be found to utilize them properly the potential contribution would be most significant. The schemes also have value in the fight against the tsetse fly. By eliminating the bush, the breeding grounds of the fly are removed; if the cleared regions can be gradually expanded, man will have ousted the fly from considerable areas. Furthermore, even the negative information gained is valuable in the better understanding of the potentialities of vast sections of the continent.

Irrigation Schemes. For the future, perhaps the greatest possibility for upgrading areas within the eastern plateau region is the control of its rivers and the extension of irrigation farming. This will not be an easy matter, however, because of the cost of storage dams required, and because not all of the floodplain soils are rich alluvials. There is some representation of saline soils and some soils are mixed with sands and gravels.

In Kenya, small areas have been brought under irrigation in the Tana Valley. The FAO, under a grant of $1.58 million made by the U.N. Special Fund and the Kenya government, is conducting a three-year survey of the irrigation potential of the lower Tana, which is probably the most suitable region in Kenya for large-scale irrigation. It has been estimated that about 300,000 acres might be developed to provide a livelihood for 65,000–75,000 families and a gross production of $67.2 million, of which $42 million would come from cotton.

Encouraging success is reported from the Mwea-Tebere irrigation scheme 20 miles southeast of Embu on a tributary of the Tana, where about 1,250 families are developing two 7,500-acre blocks. Yields of rice after less than three years of operation have averaged over two tons per acre. Essentially a settlement scheme, this project had cost about $2 million to 1962 and made its first profit in 1961. Each tenant farms four acres including one of rice on a rigid schedule set by the manager. Ground is prepared by machine, the tenants performing all other tasks and paying for the water on a graduating scale as their plots are developed. Problems have included occasional attacks by quelea-quelea birds, some incidence of bilharzia, sale of a substantial part of the harvest on the black market, and sharing of plots and houses on a scale which prohibits the tenant from realizing the full advantages of the scheme.

The best opportunities for extending irrigation in Tanganyika also exist on the rivers flowing across the eastern low plateaus: the Pangani, the Kilombero-Great Ruaha-Rufiji system, and the Ruvumu, which forms the border with Mozambique. The Pangani Basin, draining from the high-rainfall Kilimanjaro-Meru area, is well situated to relieve population pressure in that region, but its waters are somewhat saline and much of its plain is doubtfully suitable for irrigation. An area of 200,000 to 300,000 acres is estimated to be subject to control in the Pangani Basin in three floodplain areas. Two 1,000-acre pilot projects were recommended in a survey completed in 1962 and French banks were reported prepared to finance one to the extent of $112,000. Soils are said to be good for rice, corn, sorghum, sesame, and, in some places, cotton. At present, the absence of flood control makes irrigation impossible.

By all odds the greatest possibilities exist in the Rufiji Basin of Tanganyika, which covers about a fifth of that country. It has been the subject of a four-year joint FAO-Tanganyikan study made at a cost of $2,035,600, which concluded that large-scale development would require an expenditure of $392 million, but that no less than 1.5 million acres could be irrigated. Achievement of such a level is regarded as a long-run goal; two stages of development costing $36.8 million were recommended for completion by 1970.

Attention in the Rufiji Basin has thus far been focused upon a pilot project at Mbarali and upon a private sugar plantation in the Kilombero Valley. The Mbarali project, which is run by the Tanganyika Agricultural Corporation, involves irrigation by 1964 of 2,000 acres split into 5-acre holdings. In 1962 canals had been completed to 1,200 acres and experiments had begun with corn, beans, and peanuts, the last giving very good yields, while crop trials with cotton were beginning.

The Kilombero has a basin of about 2,000 square miles at an average elevation of 800 feet. Studies were made there in 1928, 1951-52, and under the Rufiji Basin Survey, and it has been estimated that 400,000 to 600,000 acres of good land are available for irrigation. In 1960 the Kilombero Valley Sugar Company launched operations, planning to have 3,750 acres under cultivation by the end of 1962 and to produce 20,000 tons of sugar by 1963. Developments proceeded so satisfactorily that a decision was made in 1962 to bring yearly production to 35,000 tons as rapidly as possible. The capital requirements of $6.4 million for a 7,000-acre estate and sugar factory were provided by a Dutch corporation with experience in the Far East, by the IFC, the CDC, and the Standard Bank of South Africa. Shares were also offered to the public with preference given to applications from Tanganyika residents, and about 1,000 African shareholders have participated in the financing. The estate is situated in the Ulanga District with the mill at the north of the valley on the Great Ruaha River. About 3,000 Africans are employed on the plantation and in the factory, while local residents are being encouraged to produce sugar on a smallholder basis. Production of sugar justified construction of a branch line from the Central Railway which, it is hoped, will stimulate other developments in the valley.

It has been estimated that a total of about 4 million acres are available for irrigation in

Tanganyika, which is less than 2 percent of the whole country. Most of this is located in the east, and pressure on many of the existing good lands of Tanganyika, plus the desire to increase production of commercial crops, creates a desire to press forward with development. The high capital requirements, however, mean that it will take many years before any substantial acreage can be brought under control. The IBRD has suggested that the government should plan to be developing irrigated land at the rate of about 25,000 acres a year by 1969–70.

Farming of Wildlife. One possible solution for more effective use of the dry, tsetse-ridden low plateau as well as for many other parts of Africa might be the use of wild animals as an economic resource. A systematic offtake of wild animals for supply of meat and skins has many possible advantages. It would accomplish the following:

(1) Permit utilizing otherwise very unattractive economic areas where rain-growing is difficult if not impossible and cattle grazing precluded by their susceptibility to sleeping sickness.

(2) Utilize a resource whose value is greater than that of museum pieces.

(3) Help to preserve the very valuable tourist industry by reversing the trend toward extermination of wild animals. Tourism is the fourth largest source of revenue in Kenya. In 1962 a record number of tourists visited East Africa, spending an estimated $21.7 million, including $13.4 million in Kenya.

(4) Permit improving the protein intake in areas where there is a marked deficiency. By avoiding the inhibitions of the cattle culturalists as far as meat consumption is concerned, their diet, too, would be improved. Most wild animals have edible meat, much being as good as or better than beef. It is claimed that yields can be two to six times those from cattle per unit area because of more rapid maturing and more efficient grazing.

(5) Take advantage of the ability of wild animals to subsist on low-grade vegetation, a mixed animal population making more effective use of marginal grazing land than domestic cattle.

(6) Help in soil conservation because a variety of animals with differing feeding habits tends to keep the vegetation in balance and because there would be no cultural problem in keeping numbers in line with the carrying capacity of an area. Areas used for or opened to cattle grazing, on the other hand, are very likely to be overgrazed.

These arguments appear overwhelming but can be very misleading, particularly because of the emotional appeal attached to the preservation of the magnificent wildlife of Africa. But the key question is, is it economic? There are many difficulties associated with the farming of wild animals, including inaccessibility of many of the potentially interesting areas, the expense of hunting the animals or of directing them to convenient places for slaughtering, the problems of transportation, refrigeration, and preservation of game meat, lack of acceptability of some species, and conflict with other land uses in some areas. An over-all problem is lack of detailed knowledge. Many of the claimed advantages and disadvantages have never been carefully tested or measured. Some experience in rotating game with cattle on a four-year cycle has been had in East and South Africa and a few individuals have attempted to raise wild animals on a regular ranching basis. But scientific study is required and is beginning to be applied in a few localities. Conservators at Ngorongoro Crater, for example, are studying the use of the area by both cattle and wild animals, and hippopotamuses are being slaughtered on a regular basis on the shore of Lake Edward where a surplus has led to soil erosion and destruction of vegetation upon which other animals depend. The Nuffield Foundation is supporting a biological and actuarial assessment of the project that will not be completed for several years. But it is estimated that at least 500 tons of meat can be harvested annually from local hippopotamus herds. No problem has been faced in disposing of the meat, which is delivered to local markets by truck within hours of slaughtering.

THE EASTERN HIGHLANDS AND RIFT VALLEY SYSTEM: KENYA

This third main region is a highly complex mountain, plateau, and rift valley belt. The Eastern Rift Valley may be considered as the axis of the system. About 30 to 40 but sometimes 60 miles wide, it is well marked in Kenya and northern Tanganyika, less well so to the south. The valley, which is often at a very considerable elevation itself, is typically bordered on both sides by mountains and plateau blocks or horsts, while volcanic cones lie within it, are superimposed on the adjacent plateaus, or stand off at some distance as outliers of the system.

In southwestern Kenya are the Kenya Highlands. The floor of the Rift Valley, which lies at an elevation of 1,280 feet at Lake Rudolf in the north of the country, rises to 7,000 feet near Naivasha and falls again to 1,973 feet at Lake Magadi and 2,000 feet at Lake Natron on the Tanganyikan border. The valley is studded with volcanoes, none of those in Kenya being active. East of the Rift Valley in Kenya is the Aberdare Range, rising to about 13,000 feet; on the west the Mau Escarpment has elevations up to 10,000 feet. Lying to the northwest of the highland area and straddling the Uganda border is Mt. Elgon, 14,178 feet, while east of the Aberdares Mt. Kenya rises to 17,040 feet. The Rift System, with escarpments ranging up to 4,000 feet, has an important effect on transportation; its formidability is compounded by the fact that the plateaus bordering the valley are typically at their highest adjacent to the rift.

The involved topography of this whole highland region results in notable variety in climate, vegetation, and land use patterns, changes or successions often occurring over very short distances. But this region contains much of the quality area of Kenya, much of its most densely populated districts, the major areas of white settlement, and the vast bulk of areas producing the high-value crop exports of the country. Factors favoring the Highlands include their

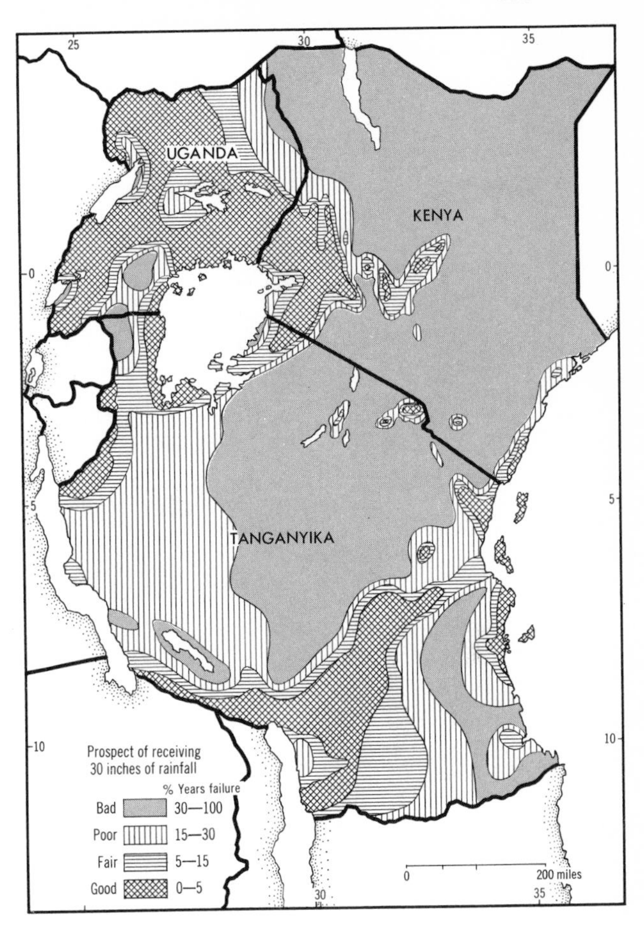

Map 72. Rainfall reliability in East Africa

greater and more certain precipitation, the general absence of the tsetse fly on the higher lands, the presence of better than average soils including some excellent volcanics, and the amelioration of temperatures and humidities, which was particularly attractive for European settlement. There are serious problems of population pressure in some sections, and soil erosion is also sometimes severe. It is estimated that 600,000 acres are in need of protection in Kenya, mostly in the highland area.

Map 72, adapted from the East African High Commission Report, clearly demonstrates the main climatic attribute of the highland zone, while Map 43 shows the favorable position with respect to the tsetse fly. The fly is not found over 6,000 feet nor in the more arid regions.

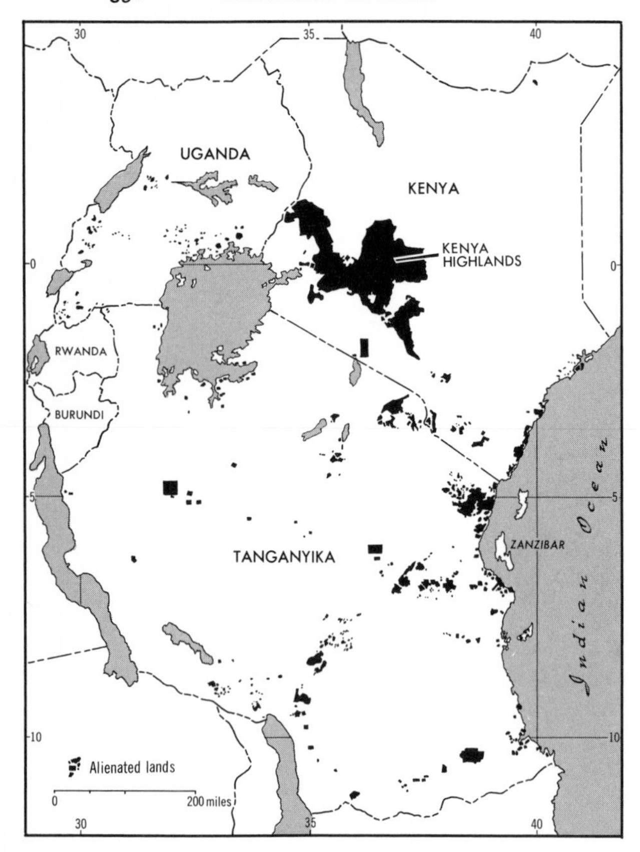

Map 73. Lands leased by or alienated to non-Africans in East Africa, 1960

Because of the major distinctions between European and African settlement patterns, it is appropriate to discuss them separately.

AGRICULTURE IN THE FORMER "WHITE HIGHLANDS." The areas of leased or alienated lands in East Africa are depicted on Map 73, showing the large, irregular zone usually called the "White Highlands" in Kenya. The whole question of reservation of lands on racial, or for that matter on tribal, lines is fraught with all kinds of moral, social, economic, and political problems. The existence of a small number of white settlers on a large block of land in Kenya was a root cause of the ugly Mau Mau revolt and has continued to exacerbate racial relations in that country. Lord Hailey summarized the position as follows in the revised *African Survey*, page 686:

Whatever other reasons may exist for the estimate by Africans of the .... government, the fact that .... Native lands passed permanently into the hands of non-Natives will always tend to colour any judgement that is formed of it. Nor will the emotion which this fact arouses permit of an objective assessment of the value which the use of the land by non-Natives has brought to the African community, however obvious this may be to the outside world.

Alienated land in Kenya totaled 12,850 square miles or 5.71 percent of the total in 1959; the alienated lands of the White Highlands totaled 11,763 square miles or 5.15 percent of the total. These figures are only of limited value, the question of quality of the lands being more important. About 41,600 square miles of Kenya are classified as having high potential, based upon an average yearly precipitation of 30 inches or over; of this total, about 7,560 square miles or 18.2 percent was in alienated lands, almost all in the White Highlands. Subtracting the forest and other national reserve land from the total of lands receiving 30 inches or more of rain, alienated lands accounted for 24.9 percent of the total available arable land.

The numbers of people involved is also a crucial factor. The total number of European and Asian farms (almost entirely European) totaled 1,890 in 1938, about 3,000 in 1952, and 3,609 in 1960. About 5,200 full-time and 1,700 part-time Europeans were employed in 1960 on these farms, which had a total area of 7,280,000 acres. This meant that fewer than 1 percent of the farmers in Kenya held about one fifth of the good farm land. Taken alone, this statement may also be somewhat misleading, because it refers primarily to ownership, not to employment. In 1959, 250,430 Africans, or 42 percent

An aerial view of European farming in the Rongai area of Nakuru District

About 1¼ million acres of former European lands are now being subdivided for African settlement.

of the total employed labor force, were engaged in agriculture. The African employees on European farms totaled 277,700 in 1960 and 254,600 in 1961. The total number of Africans residing on European farms is probably about a million. Most African laborers work on "ticket" contracts, under which the employee agrees to complete 30 days of work in a period not to exceed 36 days in return for a set wage plus food allowances, each day's work being entered on the ticket. There is also a squatter or resident labor system, under which the African contracts to work for a period of 1 to 5 years or to work for a given number of days in the year in return for the right to reside, cultivate small plots, and sometimes to keep livestock on the employer's farm. Security problems during the Mau Mau revolt caused a substantial reduction in numbers of squatters, but in mid-1959 there were still 26,000 so classified. In 1961, 18,500 "resident laborers" cultivated 80,900 acres and kept 10,700 cattle and 66,400 sheep and goats on European farms.

The history of Kenya has been replete with land disputes. The Kikuyu and other tribes place an entirely different interpretation to that of European observers on the course of events, and the evidence suggests that both parties are, to a considerable degree, correct, the conflicts having arisen from misunderstandings and different interpretations of certain legal forms. The European position is summarized by Corfield,[4] who states that "claims to alleged Kikuyu lands alienated for European settlement were the main springs of all Kikuyu political movements, subversive or otherwise, which culminated in Mau Mau," that their intense attachment to the land stemmed from the livelihood it afforded, the insurance it provided for old age, and the belief that it was the dwelling place of tribal spirits. But that the alienated lands were "stolen," as claimed by the Kikuyu, was "autosuggestion, self-deception and the propagation of patent lies."

[4] Secretary of State for the Colonies, *Historical Survey of the Origins and Growth of Mau Mau*, by F. D. Corfield (London, Her Majesty's Stationery Office, May, 1960).

Shortly before European arrival, the Kikuyu had suffered four major epidemics, causing the tribe to retreat to the Fort Hall area. When European settlement started in 1902, the "Highlands" were on the fringe of Kikuyu country, there was much vacant land, and land grants to the Europeans were made only with land not being used by Africans. But the population equilibrium of the 1890s did not last, and, as pressure increased, demands for releasing land from the reserved areas increased and land became an ever more emotional political issue.

Europeans also point to the fact that (1) the Kikuyu only consider land between 5,000 and 7,500 feet and with rainfall minima of 30–40 inches suitable for occupation and therefore that there are lands available for development within their own areas; (2) Kikuyu reserves are as good as, if not better than, land in the White Highlands; and (3) sixteen African populated districts contain land which could be more extensively as well as intensively farmed.

Africans have maintained, on the other hand, that tribal law would not permit the outright sale of land but could only authorize its use for a specific period. They were often particularly critical of holdings in the White Highlands that were either unused or only partly used. With respect to this point, a government report of December, 1960, stated that only 23,936 acres

Kikuyu children picking pyrethrum on a European farm at Molo, Kenya

Many European farms specialize in high-value cash crops. Kenya produces about two thirds of the world's pyrethrum, the extract of which is used in insect repellents.

of Kenya's European-farmed area was undeveloped and 193,708 acres underdeveloped, but that much of both categories was suitable only for pastoralism and required provision of water for that. Of the 38,831 acres unalienated in the former White Highlands, only 200 acres were considered to be suitable for agriculture and 24,718 were classified as appropriate for grazing.

But whatever the exact position may have been, historically, statistically, legally, or otherwise, it was politically impossible to continue to reserve large areas for persons of a minority race, particularly when there was considerable land pressure on adjacent tribal lands. And in November, 1960, racial criteria were finally eliminated as a feature of the White Highlands, which thereafter became a part of the Scheduled Areas.

European farms accounted for a gross production of $106 million in 1960, the last year in which figures were kept on a racial basis, while total African production was estimated at $134 million. European farms have accounted for about four fifths of the total value of exports of the country. The White Highlands were, in fact, the center of economic activity, including many of the more important modern cities and much of the industrial development. Even if the farms could be divided without effect upon urban activities, it is obvious that too drastic a change could almost literally destroy the Kenyan economy. It has been calculated, for example, that the gross production per unit area on good arable European land is 3½ times that on comparable African lands.

Table 26. European and Asian landholdings in Kenya, 1960 and 1961

Acreage	Percent of holdings		Percent of area	
	1960	*1961*	*1960*	*1961*
20–499	32.8	34.0	2.8	2.9
500–999	22.1	20.9	7.6	7.1
1,000–1,999	23.6	37.4	15.5	34.3
2,000–4,999	13.9		19.1	
5,000–49,999	7.3	7.5	44.3	44.2
50,000 and over	.3	.3	10.7	11.5
	100.0	100.1	100.0	100.0

Total acreage all farms, 1960—7,731,000
Average acreage all farms, 1960—2,142
Total number of holdings, 1960—3,609[a]
1961—3,642[b]

Sources: Colony and Protectorate of Kenya, Economics and Statistics Division, *Agricultural Census, 1961, Scheduled Areas and Coastal Strip* (Nairobi, 1962), p. 5, and *Kenya European and Asian Agricultural Census, 1960* (Nairobi, 1961), p. 3.

[a]Of the total, all but 129 were in the highlands.
[b]Includes a few Africans coming into the Scheduled Areas,

European farms may be classified in several ways. The broadest division would be into the comparatively large plantation-type farms producing much of the sisal, tea, and coffee, the generally smaller mixed farms raising livestock and various field crops, though some also grow coffee, and the ranching operations, which include most of the very large holdings. Table 26 shows the distribution of European and Asian holdings by size. These may very roughly be divided according to major interest as follows: small arable farms ranging from about 20 to 200 acres, 500; large arable farms averaging about 1,100 to 1,200 acres, 580; mixed farms averaging about 1,800 acres, 1,740; and pastoral farms averaging about 3,600 acres, 780. The last category, however, includes 10 farms exceeding 50,000 acres in size.

Table 27 shows the acreage devoted to crops and livestock in the Scheduled Areas of Kenya in 1961, when almost all holdings remained in European hands, together with the gross farm revenue by crop or livestock origin. As may be seen, crops cover about 18 percent of the utilized areas or 15.5 percent of the total area of the Scheduled Areas, but account for about 74 percent of the gross farm revenue, which totaled $101 million in 1961. Livestock products accounted for 26 percent of gross revenue; in 1961 there were 392,700 dairy cattle, 549,100 beef cattle, and 580,200 sheep on these farms.

Beef cattle ranches are found chiefly in the Laikipia District. The main interest of European dairy farms is producing milk for the towns, but increasing quantities of butter are being exported. A meat canning factory at Athi River produced about 8.5 million cans in 1960, much of which was exported to Mauritius. The problems of maintaining quality herds in this area are, of course, very great, particularly in the lower-lying dryer areas, but farmers have succeeded in maintaining European herds for some years with relative freedom from disease. There is a considerable difference of opinion regarding the comparative merits of keeping high-bred cattle or upgrading indigenous livestock. European breeds have a better milk record and are considerably heavier, but losses are relatively high. Native cattle are smaller and give less milk but are not so susceptible to disease and require far less care. Some farmers have been quite successful in selective breeding the local Boran.

The history of crop production in the White Highlands is replete with recurrent disasters. Many fortunes have been lost, regained, and lost again. But over the years a great deal has been learned about the vagaries of climate and the capacity of various soils, while new strains have been developed suited to the ecology of the area. Nonetheless, plant and animal diseases and insect pests are a problem requiring constant vigilance and continuing study in the various research and experimental stations. Crop and livestock emphases vary greatly from one area to another depending upon precipitation, soils, elevation, aspect of slope, and other factors. The major crops are briefly examined in a later section.

Table 27. Acreage and gross revenue of major crops and of livestock, Scheduled Areas, Kenya, 1961

Land use	*Acreage*		*Gross farm revenue*	
	In thousand acres	*Percent of total*	*In thousand $ U.S.*	*Percent of total*
Crops	1,200	18.1	74,595	74.2
Permanent crops				
Coffee	74.3	1.1	21,302	21.2
Tea	39.6	0.6	13,234	13.2
Sisal	272.1	4.1	11,502	11.4
Fruit	8.1	0.1	1,568	1.6
Wattle and coconuts	84.9	1.3	1,084	1.1
Temporary crops				
Cereals				
Wheat	225.8	3.4	7,580	7.5
Corn	158.3	2.4	5,026	5.0
Barley	34.6	0.5	750	0.7
Oats	24.7	0.4	216	0.2
Other temporary crops				
Pyrethrum	48.5	0.7	5,985	5.9
Sugar	43.9	0.7	2,870	2.9
Sunflower and linseed	13.6	0.2	174	0.2
Others	...	...	3,206	3.2
Uncultivated meadows and pastures	5,446.8	81.9		
Livestock			13,812	13.7
Dairy products			12,202	12.1
Total acreage above uses	6,646.8	100		
Total gross farm revenue			$100,609	100

Source: Colony and Protectorate of Kenya, Economics and Statistics Division, *Agricultural Census, 1961, Scheduled Areas and Coastal Strip* (Nairobi 1962).
... = Not available.

AFRICAN SETTLEMENT PROGRAM. On January 1, 1961, a program to purchase European farms and make them available by sale to Africans was inaugurated amidst suspicion and apprehension on the part of both Europeans and Africans, the former fearing that they would never receive full value for their farms, the latter fearful of conflicting tribal demands. The first program was unrealistic in the amount requested as down payment from Africans and was rejected by the owners because the cash payment did not permit them to liquidate their investment, finance a start elsewhere, or have assurance that they would be paid the remainder due them if an African government came to power. After some confusion, renegotiation, administrative overhaul, and other changes, the program began to be intensively applied toward the end of 1962.

The settlement program is divided into four parts:

(1) The Assisted Owner or Yeoman Scheme. Designed for men with some capital of their own and some farming experience, this scheme calls for the settlement of about 1,800 families on farms ranging from about 50 to 200 acres. Thus far it has been relatively unsuccessful, mainly because not enough Africans have the capital required. Yeoman farmers are required to pay 10 percent of the value of the land to be acquired in cash plus assets in cash or in kind equal to a third of the capital value of the farm. Facilities for loans are available from the Ministry of Land Settlement.

(2) The Low-Density Small-holder Scheme. Providing for the settlement of about 6,000 families on holdings of about 15 acres of high potential land, this scheme is also intended for men with some farming experience and working capital of their own. It is intended that participants in this scheme will earn $70 to $112 after paying loan repayment charges and providing for their own subsistence.

(3) The High-Density Small-holder Scheme. Under this scheme it is planned to settle some 12,000 families a year for five years on plots averaging 14 acres which need not be of high potential. The men need not have capital or farming experience, but it is hoped that incomes will start at about $28 yearly and reach $70 yearly after a few years. Consideration has been given to increasing the average size of holdings to ensure a more economic operation. The high-density scheme involves at present a total of 1 million acres, about a fifth being allocated each year. Individual farms would typically have two thirds of their area in grass for livestock, one sixth in cash crops, and one sixth in subsistence crops such as corn and beans.

(4) Emergency Schemes. These new schemes have mostly involved forest clearance and are designed to provide landless and destitute families some opportunity to produce subsistence crops.

In the year to July, 1963, about 221 European farms were to be purchased for all schemes, their owners being paid in full an average of about $24 per acre or a total of about $6.84 million. The total cost for purchase and development of 1,200,000 acres for all schemes is estimated at almost $84 million. Full compensation if all European holdings were purchased is estimated at $336–378 million, or at $124–156 million if plantations and ranches were excluded.

The African or other participant in the land settlement program is assisted in varying degrees to acquire a holding, usually by extension of long-term loans, while he is also to be aided by agricultural experts whose costs are paid by the government as part of the administrative costs of the whole scheme. The funds made available thus far have come mainly from the United Kingdom in the form of both loans and grants. The IBRD has made an $8.4 million loan available for the Assisted Owner Scheme, while West Germany has provided funds for development loans to high-density small holders at 3½ percent interest rather than the 6½ percent required on all other loans within the settlement schemes.

In the first years, purchases were concentrated (1) in the so-called sore thumb areas, land which had been under contention between the tribes and government; (2) along the edges of densely populated reserves; and (3) on a number of compassionate cases, that is, farms owned by elderly people, widows, and infirm people.

Only time can tell whether the land settlement schemes will work successfully, but that they face a multitude of objections and problems is unquestioned. These include:

(1) Disposition of present African residents on purchased farms. In some cases more people are supported on the European farm than will be after it is split into small holdings, resulting in a net loss as far as absorption of population is concerned. In other cases, Africans who have resided on a given farm for decades will be dispossessed and without any obvious means of support. In still other cases, the Ministry of Land Settlement has found that there were many more squatters than had been reported and that it had "bought a problem of illegal squatters and illegal fields of maize" rather than a farm which could readily be subdivided and prepared for new settlers. While numerous individual injustices are likely to occur in a large-scale settlement program, there is no question that a considerably larger total number of Africans will reside on subdivided areas than on the predecessor farms.

(2) Economic size of holding. Government officials concerned primarily with the political aspects of the land problem are understandably concerned with getting a large number of Africans on the land as rapidly as possible. This led, at first, to the adoption of holdings as small as 5 acres each. Technical agricultural experts have succeeded in making the point that a larger holding is required if any adequate return is to be expected, but the high-density schemes may still be too small. It is also obvious that the expected cash returns of most participants will be closer to those of a peasant than of a true farmer. If returns prove inadequate to permit payment of annual carrying charges, the whole program will be seriously endangered.

(3) Problems of transition. Converting from a going farm operation on a large farm to a series of small, largely subsistent, mixed holdings may obviously prove very difficult to achieve smoothly. The government wishes to take over land "in good heart and in the farming cycle," but this is not always possible. About 60 European farms had been abandoned up to the end of 1962, some being occupied thereafter by squatters and others running down before the government had taken them over for subdivision. Some operations, such as dairying with high-bred European cows, simply cannot be broken down successfully. Some farmers in Uganda are taking advantage of conditions in Kenya to purchase good quality livestock. In any case there has been a decline in both beef and dairy cattle on European farms in recent years. It has been suggested that some European farms be converted to cooperative farms, thus permitting maintenance of some unified operations, but the government has apparently felt that conditions do not now permit experimenting with a variety of organizational arrangements. It is hoped, however, that a later settlement scheme will permit experimentation with a variety of approaches.

(4) Problems of supervision and technical assistance. To be successful, the settlement scheme requires careful layout of the subdivided farm, technical assistance to the new proprietor, a certain amount of farm training, especially for those with little or no previous experience, and maintenance of the necessary scientific and advisory services after settlement has been completed. These services require a fairly substantial staff of trained agricultural workers and fairly heavy government budgetary support. But it is very doubtful whether an independent government will be prepared to allocate the needed funds and perhaps even more doubtful whether there will be enough skilled advisers and technicians. The element of time is obviously a factor of immense importance; it will take time to convert the Scheduled Areas from a rather productive European-type farming economy to thousands of small holdings without severe losses in farming efficiency and economic output. The IBRD recommended in its 1961 survey that prime consideration be given to measures aimed at retaining Kenya's non-African

farmers, specialist civil servants, and professional and technical people. African leaders have also stated that Kenya's economy would be paralyzed unless the settlement schemes were carried out carefully. But responsible politicians may not be able to withstand the demand for accelerated action on the part of a land-hungry, independent populace. Settlement has been held up in places by Kikuyu agitators claiming that land would be distributed free upon independence. Failure to continue control over the Land Freedom Army, a kind of latter-day Mau Mau, could obviously have a disastrous effect on the whole program and on Kenya's entire economic future.

(5) Problem of cash crops. A severe handicap both to the settlement programs in former European areas and to the consolidation program in African farming areas, which has developed only in the past few years, is that of finding a suitable cash crop to permit a high return on the small part of the farm devoted to other than subsistence production. Indeed, this threatens the success of both operations. Coffee and pyrethrum are perhaps the most appropriate, but Kenya's adherence to the International Coffee Agreement precludes any large-scale increase in production, while pyrethrum is also grown on a quota basis to prevent overproduction.

(6) The problem of productivity. An over-all problem which is affected by a multitude of factors is whether the fragmented farms will maintain or increase the productivity of the former European farm. This is a key question for a country with a precarious budget and a heavy physical trade imbalance. The estimate that output on good land has been $3\frac{1}{2}$ times more valuable on European than on African land suggests that at least a temporary setback must be expected. But the comparison is somewhat misleading because of the relatively small production of cash crops on African farms in the past. As they produce more of such high-value crops as coffee, tea, pyrethrum, market vegetables, and fruit the comparison should prove much more favorable.

It is impossible to predict with any sureness the outcome of the land settlement program. Not only is it difficult to foresee how successful African administrators will be in maintaining an evolutionary pace, but it is also difficult to know what percentage of European farmers will be prepared to continue in Kenya. Those who would object to remaining under any African government have probably already left. Many have offered their farms for sale, but some have either refused to sell (and this has been their prerogative) or have moved into the heart of the European area. In late 1962, about a third of all Europeans seemed to be planning to leave Kenya and a third appeared equally determined to remain. Both extremes predicted that they would be joined by the middle third.

Certain predictions may be hazarded, however. It appears likely that the big tea and sisal plantations will be kept intact because of their great importance to exports and in providing agricultural employment. Pyrethrum production can probably be shifted to African farms with relative ease. Productive livestock activities depending upon exotic breeds and skilled management will be most severely affected. Pressure may develop to switch as much coffee production as possible from European producers to African producers; indeed such a move might go a long way to save the settlement and consolidation programs from failure.

AFRICAN FARMING IN THE HIGHLANDS. The Highlands are also the major area of African farming in Kenya, accounting for about three quarters of agricultural production from African areas. Considerable differences exist among the various tribal groups and according to local physical conditions, but until recently most Africans were operating subsistence holdings and producing very little for commercial sale. Food supply in some areas was precarious; malpractices were leading to depletion of the soil and to outright erosion. Holdings were often grossly fragmented, the average number of separated plots in Kikuyuland having been 8 for a 4-acre holding. Extreme cases include a 5-acre farm split into 39 noncontiguous plots and a

Kikuyu land before land consolidation
Fragmentation of land holdings contributed to malpractices which in turn were degrading the land or leading to outright soil erosion.

Kikuyu land near Kiambu after land consolidation
The multifaceted Swynnerton Plan has literally remade the landscape over broad areas.

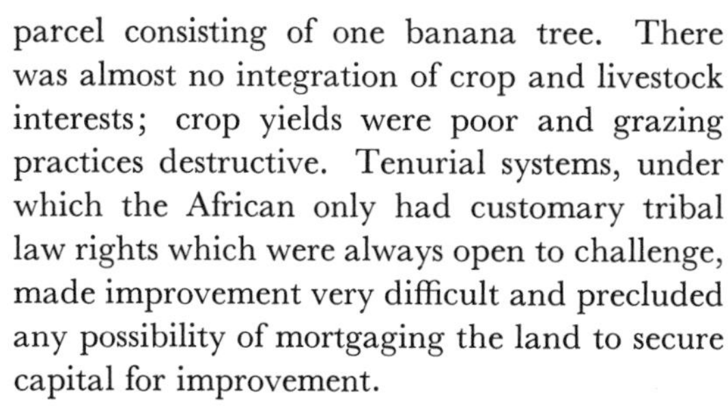

parcel consisting of one banana tree. There was almost no integration of crop and livestock interests; crop yields were poor and grazing practices destructive. Tenurial systems, under which the African only had customary tribal law rights which were always open to challenge, made improvement very difficult and precluded any possibility of mortgaging the land to secure capital for improvement.

In 1945 the African Land Development Organization was established with a $12 million allocation for a ten-year program to recondition African areas. This proved entirely inadequate to the task, and in 1954, at the height of the Mau Mau disturbances, a new five-year "Plan to Intensify the Development of African Agriculture in Kenya" was adopted, usually called the Swynnerton Plan after its author, R. J. M. Swynnerton, then Assistant Director of Agriculture. Under this program, $29.4 million was to be expended, somewhat over half being contributed by the United Kingdom, on remaking the agricultural landscape in African areas. In 1960 the IBRD made a loan of $5.6 million to Kenya to cover about a third of the cost of continuing the plan for three years.

The plan involves consolidation of holdings, introduction of individual tenure, farm planning, expansion of cash crop production, provision of rural water supplies, a livestock program, and various reclamation schemes. Some consolidation had taken place on African initiative, particularly among the Kipsigis but also in a few Kikuyu areas. But consolidation and assignment of individual tenure, which is a keystone of the whole plan, and farm planning on the scale envisaged have made this probably the most important agricultural development scheme in Africa.

Consolidation and registration of title is an involved process from adjudication of existent holdings, through layout and assignment of new holdings, marking of new boundaries and delineating them by planted hedges, preparation of maps from aerial photographs recording the new farms, to final registration of individual land claims. The rapidity with which it was accomplished in the Central Province may be partly attributed to the conditions existing during the emergency, particularly to the practice of agglomerating villages for security reasons. But the program could not have moved forward as rapidly as it did, both there and elsewhere, without the willing support of the local inhabitants. The complaint that consolidation was enforced against the will of the African does not bear examination because almost all steps are handled or approved by African committees. It has also been general practice not to institute the program until the overwhelming majority of residents have requested it. In fact, the government has been criticized by non-Kikuyu tribes for not introducing the plan in their areas as rapidly as in Kikuyuland, while visiting Africans from Uganda and Tanganyika have returned to their countries to request that similar programs be applied there.

Introduction of individual tenure is only one part of the plan. Of equal importance are the planning of farm layouts and a continuing effort to promote improved farm practices. Planned layouts require agricultural experts to arrange areas so that erosion-control practices may be implemented, water will be available, farms will be divided as equitably as possible as far as soil and other factors of productivity are concerned, and access roads will be available. Since the goal is that livestock be integrated with crop farming and that cash crops be introduced on each farm, agricultural education and information programs must be accelerated and must be backed up by continuous research. At the other end of the cycle, farmers must be assisted in marketing their output, while rigid selection is required to maintain quality standards.

Provisional figures showing the progress of the Swynnerton Plan up to June 30, 1962, as far as enclosure and registration of title are concerned, are given below.

The plan has, of course, had numerous problems and certain failures. Corruption among junior clerks in the Fort Hall District in 1960 required backtracking at considerable expense. Agitators have interfered with committees working in a few adjudication sections. More serious has been the failure on the part of Africans to register change of titles, while there is some indication that fragmentation has been renewed despite legal restriction on subdividing land below a certain size. For the future, there are some of the same worries that apply to the settlement program in the Scheduled Areas: Will it be possible to maintain the staff of technicians and advisers required to sustain the plan and improve farming practices? and will the quality standards continue to be applied? It must also be noted that the consolidation program results in there being a group of legally landless people; efforts must, therefore, be made to create opportunities elsewhere. For a time, settlement in the Scheduled Areas can meet this need, but more important in the long run is the need to develop employment opportunities in industry and other sectors of the economy. Finally, it may be asked if it would not be appropriate to give thought to conscious limitation of population growth. Average holdings of less than 10 acres are not particularly impressive in the face of a rapidly rising population.

Despite these present and potential dangers, the Swynnerton Plan stands as one of the most dynamic programs in Africa for agricultural betterment. It has literally remolded vast areas of the Kenya Highlands, and has provided a base for moving toward a more efficient and more economic farming system. A measure of its economic impact is seen in the increase in the value of produce marketed from African areas, which grew from $9.88 million in 1953 to $14.59 million in 1957 and $29.20 million in 1961.

Progress of the Swynnerton Plan as of June 30, 1962

	Enclosure		*Registration*	
	Acres	*Farms*	*Acres*	*Farms*
Central Province	1,063,919	200,473	991,285	183,266
Rift Valley Province	598,534	25,510	89,244	3,106
Nyanza Province	728,353	66,932	nil	nil
Total	2,390,806	292,915	1,080,529	186,372

Source: Figures provided by the Kenya Department of Agriculture.

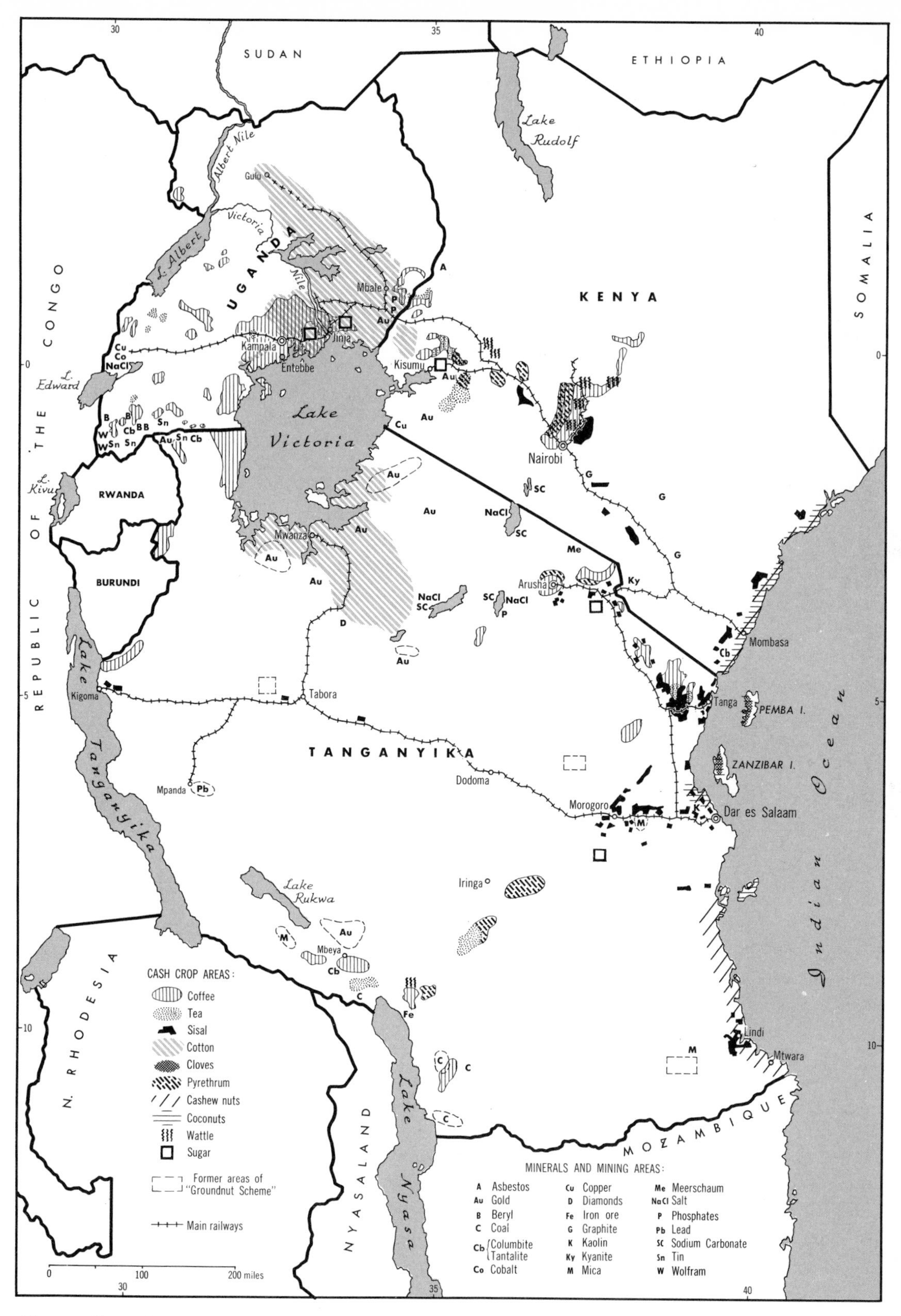

Map 74. Economic map of East Africa

Picking coffee on a European estate
Coffee ranks first among cash crops in Kenya. Production from African farms has increased rapidly since 1956.

In the last year, permanent crops accounted for about 40 percent of the total value (coffee alone for 27 percent of the total), surplus food crops (cereals, vegetables, etc.) for 22 percent, temporary industrial crops (pyrethrum, cotton, castor and other oil seeds, tobacco and sugar) for 14 percent, and livestock and dairy products for 22 percent of the total. These figures apply to all African farming in Kenya, but it is the Highlands that have had the most significant progress and that account for the lion's share of African cash crop production.

CASH CROPS FROM THE KENYA HIGHLANDS. Coffee now ranks as the most important cash crop in Kenya. Over half is grown within a radius of 50 miles north and northwest of Nairobi between elevations of 5,000 and 6,000 feet, at which elevation coffee is the cash crop par excellence (Map 74). Until 1956, Europeans produced almost all Kenya coffee exports; in fact, Africans were discouraged from producing coffee ostensibly to ensure the maintenance of quality standards. In 1946 there were 786 licensed African growers with about 318 acres in coffee; the acreage had been increased to 1,500 in 1953 when the crop first started to become of real importance. By the end of 1961, 110,000 registered African growers had planted 44,000 acres to coffee and in that year Africans accounted for about 23.5 percent of total coffee production. The average price received per ton was $1,008 as compared to $846 per ton from the Scheduled Areas, indicating that the quality was among the highest in the world and that selection was being carefully enforced. The lower price received for European-grown coffees also reflected in part the older age of their plantings.

African producers are served by 138 cooperative societies, each operating one or more coffee factories. An example of a large successful cooperative is the Ngandori Coffee Cooperative Union, formed in 1946 with 81 members. In 1962 it had 3,772 members, 5 modern coffee factories, and 2 large nurseries and was arranging for coffee spraying by teams of employees. In that year it marketed 496 tons of clean coffee valued at about $532,000; while the average receipts of members were $141 some earned as much as $2,800.

The acreage devoted to coffee on European farms was less in 1962 at 74,300 acres than it had been in 1938 when 93,722 acres were planted to coffee. Acreage was reduced by retirement of marginal lands, but production was considerably above prewar levels, being about 25,315 tons of the total Kenya production of 33,084 tons. The Kenya Planters' Cooperative Union handles about 80 percent of Kenya coffee and has about 950 members, including most of the African cooperatives. Its annual turnover of about $25 million makes it by far the biggest cooperative in Commonwealth Africa. West Germany, the United States, and the United Kingdom are the chief markets for Kenya coffee.

Kenya coffee is high-grade arabica, commanding premium prices on the world market. As noted earlier, opportunities for further expansion are restricted by world surplus production and Kenya's adherence to the International Coffee Agreement.

Tea ranks second to coffee among export

crops. Its production has been strongly concentrated around Kericho, where there are 97 registered growers and 30 factories employing about 38,000 persons of all races. The area around Limuru is also important. Tea needs an acid soil, well-distributed and heavy precipitation, and does best between 6,000 and 7,200 feet. The big push in Kenya tea production which has made that country the largest tea producer in Africa came during the 1950s and after its withdrawal from the International Tea Agreement. In 1927 Kenya exported less than 1 ton; in 1947 exports totaled 4,279 tons valued at $3.6 million; and in 1962 exports were 10,900 tons valued at $9.3 million. About a fifth of production is marketed domestically. At present, about 45,000 acres are devoted to tea, approximately 85 percent in large tea estates many of which are in the Brooke-Bond Group. Tea has characteristically been a plantation crop because of the high investment required and the greater degree of technical skill needed. A tea factory for a 1,200-acre estate may cost about $340,000, while 3,500 tea plants are planted per acre; by contrast, an acre in coffee requires only 540 plants, and only about 300 acres will justify erection of an $8,400 factory.

Kikuyu picking tea leaves at a tea estate near Limuru, Kenya
Most tea now comes from large company-owned plantations, but plans call for increasing the acreage of African tea holdings to 11,055 by 1966.

Africans were first encouraged to produce tea under a 1949 peasant tea-growing scheme, but the most spectacular increase came after 1959 under a program financed by a loan of $2.52 million from CDC, one of $594,000 from West Germany, and smaller allotments from Kenya. From 1,541 acres in 1959, the acreage in African holdings has increased to 6,400 in 1962 and is expected to reach about 11,055 acres by 1966. At that time it is hoped that a program requiring an investment of $7.14 million will permit increasing African acreage in tea to 23,250 acres. Tea may, therefore, become the number-one export of Kenya within the decade. Over 10,000 Africans now grow tea, particularly in the areas adjacent to existent plantations. Tea has also done well in the high areas along the forest edge of Mt. Kenya and the Aberdares and elsewhere where it is too cold to produce coffee. Africans tend to give individual attention to each bush and are aided by local agricultural supervisors and tea factories, while a Tea Research Institute at Timbilil Forest near Kericho is concerned with scientific problems pertaining to the whole industry.

Pyrethrum production and prices have fluctuated widely in postwar years but the trend has been generally favorable since 1955. It was

Kikuyu women being paid for picking pyrethrum on the Andersen Farm near Kijabe

thought for a time that synthetic insecticides might destroy its markets, but the ability of insects to acquire immunity to DDT has apparently given it a new lease on life. It has the advantage of being harmless to warm-blooded animals; it can be mixed in small ratios and still retain its effectiveness; and there is no evidence that insects have been able to adjust to it. Kenya produces about two thirds of the world's pyrethrum; output has increased from 1,500 tons in 1948 to 4,500 tons in 1958–59 and 10,800 tons in 1961–62. At that time, about 1,000 Europeans and 32,000 Africans were engaged in producing pyrethrum, Africans accounting for about 27.7 percent of output as compared with 10 percent in 1958. The African farmers are organized into 56 cooperatives run by African officers. In addition to the independent growers, probably about 130,000 agricultural workers get their main livelihood from pyrethrum.

Pyrethrum ranks fourth among Kenya exports. Kenya's main competitors are Japan, Yugoslavia, Tanganyika, and Congo; the African producers have the advantage that flowers yield a crop almost eight months of the year. Pyrethrum grows best at high elevations and is seldom found below 7,000 feet. Cultivation requires considerable care, but the work of picking is light and the crop can yield exceptional returns.

Some years ago, almost all output of pyrethrum was shipped as baled flowers, but the trend has been toward local extraction to reduce wastage, save on the cost of transport, and net greater return to the country. About 90 percent is sold as extract, the remainder in flower or powder form. There are now two extraction plants, one at Nairobi and one at Nakuru, the latter having been expanded in 1961.

Other cash crops produced in the Kenya Highlands include tobacco, grown mostly for local consumption; wheat, a major European cash crop grown at elevations from 7,000 to 9,000 feet; corn, usually produced in surplus by both Europeans and Africans; sisal; pineapples and other fruit; and barley, originally grown as feed for pigs, but now used for malt in brewing.

Kenya's main forests are also in the Highlands above about 5,000 feet. There is a great variety of indigenous species, but most are slow-growing so emphasis has been placed on plantings of conifers, eucalyptus, and wattle. Wattle production has been mainly an African peasant industry, though there has been a large increase in acreage by European growers. Wattle has the advantages of being a good cash crop, acting as a soil restorer, and supplying a useful wood. African production is important at higher elevations on the Aberdare slopes and on lower Mt. Kenya; the Uasin Gishu District, where the main extract factory is found at Eldoret, produces most of the European wattle. Wattle sales have suffered somewhat in recent years from competition with synthetic substitutes and with quebracho from Argentina, as well as from reduced demand following upon the use of synthetic material in shoe soles.

THE EASTERN HIGHLANDS AND RIFT VALLEY SYSTEM: TANGANYIKA

The eastern mountain system of Tanganyika is considerably more complex than that of Kenya and not so easily oriented to the Rift Valley. The *Handbook of Tanganyika*[5] notes the resemblance of its conformation to a huge number 9, the loop encircling the Masai Steppe, the tail forming a great arc to the north of Lake Nyasa. This includes the knot of mountains near Lake Nyasa where the two rift systems coalesce, usually called the Southern Highlands. Moving north the figure includes the Udzungwa or Iringa Highlands, the Rubeho Mts., the Uluguru Mts. (offset somewhat to the east), the Nguru Mts., the Handeni Hills, the Usambara Mts., the Pare Mts., and Mt. Kilimanjaro, at 19,340 ft. the highest point in Africa. Swinging around the loop we encounter Mt. Meru, the series of volcanic masses such as Loolmalasin and Ngorongoro, the Mbulu and Kondoa Ranges, the Gôgoland Hills, and the Mpwapwa Mts.

[5] John P. Moffett, ed., *Handbook of Tanganyika*, 2d ed. (Dar es Salaam, Government Printer, 1958), p. 2.

In Tanganyika the Rift Valley is well marked to about the central railway; Lakes Natron and Manyara lie within it, with Lake Eyasi in a short westward bifurcation. It is well marked again in the south, particularly along the Lake Nyasa axis. As in Kenya, the eastern highlands have a great variety of climate, vegetation, and land use patterns, and contain many of the most densely populated parts of the country, the major areas of white settlement, and the most important producing areas for high-value export crops.

AGRICULTURE IN THE TANGANYIKAN HIGHLANDS. In Tanganyika, a total of 2.14 million acres, or 0.98 percent of the total area of the country, has been leased for non-African agricultural or pastoral use. About a quarter of this is in sisal plantations, a third is devoted to grazing, three tenths is not in use, and much of the remainder is in estates in the various highlands, especially the Usambara Mountains, Mt. Meru, and Mt. Kilimanjaro in the north, but also in the Iringa Highlands and the mountains around Mbeya and Njombe in the south. Except for sisal and tea, however, non-Africans do not hold the outstanding role they occupy in the agricultural production and exports of Kenya, though an estimated 40 percent of exports by value are produced on the approximately 1 percent of the land they hold in lease.

As has already been suggested, many of the Tanganyikan highlands have a dense African population, though there are almost always opportunities for intensification of land use and in some cases opportunities of bringing additional lands under cultivation. The degree to which African agriculture has been commercialized varies widely according to tribal, climatic, soil, and other factors. Perhaps most significant is the availability of transport and distance from the sea. The north, for example, is relatively well served and contributes significantly to Tanganyikan exports; the south, possessing some excellent lands, is very remote and hence its opportunities for commercialization have been severely restricted.

A typical Chagga hut on Mt. Kilimanjaro
Coffee, the main cash crop, is grown under bananas, which are the most important subsistence crop.

The most important and perhaps most interesting highland of Tanganyika is Mt. Kilimanjaro. The indigenous Chagga have developed an intensive agriculture on the slopes of this great volcanic peak between about 3,000 and 4,500 feet and in places to about 8,000 feet. Its soils are light, moisture-holding, grey-brown volcanics of excellent fertility. Precipitation is heavy on the southwest, south, and southeast slopes; for example, the annual average at Kibosho, at an elevation of 4,850 feet, is 104 inches, while it is only 18 inches at Arusha Chini, only 20 miles to the south and east at 2,300 feet.

About 300,000 Chagga live on Mt. Kilimanjaro. They reside on small plots not usually exceeding two acres on which the staple banana, eulesine for local beer, and the cash crop coffee are grown. On the lower slopes, corn, onions, cotton, and cassava are produced. The Chagga had developed a remarkable system of irrigation on the mountain long before arrival of the European, whereby furrows, sometimes running for miles, bring water along the precipitous sides of ravines and along the contours of the mountain to the individual holdings where water distribution takes place on a carefully organized basis. The system was apparently built primarily for support of eulesine and, while the Chagga propensity for consumption of beer has been criticized, it must be admitted that it led to an amazing agricultural development and indirectly to the promotion of a relatively advanced social system. An estimated 25,000 acres of African lands are irrigated on Mt. Kilimanjaro and Mt. Meru.

The Chagga also keep cattle, which are usually stall fed on banana stems and on grass laboriously brought up by the women each day from the lower slopes several miles away. Coffee was first grown on Mt. Kilimanjaro over 50 years ago by a Catholic mission. The industrious Chagga took to its production rather rapidly and in 1925 formed the Kilimanjaro Native Coffee Union, which has since become the largest African cooperative society with 34 affiliated societies and 35,000 members. About 16,500 tons of coffee were marketed in 1963 by the KNCU, which has attempted to promote improvement in its production by various techniques including the distribution of improved seeds. Its headquarters are at Moshi in a new $560,000 building, which also serves as a community center.

There are substantial opportunities for improving the standards of coffee production by the Chagga by reducing the excessive shade provided by the present practice of growing coffee under banana trees, by proper pruning, through mulching with banana trash and grass, replacing the old stock with selected seedlings, and improving the preparation of the bean, much of which is done by inefficient individual pulping and fermentation. The quality of African-grown Kenya coffees, for example, is now superior to Chagga coffees and they command a higher market price, partly because they are prepared in central cooperative pulperies.

The population densities on Mt. Kilimanjaro are often quite high. In the Moshi district, density is over 138 per square mile; in one area it exceeds 800 per square mile. This has led to some migration to lower slope levels and, for the future, may require harnessing the Pangani River to support irrigation farming in areas adjacent to the mountain.

Mt. Meru has a somewhat comparable land use pattern to that of Mt. Kilimanjaro. Cattle in the Arusha area, however, are usually grazed around the homesteads or, when possible, sent to outlying parts of the district. The Meru Cooperative Union, Ltd. has recently installed a central pulpery for processing the local coffees.

Something over 100 European farms are found on the slopes of Mt. Kilimanjaro and Mt. Meru. The largest part of the total of 19,000 acres under coffee in non-African estates in Tanganyika is in this region. South of Moshi is Arusha Chini where about 3,000 workers are employed on a 7,500-acre irrigated sugar plantation. Several sisal plantations are also found in the area.

The Arusha District, associated with Mt. Meru, is one of three leading pyrethrum areas in the country, and in postwar years there was a small boom on European estates in production of papaya for extraction of papain, a meat tenderizer. Arusha is the site of one of the two meat processing factories of Tanganyika Packers Ltd.

Between Mt. Kilimanjaro and Korogwe and forming the northeast portion of the topographic 9 are the North Pare, South Pare, and Usambara Mountains, all fairly alike. The Usambara Mountains form a compact block about 70 miles long and from 20 to 40 miles wide whose highest elevation is 7,550 feet. Eastern Usambara has been largely alienated; coffee is the main crop, but there are also about a dozen tea estates and there has been recent experimentation with cocoa. The African sections of the Usambara Mountains are densely populated. Corn is the chief subsistence crop, though bananas and sweet potatoes are important supplementary crops; there is also a dense livestock population. The main cash crop is rice, grown in the well-watered swamps along the foot of the mountain Soil erosion reaches serious proportions in some areas on the predominantly red earth soils. The Usambara Development Scheme, introduced some years before independence, was designed to protect the area from further destruction and to determine safe but more intensive methods of utilizing the congested areas of this mountain region. Like similar schemes in other Tanganyikan highland areas, it suffered from lack of cooperation from the intended beneficiaries and has not been reinstituted after independence.

West of Mt. Meru is a group of massifs called the "Winter Highlands," a volcanic region containing Mts. Loolmalasin and Ngorongoro and, within the Rift Valley, Mt. Lengai, still active. The huge crater of Ngorongoro supports a tremendous number of wild animals since it has a good grass growth and water available year round. This region is of immense tourist interest but commercial agriculture is not well developed, except around Oldeani where some 35 European farms are situated.

The Uluguru Mountains, south of Morogoro, have population densities exceeding 400 per square mile and cultivation has been carried onto excessively steep slopes. The pilot Uluguru Land Usage Scheme, initiated in 1950, was designed to control erosion by bench terracing of annual crops and protecting river banks, to intensify agricultural production, to rationalize livestock raising by introducing the manufacture of compost and stall feeding, and to maintain the volume of water in the streams flowing from the mountains in order to protect the sisal plantations in the Morogoro District which are dependent upon them. Opposition to some of the nontraditional practices became so strong, however, that the objectives of the scheme had to be compromised after 1955.

The Iringa Highlands, running south from the loop of the 9, support about 100,000 people on about 1,250 square miles, as well as a dense livestock population. The friable soils of these highlands are easily eroded, and an effort has been made to provide grazing lands on the plains below the escarpment so that the overgrazed highlands could be given an opportunity to recuperate. Important European settlements are found near Iringa, Dabaga, and Sao Hill. A considerable amount of tea comes from the Mufindi area; flue-cured tobacco also comes mainly from Iringa, while pyrethrum is a third important European-grown crop.

In the south, the cluster of mountains at the head of Lake Nyasa belongs to both the Eastern and Central Rift Valley systems. There are great contrasts within this complex region, which is greatly disadvantaged by distance from the sea. Despite its isolation, however, commercial agriculture has developed to a degree. Europeans have tea estates in the Rungwe District south of Mbeya, coffee around Mbozi about 40 miles west of Mbeya, and pyrethrum southwest of Njombe. The Southern Highlands account for about 10 percent of the arabica coffee, a quarter of the tea, and one third of the pyrethrum of Tanganyika.

Africans are increasing their production of arabicas around Njombe and Mbeya. Near the former town is the site of the CDC-supported 44,600-acre Tanganyika Wattle Estates and of the 200,000-acre Ubena Wattle Scheme on which Africans will produce bark for a factory at Njombe. The CDC has made an investment of about $3.6 million in promoting the production of wattle in Tanganyika; the scheme began in 1949 and the first extract was produced at Njombe in 1959. Some 33,000 acres have been planted, and this acreage is to be increased in the years ahead. Africans are also participating increasingly in the production of pyrethrum in the same district, which is rapidly approaching the level of output in the Arusha and Iringa districts.

THE LAKE VICTORIA AND CENTRAL PLATEAU BASIN

A huge uplifted basin occupies the lands between the eastern highlands and the mountains and lakes of the Western Rift Zone, which is shared with Congo, Rwanda, Burundi, and Northern Rhodesia.

TANGANYIKA. In Tanganyika, this region, with an average elevation of 4,000 feet, is known as the Central Plateau and it forms the largest region of the country. Much of it is covered with *miombo* woodlands in which *Bracystegia* is the predominating species. Most of this area is either sparsely occupied or completely empty, in part because it is infested with the tsetse fly and human sleeping sickness is endemic. Precipitation is only 25 to 30 inches and is highly variable. Soils are generally poor except in the valley bottoms, where dark, heavy clays called *mbugas* are relatively fertile; they are not widely utilized, however, because it is difficult to work them with hand tools and because they are subject to seasonal flooding. A very large part of the Central Plateau is a peneplain whose monotony is relieved only by the protrusion of granitic inselberge.

That part of the Central Plateau lying south of the Central Railway has been called the "empty quarter." Around Tabora is a comparatively fertile but steppelike area which supports somewhat greater densities with peanuts and castor beans as the main cash crops. At Urambo, west of Tabora on the Central Railway, is the third area originally assigned to the Tanganyika Groundnut Scheme. Here the Tanganyika Agricultural Corporation does not farm itself, all land being leased to tenants, but does provide a central workshop and a tobacco sales floor. The main cash crop is flue-cured tobacco. Tenancies are operated on three scales: ten Europeans and one Asian have large holdings averaging 1,200 acres of cleared land; eight Africans have medium-sized holdings with 150–200 acres of cleared land; and there are a number of small, 20- to 40-acre holdings. The large holdings, which each have about 60 acres of tobacco, produced tobacco to the value of $284,200 in 1961. The medium-sized holdings, with 15 to 20 acres in tobacco, sold $45,070 worth in 1961; the best of these tenants had yields superior to those on the European holdings, the worst three had yields only one-third as high.

The *miombo* woodlands of the Central Plateau produce some *mwinga* timber plus gums, honey, beeswax, and fibers. Tanganyika is the world's largest exporter of beeswax. It is not a richly forested country, however, having only about 2 percent of its total area in high forests. In 1960, CD and W granted that country about $1.4 million for various afforestation schemes, including the planting of 16,000 acres of pine, cypress, and teak, a forest survey, and the promotion of natural forest regeneration.

Towards Lake Victoria, which lies at an elevation of about 3,717 feet, is the "cultivation steppe," a large, almost treeless area which has been cleared by the Sukuma. This area is better watered and is one of the more densely populated regions of the country, having over a million Africans on about 20,000 square miles. Overcrowding has worn out some of the lands and the amount of comparable new land available is limited. In recent years the Sukuma have been increasing the production of cotton with some rapidity, the 1962 total having been a record of 192,000 bales. The Lake Province accounts for about 80 percent of the cotton produced in Tanganyika, with exports ranging around $15–21 million yearly. Yields are low, however, and the quality would be improved by more efficient handling and ginning. Experts have demonstrated that yields could be doubled by early planting, tie-ridging to prevent erosion and to conserve moisture, and application of manure and chemical fertilizers, but the African farmer has been slow to adopt these practices despite their proved economic value.

About half of the area occupied by the group of Bantu tribes which united in the Sukumaland federation was included in the Sukumaland Development Scheme, designed to rehabilitate the region largely on a self-help basis through the adoption of soil preservation practices, improved farming techniques, control of livestock numbers, and the construction of dams and hafirs for water storage. This scheme, which was the largest Tanganyikan development project in pre-independence years, also involved the opening of about 8,000 square miles of unoccupied land by bush clearance.

Toward the west, along the Malagarasi and Ugalla river systems and near the border with Burundi, widespread swamps have repulsed settlement. But along the western side of Lake Victoria, the Bukoba District is a relatively favored part of Tanganyika. It may be divided into two major portions: a zone of rich lands along the lake shore which is well watered and supports about 80 percent of the population, and the hillier hinterland interspersed with rock outcrops which has some good soils but which has unreliable water supplies. The shore zone is the main site for the staple banana, the main subsistence crop and raw material for beer for the Haya of Bukoba. Their main cash crop is coffee, mainly robusta but including some arabica. Their production of coffee totaled 7,800 tons in 1928 and about 10,000 tons in recent years; it is marketed by the Bukoba Native Cooperative Union, to which about 90 percent of the 70,000 African growers adhere.

East of Lake Victoria, the farmers grow cotton, peanuts, rice, sesame, and corn, and carry on an extensive grazing. The huge uplifted Serengeti Plain is much drier; most of it is a game reserve, lush in the rainy season but sere and forbidding in the dry period when vast stretches are charred by grass fires.

Within Lake Victoria are a large number of islands, some of which are of considerable interest. Ukerewe Island produces cotton and rice particularly well, in part because of its favorable rainfall. The smaller Ukara Island has such great population pressures that it is the scene of some remarkably evolved and intensive agricultural practices which were developed before the arrival of Europeans. Crops are grown in accordance with a carefully planned rotation which includes the digging in of green manure crops and the provision of fodder crops for cattle. Livestock are hand fed and carefully bedded down in the huts, while their manure is composted and used on the fields. Stock numbers are rigidly controlled and when the livestock are taken through the fields they are muzzled to protect the crops. An experiment was once made to utilize these skilled farmers as demonstrators of their intensive practices on the adjacent mainland, but divorced from the necessity for such a rigorous system they soon fell into the ways used by the local farmers.

KENYA. The southwestern part of Kenya, Nyanza Province, is a part of the Lake Victoria Basin. Kisumu, on the Kavirondo Gulf, is the major lake port, handling much of the traffic for areas along both sides of the lake in all three East African countries. Nyanza Province has an average elevation of about 4,000 feet and receives from 40 to 70 inches of rain yearly. It has a dense African population, their chief cash crop being cotton, which is experiencing a slow increase in production.

Cutting sugar cane at Miwani, near Kisumu
Teams of oxen draw the trucks loaded with cane over temporary lines to the permanent tracks on which diesel engines take them to the factory. Sugar cane is a relatively new crop for Kenya.

Most of Kenya's domestically produced sugar comes from the Miwani Sugar Mills (Kenya), Ltd. which has a big new refinery near Kisumu completed in 1961 at a cost of $1.96 million. The first settlement scheme devoted to production of sugar has also been started in this district; it is planned that 3,000 to 4,000 Luo families be settled on about 20,000 acres of former European farms.

UGANDA. That portion of the Lake Victoria Basin located in Uganda includes some of the best quality lands in East Africa; indeed, it is one of the favored parts of the continent. Uganda is more heavily dependent upon agriculture than any of the East African countries; agriculture accounts for about two thirds of the gross domestic product and 90 percent of exports, and is the main occupation of about 90 percent of the population. While three fifths of the tilled land is still used for subsistence production, the value of cash crops is about 25 percent greater than the imputed value of subsistence crops. Some areas are affected by population pressure, but only about one sixth of the total available land is cultivated at any one time and this does not yield anything like its full potential.

The most favored part of the Uganda plateau is the crescent around the north end of Lake Victoria. Climatically it is favored by a relatively heavy and reliable precipitation (Map 72) and by the moderating influence of elevation. From the landform standpoint it is characterized by a seemingly endless succession of low, flat-topped hills which gradually become less pronounced as one proceeds northward. Local relief is about 500 feet; the peneplained hill tops are at elevations of about 4,300 to 4,400 feet. Soils are distinctly better than in most of tropical Africa; very typical is a catenal arrangement running from a thin covering of laterized, greyish soil on the hill tops to deep, rich, red and chocolate loam of excellent structure on the slopes, to alluvial clays that are virtually uncultivable on the valley floors, which are commonly swampy. Fortunately, it is the slope soils which cover by far the largest area. Where the land is not under cultivation the typical vegetation is a rank growth of grasses, especially the very high elephant grass. This grades into open woodlands merging into low tree-grasslands in the central part of the country.

The core area of the crescent is southern Buganda, which is the richest province of Uganda. The whole of Buganda has a population of some 2 million, or about 29 percent of Uganda's total on 23 percent of its land area. Ganda account for 55 percent of the provincial population; of the remaining population about 45 percent are Banyaruanda and 17 percent Barundi. About three fourths of these represent migrant laborers who work on the farms of the Ganda, one estimate being that half of the cash income of the average farmer is spent on hired labor. Some migrants farm their own plots rented from the Ganda. As land has gradually become less plentiful, some resentment of foreign workers and tenants has developed, but migration from Rwanda and Burundi is likely to continue heavy until such time as the Ganda become more interested in increasing their incomes and working harder to do so.

Ganda are individualist farmers, operating family farms. In accordance with the Uganda Agreement of 1900, about half of the lands of the Buganda Kingdom was allotted to notables of the tribe on a system of individual ownership. These areas, called "mailo" land from the square mile measurements employed, have since been subdivided into much smaller holdings, but many Ganda are still substantial landowners. Measures of the importance of Buganda are seen in its share of cash crop production, about 90 percent of robusta coffee, a quarter of the cotton, and 5 percent of the tea produced in the country, and in the fact that cash incomes average about twice those of the Eastern Province and four times those of the Western and Northern provinces.

The typical land use pattern over much of Buganda is as follows: (1) some grazing, but very little cultivation on the hill tops; (2) a close cultivation of the staple plantain, corn, some cassava, and sweet potatoes plus the cash crops coffee or cotton on the upper and middle slopes; this zone is also the main site of the huts or houses, which are usually surrounded by bananas; (3) some cultivation, particularly of sweet potatoes and grains on the lower slope where the soil is likely to be more acidic and sandy; and (4) papyrus swamps in the valley. There has been some experimentation with the valley clays, and with the swamps, but their potentialities are still inadequately understood.

A large number of livestock are kept in the south. While it has been typical for cattle to be herded and housed away from the cultivated area, there is a growing number of farmers who realize the value of integrated crop and livestock farming. Since 1954, an increasing acreage has been enclosed in paddocks, and this trend has been greatly stimulated by the introduction of high-yielding exotic dairy cattle from Kenya which have been obtainable at very favorable prices. In 1962 about 1,300 head of exotic cattle were in Buganda, 504 of which were imported in the previous year. Keeping such cattle requires a high standard of management and disease control, which has thus far been well maintained. It will necessitate close watching, however, and possibly some crossbreeding with more disease-resistant breeds. Foot-and-mouth disease has become a serious problem with the Nganda cattle and tick-borne diseases are also a menace; to help combat them the IBRD supplied a $280,000 loan to establish 75 dips in southeast Buganda. There would appear to be an excellent future for mixed farming, particularly for stall feeding with cut elephant grass. The Agricultural Department recommends a rotation involving three years in crops and three years in grass for grazing, but this would require some changes in land tenure before it could be fully adopted in the country. There has been a notable increase in ox-drawn plowing in recent years, particularly in the Eastern Province.

The general agricultural pattern of southern Buganda is continued eastward to southern Busoga and Bukedi and southwestward into the Bukoba District of Tanganyika. But away from the lake, conditions are not so favorable as in the fertile crescent. In the short-grass zone, finger millet and sorghum replace the plantain and corn, and cotton tends to replace coffee as the main cash crop. Cattle keeping is common, and while cattle are housed on the holding there is still little integration with tillage agriculture. North of the Buganda and Eastern provinces are Lakes Salisbury and Kioga with large expanses of swamp both around and within them. North of them, precipitation drops off gradually, particularly to the northeast. While cotton production is increasing to the north of Lake Kioga and should be stimulated by extension of the railway, the Karamoja District of the northeast is a backward part of Uganda, mindful of the grazing areas of northern Kenya. The Karamajong are primarily pastoralists, but the offtake from the area is small, having been only 22,000 of the country's record total of 690,000 head of cattle in 1960. A large meat processing factory is planned at Soroti to take cattle from the whole north, hopefully stimulating the sale from Karamoja. The livestock population of Uganda according to a 1960 census was 3.6 million cattle (about 70 percent shorthorn Zebu, 15 percent Ankole longhorn, and 15 percent intermediate types) and 3.7 million sheep and goats. Uganda is fortunate in having less than one third of its area infested with the tsetse fly. Soil erosion is a serious problem in parts of Karamoja, occasioned by the characteristically heavy showers of the rainy period, the sparse vegetation, and overgrazing. In the rest of Uganda, however, a particularly effective antierosion program has been mounted, involving especially the planting of narrow terraces with grass and, in drier areas, the preservation of buffer grass strips between cultivated fields.

A team of bullocks working in Teso, Uganda
Recent years have seen a considerable increase in the training and use of work animals in southern Uganda.

To the south and west of the fertile crescent, in western Buganda, Ankole, and much of Toro, lands become higher and more rugged. They are mostly in open grasslands with scattered bush and trees and some riverine forest. Millet is the main crop; peas, beans, peanuts, and potatoes are also important. Cattle are relatively sparse except in the two counties of Nyabushozi and Kajara in Ankole, where cattle keeping is the major occupation.

To the northwest, the Bunyoro District is fairly comparable to Buganda. Occupied by the Nyoro who have a kingdom similar to that of the Ganda, it is a fertile country of small hills and swampy valleys with a density of about 21 per square mile. Most of the Nyoro live in individual homesteads in rather closely settled areas separated from other such areas by wide stretches of uninhabited bush. Many years ago they owned great herds of cattle, but these were lost by war and disease and the Nyoro are now largely agriculturalists. The Uganda Development Corporation set up the 100,000-acre Bunyoro Ranching Scheme in 1956, starting with a herd of 5,000 head on land that had recently been cleared of tsetse fly. A reinfestation in 1960, however, delayed bringing the scheme to a viable level. Bunyoro accounts for about half of the tobacco produced in Uganda, most of it coming from the Waki Valley in the center.

Major cash crops of the Uganda Plateau. Cotton was long the prime commercial crop of Uganda. The main credit for its establishment goes to the Uganda Company, founded by wealthy supporters of the Church Missionary Society. Aided by the British Cotton Growing Association, organized in 1902 to develop alternative sources to the United States, upon which Lancashire was considered to be excessively dependent, the Uganda Company began distributing seeds to the local chiefs in 1904, when 54 bales (400 pounds each) valued at £236 were produced. By 1910–11, production had grown to 13,378 bales and cotton was accounting for about half of total exports. Between 1908 and 1914 its production spread to the Eastern Province. Rapid progress continued after World War I and exports reached 402,000 bales in 1938. This level has not been reached in post World War II years, having been 371,318 bales in 1961; the 1962 output was reduced to less than half that figure owing to disastrously poor weather conditions. In 1955 and since 1957, cotton has ranked second to coffee as the main cash crop and export of Uganda.

Over half of Uganda's cotton comes from the Eastern Province, about a quarter from Buganda, and a fifth from the Northern Province, the trend having been downward in Buganda and upward in the areas where coffee could not be grown. Coffee is more popular than cotton because it requires only about 80 man-days of work per acre per year as compared to 140 for cotton and gives yields about two to three times as great. But cotton has the advantages that it can be produced in a much broader area of Uganda and that its production can be increased, whereas coffee sales are restricted by Uganda's membership in the International Coffee Agreement. In response to an all-out government campaign, acreage planted to cotton increased from 1,516,000 in 1961 to 2,072,000 in 1962, and if comparable enthusiasm is shown in future years the goal of 500,000 bales should be met in the not too distant future. Cotton is grown exclusively by Africans on plots averaging about three quarters of an acre.

The record of cotton production has been unusual for rain-grown cotton in tropical Africa; nowhere else has that crop been so successful, though it has been tried in widespread regions. Credit must be given not only to the superior physical conditions of the country but also to the comparatively well-developed economic aspirations of indigenous producers. Yields of seed cotton averaged 294 pounds per acre in the decade to 1960, but could be considerably increased by spraying against the Lygus bug and the bollworm, and a subsidized spraying campaign has been organized. Uganda cotton is high quality with a staple longer than that of American middling and is produced relatively cheaply.

Ginning of cotton has long been handled largely by Indians, which has led to periodic difficulties as African producers resented the prices demanded and the racial dominance in the industry. Since 1952, however, 14 gins of the total of 131 have come under the ownership of African cooperatives (Map 76). Also, prices paid to the growers are fixed in advance by the government. One need is to close some of the small, inefficient gins and to disperse the gins in better relation to the producing regions and particularly with respect to the newer areas. India and Japan are normally the main markets for Uganda cotton.

Coffee was a traditional part of the Ganda farm long before it became significant as a cash crop. Its commercialization began in the 1920s and made steady if not spectacular progress in prewar years. The big boom in robusta production came in the 1950s, with production increasing from 27,000 tons in 1953 to 122,000 tons in 1961. Uganda is today the largest producer of coffee in the Commonwealth, but no further dynamic growth is to be expected because the International Coffee Agreement restricts Uganda's sales at present to 114,000 tons. What can be done is to concentrate on improving quality by more careful selection and improved processing. Taxation could also be rationalized to favor cotton rather than coffee. Of the 538,000 acres in robusta in 1961, 96 percent were in Buganda.

Other cash crops of the plateau include tobacco, sugar, tea, castor seed, peanuts, and soy beans. Uganda's sugar production doubled from 1953 to the 96,000-ton level of 1961, about 70 percent of which was consumed locally, the rest being shipped to Kenya. Until 1960, Uganda's sugar came from two large plantations started in the 1920s at Lugazi and Kakira on the fertile soils bordering Lake Victoria, the first in Buganda west of Jinja and the second in Busoga just northeast of that city. In 1960 a new plantation was established, also in the Jinja area, while overhead irrigation was applied on the 6,500-acre Kakira estate, said to be the largest area in which this type of irrigation has been installed. The estate owners have been attempting in recent years to encourage the outgrowing of cane by peasant cultivators, and have been contracting with adjacent landowners for permission to produce cane on their land in return for a share in the profits of sugar produced. The Uganda sugar estates are owned by Indians and occupy about two fifths of the acreage in non-African estates in Uganda, which was only about 98,000 acres in 1961. The total area held by non-Africans is 519 square miles or 0.68 percent of the land area of the country.

Tobacco is grown almost entirely by African small holders. In 1961 about 11 million pounds were produced on 17,000 acres, and plans are to more than double this acreage by 1965. The entire production in East Africa is purchased by the East African Tobacco Company, which allocates acreage and production quotas on the basis of the estimated requirements of the East African market. The company also provides assistance to growers and advances equipment to Master Growers, 535 of whom produce about half of the crop. Quality leaves much to be desired, while the price is well above world market levels.

Several tea estates are found in southern Buganda between Jinja and Kampala, where tea was first introduced to Uganda. This region is not as favorable ecologically as the higher lands of Mt. Elgon or the west, where the more recent developments have taken place.

Peanuts have been receiving increasing attention, especially in the Eastern Province, both as a cash and a food crop. Peanut production should be further promoted as a soil improvement measure. A $2.8 million project to irrigate 6,000 acres of bushland in the Toro District has been proposed for the intensive production of peanuts and cotton.

Minor cash crops which have received attention in recent years are cocoa, vanilla, ginger, pepper, citrus fruit, tropical fruits, and vegetables. Perhaps the most significant development in commercial production in recent years has been the growth of the domestic market for bananas and other staples and for slaughter cattle.

Uganda has a fairly well-developed lake fishing industry, with an estimated 20,000 Africans employed in fishing and fish distribution in 1960. About 5,700 craft are utilized, most of them canoes, but over 1,350 are equipped with outboard motors. Increased productivity has also resulted from replacing the traditional flax nets with nylon nets. Fish landings have increased from about 10,000 tons to 65,000 tons in 1961 valued at about $8.4 million. Lake Victoria is the main producing area, but opportunities for inshore fishing appear to be fairly restricted. The Rift Valley lakes—Albert, George, and Edward—have a combined catch about equal to that of Lake Victoria. Much of their catch is normally exported to Congo and Kenya, especially the output of two modern fish processing factories in the Lake George–Lake Edward area. Fishing only began seriously in Lake Kioga about 1960 after its crocodile population had been practically eliminated and it had been stocked with good quality fish.

THE WESTERN RIFT SYSTEM

As indicated earlier, this last zone of East Africa is shared with other nations. In Uganda it includes the Lake Albert lowlands, very hot and dry; the remote region to the west of that with elevations of 4,000–5,000 feet and precipitation of about 50 inches which produces about a quarter of the country's tobacco; Mt. Ruwenzori, which is a huge uplifted block lying within the rift and rising to 16,794 feet; Lake George and Lake Edward, along which is one of Uganda's two main game reserves; and the high land of Kigezi in the southwest corner, an upwarped shoulder of the Western Rift, culminating in the Mufumbiro volcanoes.

The area near Fort Portal is one of the leading tea producing areas of Uganda and also accounts for a portion of the arabica coffee produced. Kigezi in the extreme southwest is a continuation of the highlands of Rwanda, a deeply incised upland which is densely populated and farmed from the tops of the hills to the reclaimed swamps in the narrow valley floors, with remarkable terracing on its often extremely steep slopes. While handicapped by remoteness, this beautiful region is contributing increasing quantities of arabica to Uganda's exports.

Uganda's production of arabica is only about 7 percent that of robusta, but its value is about 14 percent of the total value of coffee exports. In 1961 the Western Province accounted for 14,000 of the 41,000 acres in arabica in the country. The Mt. Elgon area, an outlier of the Eastern Rift System, accounts for 24,000 acres of the total. Output in that area is handled by the Bugisu Native Coffee Union.

Tea has become an important export crop in recent years. The area devoted to it increased from 3,000 acres in prewar years to 19,000 acres in 1961, almost all of which came from

A scene in the Kigezi District, southwest Uganda
This deeply incised upland area is greatly disadvantaged by remoteness, but is increasing its production of arabica coffee for export.

non-African estates. Tea does extremely well in certain areas, estate yields being higher than those of India or Ceylon. Tea estates in the area are concentrated east of Fort Portal. Several are owned by Agricultural Enterprises Ltd., a subsidiary of the government-owned Uganda Development Corporation (UDC), which has a total of five tea estates in the country. The latest of the UDC estates, at Mwenge in Toro, will cover 1,000 acres and support a tea factory. Small-holder production is being promoted not only on the outgrower's own land but also on company land leased to tenants under an arrangement whereby the tenant works as a wage earner until the tea on his plot is ready for sale. The tenant may purchase the land by paying installments over a 15-year period. UDC also increases estate production by issuing shares to local governments in exchange for land. Thus the Ankole government is a minority holder in the Ankole Tea Company. This arrangement turns the land tenure system, previously an obstacle to investment, into a positive advantage, since capital expenditures are reduced by the use of shares in the purchase of land.

CDC is also participating in the development of a tea estate, this one being managed by a private company with long experience in East Africa. The value of tea production in Uganda has increased from $1.68 million in 1953 to $5.47 million in 1961 and should continue upward as immature bushes reach yielding age.

In Tanganyika, a large part of the western border is formed by Lake Tanganyika, while a series of small highlands occur along its eastern side until the large Ufipa Plateau is reached, which lies between Lake Tanganyika and Lake Rukwa. Rice and subsistence crops are produced at various points along the shore of Lake Tanganyika, particularly at Ujiji near the lake port of Kigoma. Fishing is also of some significance. Very little commerical production comes from the western highlands of Tanganyika; their extreme remoteness has militated against development.

MINERALS OF EAST AFRICA

East Africa has been relatively unimportant as a mineral producer and it was thought for some years that its potentialities were not great. But a much accelerated program of mapping and prospecting in postwar years has revealed a number of interesting bodies and there are good possibilities that other finds will be made since only a small part of the area has been thoroughly studied. It is not easy to delineate patterns in the mineral occurrences except that a roughly Y-shaped metallogenetic zone is found with the branches on either side of Lake Victoria and the stem running north-south in western Tanganyika.

TANGANYIKA

DIAMONDS. Now leading the mineral exports of East Africa, diamonds come from the Williamson mine near Shinyanga on the branch line from Mwanza to Tabora in Tanganyika (Map 74). Discovered in 1940 by a Canadian geologist who had had experience in South Africa and who spent six years exploring the country, the pipe at Mwadui is the largest ever found, an oval measuring about 3,500 by 5,000 feet, which is over three times the size of the Premier pipe in South Africa. Between 40 and 50 kimberlite pipes have been located in Tanganyika, but diamonds are associated with only a small portion of them. Mining has thus far been confined largely to simple quarrying in the gravels and soils overlying the pipe at Mwadui and in an area about 10 square miles around it, but diamonds also occur in payable quantities in the kimberlite, which is being cut at one point.

It is necessary to treat about 16 million pounds of material to obtain 1 pound of diamonds, the yield being about evenly split by weight between gem and industrial stones, with the former accounting for over four fifths of the value of sales. A large modern plant, a power station, two dams to provide adequate water, and housing and other amenities have been constructed, the operation now employing about 2,900 Africans, 58 Asians, and 310 Europeans.

After some years of negotiations during which a quantity of diamonds was stored in the Bank of England, the Williamson Mine was given a 10 percent share in the international cartel marketing diamonds, permitting its owner to become the largest individual dollar earner in the Commonwealth. After Williamson died in 1958 the company was purchased by DeBeers and the Tanganyikan government, each holding a half interest. Exports of diamonds have run about $15–16 million in recent years and can be maintained at this level for many years. They account for about three fourths of the total value of mineral output in Tanganyika. In 1962 a Belgian company obtained a license to search for diamonds in central Tanganyika.

GOLD. Long the main mineral produced in East Africa, gold came from widely dispersed localities many of which have become uneconomic in postwar years, resulting in a generally declining trend. Most of the output now comes from Tanganyika, where gold ranks second among mineral exports with a value about a quarter that of diamonds. The Kiabakari and Geita mines in the Lake Victoria area account for about 80 percent of production, but the latter has been operating at a loss in recent years. The Lupa Goldfield, northwest of Mbeya, is in decline.

OTHER MINERALS. Output of lead concentrates at Mpanda provided an export of some value in the 1950s, but the mine was closed in 1960 owing to an unexpectedly early exhaustion. A 131-mile branch line had been constructed to Mpanda in 1950; it presumably will be abandoned unless other occurrences are found in the area.

Other minerals of interest actually or potentially in Tanganyika include:

(1) Coal. Three deposits are known, of which two have been investigated by the CDC. In the Ruhuhu River Basin east of Lake Nyasa, 284 million tons of good quality noncoking coal plus 116 million tons of lower grade coals have been proved, but the remoteness of the area and the necessity for subsurface mining militate against early exploitation. The Kivira-Songwe Field near the northwestern end of Lake Nyasa has proved reserves of 20 million tons of good grade coal but somewhat inferior to that of the Ruhuhu Basin. Lastly, there is the Ufipa coal field east of Lake Tanganyika.

(2) Iron ore. The CDC also investigated a body of titaniferous iron ore in the Njombe District, known as the Liganga deposits and situated only 30 miles from coal. About 45 million tons of 49 percent metallic content were proved and there was evidence of additional deposits. Remoteness and the metallurgical problem of removing the titanium discourage mining operations.

(3) Mica. Tanganyika is a major source of mica for the Commonwealth, producing sheet mica of the highest quality. Two sorting depots are situated at Morogoro, but mica is produced in six or seven widely scattered areas. A new area south of Lake Rukwa has been opened recently.

(4) Tin and Wolfram. These minerals come in small quantities from the Bukoba District and are associated with similar ores in Rwanda.

(5) Pyrochlore. A deposit exists at Panda Hill near Mbeya and is a large potential source of columbium.

(6) Meerschaum. A discovery of this rare stone was made in 1953 in Masailand close to the Kenya border. Developed by the Tanganyika Meerschaum Corporation, it is used in the manufacture of pipes at a new factory in Arusha which replaced an earlier plant at Nairobi.

(7) Phosphates. An unusual deposit occurs at Minjingu Hill east of Lake Manyara in the Eastern Rift, apparently formed from bird guano accumulated on an island when the lake had a much greater area. Thus far, proved reserves total 10 million tons and the IBRD recommended that they be exploited for local consumption pending construction of a 70-mile extension from the railhead at Arusha.

(8) Kaolin. An extensive deposit of china clay from which a small output now comes is situated only 17 miles west of Dar es Salaam.

(9) Salt and Soda. There is a considerable production of salt from coastal pans at various

points along the coast and from brine springs at Kigoma. Soda occurs in Lake Natron, but unlike that in Lake Magadi in Kenya it is allied with common salt and is, therefore, less valuable. But the deposits of this lake and of Lakes Manyara, Balangida, and Eyasi may some day become of commercial value.

(10) Magnesite is found near Longido on the Kenya border.

(11) There are indications of copper and nickel at Nachingwea, and of deposits of graphite, garnets, gypsum, and beryl in various parts of the country. Silver is obtained as a by-product of gold and also occurs in the Mpanda ores.

KENYA

SODA. The main mineral export of Kenya is soda, produced from Lake Magadi by the Magadi Soda Company, formed in 1911 and now a subsidiary of the Imperial Chemical Industries. The raw material, known as "trona," is fairly evenly distributed over the 20-mile-long and 2-mile-wide lake and is renewed from springs probably deriving their heat from subterranean magma from the volcanoes in the area. Soda ash produced at the company's plant is used in the production of glass in world market areas; common salt is also obtained and marketed in the country. About 850 Africans and 150 Asians and Europeans are employed at Magadi; and total value of soda, soda ash, and salt was $4.93 million in 1961.

OTHER MINERALS. Other deposits in Kenya include the following:

(1) Copper. The Macalder-Nyanza Mine, opened in 1957, produces about $1 to $2 million worth of copper annually, plus some gold and silver.

(2) Gold. Output from gold mines has dwindled but some is obtained as a by-product from the Macalder-Nyanza Mine.

(3) Diatomite. Two large deposits of diatomite occur in the Gilgil area between Nairobi and Nakuru in the Rift Valley, with proved reserves of 6 million tons. The East African Diatomite Syndicate produces a small quantity.

(4) Graphite. Large deposits are known to occur near Machakos and Tsavo.

(5) Gypsum occurs near Garissa and in the Northern Frontier Province, both too far from the nearest railhead to justify exploitation.

(6) Kyanite is found between Voi and Taveta and was formerly mined in considerable quantities for conversion to mullite and the manufacture of refractory bricks. It is hoped that this industry can be rejuvenated in the near future.

(7) Asbestos is mined in a small works in West Suk and a possibly large deposit is located in the Teita Hills.

The soda ash factory of the Magadi Soda Company at Lake Magadi, Kenya
Soda ash is the main mineral export of Kenya; it is derived from "trona" drawn from the lake.

(8) Columbium and rare earths occur at Mrima Hill in the extreme southeast of the country. An estimated 56 million tons of high-grade ores occur at the surface but metallurgical difficulties stand in the way of immediate production. Another deposit occurs near Muhoroni in Nyanza Province.

(9) Oil and natural gas. Prospecting along the coast has thus far proved unsuccessful, as it also has in Tanganyika and Zanzibar.

UGANDA

COPPER AND COBALT. The most important mine in Uganda is the Kilembe copper-cobalt mine in the foothills of the Ruwenzori, the main reason for extending the railway west to Kasese. Mining began in 1948, but operations were not

The Kilembe Copper Mine, Uganda
This is Uganda's most important mine and is situated in the foothills of the Ruwenzori Mountains.

The Kilembe Copper Mine's smelting plant at Jinja, Uganda
This plant uses about half of the power consumed in Uganda and is situated at Jinja because of the low-cost electricity available from the Owen Falls installation.

fully developed until 1956 when the rail line was completed and the copper was first smelted at Jinja. The ore has a 1.8 percent copper and an 0.14 percent cobalt content. Most of it is concentrated to a 27 percent product before railing to Jinja, though some of the oxides are rich enough to permit direct shipment. The processing of cobalt has not yet begun, over 100,000 tons of concentrate assaying 1.1 percent cobalt having been stockpiled at Kasese. The company has installed its own 5,800-kw hydroelectric station on the Mobuku River in the area.

Smelting takes place at Jinja because of the low-cost power available from the Owen Falls Dam, the electric smelter being the most important consumer of electricity in Uganda. Having one of the largest and most modern electric furnaces in the world, the Jinja smelter produces 99.3 percent blister copper containing minor amounts of nickel, gold, and silver. Exports of copper were valued at $10.1 million in 1962, making it the third ranking export of Uganda. Proven reserves have been declining and will be exhausted by 1969, yet the company has had some difficulty in obtaining further exploration rights. From 1948 to 1962, capital expenditures in copper production have exceeded $25.2 million. Kilembe Mines Ltd. is owned 70 percent by Venture of Canada, 20 percent by CDC, and 10 percent by the Uganda Development Corporation. It employs about 4,500 people, many of whom are from Kenya and Tanganyika.

PHOSPHATES. Sukulu Mines Ltd. has one of the most promising deposits thus far discovered in Uganda and one of the largest phosphate deposits in the Commonwealth. Situated in the Sukulu Hills not far from Tororo, the rock contains apatite, pyrochlore, and some magnetite. Production began in 1962 but only to supply the domestic market. An output of about 400,000 tons of apatite a year would be required for economic export; markets for such a level could easily be obtained if the reserve were situated on the coast but may not develop for this particular mine for a decade or two.

OTHER MINERALS. Much of Uganda remains to be prospected, but some other minerals are produced in small quantities and other bodies are known to exist. Beryllium has witnessed an increase in output from $11,760 in 1954 to $285,600 in 1961. To date it has been hand picked, but recent discovery of large deposits at Ishasha in Kigezi makes practicable the provision of flotation plants. Tin and wolfram are also produced, especially when the market price is favorable. An iron ore deposit occurs in Kigezi but is too remote to justify development. Uganda has recently been attempting to attract capital to develop what is considered to be a favorable kaolin deposit.

INDUSTRY IN EAST AFRICA

Kenya has enjoyed the greatest development of manufacturing industries of the four East African countries, particularly of market-oriented establishments, almost all of which have been introductions of the postwar years. Data on manufacturing in all the countries are less meaningful than they might be because of such practices as including mining, construction, handicraft activities, and total employees of tea and sisal estates in various summaries of industrial activity. The following figures are nonetheless of some value in assessing the actual and comparative importance of manufacturing in East Africa.

In Kenya, the contribution of manufacturing to the gross domestic product was estimated at $39.5 million in 1954 and $64.4 million in 1962, when it accounted for about 10 percent of the total. Manufacturing and repairs accounted for 7.2 percent of the total employed workers on June 30, 1961. Most industry is small scale. According to a 1957 survey of industry,[6] 70 percent of establishments employed fewer than 20 people. Sixteen establishments employed over 1,000, twenty-six over 500. If those employing fewer than 5 are excluded, it is estimated that establishments employing over 50 accounted for about three fourths of total employment and 77.4 percent of industrial production in 1957.

Tanganyika ranks second in industrial development among the East African countries. At the end of 1960, some 2,631 non-Africans and 18,349 Africans were employed in manufacturing, including electricity and water supply.[7] Illustrative of the difficulties of assessing manufacturing development is the inclusion in the official abstract of a second table entitled "Particulars of Factories . . . by Industry and Number Employed," which gives factory employment as 83,473. That this is grossly exaggerated is indicated by the inclusion of 29,767 persons employed in sisal "processing" and of many service rather than factory occupations. This second table gives the number of factories in Tanganyika on December 31, 1960, as 4,917, but 1,442 were without power. Included are 1,258 flour milling factories, most of which could scarcely merit the title. A 1958 estimate gives the number of manufacturing establishments and electric plants as 286, which is probably a reasonably accurate measure of the number of modern factories.

In Uganda, mining, processing of agricultural produce, and manufacturing contributed an estimated 9.2 percent to the gross domestic product in 1955 and 7.8 percent in 1960 when their contribution totaled $33.3 million. In 1960 employment of Africans in these same activities was 36,800 or 16.0 percent of the total African wage employees.

Zanzibar has very little industry other than the processing of raw materials, of which the clove oil plant is most important.

INDUSTRIAL REPRESENTATION AND DISTRIBUTION

Table 28 shows the number of plants in each of the major East African countries by type of industry for the latest year available, the number of employees in Kenya and Tanganyika,

[6] Colony and Protectorate of Kenya, Ministry of Commerce, Industry, and Communications, *Survey of Industrial Production, 1957* (Nairobi, Government Printer, 1959).

[7] Tanganyika, *Statistical Abstract, 1961* (Dar es Salaam, Government Printer, 1962), p. 2.

Table 28. Selected data on industrial development in East Africa

Industry	*Uganda*	*Tanganyika*			*Kenya*		
	Number of plants 1957	*Number of plants*		*Number employed 1960*	*Number of plants 1957*	*Number employed 1957*	*Gross production (in thousand $) 1957*
		With power 1960	*No power 1960*				
RAW MATERIAL PROCESSING							
Coffee processing	53	120	26	1,585	7	258	1,285
Tea packing	5	19		1,007	...	...	
Grain milling	186	1,354	8	8,182	53	2,505	19,900
Vegetable oil processing	40	93	3	1,383			
Sugar, fats	20	66		1,313	12	2,551	5,216
Canned fruits and vegs.		8		1,411	4	863	1,820
Cotton ginning	92	43		4,637	...	...	...
Sisal, kapok, jute, coir	2	255	2	30,220	3	1,522	2,005
Misc. crop processing		46	52	3,460			
Meat products		3		28	12	1,561	8,294
Dairy products	6	12	2	224	18	688	6,261
Leather and goods	1	8	37	874	7	305	935
Fish	2	1		98			
MARKET-ORIENTED INDUSTRIES							
Bakery products	21	28	58	553	48	1,284	4,480
Confectionery	3	8	1	158	7	117	280
Misc. food industries	2	7		105			
Beer	2	2		312	13	1,844	11,676
Carbonated beverages	20	32	26	454	31	1,150	2,850
Tobacco	1				1	1,120	18,026
Soap	43	37	19	558	18	451	2,685
Clothing and textiles	2	6		445	82	1,517	4,068
Shoes		4	120	390	47	933	2,475
Sawn timber	24	101	2	3,163	75	8,150	4,388
Joinery	57	317	77	4,110	33	728	1,039
Furniture	68				107	1,463	2,447
Clay and concrete products	30	22	10	1,156	20	1,929	1,859
Cement and other mineral products	2				19	1,642	7,932
Paper bags and boxes					6	345	1,680
Pharmaceuticals	1	1		13			
Other chemical products	2	8	1	286	32	3,093	10,794
Metal products	12	6		338	71	2,395	7,896
Machinery, incl. repair	49	40	43	597	42	1,525	3,170
Shipbuilding and rolling stock repair		22	2	2,816	9	6,482	7,190
Motor box bodies	6				16	383	907
Vehicle repair	104	227	50	4,644	156	4,355	8,579
Misc. mnfg.	5				22	284	1,005
Printing and publishing	25	36	4	845	60	2,148	6,280
Retreading tires	5	6		69	7	222	963
Electricity	8	35		474	10	2,382	9,088

N.B. Note the reservations regarding these data given in the text.

Sources: Uganda: Data provided by Uganda Development Corporation; Tanganyika: Ministry of Commerce and Industry *Commerce and Industry in Tanganyika Dec. 1961* (Dar es Salaam, Government Printer, 1962), pp, 91–92; Colony and Protectorate of Kenya, Ministry of Commerce and Industry, *Commerce and Industry in Kenya, 1961* (Nairobi, Government Printer, 1962).

... = Not available.

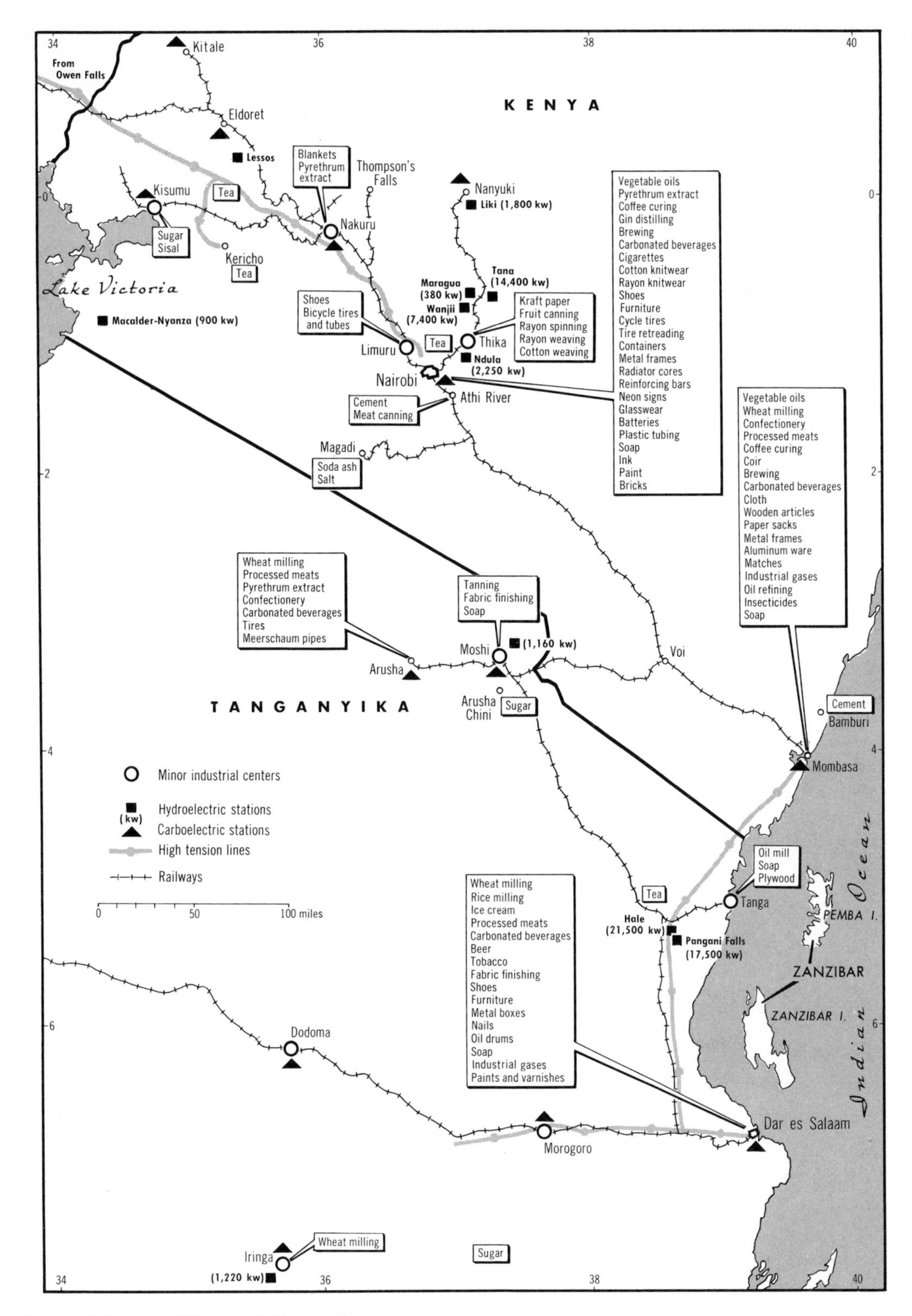

Map 75. Industries of Kenya and Tanganyika

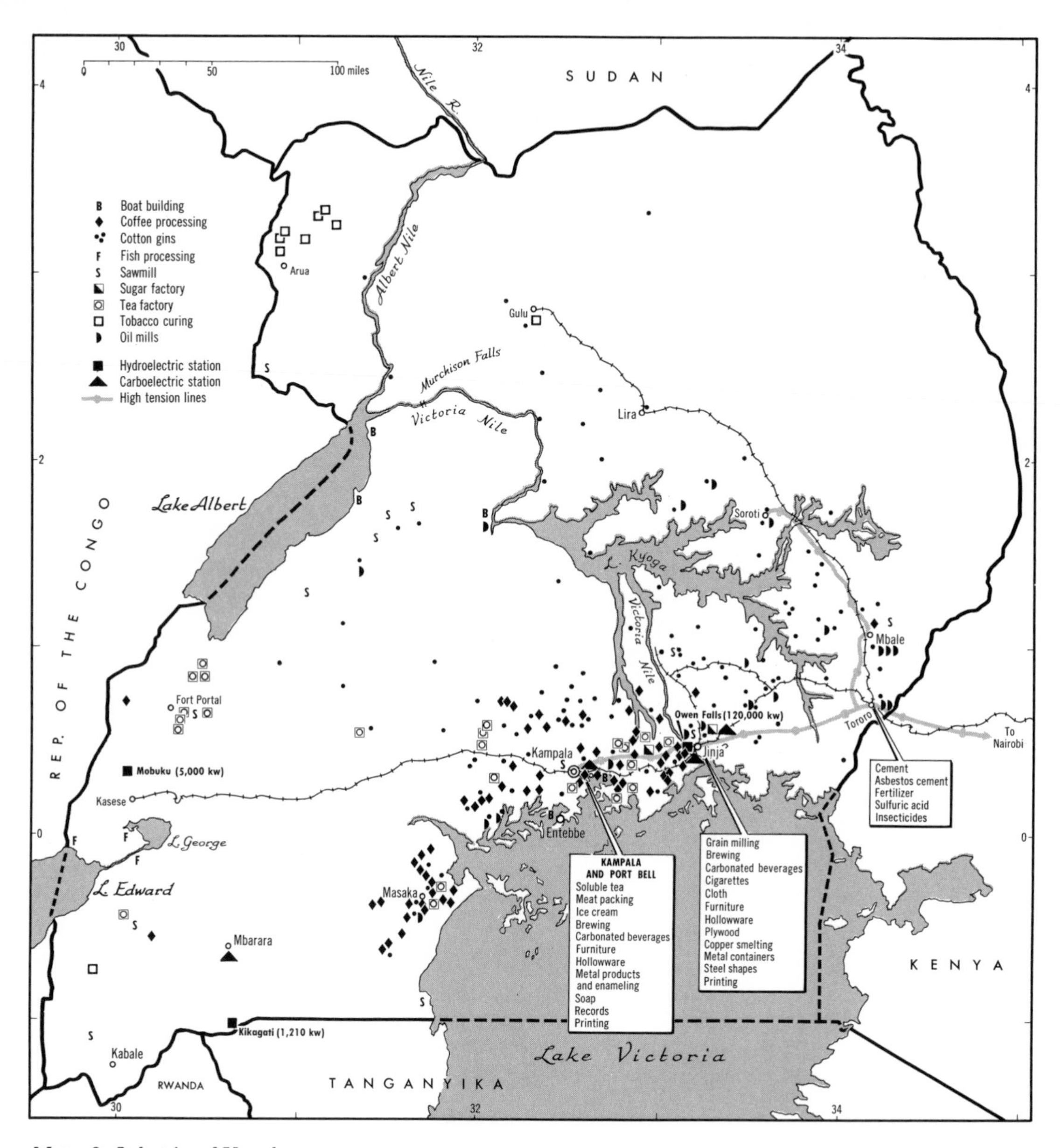

Map 76. Industries of Uganda

and the estimated value of gross production for Kenya. All of the reservations noted above must be applied to this table, plus the caution that it has been derived from three different sources whose method of collection and definition of terms were not the same.

A feature of importance as far as types of industry are concerned is the importance of tea, sisal, and sugar factories among the raw material processing factories. These are often large-scale factories which require a substantial investment, and stand very much in contrast with the usually small-scale and widely dispersed coffee processing installations and the cotton gins (Maps 75 and 76). The two sugar mills in Uganda are among the four or five largest plants in the country. An exception to the rule with respect to coffee plants is the $2.24 million coffee curing plant at Nairobi.

Also of interest is the building chemical complex of the Tororo Industrial Chemical and Fertilizers, Ltd. at Tororo, Uganda, which began operating in 1962. Managed by a subsidiary of Imperial Chemical Industries, this installation will produce about 25,000 tons of superphosphate, 10,000 tons of sulfuric acid, niobium concentrates from the apatite tailings of Sukulu, and "partly manufactured" cotton insecticides to the extent of 75,000 gallons yearly. A major concern at these relatively low levels of production is the high cost of electricity.

In the market-oriented group, the breweries, cement plants, and railway workshops are the larger scale plants, and will soon be joined by a big petroleum refinery at Changamwe, outside of Mombasa.

Of particular interest in the metal and metal fabricating group are small steel-rolling mills at Jinja, Mombasa, and near Nairobi, and several aluminum product factories, including a planned $3 million plant of Aluminium Ltd. at Mombasa.

The clothing and textile industry has had a particularly vigorous growth in recent years, especially in Kenya and Uganda. Kenya has a considerable number of small clothing factories, plus larger plants at Mombasa, Nairobi, Thika, and Nakuru, the last producing blankets. In Uganda, the factory of Nyanza Textile Industries, Ltd. (Nytil) at Jinja is one of that country's leading manufacturing establishments. Operating at a loss from 1952 to 1958, it has since expanded greatly and normally operates on a three-shift basis. Its profit in 1961 despite 78 work stoppages was about $840,000. Started with an investment of $1.8 million, the factory has a capacity that was doubled in 1962 at a cost of $2.8 million and is now about 28–30 million yards a year. Nytil first produced grey cloth, gradually moved to processed cloth, and is considering diversification into prints. About 2,500 people are employed at the mill. Two Bata Shoe factories are situated in East Africa, one at Dar es Salaam, the other at Limuru in Kenya, where cycle tires are also produced.

Uganda has one largely power-oriented plant, namely the Kilembe Mines copper smelter at Jinja. Other plants at that city may have been attracted in part by low-cost power, but are not accurately described as power-oriented establishments. The pipe factory of Tanganyika Meerschaum Corporation at Arusha is almost unique among plants in tropical Africa in making and exporting a product requiring high skill in its manufacture.

The distributional pattern of industry in East Africa is roughly comparable to that of other tropical African countries, raw material processing being widely scattered, and market-oriented industries being heavily concentrated in a limited number of cities, mainly the capitals and major ports. Nairobi is the main manufacturing center in East Africa. Within Kenya

The cotton textile mill of Nyanza Textiles (Nytil) at Jinja, Uganda

About 2,000 people are employed at this mill, which is one of the few large factories in Uganda.

Mombasa also has an impressive development, while Thika and Limuru are significant smaller centers because of their textile and shoe factories respectively. In 1957 Nairobi was credited with 60.5 percent of industrial employment and 58.5 percent of the industrial establishments in the country; the comparable figures for Mombasa were 21.0 percent and 22.5 percent.

In Tanganyika, Dar es Salaam is the leading center, while Arusha appears to be developing as the second main manufacturing center. Arusha has a relatively good situation with respect to the well-developed northern part of Tanganyika and also for marketing in the other two territories. In Uganda, Jinja has developed as the major industrial city, though Kampala has a larger number of small establishments. Tororo occupies a special position because of its cement and chemical works.

Pineapples being canned at a factory in Kenya
An example of a raw material oriented industry.

FACTORS INFLUENCING FUTURE INDUSTRIAL DEVELOPMENT

RAW MATERIALS. Looking briefly at the elements affecting the growth of manufacturing, it may first be noted that East Africa has a reasonably favorable raw material position, including production of a wide range of food and industrial raw materials from the vegetable realm, fish and forestry resources which could be more intensively developed, and a rather diverse group of minerals including coal and iron which might in the long run support an iron and steel development.

ENERGY. The energy position is somewhat spotty. Most of the coal is of only moderate grade and is located in very remote areas of Tanganyika which are otherwise not attractive for manufacturing development. Completion of the Shell-BP petroleum refinery at Mombasa in 1964 will result in savings on imported petroleum, and it may also be noted that East Africa is favorably situated with respect to Middle East sources. It is still possible, of course, that domestic oil will be found, but results have thus far been disappointing. In Kenya, a study made of the geothermal power resources in parts of the Rift Valley indicated that there was inadequate steam pressure to justify development. Some steam jets have been tapped for local farm use.

At present, hydroelectric resources are the main indigenous source of power and hold the greatest interest for the years immediately ahead. Uganda has had the most significant development—the Owen Falls Dam at the outlet of Lake Victoria (Map 76). Inaugurated in 1954, the dam has a capacity that is now 120,000 kw and that can be increased to 150,000 kw. The Owen Falls dam and plant will have a final cost of about $46.2 million, which, at about $308 per kw of installed capacity, compares favorably with most postwar installations.

About half of the power consumed in Uganda is taken by the copper smelter, Nytil, and the cement plant at Tororo. But the industrial build-up that it had been hoped would be attracted by cheap power did not materialize. In order to utilize the surplus capacity a substantial fraction of output, 41.7 percent in 1962, is sold to Kenya, being transmitted as far as 300 miles to Nairobi. And in 1961 the World Bank made a loan of $8.4 million to the Uganda

Electricity Board to help finance new distribution schemes within Uganda to broaden the market for Owen Falls power. If Kenya were to proceed with development of its Seven Forks scheme, replacing Uganda power from that source, Uganda would again be faced with a substantial surplus.

When the capacity of Owen Falls is fully utilized it will be possible to develop a 180,000-kw plant at Bujugali, just 4½ miles downstream from Owen Falls, for which preliminary plans have been prepared. An additional 275,000 kw is available on the Nile from there to Lake Kioga and about 1,390,000 kw between Lake Kioga and Lake Albert. About half of the latter capacity is sited at Murchison Falls, where the river drops 269 feet through a remarkably narrow passage.

Uganda also has a small hydro plant at Kikagati on the Kagera River, the capacity of which was increased to 1,200 kw in 1961. The Kilembe Mines have the third existing hydroelectric plant in Uganda, a 6,000-kw installation at Mobuku. While the history of hydroelectric production in Uganda has not been entirely successful, the country has witnessed an increase from 28.5 million kwh in 1951 to 453.1 million kwh in 1961, 99.1 percent of which was from Owen Falls.

Kenya is not so favorably endowed in hydroelectric potential, and the characteristic great seasonal changes in flow would require construction of storage dams instead of merely the head-creating dams required on the Nile. Hydroelectricity could nonetheless make an important contribution to the power economy of the country. The Tana and its tributaries have the greatest potential, and a number of small installations have already been constructed. The Seven Forks project could harness 240,000 kw on the Tana in three stages, while about 130,000 kw could be developed at five sites below that. Political uncertainties and a possible reduction in electricity consumption attendant upon the emigration of numerous Europeans have delayed proceeding with any large-scale project.

At the present time, Kenya receives about 52 percent of its electricity requirements from Uganda and 9 percent from Tanganyika (Map 75). Ten small hydropower stations with a total capacity of 27,290 kw provide two thirds of the 39 percent which is domestically produced, the remainder coming from thermal stations. With completion of a new thermal plant at Kipevu, the Mombasa region will no longer import power from Tanganyika.

In Tanganyika, there is a 17,500-kw plant partially utilizing the Grand Pangani Falls on the Pangani River and a 21,500-kw plant at Hale, five miles upstream. The Hale Project, involving an expense of about $15.4 million, was begun in 1961 and will be completed by 1965. A 173-mile transmission line will carry power from it to Dar es Salaam. Following closely upon the Hale plant will be a small 8,560-kw station on an upstream tributary to serve the Moshi-Arusha area. Small stations exist to serve Mbeya, Iringa, and Moshi, while most additional sites in Tanganyika could support only relatively small developments.

LABOR. The labor situation differs from most of the areas thus far studied in the availability of Indian artisans and workers, an advantage in the supply of semiskilled labor. The surplus of labor available in some of the urban centers may also be considered an advantage from the standpoint of ready availability of unskilled workers. There have been some problems associated with wildcat strikes and unrealistic union demands, but the general labor position appears to be satisfactory at the present time.

MARKET. The market situation has important advantages and disadvantages. From the standpoint of numbers, none of the countries have a large market, but, if a federation is created or if a customs union is maintained, a manufacturer catering to the domestic market would have a total market of about 27 million. In the past, Kenya has gotten a disproportionate share of the market-oriented industries moving to East Africa, which has the disadvantage for the other countries of raising the price for

The Athi River cement plant near Nairobi, Kenya
This is one of the two cement plants of that country, the second being situated near Mombasa. Capacity permits a considerable export to Tanganyika and Mauritius.

protected items without much offsetting benefit from enlarged employment opportunities. If a federation is created, it is likely that some arrangements will be made to ensure that Uganda and Tanganyika share in the build-up of consumer industries.

The market is not particularly favored from the standpoint of purchasing power, since average incomes are quite low, having been estimated at $66.6 per head in 1959. The non-Africans clustered in the Kenya Highlands do have relatively high average incomes, justifying the existence of some plants which would otherwise have difficulty in operating. While industry has stood up well in face of the exodus of Europeans that has occurred thus far, any really large-scale emigration would have a serious impact on many plants. Some industries have also been sustained by heavy government expenditures, which may not be continued on such a scale in the years ahead. This applies in particular to the construction industry.

The wide dispersion of population in East Africa and the inadequate transport links with some remote areas are, of course, disadvantageous as far as marketing of manufactured produce is concerned and are only partially offset by the population concentrations noted earlier and by the rapidly mushrooming cities.

CAPITAL. With regard to capital, East Africa will remain heavily dependent on outside sources for its industrial build-up, though many plant extensions have been locally financed and a number of wealthy Indians have capital available for local investment. The big unknown, as far as manufacturing development is concerned, is the future political climate, particularly in Kenya. There has been a flight of capital from all countries, and it could grow to far more serious proportions. On the other hand, some local and foreign investors are proceeding with plans for expanding the capacity of present plants or the introduction of new establishments.

While almost all industrial development in Kenya has been financed from private sources, government has been important in Tanganyika and especially in Uganda in the advance of manufacturing. In Tanganyika, the government is involved, for example, in the Tanganyika Packers Ltd., with two meat processing plants, the Tanganyika Meerschaum Corporation, and a new plywood plant at Tanga. Indians have also played a significant role in starting new industries in Tanganyika.

In Uganda, the two major capital sources stimulating industrial development are the Uganda Development Corporation (UDC) and Muljibhai Madhvani and Company, whose major interest had previously been in sugar. Madhvani and a second Indian source, the Mehta group, are the main providers of private local capital in Uganda. The Madhvani company has the largest soap mill in the country, is investing about \$2¼ million in the steel-rolling mill at Jinja, and is considering participation in the manufacture of matches, pulp and paper from papyrus, and distilled spirits. Mehta owns the Ugma Steel and Engineering Corporation concerned with the manufacture of steel tubes and agricultural implements. Both of these groups tend to focus their interests in the Jinja area.

The UDC is a semiautonomous government body concerned with a great variety of development projects in Uganda. At the end of 1961 the Uganda government had an investment of \$23.1 million in UDC, which had a gross turnover in 1961 of \$23.6 million. The Corporation finances its own expenses and pays no dividends though it has consistently shown a profit. At the end of 1961 its holdings were divided as follows: textiles (Nytil)—27.5 percent; building materials (Uganda Cement Industries, where a considerable capital write-off has been necessary, and Universal Asbestos Manufacturing Company, both at Tororo)—20.6 percent; agricultural enterprises—16.4 percent; mining (Kilembe Mines)—10.6 percent; property—9.6 percent; hotels—8.0 percent; enamelware (Uganda Metal Products and Enamelling Company at Port Bell)—3.2 percent; food (fish marketing at Kasenyi and grain milling at Jinja)—2.9 percent; fertilizers (Tororo)—1.2 percent. The UDC has aided small industries such as a Mugandan shoe factory producing 5 to 10 pairs a day, coffee roasting and grinding, and boat building. It has been criticized for devoting an excessive part of its capital to industry to the detriment of agriculture, but more recent investments have recognized the desirability of developing agriculture as a precondition to industrial growth and the attractiveness of tea as a profitable investment. In any case, the UDC has helped to attract additional capital, has assisted in diversifying the economy, and has started several activities which might otherwise not have appeared for many years.

TRADE

Table 29 shows the major foreign exports of East African countries in 1962, the trade among East African countries, and the growth of imports and exports at selected years from 1938 to 1962. Major characteristics of the trade position include the rather broad range of exports for Kenya and Tanganyika, but the high concentration of Uganda on coffee, cotton, and copper; the relatively high level of exports achieved by Uganda in relation to its size and population; the high dependence upon agricultural exports of all three countries; the markedly unfavorable imbalance in the external trade of Kenya, which is only partly offset by its favorable balance in the internal trade of East Africa; and the favorable balances of Tanganyika and Uganda, particularly the latter. The export economy in all three territories is a very important part of the total economy.

Table 29. Trade data for East Africa, 1938–1962

A. EXPORTS BY COMMODITY, 1962 (*in million $ U.S.*)

	Kenya	*Uganda*	*Tanganyika*	*Total*
Coffee	29.7	56.5	18.4	104.6
Sisal	12.1		44.1	56.2
Cotton	1.2	23.1	20.7	45.0
Tea	14.5	5.6	4.5	24.6
Diamonds			15.2	15.2
Meat products	7.7		6.5	14.2
Hides, skins, wool	5.3	3.3	4.2	12.8
Copper	1.3	10.1		11.4
Pyrethrum	8.9		.7	9.6
Oil seeds	.9	1.5	5.6	8.0
Grain	2.8	2.4	3.3	8.5
Cashew nuts			6.5	6.5
Gold			3.6	3.6
Sodium carbonate	3.5			3.5
Wattle products	2.4		1.2	3.6
Butter and ghee	2.6			2.6
Beans, peas, pulses			2.2	2.2
Pineapples	1.9			1.9
Cement	1.3			1.3
Wood			.7	.7
Other	9.9	2.8	6.2	18.9
Total	106.0	105.3	143.6	354.9

B. IMPORTS AND EXPORTS, SELECTED YEARS, 1938–1962 (*in million $ U.S.*)

	Kenya		*Uganda*		*Tanganyika*		*Total*	
	Imports	*Exports*	*Imports*	*Exports*	*Imports*	*Exports*	*Imports*	*Exports*
1938[a]	35	40			14	15	49	55
1948[a]	155	105			81	63	236	168
1952	166	83	68	134	105	130	339	347
1958	170	93	76	130	94	121	340	344
1961	193	116	74	116	111	138	388	370
1962	195	106	73	105	111	144	379	355

[a] Kenya and Uganda combined.

C. INTRA-EAST AFRICAN TRADE BY COMMODITY OR GROUP, 1962 (*in million $ U.S.*)

	Kenya to		*Tanganyika to*		*Uganda to*		
	Tanganyika	*Uganda*	*Kenya*	*Uganda*	*Kenya*	*Tanganyika*	*Total*
Animal products	1.69	2.17	.30	.17	.46	.05	4.84
Grain products	2.33	2.12	.57	.07	.34	.38	5.81
Sugar	.07	.16	.07		4.66	.06	5.02
Tea	1.55	.16	.05		.25	.01	2.02
Beer	1.54	.29			.01	.22	2.06
Other food	2.30	1.51	1.69	.24	.58	.14	6.46
Tobacco and products	3.60	1.92	.19	.03	2.28	.77	8.79
Industrial raw materials	.27	.30	.72	.31	.18	.04	1.82
Oils and fats	.40	.16	.41	.27	2.03	.34	3.61
Electricity			.14		.89		1.03
Chemicals	2.74	3.03	.11	.01	.27	.15	6.31
Other mnfg. goods	11.14	8.06	1.23	.13	3.11	2.46	26.13
Other	.42	.34			.02	.05	.83
Total	28.05	20.22	5.48	1.23	15.08	4.67	74.73

Sources: East Africa Common Services Organization, East African Statistical Department, *Economic and Statistical Review* (March, 1963); U.N., *Statistical Yearbook, 1962* (New York, 1963).

Part Six SOUTH-CENTRAL AFRICA

Long-hole percussion drilling at the Mufulira mine in the Northern Rhodesia Copperbelt

CHAPTER TWENTY

The Rhodesias and Nyasaland

Northern Rhodesia, Southern Rhodesia, and Nyasaland, often referred to as British Central Africa, became members of the Federation of Rhodesia and Nyasaland on September 3, 1953. The Federation's expressed policy was that of racial partnership in both the political and the economic spheres. And much was done in the ensuing ten years which was consonant with that goal, including an increased African political representation, greatly expanded betterment programs for African farming, removal of racial criteria for some landownership in Southern Rhodesian cities and agricultural areas, an increased elimination of the "color bar" in education and employment, including the bar imposed by European mineworkers on the Copperbelt of Northern Rhodesia, and opening of most public facilities such as hotels, restaurants, and swimming pools to persons of all races. But much remained to be done: European trade unions were still offering opposition to weakening the industrial color bar, only Africans were required to carry identification certificates, much land was still apportioned on a racial basis, and there continued to be many written and unwritten economic and social impediments to African advancement.

By 1960 it had become apparent that federation was not to be, at least while a white minority continued to dominate the political scene in Southern Rhodesia, and the British government announced in December, 1962, that Nyasaland and in March, 1963, that Northern Rhodesia would be permitted to withdraw from the Federation when they became self-governing. In July, 1963, the complex process of arranging for the breakup of the Federation began at a Victoria Falls conference, and dissolution took place on December 31, 1963.

In the meantime, there had been a series of conferences devoted to the constitutions of the individual countries. Nyasaland was the first to receive a new constitution, and in August, 1961, its legislative council had, for the first time, a majority of Africans. Northern Rhodesia got a majority of Africans in its legislature a few months later. Both countries were expected to become independent by 1965. Both had seen considerable unrest and violence in the previous few years; Nyasaland had a relatively peaceful devolution, however, once the die had been cast, while Northern Rhodesia, with two rival political parties, had continuing serious difficulties even after the country was firmly on the road to independence. Nyasaland is expected to become Malawi and Northern Rhodesia to adopt the name Zambia when they become independent nations.

Southern Rhodesia is obviously the focus of the most difficult problems. Classed as a "self-governing colony," it has a white minority that has been accustomed to governing itself for almost 40 years and to operating from a position of dominance vis-à-vis the African. Most Europeans have realized that they would eventually lose this dominant role, but there was wide difference of opinion regarding how rapid the evolution should be. The past few years have contained a series of powerful shocks to them: the occurrence in 1960 of the first African death from the forces of law since 1897, a deadlocked constitutional situation, rapid political advances

The Zambezi River in southern Barotseland in the western part of Northern Rhodesia

in the two northern territories, the end of the Federation, and sporadic violence and sabotage in various parts of the country. More rigid security legislation has failed to suppress the growingly insistent demands of Africans for power.

Some observers have predicted that the Southern Rhodesian whites would declare their independence, others that they would join with South Africa and form a northern extension of apartheid. It seems more likely that a series of shocks will continue, that Europeans will emigrate in increasing numbers, and that arrangements will be made for a constitution which will bring an African majority to power. After this step has been taken, and it is more difficult than in Kenya because of the self-governing status of the country, only those Europeans would remain who were willing to be governed by an African majority or who were in the country in some temporary capacity. When this does occur, probably within a few years, Africans in all three countries may find a renewed interest in federation. Southern Rhodesia would probably be named Zimbabwe.

In several ways, the Federation had the most advanced economy of any part of tropical Africa, and its rate of growth in many postwar years was as rapid as any political entity in the world. While there was slackening in the rate of growth beginning in 1957, the year 1961 saw a new high of $1,572 million in the gross domestic product, an increase in manufacturing output of 5½ percent, a new record in volume of mineral production, and, despite an unfavorable season weatherwise, a new high in sales of the prime agricultural export, tobacco. In 1962 there were records in balance of exports over imports, Nyasaland tobacco production, and output of electricity. But the trends that had begun to appear a few years earlier showed more clearly, and 1962 was, on the whole, a year of stagnancy if not regression. It saw a substantial fall in the value of product of the mining sector, a continued rapid drop in building and construction, and a slight fall in the value of product of manufacturing. There was a 15 percent drop in investment expenditure, gross operating profits of the business sector fell sharply, the gross national income per capita fell from $159.60 in 1961 to $154.00 in 1962, and, perhaps most serious, there was a decline in the total number of employees estimated at 3 percent.

Despite serious political and economic uncertainties, however, there were plans in 1963 for new enterprises. In agriculture, the output of citrus fruits, tea, sugar, peanuts, butter and cheese, and other products was expanding with force. In mining, while world consumption and prices are temporarily depressed, there are good prospects for expansion of copper production in Northern Rhodesia and of a variety of minerals in Southern Rhodesia. In manufacturing, favorable developments include the construction of new plants such as a petroleum refinery, glass bottle factory, and plywood plant, and plans for a variety of new establishments, particularly in Northern Rhodesia. But the continuing political uncertainties make short-run prediction extremely hazardous, particularly for Southern Rhodesia.

ECONOMIC GAINS AND LOSSES FROM FEDERATION

There has been strong difference of opinion regarding the economic value and justification of federation and regarding the economic effects that will result from its dissolution. Southern Rhodesia derived the greatest benefit. Federal tariffs on industrial products aided it the most because it had the largest industrial complex, though manufacturing's contribution to the gross domestic product grew at about the same rate in all three countries from 1954 to 1960. Salisbury gained by placement there of the federal government, the main offices of the copper companies (moved to Lusaka in 1963), insurance companies, banks, and building societies. Southern Rhodesia also probably gained by the greater attractiveness of the Federation to outside investors, backed as it was by the huge resources of the copper industry. It has recently been estimated that about $78.4 million of its cash economy was involved with the Federation, that about a third of its manufactured produce is normally marketed in Northern Rhodesia, and that about 45,000 people owed their jobs to the Federation.

Just how great Southern Rhodesia's losses will be from abandonment of federation will depend on what functions continue to be handled on a joint basis and how protective Northern Rhodesia and Nyasaland decide to be. Certain functions must be handled by some kind of a common services organization if all three countries are not to suffer: railway transport, Kariba power, communications, currency regulation, etc.

Nyasaland gained in two major ways from federation. First, it received an annual subsidy which was relatively large in relation to the total revenues at the disposal of the Nyasaland government. In 1961 it was estimated to have received $9.3 million, or 40.5 percent of its recurrent expenditures, from federal sources. Second, many migrant workers were employed in the two Rhodesias. Money injected into the Nyasaland economy during 1958 because of migrant laborers working within the Federation was estimated at $1.37 million exclusive of sums brought back personally or mailed back by the migrant workers. In 1960 about 130,000 Nyasas were employed in the Federation outside Nyasaland, and any marked reduction in this number would greatly influence the economy of the country. The breakup of the Federation does not necessarily mean that these jobs will be lost, but two independent Rhodesias might be expected to favor employment of their own nationals, particularly in the event of depressed conditions. Nyasaland did not gain greatly from sales of its produce to the Rhodesias except in the case of cotton.

Nyasaland probably lost through the imposition of federal tariffs on imported manufactured goods, which required paying higher prices for certain articles, reduced government revenue on imported goods, and made it impossible to protect its own infant industries. On the other hand, there was an offsetting gain in increased opportunities for Nyasas to find employment in Southern Rhodesian industry.

Northern Rhodesia probably gained the least through federation, because a portion of its revenues from copper was diverted to the other two countries. However, since it has the most nearly one-product economy of the three, it probably gained from the greater stability in revenue of the more diversified Federation. Its common interests with Southern Rhodesia in transportation and Zambezi power have already been noted.

The economies of the three parties to the Federation were not sufficiently advanced to take full advantage of the opportunities it represented. As they matured, the benefits of a larger and unified market, of greater diversification, of increased interdependence, of centralized planning, of certain common services, and of easier attraction of outside capital would have increased. Just how severe the losses from its breakup will be depends on how rigidly nationalistic the individual countries become. But dissolution of the Federation must be expected to reduce confidence in the area on the part of domestic and foreign investment sources and, at least temporarily, to limit the opportunities for interregional exchange of persons, goods, and services.

THE DEMOGRAPHIC BACKGROUND

Since the population make-up is of such overwhelming importance politically and economically, it is well to examine it in some detail. The total population of the Federation was estimated to be 9,491,600 at the end of 1962 (Table 30), 96.3 percent of whom were Africans. Southern Rhodesia had 41.4 percent of the total, Nyasaland 31.4 percent, and Northern Rhodesia 27.2 percent. Nyasaland had by far the greatest density; subtracting its water surface, its density was 80.6 per square mile in 1962. Southern Rhodesia had about 26.2 per square mile, and Northern Rhodesia had only 9.0 per square mile in 1962. The Nyasaland density is high for Africa; the Cholo and Mlanje Highlands in that country have densities over 200 and pockets with the exceptional density of 800 per square mile. In Northern Rhodesia, some of the Lake Bangweulu islands have densities of over 325 per square mile. In much wider areas of all three countries there is overpopulation, given the present agricultural systems.

Population growth is difficult to measure because of inadequacy of statistics, but the present crude rates of increase of all races are high, those of the Africans ranging from an estimated 2.2 percent in Nyasaland to 2.5 percent in Northern Rhodesia and 3.0 percent in Southern Rhodesia. Progressively improving health and sanitary conditions will probably result in sharper increases in the rates of growth in the years ahead.

In March, 1963, there were an estimated 976,000 wage earners in the money economy, about 64 percent in Southern Rhodesia, 23

Table 30. Area and population of the Rhodesias and Nyasaland by racial groups for selected years, 1954–1962

		Federation	*Southern Rhodesia*	*Northern Rhodesia*	*Nyasaland*
Area, in square miles		486,973	150,333	287,640	49,000[a]
Population, in thousands					
Total	1954[b]	7,162.5	2,610.0	2,068.8	2,483.7
	1961[b]	8,634.7	3,198.8	2,514.8	2,921.1
	1962[c]	9,491.6	3,931.7	2,577.6	2,982.3
African	1954	6,920	2,440	2,010	2,470
	1961	8,290	2,960[d]	2,430	2,900
	1962	9,140	3,690	2,490	2,960
European	1954	216.2	158	53	5.2
	1961	304.9	221	75	8.9
	1962	309.4	223	77	9.4
Asian	1954	16.7	4.8	4.4	7.5
	1961	25.7	7.1	7.9	10.7
	1962	27.2	7.5	8.4	11.3
Coloured	1954	9.6	7.2	1.4	1.0
	1961	14.1	10.7	1.9	1.5
	1962	15.0	11.2	2.2	1.6

Source: Federation of Rhodesia and Nyasaland, Central Statistical Office, *Monthly Digest of Statistics* (August, 1962), p. 1; (May, 1963), p. 1.

[a] Includes about 12,000 square miles of water surface.

[b] 1954 estimates for June 30; 1961 and 1962 estimates for December 31.

[c] 1962 figures are preliminary.

[d] Preliminary figures from the April-May, 1962, census of Africans in Southern Rhodesia indicate that this figure was too low, the population at the time of the census having been 3,610,000.

Table 31. Industrial distribution of African and non-African employees in the Rhodesias and Nyasaland, March, 1963 (in thousands)

	Northern Rhodesia		*Southern Rhodesia*		*Nyasaland*	
	African	*Non-African*	*African*	*Non-African*	*African*	*Non-African*
Agriculture, forestry, and fishing	36	0.7	275	4.4	56	0.4
Mining and quarrying	40	8.3	41	2.6		
Manufacturing	15	2.6	69	15.9	6	0.5
Construction	21	1.9	31	5.9	14	0.4
Electricity, water, sewage	2	.3	5	1.3	1	0.1
Commerce	15	6.5	34	25.1	11	1.7
Transport and communications	9	3.0	15	9.7	6	0.4
Domestic services	36	9.2 (Domestic and other services)	95	24.1 (Domestic and other services)	9	2.2 (Domestic and other services)
Other services	47		62		25	
Total	221	32.5	627	89.0	128	5.7

Source: Federation of Rhodesia and Nyasaland, *Monthly Digest of Statistics* (July, 1963), pp. 6–9.

percent in Northern Rhodesia, and 13 percent in Nyasaland. These figures include about 140,000 temporary workers from neighboring countries, especially Mozambique, while there are an estimated 100,000 Africans from the Federation working abroad, mainly in the Republic of South Africa and the Congo. Table 31 shows the industrial distribution of Africans and non-Africans in March, 1963. Since the vast bulk of jobs are in the cities or in European farming areas, large numbers of Africans must migrate from the reserves or from one territory to another. It is estimated, in fact, that over a third of the able-bodied men in Nyasaland work outside the protectorate at any one time. In 1960 there were an estimated 159,500 Nyasa males working outside Nyasaland, including 113,000 in Southern Rhodesia, 28,000 in South Africa, and 17,000 in Northern Rhodesia, while 36,400 left Nyasaland in 1961 to work in Southern Rhodesia. Some of the migration has been more than temporary; over a third of the Nyasas and half of the Northern Rhodesians in employment in Southern Rhodesia in 1956 had been away at least eight years.

While only about one million Africans are wage earners, it is estimated that all forms of economic activity involve about two thirds of the African population in the money economy of the Federation.

The European population increased much more rapidly than the African until recent years, but still represented only 3.3 percent of the total in 1962. The greatest increase came in the 1950s, which saw a growth from 179,040 in 1951 to 291,000 in 1959; after that the rate of increase slowed and the estimated population at the end of 1962 was 310,000. Europeans are very unevenly distributed among and within the three territories: Nyasaland has only 3.0 percent of the total, Northern Rhodesia has 24.9 percent, and Southern Rhodesia 72.1 percent.

Immigration was more important than natural growth in expanding the European populace. Strong preference was extended in immigration quotas and in assisted immigration to European citizens of the Commonwealth and especially to citizens of the United Kingdom. In the period 1938–52 approximately 96 percent of non-African immigrants were from the Commonwealth, about half from the British Isles and about 40 percent from the Union of South Africa. By 1958, however, the percent of non-Commonwealth immigrants had increased to 15. As of September, 1961, Europeans born in the Federation comprised 38.9 percent of the total European population; those born in South Africa totaled 24.6 percent, and those in the British Isles 24.0 percent. The number of Afrikaner immigrants is considered to be a critical factor, but the strength of the nucleus of the Afrikaners on the Copperbelt is greatly reduced because the South African citizen does not have a vote in Northern Rhodesia.

Immigration continued heavy until 1957, after which there was a marked decline, occasioned in part by the somewhat depressed conditions in the copper industry, but later more by increased concern regarding the political future of the European in the Federation. Not all of the immigrants have been satisfied to remain in the area, and there has been a fairly strong emigration in some years. But in 1961, for the first time in many years, there was a net emigration of 1,241 non-Africans. In 1962 net emigration was 1,883, and it was 6,070 in the first nine months of 1963. It is not unlikely that this trend will continue for some years; indeed it has been suggested that European farmers should be deliberately bought out, following the example of Kenya, to reduce the dimension of future tension. Of course, many government employees cannot be considered permanent residents, as they often retire at an early age and leave the area. From the economic standpoint, however, any large exodus of Europeans would have a strongly depressing effect on the economy and substantially reduce the opportunities for African employment and improvement of the infrastructure.

There were some 127,300 non-Africans working in the Federation in 1963, 70.0 percent in Southern Rhodesia, 25.5 percent in Northern Rhodesia, and 4.5 percent in Nyasaland. A marked characteristic of the European population is its heavy concentration in urban areas. Over a fifth of the Europeans actively engaged in Northern Rhodesia in 1961 were employed by the Copperbelt mining companies, and in December, 1962, 52,800 of the total of 87,600 non-Africans resided in the seven main towns on the belt. In Southern Rhodesia, 138,850 of the 220,610 Europeans in 1961 resided in the cities of Salisbury and Bulawayo alone. For the Federation as a whole, 75.3 percent of the total non-African population in 1962 was to be found in the nineteen largest cities. African migration to the cities is also increasing rapidly, creating severe housing problems which are requiring ever-increasing expenditure. The population of Africans in Salisbury increased from an estimated 104,000 in 1951 to 217,000 in 1962, the comparable figures for Bulawayo being 90,000 and 155,000. Application of the Native Land Husbandry Act in rural areas of Southern Rhodesia has resulted in increasing the landless class and will contribute to the future growth of urban communities.

The Federation had a relatively small Asian population, totaling only 27,200 in 1962, and about 15,000 "Coloured" people or persons of mixed races. The economic contribution of both these groups is considerably greater than the 0.5 percent of the total population they represent.

THE PHYSICAL BACKGROUND

The total area of the Federation was 486,973 square miles; Northern Rhodesia accounted for almost three fifths of the total, Southern Rhodesia for about three tenths, and Nyasaland for about one tenth. The land of the Rhodesias is mostly on the plateau of Central Africa (Map 77). Average elevations in Northern Rhodesia range between 3,000 and 5,000 feet above sea level, the greater part of the plateau being between 3,000 and 4,000 feet. Shallow swamps and lakes, such as Lake Bangweulu and the Kafue Flats, cover large areas of the flattish plateau surfaces. In many localities the level of the plateau is broken by hills, sometimes occurring as chains which develop into areas of more rugged country. The Muchinga Mountains, west of the Luangwa trough, form part of the great escarpment and have individual peaks rising to about 8,000 feet. The Luangwa trough itself is believed to be an ancient depression and is covered with sedimentary formations in contrast to the bulk of the plateau area. In the northeast is a mountainous area associated with the Lake Nyasa Rift Zone and isolated from the rest of the country by the low-lying, unhealthy Luangwa Valley.

In Southern Rhodesia, a belt of generally level land above 4,000 feet runs nearly across the country from northeast to southwest. This area, about one fifth of the country, contains most of the European population and the densest African settlement as well. It is the physical and economic backbone of the country. From this region of highveld the land drops off through a broad, more heavily eroded, middle veld to the lowveld of the Zambezi Valley in the northwest and of the Limpopo and Sabi basins in the southeast. The margins of these troughs are everywhere marked by higher, rugged terrain, while the relief is gentle on the soft rocks of the troughs themselves. The Zambezi trough is deep and rather narrow, with very steep sides. Largely because of aridity and insect pests it is just beginning to be developed. The southeastern lowveld is considerably broader and also largely undeveloped. The eastern border of Southern Rhodesia is marked by mountain country, whose continuity is broken by a gap at Umtali.

Nyasaland, a strip of land 520 miles long and 50 to 110 miles wide, is composed mainly of plateaus and highlands ranging from 3,300 to 10,000 feet, plus a portion of the Great Rift Valley occupied by Lake Nyasa in the north and by the Shire River in the south. The 360-mile-long Lake Nyasa stands at an elevation of about 1,565 feet, while the lower Shire Valley is only 100 to 300 feet above sea level.

The presence of much high land in the Federation moderates the climate, making it attractive for white settlement and permitting a broad range of crops. Lowland tropical crops may be grown in the troughs, though this would often require irrigation, while other tropical, subtropical, and middle-latitude crops give potentially great diversity to the highveld and to the highland areas. The landform features do not present the difficulties of overland movement characteristic of East Africa, as is revealed in the less accidented profile of the Rhodesia Railways' main line or in the newer line to Lourenço Marques.

THE INFRASTRUCTURE: TRANSPORT

NORTHERN AND SOUTHERN RHODESIA

Because of the pervasive influence of transportation and power, it is desirable to survey these factors before turning to agriculture, mining, and industry.

RAILWAY DEVELOPMENT. The backbone of the transport system of the two Rhodesias is the Rhodesia Railways, whose older main line runs 1,270 miles from the Mozambique border near Umtali to Salisbury, Bulawayo, Livingstone, Lusaka, the Copperbelt, and the Congo border. This somewhat devious route may be readily explained by a glance at a map of the area showing relief (Map 77); in so far as possible the main line keeps to the higher plateau levels and crosses the Zambezi just below but at the crest level of Victoria Falls where the river is confined in a narrow gorge which could readily be bridged.

For many years, Beira, to which the main line leads in Mozambique, was the gateway for the overseas traffic of the Rhodesias; before 1955 it normally handled 65 percent of the total external trade by value of British Central Africa and 80 percent of the total overseas trade. Severe congestion at Beira and on the Rhodesian line made it necessary to seek a second outlet, and in 1955 a line was opened to the southern Mozambique port of Lourenço Marques, which had the further attraction of available capacity. This Pafuri Link or Limpopo Line, totaling 248 miles in Southern Rhodesia, greatly relieved pressure on the railway and on Beira and also opened up a hitherto undeveloped part of Southern Rhodesia. Its traffic has increased steadily and was 1,419,000 tons or about 32 percent of total external rail movements in 1961.

The first rail line to the Rhodesias came northward from South Africa via Bechuanaland to Bulawayo, and this line remains the only direct rail link with the Republic of South Africa. The 398-mile section in Bechuanaland is owned by the Rhodesia Railways, which works the northern half from the Rhodesian border to Mahalapye, the remaining section being worked by the South African Railways. South African ports are too far distant to be very attractive for Rhodesian overseas traffic, though they always handle some import cargoes. The connection is more important in traffic between the Rhodesias and the Republic of South Africa, which is one of the few inter-African movements of real significance.

Rhodesia Railways is also connected via the BCK and the Benguela Railway to Lobito, but this line has never handled the Rhodesian traffic that might have been expected in view of the considerable distances saved on land and sea

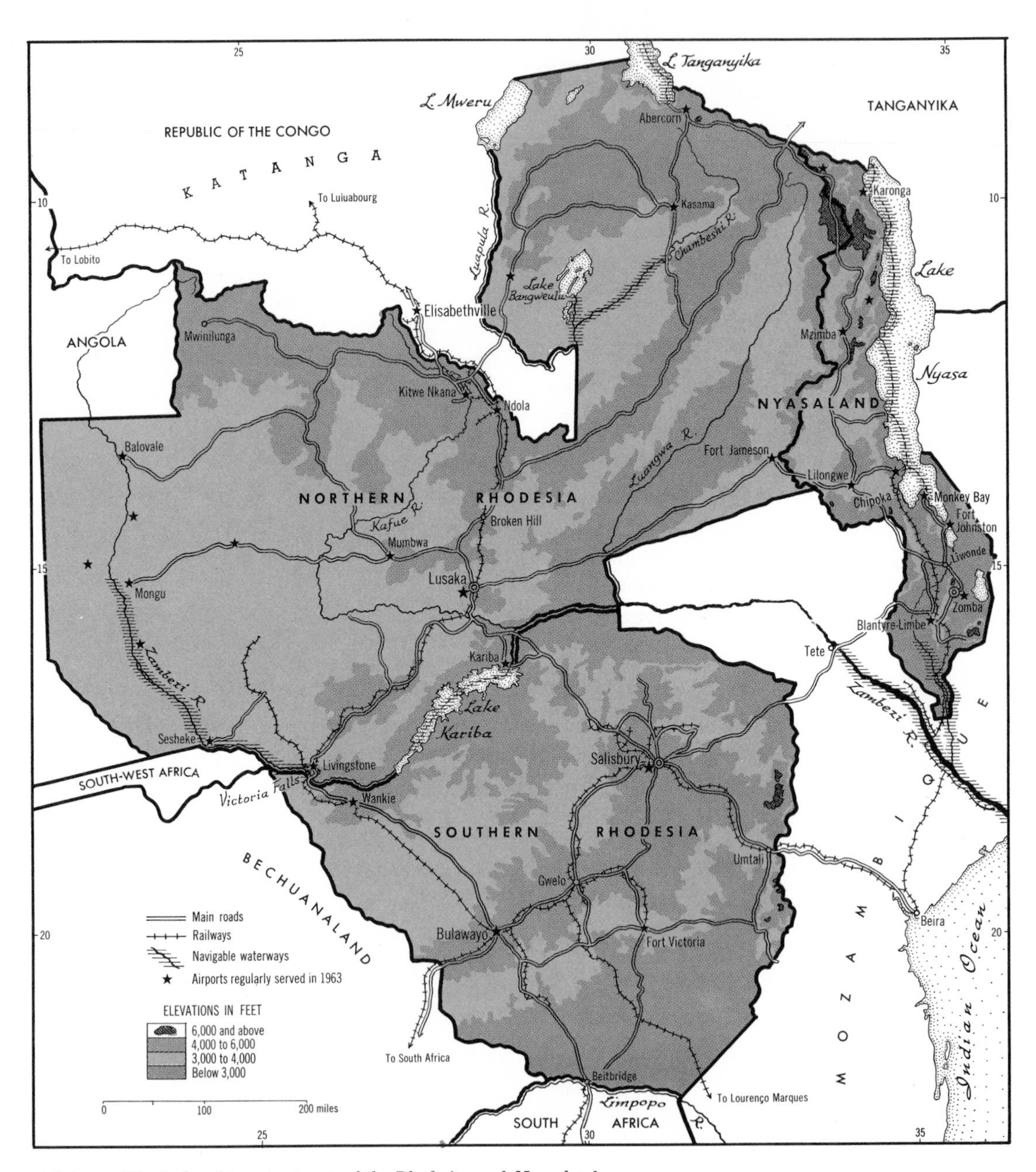

Map 77. Physical and transport map of the Rhodesias and Nyasaland

routes from Northern Rhodesia. In the 1950s, considerable tonnages of coal were brought to the Copperbelt on this line owing to the inability either of Wankie to mine adequate coal or of the Rhodesia Railways to move enough of it to the copper complex. But copper was first exported via this route only in February, 1957, after the Bulawayo Conference had agreed partially to release the Copperbelt from long-standing commitments to use the Rhodesia Railways to the east. A new agreement between the copper companies and Rhodesia Railways in 1960 again reduced the use of the western outlet, the companies having been extended a lower rate on their shipments to the east in return for an agreement to move at least 600,000 tons over the Rhodesia Railways and not more than 36,000 tons over the Katanga-Benguela route. In the 1961 operating year, only 21,708 tons of Northern Rhodesia copper moved via Lobito; 572,095 tons moved via Mozambique ports, and 16,763 tons went to the Republic of South Africa. While the routes to the east are anachronistic in terms of direction and distance, they do have the advantages of supporting the domestic lines and saving expenditure of foreign exchange.

Other foreign links with the Rhodesia Railways have been studied and proposed. A connection from the line in Northern Rhodesia via the northeastern lobe of that country to a rail line in Tanganyika was not approved because of its high cost in relation to the estimated traffic that might be generated by it. The Rhodesian system has not been connected to the South African Railways in the 100-mile gap between West Nicholson and Beit Bridge in part because of Rhodesian desires not to strengthen ties between the two areas, in part because it is believed that the present connection via Bechuanaland is adequate without expending the $5.6 million that would be needed for the Beit Bridge link.

There has been sporadic interest regarding a new line to the Atlantic, either to a port in South-West Africa or to Baía dos Tigres, Moçâmedes, or Lobito in Angola, the last involving a link to the Benguela Railway not passing through the Congo. The most likely such connection would be to Moçâmedes. The Portuguese have already extended the line quite far inland from that port and are interested in carrying it to the Rhodesian border; the Rhodesian portion would probably run from about 10 miles north of Livingstone to the Kwando River. Most of the route would be comparatively easy, only one large bridge being required to cross the Zambezi near Katimo Mo-lilo. This 210-mile link would cost about $65.8 million, according to a study made in 1958. An independent Northern Rhodesia would not authorize such a link so long as Angola is Portuguese.

Additional proposals have been made for new internal lines in the Rhodesias. A saving of 175 miles on shipments from Northern Rhodesia and southwestern Southern Rhodesia could be effected by connecting the existing Gwelo-Umvuma branch in Southern Rhodesia to the main line at Odzi near Umtali, which would also reduce congestion by bypassing Salisbury and bring rail service to the upper Sabi River. A link from Sinoia in Southern Rhodesia to Kafue in Northern Rhodesia would reduce the distance from Lusaka and the Copperbelt to Salisbury and Beira by 500 miles but would follow a difficult route across the Zambezi Valley.

In addition to the need for new lines, there have been and continue to be heavy requirements for improvements on the existing line and to the locomotive park and rolling stock. The 1,250 miles from Umtali to Ndola have been relain with 100-pound track. New diesel-electric and powerful Beyer-Garratt articulated steam locomotives have been purchased and several thousand wagons have been added to the rolling stock. A centralized traffic control system now operates over much of the line, said to be the longest such system in the world. But if traffic continues to grow as it has in the past, additional heavy expenditure will be required to enlarge the capacity of the railways and some sections may have to be double-tracked.

Total freight traffic on the Rhodesia Railways has increased from 2.9 million tons in 1938–39

A strip road in Southern Rhodesia
These hazardous roads have been largely replaced by high-standard paved highways in recent years.

to 8.4 million tons in 1954 and 11.8 million tons in 1962. Coal and coke, almost all from Wankie, normally represent the largest tonnage (23.9 percent of the total in 1962), while other minerals accounted for about 27.8 percent of the total. Passenger traffic was 4.1 million in 1962.

Two criticisms have frequently been made regarding the Rhodesia Railways: one, the lack of farsightedness in calculating the future demands on the lines, which helped to explain the fairly chronic pressure on existing capacities in the 1950s; the other, the rigid color bar in railway employment. The latter was finally removed in 1960 when the European union agreed to its abolition provided that there would be no lowering of work standards in adoption of the principle of the rate for the job.

ROADS. The trunk roads of the Rhodesias parallel the rail line, with numerous feeders acting to some extent as branch lines. The Great North Road from Kapiri Mposhi through the relatively neglected eastern lobe of Northern Rhodesia to Tanganyika has been improved and is the chief transport artery in that region. Contact with this part of Northern Rhodesia is somewhat handicapped by the extension into the country of the Katanga pedicle of the Congo and by the presence of the Luangwa trough. Contact between Nyasaland and Southern Rhodesia is similarly affected by the extension of Mozambique territory up the Zambezi Valley. Motor services are operated by the Rhodesia Railways on about 5,700 of the 36,270 miles of road in Southern Rhodesia and regular services are also run on a substantial percent of the 19,853 miles in Northern Rhodesia, but most road haulers operate in confined areas around the main centers. Competition with the railways is avoided by restrictions on length of haul and by agreements between the railways and long-distance road haulers. The two Rhodesias have an unusual length of paved roads, but most roads are still precarious in the rainy season and there is still a considerable mileage of the somewhat hazardous strip roads in Southern Rhodesia. The vehicle park, totaling 226,289 in 1961, is also unusually large for tropical Africa.

WATERWAYS. Waterways are of little significance in the Rhodesias. There is regular barge traffic on the Zambezi above Victoria Falls to Mongu in Barotseland; the waters of Lake Bangweulu are used for local traffic and are connected by a 200-mile, four-foot-deep channel to Kapalala at the border of the Katanga pedicle on the Luapula River and to Mbati on the Chambezi River; and some trade of the Abercorn area in the extreme north moves via Mpulungu on Lake Tanganyika to Kigoma on steamers operated by the East African Railways. Lake Kariba provides a new waterway for the Rhodesias, stretching some 175 miles upstream from the dam, but it will probably have greater interest for tourism and fishing than for transport.

AIRWAYS. The government-owned Central African Airways provides air coverage within the territory and to adjacent countries. Measured by miles flown in civil aviation, the airways of the Federation rank second to the Republic of South Africa on the African continent. The main airport is at Salisbury; there are five other major termini and 168 smaller fields.

NYASALAND

Nyasaland is served by one rail line running from Salima near Lake Nyasa to Beira and having a connection to the lake port of Chipoka. In 1962 the Nyasaland Railways carried 612,500 passengers and 935,500 tons of freight. Lake Nyasa is the most important inland waterway of the Federation, but tonnage carried on the ships, operated by the Nyasaland Railways, is still very low, totaling only 12,000 to 16,000 tons a year. Lake transport has been hindered by the comparative scarcity of natural harbors and of good connecting roads from the hinterland. Only Nkata Bay and Chipoka have good port facilities but the latter, which is the present rail-lake terminus, has poor site features. Monkey Bay, at the tip of the peninsula which separates the two southern arms of Lake Nyasa, is now the base for lake steamers and has a far better harbor. But the level of lake traffic discourages expenditure on a 42-mile link that would be required to tie it to the main line. A second difficulty in use of the lake has been shifts in its level of as much as 20 feet, but these have been reduced by erection of a bund intended to stabilize its level at Liwonde on the Upper Shire. There are about 6,896 miles of motor roads in Nyasaland, with only the main road from Mlanje through Blantyre and Zomba to Liwonde being paved. The north-south trunk road, which has been improved, is the main route.

THE INFRASTRUCTURE: ENERGY

With completion of the Kariba Dam, the Rhodesias moved into a comparatively favorable energy position. But the shortage of adequate fuel and power had often been a severe problem in the decade and a half after World War II. At one period it was the Wankie Collieries which could not produce enough; at another it was the railways which could not move the quantities required. Shortages of coal and coke on the Copperbelt made it necessary to burn large quantities of wood, which was estimated to cost three times as much as coal and which led to denudation of the forest cover over wide sections. Coal was also imported from South Africa and America via the Benguela and BCK railways. Elsewhere, the shortage of fuel made it necessary to ration electricity and hence undoubtedly acted as something of a damper to industrial expansion.

But these shortages of fuel and power were not occasioned by a shortage of reserves. All three countries have coal; there are excellent possibilities for further development of hydroelectric resources, and, for the future, there may be sizable deposits of uranium ores. Knowledge regarding the extent of coal deposits and hydroelectric resources is still sketchy, but enough is known to indicate that the power and fuel position is quite adequate to support a greatly expanded economy, and that the area compares favorably with most African countries in this regard.

COAL

Until the 1960s, the major source of energy in the Federation was the Wankie Collieries (Map 82), 200 miles northwest of Bulawayo and 68 miles southeast of Victoria Falls on the main line. Proved reserves around Wankie are given at 892 million tons of low-ash coking-quality coal and 335 million tons of poorer quality coal; possible reserves total 412 million tons. Much of the Wankie coal lies close to the surface; the main seam varies in thickness from 11 to 34 feet and is worked easily from inclined shafts at depths varying from 80 to 200 feet. Mining began at Wankie in 1903 and reached an output of 1 million tons in 1927, 2 million tons in 1949, and a record of 4.2 million tons in 1957. Output, now confined to two collieries with a capacity of 4.5 million tons, was expected to decline with the beginning of transmission from Kariba

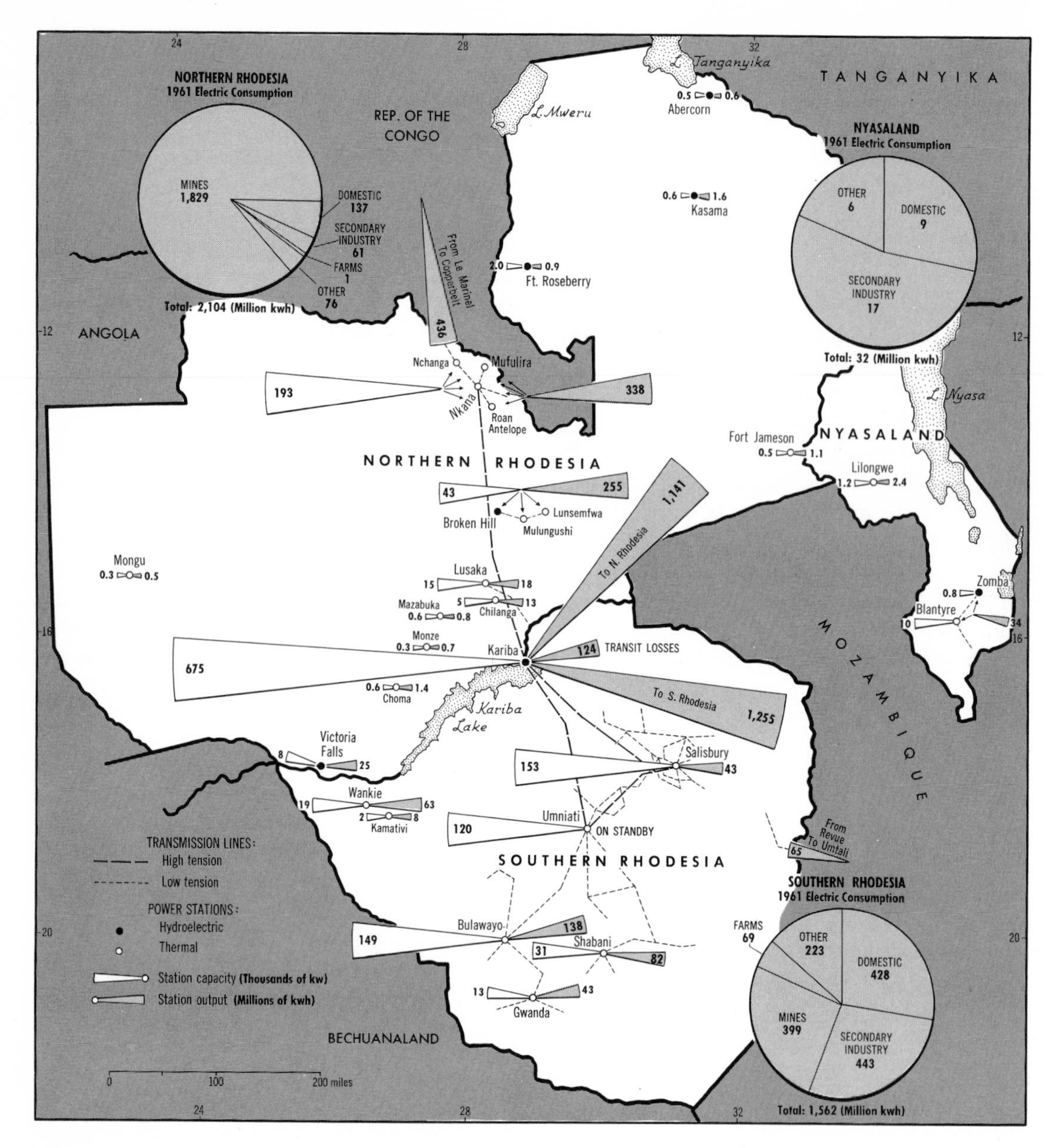

Map 78. The electrical energy position of the Rhodesias and Nyasaland, 1961–1962

and in fact did fall to 2.92 million tons in 1962. Wankie Collieries employed about 450 Europeans and 6,240 Africans in 1961, producing coke, by-products, and firebricks in addition to coal. Coal is mined at Wankie at exceptionally low cost, the price at pit head being $2.80 in 1961 and 1962 until it was raised to $3.08 in November, 1962.

Southern Rhodesia also has coal reserves in the Sebungwe area northeast of Wankie and in the Sabi Valley. The latter area has about 5 billion tons of proved reserves, by far the largest in the country, and has seams averaging 46 feet in thickness, but its coals have the highest ash content of all the Southern Rhodesian coals, averaging about 35 percent. The limited known reserves of high-quality coal in the colony suggest that consideration be given to its rational exploitation, and make somewhat questionable efforts that have been made, albeit unsuccessfully, to sustain output by securing large-scale foreign outlets.

Coal has also been found in Northern Rhodesia north of the Zambezi, but most fields appear to have coals of 22 to 30 percent ash content and narrow seams. Nyasaland has several deposits, chiefly of mediocre coals. In total, the coal reserves of the Federation are probably immense, certainly much greater than the 7.25 billion tons officially listed as "proved reserves." Although it is unlikely that more than a small percentage will prove to be of coking quality, these reserves appear to give the countries greater possibilities than other tropical African countries for developing an integrated industrial economy.

HYDROELECTRIC POWER

The hydroelectric potential of the area is very great. The markedly seasonal regime of even the larger rivers is a handicap, but the very considerable potential heads and some excellent sites for storage are compensating factors. The Kariba Dam and plant on the Zambezi is now the main source of power in the Federation and the largest existing hydroelectric installation in Africa (Map 78). The flow of the Zambezi River varied at Kariba from 15,000 to 200,000 cusecs before control, hence the need for a large capacity lake, met by construction of a 420-foot-high dam, 1,900 feet across at the top. Lake Kariba, averaging about 12 miles in width, covers about 2,000 square miles and required several years to be filled. The lake itself, the largest man-made lake in the world, is a new resource; several harbors are being established for recreation and support of a fishing industry for which the lake is being stocked with bream. In a six-month period in 1961, recorded shipments of fish from the lake totaled over 500 tons. A problem which has arisen and still awaits solution is eradication of a fernlike floating weed, *Salvinia auriculata* or "Kariba weed," which should not, however, interfere with power-generation.

The Kariba Dam on the Zambezi River
Africa's largest hydroelectric project, Kariba now has a capacity of 675,000 kw, which can be raised to 1,575,000 kw. In 1962 it produced 65 percent of total electricity in the Rhodesias and Nyasaland.

At present there is one underground power plant in the right bank below the dam with a developed capacity of 675,000 kw when the reservoir is filled. Later a 900,000-kw plant will be constructed within the north bank, but this will probably not be needed before 1970. The Kariba Project, which was adopted in 1955 and officially inaugurated in 1960, represents one of the greatest investments in African development, involving a total expenditure of about $223 million for the first stage. Kariba is connected by a 330-kv transmission system to areas accounting for 87 percent of the total consumption of electricity in the Federation, including the Copperbelt and the highveld of Southern Rhodesia. In 1962 Kariba accounted for 65.2 percent of total electricity produced in the Federation, a percentage which is likely to increase as enlarged output permits closing down or reducing the output of carboelectric stations. About 48 percent of its output in that year was transmitted to Northern Rhodesia, particularly to the Copperbelt, and 52 percent to electricity grids serving the highveld areas of Southern Rhodesia.

No sensational reduction in the cost of power to consumers has occurred in the Rhodesias as a result of Kariba coming on stream, because of the commitment to pay off the indebtedness incurred in a relatively short period of years. The cost of power should decline 44 percent from the 1961 level, when it was slightly below the average cost of electricity in the United States, by 1971, and considerably more by 1981, but it will be some years before electricity will be sufficiently cheap to attract power-oriented industrial establishments.

Kariba weed (Salvinia auriculata), *a fernlike weed which has grown rapidly on Lake Kariba*
While no solution has been found for this problem, it is not expected to interfere with power generation.

It may be questioned why the natural site of Victoria Falls was not first developed before turning to a project requiring the construction of an expensive storage and head-creating dam. There were three objections to developing power at Victoria Falls: (1) the fear of destroying the beauty of a site with very considerable value to the tourist industry; (2) the great fluctuation in flow over the Falls, the mean maximum flow being about ten times the mean minimum flow; and (3) the considerably greater distance of the Falls from major consuming centers. A small 8,000-kw plant now serves the local communities near Victoria Falls and a study has been undertaken regarding the advisability of placing a new plant close to the present installation in the Third Gorge, this plant to have an initial capacity of 6,000 kw and an eventual capacity of 12,000 kw. A second, more ambitious scheme would involve construction of a 100,000-kw plant in the Fifth Gorge, power from which might be consumed in a nitrogenous fertilizer plant at Livingstone. Finally, if a site can be found above the Falls suitable for storage it would be possible to develop perhaps an additional 200,000 kw at the Falls without affecting its beauty, and indeed probably contributing to it.

There are a number of other hydroelectric plants in being at the present time. Plants on the Lunsemfwa and Mulungushi rivers with a total capacity of 36,700 kw meet the bulk of needs at Broken Hill, Northern Rhodesia. Three small plants have recently been constructed at a cost of $2.8 million elsewhere in Northern Rhodesia: 2,000 kw at Fort Roseberry, 900 kw at Kasama, and 500 kw at Abercorn. In Nyasaland, Zomba has a 750-kw station.

There are numerous other sites that may later be developed in the Federation, notably on the Kafue, the Shire, the Zambezi, and the Chambezi headstream of the Congo. The Kafue would probably be the next major development after Stage 2 of the Kariba Project has been completed. Preliminary studies indicate that the installations would be a 200- to 300-foot-high storage dam 240 miles upstream from the Kafue Gorge at the Meshi Teshi gap, a small dam at the head of the gorge, and two power stations in the gorge. The river drops 1,964 feet in 12½ miles in the gorge and the total capacity developed would be about 1.2 million kw.

In addition to Kariba and Victoria Falls, it is estimated that 175,000 to 520,000 kw could be developed on the Zambezi northeast of Wankie, and about 1 million kw in the Marata Gorge downstream from Kariba. In Nyasaland, a survey of the Nkula Falls site on the Shire River indicated that about 20,000 kw could be developed to serve Blantyre-Limbe-Lilongwe at a cost of about $8.4 million. The Federation was prepared to proceed with this scheme, but the Nyasaland government refused to accept aid from the Federation in view of its intention to secede upon independence. In 1963, however, the Nyasaland government was proceeding with a somewhat restricted development at Nkula Falls, financed partly by a $2.8 million grant from the CDC. A total of about 250,000 kw could be developed on the Shire River.

There is, then, no reason for this area to be short of fuel and power for many years. And despite shortages that have existed, the Rhodesias have long compared very favorably with other African countries in production and consumption of electricity (Chart 3). Map 78 shows the capacity and output of electric stations in the Federation in 1961–62. In addition to the hydroelectric installations, there are large carboelectric plants on the Copperbelt and at Umniati, Salisbury, and Bulawayo. Umniati is now on a standby basis and the others are being operated at well below capacity since Kariba power can meet the needs of the areas they serve. The Copperbelt has received power from Le Marinel station in Congo in recent years under agreement with UMHK, while some electricity is also imported from Mozambique to the Umtali area and a very small amount from Messina in South Africa to Beit Bridge. The amount of electricity contracted to be received from Mozambique was based on optimistic projections of growing needs, resulting in Umtali's being obligated to pay for more electricity than it has required in recent years. Electricity sent out by all undertakings serving the Federation in 1961–62 totaled 4,198 million kwh, of which 65.2 percent was generated at Kariba, 15 percent in the rest of Northern Rhodesia, 6 percent in the rest of Southern Rhodesia, and 0.9 percent in Nyasaland, while 11.2 percent was imported from Le Marinel in Congo and 1.7 percent came from Revue in Mozambique. The increase in production has been very rapid, moving from under 500 million kwh in 1938 to 2,460 million kwh in 1955 and 4,198 million kwh in 1962.

PETROLEUM

There are no known deposits of petroleum in the Federation nor are the geological formations encouraging. The success of South Africa's oil-from-coal plant at Sasolburg near Vereeniging has been watched with interest with the thought of possible duplication on one of Southern Rhodesia's coal fields, but preliminary investigations suggested that such a plant would not be feasible as yet. The erection of a large refinery near Umtali will also militate against such a development and will somewhat reduce the expenditure of exchange on imported petroleum products.

AGRICULTURE

THE PHYSICAL BASE

It takes but a brief examination to reveal the relative poorness of the Rhodesias and Nyasaland for intensive agricultural pursuits. The basic physical handicaps are the climatic and soil characteristics. The highly seasonal pattern of precipitation, with rainfall almost entirely confined to the summer, means that cropping is also confined to this season unless irrigation can be applied. Over most of the area rain begins about the end of November and ends in March or April, though the rains start somewhat earlier in the northwest of Northern Rhodesia and last longer in northern Nyasaland. The mountainous sections also have an atypical distributional pattern, rain falling in most months of the year, particularly on the eastern and southeastern slopes. A second major climatic handicap is the relatively small total precipitation over the bulk of the region, and this is the main determinant in land use.

The mean precipitation in Southern Rhodesia is 26.1 inches, though the highlands on the eastern borders receive as much as 100 inches. Extensive areas in the south of that country and in the Limpopo Valley receive only 12 to 16 inches. In Northern Rhodesia, the average precipitation is 40.3 inches, being higher toward the north and lower particularly in the Luangwa and Zambezi valleys. Nyasaland has a mean rainfall of 41.7 inches but greater variation than either of the other countries. The highlands average about 60 inches, the lowlands 30 inches, and much of the country has a climate similar to and better than that of the eastern districts of Southern Rhodesia.

A third factor is the high degree of unreliability in rainfall; the rains are unreliable in their onset, their duration, their distribution within the season, and their total amount. This is reflected in a wide variation in crop yields and in the carrying capacity of pastureland. Yields of the staple food crop, corn, fluctuate widely, and consequently foreign and internal movements vary sharply from year to year. Low yields are not only a result of low precipitation, but may be occasioned by excessively wet seasons.

Precipitation varies considerably with altitude, aspect, and latitudinal position. These differences now explain the localization of such crops as tea, tobacco, and sugar and will lead in the future to more clearly defined agricultural regions than now exist. The atypical areas, such as the lower lands of the Zambezi, Shire, and Sabi rivers, or the higher lands of Nyasaland and eastern Southern Rhodesia, will be looked to for specialized production to bring greater productivity and variety to the agricultural pattern.

Temperature characteristics are, in contrast to precipitation, unusually favorable. High temperatures usually associated with the tropics are considerably modified on the plateaus, and the light ground frosts which are likely during the winter at higher altitudes impose few limitations on the range of crops which may be grown. On the other hand, the prevailing high temperatures below 2,000 feet permit the production of such tropical lowland crops as sugar.

Although soil surveys are as yet entirely inadequate to permit any sound quantitative judgments, it is generally accepted that by far the larger part of the area has mediocre soils. There is a widespread deficiency of available phosphates, the nitrogen reserves are quickly depleted, and the structure of most soils tends to deteriorate rapidly when they are subjected to cultivation. Loss of structure is in turn followed by a sharp decline in productivity and by increased susceptibility to erosion. In general, the soils derived from the ancient rocks of the plateau are shallow and infertile, while the soils of the lowlands and valleys are potentially more productive.

Southern Rhodesian soils vary from fertile red clays to far more prevalent sandy soils of low basic fertility which are, however, quite suitable for flue-cured tobacco. European farmers have also, through better rotational practices, greater application of fertilizer, and more interest in mixed agriculture, learned how to preserve and even improve their inherently poor soils. Soils in Northern Rhodesia are for the most part highly leached and shallow on the plateaus or deep, loose Kalahari sands of low productivity. The most fertile soils are the "upper valley soils" found mainly in the lower Kafue basin between Pemba and Broken Hill and the "lake basin soils" of the northeast, which carry a dense agricultural population.

Nyasaland has some of the best soils of the

Federation, particularly in the Lower Shire Valley, in the Cholo and Mlanje Highlands, and on the Lilongwe Plain. But large areas of stony, shallow soils exist in the Northern Province and in the Central Shire area.

The primary result of the combination of soils and climates is that only a very small part of the area is favorable for intensive arable-mixed farming, while the bulk of the area, about three fifths, has too low and undependable precipitation for reliable crop production and is suitable only for grazing. Some of the dryer, warmer areas are, however, the best for irrigation agriculture. It is safe to say that the most important physical problem facing the three countries is proper utilization of their land surface. But a speedy solution cannot be expected and, in the meantime, some existing land practices as well as certain economic forces are not conducive to the maintenance of even the present level of quality.

Insect and disease attacks are also continuing problems. About five eighths of Northern Rhodesia is tsetse-ridden; Nyasaland and Southern Rhodesia are more fortunate, the latter being about nine-tenths tsetse-free. Cotton production in Southern Rhodesia has been severely cut back by plant disease, and the existence of countless termitaria is another problem of considerable dimension.

THE DIVISION OF LANDS

The division of land between Africans and Europeans is a subject of intense concern to Africans, dominating political discussions, even among the urbanized Africans. The allocation of lands has caused friction in Nyasaland and is a subject of growing seriousness in Southern Rhodesia. The amount of land reserved for Europeans varies greatly from country to country (Table 32), and changes are now taking place which presage important alterations in land distribution in the years ahead. Southern Rhodesia, which had the largest percentage of alienated lands, some 49.4 percent of the total area of the country in 1960, amended its Land Apportionment Act in 1961 to set up 5.26 million acres as unreserved land accessible on a nonracial basis and to create an Unreserved Land Board to handle the selling or leasing of land among racial groups. The government purchased a large company holding as a first

Table 32. Land allocation in the Federation, 1961

	Federation		*Northern Rhodesia*		*Southern Rhodesia*		*Nyasaland*	
	In thousand acres	*Percent*	*In thousand acres*	*Percent*	*In thousand acres*	*Percent*	*In thousand acres*	*Percent*
Total area	304,303	100	184,090	100	96,610	100	23,603[a]	100
Assigned to Africans	237,783	78.1	173,676[b]	94.3	43,774	45.3	20,333	86.2
Assigned to Europeans	43,042	14.2	5,576[c]	3.1	36,784	38.1	682	2.9
Other	23,478	7.7	4,838	2.6	16,052[d]	16.6	2,588	10.9

Source: For Northern Rhodesia and Nyasaland, derived from Advisory Committee on the Review of the Constitution of the Federation of Rhodesia and Nyasaland, *Report*: *Appendix VI. Survey of Developments since 1953*, Cmnd. 1149. (London, Her Majesty's Stationery Office, 1960), pp. 234, 246. For Southern Rhodesia, *Report of the Advisory Committee: Development of the Economic Resources of Southern Rhodesia with Particular Reference to the Role of African Agriculture* (Salisbury, Government Printer, 1962), p. 141.

[a] Land area.

[b] Includes 29,427,000 acres in Barotseland, 34,713,000 acres in African reserves, and 109,536,000 acres in native trust land.

[c] Includes 3,508,000 acres of Crown Land in freehold and 2,069,000 acres in leasehold. Africans were not prescribed by law from buying Crown Land but had not successfully applied for any as of 1961.

[d] Includes 2,308,000 acres of forest area and forest reserves, 4,208,000 acres in national parks, 4,276,000 acres in nonhunting reserves, and 5,260,000 acres in unreserved land.

major step in securing additional land space for distribution to Africans. While some whites considered the Land Apportionment Act as the cornerstone of society, it is obviously unrealistic to allocate almost half the country to about 6 percent of the population, especially since there is inadequate land to apportion into economic holdings in the African areas, and it can only be a matter of time before the act is totally repealed. The amount of land in the two Rhodesias listed as assigned to Europeans in 1962 is, it should be noted, somewhat misleading because part of it has not been allocated and part of what has been allocated is either not occupied or remains undeveloped. For example, about one third of the alienated land in Southern Rhodesia in 1960 had not been assigned and about one sixth of what had been assigned was not actually in farm holdings.

EUROPEAN FARMING

A more meaningful conception of the status of European farming may be derived from the number of farmers and farm holdings, from the areas under cultivation, and from the estimated gross value of crop and livestock production from European farms, the last shown in Table 33. In 1956 only about 9,000 Europeans were operating or employed on Federation farms, cultivating about 80,000 acres in Nyasaland, 207,500 acres in Northern Rhodesia, and 820,000 acres in Southern Rhodesia. The total area held by European farmers in Southern Rhodesia in 1960 was 34.5 million acres, most of this being in large ranches.

Southern Rhodesian farms vary greatly in size, as is seen from the following figures, compiled in 1960:

Size of holding in acres	*Number of farms*	*Percent of total area in European farms*
1,000 and below	2,100	2.2
1,001–5,000	3,564	26.5
5,001–20,000	1,156	30.4
20,001 and above	244	40.9

The sharp contrast between the large European farm and the African holding, averaging about 8 acres, is excessive, irrespective of ability or contribution to the economy. In fact, there is ample opportunity to enlarge African holdings without any serious impact on European farming, as is suggested by the following statement which appeared in a recent government publication:

> In the areas of good soil and rainfall the vast majority of farms (European) were far too large for there to be any reasonable expectation of the occupiers ever utilizing their land resources to the full, and this survey showed that it was exceptional for farms, even in good cash-cropping areas, to show an average utilization of more than half their potential arable.[1]

Despite this criticism, however, European farmers must be credited with a most significant contribution to the Rhodesian or Nyasaland economies. Their output of flue-cured tobacco was the second-ranking export by value in the Federation, and they accounted in 1962 for an estimated 68.3 percent of the gross value of crop and livestock products in Southern Rhodesia or 50.0 percent of the gross value for the whole Federation. European farms produced 83.4 percent of cash crops in 1962.

The bulk of European holdings in Southern Rhodesia are on the highveld (Map 79), which is the most favorable land climatically and economically. The more important producing regions are around Salisbury and in the Eastern District, though the largest holdings are in the less favored parts of the country.

In Northern Rhodesia, about 1,185 European farmers holding 3.79 million acres account for about 70 percent of the marketed agricultural production of the country. Most of them are situated in a compact belt along the rail line from Livingstone to the Copperbelt, though a few are found around Abercorn in the extreme north and around Fort Jameson near the Nyasaland border. In Nyasaland the main European areas are in the Cholo and Mlanje districts. European estates account for almost all of the tea and tung oil produced in Nyasaland and for part of the tobacco and coffee.

[1] Federation of Rhodesia and Nyasaland, *An Agricultural Survey of Southern Rhodesia, Part II—Agro-Economic Survey* (Salisbury, Government Printer, 1960), p. 90.

Table 33. Estimated gross value of crop and livestock production in the Rhodesias and Nyasaland, 1962

	Southern Rhodesia		*Northern Rhodesia*		*Nyasaland*	
	In million $	*Percent*	*In million $*	*Percent*	*In million $*	*Percent*
European farms	157	68.3	19	26.4	16	20.5
African farms						
Sales	13	5.6	8	11.1	14	18.0
Subsistence	63	26.1	45	62.5	48	61.5
Total	233	100	72	100	78	100

Source: Federation of Rhodesia and Nyasaland, Ministry of Economic Affairs, *Economic Report, 1963* (Salisbury, Government Printer, 1963), p. 64.

Practices on many of the European farms still leave much to be desired. Some have made little effort to develop soil-conserving practices and farming systems. The application of fertilizer is typically low. Emphasis on corn or tobacco on many farms is carried to the point of monoculture. But a very substantial improvement has been made on the better farms in recent years, particularly through the practice of grass ley farming involving 3 or 4 years in grass for each year in tobacco or corn. Attention has been given to the development of special grasses suitable for pasturage, these grasses improving the friability of the soil, preventing erosion, and, with adequate fertilization, maintaining or even improving the productivity of the land.

AFRICAN FARMING

INDIGENOUS SYSTEMS. African farming, until very recently, followed traditional practices almost everywhere. Some native systems display a keen sense of the relations between the character of the soil and the natural vegetation that grows on it. For example, a "soil selection" system is practiced in Barotseland in which there are at least six distinct and specialized garden types on which the crops grown, the soil treatment, and the periods of cultivation and fallow vary according to the fertility and regenerative capacity of the soil.

A second example is *chitemene* cultivation, practiced in considerable areas of the Rhodesias. There are many varieties of *chitemene*, but the essential feature is the practice of lopping branches or felling trees over a wide area surrounding the actual garden and then burning them on the garden.[2] Burning destroys weeds, makes clay soils more friable, and provides a fertilizing ash. Given static conditions, these and other systems can be considered as somewhat ingenious adaptations to the environment.

Modern practices and conditions, however, have often led to the degeneration of the

[2] Colin G. Trapnell, *The Soils, Vegetation and Agriculture of North-eastern Rhodesia* (Lusaka, Government Printer 1953), p. 36.

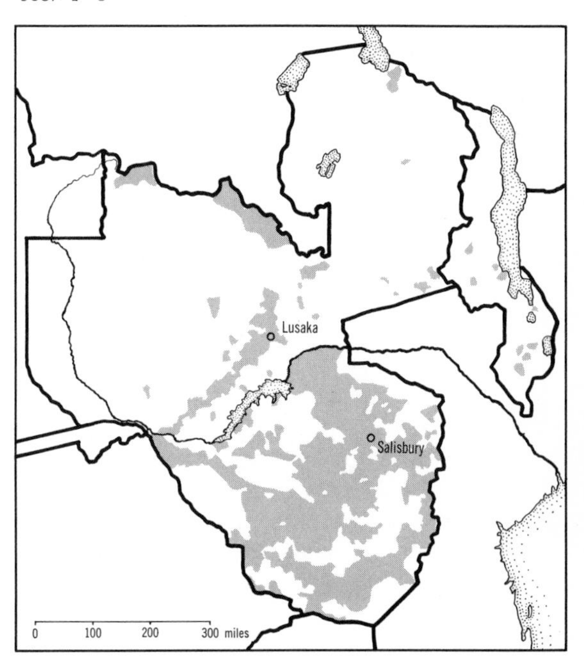

Map 79. Areas of European farming or concessions in the Rhodesias and Nyasaland

traditional native systems, not all of which are good examples of proper land husbandry in any case. Partly because of the absence in the rural areas of from 40 to 70 percent of the able-bodied males, who migrate to the mines, industries, and European farms and households, annual garden extensions have often been abandoned, even when there is more than ample land. Secondary crops are often neglected to the detriment of nutritional standards. In some areas, degeneration has resulted from the expansion of population and the consequent shortening of the period in bush or grass fallow, which should probably be close to 20 years on the old rock soils. These phenomena are by no means confined to these countries; to an extent they represent a largely inevitable effect of the introduction of a modern economy. But the degradation of large areas is a problem of major importance requiring appropriate steps to offset its deleterious effects. An increased disharmony between rural and urban areas could otherwise prove to be a serious barrier to continued development in any sphere. Farming in African areas must also be seen in the light of a rapidly expanding population and of already existent overcrowding, especially in Nyasaland.

DEVELOPMENT PROGRAMS. Until relatively recently, the attention given to improving African farming was entirely inadequate. A handful of European advisers worked mightily to encourage better practices but could not have been expected to bring about changes of the order required. More recently, numerous efforts and several large-scale programs have been adopted or proposed to upgrade the standards of African agriculture, to bring it more rapidly into the money economy, and, indeed, to remake the whole farming landscape.

Chitemene *agriculture in Northern Rhodesia*
Branches are cut from trees over a wide area, collected in piles, and burned to provide fertilization for a garden patch.

Southern Rhodesia. Southern Rhodesia has had the most dynamic program under its African Land Husbandry Act, passed in 1951 but intensively applied only in the later 1950s. Unfortunately, this program ran into serious political and social difficulties and was about at a standstill in 1962. The goal of this program was to transform some 30 million acres of African lands in about 155 reserve and special areas of great areal and physical variety, by substituting a system of improved commercial farming for the traditional systems of land holdings and the primitive methods of self-subsistent, shifting agriculture.[3] The new system was to involve the granting of individual arable and grazing rights and the directed application of minimum standards of good husbandry including contour terracing, crop rotation, manuring, and improvement of livestock. A typical application was supposed to involve (1) surveying the area; (2) allocation of blocks of land to be tilled, their shape and size depending on soil, landform, demographic, and other characteristics; (3) instruction to the farmers by Land Development Officers with respect to crops and farming practices; (4) assignment of land unsuitable for cropping to the grazing of cattle and goats, whose numbers were restricted to prevent overgrazing; the typical pattern was for an arable block to be surrounded by grazing areas divided so as to permit the upgrading of livestock; each family head had about 50 acres in grazing land; (5) relocation of dwellings into villages on new and permanent sites, with an effort being made to encourage the erection of higher-standard

[3] See Barry N. Floyd, "Land Apportionment in Southern Rhodesia," *The Geographical Review* (October, 1962), pp. 566–82.

homes; (6) development of a conservational system including provision of contour banks, drainage channels, and access paths; and (7) assignment of individual holdings to each family. Normally, each family head was allotted 8 to 15 acres consisting of several linear fields bounded by contour banks.

Such an ambitious program, involving an expenditure of over $55 million from 1952 to 1962, could not have been entirely successful in a brief span of years. In fact, the whole program foundered seriously after a few years of intensive application and in 1961 was essentially halted pending new legislation and a revised program. Failure was not directly attributable to the program itself but rather reflected the whole picture of land allocation in Southern Rhodesia. The program was, in effect, hamstrung by the Land Apportionment Act, which meant that individual holdings were often just adequate to be considered an economic unit and that many thousands of people could not be assigned land even on a tight schedule. In Matabeleland, for example, it was estimated that there were about 100,000 people and 110,000 cattle for which no provision could be made.[4] It had been envisaged that whatever surplus of people were not accommodated on individual holdings would be readily absorbed in expanding industry and other nonagricultural employment, but, in fact, employment of Africans declined at the crucial point owing mainly to the slackening pace of economic development. Rather than opportunities for additional employment being provided in the cities, numerous people from the cities were thrown back on the land. As the African traditionally looks upon tribal land as his main source of security, he could not accept the fact that no allocation could be made to him, and the government was forced to alter its original regulations accordingly. Nor was the African willing to accept the necessity for reduction of cattle numbers, and the government was forced to modify its method of counting cattle to permit a heavier stocking. Asked to make two very drastic and major changes in his attitude toward land and toward cattle and aware of the marked contrast between his congested areas and the underdeveloped European farm lands, the African, not surprisingly, responded readily to political exhortations to ignore or disobey the act.

Other faults of the program were that too much emphasis was given to allocating land and too little to extension work after the assignment of individual tenure, that there was considerable dishonesty on the part of African land authorities with respect to the original allocations, that there was inadequate availability of credit to permit proper development of the new holdings, and that some layouts were too hastily and hence erroneously made. An unfortunate and unforeseen difficulty was encountered in the promotion of Turkish tobacco as a cash crop; eminently suitable from the technical standpoint for peasant cultivators, it was seriously affected by a plant disease and the number of African growers declined from 4,444 in 1959–60 to 570 in 1960–61.

Despite the many criticisms that have been made of the African Land Husbandry Act, it did contain many beneficial aspects. It involved important conservational features, both for tilled areas and for the veld used only for grazing; it eliminated fragmentation of holdings; it was designed to husband the all-important water resources; and it involved efforts to improve crop production. Furthermore, the fact that grazing control and assignment of individual tenure were resented does not mean that they were not needed and not beneficial. In fact, there is evidence that individual holdings are being increasingly accepted in some areas.

The achievements of the land husbandry program are difficult to assess at this point. By 1962, about 15.4 million acres or about three fourths of the total allocations had been completed and, despite some sabotaging of conservation layouts, important progress had been made in the application of sound land husbandry techniques. Given an assignment of additional lands

[4] J. R. V. Prescott, "Overpopulation and Overstocking in the Native Areas of Matabeleland," *The Geographical Journal* (June, 1961), p. 222.

and a greater effort to work cooperatively with the African, there could be much long-term gain resulting from the program.

In addition to the African reserve areas, Southern Rhodesia has 8.1 million acres of Native Purchase Areas which are supposed to be available for dividing into freehold farms of 50 to 350 acres. These farms may be purchased by "master farmers" who have demonstrated their farming abilities or by farmers who successfully complete a two-year training program. Unfortunately, some 25,000 unqualified families have been permitted to occupy some of this land and to farm in the traditional way, thus reducing the acreage available for the several thousand applicants on the waiting list to purchase farms. In 1962, however, a 500,000-acre ranch estate was purchased by the government to provide land for between 1,000 and 1,300 would-be purchasers. By the end of 1958, 5,683 farmers had purchased 560,222 acres in the Native Purchase Areas.

It may be questioned whether adequate attention has been accorded to the African farmers in the Purchase areas. These are likely to include a large percentage of the more advanced African farmers, of those who have shown a willingness to adopt modern techniques; more extension work with them might, therefore, prove rewarding.

In 1959–60 a sample survey of African agriculture in Southern Rhodesia was carried out which produced such surprising results that they were not published until 1962 pending a recheck for accuracy. Most unexpected among the findings were the relatively high yields of corn and peanuts obtained by African farmers. Whereas it had been generally accepted that yields were from a third to a half of average yields on European farms, they were measured on the farms surveyed at 72.7 percent of European yields for corn and almost the same yield for peanuts. Other interesting results included the large number of African farmers who were found to have paid employees and the considerable variation in size of area cropped. Indeed, one quarter of the farmers surveyed had 60 percent of the cultivated area. This survey has stimulated much interest in Southern Rhodesia. It suggests that more such studies are required, that Africans may be marketing corn in much greater quantities than previously estimated, and that numerous farmers are displaying a greater degree of initiative than heretofore accepted. It has also had the desirable effect of winning new support for combining European and African farming unions, marketing arrangements, and agricultural services.

Northern Rhodesia. Northern Rhodesian schemes for African farmers have been of a more restricted character. The agricultural department notes that there has been a remarkable development of African farms run on improved lines in accordance with the advice of government officials, that there have been marked improvements in native cattle, and that there is an increasing demand for individual title to lands. By 1960 some 400 Africans had qualified as Master Farmers. In the Fort Jameson district of the Eastern Province, where there is considerable overcrowding, a resettlement scheme has been applied costing some $260,400 in five years. Involving the resettlement of 50 villages and 500 individual farmers, the scheme includes provision of dams, wells, roads, tsetse control, and improved farming in the new areas.

In 1957 an Impact Scheme was launched in the Northern and Luapula provinces designed to speed up the process of rural development. Involving the expenditure of $5.6 million over a four-year period on a limited area, where about half of the able-bodied males are normally working on the Copperbelt, this scheme aimed to establish stable rural communities based on agriculture and fishing with attention being given to improvement of marketing, crop production, communications, forestry, fishing on Lakes Mweru and Tanganyika, and to the development of other rural industries. The scheme has not been entirely successful, probably because it expected to achieve too much in too short a period and failed to elicit support of the local populace.

But resettlement and impact schemes are

likely to be very costly and applicable only to restricted areas, leaving the vast bulk of African rural areas largely untouched. Realizing that more rapid improvements were necessary on a widespread basis, Northern Rhodesia has developed a plan to raise the economic status of the African population in a program somewhat similar to that of Southern Rhodesia. The program was first proposed in mid-1961, and it was estimated that $56 million to $92.4 million would be required in a four-year period to implement it. As this was considered an unobtainable amount, a $19 million four-year working program has been developed to help about 50,000 African peasant farmers raise their living standards above the subsistence level.

Nyasaland. In Nyasaland the traditional form of tenure and traditional farming remain strongly entrenched. For over two thirds of the Africans the tenurial arrangements involve the husband's moving to his wife's village upon marriage, matrilineal inheritance, and land allocation by village headmen. This system has broken down under the force of modern circumstances, but only to a limited degree. There has been a Master Farmer Scheme with over 700 farmers registered in 1961 and some consolidation of holdings under Land Reorganization Schemes, but most experts who have examined the Nyasaland position feel that much more pervasive improvements must be made and particularly that real advances cannot be expected unless individual tenure is applied.

A special problem in Nyasaland exists in the Southern Province, particularly in the Cholo and Mlanje districts, where much of the population lived on European estates until recently. A system called "thangata," which involved some security of tenure in return for either payment of rent or by working, led to much political unrest. The government has attempted to meet the problem by buying land and by resettlement. In 1946 some 173,000 Africans, including a large number who had migrated from Mozambique between 1900 and 1940, were associated with "thangata"; by 1960 this number had been reduced to 18,000. In the period 1953 to 1961 European holdings were reduced by government purchase from 3.9 to 2.9 percent of the total area of the country.

CROPS

CORN. Corn occupies the largest acreage on both European and African farms in the area. Some of it is used as cattle feed, but most of it is used or sold to provide the main staple African food. In 1961 the production totaled 714,000 tons in Southern Rhodesia, 238,000 tons in Northern Rhodesia, and 116,000 tons in Nyasaland, about three fourths of the total coming from European farms. In recent years there has been a substantial surplus, much of which has been exported at a loss. The surplus is explained in considerable part by an increased average yield; in Southern Rhodesia, yields on European farms, nearly all of which plant hybrid corn, increased from 1,200 pounds per acre to over 2,800 pounds per acre in a few years, while some of the better farms are getting 8,000 pounds per acre. Corn has played a very important role in the promotion of European farming in the Rhodesias; by subsidizing its price, the government aided farmers in paying off their debts and capitalizing their farms. In 1957, for example, the European farmer in Northern Rhodesia received 40 shillings per bag, which was about 30 percent above world prices; Africans received 30 shillings per bag with an additional 10 shillings going to an African Betterment Fund. The subsidization of corn production has, however, gradually led to distortions in marketing arrangements which require correction, while the difference in prices paid for European and African corn has resulted in misunderstanding and resentment on the part of African farmers.

TOBACCO. Tobacco is by all odds the main cash crop of the three countries. The very large increase in production in postwar years, one of the most spectacular in agricultural crops in Africa, was stimulated by ensured sales in the British market, where dollar shortages required sharp reductions of American tobacco imports, and also by the acceptability of tobaccos grown.

Tobacco auctions at Salisbury, Southern Rhodesia
Salisbury has become the leading tobacco mart in the world and its auction floors compare favorably in modernity of equipment with those of the United States.

Under the first British purchase contract, the 1948 London Agreement, United Kingdom buyers contracted to take two thirds of the Southern Rhodesian crop of flue-cured leaf up to 70 million pounds a year for five years, subject to specific price and quality. More recently the agreement market in Britain has been 90 million pounds per year, and the Federation has also been successful in finding markets in 40 other countries. Production of flue-cured tobacco in the Federation increased from about 43 million pounds immediately after the war to a record of 236 million pounds in 1961, the value of sales increasing from about $15.5 million to $93.2 million in the same period and to a record $95.8 million in 1962. In 1961 the Federation accounted for 83 percent of the total tobacco exports from Africa and about an eighth of total world exports; in production it accounted for 63.5 percent of African tobacco and about 3.1 percent of world output. Tobacco exports ranked second to copper by value among Federation exports, having been 19.6 percent of the total in 1962 (Table 34). While earlier postwar production of tobacco tended to be monocultural, and tobacco makes heavy demands upon the soil, farmers are now tending to follow better rotations, particularly with grass leys, and to apply compensating fertilization. Yields of flue-cured tobacco increased from 550 pounds per acre in 1953 to 1,031 pounds per acre in 1962.

A barn for flue-cured tobacco in Southern Rhodesia
The Rhodesias and Nyasaland saw a spectacular increase in tobacco production in postwar years, partly because of British efforts to save hard currency by purchasing tobacco grown in the Commonwealth.

Almost all of the flue-cured tobacco, which represents the largest segment of tobacco produced, is grown on European farms, mostly in the northern highveld of Southern Rhodesia, but also along the line-of-rail and in the Fort Jameson area of Northern Rhodesia, in the Southern Province of Nyasaland, and at Kasungu in Nyasaland's Central Province (Map 80). In the area defined as the Southwestern District, that is, Southern Rhodesia and the line-of-rail in Northern Rhodesia, there were 3,145 registered growers of flue-cured tobacco in 1961; their output is marketed in very modern auction floors at Salisbury, which now rates as the world's largest tobacco mart. In northeastern Northern Rhodesia and Nyasaland there were only 93 flue-cured growers in 1961; their leaf is sold at Limbe in Nyasaland. Only about three Africans produce flue-cured tobacco, mainly because it requires a substantial amount of fixed and working capital, but efforts may be intensified to assist Africans to produce this higher value leaf. Profits are somewhat erratic from year to year, but have generally been reasonably satisfactory and sometimes excellent. In 1961–62 the average net profit was estimated

Table 34. Selected data on the trade of the Federation, 1954–1962 (in thousands of dollars)

Main exports	*1954*	*1961*	*1962*
Metals and minerals			
Copper	242,270	315,333	312,728
Asbestos	18,130	23,638	21,378
Gold	18,332	19,855	19,166
Chrome and ferrochrome	8,047	11,542	10,094
Pig iron and steel	53	7,062	8,571
Zinc	5,872	5,247	6,784
Lead	3,444	2,038	2,008
Cobalt	4,645	1,814	2,982
Manganese ore	140	1,324	1,288
Tin	—	1,257	1,428
Coal	115	902	711
Lithium ores and salts	571	538	714
Total	301,619	390,550	387,852
Agricultural products			
Tobacco	69,765	117,510	114,708
Corn	1,271	12,709	17,598
Tea	7,700	12,354	10,024
Meat and products	3,998	9,206	10,424
Peanuts	1,145	4,164	6,687
Cattle hides	3,030	2,652	2,450
Wattle extract	—	1,212	1,467
Cotton	1,291	588	529
Total	88,200	160,395	163,887
Other			
Apparel	7,112	3,732	3,968
Cigarettes	887	1,540	1,985
Radios and parts	1,165	1,229	2,036
Footwear	871	1,154	980
Other domestic exports	21,045	21,890	25,760
Total	31,080	29,545	34,729
Total domestic exports	420,899	580,490	586,468
Re-exports	8,571	18,348	19,342
Total exports	429,470	598,838	605,810
Total imports	350,812	434,017	400,386

Source: Federation of Rhodesia and Nyasaland, Ministry of Economic Affairs, *Economic Report, 1962* (Salisbury, Government Printing and Stationery, 1962), pp. 40–42; *Economic Report, 1963*, pp. 33–34.
— = None or negligible.

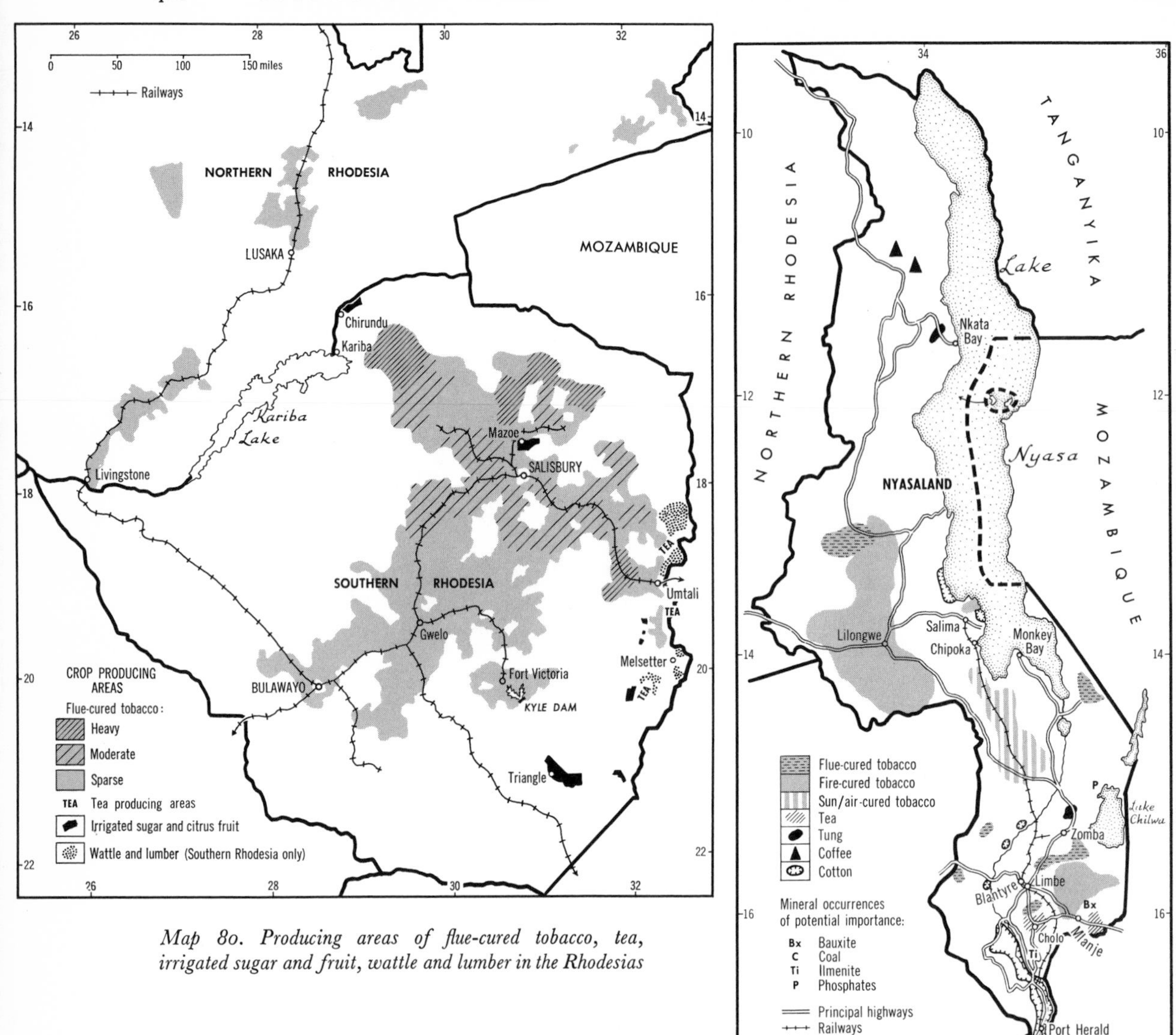

Map 80. Producing areas of flue-cured tobacco, tea, irrigated sugar and fruit, wattle and lumber in the Rhodesias

Map 81. Economic map of Nyasaland

to be $5,390 for Rhodesian tobacco growers, or somewhere between 4 and 5 percent of invested capital. Flue-cured tobacco grows best on light, sandy soils of relatively low fertility in areas with about 25 inches of rain and between about 3,000 and 4,000 feet elevations. There is much land available for expanding tobacco production, the only limitation at the present time being the size of the market.

Western fire-cured tobacco, usually sold at less than half the price per pound for Virginia flue-cured, is mainly produced by Africans in Nyasaland (Map 81), and provides a substantial part of the pipe tobacco consumed in the United Kingdom. Yields fluctuate considerably depending on the season, but the amount marketed now runs at about 21 to 26 million pounds. While 1961 saw an unusual drop to 15.6 million pounds, the 1962 sales were a record. In fact, the volume of all types of tobacco sold at Limbe in the 1961–62 season, including some leaf from northeastern Northern Rhodesia, totaled a record 38.7 million pounds valued at $10.6 million, up 9.9 million pounds and $2.8 million from the previous year.

Turkish tobacco comes mainly from Southern Rhodesia; in 1960 about 70 percent was produced by 120 European growers and the remainder by 4,417 African growers. It is considered particularly suitable for African production and was being actively promoted as a cash crop under the land husbandry program until the incidence of disease discouraged hopes for a major expansion in production. About three fifths of the Turkish tobacco produced in Northern Rhodesia came from African farms in 1960. Burley tobacco is produced by Europeans and Africans in Nyasaland and in the Eastern Province of Northern Rhodesia. In 1963 a large-scale scheme to boost African production of tobacco in Northern Rhodesia was under investigation calling for the installation of 500 growers on an area where production would be supervised by one European and several African technicians. Based upon a planned output of 550,000 pounds, returns to the individual farmers would vary from an estimated $168 to $236 per annum.

TEA. Tea ranks second among agricultural exports, over 90 percent of production coming from Nyasaland, where output is about evenly split between the Cholo and Mlanje Highlands. About 29,000 acres are planted to tea in that country with about 3,000 acres not yet bearing in the main regions and 105 acres not yet mature in a new area near Nkata Bay in the Northern Province. Some of the additional 21,000 acres considered suitable for tea production in Nyasaland are held by Africans, which suggests that out-growing programs might be appropriate. Almost all tea now comes from European estates, which employ about 30,000 Africans. There are 29 tea factories in Nyasaland, whose exports increased from 13.4 million pounds valued at

A tea estate near Mlanje, Nyasaland
About 30,000 Africans are employed on tea estates in Nyasaland, which has 29,000 acres planted to tea.

$4.4 million in 1953 to a record 30.0 million pounds and $12.3 million in 1961. Most of the exports go to the United Kingdom.

Southern Rhodesia has a much smaller but burgeoning tea area in the Eastern Highlands. About 3,900 acres are planted to tea in the Umtali and Chipinga districts and also at Inyanga. Output totaled 2.4 million pounds in 1961 valued at $1.2 million and was mainly marketed domestically; it could well be quintupled by 1975. There are now two tea factories in the colony.

PEANUTS. Peanuts have recently become the third export of Nyasaland. In 1962 a record crop of 36,270 short tons was produced there, nearly all by Africans. Export peanuts also come from northeastern Northern Rhodesia, which has seen a marked rise in production to 16,920 tons in 1962. Despite an increased production in Southern Rhodesia, that country is still importing substantial tonnages of peanuts to fulfill its requirements for vegetable oils.

COTTON. Cotton is an important African crop in the Southern Province of Nyasaland, 1962 having seen a record production of 19,030 short tons with farmers receiving over $1.7 million for its sale. Cotton was a fairly major crop at one time in Southern Rhodesia, but pests all but destroyed it. Production of seed cotton was 1,492 tons in 1961, but with the discontinuance of the Sabi Tanganda Estate in the Sabi Valley this figure was cut to 635 tons in 1962. It is hoped that research in progress will develop effective methods of combating cotton pests so that imports of cotton, now running at about 1,000 tons annually, can be reduced. Local experts feel that the Tanganda estate abandoned production just as most of its problems had finally been met and that the Sabi Valley will eventually be an important producer of cotton.

TUNG OIL. In early postwar years it was hoped that Nyasaland could become an important exporter of tung oil. Estates were developed in the Cholo, Zomba, and Blantyre districts and by the Colonial Development Corporation in the Vipya Highlands of the Northern Province, but low prices and reduced demands have discouraged expansion and there has been a contraction of acreage from 19,000 in 1956 to 15,069 acres in 1961. Oil is extracted at two plants in the south and at Mzuzu in the north. Tung fits in well with tea production, helping to sustain a fairly even labor demand.

SUGAR. A considerable expansion is occurring in sugar production, which met only 10 percent of federal needs in 1959. In that year, 8,730 acres were under sugar, of which about 55 percent was producing. In 1962 about 37,000 tons of sugar were produced in Southern Rhodesia at three estates, from 3,500 acres at Chirundu in the Zambezi Valley, 3,500 acres at Hippo Valley, and 18,000 acres on the Triangle Sugar Estates in the southern lowveld. With expansions at these three estates, it was expected that the Federation would be self-sufficient in sugar by 1963, and become a net exporter shortly thereafter.

CITRUS FRUITS. Several large estates in Southern Rhodesia meet the domestic demand for citrus fruits and provide a small surplus for export. The Mazoe Estate has produced over 60 percent of the fruit grown annually. An increase of 3,000 acres will almost treble its output; this will involve raising the Mazoe Dam 10 feet to increase storage from 18,000 to 28,000 acre feet and adding 10 miles to the present 22-mile canal. Costing about $1.12 million, these changes will make Mazoe the second largest privately owned citrus estate in the world. The Hippo Valley Estate, which now has about 800 acres in citrus, is slated to become the largest citrus estate in the area with a gross turnover of $56 million yearly by 1970 from 100,000 trees. The Hippo Valley Estate represents an investment of $5.6 million and is providing employment for about 3,000 Africans and 60 Europeans. In addition to its interest in citrus fruit and sugar, the estate is experimenting with corn, sorghum, and cotton.

OTHER CROPS. Additional crops are of much less importance commercially. African production of coffee is being encouraged in the Ikumbi area of northeastern Southern Rhodesia. A

Rhodesian Selection Trust offer of $252,000 to stimulate production of arabica coffee in Nyasaland was rejected during the period of political tension in that country. At present, a small production from around Rumpi in Nyasaland is trucked all the way across Tanganyika for marketing at Moshi, the resulting low returns having been somewhat discouraging. It has been recommended that 7,200 acres of arabica coffee be planted in Southern Rhodesia in the next 15 years, but only limited areas of the country are suitable for its production.

Cocoa is being grown on an experimental basis in the lower Shire Valley in Nyasaland. While further trials are necessary before its future can be assessed, it has been estimated that a production valued at $2.8 million yearly could be obtained in the Elephant Marsh area. The crop now grown is said to be the only cocoa in the world grown under irrigation.

Some rice produced by Africans in Nyasaland is sold in the guaranteed markets of the other countries, but any extension would require additional water control, and an $11.2 million rice irrigation scheme in the Port Herald District has recently been given up owing to apathy and opposition from the intended beneficiaries. Potatoes are produced by Europeans in the Rhodesias, especially in the Salisbury District, and by Africans in Nyasaland. Crops which should be more intensively pushed include sorghum, peanuts, soya beans, market vegetables, and sunflower, which greatly increases yields when rotated with corn and provides a valuable cattle feed.

High-bred Hereford cattle on a highveld farm in Southern Rhodesia

Beef production has been increasing rapidly in recent years, which have seen a marked improvement in practices, particularly in the provision of supplementary feed in the dry period.

LIVESTOCK INTERESTS

The Federation has witnessed some increase in livestock production in recent years under the stimulus of a guaranteed market at minimum prices set by the Cold Storage Commission in Southern Rhodesia and Nyasaland. In 1961, 462,000 cattle were slaughtered as compared with 315,657 in 1952. Production of milk on dairy farms has outstripped the demand in Southern Rhodesia, promoting the output of butter and cheese. But butter is more costly to produce locally than to import, and the area continues dependent on foreign sources for about a third of consumption. A new dried whole milk factory at Salisbury may absorb some of the surplus milk in the years ahead.

About 5,000 cattle producers in the Federation employ approximately 30,000 people, the average herd being between 500 and 1,000 head. In 1962 there were an estimated 5.4 million cattle, about a third owned by Europeans. The hardy Africander cattle is preferred in many areas, though there has been increasingly successful crossbreeding with European cattle or maintenance of purely European breeds. There is considerable room for expansion in livestock production. The major problems include a very low average calving rate, which could be rapidly improved, however, by supplying small amounts of supplementary feed; intensification of bush vegetation, the control of which could increase capacity by 50 percent; and the poor quality of grasses available in the dry period, which helps to explain the trend toward smaller scale, more intensive practices and toward production

The Nyanyadzi irrigation area in eastern Southern Rhodesia
This is one of nine schemes developed for African farmers in the Sabi Valley and Manicaland.

of lucerne and other supplementary feed on a year-round basis on some of the better farms. Africans own over half of the 494,000 sheep, two thirds of the 24,000 pigs, and almost all of the 1 million goats in the three countries.

It is believed that exports of meat to the United Kingdom could be greatly increased if a more continuous supply could be effected and if there were regular and adequate shipping space available. In any case, the livestock industry is viewed as a sound and stabilizing part of the Federation's agricultural picture. Since no less than 80 percent of the land of Southern Rhodesia, which now accounts for four fifths of total slaughter cattle, is considered best for livestock production, that country should be a bigger beef producer and exporter than it is.

AGRICULTURAL NEEDS

The agricultural and land-use problems of the Federation are now the subject of numerous development programs, but remain too serious to justify complacency. Except in highly specialized areas, future emphases in areas suitable for cropping should probably be on mixed farming, because, with poor soils, any transformation to permanent cultivation will require composting with cattle manure. Furthermore, the general physical quality of the three countries suggests that livestock farming must eventually assume a much more important part in their economies, primarily because of the climatic limitations on tillage agriculture. It is reasonable to predict that progress in combating trypanosomiasis and its carrier, the tsetse fly, will open up vast areas where grazing is now precluded. Methods of controlling the fly in the Rhodesias differ somewhat from those in East Africa, as it is considered that bush clearance is impractical. Discriminative spraying with dieldrin has been effective on an experimental basis, while game destruction has opened wide areas for grazing without any serious effect on total game reserves.

The need to improve soils also places emphasis on the possibilities of increasing the application of artificial fertilizers. Phosphatic fertilizers may be made available in the future from deposits of apatite either at Dorowa in Southern Rhodesia or at Tundulu Hills in Nyasaland, while nitrogenous fertilizers might be produced by fixation, using power from one of the proposed hydroelectric developments. It has been found that in the medium and higher rainfall areas, crops and pastures respond very well to generous applications of nitrogenous fertilizer. A superphosphate plant now exists at Salisbury and there is production of nitrogenous fertilizers as a by-product of coke oven operations at Redcliff.

Meteorological, soil, and ecological surveys will disclose the capabilities of lands at present but little used. In particular, lowland areas with sedimentary rock or alluvial floors, such as the Luangwa trough in Northern Rhodesia, need studying. Even the plateau soils vary considerably, while the soils of Nyasaland have greater variety than those of the Rhodesias. The better areas in all three countries need careful delineation.

IRRIGATION DEVELOPMENTS AND POTENTIALITIES. The general shortage of water, particularly during the winter months, makes obvious the desirability of studying irrigation potentialities, which are not inconsiderable. Southern Rhodesia has by far the most advanced program of water control. Its largest project to date is the Kyle Dam, completed in 1960 in the Fort Victoria district. With a storage capacity of 256 billion gallons, or about five sixths of the total for all dams in the colony excluding Kariba, it supplies water to the Hippo Valley and Triangle estates. The Bangala Dam, 60 miles south of the Kyle Dam, increases the amount of water available for the Hippo Valley Estate. In 1960–61 a total of 54,000 acres were under irrigation on European holdings in Southern Rhodesia, while 4,669 acres were irrigated in nine schemes in the Sabi Valley and Manicaland supporting 1,376 African families. It has been estimated that a total of 982,000 acres is irrigable in Southern Rhodesia, over 90 percent of which would fall within three large projects—Sabi Ruzawi, Hunyani, and Zambezi. Attention is now being given to starting a long-range program to develop 340,000 acres in the Sabi Valley. In addition to irrigation projects, there is a relatively advanced program of water control in Southern Rhodesia. From 1955 to 1961, some 2,871 small dams with a total capacity of 18.6 billion gallons were constructed in Southern Rhodesia on European farms, while a total of 886 dams with a capacity of 25.2 billion gallons were in being on African areas in mid-1961. Thousands of boreholes and wells have also been sunk. Nonetheless, the Southern Rhodesian water control program is still at a beginning stage and many opportunities remain for improving water conservation.

The Kariba Dam will permit the irrigation of sizable areas in the two Rhodesias along the Zambezi Valley. In Northern Rhodesia there are interesting possibilities for irrigating extensive lands for sugar, rice, and other crops in the Luangwa Valley. On the plateau surface, increasing attention will be given to the potentialities of the swampy and seasonally flooded areas, both the very large ones and the smaller *dambos* and *vleis*, areas of impeded drainage. The seven largest swamps and adjacent plains in Northern Rhodesia total 13,754 square miles, or no less than 6 percent of the country. Just what the appropriate combination of uses should be in these areas will not be known until they have been much more thoroughly studied, but it is reasonable to believe that, with their apparently superior soils and with an excess of water, the effects of proper control will be highly rewarding. A pilot farm, financed by the Rhodesian Selection Trust group of copper mining companies, was one of the first projects devoted to research and development of such areas. It is situated in the better-known eastern part of the Kafue Flats, where there is a total of 1,300,000 acres subject to annual inundation. A firm of Dutch consultants hired for the

Huts and woodlands at Nyanyadzi
This illustrates the nature of the area before irrigation water is applied.

investigation has estimated that a dam at Meshi Teshi, after allowing for hydroelectric developments, could irrigate 450,000 acres and still leave two thirds of the Flats free for grazing or for preservation of the abundant wildlife. At a 700-acre experimental farm near Mazabuka three systems of maintaining the correct moisture balance are being studied: gravitational distribution, pump spraying, and underground seepage canals.

In 1961 the U.N. Special Fund granted about $600,000 to continue investigations on the Kafue Flats, including studies of the suitability of soils for irrigation, polder farming, cattle production, and fish and wildlife resources. In 1962 it was reported that wheat, barley, and potatoes had proved to be excellent winter crops, and that cotton, sunflower, peanuts, and kenaf had high yields in summer. It is also believed that the alternate wetting and drying produced by irrigation has a beneficial effect on the soil. In 1963 one of the dikes protecting the experimental area was breached by unusually high water, interrupting work for the year. Recently a $9.8 million scheme has been proposed by the managing company, patterned in part on the Gezira Scheme, that calls for polderization of 20,000 acres. It is estimated that the gross annual production of the scheme would be valued at $3.9 million, which, at 40 percent of the invested capital, would rate favorably as compared to the 30 percent which the World Bank has suggested as required to justify an irrigation scheme. About 14,000 people would be supported on the polder, average incomes varying from an estimated $314 for a tenant holding six acres to $941 for more experienced farmers on 18-acre plots.

The Lower Shire Valley contains the bulk of lands in Nyasaland of interest from the standpoint of irrigation. About 28,000 acres could be irrigated in small sites along the river, while a dam on the middle Shire could control about 150,000 acres of reclaimed swamp lands. The cost of the latter scheme has thus far discouraged its adoption. But the fertile soils of the region, the multiple purposes of such a dam, and the land pressure in southern Nyasaland suggest that its development will be undertaken in the not too distant future.

FISHING AND FORESTRY

FISHING

A rather special interest in the production of food attaches to fishing. It is carried on to some extent in all the larger lakes and swamps, but would appear to be capable of very great extension, which would be highly beneficial to a populace with a diet generally deficient in proteins and calcium. Northern Rhodesia has the greatest interest in fishing, with about 24,000 long tons a year being marketed. The river swamps and lagoons of the Kafue Flats between Meshi Teshi and the Kafue Gorge are the most important producing area; Lakes Mweru, Bangweulu, and Tanganyika are also important. Largely an African industry, fishing is the mainstay of some districts. It is being aided by the government through the promotion of more modern distributional facilities, loans to fishermen for purchase of boats and nets, and support of a boat building school on Lake Mweru. Lake Kariba, being stocked with bream, should become an important source of fish for the two Rhodesias; the agreed catch for 1962 was 8,000 tons. The Southern Rhodesian fish catch is small scale, coming mainly from thousands of fishponds.

In Nyasaland, the output of non-African commercial fishing concerns was 4,360 tons in 1958, while Africans marketed an estimated 4,000 tons in the same year. Lake Nyasa is the main source of fish, but there is evidence that it has been overfished in recent years in the south, and in 1962 gill nets were introduced in place of ring nets to permit small fish to escape; the total catch in 1962 was 12,100 tons.

FORESTRY

Northern Rhodesia also has the greatest reserves of timber of the three countries, being over half-covered with deciduous woodlands, but the quality of most trees leaves much to be desired.

About 5 percent of the country is in forest reserves, an area which should probably be quadrupled. Exploitation is largely in the hands of private enterprise. The Zambezi-Sawmills Ltd., with a large sawmill in the Livingstone area, produces about 2 million cubic feet of Rhodesian "teak" logs yearly, mostly for railroad ties and mining timbers but also for parquet flooring and furniture. The Rhodesia-Congo Border Timber Company supplied very large quantities to the mining industries when coal was in short supply but now produces much smaller quantities. This company opened a new sawmill at Mikutuma in 1961. Afforestation is being carried out in five main areas in Northern Rhodesia, including the deforested areas around the Copperbelt. It has recently been estimated that the forest industry of that country could be built into a $2½ million industry.

Southern Rhodesian forestry output comes mainly from afforested areas, and plantings of exotic conifers, eucalyptus, and wattle are of increasing importance. It is hoped that a $5.6 million wattle industry can be developed, wattle having been planted on large acreages in the eastern districts. There are two modern extract factories, at Melsetter and Umtali. Umtali is also the site of a new $560,000 box factory, opened in 1962 as part of a proposed $28 million investment of the British South Africa Company in the Rhodesian timber industry, and of a $2.1 million newsprint plant opened in 1962, the first such plant in the Federation and capable of meeting the total requirements of the area at an estimated saving of $1.2 million yearly in foreign exchange. An $11.2 million paper mill is planned at Odzi in the east which would be supplied by a $1.7–2.2 million canal leading from pine forests on the mountain sides. Pine takes only 6 to 10 years to reach pulping size compared to 30 years in Sweden. The Italian Snia Viscosa Company plans an initial minimum production of 25,000 tons of newsprint and kraft paper for the federal market valued at $5.6 million yearly.

In Nyasaland, much of the original forests have been destroyed, but about 19 percent of the country is still forested. Mlanje cedar, a magnificent and unique tree, which is found in only one area, has furnished most of the durable building material produced in the past half-century.

THE MINERAL INDUSTRY

The two Rhodesias produce a wide range of important minerals and their output of copper, cobalt, asbestos, chrome, and petalite is of world significance. Other minerals are of less importance in international trade, but are of considerable actual and very great potential value to the area. The mineral industry occupies an outstanding position in the economy of Northern Rhodesia, accounting for over 95 percent of the total value of exports, providing the principal source of employment for both Africans and Europeans, and yielding well over half of the total revenue of government. Northern Rhodesia accounts for over three fourths of the value of mineral output in the area. In Southern Rhodesia, the mineral industry is relatively less significant. It is marked by greater diversity in minerals produced and in the size of operation. Nyasaland has practically no mineral industry, though a number of minerals are known to exist. In the Federation as a whole, minerals accounted for two thirds of domestic exports

Aerial view of Chibuluma, one of the large mining communities of the Copperbelt
Mine and concentration plants are in the foreground, housing for African workers beyond.

in 1962 and for about 8.3 percent of those economically employed in March, 1963. In 1962, a relatively poor year for minerals, mining contributed 20.9 percent to the gross domestic product as compared to 21.8 percent for agriculture and 10.3 percent for manufacturing.

The Rhodesias are extremely fortunate to have a large part of what is probably the world's greatest metallogenetic zone, running discontinuously from the Katanga to the Bushveld Complex of the Republic of South Africa. But there are, of course, accompanying problems. The evils of excessive migration with the resultant decline of African farming standards are particularly notable. The high dependence upon products whose world prices have fluctuated notoriously is another problem. But most serious of all has been the racial and political tension created by various color bars in employment. Finally, it can never be forgotten that however great reserves may be, one is dealing with a wasting resource.

THE NORTHERN RHODESIAN COPPERBELT

The Copperbelt mining and metallurgical operations are by far the most important in the Rhodesias, in fact among metallic mineral producers they rate second only to the South African gold industry on the continent. In recent years the Copperbelt has ranked after the United States among free-world copper producers, accounting for about 13 to 18 percent

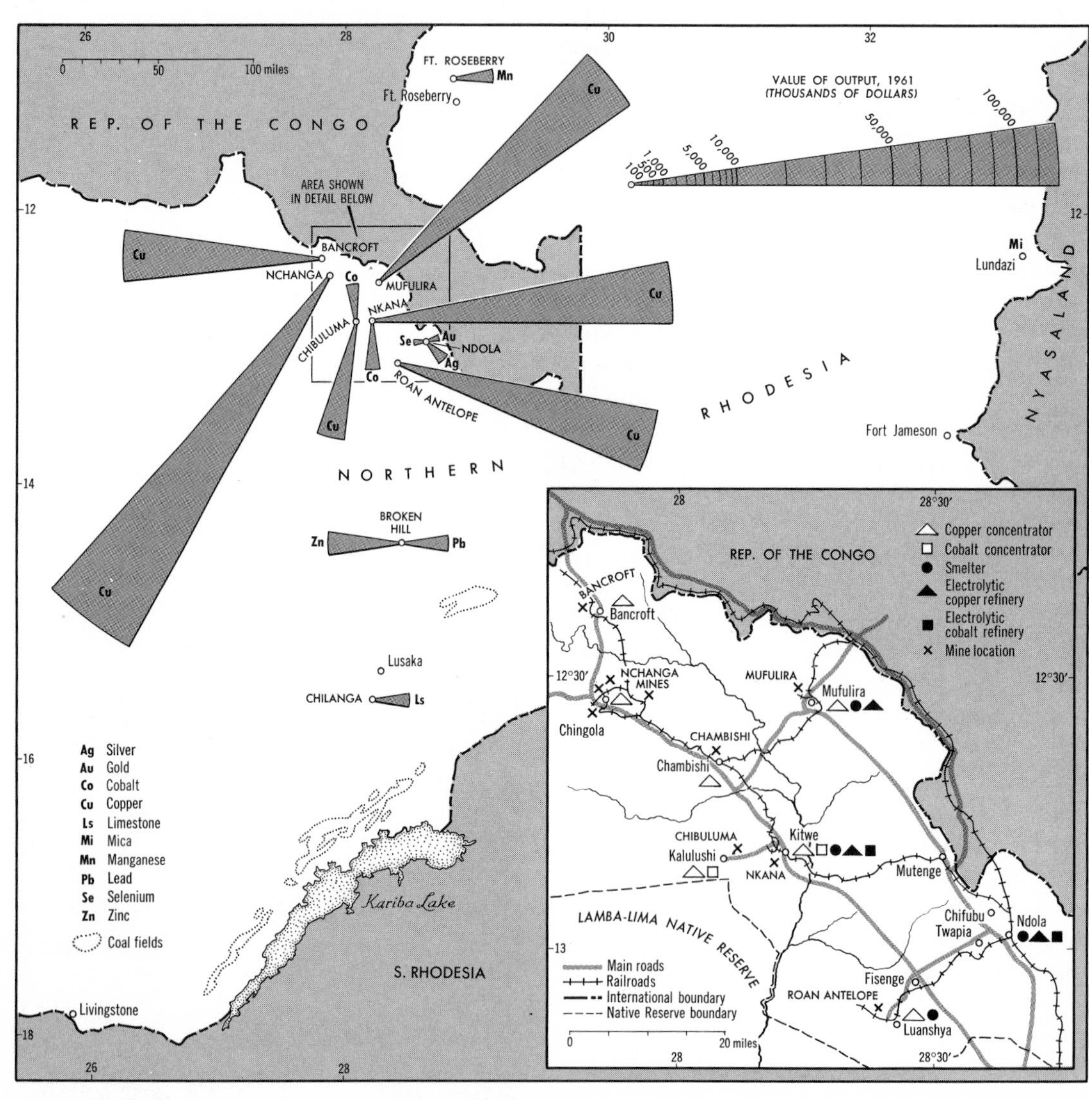

Map 82. Mining in the Rhodesias Above: Northern Rhodesia Opposite: Southern Rhodesia

of non-Communist production. In 1961, a relatively poor year, it accounted for 57.4 percent of total Federation exports, 15 percent of its net domestic output, and 24.8 percent of the Federation's budget income by direct and indirect tax payments. These figures fluctuate according to the price of world copper, variations in the net operating profits of the copper companies having been the principal cause of year-to-year changes in the Federation economy. The copper industry, which had 7,641 European and 39,036 African employees in 1961, normally accounted for about one third of African and two thirds of European employment in Federation mining. The total population of the seven main Copperbelt towns in 1961 was about 325,000 Africans, 42,000 Europeans, and 1,000 Asians. The capital investment in the copper industry and associated towns was estimated at $700 million in 1959.

Copper mining began on the present Copperbelt in 1921 at Nkana. Map 82 shows the relative importance of the present mines. The Mufulira mine now ranks second only to Chile's El Teniente among underground copper mines. Expansion programs are now under way at Nchanga and Bancroft, RST is spending $21 million to develop an ore body at Chambishi, and other bodies are known to exist.

The Copperbelt ores milled ranged in copper content from about 1.85 to 5.12 percent from mine to mine in 1960, which compares with an

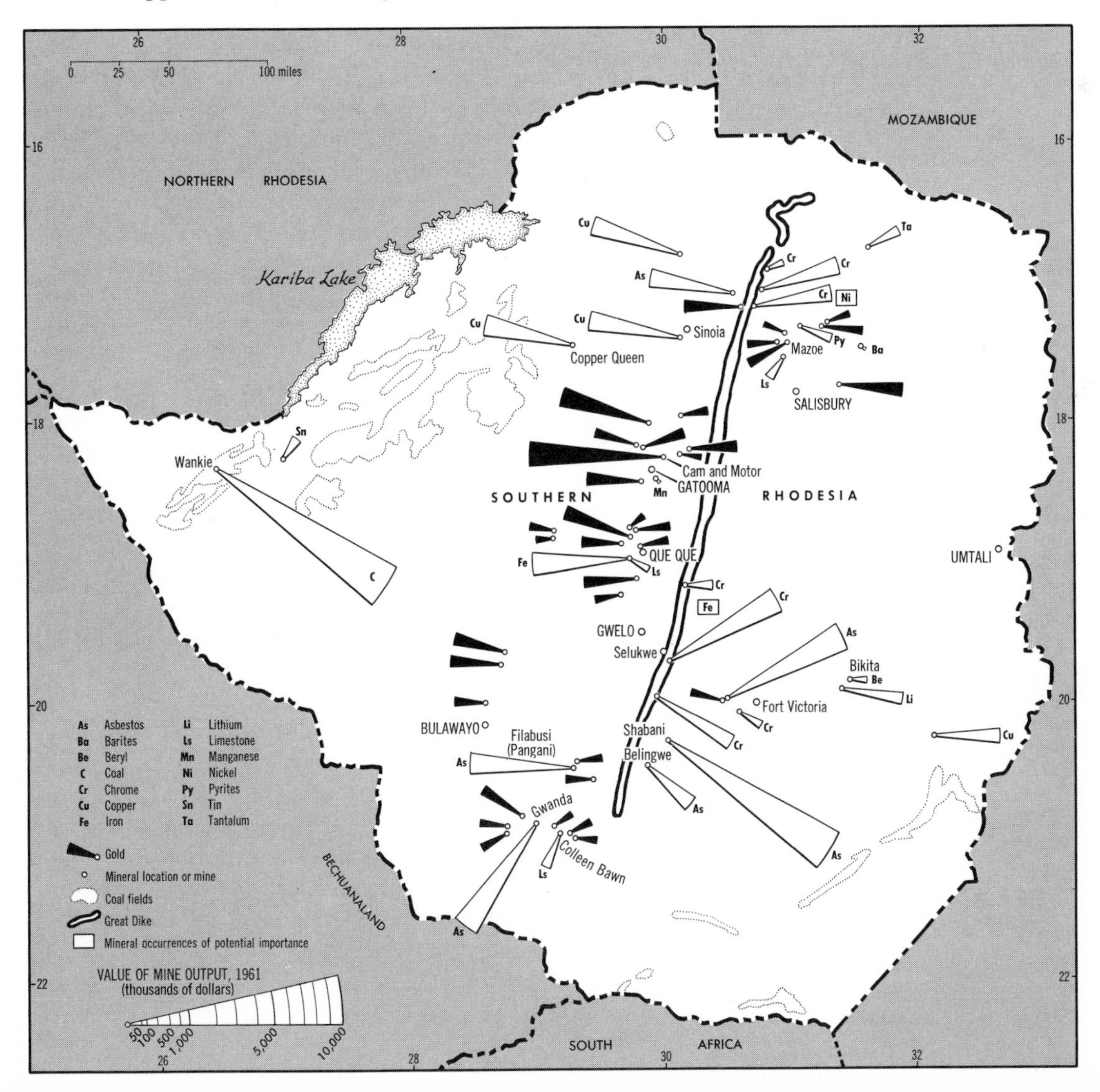

average of less than 1 percent in the United States. Chibuluma and Rhokana ores contain cobalt, production of which accounted for about 1 percent of the value of Northern Rhodesian mineral output in 1962. Ore hoisted has increased from 15.6 million short tons in 1958 to 24 million tons in 1961; copper production totaled 213,615 long tons in 1948, 375,079 long tons in 1958, and 558,789 long tons in 1961. Proved reserves are adequate to sustain production for 25 to 30 years, but new reserves proved each year usually exceed ores mined. Inferred ores are very large, adequate to sustain mining for at least 70 years. The area on the Copperbelt potentially mineralized but still undrilled is enormous, while intensive prospecting is also being extended to other parts of the country.

Copper smelters are situated at Ndola, Mufulira, Nkana, and Roan Antelope, and electrolytic refineries are situated at Nkana, Mufulira, and Ndola, the last also having a cobalt refinery opened in 1958. From 1954 to 1962 the proportion of electrolytic copper production increased from 46 to 79 percent of total production, almost all the remainder being blister copper. The proportion of electrolytic copper is increasing as additional electricity becomes available from Kariba. In 1961 about 93 percent of shipments were railed to Mozambique ports, 3.6 percent to Lobito, 2.7 percent to the Republic of South Africa, and the remainder to domestic destinations. Lourenço Marques is likely to increase its share of mineral exports from the Rhodesias partly because of congestion at Beira but mainly because it can take larger ore carriers.

The surface plant at Mufulira
The Mufulira mine now ranks second only to Chile's El Teniente among underground copper mines.

The Copperbelt has had development problems comparable to those of the Katanga area, some of which have already been noted. In power supply, for example, the shortage of coal led to felling more than a quarter million acres of Copperbelt woodlands in the 1950s. In 1956 a 320-mile line permitted Le Marinel plant in Katanga to provide about 40 percent of the belt's energy needs, while today Kariba and Le Marinel supply almost all requirements. The amount of power consumed on the Copperbelt was almost equal to that consumed in the remainder of the Federation in 1962.

Of greatest concern in recent years has been the relations between Africans and Europeans. European union and staff associations, recognized since 1937 and 1941, have been very influential in the industry and have provided the chief stumbling block to improved relations through their insistence on racially based job specifications. Formal African employee representation began in 1942 with a system of tribal representation and progressed through "boss boy's committees," more fully representative committees, and separate unions to the amalgamated Northern Rhodesian African Mineworkers' Union in 1949. After many years of extremely difficult negotiations, an agreement was reached in 1955 whereby almost 1,000 posts in 22 categories were transferred to Africans; by 1959, 297 Africans had been promoted to more advanced jobs and 318 were in training or waiting vacancies. After additional lengthy discussions, the European mineworkers finally voted in late 1960 to end the color bar.

A second labor problem is that of stabilizing labor on the Copperbelt. At the end of 1961 the average length of services of African employees was 5.6 years, with 39.4 percent having worked for less than two years. Efforts to encourage stability include increased provision of housing for married couples, encouraging workers to bring their families, payment of vacation travel and long-service bonuses, pension and leave schemes, and higher-than-average wages. The companies would prefer that labor be stabilized without causing excessive urbanization and that those living in mine housing would return to tribal areas on retirement, but whether this can be expected after employees have partially or fully severed contacts with their original areas is questionable. About 25 percent of African employees come from outside Northern Rhodesia.

An additional problem is associated with the present distribution of tax and royalty payments. As has already been noted, Northern Rhodesian politicians are jealous of the revenues from copper now going to other parts of the Federation and are likely to take steps toward reducing this drain when independence is achieved. They may also wish to renegotiate the agreement with the British South Africa Company, guaranteed by the British and Rhodesian governments, whereby that company receives a royalty on every ton of ore removed from the ground. Based on agreements made with African chiefs between 1895 and 1900, the companies' net earnings from them in the five-year period to September, 1960, totaled $140 million. Though the agreements are scheduled to expire in 1986, it is not unlikely that an African government will seek to discontinue or reduce them shortly after independence.

OTHER MINERALS IN NORTHERN RHODESIA

The other important minerals produced in Northern Rhodesia include:

(1) Lead and zinc, mined at Broken Hill, south of the Copperbelt. Reserves estimated at 6.38 million tons in 1961 are adequate for many years of production, while there are several known ore bodies, including the Star Zinc body, in the general area that have not as yet been touched. Production ranges around 15,000 short tons of lead and 30,000 to 34,000 short tons of zinc yearly with a small by-product yield of cadmium and silver. In 1961, 433 Europeans and 1,828 Africans were employed at Broken Hill. Modern concentrators and smelters and a refinery are situated at Broken Hill powered by company-owned hydroelectric plants on the Lunsemfwa and Mulungushi rivers. In 1962 a $15.1 million smelting furnace was installed which is expected to increase production to 55,000 tons of zinc and 28,000 tons of lead annually, partly by extracting a higher percentage of metal from the ore and partly by the reworking of mine dumps.

(2) Manganese, procured from seven small mines in Central and Luapula provinces, the largest in the Fort Rosebery district.

(3) Uranium, produced by the Rhokana Corporation from near the southern end of its Mindola copper body.

(4) Gold and selenium, obtained as by-products from electrolytic refinery slimes.

(5) Mica, coming from seven small mines in the Fort Jameson district.

(6) Limestone.

Other mineral occurrences include a pyrite deposit near Lusaka which may be opened up for use in the smelting operations at Nkana, a 100,000-ton reserve of quartz sand at Kapiri Mposhi, beryl, and amethyst. The evidence suggests, however, that copper will long be the dominant mineral production from Northern Rhodesia; certainly its occurrences are particularly widespread. Barotseland has not so far been investigated, creating a large empty area on the mineral map of the country.

THE MINING POSITION IN SOUTHERN RHODESIA

Mining began in Southern Rhodesia long before arrival of the European, some 4,000 ancient workings having been found from which an estimated 2 million ounces of gold were removed by pre-European miners. The discovery of gold by Europeans in 1865 and later was the main reason for occupation of the colony, some 68,000 claims having been recorded by 1894, and, with the exception of one year, gold remained the first interest in Southern Rhodesian mining until 1948, when base minerals surpassed the value of its output. Today, base minerals have a value two and a half times that of gold and the gap is likely to widen in the years ahead. About thirty

The Shabani asbestos mine, Southern Rhodesia
This is the largest asbestos operation in Southern Rhodesia, which ranks third among world producers.

Ore shaft headgear and mill at Shabani
Asbestos ranks first among the mineral exports of Southern Rhodesia.

minerals, metallic and nonmetallic, are now produced in Southern Rhodesia of which five—asbestos, gold, coal, copper, and chrome—account for over 90 percent of the total value of mineral production. The 383 producing mines and their associated works employed 2,763 Europeans and 48,065 Africans in 1961, consumed about 25 percent of the electricity in the country, and accounted for about 12.3 percent of Federation exports. The much smaller scale of Southern Rhodesian mining as compared to that on the Copperbelt is revealed by the fact that almost a third of the mines employ under ten people, while only nine had over 1,000 employees in 1961. Almost 70 percent of African employees are aliens, a quarter of the total labor force coming from Nyasaland, a fifth from Mozambique, and 18.6 percent from Northern Rhodesia.

Rogers has described the location of Southern Rhodesian minerals as follows:

> The central feature of mineral distribution in Southern Rhodesia is the Great Dyke, which appears as a range of hills stretching for 350 miles north-south through the middle of the Colony. Within it are vast reserves of high grade chrome; it also contains platinum and nickel, but in such a form that no economic process of extraction has yet been evolved. Along either side of the Dyke, like islands in a sea of granite, are the gold belts. Richer on the west side, they extend in less regular form as far as Umtali, in the east. In the lower lying areas on the boundaries of Southern Rhodesia, are the coalfields.
>
> Asbestos and chrome are associated with the Great Dyke, but the other base minerals are widely scattered. North of Sinoia is a rich area of copper and mica fields; east of Fort Victoria are the lithium fields and phosphate deposits; the tin fields lie southeast of Wankie, and there are extensive deposits of iron ore near Que Que and in the Bukwe Mountains, by the Lourenço Marques railway line.[5]

GOLD. From occupation of the colony up to 1961, gold accounted for 51.7 percent of the total value of mineral production—$1.3 billion. There are still about 265 working mines, but the bulk of output comes from twelve major ones, the outstanding mine being the Cam and

[5] Pat Rogers, "Mining in Southern Rhodesia—Unfinished Saga," *Horizon* (May, 1961), p. 12.

Motor Mine near Gatooma, which, at 6,500 feet, is the deepest mine in the Rhodesias. Most of the gold bodies are small, heavily faulted, and widely scattered; a large number of small workings have closed in postwar years, and the trend is toward consolidation of existing mines. Gold mining is, then, in a somewhat depressed state, though some mines have been aided by the subsidized custom roasting plant which the government maintains at Que Que.

ASBESTOS. Mined since 1908, asbestos now ranks first by value among Southern Rhodesian minerals. That country leads in world production of top-grade chrysotile asbestos, but is third in total production. There is a large-scale working at Shabani, a smaller one at Mashaba, 35 miles distant, and 13 other producing companies. Success in increasing sales of asbestos in recent years has helped to stimulate a $7.6 million development scheme at Pangani Asbestos Mine near Filabusi which, it is hoped, will increase sales by about $2.8 million yearly. In 1960 about 720 Europeans and 10,700 Africans were employed in mining asbestos.

CHROME. Chrome ore normally ranks third among the colony's minerals, but fell to fifth place in 1962 owing to increased competition from Soviet mines. About 19 mines, of which Selukwe Peak is the largest, produce chrome ore, the total reserves being very large. A small ferrochrome plant producing low-carbon ferrochrome is located at Gwelo, but the high cost of electricity forced it to shut down in the late 1950s. Following an additional investment and the promise of lower-cost power from Kariba it has again been in operation since 1961, while a 12,000-ton, $2.8 million ferrochrome plant was opened at Que Que in 1962. Established since 1906, the chrome mining industry has been a major supplier of high-quality metallurgical grade chromite to the ferrochrome industry of the United States.

COPPER. Some copper was mined in earlier years in Southern Rhodesia, but that mineral has only become important in recent years, and four major mines—Umkondo, Mangula, Alaska, and Copper Queen—now account for about 11 percent by value of Southern Rhodesian mineral output.

IRON ORE. Resources of iron ore are of particular significance because of their impact on possibilities of sustaining an iron and steel industry within the country. Occurrences are widespread and reserves are estimated to be at least a billion tons of 56 to 64 percent metal content. The largest high-grade reserves are found at Bukwe near the rail line to Lourenço Marques, and another large deposit is under study at Chikurbi near Salisbury. All iron ore mined until 1962 came from Redcliff, immediately adjacent to the iron and steel mill. Proved reserves of 50 percent or better ore within a radius of 12 miles of Redcliff are given as 30 million tons, while possible reserves are three or four times as large. Efforts made to interest foreign countries in the development of iron ore for export having been successful, a new opencast mine at Beacon Tor near Que Que began exporting ore to Japan in 1962 at a level of 250,000 tons a year. This ore is sold at the remarkably low cost of $1.68 a ton delivered to the rail station.

OTHER MINERALS. Southern Rhodesia produces a variety of other minerals of lesser importance, including:

(1) Petalite, a lithium ore, mined at the Bikita deposits in the Fort Victoria area, said to be the largest mine and proven deposit in the free world, containing 3.6 percent lithium oxide as compared with 1 or 2 percent in most fields. Production of ores, which were shipped raw after roasting, increased from 3,700 tons in 1951 to 109,000 tons in 1957, but declined to 55,000 tons in 1961. Mining is now shifting to underground workings and a concentrating plant has been constructed. The Bikita ores also yield a large part of the beryl produced in Southern Rhodesia, though there are also 30 small beryl mines in the Salisbury District.

(2) Tin, known in several localities, but mined primarily at the Kamativi Mines near Wankie. In 1961 the Beryl Rose Mine north of Mt. Darwin close to the Zambezi Valley was developed to produce tantalum and tin.

(3) Noncrystalline corundum, of which Southern Rhodesia is the world's largest supplier.

(4) Nickel, from Bindura in the Mazoe Valley.

(5) Iron pyrites, produced in the Salisbury District to support domestic production of sulfuric acid.

(6) Magnesite, from one mine in the Gatooma area.

(7) Limestone.

(8) Barites, from the Dodge Mine at Shamva, believed to be the world's largest high-grade body of barium.

(9) By-products of gold mining—antimony, arsenic, and silver.

Other minerals known to occur include caesium, columbium, diamonds, emeralds, fluorspar, graphite, gypsum, phosphates, platinum, quartz, tungsten, uranium, and vermiculite.

MINERALS IN NYASALAND

In Nyasaland there is a 65-million-ton reserve of bauxite of 42.7 percent alumina content on Mt. Mlanje (Map 81), which has suggested the possibility of refining aluminum, using power from the proposed Shire Project. Other minerals known to exist, in addition to coal which has already been noted, are columbium, corundum, graphite, iron ore, kyanite, limestone (adequate to support a cement mill at Blantyre), manganese, mica, phosphates (a large deposit of high-grade apatite is found 60 miles from the railway at Tundulu Hills south of Lake Chilwa), monazite, titanium (a deposit in the Shire Valley could prove to be Nyasaland's most important mineral prospect), radioactive minerals, and vermiculite. Unfortunately, most of these deposits are small and low grade, while location militates against opening up some of the more interesting bodies.

Table 35. Selected data regarding manufacturing development in the Rhodesias and Nyasaland, 1955–1962

Area	*Year*	*Index of industrial production*	*Number of establishments*	*Gross output (in million $)*	*Total number of employees (in thousands)*	*Total wages and salaries (in million $)*
Federation	1955	69.5	1,003	264	92	53
	1959	100.0	1,319	409	113	84
	1960	106.4		440	145	105
	1961	109.6	1,363	465	136	101
	1962	106.7				
Southern Rhodesia	1938		299	25	18	7
	1947		430	84	41	17
	1955		709	216	70	44
	1959		967	336	85	69
	1961		1,059		97	
Northern Rhodesia	1947		74	6	6	1
	1955		219	36	15	8
	1959		254	54	17	12
	1961		241		25	
Nyasaland	1955		75	12	7	1
	1959		98	19	11	3
	1961		63		14	

Sources: Federation of Rhodesia and Nyasaland, Central Statistical Office, *The Censuses of Production of the Federation of Rhodesia and Nyasaland, 1958–1959* (Salisbury, Government Printer, September, 1961), p. 12; *Report of the Secretary to the Ministry of Commerce and Industry for the Year Ended 31st December 1961* (Salisbury, Government Printer, 1962), pp. 16–17; *Monthly Digest of Statistics, August, 1962* (Salisbury, Government Printer, September, 1962), p. 39; Central Statistical Office, *Preliminary Results of Federal Censuses of Population and of Employees: (1) Industrial and Racial Distribution of Employees* (Salisbury Central Statistical Office, March, 1962), pp. 3–6, 12–15; unpublished data, Ministry of Commerce and Industry.

MANUFACTURING IN THE FEDERATION

In secondary industry the Federation is, as might be expected, in an early stage of development. Industry in Nyasaland is confined almost entirely to the primary processing of agricultural produce; that of Northern Rhodesia is concerned chiefly with the concentration, smelting, and refining of minerals; but Southern Rhodesia displays surprising industrial variety, with some representation in most important fields. Southern Rhodesia accounted for about 72 percent of employment and 82 percent of the gross output in manufacturing in the Federation. An indication of the rapid progress made in Southern Rhodesia is revealed by figures on gross value of production, which rose from $14.3 million in 1938 to $173 million in 1953 and $244 million in 1957; in the Federation, the gross output increased from $263 million in 1955 to an estimated $465 million in 1961. As was indicated in Table 31, manufacturing employed about 90,000 Africans or 9.2 percent of the total employed in the Federation in March, 1963. Its contribution to the federal gross domestic product increased from 8.2 percent in 1954 to 10.3 percent in 1962.

Table 35 summarizes certain features of industrial growth in the Federation. Certainly, manufacturing is more advanced than in any other tropical African country, though it compares unfavorably with that of South Africa. And much of industry is still small scale, overlocalized, and under capitalized. In 1958, for example, only one tenth of the plants classified as manufacturing establishments had over 200 employees; these 120 plants employed 55 percent of the total workers and accounted for 54 percent of the gross output in industry.

THE LOCATION OF INDUSTRY

With regard to the location of industry, primary processing of mineral and agricultural raw materials is typically close to the producing areas. Other manufacturing is heavily concentrated at Salisbury and Bulawayo. In 1957 Salisbury accounted for an estimated 41.8 percent of the gross value of manufactured output in Southern

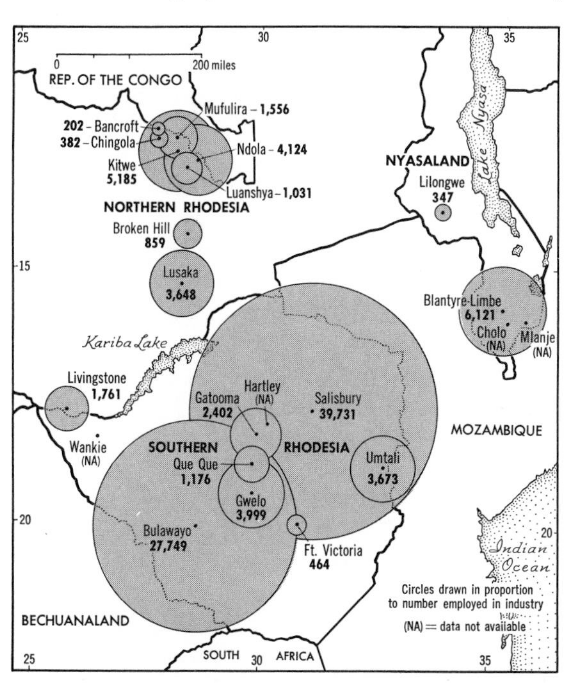

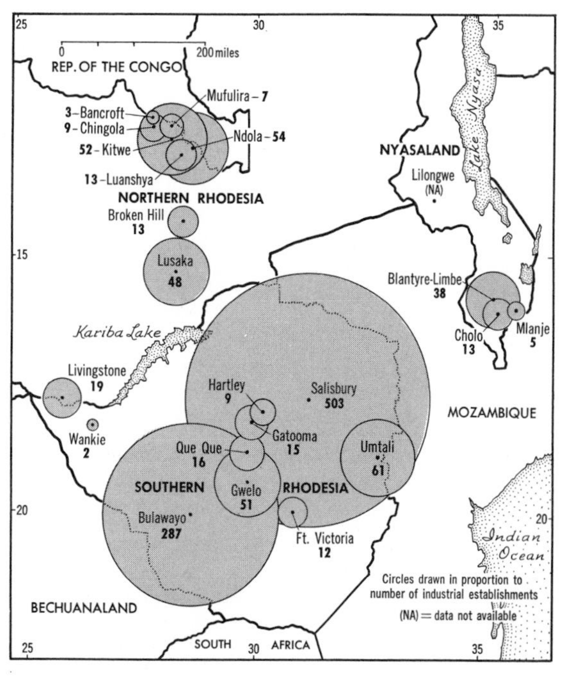

Map 83. The relative importance of industrial cities in the Rhodesias and Nyasaland, 1961

(a) By number of employees *(b) By number of manufacturing establishments*

Rhodesia, Bulawayo for 36.9 percent.[6] The midland towns of Gwelo, Que Que, Gatooma, and Hartley accounted for 12.5 percent of the gross value and Umtali in the east, the fourth ranking town, for 3.8 percent. Thus, these seven communities provided 95 percent of the total value of manufactured output. Lusaka, Ndola, and Kitwe are the main centers in Northern Rhodesia but do not begin to compare with the two main Southern Rhodesian centers; Blantyre-Limbe is the focus of the very small modern industrial build-up in Nyasaland. Map 83 shows the relative importance of the industrial towns of the Federation as measured by numbers employed in industry and number of manufacturing establishments in 1961. In that year, Southern Rhodesia accounted for about 77.7 percent of the total number of manufacturing plants in the Federation, Northern Rhodesia for 17.7 percent, and Nyasaland for 4.6 percent. In numbers employed in manufacturing, Southern Rhodesia accounted for about 71.3 percent of the total, Northern Rhodesia for 18.4 percent, and Nyasaland for 10.3 percent. These figures must all be taken as approximate; it is likely, for example, that nonmanufacturing employees of tea plantations exaggerate the importance of Nyasaland.[7]

With respect to the future distribution of industry, the most significant factor in the short run will be whether some kind of customs union is maintained among the three countries. There is no question but that Southern Rhodesia has the favored location for serving a unified market and it would be likely to retain its dominant position in manufacturing under a customs union. An effort would probably have to be made for political reasons to stimulate some industrial growth in Northern Rhodesia and Nyasaland, but no very large-scale development may be expected or is justified in the latter. A four-man team from Oxford University estimated in 1961 that an industrial investment of about $2.8 million could be justified in Nyasaland, with the main opportunities being in textiles and clothing, small-scale engineering, canning of fruits and fish, and brewing. The Nyasaland Ministry of Finance has stated that a manufacturing investment of about double that figure would be appropriate.

STIMULANTS TO INDUSTRIAL DEVELOPMENT

A number of influences have encouraged the rise of manufacturing in the Federation, including the high cost of importing goods to this landlocked area, the inability to obtain goods during the war and early postwar years, and the wish to provide employment for increased numbers of immigrants. The facts that agriculture could not be expected to absorb really large numbers of Europeans and that the European population is highly urbanized place greater emphasis on industrial development than might

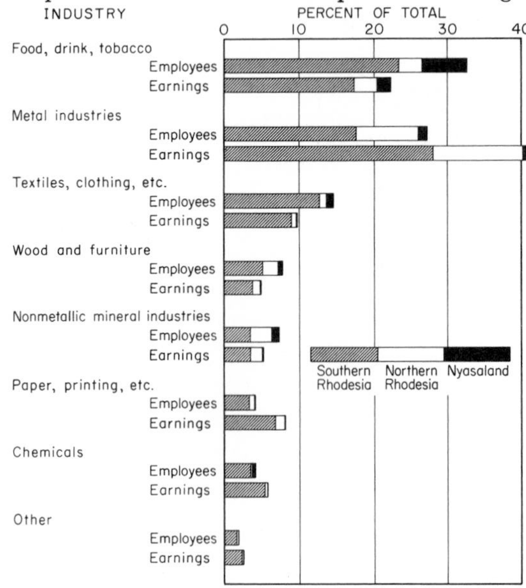

Chart 4. The relative importance of industrial groups in the Rhodesias and Nyasaland as measured by percent of total employees and earnings, 1961

[6] Leonard Tow, *The Manufacturing Economy of Southern Rhodesia, Problems and Prospects* (Washington, National Research Council, 1960), p. 79.

[7] In 1963 a revised industrial classification was developed moving all tea estate workers and tobacco graders from "manufacturing" to "agriculture." This and other changes resulted in a reduction of Africans employed in manufacturing as compared with the previous index of 10,800 and an increase of non-Africans employed in manufacturing of 130. (*Monthly Digest of Statistics*, July, 1963 pp. 6, 8.) Table 31 uses the new classification; Table 35 and Map 83 are based upon the earlier classification.

Table 36. Types of industry in the Rhodesias and Nyasaland by number and location of individual plants, 1961

	1	2	3	4	5	6	7	8	9	10	11	12	13	14	15	16	17	18	19	20	21	
	Animal and dairy products	*Agric. and vegetable products*	*Preserved food, excl. 1*	*Beer, spirits, soft drinks*	*Cigarettes and tobacco*	*Textiles, rope, canvas*	*Clothing*	*Leather products*	*Timber and products, excl. 10 and 11*	*Furniture*	*Pulp and paper products*	*Printing and publishing*	*Rubber products*	*Chemicals*	*Plastics*	*Bldg. materials and accessories*	*Basic metals*	*Metal products, excl. 19 and 20*	*Machinery*	*Transport equipment*	*Miscellaneous*	*Total*
Southern Rhodesia																						
Salisbury	6	10	17	13	4	9	42	4	40	51	11	34	6	40	7	60	4	70	38	21	16	503
Bulawayo	2	5	8	5	1	10	55	2	25	21	6	14	6	18	2	19	8	49	14	7	10	287
Umtali	1	3	3	2		2	4	1	11	4	2	2		2	1	2		8	1	8	4	61
Gwelo	1	1	1	1			5	1	4	2		2	2			7	4	9	2	6	3	51
Que Que		1					2		2			1				1	3	4		2		16
Gatooma						4	1		1			1				2	1	3	2			15
Fort Victoria		2		1			1		1				1			2		1	1	2		12
Hartley		1				1	1						1			1		2		2		9
Northern Rhodesia																						
Ndola		3	2	2		1	9	1	3	5	1	5	2	1		8	1	5	1	2	2	54
Kitwe	1	3	2	1					6	2		1	4	1	1	7	1	12	6	2	2	52
Lusaka	1	3		2			5		3	4		1	2	1	1	9		11	1	3	1	48
Livingstone				1		1	3		5	1		1	1	1		2		1		1	1	19
Broken Hill	1	3		1			2					2		1		2	1					13
Luanshya	1	1					1		1	2								5	1	1		13
Chingola	1											1				4	1	2				9
Mufulira	1											1				3		2				7
Nyasaland																						
Blantyre-Limbe	1	9	1	1		2			5	5		2	1	2		4		4			1	38
Cholo		9			1	2														1		13
Other than above towns[a]	3	42	2	4	1	2	14	2	8	7		4	1	4		11		29	4	5		143
Total	20	96	36	34	7	34	145	11	115	104	20	72	27	71	12	144	24	217	71	63	40	1363

N.B. There is a limited exaggeration in total number of plants resulting from some factories being recorded as producing goods under several categories.
Source: Unpublished data from Federation of Rhodesia and Nyasaland, Ministry of Commerce and Industry, 1962.
[a] Not differentiated by territory.

otherwise be expected. The government has participated directly in founding certain industries, including cotton spinning and iron and steel, and has attempted to stimulate industrial growth in other ways. The first Federal Customs Tariff, dated July, 1955 was designed to encourage and help new enterprises, and later increases have been made to favor specific industries, a major increase having been made in September, 1962. Opinion differs regarding the value of governmental assistance, some assessing the aid as unusual, others criticizing the absence of a relatively progressive government policy towards industry. Excessive weight has probably been given to tariff protection, which, in view of the limited size of the market, may result in misplacing the emphasis in manufacturing developments.

SEGMENTS OF INDUSTRY

The relative importance of individual manufacturing groups in the Federation is somewhat distorted by the inclusion of certain industries which might more meaningfully be defined as service establishments, some excessively small shops, and total employees of some companies which are engaged in other activities besides manufacturing. Chart 4 shows the relative importance of manufacturing groups as measured (1) by percentage of numbers employed as of September, 1961, when the total was 136,308 and (2) by percentage of total earnings excluding less-frequent bonuses and allowances for the month preceding the September census, when the total wage bill for manufacturing industry was at the annual rate of $100.0 million.

Interior of a large brewery at Bulawayo

Table 36 shows the number of plants by category found in the Federation and its manufacturing centers in 1961, again revealing the dominance of Salisbury and Bulawayo, and suggesting the small-scale character of many industries. It does show, however, a relatively broad diversification and a much-above-average representation of market-oriented establishments.

The food, drink, and tobacco products industries rank first in numbers employed, but second in total earnings of employees and in number of establishments, most of which are quite small. Animal and dairy products factories include six ice-cream plants, cheese and butter factories, and plants producing canned meats including a large new pig-processing works near Salisbury. The agricultural and vegetable produce category includes 55 corn meal factories, most of which are located outside of the main industrial centers; 28 tea factories, mainly in the Mlanje and Cholo Highlands of Nyasaland; large sugar factories at the Hippo Valley, Triangle, and Chirundu estates; and six flour mills, several of which were considerably expanded in 1961. Preserved food works include a $1.12 million canning factory at Bulawayo with a capacity of 30 million cans a year, four fruit-juice factories, and thirteen confectionery producers. Brewing is confined to a small number of large plants at Salisbury, Bulawayo, and Kitwe, but carbonated beverages are produced in twenty-four widely scattered and often very small plants. Two European brewing companies were negotiating in 1962 for the establishment of new breweries at Salisbury. The largest cigarette factory is a $1.4 million plant at Salisbury.

The textile and clothing industries have expanded with considerable force, their output having nearly doubled from 1955 to 1959. Textile mills now supply about half of the needs of the Federation for cloth and a new spinning mill at Salisbury has increased capacity substantially. The Gatooma cotton textile factory, the first major component in the industry, was erected by the government when ocean shipping was scarce. A half-dozen other weaving plants have since been constructed, and the Gatooma mill was sold to private interests in 1959. The textile industry has had greater difficulty in competing with foreign imports than the clothing industry and has recently asked for increased tariffs to protect it from "unorthodox overseas competition." Some 140 clothing factories, of which 55 are in Bulawayo and 42 are in Salisbury, employ over 10,000 persons and produce a diversified range of products, though shirts, dresses, and pants are the main items. This industry tends to be small scale and low-wage; it is claimed that it can produce articles of comparable quality to those imported at from 20 to 30 percent below the price of imported goods. A jute mill erected at Umtali in postwar years proved uneconomic and was forced to close after a few years of operation.

The most important leather goods factory is the very modern Rhodesian Bata Shoe Company, Ltd. plant at Gwelo, said to be the largest shoe factory in southern Africa. Bata intends to build a second shoe factory at Lusaka in Northern Rhodesia. Timber and timber products produced include blinds, boxes, doors, parquet flooring, plywood, and rail ties. The number of factories in this category is unduly swelled by the inclusion of 61 joinery firms, most of which are very small. Furniture factories also tend to be small and rather widely dispersed; included in this category are 34 firms producing metal furniture, 52 producing wooden furniture, and 8 producing both, while the remaining 10 firms produce mattresses. The pulp and paper products industry was briefly touched upon under forestry; it also includes factories in the main cities producing various stationery items. Printing and publishing appear relatively more important than they are when measured by number of establishments, for these include 46 letterpresses mostly of only local importance.

Twenty-two of the twenty-seven plants producing rubber products are retreading and vulcanizing establishments. The most important factory in this category is the Dunlop (Rhodesia) Ltd. tire factory at Bulawayo, now employing about 1,000 workers. This $4.2 million plant was unable to operate at a profit until given additional tariff protection in 1961.

The chemical industry is represented by plants producing fertilizers, oil and soap, paints and polishes, matches, explosives, acids, pharmaceuticals, and oxygen. The Sir Alexander Gibb report of 1960 strongly recommended that a large nitrogen plant be erected in the Federation, and study is in progress with respect to the most suitable process and site. Political considerations appeared in 1962 to favor a site in Northern Rhodesia, either at Kitwe or at Livingstone, but collapse of the Federation presents an entirely new set of considerations. A request for tariff action to protect a proposed $2.8 million phosphatic fertilizer factory at Dorowa was refused in 1961 and the project was shelved. Prolonged negotiations with respect to the erection of an oil refinery in the Federation finally led to construction of a $42 million plant at Umtali which will be capable of providing all products except aviation fuel and lubricating oils at no higher prices than those previously existing. It is hoped that transmission of crude oil by pipeline from Beira can be effected at slightly below half the present cost by tank car. British and American interests were strongly at odds regarding the justification for a local refinery, the British claiming that it would aggravate unemployment, cost the railways $840,000 a year in lost revenue, create a monopolistic situation, be too small to achieve desirable economies in scale, and prevent the Federation from taking full advantage of excess

A ferrochrome plant at Gwelo
The Southern Rhodesian chrome industry has been hurt in recent years by increased competition from the USSR.

refinery capacity in the world. The twelve manufacturers in the plastics field produce a wide variety of products from bags and pipes to household goods and rainwear.

The largest number of building material plants are brickworks, of which there were 64 in 1961. These tend to be small and widely scattered because of the low value per unit weight of their product. Cement mills are found at Salisbury, Bulawayo, and Colleen Bawn in Southern Rhodesia, Chilanga in Northern Rhodesia, and Blantyre in Nyasaland, but the Chilanga plant was forced to close down in 1960 after the demand at Kariba had been met. The decline in construction due to political uncertainties has depressed the whole building materials industry sharply in recent years.

In the metal and metal-fabricated section there is wider representation than in any African country except South Africa. The basic metals category includes 13 castings works, the important ferrochrome plants previously noted, and a producer of lead pipes. Most important, however, are the iron and steel mills of the Rhodesian Iron and Steel Company, Ltd. (Riscom) at Redcliff near Que Que and at Bulawayo. The mill at Redcliff was begun during the war and "held together by hairpins and paper clips"; its small scale made economic operations very difficult despite government assistance. When acquired from the government by a private syndicate in 1957, the Redcliff works consisted of two 240-ton blast furnaces, two 225-ton open-hearth steel furnaces, and 10-inch and 20-inch rolling mills. In 1956 it produced 63,000 tons of ingot steel. Under a $25.2 million expansion program, a new 650-ton blast furnace, new open-hearth furnaces, and improved rolling mill facilities were provided in 1962, when 600 Europeans and 1,900 Africans were employed. Output in 1961 was 216,300 tons of pig and 90,800 tons of ingot steel. Iron ore is secured almost at the site at about 75¢ a ton, limestone is quarried at an adjacent hill, and coal is railed from Wankie, though it could be obtained at a distance of no more than 100 miles. The Bulawayo works of Riscom include an electric furnace, a rolling mill, and a forging plant. Despite the exceptionally low cost of raw materials and low labor wages, Riscom has had difficulty in competing with imports because of its small scale, and the company had a net loss of about $400,000 in 1960. A second major drawback is the site of the Redcliff works, the limestone and iron quarries and the mill all being situated in a constricted valley with only limited flat space available. If sufficient foreign orders could be obtained for pig iron, however, the company could probably greatly rationalize its operations and improve its profit position. In 1962–63 negotiations were being carried on with the Kawasaki Steel Corporation of Japan with a view to possible export of 400,000 tons of pig and 700,000 tons of iron ore over a ten-year period. Involving an expenditure of about $12.6 million, the project would require adding a 1,000-ton-capacity blast furnace at Redcliff and installing mining equipment at Bukwe.

Metal products coming from Federation plants include aluminum goods, drums, chains, doors and windows, fencing, nails, sheet metal products, and stoves. Machinery produced includes agricultural implements, pumps, electrical appliances, refrigeration equipment, and radios. Bulawayo is the main center for the metal-fabricated, mechanical, and electrical goods industries, which rank as the number-one segment of manufacturing in that city. Its two radio producers have succeeded in marketing a considerable output in adjacent countries. Television sets are also assembled in Bulawayo, transmission having begun at Salisbury and Bulawayo in 1961–62.

The category of transport equipment includes 17 boat and barge builders, 18 bus and car body works, 1 bicycle assembly plant, and 5 automobile assembly plants. Only the assembly plants are modern, relatively large-scale establishments. Salisbury (Rover Company, Ford Motor Company, and the Rootes Group) and Umtali (British Motor Corporation cars and bicycles) are the main centers, but a Jeep assembly plant has recently been opened in Lusaka.

Finally, miscellaneous industries include producers of baskets and brushes, glass (Umtali has a $900,000 glass factory, and a $1 million glass container plant was opened at Gwelo in 1963), gramophone records (it is claimed that 90 percent of those used in the Rhodesias and Nyasaland are produced by a Bulawayo firm), jewelry, and toys.

The Rhodesian Iron and Steel Company plant at Redcliff
This steel mill has an exceptionally favorable raw material position, but its small scale has made economic operation difficult.

THE FUTURE GROWTH OF MANUFACTURING

The future growth of manufacturing in the area will depend upon the availability of markets, labor, power, raw materials, and capital, with political developments having a strong influence on several of these factors. A brief assessment of each of these will show some of the strengths and weaknesses of the area with regard to industry.

MARKET. The weakness of the market would appear to set definite limits on the size of the industrial establishment. Even if the European population, with a high average income, were to quadruple, it would still be too small to support many types of industrial enterprises. This provides a strong argument for working to raise the African standard of living, for it is only the indigenous populace that can provide a potentially large domestic market. In 1961 the average earnings of the 984,010 African employees in the Federation were $280 as compared with $3,433 for the 121,800 European employees.

The advantages of the Federation market have included the high purchasing power of many Europeans, the demand stimulated by large and small development and construction projects (now temporarily depressed), the fact that about an eighth of all the Africans of Rhodesia and Nyasaland are wage earners, and the very considerable geographic concentration of the two richest market regions—the high veld of Southern Rhodesia and the Copperbelt of Northern Rhodesia. These two regions contain a high proportion of all wage earners in the three countries. The Copperbelt has a large number of the best-paid employees in the Rhodesias, since average earnings in mining are 70 percent above the average for Europeans and 88 percent above the average for Africans. Finally, while the average income of the African is low, the aggregate purchasing power is adequate to absorb substantial quantities of clothing, shoes, bicycles, furniture, and so on.

It does not now appear that opportunities for export of manufactured products are great, except for items semiprocessed from domestically produced agricultural and mineral raw materials. Some textiles and clothing items are exported to the Republic of South Africa, but that country's desire to foster its own industry does not suggest that the Rhodesias will be permitted to secure a very large slice of the Republic market. The Federation of Rhodesian Industry has suggested that some items may be produced at lower cost in the Rhodesias than in the Republic because of the less restrictive policies of the former with regard to employment of Africans in manufacturing, and that these items might, therefore, secure a market in the Republic. Adjacent areas may absorb some produce, such as shoes, clothing, and electrical goods, but several of them have plans for their own industrial development, while sales to overseas markets are hampered by the interior continental position of the area. On the other hand, the favorable raw material position of its iron and steel industry and its relatively better developed metal fabricating industry may permit Southern Rhodesia to market mechanical and metal items in adjacent countries and iron and steel abroad as the industry becomes better rationalized.

LABOR. Regarding labor, the rapidly increasing population provides an adequate supply. Complaints of labor shortages during the 1950s were scarcely consonant with the prodigal use of labor, while with the slowing pace of economic development a fairly troublesome unemployment problem has recently developed in Southern Rhodesia and Nyasaland. This will probably result in increasing restrictions being imposed on migrants from other countries, and Southern Rhodesian authorities have stated that independent Nyasaland's laborers are to be treated as aliens. In 1961, 45 percent of the Africans employed in Southern Rhodesia were from outside that country; Northern Rhodesia had 17 percent and Nyasaland 6 percent of its workers from other countries.

The system of landownership in Southern Rhodesia has forced the industrialist to adapt his operations to the employment of migratory labor because the African worker, not permitted to settle in European areas, was obliged to keep one foot in the reserve. Not surprisingly, labor turnover rates were high and productivity low. It was possible for a manufacturer to stabilize his labor force partially by providing his own township for African employees, but this was likely to increase capital requirements by about 25 percent. Recently this situation has been improved by extension of legal rights to purchase of urban land by Africans, while the governments have adopted much more ambitious programs for providing African housing. The greater stability of settled workers has been revealed on numerous occasions, not only in manufacturing, but in mining and other occupations. There has also been considerable progress in improving productivity in recent years, the domestic production per head of population in Southern Rhodesia having increased from $157 in 1953 to $199 in 1958 and $263 in 1961.

Shortages of artisans, skilled workers, and managers are likely to be more restrictive in the future than shortages of unskilled and semiskilled labor, though the Rhodesians do not have the same limitations in this regard that exist in most tropical African countries. Further relaxation of the color bar would help this situation, both by permitting the rise of Africans who are willing and able to absorb the necessary training, and by freeing Europeans from less important jobs so they could make a greater contribution to the economy. In Northern Rhodesia, it has been suggested that some industries have been deterred from moving to the Copperbelt by the necessity to meet the wages paid by the mining companies, but the heavily concentrated and relatively wealthy market appears to have more than offset this consideration.

An absolute essential is to remove the remnants of racial restriction in industrial employment, which all too clearly contradict claims of aiding African advancement. As in our own country, it is usually just those people who claim the Negro is incapable of handling jobs beyond a given level who are most insistent on seeing that he does not get the opportunity.

Labor unrest has been a problem of serious dimensions in the mining industry, but has not thus far been serious in manufacturing. African unions are youthful and inexperienced, however, hence it is not unrealistic to expect that manufacturers will face both responsible and irresponsible labor action.

RAW MATERIALS AND ENERGY. Turning to the raw material, fuel, and power position of the Rhodesias as it may affect industrial development, we recall the substantial hydroelectric and reasonably favorable coal resources of the area. They permit envisaging the development of a more rounded industrial economy than may be practicable in most African areas. The exceptionally low cost of coal must also be noted.

The area is well endowed from the standpoint of industrial raw materials. In agriculture, the production of cotton, vegetable oils, tobacco, food crops, and livestock may be expanded, while physical characteristics permit the introduction of other crops providing industrial raw materials. The opportunities in forestry are also substantial so long as a sufficiently vigorous afforestation program is sustained. Mineral raw materials are tremendous and varied, but, for many years, greater importance will attach to them as exports rather than as raw materials for industry. One shortage which will require increasing attention is that of water supplies for domestic and industrial use on the high veld of Southern Rhodesia. Water is now high cost and no community has large untapped reserves.

CAPITAL. From the standpoint of availability of capital, the Federation was one of the most attractive African areas for foreign investment in postwar years, though the greater part of the funds went into transportation, power, and mining rather than to secondary industry. In more recent years there was a decline of outside investments and a relative increase in domestically generated capital investments. The ratio of investment to gross national product was very large, though political conditions led to a considerable sloughing off in more recent years.

The Rhodesias and Nyasaland, in conclusion, have excellent potentialities for economic expansion. The weakest physical link is the agricultural base, though even here the opportunities are very great. The remarkable metallogenetic zone of the Copperbelt and other substantial mineral resources can readily be further exploited to yield exchange and provide industrial raw materials. There is room for expansion in many secondary industries, and there is a power, fuel, and raw material base adequate to justify a fully integrated manufacturing economy.

The key question is whether the political problems of the area will be resolved with sufficient rapidity to prevent a serious disruption of the economy. Unlike Kenya, there is plenty of room for both European and African farmers, the skills of the Europeans in mining and industry are required, and the countries should not permit their comparatively well-developed national and federal services to be dismantled. There are risks, of course, in a rapid devolution of power, but the risks in clinging to power appear far more dangerous and the opportunities created by devolving it far more rewarding. Indeed, the area has a physical and human resource complex which would permit its rapidly outpacing the other countries of tropical Africa.

CHAPTER TWENTY-ONE

Angola and Mozambique

Political uncertainties in Portuguese Africa make it somewhat difficult to assess the short-term possibilities for economic advance. In February, 1961, an uprising of serious proportions began in Angola, spreading over wide sections of the north; it resulted in the deaths of about 1,500 to 2,000 Europeans and 30,000 to 50,000 Africans, the flight of 250,000 to 300,000 Angolans to Congo, and considerable destruction of coffee plantations, houses, villages, roads, and bridges. The most intense phase of the revolt ended after about six months, but sporadic fighting continued well into 1962. Portugal met the revolt by bringing about 35,000 troops from the metropole, who gradually brought most of the affected area under control. In 1963 Africans returning from the bush or abroad were being put into villages of about 3,000 inhabitants, the size being considered appropriate both for introduction of social improvements and for maintenance of security. Those who failed to pass a rigid screening were reported being sent to the south, where they were treated as outcasts by the indigenous tribes.

In the meantime, two governments-in-exile have been set up, some African governments have recognized one of them, Angolans are said to be training in several countries for a renewed revolt or sustained guerrilla action, and independent African governments have intensified their demands for a boycott of Portugal and for punitive action by the U.N. While Mozambique had not undergone comparable unrest, it, too, had a government-in-exile and had all of the symptoms of a threatening political revolt.

Portugal has maintained that its territories in Africa are provinces of Portugal, not colonies. But this claim is largely semantic, for there are numerous contrasts in the political, social, and economic administration of the metropole and the overseas provinces, and many characteristics of colonialism are strongly in evidence in the latter.

The explanations for the lack of success of Portuguese policies in Africa are partly the nature of these policies, partly the failure to recognize the accelerating political changes that have characterized the continent in postwar years, and partly Portugal's inability to finance the development that would be required. The effect, if not the intent, has been preservation to a large degree of the status quo.

The Portuguese firmly believe that through work the African's physical, mental, and moral standards will be raised. Accordingly, unless engaged in full-time cultivation of marketable crops, all adult male Africans were required until recently to work in gainful employment for at least six months a year. This led to abuses sometimes no different from forced labor. Reforms instituted before the revolt were not adequate to halt a large-scale emigration to escape the labor requirement, but in late 1962 the first phase of a completely overhauled labor law was applied, stipulating minimum wages, maximum hours, and improved conditions for rural workers.

Portuguese policies are avowedly paternalistic, but the benefits extended to the Africans have been less than impressive. Wages are relatively low and have not always kept pace with inflation; only about 3 percent of the populace is literate; health facilities are seldom provided outside the more important communities. Again, the Angolan revolt has led to reforms; an effort was made to double the school population in 1962, universities were started in Angola and Mozambique in 1963, and funds for medical facilities were greatly increased.

Special pride is taken by Portugal in the lack of racialism in the approach to its overseas provinces, and it is true that there is a substantial number of persons of mixed race in her African provinces. It has also been possible for Africans to acquire equality of status with Europeans by learning Portuguese and forsaking tribal ties and customs. But in 1960, only about 35,000 Africans in Angola and 6,500 in Mozambique had chosen to become assimilated, though some additional thousands probably could have qualified if they had not wished to retain the preferred tax position of the *indigenato*. Nor can it be accepted without important reservations that the Portuguese white is without prejudice. With the rapid build-up of the European population in Angola and Mozambique in recent years, there has been increased evidence of racialism, and migrants from the lower strata of Portuguese society have taken a larger percentage of the jobs normally handled by Africans in other countries.

The political and financial status of Portugal helps to explain its failure to effect greater advances in Africa. One of the poorest countries in Europe, it is characterized by a considerable degree of rural underemployment. Politically, the country has seen little change since the 1920s; opposition is no more welcome or tolerated in the metropole than it is overseas. Despite its own inability to provide development capital in adequate amounts, Portugal has been very chary of accepting outside aid or investment in Africa, partly for fear of reducing its authority in the overseas provinces. These areas have also been important economically to Portugal, and there was the desire to ensure that as much as possible of the earnings from them accrue to the metropole rather than to other investors. Angola and Mozambique together buy about a quarter of Portugese exports. Angola is particularly important as an earner of dollar exchange for the escudo bloc; in 1961 only 19 percent of its exports went to Portugal, while 47 percent of its imports came from the metropole. Mozambique receives a substantial amount of foreign exchange through its very important transit traffic, tourism, and payments on contract labor working in the Rhodesias and South Africa.

Despite a record which is subject to justifiable criticism, it should be noted that both Angola and Mozambique have witnessed marked economic advances in postwar years in terms of development of their infrastructures and output of goods and services. Their share of world imports and exports increased about 31 percent and 55 percent respectively from 1938 to 1961. In postwar years Angola saw a big boom in coffee exports, the introduction of diversified mining, marked increases in the transit traffic handled by Lobito, and a not inconsequential industrial build-up. Mozambique benefited even more from transit trade, while its export of cotton and other agricultural products increased substantially. By 1964 both provinces had significant hydroelectric and irrigation projects in being and under development, there had been notable improvements in their transport facilities, and some previously almost untouched interior areas were increasingly being brought into the modern economy. True, a disproportionate share of development funds had been spent on projects of prime interest to Europeans, but at least the base for further and more widespread advances had been vastly improved.

As a consequence of the Angola revolt, Portugal has announced plans for constitutional and other reforms in its relations with the overseas territories. The constitutional changes call for extension of greater authority to the provincial governments, suppression of the *indigenato* system, and granting of citizenship to all residents, though the vote was to be limited to those Africans who could read and write Portuguese and pay $7 yearly in taxes. In the economic sphere, reforms have included the introduction of collective bargaining, changes in the laws governing land rights, control of the discriminatory cotton marketing arrangements, and inauguration of a common market between Portugal and its overseas provinces. The new trade arrangements call for elimination of all Portuguese barriers except on some competing agricultural produce by 1964 and removal of provincial barriers to Portuguese produce by the end of 1971. There has also been a very sharp increase in development expenditures, the 1961 allotment having been raised from $28.6 to $59.3 million. In June, 1962, Angola's big businesses, which had been in a sacrosanct realm, found their profits taxed for the first time.

Whether these changes have come in time and whether they are sufficient is highly questionable. They do, however, represent welcome changes and probably only the first of a series which will bring Portuguese Africa more closely in line with other countries on that continent. There is a serious dilemma present, however, which will make the coming years particularly difficult. Angola and Mozambique are even less prepared for independence than Congo from the standpoint of the number of educated Africans, yet the pressure for independence from within and from without is bound to accelerate. Without a markedly expanded effort in the social sphere, which would have to involve assistance from non-Portuguese sources, it is difficult to see how a reasonably smooth transition can be accomplished.

ANGOLA

Angola is a roughly rectangular country with an area of 481,226 square miles and a coast line about 1,031 miles in length. It is about equivalent in size to Texas, California, and Arizona combined, or to Iberia, France, and Belgium and is fourteen times as large as the metropole.

PHYSICAL BACKGROUND

The vast bulk of Angola is an extension of the central African plateau which drops off to the Atlantic coast in two steps, widely spaced in the north, closer in the center, but almost joining in the south.

The coastal plain, with elevations to 1,300 feet, varies in width from about 12 to 100 miles, being greatest in the lower valley of the Cuanza River just southeast of the capital. The presence of the cool, northward-flowing Benguela Current offshore moderates temperatures along the coast and reduces precipitation markedly. At Cabinda in the north the average rainfall is 25.4 inches, at Luanda it is 13.3 inches, at Lobito 10.5 inches, and at Moçâmedes only 2 inches. While these amounts limit rain-grown crops, there are opportunities for irrigation agriculture, which is further advantaged by the existence of some good soils along the river valleys.

The transitional lands and escarpments, ranging from 1,300 to about 3,300 feet in elevation, are varied in depth and aspect. In the north, the rise to the main plateau is gradual; in the central and southern sections, it is quite abrupt. Orographic precipitation contributes to the presence of a profuse vegetation in the north, which gradually evolves toward the south to savanna and steppe patterns.

The plateau itself has elevations from about 3,300 to 5,000 feet in the north and south except in the high Humpata Mountains in the south near Sá da Bandeira, but swells in the center to general elevations of 7,000 and 8,000 feet and over, especially along its western edge. The latitudinal position becomes dominant in setting the rainfall pattern, tropical rainy climate existing in the north and in the Cabinda Enclave, tropical highland savanna in the center, and highland steppe in the south. Annual precipitation is about 60 inches in the north, 40–60 inches in the center, and 25–40 inches in the south. There are two well-marked seasons, the rainy season roughly from September to April, and the cooler, drier "Cacimbo" from May to September. The northern plateau is suitable for tropical crops such as coffee, oil palm, and cotton; inland from Lobito, the Benguela-Bié Plateau is appropriate for corn, peanuts, sisal, etc.; the southern Huila Plateau is mainly cattle country, the southeastern Cuando-Duango area consisting of seemingly limitless stretches of sandy wastes interspersed with somewhat higher areas covered with thin forests. Temperatures on the plateau are everywhere moderated by elevation, making large parts attractive for European settlement.

POPULATION

The population of Angola was estimated at 4.87 million in 1961, including about 200,000 Europeans, an increase from 44,000 in 1940 and 79,000 in 1950. There are two main ethnic groups among the Africans: some Khoisan, believed to be descended from aboriginal races, and over 90 Bantu-speaking tribes who comprise the vast bulk of the population. In sharp contrast with most tropical African areas, many Europeans are small holders, petty operators, and even unskilled laborers. On several agricultural projects both here and in Mozambique, European farmers are not permitted to use African labor.

The over-all density was only 10.1 per square mile in 1961 but it is, of course, variable from area to area. About a quarter of the country has only about 1.3 per square mile, the eastern and southern regions having the lowest densities. The density is approximately 25 per square mile on a third of the territory. Urbanization is not pronounced, but Luanda has seen a dynamic build-up in postwar years and had a population in 1958 comprised of about 40,000 Europeans, 12,500 persons of mixed blood, and 175,000–180,000 Africans.

LAND USE REGIONS

Angola's economy is heavily dependent on extractive activities, of which agriculture is dominant. A number of broad land use regions can be delineated with differing economic and crop emphases.

THE CABINDA ENCLAVE. Measuring 2,794 square miles in area, Cabinda may be considered as a distinct region not only because of its separation from the rest of Angola but because of its significance in production of tropical timber (Map 84). All of the timber exported from Angola comes from Cabinda, forests covering the bulk of the interior and 84 percent of the whole enclave, where precipitation exceeds 50 to 60 inches a year. Its prewar economy was poorly developed owing to lack of finances, shortages of manpower, and transport deficiencies. Postwar years saw the first intensive exploitation of the forests, a peak export of 73,813 tons valued at $3.2 million having been reached in 1958, with an additional 10,000 tons being shipped to other Angolan areas. Over half of timber exports, which account for about 65 percent of the value and 90 percent of the volume of exports, are in logs, about three eighths in rail ties, and one twelfth in sawn lumber. Some 50 loggers and 18 mills are operated in Cabinda, most of their production being exported through the lighterage port of the district's main town, Cabinda. Coffee, palm products, and other crops account for the remaining 35 percent of enclave exports.

NORTHERN ANGOLA. The northern section of Angola has a relatively undeveloped coastal lowland, a fairly broad and variable-surfaced subplateau which drops into the Cuango Valley on the east, and a plateau which is less extensive than in central and southern Angola. The vegetation is steppelike on the coast, luxuriant on the subplateau, and sparser on the somewhat monotonous plateau, which has only small areas of workable timber.

The economic mainstay of the north is coffee, most of which is produced at elevations ranging from 1,300 to 5,000 feet. Coffee has been the prime export of Angola (Table 38); indeed it normally ranks as the leading earner of foreign exchange in the entire escudo area. It enjoyed a remarkable boom in postwar years, acreage in coffee having risen from 88,000 in 1938 to 663,000 in 1957; production increased from 19,000 tons in prewar years to an average of 48,900 tons in the period 1946 to 1951, 78,000 tons in 1959, and 185,000 tons in 1962. In 1962 coffee accounted for 43.7 percent of the total value of exports from Angola, which has ranked as Africa's leading coffee producer in recent years. Like other African countries, it is

A coffee estate in the Dembos region
Angola ranked as Africa's leading coffee producer in 1962.

now plagued with a surplus production. Despite the revolt, Angola harvested a record crop in 1961, though some 15 percent of the predicted output was lost; its 1962 output was up one third from the 1961 level. Europeans normally produce about three fourths of Angolan coffee, but the African share has been increasing. In 1957 about 400 European growers had 500 plantations, but one large company was responsible for about a quarter of total production. Small *fazendéiro* going into coffee production were usually granted 125 to 250 acres, to which they could secure title if 10 percent had been developed in five years.

The main coffee producing areas in Angola are on the Uige Plateau. The mountains around Carmona are dotted with fazendas of European colons and this town had a very rapid growth in the 1950s as a result of the coffee boom. A second concentration of coffee estates is around Gabela inland from Porto Amboím, while arabica coffee is produced on the highlands along the Benguela Railway.

Most of Angolan coffee is good-grade robusta, commanding a higher price than most African robustas on the world market. Plantings of arabica in the vicinity of Moderna and at Ganda on the southern edge of the central zone will increase the share of arabica in future years.

The Junta de Exportaçao do Cafe, one of several similar commodity boards in Angola and Mozambique, plays an important role in coffee production, maintaining a large experimental farm near Carmona, providing free seedlings, advising the planters, and establishing coffee preparation plants.

Medium-staple cotton, produced under a system of zone concessions accorded to private companies, is grown in small patches by about 60,000 Africans in the northern coastal area and along the Luanda railway, the Catete and Malange districts being important. Concessionaires were charged with assisting and advising the African growers, providing selected seed, purchasing the crop, ginning, baling, and shipping the product. Prices were fixed by the government, and were typically below world market prices, in order to favor the metropolitan textile industry. After a growers' strike in the Cassange area in 1961 to protest the low prices, legislation was enacted to correct the situation. It is now hoped that output will increase from the present level of about 19,000 tons to 40,000 tons yearly.

Sugar is grown along the lower courses of several rivers in Angola, both in the north and in the center, there being about 37,500 acres devoted to this crop. Four firms hold exclusive concessions; domestic and export prices are controlled; and shipments to Portugal are regulated by a quota system. The main producing areas in the north are in the lower Dande and Cuanza valleys relatively near Luanda. A $7 million project of the Cuanza Sugar Company to form *colonatos* of growers and construct a factory has been postponed by the company's failure to amass sufficient capital support.

An important irrigation project is planned for the lower Cuanza Valley, about 18 miles from Luanda. In the first stage, which is based upon the Cambambe Dam now under construction, 250,000 acres will be drained, irrigated by pumps, and brought under flood control. Eventually, about 750,000 acres may be controlled. A considerable part of the first lands will be used to produce foodstuffs for the capital.

The M'Bridge River Basin is the site of a

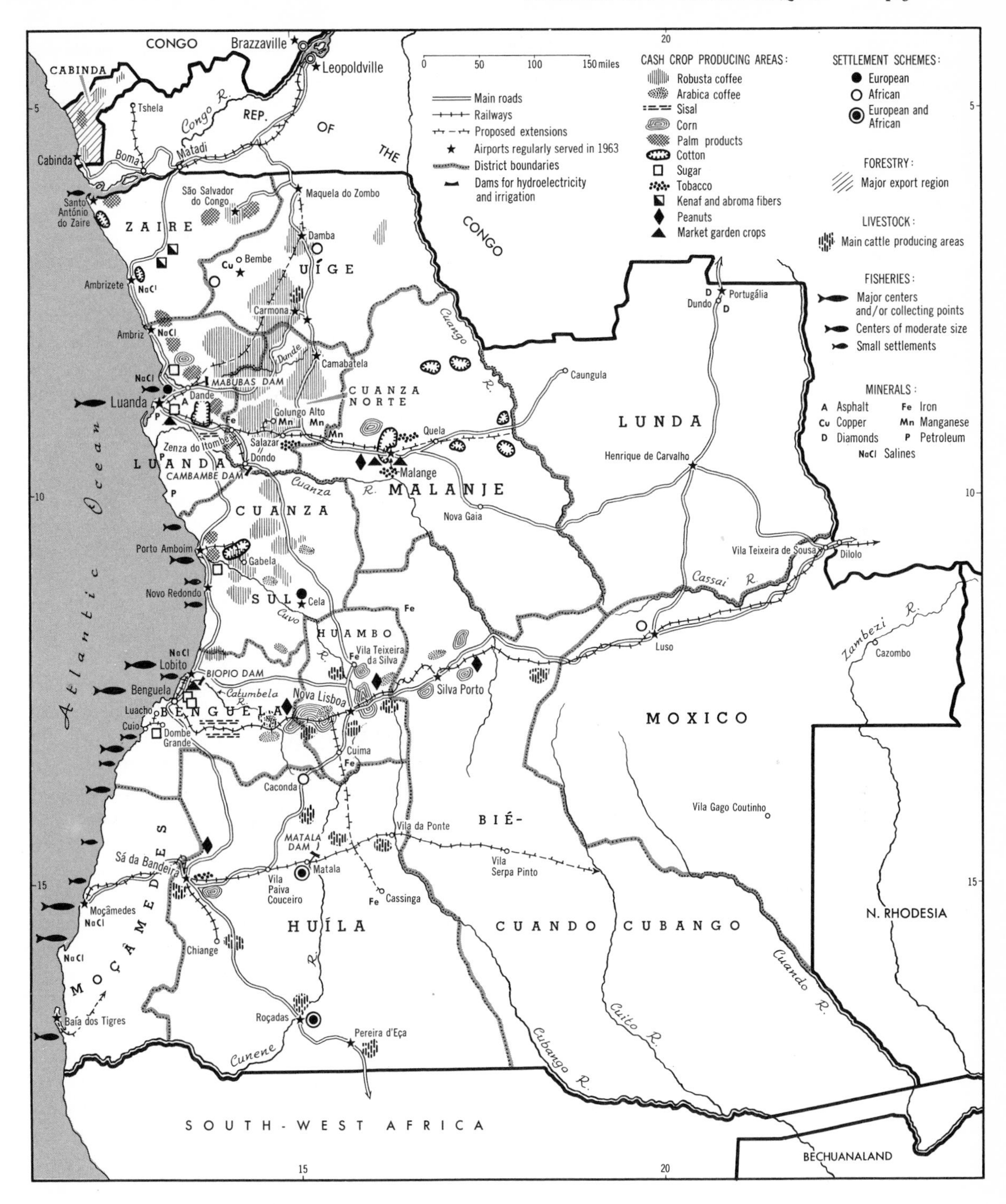

Map 84. Economic map of Angola

concession of the large Portuguese corporation, Companhia Uniao Fabril. The chief interests on its 75,000-acre holding are kenaf and abroma fibers, but 1,200 acres of coffee and 6,000 acres of coconuts are also planned.

The northern region also produces palm products, cassava, and other tropical crops, but only in relatively small quantities. The area around Malange ships a considerable amount of market garden crops to the urban areas of Luanda, while tobacco is produced by Europeans in the same area and by Africans around Lucala, most of the production being taken by tobacco factories in the capital. Plans call for developing an export of bananas totaling about 100,000 tons by 1967.

MIDDLE ANGOLA. The coastal plain is quite narrow in this section of the country, but sugar plantations are found near Catumbela and in the Caporolo Valley which drains into the Atlantic at Cuio. The central uplands, which contain the highest part of the country, form the Angolan watershed between the Congo-Atlantic and the Zambezi-Okavango river systems. Precipitation is quite high on the more elevated parts of the Bié Plateau, but gradually diminishes to the interior.

In the main producing belt, along the Benguela Railway, the land is rolling to extremely hilly with scattered inselberge and rough, infertile hillsides. Sisal, which ranks as the second export crop by value, is produced on European estates along the line, with Cubal being one of the principal centers. Angola ranks second to Tanganyika among African producers, but third after Brazil among world producers of sisal. Approximately 306,000 acres are planted to sisal, with about four fifths producing.

Corn, the third crop export, also comes mainly from the line of rail on the Benguela Plateau, though some comes from the Malange area in the north. The corn belt of the Benguela Plateau has moderately heavy red soil of low fertility which is permitted to revert to bush after a few years of cultivation. About 95 percent of production comes from African farms. Yields of corn are about 10 to 12 bushels per acre on the Benguela-Bié plateaus as compared to 20 to 25 bushels per acre in the Malange region, and total production fluctuates greatly depending on seasonal conditions.

As noted earlier, arabica coffee is also grown along the rail belt. Peanuts, sesame, wheat, beans, and peas are also produced in this section of the country, while Europeans produce some tobacco at Cela. Beeswax is collected in the interior from crude barrel-shaped, bark hives fastened in the trees. While three honey and wax crops can be collected annually, there is considerable loss owing to the crude methods employed.

Livestock are relatively less important than in the south, but a $1.12 million plant is under construction at Nova Lisboa which will produce an unusual variety of animal products from canned meat, soups, and soap, to pharmaceuticals and fertilizers.

SOUTHERN ANGOLA. The main agricultural concern of southern Angola is livestock raising, which has been only slightly commercialized. The most important area is on the plateau in southwestern Angola in a zone extending from Vila Pereira d'Eca northward to the Benguela Railway. Cattle, of which there are an estimated 1¼ million head, are the prime interest of many tribes in Angola, but adherence to a cattle culture, low prices fixed by the government on livestock products, and long distances to shipping and marketing points have militated against any sizable commercial development. Some wells have been bored in the southern livestock area, and a modern abattoir and deep-freeze plant has been constructed at Sá da Bandeira where a few European ranches are located. A new refrigeration and storage plant has also just been completed at Moçâmedes, while a large German-owned firm has installed a ranch near Vila da Ponte to raise cattle for corned beef. The government has also developed plans to organize African livestock into several large tribal ranches to permit better use of the available feed and water supplies, but many years will be required to realize the very substantial potentialities that exist in the country.

SETTLEMENT SCHEMES

A considerable effort, particularly under the two six-year development plans initiated in 1953, has been concentrated on agricultural settlement schemes in various parts of the country. The most important of the European settlement projects are at Cela, in a well-watered valley east of Novo Redondo, and around Matala in the middle Cunene Valley. The Cela Scheme was begun in 1952, and by 1962 some 400 Portuguese families had been settled in villages in the area. The government prepares the land for each farm and constructs the villages in typical Portuguese style. Original farms had 15 acres of irrigated land reclaimed from swamp, 30 acres of nonirrigated land, and 100 acres for grazing; later, farms with 100 acres of cropland to be worked with the aid of tractors have been allotted, while in 1960 the distribution of holdings with 40 acres of irrigated land and 220 acres for grazing was begun. The smaller farms cost about $4,500–$5,000 and are made available to poorer immigrants with the assistance of 25-year, low-cost mortgages. The colony maintains tractor and machinery pools, but much of the work is done with oxen. The peasants are not permitted to have African workers or servants.

Crops grown at Cela include rice, coffee, wheat, peanuts, corn, potatoes, fruits, vegetables, and tobacco, but the main specialization will probably be on dairy and beef cattle. In 1959, 200 head of Danish cattle were imported to serve as a nucleus of the dairy herd and an additional 1,700 head were to be imported; the entire herd totaled 6,000 cattle in 1960. A small butter and cheese plant has been constructed at St. Mamede.

It is difficult to assess the value of this and other settlement schemes. Some poor settlers have had great difficulty in establishing themselves, others have found the holdings too small to permit a satisfactory income, while another criticism has been the failure to establish the necessary processing facilities. Instituted partly to relieve the demographic pressure in Portugal, the schemes appear to make only a minor contribution in relation to the population increase there of about 72,000 yearly. The cost per family may also be questioned in the light of pressing budgetary demands in other spheres, while the whole future of white settlement in Africa cannot help but give concern for the position of these colons.

The Matala Scheme, an irrigation settlement project on the middle Cunene, is planned to be the largest colonization scheme in Angola, and may involve a total expenditure of $30 million. By 1962 about 400 European and African families of a planned eventual total of 8,000 had been installed in five villages near Matala on the Moçâmedes rail line. A canal takes off from the Cunene Dam, follows the contour of the valley, and irrigates a relatively narrow band along the river. The major crop emphasis is to be tobacco for export; wheat and some vegetables are also grown. The administration of this scheme is similar to that at Cela. Later, an area further south near Fort Roçadas may be developed for irrigated farming.

Several African settlement schemes were also introduced in the 1950s, two of the largest being in the Loge Valley and at 31 de Janeiro in the north. Both were overrun during the rebellion but resumed activities later. The Loge Valley scheme, situated 90 miles northwest of Carmona, has been allotted 20,000 acres, but most of this has not yet been planted. Europeans handle most of the plowing and cultivating, which is done by machine, and direct the planting program. Coffee occupies about 70 percent of the acreage, palms about 2 percent, the rest being devoted to subsistence peanuts, cassava, beans, and corn. Africans are responsible for some of the cultivation, for all of the harvesting, and for the care of poultry and livestock.

The 31 de Janeiro scheme is situated southeast of Damba in a previously almost uninhabited area. Here 1,150 Africans, 185 of whom are family heads, have cleared about 1,250 acres of a planned 5,500 acres. Europeans build the roads required, contour plow and terrace the fields, direct the mechanical preparation of the fields, and instruct the African peasants on appropriate use of the land. Cassava is the chief subsistence and cash crop; corn, peanuts, vegetables, and fruit are also grown. It is possible that Portuguese immigrants will also be settled on this scheme.

Other settlement schemes are situated in the Moxico District near Luso and in the Bengo River Valley, just north of Luanda. The last is being prepared to produce vegetables, fruit, and cattle for the Luanda market.

The possibilities for developing Angolan agriculture are enormous. It is estimated that less than 2 percent of the country is planted to field and tree crops, while probably at least 50 percent could be so used. Irrigation can be extended greatly in the areas now being brought under control and elsewhere. And there are wide opportunities for the improvement and extension of commercial livestock production.

FISHING

Angola ranks among the leading nations in Africa in fishing, products from this industry ranking third among exports with about 6–9 percent of their total value. A great string of coastal settlements are engaged in fishing (Map 84) and may be classified into three categories: (1) the main collection centers—Moçâmedes, Benguela, and Luanda; (2) several fairly spacious harbors which shelter larger fleets and installations and which ship all or part of their catch directly overseas; and (3) a series of small hamlets which treat their own catch but deliver the processed fish to regional collecting centers. While fishing was established in Angola in the early nineteenth century, it was not until the 1950s that the big expansion occurred, but the bubble burst in the late 1950s with an unexplained reduction in the numbers of fish moving along the coast.

Fish drying at a small company plant near Benguela
Angola is one of the leading African nations in fish catches, but the industry is small scale and uses little modern equipment.

Angola is advantaged by the existence of the Benguela Current, which, like other cool ocean currents, normally has a large fish population, and by the existence of continental shelves considerably larger than for most of Africa. But its industry does not compare in modernity with those of the Republic of South Africa or South-West Africa, there being no special loading and unloading installations and poorly represented canning and freezing establishments. The first modern trawler was not acquired until mid-1962. Most of the fishermen are Portuguese, but many Africans are employed in the shore installations. Over four fifths of the marketed products are fish meal and fish oil, about a sixth is sun-cured, the small remaining percentage being sold fresh or canned.

The southern coastal stretches are most important in fishing. Porto Alexandre, Moçâmedes, Baía dos Tigres, and Luciras are the main centers in that order, but many small fishing points are strung out along the dry coast and, like an archipelago of small islands, maintain contact with the rest of the country only by sea. Benguela is the main fisheries center along the central coast and collects all of the fish products of the main central belt south of Lobito, where Baia Farta is of particular importance. Porto Amboím and Novo Redondo, about midway along the Angolan coast, have a minor representation. Although it is advantaged by a good offshore shelf, this section of the coast does not have as great fish resources. Finally, there is a substantial, though largely unrecorded, fish catch at Luanda, much of which is sold fresh to the urban community. This is the only area where Africans, the Mussorongos, engage in ocean fishing.

MINING IN ANGOLA

Except for diamonds, mining has only become important in Angola in postwar years. Large areas of the country have still not been well prospected, and the geology of the country gives hope that valuable resources remain to be discovered, particularly along the Congo-Rhodesia borders. Diamonds have long been the most valuable mineral. In the period 1920–40, they were the main financial support of the territory and they still rank second only to coffee. In 1961 they accounted for 17.1 percent of total exports, when a record of 1,147,000 metric carats was produced. About 600 Europeans and 24,250 Africans are employed in the Diamang workings near Dundo in the remote northeast near the Congo border. Output from the alluvial workings is mainly industrial stones. Owned mainly by Belgian and British interests, Diamang is the largest private employer of African labor in Angola. Under long-term contracts it had exclusive prospecting rights over a large area and was exempt from taxes, but in 1955 the Portuguese government's share of capital stock in the company was increased from 5 to 11 percent and its share of annual profits was increased by $450,000. In 1961 Diamang agreed to loan $3.67 million to the Angolan government for its economic development program.

Iron ore ranks second to diamonds. First produced in 1956, iron ore increased in output to 471,000 tons (iron content) in 1961. The Lobito Mineral Company mines iron ore at Cuíma, Teixeira da Silva, Andulo, and Cassinga. Output from Cuíma, which is 36 miles south of Nova Lisboa, was trucked to the Benguela Railway until a 41-mile branch was completed in 1962 to Robert Williams Station.

A diamond washing plant near Dundo
The diamond industry, employing about 24,250 Africans and 600 Europeans, accounts for about a sixth of Angola's exports.

The Cuíma iron ore and the Cassinga deposit, about 300 miles from Moçâmedes, are the focus of a $45.5 million project to be financed by an international consortium including Krupp of Germany. Included in the project are new mining equipment, a branch line from the Moçâmedes line, improvement of that line, and construction of special port facilities at Moçâmedes. Output at Cassinga is slated to reach 4 million tons within three years. The Angolan Mining Company produces a small amount of iron ore near Malange in the north.

Petroleum was discovered in Angola in the mid-1950s on the coastal plain near Luanda and about 90 miles south of that city. Exploration continues along that coast, eight new producing wells having been drilled in 1961 about 43 miles south of the capital. Output increased from 9,000 metric tons in 1956 to 104,000 metric tons in 1961 and 471,000 tons in 1962. In 1958 the Belgian firm Petrofina, which has developed the Angolan resources, constructed a 100,000-ton refinery at Luanda which treats all of the crude oil produced. Its capacity was doubled in 1960 and raised to 500,000 tons in 1962, adequate to meet the present needs of Angola. Exploration in the Cabinda Enclave by a subsidiary of Gulf Oil was discontinued in 1961, whether because of the revolt or discouraging results is not entirely clear.

Manganese is the only other mineral now produced in significant quantities, output having been 9,700 metric tons (manganese content) in 1961, a poor year. Mining takes place in the Malange area, particularly from a bench mine at Quitota, but promising deposits have been found in a wide belt in the north. Copper is mined and smelted in small quantities at Mavoio near Bembe and trucked to Luanda for export; a larger investment would be required to expand capacity. Other interesting copper deposits are reported to occur south of Benguela at Quelengues and near Moçâmedes.

A search has been made to uncover bauxite reserves adequate to feed a 50,000-ton aluminum refinery proposed to utilize power from Cambambe, but no finds have as yet been reported. Asphaltic rock is mined at Cacuaco, near Luanda. Salt is produced at many points along the coast, most of the output being consumed domestically. A large deposit of phosphates is known to exist in the Cabinda Enclave, and a 500-million-ton reserve of lignite has been reported near Luso on the central plateau.

INDUSTRY IN ANGOLA

The pattern of manufacturing development in Angola is quite comparable to that of other tropical African countries. Raw material processing is still most important and has increased with the build-up of agricultural, forestry, and mineral output. But consumer-oriented industries have witnessed the greatest relative increase in postwar years. Table 37 shows the industries existing in 1963, indicating that Luanda is the most important center for plants catering to the domestic market. That city, in fact, has about 20 percent of all capital invested in manufacturing. Most establishments are small, but the Texteng cotton mill employs about 1,000 people and has a yearly output of about $1.2 million. The Cuca brewery, with a production of 7 million liters of beer annually, the Secil cement plant with a capacity of 290,000 tons a year, and a $5.3 million tire factory at nearby Cacuaco are other larger plants.

The Biopio hydroelectric station
This 14,000-kw installation serves the Lobito-Benguela region.

Hope for a continuing growth of industry is based in part on hydroelectric developments. The largest project is that on the Cuanza River at Cambambe (Map 84), about 110 miles east of Luanda. This river drops 3,300 feet in a 60-mile stretch, and the Cambambe Dam, soon to be completed about six miles above Dondo, represents the first stage of its harnessing. A 279-foot-high dam will permit utilizing a 374-foot head, and the underground power station will contain four 65,000-kw sets for a total capacity when completed of 260,000 kw, one of the larger developments in Africa. In the future, four other dams further upstream could bring the total capacity on the Cuanza to 2.28 million kw.

Power from Cambambe is transmitted to Luanda. Large-scale consumers are not yet in being, which will mean that there will be a surplus capacity for some time. Plans for a 50,000-ton aluminum refinery have had to be postponed because of the failure to attract sufficient capital. Other industries that have been proposed include a ferroalloy plant and a nitrogen fertilizer installation. The Cambambe Dam will also permit irrigation of about 250,000 acres in the lower Cuanza.

A 14,000-kw plant serving the Lobito-Benguela area is situated at Biopio, 20 miles from

Table 37. Manufactured products from the main industrial centers of Angola and Mozambique

Angola		*Mozambique*	
Luanda	*Lobito*	*Lourenço Marques and Matola*	*Beira and Dondo*
Edible oils	Cloth bags	Foods	Edible oils
Fruit preserves	Agricultural implements	Flour	Flour
Candy	Metal frames	Biscuits	Beer
Flour and starch	Plastic articles	Carbonated beverages	Carbonated beverages
Bread	Cement	Tobacco products	Tobacco products
Biscuits		Plywood and veneer	Sacks
Macaroni		Aluminum ware	Soap
Beer	*Malange*	Plastic articles	Industrial gases
Carbonated beverages		Soap	Wax polishes
Tobacco products	Oil extraction	Paint and varnish	Paint
Cloth	Starch	Petroleum products	Aluminum ware
Blankets	Flour	Cement	Electric cable and wire
Pharmaceutical cotton		Bricks and tiles	Cement
Knitwear	*Alto Catumbela*	Metal drums	Fibro-cement
Underwear		Metal files, nails	Bricks and tiles
Fish nets and cords	Wood pulp	Paper bags	
Jute bags	Sacks		
Rubber shoes			*Vila Pery*
Wooden articles			
Aluminum ware			Cloth
Plastic articles			Blankets
Furniture			Sacks
Pharmaceuticals			Fruit preserves
Soap			
Industrial gases			
Tires			
Explosives			
Plastics			
Petroleum products			
Cement			
Bricks and tiles			
Cement blocks			
Printing			
Paper and cardboard			
Small boats			

the latter city. A 72-foot dam has been constructed at Matala on the Cunene River developing a capacity of 27,200 kw. Electricity is transmitted to Sá da Bandeira and Moçâmedes from this site. The dam at Matala serves also as a bridge for the Moçâmedes rail line, but its main function is to store water for the settlement project previously noted. Recent experience indicates, however, that there is inadequate control to sustain either the irrigation or the power projects, requiring that a second dam be built further upstream. Eventually, a 400-foot head could be developed at the Ruacana Falls near the border with South-West Africa.

Diamang has its own 10,000-kw plant at Dundo, and the Benguela Railway has a small

1,250-kw installation near Nova Lisboa. A 50,000-kw station is planned for the Lomaum Rapids near Alto Catumbela; the dam is needed to protect the Biopio Plant, which was inundated in 1961 for some weeks, while the power will be partially used in a new cellulose mill at Alto Catumbela. Small hydro stations are planned for the Cela and Bengo River colonization projects.

Other possibilities for hydroelectric production exist in the far north and on the Lucala River. The potential in the north is less interesting than that further south because of the opportunities for irrigation developments in the latter. The Duque de Bragança Falls on the Lucala River could be developed at low cost, though the desire to retain the scenic beauty of the Falls will impose some limitations. The Oeiras Rapids on the same river have a big potential and could permit the irrigation of about 225,000 acres, but their remoteness is something of a disadvantage.

In addition to the hydroelectricity, other sources of power in Angola are petroleum, a tiny production of coal from southeast of Luanda, wood, and bagasse and alcohol from the sugar factories. The consumption of electricity has expanded with great rapidity in postwar years, having been 22.5 million kwh in 1947 and 142.6 million kwh in 1960.

Angola faces the same problems noted for other African countries in its continuing drive to industrialize, perhaps in a somewhat greater measure. Portugal has shown considerable acumen in the use of its capital, but the amounts available for investment from within its overseas provinces or from the metropole are scarcely adequate for the development of these large territories. About $101.3 million in public capital was expended under the 1953–58 plan and $252 million was budgeted for the 1959–64 program. Of the first amount, $72 million came from Portugal, the rest from the Angolan Development Fund, started in 1938. Under the second plan, $165 million was scheduled as the metropole's contribution. Complaints of a labor shortage in Angola are not entirely justified

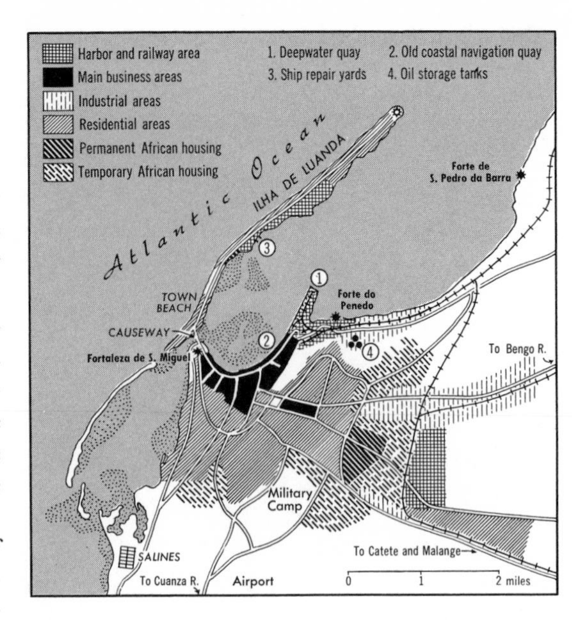

Map 85. The port of Luanda (after van Dongen)

since several tens of thousands of Africans migrate for work to other countries. The market position is less favorable than that of many African countries because the Angolan population is relatively small, is widely dispersed, and has a very low average income, and because the metropole, with only 9 million people, also has a relatively small purchasing capacity.

TRANSPORTATION IN ANGOLA

One usually thinks of transportation as just a part of the domestic infrastructure of an African country, but in Angola and also in Mozambique railways and ports are also significant as earners of foreign exchange through the handling of transit shipments for a number of the most highly developed interior areas of the continent. Both territories are also unusually favored, especially by African standards, in the existence of a number of excellent harbors along their rather lengthy coastal stretches. While Angola has only one rail line and one port now handling transit shipments, there are long-run possibilities for increasing such movements, both for Congo and for the Rhodesias. The main features of Angolan transport may be summarized by noting the ports and their connecting routeways, starting in the north.

Angola has most of the southern bank of the maritime Congo River and maintains a small port establishment at Antonio do Zaire, downstream from Matadi. Its hinterland is not now productive, and Congo did not choose to seek the development of a port in Angolan territory on the lower Congo as a possible extension for the congested Matadi, hence it remains as a minor installation. North and south of Luanda, a number of small lighterage ports tap a portion of the coffee trade of northern Angola—Ambriz, Ambrizete, and Porto Amboím. The last has an 80-mile rail line extending to Gabela.

Luanda has a large natural harbor protected by a long sandy island now joined to the mainland by a concrete causeway (Map 85). Deepwater facilities were first provided in 1945 when the present rectangular pier was completed, giving access to five large and two small oceangoing vessels. With a traffic tonnage of 752,000 in 1961, Luanda ranks second to Lobito in tonnage and value handled but first in the value of domestic traffic. It exports about 80 percent of the country's coffee, a third of its sugar, all of the cotton shipped, and some of the sisal, palm products, tobacco, and rice produced in its hinterland. The large European population of this capital city accounts for the high proportion of imported goods moving to Luanda. Prospective mining and industrial developments dependent upon the port led to plans under the second six-year plan (1959–64) for a $5 million port extension program including new deepwater, cabotage, and fishing facilities.

The railway serving Luanda was started in 1886 and reached its present terminus of Malange, 263 miles inland, in 1909. This line largely replaced the Cuanza River, which had been important as a national traffic artery, and in 1957 the branch from Viana to the river port of Bom Jesus was finally lifted. The line, originally meter-gauge, has recently been changed to standard 3-foot–6-inch gauge. Despite this and other improvements, the line is still in a relatively poor state and operates at only about half of capacity, in part because of the low traffic from the hinterland, in part because of sharply increased competition from road haulers. The hinterland has, however, seen new products brought forward in successive decades, sugar in the 1920s, almost all from Bom Jesus, cotton in the 1930s, sisal in the 1940s, coffee mainly in the 1950s, and, more recently, minerals—iron ore and manganese. For many years there was talk of extending the line into Congo to permit Luanda to participate in transit traffic for that country. The new Congo District Railway is being extended toward the Uíge Plateau and may eventually be tied to the Leopoldville-Matadi line, but disputes regarding the most suitable route and political uncertainties have slowed its construction.

Lobito's harbor, about midway along the coast, is protected by one of the sandspits that are

The main pier at Luanda
In the background is the spitlike island which protects the harbor, Angola's second ranking ocean terminus.

among the most striking features of the Angolan coast. It now has accommodations for eight ocean-going vessels at two deepwater quays arranged in an L-shape, plus facilities for coastal vessels at the head of the 3-mile bay. Recent installation of a mechanical ore loader has increased the capacity of Lobito from 2 to 3.5 million metric tons.

The Benguela Railway permits Lobito to rank as the second port in tonnage traffic to and from the Congo. Started in 1903, it reached the 300-mile point in 1914, when the war interrupted construction; resumed in 1920, the line was completed to the border in 1928 and finally connected with the BCK in 1931. Extending 838 miles from Lobito to the border, the Benguela Railway follows a difficult route to the plateau, climbing 3,000 feet in 37 miles, dropping to 1,770 feet 16 miles beyond, and then ascending to 6,082 feet 240 miles from Lobito. Gradients reach 2.5 percent and some curves have rather short radii, but the private Benguela Railway Company has maintained and improved the line to keep pace with greatly increased traffic in postwar years. Wood is still used as a major fuel, the company having planted about 85 million trees in softwood plantations of eucalyptus stretching for many miles along the line. About 16 million new trees are planted each year.

The potentialities of the Benguela line and of Lobito were largely unused until the 1950s because of Belgian preference for the national route in Congo and long-standing agreement of the Northern Rhodesian copper companies to use the Rhodesia Railways. Congestion on the route to Matadi, plus the obvious advantage of eliminating rail-river transshipments, finally led to much heavier use of the direct line from Katanga to the coast. In 1961 Lobito handled some 763,000 tons of transit traffic including 620,000 tons of minerals and metals. Copper traffic from Northern Rhodesia increased for a few years upon expiry of the agreement with the Rhodesia Railways, but a new contract in 1961 again reduced this movement severely. The distance advantage of the Lobito route is substantial, the mileage from Elisabethville to London being 6,359 miles, as compared to 8,969 miles via Lourenço Marques, 8,818 miles via Beira and the Suez Canal, or 9,255 miles via Beira and the Cape. Lobito handles somewhat over two fifths of domestic shipments by tonnage and somewhat less than one fifth by value of domestic shipments.

Moçâmedes ranks as Angola's third major port, though its traffic is far below that of Lobito or Luanda and consists mainly of fish products. Situated in a fairly open bay with several inner indentations, it was first provided with deepwater facilities in 1954–57. Now having a 1,260-foot quay with 34-foot alongside depths, it is scheduled to have an additional 4,050 feet with lesser depths, plus storage facilities and mechanical loading gear for iron ore coming from Cassinga.

The rail line from Moçâmedes was constructed on the 155-mile stretch to Sá da Bandeira between 1905 and 1923. In recent years it has been extended to Cuchi, 468 miles from the coast and about 400 miles from the Rhodesian border. The town of Moçâmedes had a population of 4,500 Europeans, 2,500 Africans, and 360 persons of mixed blood in 1958, an unusual preponderance of Europeans, explained primarily by the importance of the fishing industry. Moçâmedes was particularly hurt by the depression in that industry in recent years.

Other harbors of southern Angola are only partially developed, and the aridity of their hinterlands does not encourage enlarged facilities. Porto Alexandre, which has an excellent harbor enclosed by a 3.2-mile sandspit, is the leading single fishing center of Angola. In 1958 there were 20 fish meal and oil plants in the vicinity, and 6 boat construction firms. Luçiras also has a large deep harbor, but supports only a small fish industry. Baía dos Tigres in the extreme south has a vast harbor measuring 12 square miles, again protected by a sandspit. It was surveyed in 1954–55 as a possible alternative head to Moçâmedes for future transit traffic from the Rhodesias, but the traffic at the latter port would have to increase considerably to justify investment at Baía dos Tigres.

Navigable waterways are of very minor importance in Angola. The Cuanza River is navigable for 120 miles for boats drawing up to 8 feet but the Luanda rail line has largely replaced it. The lower Dande is used on a 40-mile stretch to transport raw sugar and palm products from large plantations to the lighterage port of Barra do Dande. The Bengo, Loge, and M'Bridge rivers can be ascended 31, 15, and 14 miles respectively by small boats.

The roads of Angola are very inadequate and many are in poor condition, except in the vicinity of the major towns. Nonetheless, there has been an increasing carriage of goods by road, particularly in the north. The revolt revealed very clearly the paucity of good roads and led to adoption of a crash program to bring the total of all-weather roads to about 10,000 miles. The poor state of the roads has encouraged the use of internal airways, especially to Carmona and other points not served by railways.

MOZAMBIQUE

Despite contact with Portugal dating from discovery in 1489 and established presence since 1498, Mozambique is one of the less developed of African nations. It is, however, somewhat erroneous to equate presence with interest in the area. Except for extraction of gold and silver from the mines of Manica, development of Mozambique itself did not begin until four centuries after the first contacts, this lack of interest being explained by Portugal's greater concern with the lucrative Indian trade and with the colonization of Brazil, the presence of warlike tribes in Mozambique, the competitive Arab influence on the coast, and the lack of capital.

ECONOMIC-GEOGRAPHIC KEYNOTES

RELATIVE LACK OF DEVELOPMENT. The relative underdevelopment of Mozambique is revealed in a variety of ways: by the existence of some large, almost untouched areas, by a very inadequate infrastructure except for a few favored areas, by the low wage level and average income of the inhabitants, and by the low level of exports. In no commodity does Mozambique have a really significant production or export (Table 38); it ranks fifth among African countries in production of its major export, cotton.

LOW DEVELOPMENT OF NONAGRICULTURAL PRODUCTION. A second keynote is the very high dependence upon agriculture among domestic economic activities. Vegetable products account for over 90 percent of total exports by value, and about 93 percent of Africans within the province are engaged in agriculture. Other segments of the economy are only meagerly represented.

Mining. In mining, for example, coal is the only mineral produced in significant quantities, output having been 321,000 tons in 1961. Mining of coal takes place in the Moatize field near Tete in the Zambezi Valley where easily accessible, good quality reserves are estimated at 700 million tons (Map 86). Coal has also been found near the Limpopo Railway and surface deposits with a 60-foot seam are reported at Maniamba in the Nyasa Basin. Other minerals produced in small quantities include asbestos, bauxite, beryl, bismuth, columbo-tantalite, diatomite, ilmenite, gold, mica, and salt. Additional minerals known to exist include chrome; copper; corundum; graphite, occurring in a 240-mile belt along the coast from Antonio Enes to Nacala and in Angonia; iron ore, found at Sena and Tete, but whose high titanium content discourages exploitation; graphite; nickel; radioactive minerals, again in the Tete district; tin; and zircon. The Mozambique Gulf Oil Company has been prospecting along the coast for some years; in 1961 two gas finds were made north and south of the Save River and a decision was taken to increase exploration expenditures to $15 million in the years to 1967.

Fishing. This industry is also poorly represented, although resources in the Mozambique channel are probably adequate to sustain a much larger fleet. Except for export of some shrimp to South Africa, the catch of about 4,000–5,000 tons is almost exclusively for local consumption, mainly in Lourenço Marques. About 24 motor vessels and 3,038 sail- and rowboats are engaged in the fishing industry.

Manufacturing. Modern manufacturing is also meagerly represented, though there has been some build-up of market-oriented industries in the last decade, particularly at Lourenço Marques and Beira. Table 37 shows the types of industry represented, except for those processing agricultural commodities located in the producing districts. Almost all establishments are quite small with the exception of three sugar mills, the cement mills, the oil refinery at Lourenço Marques with a capacity of about 500,000 tons, the breweries, and the textile mill at Vila Pery.

Table 38. Major exports of Angola and Mozambique, 1961; imports and exports in selected years, 1938–1962

Angola		Mozambique	
Commodity	*1961 exports (in million $)*	*Commodity*	*1961 exports (in million $)*
Coffee	48.73	Cotton	24.00
Diamonds	23.09	Cashew nuts	11.83
Sisal	11.07	Sugar	11.30
Fish products	8.64	Coconut products	9.29
Corn	7.83	Tea	8.10
Iron ore	4.99	Oilseeds and cakes	6.74
Sugar	3.38	Sisal	5.64
Cassava	3.12	Logs and lumber	4.03
Palm products	2.80	Tobacco	.73
Logs and lumber	2.57	Bananas	.45
Cotton	2.43	Coal	.31
Coconut products	1.89	Other	6.21
Petroleum	1.49	Total	88.63
Beans and peas	.99		
Beeswax	.69		
Manganese	.48		
Peanut products	.45		
Copper	.41		
Other	9.69		
Total	134.74		

	Angola		Mozambique	
Year	*Exports (in million $)*	*Imports (in million $)*	*Exports (in million $)*	*Imports (in million $)*
1938	15	10	8	22
1948	60	49	40	71
1958	128	130	71	115
1960	124	128	73	127
1961	135	114	89	129
1962	148	136	91	136

Sources: Provincial Trade Reports, 1961; U.N., *Statistical Yearbook, 1961* (New York, 1962); *Monthly Bulletin of Statistics* (August, 1963).

Development at Vila Pery is based upon harnessing of the Revue River at Mavudzi. The hydroelectric station there supplies Beira, Vila Pery, and other towns along the railway, and transmits power to Umtali in Southern Rhodesia. The textile mill at Vila Pery consumes about 2,100 tons of cotton in the production of cloth, blankets, and sacks.

THE ASSETS OF LOCATION. A third keynote is the importance of the location of Mozambique with respect to the highly productive Rhodesias and the Transvaal. The province capitalizes on this asset in three main ways: through transit traffic on its railways and at the ports of Lourenço Marques and Beira, through receipts of Africans migrating to the Rhodesias and the Republic of South Africa for employment, and through the tourist industry which attracts some thousands of people from these countries, particularly in the winter months. Mozambique's physical trade balance is very unfavorable, but earnings from these activities have until recently permitted achievement of a favorable balance of payments.

The railways and ports of Mozambique are by far the largest revenue earners in the province. Port charges usually contribute about 40 percent as much as commodity exports to receipts of international payments. The two main ports contribute over a fifth. Beira alone accounts for about twice the annual gross receipts of Lisbon. In addition to its strategic location, the province is also advantaged by an irregular coastline with four harbors fairly well spaced along its 1,700 miles which can be entered by average deep-sea vessels—Lourenço Marques, Beira, Nacala, and Porto Amelia. Elsewhere, however, the coastal waters are shallow and coral reefs often inhibit inshore movement.

The Mozambique Administration of Harbors, Railways, and Transport Services owns and operates most of the railways, harbors, airlines, and highway transport in the territory. It also maintains motor repair shops, coal handling equipment at Lourenço Marques, and large fruit cold-storage and fish refrigerating facilities at the capital. Its special highway transport services operate regularly on about 3,000 miles of routes and, during the harvest period, on practically all roads serving areas which produce export crops.

While marked attention has been given to developing and modernizing the rail and port facilities handling transit traffic, the internal transport net has been relatively neglected. Roads are characteristically poor and there is only a sparse network, but fears engendered by

Humping at the marshaling yards of Lourenço Marques
The railways and ports of Mozambique are the largest earners of revenue in the province, handling a large traffic tonnage for the Rhodesias, Nyasaland, and South Africa.

the Angola revolt have led to a greatly accelerated road building program. The most important job involves construction of a first-class road linking Lourenço Marques and Beira. Military considerations have also dictated the construction of new airports. The transport administration's DETA airways operates internal services from 15 airports and international services from Lourenço Marques, Beira, and Lumbo.

Migrant labor earnings are another important source of income for the country and an exchange earner for the government, about 6 percent of international payments receipts being derived from immigrant remittances. About 65,000–115,000 Africans (85,387 in 1961) are recruited yearly for the South African mines under the Mozambique Convention first signed in 1909 and continued under later modifications. Recruitment is handled by the Witwatersrand Native Labour Association, which is responsible for the worker from the signing of the contract to the return to his village. Portuguese labor officials have offices on the Rand. Under these arrangements, a portion of the pay of Mozambique Africans is withheld and paid to the Mozambique government in gold; the government then pays the returning workers in local currency. Mozambique gains not only in exchange but through the expenditure of withheld earnings in Mozambique, and from several fees charged to the contract workers. In addition to the laborers recruited for the Rand mines, an estimated 200,000 Africans voluntarily migrate to work in the Republic, some clandestinely. About 150,000 to 160,000 move yearly to the two Rhodesias. While these migrant laborers make a significant contribution to Mozambique income and currency exchange, the system has a somewhat unpalatable exploitative character and is objectionable in that it treats laborers as commodities subject to barter and in that the absence of some 450,000 or more able-bodied males must reduce the possibilities of developing the domestic economy to a considerable degree. The fact that earlier abuses have been progressively eliminated and that most laborers apparently look upon work on the Rand as an adventurous way of proving one's manhood does not entirely offset the undesirable aspects of the system.

PHYSICAL OVERVIEW

With an area of 302,328 square miles, Mozambique is seven times the size of Portugal and about as large as Texas. It is about 1,220 miles long and varies in width from 50 to 718 miles. Topographically, it may be broadly divided into three zones: (1) the coastal belt, one of the largest in Africa and covering about 42 percent of the country; narrow in the north, it widens constantly to the south, extends far inland in the Zambezi Valley, and includes most of the country south of Beira; the line of the great rift valley ends at the coast and is marked in Mozambique in the Shire Valley; (2) a transitional zone of hills and low plateaus ranging from about 500 to 2,000 feet in elevation and covering about 29 percent of the country; and (3) plateau and highland regions with average elevations of 3,000 feet, composed mainly of granitic and gneissic rocks. Most of the north between the lower Zambezi, Lake Nyasa, and the coast is part of this zone; it is also represented in extensions of the Rhodesian highlands along the border of Southern Rhodesia. In the extreme south, only a narrow fringe of hills exists along the border. A few isolated ranges rise above 4,500 feet, especially east of Lake Nyasa; the maximum elevation is 7,865 feet.

Rainfall is heaviest toward the north and at higher elevations (Map 4). There are two well-marked seasons: the cool, dry period from April to September, and the hot, rainy period from October to March. Most of the country would be classified as tropical savanna, though conditions are more steppelike in the low south and in the Zambezi Valley. The vegetation is characterized by grassy cover with scattered trees; only in some of the well-watered highlands and in the more humid back country of Beira are denser stands of timber found. Most of the soils of Mozambique are poor and sandy, but rich alluvials exist in several major river valleys and deltas, presenting attractive potentialities when river control has been effected.

POPULATION

The population of Mozambique was estimated to be 6.7 million in 1961, 96 percent of whom were Africans. Almost all of Bantu stock, the Africans are divided into twelve major and over thirty-four lesser tribes; twelve major languages are spoken, each subdivided into several dialects. The European population of Mozambique has been increasing rapidly in postwar years. In 1940 Europeans totaled 27,438; their numbers were placed at 66,000 in 1955 and 103,000 in 1960. They are heavily concentrated in the urban communities, with about 50 percent in Lourenço Marques and Beira. Other non-Africans include about 34,000 persons of mixed race, 17,000 Indians, and 2,500 Chinese. Following the take-over of Goa by India, several hundred Indians were repatriated from Mozambique and others interned; all of the internees were reported to have been released by the end of 1961.

The *indigenato* system was officially ended in Mozambique in September, 1961, but the *de facto* position of the African has not been sensibly altered as a result. In a 1962 election in which there were 29,000 eligible voters, for example, 24,000 people actually voted and only 200 of these were Africans. In 1960 the number of assimilated Africans was only 6,500. It is now Portuguese policy that racial intermarriage be promoted in Mozambique to bring about a truly nonracial state. Officials admit that the long-time Mozambique European objects to intermarriage, but they believe that many of the bachelors among the large number of peasants to be brought from Portugal will select African wives.

The most densely populated areas of the country are in the southern coastal stretch, parts of the Zambezi Valley, the pastoral Angonia Highlands, and the northern seaboard. Parts of the southern interior and the Save River area are practically empty, and much of the central and northern inland regions are also sparsely populated.

LAND USE REGIONS

The physical attributes of Mozambique are such that approximately a third of the country is considered suitable for tillage agriculture. At present only about 1 percent is cultivated. Africans farm an estimated 1,250,000 acres, most of which are devoted to subsistence crops. Most of them practice a shifting agriculture in burnt clearings, typically own no cattle, and farm only the minimum required. The main subsistence crops are corn, peas, manioc, sesame, and a variety of vegetables. Among cash crops, Africans account for all of the output of cotton and most of the rice. They also collect a variety of uncultivated products: cashew nuts, castor seeds, coconuts, jute, mufurra nut (an indigenous source of nonedible oil for soap), mangrove bark, and rubber. There are about 1.1 million cattle in the country, mostly in the tsetse-free south.

The European or so-called organized agriculture is concentrated on a variety of cash crops: sugar, sisal, tea, copra, corn, tobacco, citrus fruit, bananas, vegetables, and flowers. There are about 1,500 European holdings, 85 percent of which are owned by individual farmers, the rest by companies. Holdings total 3 million acres in extent, but less than a sixth of that is cultivated.

THE NORTH. The area north of the Zambezi Valley may be taken as one broad land use region. Long undeveloped except for sisal estates along the coast and copra at Quelimane, it has more recently become the main agricultural region of the country (Map 86), accounting for three fourths of cotton production, four fifths of cashew nut and peanut sales, nearly all of the cassava and potatoes marketed, much of the rice, all of the tea, and smaller quantities of a great variety of other crops including kapok, bananas, jute, sunflower, peas, vegetables, tobacco, and wheat.

The extreme northern districts are less developed than the districts of Moçambique and

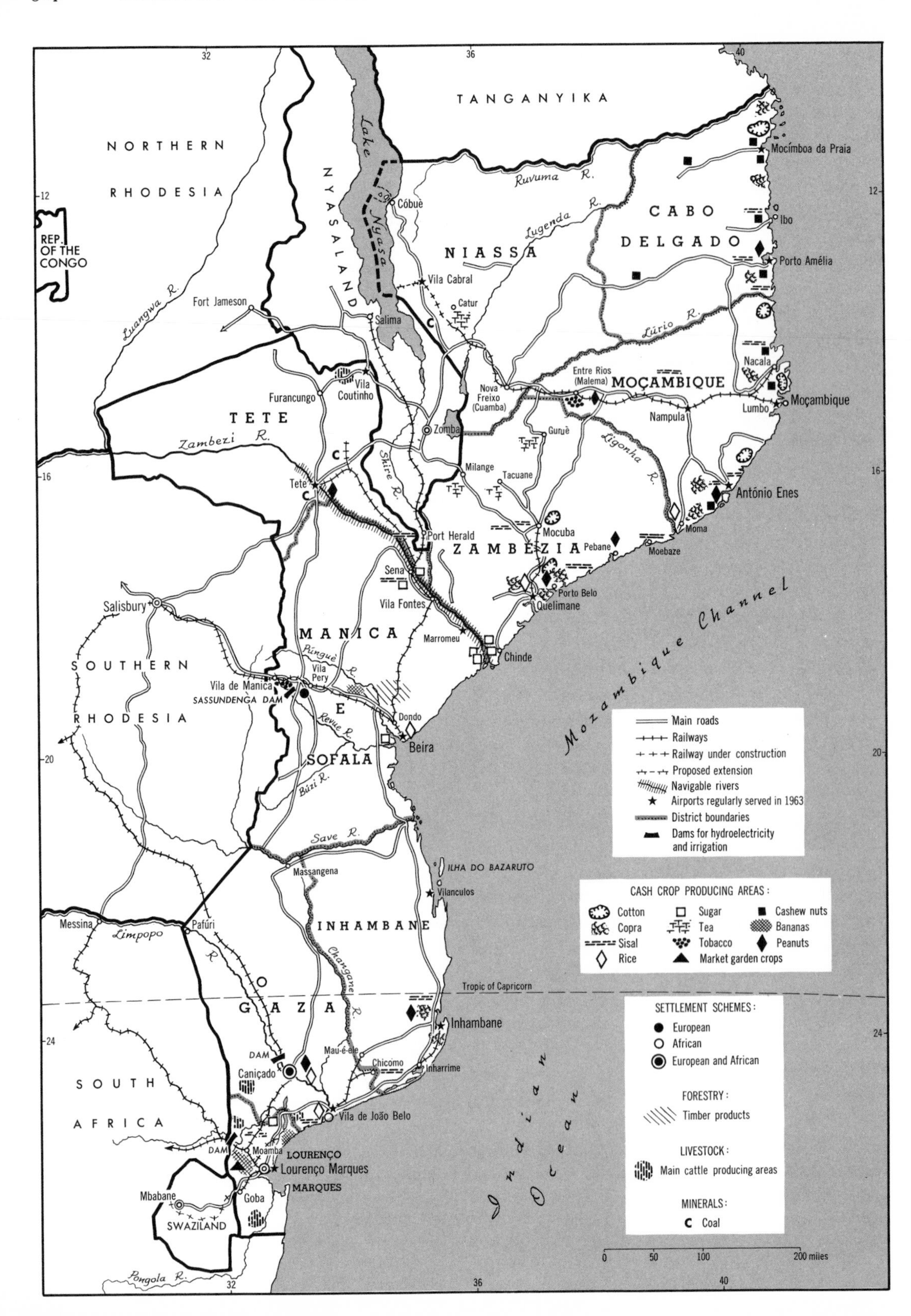

Map 86. Economic map of Mozambique

Zambezia, except for scattered localities along the coast. Eventually they could be comparably productive. This region possesses in Pemba Bay one of the finest natural harbors on the east African coast, but the low traffic moving through Porto Amelia on its southern shore is a measure of the generally low existing development. Possessing a T-shaped quay capable of accepting one large vessel and one coaster, Porto Amelia handled only 52,000 tons in 1961.

It is the hinterland of Nacala that has seen the most dynamic developments in the north. The first center of Portuguese influence in the area was the town of Moçambique, founded in 1508, for centuries a military establishment and a revictualing and refitting center, and capital of Portuguese East Africa until 1898. Situated on a small coral island three miles from shore, it is now of more historic than economic importance. The lands lying in the interior of the mainland remained virtually untouched for over 400 years. In 1924 a 1.067-meter-gauge line was begun from Lumbo on the mainland opposite Moçambique Island and completed to Nampula in 1932. As the years progressed it became increasingly clear that neither the island nor Lumbo had adequate facilities for modern port installations, and attention was focused upon Nacala. In the 1950s the town of Nacala was moved to the eastern side of an extension of Fernão Veloso Bay, where level land and good offshore depths provided excellent site features. The bay and its extension offer an enormous harborage and provide complete protection even from cyclones which periodically visit the area. A short deepwater berth was completed in 1957 at Nacala, but by mid-1962 a new wharf permitted the largest ocean freighters on this run to be accepted.

Nacala has also become the seaward terminus of the northern rail line, which has been extended inland almost to Catur, 450 miles from Nacala. A proposal that this line be connected with the Nyasaland Railway did not meet with favor because that line, always precariously sustained, feared the loss of part of its relatively meager traffic. It is planned, therefore, that the line be extended to Metangula on Lake Nyasa and that it cater almost entirely to domestic traffic, including that gathered from the Mozambique shores of the lake.

A more intensive development of the Nacala hinterland began only in postwar years. Four large concessionaires promoted the African production of cotton under a system comparable to that in Angola, and the government provided more technical advice to the African growers. In 1961 cotton production was freed by regulation of administrative authority over growers and by removal of the price stipulations favoring Portuguese textile manufacturers. These changes may result in increased sales to Southern Rhodesia and South Africa. Cotton production increased from an average of 29,000 tons in 1948–52 to an average of about 40,000 tons in 1958–61. The 1961 yields were reduced because of heavy rains and insect damage. Cotton growing employs an estimated 560,000 families in the entire country. Large additional areas are suitable for its production.

Most of the country's cashew nuts, the third crop export, are produced in the north, particularly along the coast. They are bartered with storekeeper-collectors and, except for a small quantity processed in a Lourenço Marques factory, are exported to India for decortication. In 1962 a Portuguese-Italian company with strong FIAT representation was reported to be seeking authorization to establish one or more plants in Mozambique to deshell cashew nuts using a new machine developed in Italy. If these machines prove successful, Mozambique would receive a substantially higher return for its cashew nut exports. Other important crops produced mainly by Africans in the north are rice and peanuts.

European estates have long produced sisal, and there are now some 22 plantations with about 125,000 acres in sisal scattered along the coast. Sisal is the only significant dollar earner among Mozambique exports, but its production is less than half that of Angola. A development of increasing significance has been the colonization of several interior highland areas by

Portuguese farmers, whose main cash crops are tea and tobacco.

Tea comes from the Milange, Tacuane, and Gurue areas, a portion of the crop being exported. Acreage under tea increased from 13,000 acres in 1956 to over 40,000 in 1960; production reached a record 10,200 metric tons in 1961. About 40,000 Africans are employed on tea estates, two thirds on six-month contracts, one third on a yearly basis. There are large additional acreages suitable for tea production, not only in the present areas but in the high-lying, high rainfall lands bordering Lake Nyasa.

Tobacco is produced on European farms around Malema on the Nacala line, where a new factory has been built to encourage expanded output. Ecological conditions are similar to those of the Southern Rhodesia highveld and the area could greatly increase production.

The northern lands behind Quelimane may be considered as a subregion. Situated 12 miles upstream from the mouth of the Rio dos Bons Sinais, Quelimane has a quay for coastal vessels and serves one of the most developed agricultural regions of Mozambique, including the tea area already noted. It is the terminus of an 89-mile line to Mocuba supplemented by over 1,200 route miles of Mozambique Railways motor services. A 4-million-tree coconut plantation near Quelimane, said to be the largest in the world, has two thirds of the coconut palms in the Zambezia district. Copra normally ranks third among Mozambique exports; shipments of oil will increase upon completion of a $700,000 oil press financed by the German Krupp concern. There are also about 10,600 acres in sisal along the Zambezia coast, some being shipped from minor ports to Lourenço Marques and Beira for export.

CENTRAL MOZAMBIQUE. The districts of Manica e Sofala and Tete are in the hinterland of Beira. Production from the domestic area is, however, greatly overshadowed by the importance of Beira and its connecting railways in transit traffic for the Rhodesias and Nyasaland. Beira was severely congested in the first postwar decade, but a 1950 convention between the United Kingdom and Portugal guaranteeing a flow adequate to justify port expansion led to new construction, which has, together with the new line to Lourenço Marques, helped to meet the increasing demands of the extranational hinterland, though Beira was still somewhat congested in 1961–62.

Beira, located at the confluence of the Púnguè and Buzi rivers fifteen miles from the mouth of the Púnguè, has a mediocre physical site. Shipping is disadvantaged by shallow coastal waters, sand banks, and a constricting bar in the river's mouth, restricted depths at low tide in the

Tea production near Gurue
About 40,000 Africans are employed on tea estates in the highlands of northern Mozambique.

harbor, silting, and by an 18- to 23-foot tidal range which aids entry into the harbor but increases the problems of working at the piers. On land there is the additional difficulty of an unstable surface which requires that all buildings be constructed on piles. Beira now has 2,712 feet of deepwater quays; two new spaces were completed in 1962, and two additional berths are under construction. Ore carriers picking up chrome from Southern Rhodesia are loaded by a $950,000 bulk mechanical installation at a T-shaped pier which is also used for discharging of petroleum tankers. There is also a 1,471-foot lighterage wharf and unimproved quayage for small coastal vessels. Lighters are rather intensively used at Beira. Traffic at Beira totaled 3.31 million tons in 1961.

The railway to Southern Rhodesia was first constructed in 1893–96 as a 0.60-meter-gauge line from a point 50 miles upstream from Beira to the border, tugs and lighters working the river from rudimentary facilities at Beira. In 1897 the line was connected across the Púnguè Flats to Beira and two years later it reached Salisbury. As the railway from the south was 3-foot–6-inch gauge, the Beira line had almost immediately to be relaid, and the opportunity was taken to enlarge the excessively sharp curve radii and to realign some of the steeper sections. The hilly section, rising to 3,500 feet at the Rhodesian border, still follows a poor trajectory, and beginning in 1961 several sections were being realigned as part of a $35 million program to improve Beira and the railway to Southern Rhodesia. A crude petroleum pipeline is also to be constructed from Beira to Umtali.

The Nyasaland line was begun in 1907; by 1915 it had been brought from Blantyre to the north bank of the Zambezi River, which was navigable to Chinde, a small port at the river's mouth. After World War I, a line was built from Dondo not far inland on the Beira line to the southern bank of the Zambezi about 25 miles below the terminus of the line from the northern bank; the two segments were finally linked in 1935 after a long bridge had been constructed across the river giving a total of

A coconut plantation near Quelimane
This plantation is said to be the largest coconut plantation in the world.

175 miles of track from Beira to the Nyasaland border. The vast bulk of imports and exports of Nyasaland now moves via Beira. A 173-mile branch, built between 1939 and 1949, runs from Dona Ana, on the line to Nyasaland, to Tete, and is used mainly for hauling coal from the Moatize field.

The Beira area has had a considerable build-up of industry in postwar years, attracted in part by low-cost hydroelectric power from the Mavudzi plant on the Revue River 23 miles from Vila Pery and 110 miles from Beira (Map 86).

The domestic hinterland of Beira is the leading forestry and mining area of the country. About 10 percent of the country has exploitable forests, there being about 157 concessionaires with 1 million acres of high forests plus $2\frac{1}{2}$ million acres of mangrove concessions. The main forest area of central Mozambique lies along the Nyasaland line north and south of Inhaminga. The main products are railway ties, parquet flooring, and hardwood logs; about 40 percent of provincial output is exported, three quarters to the Republic of South Africa and the Rhodesias.

The bulk of Beira's hinterland is sparsely settled, the two districts of Manica e Sofala and Tete having an average density of about 13 per square mile in 1960. Little effort was made to develop it before 1948. The remote Tete district is still largely undeveloped except for coal mining, though a small amount of African produce moves down the Zambezi by canoe and barge. That river is navigable for 9 months a year from 37 miles above Tete to Chinde near its mouth.

The British-owned Sena sugar estates are situated on the Zambezi and ship about 60,000 tons of sugar yearly to Chinde. This is one of the three large sugar plantations which have accounted for all of Mozambique's sugar production. The Zambezi Valley will eventually be one of the most productive parts of Mozambique; its potentialities have been the subject of study for some years by a special mission which issued a preliminary report in 1963 suggesting a multimillion dollar, multipurpose development project. Proposed mineral production would include a million tons of iron ore yearly, half from Messeca and half from Luendi; 2 million tons of coal a year; 4 million tons of titanium and magnetite from Macuédua; and unspecified quantities of copper from Massamba and Chidué and fluorite from Macossa. Priority would be given to production of coke and other by-products from coal.

A crude cattle dip in the Zambezi Valley
A long-range multipronged scheme for agricultural, mining, and industrial development has been prepared for the Zambezi Valley, but most of this potentially productive area is now sparsely populated and is meagerly commercialized.

The first phase would also include construction of a $7 million dam at Caora-Bassa which would regulate the water for irrigation, improve navigation on the river, and permit an output of 6 million kwh yearly. The proposed agricultural program would begin with the development of 320,000 acres, which would support an estimated 67,000 Portuguese (13,500 families) and 60,000 Mozambiqui. The major crops would be sugar, cotton, tobacco, citrus fruit, corn, and rice. Additional uses would be for plantations of pine, eucalyptus, and acacias, and for ranching. The estimated cost of the first phase of this ambitious project is $140 million. Both the large amount required and the lack of any obvious connection among some of the parts of this project suggest that it will not be adopted speedily and probably only on a piecemeal basis. Claims that the Zambezi Valley is suitable for European settlement may also be open to question.

The river valleys and flats near Beira are the scene of several more intensive agricultural developments. One of the large sugar estates is situated near the mouth of the Buzi River, while plans call for a new plantation on the Púnguè River flats 35 miles northwest of Beira. This project, which started in 1961, calls for operation of a holding worked by Portuguese settlers which would produce 60,000 tons a year. Each family head would direct five African workers and have a tractor and driver at his disposal, receiving an estimated $7,000 a year for his services. In 1963 it appeared that the company financing this scheme was having some difficulty in raising capital for the sugar factory.

On the Manica-Sofala plateau west of Beira only a thin veneer of agricultural colonists are found despite the availability of an estimated 15 million acres suitable for agriculture, especially in the Chimoio uplands. The Chimoio region, centered on Vila Pery, is the site of a colonization scheme of some interest. The government plans to settle 200 to 300 Portuguese families on 75,000 acres there. Each settler will be provided with 1,250 acres of land, a house and barn, a tractor and other implements, seeds, ten workers, and a monthly salary in return for a share in the major cash crop, which may be sisal or kenaf. Corn is the outstanding crop from European farms now on the plateau, but some oilseeds and cake, fruit, vegetables, and sisal, and small quantities of wheat and rice are also shipped, while settlers at Zonue in the Revue Valley appear to be doing well with tobacco. Africans produce some cotton in the Gorongoza and Chimoio areas.

South of Beira to the Save River there is practically a no man's land except for coastal fishing villages marketing their catch in that city. The main road being constructed between Beira and Lourenço Marques may open up new possibilities in this region, while the proposed connecting rail line from Mapai on the Limpopo River to Vila Pery on the Beira Railway would help to open the interior.

THE SOUTH. That part of Mozambique south of the Save River is again dominated by a transport-industrial center, Lourenço Marques, the very much off-center capital of the province. That port is one of the major gateways for the Transvaal and, since 1955, for the Rhodesias. Situated in the deep, well-protected Delagoa Bay, it has had deepwater facilities since as early as 1903. It now has 7,290 feet of quays capable of accommodating 15 ocean-going vessels with an additional 1,000 feet under construction, two electric coal loaders with a combined capacity of 10,000 tons a day, and large cold-storage facilities for fruit. Matola, four miles up the estuary, has a petroleum refinery and bulk storage facilities, and lumber wharves. New mechanical ore-loading gear is being installed there for handling of iron ore to be shipped to Japan from Swaziland. In 1962 the harbor was being dredged to permit access by 60,000-ton ore carriers to this installation. A high percentage of Lourenço Marques's traffic, which was 7.1 million tons in 1961, is in bulk commodities—coal and metallic minerals among exports, petroleum and timber among imports.

Lourenço Marques is important in the handling of South African traffic not only because it is the nearest port to the highly productive Transvaal but also because of the Mozambique Convention. The present version of this agreement guarantees that a minimum of 47.5 percent of transit traffic destined for a region defined as the "competitive area" enclosed between the stations of Pretoria, Springs, Germiston, Vereeniging, and Klerksdorp will pass through Lourenço Marques. In return, the gold mining industry, which has had an almost chronic shortage of African labor until very recently, is permitted to recruit 65,000 to 80,000 Africans from that part of Mozambique south of 22° S for one year's work on the Rand. In postwar years Lourenço Marques often exceeded its stipulated share of transit traffic owing to congestion on the South African Railways. It ranks as the third importing point for the Republic.

The most important rail line from Lourenço Marques is the 57-mile Ressano-Garcia line, linked in 1894 to the South African Railways. Laid with 120-pound rails because of its heavy mineral traffic, the line has a capacity of about 4½ million tons which could readily be raised if necessary. The 395-mile rail from Lourenço Marques to Johannesburg is 99 miles shorter than the line from the latter city to Durban, 319 miles less than that to Port Elizabeth, and 561 miles shorter than the railway to Capetown. The second important international line takes off from the line to the Republic at Moamba, runs northward to Guija on the Limpopo River, and follows that valley into Southern Rhodesia. Its length within Mozambique is 331 miles. Completed in 1955, it has handled an increasing share of Rhodesian traffic in succeeding years.

A third international link was completed in 1962 when the short line to Goba was taken to the Swaziland border for connection with the railway being constructed across that country.

Portuguese peasants working on a settlement scheme in the Limpopo Valley

The Goba line, which was originally planned as a second connection with the Transvaal, also serves the fertile Umbeluzi Valley in Mozambique. A fourth, 19-mile line extends to Marracuene, serving banana plantations near Vila Luiza and Manhica on the Incomati River. It is possible that this line may be extended 150 miles northward to stimulate development of farming and grazing in southern Mozambique.

The city of Lourenço Marques had an estimated population of 184,000 in 1961, including half of the *civilizado* of the province. In addition to its great importance as a transport center, it is the main governmental, commercial, and manufacturing city of the country and the focus of an important tourist industry as well.

In southern Mozambique the most fertile agricultural zones are found in the valleys of the Limpopo, Incomati, and Umbeluzi rivers. Dairying, market gardening, and cotton raising are carried on near Lourenço Marques. Plantations of pine, cyprus, and eucalyptus are being developed in the north of the Lourenço Marques district.

The country's third large sugar plantation is situated at Xinavane on the Incomati River, producing about 25,000 tons of sugar yearly, and Portuguese farms produce bananas in the same valley. Most of these bananas have been sold in South Africa, but that market has become increasingly saturated by domestic production that has depressed output in Mozambique. Several development schemes have been proposed for the Incomati, but little progress had been recorded on them as of mid-1963. The Incomati-Movene Scheme involves harnessing of the Incomati River by a dam just inside the Mozambique border, diversion of part of the waters via a 20-mile tunnel into the Movene Valley, and irrigation of 120,000 acres for the support of 12,000 families for whom wheat would be the principal crop. Plans to settle the right bank of the Incomati River were reported progressing in 1962, but efforts appeared to be confined to apportionment of 116 strips of land to African

Grain fields in the Limpopo settlement scheme
The economic contribution of this scheme has thus far been low in relation to the investment involved.

peasants in the region between Moamba and Chinhanquanine.

The Limpopo Valley is the scene of the most important settlement project in being, started in 1953. The original goal was to settle about 30,000 Europeans and 60,000 Africans, but the scheme has faced numerous difficulties, and emphasis appeared to be shifting elsewhere after 1960. Some $30 million had been spent to 1961 with relatively little progress to show for it. Control of the Limpopo began with construction in 1956 of the 2,280-foot-long, 42-foot-high dam whose surface is used by the rail line to the Rhodesias, permitting the irrigation of 75,000 acres and agricultural use of over a half-million acres.

Each settler in the Limpopo Scheme was provided with a three-room house, stable, and storehouse, a poultry yard and large garden, and allotments of irrigated and dry land. A man with one or two children received 10 acres of irrigated land; each additional child raised the allotment 2½ acres up to a total of 25 acres. Each village of 40 settlers also had about 50 acres of common irrigated land for production of fodder and 2,400 acres of common grazing land which was fenced and provided with a stock watering supply. In return for each holding the state receives a sixth of the farm produce; it is also prepared to provide loans for furniture, livestock, equipment, seeds, and one year's provisions.

In addition to crop and livestock production, the scheme has attempted to promote raising of fish and had planted an estimated 4.2 million trees by 1962. In that year, 811 European and 315 indigenous families had been settled. The scheme had 57 tractors and 16 bulldozers available; its livestock included 971 cows, 4,812 working oxen, 1,181 pigs, and 545 goats. The total value of agricultural produce sold in 1962 was about $465,000, with the rice crop alone accounting for an estimated $347,000.

Difficulties encountered have included the contraction of a variety of diseases (a sixth of the men were reported to have bilharzia in 1962, while the incidence of malaria and tuberculosis was also high), an oppressive climate, floods, inadequate holdings, overcrowded housing, and problems of marketing the surplus production. By 1962 the number of peasants coming from Portugal had slowed materially, while some had given up and moved to Lourenço Marques, contributing to a growing unemployment problem. As far as the government is concerned, its expenditures had totaled $10,025 per family; its returns were only about $77,000 in 1962. A striking feature of the Portuguese settlement schemes is their close patterning of farming in Portugal; most settlers are peasant farmers who have a largely subsistent operation. Their contribution to the provincial economies of either Mozambique or Angola are not particularly impressive, especially when viewed against the very large capital expenditures.

The Limpopo Valley has one of the larger concentrations of cattle in the country, mostly Landim and Africander breeds held by Africans. They are poorly commercialized at the present time.

Near Vila de João Belo, at the mouth of the Limpopo, is the Inhamissa Scheme, a government cooperative for Africans. This scheme has had much more favorable results than the other settlement projects of Mozambique. Eventually some 20,000 acres of reclaimed marshland are to be divided into 10-acre family farms producing rice, corn, beans, peanuts, cassava, and bananas.

Vila de João Belo is the head of a short rail line; its harbor has been deteriorating rapidly through deposition of silt. That town and Inhambane, further north along the coast, are the main centers of the Inhambane and Gaza districts. Inhambane is also the terminus of a short rail line and has a harbor equipped with a modern lighterage pier. Both small ports are tributary to Lourenço Marques, through which their trade is transited. They ship a great variety of produce, including cotton, rice, cashew nuts, peanuts, timber, tobacco, sisal, and corn.

It is apparent that Mozambique has excellent possibilities for extension and intensification of agricultural pursuits. While the desire to push European settlement is understandable in relation to the situation in Portugal, it would seem desirable and necessary that greater attention be given to African advancement in the province.

For Portuguese Africa as a whole, the prime necessity is for a greater sensitivity to the needs and aspirations of the African. There is within the Portuguese policies the possibility of working toward a multiracial society comparable to that of Brazil, but the remaining elements of repression and neglect would have to be replaced by greater concern for the overwhelming portion of the populace. This will require markedly increased expenditures for social and economic advance and a wider adherence to the avowed principles of Portuguese policy. It seems questionable whether there will be time for such changes given the present African climate.

Part Seven SOUTHERN AFRICA

Part of the Johannesburg skyline, with gold mine slag heaps in the background

CHAPTER TWENTY-TWO

The Republic of South Africa

South Africa is a land of contrast, a land of paradox and contradictions, a land of great problems and great promise. Economically, it stands head and shoulders above other African countries; politically, it has brought upon itself the calumny of much of the world and appears to many observers to be determinedly set upon a course of self-destruction.

MEASURES OF ECONOMIC IMPORTANCE

The Republic's wealth is a tribute, on the one hand, to the great richness of its underground resources and, on the other, to the ability of its people, particularly its dominant white minority. Its achievements have, however, required the contributions of all of its racial groups working in a kind of unequal partnership which, all too often, goes unrecognized. The net national income in 1960–61 was $5,980 million, which represented an increase of about 450 percent in the 43 years from 1918–19. The gross national product in 1963 was estimated at about $8,600 million. The national income per head is about twice the African average and half again as high as that of the second ranking country. With about 7 percent of the total population of Africa, South Africa accounts for approximately a quarter of the output of goods and services on the continent.

The outstanding economic position of the Republic may be further measured by looking briefly at the individual sectors of the economy, In mining, it produces about 43 percent of the total value of African minerals. It mines some two thirds of the free world's gold, ranks first in the output of platinum, chrome, antimony, and manganese, second in asbestos, and third in uranium. It produces about 80 percent of the coal mined in Africa.

Agriculturally, despite numerous physical handicaps, South Africa leads the continent in the production of corn, sugar cane, and wool, ranks second in cattle and tobacco, third in citrus fruit, and fourth in wheat. With about 7 percent of the land surface and 10 percent of the population of sub-Saharan African, it raises about one fifth of the food of that area. South Africa also ranks as the leading fishing nation on the continent.

South Africa has a far more diversified and developed industrial sector than any other African country. Manufacturing has increased its share of the national income from 9.4 percent in 1919 to 24.6 percent in 1959. The Republic generates twice as much electric power as the rest of sub-Saharan Africa combined. It has the only well-developed iron and steel industry on the continent, and supplies a greater percentage of its needs for manufactured goods than any other African country.

In the field of transport, South African Railways handles over half of the total railway freight of Africa. That country possesses the only real rail network on the continent, which includes the longest electrified lines outside of Europe and North America. Its road system, including over 8,700 miles of paved highways, is also superior, and the country has some 40 percent of the motor vehicles registered on the continent.

Table 39. Estimated population of South Africa by racial groups for selected years, 1904–1962

Year	Total (in thousands)	African		White		"Coloured"		Asian	
		In thousands	Percent	In thousands	Percent	In thousands	Percent	In thousands	Percent
1904	5,175	3,490	67.4	1,117	21.6	445	8.6	122	2.4
1921	6,927	4,697	67.8	1,521	22.0	545	7.9	163	2.4
1936	9,588	6,596	68.8	2,003	20.9	769	8.0	220	2.3
1951	12,671	8,560	67.6	2,642	20.8	1,103	8.7	367	2.9
1960	15,841	10,808	68.2	3,068	19.4	1,488	9.4	477	3.0
1962	17,065	11,645	68.2	3,250	19.0	1,648	9.7	522	3.1

Sources: Union of South Africa, Bureau of Census and Statistics, *Union Statistics for Fifty Years, 1910–1960, Jubilee Issue* (Pretoria, Government Printer, 1960), pp. A3–A5; Republic of South Africa, *Monthly Bulletin of Statistics* (Pretoria, Government Printer, July, 1962), p. 2.

N.B. Columns may not total because of rounding.

THE RACIAL PROBLEM

Despite the evident achievements of South Africa in the economic sphere, that country faces economic uncertainties of serious dimension, most of which can be traced directly to the racial policies it has pursued in recent years. The composition of the South African population is complex, four major groups being represented, and the cleavages or distinctions among the groups are being legally sharpened with each successive year. Table 39 gives the population of racial groups for selected years. The dominant group is the whites, who now comprise about 19.0 percent of the total population, but the bulk of the whites are themselves split into two major groups—the Afrikaners, predominantly descended from Dutch and Huguenot immigrants whose first permanent settlement, at the Cape, dates from 1652, and those of British stock, who first settled in the early 1800s after Britain had taken over the Cape. According to the 1960 census, 58 percent of the Europeans in South Africa have Afrikaans as their home language, 37.3 percent have English, 1.4 percent both languages, 1.1 percent German, 0.7 percent Dutch, and 1.5 percent other languages. Of the four provinces of South Africa, only Natal has a majority of English-speaking whites. The Republic now has about two thirds of the total white population of the continent. The fundamental racial policies of the exclusively white-controlled government reflect the minority position of the "European" population and help to explain the program announced in mid-1962 calling for the attraction of 40,000 to 50,000 white immigrants a year for settlement. The avowed but scarcely attainable goals are a white population of ten million by 2000 A.D. and eventually one equal to the combined population of the other racial groups. As the net immigration of whites (Table 40), despite a surprising surge in 1962–63, is now fairly small, and as the natural rate of increase in 1961 for both Africans and Coloureds was

Table 40. Immigration and emigration of whites, South Africa, for selected periods, 1925–29 to 1962

Year	Number of immigrants	Number of emigrants	Net gain or loss
1925–29	33,546	19,994	+13,552
1930–34	20,875	13,255	+7,620
1935–39	39,006	15,969	+23,037
1940–44	8,044	10,419	−2,375
1945–49	92,835	38,520	+54,315
1950–54	80,192	61,356	+18,836
1955–59	63,057	54,522	+8,535
1960	9,789	12,612	−2,823
1961	16,309	14,903	+1,406
1962	20,916	8,945	+11,971

Sources: Union of South Africa, Bureau of Census and Statistics, *Union Statistics for Fifty Years, 1910–1960, Jubilee Issue* (Pretoria, Government Printer, 1960), p. C-7; Republic of South Africa, *Monthly Bulletin of Statistics* (Pretoria, Government Printer, July, 1962), pp. 11–12; (May, 1963), p. 13.

about double that of the whites, the goals for greatly increasing the ratio of the Europeans do not appear realistic. About four fifths of the Europeans now live in cities and towns, there having been a particularly notable influx of Afrikaans-speaking whites in recent years. Their earlier predominantly rural character was an important factor in their antipathy toward British South Africans, who dominated the nonfarm segments of the economy.

Africans, the vast majority of whom are Bantu, are the largest group, comprising 68.2 percent of the population. About 56 percent of the total African population lives outside the Bantu areas, somewhat over half of these residing in urban locations or communities, the remainder mainly on European farms. The latest demographic studies reveal a large-scale increase in the number of urban Africans, despite efforts to control the influx of Bantu into the towns. In the ten years to 1960, for example, Pretoria gained almost 80,000 and Durban 46,000. Nine major and several minor tribal groups are recognized, but detribalization has progressed rapidly in recent years. The government has been seeking to reduce the number of Bantu languages taught from seven to two; on the mines there are as many as 53 linguistic groups, which has led to the use of a language resembling Swahili. In addition to the 10.8 million South African Bantu, there are normally about 770,000 Africans from adjacent countries in the Republic, almost half of whom are employed on the gold and coal mines.

Third among the major racial groups are the "Coloureds." Derived from the admixture of Hottentots, imported slaves, whites, Africans, Asians, and other "Coloureds," they represent some 9.7 percent of the total population and live predominantly in the Cape Province, which has about 88 percent of their total number. Last are the Asians, comprising about 3.1 per cent of the total population. They are, as elsewhere in Africa, divided by racial and religious differences. Asians were brought to South Africa between 1860 and 1911 as field workers for the sugar plantations of Natal; further immigration was prohibited after 1911, but efforts to repatriate numbers of Asian residents were never successful. About 82 percent of the Asians reside in Natal, especially in Durban.

Space prohibits detailing the attributes, attitudes, and circumstances of each of the main racial groupings, but the significant point is that nowhere else on the continent are the distinctions among the groups so sharply drawn. While the white rulers of South Africa have long pursued discriminatory policies, these have become increasingly rigidified under the predominantly Afrikaner South African Nationalist government, whose goal is the separate development of the races.

The basic aim of apartheid, which is now officially called "separate development," is to secure white domination by dividing the racial groups according to living area, education, other facilities of all kinds, and even churches. Control is exercised through various laws which restrict the actions and public utterances of all groups, laws which have rather completely eroded civil and individual liberties, for white South Africans as well as others. The adoption of apartheid may be explained (*a*) by the isolation of the Afrikaner, especially after the great trek into the interior and the long period of cultural separation from changing Western thoughts; (*b*) the lack of any unifying theme or ideal in the country (even the Christian churches have long been at loggerheads); (*c*) the real force of Afrikaner nationalism, which, in religion, language, and custom, is monolithic; (*d*) the long tradition of segregation, characteristic throughout South African history; and (*e*) the existence of a large dependent populace within the country. To most South African whites, of whatever descent, it appears inconceivable that their way of life could be maintained if there were democratization; one man–one vote spells suicide to them. This dilemma explains why some people of unquestioned sincerity support apartheid, striving to justify this position by working for greater economic and social advance for the African. Indeed, one of the stated objectives of apartheid is to develop the African, and South

Africans are quick to point out the higher incomes and educational standards of the Bantu in South Africa, the substantial sums now being spent on African housing in the cities, and proposals for improvement of the economies in the reserves (see below, page 553). Thus there is repression with one hand and uplift with the other. But with the dynamically changing circumstances in the rest of Africa, this is not enough, and one looks upon the future of South Africa with very grave misgivings. Whether the now fragmented opposition to apartheid, surprisingly vocal in the press and intellectual circles, will be capable of uniting to lead toward the envolvement of more liberal policies is a serious question.

It would be grossly erroneous to conclude that apartheid is now working in the Republic. In fact, complete partition is not seriously suggested. Today, well over half the Bantu live outside the reserves; economic integration exists in the sense that these Bantu belong to the European economy while the Europeans rely upon them. Any real separation of the races would, indeed, lead to the collapse of the whole economy, which is increasingly dependent upon the African, especially in the industrial sphere. The millions now being spent on separate development and on the military and police forces represent a small part of the real cost of discrimination; the major cost stems from the brake on the whole economy resulting from restrictions on the advance of the nonwhite groups.

PRESENT ECONOMIC UNCERTAINTIES

There is no question but that the rigidifying policies of the South African government have adversely affected the economic position of the country. After the Sharpeville shootings of March, 1960, and the decision to leave the Commonwealth in March, 1961, foreign reserves, which had been $437 million in January, 1960, declined to a low of $198 million on June 16, 1961. Strict import and exchange control was applied, which, together with an increased production of gold, resulted in a remarkable increase in gold and foreign exchange reserves to a 14-year high of $594 million in July, 1962, and to $627 million in July, 1963. The South African economy had displayed a considerable resilience, but the long-term shadows remained and the prediction made by the Cape Town *Forum* in August, 1961, is probably still valid: "Just as the insupportable cost of its Algerian policy has repeatedly brought about a devaluation of the French franc, so apartheid will drain the lifeblood of our economy until the anemia is pernicious."

Other economic uncertainties in 1962 and 1963 included the somewhat decelerated rate of economic expansion in 1962, a reduced investment in industry, a net outflow of foreign capital, the long-term effect of loss of Commonwealth preference (preference was extended by Britain for one year after South African withdrawal from the Commonwealth and a 1962 treaty provided for a five-year continuance of the trading conditions existing between South Africa and the United Kingdom), the future of sugar exports following loss of South Africa's quota in the Commonwealth Sugar Agreement (bilateral agreements and fortuitous sales to the United States saved the industry from disaster), the decline in value of South African shares, an exodus of professional men, which hit university faculties particularly hard, and the imposition of boycotts on South African goods on the part of certain African nations.

H. F. Oppenheimer, chairman of the huge Anglo American Corporation of South Africa, Ltd., summarized the position as follows:

> It is idle to contend that the dislike of South Africa's policies abroad arises merely from misunderstanding .... The truth is that the fundamental principle upon which South African policy is at present based is morally unacceptable to practically all the nations of the world.... I have no doubt that at present the government is capable of controlling the situation by force ... but only at the cost of a perpetuation of racial conflict, which must become progressively more embittered. And while this conflict lasts it will be impossible to restore confidence in the future of the country, and the economy will be threatened with stagnation.

Table 41. Production and sales of South African minerals, 1961

Mineral	Units	Production (in thousand units)	Sales (in thousand units)	Value of sales (in thousand $)	Percent of total value
Gold	oz.	22,942	22,942	797,334	64.0
Uranium oxide	lbs.	10,937	9,919	110,975	8.9
Coal	tons[a]	43,613	44,628	83,562	6.7
Diamonds	carats	3,788	3,719	52,153	4.2
Asbestos	tons	195	193	31,158	2.5
Copper	tons	58	57	28,970	2.3
Manganese ore	tons	1,569	1,408	18,409	1.5
Iron ore	tons	4,473	4,109	13,546	1.1
Chrome ore	tons	990	1,015	9,255	0.7
Tin concentrate	tons	1,604	1,554	3,181	0.3
Silver	tons	5	5	2,271	0.2
Other metallic minerals (titanium, vanadium, etc.)				8,414	0.7
Other nonmetallic base minerals				12,533	1.0
Lime and limestone				11,543	0.9
Salt				2,330	0.2
Other quarry products				24,427	1.9
Other not specified				35,939	2.9
Total				$1,246,000	100

Sources: Republic of South Africa, *Monthly Bulletin of Statistics* (Pretoria, Government Printer, July, 1962), pp. 48–49; Transvaal and Orange Free State Chamber of Mines.
[a] Short tons.

MINING IN THE SOUTH AFRICAN ECONOMY

The Republic of South Africa, as has already been suggested, is one of the leading mineral producing nations of the world. The sales of all minerals from the earliest date of record to 1962 total $18.3 billion; most recent years have shown successive new records, the 1961 value of mineral sales having been an all-time high of $1.25 billion. Mining's contribution to the national income is given as 13.9 percent of the total in 1960-61, in which year a total of 619,000 persons, including 67,000 whites, were employed. These figures poorly reveal the importance of mining to the South African economy, which is more accurately suggested by the facts that minerals account for about 55 percent of the value of exports and gold alone for 38.4 percent, that much of the transport and power services were constructed in response to the needs of the mining industry, that a large segment of industry is based upon and caters directly to the mining industry, that mining indirectly permits the subsidization of a very large part of South African agriculture, and that the progress of industrial development depends largely upon the level of mineral exports.

South Africa possesses a great variety of minerals, over a score of which are produced in values exceeding a million dollars. Table 41 shows the output and volume and value of sales of South African minerals for 1961. It may be noted that the six leaders—gold, uranium oxide, coal, diamonds, asbestos, and copper—accounted for 88.6 percent of the total value of mineral sales in that year. While South Africa has been more thoroughly prospected than most African countries, there are opportunities for initiating production in known bodies not now exploited and undoubtedly for discovering new deposits and further proving known bodies.

South Africa is, indeed, a mineral storehouse, but the inevitable exhaustion that applies to any mineral body is a matter of continual concern to South Africans. It leads, on the one hand, to a tendency to minimize the significance of mining to the economy and, on the other hand, to programs designed to reduce the over-all dependence on that activity.

GOLD

IMPORTANCE TO THE ECONOMY. Gold is by all odds the most important mineral produced in South Africa, measured by value of output, and historically it has accounted for over three quarters of the total value of all South African minerals produced. In 1961, when that country produced 66.6 percent of the free world's gold, gold accounted for 38.4 percent of foreign exchange receipts from merchandise and gold exports, for about two thirds of the value of minerals produced in the Republic (including the by-products of gold production—uranium oxide, silver, etc.—the figure would be nearer three fourths), for approximately three fourths of European and African employment in mining, and for $120 million in taxes and profit shares to the government. It was estimated a few years ago that, directly or indirectly, one half of South Africa's total population was dependent on gold mining for its existence. Furthermore, production has been increasing, output having grown in value from $400 million in 1951 to $797 million in 1961 and $889 million in 1962.

Gold mining forms the main basis for the economy of the Witwatersrand (see Maps 10 and 90), with a city population alone approaching two million, and for the newer and less rounded development of the Orange Free State gold field centered upon Welkom. The large urban complex of the Rand, which has appropriately given its name to the South African monetary unit, has provided the stimulus for a very considerable part of the Republic's agricultural and manufacturing development. With the closely associated developments at Pretoria and Vereeniging, the southern Transvaal industrial district is distinctly the most important in South Africa. While that area has other attributes, industry would scarcely have started there had it not been for gold, which gives a locational orientation for a well-rounded industrial buildup that is unique in the world.

Gold mining also made it economically possible to construct railways up the difficult scarps from various coastal points, and the story of competition for the traffic of the Rand is a fascinating one in transport history. Durban and Lourenço Marques are particularly dependent upon traffic to and from the Transvaal, but Port Elizabeth and East London also share in serving the area.

Gold, like diamonds, was responsible for attracting large numbers of immigrants to the country and is a most important reason why South African whites have the fifth highest income level in the world. Gold mining has also provided ready employment for Africans, not only from the Republic but from the High Commission Territories, Mozambique, and other countries of southern Africa. While recruitment and handling of African laborers has had certain undesirable features, more especially

Surface plant and slag heaps of the Western Ultra Deep Levels gold mine It is planned that this mine be taken to a depth of 15,000 feet, which would make it the deepest in the world.

inadequate health measures in earlier years and the continued use of the compound system, it must be said that wages compare very favorably with those of tropical African countries and that increasing numbers of Africans are prepared voluntarily to migrate to the gold fields for employment.

Finally, gold has provided an extremely important stabilizing factor in the South African economy. A commodity that can be sold in international markets in whatever quantity produced at a price which does not vary in recessions obviously sustains other parts of the economy.

The high dependence of the Republic's economy on gold, however, raises certain significant questions. How long can the economy continue to rely so heavily on gold? What are the possibilities for developing a more rounded economy? The first question will be examined in the following section.

FACTORS IN THE PERMANENCE OF GOLD MINING. Gold is an exhaustible resource which must eventually give out. But the Republic's gold mines, which have led the world in gold output for 67 years, have had an unusually long life, having already outlasted most competitors. The factors which explain this unusual permanence present an uncommon array of fortuitous conditions.

Large reserves. Basically, of course, the most important factor is the vast extent of the reserves, which consist, not of easily worked out alluvials or thin, rich veins of gold, but of low-grade and relatively uniform ores contained within a conglomerate matrix and extending over a large area. The gold-bearing conglomerates occur in thin tabular sheets called reefs which occur in a sequence of sedimentary beds up to five miles thick. The main Reef Leader, varying from a few inches up to ten feet in thickness, is now the principal source of ore on the Rand. The Witwatersrand, Orange Free State, and associated gold fields (Map 87) are by far the largest cognate group of metalliferous ore deposits being mined anywhere in the world. In 1963 their 55 active mines stretched unevenly along an arc nearly 300 miles in length. The fairly uniform nature of these deposits permits the industry to plan years in advance, to maintain uniform tonnages, grade, and profits.

Availability of coal. A second factor explaining the permanence of gold mining is the fortuitous presence of coal nearby, without which it might well have been impractical to mine the gold, since large quantities of low-cost power are required. Originally, coal was obtained within the Rand itself, from Boksburg, Brakpan, and Springs, but the poor quality of this coal and the greater difficulty in its mining reduced these sources to a minor role, and the Witbank Collieries, some 90 miles to the northeast, and those south of Vereeniging in the Orange Free State now supply the vast bulk of requirements.

Adequate water supplies. Third is the availability of adequate water, which is used in very large quantities for wetting the cutting face, washing, and refining, and for industrial and domestic purposes. There have been and are certain problems associated with the supply of water in this semi-arid area, but they have thus far been successively met. Control of the Vaal River has been particularly important. In 1959 what is claimed to be the world's largest electrodialysis plant, capable of partially purifying 2.5 million gallons a day of water pumped from the mines, went into operation at the Free State Geduld Mine in response to the need to conserve water, but the cost of producing industrial water was in excess of the cost of river water and the plant has since been at least temporarily closed.

Group administration. Fourth is the organizational arrangement known as group administration which has been evolved by the mining community. Under this system, detailed comparative studies are made of every factor in costs that can be distinguished. Made available to each mine, these data permit the testing of individual operations against the average. New technological developments and scientific expertise are also shared, and cooperation is carried further in the provision of unified rail and power systems, central compressed air plants, a central refinery at Germiston said to be the most efficient in the world, and in the joint processing of

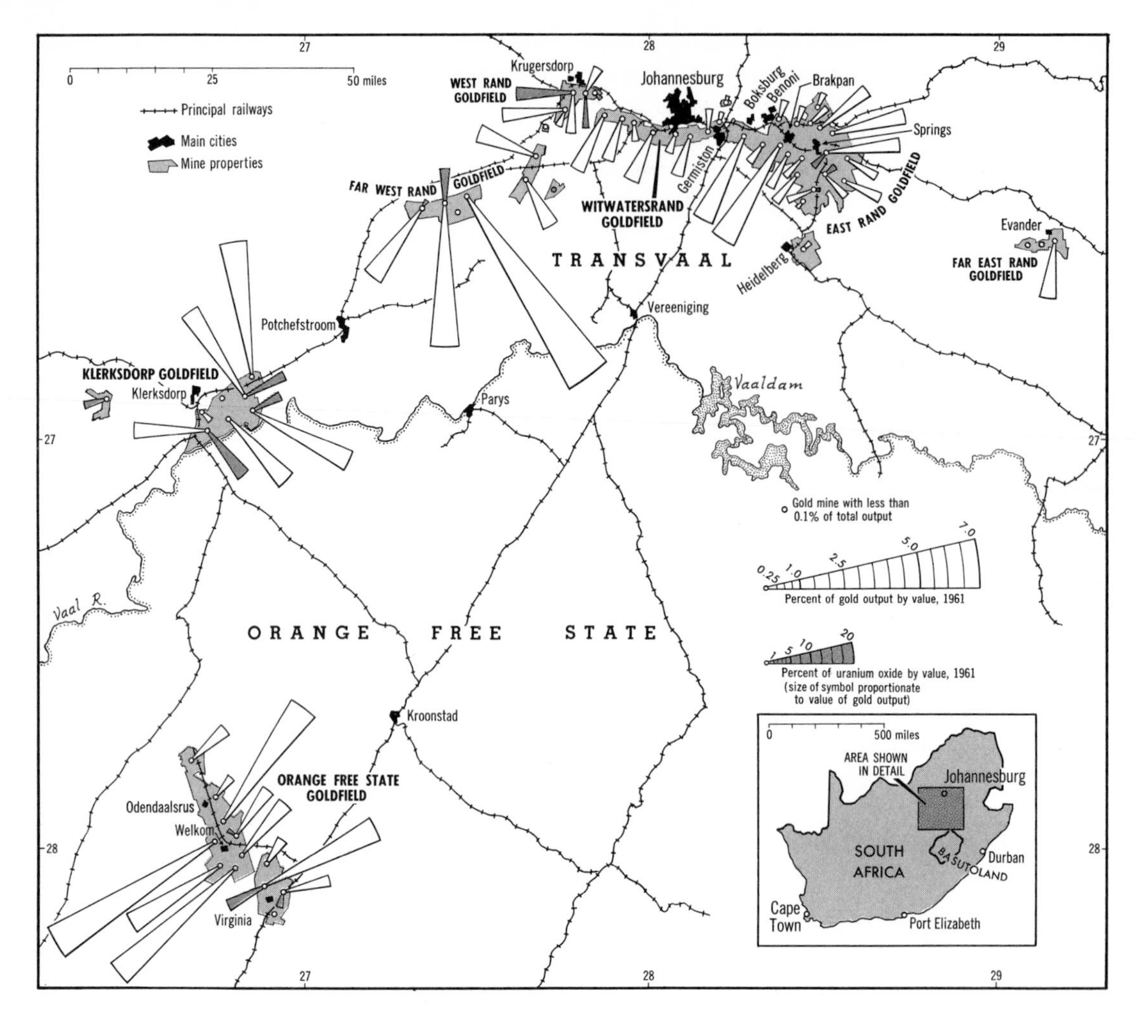

Map 87. The Transvaal and Orange Free State gold fields

by-products, especially uranium. The necessity for large amounts of capital and for making whatever savings in scale are possible helps to explain the highly developed cooperation in the industry. Opening of a new mine may require from $28 million to over $115 million. In 1960 some 66 gold mining companies, 24 coal mining companies, and 13 financial corporations were members of the Transvaal and Orange Free State Chamber of Mines, the centralizing association. The gold mining industry, then, presents a working model of a rationalized industry.

Technological improvements. Fifth has been the ability, through technological development and innovation, to meet many of the problems presented by the nature of the ore and the occurrence of the ore bodies. Briefly, these problems include:

(1) The low average grade of the ore. The total volume of ore milled in 1961 was 67.4 million tons, yielding an average of 6.506 dwts. of gold. The average yield has been increasing in recent years, largely because the Free State areas have a somewhat higher metal content. Much earlier, in 1890, invention of the cyanide process permitted winning from a quarter to half again as much gold from each ton as had previously been extracted.

(2) The great depth of workings, very few being less than 4,000 feet below the surface. Since a shaft 4 to 5 thousand feet deep may cost nearly $2.8 million, this has meant that emphasis has been placed on keeping the number of shafts sunk to the minimum. The East Rand Proprietary Mine, over 11,300 feet deep, is now the deepest mine in the world, but it is planned that the Western Deep Levels Mine will ultimately be carried to 15,000. Attention has also been given to improving shaft sinking and rock-tunneling speed and efficiency. For many years, 100 feet per month was considered the normal rate for sinking shafts and in 1940 the record speed was 454 feet per month. Only a few years ago sinking at the rate of 1,000 feet per month was considered the equivalent of the four minute mile, but an 80 man team at Buffelsfontein Mine in West Transvaal achieved 1,251 feet in one month in March, 1962. Important advances have also been made in pre-lining the shaft as it is being sunk.

(3) Difficult ventilation, occasioned by the large amount of dust, the great depths involved, and the increasing heat of the mines at lower levels. Strict control methods have drastically reduced the silicosis rate among workers and improved techniques have permitted working at depths which were impractical some years ago. Rock temperatures are likely to increase rapidly with depth; in the Orange Free State mines they are about 87° F. at 2,000 feet and 100° F. at 4,000 feet below the surface. These temperatures, combined with the characteristically wet underground condition, mean that air must be refrigerated underground.

(4) Enormous ground pressure at depth. This is today considered the most important physical problem, one that becomes more severe because of the increasing depth of workings and, in the Orange Free State, because of the friable and fissured ground encountered.

(5) Miscellaneous additional difficulties, including the narrowness of the gold reefs, the restricted ability to use gravity in removing the ore, heavy faulting in some of the new mines of the Orange Free State and Klerksdorp areas, and the need to pump large quantities of water from some of the mines, especially in the Orange Free State. Water bearing fissures were, in fact, the most serious problem faced in development work in that area. Even today many million gallons a day of fossil water are pumped to the surface. Being saline, the water cannot be readily used nor put in the river systems and is, therefore, piped to large evaporation basins which have become recreation areas and the habitat of numerous birds.

Presence of by-products. Another explanation for the ability to mine the gold ores of the Republic, and an important factor, is the existence of by-product minerals. Silver occurs in the average ratio of 1 to 10 to the weight of gold; platinum is also extracted. But most important has been the extraction, beginning in 1952, of uranium oxide, which gave a great fillip to the gold mining industry. Uranium in the gold reefs places South Africa among the leading nations of the world in reserves of fissionable ores. In 1961, 15 mines delivered slimes to concentrating plants for the extraction of uranium oxide. In the late 1950s, the sale of uranium oxide, taken mostly by the United States and British Atomic Energy Commissions, brought about 18–19 percent of the total receipts of the gold mining companies, but in 1961, exports of uranium were less than 14 percent of the total. Reduced demands for uranium oxide have led to renegotiation of contracts which stretch out the delivery of purchased amounts seven years beyond the original termination date of 1966.

Availability of low-wage labor. Finally, but by no means least important, the gold industry of the Republic owes its continuance to the availability of large numbers of low-wage laborers. If the gold reefs were situated in the United States they probably would be of interest only to students of geology; they would not be worked. While for many years it was not possible to secure an adequate supply of labor, this situation has eased considerably in recent years and has helped to explain the record outputs achieved, while a recent trend has seen a reduction in the over-all needs for labor. In 1963

African miners leaving the shaft head of a Witwatersrand gold mine
In 1963 some 377,000 Africans were employed by the South African gold mining industry.

some 377,000 Africans were employed in the gold mines, a substantial number of whom were secured from foreign areas under wage rates somewhat lower than those prevailing for Africans from the Republic.

After this brief account of the factors that explain the already long life of South Africa's gold mines, it is appropriate to ask again: How long may a high level of output be expected to continue? From the standpoint of physical reserves, one can only make a partially informed guess, because further exploration and the development of new techniques may well extend reserves considerably. We do know that the Central Main Reef, where mining began in 1886, is rather fully exploited and contains probably no more than enough ore to sustain production for another 20 to 25 years. The tonnage milled in this area declined from 1950 to 1961 by 48 percent. On the East Rand it was expected in 1962 that 13 of its 19 mines would probably close by 1970, these 13 mines accounting in 1962 for about 8.5 per cent of total gold production.

On the other hand, the Far West Rand only came into production in 1939 and its output continues to increase. The new Western Deep Levels Mine in this area, the costliest and largest mine ever sunk on the reefs (the 5-year development costs are given as $115 million), only began producing in 1962 and has an estimated life of 60 years. The West Driefontein mine in this same area is now the largest gold mine in the free world and has a higher output of gold than the mines of any country outside of South Africa except Canada. The Klerksdorp Field, farther to the southwest, is also a newer and growing field, but the most sensational development has been in the Orange Free State gold fields. Mining there began in 1948, and today about a dozen mines are in operation, accounting for 32.4 percent of total gold output in 1961. The Orange Free State reefs have the advantages of appreciably shallower depths than those now worked on the Rand and of higher gold content, but this field is relatively disadvantaged by greater faulting, a steeper geothermic gradient, and large quantities of water which must be pumped to the surface.

Since 1945 a score of new mines have been opened in all fields, twelve in the Orange Free State, and these new mines now account for over 50 percent of total output. But the number of opportunities for new developments appears to be dwindling: new mines in process of being opened declined from six in 1961 to one in 1963 and, barring new finds, the only prospects for other openings appear to be for several mines in the Far West Rand, Klerksdorp, and Evander areas.

Physically, it may be roughly estimated that a high level of production can probably be maintained for 50 years, but a peak may be reached within the next decade and, according to one expert, as early as 1967. Other informed predictions are that by 1981 only four of the

Witwatersrand mines will still be working and that a sharp contraction of output will occur after about 1988. Increased efficiency of operations, coupled with the system of taxation in being, tends to shorten the economic life of the mines. At present, tax provisions permit the developer to write off capital expenditures against profits. Until such time as profits exceed the capital spent by the mine, it is free from tax, but once this stage is reached the government claims as much as 66 percent of profits.

Economically, the mines constantly face something of a squeeze play. Wages and cost of materials gradually increase. But the industry has been able to offset these costs by greater efficiency, larger-scale techniques, sale of by-products, and because of the devaluation of 1949. The big unknown is the price of gold, which has remained at $35 an ounce since 1937. Sometimes it is possible to sell a portion of output at a premium, the black-market price having gone to $44 an ounce in the Korean crisis, but the industry cannot count on large or sustained sales at more than $35. Should it become necessary to devalue the dollar in the United States, South Africa would be greatly benefited, but official policy in the United States is thus far strongly opposed to such a move. The fact that the working profit in 1962 was $343 million on a total gold output valued at $889 million and that working costs have declined in relation to the value of output in recent years suggests that the squeeze is certainly not an unbearable one for most mines.

It is impossible to predict the effect which the course of political events will have on the gold industry. While the mining industry attempts to follow sound labor management practices and offers wages above those available in agriculture and services, it is prevented by government regulation from extending certain benefits, such as a large number of quarters for workers with families. The repressive policies of the Republic are bound to subject that country to increasing pressure, to lead to increasing resentment on the part of African workers. Fifty years may be a relatively long life for a metallic ore body; it is a very long period indeed in the present political evolution of Africa.

Even though the gold industry has reasonable prospects of carrying on for 50 years or more, the heavy dependence of the country on this production provides an uneasy and finite base for its economy. In examining the possibilities for diversification and for reducing the relative dependence on gold, it is appropriate to examine, first, the opportunities which exist through the production of other minerals. Even a cursory look reveals that the Republic is exceptionally favored in quantity and variety of mineral resources. It is, in fact, one of the greatest mineral storehouses in the world. Production of nonferrous minerals, ferroalloys, and precious stones is important on a world scale, and rescrves of the basic materials, coal and iron, are also very substantial.

DIAMONDS

The output of diamonds of South Africa and of South-West Africa is more or less fully integrated, making it appropriate to discuss the industry of the two countries together. In 1961 the value of sales was as follows in million dollars:

	Mine	*Alluvial*	*Totals*
South Africa	$35.6	$16.5	$52.1
South-West Africa		48.3	48.3
Total	$35.6	$64.8	$100.4

Taking the output of both countries, diamonds exceed the value of any other mineral except gold, and these countries have long ranked first among world producers of gem diamonds, second among producers of industrial stones.

Diamond mining played a very important role historically in southern Africa, by attracting settlement and transport and by providing large amounts of capital for other enterprises, including the production of gold, copper, and citrus fruit, and for opening up of the Rhodesias. In South-West Africa it is the leading economic activity, measured by value of output.

Diamonds are produced under quite varying

circumstances. The more important deposits in South Africa occur in volcanic kimberlite pipes, the main groups of which are centered on Kimberley, Pretoria, Jagersfontein, Koffiefontein, and Postmasburg. Only about a sixth of the more than 150 pipes thus far discovered contain diamonds in workable quantities and the bulk of production has come from seven pipes. The pipes vary greatly in size, the largest being the Premier Mine, 25 miles east of Pretoria, which covered 78 acres at the surface; it is now mined from below ground and has been worked to a depth of over 3,500 feet. This was the source of the 3,025.75 carat Cullinan Diamond.

Alluvial diamonds in South Africa are won in the valleys of the Orange, Vaal, and Hartz rivers between Prieska and Potchefstroom, in the districts of Lichtenburg and Ventersdorp in the West Transvaal, and on the coast of Namaqualand. In 1963 the Komaggas field in Namaqualand, which had been closed for 35 years, was opened for diamond prospecting.

The "Big Hole" at Kimberley
Diamonds were mined from the surface to a depth of 3,600 feet in the years 1871–1914, creating the largest man-made hole in the world. The diamond pipe is now mined from underground.

In South-West Africa, the major areas exploited are along the marine terraces at Oranjemund and Bogenfels, though the so-called Diamond Coast runs north as far as Conception Bay. In the mid-fifties a new field was discovered about 170 miles south of the Cunene River, while in 1962 and 1963 the world's first two sea-going diamond suction-dredges began working the Chameis Bay area of South-West Africa, about 60 miles north of the Orange River mouth. Results have been very encouraging and have led to expressions of interest by several other companies, including Tidewater Oil. It has been estimated that the Chameis Reef alone contains 14 million carats.

The average South African diamond mine moves about 30 million parts of ground to secure 1 part diamond; in the South-West African alluvials the ratio may be nearer 100 million to 1, though the offshore ratio appears to be much more favorable. South-West Africa is notable for the high proportion of gem stones recovered, especially in the 60-mile stretch north of the Orange River. That country wins 90 percent gem stones as compared to a world average of 22 percent, permitting it to rank as the most important single source of quality gem diamonds in the world. The South African proportion is 40 gem to 60 industrial. Gem stones account for about 70 percent of the total value of all diamonds sold on the world market.

While the history of diamond mining is replete with difficult periods and lengthy closings of numerous mines, the war and postwar years have been highly favorable and have witnessed repeated broken records. Fears of overproduction continue, particularly in view of the numerous new fields opened in various parts of the world in recent years, but the Diamond Producers Association apportions production among its members and two international corporations handle and carefully control the international sale of gem and industrial diamonds. DeBeers produces almost all of the South-West African diamonds and about 81 percent of South African diamonds, measured by weight. A second major concern of the diamond industry has been the production of synthetic boart, first achieved by General Electric in the United States in 1955. Not to be left at the post, DeBeers opened a synthetic diamond plant at Springs in 1961. Some 49 establishments in South Agrica are engaged in the cutting and polishing of diamonds, and exports of these diamonds exceed the value of rough diamond shipments.

COAL

While gold and diamonds are primarily important as earners of foreign exchange, coal is of enormous actual and potential significance as an energy base for the South African economy. Production of coal totaled 48.0 million tons in 1961–62, permitting South Africa to rank as the world's ninth largest producer. By value of output, coal ranks third among the Republic's minerals, with a total value in 1962 of $91.1 million.

The known reserves of coal were given in 1962 at 75 billion tons, while total reserves have been estimated at 223 billion tons. Seams are characteristically near the surface, the maximum depth of working now being only about 800 feet, and are generally horizontal, so that gently inclined shafts are usually used and coal is often removed by conveyor belts. Seams are rather thick, up to 50 feet in the Transvaal, but are thinner and more interrupted by faulting and volcanic instrusives in Natal. Mining is carried on largely by the room-and-pillar method and, while some operations are largely mechanized, there is very little use of continuous mining machines. The Sigma Colliery of the South African Coal, Oil and Gas Corporation (SASOL)

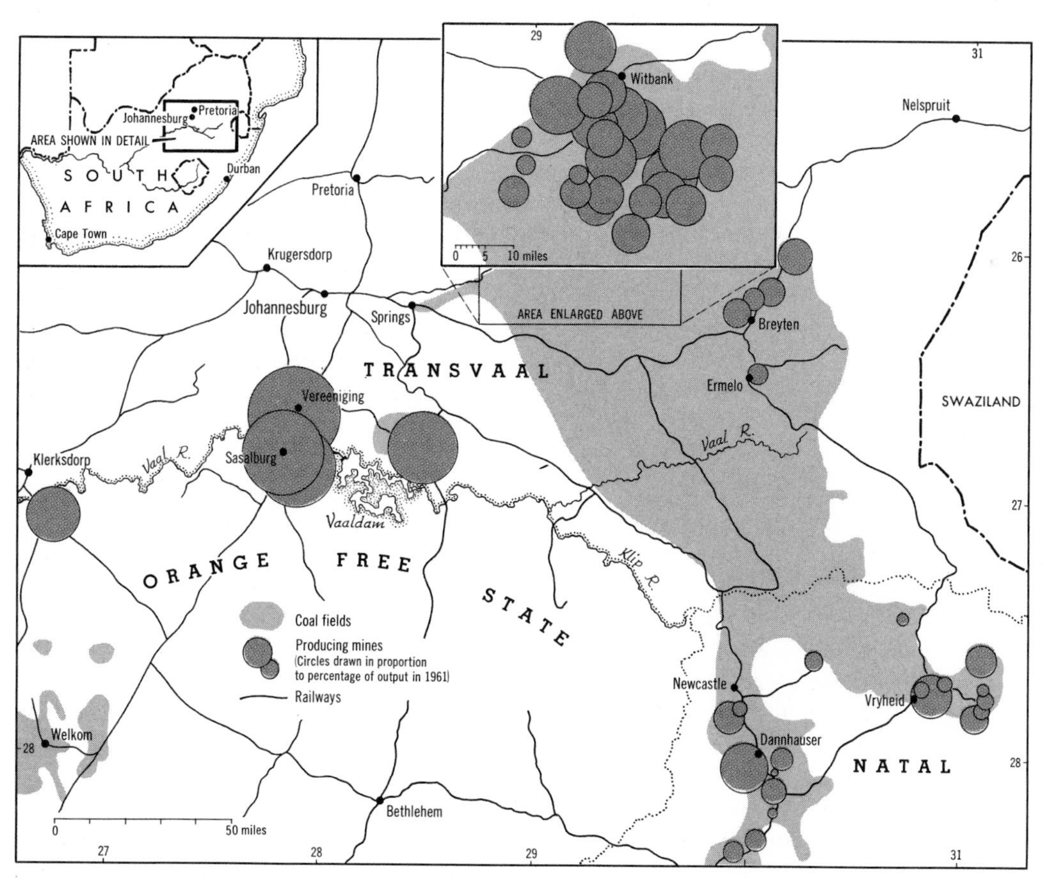

Map 88. Producing coal fields and collieries of South Africa

is one of the few fully mechanized coal mines, and achieved an output per man-shift of about 14 tons in 1961 as compared to about 3.5 tons in conventional mines.

While the mode of occurrence of South African coals is generally very favorable, this advantage is somewhat offset by the relatively poor quality of the bulk of the reserves. Most coal has a low calorific value and a high ash content and only a small percent of the proved coal is of coking quality (280 million tons, in the Natal field). A number of fields have not yet been systematically explored, however, and one of these, the Waterberg area of the northwest Transvaal, which is now being studied by the South African Iron and Steel Corporation, is credited with coking reserves of about 6 billion tons.

About 60 collieries are now operating, employing about 72,000 people in 1962 including 58,000 Africans, some 40 percent of whom were from Mozambique. Coal is produced at exceptionally low cost, the average having been only $1.65 per ton in 1961, or less than one-third the average cost of American coal. In 1962 the price for Transvaal and Orange Free State coal, which is somewhat below that for the more valuable, less easily mined Natal coal, was increased to from $1.48 to $1.75 per ton to all consumers except the South African Iron and Steel Industrial Corporation and the Electricity Supply Commission. This very low-cost fuel is of great importance to the South African economy, particularly to the mining, iron and steel, oil-from-coal, cement, and transport industries. Railways and power stations consume about three fifths of the coal mined, the mining industry in turn using over half of the electricity produced.

The largest reserves of coal are in the Transvaal, where the main producing area is on the highveld around Witbank (Map 88). In 1961–62 Transvaal accounted for about three fifths of total Republic output by tonnage. This field, and the field near the Vaal River both in the Transvaal and the Orange Free State, are very favorably situated with respect to the gold fields and the country's main industrial region. The main field in the Orange Free State, which accounts for about a quarter of total production, is centered on Sasolburg. Natal, which has the only coking coal production, accounts for about a seventh of total coal output. The center of this province's field is about 275 miles from Durban, while the Witbank field is 276 miles from Lourenço Marques. Coal was exported after World War II to Europe, South America, Asia, and Australia, but transport shortages in South Africa made it impossible to sustain the level, and exports were greatly reduced until recent years when about a million tons a year have been dispatched to markets as widely scattered as Burma, Israel, and South America.

No oil has been found in the Republic nor could more than a small fraction of the area be expected to contain petroleum. A contract for exploration near the Angola border of South-West Africa was reported in late 1961, and a German-financed company plans to spend $36.4 million (in five years) on oil exploration over 300,000 square miles of the Karroo Basin in South Africa.

OTHER MINERALS

A great variety of other minerals are produced in South Africa, as seen in Table 41 and Map 89. While some are used primarily in the country, such as the various quarry products and iron ore, and some are partly consumed domestically, such as copper, asbestos, and manganese, the most important function of these minerals is the earning of foreign exchange. In 1961, exports of minerals other than gold, uranium, and diamonds totaled $153 million or 7.6 percent of the total value of exports. In many years, exports could have been greater had the railways been able to handle larger tonnages, while the distance from port of some bodies is a factor decreasing their competitiveness. The bulk of a number of these minerals has been important in justifying the construction of a relatively superior rail system and of special facilities in the main ports.

The most important mineral region outside the gold reefs and diamond areas is the so-called Bushveld Complex in the Transvaal, one of the

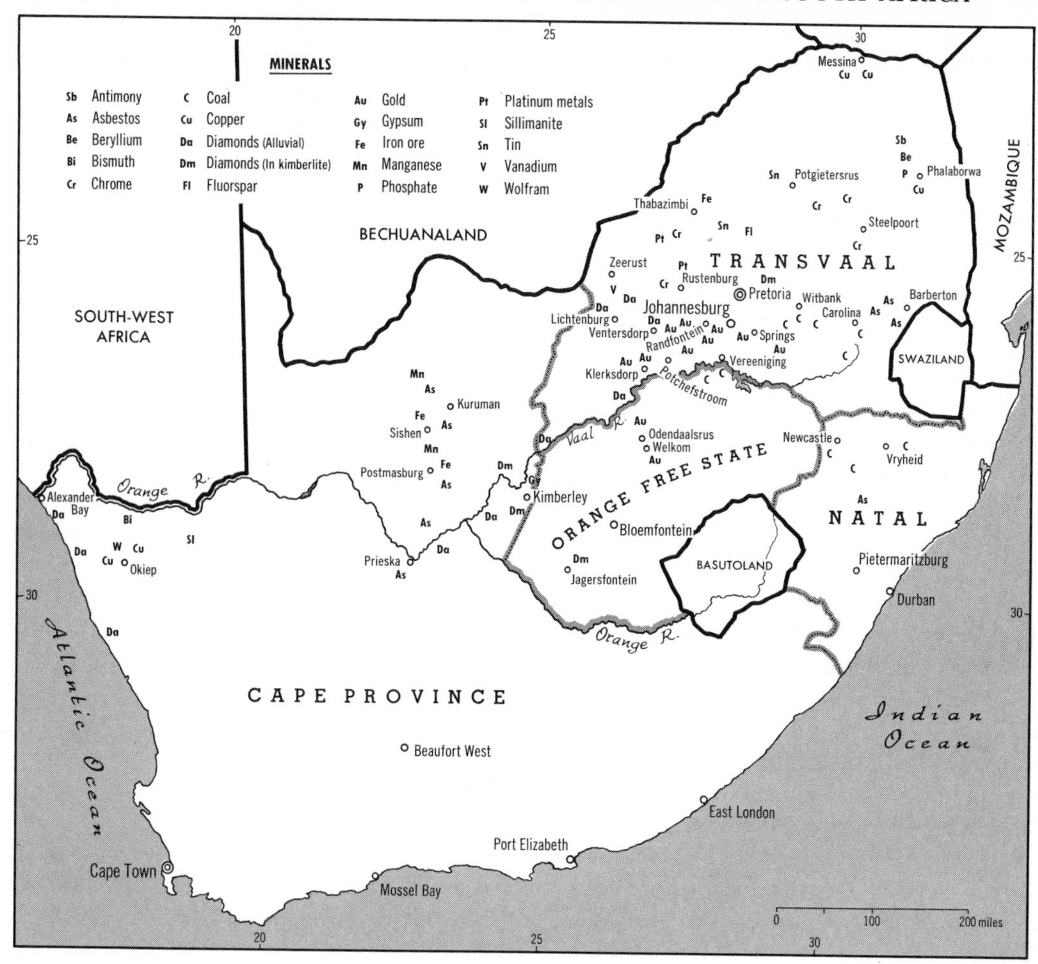

Map 89. Location of main mineral producing areas in South Africa

most remarkable mineralized areas in the world This area contains multiple occurrences, often along well-defined lines, of many minerals, including chrome, copper, platinum, nickel, magnesium, asbestos, iron, tin, bismuth, manganese, and vanadium. Other important mineralized regions include the zone from Prieska to Postmasburg and beyond in the northern Cape Province, and the region around O'okiep in the Namaqualand section of the Cape. Relatively little mining now occurs south of about the 30° S parallel.

Among the precious metals produced in South Africa, osmiridium and silver come from the Rand mines. South Africa is the world's leading producer of platinum, with the mine operating in the Rustenburg District being the largest single platinum producer in the free world. All of the main deposits, which contain enormous reserves, are in the Transvaal. Current statistics of output and sales are not available, but sales are probably valued somewhat below the mid-fifties range of $17 to $23 million because slackened demand has reduced operations to well below capacity.

Among the base metallic minerals, copper takes pride of place and ranks by value as the sixth most important mineral produced in the Republic. The leading mines are in two areas: near Messina in the northern Transvaal close to the Rhodesian border, which is noted for exceptionally pure ores, and around O'okiep in Namaqualand, Cape Province. In 1963, a $104 million venture was announced for Phalaborwa in the Transvaal lowveld, adjacent to a vermiculite mine. This operation is unique among African copper mines in the low percent of metallic content of the ores, which average only 0.69 percent. The ability to use very large-scale equipment in surface operations explains the possibility of exploiting these ores. An output of 80,000 tons of blister copper is planned for five years, starting about 1966, then production of about 68,000 tons a year for about 21 years, when any further extraction would probably require going underground.

Manganese ranks after copper, South Africa being second or third world producer of this most important additive to steel. The bulk of ores in the Republic are of low grade, averaging 40 to 48 percent metal content, but they have the advantage of being very hard, which minimizes disintegration in handling or under long storage. Production of manganese for carbon steel comes from the great Postmasburg deposits, 100 miles west of Kimberley, and from west of Kuruman, both in the Cape Province; manganese dioxode used in the extraction of uranium oxide is supplied from scattered workings over a large area in the western Transvaal. Some manganese is consumed in the Republic's ferromanganese plants before export. The Newcastle plant has a capacity of 30,000 tons a year; the Cato Ridge plant near Durban has recently been doubled to a capacity of 100,000 tons.

There are fairly large reserves of high-grade iron ore and enormous reserves of low-grade ore with a high silica content. Proved and probable reserves are given as 1.3 billion tons of high-grade ores and 6 billion tons of low-grade ores; possible reserves are listed at 2,000 billion tons, and there is an estimated reserve of titaniferrous iron ore of 2.2 billion tons. The most important deposits are in the Rustenburg (Transvaal) and Postmasburg (Cape Province) areas, with the bulk of production coming from Thabazimbi ("mountain of iron") in the former district and Sishen in the latter. High-grade hematite ore of 57 to 65 percent metal content and very low sulfur and phosphorous impurity is mined at Thabazimbi by opencast methods from a body with estimated reserves of 120 million tons. The cost of mining iron ore is exceptionally low, ranging around $2.00 per ton or only about a sixth of ore costs in the United States, In 1962 a contract was concluded with four Japanese steel firms for the delivery of four million tons of ore over a 10-year period beginning in 1963 from a mine in the Postmasburg area.

Other metallic minerals of some significance include:

(1) Antimony from the Letaba district, Eastern Transvaal. South Africa was the world's leading producer until 1958, when it lost this position to China.

(2) Chrome ore, from various places in the Lydenburg and Rustenburg sections of Transvaal, which may have the world's largest reserves. Construction of an $8.4 million ferrochrome plant at Witbank may further stimulate sales of chrome.

(3) Tin, which is produced at six mines in the Transvaal bushveld. Deposits tend to be scattered and limited in extent but output has increased rapidly in the last decade. A refinery at Zaaiplaats smelted 862 tons in 1961, but tin concentrates are also exported.

(4) Titanium, coming from sands at Umgababa on the south coast of Natal.

(5) Vanadium, which comes from very large reserves in the Bushveld Complex.

Nonmetallic minerals of importance include andalusite and sillimanite, used in the manufacture of refractories and for certain porcelainware; asbestos, one of South Africa's leading exports, coming mainly from the Pietersburg and Lydenburg districts of the northern Transvaal and from near Kuruman in Cape Province; a variety of quarry products, of which materials for the manufacture of cement are most important; fluorspar, used mainly as a flux in the steel industry; and phosphates, largely from Phalaborwa in the Transvaal lowveld.

It may be concluded that South Africa has an

enviable position in the variety and quantity of its mineral resources. That country would certainly appear to have the greatest opportunities in Africa from the raw material standpoint to develop metal and metal fabricating industries. Particularly significant are its reserves of coal and iron ore; while the shortage of coking coal may be a long-run handicap, it is possible that new processes will have been initiated by the time a serious shortage is reached.

INDUSTRY IN THE REPUBLIC

In order to understand the potentialities for industry's reducing the dependence upon gold, one must examine the present state of development and analyze the attributes and deficiencies of the physical and socioeconomic environment of South African industry.

IMPORTANCE IN THE ECONOMY

According to official statistics, private manufacturing accounted for 23.8 percent of national income in 1960–61 as compared with 13.9 percent for mining and 10.8 percent for agriculture fishing, and forestry. The comparable figure for manufacturing in 1939 was 17.7 percent, suggesting the dynamic growth that industry has enjoyed in postwar years. The gross value of industrial production increased from less than $560 million in 1939 to $3,163 million in 1953 and $4,700 million in 1963. As indicated earlier, however, these figures somewhat exaggerate the relative importance of manufacturing; they include the processing of minerals, construction, and a number of establishments which might more appropriately be listed under services. Also, a sizable part of the present industrial plant caters directly to the mining industry and would simply not exist if mining were not so important. Furthermore, industry is still a net consumer of foreign exchange, whose earnings are largely dependent on mineral and agricultural products.

However, manufacturing has made and continues to make very real strides, and for much of the postwar period advanced at a rate which compared favourably with any world area. Employment in industry (including construction) increased from 307,000 in 1938 to 732,000 in 1954–55 and 808,000 in 1962. The number of private industrial establishments grew from 9,825 in 1937–38 to over 14,300 in 1959–60. Nor has expansion been confined to a few selected branches of industry; it has involved a diverse growth, including such industries as foodstuffs, iron and steel, metal fabrication, chemicals, textiles and clothing, shoes, paper, chemicals, and many others. South Africa is by far the most industralized country of Africa, the only one with a rather well-rounded manufacturing economy. The most notable deficiencies are in the production of machine tools, vehicles, machinery, and newsprint, where there continues to be heavy dependence on imported goods. These gaps prevent the Republic from having a fully integrated industrial establishment.

MAJOR INDUSTRIAL GROUPS

Table 42 gives certain key data for the major manufacturing industries in South Africa. If all phases of the metal and metal fabricating industry are combined, this branch of manufacturing ranks first in employment, with about 36.1 percent of the total in 1961, though, with 37.7 percent of the total gross value of output from manufacturing, it falls slightly below the food, beverage, and tobacco industries. The high importance of the metal industries is unique on the continent.

The Republic is particularly favored by the possession of a number of modern steel mills which produce pig and steel at very low cost. The two major plants are nationally owned and managed by the South African Iron and Steel Industrial Corporation (ISCOR). Pretoria, the original center, now has a plant with a capacity of 1.1 million tons. It receives coal from Witbank, 66 miles distant, and from Natal, where ISCOR has a wholly-owned mine near Dannhauser, 252 miles away. Iron ore comes mainly from Thabazimbi, 150 miles northwest of Pretoria. The Vanderbijlpark installation is newer and larger, having been opened in 1951 and having a steel capacity of 1.25 million tons. Located just west of the important steel fabricating center of Vereeniging and within the gold-bearing arc, it secures coking coal from Natal, lower grade coal and electric power from the mines and pit-head stations in the immediate vicinity, and iron ore mostly from Sishen in the Cape Province, but also from Thabazimbi. Both Pretoria and Vanderbijlpark are very well situated with respect to the country's leading industrial area and to the great markets of the mining industry.

South Africa also has several nonintegrated pig and steel plants. The Union Steel Corporation (USCO), the oldest member of the steel group and an autonomous company in which ISCOR holds a controlling interest, has two steel mills at Vereeniging. The first of these, the Vaal Works, has three open-hearth furnaces and three electric furnaces and relies mainly on scrap as its raw material. The second, the Klip Works, produces special steels in six electric furnaces, including those used by the mining industry for drilling. The two works ship out about 170,000 tons of high-value steel a year. African Metals Corporation (AMCOR) produces about 260,000

Table 42. South African private industry: Employment, number of establishments, and gross value of output by major groups

Industrial category	*Employment, 1961*		*Number of establishments, 1959–60*	*Gross value of output, 1959–60 (in million $)*
	White	*All other*		
Metal and mechanical				
Basic metal	17,900	17,300	121	280
Metal products	24,900	54,100		
Machinery	18,300	18,200	2,650	683
Electrical machinery	11,900	13,400		
Transport equipment	35,800	38,600		
Subtotal	108,800	141,600	2,771	963
Textiles, clothing, and footwear				
Textiles	4,900	31,800		
Clothing and footwear	13,500	58,700		
Subtotal	18,400	90,500	1,869	471
Food, beverages, and tobacco				
Food	17,600	78,700		
Beverages and tobacco	5,000	11,700		
Subtotal	22,600	90,400	1,889	994
Chemicals				
General chemicals	13,800	24,100	419	344
Petroleum and coal products	2,800	3,300	43	107
Subtotal	16,600	27,400	462	451
Other				
Nonmetal mineral products	8,700	48,100	792	189
Furniture, wood and cork	9,300	44,100	1,128	147
Paper, printing	16,900	20,500	661	201
Leather, excluding footwear and rubber	4,600	9,600	64	46
Miscellaneous	4,200	9,600	600	88
Subtotal	43,700	131,900	3,245	671
Total	210,100	481,800	10,236	3,550

Sources: Republic of South Africa, *Industrial Census, 1959–60*, Special Report No. 250 (Pretoria, Government Printer 1962), pp. 12–16; *Monthly Bulletin of Statistics* (July, 1962).

Aerial view of the South African Iron and Steel Industrial Corporation (ISCOR) plant near Pretoria
Output of steel in South Africa was 2.64 million tons in 1962; plans call for a capacity of 4 million tons by 1972.

Tractor assembly at a Port Elizabeth plant
South Africa has ten vehicle assembly plants.

tons of pig iron at its Newcastle, Natal, works and a large part of the country's ferroalloys at Newcastle, Witbank, and Kookfontein. The Newcastle plant is the site of a large new blast furnace erected at a cost of $25 million, constructed to permit meeting a contract with the Yawata Iron and Steel Company calling for delivery of 500,000 tons of pig iron a year for a period of ten years.

Output of steel in South Africa increased from about 344,000 tons in 1938–39 to 2,640,000 tons in 1962. In the latter year, pig iron production was 2.41 million tons; ferroalloy production was 200,000 tons, a more than threefold increase since 1957. In 1962 a multimillion dollar eight-year expansion program was begun by ISCOR with the ultimate goal of increasing its steel capacity to about 3.85 million tons, the major additions to be made at Vanderbijlpark. As the country now produces only about 76 percent of domestic steel requirements, this expansion, as well as AMCOR's expansion at Newcastle, would appear to be well justified. The exceptionally low cost of South African pig iron and steel may also result in capturing additional foreign markets in the years ahead.

The metal products, machinery, electrical goods, and transport equipment industries are of growing importance in the Republic. The establishment in 1945 of the Vanderbijl Engineering Corporation, with a large foundry for light and heavy castings, and machine, welding, fabricating, and forging shops, greatly widened the scope for producing industrial and mining equipment. Of particular interest also is the automotive assembly industry, one of the most modern of the Republic's manufacturing segments, in which 10 plants assemble several dozen makes of cars and trucks, thus saving substantial transport costs as well as foreign exchange. However, only about a fifth of materials consumed by the industry are now produced in South Africa, though new plants promise to increase the share considerably. The variety of metal products in South Africa is far greater than for any other African country, including a range of machinery and electrical goods which is unusual. Nonetheless, the product emphasis still reveals a youthful economy.

The production of food, beverages, and tobacco products is the second ranking group of industries in employment, first in gross value of output. This group depends largely upon South African raw materials and upon the domestic market, but there is an important export of sugar, wine, canned fruits, and fishing products. On the whole it is competently organized, but could benefit substantially from a broader domestic market, from more progressive enterprise in food distribution, and from continued attention to attractive presentation.

The clothing and textile industry ranks third among manufacturing groups and the value of textile production increased 8½-fold in the period 1947–59. There are over 700 clothing factories and 298 textile mills in the Republic producing a wide range of textiles and garments. While the industry cannot supply as wide a range or as high quality goods as can be imported, it does readily compete in price and quality for the goods produced. Of especial importance in recent years has been the opening of a large rayon factory at Umkomaas, Natal, and of a big spinning and weaving plant at Pinetown, Natal, for the production of heavier drills and denims. Both the textile and the clothing industries are generally well equipped and operate efficiently. The ratio of nonwhite to white employees is particularly high in this group, having been about 5 to 1 in 1961 as compared to about 1.3 to 1 in the metal and metal fabricating industries and about 2.3 to 1 for all manufacturing industries in the Republic.

The chemical industry owes its importance largely to the demand from the mines for explosives and chemicals, but also to the need for fertilizers in agriculture. With the construction of the government-owned coal-from-oil plant at Sasolburg it also became possible to install several petrochemical factories, and a synthetic rubber plant costing $12.6 million was started there in 1962. Fisons already has a $7 million fertilizer plant at Sasolburg and has contracted to open a nitrogenous fertilizer plant using nitrogen gas from the SASOL plant that was formerly wasted. Still another plant for Sasolburg will be an African Explosives and Chemical Corporation installation to produce polythene, arctona, nylon 6, and cyanide using raw materials from SASOL. Three large petroleum refineries are situated in the Republic, including a new $70 million Shell refinery at Durban.

THE LOCATION OF SOUTH AFRICAN INDUSTRY

The distributional pattern of South African industry is a relatively simple one, consisting of one well-recognized district in southern Transvaal and a series of nodes associated with the major coastal cities. Map 90 depicts the relative importance of regional centers as measured by numbers employed in 1956–57, the latest census for which district figures have been compiled.

The Southern Transvaal Industrial District has been described as having a cruciform shape with each axis about 80 miles in length and with some signs of its evolving to a diamondlike pattern.[1] This district, which contains over three million people including a million whites, has three major nuclei—Pretoria, Johannesburg and

[1] T. J. D. Fair and E. W. N. Mallows, "The Southern Transvaal," *The Town Planning Review* (July, 1959), pp. 125–38.

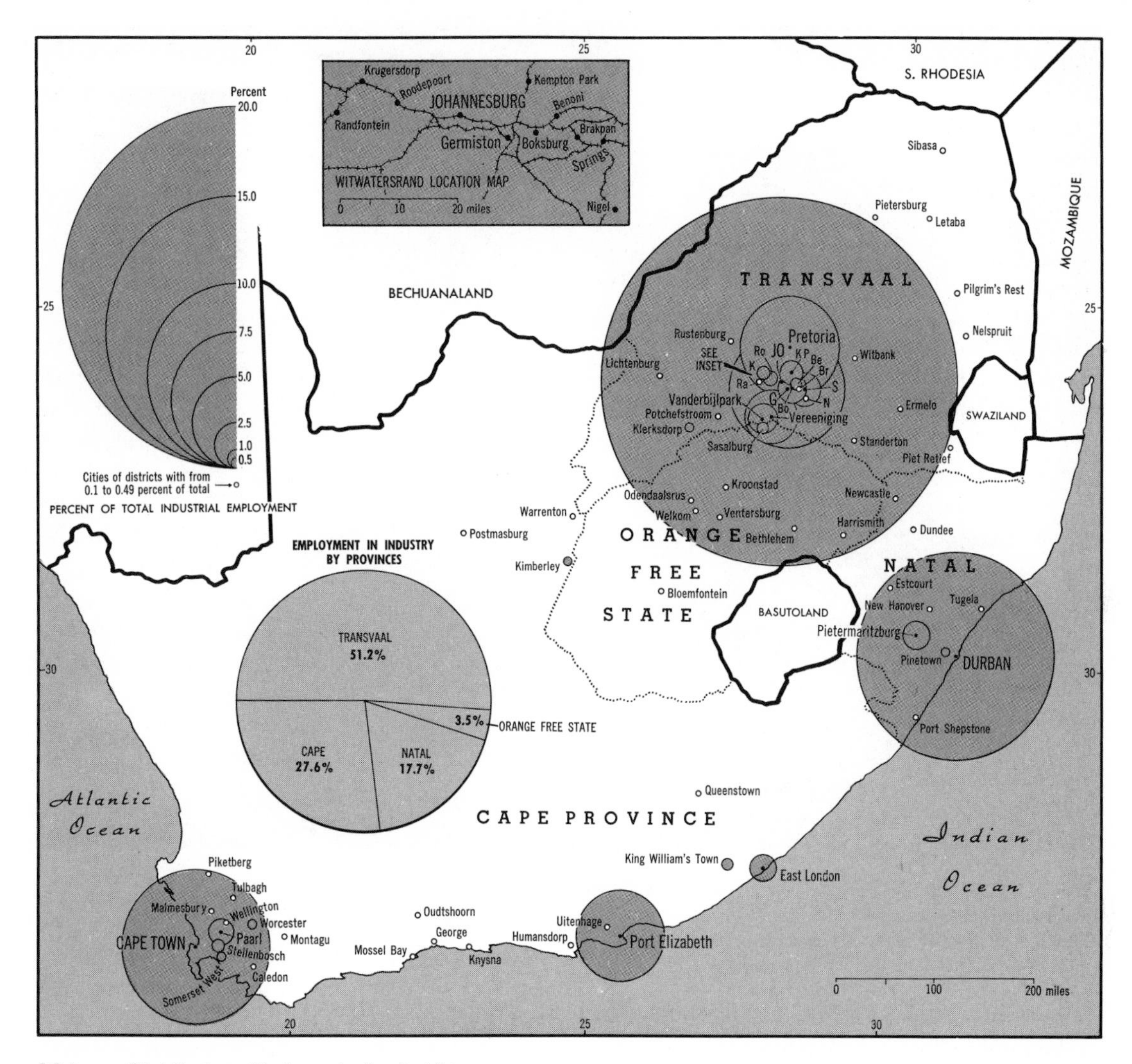

Map 90. Distribution of industry in South Africa

the inner zone of the Rand, and Vereeniging–Vanderbijlpark—all important in manufacturing but also representing respectively the chief government, financial, and heavy industrial centers of the Republic. The Southern Transvaal accounts for about three eighths of the country's industrial establishments, for over two fifths of the gross output in manufacturing, and for 43.3 percent of the African and 49.1 percent of the white labor force in secondary industry. Johannesburg alone is credited with 20.0 percent of the gross output of industry in the Republic. It has also witnessed the most rapid growth in manufacturing of all the industrial districts. There are numerous explanations for the dominant position of the Southern Transvaal Industrial District: foremost is its position with respect to the enormous market of the gold mining industry, but it is also well centered with respect to other mining communities, the large conurbations of the area, and even with respect to the national market. The availability of coal and cheap carboelectric power is a second major advantage, while of lesser significance are the

Aerial view of Cape Town with Table Mountain in the background
Cape Town accounts for an estimated 15.5 percent of South Africa's gross industrial output.

availability of labor and the existence of a distance tariff in this inland industrial region. The chief disadvantage of the district is the long distance from domestic ports, compensated in part by the relative nearness to Lourenço Marques, which, under the terms of the Mozambique Convention, must handle 47.5 percent of the tonnage of merchandise imports into the area bounded by a line connecting the freight stations serving Pretoria, Springs, Vereeniging, Klerksdorp, Welverdiend, and Krugersdorp. In the long run, the supply of water could become a more serious problem; it has already required rather substantial capital works programs. And the relatively declining position of the Rand in gold mining also raises interesting questions with respect to long-range industrial location. While this district is particularly important in the iron and steel, metal and engineering, and chemical industries, it also has sizable representation in the other major groups of South African industry.

Among the coastal centers, Cape Town and its satellite communities rank first with about 15.5 percent of gross industrial output. The Western Cape District is important in the manufacture of foodstuffs, wines, tobacco products, textiles and clothing, and furniture, and in 1962 construction began on the Republic's third major oil refinery, a $30.8 million Caltex plant about seven miles from the Cape Town docks.

Durban and Pinetown account for about 14.9 percent of the gross industrial output of the Republic. The more important industries here include sugar refining, rubber goods, chemicals, tanning, rayon textiles, and oil refining, for which there are two major plants. Port Elizabeth and Uitenhage produce an estimated 4.9 percent of the Republic's industrial goods. The assembly of motor vehicles and production of tires are of especial importance, while Port Elizabeth is also a growing textile center. East London, the other major port, is of only minor significance, with about 1.3 percent of total industrial output. The remainder of South African industry is scattered and usually consists of raw material oriented establishments or service and construction "industries." At the last industrial census Transvaal accounted for 50.1 percent of gross industrial output, Cape Province for 26.0 percent, Natal for 20.6 percent, and the Orange Free State for only 3.3 percent.

It is government policy that industry be encouraged to disperse more widely and, as an integral part of its apartheid program, that industry be established in localities immediately adjacent to African reserves, thus permitting the use of African labor without migration to European urban areas. Certain transportation and tax incentives are offered to encourage such industrial placements, which would have the additional advantage of access to the lowest wage labor in the Republic and, in a limited number of cases, to raw materials. In a few places the location of reserves means that border industries can readily fit into the existent pattern of industrial development, such as at Pretoria, Durban, and Ladysmith, but the major locational factor suggested is almost entirely artificial and the number of misplaced plants would probably greatly exceed the number suitably located. Furthermore, dispersal would be entirely contrary to the trend of the last decades, which has been, for a variety of cogent reasons, toward greater concentrations in readily defined industrial districts.

FACTORS INFLUENCING INDUSTRIAL GROWTH: THE PHYSICAL CONDITIONERS

The foregoing brief review of South African industry will permit a better understanding of the major factors which affect and which will influence the further development of industry in that country.

RAW MATERIALS. First, from the standpoint of raw materials it need not be reiterated that the mineral position is, on the whole, excellent, comparing very favorably with most other countries in the world. Of greatest importance is the ability to produce low-cost steel, but there are numerous opportunities for the further processing of many minerals, both for domestic consumption and for export. The position with respect to agricultural raw materials is much less favorable, though such products as wool, corn, sugar, oils, wine, and fruits do support sizable establishments. Cotton may also increase in importance if effective disease and pest control is achieved. The fisheries of South Africa support a growing fish meal, oil, and canning industry and can be further rationalized. The forest resource picture is not impressive, though wattle exports are important and output from exotic plantations will doubtless support an enlarging pulp, paper, and cellulose industry.

ENERGY. The energy position of the Republic is characterized by the dominance of one superior resource, outstanding not because of quality but because of the very attractive price at which it is produced. While the coal industry itself is concerned with narrowing profit margins and the scarcity of African labor, and favors an increase in the government-controlled price of coal, the pit-head cost of coal is so low by world standards that some increase would probably not seriously affect either the ability to export or the well-being of Republic industry. An unusual feature of the energy consumption complex of South Africa is the persistently dominant position of coal; South Africa is the only developed country where this has held true in postwar years.

In 1961, 69.4 percent of the electricity generated in the Republic was produced by the government-owned Electricity Supply Commission (ESCOM), 18.7 percent came from municipal stations, and 11.9 percent from plants owned by private mines and industries. Total electricity generated in South Africa has increased from 9,259 million kwh in 1948 to 24,556 million kwh in 1961. Almost all electricity comes from carbo-electric stations, some of which have a very large capacity. The new Komati station in eastern Transvaal, with a capacity of 1 million kw, is the largest thermal station in Africa. ESCOM's 28 plants claim the lowest cost of stream-generated electric power in the world, the average sale price having been 0.3691¢ U.S. in 1961, a figure which compares favorably with many hydroelectric stations in other parts of the world. The mines consumed 51.4 percent of ESCOM's sales in that year, with gold and uranium producers taking 93 percent of that. The low cost of electricity is traceable to three main factors: the ease and low cost of coal mining (in 1961, the lowest cost coal at ESCOM stations was $1.30 per short ton at the Vaal station, the highest cost was $6.66 a ton at Hex River in the western Cape), the low wages of labor, and the ability to effect savings in scale because of the large demands of mining and industry for electric power.

The SASOL oil-from-coal plant at Sasolburg
Based upon extremely low-cost coal, this plant is the world's largest such establishment. Sasolburg is rapidly becoming the leading chemical center of South Africa with the construction of additional carbo- and petrochemical plants.

In order to reduce its dependence upon the Middle East and to save on expenditure of foreign exchange, the South African government constructed the world's largest oil-from-coal plant in 1955 at Sasolburg, 14 miles south of Vereeniging, and just 1½ miles by conveyor belt from its wholly owned Sigma Colliery. It was expected that the extremely low cost of coal at the plant, less than half the national average, plus the high delivered cost of imported petroleum to the southern Transvaal market, would ensure the success of the plant, but technical difficulties in the first years prevented achieving anywhere near the designed capacity of 60 million gallons of all products. However, turnover of the plant, run by the South African Coal, Oil and Gas Corporation (SASOL), increased from $1.86 million in 1955 to $25.1 million in 1960–61. While the profits of $3.63 million in 1961 and $5.05 million in 1962 do not represent a very good rate of return on the $134 million investment in the plant, they indicate that earlier running-in problems have been met. In 1961 it was announced that the plant would be doubled in a seven-year program costing $84 million, but a later assessment led to postponement of this project in favor of devoting capital to a $53 million petrochemical program using imported petroleum, at least temporarily. It is not unlikely that a pipeline will be constructed from Durban to Johannesburg via Sasolburg to provide the needed crude oil and to relieve pressure on the railways.

Hydropower resources of the Republic are not very great and few hydroelectric stations have been constructed. Some of the relatively short rivers flowing eastward present interesting possibilities for development, as do the higher tributaries of the Orange. But the low precipitation over the bulk of the country, its highly seasonal character, and the general absence of attractive storage sites reduce the possibilities despite the average high elevation of the area.

For the future, the great resources of uranium

provide a more than ample base for the nuclear-electric industry, but the low cost of carbo-electricity will probably mean that South Africa will postpone interest in this new source of energy for some decades.

WATER SUPPLY. As suggested in the discussion of the Southern Transvaal Industrial District, water supply is a subject of some concern with respect to South African industry. In the decade to 1958, some $150 million was spent in South Africa on water conservation and increasing allocations will have to be made to meet requirements in the years ahead. Greater attention will have to be given to the treatment of sewage and of industrial effluents to secure industrial water, to the more careful utilization or even reduction of water now used for irrigation, and to various schemes to divert water into the river systems best capable of serving the industrial communities. The shortage of water on the plateau may also influence certain industries to locate along the coast, especially in Natal, the wettest of South African provinces.

OTHER PHYSICAL CONDITIONERS. An additional physical factor which has some influence on South African industry is the location of the country at the extermity of the continent in a position of partial isolation. While increasing the expense of delivery from supply points and the cost of shipping to world markets, the distance from the major manufacturing centers of the Northern Hemisphere also acts as a kind of protection for some South African industries. The configuration of the country also tends to increase the costs of transport, as does the scattered nature of industrial centers and the internal position of the southern Transvaal.

FACTORS INFLUENCING INDUSTRIAL GROWTH: THE NONPHYSICAL CONDITIONERS

MARKET. As to the nonphysical influences on South African industry, perhaps the most important limiting factor is the restricted size of the domestic market. While the white population has a relatively very high standard, the Bantu populace has a total income somewhere between 25 and 30 percent of the national income, and individual African cash incomes are not adequate to stimulate a great variety of plants which might otherwise be justified. Furthermore, most South African political and economic policies work toward a continued low standard for the African worker. The Republic's Industrial Development Corporation, in fact, has predicted that the average non-European income will increase only about 24.5 percent between 1960–61 and 1975–76, while European incomes would rise in the same period by 28.3 percent.

Important in developing the domestic market for specific South African manufactures has been the government policy of tariff protection pursued since 1925, which has stimulated the development of such industries as auto assembly, tire production, some textiles, petroleum refining, and the SASOL oil-from-coal project.

The restricted size of the domestic market naturally leads to the examination of possibilities of catering to foreign markets. Within Africa, the largest available market would appear to be in the Rhodesias, but, as has been seen, these countries have pretensions to integrated industrialization themselves and will doubtless continue to protect their rising industries against South African imports. Nonetheless, exports to other African countries which, unlike exports of the Republic to the more highly industrialized countries, consist mainly of manufactured goods total about a fifth of merchandise exports. And, just as trade has increased among the leading industrial nations of the world, so should the opportunity for interchange among African nations improve as their economies develop. South Africa could assume a position of leadership in certain phases of supply, particularly of iron and steel and metal-fabricated items. But the racial policies of the Republic are likely to restrict realization of the potentialities; these policies are increasingly resented by African nations, which have called for one or another form of restriction on trade with the Republic. As for markets outside Africa, the greatest opportunities would appear to lie in the sale of pig iron and steel and in semiprocessed metals such as ferromanganese and ferrochrome. Despite the low wages of its African labor, the Republic cannot compete on a price basis in the field of textiles with such producers as Japan and Hong Kong.

HUMAN RESOURCES. From the standpoint of human resources, there is a sharp dichotomy between white and nonwhite. Whites receive excellent wages and fill all of the managerial and skilled labor jobs, plus most of the semiskilled positions. Africans provide the unskilled and some of the semiskilled labor and receive wages that, irrespective of productivity, bear little relation to those of the whites. The total salaries and wages in manufacturing industry in 1961 were $558 million for the 210,100 whites employed, $187 million for the 356,400 Africans, and $101 million for the 125,400 Asian and Coloured employees.

Advantages in the labor-management area as far as industrial development is concerned would include the low wages of Bantu, Asian, and Coloured labor, which permit exceptionally low-cost production of certain items such as coal, steel, and power and competitive pricing in many consumer goods despite a lower productivity than that of competing nations. Wages are, however, higher than in adjacent African countries and this gives a second advantage—the ability to attract large numbers of workers from extranational areas. Some South Africans see this dependence upon foreign workers as a kind of safety valve, for unemployment in the country could be eliminated in future recessions simply by restricting immigration of laborers. Another advantage is the fact that much of the nonwhite labor of South Africa is more evolved and more experienced than that of other African countries, hence the skill, though still low, is relatively favorable. Finally, an advantage is the existence of the largest number of whites in any African country, people who are familiar with the modern, machine civilization and capable of moving into industry with relative ease.

Unfortunately, the disadvantages in the labor-management sphere are equally if not more impressive. Possibly the most immediate bottleneck to industrial expansion is the shortage of managerial talent and of skilled labor. This shortage may be attributed in part to the dynamic expansion of manufacturing in postwar years, but it also reflects the policy of restricting the advance of the bulk of the population and thus markedly reducing the pool from which skill might be obtained. In most postwar years there has also been an outright shortage of workers in industry, recruitment of labor having failed to keep pace with requirements. The shortfall has never been as serious in industry, however, as in farming, where the lowest wages are paid, or as in mining, which often had difficulty in competing with the more attractive industrial jobs. Of course, the shortage of labor is not without its advantages, at least from the social standpoint. It has led to the provision of better housing and food in order competitively to attract the African; it has encouraged the use of labour-saving equipment and hence improved productivity on the farm and in the mines and factories; it has forced the upgrading of the African in the face of laws designed to restrict his relative progress; and it has created pressure to raise wages of the non-Europeans.

The shortage of semiskilled workers could be alleviated if more non-Europeans were admitted to such jobs. In fact, this has been occurring despite traditional South African social customs and the official policies of controlling the flow of nonwhites to industrial areas and of reserving specific jobs for members of the white race. The movement of black labor in the Union is heavily controlled by a mass of legal restrictions which are increasing in scope and severity, and the Bantu is forbidden to join a union with powers of collective bargaining. But the government has not actually been able to enforce the rules that are on the books, since to do so would fatally cripple a large part of South African industry. An order in 1957 allotting 40,000 of 48,000 jobs in the clothing industry to whites was met with such protests on the part of European owners that the industry was almost immediately exempted from applying the quota established; to have done so would literally have ruined the industry, whose percentage of whites was only 11.4 percent at the time of the determination. But the principle of job reservation remains as a threat to the orderly development of the Republic's manufacturing establishment.

The restrictions imposed upon Bantu, Asian, and Coloured labor stem mainly from the fear that whites will somehow be deprived of job opportunities, that the size of the pie is limited and, therefore, that any gain by one racial group is at the expense of another. The European, in defending the wish to preserve his position, may point to the fact that the proportion of African labor in industry increased from 44 percent in the years 1924 to 1930 to 57.1 percent in 1955–56 while the proportion of Europeans declined from 36.3 percent to 25.6 percent in the same period, but in fact the numbers of Europeans employed in secondary industry increased from 69,800 in 1929 to 117,100 in 1938 to over 200,000 in the 1950s. The increasing proportion of Africans employed in industry has not been at the expense of Europeans; it has been a requisite for the expansion of industry. Any attempts to freeze the status quo in employment or to rigidify racial employment quotas in specific industries can only delay the further expansion of manufacturing.[2] It should be stated that many industrialists, as well as the leading mining interests, are far in advance of government in their attitude towards non-European wages and employment.

The other disadvantages of the labor position in the Republic are similar to those outlined for most of Africa under the discussion of industry in West Africa—impermanence, instability, low productivity, and so forth. Despite certain measures to reduce these deficiencies, many Republic laws must have the effect of sustaining them. South African efforts to maintain the status quo in employment relations are not only directly contradictory to any sound economic reasoning, they are fraught with the most serious long-run dangers for that country, while the effective contributions of all races could yield most promising rewards.

CAPITAL. The situation with respect to capital supplies has, at least until recently, been quite favorable for the development of South African industry. Profits from mining have been used in part to develop industry and the country has been capable of generating a much higher percentage of its capital requirements than other African countries. But domestic funds have not flowed from one industry to another as freely as in other industrial nations, while the local investor is more prone to favor building societies or agriculture.

Foreign investment has been substantial in South Africa, having totaled over $3,900 million at the end of 1956, but the rate of capital inflow decreased sharply in succeeding years for a variety of reasons but primarily because of the fear that the racial policies of the country would sooner or later lead to serious difficulties. Much foreign investment is in the form of fixed assets, however, and cannot readily be withdrawn. In 1960 the foreign investment stood at approximately $4,275 million.

Even before the decline in the rate of foreign investment the South African government took steps through the Industrial Development Corporation (IDC) to harness risk capital for promotion of industry. In 1960 IDC held a portfolio of $182 million in industry. The government has also invested directly in ISCOR, SASOL, FOSKOR (formed to develop large apatite deposits occurring in the Phalaborwa area of the Transvaal lowveld), SAICCOR (which participated in the construction of a $23.8 million rayon pulp plant at Umkomaas, Natal, in partnership with the IDC, Courtaulds of Britain, and Snia Viscosa of Italy, who later sold out to Courtaulds), and in the Bantu Investment Corporation, designed, with a capital of $1.4 million, to promote industrial and other undertakings on the part of Africans in the reserves.

To conclude this section on industry, it may be said that South Africa has very substantial

[2] See Sheila T. van der Horst, "The Economic Implications of Political Democracy: The Road to Economic Progress," Supplement to *Optima* (June, 1960), 50 pp.

opportunities in the industrial realm, but that it is not likely to realize them unless the bulk of its population is freed from the mass of restrictions curbing its advance and until its nonwhite population provides a more powerful market for South African manufactures.

AGRICULTURE

Agriculture appears to be the potential weak link in the South African economy. Development in some regions is impressive and there are potentialities for intensification and extension, but agriculture cannot be expected to replace gold or to provide the answer to the need for an expanding, more diversified economy. And, despite substantial improvements that have been made in the farming sector, its relative importance has declined and its index of production reveals a considerably slower rate of growth than that of other sectors. In 1960–61, agriculture, forestry, and fishing accounted for an estimated 10.8 percent of the total geographical income. Agriculture remains, however, the most important single source of employment with about 112,000 white farmers, 816,000 regular employees engaged on farm work, and 146,000 domestic servants employed on farms. The total population on European farms is about 410,000 whites and 2,500,000 nonwhites, while if the country is taken as a unit about half of the total population is still sustained by farming.

THE PHYSICAL BASE

The most important explanation for the limited potentialities of South African farming is the difficulty of the physical environment, especially the deficiencies of climate and soils, but also the nature of the landforms, particularly in the more favored climate regions.

TOPOGRAPHY. While it is possible to distinguish scores of landform regions in South Africa, the over-all pattern consists of a narrow coastal belt on the west, south, and east which rises sharply inland to the great interior plateau varying in elevation from about 3,000 to 6,000 feet. The plateau is characteristically bounded by a chain of mountains which form the outward facing escarpments and which are highest on the east, where the Drakensberg Range has isolated peaks reaching 10,000 feet. At the base of the escarpment is the lowveld, generally below 1,800 feet, and in some places intermediate steps on slopes provide a middle veld. The plateau

Part of the Drakensberg Range
Extending along the east and rising, often abruptly, to elevations of as much as 10,000 feet, this range is a formidable impediment on the routes between the coast and the interior plateau.

surface is mostly a great plains area, varied in parts by broken country and by steep-sided, flat-topped masses. It may be divided into three major subregions: (1) the Cape middle veld, with elevations between 2,000 and 4,000 feet, relatively smooth, and quite dry; (2) the highveld, from 4,000 to 6,000 feet except for sections in the east; the even surface of this region is broken only by a few low ranges and numerous small inselberges, called koppies; and (3) the Transvaal plateau basin, actually a continuation of the highveld.

Taken alone, the landform factor is not too unfavorable, the vast plateau surface permitting ease of movement over much of the country. But the form of South Africa as a great uplifted basin restricts the area in desirable coastal lowlands; confines the favorable Mediterranean climate to a very small section below the Karroo escarpment in the southwest, an area further limited by the folded mountains of that region; similarly restricts the potentially highly productive humid subtropical region to the east so that this most propitious climate occurs in large part in areas possessing landforms unsuitable for agricultural activity; and means that the best landform area is in the rain-shadow of the uplifted plateau edges. Other disadvantages of the topography which influence all aspects of the economy include the difficulty of building and the high cost of operating transport lines from coastal points to the interior, and the lack of any navigable streams in the country.

CLIMATE. In a single-factor analysis, it is climate which presents the most severe limitations to agricultural intensity in South Africa, though climate is obviously greatly influenced by the topography. Climate types vary from dry subtropical or Mediterranean in the south-west, a favored region for fruit, wheat, the vine, and tobacco, to humid subtropical along the east, suitable for a great variety of crops, to subtropical and tropical semiarid and arid regions over the bulk of the interior.

Precipitation varies from 4 to 6 inches in the west to over 70 inches in very small portions on the eastern side of the mountains. Only 2.8 percent of the country has an average of over 40 inches of precipitation, only 10.2 percent has over 30 inches, the amount needed for intensive farming with the rates of evaporation characteristic of the country. An additional 11.4 percent has between 25 and 30 inches, which means that only 21.6 percent has annual rainfall adequate to support successful crop production. At the other extreme, 30.3 percent has less than 10 inches, 64.7 percent less than 20 inches, and 78.4 percent less than 25 inches. Aridity is, then, the keynote of much of South African climate. It may be further measured by the low runoff, only 8 percent as compared with 57 percent in the Netherlands or 31.5 percent in the Thames Valley. Other disadvantages of the climate include the high variability in rainfall, the occurrence of violent storms in the rainy season which contribute to the serious soil erosion problem, and the high seasonality of rainfall. Over 85 percent of precipitation occurs in the months from October to April, with virtually no rain falling the rest of the year over the bulk of the country. Exceptions to this generalization occur in the small Mediterranean region, where rainfall maxima are in winter, and on the south and east coasts where rain falls year round though with increasingly marked summer maxima toward the north.

From the standpoint of temperature there is a remarkable uniformity of mean annual temperatures over the greater part of the country, an effect of the plateau structure of the country. The most striking differences in mean annual temperature are between those of the west coast, affected by the cold Benguela Current, and those of the east coast, influenced by the warm Mozambique Current. On the other hand, there are considerable differences in the annual temperature ranges, with greater extremes occurring in the inland locations. Sharp frosts occur in most of the area once or more times in the winter, while high summer temperatures reduce the effectiveness of the rainfall. On the highveld the winter cold and increased diurnal and annual ranges of temperature limit the production of tropical fruit, while winters are seldom sufficiently cold to permit the growth of middle latitude deciduous fruit. Yields of corn on the plateau are reduced by the short growing season, by extremes of temperature and humidity, and by the occurrence of periodic droughts.

SOILS. In general, the soils of South Africa are relatively poor and difficult to manage. There is often a serious deficiency in phosphorus, humus content is low, soils mechanically weathered from ancient rocks are liable to compaction, there is much leaching in the rainy season, termites and grass fires have deleterious effects, and large areas are stony or mountainous. Elevation, steepness of slope, and rainfall characteristics lead to much soil erosion with losses estimated at 300 to 400 million tons of soil annually. Despite the difficulties of soil management, progress has been made in the scientific understanding and treatment of soils and since 1946 there has been a multipronged soil conservation program which has been increasingly effective in preventing erosion, in upgrading the vegetational cover, and in preventing losses through inadequate water control.

It is clear, then, that South African agriculture is faced with numerous and difficult physical problems. The combined deficiencies result in reducing the really favorable areas—as to climate, landform, and soil—to only about 10 percent of the total area. While it has frequently been suggested that Natal would someday be the garden province, even this climatically favored region is mostly one of medium or low agricultural productivity and stands today as a deficit producing area. Good quality lands in Natal are confined to only 5 percent of the total, with the best areas found in the 5- to 20-mile-wide coastal belt; 70 percent is classed as having moderate capacity and 25 percent as possessing only very limited potentialities.

Merino sheep at Maclear, Cape Province
Aridity over most of South Africa limits the extension of tillage agriculture and about 90 percent of the country is used for stock breeding purposes. Wool ranks second to gold among the Republic's exports.

THE NATURE OF AGRICULTURE

THE IMPORTANCE OF PASTORALISM. The average low capacity of the land in the Republic explains the high importance of extensive grazing, the predominance of pastoralism in the agricultural scene, and the fact that wool is the most important surplus product from the land. From the early days, cattle and sheep raising have been the principal interests of the rural population, with the main pastoral products being wool, mohair, cattle hides, sheep and lamb skins, and goat and kid skins. Even today, nearly 90 percent of the country's total area is used for stock breeding purposes, and animal husbandry accounts for about 45 percent of the total annual gross value of agricultural production. This does represent a reduction from about 73 percent of the gross value of agriculture in 1917-18. Difficulties in livestock grazing are considerable, including the low carrying capacity of the drier regions, losses which are sustained in drought years, the difficulty of improving the veld grasses, and the prevalence of animal diseases in the hotter areas. In the northwest Cape, where rainfall is below 6 inches a year, about 66 acres are required to maintain one head of cattle or 11 acres for one sheep; in the vast Karroo, with from 6 to 10 inches of rain yearly, from 4½ to 12 acres are required per sheep though it is considered that there is substantial scope for increasing the capacity by veld improvement and provision for supplementary feeding; there are similar possibilities in the semiarid areas of the northern Cape, southwest Orange Free State, and the northern Transvaal.

Wool is the most important pastoral product and ranks second only to gold among the country's exports. The present sheep population is about 38 million, of which about 3.8 million are owned by non-Europeans. Approximately 85 percent of the sheep are wooled and 84 percent of these are merinos, South Africa producing about a seventh of the world's merino clip. The arid Great Karroo is the homeland of the South African merino sheep and Cape Province has about 65 percent of the sheep population of the country; the Orange Free State ranks second with 22 percent. About 90 percent of the wool clip is exported, the United Kingdom normally taking about a quarter and France following in importance. The marked fluctuations in wool prices result in greatly varied annual earnings, the peak having been reached in 1950–51 with a total value of clip of $254 million; the 1960–61 clip was valued at $126.7 million. Average wool yields per sheep have gradually increased from about 6.2 pounds in 1931 to 7.5 pounds in 1939 and about 8.5 pounds since 1950.

The center of the mohair industry is the eastern Cape Province. At present, the mohair goat population is about 875,000 and the annual mohair production runs around 7.5 million pounds, including about 1 million pounds from Basutoland. This is the third largest production in the world. Prices have improved substantially in recent years, permitting an increase in the value of exports from $5.0 million in 1957–58 to $8.5 million in 1960–61.

The beef industry of South Africa is based primarily upon Africander cattle, an indigenous breed well adjusted to local conditions and also a good draft animal, but other breeds are also raised, particularly Friesland, Jersey, and Shorthorn types. Bantu own about 42 percent of the approximately 12 million head. Production, which is mainly on an extensive basis from the veld, is not adequate to meet domestic needs, so that South Africa imports a substantial number of slaughter cattle from adjacent territories. Numerous European breeds of cattle are kept on intensive dairy farms whose output has increased greatly over prewar years; dairy products also come from multipurpose cattle kept on the natural grazing. Ostriches are now raised only in the Oudtshoorn district; whereas the ostrich population was about 780,000 in 1920, it was only 30,000 to 40,000 in 1962.

TILLAGE AGRICULTURE. Fifty years ago South Africa was unable to feed itself despite the fact that farming had been the traditional occupation for over 250 years. Today it produces most of its food requirements and about 25 to 30 percent of the agricultural raw materials consumed by secondary industry, and derives about a quarter of its total export earnings from crop and livestock products. Production of practically all important agricultural and pastoral products is substantially above local demand (except for wheat, cotton, and occasionally meat), which results in large quantities being exported, often at a substantial loss.

Practices in tillage farming remained poor for many years, the average farmer lacking a tradition or skill in this activity. But important changes have occurred in recent decades and particularly during and after World War II. In the past decade, the value of agricultural production has increased about 50 percent, the revolution in agriculture being characterized by a great increase in mechanization (the number of tractors rising from 6,019 in 1937 to 22,292

Africander bulls on a stud farm in the Orange Free State
The beef industry of South Africa is based primarily upon this indigenous breed.

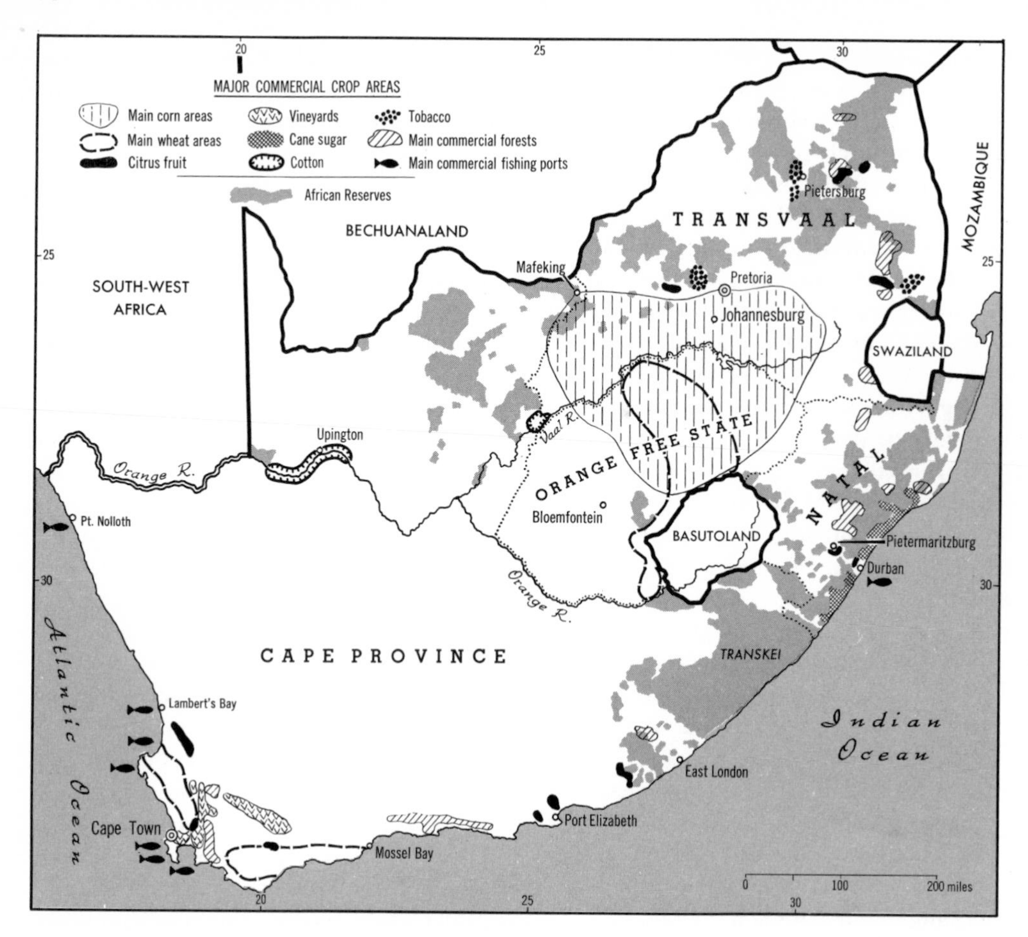

Map 91. Major commercial crop, forestry, and fishery areas of South Africa; location of African reserves

Plowing a field in the "maize triangle" of the highveld
Corn is the main field crop in South Africa and is now produced in surplus. The number of tractors in use increased from 6,019 in 1937 to 106,374 in 1958.

in 1946 and 106,374 in mid-1958), a considerable replacement of oxen by beef and dairy cattle, greater attention to pasture improvement and rotational cropping, more regional specialization, increased application of fertilizer, and a reduction in the average size of farms except in the semiarid Karroo and the arid Kalahari. Standards of Bantu farming remain very low and are only now being given serious attention; average holdings in the reserves are extremely small.

A feature of South African agriculture is the controlled marketing of a variety of crops and livestock products. Some 17 control boards regulate approximately 70 per cent of the total value of all agricultural produce marketed. Most products exported, not including wool, are sold at a loss, sometimes at a substantial cost to the government. This suggests again the dependence upon mining from which the subsidies must in large part be indirectly extracted.

MAJOR CROPS. The principal field crops of South Africa are corn, wheat, oats, barley, rye, potatoes, sugar, peanuts, and tobacco, with corn accounting for about 71.4 percent of the total cropped area of 10.5 million acres and 45 percent of the European tilled areas. Corn is the main staple food of the Bantu population and has growing importance as a fodder crop. The most important corn area is the so-called maize triangle (Map 91), extending on the highveld prairie soils below 4,000 feet from Mafeking and Vryburg in the northwest to Ermelo in the east and Wepener in the south. This region is rather sharply delineated, on the west by the 20-inch isohyet, on the north by broken country and reduced effectiveness of precipitation, and on the east by the lower temperatures and moister summers as elevation increases towards the Drakensberg Escarpment. Corn is also grown by both Europeans and Africans in the eastern areas below the Drakensberg. While practices have been deficient in the past and yields low, greater use of hybrid seed, attention to control of weeds, insect pests, and diseases, some reduction in monocultural practices, and improved fertilizing have brought average yields from about 472 pounds per acre in 1949–50 to about 755 pounds per acre in 1960–61. Total production was about 5.4 million tons in 1961–62, which, it is stated, could readily be increased to 6.0 million tons by continual application of improved practices. But this would be about double the domestic consumption and, as the export of each ton involved a loss of about $3.50 to $4.00 to the Stabilization Fund, the government was forced in 1962 to reduce the price to producers and thus discourage further expansion.

Wheat is a winter crop grown in the southwest Cape region, in the irrigated valleys of the Transvaal bushveld, and in the eastern part of the Orange Free State. Production costs are high and yields low, varying from 2½ to 10 bushels per acre. Sorghum, usually called kaffir corn, is also produced in surplus, consumption amounting to about 160 thousand tons yearly and the surplus to 68,000 to 190,000 tons. African farmers produce about half of the crop, which is used chiefly for brewing Kaffirbeer, a nutritiously rich and alcoholically weak drink.

Sugar cane is grown in the coastal belt of Natal and in a small section of the Transvaal on the Pongola River, some 600,000 acres being devoted to this crop. The main belt stretches from about 90 miles south to 170 miles north of Durban and inland mostly within 7 or 8 miles from the sea. Eighteen mills process the cane, most of them also being involved in its production. Sugar output could be greatly increased in the north if irrigation were provided and, more important, if a market could be obtained. But South Africa is a fairly marginal producer owing to only minimally satisfactory climatic conditions, a two-year maturing period, and the practice of growing cane on slopes where machines cannot be used. Nonetheless, there has been a marked improvement in yields, which increased by 35 per cent in the decade to 1959.

Of the approximately 4,700 cane growers,

Sugar-cane fields in Natal Province
About 600,000 acres in the coastal belt of Natal are planted to cane. The rugged terrain makes it difficult to introduce mechanization.

about 47 percent are Bantu, 30 percent Asian, and 23 percent European, the last accounting for about 85 percent of total output. Beginning in 1951, the United Kingdom took a fixed amount of sugar at a prearranged price each year, the Swaziland quota being integrated with that of South Africa. Following withdrawal from the Commonwealth, South Africa lost its quota, but a bilateral agreement ensured the sale of a somewhat reduced amount for a five-year period ending in 1966; the price received will also be somewhat lower but still above the world price. South Africa also benefited in 1962 from sales to the United States, resulting from manipulations with respect to Cuba's previous share of the American market.

Fruits are of considerable importance in specialized areas. Citrus orchards, which represent a $112 million investment, are found in such widely scattered areas as the western Cape, the coastal areas of the eastern Cape, around and inland from Durban in Natal, and in north, west, and eastern Transvaal. The Zebediela Estate in northern Transvaal is said to be the largest citrus estate in the world with close to one million trees planted in 1961. The citrus industry is highly organized on a cooperative basis and is greatly advantaged by off-season production with respect to the markets of the Northern Hemisphere. Like many other crops, the production of citrus fruit has been increasing somewhat more rapidly than the market justifies and in some years a portion of the crop has been sold at nonremunerative prices or has been dumped. Citrus exports, which take about three fourths of production, rank second only to corn among crop exports. Deciduous fruits come mainly from the Mediterranean region of the Cape; about half of the $56 million worth produced is exported, predominantly to Britain. Tropical fruits such as bananas, pineapples, mangoes, and papayas are grown on the coastal belt of the eastern Cape and Natal and in the lowveld of Transvaal under irrigation.

Viticulture is confined commercially to the southwest Cape where about 160,000 acres have been planted to the vine. Paarl is the main center and headquarters for the 4,500-member Cooperative Winegrowers Association (KWV), which regulates the supply of wine to the domestic market and has succeeded in enlarging the overseas market as well. The better quality wines are generally produced in the coastal belt on slightly acidic slope soils of moderate fertility and generally without irrigation. In the second main belt, along the Little Karroo, which stretches from the first mountain range to the Swartberg, the vine is grown under irrigation

A citrus farm in the Rustenberg area
About three fourths of citrus production is exported, permitting citrus fruit to rank after corn among crop exports. South Africa is advantaged in European markets by delivery in the off-season.

Vineyards near Worcester in the small dry-subtropical belt near Cape Town
About 160,000 acres are devoted to the vine and wine is South Africa's oldest export.

on rich alluvial soils and yields a sweet wine, rather than the more delicate, dry wines of the coast. Marked soil and climatic differences result in a notable variety of wines being produced within a remarkably circumscribed area. Wine is South Africa's oldest export, the first grapes having been pressed in 1859. At present, some 70 million gallons of wine are produced, with exports amounting to about 3.5 million gallons of wine and 0.5 million gallons of brandy with a total value of about $5 million. Again, there has been overproduction in recent years and the loss of Commonwealth Preference may further restrict foreign sales, but consumption of South African wine has been increasing rapidly in the United Kingdom and this may offset the less favorable factors.

Tobacco is grown fairly widely, but the main producing regions are north and west of Pretoria. South Africa changed from a deficit producer to a surplus producer in postwar years, output having increased from 30 million pounds in 1946–47 to 56 million pounds in 1961 when consumption totaled about 50 million pounds. Virginia-type tobaccos represent 97 percent of the total crop.

Over half of the cotton produced in the country is grown along the Orange River between Upington and Buchuberg. Other producing areas include the Vaal-Hartz Irrigation Scheme, the eastern Transvaal lowveld, the northern Transvaal, and the Natal, Zululand, and Swaziland areas. Production, which has ranged around 5,250 to 7,500 tons in recent years, meets about a third of domestic needs. Ginning is handled in five plants.

While South Africa is not favored physically for intensive agriculture, it is obvious that under the present population and marketing conditions there is more than adequate ability to meet demands for most commodities. And, as farming standards improve, there are opportunities for substantially greater yields on much of the area farmed at present. Eventually, however, much greater attention will have to be paid to rationalizing agriculture, to the upgrading of pasture, to the control of soil erosion, and to the extension of irrigation, including irrigation in humid regions. Particularly important, and of pressing urgency, is the need to improve all manner of land use practices in the reserve areas, while a better standard of living among the African population would quickly absorb some of the apparent surplus which now plagues organized agriculture.

IRRIGATION DEVELOPMENTS. Since water is the most serious shortage in South African agriculture, it is not surprising that increasing attention is being given to development of irrigation projects. The largest single irrigation scheme is now above the junction of the Vaal and Hartz

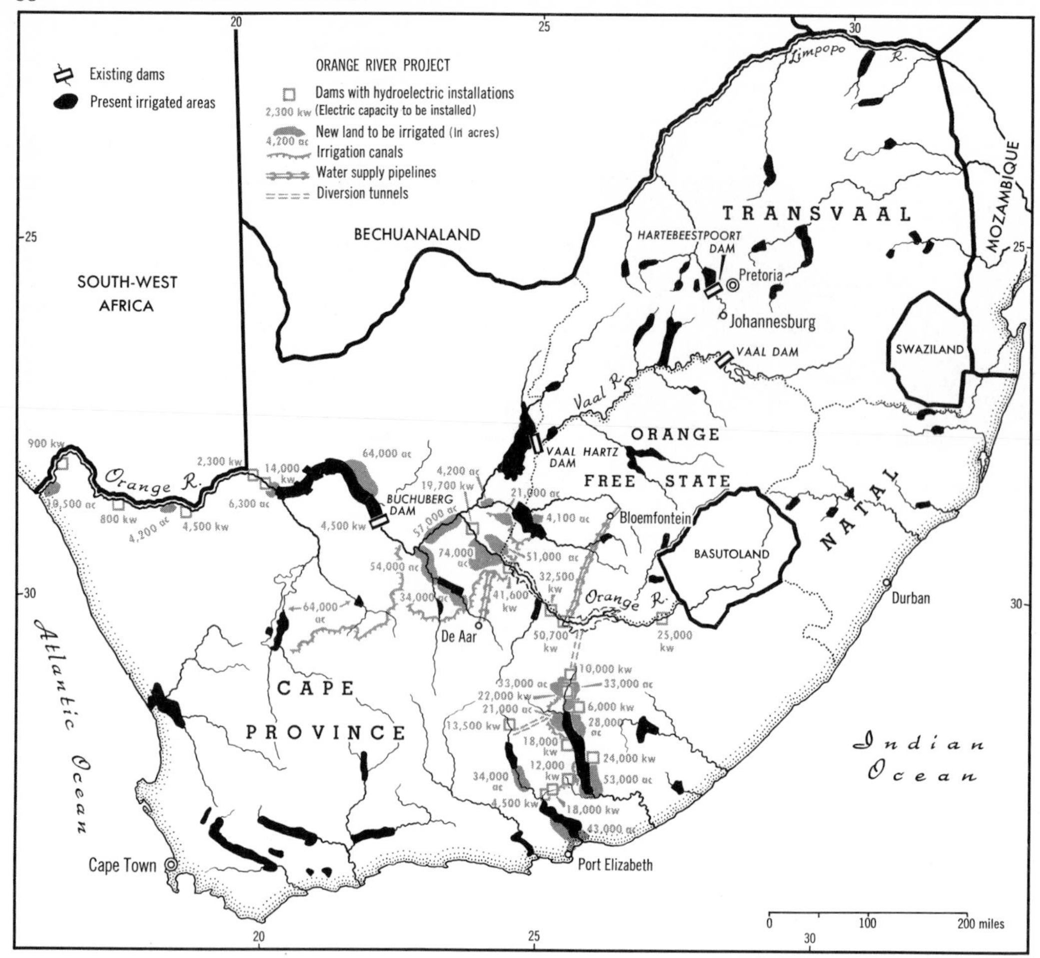

Map 92. Present irrigated areas in South Africa; details of the proposed Orange River Scheme

rivers below the Vaalhartz Dam, where water is taken from the Vaal River through a 34-foot-deep, two-mile-long cut to the Hartz River and then used to irrigate about 86,000 acres of which 20,000 acres are in the Taungs African Reserve (Map 92). The Hartebeestpoort Dam near Pretoria also feeds one of the largest irrigation schemes, and a $53 million project is under development near the Transvaal-Natal border on the Pongola River which will control nearly 150,000 acres. Other irrigation areas include the ones up- and downstream from Upington on the Orange River irrigated by the Buchuberg Dam and totaling about 38,160 acres, about 80,560 acres irrigated along the Vaal River, 55,000 acres on the Limpopo, and 15,000 acres on the Bushman and Mooi tributaries of the Tugela.

The area now irrigated totals an estimated 1.4 million acres, of which 260,000 acres are controlled by sixteen major state-built dams serving 6,000 farmers, 490,000 acres fall under 182 cooperative irrigation boards serving 8,800 farmers, and about 660,000 acres have been brought under irrigation by individual farmers. Not all of this irrigation is intensive, some acreages being subject only to supplementary or seasonal watering.

The opportunities for further irrigation are at best quite limited because only 8 percent of total rainfall ever reaches the rivers and because large quantities of available water must be developed to supply industrial, mining, and domestic requirements rather than be used for irrigation. The country's largest storage dam, the Vaal Dam, about 60 miles southeast of Johannesburg, for example, is used mainly to supply the mining and industrial areas of the Transvaal and the Orange Free State. Indeed, it is not unlikely that in specific areas there will be pressure within a few decades to buy out existing irrigation rights in order to secure additional quantities of water for nonagricultural purposes.

Additional difficulties facing the development of irrigation stem from the lack of suitable sites; characteristically, either a very high dam or a dam which is likely to flood extensive areas is needed. There are no natural lakes in which water can be stored. Furthermore, there are no large underground basins, and it appears that water is now being drawn from subterranean sources more rapidly than it is being replenished, which is a source of serious concern for several irrigated areas. Nor can reuse of industrial water or the partial demineralization of brackish waters provide more than a minimal part of South Africa's water needs.

In 1962 the government announced plans for the most ambitious water control scheme thus far considered—a multistage, multipurpose plan to harness the waters of the 1,300-mile Orange River, South Africa's most important river, whose basin covers about half of the country (Map 92). The entire project is expected to take 30 years to complete and to cost about $630 million, the first phase involving an expenditure of over $150 million. When the project is completed, twelve dams and weirs, of which three will be major, will comprise the main features of this scheme. Some water will be diverted from the Orange to the Fish and Sundays rivers by 51-mile and 32-mile tunnels, because insufficient land with irrigable soil exists in the catchment of the Orange River, while the Fish and Sundays valleys have an urgent need for supplementary water and large areas available for further irrigation. Ultimately, some 756,000 acres will be brought under irrigation, about 70 percent in the Orange Basin, the rest in the other basins. The main dam at Ruigte, which will be 260 feet high and 2,130 feet long in the first phase, can be raised subsequently to give adequate regulatory capacity and to offset the accumulation of silt; its capacity will be double that of the Vaal Dam.

While the main purpose of the Orange River Project is to extend the area under irrigation, it will also involve the installation of 20 hydroelectric stations with a total eventual capacity of 199,600 kw, about one sixth of which must be used for pumping water. In addition, some 100 million gallons a day will be pumped to cities and towns, including Bloemfontein, Kimberley, and Port Elizabeth.

It is estimated that the country's agricultural production will be increased $160 million annually by the Orange River Project, and that the project may permit achieving self-sufficiency in cotton and wheat. The first phase of the scheme will involve construction of two major dams, the Orange–Fish tunnel, pipelines to two cities, and large irrigation systems.

The problems inherent in water control schemes in South Africa are well illustrated by the Orange River Project. The characteristic relatively small runoff is seen in the mean annual discharge at the Orange mouth of 9,116,000 acre feet from a catchment area of 328,000 square miles. The aridity of large parts of the country is illustrated by the fact that over 98 percent of runoff is contributed by the 113,000 square miles of the Vaal and Upper Orange. The problem of competing uses is seen in the decision to reserve all waters of the Vaal for its catchment and of the Caledon for the Orange Free State. The relative poverty of the country in hydroelectric resources is also illustrated, for the combined capacity of the 20 installations will be only a fifth of the capacity of the new Komati coal-fired plant. Finally, it may be noted that the costs-to-benefits ratio of the Orange River Project is not particularly favorable.

THE AFRICAN RESERVES

THE PRESENT POSITION. The sharply contrasting and special position of the African reserves

A typical Zulu kraal near Mahashini, northern Natal
African reserves cover about 13 percent of South Africa and have an average density of about 87 per square mile, as compared with about 30 per square mile for the remainder of the country.

makes it essential to examine the conditions that now prevail in these areas and the plans which are being developed regarding them. In 1962 there were 264 areas in South Africa reserved for residence by Africans (Map 91). Covering about 13 percent of the country, they are considered the homeland of all Africans, who comprise 68.2 percent of the total population. However, the estimated actual population of the reserves is 4.76 million, the remaining Africans being found in European farming areas or in the urban communities. The actual population gives a density of about 87 per square mile as compared with about 30 for the remainder of the country.

The reserves vary in size from 16,000 square miles for the Transkei, larger than Switzerland, to small bits of isolated blocks. Their physical conditions also vary enormously. The largest reserves are in the better watered areas along the east coast; in fact, 76 percent of their total area is in regions receiving 20 inches or more of rain yearly as compared with 35 percent for the country as a whole, but a substantial portion is located in the semiarid regions along the north and northwest. And the moister Transkei and Natal reserves are, unfortunately, situated in the regions of roughest topography in the Republic, with only 11 percent and 23 percent of their areas classified as flat to gently undulating. The reserves are characterized by the general absence of large towns, scarce mineral resources except for asbestos, platinum, and chrome, very limited development of manufacturing, and an entirely inadequate infrastructure.

From the land use standpoint the keynote is overpopulation of people and livestock, and there is little doubt that the carrying capacity has been deteriorating in recent decades. Holdings are too small to permit modern farming practices or to support a peasant farmer and his family. The reserves do not produce adequate food to support their inhabitants and are thus dependent upon supplies from the European areas. The Tomlinson Commission estimated in 1956 that about half the population of the reserves needed to be taken off the land, and developments to date do not justify reducing this estimate.

Other problems pertaining to the reserves are comparable to those of other regions of sub-Saharan Africa: the deficiencies of tribal tenure, of communal grazing, of excessive dependence upon the work of women, and of backward

A view in the Transkei, South Africa's largest African reserve
This reserve is being used as a model in the development of Bantustans, which are to be partly administered by African authorities. Overgrazing and overcropping have led to serious erosion problems in much of the Transkei.

farming techniques. What is needed is a multifaceted program of resettlement and agricultural modernization and the provision of opportunities for employment outside of farming.

PLANS FOR BANTU STATES. The South African response to these problems closely reflects the official policy of separate development. It calls for consolidating the 264 separated reserves into an undetermined number of so-called Bantustans reserved for residence by Africans and each hopefully inspiring the love and loyalty of members of the major tribal group inhabiting them or absent from them in other parts of the country. Earlier, tentative maps of the Bantustans carried a footnote reading, "Inclusion of protectorates within these areas is here assumed," making density figures appear somewhat more attractive, but the impropriety of thus including land outside the Republic was soon appreciated.

In 1961 the government launched a five-year development plan for the Bantu areas, estimated to involve a total expenditure of $160 million by 1966. The largest segment of proposed spending, 67.5 percent of the total, is allocated for housing and village construction. Some 81,505 houses are to be built, over half in Natal. In so far as possible, Bantu are to be the contractors and workers and they may also take long-term loans from the Bantu Investment Corporation to build their own homes. The program also calls for placing 32,000 acres under irrigation, afforesting 117,500 acres, putting 21,000 acres under fiber cultivation, and improving the infrastructure of roads, water supply, and power.

Consolidation of the reserves into aggregated blocks involves the purchase of some land from private owners and the allocation of state-owned land to the separate Bantustans. By mid-1962 only 2.8 million acres remained to be secured before the stated goal of a total area of 41.1 million acres had been achieved. In addition to consolidation of the reserves it is also intended that 444 so-called Black Spots, where Africans have settled in European areas, will be eliminated.

Political changes are also proposed for the Bantustans, where a degree of African rule will be extended. "Bantu Authorities" will have power to impose taxation, but the European government will retain control over external affairs, defense, certain aspects of the administration of justice, posts and telegraphs, railways and harbors, immigration, currency, public laws, and customs and excise.

The Transkei has received the greatest attention to date under the development program and is considered to be a kind of model for other Bantustans. The first Bantu Authority was set up there in 1959, a degree of home rule was extended in 1962, and a representative assembly was elected in 1963, composed of 45 elected members, four Paramount Chiefs, and 60 other chiefs. Revenue from all direct taxes now paid to state, provincial, and territorial authorities and taxes paid by territorial citizens outside the reserve will accrue to the Transkei, which will be granted additional sums by the Republican government.

The Transkei is slated to receive about 17 percent of the new African homes under the development plan and work has begun on the irrigation of 12,000 acres in that territory. There are, without doubt, substantial opportunities for improving conditions and land use in the Transkei, but the program cannot be expected to make it economically viable unless manufacturing establishments move to it or to the border areas in substantial numbers.

Just what impact the development of Bantustans will have upon the evolving social, economic, and political situation in South Africa is difficult to predict at this juncture. Very considerable unrest occurred in Pondoland in 1960–61, there were almost immediate demands for further assignment of authority or for the granting of complete independence, there has been pressure to reduce the proportion of chiefs to elected representatives in the assembly, and a problem of potentially serious dimensions is the frustration of the 250 university graduates in the Transkei who lack any real degree of free expression.

Proponents of Bantustans see them as a logical fulfillment of "constructive" apartheid, as proof that the whites are concerned with enlarging the opportunities for African advancement, and as an answer to foreign critics of South African racial policies. Some South Africans consider that the proposed programs extend too great authority to the African who, they maintain, will inevitably misuse it, while other white South Africans resent being taxed for support of the program. Liberal critics of the Bantustans, on the other hand, see them as simply an extension of the uneconomic and impractical apartheid system. Specifically, it is claimed that their promotion will stunt normal economic growth by restricting markets, that the restriction of industrialization in the reserves to that which can be started by African entrepreneurs will greatly limit development, that the national economy will be fragmented rather than desirably unified, that the cooperation of the races, upon which the country's prosperity has been based, will be greatly reduced, and that the system will fail to satisfy world opinion because it is not democratic and does not represent an equitable allotment of resources.

One of the real tests of the program will be whether enough employment opportunities are created in or adjacent to the Bantustans to absorb the surplus population within them. As has already been suggested, this seems unlikely to occur. As Drs. Fair and Green state:

> . . . while a policy of industrial dispersal is more vigorously advocated in South Africa than anywhere else in sub-Saharan Africa, it is in this very country that the urban and industrial tide of concentration is running the strongest, and that the gap between the levels of development of the more backward areas and of the more advanced economic islands is most clearly discernible.[3]

Finally, the plan for development of the Bantustans does nothing toward solving the problem of Africans in the urban communities. The government points with pride toward the improvement of housing and amenities in the African townships in recent years, a total of $280 million of government funds having been spent on rehousing the urban Bantu in the ten years to 1962 in addition to large municipally sponsored housing projects. An indication of the magnitude of the problem faced is suggested by the rapid increase of Bantu in urban areas—from about 900,000 in 1938 to 1,689,053 in 1946 and 2,622,872 in 1957. But the continuance and increasing severity of racial discrimination in these urban areas robs the whole program of being the sincerely positive program its initiators would like to have it considered.

Despite the criticisms that apply to the organization of Bantu states, the program for the economic betterment of the Bantu reserves represents the first major effort to work toward a more rational use of their resources, and this must bring some lasting benefits. Furthermore,

[3] T. J. D. Fair and L. P. Green, "Development of the 'Bantu Homelands,'" *Optima* (March, 1962), p. 10.

it indicates that the present government accepts that *baaskap* (boss-ship) cannot work and that a white minority cannot perpetually rule four times their number of African, Coloured, and Asian peoples. As Munger points out, the Transkei political changes "do represent a significant advance in the psychological conditioning of white opinion."[4]

FORESTRY AND FISHERIES

FORESTRY

The national timber resources of South Africa are very limited. Scrub forests exist, chiefly along the east coast, and acacia forests cover extensive areas but the only indigenous high forests are confined to the constant rainfall area in the south and to the seaward slopes of the mountains, occupying altogether only about 0.2 percent (515,000 acres) of the country. The slow rate of growth of many indigenous species and the desire to reduce expenditure on timber imports have led to a vigorous afforestation program utilizing exotic species, the total area in plantations now being almost four times greater than that covered by natural high forests. By 1980 it is expected that about 3 million acres will be covered by forest plantations, but opportunities for further extension are not great.

The most important tree economically is the black wattle, cut by over a thousand growers from plantations covering about 780,000 acres, chiefly in the so-called mist belt of Natal at elevations ranging from 2,000 to 4,500 feet. Pietermaritzburg is the main center and has the largest of nine wattle extract factories. South Africa ranks first in the world in the production of wattle extract. Most exports are in the form of a solid concentrate, but some dried bark is also sold abroad. Exports of extract and bark were valued at $2.85 million in 1961, a reduction from the previous year's exports of $3.37 million, in large part the result of a price war with the Argentinian manufacturers of quebracho. The remainder of the tree is used for pit props, as fuel, and for the manufacture of chipboards.

Eucalyptus plantations, covering about 360,000 acres, are especially important for the mines. There is a growing acreage under conifers, now totaling some 700,000 acres, and a small area in poplar, used for matchsticks. Comparatively new industries in the Republic are pulp mills, the Enstra and Tugela mills of the South African Pulp and Paper Industries Ltd. having an output of about 100,000 tons in 1961. The rayon pulp mill at Umkomaas, previously noted, uses eucalyptus, and exports most of its production. The local timber industry supplies only about 40 percent of the country's total requirement of about 20.5 million cubic feet per year.

FISHERIES

South Africa ranks as the largest producer of fish and fish products in Africa and in the Southern Hemisphere. Together with the fishing industry of South-West Africa, with which it is closely integrated, there is a capital investment of $56 million in boats, buildings, and factories and an employed force of 7,500 fishermen and 20,000 other workers. The fleet includes 200 large diesel vessels, 70 steam and motor trawlers, and 470 smaller line and rock lobster boats. Fishing is carried on all along the extended coast of South and South-West Africa with concentrations along the southwest Cape and along the coast of South-West Africa, the Atlantic side being favored by the cool Benguela Current. Rock lobsters, found between low water and depths of 20 to 25 fathoms northward to Luderitz, have a particularly high value, but the practice of catching excessively small lobsters presents something of a threat to the future of this industry. South Africa engaged in whaling operations in the Antarctic for about 25 years to 1957, when its one factory ship was sold to Japan; offshore whaling is carried on from Durban and Saldanha Bay in the winter. In 1961, ten whale catchers aided by two spotter aircraft participated in this branch of the industry.

[4] Edwin S. Munger, "Transkei Independence: Fact or Fantasy?" *Africa Report* (May, 1962), p. 6.

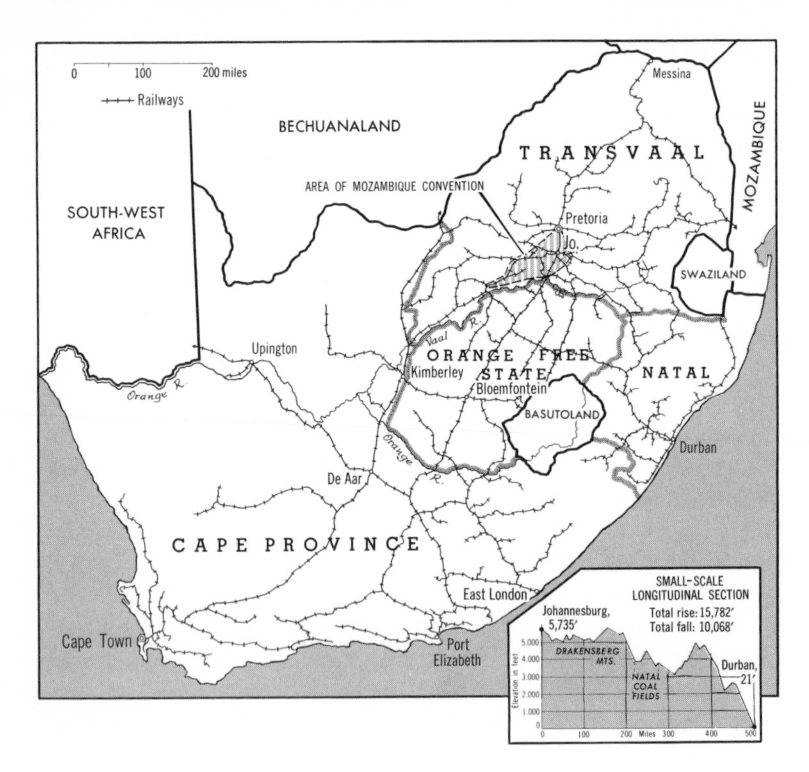

Map 93. South African transport —railways

The total fish catch has grown rapidly, being over ten times the prewar level and breaking records in five successive years to 1963. Exports of fish and whale products were valued at over $64 million in 1961 with the most important products being canned pilchards (one third of total value), fish meal (a fifth), rock lobster products (a sixth), and fish and whale oil (an eighth). Fish meal is used mainly in livestock feeds; oils are used in the production of edible oils and fats, paints, and varnishes.

The Blue Train in the Hex River valley on the main line between Cape Town and Johannesburg
Railways provide the backbone of the South African transport system, partly because they are shielded from competition by regulations on road haulers.

TRANSPORTATION AND TRADE

TRANSPORTATION

Reference has already been made to certain of the features of South African transport, so that only a brief summary is required at this point. The railways provide the dominant form of inland transport, in large part because of the considerable importance of bulk mineral and agricultural commodities and the substantial distances separating producing areas from ports

Map 94. South African transport —roads

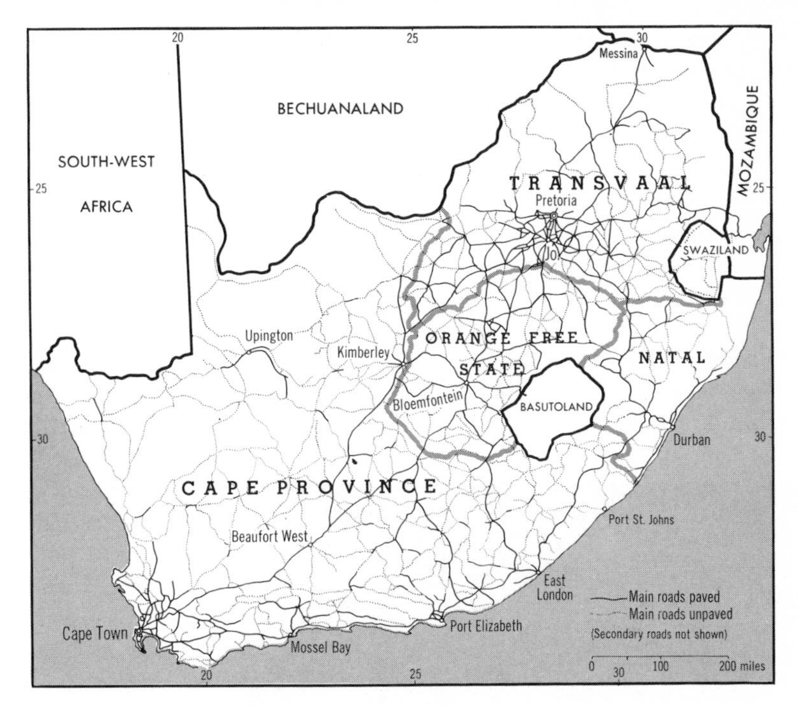

and consuming regions, but also because they have been favored by rigid restrictions on highway competition. With some 13,608 route miles of line, South Africa has at least a rudimentary network (Map 93) connecting all of the major cities and towns and possessing links with South-West Africa, the Rhodesias, and Mozambique. Freight hauled has increased from 37.8 million tons in 1939 to 89.2 million tons in 1961. The state-owned South Africa Railways also maintains regular highway services on routes totaling 31,530 miles and carrying about 4 million tons of freight yearly.

So great was the expansion of traffic in postwar years that the railways found increasing difficulty in handling the tonnage offered and a major crisis had developed by 1954. Despite an accelerated investment program, involving an expenditure of $1.82 billion in the 15 years to mid-1962 for purchase of additional power and rolling stock, electrification of some of the lines, double-tracking in a few places, and other modernization programs, the railways were unable to lift about 5 million tons a year in 1957 and 1958 and, despite a record tonnage hauled in 1961, were still having difficulty in meeting all the requirements. The carriage of coal, lumber, and manganese was particularly limited in some years, but the greatest complaints have come from industrialists who object that the system of priorities adopted and the rating policies favoring agricultural commodities and bulk ores have operated to their disadvantage in competing with foreign manufactures. The railways do, however, operate at a profit, in contrast to many of the lines of tropical Africa, the surplus of $28 million in 1960–61 having been a record.

The Republic also has approximately 200,000 miles of roads, of which about 8,700 are paved (Map 94). Despite the restrictions on road haulage which would compete with the railways, there has been sufficient need for urban and intercity freight traffic to justify an increase of commercial vehicles, excluding buses, from 138,000 in 1951 to 235,000 in 1960. The South African Railways fleet accounted for less than 1 percent of this number. The total registration of motor vehicles in 1960 was 1,237,000.

An extensive network of domestic air services

is operated by the regular services of the South African airways. International flights to Europe have recently been restricted to routes via Portuguese areas because of denial of landing rights in independent African countries. A particular feature of air traffic in South Africa is the special service run by the Witwatersrand Native Labour Association (WNLA) to pick up and return African mineworkers from such areas as Bechuanaland, Northern Rhodesia, and Nyasaland. Inaugurated in 1952, the WNLA air service now operates regularly on seven different routes radiating from the main airport at

The central business district and port of Durban
Durban is the leading port of Africa, handling about 10 million tons of cargo annually. The narrow entrance to the harbor is seen in the extreme left background.

Francistown; in 1961 it carried 110,000 passengers. The WNLA also operates an integrated service of canoes, river and lake craft, trucks, and buses, and has contributed to the construction of roads in the remote areas from which labor is recruited.

The ports of South Africa are fairly well spaced along the coast, but none of them are first-class natural harbors and all have had to be more or less extensively improved to handle modern vessels and rapidly increasing tonnages. Because of its position as the domestic port nearest to the highly productive areas of the Transvaal, Durban takes pride of place among South African ports, handling almost half of inbound cargo and over half of exports moving via these ports. Its total freight traffic has increased from 4.8 million tons in 1938 to 10.1 million tons in 1961, making it the leading port on the continent. Durban now has a fine, almost landlocked bay covering 4,122 acres and accessible by a channel with minimum depths of 40 feet; the bay was formerly covered largely by mangrove swamps and was partially closed by a sand bar. The port facilities include 8,462 yards of wharfage with alongside depths exceeding 30 feet, 1,285 yards of quay space with lesser depths, special mechanical coal and ore handling gear, large cold stores, and a sizable drydock. As already noted, Durban is forced to share with other ports the rich traffic of the Transvaal, with Lourenço Marques because that port is 119 miles closer to Johannesburg and because of the Mozambique Convention, with Port Elizabeth and East London partly because of necessity to employ all available rail lines in view of the pressure upon the railways in postwar years. In 1960–61 the South African Railways forwarded 2.27 million tons to the Mozambique railways and received 1.34 million tons. The vast bulk of this tonnage was in transit through Lourenço Marques.

Cape Town ranks second to Durban among South African ports. It handled 4.7 million tons in 1961, comprising close to a quarter of both imports and exports moving through domestic ports. Its position near the tip of the continent and as the main passenger port results in a greater number of ship entries than for Durban. Forty deepwater vessels can be berthed in the docks at Table Bay, which has large pre-cooling stores and grain elevators as well as the largest drydock in the Southern Hemisphere. Material dredged from the harbor has been used to create a large foreshore area which contains adequate new space for port activity as well as for extension of the city's business district.

Port Elizabeth, handling some 2 million tons of South African port traffic, has long enjoyed a reputation as the country's most efficient harbor.

Expected increases in traffic, especially of manganese and iron ores, have led to the recent provision of fully mechanized ore loading facilities which have added about 1.5 million tons to the capacity of the port. This and other improvements permit the port to accept 45,000-ton ore carriers and to have a total capacity of about 4 million tons a year. East London, Mossel Bay, and Port Nolloth are the only other South African ports of any importance. East London, the only river port in the Republic, has recently been improved by the construction of a turning basin at the mouth, the dimensions of which previously restricted movements into and out of the port.

TRADE

Numerous factors influencing domestic and foreign trade of the Republic have been touched upon in previous sections. Suffice it to note, in conclusion, that South Africa accounts at present for about 21 percent of total African imports and 28 percent of its exports. Only a worsening political situation would have a profound influence on the level of trade, though losses in specific products such as fruit, wine, and sugar may result from the end of preference arrangements with the Commonwealth and from the evolving position of the European Economic Community and its overseas associates. Exports of the more important commodities for 1961 are shown in Table 43.

Cape Town Harbor in Table Bay
Material dredged from the bay to provide the large new dock on the right has been used to fill in a foreshore area which is the site of several large new office buildings.

Table 43. Major exports of South Africa, 1961; total exports and imports, 1938–1962

Minerals and metals	*1961 exports (in million $)*	*Agricultural products*	*1961 exports (in million $)*
Gold	685.7	*Animal products*	
Diamonds	117.2	Wool	153.1
Atomic energy material	111.1	Hides and skins	32.1
Copper ore and ingots	36.2	Angora hair	10.9
Asbestos	33.0	Meat	9.6
Ferroalloys	20.9	Butter	9.3
Manganese ore	16.1	Eggs	4.1
Lead ore and concentrate	15.3		
Chrome ore	8.3	*Crops*	
Coal	7.2	Citrus fruit	26.4
Iron ore	5.5	Other fruit	65.3
Vanadium oxide	5.0	Fruit juices	3.4
Andalusite and sillimanite	4.2	Wines	4.9
Antimony concentrate	3.1	Other beverages	2.6
		Corn and products	58.3
Manufactures		Sugar	23.5
		Peanuts and oil	19.2
Motor vehicles	53.4	Tobacco and mnfgs.	3.7
Iron and steel	29.6	Sorghum	3.6
Machinery	26.5	Other nonedible agricultural products	13.1
Railway material	3.3	Other foodstuffs	27.4
Other metal products	26.5		
Explosives	7.2	*Fishery products*	
Furnace oils	6.2	Fish	41.3
Insecticides	3.0	Fish meal	14.9
Other chemicals	19.8	Whale and fish oil	8.1
Clothing	6.6		
Other textile products	9.2	*Forest products*	
Shoes	3.4	Pulp	13.4
Tires and tubes	4.7	Wattle bark extract	9.1
Other leather and rubber	3.8		
Wood products	5.3	*Miscellaneous*	27.1
Books, paper, stationery	8.0	*Re-exports*	142.8
Jewelry, etc.	1.4	*Total*	2,013.9

	Exports (in million $)			*Total imports (in million $)*
	Merchandise	*Gold*	*Total*	
1938	163	355	518	464
1948	557	654	1,211	1,424
1958	1,096	621	1,717	1,555
1960	1,238	802	2,040	1,555
1961	1,328	686	2,014	1,406
1962	1,324	891	2,215	1,434

Sources: Republic of South Africa, *Monthly Bulletin of Statistics* (July, 1962), pp. 62–64; (May, 1963), pp. 57–59; U.N., *Statistical Yearbook, 1962* (New York, 1963); U.N., *Monthly Bulletin of Statistics* (May, 1963).

CHAPTER TWENTY-THREE

South-West Africa

South-West Africa, a German colony from 1892 until World War I, was then mandated to South Africa by the League of Nations and has since been administered largely as an integral part of that country. The United Nations lists it as a "former mandated area," because South Africa has refused to recognize any trusteeship obligations, while the U.N. has refused to recognize its incorporation into the Republic. Following a long series of efforts by the U.N. and much bitter criticism of South African policies respecting the territory, the U.N. was finally permitted to send a team of observers there in 1962. The most serious criticisms that may be made of the administration of the territory are comparable to those directed at South Africa itself: imposition of apartheid, and failure to give adequate attention to the advance of its nonwhite populace. As will be seen, the vast bulk of development investments have pertained to European mining, fishing, and agriculture, while the non-European has played the usual role of migrant worker. Internally, the country was divided until 1961 into a Police Zone in the southern two thirds, where most of the land is European-owned, and the Native Territories of Ovamboland, the Kaokoveld, and Okavango, in the northern third, which were administered by the traditional system of indirect rule through local chiefs. While the Police Zone was extended to the north in 1961, this has made little actual difference thus far in local administration.

South-West Africa has an area of 317,725 square miles, about the size of France and the United Kingdom combined. This excludes the Walvis Bay region, a 434-square-mile enclave administered by South-West Africa, but actually part of the Cape Province. The population of the territory was estimated in the 1960 census to be 525,064, comprised of 73,154 whites, 427,980 Africans, and 23,930 "Coloureds"; its mid-1961 population is given as 534,000. The largest number of whites are Afrikaans-speaking; the German-speaking population ranks second while the English-speaking inhabitants are a relatively small group.

The African population includes about 10,000 to 15,000 primitive, nomadic Bushmen and about 30,000 Nama, or Hottentots. The Bushmen are now largely confined to the northeast and semidesert areas along the Bechuanaland border, while the Hottentots live either on reserves in the south or on European farms and in the towns. The largest of the Bantu tribal groups, the Ovambo, has some 255,000 members living in the north and about 35,000 in the predominantly European areas, where they work under 18-month contracts administered by the South-West Africa Native Labour Association. Best organized of the several Bantu tribes, they provide the largest number of laborers for farming and the mines. The Berg Damara and Hereros, other Bantu groups, have reserves in the south; each tribe numbers about 30,000, but the Hereros were a larger group until being decimated in a revolt against the Germans in 1893.

South-West Africa has an over-all density under 2 per square mile, but large parts are almost uninhabited, including the coastal Namib Desert (except for the ports and diamond-mining centers), the steppelands of the east, and the Etosha Pan Game Reserve in the southern part of the northern plain. The more heavily populated regions are the central uplands, containing a substantial portion of the European population and the capital city of Windhoek with a 1960 population of 35,000, including 19,000 whites.

PHYSICAL CONDITIONS

Most of South-West Africa is part of the great plateau of South Africa, with an average elevation of about 3,600 feet interspersed with broken mountain masses ranging from 6,000 to 8,000 feet and extending with interruptions from the southwest to the Kaokoveld Mountains. The plateau area swells towards the center of the country, having elevations of 4,000 to 5,000 feet around Windhoek, and subsides into a vast alluvial plain in the north, about 2,000 to 3,000 feet above sea level. A thousand-mile-long coastal plain extends the entire length of the country and inland from 60 to 100 miles.

The country is largely arid and semiarid. The Namib Desert along the coast is one of the driest in the world, with averages of less than one inch of precipitation yearly. Inland, rainfall increases from 3 to 6 inches in the dry Namaqualand in the south to 14–16 inches in the center, and about 22 inches in the north. As is usual in dry areas, rainfall is highly unreliable, and the economy suffered severely from a drought lasting six years into 1962. As rainfall is often inadequate, underground water is tapped where possible. Ranchers must often construct relatively large dams to hold surface runoff, and, since precipitation varies greatly from year to year, efforts must frequently be made to store adequate stock water for more than one year. Water is also obtained from the perennial rivers such as the Orange, Okavango, and Cunene, and by tapping the water flowing beneath the surface in the sandy beds of seasonal streams. In the Caprivi strip, the Zambezi, Chobe, and Kwando are perennial streams, and extensive marshy areas occur along the last, but no modern developments have occurred in this extremely remote area. Vegetation consists mainly of a variety of grasses and bushes, particularly the thornbush.

AGRICULTURE

Grazing is the most characteristic occupation of South-West Africa. Sheep and goats predominate in the south, with the karakul sheep being of particular importance. Introduced early in the century, karakul sheep provide one of the main exports of the country in the form of pelts used mostly in the United States for the production of Persian lamb "furs." The slaughtering of lambs when only a day old reduces the drain on the ewes and helps to explain the ability to maintain flocks in an area so arid. Export of karakul pelts, in which South-West Africa leads the world, increased from about 10,000 in 1926 to 1.58 million in 1939 and 2.35 million in 1962, when exports were valued at a record $17.7 million.

Cattle assume importance in the center and the north, and the eastern region has "undergone a most remarkable transformation"[1] in recent decades through the introduction of cattle ranches which secure necessary water from deep wells. Of the total of about 5,500 European farmers in the country, about 3,000 are engaged in cattle ranching. A great variety of breeds are kept, including the Texas Brahman, the Africander, and European breeds such as the Aberdeen Angus and Brown Swiss. Moderate amounts of dairy products and beef are sold, mainly in the Republic. In 1959 a record of 310,795 head were exported from the territory, valued at about $24 million, but the persistent drought mentioned earlier greatly reduced shipments in 1961 and 1962. By 1962, it was also estimated that the number of cattle held by Africans in the north had decreased by two thirds.

Tillage agriculture is relatively limited, as is to be expected in so dry a country. Around Grootfontein and Otjiwarongo in the north, where rainfall averages about 20 to 24 inches, some corn, wheat, potatoes, and beans can be grown in better years, the corn silage being used to help maintain dairy herds. The Ovambo plant raingrown millet and sorghum in a belt about 100 miles wide along the northern border.

[1] Richard F. Logan, "South West Africa," *Focus* (November, 1960), p. 5.

Some opportunities exist in scattered areas for further tapping of ground water and control of surface runoff. A plan was announced in 1961 to harness the Cunene River on the Angola border for hydroelectric and irrigation development on behalf of the Ovambo. Known as the Ovambo Canal Scheme, it would involve constructing a 60-mile canal preferably starting from inside Angola and installing two hydroelectric stations, one at Ericson's Drift, 20 miles inside Angola, and the other larger one on the border at Ruacana Falls. The necessity for international agreement may delay fruition of this scheme. Other water control projects include the Swakop Dam near Okahandja for supplying water to Windhoek, not yet started, and the Mariental State Water and Irrigation Scheme on the Fish River. The major engineering feature of this scheme is the Hardap Dam, completed in 1962 at a cost of $5 million, and representing the third largest irrigation dam in southern Africa, giving control over 7,400 acres which will be divided into about 150 European farms. Later, a 460-kw hydroelectric station will be installed. The Okavango River could also be used for irrigation, but its extreme remoteness has not encouraged development or study.

FISHING

Fishing ranks third after mining and agriculture in economic importance, fifty-six firms employing over 200 Europeans and 3,500 non-Europeans. Walvis Bay, where pilchards, whitefish, and snoek are the main catch, and Luderitz, which is the main lobster center, are the chief fishing ports. The catch of pilchards is controlled more by quota prescribed by the government than by the quantity of fish available. The industry has had no difficulty in catching up to the record quotas assigned in recent years—378,000 tons in 1961, and 435,000 tons in 1962. The 1963 quota was set at 540,000 tons.

The rock lobster industry has also had great success in increasing its catch and sales. The 1962 catch was a record 15.9 million pounds, up 3 million pounds over 1961, and was valued at

Karakul sheep resting under a tree
Pelts, which are used for Persian lamb coats, are one of the main exports of South-West Africa, which leads the world in their production.

Cattle at an artificial watering reservoir in the Ommetjette African Reserve
Aridity over most of the country makes grazing the most characteristic occupation.

Collection of grain for famine stores
A drought lasting six years finally ended in 1962; while it was unusually long, droughts occur irregularly but certainly over most of the country.

about $4.5 million. The total value of all fish products in 1961 was $31.9 million.

MINING

Mining dominates the economy of South-West Africa in terms of value of production, exports, and in wage employees. The diamond industry, closely integrated with that of South Africa, is discussed under that country. Diamonds provided almost two thirds of the estimated value of total mineral exports from South-West Africa in 1961.

Copper, lead, zinc, and by-products are mined at Tsumeb in the northeast. This operation was begun by the Germans in 1908, closed in 1940, and reopened on a larger scale after purchase by American interests in 1946. The ores at Tsumeb, which is one of the principal base metal mines in the world, have a combined copper, lead, and zinc content of about 21 percent; output of zinc and lead makes the mine the largest producer of these metals in Africa. A smaller mine owned by the same interests began production in 1962 at Kombat, 65 miles from Tsumeb. It has 3.4 million tons of proven and probable reserves of ore averaging 2.8 percent copper and 2.9 percent lead.

Until recently, much of the output from Tsumeb was shipped as concentrates, but under a $25 million investment program several smelters and other plants are being placed at the site. A copper smelter, which smelts concentrates from Tsumeb and Kombat, was completed in 1962, a lead smelter and refining plant in 1963; specialized plants for germanium, arsenic, and ultimately cadmium are also included in the program. Tsumeb employs about 600 Europeans and 2,500 Africans. Lead, zinc, and vanadium are also mined at Berg Aukas.

Tsumeb, a copper mining town in the northeast
Surface workings of the mine are seen in the foreground. Mining dominates the money economy of South-West Africa.

Other minerals produced in South-West Africa include manganese at Otjosundu, lithium ores near Karibib, tungsten at Krantzberg and Brandberg, plus tin, fluorspar, and salt, while a variety of other minerals are known to occur. An investigation for oil is now under way, and a coal deposit is being studied east of Grootfontein.

INDUSTRY

Such industry as exists in South-West Africa is associated mainly with mining, fishing, and agricultural activities. A few market-oriented plants produce such commodities as beer and mineral waters, clothing, soap, brushes, and bricks and tiles.

TRANSPORTATION AND TRADE

Considering the relative poverty of its surface, South-West Africa has a surprisingly good transport net. The main rail line, linked with Upington in the Republic, runs more or less north-south on the plateau; western links connect it with the ports of Luderitz and Walvis Bay, while branch lines run to mining communities and eastward to the ranching country centered on Gobabis. Recent conversion of 353 miles of 2-foot gauge line in the north has brought the total length of standard 3-foot–6-inch track to about 1,467 miles. The railways, which now use diesel traction exclusively, are operated as part of the South African system.

Regular motor services run by the rail administration operate on about 3,300 route miles. The road mileage consists of about 34,000 miles of dirt and gravel roads and 187 miles of paved road, but it is planned that 1,400 miles will be paved by about 1980. Expenditure on roads has increased by more than 10 times in the last decade; the number of cars now exceeds 30,000.

Walvis Bay, a natural harbor, handles the bulk of territorial traffic. It suffered serious congestion until 1961, when a new wharf was completed, nearly trebling the cargo handling capacity. Accommodations now include a 4,600-foot quay for eight freighters, and a new tanker berth; mechanical gear includes many cranes and an ore loader for concentrates from Tsumeb. In 1961 Walvis Bay shipped 596,000 short tons and landed 311,000 short tons.

Luderitz, with an artificial harbor partially protected by a 493-foot jetty, is the only other port of importance. Only fishing vessels and shallow-draught coasters can be accommodated. It is the base for the rock lobster fleet.

Since 1955, trade figures for South-West Africa have been integrated with those of the Republic, so that it is impossible to more than estimate total shipments or receipts. The value of imports through territorial ports is about $18 to $23 million yearly; the value of exports at these ports is about $56 million a year. Total exports may, however, be nearer $120 million and total imports about $80 million, giving an exceptionally favorable physical balance.

Relatively unknown and little visited, restricted by inadequate precipitation and periodic drought, South-West Africa nonetheless compares favorably with many African countries in the level of its economic development. The modernity and cosmopolitan character of its towns and the relative excellence of its infrastructure have impressed even critical observers. It does, however, possess some of the same difficult racial problems as those of its mentor, the Republic, and has applied almost the same system of apartheid in attempting to meet them.

CHAPTER TWENTY-FOUR

The High Commission Territories

Bechuanaland, Basutoland, and Swaziland are three sharply contrasting countries, appropriately linked only because of their common political classification as High Commission Territories. Each is administered separately, however, under resident commissioners responsible to the British High Commissioner and, since 1961, to the Colonial Office. While their histories differ greatly, they have the common feature of requested protection from the British Crown. Their positions vis-à-vis the Republic of South Africa are also the same: the 1909 South African Act promised that they would eventually be transferred to that country but only after consultation with the people. The South African government attempted to promote this transferral on several occasions, but such a move would not be countenanced by the indigenous inhabitants and would be politically unacceptable to the British Parliament so long as the present racial policies of the Republic persist.

The three territories were long neglected economically and politically. Bechuanaland did not acquire an adequate administrative staff until 1954, and ordinary and development expenditures by government were still only about $8.93 million in 1962–63, which, however, represented an increase from $1.89 million in 1949–50. Basutoland still has an inadequate staff, particularly in view of its serious population and soil erosion problems. Its government expenditure increased from $2.85 million in 1949–50 to $6.24 million in 1959–60. Swaziland is considerably better endowed than the other two territories; while its regular and development expenditures, totaling $1.90 million in 1949–50 and $11.45 million in 1961–62, were not substantially larger than those of Bechuanaland and Basutoland, there has been a much greater investment of private capital in that territory.

The three territories had elected legislative councils only in 1960–61, but the High Commissioner still retains authority over such matters as defense, external affairs, internal security, and public service. Further steps toward self-rule will follow, perhaps to independence by 1965, but the territories may wish to retain some ties with Britain as protection in their relations with the Republic. Suggestions that the three countries attempt to seek economic independence from the Republic appear to be most unrealistic except possibly for Swaziland; in fact, it may be expected that interdependence with that country will increase as their economies develop.

BECHUANALAND

Bechuanaland Protectorate is a huge semiarid plateau averaging about 3,000 feet above sea level, hilly and broken in the east but gently undulating to flat over the bulk of its 222,000 square miles. The eastern region has the most favorable rainfall and agricultural potential and the bulk of the population; rainfall averages about 18 to 22 inches as compared to 12 inches or less in the drier west. The largest part of the country is Kalahari sand veld (Map 95), much of which is uninhabited. Two areas in the west are of somewhat greater interest: the region around Ghanzi, where a number of European farms are situated on a limestone ridge relatively well supplied with water; and the area around

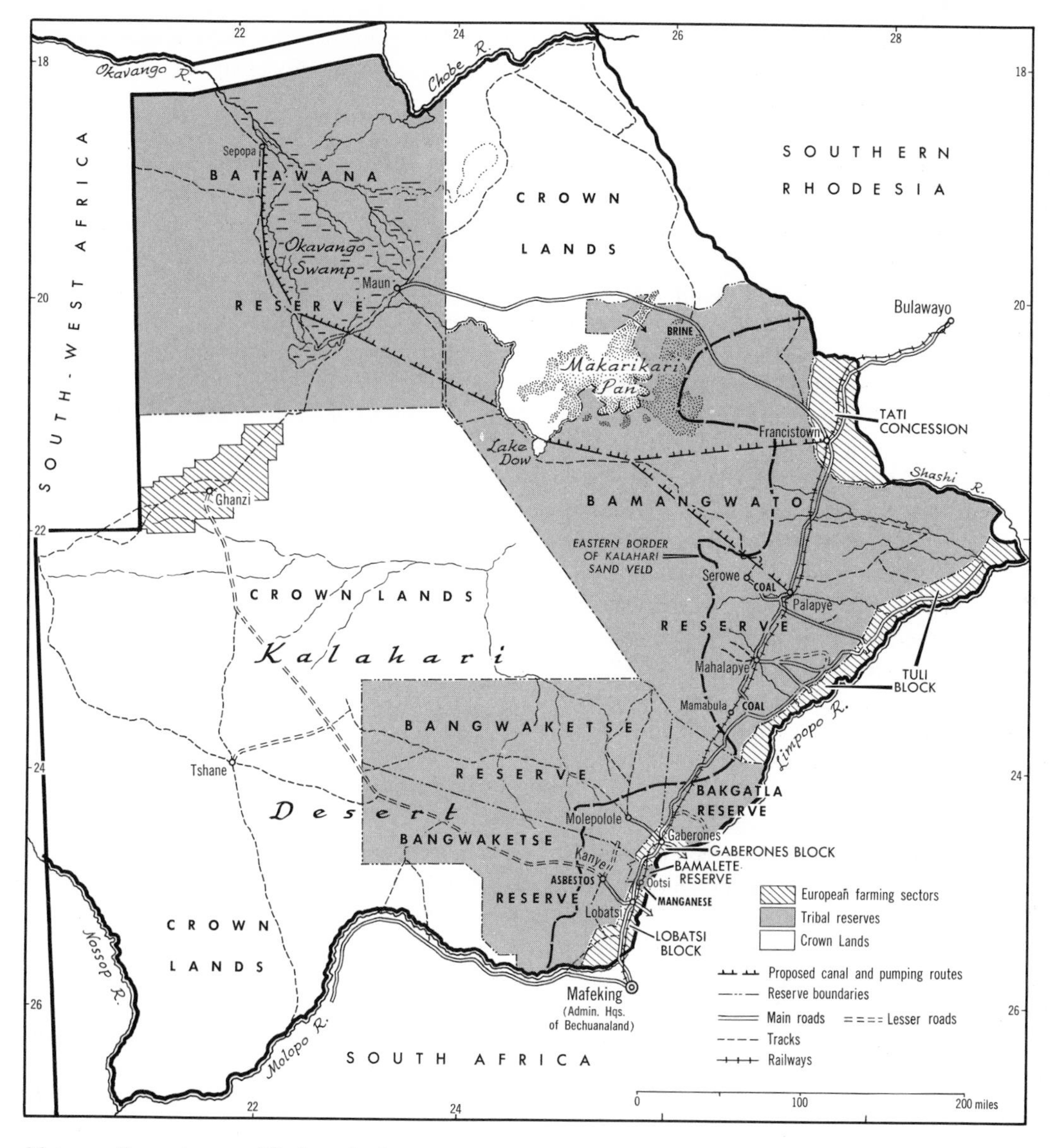

Map 95. Economic map of Bechuanaland

Maun on the edge of the Okavango Swamps, primarily a cattle raising region.

The outstanding keynote of Bechuanaland is aridity, which affects practically every aspect of its economic development. Three examples may be given as illustrations:

(1) Water supplies are so short in the two principal towns that the government seat could not readily be moved from its present anomalous situation at Mafeking, 17 miles outside of the Protectorate and in the Republic, which is no longer even associated through the Commonwealth. Nonetheless, it has been decided to move the capital to Gaberones, which will require construction of a dam to increase the water available.

(2) Large parts of the Kalahari are described as so highly sensitive that they should be closed

to all livestock development. A. L. du Toit is credited in a recent study as comparing the soil and vegetation of the Kalahari "in their delicacy to the skin on the face of a beautiful woman: once destroyed never replaceable."[1]

(3) The third example comes from Debenham[2] and suggests the lengths to which Bushmen will go to secure water. After finding a certain plant which indicates damp sand, a woman proceeds to scrape a hole in the sand to arm's length, then takes a grass stem or hollow reed, surrounds its end with fine roots or grass, and places that end in the bottom of the hole. The sand is then carefully replaced around the reed and firmly tamped down. After an hour or two the woman begins to suck through the tube and in another hour or two the water begins to rise in the reed. With a second straw she expels it into one end of an ostrich egg. A number of these are filled, sealed with clay, and buried as reserves for dry weather.

Most of the Bechuanaland population is made up of eight main Bantu-speaking tribes but there are a number of other smaller groups including Bushman or Sarwa. About 80 percent of the people live near the rail line which traverses the country all along the east. This region is studded with a number of large villages, of which Kanye and Serowe have as many as 20,000 persons during part of the year but are practically empty at other times. Farming lands up to 30 miles away are worked with these villages as bases, while herdboys may be tending the family herd 100 miles away on the other side. In the northwest, people live in small settlements on islets in the swamp or along the main water-courses. All but 17,000 Africans live in tribal reserves. About 3,200 Europeans reside in Bechuanaland, including a number of farmers and ranchers in the Lobatsi, Gaberones, and Tuli blocks, and the Tati Concession in the east, along the Molopo River in the south, and on the Ghanzi Farms in the west. Lobatsi and Francistown are the largest towns in the Protectorate.

[1] *Basutoland, Bechuanaland Protectorate and Swaziland: Report of an Economic Survey Mission* (London, Her Majesty's Stationery Office, 1960), p. 18.

[2] Frank Debenham, "The Kalahari Today," *The Geographical Journal* (March, 1952), pp. 18–19.

GRAZING

Owing to aridity, Bechuanaland is predominantly a grazing country, with animal products providing by far the greatest share of income. The three High Commission Territories are in customs union with South Africa so that only rough estimates of exports can be made and import figures are not available, but Table 44 reveals that animal products accounted for an estimated 71 percent of exports in 1961. About 90 percent of the estimated 1,325,000 head of cattle in 1960 were owned by Africans, some herds being very large. The veld generally provides good grazing but at a low carrying capacity, perhaps one head per 20 acres in the more favored southeast and one head per 50 acres in the Kalahari. Actually, only about a sixth of the country is now used for grazing, partly because of reserve boundaries, partly because there are inadequate watering points in many areas. The present situation is characterized by an excess of cattle on the lands in use and too great a concentration around available watering places. While there is increasing willingness to sell cattle, the tribes still adhere to a cattle culture and are more interested in numbers than in quality. Disease problems are acute, foot-and-mouth disease causing periodic sealing of parts or all of the territory from outside markets, and

Table 44. Estimated exports of Bechuanaland, 1961

	1961 exports	
Product	*In thousand $*	*Percent*
Cattle	5,303	55.0
Hides and skins	773	8.0
Sorghum	752	7.8
Abattoir by-products	731	7.6
Manganese	806	8.3
Asbestos	477	5.0
Other	804	8.3
Total	9,646	100.0

Source: High Commissioner's Office, Cape Town.

the tsetse fly appears to be advancing in parts of the northwest.

Several programs have been instituted in recent years to improve this general position. From 1946 to 1952, some 663 successful bores were drilled by the government and over 600 by private interests, with about 80 bores now being sunk annually; over 70 dams have also been constructed. Efforts are being made to establish control of the number of cattle at each watering point and to increase the offtake of cattle. The Kgatla have regulated their herds for some years and the Kwena have recently instituted grazing regulations, but in neither case is the control sufficiently rigid or well related to carrying capacity. Disease control is sought by fencing, dipping, etc., and by an anti-tsetse campaign in the west. A marked improvement came in 1954 with construction of an abattoir at Lobatsi which now handles about 80–90 percent of the total cattle exported, and the CDC supported the establishment of an adjoining meat cannery in 1961. Most of Bechuanaland's cattle exports go to the Republic, the Rhodesias, and Congo but, since 1958, some success has been had in securing overseas markets. Some cattle are walked over long distances to Lobatsi or to outside markets; here the effort is to improve the routes by provision of additional watering points.

Experts maintain that there are considerable opportunities for expanding the livestock industry of Bechuanaland, partly through better control in existing areas, partly by extending grazing to the large sections not now used. Water development sets the limits of expansion, but neither the surface nor subsurface resources are as yet well mapped. Construction of a large number of small conservation dams would probably be most beneficial. Additional underground resources undoubtedly exist, but chances of finding a really substantial supply are slim. A part of the water is of fossil origin and indications are that some areas are already overusing the available supplies.

The largest amount of unused water in the Protectorate is lost in the Okavango Swamps of the northwest. Possible control of this water has been the subject of speculation and investigation for many years, but no study has as yet been sufficiently precise to justify proceeding with development. The Okavango River, second only to the Zambesi in southern Africa, rises in Angola and brings a mean annual flow into Bechuanaland of about 6.3 million acre feet. From near the border, the river runs 90 miles in a wide, papyrus-covered valley, then divides into two main streams flowing into either side of the swamp (Map 95). The roughly triangular swamp totals about 4,000 square miles. Its upper part is permanent and largely covered by papyrus; the remainder fills up annually, while varying quantities of water flow seasonally along the Botletle River 160 miles to Lake Dow and thence into the Makarikari Pan. The vast bulk of water from the Okavango River is lost through evaporation and transpiration in the swamps. The Brind Plan calls for clearing the eastern defluent of the swamp and directing more water into the Thamalkane and Botletle rivers for storage to sustain irrigation farming. It has also been suggested that a canal could be built along the western and southern borders carrying 500 to 1,000 cusecs all year, and that part of this water might be led and pumped across the country to Francistown and Palapye. Since the Okavango contains the only large concentration of water in Bechuanaland, it must sooner or later be developed, but topographic, hydrographic, soil, and crop studies are first required.

TILLAGE AGRICULTURE

It is estimated that about 8 million acres of Bechuanaland are potentially arable, or 5.6 percent of the whole. At present, only about 400,000 acres or 5 percent of the potential is actually farmed. The main crops are corn and sorghum; there is normally a net import of the former and a net export of the latter. Yields vary widely according to the amount and distribution of precipitation. Cow peas, beans, and small quantities of millet and peanuts are exported. The total value of crop production is estimated at about $2.8 million yearly, the largest share coming from African dryland farms.

In an effort to upgrade African agricultural standards the Pupil Farmers Agricultural Extension Scheme was introduced in 1947, under which the Department of Agriculture supplies improved seed, fertilizer, insecticides and fungicides, and implements to cooperators who agree to follow the advice of demonstrator farmers for a training period of 3 or 4 years. The implements are withdrawn during the training period and the farmer is encouraged to purchase his own replacements. Agricultural Extension Officers work closely with from 7 to 16 demonstrators and each demonstrator is assigned up to 10 cooperating trainee farmers. There are now over threescore demonstrators and about 500 plots in the scheme, which appears to be well adapted to a situation in which there are limited funds available for expenditure.

Most of the European farmers in Bechuanaland are primarily interested in ranching. Some of them, especially those in the Ghanzi District, have a relatively important production of dairy products, and the Francistown plant produces butter valued at about $240,000 a year. Most of the lands thus far brought under irrigation are on European farms, and further opportunities exist for irrigating some excellent soils in the Tuli Block and, on a much smaller area, in the Tati Concession. Some lands on the Bechuanaland and South African sides of the Limpopo are supplied from privately constructed weirs across the river, but further development on this river, which ranks second to the Okavango in potential, would require a storage dam. The recently completed Notwani Dam, with a capacity of 430 million gallons, supplies water for the railway and for the Gaberones Block. A small but profitable 200-acre irrigation scheme was instituted in 1939 at Mogobane, 23 miles from Lobatsi, to produce famine-relief crops for the local tribe.

LABOR MIGRATION

Ranking second to agriculture as a source of income to the Protectorate are the returns from labor migration, which began as early as 1871 with workers going to the Kimberley diamond mines. Today, about 20,000 Africans or a fifth of the adult male population are absent from the territory at any one time, the normal absence being 9 months and the legal limit 18 months. Many workers return four or five times to the Rand. Benefits to the Protectorate from deferred pay, remittances, and taxation of migrants total an estimated $2.8 million yearly.

Labor migration to South Africa is also important to the economies of Basutoland and Swaziland, but the sharply contrasting political trends in the High Commission Territories and the Republic threaten to interfere seriously with this movement. South Africa strongly resents the use of Basutoland, an enclave entirely surrounded by the Republic, as a place of refuge for local dissidents; a stream of refugees also passes through Bechuanaland on their way to the independent African states to the north. South Africa has taken increasingly rigid measures in the last few years to eliminate these movements. Residents of the territories, who previously migrated without formality, must now carry passports and medical certificates and are fingerprinted at the border. South Africa has also stated that immigration from the territories may be controlled to reduce any unemployment problem faced by the Republic, while some of the people from the High Commission Territories who have lived for many years in South Africa may be forced to return to them every two years to reapply for permission to work in South Africa. Basutoland would be most severely hurt by any marked reduction in migrants, and has little that it can do to retaliate. Bechuanaland may require presentation of travel documents by white South Africans and could introduce restrictions on those now farming or working in that territory. Swaziland has ample opportunities to absorb its own workers and might even be advantaged by restrictions on employment of migrant workers in South Africa. Benefits to the Bechuanaland Protectorate from the deferred pay remittances and taxes of migrants total an estimated $2.8 million yearly.

MINING

Mineral output is of minor but increasing significance, mineral exports having been a record $1.28 million in 1961, and the greatly intensified prospecting of recent years may reveal bodies of great importance for the future. At present, there is a small output of asbestos at Ngwatketse (exports in 1961 were valued at $477,000) (Map 95), an increasing production of manganese ore (1961 exports valued at $806,000), and a very small production of gold and silver. Mining of manganese takes place at the Kwagkwe Hill area, about 23 miles northwest of Lobatsi, where a separation plant was installed in 1960. Mining of manganese at Ramoutsa was discontinued in 1958, but ore bodies are now under study at Ootsi Mountain, both of these localities being not far north of Lobatsi.

Considerable interest attaches to coal deposits in Bechuanaland. To date, two main exploitable seams have been examined, one at Mamabule, 35 miles south of Mahalapye on the rail line, the other west of Palapye. Large reserves of good medium, South African-quality coal capable of being mined from the surface have been proved. Export coal would have to be beneficiated, however, and an ensured market of at least 500,000 tons annually would be required to justify the cost of large-scale mining equipment, totaling at least $5.2 million, while at present the estimated market is only about 258,000 tons. High-grade hematite is reported to occur in the same area.

Rhodesian Selection Trust through its subsidiary Bamangwato Concessions has been studying extensive brine deposits in the delta of the Nata River north of the Makarikari Pan, copper at the Bushman mine 75 miles west of Francistown, and a nickel occurrence. In 1962 it was reported planning to spend $5.6 million to produce 60,000 tons of sodium carbonate a year, pumping concentrated brine from the Nata River via a 10-inch, about 110-mile pipeline to the railroad 10 miles south of Francistown. Finally, an extensive concession was made in 1961 to Mobil Oil, Southern Africa, Ltd., which is conducting preliminary geophysical work near the South-West Africa border.

INDUSTRY

Only a very few manufacturing plants exist in the Protectorate, nor can any large development be expected. Lobatsi has the abattoir already mentioned, plus a corn mill, a malt factory, and soap works. Francistown has a creamery, a bonemeal factory, and a hides and skins depot. These two are the only towns with community electric plants, but demand exceeds supply and the scarcity of water militates against further steam power plants.

TRANSPORT AND TRADE

The limited budget of Bechuanaland, $9.3 million in 1961, does not permit much expenditure on transport lines. The Protectorate does benefit from its position between the Republic and the Rhodesias and the existence of the only line directly connecting these two areas, 394 miles in length. An adequate gravel road parallels the railway across the more developed eastern districts. Aside from this road, service links in the European districts, and routes to Ghanzi and Maun in the west, roads are practically nonexistent. Ghanzi, in particular, suffers from remoteness, cattle having to be trekked 400 miles over a difficult route to Lobatsi. It has been recommended that this area be connected by an improved road to the railhead of Gobabis in South-West Africa, a distance of 180 miles, 130 of which are within Bechuanaland. Regular air services serve Lobatsi, Maun, Francistown, and Ghanzi.

Table 44 gives the main exports of the Protectorate for 1961. South Africa is Bechuanaland's main trading partner, but overseas sales of beef have increased in recent years. No figures are available for imports of Bechuanaland, but most arrive from South Africa, with which the Protectorate has a customs union.

BASUTOLAND

Basutoland, having an area of 11,716 square miles, is situated on the western watershed of the

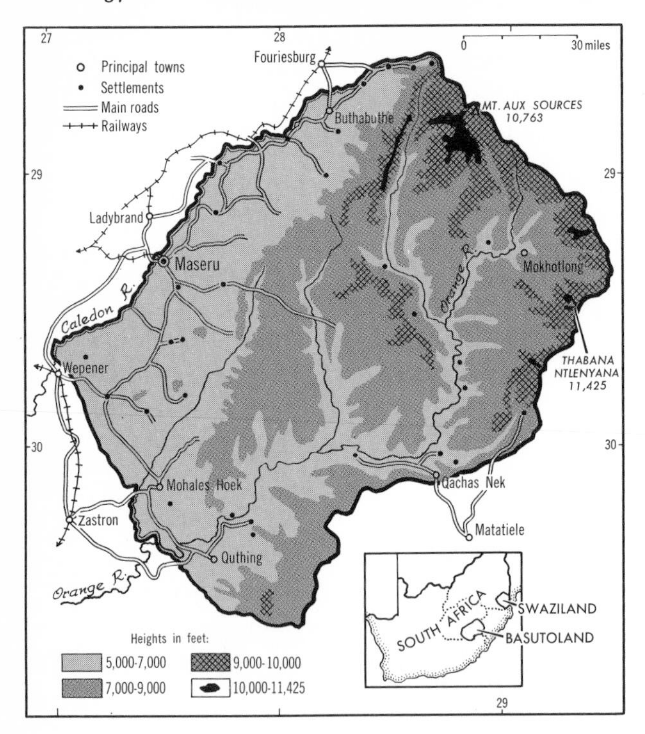

Map 96. Physical and transport map of Basutoland

great Drakensberg Escarpment entirely surrounded by Republic territory (Map 96). It may be divided into three lowland and two highland topographic regions in the ratio of about 1:4 in area covered. On the west is a border lowland characterized by soil impoverishment and severe erosion but possessing a considerable proportion of uncultivated arable lands in places below 5,000 feet. Extending east of this zone is a more fertile, less arid lowland belt between about 5,000 and 6,000 feet elevation interrupted by sandstone plateaus. These first two zones contain about two thirds of the population (about 734,000 in 1963 including about 3,000 non-Africans) and the main crop producing area. The third lowland area is a long wedge along the Orange Valley in the southern part of the mountain zone. The highland region consists of (1) a foothill zone between the lowlands and the Maluti Mountains, rolling country between 6,000 and 7,000 feet interrupted by mountain spurs and river valleys. In the valleys and on the flatter areas, rich volcanic soils provide some of the best soils of the territory and erosion is not so advanced as in the west. Agriculture is, however, less developed than in the lowlands. (2) The mountain zone, mostly above 8,000 feet and attaining elevations exceeding 11,000 feet. Its deep valleys, separated by uplands and steep ridges, are fairly densely populated; the lands above 8,000 feet are traditional "cattle post" country, formerly used exculsively for summer grazing. Population pressure is leading to increasing settlement and arable farming in this zone. The short growing season and highly erodible thin soils are severe handicaps to agriculture, and in places the soils have been completely removed.

Temperature and precipitation vary greatly from region to region and within individual regions according to elevation and aspect of slope. Concentrated in a few months, rainfall is quite variable, yearly averages ranging from 75 inches along the scarp to 25–30 inches in the lowlands. The incidence of frost is erratic but may often be disastrous; hail is a summer hazard in all districts. The natural vegetation of Basutoland is grass; most of the trees that do exist have been planted in connection with gully control.

The bulk of the population are Basuto (or Basotho), a Bantu tribe, and all of the land is held in trust for the Basuto nation by the Paramount Chief and may not be alienated. There are no European-held lands, the bulk of the European population being in government, missions, and commerce.

AGRICULTURE

A keynote of Basutoland is the severe erosion problem which, despite one of the more dynamic control programs in Africa, still threatens to destroy much of the country's most valuable heritage. Steep slopes, inadequate grass cover, thin, erodible soils, downpours in the rainy season, and overstocking all contribute to erosion. While erosion is most severe in the lowland areas, control must be instituted in all regions because poorly sited plots and overgrazing in the highlands are a threat not only to those zones but to the lands below them. Control programs involve terracing, grass stripping, construction of dams, planting of trees to arrest gullying, and limitation of grazing rights. Control is much more than a physical problem. It is a social problem in that some required measures are resented by the populace, such as village relocation, closure of areas for recuperation, and stipulated distribution of livestock. It is an economic problem because the government does not have adequate funds to mount a campaign of sufficient proportions to gain really effective control. As was stated in the Department of Agriculture Annual Report for 1960, "the bulldozer is no longer the kingpin of the operation. We are now facing up more to the human problem rather than the mechanical."

Basutoland is mainly a grazing country, with wool and mohair comprising about 60 percent of the total value of exports. One report described the livestock of Basutoland as "a heterogeneous collection of beasts showing signs of every conceivable strain." Yields are characteristically low and of relatively poor quality; the lambing rate for sheep and goats is very low, in large part owing to overgrazing, particularly in the winter when the value of the grazings declines rapidly after the first frost. Improvement is sought in part by the sale at subsidized prices of imported first-class Merino and Angora rams. Up to 500 Merino and 400 Angora rams are purchased in the Republic at about $28 each and sold at $14 each. In the case of wool, these ram importations, totaling almost 17,000 in the period 1935–62, are estimated to have resulted in a reduction of the undesirable coarse and colored wool marketed from 33 percent of the total in 1935 to a low of 4 percent in 1958 and 5 to 10 percent in the years to 1962. But Basuto graziers prevent realization of the full benefit of this program by periodically breeding with low-class crossbred sheep and goats, which increases the hardiness of the animals but decreases the quality of the wool and mohair.

Improvements are also needed in grading, management of the clip, and in marketing. But no real advance can be expected until an effective grazing control program has been adopted, which means abandonment of communal grazing and provision for some supplementary feeding in the dry winter months. According to the 1961 animal census, there were then 380,000 cattle, 1,230,000 sheep, 600,000 goats, 90,000 horses, and 50,000 donkeys in the country; except for goats there has been a small, not entirely understood, decrease in numbers from 1938 or 1952 totals. In addition to wool and mohair, there is an export of live animals, hides, and skins, but the value of live animal imports exceeds that of exports, an

Corn fields and gully erosion in the western lowlands of Basutoland
Despite substantial efforts to protect the land, Basutoland continues to have one of the most serious soil erosion problems in Africa.

obviously unhealthy condition for a country which climatically and geographically should be a fairly large livestock exporter. An effort is being made to improve the cattle by importation of Swiss bulls, considered appropriate triple-purpose animals to meet the requirements of meat, milk, and draft power. It is also hoped that it will be possible to set up 45 to 50 livestock improvement centers, each of which will contain a small clinic, stables for rams and stallions, wool sheds, and hide preparation facilities.

About 12 to 13 percent of the territory is used for tillage agriculture, including about 40 percent of the lowlands and about 6 percent of the highlands. The main crop and foodstuff is corn, but it is normally necessary to import from 10,000 to 25,000 tons to meet local requirements. Sorghum, wheat, potatoes, and a few fruits and vegetables are other subsistence crops. The total value of crop production is estimated at $11 to $14 million yearly, of which about 6 percent is exported, wheat and pulses accounting for nine tenths of the total. The typical farmer tills 5 to 7 acres, often in scattered holdings to ensure a fair distribution of the different soils. About one out of fourteen Basuto is landless. Yields are characteristically low, but are capable of considerable increase under proper practices and also under the stimulus of a system of individual tenure, which has been strongly recommended to encourage capital improvements and progressive farming.

The government has been attempting to instill better practices by a Progressive Farmer's Scheme, to which about 800 farmers now belong, and by promotion of cooperatives, which had 2,700 members in 1960. In both cases expansion was limited only by the size of the training staff, it being estimated that only about a third of the field advisers are really fully adequate for extension work. A special prototype land use scheme, instituted at Taung in an overgrazed and eroded lowland area to develop methods for safeguarding the land and improving output, proved that its techniques were effective but lack of acceptance by the local farmers in 1960 resulted in rapid deterioration of the veld to its previous poor condition. It involved closing lands to permit restoration of the grass cover, construction of siltation dams, soil erosion control, and establishing grazing and tillage practices designed to maintain fertility of the soil. The future will, however, probably see much more effort devoted to multipurpose land use programs.

LABOR MIGRATION

While there are potentialities for improving and intensifying agriculture in Basutoland, the area simply could not support the present population at a favorable standard unless it were possible to develop secondary occupations. It is not surprising, therefore, to find that Basutoland has the highest dependence of the three High Commission Territories on labor migration to the Republic. About 130,000 Basuto, including 80,000 adult males (43 percent of the total), are absent at any given time, mainly working on the Rand and Orange Free State mines where they are valued particularly in development work. In 1960 about $2.16 million came into the territory through deferred pay and remittances; and $224,000 accrued to the government in recruiting taxes and fees. The high dependence on migrant labor earnings contains certain dangers, for influx control measures in the Republic could have a quite serious effect on the economy.

WATER RESOURCES

Basutoland is a well-watered country, the source of a number of perennial streams, including the Orange River, flowing into the Republic. At present, there is practically no irrigation and the scope for its application in Basutoland is not great. Hydroelectric potentialities are, however, very substantial. The most effective development appears to involve diverting the flow of the upper tributaries of the Orange westward into the steep valleys running towards the Caledon. Three schemes following this pattern have been proposed, of which the Oxbow Scheme has received the greatest attention. This project could be developed in successive

A Basuto hamlet near Maseru
The poverty of Basutoland's physical resources gives it heavy dependence on migratory labor, and Basuto workers are favored for certain jobs on the South African mines.

stages: (1) constitution of a run-of-river dam with small storage capacity and a temporary power station; this step, costing about $6 million, would develop a head of 1,950 feet to produce an estimated 44 million kwh annually; (2) diversion of water from three additional streams; (3) construction of tunnels and of an upper power station; (4) completion of the Ox-bow storage dam; and (5) construction of a large power station. The completed scheme would involve a capital expenditure of about $40.3 million and produce about 418 million kwh yearly. The other two schemes are the Kau River Scheme, costing $34–42 million to develop 350 million kwh, and the Semena River Scheme, involving an investment of $126 to $140 million to permit production of 1,000 million kwh. In all cases the bulk of the power would presumably be sold to the Republic, while additional revenue would be derived from delivery of regulated water to the South African border.

MINERALS AND INDUSTRY

Prospects for development of mining in Basutoland appear to be poor. Occasional alluvial diamonds have been found and numerous claims were made by Basuto diggers in 1961–62 north of Mokhotlong. Pipes and fissures of kimberlite have been located, but after four years of prospecting it appeared in 1962 that none could be developed economically. Almost no industry exists in the territory, except for brick works and two mission printing presses. It was announced in 1962 that a group of South African industrialists were interested in launching twelve new industries. Difficulties encountered with respect to securing an adequate assurance of long-run tenure on the plant site were removed in 1963 by the provision of an industrial estate at Maseru.

TRANSPORT AND TRADE

With its very difficult topography, it is not surprising that Basutoland has a poorly developed transport network, but the emptiness of the road map as compared to surrounding areas is not entirely attributable to this factor. Maseru, the capital, is the only town served by rail, from a one-mile branch of the Bloemfontein-Durban line. There are about 228 miles classified as "main" roads, chiefly in the lowlands, but they are not always traversable in the rains and require graveling to bring them up to a satisfactory standard. An additional 728 miles of road of varying standards exist, plus 164 miles of jeepable tracks. Countless miles of bridal trails provide the only access to much of the highland areas; the Basuto using them ride ponies, donkeys, oxen, horses, and an increasing number of mules. The Basuto pony was once considered a valuable animal, but selective offtaking for sale and poor breeding practices have left a degraded animal today. A local airline, Basutair Limited, maintains service from Maseru to five towns, the journey across the country to Mokhotlong taking one hour as compared to six days on horseback. Charter flights may be made to 28 airstrips and a company helicopter has been used intensively in connection with prospecting for diamonds.

Accurate data are not available on the trade of Basutoland. Its exports are believed to have totaled about $3 to $5 million yearly in recent years, which has been only about 45 to 55 percent of imports. In 1961 wool accounted for $1,233,400 and mohair for $886,200. In each case there is a good deal of unrecorded exports, smuggled across the border to avoid the direct export tax of $0.021 a pound on wool and $0.049 a pound on mohair. Corn from the Republic is smuggled back to avoid paying the levy of $0.73 a bag. Other exports include hides and skins, wheat, peas and beans, and sorghum. Recorded corn imports averaged 13,100 tons in the decade to 1961, which was very much greater than the exports of grains.

SWAZILAND

Swaziland is the smallest (6,704 square miles and maximum dimensions of 90 by 120 miles), the richest, and the most complex of the High Commission Territories. Situated, in contrast to Basutoland, on the eastern watershed, it may be divided topographically into four distinct regions, each running from north to south. (Map 97). On the west is the highveld, a northeasterly extension of the Drakensberg, occupying about 45 percent of the country. With general elevations of 3,500 to 5,000 feet and maxima of 6,000 feet, this region records some of the highest rainfall averages in southern Africa, ranging from 45 to 73 inches and over. Frosts, usually light but occasionally severe, occur in this zone. It is a wide belt of granite-based, broken, heavily dissected country used for grazing and dryland farming and to support a number of important postwar forestry plantations.

Second is the middle veld with elevations ranging from about 2,700 to 1,300 feet and comprising about 25 percent of the country. Its surface is undulating to more markedly rolling and is dissected at intervals by eastward flowing streams. Precipitation averages about 30 to 40 inches and occasional light frosts occur. The grazing potential of this zone is superior to that of the highveld, but its "sourveld" grasses are not highly palatable and about 6 to 8 acres are required to support one head of cattle. Rain-grown crops give fair to good yields in favorable seasons but unsatisfactory yields in drier years. A great range of tropical, subtropical, and middle latitude crops can be grown in this zone under irrigation.

Third, the lowveld, with average elevations of about 500 to 1,000 feet, covers about 21 percent of the country. Most of it is gently undulating acacia bushveld, but occasional ridges and hills give elevations of as much as 2,300 feet. Rainfall is only 20 to 30 inches, which will support only grazing or the production of hardy annuals such as sorghum and millet; temperatures are rather high. The presence of some very good alluvial and basaltic soils and of a number of transversing streams provides attractive features for irrigation, whose potential has only begun to be exploited in postwar years. Again, the range of possible crops is considerable.

The last region is the Lebombo Plateau, covering the remaining 9 percent. It is an undulating to rolling, narrow plateau with elevations of 1,500 to 2,700 feet dropping off abruptly into the eastern lowveld and dissected by the three main streams leaving the country. Precipitation of about 33 inches permits the support of good pastures.

DISTRIBUTION OF THE LAND AND POPULATION

A complex position with respect to landownership is superimposed on the relatively simple

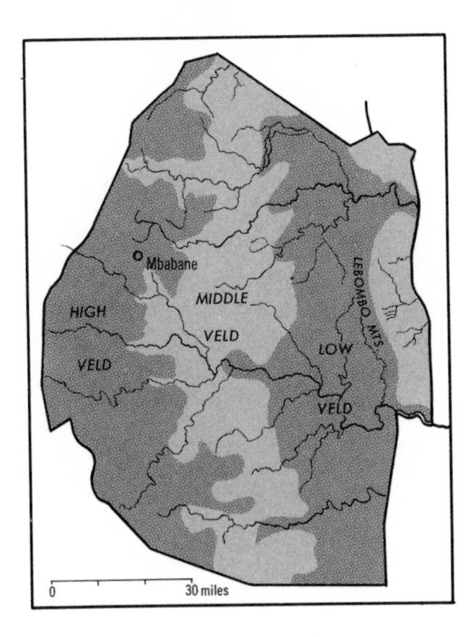

Map 97. Physical regions of Swaziland

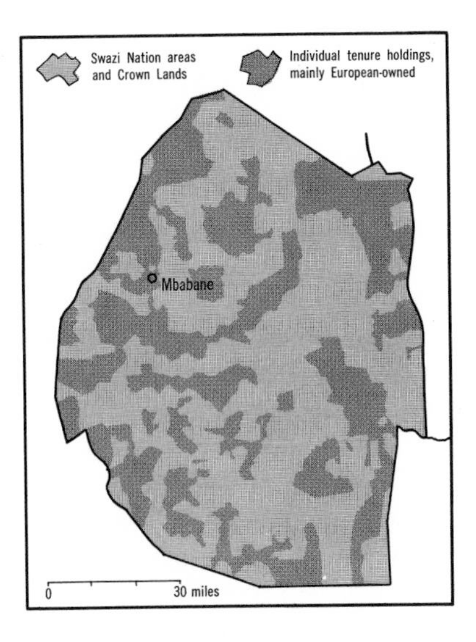

Map 98. Distribution of landholdings in Swaziland

topographic pattern. It stems from the recklessness of the Swazi king Mbandzeni, who, in the period 1880–90, granted all manner of concessions, including one for the sale of buttons, and sometimes three or four deep as far as land rights were concerned. These were fairly well sorted out in the Proclamation of 1907, and additional lands have since been credited to the Swazi, who now hold about 52.6 percent of the territory. Individually owned lands, held mainly by Europeans, comprise 44.4 percent of the total, most of the remainder being in Crown lands.

The Swazi and European holdings are intricately interwoven (Map 98), which results in land use patterns showing sharp contrasts from section to section within each major zone and in comparable differences in population densities. The population of Swaziland was estimated at 275,000 in mid-1962, about 96 percent of whom were Africans. These are mostly the Bantu Swazi, who have retained a strong tribal cohesion. The European population has grown rapidly in postwar years, from 3,201 in 1946 to about 7,800 in 1961, when there were an estimated 1,600 Eurafricans. The density of population on the 35 separate blocks of African-held land is about six times as great as on the European areas, but pressure on the land is not excessive. The division of lands has led to repeated complaints by the Swazi, complaints which may be intensified because all of the main developments in recent years in mining, forestry, irrigation, commerce, and industry have been focused in the European enclaves.

AGRICULTURE

The Swazis are traditionally cattle culturalists but have increasingly accepted the commercial value of their cattle. According to the 1961 animal census, there were about 635,000 cattle, 219,000 goats, and 38,000 sheep in the territory in that year, with non-Africans holding about a quarter of the cattle and sheep. Most of the African and some of the less skillfully used European lands are overgrazed, which has led to erosion problems, much less serious than those of Basutoland but still requiring attention. The government has attempted to meet the problem through a number of resettlement schemes somewhat comparable to those in Basutoland. While first resented by the Swazi, these schemes now appear to be making reasonable headway. Something under a tenth of the country is devoted to the wintering of about 157,000 sheep from the Transvaal.

Landscape in the highveld of Swaziland
Trek sheep are grazed over much of the highveld. Part of the Havelock Asbestos Mine is seen in the middle distance.

A considerable variety of rain-grown crops is found in Swaziland. Corn is the staple food and dominant crop, occupying 70 to 85 percent of tilled lands except in the lowveld where sorghum is more important; millet, potatoes, legumes, peanuts, vegetables, tobacco, cotton, and such fruits as avacado, mango, pineapple, and banana are also grown. Of these, the three most important cash crops are cotton, pineapples, and tobacco. Despite record crops of corn in recent years, the country remains a net importer. The opportunities for extending cultivation, which occupies only 8.8 percent of the total area, are substantial.

While the overwhelming proportion of the land is still used for rain-grown crops and grazing, the past decade has seen dynamic development of irrigation farming and there are substantial opportunities for its extension. About 50,000 acres are now under irrigation, over two thirds of which is in four major schemes. Most important is the Swaziland Irrigation Scheme (SIS), in the northern extreme of the lowveld (Map 99), started by the CDC in 1950. An 833-foot-long weir across the Komati River and a gravity canal 41 miles long were completed in 1956 at a cost of $2.8 million and now control 16,000 acres, which may later be increased by 19,000 acres. The CDC, two private operators, and the Swazi nation each have areas under irrigation. Sugar, rice, and citrus fruits are the main crops. Sugar production supports a new 40,000-ton-capacity mill at Hlume, which is allotted a quota in accordance with a Swaziland–South African agreement. Beginning in 1964, Swaziland's share of total domestic and foreign sales of sugar from the two countries will be increased to 8.5 percent, which will permit an output for all of Swaziland estimated at 90,000 tons yearly. Exports were nil in 1958 and 54,500 tons in 1961, when the total area in cane in Swaziland had increased to 19,000 acres.

In 1962 a $716,000 land settlement scheme for the SIS area, building upon the experience from a pilot project begun there in 1960, was announced. Known as the Vuvulane Irrigated Farms, the project will have three types of farms: 8-acre small-holder leaseholds for Swazi family farms, 60-acre sugar farms available for mortgage purchase, and 100-acre freehold farms available to Europeans or Swazis.

The other important irrigation schemes are:

(1) The Big Bend, on the Great Usutu River in the lowveld, where 10,000 acres are irrigated by a pump-fed canal and where a crop pattern comparable to that of the SIS is followed. This area also has a 40,000-ton-capacity sugar mill.

(2) The Ngonini Estates in the lower elevations of the Piggs Peak district, growing bananas and citrus fruit on 1,200 acres.

(3) The Malkerns Irrigation Scheme on the Great Usutu River in the middle veld. Some 7,500 acres are now irrigated on 35 European

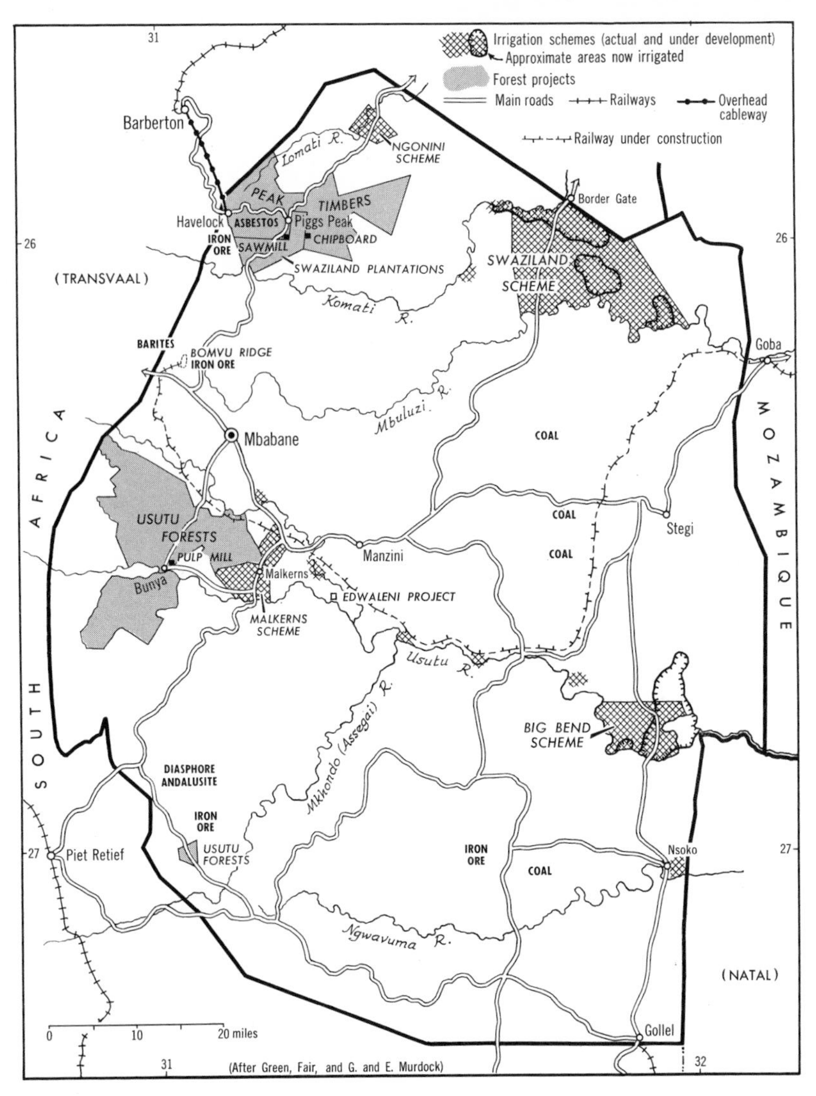

Map 99. Economic map of Swaziland

farms, 2,050 acres on African land, and 500 acres on government land in this area. Citrus fruit is of increasing importance in this scheme, which had the largest share of the country's 445,000 citrus trees in 1962. Only 6 percent of these had reached bearing age in that year; it is estimated that sales of citrus fruit will total $13 million in 1970. It is also hoped that increasing production of fruits and vegetables in the Malkerns area will help to sustain a cannery there, which has had difficulty in operating successfully with rain-grown pineapples produced in the district.

FORESTRY

Three large plantations of pine and eucalyptus covering about 200,000 acres have been developed in postwar years, all in the highveld, where the rate of growth is one of the most rapid in the world. It is estimated that pulpwood can be grown on a 15-year rotation. The most important plantation is the 95,000 acres of pine of the Usutu Forests, said to be the second largest man-made forest in the world. Owned by CDC and Courtaulds, it began supporting production of an unbleached sulphate pulp mill at Bunya in

1962. Representing an investment of $11.2 million, this plant will produce 100,000 tons of pulp yearly when operating at full capacity for export via Lourenço Marques, adding an estimated $9.8 million to annual export earnings. About 300 Europeans and 2,500 Africans are employed by Usutu Forests.

In the north, Peak Timbers and Swaziland Plantations have planted 66,000 acres and 10,000 acres on contiguous areas in the Piggs Peak district. Peak Timbers now has a sawmill and a factory using thinnings to produce chipboard, but has not yet secured adequate markets to permit full-scale operation. Boxing materials are cut at the Swaziland Plantations. The northern forests are handicapped by inadequate transport connections. The regions now occupied by all of the forest plantations were previously used for the winter grazing of trek sheep from South Africa, the new use representing a far greater contribution to the Swaziland economy.

MINERALS

One mineral, asbestos, has until recently accounted for over half of Swaziland's exports by value. In 1961 its share of exports had declined to 43.5 percent of the total, but mining of asbestos was still the leading economic activity in the country and contributed over 60 percent of government revenue obtained from income taxes. It is produced at the Havelock Mine in the Piggs Peak area (Map 99), said to be one of the five largest mines in the world, moved by a 12½-mile aerial ropeway to Barberton in the Union, and railed from there to Lourenço Marques. The mine employs about 150 Europeans and 1,500 Africans. Opportunities for maintaining and increasing the production of asbestos are excellent, as both the present producer and additional concession holders have proved large new reserves in the same area.

Interest has been focused in recent years upon a deposit belonging to the Anglo-American group of 62.6 percent iron ore at Ngwenya near the Transvaal border northwest of Mbabane. About 35 million tons of ore have been proved that can be mined from the surface, and in 1961 it was possible to start preparatory work at the site after an agreement valued at $112 million had been concluded with the Yawata and Fuji Iron and Steel Companies of Japan for the delivery of 12 million tons of ore over a ten-year period starting in 1965. This contract will have an immense impact on the Swazi economy because it has justified the construction of a rail line across the country which should benefit many activities in addition to iron mining.

Swaziland also has anthracite and semi-anthracite coal (low-volatile bituminous) occurring in minable seams on the eastern edge of the lowveld and extending for 90 miles right through the territory. Two sites have been examined in detail: one west of Stegi, the other near Maloma, where a considerable amount of underground development has taken place. A very small output is now hauled by road to the railhead at Gollel in the southeast corner, but it is hoped that production of about 60,000 tons a year will begin in the near future, slightly over half going to the new railway and additional tonnages supplying the two sugar mills. The low-grade coal will be the first mined, solely because of its more favorable location, but the anthracite coal is bound to attract interest sooner or later because it probably ranks with the best coals of southern Africa.

Other minerals produced include gold, tin, diaspore, barites, and pyrophyllite. Mining of gold in Swaziland was one of the earliest mining ventures in southern Africa; output was discontinued from 1953 to 1960 but a resurvey of old workings in the Piggs Peak area encouraged new operations leading to an output valued at about $33,600 in 1961. In 1962 some rather spectacular findings opened the possibility of attracting quite a large operation to the territory, and, since serious prospecting only started in 1961, the hopes are high for additional finds. Tin comes from near Mbabane and the other minerals from the southwest. In 1960 a deposit of copper-nickel-cobalt ore was discovered at Mhlambanyate, and a big manganiferous iron ore find has also recently been made,

Part of the Peak Timbers plantation in the Piggs Peak district of Swaziland
About 200,000 acres have been planted in three pine and eucalyptus plantations in the highveld. Peak Timbers has a sawmill and chipboard factory, while the Usutu Forests will be used for production of pulp.

unfortunately in a rather remote location. Additional possibilities include the development of high-grade kaolin and of pyrites.

INDUSTRY

Almost all of the industrial development in Swaziland is associated with processing of extractive products. Plants include the large works at the Havelock Mine, the three forest product establishments previously noted, the Malkerns cannery, the two new sugar mills, and a maize mill and malt house at Manzini (formerly Bremersdorp).

Swaziland has favorable conditions for hydroelectric development. Several of its important streams enter the territory in deep gorges at elevations of 3,500 to 4,500 feet, and flow across the country to leave at elevations of about 500 feet. Five small stations are now in being and in mid-1963 the IBRD arranged a loan to help finance a $6 million electrical installation 10 miles from Manzini. A 1,000-kw thermoelectric plant will be constructed to meet immediate needs, but the main plant will be a 10,000-kw hydroelectric station on the Little Usutu River. About half of the output will be consumed by the iron mining company and the Usutu pulp mill; the remainder will be transmitted to the main towns of Mbabane and Manzini, which have had a serious shortfall in production in recent years, to the new railroad town of Sidvodokvo, and to the Big Bend for pump irrigation. For the future, about 30,000 kw could be developed by diverting water from the Great Usutu, while about 225,000 kw could be harnessed by 13 stations on the Great Usutu. Many hydroelectric schemes will also increase the opportunities for irrigation farming.

It is possible that a labor shortage will develop in Swaziland if the variety of mining, agricultural, and other projects which contain interesting potentialities attract investment. In 1961 employers with over 50 employees had 17,049 wage earners including about 3,000 foreign Africans. Some leeway exists in the migrant labor which now goes to the Union; in 1961 about 6,900 Swazis were so engaged, contributing about $277,000 in deferred pay and family remittances, $315,000 in cash and goods brought back, and $22,000 in taxes to the territorial economy. The government would like to discourage further migration, for all of the able-bodied males will be needed in the country for rail and road construction and other enterprises.

TRANSPORTATION AND TRADE

A glance at Map 93 will reveal the somewhat isolated position of Swaziland with respect to railway service. This situation will improve immensely with completion of the 140-mile line across the country from Bomvu through some of the most productive parts of the territory to Goba in Mozambique. This line will serve the proposed iron mine, the Usutu Forests, the important Malkerns agricultural area, coal production at Mpaka, and may later be tied by short branches to Mbabane and Manzini.

There are now 1,200 miles of roads about half being classed as trunk or main roads. A road between Mbabane and Manzini and the branch road from the Usutu pulp mill are paved while a first-class road across the country is now being laid. The territory got its first airport in 1961 at Matsapa, four miles from Manzini.

Green and Fair see the Mbabane-Manzini zone as the leading economic axis in Swaziland, serving important development areas in both the middle and the high velds. Mbabane, the capital and largest town, has a population of about 5,500 including 1,300 Europeans; Manzini, with 4,300 including 1,200 Europeans, is increasingly becoming the territory's commercial hub and is an embryonic industrial center.

Data regarding the trade of Swaziland are given in Table 45. South Africa has characteristically been the major consumer and supplier of Swazi shipments except for asbestos exports, but its share may be expected to decline sharply with new mineral and agricultural developments.

Table 45. Exports of Swaziland, 1955, 1961 (in thousand dollars)

Product	*1955*	*1961*
Asbestos	...[a]	8,120
Sugar	nil	5,162
Cattle	883	1,774
Cotton	624	1,007
Timber products	28	906
Rice	400	545
Pineapples, canned	15	216
Citrus fruit	10	189
Other fruit	38	171
Butter	196	153
Hides and skins	76	104
Tobacco	84	67
Wattle bark	130	35
Other		269
Total		18,718

Sources: Swaziland, "Current Economic Position and Prospects of Swaziland" (June 22, 1962, mimeographed), Table I; Swaziland, *Annual Report of the Department of Land Utilization, 1961*, I, 15.

... = Not available.

[a] 1957 exports were $6,860,000.

Part Eight MADAGASCAR AND THE MASCARENES

A village in the Betsimitatatra Plain near Tananarive, Madagascar

Madagascar

This "continent of the Indian Ocean" has many of the characteristics and problems of Africa, of which it is the largest appurtenance, yet it has distinctive physical, cultural, and economic features which give it peculiar interest.[1] Madagascar owes its distinctiveness in considerable part to the Malayo-Polynesian origin of a substantial part of its populace, to the isolating influence of its location, and to its island character.

Likened to the imprint of a left foot in the sand, the "Grand Isle" stretches for almost 1,000 miles as a giant breakwater off the coast of Mozambique, from which it is separated by the 250- to 500-mile-wide Mozambique Channel. Averaging about 230 miles across and with a maximum width of 360 miles, Madagascar has an area of 227,736 square miles, making it equivalent to the British Isles, West Germany, and Belgium combined, or about 3½ times the size of New England. It is the world's fourth largest Island. Madagascar's population in 1963 was about 5,850,000, all but about 2 percent of whom were Malagasy. Measured by the production and consumption of energy, the development of land transport, and the level of international trade, Madagascar rates with such less-developed African countries as Sierra Leone, Ethiopia, and Mozambique. Its mining and manufacturing industries compare unfavorably with most tropical African countries.

THE PHYSICAL MILIEU

The location of Madagascar helps to explain its isolation, the development of independent species of flora and fauna and the absence of other species common to Africa, the rather unusual crop emphases of the country, and some of the contrasts in cultural practices. Some islands are located in the stream of world movements and their interests are more universal than insular, but Madagascar's location has tended to minimize its contact with the outside world. Contributing to this isolation have been the inhospitable nature of much of the coast and the fact that the most highly developed group, the Merina, who might have been expected to develop trade, deliberately isolated themselves in the center of the island and long discouraged contacts with surrounding peoples.

There were a few early attempts at settlement and at establishing commercial posts. The French Société de l'Orient tried to start a colony at Sainte Luce, 25 miles north of Fort Dauphin, in 1642, but after 27 of the party of 89 were lost in the first month, the colony was moved to the healthier Fort Dauphin. Following a long series of misfortunes, violence among the settlers, wars against the natives, pillage, and reciprocal massacres, the colony was abandoned in 1674. At the end of that century, a French pirate founded the colony of Libertalia at Diégo-Suarez, and about 1720 Ile Sainte Marie off the east coast

[1] A substantial portion of this chapter is an updating of the author's article, "The Economic Geography of Madagascar," appearing in *Tidjschrift voor Economische en Sociale Geografie* (July–August, 1957), pp. 161–72, and of "Madagascar and Tropical Africa—Similarities and Contrasts," in William A. Hance, *African Economic Development* (New York, Harper, 1958). The author thanks the editor of *Tijdschrift* and the Council on Foreign Relations for permission to use these writings.

was acquired by the son of an English freebooter and a local chief's daughter. Their daughter Bety ceded this island to France in 1750, and a decade earlier the little island of Nossi-Bé on the northwest had become a protectorate.

But most ships sailing to the Orient passed by Madagascar, whose participation in world trade was insignificant. Opening of the Suez Canal made the island even less important, though the French did establish their prime naval base in the Indian Ocean in the magnificent harbor of Diégo-Suarez. The island's location acquired greater significance in World War II with the closing of the Mediterranean route. After the local government had sided with Vichy upon the fall of France, the British felt it necessary to invade the island to prevent its falling into the hands of the Japanese. An enemy submarine base at Diégo-Suarez would have provided a formidable threat to the Middle East supply lines around the Cape.

The generally isolating influence of its location removed Madagascar to a considerable degree from the flood of journalists, officials, tourists, academicians, and businessmen who invaded Africa in postwar years. The French colonial government enjoyed an amazing degree of privacy in Madagascar. A revolt in 1947–48 went almost uncovered in the world press, though it resulted in far more deaths than the Mau Mau uprising in Kenya. And only a handful of non-French scholars have made special studies of the island.

The element of isolation, however, should not be overstressed; to some degree it has been used as a convenient rationalization for failure to achieve a more satisfactory economic development. It is true that the island lies off the beaten track, but it is served by several liner and regular freight services. If isolation were really as severe a handicap as it is said to be, Mauritius, which is several days further away from Europe on the same services, should be equally undeveloped, but, in fact, it has exports about three-quarters those of Madagascar from an area less than a third of 1 percent as great.

LANDFORMS

The geology of Madagascar determines the larger topographic regions; it divides the island into two main zones, a highland region composed largely of Archean granites, and the western plain of almost undisturbed sedimentary rocks dipping gently towards the Mozambique Channel and occupying about a quarter of the total area. From the topographic standpoint, the dominant feature is the great central highland which extends 720 miles north and south with a maximum width of about 240 miles (Map 100). This area is usually called the "central plateau," which conveys a highly erroneous impression of its surface features. Although the hills often appear to have a fairly uniform elevation and although they rise from the Archean base that is substantially elevated above sea level, the area is profoundly cut by valleys and the great bulk of it is in slope. It is more accurate to think of this important region as a high-based hill-land.

Rising above the average altitudes of 3,900 to 4,600 feet are three principal masses: Tsaratanana in the north, whose summit of volcanic rock rises to 9,449 feet; Ankaratra, an enormous volcanic massif with elevations of 7,000–8,000 feet in the center of the country and following the general grain of the highlands; and Andringitra, a vast denuded granite mass rising to 8,700 feet south of Ambalavao. The highland area is generally higher in the east, where it drops off abruptly in one or two steps to the eastern coastal zone. Between the two scarps at about the middle of the island are some fairly extensive flattish areas, the Mangoro and Lake Alaotra basins.

From the standpoint of human use, the Madagascan uplands are a more difficult region than the African plateau. There are the same difficulties of approach, the same fringing scarps, and the same lack of navigable streams that long repelled the opening up of Africa. But even when the heights are attained, the inhibiting influences of the landforms continue. Roads are constructed with difficulty; with the aim

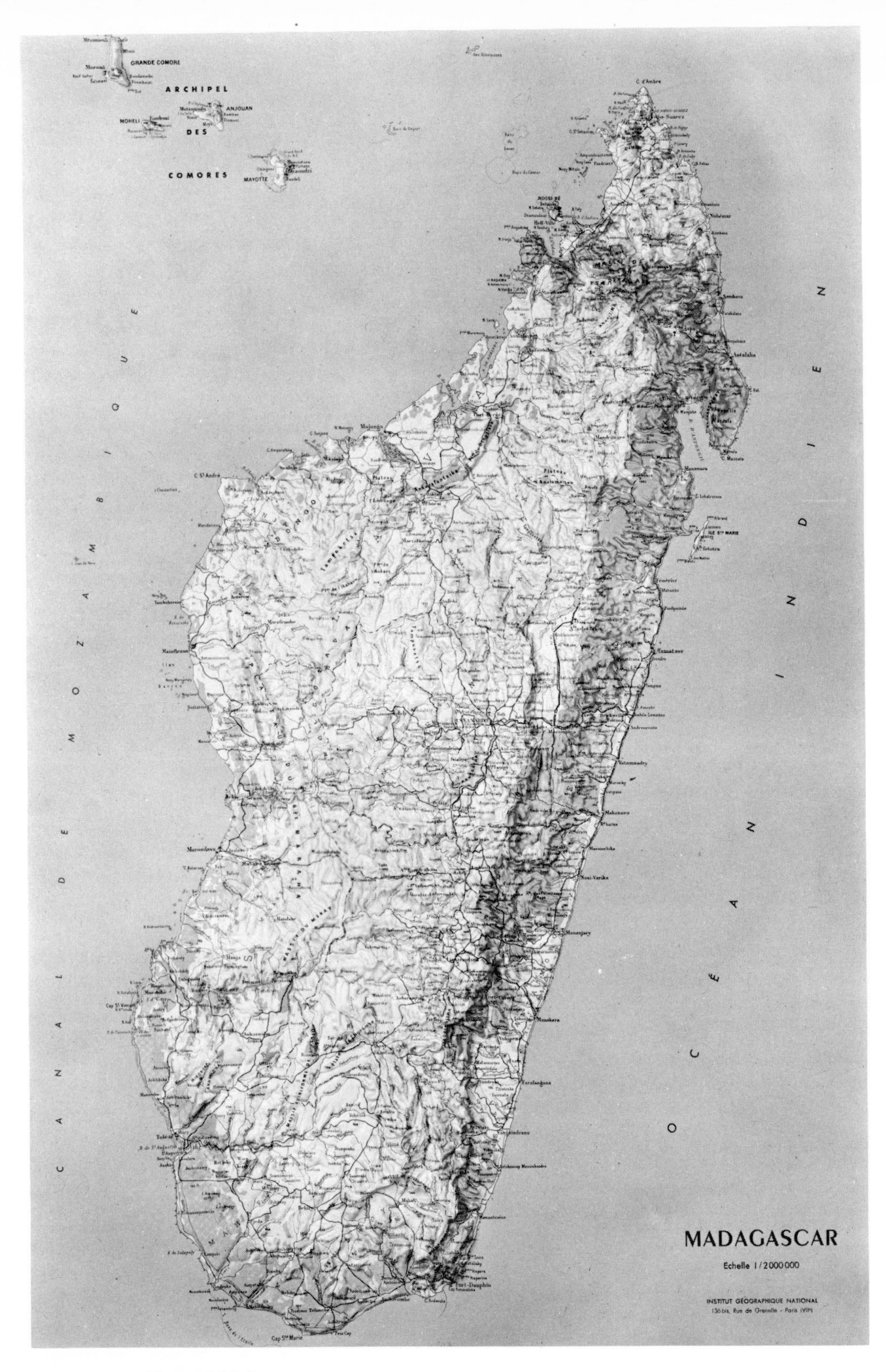

Map 100. Landforms of Madagascar
Reproduced by permission of the Institut Nationale Géographique de France

of reducing expenditure on bridges they meander endlessly along the fairly even crests of the dissected hills. Soil erosion occurs more readily, and is more difficult to control; use of the sloping surfaces for agriculture is not attractive. On the other hand, there is perhaps an advantage in the more rapid accumulation of water in the valleys, which may then be controlled for the intensive cultivation of paddy rice.

The eastern coastal zone, only 10 to 50 miles wide, is composed of downfaulted segments of the island's Archean massif fringed by flat, low-lying swampland resting on Quaternary deposits. A series of lagoons lie behind the very narrow belt of sand which extends in a remarkably straight line along the coast from Fenerive almost to Fort Dauphin, while one or more coral reefs, usually submerged, lie immediately off the coast. A final scarp or series of scarps, lying below the sea, leads to enormous depths very close to the island mass.

On the western side of the island a 60- to 120-mile-wide belt of plains and low plateaus dips gently toward the channel, while a series of more or less well-marked cuestas face the central highlands, from which the area often is separated by a profoundly eroded scarp zone, known in the center as the Bongo Lava.

The smaller features of the coastal areas of Madagascar have many of the same inhibiting features of the African coasts. On the east, there are only two sizable indentations: Diégo-Suarez in the extreme north and Antongil Bay. Diégo's usefulness is greatly reduced by its location at the narrower extremity of the island and by its small hinterland, restricted by difficult landforms to the south. Antongil Bay is open to the prevailing winds. From Foulpointe almost to Fort Dauphin, a distance of about 600 miles, the east coast is remarkably straight, the absence of indentations and protected bays forcing the use of inadequate and often dangerous open roadsteads. The only respectable east coast port, Tamatave, is partly artificial. Its protection is inadequate, however, and a seiche, or rhythmical motion, develops in the harbor even with winds of moderate intensity. River mouths along this coast are offset, and are clogged with shifting bars; they are used by lighters but ocean-going vessels must stand offshore in a characteristically heavy sea. Offshore coral reefs further endanger loading and unloading operations.

The west coast, which, with its gently dipping sediments, is quite unlike the typical African coastal zone and more like those of the continents facing the North Atlantic, is considerably more attractive, but even there the larger river mouths and deltas are unreliable because of rapid silting. Efforts to construct a deepwater port at Majunga, for example, have been frustrated by silting behind a kilometer-long dike which reduced depths from 36 feet to as little as 3 feet in a ten-year period.

The topographic features of both coasts and of the interior of Madagascar have been largely responsible for the division of the island into many economic subregions (inset Map 103) whose contact with one another is often very tenuous. The central highlands are tied to the east coast by two rail lines and by a number of mediocre roads, while the unusual Canal des Pangalanes, connecting a series of littoral lagoons, unites some areas of the east coast. But long stretches on both sides of the island function more like island archipelagoes than as parts of the same land mass. One sees, as a consequence and on a reduced scale, the same sort of concentration of economic activity in coastal and highland "islands" that is discernible on the continent.

CLIMATE

Madagascar is entirely tropical, its major climatic features being controlled most strongly by its position in the prevailing easterlies of the Southern Hemisphere and by its relief. Rain is conditioned by three principal winds: the prevailing easterlies, the "monsoon" of Mozambique, and winds coming from the high pressure areas to the south. The easterlies blow all year on Madagascar and, abetted by the orographic factor on the east-facing scarps, give the east coast heavy precipitation (Map 2). Split somewhat by the island's relief, these winds form two branches, the northern one passing Cap d'Ambre and returning to strike the northwest coast. This contributes, especially in winter, to giving the northwest a climate analogous to that of the east coast. The southern branch arrives well weakened at Fort Dauphin and scarcely penetrates westward from that point, there being a very sharp isohyet gradient at the southern tip of the island. The prevailing easterlies that pass over the central highlands become strongly drying in winter, creating a foehn which accentuates the dry season.

The "monsoon" of Mozambique, coming from the northwest, brings sometimes violent summer rains to the northwestern coast, particularly northwest of Majunga. This is the second factor giving the northwest coast a climate comparable to that of the east. Winds from the middle latitude highs chiefly affect the island south of the Tropic of Capricorn, bringing cold weather and occasional rain.

Altitude plays the dominant role in temperature distribution. The central highlands enjoy a highly moderate climate; the east and northwest coasts are continuously hot, and the west displays a continental influence in its greater temperature ranges.

The island may be divided into four main climate regions. First, a tropical rainy climate zone runs almost the full length of the east coast and along the northwest coast as well. Constantly hot and humid, this area has a climate analogous to that of the Congo Basin or the Guinea Coast. Second, the central highlands have a tropical highland climate, comparable with the climate of upland parts of Kenya or Tanganyika. Third, a tropical savanna climate region runs along the west and across the northern tip of the island with a well-marked dry period in the winter, but with precipitation in most months of the year. Lastly, a tropical steppe climate prevails in the southwest. The west and south, especially, suffer from irregularity of precipitation and from alternating excessive aridity and torrential rains. But even parts of the east coast suffer from the uneven distribution of precipitation: high rains in October and November cause the coffee flowers to fall; heavy rain in July inhibits the drying of vanilla and coffee; dryness in January-February causes low rice yields, while damaging floods are common.

The climate regime of Madagascar permits production of the same tropical crops that are produced in Africa, though the emphases are quite different. Palm products, the great staple agricultural exports of Congo and Nigeria, are almost absent, cocoa is produced in very small quantities, and interest in cotton is just beginning. But almost all the other crops of tropical Africa are included in the list of exports, and the island enjoys a nearly unique position in production of vanilla and certain essential oils.

One additional feature of the climate must be mentioned, the frequency of hurricanes, one or more of which visit the island each year. The east coast is most severely and regularly hit, but the west coast and highland areas are by no means immune. East coast cities, farms, and transport facilities are periodically severely affected, while the prevalence of hurricanes and, indeed, of generally high winds is another of the many disadvantages of the east coast ports. These disturbances account for the absence of Arab dhows in the coastal and international traffic of the east coast, while a considerable number of these vessels engage in the carriage of freight along the west. And it is estimated that bad weather and heavy seas account for over half of the days lost by ships operating in Madagascar waters. The most severe losses from hurricanes occurred in 1929 when Tamatave was virtually destroyed, in 1949 when the Moromamy (Brickaville) bridge of the main rail line was washed away, interrupting traffic for six months, in 1953 when 75 percent of the buildings in the less-frequented west coast port of Majunga were damaged, in 1955–56 when nine hurricanes hit the east coast of the island, and in 1960 when five severe storms within five weeks caused 150 deaths and destruction estimated at $12.3 million, and resulted in a marked

Erosion control applied in a gully east of Lake Alaotra
Soil erosion is a problem of immense proportions in the highlands of Madagascar. Only the planting of trees has proved effective in preventing extension of gullies such as this.

decline of valuable coffee, vanilla, and clove exports.

SOILS

Madagascar has been described as having "the color and fertility of a brick"; indeed it is sometimes called the Red Isle. Latosols, the curse of the tropics, cover not only the bulk of the rainy tropical east coast but also most of the highlands and part of the savanna area, where somewhat better soils might be expected. They explain the practice of shifting agriculture in the east, where it is known as *tavy*.

Much of the sedimentary area is also disadvantaged by poor soils, being covered by an infertile skin of clayey sand. Nonetheless, the best regional soils are found in great concentric arcs in the dryer western savanna and in the limestone Mahafaly plateau in the south where, unfortunately, precipitation is most deficient and erratic. There are some good to excellent azonal soils, including those of volcanic origin in the Lake Itasy area west of Tananarive, the Antsirabe region to the south, and on the island of Nossi-Bé, as well as alluvials in the short valleys of the east and along the greater but more irregular streams of the west.

In view of the generally deficient soils, it is perhaps fortunate that the prevailing agriculture of the highlands is confined to the usually small valley bottoms, and that it is centered upon cultivation of paddy rice. Here is found the accumulation of the somewhat better top soil, while paddy farming results in far less drain on the soil. On the east coast, alluvial soils have frequently been utilized for paddies and a considerable portion of the population is dependent upon them. There is sometimes an almost continuous string of villages along the lower valleys. On the west coast, development of the valleys and use of their fertile soils is much more haphazard, though some of the more important postwar projects have been located with primary reference to the soil factor.

Soil erosion is a problem of immense proportions on Madagascar, particularly on the central highlands, where bright red gashes scar the landscape over very wide areas. The major cause of erosion in the highlands is not farming of the slopelands, which is uncommon unless rice terraces are laboriously constructed, but the almost complete removal of the natural forest by deliberate firing, and subsequent overgrazing of the grasslands. There are few regions on the continent where soil erosion has been as severe as it is in central Madagascar.

THE FLORA AND FAUNA

The vegetation of Madagascar shows primary response to the climatic pattern, but misuse by man has degraded it over perhaps 70 percent of the island's surface. Most of the species are African, but those that are unique to Madagascar give some vegetational landscapes a fascinating appearance. The east coast and scarp zones and the northwest, except in the swampy littoral and where man has cut the forest commercially or for subsistence farming, have tropical rainforests with closely spaced trees of average height and with numerous species represented. These forests are variously estimated to cover from 10 to 13.5 percent of the island. Areas of *savoka* or secondary woodland, however, are greater than those of virgin forest.

The central highlands were covered not many centuries ago with forest, but man-lit fires have destroyed all but a few remnants in inaccessible parts, and now this region is covered largely with grasses of only mediocre nutritive value. There is a program of reforestation with mimosas, pine, and, above all, eucalypts, but it has only begun to reduce the huge denuded areas of the central region. The west and south have greatly variable vegetation types, sometimes low grasslands, often some type of bush country with surprising thickness despite the greater aridity. Finally, about 1,000 square miles of mangrove forests fringe the west coast.

Like the flora of Madagascar, the fauna has numerous African species and others of domestic evolution. There is a complete absence of the big game that characterizes Africa, the largest wild animals being the crocodile and the lemur, whose presence almost gave the name Lemuria to the island continent. Snakes are seen more often in Madagascar than in Africa, but none of them are poisonous.

Insects are of greater significance. Until recently, the east coast had an unsavory reputation as a highly malarious region, but a remarkable campaign, involving the spraying of every house and hut on the island at least once a year and the free dispensing of nivaquine in schools, has virtually eliminated *Anopheles Funestus* from the highlands and greatly reduced the prevalence of *Anopheles Gambiae* on the coasts. So successful was the campaign that malaria had been practically arrested on the entire island by 1955. The effect of this sudden great improvement in health conditions was almost immediately apparent in the increasing rate of population growth, which was almost nil in 1946 but is now probably at least 2.8 percent.

Locusts are one of the worst pests of the island. Crop production is constantly threatened by invasions of these insects from the arid regions of the south. Dusting, mainly from helicopters, has been successful in combating locusts, but they remain a considerable menace. The absence of one insect on Madagascar is worthy of note—the tsetse fly—a blessing that has not

A government worker about to spray a hut near Fort Dauphin with DDT
A very successful antimalarial campaign resulted in a dynamic increase in the rate of population growth in postwar years.

Household articles removed before spraying takes place
With the exception of a few pieces of furniture, this represents the total worldly possessions of the inhabitant.

been fully appreciated. This permits the working out of systems of agriculture which are not now applicable in large parts of the continent, but which may be of great benefit when some method of fly control has been discovered. Experiments at the Ivaloina Agricultural Station in the rainforest area north of Tamatave indicate that a rather satisfactory system of mixed agriculture is possible.

THE POPULATION OF MADAGASCAR

The estimated population of the Malagasy Republic in 1962 was 5,657,601. Until about 1948 the keynotes of the demographic pattern were low density and a slow rate of growth if not stagnation. For long, a high death rate nearly canceled a high birth rate. The high death rate was explained by malnutrition, disease, unhygienic conditions, and intertribal warfare. Certain cultural features have also contributed to the high death rate; the Malagasy have a profound fatalism and resignation regarding death.

But recent years have seen a highly dynamic change in population growth. Improved health measures and disease control, particularly the antimalaria campaign previously noted, have contributed to an increased birth rate and a lowered death rate. The increase in population was only 10,978 in 1946; by 1955 it was 102,627, and in 1961 it was about 184,000. This demographic boom is bound to have a striking impact on the economy of Madagascar, but adjustments to it have been slow in materializing.

The population density of Madagascar was 24.8 per square mile in 1962, but there are sharp differences between the area around Tananarive and portions of the east coast with densities of over 120 per square mile and the west and south with densities as low as 3 to 6 per square mile (Map 101). Nor are the more favored areas always the more densely populated. Tananarive, with a population of about 250,000 in 1961, is the only real city on the island.

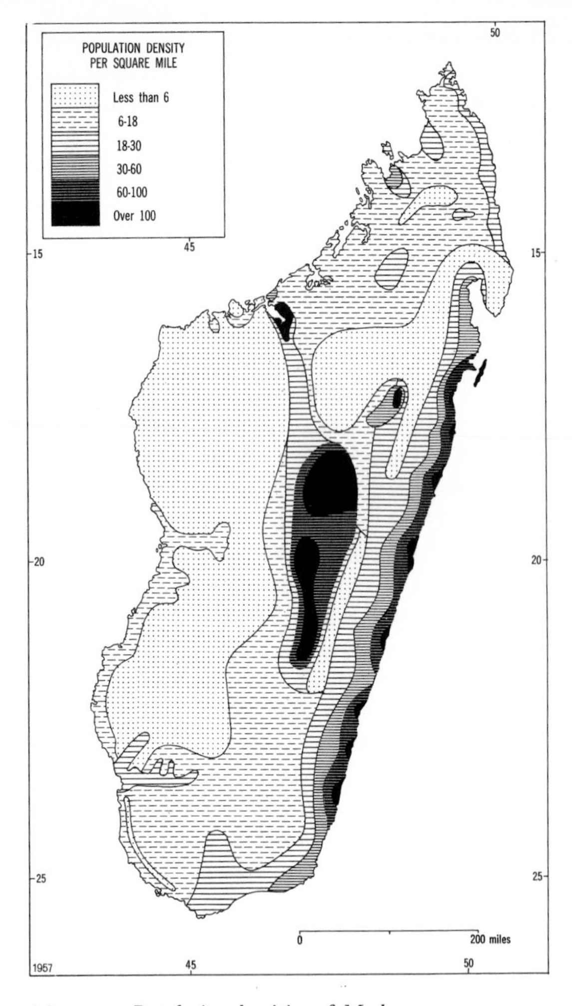

Map 101. Population densities of Madagascar

THE INDIGENOUS PEOPLE OF THE ISLAND

A total of 97.8 percent of the population of Madagascar are Malagasy. Most writings have followed the theory that the bulk of the population is descended from immigrants who came across the Indian Ocean bringing with them the language which later developed into Malgache, rice, and many culture traits which are still common to Madagascar and Indonesia. The Negroid characteristics of most of the Malagasy were said to be derived from the Negroes of Melanesia.

A second main theory of long standing is that Madagascar was populated by Africans long before the arrival of the Indonesians, and that the latter imposed their language and many culture traits after subjugating the Negroes. The inclusion of many Bantu words in the Malgache language is cited as supporting evidence. Less widely accepted theories are that the Negroes of Madagascar represent an independent migration from Asia and that Indonesian-Polynesian migrants came via the Horn of Africa, bringing Africans from there to the island.

It seems most likely that none of these theories are accurate. There is no question that the Merina originated in the East, probably in Indonesia, and they probably came to Madagascar Kon-Tiki style. But the Malagasy Negroids, who make up most of the other tribes, are quite likely of Bantu-Swahili origin and may have come from East Africa, using the islands of the Comores Archipelago as stepping-stones. Many of the customs of the coastal tribes, especially the attitudes of pastoral tribes toward their cattle, appear closely related to those of African graziers. And there are a substantial number of words in Malgache which have a Bantu or Swahili origin.

There has undoubtedly been a considerable mixture of the various indigenous Malagasy. Even the Merina must have a strong African element, for many people apparently claim to belong to this tribe who have only a minimal racial connection. The Merina do, however, retain the appearance of Indonesians very strongly. The Betsileo, sometimes called the southern Hova (an incorrect term for the Merina, because it applies only to one of their four main castes), have the greatest similarity to the Merina; the Betsimisaraka follow. These three tribes have estimated populations of 1,400,000 (Merina), 800,000 (Betsileo), and 700,000 (Betsimisaraka), or about half of the total population. But the coastal tribes have relatively little mixture with the Merina. They are split into about fifteen major groups.

Closely associated with the problem of their origins is the question of the degree of unity among the Malagasy people. Some observers describe it as remarkable, noting that the indigenous patterns of social organization and religion were everywhere fundamentally the same. Other observers say that the Malagasy differ as widely as the Russians and Spaniards and that various dialects of Malgache are unintelligible to those speaking other dialects.

There is considerable political rivalry between the more evolved Merina and the coastal tribes. Before the Europeans arrived, the Merina had a detailed history, advanced governmental forms, and a fairly well-developed exchange economy, and were practicing a highly organized, intensive agriculture not found in sub-Saharan Africa. Today, their standards of dress and housing are superior; they have the highest literacy rate and the largest number of educated people of the Malagasy tribes. An estimated 10,000 Merina could read and write in 1836; today

A Merina village near Tananarive
The Merina comprise the most evolved tribe of Madagascar. Originating centuries ago in southeast Asia, they introduced a paddy rice culture and the Malgache language to the island.

about 75 percent of their children are attending school as compared with about 30 to 40 percent for the whole island. The Merina hold most of the positions in the government; they are the clerks, the technicians, and the artisans of the island and not only in their traditional area of Tananarive Province. As might be expected, many of the other tribes resent the Merina, and, since they outnumber the Merina, hold most of the ministerial posts in the government. Despite these tribal rivalries, however, Madagascar does appear to have stronger unifying influences than most African countries, particularly the common language and a somewhat greater feeling of national consciousness than that possessed by many African tribes.

THE NONINDIGENOUS POPULATION

The non-Malagasy population of Madagascar in 1962 consisted of 51,856 Europeans, 40,377 Comoriens, 13,233 Indians, and 8,901 Chinese. In assessing the contribution of "Europeans" to Madagascar it is important to note that a substantial number of those classified as French are Creoles from Réunion or Mauritius, many of whom are small colons, foremen, operators of mechanical equipment, and small merchants. They do not pull the same weight, man for man, as the Frenchmen from France; although they dominate such nonplantation European farming as there is on Madagascar, their practices have been characterized by small scale of operation, small capital investment, and previously by exploitative sharecropping systems. After the revolt, the French gave considerably greater attention to assisting Malagasy agriculture rather than favoring the "French" settlers and also adopted a new firmness toward demands of the small colons.

The French-born Europeans are still present in Madagascar in considerable numbers. While those working for the government are being rapidly replaced by Malagasy, the French continue to be heavily represented in education, missions, plantations, industry, and the larger commercial institutions.

The Indians, who include Muslims and Hindus, are often petty merchants, and are found particularly along the west coast. Others are masons, carpenters, ironworkers, and jewelers. The original Chinese on Madagascar were mainly Cantonese brought in to work on the Tananarive-Côte Est Railway in the first decade of the present century. A large number of them are now small merchants, located especially on the east coast and in the central highlands. The fact that only an eighth of the total Chinese are women reflects the fact that Chinese often take Malagasy women for their wives. Of the other nonindigenous people, Arabs are of some importance in the Majunga area, several hundred Greeks are scattered throughout the island, and British and Americans are well represented in the mission field.

As in other parts of Africa, the Asian peoples are frequently accused of sharp practices, such as paying illicit prices for collection of Malagasy-produced crops and lending money at usurious rates. As the small merchants purchase most of their goods from the three largest European trading companies, the heirarchy of merchants and other middlemen is often a heavy burden on production and commerce. However, the Malagasy have not been willing to enter the commercial field, and it is not easy to see how some of the remote areas of the island would be served without the Asians. To some they appear not as exploiters but as indispensable intermediaries. The dominant position of the several minority groups on Madagascar is indicated by the estimate that they account for about 85 percent of the 3,541 private employers on the island. About three fourths of the nonindigenous population of Madagascar lives in the eight largest towns, over a third in Tananarive alone. The capital, in fact, is the Paris of Madagascar, there being a high concentration of cultural, commercial, industrial, and political institutions in the city.

MAJOR LAND USE REGIONS

Over 93 percent of the Malagasy are dependent upon agriculture, which is still very largely concerned with subsistence production. The major uses of the cultivated lands, which total only about 3 percent of the island's surface, were estimated as shown in Table 46 in 1962.

Table 46. Major uses of the cultivated areas on Madagascar, 1962 (in thousands of acres)

Total cultivated surface		6,900
Irrigated		1,625
Rice	1,575	
Field crops		1,925
Manioc	750	
Mountain rice	250	
Peanuts	87	
Sisal	40	
Tree crops		687
Coffee	488	
Cloves	80	
Vanilla	12	
Fallow		2,663

Source: Malagasy Ministry of Agriculture.

Madagascar has an unusual variety of both subsistence and cash crops, which may be revealed by the following listing:

(1) Food crops: rice, manioc, corn, beans, peanuts, potatoes, taro, sorghum, bananas, sugar, and other vegetables and fruits.
(2) Vegetable oils: coconut, castor, candlenut, peanut, tung.
(3) Fibers: sisal, raffia, paka, cotton.
(4) Stimulants: coffee, tobacco.
(5) Perfumes, spices, etc.: ylang-ylang, lemon grass, cloves, pepper, vanilla.

The crops which are partly or entirely commercialized, classified on the basis of producer and destination, are as follows:

(1) Grown exclusively on European holdings primarily for export: sisal, tung oil, pepper, ylang-ylang, lemon grass, cocoa.
(2) Grown exclusively by Malagasy and having a considerable export: beans, raffia, oil-bearing seeds.
(3) Grown by Europeans and Malagasy and having a considerable export: coffee, tobacco, cloves, vanilla, sugar, manioc, rice, peanuts.
(4) Grown principally for food, mainly by Malagasy, but with some European production: rice, manioc, corn, peanuts, potatoes, market garden crops, taro, sorghum, bananas.

The island has a substantial and increasing livestock population, though it is not anywhere near as well commercialized as it should be. In 1962 it was estimated that there were 7,600,000 cattle, 406,000 pigs, 385,000 sheep, and 380,000 goats. The dependence of Madagascar on exports of agricultural origin is very high, running close to 95 percent of the total (Table 48). Farming and animal husbandry accounted for an estimated 54.6 percent of the national income in 1960.

THE CENTRAL HIGHLANDS

The heart of the country is the central highland region (inset, Map 102), particularly the section stretching from the Tananarive region to that around Fianarantsoa. Despite the difficult landforms and generally poor soils, this is the most populous part of the country, having about two fifths of the total population. About 2 million are the more advanced, relatively industrious Merina and Betsileo.

The two major concerns of the highland farmer are rice and beef cattle. Many of the valleys, often quite narrow, have been laboriously prepared for rice paddies to provide the staple food, the highlands having over half of the 1,625,000 irrigated acres on the island. Sometimes terraces have been constructed that are reminiscent of those of Indonesia, the Betsileo having the reputation of constructing the finest ones on the steepest slopes.

There are few large plains, the two most important being the Betsimitatatra Plain around Tananarive and the Lake Alaotra Basin on the intermediate level between the two eastern scarps. The former has been completely developed, though there are possibilities for better water control, and some paddies which have been abandoned could be rewon by controlling

Rice terraces near Antsirabe
The Betsileo tribe has constructed the finest rice terraces on the island, partly because of the small extent of plains available for development.

the water hyacinth and by fertilization. The more sparsely populated Lake Alaotra Basin, in contrast, is still in the early stages of development. A large part of the basin is occupied by a shallow lake and surrounding marshes. It is estimated that the utilized area can be more than doubled to about 270,000 acres. Considered to be the most favorable place for intensive, mechanized cultivation of rice on the island, the area has been the scene of a major effort to help increase the exports of rice and manioc.

Rice, which is the major subsistence crop of Madagascar, is grown as a paddy crop wherever possible. Yields are low and practices poor; rice is rarely planted in rows, rotated, or fertilized, practices which could give considerably more satisfactory results.

Although rice is particularly important on the highlands, there is a remarkable variety of other crops produced, particularly around the capital. The moderate climate permits production of tropical, subtropical, and middle latitude crops, and the great Zoma at Tananarive is undoubtedly one of the finest markets in the tropics. There are a number of small, specialized zones of crop production: around Lake Itasy, west of Tananarive, volcanic soils have permitted production of industrial crops such as peanuts, tobacco, arabica coffee, and tung oil; the high area around Antsirabe and Fianarantsoa produces coffee, tobacco, and the white potato; the Lake Alaotra Basin and the Mangoro Valley produce manioc, with much of the output of European estates, whose yields are 5 to 7 times the average, being used to manufacture tapioca.

The variety of crops grown on the highlands should not permit one to lose sight of the importance of grazing. Over three fifths of the island is used for grazing, but little care is taken of the cattle, most of which are Zebu, and there is almost no selective breeding. Although the meat is excellent to eat, yields are mediocre. Cattle are used in the highlands for drawing carts and for trampling the rice paddies preparatory to planting, but most are left to fend for themselves on the seasonally inadequate grass slopes of the region. The number of cattle was declining seriously in the 1950s owing to poor practices and a tax which discouraged increasing herds. This trend has now apparently been reversed, but exports have not increased proportionately, and Madagascar is far from deserving the title it is sometimes given of "Ile de Boeuf."

For the future, the two great needs of the

highland area are to rationalize livestock practices and to intensify use of the hilltops and slopes. Although there are valleys that have not been developed for rice cultivation, and numerous ways in which those that are developed can be improved, there is a definite limit to the possibilities of extending paddies in the difficult highland area. The rapidly expanding population now requires that attention be given to cropping on the slopes, now predominantly in grass, without increasing the already serious soil erosion. Experimental work, particularly at the Lake Alaotra Agricultural Research Station, indicates that by reforesting the steeper areas and by planting crops on the contour and in appropriate rotation, a type of mixed farming can be practiced that is far more intensive than the present nonintegrated system of rice in the valleys and cattle on the hills.

The central highlands have the best road network on the island, and the two rail lines have their interior termini in the Merina and Betsileo countries. Not only is this area the greatest consumer of imported goods, but it is also the focus of a well-developed local exchange economy. Rather disfavored from the physical standpoint, the central highland region is distinctly favored from the human standpoint, and there are numerous opportunities for improving and intensifying its agricultural production.

THE EAST COAST REGION

The second region, that of the east coast, also has a fairly dense population. Its wealth lies not in its soil, nor in the quality of its landforms, but in the rainfall regime which gives it a tropical rainy climate. The region may be divided into three north-south zones: the coast littoral, low and flat, with alluvials present to an important extent; a zone of foothills; and the scarp zone, a difficult barrier which is largely in forest. Paddy rice is produced in the lower valleys of the coastal zone, and hill rice is grown in the foothills and slopes of the scarp zone as the major subsistence crop, but corn and manioc are grown on the drier soils.

Zebu cattle on the hills near Arivonimamo
Very little effort has been made to integrate crop and livestock farming, and Madagascar has not taken advantage of the absence of the tsetse fly as well as it might have.

Robusta coffee, which is the leading Madagascan export, accounting for about 30 percent of the total value of exports in recent years, is the principal cash crop (Map 102). Its production is estimated to provide a living to eighty thousand indigenous planters plus a number of small colons. Production of coffee did not enjoy a comparable increase to that experienced by other African countries in postwar years. While Madagascar accounted for about 10 percent of Africa's exportable coffee in 1950–55, its share was only 5.6 percent in 1961–63. Explanations for this situation include the failure to replace old bushes, the destruction of plants in the 1960 hurricanes, and the inflated costs of production. A program was begun in 1953 to subsidize the replacement of overmature bushes, create numerous nurseries, improve the quality of the crop, and increase production from about 34,000 to 75,000 tons. The last goal was not achieved, maximum exportable output to 1963 having been about 50,000 tons. Receipts have fallen in recent years owing to lower market prices and reduced premium prices paid by France, while Madagascar's membership in the International Coffee Agreement limits the opportunities for further expansion.

In addition to coffee, the east coast produces such cash crops as cloves (especially on Ile

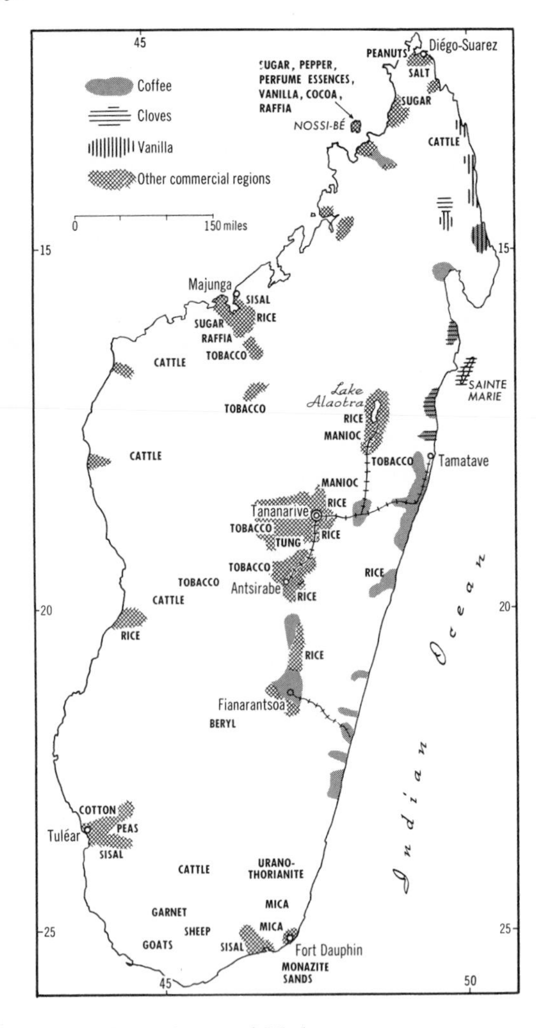

Map 102. Economic map of Madagascar

Hill rice in an east coast valley near Tamatave
Small huts and platforms in the fields are used by children who attempt to reduce the depredations of birds.

Ste. Marie), vanilla (notably in the Antalaha area), sugar (near Tamatave), and pepper. Madagascar is the leading producer of vanilla, this crop being one of the few dollar-earners exported from the island. Competition from vanillin, which is made from cloves, tends to keep the sales of vanilla to a relatively small amount, though there are sharp fluctuations in the international vanilla trade. Madagascar produces about 30 percent of the world's cloves as compared with about 70 percent from Zanzibar and Pemba. Overproduction in recent years has led to cooperation betweeen these two producers to protect the market.

Both the Malagasy and the Creole systems of farming in the eastern region are backward and destructive and have led to soil degradation if not outright erosion. The agricultural station at Ivaloina, north of Tamatave, has worked out what may be the future use of the area: rewooding of the impoverished slopes, construction of numerous tilapia ponds in the smaller valleys, pastures and rice paddies in the lower alluvial flats, and coffee cultivation on the slightly higher, better drained lands along the rivers. As noted earlier, the possibility of developing a mixed agriculture in a rainforest area, where it would be precluded in Africa by the presence of the tsetse fly, presents a fascinating opportunity to study techniques that may later be applied to the continent.

Communications are a difficult problem in much of this east coast region. North-south roads are interrupted constantly by the many rivers flowing off the drenched eastern slopes. The roads do not generally penetrate far inland in the valleys, so many potentially productive areas are not open. The coast is highly inhospitable, with a general absence of protected harbors, typically high seas, and occasional dangerous weather. In the Andapa area towards the north, roads are so poor that the produce is flown out and even staples such as rice are delivered to the region by air. Nonetheless, the island's most important port, Tamatave, is situated on this coast, and the island's railways terminate at Tamatave and Manakara.

THE NORTH AND NORTHWEST REGIONS

In the extreme north there is a small region around Diégo-Suarez which has a savanna rather than a tropical rainy climate. Some corn, peanuts, and beef are produced locally, and salines near Diégo provide most of the domestic requirements of salt, but the hinterland of that port is quite restricted by topography and it is mainly used for transshipment between coastal and overseas vessels.

In the northwest, as has been noted, there is an enclave of rainy tropical climate. One of the most important economic parts of this region is the volcanic island of Nossi-Bé, which was long a center of colonization. Its major products are sugar, pepper, vanilla, and perfume essences, especially ylang-ylang and lemon grass. Madagascar is the only important producer of pepper in Africa, but, although its output has increased from 400,000 pounds in 1935–39 to 3,000,000 pounds in 1962, it still accounts for only about 1.9 percent of world production. Nossi-Bé accounts for most of the island's pepper output; the vine is typically grown on shade trees in coffee and cocoa plantations.

Along the mainland coast of the northwest are two very rich valleys which have witnessed substantial development in the past decade. The fertile and extensive alluvial plain of the North Mahavavy is the site of a large mechanized sugar development employing several hundred Europeans and over 3,000 Malagasy. Sugar production has increased sharply since this plantation opened in 1954, permitting it to rank as the island's third or fourth ranking export by value. Opportunities for expanded output are restricted by the size of the domestic market and by the quota for sugar in France, which pays premium prices for imports from Madagascar, Réunion, and other franc zone producers.

The Sambirano Valley is the second very rich alluvial zone, its soils being derived from the high, volcanic mass of Tsaratanana. It produces coffee, cocoa, coconuts, sugar, essential oils, pepper, palm oil, manioc, and staple rice. The several parts of the north and northwest are more readily tied with each other by coastal vessel than by road, while Nossi-Bé and Diégo-Suarez are regular ports of call on the two liner routes to the island.

THE WESTERN AND SOUTHERN REGIONS

The western region is a savanna area, while the southern area is steppelike with a long, rigorous dry season and occasional yet certain droughts which lead to great losses of livestock and human suffering. Composed of a long series of dry plains and low plateaus cut by large and small valleys, both areas contain the best regional soils on the island (still not very good, however), as well as some excellent alluvials. In direct contrast to the east coast, where rainfall is the chief physical attribute, the major shortcoming of this great area is the meager and irregular precipitation.

Regionally, this is pastoral country, cattle being the main interest of the tribes, grouped under the name Sakalava in the west, with the Mahafaly, Antandroy, Antanosy, and Bara being the major southern tribes. These people were the least affected by the European presence, and the area is the least important economic region. Its advance is impeded also by the sparse network and poor quality of its roads.

Cattle raising suffers from physical difficulties, from malpractices, of which grass firing is the worst, and from cultural attitudes. Many of the tribes are more concerned with their cattle as instruments of ceremony than as suppliers of food or sources of wealth. Cattle thievery is an honored custom among some tribes, indeed almost a necessity if a young man is to be acceptable as a husband. Corralling the cattle at night to prevent their being stolen often takes place in unhealthy conditions leading to a high incidence of tuberculosis. There has been strong disincentive, then, on the part of even the more evolved to attempt improvement of their practices. Recently the government has succeeded in cutting down on cattle thievery by the imposition of more severe punishments. The government is also aiding the industry by selective breeding and the provision of about 60 wells in the south.

Despite the difficulties, there is an export of animal products from all the west coast ports. Some goats are raised in the south, producing micro-deserts around the settlements. At Ampanihy, an effort has been made to develop a rug and drape industry in the government-subsidized Maison de Mohair.

Such intensive activity as there is in this region is found in the large and small valleys, where there are many additional opportunities for intensifying production, though control works will be required in some cases. In the valleys near Majunga there is an important output of rice, the island's largest and best-quality raffia production, and less important yields of tobacco and sugar. The Betsiboka Valley is potentially one of the richest regions of the island.

Around Morandava and Tuléar, rice, lima beans, vegetables, and corn are the chief interests, while Virginia tobacco is grown in the high valley of the Tsiribihina. Efforts made to introduce cotton in the Fiherenana Valley near Tuléar and elsewhere have been slowed by plant disease problems, but hopes remain high that high-quality cotton will one day become a major export. An important postwar introduction has been that of large European sisal estates in the Mandrare Valley of the south, the fiber being exported via Fort Dauphin. About 25,000 people are employed in producing sisal. Some castor seed is produced around Ambovombé.

Goats near Ampanihy, southern Madagascar
Their grazing has resulted in formation of a micro-desert around the village.

There is, then, great variety among the regions of Madagascar, far greater than can be conveyed in this brief discussion. Perhaps the most common characteristic is the great concentration of activity in the valleys of all the regions and the very extensive use of the vast surrounding areas. Contact from one region to another and within regions is often very tenuous.

FISHING AND FORESTRY

The fishing industry is poorly developed on Madagascar. The Vezo engage in sea and lagoon fishing along the west, particularly from Tuléar, but they operate only from pirogues and have only a small surplus production. Studies of the potentialities of fishing in the Mozambique Channel indicate that a substantial yield is possible; studies are now under way on the opportunities for shrimp trawling and lobster fishing. Recent agreements have been concluded with the Japanese and Chinese to assist in the development of tuna fishing from Majunga and Diégo-Suarez. Fresh-water fish are caught in many of the rivers, in Lake Alaotra, and in the rice paddies, but there is no organized industry nor any commercialization beyond strictly local markets. It is ironic that an island with more cattle than humans and with substantial opportunities for increasing the catch of fish should be plagued by a widespread protein deficiency.

Madagascar's forests are mainly found along the east and northwest, often on steep land and in areas which are not easily accessible. Some of its unique species have great beauty, but have been cut excessively and tend to be very slow growing. In 1961 a South African company contracted to develop an export of 100,000 cubic meters of various woods yearly, but at present Madagascar is a net importer of forest products. Afforestation began in the 1930s but has not been as intensive as it should have been, from the standpoint of either erosion control or supply of lumber and fuel.

MINING ON MADAGASCAR

Madagascar did not have a modern geological service until the 1950s, so the mineral resources of the island are still very incompletely known. Mica, graphite, and uranothorianite are the three most important minerals produced, but they account for only about 5 percent of the total value of exports, and mining accounts for only about 1 percent of the national income. More recent studies indicate that Madagascar has a large variety of minerals and that it could sustain a production considerably above present levels.

The numerous intrusive granitic masses in the ancient crystallines that cover the largest part of the island play an essential role in mineralization. In the last stage of their formation, pegmatites were formed containing a great variety of minerals including mica, beryl, tourmaline, quartz, precious stones, uranium, tantalum, cerium, and others. Unhappily, the deposits are usually small, scattered, discontinuous, and unimportant. The island's graphite deposits were formed when the basement rock was metamorphosed, transforming materials that were rich in carbon. Iron occurs abundantly in the form of magnetites in the crystalline rock.

In the secondary rocks of the west, the most interesting known deposit is the Sakoa coal basin in the southwest. The coal occurs in a few beds varying from 6 to 22 feet in thickness; its quality is variable, but some coking coal has been found. But reserves are relatively small and most of them are noncoking, high ash content, mediocre coals. Efforts to attract investment to open up the field have thus far been unsuccessful; in 1962 a new study was reported on the feasibility of developing a carbo-chemical complex with main emphasis on nitrogenous fertilizers. Prospecting for petroleum has been carried on in the western sedimentaries but no favorable reports have been issued. Exploration has recently been switched from the Morandava area to the Majunga Basin.

Woman splitting mica at Fort Dauphin
Mica is one of the three main minerals produced on Madagascar; about 6,000 persons are employed in its mining and splitting.

The total value of Madagascar's mineral exports was only $4.7 million in 1961, with the three main minerals accounting for about seven eighths of the total. Mica comes from about 20 exploitations north of Fort Dauphin, each producing from 15 to 300 tons yearly. About 6,000 persons are employed in producing mica, including many women who are expert at the splitting operation.

Graphite is produced at five sites near the coast south of Tamatave and at two sites near Moramanga, all of them not far from the Tananarive-Côte Est Railway. Reserves of graphite are very large and very scattered. The availability of transport plays a key role in determining what deposits are worked, but a narrowing world market discourages opening additional mines.

Madagascar began producing uranothorianite in 1955 and five companies are now engaged in its mining in the Fort Dauphin area; their output is purchased by the French Atomic

Energy Commission, which owns and operates two concentration plants at Ambatomika. A larger production was expected to begin in 1963 from deposits at Ambindandrakemba and Belafa.

Other minerals produced in Madagascar, all in small quantities, are, in order of value of exports in 1961:

(1) Industrial beryl. The 1961 exports of 673 tons were a record. An intensive search has recently been made to find additional reserves, but most known deposits are quite small.

(2) Chromite. First produced in 1961, chromite comes from a small deposit a few miles northwest of Tamatave. An output of 20,000 tons a year is planned for this mine, while a larger deposit at Andriamena may be developed by Ugine if a 75-mile road is constructed by the government to the Lake Alaotra branch of the main rail line. Still another deposit is under study at Beriana.

(3) Monazite. A small plant at Antete near Fort Dauphin extracts monazite from beach sands. Plans call for increasing production from the 463 tons of 1961 to about 1,500 tons a year. About 15,000–20,000 tons of ilmenite could also be produced at this operation if transport problems could be solved.

Sorting garnets at a small mine near Ampanihy
Small-scale operation is characteristic of most Malagasy mining.

(4) Quartz. Reserves are large but of marginal interest.

(5) Columbo-tantalite.

(6) Semiprecious stones.

(7) Garnet. Almost all production comes from a small surface mine near Ampanihy.

Other minerals which have been under study include iron ore, bauxite, nickel (at Valorozo) manganese, copper, and lead.

THE INDUSTRIAL ECONOMY

Manufacturing accounts for less than 3 percent of the national income of Madagascar. About 22,000 people are employed in this segment of the economy. With 1950 as the base year, the index of value added by manufacturing was 262 in 1960, but this seemingly very rapid buildup may be explained by increases in only a limited number of industries plus the introduction of several entirely new plants.

Madagascar has a rather well-developed handicraft industry, especially in the highlands. Modern industry is concerned particularly with the primary processing of raw materials for export; only a few plants produce finished articles for the domestic market. Table 47 presents information on the modern manufacturing plants of Madagascar, revealing their relatively narrow range, low output, and overcapacity in several fields.

The chief disadvantage for increasing industry is the small size of market both in numbers and in purchasing power. While about 205,000 employees in the wage sector have an average income of about $400 a year, the vast bulk of the population has incomes below $40 a year. The effective market is probably less than a tenth of the population and departure of numerous French civil servants has tended further to depress the market. The scattered character of the market and poor internal communications contribute to the difficulties in this sphere. Other problems include the high cost of energy, inadequate capital, lack of skill and managerial ability, and local inflation.

Madagascar has advantages for the development of industry: substantial hydroelectric

Table 47. Data regarding manufacturing industries in Madagascar, 1961–1962

Industry	*Number of plants*	*Number employed*	*Output 1961*	*Location of plants*	*Comments*
Rice mills	77	2,400	160,000 M.T.	Scattered; mainly Tananarive, Lake Alaotra, Fianandrantsoa areas	Treat only c. $\frac{1}{5}$ of rice production; operate at c. $\frac{1}{2}$ capacity
Sugar factories	4	1,500	86,000 M.T.	Ambilobé, Namakia, Moromamy, Nossi-Bé	Ambilobé accounts for c. $\frac{1}{2}$ production; output up c. $6\frac{1}{2}$ times in decade to 1960
Oil and soap mills	15		2,104 M.T. oil 1,567 M.T. soap		Peanut oil main raw material; operate at c. $\frac{1}{2}$ capacity
Tapioca	8	1,500	5,773 M.T.	Especially Lake Alaotra area	
Meat conserves	6	1,600–1,900	4,000 M.T.	Tananarive, Majunga, Tuléar, Tamatave, Fianarantsoa	Output c. 40 percent of capacity
Tung processing	1			Lac Itasy region	Entire output exported
Sisal decortication				Mandrare River area	
Tanning					
Brewing	1	130	12,500 hl.	Antsirabe	Satisfies about one quarter of consumption; expansion planned
Carbonated beverages	4	17	60,000 hl.	Scattered, largest at Tananarive	Satisfies about 95 percent of consumption
Chocolate candy	1			Tananarive	
Fruit juice	1			Mananjary	
Cotton cloth	1	c. 700	1,208 M.T.	Antsirabe	Expansion planned
Knitted goods	1	100	700,000 pieces	Tananarive	
Men's clothing	1		300,000 pieces		
Blankets	1		c. 900 M.T.		
Sacks, twine, etc.	2			Majunga, Fort Dauphin	Majunga plant produces 3,400 tons of sacks, employs about 550
Cement	1		21,000 M.T.	Amboanio, near Majunga	Output c. $\frac{2}{3}$ of capacity; plan expansion. Plan new mill at Moramanga
Shoes	1	150	200,000 pr.	Tananarive	A Bata factory
Cigarettes			547 M.T.	Antsirabe only modern plant	Largest of several employs 250
Metal containers	1			Tamatave	
Auto assembly	1	128		Tananarive	Opened 1962; capacity 4 vehicles a day; Citroen and Renault
Radio assembly				Tananarive	
Oxygen and acetylene	3	70		Tananarive, Diégo-Suarez, Ampandandrava	
Plastic materials	1	25–35		Near Tananarive	Started in 1962
Pharmaceuticals	1	50		Near Tananarive	Started in 1962
Storage batteries	1			Tananarive	

resources; some coal; and a labor supply which is perhaps superior to that of many African areas, the Merina having displayed excellent aptitude in modern machine techniques and being more stabilized than many African workers.

No rapid expansion in manufacturing may be expected, however, despite these advantages and a favorable investment code promulgated in 1961 which provides for a variety of fiscal, customs, tax, and legal incentives for new industries. The government has recently estimated that only about 5 percent of imports could be readily replaced by goods produced in Madagascar, but that an additional 27 percent could be replaced by domestic manufactures over a longer period given sufficient capital.

ELECTRIC POWER

Madagascar rates low in the list of African countries in production and consumption of energy, not because it does not have substantial resources. Installed capacity in 1961 was 69,400 kw and production 113.2 million kwh. The production represents an increase from 40 million kwh in 1950, which means that the rate of growth has been well below the African average.

There are about 25 thermoelectric plants and 8 hydroelectric plants on the island. Only one of the latter plants is important, the 12,000-kw Mandraka station 30 miles east of Tananarive. Although the plant has been in being for some years, production is still far below capacity of this installation. Electricity is generally high cost and is publicly available only in the larger towns. In Tananarive, despite a substantial surplus available, the suburbs have not been electrified and rates are considered too high for more than a quarter of the Malagasy homes in the city itself. Even so, the capital accounts for about half of total consumption of electricity on the island. Additional developments are not likely while a surplus exists, but the substantial hydroelectric potential of Madagascar is a resource of considerable value for the future. Preliminary studies have been made of the Fatita, Ikopa, and Betsiboka rivers for possible development.

TRANSPORT DEVELOPMENT

Madagascar's transport complex[2] consists of a scanty road system, 528 miles of railways in two lines, a rather unusual but neither wide nor deep canal along much of the east coast, a remarkable air network, and 17 ports, 13 of which figure in international trade. The pattern reflects the underdevelopment and insularity of the country.

ROADS

The compact shape of Madagascar, the lack of navigable streams and coastal indentations, and the lack of justification for building additional rail lines contribute to the need for an adequate road net if the island is to be developed economically. But the existing network is rudimentary (Map 103); there are about 16,000 miles of road, or one mile for every 14 square miles of area. Only 4,500 miles are all-weather but about 1,200 miles are paved. Fully seven tenths of the roads are of irregular practicality; even the main roads are tortuous and rough except for stretches near the larger cities. In the rainy season washouts are common; *radiers*, or partly submerged concrete fords, may be dangerous or impassable; ferry service is abandoned or interrupted; roads become pitted and ravined, and many are impassable or at best only jeepable.

The road pattern is simple, consisting of a somewhat distorted and not fully articulated backbone running the length of the island with occasional ribs extending outward to the more important ports. Normally, even parts of the dorsal road are in poor condition, especially in the north, the province of Diégo-Suarez not being tied to the rest of the country by any permanent road. The worst-served part of the

[2] The author thanks the American Geographical Society for permission to use material from his article, "Transportation in Madagascar," in *The Geographical Review* (January, 1958), pp. 45–69.

Map 103. Transport in Madagascar
Inset Map: Major economic regions
Lower Inset: Profiles of main rail lines

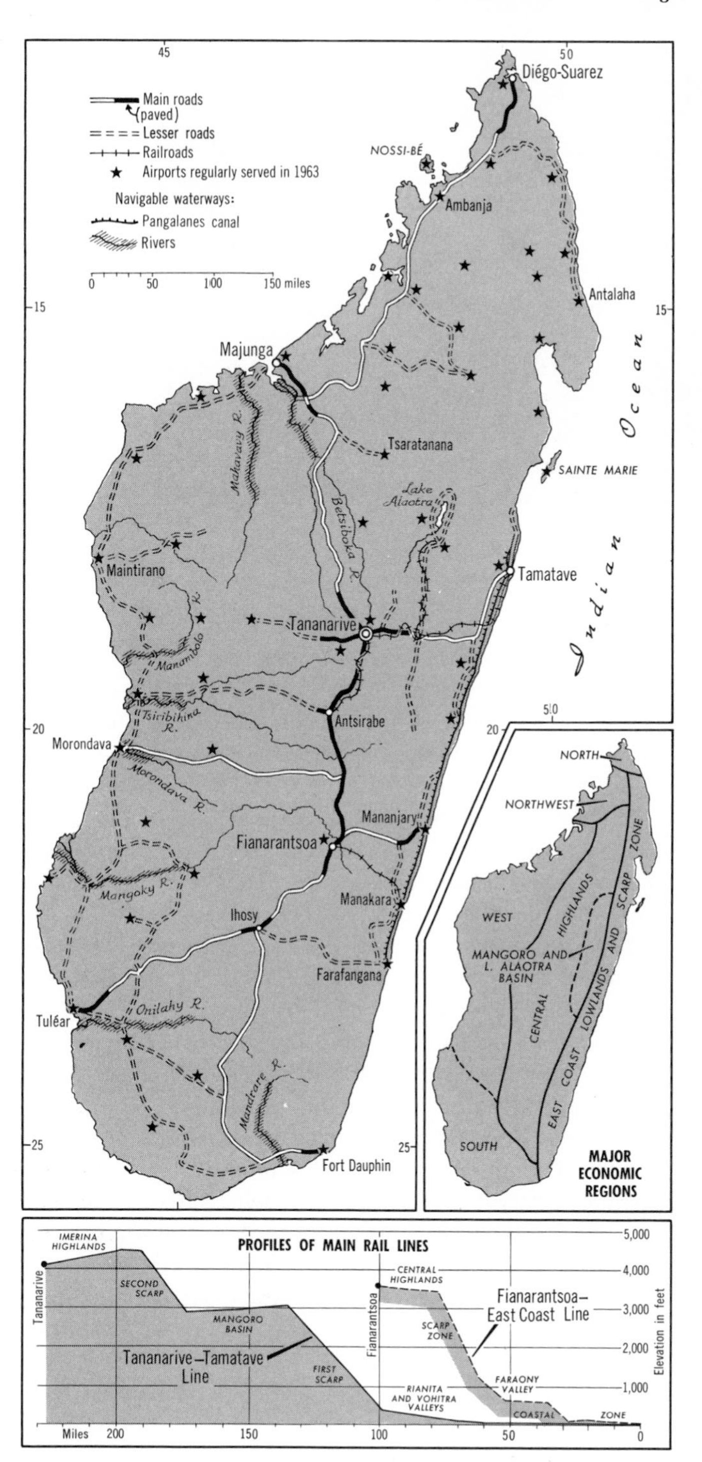

Two-wheeled bullock-drawn carts near Tananarive
These carts are commonly used on the highlands for bringing produce to the markets.

island extends almost 300 miles northward from Lake Alaotra and includes the Andapa Basin, which is accessible only by air. The best road system is in the Merina and Betsileo country of the central highlands.

In 1962 Madagascar had an estimated 50,000 vehicles, about half of which were in Tananarive Province and three eighths in the capital itself. Long-distance traffic is poorly developed, partly because of restrictions on the Tananarive–Tamatave road forbidding its use to trucks of over 2½ tons in order to retain traffic for the railway. There is a fairly significant truck movement between Majunga and Tananarive, regular bus services from the capital to Majunga, Fianarantsoa, Tuléar, and Fort Dauphin, and a rather complete service, especially in the more populated parts of the country, of *taxis brousses*, or bush buses. Two-wheeled carts drawn by bullocks are a common sight on the roads of the highlands, especially around the cities and on market days. The ricksha, or, as it is called in Madagascar, the *pousse-pousse*, is used in the large cities.

THE RAILROADS

The main rail line of Madagascar is the Tananarive–Côte Est Railway (TCE) connecting the capital with the major port Tamatave (Map 103), and having branches serving the Lake Alaotra Basin and the secondary highland center of Antsirabe. The second line, the Fianarantsoa–Côte Est Railway (FCE), connects the capital of the Betsileo country in the highlands with Manakara, an open-roadstead port. Both railways are single track, one meter in width, and completely dieselized since 1955.

Carrying about 530,000 tons a year, the railways handle about two fifths of total imports and one fifth of exports. The higher percentage of import traffic reflects the strong consumption power of Tananarive, which is also revealed by the fact that upline traffic on the TCE, which accounted for 77.4 percent of total railway ton-kilometers in 1961, is three times the downline movement.

The TCE was constructed from 1901 to 1913 and the FCE from 1926 to 1936, the slowness explained in part by the difficult topography. Both lines must surmount difficult scarps; minimum curve radii are only 80 meters; maximum gradients are 2.5 percent on the TCE and 3.5 percent on the FCE; and numerous tunnels, culverts, and bridges were required. The expense of running these lines is heavy, especially for the short, difficult, low-traffic FCE. Modernizations and rationalizations have improved efficiency, the number of employees (3,275) in 1961 having been 15 percent below 1955 and 33 percent below the 1938 level when traffic was about half as great. Unfortunately, rates are also very high, and help to explain the high cost of living at Tananarive. It costs about one-third to one-half as much to ship goods the 229 miles from Tamatave to the capital as it does the many thousands of miles from New York to Tamatave. Nonetheless, the lines have operated at a loss in recent years.

At present there is little discussion of constructing new lines or new branch lines. It has been suggested that a line running south from Moramanga might stimulate forest and agricultural development in the Mangoro Shelf, but the existence of a reasonably good road discouraged such an extension. It was also noted that joining the two systems by a 149-mile link from Antsirabe to Fianarantsoa would result in savings through consolidated maintenance in the excellent shops at Tananarive and through greater flexibility in use of equipment, but the small amount of traffic on the FCE line did not encourage further rail construction to the Betsileo country.

INLAND WATERWAYS

Few of the rivers of Madagascar are of more than local importance in the carriage of goods. Those of the east coast are interrupted by rapids, and those that flow into the Mozambique Channel are intermittent, seasonal, and plagued by shifting channels. Only the Betsiboka, which is navigable for 128 miles, is fairly heavily used, on its first 50 miles. On the central highlands the irrigation and drainage channels of the Betsimitatatra Plain are used by pirogues, and a few light barges are employed on Lake Alaotra.

The most interesting inland waterway is the Pangalanes Canal, which runs for about 400 miles along the east coast from Foulpointe to Farafangana, connecting a series of lagoons by cutting across the sills, or "pangalanes," that separate them. Before the French arrived, the Malagasy had made some links to permit the passage of dugout canoes; further canalization was carried on in the first years of colonial administration and after World War II. But the canal has never fulfilled its promise, and a recent decision has been taken to construct an improved road along the east coast which will probably spell the end of efforts to widen and deepen the canal.

PORTS

The international trade handled by Madagascar ports in 1961 was 700,000 tons, a rather feeble tonnage considering the size of the island and the fact that it has more ports than any other African country. Thirteen ports figure in international traffic and an additional four in coastal shipments. The leading port, Tamatave, handles no less than 50 percent of overseas cargo and 41 percent of total port traffic. The top six ports handle 86 percent of total port movements.

Only Tamatave can be considered a modern port; only Tamatave, Diégo-Suarez, and Tuléar have some kind of deepwater quay. Many ports are no more than poor lighterage harbors with no protection for ships at anchor and with minimal shore and floating installations. This does not mean that there are harbors just waiting to be converted into modern ports. On the contrary, the island is noted for the absence of indentations, especially on the east coast, while the west coast has other physical difficulties. It is ironical that Madagascar possesses one of the finest natural harbors in the world at Diégo-Suarez, situated where it is of minor utility to the island. The greatest need for improved facilities is at Majunga, the second main port of the island.

There is a long list of explanations for the relatively low tonnage handled in the ensemble of Malagasy ports and their relative lack of development. Basic is the underdeveloped economy of the country; a somewhat offsetting factor, however, is the fairly advanced exchange economy of the Merina and Betsileo, who produce an unusual variety of food products, their chief building materials, and numerous handicraft goods, thus reducing somewhat the necessity for international exchange. Another important explanation is the character of Malagasy exports, many of which are of high value in relation to their bulk and which do not include any high-tonnage, high-bulk mineral exports (total mineral exports were about 17,000 tons in 1960 and 27,000 tons in 1961). Physical difficulties have likewise played a part: the extremely straight east coast, presence of coastal reefs, characteristically rough seas on the Indian Ocean coast, and inaccessible river mouths. Also, only a few ports have sizable hinterlands—Tamatave, Majunga, Manakara, Tuléar, and Fort Dauphin. Two others benefit considerably from coastal trade though their hinterlands are not extensive—Nossi-Bé and Diégo-Suarez. The remaining ports serve restricted areas only, and some would certainly not exist if better land communications were available. Finally, the dispersion of activity among Malagasy ports means that maintenance and development funds must be divided and that only Tamatave gets adequate support to permit really first-class operation.

Suggestions have been made since 1933 that overseas shipments be concentrated in a few ports, but, given the present road network and the isolation of many producing regions, Madagascar could not exist now without numerous outlets to the sea. After completion of the improved east coast road, it is planned that overseas traffic there be confined to Tamatave, Manakara, and Fort Dauphin.

Like several African nations, Madagascar plans to have its own merchant marine. In 1960 the Malagasy Navigation Company was formed and now has two coastal vessels totaling 3,100 tons; in 1962 the Malagasy Society for Ocean Transport was organized with the intention of acquiring vessels to operate in international services.

AIR TRANSPORT

Madagascar has an unusually well-developed air transportation complex. It possesses 174 airdromes plus several hundred emergency landing strips; 58 airports are regularly served, giving the island one of the densest airline nets in Africa. Improvement of this branch of transport was a major feature of postwar plans, and the French spent far more on its airways in relation to area and population than it did in other French territories. The present government has carried on this interest and has participated in the construction of jet strips at Arivonimamo, 30 miles from Tananarive and the international airport for the capital, and at Majunga. A Malagasy airline, Madair, has taken over the internal lines formerly handled by Air France and Air Madagascar.

Explanations for the strong position of aviation in Madagascar include the greater ease of laying out a network of airstrips than constructing even a minimal road system and military-strategic considerations, including maintenance of internal security with a smaller force than would otherwise be necessary and protection of the naval base at Diégo-Suarez. A close study might reveal, however, that the air system is also somewhat of a luxury for a poor country, that the economy might be better aided by coming down to earth.

Table 48. Main exports of Madagascar, 1938, 1955, and 1961; total imports and exports in selected years, 1938–1962

	Percent of exports by value		
Commodity	*1938*	*1955*	*1961*
Coffee	31.9	43.4	30.0
Vanilla	9.1	5.0	10.2
Sugar		—	6.6
Rice	2.0	8.6	6.4
Clove products	4.6	4.5	6.2
Meats		2.8	4.4
Raffia	3.5	3.5	4.0
Tobacco	0.8	6.7	3.9
Lima beans	2.6	2.2	3.5
Sisal	0.1	2.4	2.9
Peanuts		2.2	2.9
Pepper		1.5	2.5
Hides and skins		1.6	2.3
Mica	3.5	0.9	2.2
Graphite	2.2	3.2	1.9
Uranothorianite		—	1.5
Other minerals		...	0.8
Others	39.7	11.5	7.8
Total	100.0	100.0	100.0

Year	*Exports (in million $)*	*Imports (in million $)*	*Exports as percent of imports*
1938	23.6	17.4	135.7
1948	50.0	77.7	64.4
1952	93.6	133.6	70.1
1954	92.4	137.4	67.3
1956	93.1	132.0	70.5
1958	82.6	108.4	76.2
1960	78.1	112.9	69.3
1961	75.4	104.2	72.4
1962	94	122	77.0

Sources: Madagascar, *Statistiques du Commerce Exterieur de Madagascar, 1960; Bulletin de Madagascar* (March, 1963); U.N., *Monthly Bulletin of Statistics* (August, 1963).
... = Not available.
— = None or negligible.

INTERNATIONAL TRADE

Perhaps the most important feature of the international trade position in Madagascar is the marked imbalance, imports being substantially greater than exports, as indicated in Table 48. If this reflected a high level of investment for the economic development of the island it would not be disturbing, but it does not. Capital goods imports have actually declined in recent years, there has been a flight of capital, and many major exports have displayed stagnancy or even regression in the last few years, not only in value but in volume of exports. Total international payments are balanced mainly by French subventions, upon which the country depends for covering all of the development budget and part of the ordinary budget. French aid was about $27 million in 1960; other aid was received from the EEC (about $5 million a year), the United States ($547,000 in 1961), and various U.N. agencies.

France has always been the predominant supplier and purchaser of Madagascan goods, for the same reasons that explain the comparable patterns for other former French territories. France takes Malagasy coffee, rice, and sisal at subsidized prices which are supposed to be suppressed in the coming years; France has in turn been favored by tariff and quota preferences. Inflated costs in Madagascar will make the period of adjustment to lower prices a difficult one, but a more rational set of prices may prove to be a desirable cathartic for the stagnating economy of the island.

In 1955 the chief provincial administrator of the province of Tamatave summarized the economic problems of Madagascar as follows:

> We suffer from a serious imbalance in accounts, from stagnation of certain products, from regression in certain activities, from a disequilibrium between consumption and production, from an increase in operating costs, from costs of production above the level of world prices, from inflation, from the proliferation of intermediaries.[3]

It is somewhat depressing that so little has been accomplished in the ensuing eight years to meet any of these problems; indeed, some of them appear to have deepened.

[3] *Bulletin de Madagascar* (February, 1956), p. 151.

The Mascarenes

Lying some 400 and 500 miles east of Madagascar in the Indian Ocean are Réunion and Mauritius, collectively called the Mascarene Islands. Both are volcanic in origin, with activity still occurring on Réunion. Both are sugar islands facing increasing problems of extreme population pressure.

MAURITIUS

Mauritius was discovered by Portuguese explorers in the early sixteenth century but it had been used for shelter by Arabs and Malays for centuries before. Uninhabited and largely forest covered, it was first settled by the Dutch in the seventeenth century but was abandoned in 1710. In 1715 France claimed the island and renamed it Ile de France; the first permanent French settlement dates from 1722. Sugar soon became the major interest; by 1797 the population had increased to about 60,000, including 50,000 slaves from Africa and Madagascar. Seized by the British in the Napoleonic Wars, it was formally ceded to them in 1814 and has since been a colony. The island now has a representative and largely responsible government with a legislative body elected by universal adult suffrage, and will probably reach independence in the not too distant future.

PHYSICAL CONDITIONS

With an area of 720 square miles, Mauritius is roughly oval in shape and composed of basalt and its varieties (Map 104). The land rises from a coastal belt fringed with lagoons and coral reefs to a central plateau with elevations of 900 to 1,900 feet. The central lands are bounded on all but the east by mountains which were probably the rim of a great volcano and whose maximum elevations are about 2,500 to 2,700 feet.

Situated in the latitude of the prevailing southeasterlies, Mauritius has temperatures moderated by its oceanic position and the trade winds. It may be divided into three major climatic zones: (1) the subhumid coastal belt, covering about 22 percent of the island, which has rainfall of 35 to 50 inches; the 10 percent of total cane lands in this belt are dependent on irrigation; (2) the humid middle belt, about 43 percent of the island, which rises to about 600 feet on the windward side and 1,200 feet on the leeward side, and has 50 to 100 inches of rainfall; this belt contains about 65 percent of the cane lands; and (3) the superhumid zones of the central plateau, lying above the second zone, having rainfall from 100 to 200 inches, and containing about 25 percent of the area planted to cane on about 35 percent of the total area of the island. Mauritius lies in the belt of maximum cyclonic disturbances and is periodically damaged by severe storms. The worst in history, with wind velocities of 160 miles per hour, struck in 1960, when well over half of the houses were damaged or destroyed and substantial portions of the sugar, tea, and tobacco crops were lost. Exports of sugar in that year were cut to only 40.7 percent of the previous year's shipments. In late 1961 and early 1962 no fewer than 14 tropical cyclones passed in the vicinity of Mauritius and one caused a loss of about 15 percent of the crop.

The soils of Mauritius are somewhat like those of Hawaii but vary from clayey to gravelly in texture. Much of the area was originally strewn with large boulders and stones; the lands from which these have been removed are called "terre franche," but the process is still not completed.

THE PEOPLE OF MAURITIUS

A great diversity and mixture of races inhabit the island. The descendants of the early French settlers and of Afro-Malagasy slaves, who have mixed to a greater or lesser degree, are classified as the "general population"; they comprise about 29 percent of the population. The majority group is now the Indians, most of whom are descended from indentured laborers brought to Mauritius after the abolition of slavery in 1835. Totaling about 67 percent of the population, they are divided in the ratio of about 4 to 1 between Hindus and Muslims. Persons of Chinese extraction comprise about 3½ percent of the population.

From the standpoint of major economic activities, the owners and senior staff of the large sugar estates are mainly descendants of the original French settlers. "Creoles," of mixed origin, are largely urban dwellers, and are important in commerce and the civil service. Indians are mainly laborers or owners of small holdings producing sugar. The Chinese are mostly shopkeepers. The formidable mixture of peoples is reflected in religious, linguistic, and other cultural differences, which often play a potent role in the political field. English is the official language; French is spoken by most of the educated people; "Creole," a French patois, is the lingua franca; and there are several Indian languages and Chinese. Language requirements in the local schools perpetuate the diversity, usually resulting in an inadequate command of any language. A second element of the school system criticized for many years is its excessively academic orientation, which has contributed to the prejudice against agricultural work of a large percentage of school leavers.

THE POPULATION PROBLEM

The outstanding problem of Mauritius is that of overpopulation. The over-all density was 696 per square mile in 1952 and 944 per square mile in 1962. Densities on the central plateau are about 1,650 per square mile, while about 35 or 40 percent of the population lives in the towns. The frightening aspect of the problem is revealed upon examination of the trends in natural increase (Table 49). In the period 1881–1944 the average annual rate of increase was less than half of 1 percent; it reached 2.26 percent in 1944–52 and is now about 3 percent per annum. The recency of the explosion is explained in considerable part by the eradication of malaria, which resulted in a 32 percent reduction in the death rate in one year. Whereas deaths from malaria totaled 3,534 or 23.1 percent of total deaths in 1945, there was only

Table 49. Demographic statistics for Mauritius, selected years, 1938–1962

Year	*Estimated population (in thousands)*	*Birth rate per M*	*Death rate per M*	*Natural increase (in percent)*	*Infant mortality rate per M*	*Maternal mortality rate per M*
1938	402	33.4	29.9	0.35	162.5	11.38
1943	417	33.1	25.9	0.72	141.5	5.14
1950	465	49.7	13.9	3.58	76.3	3.51
1955	549	41.8	12.9	2.89	67.2	1.47
1960	639	39.6	11.3	2.83	69.5	1.66
1961	656	39.8	9.9	2.99	62.0	1.14
1962	680					

Sources: Colony of Mauritius, *Mauritius, 1961* (London, Her Majesty's Stationery Office), p. 63; census of June 30 1962; U.N., *Demographic Yearbooks, 1949–50, 1961*.

one death from malaria in the years 1956 through 1962. Similarly, deaths from infective and parasitic diseases declined from 4,052 in 1948 to 320 in 1961. The Titmuss Report estimated that the population would reach 951,000 by 1972 and, given a continuance of the present trends, nearly 3 million by 2000, a prospect that amounts to "economic, social and political disaster."[1]

Evidence already suggests that there is overpopulation. The real national income per capita has begun to decline in the last decade; the sugar industry has not absorbed a larger number of workers in postwar years despite a marked increase in output; unemployment is increasing and was estimated to be 15.1 percent in 1958; a high proportion of manual laborers suffer from anemia; dietal standards are inadequate; and housing standards in the overcrowded towns are sometimes abominable.

As each year progresses, the problem is likely to become more serious. The working population will increase 50 percent in 15 years; the numbers below 15 years of age will require vastly increased educational and social services. The Titmuss Report concludes that without drastic action there will be further reductions in living standards, severe unemployment, and a breakdown in the administration of public assistance.

AGRICULTURE

About 220,000 acres or 48 percent of the island is cultivated, all but 20,000 acres to cane sugar. Food crops occupy less than 4 percent of the cultivated area, Mauritius having a high dependence on imported foods, particularly rice. Of the 107,000 persons employed in 1961, 65.4 percent were in agriculture, which accounts for over 99 percent of exports by value.

SUGAR. The economy of Mauritius is dominated by sugar. In 1961, sugar accounted for an estimated 63 percent of the employed population and, with its by-product molasses, accounted for 97.5 percent of the total value of exports. Cane occupies about 43.5 percent of the whole island and 91 percent of the cultivated area. About 51 percent of the acreage in sugar cane is owned and cultivated by 25 millers; 4 percent is owned by millers but cultivated by 2,718 tenants; 45 percent is owned and cultivated by freehold planters, most of whom are Indians. About 95 percent of the 18,851 freehold planters have under 10.4 acres, the average small holding being about 4.7 acres. The large estates are highly organized and efficiently run; operations on them have been increasingly mechanized and chemical weeding is characteristic. Attention to selection of better varieties, to fertilization, and, where necessary, to irrigation has resulted in yields of 32.2 tons of cane per acre, slightly over twice the yields from small holdings. The Mauritius Sugar Research Institute supported entirely by the industry, has an excellent record of research and development work.

In 1958, 82 percent of the labor force employed on the large estates consisted of daily task workers hired and paid through some 1,200 job contractors. The lower wages required, the fact that housing and other amenities need not be provided, and the highly seasonal character of work in the cane fields all result in preference for daily workers. Several anomalies exist in the labor situation: (1) the tendency toward agglomeration of holdings, which is likely to reduce the need in face of a rapidly growing labor force; and (2) an actual shortage of labor reported by the estates despite an increased rate of unemployment. The second of these is explained in considerable part by the unwillingness to accept manual labor; it may also reflect poor health standards, which also help to explain a very high rate of absenteeism. The shortage of workers encourages continued application of labor-saving machine techniques and chemical weeding. Also contributing to these trends has been the success of labor unions in securing an increase of 40 percent in wage rates for sugar work between 1956 and 1959. The Meade Report viewed any further wage increases

[1] Richard M. Titmuss and Brian Abel-Smith, *Social Policies and Population Growth in Mauritius* (London, Methuen, 1961), p. 237.

as a threat to employment opportunities for the future, not only in estate work but in many aspects of the island's economy.[2]

Sugar is milled in 22 plants, each serving a delimited area. A century ago there were 260 mills, but it has been the policy to centralize processing to permit greater efficiency. All producers contribute to a Cyclone and Drought Insurance Fund, whose substantial reserves were largely depleted following the 1960 storms. Production of sugar has increased from 267,000 metric tons in 1929–48 to 457,000 in 1950 and 580,000 in 1959. The 1960 crop was only 236,000 tons, owing to cyclone damage, but the 1961 crop recovered to 553,000 tons. The 115 percent increase from 1929–48 to 1959 was achieved with only a 49 percent increase in area planted. Production could be increased to 750,000 tons in a relatively few years, but market capacities might not justify this level.

At present, the sugar exports of Mauritius are largely set by the International Sugar Agreement and the Commonwealth Sugar Agreement. In 1959 limits were 359,000 metric tons to the United Kingdom at a relatively high "negotiated price"; 118,000 metric tons to Commonwealth preference markets (mostly Canada and the United Kingdom) at the relatively low world price plus the value of preference tariffs; 41,000 metric tons to non-Commonwealth markets at world prices; and a proportionate share of any shortfall from Commonwealth producers, not likely to be significant in future years. The domestic market takes about 23,000 tons. Mauritius may receive some quota increases as sugar consumption expands, and should produce in excess of quotas to permit the build-up of stocks as cyclone insurance, but there may be a period when some limitation on production will be required. The high dependence on sugar exports is revealed not only in their share of total exports but by the fact that exports account for an estimated 47.5 percent of the gross national product and

[2] J. E. Meade *et al.*, *The Economic and Social Structure of Mauritius* (London, Methuen, 1961).

Sugar cane near Mahebourg, Mauritius
Sugar and its by-products account for about 97.5 percent of Mauritius exports. Its production involves about 63 percent of the employed population.

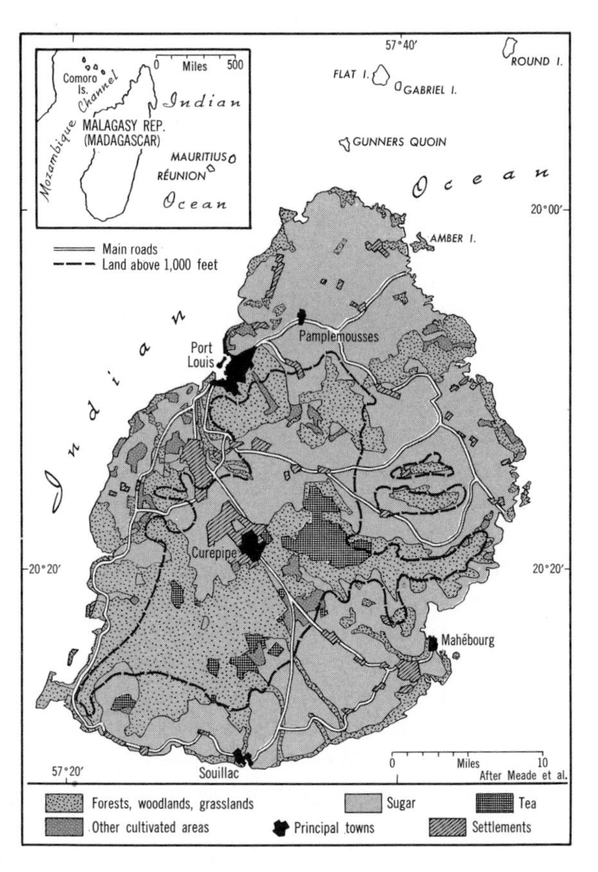

Map 104. Economic map of Mauritius

imports for 40.4 percent of gross domestic expenditure.

OTHER CROPS. The only other export crop of significance is tea, grown in areas not particularly suitable for cane. Tea has been produced for years, but only recently has it been promoted. The 1961 exports were 1,275 tons, about 56 percent of production. Plans call for increasing the average from about 6,000 acres to about 8,500 or 9,000 acres by 1965 and eventually to 15,000 acres. The government is preparing and planting about 2,500 acres which will be leased to tenants when the bushes have matured. It has also participated in the construction of tea factories, of which there are now seven.

Other cash crops include ginger, of which there is a small export; tobacco, grown by about 5,000 farmers on about 800 acres for sale to two cigarette factories selling to the domestic market; and aloe, or Mauritius hemp, a fiber which resembles sisal. Production of aloe was promoted to supply a government bag factory and to cut down on imported sacks used by the sugar industry; there is usually a shortfall in production and the factory has long operated at a loss. It has been demonstrated that Mauritius could produce a variety of crops yielding a greater return than sugar, but experience and the existence of a guaranteed market and price for the sugar have created an overweening interest in it.

A considerable share of the island not now used for agriculture is too steep, bouldery or thin-soiled to warrant cultivation, but some land is available for reclamation at a high cost, perhaps $420 per acre. Some of the forested area could also be used for tea production. A detailed land use survey is being compiled to permit assessing the best use for every acre on the island.

LIVESTOCK INTEREST. Livestock are of minor importance on Mauritius, the herd of cattle being about 40,000. Imports of animals on the hoof from Madagascar and of livestock products from various sources are large and have been increasing. An effort has been made to upgrade the peasant-owned dairy cows by use of selected Creole bulls; cows are typically stall fed on grasses collected from wastelands or on cane tops.

OTHER ECONOMIC SECTORS

FISHING. About 2,600 fishermen with 1,800 light fishing boats operate in the lagoons and nearshore waters of Mauritius, their total catch being about 2,000 tons. A recent effort has been made to advance the farming of freshwater fish.

INDUSTRY. Raw material processing establishments dominate the industrial pattern of Mauritius, including 22 sugar mills, 7 tea factories, 12 fiber decorticators and 1 sack factory, a modern sawmill, a tannery, and producers of edible oil. There has been some success in attracting market-oriented establishments, which are now represented by manufacturers of carbonated beverages, dairy products, cigarettes, wood and steel furniture, spring mattresses, metal doors and windows, boot polish, matches, paints, car batteries, lime and bricks.

Most Mauritian plants are small, rather primitive, and precariously economic. The Meade Report suggested that Mauritius work toward the Hong Kong pattern, but almost the only similarity at present between the two islands is overpopulation. Technical training, skilled labor, capital, and willing entrepreneurs are sadly lacking in Mauritius.

ENERGY PRODUCTION. Electricity output has increased rapidly in recent years, having been 16 million kwh in 1948 and 63 million kwh in 1961. In the latter year, seven small hydroelectric stations with a combined capacity of 16,540 kw accounted for less than a third of production. The share from hydro plants was reduced by unusually low rainfall. Three main reservoirs which store water for power production, irrigation, and domestic water supply are situated at elevations ranging from 1,625 to 1,900 feet. None of the island streams are large, but it is often possible to develop a very substantial head for hydroelectric production. Both additional hydro and thermal stations are being constructed to meet the growing demand.

TRANSPORTATION. Mauritius has a well-developed road net, most of which is paved and well maintained. Heavy traffic has been required to use the government railway, a 77-mile line which long operated at a loss and was finally to be closed in 1964. This will require widening and improving the standard of some of the island's light roads.

The only port of significance is Port Louis, the capital, which has one berth for vessels drawing no more than 30 feet and another with 17-foot alongside depths, but most vessels lie in the harbor to be loaded by lighter. Mauritius is well served with liners and has frequent air connections with Africa, Europe, and Australia.

RÉUNION

Réunion is like Mauritius in its volcanic origin, its population make-up, its heavy dependence on sugar, and its high population density. Discovered in the early sixteenth century by Portuguese navigators, it, too, was uninhabited. French colonists settled the island, then called Bourbon, beginning in the seventeenth century; by 1665 only 12 had arrived but the population was 4,000 in 1725. Africans and Malagasy were brought to work the sugar estates; later Malays, Annamese, Chinese, and especially Malabar Indians were brought to the islands as laborers. During the French Revolution the

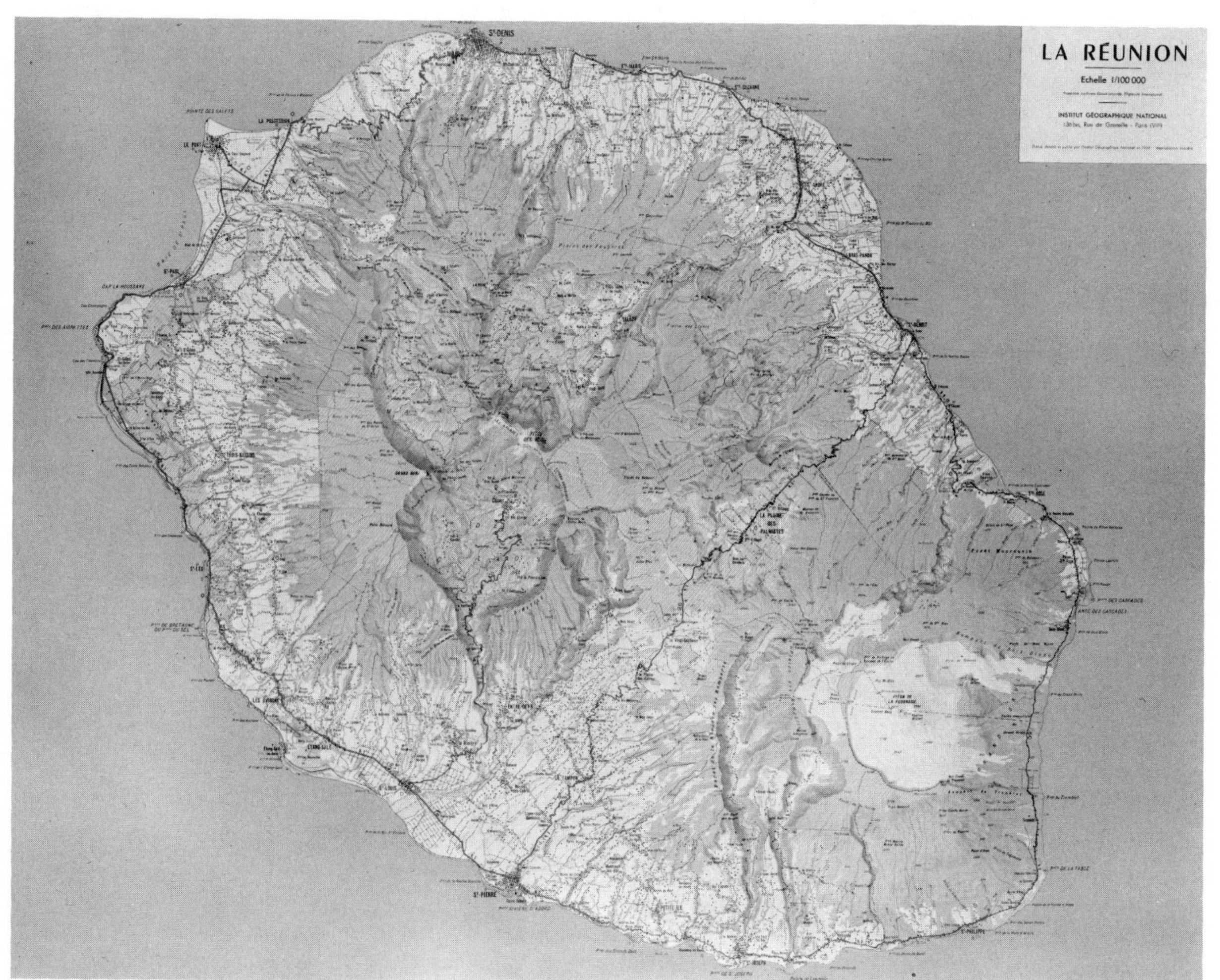

Map 105. Landforms of Réunion
Reproduced by permission of the Institut Nationale Géographique de France

island acquired its present name. It is now an overseas department of France with its own General Council acting on financial and budgetary matters.

PHYSICAL BACKGROUND

Réunion has an area of 969 square miles and is roughly oval in shape, measuring about 44 by 28 miles. Two volcanic masses dominate the scene, the largest rising to 10,060 feet in Piton des Neiges (Map 105). Three enormous cirques lie on the flanks of the dormant cone. These depressions and the canyons leading from them are walled by almost perpendicular basaltic cliffs often of spectacular height. The second and younger massif, Le Volcan, rises to 8,612 feet and is still active. The richest part of the island is the 1- to 7-mile-wide coastal strip of more gently sloping lands encircling the central massifs.

There is a sharp contrast climatically between the windward and leeward sides of the island. At Rivière de L'Est on the windward side, for example, precipitation is about 223 inches, while at Le Port on the lee it is only 35 inches.

POPULATION

Réunion probably has an even more heterodox population than Mauritius, people having been brought to the island from Africa, Madagascar, the Comores, Yemen, India, Java, China, and elsewhere, and there appears to have been a greater intermixture of the various races and people than on the sister island. Réunion does not have as great a density (357 per square mile in 1961) as Mauritius, but since a larger part of the island is unusable there is still a very marked pressure on the land.

Réunion's population has grown from about 260,000 in 1946 to 346,000 in 1961. Both its death rate and its birth rate are higher than those of Mauritius but the same general demographic trends are apparent. The death rate declined from 29.6 in 1948 to 11.6 in 1960; the crude rate of increase grew from 1.30 percent to 3.27 percent in 1960. While one might have expected to see a substantial migration from the island to France, the cost of such a trip is prohibitive for most of the population.

AGRICULTURE

Réunion's dependence upon agriculture is even heavier than that of the other main Mascarene island, but its reliance upon sugar is somewhat lower. Before 1790, sugar was produced only in small estates, but by 1865 practically all of the utilizable area had been taken up by large plantations, and one large estate accounted for an eighth of the cultivated area on the island.

Today, slightly less than a fifth of the island or about 120,000 acres is cultivated, of which about 70 percent is in sugar cane. Holdings totaled 7,039 in 1953, at which time those under 12½ acres comprised 72 percent of the total number, those between 12½ and 50 acres 19 percent, those from 50 to 250 acres 6.5 percent, and those over 250 acres accounted for 2.4 percent of the total. There was a substantially larger number of planters than holdings since *metayage*, or sharecropping, is fairly common. In 1960, for example, there were an estimated 21,000 planters.

Production of sugar has been increasing with the assistance of the Technical Center for Sugar Research and the Selection Station. In 1962 exports totaled 216,000 tons; they usually comprise about 80 percent of total exports by value. Cane is treated in a dozen mills, most of which are owned by three trusts which handle the bulk of production. Most sugar exports are sold to France under guaranteed quotas and prices, but some is sold in widely scattered markets at lower prices.

The second ranking export of Réunion is perfume essences. In 1961 they accounted for 16.3 percent of total exports by value; their weight was less than 0.05 percent of the total volume of exports. Geranium oil is most important; it is produced at elevations on the leeward side of the island where about 12,350 acres are devoted to the crop. Other essences of lesser value are ylang-ylang and vetiver. Vanilla is the only other export of significance; it has declined in importance to the present level of about 1.4 percent of total exports.

Other cash crops grown on the island include tobacco; tea, grown on an experimental basis on about 500 acres; and market garden crops. Réunion is highly dependent on imports for its food supply, but does produce enough corn to satisfy somewhat under half of its needs.

OTHER ECONOMIC SECTORS

Approximately 500 to 600 fishermen using 220 small craft are engaged in fishing on the coasts of Réunion, their total catch being only about 400 tons a year.

Industry is meagerly developed. In addition to the sugar factories, which are well equipped with modern machinery, and associated rum distilling plants, there are only a few shops producing handicraft and semihandicraft items.

Electricity is supplied by three diesel and two small hydroelectric plants, but a grid system covers almost all of the base of the island. Total capacity is about 8,500 kw, the new Langevin River station having the largest part of the total, 3,600 kw. It utilizes a head of about 799 feet. Additional sites for small plants are numerous and study is in progress on the Marsouins River.

Réunion has about 1,240 miles of main and secondary roads, 420 miles of which are paved. Until recently the road from the capital to Le Port followed a tortuous course, rising to 2,050 feet to cross a ridge which ends in steep cliffs at the sea, but abandonment of the islands 79-mile railway has permitted the building of a road around the coast using the tunnels and galleries originally constructed for the railway.

The only port on the island is Le Port des Galets, which can take the largest vessels used on the service to Madagascar and the Mascarenes, but which has a narrow, right-angle turn at the entrance requiring that ships be roped in from the shore. The port is an artificial basin cut in a low-lying gravel point on the northwest of the island.

The foreign trade of Réunion has been noted in the past decade for a remarkably even export

A sugar factory at Sainte Marie, Réunion
Réunion's dependence on sugar is lower than that of Mauritius, but sugar and its products still account for about 80 percent of the total.

The vanilla bean growing on a small farm on Réunion
Vanilla extract is a minor export of the island.

value of about $34 million yearly but an increasing value of imports which averaged $40 million in the quinquennium to 1957 and $50 million in the five years to 1962. As an overseas department of France, Réunion is aided by Fidom (Investment Fund for Overseas Departments) and by direct subventions from several French ministries as well as by the development fund of EEC. Major goals of the four-year plan (1962–65) are to encourage emigration, stimulate production of crops other than sugar, and assist in the development of nonagricultural activities, particularly manufacturing and tourism.

Bibliography

CHAPTERS I–V: INTRODUCTION

Barbour, Kenneth M., and R. M. Prothero, eds. Essays on African Population. London, Routledge and Kegan Paul, 1961.

Barclays Bank D.C.O. *Overseas Review.*

Bennett, Merrill K. "An Agroclimatic Mapping of Africa," *Food Research Institute Studies*, November, 1962, pp. 195–216.

Blondel, F., and F. Callot. "Evaluation de la Production Minière en 1958," *Annales des Mines*, May, 1961.

Bohannon, Paul J., and George Dalton, eds. Markets in Africa. Evanston, Northwestern University Press, 1962.

Bulletin de l'Institut Français d'Afrique Noire.

Carter, Gwendolen M., ed. African One-Party States. Ithaca, Cornell University Press, 1962.

Deffontaines, Pierre, ed. Géographie Universelle Larousse. Vol. II: Afrique, Asie Peninsulaire, Océanie, Paris, Larousse, 1959.

Deshler, Walter. "Cattle in Africa: Distribution, Types, and Problems," *The Geographical Review*, January, 1963, pp. 52–58.

Europe France Outremer.

Goldschmidt, Walter, ed. The United States and Africa. 2d ed., revised. New York, Praeger, 1963.

Gourou, Pierre. The Tropical World. 3d ed. Translated by E. D. Laborde. London, Longmans, Green, 1961.

Greenberg, Joseph H. The Languages of Africa. Bloomington, Indiana University Research Center in Anthropology, Folklore, and Linguistics, 1963.

Hailey, Lord. An African Survey (revised 1956). London, Oxford University Press, 1957.

Hamdan, G. "The Political Map of the New Africa," *The Geographical Review*, July, 1963, pp. 418–39.

Hance, William A. African Economic Development. New York, Harper, for the Council on Foreign Relations, 1958.

Hodgkin, Thomas. Nationalism in Colonial Africa. London, Frederick Muller, 1956.

Industries et Travaux d'Outremer.

International African Institute. *Africa.*

Jones, William O. "The Food and Agricultural Economies of Tropical Africa: A Summary View," *Food Research Institute Studies*, February, 1961.

Kimble, George H. T. Tropical Africa. 2 vols. New York, The Twentieth Century Fund, 1960.

Kool, Rudolf. Tropical Agriculture and Economic Development. Wageningen, Netherlands, H. Veenam and Zonen N. V., 1960.

Lorimer, Frank. Demographic Information on Tropical Africa. Boston, Boston University Press, 1961.

Murdock, George P. Africa: Its People and Their Culture History. New York, McGraw-Hill, 1960.

Oliver, Roland A., and John D. Fage. A Short History of Africa. 2 vols. Harmondsworth, Middlesex, 1962.

Ottenberg, Simon, and Phoebe Ottenberg, eds. Culture and Societies of Africa. New York, Random House, 1960.

Phillips, John. The Development of Agriculture and Forestry in the Tropics: Patterns, Problems and Promise. London, Faber and Faber, 1961.

Royal African Society. *African Affairs.*

Stamp, L. Dudley. Africa: A Study in Tropical Development. New York, Wiley, 1953.

The United Africa Company Ltd. *Statistical and Economic Review.*

United Nations. Department of Economic and Social Affairs.

——Economic Survey of Africa since 1950. New York, 1959.

——*Economic Bulletin for Africa.*

——Economic Commission for Africa. Economic and Social Consequences of Racial Discriminatory Practices. Addis Ababa, January, 1962.

————Industrial Growth in Africa: A Survey and Outlook. Addis Ababa, December, 1962.

——Educational, Scientific, and Cultural Organization. Social Implications of Industrialization and Urbanization in Africa South of the Sahara. Paris, 1956.

——Food and Agriculture Organization. FAO Africa Survey, Report on the Possibilities of

African Rural Development in Relation to Economic and Social Growth. Rome, 1961.
——International Labour Office. African Labour Survey. Geneva, 1958.
United States. Department of Commerce. World Trade Information Service. *Economic Reports*.
Wernstedt, Frederick L. World Climatic Data: Africa. University Park, Pa., Department of Geography, Pennsylvania State University, 1960?
Woodtli, Robert. L'Europe et l'Afrique. Vol. I; Le Potentiel Minéral Africain. Lausanne, Centre des Recherches Européennes, 1961.
Worthington, Edgar B. Science in the Development of Africa. London, Commission for Technical Cooperation in Africa South of the Sahara, 1958.

CHAPTER VI: THE MAGHRIB AND NORTHWEST AFRICA

Ardant, Gabriel. La Tunisie d'Aujourd'hui et de Demain. Paris, Calmann-Levy, 1961.
Barbour, Nevill, ed. A Survey of North West Africa (The Maghrib). London, Oxford University Press, 1959.
Blottière, Jean E. L'Algérie. Paris, Société d'Editions Géographiques, Maritimes, et Coloniales, 1948.
Capot-Rey, Robert. Le Sahara Français. Paris, Presses Universitaires de France, 1953.
Coindreau, Roger, and Charles Penz. Le Maroc. Paris, Société d'Editions Géographique, Maritimes, et Coloniales, 1949.
Despois, Jean. L'Afrique du Nord. Paris, Presses Universitaires de France, 1949.
——La Tunisie Orientale. Algiers, Faculté des Lettres, 1955.
——La Tunisie: Ses Régions. Paris, Armand Colin, 1961.
Gallagher, Charles F. "Tunisia," in Gwendolen M. Carter, ed., African One-Party States. Ithaca, Cornell University Press, 1962.
Gallissot, René. L'Économie de l'Afrique du Nord. Paris, Presses Universitaires de France, 1961.
Gautier, Émile-Felix. Sahara: The Great Desert. Translated by Dorothy F. Mayhew. New York, Columbia University Press, 1935.
Gendarme, René. L'Économie de l'Algérie. Paris, Armand Colin, 1959.
Holm, Henrietta M. The Agricultural Economy of Algeria. U.S. Department of Agriculture, Foreign Agricultural Service (FAS-M-38), July, 1958.
Institut Scientifique Chérifien. Atlas du Maroc. Rabat, various years, 1954–.
Joly, Fernand *et al.* Géographie du Maroc. Paris, Delagrave, 1949.
Meigs, Peveril. "Outlook for Arid North Africa: The Sahara," *Focus*, Vol. V, No. 4 (1954).
Mikesell, Marvin W. Northern Morocco: A Cultural Geography. Berkeley, University of California Press, 1961.
Raymond, André. La Tunisie. Paris, Presses Universitaires de France, 1961.
Thomas, Benjamin. Trade Routes of Algeria and the Sahara. Los Angeles, University of California Press, 1957.
Zartman, I. William. "The Sahara—Bridge or Barrier," *International Conciliation*, No. 541, January, 1963.

CHAPTER VII: LIBYA

Higgins, Benjamin H. The Economic and Social Development of Libya. New York, United Nations, 1953.
International Bank for Reconstruction and Development. The Economic Development of Libya. Baltimore, Johns Hopkins University Press, 1960.
Lockwood, Agnese N. "Libya, Building a Desert Economy," *International Conciliation*, No. 512, March, 1957.
Owen, Roger. Libya, a Brief Political and Economic Survey. London, Oxford University Press, May, 1961.
Villard, Henry S. Libya—The New Arab Kingdom in North Africa. Ithaca, Cornell University Press, 1956.

CHAPTER VIII: EGYPT

Ayrout, Henry. The Fellaheen. Translated by John Alden Williams. Boston, Beacon Press, 1963.
Harbison, Frederick, and Abdel Kader Ibrahim. Human Resources for Egyptian Enterprise. New York, McGraw-Hill, 1958.
Harris, George L., ed. Egypt. New Haven, Human Relations Area Files, 1957.
Hurst, Harold E. The Nile: A General Account of the River and the Utilization of Its Waters. London, Constable, 1952.
Issawi, Charles. Egypt in Revolution: An Economic Analysis. New York, Oxford University Press, 1963.
Lacouture, Jean, and Simonne Lacouture. Egypt in Transition. Translated by Francis Scarfe. New York, Criterion Books, 1959.
Oxford Regional Economic Atlas, the Middle East and North Africa. London, Oxford University Press, 1960.
Platt, Raye R., and Mohammed B. Hefny. Egypt: A Compendium. New York, The American Geographical Society, 1958.
United Nations Department of Economic and Social Affairs. The Development of Manufacturing

Industry in Egypt, Israel and Turkey. New York, 1958.

CHAPTER IX: THE SUDAN

Barbour, Kenneth M. The Republic of the Sudan: A Regional Geography. London, University of London Press, 1961.
Gaitskell, Arthur. Gezira: A Story of Development in the Sudan. London, Faber and Faber, 1959.
Hance, William A. "The Gezira: An Example in Development," *The Geographical Review*, April, 1954, pp. 253–70.
Lebon, J. H. G., and V. C. Robertson. "The Jebel Marra, Darfur, and Its Region," *The Geographical Journal*, March, 1961, pp. 30–49.
Schlippe, Pierre de. Shifting Agriculture in Africa: The Zande System of Agriculture. London, Routledge and Kegan Paul, 1956.
Sudan, Republic of the. Department of Agriculture. Agricultural Economics Division. Agricultural Statistics, 1960–61. Khartoum, October, 1962.
——Department of Statistics. National Income of Sudan, 1955/56–1959/60 (with Preliminary Estimates for 1960/61). Khartoum, April, 1962.
Sudan Almanac.
Sudanese Economist.
Tothill, John D., ed. Agriculture in the Sudan, Being a Handbook of Agriculture as Practised in the Anglo-Egyptian Sudan. London, Oxford University Press, 1948.

CHAPTERS X–XIII: WEST AFRICA

Anyane, Seth La. Ghana Agriculture: Its Economic Development from Early Times to the Middle of the Twentieth Century. London, Oxford University Press, 1963.
Banque Centrale des Etats de l'Afrique de l'Ouest. *Notes d'Information et Statistiques.*
——Togo, 1960. Paris, 1961.
Bauer, Peter T. West African Trade. Cambridge, Cambridge University Press, 1954.
Boateng, E. A. A Geography of Ghana. Cambridge, Cambridge University Press, 1959.
Buchanan, Keith M., and John C. Pugh. Land and People in Nigeria. London, University of London Press, 1955.
Church, R. J. Harrison. West Africa: A Study of the Environment and of Man's Use of It. 3d ed. New York, Wiley, 1961.
Cox-George, Noah A. Finance and Development in West Africa. London, Dobson, 1961.
——Report on African Participation in the Commerce of Sierra Leone. Freetown, Government Printer, 1958.
Forde, Daryll, and Richenda Scott. The Native Economies of Nigeria. London, Faber and Faber, 1946.
France. Mission Socio-économique du Soudan. Enquête Agricole dans le Delta Central Nigérien (Zone Inondée—Office du Niger), by Roger Caillol. Paris?, 1959.
——Secrétariat Général du Gouvernement, Direction de la Documentation. *Notes et Etudes Documentaires.*
No. 2,588, November 7, 1959. La République de Côte d'Ivoire.
No. 2,620, December 31, 1959. République du Dahomey
No. 2,638, February 26, 1960. La République du Niger.
No. 2,693, August 19, 1960. La République de Haute-Volta.
No. 2,706, October 5, 1960. La République du Togo.
No. 2,739, January 13, 1961. La République du Mali.
Galletti, R. *et al.* Nigerian Cocoa Farmers: An Economic Survey of Yoruba Cocoa Farming Families. London, Oxford University Press, 1955.
Hawkins, Edward K. Road Transport in Nigeria: A Study of African Enterprise. London, Oxford University Press, 1958.
Hill, Polly. The Gold Coast Cocoa Farmer: A Preliminary Survey. London, Oxford University Press, 1957.
Hodder, B. W. Togo: West African Republic. London, Longmans, Green, forthcoming.
International Bank for Reconstruction and Development. The Economic Development of Nigeria. Baltimore, Johns Hopkins University Press, 1955.
Irvine, Frederick. A Text-book of West African Agriculture, Soils and Crops. 2d ed. New York, Oxford University Press, 1953.
Jack, Daniel T. Economic Survey of Sierra Leone. Freetown, Government Printer, 1958.
Johnston, Bruce F. The Staple Food Economies of Western Tropical Africa. Stanford, Stanford University Press, 1958.
Nigeria. Federal Ministry of Commerce and Industry. Handbook of Commerce and Industry in Nigeria. Lagos, Government Printer, 1961.
Petch, George A. Economic Development and Modern West Africa. London, University of London Press, 1961.
Richard-Molard, Jacques. Afrique Occidentale Française. Paris, Editions Berger-Levrault, 1956.
Royal Institute of International Affairs. Nigeria, the Political and Economic Background. London, Oxford University Press, 1960.

Stapelton, G. Brian. The Wealth of Nigeria. London, Oxford University Press, 1958.

Taylor, Wayne C. The Firestone Plantations in Liberia. Washington, National Planning Association, 1956.

Thompson, Virginia, and Richard Adloff. French West Africa. London, Allen and Unwin, 1958.

United Nations Economic Commission for Africa. Transport Problems in Relation to Economic Development in West Africa. Addis Ababa, December 6, 1960.

Wells, Frederick A. Studies in Industrialization: Nigeria and the Cameroons. London, Oxford University Press, 1962.

Wills, J. Brian, ed. Agriculture and Land Use in Ghana. London, Oxford University Press for the Ghana Ministry of Food and Agriculture, 1962.

CHAPTER XIV: MIDDLE AFRICA FROM CHAD TO CONGO (BRAZZAVILLE)

Ardener, Edwin, Shirley Ardener, and W. A. Warmington. Plantation and Village in the Cameroons. London, Oxford University Press, 1960.

Berrill, Kenneth. Short Economic Survey of the Southern Cameroons. Mimeographed, August 25, 1960.

Billard, Pierre. La Circulation dans le Sud Cameroun. Lyon, Imprimerie des Beaux-Arts, 1961.

"Le Cameroun Fédéral," *Europe France Outremer*, No. 398, March 1, 1963.

Church, R. J. Harrison. "Spanish Guinea," *West Africa*, March 8, April 5, April 19, 1952.

Encyclopédie de l'Union Française, L'Encyclopédie Coloniale et Maritime: Afrique Equatoriale Française, Paris, 1950.

France. Secrétariat Général du Gouvernement, Direction de la Documentation. *Notes et Etudes Documentaires*

No. 2,696, August 31, 1960. La République du Tchad.

No. 2,732, December, 17, 1960. La République du Congo.

No. 2,733, December 19, 1960. La République Centrafricaine.

No. 2,741, January 19, 1961. La République du Cameroun.

No. 2,795, July 10, 1961. La République Gabonaise.

"Le Kouilou," *Industries et Travaux d'Outremer*, September, 1958, pp. 487–583.

Société d'Etudes pour le Développement Economiques et Social. Rapport sur les Possibilitiés de Développement Industriel du Cameroun. Paris, January, 1960.

Tardits, Claude. Les Populations Bamiléké de l'Ouest Cameroun. Paris, Editions Berger-Levrault, 1960.

Thompson, Virginia, and Richard Adloff. The Emerging States of French Equatorial Africa. Stanford, Stanford University Press, 1960.

Trézenem, Edouard. L'Afrique Equatoriale Française. Paris, Société d'Editions Géographiques, Maritimes, et Coloniales, 1955.

United Kingdom. Colonial Office. Cameroons under United Kingdom Administration, Report for the Year 1959. London, Her Majesty's Stationery Office, 1961. Also see Report for the Year 1958.

Ziéglé, Henri. Afrique Equatoriale Française. Paris, Editions Berger-Levrault, 1952.

CHAPTER XV: CONGO (LEOPOLDVILLE)

Académie Royale des Sciences d'Outre-Mer. Livre Blanc. 3 vols. Brussels, 1963.

Belgian Congo and Ruanda-Urundi Information and Public Relations Office. Belgian Congo. 2 vols. Brussels, Inforcongo, 1960.

Belgium. Direction de l'Agriculture. Volume Jubilaire du Bulletin Agricole du Congo Belge et du Ruanda-Urundi, 1910–1960. Brussels, 1961.

Bezy, Fernand. Problèmes, Structurels de l'Économie Congolaise. Louvain, Editions E. Nauwelaerts, 1957.

Campus, Fernand. L'Aménagement Hydroélectrique du Fleuve Congo à Inga. Brussels, A.R.S.C., 1958.

Fabri, Marcel, and Jean Mayer. La Population Futur du Congo. Brussels, Centre d'Etudes des Problèmes Sociaux, 1960.

Federation of Congolese Enterprises. The Congolese Economy on the Eve of Independence. Brussels, 1960.

Hance, William A., and Irene S. van Dongen. "Matadi, Focus of Belgian African Transport," *Annals of the Association of American Geographers*, March, 1958, pp. 41–72.

Merriam, Alan. Congo: Background of Conflict. Evanston, Northwestern University Press, 1961.

Michaels, A., and N. Lande. Notre Colonie: Géographie et Notice Historique. 6th ed. Brussels, Edition Universelle S.A., 1951.

"Plantations in Africa," The United Africa Company *Statistical and Economic Review*, March, 1952, pp. 1–50.

Robert, Maurice. Le Congo Physique. 3d ed., revised. Liége, H. Vaillant-Carmanne, 1946.

Skinner, Snider W. The Agricultural Economy of the Belgian Congo and Ruanda-Urundi. U.S. Department of Agriculture, Foreign Agricultural Service, June, 1960.

L'Union Minière du Haut-Katanga. Union Minière du Haut-Katanga, 1906–1956. Brussels, Editions Louis Cuypers, 1957.

Van den Abeele, Marcel, and René, Vandenput. Les Principales Cultures du Congo Belge. 3d ed. Brussels, Ministère des Colonies, Direction de l'Agriculture, des Forêts, et de l'Elevage, 1956.

CHAPTER XVI: RWANDA AND BURUNDI

Leurquin, Phillippe. Le Niveau de Vie des Populations Rurales du Ruanda-Urundi. Louvain, Editions E. Nauwelaerts, 1960.

Marqet. Jacques J. The Premise of Inequality in Ruanda: A Study of Political Relations in a Central African Kingdom. London, Oxford University Press, 1961.

Ruanda-Urundi. Geography, Economy I and II, and Social Achievements. Four pamphlets translated from the French by Goldie Blankoff-Scarr. Brussels, Inforcongo, 1960.

Le Ruanda-Urundi. Brussels, Office of Information . . . for Congo and Ruanda-Urundi, 1958.

United Nations. The Population of Ruanda-Urundi. New York, 1953.

CHAPTER XVII: ETHIOPIA

Dubois, Hubert P. Cheminot de Djibouti à Addis-Ababa. Paris, Librarie Académique Perrin, 1959.

Geiger, Theodore. TWA's Services to Ethiopia. Washington, National Planning Association, April, 1959.

Huffnagel, H. P. Agriculture in Ethiopia. Rome, F.A.O., 1961.

Imperial Ethiopian Government. Ministry of Commerce and Industry. *Ethiopian Economic Review.*

Johnston, Martin. "Addis Ababa from the Air," *Ethiopian Observer*, VI, No. 1 (1962), 17–32.

Last, G. C. "Introductory Notes on the Geography of Ethiopia," *Ethiopian Observer*, VI, No. 2 (1962), 82–134.

Lipsky, George A. Ethiopia: Its People, Its Society, Its Culture. New Haven, Human Relations Area Files, 1962.

Luther, Ernest W. Ethiopia Today. Stanford, Stanford University Press, 1958.

Mariam, Mesfin W. "An Estimate of the Population of Ethiopia," *Ethiopian Observer*, V, No. 2 (1961), 135–42.

Simoons, Frederick J. North-West Ethiopia, Peoples and Economy. Madison, University of Wisconsin Press, 1960.

State Bank of Ethiopia. *Report on Economic Conditions and Market Trends*, various issues.

Ullendorff, Edward. The Ethiopians: An Introduction to Country and People. London, Oxford University Press, 1960.

CHAPTER XVIII: SOMALIA

Castagno, Alphonso A., Jr. "Somalia," *International Conciliation*, No. 522 (March, 1959), pp. 339–400.

——"The Somali Republic in Transition," *Africa Report*, December, 1962, pp. 7–10.

International Bank for Reconstruction and Development. The Economy of the Trust Territory of Somalia. Washington, 1957.

Italy. Ministry of Foreign Affairs. Report of the Italian Government to the General Assembly on the Trust Territory of Somalia. Rome, 1958.

Karp, Mark. The Economics of Trusteeship in Somalia. Boston, Boston University Press, 1960.

Lewis, I. M. Peoples of the Horn of Africa: Somali, Afar, and Saho. London, International African Institute, 1955.

CHAPTER XIX: EAST AFRICA

Crofts, R. A. Zanzibar Clove Industry. Zanzibar, Government Printer, 1959.

Economist Intelligence Unit. The Economy of East Africa: A Study of Trends. Nairobi, The English Press Ltd., 1955.

Elkan, Walter. The Economic Development of Uganda. London, Oxford University Press, 1961.

Hill, John F. R., and John P. Moffett. Tanganyika: A Review of Its Resources and Their Development. London, Jarrold, 1955.

Hill, Mervyn F. Permanent Way. 2 vols. Nairobi, East African Railways and Harbours, 1949–57.

Hollingsworth, Lawrence W. The Asians in East Africa. London, Macmillan and Co., Ltd., 1960.

Homan, Derek. Kenya's Second Revolution: The Story of Agrarian Reform in the African Areas. Unpublished manuscript, 1961.

Hoyle, B. S. "The Economic Expansion of Jinja, Uganda," *The Geographical Review*, July, 1963, pp. 377–88.

Huxley, Elspeth. A New Earth. New York, Morrow, 1960.

——No Easy Way: A History of the Kenya Farmer's Association and UNGA Limited. Nairobi, East African Standard, Ltd., 1957.

International Bank for Reconstruction and Development. The Economic Development of Kenya. Baltimore, Johns Hopkins University Press, 1963.

——The Economic Development of Tanganyika. Baltimore, Johns Hopkins University Press, 1961.

——The Economic Development of Uganda. Baltimore, Johns Hopkins University Press, 1962.

Kenya, Colony and Protectorate of. Ministry of Agriculture. African Land Development in Kenya. Nairobi, Government Printer, 1962.
——Ministry of Commerce, Industry, and Communications. Commerce and Industry in Kenya, 1961. Nairobi, Government Printer, 1961.
——Survey of Industrial Production, 1957. Nairobi, Government Printer, 1959.
Little, Arthur D., Inc. Tanganyika Industrial Development: A Preliminary Study of Bases for the Expansion of Industrial Processing Activities. Dar es Salaam, Government Printer, December, 1961.
McMaster, David N. A Subsistence Crop Geography of Uganda. Bude, England, Geographical Publications Ltd., 1962.
Middleton, John. Land Tenure in Zanzibar. London, Her Majesty's Stationery Office, 1961.
Moffett, John P., ed. Handbook of Tanganyika. 2d ed. Dar es Salaam, Government Printer, 1958.
Morgan, W. T. W. "The 'White Highlands' of Kenya," *The Geographical Journal*, June, 1963, pp. 140–55.
Oliver, Roland, and Gervase Mathew. History of East Africa. Vol. I. London, Oxford University Press, 1963.
Swynnerton, R. J. M. "Agricultural Advances in Eastern Africa," *African Affairs*, July, 1962, pp. 201–15.
Tanganyika. Ministry of Commerce and Industry. Commerce and Industry in Tanganyika. Dar es Salaam, Government Printer, December, 1961.
Tothill, John D., ed. Agriculture in Uganda. London, Oxford University Press, 1940.
Uganda. Department of Lands and Surveys. Atlas of Uganda. Kampala, Government Printer, 1962.
Wrigley, C. C. Crops and Wealth in Uganda: A Short Agrarian History. Kampala, East African Institute of Social Research, 1959.
Zanzibar Protectorate. Report and Recommendations on the Present Position and Future Prospects of Agriculture in the Zanzibar Protectorate. Zanzibar, Government Printer, 1959.
——Report on the Economic Development of the Zanzibar Protectorate, by P. Selwyn and T. Y. Watson. Zanzibar, Government Printer, 1962.

CHAPTER XX: THE RHODESIAS AND NYASALAND

Anderson, R. *et al.* An Agricultural Survey of Southern Rhodesia. Part II: Agro-Economic Survey. Salisbury, Government Printer, 1961.
Barber, William J. The Economy of British Central Africa. London, Oxford University Press, 1961.
Brelsford, William V., ed. Handbook to the Federation of Rhodesia and Nyasaland. London, Cassell, 1960.
Duff, C. E. Regional Survey of the Copperbelt. Lusaka, Government Printer, 1959.
Federation of Rhodesia and Nyasaland. Ministry of Economic Affairs. Economic Report, 1963. Salisbury, Government Printer, 1963.
Floyd, Barry N. "Land Apportionment in Southern Rhodesia," *The Geographical Review*, October, 1962, pp. 566–82.
Hazelwood, Arthur, and P. D. Henderson. Nyasaland: The Economics of Federation. Oxford, Basil Blackwell, 1960.
Jack, D. T., chairman. Report on an Economic Survey of Nyasaland, 1958–1959. Salisbury, Government Printer, 1959.
Nyasaland. Natural Resources Department. The Natural Resources of Nyasaland. Zomba, Government Printer, 1960.
Prescott, J. R. V. "Population Distribution in Southern Rhodesia," *The Geographical Review*, October, 1962, pp. 559–65.
Tow, Leonard. The Manufacturing Economy of Southern Rhodesia, Problems and Prospects. Washington, National Academy of Sciences, National Research Council, 1960.
Trapnell, Colin G. The Soils, Vegetation and Agriculture of North-eastern Rhodesia. Lusaka, Government Printer, 1953.
Trapnell, Colin G., and J. N. Clothier. The Soils, Vegetation and Agricultural Systems of North-western Rhodesia. Lusaka, Government Printer, 1937.
Vincent, V. *et al.* An Agricultural Survey of Southern Rhodesia. Part I: Agro-Ecological Survey. Salisbury, Government Printer, 1960.
Williams, Stuart. The Distribution of the African Population of Northern Rhodesia. Lusaka, Rhodes-Livingstone Communication Paper No. 24, 1962.

CHAPTER XXI: ANGOLA AND MOZAMBIQUE

Duffy, James. Portugal's African Territories: Present Realities. New York, Carnegie Endowment for International Peace, Occasional Paper No. 1, 1962.
——Portuguese Africa. Cambridge, Harvard University Press, 1959.
Egerton, Frederick C. C. Angola in Perspective. London, Routledge and Kegan Paul, 1957.
Hammond, Richard J. Portugal's African Problem: Some Economic Facets. New York, Carnegie Endowment for International Peace, Occasional Paper No. 2, 1962.
Hance, William A., and Irene S. van Dongen. "Beira, Mozambique Gateway to Central Africa,"

Annals of the Association of American Geographers, December, 1957, pp. 307–35.
——"Lourenço Marques in Delagoa Bay," *Economic Geography*, July, 1957, pp. 238–56.
Van Dongen, Irene S. "The Port of Luanda in the Economy of Angola," *Boletim da Sociedade de Geografia de Lisboa*, January–March, 1960, pp. 3–43.

CHAPTER XXII: THE REPUBLIC OF SOUTH AFRICA

Board, C. *et al.* The Border Region, Natural Environment and Land Use in the Eastern Cape. Cape Town, Oxford University Press, 1962.
Cole, Monica M. South Africa. New York, E. P. Dutton & Co., Inc., 1961.
De Blij, Harm J. Africa South. Evanston, Northwestern University Press, 1962.
Fair, T. J. D., and L. P. Green. "Development of the 'Bantu Homelands,'" *Optima*, March, 1962, pp. 7–19.
Green, L. P., and T. J. D. Fair. Development in Africa: A Study in Regional Analysis with Special Reference to Southern Africa. Johannesburg, Witwatersrand University Press, 1962.
Houghton, D. Hobart. "Economic Dangers of Separate Bantu Development," *Optima*, December. 1959, pp. 188–98.
Norval, A. J. A Quarter of a Century of Industrial Progress in South Africa. Cape Town, Juta and Co., Ltd., 1962.
Republic of South Africa. South Africa, 1963. Pretoria, Government Printer, 1963.
Sauer, P. O. "Water for South Africa," *Optima*, December, 1956, pp. 95–100.
South African Railways. A Century of Progress, 1860–1960. Johannesburg, Da Gama Publications, Ltd., 1960.
Talbot, A. M., and W. J. Talbot, eds. Atlas of South Africa. Pretoria, Government Printer, 1960.
Union of South Africa. Bureau of Census and Statistics. Union Statistics for Fifty Years. Pretoria, Government Printer, 1960.
——Department of Mines, Geological Survey. The Mineral Resources of the Union of South Africa. 4th ed. Pretoria, Government Printer, 1959.
——*Farming in South Africa.* Official Journal of the Department of Agriculture, Special van Riebeeck Number, March, 1952; 1910–1960 Festival Issue, May, 1960.
——Report of Commission of Inquiry into European Occupancy of the Rural Areas. Pretoria, Government Printer, 1959.
——Summary of the Report of the Commission for the Socio-Economic Development of the Bantu Areas within the Union of South Africa. Pretoria, Government Printer, 1955.
Wellington, John H. Southern Africa: A Geographical Study. 2 vols. London, Cambridge University Press, 1955.
Williams, Owen. "Sugar Growing and Processing in the Union of South Africa," *Economic Geography*, October, 1959, pp. 356–66.

CHAPTER XXIII: SOUTH-WEST AFRICA

De Blij, Harm J. "Notes on the Geography of South West Africa," *Journal of Geography*, October, 1958, pp. 333–41.
Logan, Richard F. The Central Namib Desert, South West Africa. Washington, National Academy of Sciences, National Research Council, 1960.
——"South West Africa," *Focus*, November, 1960, pp. 1–6.

CHAPTER XXIV: THE HIGH COMMISSION TERRITORIES

Ashton, Hugh. The Basuto. New York, Oxford University Press, 1952.
Basutoland, Bechuanaland Protectorate, and Swaziland. Report of an Economic Survey Mission. London, Her Majesty's Stationery Office, 1960.
Debenham, Frank. Kalahari Sands. London, G. Bell, 1953.
Dundas, Sir Charles, and Hugh Ashton. Problem Territories of Southern Africa, Basutoland, Bechuanaland, Swaziland. Cape Town, South African Institute of International Affairs, 1952.
Green, L. P., and T. J. D. Fair. "Preparing for Swaziland's Future Economic Growth," *Optima*, December, 1960, pp. 194–206.
Sillery, A. The Bechuanaland Protectorate. New York, Oxford University Press, 1952.
University of Natal. Experiment in Swaziland: Report of the Random Sample Survey, 1960. Durban, Institute for Social Research, University of Natal, 1962 (mimeographed).

CHAPTER XXV: MADAGASCAR

Bulletin de Madagascar.
Chevalier, Louis. Madagascar: Populations et Ressources. Paris, Presses Universitaires de France, 1952.
Deschamps, Hubert. Madagascar. Paris, Editions Berger-Levrault, 1951.
Dumont, René. Evolution des Campagnes Malgaches. Tananarive, Imprimerie Officielle, 1959.

Enterprises et Produits de Madagascar.
France. Secrétariat Général du Gouvernement, Direction de la Documentation. "La République Malgache," *Notes et Etudes Documentaires,* No. 2,737, December, 23, 1960.
Gendarme, René. L'Economie de Madagascar. Paris, Editions Cujas, 1960.
Hance, William A. "Transportation in Madagascar," *The Geographical Review,* January, 1958, pp. 45–68.
Isnard, Hildebert. Madagascar. Paris, Armand Colin, 1955.
Revue de Madagascar.

CHAPTER XXVI: MAURITIUS AND RÉUNION

Brookfield, H. C. "Problems of Monoculture and Diversification in a Sugar Island: Mauritius," *Economic Geography,* January, 1959, pp. 25–40.
Mauritius, Colony of. Report on Mauritius, 1961. London, Her Majesty's Stationery Office, 1962.
Meade, James E. *et al.* The Economic and Social Structure of Mauritius. London, Methuen, 1961.
Titmuss, Richard, and Brian Abel-Smith. Social Policies and Population Growth in Mauritius. London, Methuen, 1960.

Subject Index

Index of Geographical Names

Picture Credits

Belgo-American Development Corporation, 319, 333, 334, 336, 339
Cameroun Information, 297 lower
Casa de Portugal, 488, 493, 494, 497, 501, 506, 510
Alphonso Castagno, Jr., 366, 369, 370
Congo Information Service, 314, 316, 322, 323, 324, 327, 335
Congopresse, 5, 344, 345
East African Railways and Harbours, 1, 23, 33, 349, 383, 384, 385, 386, 387, 397, 406, 407 left, 422, 428, 430
Egyptian State Tourist Administration, 124, 135, 137, 141
Federal Information Department, Rhodesias and Nyasaland, 254, 436, 444, 447, 448, 458 upper, 461, 463, 472, 478, 480, 481
Firestone Tire and Rubber Company, 212
French Embassy Press and Information Division, 18 upper left, 22, 84 left, 86, 91, 93, 96, 99, 100, 102, 104, 106, 177, 184, 199, 210, 223, 227, 232, 269, 278, 282 upper, 285, 295, 302, 617. Photographs of the now independent countries were taken before independence.
Ghana Information Services, 185, 200, 208, 241, 255, 256 upper
Imperial Ethiopian Government, Ministry of Information, 354, 357 right, 362
Information Service of South Africa, New York, 513, 524, 526, 533 upper, 538, 544, 545, 546, 563 upper
Kenya Information Services, 396, 403, 413, 421
Ministry of Research and Information, Nigeria, 253, 257
Monrovia Port Management, 181
Moroccan Trade Information Center, 108
Northern Rhodesia Information Department, 18 upper right
Photo Aerien Verbelke, 7, 276
Photo J. Wellens, 311
Public Relations Olin, 234
Rhodesian Selection Trust, 433, 467, 470
Shell Oil Company, 189, 196 lower, 242, 244, 279
South Africa Electricity Supply Commission, 41
South African Information Service, Pretoria, 533 lower, 536, 542, 547, 548, 552, 558, 559, 563 middle and lower, 564, 575
South African Railways, 556
Sovfoto, 125
Standard Oil Company (N.J.), 75, 112, 114, 115, 117
Sudan Information Office, 145, 146, 153, 157, 158 lower, 161
Uganda Department of Information, 415, 427
United Africa Company Limited, 204, 251, 256 lower, 320
United Nations, 83 lower, 84 right
United States Agency for International Development, Nigeria, 221, 250
Author, 18 lower, 35, 43, 58, 62, 65, 83 upper, 85, 128, 129, 130, 131, 147, 148, 158 upper, 163, 174, 182, 186, 190, 192, 195, 196 upper, 198, 211, 217, 222, 236, 238, 240, 247, 282 lower, 289, 290, 297 upper, 346, 351, 357 left, 380, 388, 390, 407 right, 409, 418, 454, 458 lower, 464, 465, 492, 508, 520, 549, 553, 573, 578, 581, 583, 590, 591, 593, 596, 597, 598, 600, 601, 602, 606, 613